Visual
Tennis

DOUBLEDAY

New York   London   Toronto   Sydney   Auckland

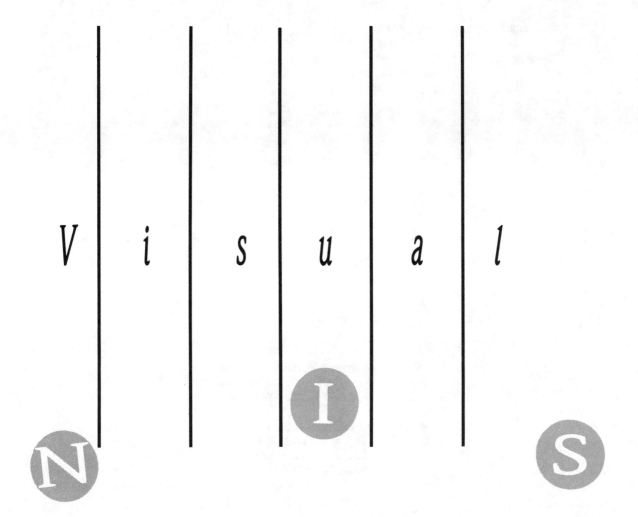

Visual

**Mental Imagery
and the Quest
for the Winning Edge**

John Yandell

Foreword by Dick Gould
Photographs by Julie Polunsky

To Cynnie and Bud

PUBLISHED BY DOUBLEDAY
a division of Bantam Doubleday Dell Publishing Group, Inc.
666 Fifth Avenue, New York, New York 10103

DOUBLEDAY and the portrayal of an anchor
with a dolphin are trademarks of Doubleday,
a division of Bantam Doubleday Dell
Publishing Group, Inc.

Library of Congress Cataloging-in-Publication Data
Yandell, John.
Visual tennis : mental imagery and the quest for the winning
edge / John Yandell. — 1st ed.
p.   cm.
1. Tennis—Psychological aspects.   2. Imagery (Psychology)
3. Visualization.   I. Title.   II. Title: Visual tennis.
GV1002.9.P75Y36   1990
796.342′01′9—dc20   89-28339
CIP

ISBN 0-385-26422-4
Copyright © 1990 by John Yandell
with photos by Julie Polunsky

CUR

Acknowledgments

It is a pleasure to acknowledge the people who have helped me in the development of the teaching system presented here. The list begins with my first tennis coach Frank Ward, who later also taught me to be a teacher, and with Bill Austin, one of the most charismatic pros I have known, who taught me to hit a backhand in one hour.

There are the numerous individuals in the Bay Area tennis community who have given me knowledge, support, and critical feedback over the years. The debt my work owes to Dick Gould is acknowledged in the text. I want to thank him personally for sharing his time and his encouragement with me so freely. Alan Davis requires recognition for giving me my first head pro job at Golden Gate Park. Without his confidence in me this book would never have been written.

I want to thank other tennis comrades. Scott Murphy, practice partner, and coaching adversary, has read parts of this book at various stages, as have Charlie Hoeveler, director of the Adidas Tennis Camps, and Weston Reese, director of tennis at the San Francisco Tennis Club. Their enthusiasm and comments have been valued. Fellow teaching pros Michael Friedman and Julie Montague have helped me, not only by reading the text, but by testing the techniques presented here on the teaching court with hundreds of tennis players. My friend Peter Pearson, a beautiful technical player and the source of many of my own spontaneous visual learning experiences, has provided continuous support and entertaining commentary throughout the course of the project.

Christine Guarnaccia of the International Tennis Hall of Fame has been an important source for video and written material on the history of the game's styles. My student Cliff West, in addition to subjecting himself to numerous experiments in teaching theory, introduced me to the joys, and occasional agonies, of modern word processing.

The photos at the heart of this book's teaching sequences need special comment. First, I want to thank my longtime creative associate Chuck Koton for shooting the test photo sequences. The images you see here are the product of the skill of my photographer, Julie Polunsky, who worked closely with me in what was probably the most intense phase of the project. I also want to thank Marty Takigawa and the other printers at HiFi laboratories in San Francisco for producing the large number of technically demanding prints on a very compressed schedule. I also feel special gratitude to my agent, Angela Miller, who, a long time ago, planted the idea for this book in my mind.

Finally, there is the team at Doubleday that made *Visual Tennis* a reality, starting with my editor, Kara Leverte. I was extremely fortunate to have, in Kara, an editor who not only knew the game of tennis and played it well herself, but someone who understood that there was something new in the concept for this book, and was willing to work at every stage to give it shape and expression. Her assistant, Marirose Ferrara, also made special efforts to facilitate the project. My designer, Carol Malcolm, performed with seeming ease the difficult task of translating a teaching process into words and pictures on printed pages. Finally, I want to acknowledge Patty Moynihan of the Doubleday marketing department, an avid player herself, for her enthusiasm for the book, and her effort to make it accessible to tennis players everywhere.

CONTENTS

Foreword by Dick Gould   3

INTRODUCTION   5

HOW VISUALIZATION WORKS   11

THE CLASSICAL STYLE   17

THE FOREHAND   27

Creating the Forehand Swing Pattern   31
Executing the Forehand   40
Muscle Memory Corrections   42
Keying the Forehand   45
Variation: The Circular Backswing   52
Variation: The Closed Face Backswing   54

THE BACKHAND   57

Creating the One-Handed Topspin
    Backhand Swing Pattern   63
Executing the One-Handed Topspin Backhand   72
Muscle Memory Corrections   74
Keying the One-Handed Topspin Backhand   77
Variation: The One-Handed Slice Backhand   84

Creating the Two-Handed Backhand Swing Pattern   87
Executing the Two-Handed Backhand   96
Muscle Memory Corrections   98
Keying the Two-Handed Backhand   101

THE RELATIONSHIP BETWEEN
TIMING AND POWER   **109**

THE VOLLEY   **113**

Creating the Forehand Volley Swing Pattern   117
Executing the Forehand Volley   126
Muscle Memory Corrections   127
Keying the Forehand Volley   130
Variation: The Underspin Forehand Volley   134

Creating the One-Handed Backhand Volley
   Swing Pattern   137
Executing the One-Handed Backhand Volley   146
Muscle Memory Corrections   147
Keying the One-Handed Backhand Volley   150
Variation: The Underspin Backhand Volley   154

Creating the Two-Handed Backhand Volley
   Swing Pattern   157
Executing the Two-Handed Backhand Volley   166
Muscle Memory Corrections   167
Keying the Two-Handed Backhand Volley   170

THE SERVE   **175**

Creating the Swing Pattern for the Basic Serve   181
Executing the Basic Serve   192
Muscle Memory Corrections   194
Keying the Basic Serve   197
Variation: The Advanced Serve   204

USING YOUR STROKE KEYS ON THE COURT   **208**

THE GRIPS   **213**

The Forehand Grips   215
The One-Handed Backhand Grip   216
The Two-Handed Backhand Grip   217
The Continental Grip   218

Foreword

Occasionally, a book comes along that has something genuinely new and exciting to say about the game of tennis. *Visual Tennis: Mental Imagery and the Quest for the Winning Edge* is one of these exceptional books.

In these pages, John Yandell presents us with a new approach to learning and playing the game. *Visual Tennis* is based on the insight, now well documented by research in sports psychology, that sports learning is naturally visual. Tennis players have always learned by watching better players, and often play far above their normal levels after doing so. *Visual Tennis* is a complete teaching system based on visual techniques.

Visual Tennis teaches you to think about your game in a different medium, in images rather than in words. In the individual chapters, Yandell provides what are among the most detailed visual models ever created for all the basic shots: groundstrokes, volleys, and serves. Each stroke is shown in full from both the front and side views, and then broken down into its key components. By mastering the key images, students learn to produce superior strokes effortlessly and automatically. Unlike many instructional books, *Visual Tennis* includes models for both the one-handed and two-handed backhands, and shows you how to decide which is right for you.

Visual Tennis goes beyond teaching basic strokes, however. Perhaps its most important contribution is to show players at all levels how to use visualization to produce their best tennis under the pressure of match play. To do this, Yandell effectively uses a system of stroke keys. By visualizing the key just before hitting a shot, the player triggers the correct execution of the stroke pattern, no matter what the situation on the court.

Of special additional value, Yandell provides an analytic comparison of the three major styles of play: the continental, the western, and the eastern, or classical. He points out the strengths and weaknesses of each, and shows that the classical strokes are the most effective for the majority of players, and also, the easiest to learn. He explains how most of the great modern players use some variation of classical strokes, and why the classical style can be used with equal success for serve and volley, the baseline game, or any combination of the two.

Would you like to play winning "A" tennis at your club? Are you a junior player who would like to move up in the junior rankings, or earn a ranking for the first time? The book states that these goals are realistic for virtually any player. Players who adopt the total visual approach often progress several ability levels, competing against and beating players who had previously seemed out of reach.

Visual Tennis has value for everyone in tennis from the beginner to the ranked tournament player. It will be of special interest to theorists of the game, and to working teaching pros who would like to produce the same results with their own students. In the Introduction, Yandell includes a critical analysis of the failures of the traditional approaches to teaching. He shows how visualization transcends the inherent limitations of most tennis instruction, by creating a teaching technology based on the way athletes actually learn.

With the publication of this book, John Yandell establishes himself as one of the most innovative tennis teachers in the country. His critically acclaimed video *The Winning Edge*, starring John McEnroe and Ivan Lendl, is a best-selling instructional tape, and is widely used by teaching pros and at tennis camps across the country. In *Visual Tennis*, Yandell sets out his theories of visual modeling in greater detail, and provides a fresh set of model stroke patterns for every aspect in the game. The images of the strokes alone make the book worthwhile. But what is more promising is the prospect that every player who uses them as part of the visualization training process has the potential to hit the ball with the same fluidity and technical precision.

I have known John for ten years, since his days as a graduate student in the humanities at Stanford. His work provides a new analytic perspective on the game. This book excites me and is highly recommended to any reader interested in discovering his or her true potential.

—DICK GOULD
MEN'S TENNIS COACH
STANFORD UNIVERSITY

INTRODUCTION

As a tennis player, has this ever happened to you? After watching great tennis, you went out and played the best tennis of your life. The match you saw may have been on television, at a pro tournament, at a club, or the public courts. Afterward, it was as if you could not miss. You had total control of the ball, and effortlessly dominated your opponent. You went to the courts the next time expecting to play the same way, but instead, the effect had disappeared.

What you experienced was the spontaneous power of visual learning. Visual learning is at the root of how great tennis players learn and play the game. Great players do this intuitively, often without consciously realizing how it occurs. The average player, however, needs help to develop this same ability in himself. Unfortunately, this is something he almost never receives, since the traditional approaches to teaching the game

are not based on visual learning, and therefore cannot cultivate this powerful natural ability in students. The result is that the majority of players have the kind of tennis experience described above only by accident, if at all.

It's not surprising that by watching other players, you absorb something from them, almost by osmosis. But why does this happen? The answer has to do with the nature of the learning process. In reality, *all* sports learning, tennis included, is essentially visual. Anyone who has learned to throw a baseball or a football, or to shoot a jump shot, can probably recall watching and imitating someone else.

The term that best describes this modeling process is *visualization*. To define it in the words of noted sports psychologist Jim Loehr, "Visualization is thinking in pictures."[1] We learn sports motions naturally, by visualizing images of

---

[1]*James E. Loehr,* Mental Toughness Training for Sports: Achieving Athletic Excellence (*Lexington, Mass: Stephen Greene Press, 1986*). *Loehr stresses the importance of visualization training in his overall approach to developing mental toughness. See pp. 105–10.*

them first. These images then become a kind of mental blueprint for the body to follow. The way John McEnroe learned to play tennis is a typical example. As McEnroe describes it, "When I was learning to play, I just watched Rod Laver and tried to do what he did."

Ivan Lendl had a similar experience as a young player. He would play much better after ball-boying matches for the top adult Czechoslovakian players. "Being on the court so close to the players I saw things, and then I would start to do them myself," he said.

Sports psychologists have demonstrated that the ability to visualize is linked to performance in almost every known sport. They have devised training programs using visualization techniques in football, basketball, baseball, track and field, skiing, and golf, to mention a few of the best-known examples. These programs systematically enhance the natural visual learning process. Visualization is now regularly incorporated into the training programs of the world's top athletes.

A recent overview of the scientific literature concluded that visualization is a proven factor in improving sports performance. How powerful? In experiments measuring improvements in sports skills, the overview concluded, visualization *by itself*, that is visualization even *without* physical practice, produced measurable improvement in performance across a wide range of motor skills.[2] If you stop to think about it, this is a rather startling conclusion. The inference is that tennis players can increase their success simply by *thinking correctly* (in pictures) about their sport, independent of practice time on the court. The study concludes that a combination of regular practice and visualization is the key to the development of the athlete's full potential.

Although the effectiveness of visualization has been demonstrated in research, and visualization training has become an established aspect of Olympic and professional sports, this book is among the first programs to make the same training available to recreational and competitive athletes below the world-class level. Its purpose is to set out a teaching technology for tennis that is based on the visual learning process.

In 1985, I collaborated with John McEnroe and Ivan Lendl on the creation of *The Winning Edge*, a tennis video that also made use of the principles of visualization. In the video, McEnroe and Lendl provide visual models for the strokes and shot patterns. First they break the stroke or technique down into its key components. Then they reconstruct the motion into a fluid whole. The viewer, by visualizing as he watches the video, transfers the images into his mental imagery. These images then become the basis for forming his own shots.[3]

This book goes beyond the video in that it not only breaks down each stroke pattern into its component parts, but also offers a detailed series of checkpoints to help the tennis player turn his visual model of each stroke into a more precise physical motion. These checkpoints allow students to evaluate how closely they are following the model on a regular basis, form the basis for doing what are called "muscle memory corrections." The corrections allow any player to correct his mistakes as they actually happen, before they can become permanently ingrained in the stroke pattern. Developed by Stanford tennis coach Dick Gould and his partner Tom Chivington, muscle memory is one of the most powerful techniques ever devised for correcting technical flaws in stroke production. The process is explained in detail for each stroke in the individual chapters.

---

[2]*Deborah L. Feltz and Daniel M. Landers, "The Effects of Mental Practice on Motor Skill Learning and Performance: A Meta-analysis," Journal of Sports Psychology, 1983.*

---

[3]*A pioneering video in the field is Tennis with Stan Smith from Sybervision. The Sybervision theory is that, at least occasionally, every player hits the ball correctly. By watching the video the player is supposed to bring out this preexisting muscle memory. In reality, developing consistent stroke patterns requires a more detailed and systematic approach. Since the strokes are not broken down into their component parts, it is difficult to use the tape to form clear visual models. Many viewers also find the continuous repetition of the same images difficult to watch. However, Stan Smith's strokes are without doubt a source for many solid technical models, and I recommend the tape for the supplemental video training outlined here.*

Finally, *Visual Tennis* goes beyond the video in offering powerful techniques that can be used to produce consistent strokes under match play conditions. Each chapter provides a series of selected images or "stroke keys" that the player uses to trigger the correct technical stroke pattern. Working with the keys, a player can create his own stroke key chart for every shot. These keys provide any player with the avenue for achieving consistent stroke production, even under competitive pressure.

Currently, tennis instruction can be almost universally divided into two basic schools of thought, neither of which utilizes visual learning in a systematic way. The first, and the most dominant, is the "tennis tip" school. This school teaches the game through a series of self-contained "tips" about various aspects of the game. A common tip from this school is, for example, "Start low and finish high on your groundstrokes," or "Take a short backswing on the volley."

Perhaps you've taken lessons, or seen other players taking lessons, in which the pro offers an array of tips such as these, yet none of them seem to have a positive impact on the stroke. Trying to prepare early, for example, the student jerks the racket back, but every backswing is slightly different, and the rhythm of the motion is destroyed. Next the student tightens up his arm trying to keep a firm wrist, but this makes the contact late and jarring. He tries whipping his body through the ball at various times, but the shots are uncontrolled, and the pace fluctuates wildly. He experiments with a variety of different follow-throughs, but none of them seem to influence where the ball lands. Meanwhile, the pro constantly feeds the student more information, tries to be encouraging, but secretly wonders why teaching a basic stroke is so difficult. If this is all you have seen or experienced, then you have no way of understanding that learning to hit the tennis ball does *not* have to involve this kind of frustration.

To be fair, the leading exponents of this school have done significant research into the biomechanics of the game, and, in fact, some of their most important conclusions are cited here. Their failure has been in translating the raw data into a truly effective teaching technology. Simply put, their approach to teaching starts with the false assumption that verbal commands, or "tips," can be used successfully to teach physical motions. The truth is that they can't. In the typical lesson situation described above, the student attempts to apply a tip such as "keep your wrist firm" to his forehand. But the focus on a verbal message leads to a mechanical response and the isolation of one set of muscles, with no concept of how the "tip" relates to the stroke as a whole. When the student is unsuccessful in improving the stroke, he usually ends up blaming himself for his lack of progress and concludes that he simply lacks the ability to hit the ball well. Many teaching pros go through the course of their careers thinking that the situation described above is normal, and never question the ineffectiveness of the tennis tip method.

But other teaching pros have reacted to this experience in a different way. Rather than simply accept the futility of the tennis tip method, they have rejected it altogether in favor of a second teaching approach, what I call the "mystical" school. The mystical school responds to the inadequacy of verbal instruction by abandoning tips and analysis altogether. Instead, it focuses on the so-called "inner game," or the internal mental dialogue that occurs when you play tennis.

The mystical school teaches that it is the player's internal dialogue, either about his fears and self-doubts, or about technique that prevents the student from learning to hit the ball. The focus, in the view of the mystical school, should not be inward, but rather turned *outward*, entirely to the ball. The role of the instructor is to help students reach a kind of "mystical union" with the ball.

According to the extreme version of this school, by watching the ball, and doing literally nothing else, anyone can develop excellent strokes. The human body already "knows" how to play tennis. The art of teaching is to help the student get the mind out of the way, so that tennis can "happen."

There is no doubt that this approach

contains a powerful truth about the game of tennis, that is, that ball focus is a crucial aspect of learning and playing well. It is also correct in pointing out that verbal commands do not necessarily lead to improved technical stroke production. It correctly identifies the negative role that a player's internal mental dialogue can play in preventing good tennis. It also advocates watching the technique of superior players. But by any objective measure, this approach never leads to the development of solid stroke production for the majority of players. Because it provides no information whatsoever about the bio-mechanics of hitting tennis balls, its results are, on the whole, inferior to even the tennis tip school. The real beneficiaries of the inner game are advanced players who already have well-developed strokes, and who use its insights to improve the mental aspects of their play.[4]

The common problem with both the mystical and the tennis tip approach is that neither one offers a teaching technology based on the process by which sports learning really occurs, that is, by visual assimilation. McEnroe was not the first, or the last, young player to learn by copying great champions. In fact, the rise of various styles of play among junior and recreational players mirrors the changing styles of the players at the top of the professional game. The dominance of Jimmy Connors and Chris Evert in the 1970s established the two-handed backhand as a permanent aspect of the game. Bjorn Borg touched off a movement to heavy topspin and a defensive, baseline style of play. When John McEnroe dethroned Borg, the serve and volley style soared in popularity. This development was paralleled in the women's game by the attacking play of Martina Navratilova. When Ivan Lendl and Boris Becker moved to the top of the tennis world, suddenly the one-handed backhand came back.

There is no point in denying that tennis is a challenging sport. To play good tennis, you must execute a variety of complex physical motions with consistent precision. The most talented young players do this automatically and unconsciously, but the majority of players lack the exceptional visual learning skill necessary to do this entirely on their own. Instead, they are limited to occasional flashes of brilliance, for example, after watching the superior technique of others. To perform consistently they need help to cultivate the natural, visual learning process. But most teaching pros, despite their sincere intentions and heroic efforts, are unable to provide them that help, because the two predominant schools of instruction are not based on the real nature of sports learning. To the extent that most traditional lessons work, it is because the students either model themselves on the strokes of their teachers, or because they possess the natural ability to translate the verbal information into visual images.

Visual Tennis is based on more than ten years of teaching, coaching, and research. As a teaching pro, I have taught over ten thousand hours of lessons using the principles of visualization training. I have seen it benefit players competing at the professional level, in college, in junior tournaments, in club matches, in club tournaments, and in friendly recreational play.

In addition to my own experiences over the years with spontaneous visual learning, a second factor in the genesis of my approach goes back to the late 1970s, when I was a student at Stanford. During that time I first met men's tennis coach Dick Gould, and learned his teaching system, working as one of his recreational tennis instructors. Dick is known as the legendary coach of ten Stanford men's college championship teams. What is less well publicized is that he also runs one of the largest and most successful instructional programs in the country, teaching players at all levels, from complete beginners to nationally ranked junior players. As far as I know, Dick and his partner, Tom Chivington, the Foothill College tennis coach and the coach of touring pro Brad Gilbert,

---

[4]See Timothy Gallwey, The Inner Game of Tennis, (New York: Random House, 1974), and Inner Tennis, Playing the Game, (New York: Random House, 1976). Gallwey's discussion of ball focus was a vital contribution that changed the way the game is understood. The technology of stroke production presented here is compatible with Gallwey's concentration techniques.

were the first teachers in the country to make explicit stroke models the basis of a teaching system.

Visual Tennis has evolved, in part, from my experience with Gould's sytem. Readers who are familiar with Dick's classic book will recognize the debt my work owes him.[5] My departure is in defining the causal role of the visual dimension in the learning process, and in making it the basis for an entire teaching approach. In a certain way, this visual dimension was latent in Dick's and Tom's concept of a model stroke. In my opinion, the use of physical models worked because they activated the natural visual learning process. However, in my own extensive subsequent teaching, I found the physical models alone were often insufficient to produce consistent stroke production. Eventually, I realized that the model strokes had worked for me because they triggered *mental images* of the correct stroke patterns. The majority of players, however, needed explicit instruction in order to do this for themselves. This insight started the evolution of the visualization training system. In effect I was using Dick's stroke models to create a method that would systematically produce the kind of visual learning experiences I had had spontaneously so many times as a player.

In addition to approaching the game by emphasizing the visual dimension, this book also differs from Dick's approach in the exact form of the model strokes offered. I have altered aspects of the models for the groundstrokes and volleys. I have also created new models for the footwork on the advanced serve. These changes are based on my own teaching experience, my work with McEnroe and Lendl in making *The Winning Edge*, and on the analysis of the stroke patterns of successful players at all levels.

While it is essential to define stroke patterns precisely, what is even more essential is a technology that will turn these patterns into real tennis. In my opinion, the quality of the stroke production in recreational and competitive tennis could be drastically higher than it actually is.

Despite major investments in lessons, clinics, tennis camps, wide-body rackets, etc., far too many players have technical inconsistencies that limit their development and cause them continuous frustration. The inability of most players to improve cannot be blamed on the players themselves, or on the efforts of their instructors. Rather, it lies in the nature of tennis instruction itself.

Of course there are physical differences between players—some have better hand-eye coordination, or are stronger, faster, or more mentally determined. These factors may set some upper limit on a player's development, but frequently, they do not come into play in deciding matches. This is because technique tends to determine the outcome of most matches below the very highest levels of play. But superior technique is something that virtually every player can develop. It is a matter of approaching the game with the right instructional principles, and making the effort to put them into practice.

What kind of results can you achieve using the system presented here? I have found that any club player who follows the principles in this book can learn to compete at the "A" level, and that any junior player can improve a minimum of ten places in the sectional rankings, or achieve a ranking for the first time. Usually this can be accomplished within a period of one year or less, if a player is willing to dedicate himself to the process.

There is a causal relationship between the use of visual images and the proper execution of physical strokes. If you follow the program outlined in this book, you will be able to duplicate the magic that most tennis players experience only by accident. You will learn to play with a classical style that is technically sound, physically effortless, and aesthetically pleasing. You will develop the ability to hit with pace, depth, spin, and precise ball control. In short, you will learn to play the best tennis of your life for the rest of your life.

---

[5]*Dick Gould, Tennis Anyone? 4th ed. (Palo Alto, Calif.: Mayfield, 1988). This book is the best introduction to all aspects of the game ever written.*

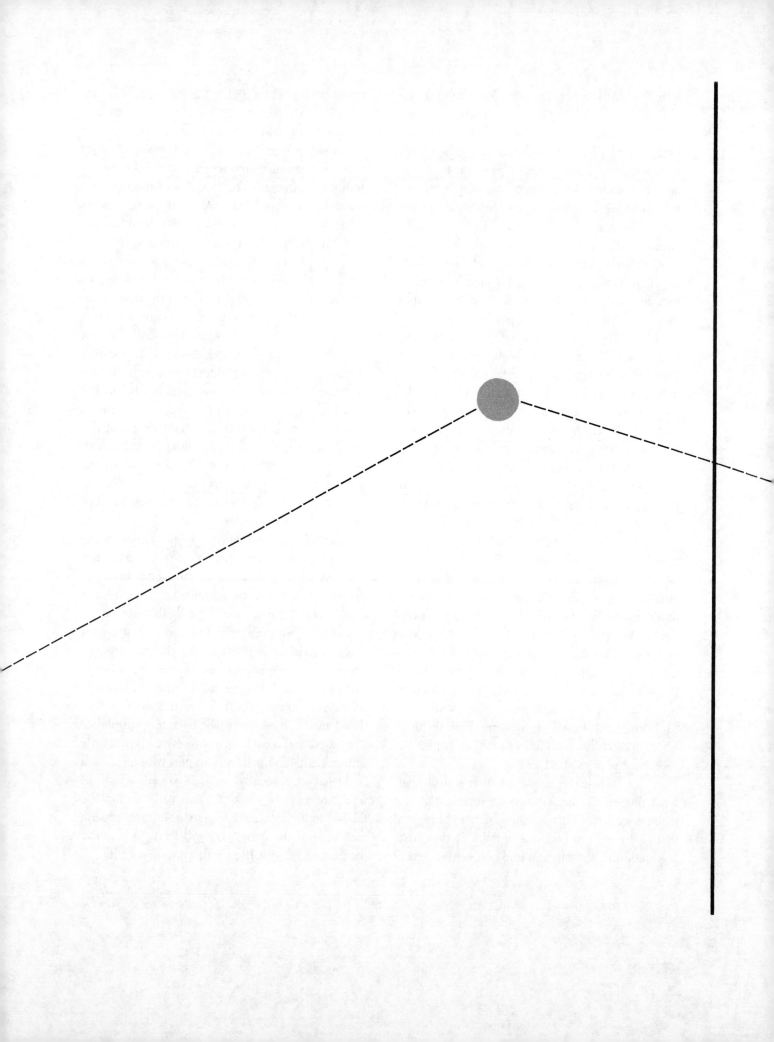

HOW VISUALIZATION WORKS

I f you study tennis below the pro level, you will come to the conclusion that the majority of points, and therefore the majority of matches, are lost, rather than won. Specifically, most points are lost on errors, and primarily, on unforced errors. An unforced error means that a player fails to hit the ball over the net and in the court on a basic shot. The error was not forced by pressure from the opponent, it was a breakdown in stroke production on what should have been a routine stroke. A study of club matches showed that, on the average, if the player who lost the match had gotten just one more shot over the net in every point, he would have ended up winning the match instead.

Unforced errors occur for two principle reasons: first, most players have too much variation in their basic stroke technique from ball to ball, and second, they attempt to hit too many shots that are too good, either winners in impossible situations or shots hit with far more velocity than is actually necessary to win the point.

If you watch the top players you will notice they rarely make these kinds of errors. Most points in professional tennis are won, not lost. They are decided by winners or forcing shots, not unforced errors. This is primarily due to the remarkable consistency of these players' stroke patterns. In pro tennis, you see shot after shot executed with unfailing technical precision, despite ball velocities that often exceed 100 miles per hour.

To their credit, club players and junior tournament players often recognize that it is the lack of consistent strokes that causes their errors and limits their performance. They try to correct this through lessons, but, too frequently, without noticeable success. Lessons usually do not produce good stroke technique because the major schools of tennis instruction do not work with the visual learning process.

Visualization training offers the tennis player the opportunity to learn to hit any shot in the game with a high degree of technical precision, and to do so consistently under the pressure of competitive play. Until you have experienced the satisfaction of hitting short balls for winners on a routine basis, or passing down the line consistently on the backhand side, or putting together a series of dominating serve and volley points, you cannot truly appreciate visualization training's power and value.

The chapters that follow outline an approach for hitting all the basic shots: the groundstrokes, the volleys, and the serve. In the backhand chapter, there are sections on hitting with one hand or two, as well as a discussion of how to determine which stroke you should develop. The chapters are designed to be used together, or independently, so that a player can work on one or more individual strokes.

Each chapter begins by providing the player with a *model stroke*. This model has both a *visual* and a *physical* component. To learn a given stroke it is necessary to master both the visual and the physical aspects of the model. This means learning to visualize a technically perfect stroke, and at the same time, to swing the racket according to the image. The role of the visual model is crucial for one simple reason: if you cannot *see* youself swing the racket correctly in your own mind, you will be unable to swing it correctly on the court. Learning a clear mental model gives the body the information it needs to hit the shot, and to hit it the same way on every ball.

In each chapter, you will learn to master the visual and physical models simultaneously. To do this, the strokes will first be broken down into several component parts, what I call the "still frames." By putting the four still frames together, the player learns to execute the swing physically. Simultaneously, he learns to visualize the swing in his mind's eye. The goal is for the two models to correspond as precisely as possible.

At first, this procedure of dividing the strokes into still frames and checkpoints may seem somewhat complex and difficult to learn. Actually, in the long run, the opposite is true. It may sound simpler just to say "Swing low to high on the forehand," and leave it at that, but what does a statement like this really mean? The racket can be in at least four or five different positions on the turn, all of which could be considered "low." But which one, if any, will be correct? Where exactly, does the racket head point? How far back does it go? What position is the arm in? Where are the shoulders and legs?

The purpose of the still frames and the checkpoints is to define exactly where the body and racket are positioned at each stage of the stroke. In the long run this will lead to simplicity, not confusion. The goal is to use the checkpoints to learn what the correct positions actually feel like physically, and more importantly, what they *look* like in the mind's eye. This is done through a series of successive, gradual approximations, working with the checkpoints until the model stroke pattern becomes natural. The goal is not to instantly memorize a long list of information about each stroke, but rather to create deep muscle memory of excellent technical stroke patterns. The checkpoints are only guides to help you see and feel what correct stroke patterns are really like. Used correctly, what you should remember is not only the checkpoints themselves, but the feeling and the image of what the stroke is like when the checkpoints are correct. If you take the time to work with the checkpoints until they are comfortable—it will more than pay off in the quality of your tennis.

After learning the still frames and putting them together into practice swings, the second aspect of developing the model stroke is hitting balls in what is called *controlled drill*. A basic principle of visualization training is that it is *literally impossible* to learn or correct stroke patterns in competitive play, or even in a normal rally. Controlled drill means that the player uses either a partner, a teaching pro, or, if possible, a ball machine to feed him practice balls. At first, the balls should be hit *with low to moderate pace.* They should also come directly to the player, allowing him to execute the stroke *without* having to move. Working in controlled drill allows the player to concentrate entirely on the correct execution of the stroke and the development of his visualization skills.

The controlled drill is also critical because it allows the player to learn the process of *muscle memory correction.* Muscle memory corrections are a central part of the visualization learning process, because they allow a player to correct his mistakes *literally as they happen.* To do a muscle memory correction, the player learns to freeze at the end of a given stroke in what is known as the "statueman" (or "statuewoman") position. By freezing in the statueman position, the player can carefully evaluate the accuracy of the stroke pattern. He does this by comparing his *actual* finish position to the checkpoints for the model stroke. The player than makes a *muscle memory correction* by physically adjusting from his statueman position to the correct position.

Muscle memory work is one of the most powerful aspects of the visualization process. Doing muscle memory corrections eliminates a primary failure in traditional lessons. This occurs when the student makes a technical mistake, and then without correcting, simply recovers to the ready position. The pro points out the error, but the student makes the same error on the next ball, or often makes a new error trying to correct the old error. This pattern can repeat itself to the point of absurdity: the pro gives the same tip over and over, the player goes back and forth from one error to another, but no fundamental change occurs. Muscle memory correction gives the tennis player—and the teaching pro—a way to break this unproductive cycle. It is the only technique that gives the player a physical demonstration of how far his stroke deviated from the correct pattern, and what it actually takes to correct the error.

An indispensable part of developing your strokes and learning the muscle memory cor-

rection process is seeing your tennis on video. You can accomplish this by using a home video camera, or better, by working with a pro that makes extensive use of video in his teaching. No amount of verbal description can take the place of the direct visual feedback video provides. It creates a clarity that is impossible to achieve in any other fashion. Research has shown that almost all sports learning accelerates rapidly with the addition of video. For some students, I find that viewing themselves regularly on video is the most powerful single aspect of the entire visualization training process.

The long-term goal of the visualization training process is to create a stroke that is so solid and consistent that you can execute it virtually indefinitely, first in controlled drill, then in rallies, and finally, under the pressures of competitive play. *Visual Tennis* teaches every player how to do this by helping him develop a system of personal stroke keys.

A stroke key is one aspect of an overall stroke pattern, or more precisely, an image of one aspect of the stroke. By holding the image of the key in the mind's eye while he hits the ball, the player activates the entire stroke pattern. The key provides the player with a mental blueprint to follow in making the swing. Properly developed, the key system gives the player a reliable, automatic method for executing the correct technical stroke pattern.

A stroke key can be any part of the image of the overall stroke. It can be an image of one of the four still frames, or one or more of the checkpoints. On the groundstrokes, for example, I have found that the most effective key is some variation of the image of the finish position. The key can also be a moving image, a kind of mini-movie of the *entire* stroke. In the chapters that follow you will learn how to develop and test various keys, how to determine which keys are effective, or "active," in your game. A final section shows you how to create your own stroke key chart for each stroke. Using stroke keys allows any player to correct even difficult problems in preparation and timing, the kinds of problems that are especially resistant to change in traditional lessons.

Because stroke keys are pictures, they bypass the paralysis and confusion caused by words and verbal commands. The fact is that tennis happens too fast to think about in words. But pure imagery can flow through the mind at the speed your body actually moves on the court. Stroke keys are the perfect medium to guide the complicated interplay between mind and body required to play great tennis.

There is also a related major additional benefit. Developing and using a system of personal stroke keys provide the antidote to the universal sports phenomenon of "choking." Stroke keys can eliminate choking because they give the player a way to keep the mind focused even in very tense situations. Focusing on an active stroke key blocks the entry of distracting thoughts and fears. This intrusion of unwanted internal verbal dialogue is what causes unforced errors on easy balls. Typically, confronted with an open shot, a player tells himself something along the lines of "I *have* to make this shot," or "Good players always make these," etc. Ironically, this kind of expectation creates so much pressure that it almost guarantees the player will make the error he is so desperate to avoid.

The first step in overcoming this fear is often simply admitting it exists. A great many players deny they are afraid, and thus are incapable of addressing the problem. It is important in playing competitively, no matter what the level, to accept the natural fear that goes with pressure, and to give yourself permission to miss easy shots until you become comfortable in the situation. If you are willing to do this, the fear will gradually decrease to a level at which it can be controlled. [1]

In addition to developing your stroke patterns, doing muscle memory corrections, and creating your own system of personal keys, the final aspect of visualization training is doing vis-ualization work *away* from the court. As noted above, research studies have demonstrated the value of this form of mental practice in improving sports performance. In fact, visualization is so powerful that it can produce improved performance even without physical practice. However, the maximum benefit occurs when mental and physical practice are used in combination.

The procedure for doing off-court visualizations is simple: sit down and close your eyes. Some people prefer to do visual work in a quiet, or even a dark environment, others do it to music. Eastern European trainers have their athletes lies down, listen to classical music, and then visualize perfect performances in their individual sports. Whether you lie down or listen to music, the important thing is to be relaxed, comfortable, and motivated. If you have trouble sitting still, it can help to actually get up and swing the racket physically while doing the visualizations.

Starting with one stroke, see yourself execute it perfectly, following the models shown in the individual chapters. Give the image as much detail as possible. Try to see your entire body and your racket. See the brand name on your racket, tennis shoes, tennis clothes, etc. Try visualizing in color if you do not normally do so. Visualize the swing at different speeds. Start in slow motion, and gradually work up to the speed of your swing in actual play. Add the sound of the ball striking the center of the sweet spot. Now shift to the system of personal stroke keys you have devised for the stroke. Focus on each individual key in the context of the overall stroke. Visualize each of your keys. Now repeat the same procedure for each of your other strokes.

As you advance as a player, you can start to visualize shot combinations as well as basic strokes. See yourself hit a forehand, then a backhand, then a forehand, etc. Then put together imaginary points—a serve followed by a winning

---

[1] *This is the point made by Allen Fox in his indispensable book* If I'm the Better Player, Why Can't I Win? *(New York: Simon and Schuster, 1979). It explains how great players accept their fear of choking, and how you can reframe court situations to do this yourself. The book is one of the best analyses ever written of competitive sports psychology, and is probably a prerequisite for certain players in developing their stroke key system.*

first volley, or a return of serve followed by a passing shot. Put together patterns that are typical of the kinds of points you play, or would like to play, in matches. Visualize the combinations that are your strengths, and especially, your weaknesses. (For example, if you have trouble making low first volleys on your forehand, or hitting backhand groundstrokes down the line, see yourself executing a series of these shots.)

Although still outside the mainstream of tennis instructional theory, visualization techniques have recently gained attention as part of the growing interest in sports psychology, and are the subject of a growing number of articles in the tennis press. Typically, these articles advise a player to work on a troublesome shot by "imagining yourself hitting the shot perfectly." The problem with this advice, however, is that it assumes the player knows what a "perfect" shot looks like in the first place. In fact, if the player could see the stroke clearly in his mind's eye, he would probably not need advice on how to improve it through visualization. Worse, by following this advice, he may actually reinforce his technical problems by visualizing flawed technique.

To be truly effective, visualization training must first show the player how to construct a superior technical image of the stroke. Only then can the player benefit from visual practice in any systematic or meaningful way. This is why the majority of this book is dedicated to construction of technical models and stroke keys for each stroke.

A final dimension of a complete visual training program is the use of video images. This means watching video of good stroke technique in order to reinforce your own visual models. Video is also a source of timing, rhythm, and inspiration. Most players have discovered the value of watching great tennis on their own. This same effect should be systematically cultivated. *The Wining Edge* is an example of an instructional video designed to enhance visual modeling, as is *Tennis* with Stan Smith from Sybervision. Taping television matches is a limitless source of additional images.

In addition, I have created a video version of *Visual Tennis*. This video provides clear models for strokes that are unavailable on other instructional videos. These include the straight backswing forehand, the two-handed backhand, the two-handed backhand volley, and the basic serve. Although both the book and the video are designed to be used independently, most students will find it more effective to use them together.

Finally, I recommend that every student make his own personal visual modeling video, if possible. Again, using a home video camera or working with your pro, record a series of perfect practice swings. Do a statueman at the end of each swing to emphasize the checkpoints. Do perfect freeze frames of each aspect of the stroke. Now practice executing the models hitting balls in the controlled drill, preferably against a ball machine.

How much visual practice should the average player do away from the court? This is a question that every player has to answer for himself based on his own experience. Research suggests that the optimum ratio may be as high as an hour of visualization for every three hours spent on the court. If this ratio is correct, it means that it is almost impossible for the average player to do too much visualization.

As a start, try one session of visual practice for every session of actual play. For example, if you play three times a week, have three visualization sessions. Try doing pure visualization in two, and watching video in the other. Start with five to ten minutes of pure visualization, and ten to fifteen minutes of video. If you wish, you can build up the length of your sessions from there. By experimentation, and by working with your pro, find the combinations that keep your interest and enhance the quality and your enjoyment of the game.

THE
CLASSICAL
STYLE

Visual Tennis is based on the creation of a series of model strokes. These models could be drawn from any of three predominant styles in the game: the continental style, the western style, or the eastern or classical style. The models I have chosen are of the classical style. This does not mean that the principles of visualization training cannot be applied to either the continental style or the western style. Players who want to play either continental or western tennis could follow the principles outlined in this book simply by creating their own visual models using video and/or still photos of players using those styles.

However, for the majority of players, the classical style will be by far the easiest of the three to develop, and also the most productive in terms of competitive results and aesthetic satisfaction. There are two compelling reasons for this: first, the classical style is *mechanically simpler*, and second, it is more *strategically flexible*.

Compared with continental or western strokes, classical stroke patterns have the fewest number of variables to master, and thus are easier to learn, and also to execute consistently, especially under pressure. The primary technical difference between the three styles is that classical strokes require a minimum use of wrist to execute correctly. This stems from the differences in the forehand grip. With the grip for the continental forehand, part of the palm of the hand is placed *on top* of the racket. At the other extreme, a western forehand grip places part of the palm of the hand *underneath* the racket handle. But the classical forehand grip places almost all of the palm of the hand *behind* the racket, so the palm and the racket head are parallel and naturally aligned.

The grip plays a crucial role in the nature of the forehand stroke because the grip dictates the role of the wrist in the execution of the stroke. Wrist motion is by far the most difficult factor to control in any tennis shot, and is responsible for a majority of technical errors on the forehand. Because of the grip, both the continental and the western forehands require that the wrist be released through the contact with the ball. By releasing the wrist, the player in either of these alternate styles accelerates the racket head upward through the ball, producing topspin.

High-speed photographic studies have shown that whatever style you play, the racket face *must* be vertical at contact to produce spin and ball control. When the wrist is released in the course of the swing, achieving this vertical racket position requires almost perfect timing. Even a slight error in the wrist release can result in the loss of racket head control, and thus, an unforced error. This problem is eliminated in the classical style in which the wrist is not usually released until after impact, if at all.

This is not to say that literally every tennis player should follow the classical style. There are certain advantages to the continental and the western games. Continental strokes are based on taking the ball on the rise. By hitting the ball on the rise, players generate additional pace from the speed of the ball as it accelerates upward off the court. At the same time, by taking the ball earlier, they cut down the time the opponent has to recover from his shot, and react to the next ball. Continental tennis is well suited to fast court surfaces, most notably grass, and to playing the serve and volley game.

At the other end of the spectrum, the western style is often superior on slower surfaces, especially clay. The western style relies on large looping swing patterns that produce exaggerated topspin. Generally, western-style players allow the ball to drop slightly below the top of the bounce before making contact. This allows them the extra time necessary for making the exaggerated western swings. If he has truly mastered this heavy topspin style, the western player is very difficult to outrally, and his groundstrokes are superior to hitting passing shots because of the dipping action caused by the additional topspin.

Despite the undeniable successes recorded by players in both these technical traditions, the difficulties of the western and continental styles are prohibitive for the majority of recreational, and even tournament players. Because of the central role of the wrist release, playing continental or western tennis well requires vastly superior hand-eye coordination. It also requires significantly more practice to develop and maintain. Few players have the phenomenal timing that allows John McEnroe to hit every ball on the rise. Fewer still have the time and determination of a Bjorn Borg, who spent four hours a day hitting against a wall to perfect his forehand wrist roll. Compared with these styles, the classical style can be learned much more quickly by players regardless of natural ability and available practice time.

An additional advantage is that with classical strokes it is possible to hit the ball equally well on the rise, at the top of the bounce, or, slightly on the way down. Classical players can take the ball early on every shot as do Jimmy Connors and Andre Agassi. They can play it just after the top of the bounce the way Chris Evert does. Or they can vary their timing to the court and the opponent following the style of Ivan Lendl, who takes the ball early in some matches, and lets it drop slightly in others. Most recreational and even tournament players will naturally tend to hit the ball as it drops, but there are exceptions at all levels of the game. With classical strokes, every player can experiment with the timing of the strokes for himself.

In addition to its technical simplicity, the second major advantage of the classical style is its strategic flexibility. Most players lack the ability to play winning serve and volley tennis against every opponent. Conversely, baseliners have difficulty winning points quickly on faster courts, especially against weaker players. Most players maximize their success by playing a combination of attacking and backcourt tennis. Against some opponents, they should take the net at every opportunity. Other opponents should be played primarily from the backcourt. Most matches, however, require you to mix these two styles depending on the situation. The goal is to use your relative strengths against the relative weaknesses of each opponent. Thus, your strategy should be chosen for its effectiveness against a given opponent, on a given court, on a given day. This mix of attacking and baseline strategies is called the all-court game.

Compared with continental or western tennis, the classical style is much better suited to playing the all-court game. It is possible to attack or to defend in any combination, and with equal success, if you play classical tennis. This is particularly true on hard court surfaces, which have become the standard in the United States, and, increasingly, around the world.

It is this dual advantage of strategic flexibility and technical simplicity that makes the classical style the best choice for the majority of players at all levels. This conclusion does not imply that classical players cannot learn from players using a different style. All players should try to imitate the fabulous shoulder turns on the groundstrokes of a McEnroe or a Borg. Despite his continental groundstrokes, McEnroe's volleys are perfect technical models for classical players. The same could be said of the service motion of many western-style players, including Borg. However, classical strokes offer a simpler and more effective overall approach to playing your best tennis.

How do classical-style players stand in comparison with champions of the two other styles, and what players can we draw on to create the models for classical strokes? It is fair to say that over time, and particularly in the modern era, classical tennis has been the dominant style, with more great champions to serve as technical models than the other two styles combined.

The origins of the classical style in tennis go back to Bill Tilden, who dethroned the western-style champion Bill Johnston as the world's top player in the 1920s. Tilden dominated the game in his era more completely than any player since, winning the U.S. title seven times and Wimbledon three times, the last Wimbledon title coming in 1930 when Tilden was thirty-seven. Tilden was immediately followed by a second dominant classical champion, Ellsworth Vines, a powerful all-court player, also a winner at Wimbledon and twice U.S. champion in 1931 and 1932. Then came Don Budge, a flawless stylist, and the player who defined the Grand Slam of tennis by winning Wimbledon, the French, the American, and the Australian titles in a single year for the first time in 1938. The next great classical champion was Jack Kramer, the dominant force in tennis in the 1940s, who also established the serve and volley strategy as a permanent aspect of the modern game.

Ken Rosewall, Tony Trabert, and John Newcombe are among the other outstanding classical players who have found their places in tennis history. Rosewall, who won five major singles titles, possessed a backhand that was the virtual archetype of the one-handed underspin drive. Trabert, who had an extremely solid all-around classical game, hit the ball with more depth and topspin than other players of his era, and in 1955, won three of the four Grand Slam legs, missing only the Australian title. Newcombe, who won the U.S. title twice and Wimbledon three times, used classical strokes to play an extremely aggressive serve and volley game. His forehand, with its loop backswing, minimal use of wrist, and smooth high finish, still remains one of the best models for that variation of the stroke.

In the history of the women's game, the dominance of the classical style is even more pronounced. Alice Marble, Helen Wills Moody, Maureen Connolly, Margaret Court, and Billie Jean King are all outstanding examples of players with classical stroke patterns. They also are the greatest players in the women's game before the Open era. Only Suzanne Lenglen, the athletic French champion of the 1920s played with a different technical style, the continental. There has yet to be a great women's champion with western strokes.

The classical women's champions use

a mixture of strategies, as did their male counterparts. Thus, Alice Marble, who played the serve and volley in the 1930s, as well as Margaret Court and Billie Jean King all adapted classical technique to an attacking style. Maureen Connolly, and Helen Wills Moody, on the other hand, achieved equal success playing classical tennis from the baseline.

With the beginning of modern professional tennis, the definition of who is a classical player becomes more complex for several reasons, including the introduction of the two-handed backhand as a dominant stroke, the advent of heavy or exaggerated topspin, and the dramatically increased shot velocity with the evolution of racket technology. Yet the majority of the great players in the 1970s and 1980s can still be clearly identified by their classical technical strokes. The list includes top men players such as Stan Smith, Vitas Gerulaitis, Sandy Mayer, and Brian Gottfried. Among the women, examples are Virginia Wade, Hana Mandlikova, and Tracy Austin.

The list also includes four players who have dominated the game in the 1980s: Chris Evert, Jimmy Connors, Martina Navratilova, and Ivan Lendl. Most recently we can add Steffi Graf, Michael Chang, and Andre Agassi to the list of great classical players.

In some respects, the games of these modern classical players could not appear to be more varied. Chris Evert is the prototype of the ultra-steady, two-handed baseliner. Martina Navratilova is one of the great pure serve and volley players. Jimmy Connors hits the ball early and almost completely flat. His game is based on natural aggressiveness and incredible shot making. Ivan Lendl is known for his power, topspin, and consistency, a combination that allows him to win on a variety of court surfaces. Steffi Graf plays primarily from the baseline with a one-handed backhand, but hits the ball harder than any other woman currently in the game. Agassi is every bit as aggressive as Connors, but hits the ball with more topspin, and possibly, with even more pace.

What is not usually recognized is that all these champions have basic technical similarities that place them within the bounds of the classical tradition. Their variations in strategy of play only demonstrate the supreme versatility of classical stroke production. The way these players strike the ball gives them more in common with one another than with other players who may play a similar strategic style. As we have just seen, classical tennis is not defined by strategy. It is equally well suited to the baseline or the attacking game. Neither is it defined by the nature and amount of spin a player uses. A player may hit various shots with topspin, with underspin, or hit them flat, and still play classical tennis. Playing within the classical style it is possible to hit the ball as flat as Connors, with a moderate degree of topspin as Evert, Navratilova, Agassi, and Graf do, or with heavier topspin as does Lendl. Further, it is possible to play classical tennis with either the one-handed or two-handed backhand.

Rather than strategy or spin, the classical style can best be defined in terms of more basic factors of grip and bio-mechanics of stroke production. At base, the strokes of all great classical players share five elements in common:

1. Some version of an eastern forehand grip. This is combined with an eastern or continental backhand grip for the one-handed backhand, or a left-handed forehand grip for the two-handed backhand.

2. The use of compact swing patterns with a minimum of wrist and with the hitting arm close to the body.

3. Vertical swing planes, with the racket perpendicular to the court, and smooth, high follow-throughs.

All of the players mentioned above use variations of the eastern forehand grip. Evert and Navratilova are close to having "pure" eastern grips, while Connors, Graf, Agassi, and Lendl all have various versions of the "modified" eastern grip that rotates the palm position slightly downward toward the underside of the racket. None of these players rotate the palm far enough, however, to reach the extreme position of the western grip, where the palm is turned under the racket handle. All have the bulk of their palms squarely positioned behind the racket handle, and this position is the basis for a classical forehand stroke.

The second component of the classical forehand is the use of a compact swing pattern, which eliminates, or minimizes, the role of the wrist. The role of the wrist in stroke production is one of the most widely misunderstood aspects of the game, and the subject of contradictory advice. A common tennis tip advises every player to "keep a firm wrist" on the forehand. But an equally popular school of thought argues that the wrist should be released at contact to generate additional racket head speed.

As the photos in the forehand chapter demonstrate, both these views are an inaccurate description of the wrist position on a good classical forehand. One of the distinguishing characteristics of the forehand swing of classical players is not a stiff or "firm" wrist. Rather, the wrist is slightly laid back at contact with the ball. Keeping a firm wrist implies that the wrist and arm should stay straight in line on the forehand. This will cause the hit to be late, make the swing stiff, and dramatically reduce both power and spin. On the other hand, releasing the wrist through the contact will lead to a loss of racket head control, reduced body leverage, and thus a loss in shot velocity.

In the forehand turn position for each of the players identified above, the elbow is slightly tucked in toward the waist, and the wrist is at an angle to the forearm, laid back so that the racket points vertically at the rear fence of the court. This arm position is called the double bend position. The arm stays in this double bend position— elbow in, wrist back—at the contact point, all the way through to the finish position. This arm position creates what is known as a "compact" swing pattern. In the compact swing, the arm and body move together in unison. The arm stays in, and this eliminates the common error of using too large a swing. The double bend position keeps the classical player from using too much backswing and/ or a rolled, uncontrolled followthrough.

If the wrist releases at all in the classical swing, it is as a relaxation response, and this occurs after the contact with the ball. The fact is that it is impossible to make early contact with the ball on a classical forehand unless the wrist is at least somewhat laid back. For the sake of simplicity, the models presented here demonstrate the wrist staying in this position throughout the stroke. The vast majority of players, I have found, only invite inconsistency and loss of power with any variety of wrist movement in their basic stroke pattern. In the classical forehand, the wrist is released at contact only as a last resort, for example, when running wide and stretching to get the racket on the ball, or to hit topspin when the ball is short or very low. Commentators who state that Ivan Lendl has a "wristy" forehand have never closely examined still frames of his stroke pattern. What often misleads observers is Lendl's closed face backswing. As we shall see in the chapter on the forehand, this is actually a technical advance in the nature of the backswing. It allows Lendl to maintain the essential elements of the classical forehand while hitting with as much or more velocity than any player in the game.

The third factor going into a classical stroke is the nature of the swing plane. Unlike the continental and western forehands, where the face of the racket turns over during the course of the swing, the classical forehand is based on a *vertical swing path*. This means that the racket head stays vertical, or *perpendicular*, to the court surface from ready position all the way through to the finish. Even if the wrist relaxes on the followthrough, it never turns the racket face over in relation to the plane of the court.

Topspin is a natural aspect of the classical stroke because the racket face starts below the contact point with the ball, and is accelerating upward at contact. This upward acceleration causes the racket face to brush upward across the back side of the ball, and the ball to rotate over itself, that is, to rotate with topspin, as it travels back toward the opponent. With a vertical swing path, the classical player can produce natural topspin. This means that topspin results automatically from the proper execution of the stroke without extra or conscious effort. This contrasts with the continental or western forehand (as well as an improperly hit eastern forehand) where topspin is generated by releasing the wrist at contact to increase racket head acceleration.

Another advantage of the classical style is that it not only allows a player to produce natural topspin, it allows him to vary the amount of topspin without changing his basic stroke. By accelerating the racket upward more sharply at contact, the player increases the brushing effect on the back of the ball, and this creates additional spin. Conversely, by moving the racket head through the ball on a slightly straighter line, the player can decrease the amount of spin, hitting the ball with a flatter trajectory.

A crucial aspect in generating this natural topspin is a high, complete followthrough. A logical question asked by students is: why worry about the followthrough when the ball is already off the strings? The answer is that the followthrough determines how the racket is moving at the contact, and is a crucial factor in the nature of the stroke. As discussed in detail in the individual stroke chapters, a full, high followthrough means that the racket will be accelerating at the contact point, and this acceleration is what produces pace as well as topspin.

The fourth factor that defines the classical style is the role of body leverage, the shoulders and the legs, in producing the stroke. The legendary tennis instructor Tom Stow, who coached Don Budge when he won the first Grand Slam, was once asked to reduce tennis to three words. His reply was: "Turn your shoulders." Allowed three more words, he might have added: "Coil your legs." The shoulders and the legs, rather than an exaggerated swing, are the key to maximizing power in classical tennis. Thus, in the preparation for the stroke, the position of the body at the turn is critical. As we will see in the sequence photos that follow, the shoulders must be turned fully sideways so that they are perpendicular to the net. Next, as the player steps into the shot, the knees should be fully coiled just prior to the start of the foreswing. If the shoulders are turned and the knees coiled before the racket starts forward, the classical player will automatically produce great body leverage. The rotation of the shoulders and the uncoiling of the legs will generate increased acceleration of the racket head as it moves toward the ball. This will be translated into shot velocity and topspin.

This brings us to the fifth and final characteristic of classical players—their relaxed, fluid appearance. They make playing great tennis look effortless. The reason for this is rooted in the nature of the classical style. Classical players appear to be working less hard because they minimize mechanical variables and maximize body leverage. Classical players generate effortless power, and play with an understated ease. Classical strokes are simply more efficient—there is less to do to hit the ball correctly. If you master classical stroke patterns, your game will take on this appearance, and it will have a corresponding feel. You cannot really understand the physical and aesthetic pleasure of playing this kind of tennis until you have played it yourself.

In the following chapters this is what you will learn how to do. Each chapter sets out a model for the particular stroke. In some cases, there is a basic model, and then one or more variations. On the forehand, for example, the basic forehand model uses a straight backswing, but the circular backswing and the closed face backswing developed by Ivan Lendl are presented as variations. On the backhand, there are models for the one-handed topspin backhand, the one-handed slice backhand variation, and the two-handed backhand. Furthermore, each chapter discusses how to decide which particular model, or models, to incorporate into your own game.

What I have done in the individual chapters is to try to strip away the personal variations each player develops and reduce the stroke patterns to the fewest number of possible elements. This approach provides the cleanest possible models for each stroke, models that each player can absorb and synthesize into a stroke pattern marked with his own personality and flair. If you observe players trained in the visualization system, you will see that their strokes share the basic technical elements presented here, and are usually highly reliable and effective, but no two look exactly the same. There are going to be differences in the exact length and shape of the swing, and in the amount of body rotation, spin, pace, leg action, etc., but these all are differences that fall within the boundaries of the classical tradition.

The reality is that no player will ever execute the model stroke with absolute perfection on a regular basis. The model stroke serves only as an ideal that students should strive to approximate. Its great value is in giving every player a precise image of what he is trying to do. On the court, a player who can execute his stroke models with 80 to 90 percent accuracy will play consistently excellent tennis, and, over time, develop his full potential for the game.

Despite the stroke variations and the flexibility of the models presented here, it is more than possible that other players and teaching pros will have different definitions of the "correct" classical stroke patterns. For example, some pros may disagree with my view on the acceptable range of forehand grips, or they may advocate a more extreme grip on the one-handed backhand. Others might advocate a larger, less compact backswing on the basic forehand model, or argue that the backhand backswing should be taught from the beginning with an upward looping motion. They may disagree with my belief in the necessity of a high service toss, or the footwork I advocate on the advanced serve. They may reject my emphasis on the role of shoulder rotation in the volley. Others may feel my stroke models place too much emphasis on the length and precision of the followthrough, or they may disagree with my view on an absolute minimum use of wrist.

This list undoubtedly does not exhaust the points of potential critical disagreement. In my opinion, however, none of these objections should distract from the fundamental question posed by this book—the issue of how best to teach the game. I believe that the models I have chosen provide the simplest choices for teaching sound technical strokes, and doing it in the shortest possible time. I also believe that the superiority of the models I have chosen can be easily demonstrated by working with students on the teaching court, and I encourage other teachers to prove this to themselves. But to those who choose to define classical stroke patterns differently, I say that visualization teaching technology provides the best possible chance for actually putting them into practice, as it is the only approach that works with the body's natural learning process.

The fact is that the majority of players already use some version of the classical grips, and the majority of teaching pros profess to teach some version of classical stroke patterns. The problem most players face is not in choosing how they hold the racket, or how they would like to hit the ball, but in translating those choices into effective, consistent strokes. If you go to most tennis clubs, it is common to see players gripping the racket correctly, but stroking the ball quite poorly, due to inconsistent swing patterns, inadequate shoulder turns, uncontrolled wrist action, late contact, poor leg work, or some combination of all of the above.

The failure of most players to play better lies not so much in the players themselves, or in the efforts of their instructors, but rather, in the nature of tennis instruction itself. Visualization training overcomes this fundamental weakness by approaching the game in the same way that great players have always done—instinctively, naturally, visually.

THE FOREHAND

The forehand is the most basic shot in tennis, and the stroke most players learn first. Typically, it becomes at least somewhat consistent fairly quickly, and develops into their best shot. At higher levels of play, however, this tendency is frequently reversed. Top players are often more inconsistent on the forehand side. A well-known television commentator once remarked that there were only four players in the world with good forehands. A similar pattern can also occur in recreational tennis and sectional tournament play. As a player improves and faces better competition, his forehand becomes less reliable than his backhand. How can this phenomenon be explained? More importantly, how can a player build a reliable forehand that will hold up no matter how advanced his level of play may become?

The answers to these questions lie in the technical nature of the stroke. While there is no doubt that a forehand is an easier motion for most players to learn, in some respects it is actually a more technically complex shot than the backhand, due to the position of the shoulders. To make a correct swing on the forehand, it is necessary first to turn the shoulders perpendicular to the net, and then, to rotate them back a full ninety degrees, to parallel with the net. This rotation, while relatively easy with low paced balls hit by beginning and intermediate players, becomes more and more difficult to achieve as the velocity of the rallies increases at higher levels of play. There is a common tendency for players at higher levels to abandon correct coordination of the body rotation and to rely more and more on the arm and wrist to execute the shot. This leads to inconsistency on the forehand side. This is also frequently true with recreational players who learn to get the ball over the net using the arm and wrist.

As they improve, and face better players, they are unable to execute the stroke consistently and make numerous unforced errors when they try to rely on wrist action to generate velocity and hit forcing shots.

Most of the truly great players have developed forehands that maximize the use of body leverage and minimize the role of the arm and wrist—players such as Ivan Lendl, Andre Agassi, Steffi Graf, and Chris Evert. Even the players who play with a western or continental style, Bjorn Borg, Boris Becker, or John McEnroe, have forehands that are built on superior shoulder rotation, and use of the legs for power. In this chapter you will learn a stroke model which relies on body leverage and a minimum of arm and wrist motion to execute. If you use the principles of visualization to master the forehand bio-mechanics, you will build a stroke that will be consistent and powerful at any level of play.

The classical forehand stroke demonstrated here can be hit well with either of two variations on the same basic eastern grip, as demonstrated in the grip chapter. I call these the classic eastern and the modified eastern. Both grips place the bulk of the palm of the hand directly *behind* the racket handle. Players such as Chris Evert and Martina Navratilova are close to the pure eastern grip, with Martina's grip verging on a mild continental. Lendl, Agassi, Graf, and Jimmy Connors, on the other hand, have modified eastern grips, which are rotated slightly downward toward the western.

Is there a relationship between the variations in the classical grip and the spin the player produces? Both Evert and Navratilova hit with moderate topspin, while Lendl and Agassi have heavier ball rotation. This would suggest that to achieve more spin, a player should shift toward the modified eastern. Connors, however, also uses the modified eastern grip, and he hits the ball almost completely flat. While it is true that grip plays a role in the degree of spin, it is only one factor. More important is the actual swing path the racket takes. Topspin comes from the rapid

upward acceleration of the racket face at ball contact. Thus, the correct, low racket position at the start of the foreswing is crucial to generate ball rotation. Unless the player masters a consistent stroke pattern incorporating this, he will never hit topspin consistently, no matter which grip he uses.

The primary factor, then, in deciding on your own forehand grip is not spin, but rather what feels comfortable, and what produces consistent results. If you are unsure, begin by trying the classical, or pure eastern grip. Then slide your grip slightly downward to the modified eastern position, and experiment with it. Most players, I find, tend to be more comfortable with this modified version. In terms of the stroke pattern, either can be the basis of a correct technical stroke, so it is up to you, in conjunction with your teaching pro, to find the variation you prefer.

The other major variable in the classical forehand swing pattern is the backswing. Should you learn the stroke with a simple, straight backswing, or with a circular loop, as is commonly taught by teaching pros? From the purely theoretical point of view, it could be argued that the loop is superior. This is because, with the loop, the racket head is in continuous motion. It travels in a circular path, and thus, there is unbroken acceleration toward ball contact. With the straight backswing, there is a slight pause, because, when the racket goes straight back, it must then stop, shift directions, and then start forward to the ball. Theoretically, then, the loop should generate slightly more racket head speed, and also be more fluid and rhythmic.

In my experience, however, the "theoretical" advantage of the loop rarely results in better forehands. The reverse is usually the case. Players who are taught the loop seem always to exaggerate the motion. Typically, the circular backswing becomes too large and too time consuming. The player often ends up with a gigantic swing, flailing at the ball with his arm and wrist, generating only a fraction of his potential power, and making far more than his share of unforced errors. Remember that a fundamental aspect of classical tennis is the use of *body leverage* to produce ball velocity. As we will see when we turn to the model stroke, this means that the arm must stay in the double bend position, and remain fairly close to the body throughout the stroke. This allows the shoulders and legs to play a central role in the stroke. The circular backswing tends to reduce or eliminate these crucial elements. With a large, circular swing, the arm and racket tend to move independently, instead of in smooth coordination with the rest of the body.

The straight backswing preserves the coordination of all the stroke elements in the forehand. It is also far simpler to learn. The most crucial aspect of the backswing is the position of the racket head at the moment it starts forward to the ball. With the straight motion, the racket head goes directly to the correct position, low and close to the body. Beginners feel the strength of this racket position almost immediately. Players who learn the loop often never master this correct arm and racket position, and are unable to hit up on the ball to develop topspin.

For these reasons, the primary model in this chapter is the straight backswing. If you closely observe players such as Evert and Connors, two good examples of this variety of the stroke, you will notice something interesting: although the backswing is beautifully compact, the racket head never actually stops moving. There is a small elliptical loop as the racket changes direction from backward to forward. By focusing on a straight backswing, most players will naturally develop this minimal looping motion, which preserves racket head speed and aids rhythm and timing. Stressing the full circular loop, on the other hand, will destroy other important basic elements in the stroke, and create problems that are difficult to correct later.

Having said this, I am also presenting two other versions of the backswing as *variations*. The first is the larger, classical loop discussed above. This is shown for two reasons. First, a certain percentage of players will naturally, on their own, progress from the straight backswing to the loop. If the basic mechanics of the stroke are sound, this will not cause problems, and in fact, may add slightly greater racket head speed. If this motion is natural, and producing solid stroke production, it would be counterproductive to force an arbitrary change to the straight backswing. Also, players who have learned the loop originally, but are now struggling with the stroke, sometimes do better by correcting a faulty loop, rather than trying to change to the straight backswing.

The second backswing variation presented here is the closed face loop. This is the backswing developed by Ivan Lendl. His forehand will go down as one of the best in the history of tennis. It is a model of technical excellence, power, consistency, and ball control. Yet many players, teaching pros, and commentators think of it as an unorthodox, and even idiosyncratic shot. However, I believe Lendl's forehand represents an advance in the evolution of the classical style.

The closed face backswing has mesmerized and confused most observers so that they fail to note the crucial elements the stroke shares in common with other classical forehands. These include the tremendous application of body leverage through shoulder rotation and the uncoiling of the legs, and also the double bend position of the hitting arm. A common criticism of Lendl's stroke pattern is that it is "wristy." However, still frame analysis clearly shows that he makes contact with the wrist laid back, and the elbow tucked in toward the waist—the double bend arm position associated with the classical forehand swing pattern. The wrist release, if any, comes after the ball is off the strings, and is a relaxation response at the end of the followthrough, rather than a part of the actual bio-mechanics of the stroke. As outlined in the introduction, one characteristic of any classical stroke pattern is a vertical swing plane. Lendl's closed face backswing preserves this element as well. While it is true that the face is closed through the course of the backswing, it quickly becomes vertical as it approaches contact, a position that is maintained in the course of the followthrough.

This closed face backswing is a technical advance in three respects. First, it eliminates the major danger of the open face loop, the tendency for the arm to move independently, and thus, reduce the use of body leverage in the stroke. With the face closed, the elbow is literally forced in toward the body at the completion of the backswing, so that the arm is in the correct position and the shot can be generated with the hitting arm, shoulders, and legs working in unison. Second, by closing the face, Lendl makes the circular backswing motion much more compact than with the larger traditional loop. The racket still travels in a circular path, picking up additional racket head speed, but since the circle is smaller, the path is much shorter. This allows Lendl to execute the entire stroke more rapidly, an advantage given the extremely high ball velocity of modern pro tennis.

With the large loop, some players, even at the recreational level, are unable to get the racket around to contact in time, causing their forehands to break down against powerful opponents. With the closed face backswing, the player can generate as much or more racket head speed as with the large loop, but do so in less time, ensuring early contact.

The third advantage to the closed face loop is the production of greater topspin. As the sequence photos of this backswing show, the position of the racket at the completion of the backswing is *lower* than either the straight backswing, or the traditional loop. This means that as the racket starts forward to the contact, the angle of the swing plane is steeper. Since the racket is moving upward more sharply at the contact point, the brushing effect on the backside of the ball is greater, and thus, the stroke will have increased topspin. Using the closed face backswing Lendl has maximized the amount of topspin that can be generated within the technical boundaries of the classical style.

This conclusion does not imply, however, that all or even most recreational players should adopt the closed face loop. As noted, for a beginner, the straight backswing is by far the easiest to master. It simply has the fewest variables, and is likely to lead to solid forehand stroke production in the shortest period of time. However, for advanced players, or for players who are struggling with a traditional loop backswing, the closed face is a potential option. If you are late at contact with your looped forehand or, if your stroke lacks power, experiment with the closed face. Properly executed, it will maximize your body leverage, as well as produce greater consistency.

Whichever backswing you develop, your forehand should preserve the crucial technical elements of classical stroke production. The classical forehand allows you to hit a stroke with superior pace and consistency, with the minimum number of technical variables. This will allow you to maintain a high level of execution as you improve and advance to higher and higher levels of recreational or competitive play. The following teaching progressions will show you how to do this for yourself.

CREATING THE FOREHAND SWING PATTERN

In the following sections, you will learn to hit the forehand using the principles of visualization training. Through a combination of special sequence photos and text, you will create a precise *physical* and *visual* model. This model will become your personal blueprint for developing the stroke.

First, the forehand is presented from the front view and broken down into its component parts. Accompanying this sequence is a description of the genereal technical characteristics of the stroke. Then the stroke is shown simultaneously from both the front and the side views. In these two sequences, the four key still frames are identified. These still frames will become the building blocks for learning the model stroke. They are:

1. **The Ready Position**
2. **The Turn**
3. **The Contact Point**
4. **The Finish Position**

If you observe the still frames in the context of the overall stroke pattern, you will see that passing through each of the still frames correctly will guarantee that the entire swing pattern is correct as well. In simple terms, if the swing is correct at the Ready Position, at the Turn, at the Contact Point, and at the Finish Position, it will *have* to be correct at every point in between as well.

In the following section, you will then learn how to master each of the four still frames individually, through a series of detailed checkpoints. Then you will put the correct still frames together into a complete forehand swing pattern. After, you will learn how to do muscle memory corrections, allowing you to correct your mistakes as they occur in the learning process. Finally, you will learn to create your own personal system of stroke keys for the forehand that will allow you to hit the stroke consistently in rallies and in match play.

The basic learning progressions are demonstrated with the straight backswing, which, as discussed in the introduction to this chapter, is the simplest, most reliable, and easiest to learn. In addition, however, the two backswing variations discussed above are included: the circular backswing, and the closed face circular backswing. There are also stroke keys for both variations.

1	2	3	4	5
READY POSITION	START OF TURN	THE TURN	STEP TO BALL	START OF SWING

Characteristics of the Forehand
FRONT VIEW

○ ○

Grip: The forehand begins with an eastern grip which places as much of the palm of the hand as possible directly *behind* the face of the racket. This can be seen in Frame 2, above, and also in Frame 6, where the hand is squarely supporting the racket face at contact. The proper grip ensures that the stroke will be hit with the minimum number of variables, and this simplicity is the key to consistent execution. If you are unsure about how to achieve the correct grip, the two major classical variations are demonstrated in the grip chapter.

Minimum Use of Wrist: The forehand is executed with virtually no wrist movement throughout the course of the stroke. Instead, the arm and wrist are already in the double bend position in the Ready Position (Frame 1), with the wrist slightly laid back and the elbow tucked in toward the waist. This position is maintained at the Turn (Frame 3), at the Contact Point (Frame 6), all the way through to the Finish Position (Frame 9). This distinguishes the classical forehand from both the western

6
CONTACT POINT

7
START OF FOLLOWTHROUGH

8
FOLLOWTHROUGH

9
FINISH POSITION

and the continental, which rely on the release of the wrist at impact. If the wrist releases at all in the classical stroke, it is as a relaxation response that begins near or after the Finish Position shown above. For the purposes of the model, the correct laid back position is shown here throughout the course of the stroke.

Vertical Swing Path: In the classical forehand swing pattern, the racket face remains *vertical*, or perpendicular, to the court surface throughout the course of the motion. In the Ready Position (Frame 1), the racket starts in the correct vertical position. This is maintained as the motion starts (Frame 2). At the completion of the Turn (Frame 3), the racket face is still straight up and down. This position is maintained throughout the course of the forward swing as well, at the Contact Point (Frame 6), all the way to the Finish Position (Frame 9).

Natural Topspin and Power: With a vertical swing plane the forehand stroke will produce natural topspin and shot velocity. These are generated by the swing path, the rotation of the shoulders, and the uncoiling of the legs. In the Ready Position (Frame 1), the shoulders start parallel to the net. At the Turn (Frame 3), they have rotated ninety degrees and are perpendicular. At the Contact Point (Frame 6) they are rotating back into the ball, until they are again parallel to the net at the Finish Position (Frame 9). In the Ready Position (Frame 1), the knees are flexed. At the Step to Ball (Frame 4), they are fully coiled. At the Contact Point (Frame 6), the knees uncoil into the shot, remaining slightly flexed in the Finish Position (Frame 9). This body rotation, combined with the uncoiling of the legs, causes the racket face to accelerate sharply, brushing up the backside of the ball at contact, generating power and spin.

Forehand: Four Key Still Frames
SIDE VIEW

○○○○○○○○○○○○○○○○○○○○○○○○○○○○○

STILL FRAME #1   **STILL FRAME #2**

READY POSITION   **START OF TURN**   **THE TURN**   **STEP TO BALL**

Forehand: Four Key Still Frames
FRONT VIEW

○○○○○○○○○○○○○○○○○○○○○○○○○○○○○

STILL FRAME #1   **STILL FRAME #2**

READY POSITION   **START OF TURN**   **THE TURN**   **STEP TO BALL**

STILL FRAME #4

STILL FRAME #3

START OF SWING   CONTACT POINT   FOLLOWTHROUGH   FINISH POSITION

STILL
FRAME #4

STILL FRAME #3

START OF SWING   CONTACT POINT   FOLLOWTHROUGH   FINISH POSITION

Still Frame 1
The Ready Position

○ ○ ○ ○ ○ ○ ○ ○ ○ ○ ○ ○ ○ ○

Checkpoints:

1. The Shoulders: The shoulders are parallel to the net in the Ready Position. The upper body is straight up and down from the waist. The bend is in the knees, not at the waist.

2. The Hitting Arm: The hitting arm is already in the double bend position. This means that the elbow is tucked in toward the waist, and the wrist is slightly laid back.

3. The Racket: The racket is slightly below waist level. It points directly at the net, and the face of the racket is perpendicular to the court surface.

4. The Legs: The legs are shoulder width apart, or slightly wider. The knees are flexed, and the weight is slightly forward on the balls of the feet.

Establish the Ready Position physically using the checkpoints, then create the visual image.

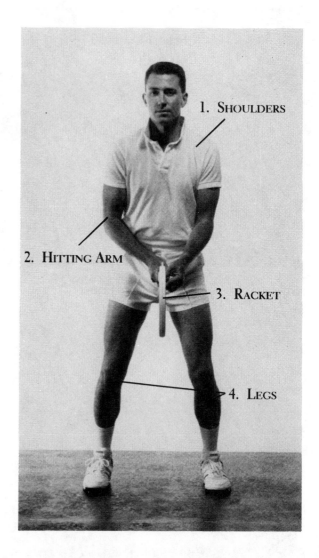

1. SHOULDERS

2. HITTING ARM

3. RACKET

4. LEGS

Still Frame 2
The Turn Position

○ ○ ○ ○ ○ ○ ○ ○ ○ ○ ○ ○ ○

Checkpoints:

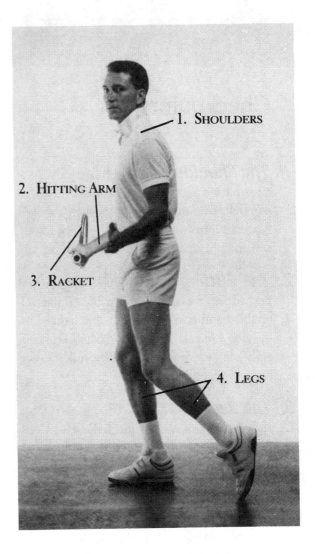

1. SHOULDERS

2. HITTING ARM

3. RACKET

4. LEGS

1. *The Shoulders:* The shoulders have rotated ninety degrees, moving from parallel to perpendicular to the net. The left shoulder is pointing directly at the net. The head is turned slightly to follow the oncoming ball.

2. *The Hitting Arm:* The hitting arm has rotated with the shoulders and remains in the double bend position. The elbow is tucked in toward the waist, and the wrist is laid back. This arm position naturally places the racket slightly below waist level.

3. *The Racket:* The racket has traveled straight back along a line, until the head points directly at the back fence. The *shaft* of the racket is parallel to the court. The butt of the racket is visible to the opponent. The *face* of the racket is still perpendicular to the court.

4. *The Legs:* Both feet have pivoted sideways and are pointing to the side fence. The weight is on the right pivot foot, and the left toes are used for balance. The knees are still flexed.

Move from the Ready Position to the Turn and establish the position physically using the checkpoints, then create the visual image.

Still Frame 3
The Contact Point

○ ○ ○ ○ ○ ○ ○ ○ ○ ○ ○ ○ ○ ○

Checkpoints:

1. ***The Shoulders:*** The right shoulder has :
tated back roughly halfway toward the origin
parallel position, and is positioned solidly l
hind the arm and racket. The upper body
still straight up and down at the waist.

2. ***The Hitting Arm:*** The hitting arm l
pushed the racket forward to the contact. T
double bend position remains unchanged, w
the elbow in and the wrist laid back. This crea
early contact, and ensures the full transfer
body leverage into the ball.

3. ***The Racket:*** The racket has moved forwa
and slightly upward to the ball. The Cont
Point is early, well in front of the front leg. T
shaft of the racket is still parallel, and the *fi*
perpendicular to the court surface.

4. ***The Legs:*** The left front foot has stepp
forward into the ball, so that the tips of the t
are parallel along the edge of a straight li
The weight is transferred forward to the left fo
and the knees are still bent, but have uncoi
slightly into the ball.

Move from the Ready Position to the Turn, ;
forward to the Contact Point. Establish the ,
sition physically using the checkpoints, then
create the visual image.

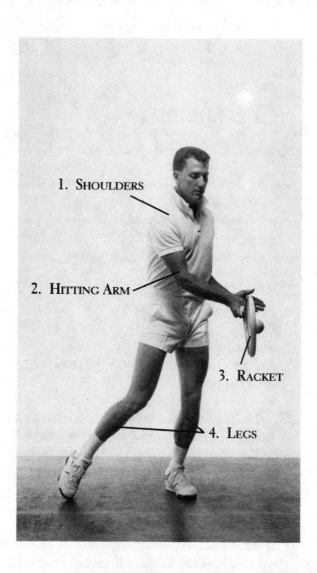

1. SHOULDERS

2. HITTING ARM

3. RACKET

4. LEGS

Still Frame 4
The Finish Position

○ ○ ○ ○ ○ ○ ○ ○ ○ ○ ○ ○ ○ ○ ○ ○

Checkpoints:

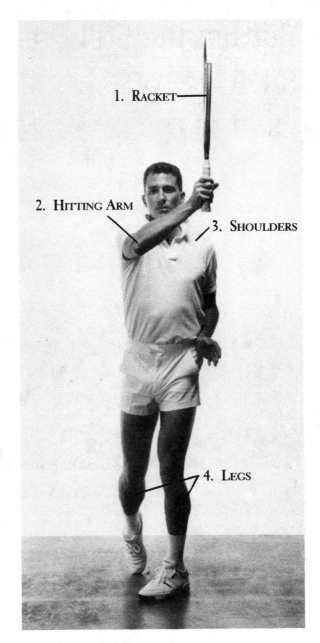

1. RACKET

2. HITTING ARM

3. SHOULDERS

4. LEGS

1. The Racket: The racket has accelerated all the way to the Finish Position. The wrist is at eye level. The shaft of the racket is straight up and down with the butt of the racket pointing down at the court. The face of the racket is perpendicular to the left shoulder and to the net.

2. The Hitting Arm: At the finish, the hitting arm is still in the double bend position, with the elbow about thirty degrees from parallel to the court. The wrist remains slightly laid back, and has not released at impact, or through the course of the followthrough.

3. The Shoulders: The shoulders have rotated a full ninety degrees until they are once again parallel to the net. The upper body is still straight up and down from the waist.

4. The Legs: The weight is now fully forward on the left front foot, and the right toes are used for balance. The knees have uncoiled into the ball, but remain slightly flexed.

Move from the Ready Position to the Turn, the Contact, and then forward to the Finish. Establish the position physically using the checkpoints, then create the visual image.

Putting the Still Frames Together
SIDE VIEW

○ ○

READY POSITION THE TURN CONTACT POINT FINISH POSITION

Executing the Forehand

Once you have learned the still frames and the checkpoints, you can put them together into a full swing pattern. The four still frames and their corresponding mental images are the key elements you must have to develop superior stroke production. Using them, you will teach your body to execute the motion effortlessly and automatically. Your goal is to execute the swing over and over until you pass through each of the still frames correctly on every repetition. This is called building *muscle memory*.

Building your muscle memory is a three-step process. First, you should practice the forehand swing *without* actually hitting balls. If possible, do this in front of a full-length mirror. Start with one swing, and build up to ten perfect swings. Make sure that you pass through each of the still frames correctly. If you are unsure, stop and refer to the checkpoints. You can also refer to the full stroke sequences at the beginning of the chapter to improve your feel for the overall motion. You may find that the model images of the still frames will spontaneously come to mind, guiding the motion. If you are struggling with a particular aspect of the motion, go back and re-create it physically and visually for yourself. Doing regular practice swings is particularly vital for beginning players.

The second method for creating muscle memory is hitting balls in *controlled drill*. A fundamental principle of visualization training is that it is impossible to develop or correct a stroke by playing games, or even by rallying. To make the process work you must have controlled conditions. This means having the opportunity to hit a stream of well-placed balls, coming at low to moderate speed. Also, the balls in controlled drill should come directly to you, and should not require extensive footwork to reach and set up for.

You can create controlled drill by working with a practice partner, or with a teaching pro, who can also help monitor your progress. However, the best way to work in controlled drill is with a ball machine rented at a club or public tennis center. The advantage of the ball machine is the great precision of the ball placement, something that rapidly facilitates the development of muscle memory.

If you are a beginner, or if at first you find it difficult to execute the entire motion, start in the Turn Position, with the racket already back and the body aligned according to the checkpoints. Once you are able to execute the stroke then begin from the Ready Position, and develop the full motion.

Work in controlled drill until you can hit ten strokes according to the model. As you hit balls, you should also do muscle memory corrections, as explained in the next section. These will allow you to monitor the technical progress of your stroke. When you can hit ten strokes with real precision, increase the speed of the balls, and the number of repetitions.

The next step in controlled drill is to add footwork, or movement to the ball. When the ball does not come directly to you—as it almost never does in a match—your goal is to beat the ball to where it is going and to set up for the stroke as if it had come to you in the first place. There are two crucial aspects to accomplishing this. The first is to turn immediately, before actually moving to the ball. This means getting the shoulders sideways to the net and the racket all the way back. Players who do not prepare first, but simply take off after the ball, often get there in time, but then must rush to finish the backswing. This makes them late at the contact, and, as a consequence, they almost never learn to execute a solid stroke. In addition, without the full shoulder turn, they may lose significant power, even if the racket preparation is correct. This is why it is crucial to turn immediately. With practice, a player may naturally start to spread the racket preparation over the duration of the movement, but this is not necessary, and is virtually impossible to achieve at the beginning. In order to learn correct preparation, the player should start with an immediate, full turn prior to any movement to the ball.

The second step in learning footwork is to move by taking short, choppy steps. The small steps allow you to position yourself precisely to the ball. Players who take large, awkward steps are either too close to the ball at contact, or too far away. Short steps allow you to control the intervals of your movement so that you can position yourself to step parallel, directly into the shot. For the split second of the hit, you should be set, with your weight forward on the front foot. Do not step through the stroke with the back foot, or allow the motion to rotate you off your base. You can analyze your footwork by doing muscle memory corrections as explained in the next section. After the stroke, return immediately to the Ready Position, and slide step back to the center of the court.

As with the basic stroke, develop your footwork working with a ball machine, if possible. Start by moving two or three steps to the ball, and gradually increase the distance. Make your movement to the ball wider and wider until you can cover both corners of the court. As you work on moving to wider balls, you will find that the length of your steps will naturally increase, but that you will come back to the small choppy steps when you reach the ball and set up to step into the shot. Next you should progress to rallies, and finally, match play. The last section of this chapter will show you how to develop and use stroke keys to execute the stroke under competitive pressure. If you find that your execution is breaking down in matches, go back to controlled drill until your confidence and consistency return.

The third technique for developing your muscle memory is pure visualization, or practicing visualizing your stroke away from the court. As explained in the Introduction, you can practice visualizations by allocating specific practice time to sit down and do them, or you can simply make use of spare moments in the course of your day. Whenever you find your mind turning to your tennis game, take the opportunity to work on your visual models. Visualize yourself executing a perfect forehand. In your mind's eye, see yourself pass through each still frame, and make sure the checkpoints are correct. Work up to ten visual repetitions. Supplement this visual work by watching video of high-quality forehand stroke execution. You can use existing instructional tapes and also tape matches of top professional players. The *Visual Tennis* video is designed specifically to enhance this modeling process.

Muscle Memory Corrections

○ ○

Muscle memory corrections are a crucial aspect in the development of a technically sound forehand stroke pattern. Accordingly, they should be a regular part of your work in controlled drill.

What, exactly, is a muscle memory correction? It is a simple procedure that allows you to recognize and correct your errors as they happen, before you can repeat them and they become ingrained in your stroke pattern.

To make a muscle memory correction, you simply freeze at the end of the stroke in your followthrough position. Do not recover for the next shot. Instead, stop exactly where the stroke finished, and be statueman.

From the statueman position, you now compare your actual finish with the checkpoints for the correct Finish Position. How does your stroke compare with the checkpoints for the racket, the hitting arm, the shoulders, and the legs? Note any differences. Now, simply adjust your body and racket from wherever they actually are to the corrected Finish Position. This is a muscle memory correction. The muscle memory correction process allows your muscles literally to feel the difference between what you did and what you were trying to do, that is, to execute the swing correctly according to the model.

By making a muscle memory correction after the stroke, you increase the probability that your *next* stroke will be correct or, at least, approximate the model more closely. By doing regular corrections in controlled drill, you will eventually bring the two in line, so that the stroke follows the model on a consistent basis. You will also find that you are hitting the stroke solidly and effortlessly. If, on the other hand, you hit a lot of forehands in controlled drill or rallies without making corrections, you will reinforce your errors, creating tendencies that will be more difficult to correct later. In developing your muscle memory corrections, you should make extensive use of video. By watching videos of your actual stroke production, you will not only see how you are deviating from your model, you will develop a much clearer image of the model stroke itself.

The following sequences show you how to do muscle memory corrections for the most common types of forehand errors: errors in the position of the racket or the hitting arm, and errors in leg position. Using the checkpoints, you can diagnose other errors that differ from the ones shown below. These examples, however, will show you how the muscle memory correction process actually works on the court.

Muscle Memory Corrections:
Racket and Hitting Arm

The following sequences demonstrate the three most common errors in the followthrough on the forehand. Each error involves incorrect positioning of the racket and the hitting arm. By freezing in the statueman position at the end of the stroke, these errors can be corrected before they become ingrained in your stroke pattern. To make the correction, compare the actual position of your arm and racket to the checkpoints for the correct forehand finish. Then simply reposition the racket as shown below.

The first error shown is a short swing, or the lack of a complete followthrough. Typically, this will result in hitting long, and in a lack of consistent topspin. The second error is releasing the wrist at contact. This results in a loss of body leverage and thus power, and also in a loss of control of shot direction. The third error is turning the racket over. Although this sometimes produces heavy topspin, it also causes great inconsistency and a high percentage of unforced errors. By correcting these, and any other errors, in controlled drill, you will develop a consistent, technically superior followthrough, a central component in hitting the forehand well.

STATUEMAN
Short Followthrough
and Correction

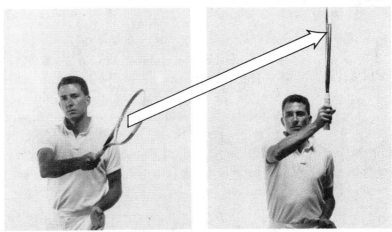

ERROR: SHORT FOLLOWTHROUGH   CORRECTED FINISH POSITION

STATUEMAN
Wrist Release and
Correction

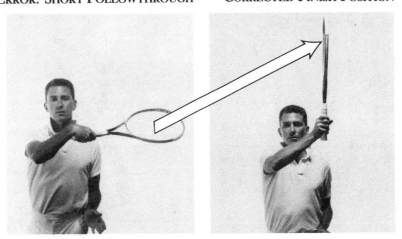

ERROR: WRIST RELEASE AT FINISH   CORRECTED FINISH POSITION

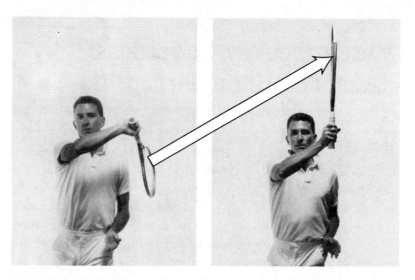

STATUEMAN
Turning the Racket
Over and Correction

ERROR: RACKET HEAD TURNED OVER AT FINISH   CORRECTED FINISH POSITION

Muscle Memory Correction:
Leg Position

The sequence below shows the most common error in leg position at the finish of the forehand: finishing with an open stance. This error is caused either by an incorrect step to the ball, or by allowing the swing to rotate the front foot off the court during the course of the swing. In either case, the player finishes the shot with an open stance, makes late contact with the ball, and loses both body leverage and control of the shot. To correct this error, freeze in the statueman position. Now, referring to the checkpoints for the legs at the finish, simply adjust your body to the correct position. Note that the tips of the toes of *both* feet should be parallel along a straight line, with the knees slightly flexed, as shown in the second photo of the correct position.

STATUEMAN
Open Stance
and Correction

ERROR: OPEN STANCE AT FINISH POSITION   CORRECTED FINISH POSITION

KEYING THE FOREHAND

The purpose of the visualization process is to help you develop a forehand that will be reliable, especially under pressure. Most forehand errors result from a breakdown in basic stroke production. If you watch most players, you will see that the level of stroke execution varies considerably from one ball to the next. When the stroke deviates too far from the correct swing pattern, it breaks down, producing an error.

The visualization training system overcomes this fundamental problem by creating a system of personal *stroke keys*. A stroke key is a single visual element of the stroke pattern that is used to activate the *entire* stroke. The process for using a stroke key is simple: in the split second before hitting the shot, the player visualizes *the image of the key*. By holding this mental image in mind, the player triggers the execution of the whole stroke pattern. The key functions as a kind of mental blueprint, which the body then naturally follows. By mastering the still frames, and learning to execute the forehand stroke in controlled drill, you have laid the groundwork for creating your stroke keys.

The following section outlines a half dozen of the most effective keys for this stroke. Determining which of these keys are most useful for your game is something you must do by trial and error. Theoretically, an image of any part of the stroke could be an effective key. Each of the four still frames is a potential key, as are the individual *checkpoints* for each of the still frames. By working in controlled drill, you must determine whether a given key consistently activates your forehand stroke. If it does, the key is an *active key*.

In my experience, the single most powerful key for the forehand is the image of the Finish Position. Thus, the image of the Finish Position is the first forehand key presented here, and the first key you should test for yourself. First, do a practice swing and freeze in the Finish Position. Make sure each of the checkpoints is correct. Now close your eyes, and visualize yourself in the correct Finish Position. You will probably see yourself in your mind's eye from over your shoulder and from slightly behind, and also, from about the waist up. This is what I call the *player's perspective*. The image of the Finish Position, as well as several of the other keys, are therefore presented from this viewpoint. As you see the image of the finish in your mind, give it as much detail as possible. This image will now become the blueprint for the execution of the correct stroke.

Now, test the key by working in controlled drill. As the oncoming ball approaches, visualize your image of the Finish Position. Hold the picture in your mind's eye, and as you swing, make *the real racket* overlap the image. You will find that the image will function as a magnet, attracting the racket to the correct Finish Position. As you hit balls, work to make the racket and the image correspond as precisely as possible. Monitor your success in doing this with muscle memory corrections. Until you work with the finish key, there is no way to understand how powerful it is, or how consistent it can make your stroke execution. Once the key is solid in controlled drill, you can test it in rallies and then matches.

You may want to experiment with slight variations of the finish key by focusing on one or more of the checkpoints, such as the double bend arm position, or the wrist at eye level, etc. Test each variation in the same fashion described above. As the oncoming ball approaches, visualize the image of the key. Make your real arm, racket, wrist, etc., overlap the image. Do this for ten to twenty balls. If the stroke pattern improves, then this key is *active* for you, and you should add it to your stroke key chart.

As noted in the introduction, a second major source of unforced errors on any stroke is the tendency to overhit the ball, usually in the attempt to hit a winner. When most players have an opening to win a point, they regularly try to hit the ball too hard, often ending up with an unforced error. This is particularly true on the forehand, which most players consider to be their best weapon. The tendency can be attributed to overexcitement, but also to a fallacy in the way players think about the stroke. It is a common assumption that using more muscle will lead to more ball velocity, and hence the belief that to hit a winner you should hit the ball as hard as possible.

In terms of the physics of the stroke, the truth is completely the reverse. When players overhit the forehand, they associate the higher level of muscle tension they feel in their arms with a harder shot. But if we examine what is happening to the racket at contact, we can see this is not the case. When a player muscles the ball, he tenses his arm and takes a shorter stroke, concentrating on the contact point and reducing the length of the followthrough. But with this tense, short followthrough, the racket is actually *decelerating* as it approaches the ball, since the swing comes to a stop shortly after contact. Because it is the speed of the racket head that imparts velocity and spin, the use of excess muscle creates the opposite effect from what the player intends. It slows down the racket at contact. Without topspin to give the shot an arcing flight, he is also more likely to hit the ball either into the net or out of the court. Unfortunately, our nerve endings do not extend into the racket head. Thus, there is no way for the players to feel directly what is happening at the moment of ball contact. We can feel only what is happening in our hitting arm, not in the racket head itself. Too many players make the mistake of associating muscle tension in the arm with racket head speed.

In reality, by relaxing and stroking to the correct Finish Position, the player ensures that the racket head acceleration will be maximized. This will, in turn, maximize both pace shot velocity and ball rotation. The role of the followthrough in generating power explains the effortless quality that we associate with the strokes of the great pro players. They hit the ball with tremendous velocity, yet their strokes seem fluid and effortless. This is because they rely on good technical execution, rather than on brute force. They maintain a certain level of relaxation, even under great pressure. This allows their rackets to do the work through natural acceleration. When players ask me how to hit the ball harder, the answer is to relax, and execute the stroke. If the Finish Position is correct, then the racket will generate pace naturally and automatically. Beyond this, additional velocity comes from the legs, as will be explained below.

In addition to the Finish Position key, there are two other basic keys for the forehand. These are the image of the turn and the image of the contact point. If you have difficulty with either of these aspects of the stroke, these keys will eliminate the problem. For some players, they may also prove as effective, or even more effective, than the Finish Position in activating the entire stroke pattern. You should experiment with them in controlled drill to determine if this is true for your game.

Finally, there are three supplemental forehand keys. The first shows you how to key the stroke by visualizing the palm of the hand as the face of the racket. For many players, this key will be helpful in eliminating wrist release at contact, and also, in coordinating the proper roles of the shoulders and hitting arm throughout the stroke. The last two keys are more advanced. The first demonstrates the role of the legs in generating additional power. The second key shows you how to create additional topspin by hitting up on the ball more sharply at contact. Experiment with these keys when the bio-mechanics of the basic stroke pattern are solid.

One important aspect of developing your keys is correlating specific keys with your most frequent errors. The ultimate benefit of the stroke key system is that it teaches every player to understand the types of mistakes he makes and how to correct them on the court. What are your tendencies, and what are the counteracting keys? This process is called *tendency analysis*. For example, if you or your teaching pro discover that your contact is consistently late, you will want to work extensively with the image of the contact point as a key. Or, similarly, if you find that you are having difficulty with the preparation of the racket and/or the body position, you should create a key using the image of the Turn.

As you experiment with developing and refining your keys, systematize them into a personal stroke key chart. In the last section of the book, I include a sample chart to serve as a model. The chart has two parts. First it identifies up to four keys that are usually active on the stroke. Second, it provides tendency analysis. In this section, the player lists his typical errors, and with them the counteracting keys he has developed for each tendency.

One of the great difficulties most players face in actually playing the game is knowing what to think on the court. Often they are consumed by negative thoughts about their own game, about their opponent, or about strategic situations that occur in the course of a match. Worse, their minds often wander to something else entirely—to virtually any topic other than tennis. It is important in tennis that the mind be continually focused during play. Great players concentrate almost instinctively. As noted, some previsualize their shots spontaneously, others, have made it into a conscious technique. Unfortunately, this is rarely the case below the top levels of the game. Many players do not realize that they are not really concentrating, and most teaching pros have no systematic approach for teaching mental focus.

The stroke key system provides a framework for overcoming these problems and creating concentration on the court. Since it is based on a series of images, the entire system is *nonverbal*. As noted in the Introduction, the game simply moves more quickly than a human being can think, at least in words. The images of stroke keys provide a method for producing consistently high-quality tennis because they can flow through the mind at the same speed the game is actually played on the court.

The learning procedure for creating your stroke keys is identical to that for mastering the still frames. First, establish the position physically, referring to the checkpoints that accompany the image. Next, close your eyes and create an image of the position in your mind's eye, giving it as much detail as possible. Notice how the position feels physically, and make the image and the feeling correspond in your mind. Now test the key in controlled drill. As the ball approaches, hold the image of the key in mind; as you swing, make your racket, hitting arm, shoulders, etc., overlap the image of the key. Determine whether the key is active, and if so, add it to your personal stroke key chart.

Keying the Forehand: The Finish Position from the Player's Perspective

○ ○ ○ ○ ○ ○ ○ ○ ○ ○ ○ ○ ○ ○ ○ ○ ○ ○

As discussed above, the image of the Finish Position is the single most effective key to activate the forehand for most players. If the finish is correct, then the entire stroke pattern is usually correct as well. The finish key also eliminates the tendency to overhit on the forehand, and actually maximizes pace and topspin.

      The finish image is presented from the player's perspective—how most players actually see themselves in their mind's eye, from over the shoulder, and slightly behind. Note the checkpoints for the stroke: the wrist at eye level, the hitting arm in the double bend position, the shaft of the racket vertical to the court, and the face of the racket perpendicular to the left shoulder. Establish the position physically, then create the image. Test the key in controlled drill.

Keying the Forehand: The Turn Position from the Player's Perspective

○ ○ ○ ○ ○ ○ ○ ○ ○ ○ ○ ○ ○ ○ ○ ○ ○

One of the most difficult problems for any player to correct is an error in the Turn Position. If the Turn is incorrect, it leads to late contact and poor body leverage. Doing muscle memory corrections at the end of the stroke does not reveal or correct this error. The solution is to key on an image of the

Turn. By holding the image of the Turn at the start of the stroke, the player can guide his body and racket into the correct position, quickly correcting a serious technical flaw.

The image shown here is, again, from the player's perspective, over the shoulder, the way that most players visualize themselves. Note that the shoulders are fully turned. The racket head points straight back to the back fence. The shaft of the racket is parallel to the court, and the face of the racket is perpendicular. The arm is in the double bend position. Establish the position physically, and create the mental image. Now test the key in controlled drill.

Keying the Forehand: The Contact Point from the Player's Perspective

○ ○ ○ ○ ○ ○ ○ ○ ○ ○ ○ ○ ○ ○ ○ ○

Although the correct finish will usually produce an early Contact Point, some players find that the image of the contact itself is a more effective key for the forehand. If late contact is a tendency, this key will correct it.

Early contact ensures that the stroke will have the maximum body leverage, and hence, shot velocity. Early contact is also what gives the shot a solid and effortless feeling. Again, the key is created from the player's perspective. Note the checkpoints. First, the racket is well in front of the front leg. The wrist is slightly laid back with the elbow in toward the waist. The shaft of the racket is horizontal, and the face of the racket is perpendicular to the court. Establish the position physically and then create the mental image. Test the key in controlled drill.

Keying the Forehand:
The Palm of the
Hand Is the
Face of the Racket

○ ○ ○ ○ ○ ○ ○ ○ ○ ○ ○ ○ ○ ○ ○ ○ ○ ○

THE SEQUENCE ABOVE SHOWS THE IMAGE OF THE PALM AS THE FACE OF THE RACKET AT THE TURN, THE CONTACT POINT, AND THE FINISH POSITION.

One of the most common technical errors on the forehand is releasing the wrist at contact. This tendency detaches the racket head from the body and destroys the power and consistency of the shot. To correct this tendency, visualize the palm of the hand as the face of the racket. This will keep the wrist slightly laid back throughout the swing. Establish the physical position for each of the three frames above, then create the visual image. Test the key in controlled drill by visualizing a still image of the palm at one of the three key frames, or a mini-movie of the entire motion.

50

Keying the Forehand: Using the Legs for Power and Topspin

○ ○ ○ ○ ○ ○ ○ ○ ○ ○ ○ ○ ○ ○ ○ ○ ○ ○

If you have developed your forehand properly, you should already be getting leg leverage in your shot. This key will show you how to increase it to its full potential.

The front thigh muscle, or the quadricep, is the strongest muscle in the body. When you bend the knees at the step to ball, you coil the quadricep as if it were a spring. As the racket sweeps forward to the Contact Point, the spring uncoils into the shot. By increasing your knee bend, you can increase this uncoiling effect at contact. This increases the acceleration and the brushing action of the racket face on the ball. The result is more pace and topspin. The stroke will feel effortless and the swing will still be smooth and relaxed, but will have noticeably more velocity and ball rotation. Create the physical position shown above by maximizing your knee bend at the step to the ball. Then create the visual image. Test the key in controlled drill.

Keying the Forehand: Hitting Up on the Ball for Topspin

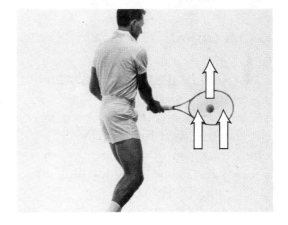

○ ○ ○ ○ ○ ○ ○ ○ ○ ○ ○ ○ ○ ○ ○ ○ ○

The forehand swing pattern you have developed is designed to produce topspin automatically. If the racket face is vertical to the court at contact, the strings will brush the back side of the ball, causing the ball to rotate over itself. But the ability to hit up on the ball, and therefore the amount of topspin generated, can be increased using this key. As you improve and face players who hit with more velocity, you will find you need additional spin to control the ball and keep it in the court. The only change required to alter the amount of spin is a slight increase in the steepness of the swing plane. The racket face should remain vertical, but move more sharply upward at contact, as the arrows show. Establish the physical position shown above, and create a visual image of hitting up, with the racket brushing the face of the ball. Test the key in controlled drill.

Variation:
The Circular Backswing

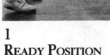

1
READY POSITION

2   3
PATH OF THE CIRCULAR BACKSWING

4
THE TURN

Advantages of the Circular Backswing: As noted at the start of the forehand chapter, the circular backswing, at least in theory, generates more racket head speed because the racket is in continuous motion along the path of a circle, rather than stopping at the end of the backswing. Instead of taking the racket back directly along a line to the Turn Position, the path of this backswing is in a semicircular loop. As the shoulder turn starts, the racket moves *upward* from the Ready Position along a curved arc (Frame 2). At the highest point, the tip of the racket is roughly even with the top of the head (Frame 3). The racket then descends along the same arc to the Turn Position (Frame 4). Thus the backswing has traced the circumference of a half circle. Some players will develop this larger looping motion naturally, and execute the forehand well using it. Also, players who were taught the loop initially, but find that it is now causing problems, may find it easier to correct the flaws than to change to a straight backswing.

Similarities to Straight Backswing: Note that during the course of the circular motion, the elbow stays bent, tucked in toward the waist. At the completion of the Turn (Frame 5), the racket is in virtually the same position as in the straight backswing; it has simply arrived there by an alternate route. Once the Turn is complete, the forward motion of the stroke follows the same path as in the straight backswing. Thus the stroke has the same general technical characteristics and bio-mechanical simplicity as the straight backswing forehand, producing natural body leverage, power, and topspin.

Keying the Circular Backswing:
The Position of the Hitting Arm

○ ○

 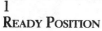  

1
READY POSITION

2
START OF THE TURN

3
THE TURN

The key to executing the circular backswing correctly is maintaining the correct hitting arm position throughout the motion. The common tendency, however, is for the arm to get out away from the body, so that it is moving independently from the body and the swing is too large. The result is a backswing that takes too long to execute, contact that is late, and a stroke hit primarily with the arm, and with little body leverage.

The antidote to this tendency is to key the stroke on the hitting arm position. As the arrows in the sequence above show, the elbow should stay in, pointing toward the waist throughout the backswing. In effect, the backswing revolves around the pivot point of the elbow, so that at the completion of the turn, the hitting arm is in the perfect double bend position. The player is now in position to execute the rest of the stroke according to the classical forehand model presented above.

Create your own circular backswing key using the images above. The key can be an image of the arm position at any point in the backswing, or a mini-movie of the entire motion. Test the key in controlled drill, and, once it is solid, in rallies and match play. In addition to the specific keys for the circular backswing, the remainder of the stroke should be keyed using the same images for the straight backswing forehand. Experiment with these, as well as the backswing keys, in creating your forehand stroke key chart.

53

Variation:
The Closed Face Backswing

○○○○○○○○○○○○○○○○○○○○○○○○○○○○○

1
READY POSITION   2   3 **PATH OF THE CLOSED FACE BACKSWING**   4
                                                                                   THE TURN

Differences from the Circular Backswing: As in the circular backswing, the closed face backswing has a semicircular arc, but with two differences. First, the racket head is tilted downward in the Ready Position (Frame 1). Second, for the first two feet, the racket starts back along a straight line (Frame 2). Only then does the racket start to move upward on a circular path (Frame 3). At the highest point, the racket head is at shoulder level. From here it starts downward on the same arc, until the completion of the Turn (Frame 4). At the Turn, the face of the racket is still tilted downward. It will automatically become vertical as it approaches the ball. Players looking for more power and spin can consider trying the closed face backswing, as well as players struggling to correct problems with the classic loop.

Advantages of the Closed Face Backswing: The first advantage of the closed face backswing is that it is more compact than the classical loop. With the closed face, the racket comes up to about shoulder level at the highest point, versus the classical loop, which reaches the top of the head or higher. This means that the stroke can be executed more quickly, because the racket travels a shorter distance. Yet because the motion is still circular, the acceleration is continuous, and thus produces increased racket head speed and shot velocity. The second advantage of the closed face loop is that it produces more topspin. This is because, at the completion of the backswing, the racket head is lower (Frame 4). This produces a steeper swing plane, more brushing effect at contact, and thus, more ball rotation.

Keying the Closed Face Backswing: Closing the Racket Face

○ ○

1	2	3
READY POSITION	**START OF TURN**	**THE TURN**

The key to executing this backswing is achieving the correct racket face position at the start of the stroke. Although Ivan Lendl keeps his racket vertical in the Ready Position, a player working on this variation can ensure that the motion starts correctly by waiting for the ball with the racket face already closed, at about forty-five degrees to the court. As the arrows show, the face remains closed as the racket goes back (Frame 2), then up and around, and down to the Turn (Frame 3). Note that as the racket starts up on the circular part of the motion, the elbow moves up and away from the waist. However, if the face remains closed, the elbow will automatically be forced back in toward the waist at the completion of the backswing. This will ensure the preservation of body leverage in the stroke.

Use the images above to create your own key, or keys, for the closed face backswing. An active key can be an image of the racket face closed at the start, at any part of the motion, or a mini-movie of the entire motion. It could also be the correct double bend position of the arm, with the elbow in to the waist and the face still slightly closed at the completion of the backswing.

Test each key in controlled drill, and once it is solid, move on to rallies and match play. In addition to the backswing keys noted here, the remainder of the stroke should be keyed on the same images as the straight backswing forehand. Compile your keys into your forehand stroke key chart.

55

THE BACKHAND

As we have seen, it is possible to play classical tennis with either a one-handed or a two-handed backhand. The question every player has to answer is: which stroke will work best in my game?

In discussing the relative advantages of the two strokes, there are two factors to consider. The first consideration is strategic: which backhand is better suited to my style of play? The second consideration is practical: which backhand can I develop and learn to execute most quickly?

Turning first to the strategic question, there are pluses and minuses on both sides, but generally, the one-handed is better suited for attacking tennis, and the two-handed for baseline play.

Although it is possible to volley well with two hands once you are at the net, the two-handed backhand is, usually, a liability on approach shots and in the mid-court game. This is due to the difficulty of hitting low volleys with two hands, and also, the greater difficulty of hitting with slice. Without slice, two-handers are simply less effective on short balls, low balls, approach shots, and first volleys. In these situations, to get the racket head under the ball, the two-hander has to push the ball up into the air, making a weaker and more defensive shot.

The one-handed backhand, on the other hand, is supremely versatile in the attacking game. A one-handed player can take a low ball, or a short ball, hit a sliced approach shot, and follow it to the net. Because of this ability to hit with underspin, as well as the slightly extended reach, the one-handed backhand is also superior on low volleys and half-volleys. The key to playing attacking tennis is to be able to make these difficult half-court volleys, and these require the use of slice to get the ball up over the net and down inside the baseline.

Two-handed players who are determined to slice effectively are forced to develop a separate one-handed shot. Bjorn Borg and Mats Wilander, two of the greatest two-handers of all time, both developed a one-handed slice to overcome the limitations of the two-handed style. But this alternative is difficult for most players. The bio-mechanics of the two strokes are so different that going back and forth between them requires tremendous mental and physical flexibility. Few players who try to combine the two-handed drive with a one-handed slice ever succeed in producing both backhands consistently. Thus, throughout the history of the game, it is not surprising to discover that the great serve and volley players have all played their backhands with one hand.

Conversely, almost without exception, the great two-handed players in the modern era have been baseliners. First, the two-handed shot, if properly executed, is a more powerful shot. At best one-handed players can hit their backhands with about 85 or 90 percent of the pace on their forehands. But the two-hander can be hit with at least as much and sometimes with more power than the forehand. Therefore, a two-hander will generally have more ball velocity on the backhand side than his one-handed counterpart. This makes the two-handed backhand a formidable shot in baseline rallies and on return of serve. It is not unusual for the backhand to become the stronger side for a two-hander, forcing his opponents to play to his forehand side.

Second, it is easier to hit the two-handed shot with topspin, and to vary the amount of topspin. The relative ease of producing spin makes the two-handed shot at least the equal of the one-hander for passing shots. Also, because the stroke is produced with bio-mechanics that are similar to those of the forehand, high balls are much less of a problem for the two-hander. With two hands, the player can hit up through a high ball with relative ease, producing good pace and heavy topspin. The one-handed player, by com-

parison, is forced to play most high balls with slice, and cannot usually generate the same pace as a two-hander on a comparable ball, let alone generate topspin. While it is true that the bio-mechanics of the two-handed shot make it slightly more difficult to set up for running balls, the great two-handed champions, as well as thousands of successful junior players, have proved that the reduced reach of the stroke is not a major drawback, as was once commonly thought. Actually, in a backcourt rally, all other factors being equal, the two-handed player usually has the advantage.

This is not to imply that one-handed players cannot play outstanding baseline tennis. We need look no further than Ivan Lendl to see how effective the one-handed backhand can be from the backcourt. Steffi Graf, already one of the greatest women players of all time, is another excellent example of a one-handed backhand player who wins from the backcourt. Given the success of these two players, it is hard to conclude that the one-handed backhand is always deficient in the backcourt. In fact, the one-handed style has some clear advantages of its own in backcourt play. The one-handed stroke can be hit with slice, hit flat, or hit with topspin, all with only slight variations in the basic stroke pattern. This means that in a backcourt rally the one-handed player can vary the pace and spin of the ball at will, upsetting the rhythm and neutralizing the pace of a two-handed opponent.

Just as it is impossible to claim that the one-handed backhander never wins from the baseline, it is also incorrect to assume that two-handed players never win at the net. Jimmy Connors has always mixed volleys effectively into his overall game. Chris Evert has done the same thing at various points in her career. Bjorn Borg, the quintessential baseliner, played serve and volley tennis in capturing his last Wimbledon title, beating off the challenge of the young John McEnroe. And the South African champion Frew McMillan, one of the greatest volleyers of all time, volleyed with two hands on *both* sides.

For most players, however, these types

of detailed strategic comparisons are less important than a second, more practical consideration: which shot can be developed most easily and most rapidly, and which shot will be most consistent and most effective for the individual player? In American junior tennis, the last fifteen years have seen the two-handed backhand become the dominant choice. There is a reason for this trend: for junior players, and for many adults as well, the two-handed shot is *far* easier to learn initially, and can become a reliable stroke, at times, almost immediately. The fact is that most junior players do not have the strength to hit the one-handed backhand effectively until the age of fourteen or even sixteen. With players starting at earlier and earlier ages, this can mean years of frustration trying to develop the one-handed shot. The two-handed backhand, however, requires less strength than the one-handed backhand, or the forehand for that matter, and is therefore far easier for many players to learn.

Another major drawback in learning with one hand is that a one-handed player must master hitting the ball with slice as well as with topspin. Without slice, a one-handed player is almost defenseless against a high ball to the backhand, or against a short low ball. Once mastered, the variety the slice offers becomes a strength, but attempting to master two spins simultaneously is a serious difficulty for a beginning player. Usually, it is necessary to spend months solidifying either the slice or the topspin drive before the other can be added, and this protracted learning process puts the one-handed player at a decided disadvantage in the interim.

From the point of view of the teaching pro, it is usually counterproductive to teach the one-handed backhand to juniors. Occasionally, of course, there are junior players who are exceptions, and who have the extra strength or superior timing to develop a one-handed stroke at an early age. Also, junior players who have the inclination (and the volleying ability) to play attacking tennis should consider either persevering with the one hand or switching from two hands to one as soon

as they are physically strong enough. But generally junior players at all levels are better off with a two-handed backhand because it will allow them to enjoy playing the game in the shortest period of time, and allow them to play it well. For most juniors, it is simply ridiculous to spend five or six years trying to play tennis without a backhand.

The same argument can be made for many beginning adults, particularly women. Because the two-hander is so much quicker to learn, and because it requires less strength, beginning women pick it up as quickly as the forehand. Often this is also true for experienced women players who have struggled for years with ineffective one-handed backhands. After hitting only a few balls with the two-handed shot, many find their backhand problems are solved. Any woman player who has consistent problems on the backhand side should definitely experiment with switching to two hands.

In some cases this same line of reasoning applies to male players. However, it is generally more difficult for adult men to learn with two hands. First, the two-handed backhand is technically very similar to a left-handed forehand. Therefore it requires that a player be at least somewhat ambidextrous, so that his left arm and left hand can guide the stroke. Second, it requires greater physical flexibility, because of the additional body rotation required to hit the two-handed shot, something we will discuss in detail later. While rarely a stumbling block for junior or women players, these two requirements usually make it harder for a man to develop the shot. For whatever reasons, most adult men tend to be more right-side dominant, and also, considerably less flexible than women. Thus, for beginning men, the two-handed backhand is an awkward, stiff shot, unlikely ever to become a flowing, natural stroke. The same is true for an experienced male player with a weak backhand who decides to experiment with the two-hander. Although it is worth trying two hands, the majority of men will progress more quickly toward a natural stroke if they learn to hit with one hand.

Occasionally, of course, the reverse is true. The final decision must be made based on the combined judgment of the student and the teaching pro. Usually, after a period of experimentation, the choice becomes obvious. As a rule of thumb, I start junior players by showing them the two-handed backhand. I start beginning men with one hand, and beginning women with two. If they do not make initial progress, then it is definitely worth experimenting with the alternate style, until it becomes clear which will work best for the given player.

If you choose the one-handed style, it will be necessary to learn both the topspin drive and the slice. To be a complete one-handed player, it is necessary to have both shots. In the beginning stages, however, it is impossible to learn them simultaneously. Rather, a player should work to solidify one as a basic backhand, and add the other only when this has been achieved. The question then becomes, which should you learn first? In my teaching experience, I have found most players are more comfortable learning the flat or moderate topspin drive. For this reason, I have presented the one-handed topspin drive as the basic model for learning the bio-mechanics of the stroke, and the one-handed slice as a variation.

A significant percentage of players, however, will have the natural tendency to come under the ball. There is no way to predict which will work for you. The best way is to start with the model for the topspin drive, and then see what happens. If, in learning the topspin drive, you or your pro detect that you are tending naturally to hit under the ball, then you should recognize this tendency, switch gears, and develop the slice.

Although the majority of players will gravitate to the flat or topspin drive, for the minority who have a natural affinity for slice, it may actually be an advantage. With slice you can play the ball anywhere on the court, whether it is high or low, deep or short. With the one-handed topspin drive, it is extremely difficult to come over these balls. Also, the slightly more compact nature of the slice stroke makes it possible to hit balls

when you are rushed, when you are unable to set up completely, or when you are forced to hit on the run. Again, because of the compact and versatile nature of the stroke, it is usually the basic pattern on return of serve. Ken Rosewall, who had one of the most beautiful and most effective backhands ever, hit with moderate slice and never found it necessary to come over the ball. However, I have found that it is virtually impossible, initially, to teach a player to hit the slice one-handed backhand—unless he or she shows a natural affinity for the stroke.

Most one-handers will be more comfortable with the topspin drive, and learning this first has advantages of its own. First, it can usually be hit with more pace. Because it can also be hit with varying degrees of topspin, it is superior for passing shots, and also, because of the superior pace, for forcing the play in baseline rallies.

Turning to the one-handed models themselves, some students of the game will notice that both the topspin and underspin strokes presented here have straight backswings. The objection may be raised that most experienced players do not use a straight backswing. Rather, they bend the elbow up at the start of the backswing, raising the racket head to about shoulder level first, and dropping it down only as the racket approaches the contact point. It is true that, for an advanced player, this loop backswing may offer an advantage. The looping motion helps add a rhythmic quality to the stroke, and also, it makes the motion more continuous, which may in turn produce slightly more racket head speed. Trying to perfect the loop backswing from the outset, however, is almost certain to arrest, or more likely, prevent, development of a sound overall stroke.

The problem with teaching the loop backswing is that it tends to result in an "elbow lead." This means that the player's elbow remains bent too long so that it moves through the swing *ahead* of the racket. The elbow lead is, in fact, probably the most common technical flaw among one-handed players. With the elbow leading the stroke, the contact point can never be correct. Instead it will always be disastrously late, well behind the front edge of the body. From this contact position, a player has insufficient leverage to execute a solid stroke, and produces instead a weak, uncontrolled shot.

One of the most crucial aspects of *either* one-handed shot is that the arm must be straight at contact so that the ball is played in front of the body. With the straight backswing this is much easier to achieve. The arm is in the correct hitting position already, and it is simply a matter of keeping it that way throughout the course of the swing. In contrast, the loop backswing requires that a player move his arm into the hitting position in the midst of the swing.

With all the other factors that a player must control to learn a new stroke, it is asking too much for him to start with his elbow in the wrong position. Having the arm straight at contact is far more important than any small improvement in rhythm or racket head speed stemming from a loop backswing. Usually, a player who learns to hit with the straight backswing will begin to loop naturally, once the mechanics are solid and he is hitting the shot with confidence. But since the difficulties it causes far outweigh its marginal benefits, I have excluded it from my basic models. In this respect, the backhand models are analogous to those for the forehand. Both place the arm in the correct hitting position at the start of the stroke, a position that remains unchanged throughout the movement. This eliminates unnecessary variables and is a key to consistent stroke production. If your natural inclination is toward the two-handed backhand, you will avoid, at least initially, the problem of choosing between two variations of the basic stroke. Although, as noted, there are disadvantages to hitting certain balls with two hands, it is at least possible to play everything with the basic two-handed stroke pattern. Depending upon how successful you are playing low balls and short balls, you may eventually experiment with adding the one-handed slice. But this is something mainly for advanced players to consider.

Turning to the two-handed stroke pattern itself, it should be noted that in the model presented here, both hands are used for the *entire* stroke, and remain on the racket handle at the end of the followthrough. It is true that some two-handers let go at the contact point, or shortly thereafter. Borg did this from the beginning, and Jimmy Connors has as well in the latter stages of his career, although, as a younger player, he almost always played the shot with both hands. I think it is crucial for most players to use the full two-handed stroke. In fact a case can be made that Borg's backhand was not a true two-hander, but rather a "one-handed push," since he hit it with an extreme eastern backhand grip, and used the front arm at least as much, if not more than the back arm to generate power. For the true two-hander, as we will see, the back left arm should dominate the swing. This is what makes the shot so effective and easy to learn—it is hit with biomechanics that are very similar to those of a left-handed forehand. Letting go in the middle of the swing confuses the relationship between the front and back arms in making the hit, introduces additional variables that are difficult to control, and adds no appreciable benefit to the effectiveness of the stroke. The two-handed model used here is what I call the "true" two-hander. It is the stroke used by Chris Evert, Mats Wilander, and the young Connors. It will provide you with the most consistent and effective stroke if you choose the two-handed backhand.

In the sections that follow, you will see how to hit both the one-handed and the two-handed backhands using visualization techniques. As discussed, you may need a period of experimentation, working with your teaching pro or coach, to decide which is best for you. But the basic problem most players face on the backhand side is not only deciding how many hands to use, but developing effective stroke production with *either* style. Through visualization you can create a solid technical foundation for either stroke. Some players go through their entire tennis lives living in fear of their backhands. Using the stroke patterns in this book, combined with a little hard work, your backhand can become a shot you look forward to hitting. It could even become the strength of your overall game.

CREATING THE ONE-HANDED TOPSPIN BACKHAND SWING PATTERN

As was the case with the forehand, the heart of the visual approach to learning the one-handed topspin backhand is a series of still frame sequence photos. These sequences will serve as a blueprint for creating your own swing pattern. Through visualization techniques, you will learn a precise *physical* and *visual* model of the stroke.

As with the forehand, the shot is first demonstrated from the front view, and broken down into its component parts. Accompanying this sequence is a description of the general technical characteristics of the stroke. On the next four pages, the stroke is presented simultaneously from both the front and side views. These sequences isolate the four key still frames. The still frames are:

1. **The Ready Position**
2. **The Turn**
3. **The Contact Point**
4. **The Finish Position**

By looking at the overall sequence, you can see how passing through each of the four positions correctly will guarantee that the entire swing pattern is correct. If the swing is correct at the Ready Position, at the Turn, at the Contact Point, and at the Finish Position, it will *have* to be correct at every point in between as well.

Following the same progression as with the forehand, the next section teaches you to master each of these four positions through a series of checkpoints. Then, you will put the still frames together into a complete one-handed topspin backhand swing pattern. The next section shows you how to do muscle memory corrections, eliminating your errors as they occur. Finally, you will learn how to create your own personal system of stroke keys for the one-handed topspin backhand that will allow you to hit the stroke consistently in actual play and under competitive pressure.

1	2	3	4	5
READY POSITION	START OF TURN	THE TURN	STEP TO BALL	START OF SWING

Characteristics of the One-Handed Topspin Backhand FRONT VIEW

○ ○

Grip: The one-handed topspin backhand begins with the classical eastern backhand grip. The grip shift takes place immediately at the Start of the Turn (Frame 2). If you are unsure of the correct backhand grip, it is explained in the grip chapter.

Differences from Forehand: The primary difference between the forehand and the one-handed backhand is that on the backhand the hitting shoulder is *automatically* in front when the body reaches the Turn (Frame 3). On the forehand, the hitting shoulder must rotate ninety degrees to reach the Contact Point. On the backhand, the hitting shoulder is positioned at the front edge of the body *before* the start of the swing. Hence the one-handed backhand is hit with less body rotation. The motion

6
CONTACT POINT

7
START OF
FOLLOWTHROUGH

8
FOLLOWTHROUGH

9
FINISH POSITION

is something like the swinging of a gate on a hinge. The arm and racket are the gate, locked together in one piece, swinging on the hinge of the shoulder, making it vital that the arm and racket stay *straight* throughout the entire motion.

Minimum Use of Wrist: This straight arm position means that the one-handed backhand is hit with a minimum of wrist action. The position of the wrist, once the grip is changed, remains the same throughout the motion. With the arm straight and the wrist locked at the Start of Swing (Frame 5), the contact cannot help but be in front of the body (Frame 6)

Vertical Swing Path: As with the forehand, the one-handed topspin backhand is hit with a vertical swing path. This means the racket face stays perpendicular to the court surface throughout the motion. This vertical position can be clearly seen at the Ready Position (Frame 1), the completion of the Turn (Frame 3), the Contact Point (Frame 6), and the Finish Position (Frame 9).

Natural Topspin and Power: With the racket face vertical, the one-handed player will produce natural topspin. At the Contact Point, the vertical racket face brushes upward along the back side of the ball (Frame 6). This brushing action causes the ball to rotate over itself automatically. An additional source of topspin is the uncoiling of the legs. As the player Steps to Ball (Frame 4), his knees are fully bent. At the Contact Point (Frame 6), the uncoiling happens automatically, continuing through to the Finish Position (Frame 9). This causes increased acceleration of the racket head, and maximizes the brushing effect on the ball. In addition, this uncoiling of the legs, combined with the early contact in front of the shoulder, maximizes body leverage on the ball, creating natural power and shot velocity.

One-Handed Topspin Backhand: Four Key Still Frames · SIDE VIEW

○ ○

STILL FRAME #1   **STILL FRAME #2**

READY POSITION   **START OF TURN**   **THE TURN**   **STEP TO BALL**   **START OF SWING**

One-Handed Topspin Backhand: Four Key Still Frames · FRONT VIEW

○ ○

STILL FRAME #1   **STILL FRAME #2**

READY POSITION   **START OF TURN**   **THE TURN**   **STEP TO BALL**   **START OF SWING**

STILL FRAME #3

STILL FRAME #4

CONTACT POINT   START OF FOLLOWTHROUGH   FOLLOWTHROUGH   FINISH POSITION

STILL FRAME #4

STILL FRAME #3

CONTACT POINT   START OF FOLLOWTHROUGH   FOLLOWTHROUGH   FINISH POSITION

Still Frame 1
The Ready Position

○ ○ ○ ○ ○ ○ ○ ○ ○ ○ ○ ○ ○ ○ ○

Checkpoints:

1. The Shoulders: The shoulders face the net in the Ready Position. The upper body is straight up and down from the waist. The bend is in the knees, not the waist.

2. The Hitting Arm: The hitting arm is positioned so that the elbow tucks into the waist. This is the same as for the forehand. Wait with the forehand grip.

3. The Racket: The racket is slightly below waist level. It points directly at the net. The face of the racket is perpendicular to the court surface.

4. The Legs: The legs are shoulder width apart, or slightly wider. The knees are flexed, and the weight is slightly forward on the balls of the feet.

Establish the Ready Position physically using the checkpoints, then create the mental image.

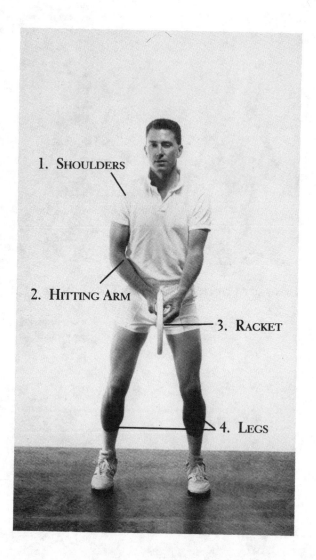

1. SHOULDERS

2. HITTING ARM

3. RACKET

4. LEGS

Still Frame 2
The Turn Position

○ ○ ○ ○ ○ ○ ○ ○ ○ ○ ○ ○ ○ ○ ○

Checkpoints:

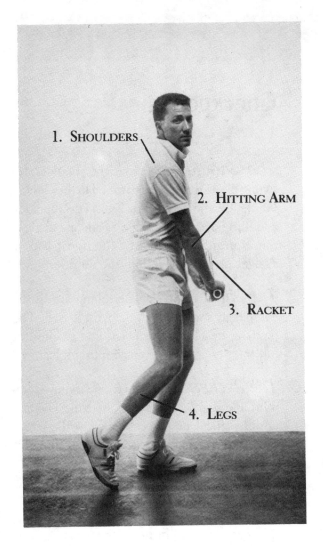

1. SHOULDERS

2. HITTING ARM

3. RACKET

4. LEGS

1. The Shoulders: The shoulders have rotated ninety degrees, and have moved from parallel to perpendicular to the net. The right shoulder is pointing directly at the net, and the head is turned slightly to follow the oncoming ball.

2. The Hitting Arm: The hitting arm is straight. The racket hand is positioned in line with the middle of the back leg. This naturally positions the racket below waist level.

3. The Racket: The racket has traveled straight back along a line until it is pointing at the back fence. The racket is horizontal, or parallel, to the court. The butt of the racket is visible to the opponent. The *face* of the racket is still perpendicular to the court.

4. The Legs: Both feet have pivoted sideways and are pointing to the side fence. The weight is on the *left* pivot foot, and the right toes are used for balance. The knees are still flexed.

Move from the Ready Position to the Turn. Establish the position physically using the checkpoints, then create the mental image.

Still Frame 3
The Contact Point

○ ○ ○ ○ ○ ○ ○ ○ ○ ○ ○ ○ ○ ○ ○

Checkpoints:

1. The Shoulders: The right shoulder has swung the arm and racket around to the Contact Point, like the hinge of a gate. The shoulders and hips have rotated slightly, and are at about ninety degrees to the net. The upper body is straight up and down from the waist.

2. The Hitting Arm: The hitting arm is still completely straight, with the wrist locked. This position creates early contact, and ensures the full transfer of body leverage into the ball.

3. The Racket: The racket face has moved forward and slightly upward to the ball. The face is still vertical or perpendicular to the court. This ensures that the racket will brush the back of the ball, creating topspin.

4. The Legs: The right foot has stepped forward to the ball, so that the toes are parallel, along the edge of a straight line. The weight is fully forward on the right foot, and the knees have started to uncoil.

Move from the Ready Position through the Turn to the Contact Point. Establish the position physically using the checkpoints, then create the mental image.

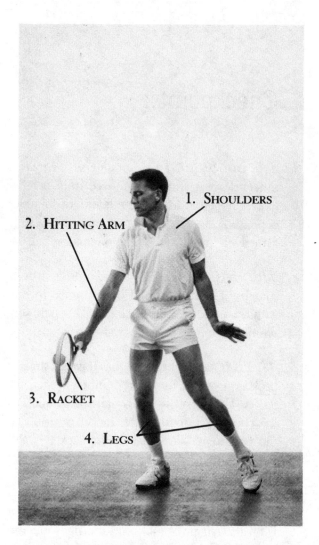

Still Frame 4
The Finish Position

○ ○ ○ ○ ○ ○ ○ ○ ○ ○ ○ ○ ○ ○ ○ ○

Checkpoints:

1. The Racket: The racket has accelerated upward to the Finish Position. The wrist is at eye level. The racket is straight up and down, with the butt pointing straight down at the court. The racket has swung about forty-five degrees past perpendicular to the net.

2. The Hitting Arm: The arm is still straight, as it has been throughout the motion. It is now in line with a line drawn across the front of the shoulders. The wrist remains locked, and has released at impact or through the course of the followthrough.

3. The Shoulders: The shoulders have rotated slightly at the finish, opening up a maximum of forty-five degrees to the net. The upper body remains straight up and down from the waist.

4. The Legs: The weight is fully forward on the right front foot. The player has come up on his left rear toes for balance. The knees have uncoiled into the ball, but remain slightly flexed.

Move from the Ready Position through the Turn to the Contact Point to the Finish Position. Establish the position physically using the checkpoints, then create the mental image.

Putting the Still Frames Together
SIDE VIEW

○ ○

READY POSITION   THE TURN   CONTACT POINT   FINISH POSITION

Executing the One-Handed Topspin Backhand

Once you are familiar with each of the key still frames and the checkpoints, you can start putting them together into practice swings. The sequence above shows you how to do this. Start in the Ready Position, move to the Turn, then to the Contact Point, and finally, the Finish Position. Make sure the checkpoints are correct at each stage. As you develop the stroke, practice the correct swing over and over, until you can execute the entire swing, automatically passing through each of the still frames correctly. This is called building muscle memory.

As noted in the forehand chapter, it is literally impossible to build good muscle memory in actual play, or even just rallying. This is true regardless of your level of play. To apply the principles of visualization properly, you must work extensively in controlled drill, hitting a steady stream of low to moderate speed balls. These balls must be well placed, and hit directly to you, so that no running is necessary to set up for the stroke. Controlled drill can be arranged by renting a ball machine at a club or public tennis center. You can also work with a practice partner, taking turns feeding balls to each other. Or you can work with a teaching pro, who can not only feed you the balls, but can help monitor your progress.

The purpose of controlled drill is to learn how to hit the stroke pattern precisely and correctly, building muscle memory and confidence. An initial goal is to hit ten one-handed topspin backhands exactly according to the model. As explained in the next section, muscle memory corrections will help you monitor your level of success in executing the stroke correctly. As soon as you are able to execute ten strokes, you can gradually increase the speed of the balls you hit, and/or the number of repetitions.

The next step in controlled drill is adding footwork, or movement to the ball. Since the ball rarely comes directly to you in a match, your goal is to beat the ball to wherever it is going and to set up for the stroke, as if it actually had come to you in the first place. As with the forehand, there are two aspects to accomplishing this. The first is making an immediate turn. This means getting the shoulders sideways to the net and the racket all the way back *before* starting the movement. Players who do not prepare first, but simply take off after the ball, often get there but rarely have time to finish the backswing once they arrive. This makes them late at the contact, and, as a consequence, they do not develop a solid, consistent stroke. Also, without the full shoulder turn, they may lose power, even if the racket preparation is correct. With practice, a player may naturally start to spread the racket preparation over the duration of the movement, but this is not necessary, and is virtually impossible to develop intentionally.

The second step in learning footwork is taking short, choppy steps. The small steps allow you to position yourself precisely to the ball. At contact, players who take large, awkward steps are invariably too close or too far away. Short steps allow you to control the intervals of your movement so that you can position yourself to step directly into the shot. For the split second of the hit, you should be set, with your weight forward on the front foot. Do not step through the stroke with the back foot, or allow the motion to rotate you off your base. You can analyze your footwork by doing muscle memory corrections as explained in the next section.

As with the basic stroke, develop your footwork working with a ball machine, if possible. Start by moving two or three steps to the ball, and gradually increase the distance. Make your movement to the ball wider and wider until you can cover both corners of the court. As you work on moving to wider balls, you will find that the length of your steps will naturally increase, but that you will come back to the small choppy steps when you reach the ball and set up for the shot. Now progress to rallies. If the stroke breaks down, return to controlled drill to reestablish the correct swing pattern.

You should also increase your muscle memory by doing practice swings away from the court. If possible, do this in front of a full-length mirror. Start in the Ready Position and execute a practice swing in super slow motion. Make sure that you pass through each of the still frames, and that the checkpoints are correct. If you are uncertain, take the time to stop and compare them with the models. Do ten perfect swings. Try to do this every day, and build up to twenty-five or even fifty swings.

A second component of building muscle memory is to practice visualizing the one-handed topspin backhand. To do this, repeat the process described above *visually*. Start in the Ready Position and see yourself execute a practice swing. Again, make sure that, in your mind, you see yourself passing through each of the still frames, and that the checkpoints are correct. Start with ten perfect swings, and as above, work up to twenty-five or fifty. If you wish, you can also do physical practice swings as you visualize.

You can do your visualization practice in other ways. Anytime you find your mind drifting to your tennis game take the opportunity to practice a few visualizations of the shot. You can do this at work, or even if you are caught in traffic. Any spare moments can be converted to working on your backhand, even if you are nowhere near a court.

The second component of off-court visualization is watching videos of good technical backhands. The *Visual Tennis* video provides you with these images, as do *The Winning Edge* and other instructional tapes.

Muscle Memory Corrections

○ ○

As with the forehand, a central aspect in the development of the one-handed topspin backhand is the process of muscle memory correction. Doing muscle memory corrections should be a regular aspect of your work in controlled drill.

Muscle memory corrections allow you to recognize and correct your errors *as they happen*, before they have the chance to repeat themselves and become habitual.

On the backhand, do your corrections as follows: at the end of the stroke, stop and freeze your body in your followthrough position. Literally freeze like a statue—do not recover after the stroke.

From the statueman position, compare your actual finish with the checkpoints for the correct Finish Position. How does your finish compare? Note the difference. Now, move your body and racket from wherever they actually are to the correct Finish Position according to the checkpoints. This process allows your muscles literally to feel the difference between what you did and what you were trying to do, execute the model stroke with a correct finish.

By making a muscle memory correction after the stroke, you dramatically increase the probability that your next backhand will be correct, or will approximate the model stroke more closely. By doing a series of corrections in controlled drill, you will eventually bring the two in line so that your stroke follows the correct pattern on a consistent basis. Conversely, if you hit a lot of backhands without correcting, you end up reinforcing your errors, and creating bad habits that will be more difficult to correct later. In working on your corrections, you should make extensive use of video. By watching video of your actual stroke production, you will not only see how you are deviating from your model, you will develop a much clearer image of the model stroke itself.

By using the muscle memory correction process, you will see radical improvements in your stroke pattern. When you are working in controlled drill, stop after approximately every five balls and do a complete muscle memory correction. As you progress, you will note that your corrections will be smaller and smaller, and that your stroke begins to follow the model more consistently. You will also notice that you are hitting the ball solidly and effortlessly.

The following sequences show you how to do muscle memory corrections for the most common one-handed topspin backhand errors. These are errors on the followthrough in the position of the racket and hitting arm, and errors in the leg position. You can diagnose your own particular errors if they differ from these by using the checkpoints.

Muscle Memory Corrections:
Followthrough

These three sequences demonstrate the three most common errors on the one-handed topspin backhand followthrough.

The first error is stopping the swing short, or the lack of a complete followthrough. The second error is the release of the wrist at contact, causing the face of the racket to turn over, rather than stay vertical. The third error is the elbow lead, in which the elbow remains bent throughout the stroke, causing late contact.

Each of these problems can be rectified by muscle memory corrections. By making these corrections in controlled drill you will develop a consistent, full followthrough, which is crucial in learning to hit the stroke consistently.

STATUEMAN
Short Followthrough
and Correction

ERROR: SHORT FOLLOWTHROUGH   CORRECTED FINISH POSITION

STATUEMAN
Wrist Release
and Correction

ERROR: WRIST RELEASED AT FINISH   CORRECTED FINISH POSITION

STATUEMAN
Elbow Lead
and Correction

ERROR: ELBOW LEAD AT FINISH POSITION   CORRECTED FINISH POSITION

Muscle Memory Correction:
Leg Position

This sequence shows the most common error in leg position on the one-handed topspin backhand. It is caused either by an incorrect step to the ball, or by rotating the front foot off the correct position during the swing. The result is that the player finishes with an open stance, making late contact, and losing both body leverage and ball control.

To correct, freeze in the statueman position. Now, referring to the checkpoints for the legs, adjust to the correct position. The tips of the toes of both feet should be parallel along a straight line, as shown in the second photo.

STATUEMAN
Open Stance
and Correction

ERROR: OPEN STANCE AT FINISH POSITION   CORRECTED FINISH POSITION

76

KEYING THE ONE-HANDED TOPSPIN BACKHAND

The goal of the visualization learning process is to develop a one-handed topspin backhand that will be consistently effective, especially under the pressures of actual play. If you observe most players' backhands, you will notice how the majority of their errors result from breakdowns in technical stroke production. Their stroke varies in the level of execution from one ball to the next. Eventually, it deviates too far from the correct pattern and breaks down, producing an error. Visualization offers a solution to this fundamental cause of inconsistency.

The crucial step in developing a reliable backhand is creating your own personal system of *stroke keys*. A stroke key is a single element taken from the stroke pattern that is used to activate the entire stroke in actual play. The process for using a key is simple: in the split second before actually hitting the shot the player *visualizes the key*. By holding this mental image in mind, the player triggers the correct execution of the entire stroke pattern.

Mastering the key still frames and learning to execute the stroke in controlled drill and in rallies are prerequisites for developing your stroke key system. Through these preliminary steps, the player develops the muscle memory that makes the use of the keys possible. Then, by using the image of the key on the court, the player triggers this reservoir of muscle memory. This gives the player a reliable method for hitting effortless, technically superior strokes in match play. The development of keys is a personal process, and must be done by trial and error over time. Theoretically, there are a dozen or more keys that could be effective. In reality, each individual will find certain keys produce the stroke almost as if by magic, while others do not.

For the one-handed topspin backhand, an active key could be the image of any one of the four still frames, or an image of any one of the checkpoints. However, as with the forehand, the single most effective key is usually an image of the Finish Position, since any stroke that finishes correctly was, in all probability, correct on its way to the finish as well.

To create the finish key, follow this procedure: do a swing and freeze in the Finish Position, making sure the checkpoints are correct. Now close your eyes and visualize yourself in that position. What I have found is that the vast majority of players will see themselves in their mind's eye from over their *opposite* shoulder. (For the backhand, this means the left shoulder.) Also, they will see themselves from about the waist up. Once you have created this image in as much detail as possible, it will become your blueprint for the stroke.

Now you are ready to test the key. Start first in controlled drill. As the oncoming ball approaches, hold your image, or blueprint, of the Finish Position in your mind. As you swing, put your actual racket directly over the *image* of the racket in the blueprint. Strive to make them overlap as perfectly as possible. With practice, you will find that the blueprint image will function almost as a magnet, attracting the racket to the correct Finish Position. Try this process for ten to twenty balls. Now evaluate the result: how well did you hit the ball? If the key produces consistently high-quality backhands, then it is an *active key* for you. Repeat the test in the rally. If it continues to be active, you are ready to try out the key in match play. You may also want to experiment with slight variations of the image, focusing, for example, on one of the checkpoints, such as "wrist at eye level," or "straight hitting arm," etc.

In addition to the Finish Position, I have provided images of the two other most effective keys for the majority of players. These are images for the Contact Point, and for the Turn, both seen from the player's perspective. If you are having difficulty with late contact, or the preparation of the racket, you should work with these keys. Some players find they are more active than the image of the Finish. Create these keys by the same process described above.

Finally, I have provided two additional keys. The first is for maintaining a straight hitting arm position throughout the course of the swing, a critical element in the one-handed backhand. The second is for increasing the roll of the legs in the shot. This key will help any player increase pace and spin once the basic bio-mechanics are solid.

As outlined for the Finish Position key above, the learning procedure for creating your stroke keys is identical to that for mastering the still frames. First, establish the position physically, referring to the checkpoints that accompany the image. Next, close your eyes and create an image of the position in your mind's eye, giving it as much detail as possible. Notice how the position feels physically, and make the image and the feeling correspond in your mind. Then test the key in controlled drill. As the ball approaches, hold the image of the key in mind, and as you swing, make your racket, hitting arm, shoulders, etc., overlap the image of the key. Once the key is solid in controlled drill, you can move on to rallies and match play.

The final step in developing your key system is tendency analysis. Each player should understand the types of mistakes he usually makes and how to correct them on the court. This means recognizing which keys counteract your most frequent types of errors.

As you experiment with developing and refining your keys, systematize them into your own stroke key chart, as explained in the final section. The chart has space for you to identify the active keys for your one-handed topspin backhand. It also has space to chart your individual tendencies, and the counteracting keys for each tendency. You can take the stroke key chart on the court with you and refer to it in matches during game changes.

As mentioned in the forehand chapter, one of the major problems most players face in matches is knowing how to think on the court, and specifically, how to maintain concentration. The stroke key system provides a method for achieving continuous focus. As noted, the game moves more quickly than human beings can think in words. Stroke keys provide a method for maintaining concentration and producing consistently high-quality tennis, because the key images can flow through the mind at the same speed the game is actually played on the court. Experiment with the keys presented here, and develop others either on your own, or in conjunction with your teaching pro. Test them in controlled drill, rallies, and in match play, and add them to your chart, updating it regularly.

Keying the One-Handed Topspin Backhand: The Finish Position from the Player's Perspective

○ ○ ○ ○ ○ ○ ○ ○ ○ ○ ○ ○ ○ ○ ○ ○ ○ ○ ○ ○

As discussed, the image of the Finish Position is usually the most powerful single key for the backhand. This is because the entire stroke pattern must be correct in order to produce a correct finish. A common question asked by students is: why is followthrough so important, if the ball is already off the strings at the Contact Point?

The answer is that the Finish Position determines *how* the racket is moving at the Contact Point, and thus the nature of the hit. The racket face must be accelerating upward and outward toward the Finish Position to create power and spin at contact. Note the checkpoints: the racket shaft is vertical, the arm straight with the wrist at eye level, and the swing has gone about forty-five degrees past perpendicular to the net. Establish the position physically, and create the mental image. Test the key in controlled drill.

Keying the One-Handed Topspin Backhand: The Turn Position from the Player's Perspective

○ ○ ○ ○ ○ ○ ○ ○ ○ ○ ○ ○ ○ ○ ○ ○ ○ ○ ○ ○

A vital aspect of the stroke is the correct execution of the Turn. The correct Turn positions the body and the racket to make a solid stroke. Many players have backhand problems that stem from an incorrect or incomplete Turn. These can be overcome by creating the key shown here. Again, this image is from the player's perspective—how most players tend to see themselves in their mind's eye. Note several key elements. The shoulders are fully turned. The racket is all the way back with the arm straight and the racket hand in the middle of the back leg. The racket face is *vertical* to the court. Establish the physical position and create the mental image. Test the key in controlled drill.

Keying the One-Handed Topspin Backhand: The Contact Point from the Player's Perspective

○ ○ ○ ○ ○ ○ ○ ○ ○ ○ ○ ○ ○ ○ ○ ○ ○ ○ ○

This image is designed to create a key for the Contact Point from the player's perspective. Although a correct Finish Position will usually result in correct contact, many players find it effective to key on the image of the Contact Point itself.

There are several important points to note. First, when the contact is well in front of the front leg the body leverage on the ball is maximized. Second the arm is straight, and the racket is horizontal to the court. From this viewpoint you can also see how continuing the swing outward and upward will result in the racket face brushing the ball, creating topspin. Establish the physical position and create the mental image. Test the key in controlled drill.

Keying the One-Handed Topspin Backhand: Straight Hitting Arm Throughout Swing

○ ○ ○ ○ ○ ○ ○ ○ ○ ○ ○ ○ ○ ○ ○ ○ ○ ○ ○ ○

THE ARROWS SHOW HOW THE HITTING ARM IS STRAIGHT AT THE TURN, THE CONTACT POINT, AND THE FINISH POSITION.

A straight hitting arm eliminates the danger of an elbow lead, and ensures that you achieve maximum body leverage on the ball. Note that the arm is already straight at the turn. From there it is only a matter of maintaining the correct alignment at the Contact Point and at the Finish Position. Establish each of the three positions shown above physically, and create the mental images. The key can be an image of the arm at any of the three positions, or a mini-movie of the entire motion. Test the key in controlled drill.

Keying the One-Handed
Topspin Backhand:
Using the Legs
for More Power and Topspin

○ ○

AT THE STEP TO BALL, MAXIMIZE YOUR KNEE BEND
TO INCREASE BALL VELOCITY AND TOPSPIN.

If you watch Ivan Lendl hit topspin backhands, you may have been struck by the tremendous leverage he gets from his legs. He has so much knee bend, occasionally he actually touches his back knee down on the court. Few players have the strength and flexibility to go down this far, but every player, once the basic stroke pattern is reliable, should try to maximize his own knee bend. By going down as far as possible and shifting the weight fully to the front (right) leg, you increase the uncoiling action of the legs into the ball at contact. This adds racket head speed and increases the natural brushing action of the strings on the ball. The result is significant additional ball velocity and topspin. Establish the position physically and create the mental image. Test the key in controlled drill.

Variation:
The One-Handed Slice Backhand
SIDE VIEW

○ ○

1	2	3	4	5
READY POSITION	**START OF TURN**	**THE TURN**	**STEP TO BALL**	**START OF SWING**

Grip: The one-handed slice backhand is hit with the same classical eastern grip as the topspin shot. Again, the grip shift takes place immediately at the start of the Turn (Frame 2). Refer to the grip chapter if you are not sure that you are using the correct grip.

Similarities to Topspin Backhand: Like the topspin version, this shot is hit with the arm straight and the wrist locked. Also, the right hitting shoulder is already in front at the completion of the Turn. The arm and racket are like a one-piece gate swinging on the hinge of the shoulder (Frame 5 through 9). The Contact is well in front of the front leg (Frame 6). Again, there is far less body rotation than on the forehand.

Differences from Topspin Backhand: The two variations of the one-handed backhand differ on two key points. First, to achieve underspin, rather than topspin, the slice backhand is hit with the racket face *slightly open*, rather than perpendicular to the court (Frame 6). Second, the backswing is slightly *higher* (Frame 3), than the topspin shot. Instead of starting below the ball, the slice backswing is made at the level of the ball, or slightly above (Frame 4). If the ball is high or low, the racket is raised or lowered accordingly. From this position, the racket face comes through the ball on a straight line, allowing the racket head to impart natural slice.

6
CONTACT POINT

7
START OF
FOLLOWTHROUGH

8
FOLLOWTHROUGH

9
FINISH POSITION

Generating Slice: To create slice, the racket must move through the Contact Point with the face slightly open, about thirty degrees to the court surface. Visualize the ball as an orange, and the face of the racket as a knife. Now, use the knife to slice off the bottom diagonal third of the ball. This will cause the strings to bite as they slide under the ball, making the ball rotate *backward* under itself, with underspin, or slice. This slicing action can be clearly seen in Frames 5 through 7. Unlike a topspin groundstroke, the slice is not hit with a vertical swing plane. However, as with a topspin forehand or backhand, the angle of the racket face to the court is set by the completion of the Turn, and then *remains unchanged* throughout the course of the swing. Compare this at the Start of Turn (Frame 2), with the Finish Position (Frame 9). This gives the shot a technical simplicity characteristic of the classical style.

Natural Power and Spin: Once the face of the racket is properly set, the underspin will be generated automatically in the course of the swing. Early contact ensures that the body weight transfers naturally into the shot. As with the case of the topspin backhand, the uncoiling of the legs will generate additional racket head speed, and additional spin and shot velocity. At the Step to Ball (Frame 4), the legs are fully coiled. At the Contact Point (Frame 6), they have released slightly into the ball, maximizing the player's body leverage on the shot.

Keying the One-Handed Slice Backhand:
The Angle of the Racket Face

○ ○

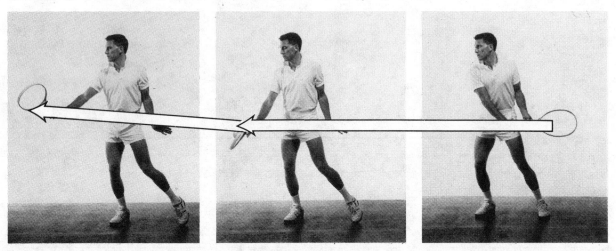

THE ANGLE OF THE RACKET FACE IS SET AT THE TURN, AND REMAINS CONSTANT THROUGH THE SWING, AT THE CONTACT POINT, AND AS THE FOLLOWTHROUGH STARTS.

The key to executing the slice variation of the one-handed backhand is to set up the racket face correctly at the completion of the Turn (Frame 1). The face should be set open at about thirty degrees to the court. The level of the racket head should be at the level of the ball, or slightly higher. Once the angle is correctly set, it remains unchanged throughout the stroke, at the Contact Point (Frame 2), and at the start of the followthrough (Frame 3). Aside from this difference, the bio-mechanics of the slice swing pattern are virtually identical with the topspin variation. The arm is straight throughout the swing, and the Contact Point itself is well in front of the front leg. Note, also, that the racket face has moved outward along the line of the shot, and only then starts upward to the Finish. It is common for players to attempt to swing sharply downward in an attempt to create slice. But this kind of radical, chopping motion will result in late contact, a loss of body leverage and pace, and a tendency for the ball to float. Instead the racket face moves through the ball on a line as shown by the arrow above. The slice is the automatic consequence of this swing plane.

Use the images above as the basis for your keys on the slice backhand. Follow the visualization process described at the start of the chapter to create an image for each of the three positions shown above. As with the topspin variation, your key can be any of the three individual frames, or a mini-movie of the entire motion. Test your keys in controlled drill, then move on to rallies and finally match play. In keying the slice backhand, you should also experiment with the keys for keeping the arm straight and increasing the knee bend presented in the section on the topspin backhand.

Do the off-court visualization work for the slice variation, just as you did in developing topspin.

CREATING THE TWO-HANDED BACKHAND SWING PATTERN

The following section demonstrates the two-handed backhand in a series of still frame photos. These sequences are the blueprint you will use to create your own swing pattern for the shot. As is the case with the forehand and the one-handed backhand, they provide the images for learning a precise *physical* and *visual* model of the stroke.

First, the stroke is broken down into its component parts from the front view, and the general technical characteristics of the stroke are described. Then, the two-handed stroke is shown simultaneously from the front and side views, and the four key still frames are isolated. As with the other groundstrokes, these four still frames are:

1. **The Ready Position**
2. **The Turn**
3. **The Contact Point**
4. **The Finish Position**

Looking at the overall sequence and the four key still frames, it is obvious that if the swing is correct at each of these points, it will be correct for the course of the whole swing as well.

Once the key frames are identified, the next section teaches you how to master each of these four still frames through a series of detailed checkpoints.

Then, the following section shows you how to put the still frames together into a smooth, continuous stroke pattern. Following this, you will see how to do muscle memory correction for the two-handed backhand, correcting your mistakes as they happen. Finally, you will see how to create your own system of stroke keys. These will allow you to execute the shot effortlessly and automatically even under competitive pressure.

1
READY POSITION

2
START OF TURN

3
THE TURN

4
STEP TO BALL

5
START OF SWING

Characteristics of the Two-Handed Backhand FRONT VIEW

○ ○ ○ ○ ○ ○ ○ ○ ○ ○ ○ ○ ○ ○ ○ ○ ○

Grip: The two-handed backhand is hit with *two* forehand grips. The right-hand forehand grip is maintained, and a second forehand grip is added on top with the left hand. The two hands are together, touching, but not overlapping, on the racket handle (Frame 2). This should be your grip in the Ready Position. An alternative is to shift the right hand to a backhand grip, making possible the later development of a one-handed slice backhand. Both variations are demonstrated in detail in the grip chapter.

Differences from One-Handed Backhand: The bio-mechanics of the two-handed shot are radically different from the one-handed. On the two-hander, the *left* arm is the hitting arm. The left hitting arm and the left shoulder dominate the swing, with the right arm adding additional, but secondary support. Thus, the two-handed shot is technically almost identical to a *left-handed* forehand. It relies on rotating the left shoulder and the left hitting arm forward to the contact (Frames 5, 6, and 7), unlike the one-handed shot, in which the right, *front* shoulder dominates the swing.

Minimum Use of Wrist: The position of the left hitting arm on the two-hander is the same

6
CONTACT POINT

7
START OF
FOLLOWTHROUGH

8
FOLLOWTHROUGH

9
FINISH POSITION

as the right hitting arm on the forehand. This means the arm is in the double bend position, with the elbow in toward the body, and the wrist slightly laid back. The arm and wrist are already in this position in the Ready Position (Frame 1). This then remains unchanged throughout the stroke, with the wrist still laid back at the Finish Position (Frame 9).

Vertical Swing Path: The two-handed backhand is hit with the racket face vertical to the court surface throughout the course of the swing, as with the forehand and the one-handed topspin backhand. The racket face is perpendicular to the court in the Ready Position (Frame 1), at the Turn (Frame 3), at the Contact Point (Frame 6), and at the Finish Position (Frame 9). This simple vertical swing path eliminates wrist and arm movement as variables in the stroke, and is a major factor in the ease of learning the two-handed backhand, and in executing it consistently.

Natural Topspin and Power: With the racket face vertical to the court as described above, the player who hits a two-handed backhand will produce topspin simply by executing the swing. The topspin is generated by the rotation of the shoulders, the upward path of the swing, and the uncoiling of the legs. At the Contact Point (Frame 6), the shoulders are rotating forward. The racket face brushes up the back side of the ball, causing the ball to rotate over itself automatically. At the Step to Ball (Frame 4), the knees are fully coiled. The knees release into the ball at the Contact Point (Frame 6), increasing the acceleration of the racket, the brushing of the strings on the ball, and hence the amount of topspin. This leg leverage, when combined with early contact and the full rotation of the body, also creates great natural power and shot velocity.

Two-Handed Backhand:
Four Key Still Frames · SIDE VIEW

○○○○○○○○○○○○○○○○○○○○○○○○○○○○○○○

STILL FRAME #1   **STILL FRAME #2**

READY POSITION   **START OF TURN**   **THE TURN**   **STEP TO BALL**   **START OF SWING**

Two-Handed Backhand:
Four Key Still Frames · FRONT VIEW

○○○○○○○○○○○○○○○○○○○○○○○○○○○○○○○

STILL FRAME #1   **STILL FRAME #2**

READY POSITION   **START OF TURN**   **THE TURN**   **STEP TO BALL**   **START OF SWING**

STILL FRAME #3

STILL FRAME #4

CONTACT POINT   START OF   FOLLOWTHROUGH   FINISH POSITION
                        FOLLOWTHROUGH

STILL FRAME #4

STILL FRAME #3

CONTACT POINT   START OF   FOLLOWTHROUGH   FINISH POSITION
                        FOLLOWTHROUGH

Still Frame 1
The Ready Position

○ ○ ○ ○ ○ ○ ○ ○ ○ ○ ○ ○ ○ ○

Checkpoints:

1. *The Shoulders:* The shoulders face the net in the Ready Position. The upper body is straight up and down from the waist. The bend is in the knees, not the waist.

2. *The Hitting Arm:* The hitting arm is positioned so that the elbow tucks into the waist. The hands are together with two forehand grips.

3. *The Racket:* The racket is slightly below waist level. It points directly at the net. The face of the racket is perpendicular to the court surface.

4. *The Legs:* The legs are shoulder width apart or slightly wider. The knees are flexed and the weight is slightly forward on the balls of the feet.

Establish the Ready Position physically using the checkpoints, then create the mental image.

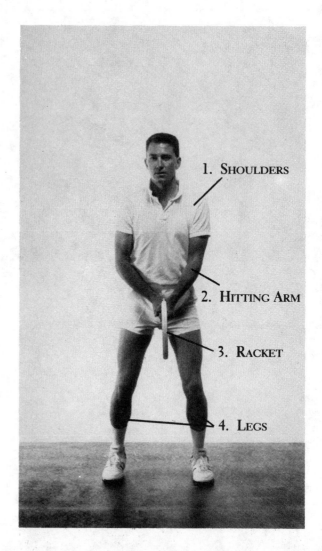

1. SHOULDERS

2. HITTING ARM

3. RACKET

4. LEGS

Still Frame 2
The Turn Position

○ ○ ○ ○ ○ ○ ○ ○ ○ ○ ○ ○ ○ ○ ○

Checkpoints:

1. The Shoulders: The shoulders have rotated ninety degrees, and are now perpendicular to the net. The right shoulder is pointing directly at the net, and the head is turned slightly to follow the oncoming ball.

2. The Hitting Arm: The back, left hitting arm is in the double bend position, elbow into the waist, wrist slightly back. The right hand is in line with the middle of the back leg.

3. The Racket: The racket has traveled straight back along a line, and points at the back fence. The *shaft* of the racket is parallel to the court surface. The butt of the racket is visible to the opponent. The *face* of the racket is perpendicular to the court.

4. The Legs: Both feet have pivoted sideways and are pointing to the side fence. The weight is on the left pivot foot, and the right toes are used for balance. The knees are still flexed.

Move from the Ready Position to the Turn. Establish the position using the checkpoints, then create the mental image.

1. SHOULDERS

2. HITTING ARM

3. RACKET

4. LEGS

Still Frame 3
The Contact Point

○ ○ ○ ○ ○ ○ ○ ○ ○ ○ ○ ○ ○ ○ ○

Checkpoints:

1. The Shoulders: The shoulders have rotated back almost halfway to their original position. The back shoulder is solidly behind the arm and racket, absorbing the impact of the hit. The upper body is still straight up and down from the waist.

2. The Hitting Arm: The hitting arm is still in the double bend position, and has brought the racket forward to the Contact Point. This position creates early contact and the full transfer of body leverage.

3. The Racket: The face has moved slightly upward to contact, creating the brushing effect for topspin. The face of the racket is perpendicular to the court, and the contact is early, in front of the front leg.

4. The Legs: The right front foot has stepped forward so the toes are parallel, along the edge of a straight line. The weight is fully forward on the right foot, and the knees have started to uncoil into the ball.

Move from the Ready Position through the Turn to the Contact Point. Establish the position physically using the checkpoints, then create the mental image.

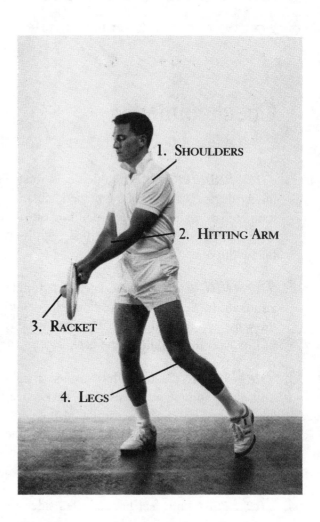

1. SHOULDERS

2. HITTING ARM

3. RACKET

4. LEGS

Still Frame 4
The Finish Position

○ ○ ○ ○ ○ ○ ○ ○ ○ ○ ○ ○ ○ ○ ○

Checkpoints:

1. The Racket: The racket has accelerated upward to the Finish Position. The left wrist is at eye level. The shaft of the racket is straight up and down, with the butt pointing directly down at the court. The edges of the frame are perpendicular to the right shoulder and to the net.

2. The Hitting Arm: The left arm finishes in the double bend position. The elbow is bent, about thirty degrees from horizontal with the court. The wrist has not released, and remains laid back. The *right* arm has collapsed at the elbow.

3. The Shoulders: The shoulders have rotated back fully parallel to the net, as they were in the Ready Position. They have rotated a full ninety degrees through the course of the shot.

4. The Legs: The weight is fully forward on the right front foot. The player has come up on his left rear toes for balance. The knees have uncoiled into the ball, but remain slightly bent.

Move from the Ready Position to the Turn, Contact, and the Finish. Establish the position physically using the checkpoints, then create the mental image.

Putting the Still Frames Together
SIDE VIEW

○ ○

READY POSITION   **THE TURN**   **CONTACT POINT**   **FINISH POSITION**

Executing the Two-Handed Backhand

After you master the four key still frames, you can start to put them together into a full swing pattern. The sequence above shows you how. Start in the Ready Position, move to the Turn, then forward to the Contact Point, and, finally, to the Finish Position. Make sure your checkpoints are correct as you pass through each still frame. You are now ready to start building your muscle memory for the stroke. This should be done in three ways.

First, practice the correct swing without actually hitting balls. Do this in front of a full-length mirror if possible. Start with one swing and build up until you can do ten perfect swings, passing through each still frame with the checkpoints correct, without having to think about it.

The second component to building muscle memory is hitting balls in controlled drill. As noted for the other strokes, controlled drill is crucial in establishing correct technical swings. Initially, you must hit balls that have low to moderate pace, and which come directly to you. As you work in controlled drill, do muscle memory corrections to measure your success. Some common corrections for the two-handed backhand are demonstrated in the next section. As with your practice swings, work in controlled drill until you can hit ten strokes with minimal or no correction. You can set up controlled drill practice by renting a ball machine, working with a practice partner or with a teaching pro. When you can hit ten strokes with real precision in controlled drill, you should increase the speed of the balls and the number of repetitions.

The next step in controlled drill is adding footwork, or movement to the ball. Your goal in moving to the ball is to set up as if the ball had come directly to you in the first place. Because it is difficult to hit the two-handed shot with an open stance, the stepup is even more important than with the other groundstrokes. At the split second of the hit, you should be set, with your weight forward on the front foot.

The two key elements in a correct set up are the same as for the forehand, or the one-handed backhand variations. The first is making an immediate turn. This means getting the shoulders sideways to the net and the racket all the way back *before* starting the movement. The second is positioning yourself to the ball with short, choppy steps. An immediate turn means that when you get to the ball you will be ready to hit, rather than having to take time to complete the backswing. Without a good turn, the player will never establish early contact, and will also lose the valuable additional body leverage that comes from the two-handed shot. With experience, players often naturally spread the racket preparation over the course of the movement, but this is not necessary and is virtually impossible to develop initially. It will happen automatically in the course of practice, if at all.

The second aspect to good movement, taking short, choppy steps, allows you to position yourself precisely so that you can step parallel into the shot. Players who take large, awkward steps are usually either too close or too far away from the ball at contact. With short steps, you control the intervals of your movement.

Develop your footwork working with a ball machine, if possible. Start by moving two or three steps to the ball, and gradually increase the distance. Make your movement to the ball wider and wider until you can cover both corners of the court. You will find that the size of your steps will naturally lengthen out, but that you will come back to the smaller steps when you actually approach the ball to set up for the shot. When you feel confident in these variations of controlled drill, progress to rallies. If the stroke breaks down, return to controlled drill to reestablish the correct swing. You can analyze errors in your footwork by doing muscle memory corrections as explained in the next section.

The third aspect of developing good muscle memory is to practice visualizing the stroke away from the court. Visualize yourself hitting a perfect two-handed shot. Again, build your repetitions up to ten, or more. You can practice your visualizations by allocating specific time to do this, or by doing them in your spare moments at work, whenever your mind drifts to your tennis. Another aspect of working visually on your backhand is to watch video. The *Visual Tennis* video is the only instructional tape with extensive images of two-handed stroke production. You can also tape players such as Chris Evert, Mats Wilander, or Andre Agassi. Another good source of video is to tape yourself executing perfect practice swings, or hitting the stroke correctly in controlled drill. Incorporate this into your overall visualization program.

Muscle Memory Corrections

○ ○

Muscle memory corrections are also a basic part of developing an effective two-handed backhand. These corrections should be a regular component of your work in controlled drill.

To review, a muscle memory correction is the simple, powerful procedure that teaches you to recognize and correct your errors *as they happen*, before they can become established habits.

They should be made as follows. At the end of the stroke, stop immediately and freeze in your Finish Position. Literally freeze like a statue—do not recover for the next shot.

From this position, compare your actual Finish Position with the checkpoints for the correct Finish Position. How does your actual position compare with the checkpoints for the racket, the hitting arm, the shoulders, and the legs? Note the difference. Now, simply move your body and racket from wherever they actually are to the correct Finish Position, according to the checkpoints. The process is vital to developing a consistent stroke because it allows your muscles literally to feel the difference between what you really did and what you were trying to do—execute the model stroke with a correct finish.

By making a muscle memory correction after the stroke, you increase the probability that your next stroke will be correct, or will approximate the model stroke more closely. By doing a series of corrections in controlled drill, you will eventually bring your actual stroke in line with the model. Conversely, if you hit a lot of backhands without muscle memory corrections, you reinforce your errors, and deepen a habit pattern that will be more difficult to correct later. In working on your corrections, you should make regular use of video. By watching video of your actual stroke production, you will not only see your errors, you will develop a much clearer image of the model stroke itself.

The following sequences show you how to do muscle memory corrections for the two most common types of errors: errors in the followthrough position of the racket, and errors in leg position. You can diagnose your own particular errors, if they differ, by using the checkpoints.

Muscle Memory Corrections:
Followthrough

These three sequences demonstrate the most common errors in the followthrough on the two-handed backhand.

The first error is making too short a swing, resulting in an incomplete followthrough. This causes a loss of ball control due to lack of topspin, and also reduced pace. The second error, releasing the racket with the left hand, causes the loss of the natural body leverage coming from the left side. It also will cause the two-handed player to have difficulty controlling the direction and depth

98

of the shot and produce many unnecessary errors. The third error is breaking the wrists at contact, causing the racket face to turn over rather than remain vertical. When the wrists break, the player tends to hit the ball late, again losing power. In addition, the sudden change in the direction of the racket head makes it hard to control the amount of spin and the trajectory of the shot.

Each of these problems can be rectified by muscle memory corrections. Freeze in the statueman position and examine the position of your actual finish, and, by using the checkpoints, reposition the racket as shown. By making these corrections in controlled drill, you will develop a consistent, full followthrough.

STATUEMAN
Short Followthrough
and Correction

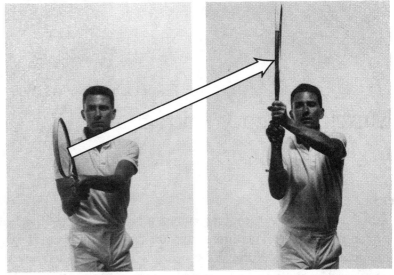

ERROR: SHORT FOLLOWTHROUGH   CORRECTED FINISH POSITION

STATUEMAN
Releasing the Left Hand
and Correction

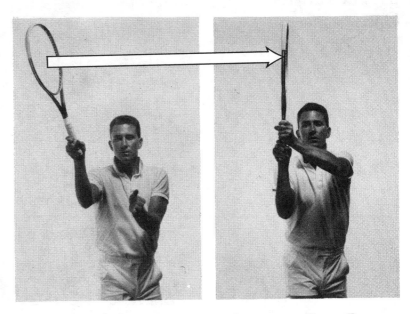

ERROR: RELEASING THE LEFT HAND   CORRECTED FINISH POSITION

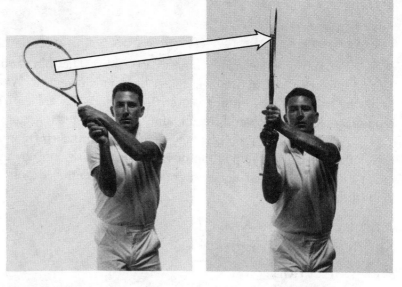

STATUEMAN
Releasing the Wrists
and Correction

ERROR: RELEASING THE WRISTS   CORRECTED FINISH POSITION

Muscle Memory Correction:
Leg Position

This sequence shows the most common problem in leg position on the two-handed backhand: finishing with an open stance. This error results either from an incorrect step to the ball, or from rotating off the front foot during the course of the swing. The result is that the contact is late behind the front edge of the body. This means a loss of body leverage, shot velocity, and ball control.

To correct this error, freeze in the statueman position. Now, referring to the checkpoints for the legs if necessary, adjust to the correct position. The tips of the toes of both feet should be parallel along a straight line, with the knees slightly flexed, as shown in the second photo.

STATUEMAN
Open Stance
and Correction

ERROR: OPEN STANCE AT FINISH POSITION   CORRECTED FINISH POSITION

KEYING
THE TWO-HANDED
BACKHAND

Once you have developed your muscle memory and are able to hit the two-handed backhand in controlled drill, you can move forward and develop your system of personal stroke keys. The purpose of the stroke key is to allow you to hit the two-handed backhand consistently in match play.

As is the case for the other groundstrokes, the image of the Finish Position is likely to be the most effective key for the two-handed backhand. Again, if the finish of the stroke is consistently correct, there is a very good chance that the entire stroke will be correct as well. The Finish Position key is the first key presented below.

Also included are the keys for the Turn and the Contact Point. If you find you have difficulty preparing correctly for the stroke, then you should work with the image of the Turn. Similarly, if you are taking the ball late, or there is an error in your position at contact causing you to lose power or ball control, experiment with the correct image of the Contact Point. Some players may also find that these keys are more effective than the Finish Position in activating the overall stroke.

The learning procedure for creating your stroke keys is identical to that for mastering the still frames. First, establish the position physically, referring to the checkpoints that accompany the image. Next, close your eyes and create an image of the position in your mind's eye, giving it as much detail as possible. Notice how the position feels physically, and make the image and the feeling correspond in your mind. Then test the key in controlled drill. As the ball approaches, hold the image of the key in your mind, and as you swing, make your racket, hitting arm, shoulders, etc., overlap the image of the key.

If you visualize the key clearly, it should function as a magnet, attracting your racket and body to the correct position. Hit ten to twenty balls in controlled drill. Rather than using the entire still frame, you may want to visualize just one aspect, such as the wrists at eye level at the Finish Position, the left hitting arm in the double bend position with the wrist laid back at contact, or the tip of the racket pointed straight back at the back fence at the Turn. Experiment with these and other aspects of the images to determine which are best for you.

In addition to these basic keys and their variations, two other more advanced keys are included. These are designed to produce more power and topspin, once the basic stroke is solidly established. The first is the use of extra knee bend. The second key is the brushing action of the racket face on the ball. Create these keys in the same fashion as the others, and test them in controlled drill first. Again, it is important that the basic stroke pattern be solid before you attempt to create additional pace and spin.

Finally, you should develop your tendency analysis for your two-handed backhand. For example, if you or your teaching pro discover that your contact is consistently late, you will want to work extensively with the image of the Contact Point as a key. Or, similarly, if you find that you are having difficulty with the preparation of the racket and/or the body position, you should create a key using the image of the Turn.

As you experiment with developing and refining your keys, systematize them into a stroke key chart. The chart, as shown in the last section of the book, has two parts. First it has space for you to identify as many as four keys that are active for your two-handed stroke. Second, it leaves space for tendency analysis. Here, the player lists his typical errors, and with them the counteracting keys he has developed. You can take the chart with you on the court, and refer to it on the game changes as necessary.

As noted in the sections on keying the other groundstrokes, a major problem most players face is maintaining concentration on the execution of their strokes. The stroke key system provides a framework for achieving this. The images of stroke keys provide a method for producing consistently high-quality tennis, because they can flow through the mind at the same speed the game is actually played on the court.

The keys presented here should be used as a guide in developing your own personal system of two-handed backhand keys. Your goal is to determine which keys are active, and which counteract your own particular tendencies. Test these keys, and others that you or your pro may create, in controlled drill, rallies, and in match play. Compile your chart from the results of this work, and update it frequently.

Keying the Two-Handed Backhand: The Finish Position from the Player's Perspective

○ ○ ○ ○ ○ ○ ○ ○ ○ ○ ○ ○ ○ ○ ○ ○

The Finish Position for the two-handed backhand is the most basic, and usually the most effective, key. If you produce a correct finish, the rest of the stroke leading up to the finish must be correct as well. If you visualize yourself in your mind's eye, you probably will see yourself from over your left shoulder. This is the visual perspective of the key as shown. Note the checkpoints: the left wrist is at eye level, the arm is still in the double bend position, and the racket is straight up and down. The front edge of the racket is perpendicular to the net, and the rear edge is perpendicular to the right shoulder. Establish the position physically and create the mental image. Test the key in controlled drill.

Keying the
Two-Handed Backhand:
The Turn Position
from the Player's
Perspective

○ ○ ○ ○ ○ ○ ○ ○ ○ ○ ○ ○ ○ ○ ○

Unless the Turn is correct on the two-handed backhand, as with any groundstroke, it will be impossible to execute a solid stroke. If you are having problems with your preparation, you should work intensively with this key. Again this key is shown from the player's perspective. Note the checkpoints: hitting arm in double bend position, with left elbow into the waist, tip of the racket pointing toward the back fence, face of the racket perpendicular to the court. The racket is also well below waist level. Establish the position physically and create the mental image. Test the key in controlled drill.

Keying the Two-Handed Backhand: The Contact Point from the Player's Perspective

○ ○ ○ ○ ○ ○ ○ ○ ○ ○ ○ ○ ○ ○ ○ ○ ○

This image is designed to help you create early contact on the two-handed backhand. Usually, a correct finish will ensure that the contact is correct as well. Many players, however, find that using the image of the contact itself is more active. If you find that you are taking the ball late, this key will solve the problem. In addition, players who want to increase their body leverage, and hence the pace of their shot, will find that taking the ball slightly farther in front will produce this result effortlessly.

This key clearly demonstrates the following elements: the shaft of the racket is horizontal, and the face of the racket is perpendicular to the court. The back left shoulder is rotating forward, driving the stroke, with the left, hitting arm in the double bend position. The weight is forward on the front foot, and the Contact well in front of the leg. Establish the position physically and create the mental image. Test the key in controlled drill.

Keying the
Two-Handed Backhand:
Using the Legs
for More Power and Topspin

○ ○

AT THE STEP TO BALL, MAXIMIZE THE KNEE BEND AND THE
WEIGHT TRANSFER TO INCREASE SHOT VELOCITY AND TOPSPIN.

One characteristic of all great two-handed players is their use of the legs in the execution of the stroke. Jimmy Connors, Chris Evert, Bjorn Borg, Mats Wilander, and recently Andre Agassi, all generate the pace of their backhand drives in great part from the legs up. By maximizing your knee bend, you guarantee that your legs will release into the shot. As the legs uncoil, they generate additional racket head speed and body leverage. This translates into power, and also, increased topspin. The use of the legs can be the difference between having a solid, consistent two-handed shot, and having the extra velocity that transforms the stroke into a weapon. As you step to the ball, shift your weight fully forward to the front foot, and go down in your knees as far as possible. Establish the position physically, and create the mental image. Test the key in controlled drill.

Keying the Two-Handed Backhand: Hitting Up on the Ball for Topspin

○ ○ ○ ○ ○ ○ ○ ○ ○ ○ ○ ○ ○ ○ ○ ○ ○ ○ ○ ○

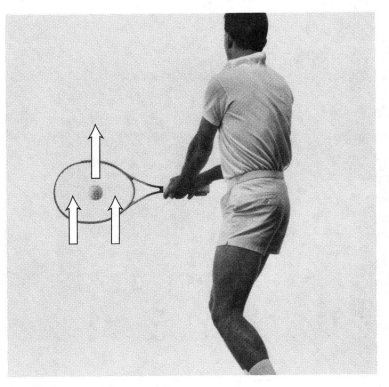

AT CONTACT, THE RACKET FACE MUST BE VERTICAL AND MOVING SHARPLY UPWARD TO GENERATE ADDITIONAL TOPSPIN.

If you hit the ball with the correct two-handed swing pattern, you should produce topspin automatically. With the racket face vertical at the contact, and accelerating upward, the strings will automatically brush up the backside of the ball and cause it to rotate over itself. As you progress as a player and hit with more pace against better opponents, you may find you need additional spin to keep the ball in the court. Topspin, by causing the ball to travel in an arc, generates additional net clearance, but also causes the ball to drop more sharply, so that it can be hit with more pace and depth without going long. Establish the key physically, and then create the mental image. Visualize the racket moving sharply upward, with the face still vertical, as shown by the arrows. Test the key in controlled drill.

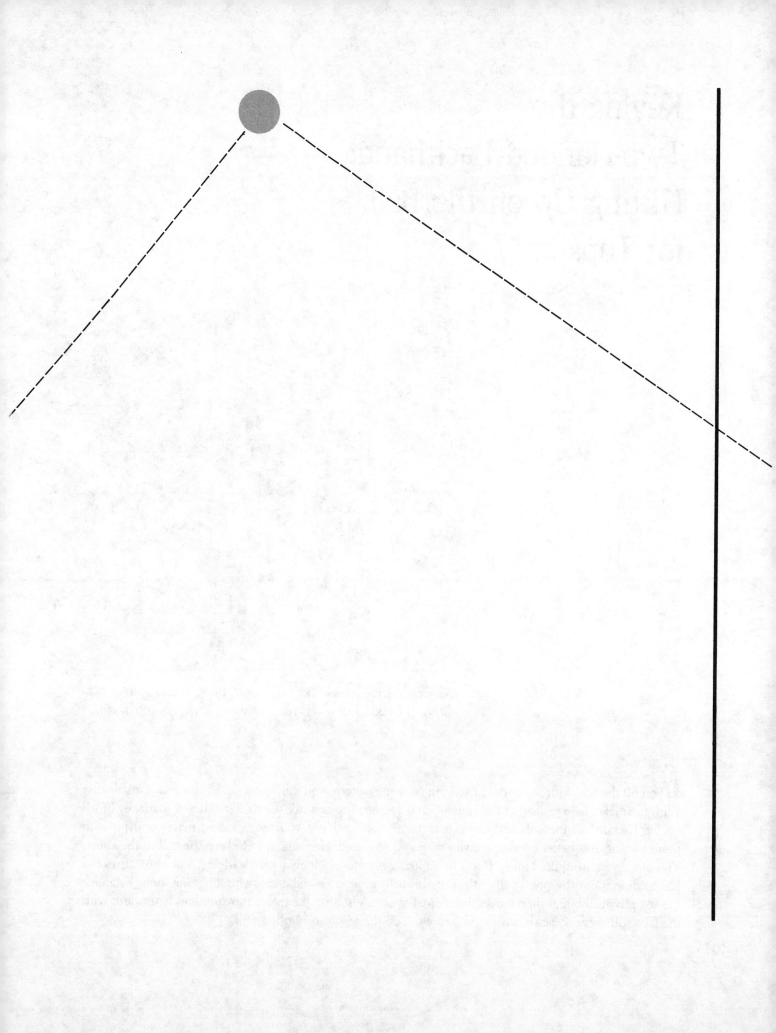

THE RELATIONSHIP BETWEEN TIMING AND POWER

As noted in the chapters on the groundstrokes, one characteristic of great classical players is their smoothness and effortless power. If you watch video of the great players, especially in slow motion, you will note that the racket flows evenly through the stroke. There is no increase in muscle tension as the racket head approaches the contact, no discrete moment when the player "strikes" ball. In fact, there is no perceptible difference between the contact point and every other point on the swing. Possibly the biggest misconception about power on the part of the average player is that hitting the ball harder takes more muscle.

Power, instead, comes from continuous racket head acceleration, and from body leverage. Body leverage is created, as explained in the stroke chapters, by shoulder rotation, by the uncoiling of the legs, and by making contact in front of the body. When the contact is in front of the body as demonstrated in the models, a player ensures that the full leverage generated by the motion will be transferred into the shot.

Therefore, as you develop your stroke patterns for your groundstrokes, you should strive to keep the rhythm of your motion even. This means, whether in controlled drill, rallies, or match play, you should let the ball set the pace. Rather than trying to increase ball velocity by swinging faster, you should imagine yourself hitting the ball back at the speed it is coming. If your technical execution is correct, you will naturally generate pace through the body leverage from the shoulders and legs.

There is a final factor that influences the power of the shot. This is the *timing* of the hit. Taking the ball on the rise, a player can generate extra velocity, without making any change in the stroke pattern itself. This is possible because by taking the ball on the rise, the shot gains velocity from the acceleration of the ball as it comes up off the court. When a tennis ball bounces, the force of hitting the court compresses the ball, partially flattening it out against the court surface. As the ball rebounds and expands back to its original size, it accelerates upward off the court, and its velocity increases. As it approaches the top of the bounce, however, it quickly starts to slow down. This deceleration continues as it reaches the top and starts to drop down. By hitting the ball on the rise, the player catches the ball when it is still accelerating, and therefore this additional velocity is automatically transferred into the shot.

It is important to distinguish here between two terms that are frequently confused. These are hitting the ball "early" and hitting the ball "in front." They are not identical and, in fact, refer to two different aspects of ball contact. Hitting the ball early refers to where the player contacts the ball in relation to the court. The "earlier" the contact, the closer the ball is to the court—the less distance it has traveled toward the top of the bounce.

Hitting in front, on the other hand, refers to where the player contacts the ball *in relation to his body*. Making contact in front, at least with classical stroke patterns, means that the contact point is in front of the edge of the body, usually with the front foot set, so that the full body leverage, from the shoulders and the legs, will be transferred into the shot. It is possible, therefore, to hit the ball in front without hitting it early. For example, the player could let the ball drop below the top of the bounce, and still position himself to strike it with a contact point in front of his body. Conversely, it is also possible to take the ball early, or on the rise, without making contact in front of the body. This is particularly true of the continental strokes. Since it is possible to hit the continental forehand equally well off the back foot, a continental player may actually make contact when the ball is already past the front edge of his body. However, he will still position himself in order to hit the ball *early*. The ball may be behind

his front foot, but he will still strike it on the rise, while it is close to the court, before it reaches the top of the bounce. Actually this is a requirement, since it is almost impossible to execute a solid continental stroke on a high ball.

As demonstrated in the groundstroke chapters, contact in front of the body is a common characteristic of all classical strokes. However, not every classical player takes the ball early. Players such as Chris Evert and Ivan Lendl usually hit the ball at the top of the bounce, or slightly on the way down. One of the great advantages of the classical style is that it allows flexible timing. Indeed, Evert and Lendl often take the ball early when the situation in a given match requires that they do. A classical player has the option to hit the ball at the top of the bounce, on the way down, or to hit it earlier, on the rise.

Early timing, or the ability to hit the ball on the rise, is a characteristic of many of the great champions in the modern game. Jimmy Connors, John McEnroe, Martina Navratilova, and Andre Agassi are players who generate power from taking the ball earlier than other players. In addition to the extra shot velocity, there is a second major advantage to early timing. By taking the ball as it comes up on the court, a player reduces the amount of time his opponent has to recover and prepare for the next shot. Not only does the opponent have to deal with a more powerful shot, he is forced to do it more quickly. If you have ever been on the court with a player of this type of timing, you are aware of the kinds of problems it can cause. The ball comes with laser-like velocity, and is on top of you, or past you, almost before you can react to it. Worst of all, the player who hits the ball early hardly looks like he is working— he is generating the extra pace simply by altering his timing, not by putting more effort into his stroke, and certainly not by using more muscle.

For players developing classical strokes, timing is a final variable with which to experiment. Rather than trying to hit the ball harder by swinging harder and muscling the ball, the classical player who wants additional power should instead experiment with hitting the ball earlier. I have found that some players, even beginners, or intermediate players with relatively poor strokes, will naturally tend to pick the ball up on the rise, without even being told to try this. Similarly, many accomplished players will consistently play the ball after the top of the bounce, and are not comfortable playing the ball early.

As with so many aspects of the game, every player must discover the exact timing that is best for his game. However, the further you progress in the game, and the higher the level of competition, the more important and valuable this ability to hit on the rise becomes. If you find that you would like more pace in your natural stroke patterns, or if you find that you are being consistently outhit by more powerful opponents, you should experiment with your timing.

As with the development of your basic strokes, start by working in controlled drill. Simply step up slightly closer to the oncoming ball, and pick it up before it gets to the top of the bounce. Keep the contact point in front and catch the ball as it is coming up off the court. You may be surprised at the marked increase in the velocity of your shot. You may also find that, initially, this velocity is more difficult to control, and that you hit more balls than usual either long or into the net. Make sure that you keep the swing smooth and relaxed, and that you follow through all the way to the finish position. You may find you need to hit up on the ball slightly more at contact to generate additional topspin to control the extra pace. Also, on the underspin backhand, you may have to hit through the ball slightly more sharply to generate more slice.

Test your early timing in controlled drill with balls hit directly to you, then add movement. If you can produce consistent strokes, progress to rallies, and finally, to matches. If you find that you have a natural affinity for early timing, you can make it a basic aspect of all your groundstrokes. Another option is to hit the ball on the rise only when you are forced to do so by your opponent.

There is no doubt that the degree of difficulty of timing every ball on the rise is much higher than letting the ball drop slightly before contact. That is why you see relatively few players who can do it consistently below the highest levels of the game. Even among the pros, many players do so only when necessity requires. One thing is certain, however: hitting the ball early is the key to producing more power, beyond the execution of a superior technical stroke pattern. If you are continually frustrated by your inability to hit with more power, this is the variable you should strive to master, rather than altering your stroke patterns, overhitting the ball, and producing needless unforced errors.

THE VOLLEY

*I*n one way, the volley is the simplest of all the basic strokes because it has the shortest swing pattern. A good technical volley has no real backswing and very little followthrough. But in another way, the volley is the most difficult. This is because when a player is at the net he is only about half as far away from his opponent, and therefore has only half the time to react and execute the stroke. Although the volley has the least complex motion, it is usually the hardest to hit successfully in matches because the player has such a brief interval.

Playing effective serve and volley tennis is the most dominating, quickest, and possibly most satisfying way to win matches. However, pure serve and volley players are probably born, rather than made. The degree of difficulty of playing serve and volley tennis is much higher than playing in the backcourt, or even playing the all-court game. In the pro game, only two great champions in the last decade, John McEnroe and Martina Navratilova, have been pure attacking players.

Few recreational players can make serve and volley their sole match strategy. But every player can learn to volley confidently using the visualization approach, and, therefore, can learn to incorporate net play into his overall strategy. This means learning to play the all-court game: coming in on short balls when appropriate, and mixing in serve and volley points against certain opponents.

The best definition I have ever heard of the volley is that it is like setting up a mirror in front of a laser beam. The goal is to redirect the laser beam in order to make a superior ball placement. It is rarely necessary to change pace or add speed to an oncoming ball to hit a winning volley. At the net, because you are half as far away from your opponent, the angles between the two players are much sharper. A ball volleyed to the sideline from the net will force a player on the baseline much wider out of the court than a groundstroke hit to the same spot. The more radical angles that are possible at the net are the key to winning placements. To hit a winning volley a player simply redirects his opponent's shots to take advantage of the superior geometry of his position.

Many players are terrified of the net because the play is so much faster there. This fear causes poor shot execution. But this situation, though fairly common, is neither necessary nor inevitable. Any player can learn to volley competently and aggressively if he approaches it correctly.

The first factor that goes into developing the volley is recognizing the crucial role of ball focus. Watching the ball as the opponent makes his shot is a prerequisite for sound volley technique. As you learn the volley in the following sections, it is crucial that you learn to react to the ball as soon as it is hit.

This is only the first step. As stated, the volley requires much less motion than a groundstroke or a serve. But the volley also differs from the other basic shots in another crucial aspect— the earlier contact point. The volley is a reaction or response shot that uses the pace of the oncoming ball. Pace on the volley comes from timing and superior body leverage. To hit the volley with the maximum velocity, therefore, the contact must be significantly further in front of the body than on the groundstrokes. This is the element the majority of recreational players fail to establish. At best, they take the ball at the front edge of the body, as they would a groundstroke. Or worse, they take a large backswing, and make contact behind the plane of the shoulders, attempting to compensate for their lack of technique by overswinging.

In fact, the foreswing on the volley *starts* at about the point where the racket is *contacting* the ball on a good groundstroke. As the racket moves forward, the correct contact point is

at least a foot further in front than a groundstroke. In professional tennis, the most aggressive and effective volleyers, players such as McEnroe and Navratilova, are also the players that make the volley look easy. This is due to their timing. By taking the ball further in front than other players, these great champions create superior body leverage. This body leverage means natural power with minimal effort, making the shot look effortless. Taking the ball early at the net is the difference between a good placement that the opponent is able to reach and play back—possibly hitting a passing shot—and a winning volley the opponent has no chance to return. Unless a player understands these differences he will never develop a consistent, effective volley.

Turning to the stroke patterns themselves, there are two major areas of dispute in the theory of the volley which must be addressed. The first is: should the player change grips at the net? The second is: should two-handed backhanders volley with one hand or two?

In my view, there is no absolute answer to the first question of whether to change grips. Jack Kramer virtually invented the serve and volley game, and he changed grips. But Rod Laver and John McEnroe, the two most devastating attacking players to follow Kramer, hit all their volleys with the same continental grip. Martina Navratilova uses the single grip as well. With the increased shot velocity in the modern era, it is probably preferable, at the pro level, to hit all volleys without grip changes.

But for most beginners, and even for some experienced players, this technique will prove much more difficult to master. Therefore, the basic volley models presented here are demonstrated with the same eastern grips as the groundstrokes. There is an additional reason for this. When first learning the volley motions, a player should learn to hit his volleys flat, without underspin, focusing on the bio-mechanics and establishing solid contact. This will happen naturally using the eastern grips.

Once the basic mechanics of the volley

are solid, however, players should experiment with the continental grip. In addition to eliminating the extra time and movement required for the grip shift, the use of the single volley grip makes it easier to hit the ball with underspin, particularly on the forehand side. Underspin gives the player more control of the ball, and is a necessity on low volleys, angled placements, and touch volleys. With the eastern forehand grip it is necessary to use the wrist to dip the racket face sharply under the ball to produce underspin. With the continental grip, however, the player can produce underspin on the forehand while still hitting through the ball on the line of the shot. The change of grip alters the angle of the racket face so that it slides under the ball automatically. The same is true to a lesser extent on the backhand volley, which also requires a slight dipping motion in the swing when hit with the eastern backhand grip, though less so than on the eastern forehand volley.

Since it is more natural to hit the underspin volleys with the continental grip, this is the grip used for the underspin variations presented here. Some players will take to the slice volley with the continental grip quite rapidly. Others, sometimes even players at higher competitive levels, are never able to hit the shot naturally, and are better off sticking with the grip switch at the net. But all players, particularly those with a preference for the attacking style, should at least test the continental grip to see if it will work better for them.

Just as was the case with the groundstroke models, I have chosen to demonstrate the one-handed volley with a straight backswing. If you watch top players, you will see that on the volley, as with the groundstrokes, they initially bend the elbow and raise the racket head as they turn to the ball. Again, this may be a source of additional rhythm and racket head speed. But for the player just trying to develop the shot, it is likely to cause insurmountable difficulties. Top players who use this mini-loop on the volley all keep the *upper* arm (from the elbow to the shoulder) even with the front edge of the shoulders. The racket

head then comes forward, in line with the upper arm, and the elbow straightens out somewhat so that the contact point is well in front of the body. Beginning volleyers who try to copy this motion, tend, however, to take the *entire* arm back beyond the plane of the body, ending up with a backswing that is closer to that for a groundstroke and far too large for a volley. This, in turn, produces late contact, the single most common technical error at the net.

It is important initially to develop the feeling of solid, early ball contact on the volley. This is accomplished most easily following the models as shown. After the correct contact point is established, most players will begin to add a little more backswing *naturally*, but this will supplement rather than undermine the fundamentals of the stroke. Trying to create a loop backswing from the beginning will reverse this effect.

As for the second major issue in the theory of the volley, the one-handed versus the two-handed debate, I believe that most two-handed groundstrokers should also learn the two-handed volley. As noted in the chapter on technical styles, it is possible to volley very well with two hands. More relevant, however, is the fact that for most two-handers, it is usually extremely difficult to learn to volley *at all* with one hand. As is the case with the groundstrokes, the bio-mechanics of the one-handed and two-handed backhand volleys are diametrically opposed. A player with no experience hitting with one hand on his groundstrokes starts learning the volley with virtually no muscle memory if he tries to learn with one hand. Making the task even more difficult, he will have to change grips for the first time in his life, and remember to do this at the net regularly, without the habit of doing it in the backcourt. On the other hand, if he has mastered the bio-mechanics of hitting a backhand groundstroke with two hands, he can quickly and naturally draw on this ability in developing a two-handed volley. He will already have developed the basic skill of hitting with the left arm and back left shoulder. The two-handed volley can then be developed as quickly as the two-handed groundstroke, and will produce excellent results mixed in an all-court singles game, and also in doubles.

As also noted in the chapter on the classical style, two-handed players tend to play primarily from the backcourt, and players who want to play attacking tennis should probably develop *both* their backhand groundstrokes and volleys with one hand. For the vast majority of players, continuity on the backhand between their bio-mechanics in the backcourt and at the net will be the best approach.

The volleys presented here are extremely compact technical models. They are based on shoulder turns, and early contact, with virtually no backswing and very little followthrough. The role of the shoulders in the volley has been generally misunderstood in instructional theory. Often the volley is described as a punching motion, implying that the arm extends outward, moving independently of the shoulders and upper body. However, if you observe the top volleyers in the game—John McEnroe, Martina Navratilova, Stefan Edberg, Boris Becker—you will see that the genesis of the motion forward to the ball

lies in the rotation of the shoulders. In terms of the bio-mechanics, this is one similarity with the groundstrokes. Compared with the groundstrokes, the amount of rotation is significantly reduced, yet it is still a primary power source, and the key to consistent execution at the high speed of match play. As we will see in the models themselves, good technical volleys have almost no independent arm movement. Instead, the racket can be positioned correctly at the turn solely by the rotation of the shoulders. The motion forward to the early contact point described above is then simply the rotation of the shoulders back toward the original position. This compact turning motion reduces the amount of time necessary to execute the volley to a minimum, and it is something that can be achieved in even the fastest exchanges at net. In contrast, the player who begins his volley motion by taking the arm back and away from the body rarely recovers in time to achieve early contact, and appears to be working very hard, or even flailing at the ball, with little or no result. Pay attention to the role of the shoulders as you develop your stroke and you will volley solidly and aggressively with an economy of motion and effort.

CREATING THE FOREHAND VOLLEY SWING PATTERN

To learn to hit the forehand volley, we will use the same progression as with the groundstrokes, starting with the still frame sequence photos. The sequences will serve as the blueprint for your own swing pattern. Through the techniques presented, you will use them to create a precise *physical* and *visual* model of the stroke.

First, the forehand volley is shown from the front view, and the general technical characteristics of the stroke are outlined. On the following pages, the stroke is shown simultaneously from the front and side views and the four key still frames are isolated. These four still frames are:

1. **The Ready Position**
2. **The Turn**
3. **The Contact Point**
4. **The Finish Position**

As with the groundstrokes, you can see that if the motion is correct at each of the still frames, it will have to be correct throughout the whole pattern. This is particularly true on the volleys because the motions are so much more compact that little that can go wrong in between if the still frame positions are right.

In the following section, each of the four still frames is individually demonstrated, with its checkpoints. You will learn how to create the still frames physically, and also to create a mental image of yourself in each position. After you have learned each still frame, you will see how to put them together into the forehand volley stroke pattern. The following section shows how to do muscle memory corrections for the most common errors. Finally, in the last section, you will learn to create a system of stroke keys to hit reliable forehand volleys under the pressure of match play.

1
READY POSITION

2
START OF TURN

3
THE TURN

Characteristics of the Forehand Volley
FRONT VIEW

○ ○

Grip: When learning the forehand volley, you should start with the same grip as on your forehand groundstroke. The forehand grip variations are discussed in the grip chapter. If, however, your groundstroke grip is an extreme version of the modified eastern, you will probably want to start with a less severe grip on the volley. This sequence is demonstrated with the classic eastern grip, clearly visible in Frame 3.

Ready Position: The forehand volley starts with a Ready Position that differs from the ground-strokes in one vital aspect—the position of the racket head. On the groundstrokes, the racket is below waist level, and points directly at the net. On the volley, the racket head is *high*. The top of the racket should be approximately even with the top of the head (Frame 1). This allows it to move to the Turn *directly* on a straight line (Frames 2 and 3), without wasting time or motion.

Compact Motion: Compared with the groundstrokes, the swing pattern on the volley is extremely brief. There is no backswing as such. Instead, the body and the racket are simply turned

4
STEP TO BALL

5
CONTACT POINT

6
FINISH POSITION

sideways to the ball. The racket face never goes further back than the front edge of the shoulders (Frame 3). Likewise, there is very little followthrough. The racket never crosses to the opposite side of the body, as on a groundstroke (Frame 6). Instead, it moves forward on the line of the shot for a maximum of one to two feet.

Minimum Use of Wrist: As is the case with the groundstrokes, the forehand volley is hit with little or no wrist. Instead, the arm is in the double bend position at the Ready Position (Frame 1), the Turn (Frame 3), the Contact Point (Frame 5), and at the Finish Position (Frame 6). Note the elbow is tucked in toward the waist, with the wrist slightly laid back.

Role of Shoulders: Properly executed, the forehand volley is hit almost entirely with shoulder rotation, with a minimum of independent arm motion. In the Ready Position, the shoulders start parallel to the net (Frame 1). At the Turn, they have turned sideways about forty-five degrees (Frame 3). This automatically positions the arm and racket correctly. From the Turn, the shoulders rotate forward, pushing the hitting arm and the racket to the Contact Point (Frame 5) and the Finish (Frame 6). This rotation provides natural body leverage.

Early Contact Point: Compared with the groundstrokes, the Contact Point is much earlier on the volley. In fact, the position of the racket at the Turn (Frame 3) is roughly the same as at the *contact* on most groundstrokes. On the volley, however, the racket then moves forward to the ball, meeting it a foot or more in front of the front edge of the body (Frame 5). This, in conjunction with shoulder rotation, maximizes the natural power of the shot. Early contact is the key to executing the forehand volley consistently, and to generating ball velocity, with little muscle effort.

Forehand Volley
Four Key Still Frames · SIDE VIEW

○○○○○○○○○○○○○○○○○○○○○○○○○○○○○○○○

STILL FRAME #1   **STILL FRAME #2**

READY POSITION   **START OF TURN**   **THE TURN**

Forehand Volley
Four Key Still Frames · FRONT VIEW

○○○○○○○○○○○○○○○○○

STILL FRAME #1   **STILL FRAME #2**

READY POSITION   **START OF TURN**   **THE TURN**

STILL FRAME #3 STILL FRAME #4

STEP TO BALL   CONTACT POINT   FINISH POSITION

STILL FRAME #3   STILL FRAME #4

 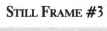 

STEP TO BALL   CONTACT POINT   FINISH POSITION

121

Still Frame 1
The Ready Position

○ ○ ○ ○ ○ ○ ○ ○ ○ ○ ○ ○ ○ ○ ○ ○

Checkpoints:

*1. **The Shoulders:*** The shoulders are parallel to the net. The upper body is straight up and down from the waist. The bend is in the knees.

*2. **The Hitting Arm:*** The hitting arm is positioned so that the elbow tucks in toward the waist. The hands are slightly above waist level. Wait with the forehand grip.

*3. **The Racket:*** The tip of the racket is even with the top of the player's head. This high racket position is a key difference between the Ready Position on the groundstrokes and that on the volley.

*4. **The Legs:*** The legs are shoulder width apart, or slightly wider. The knees are flexed, and the weight is slightly forward on the balls of the feet.

Establish the Ready Position physically using the checkpoints, then create the mental image.

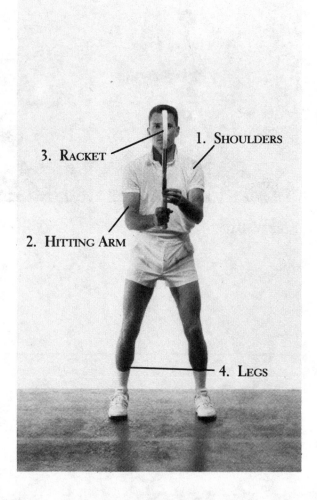

Still Frame 2
The Turn Position

○ ○ ○ ○ ○ ○ ○ ○ ○ ○ ○ ○ ○ ○

Checkpoints:

1. The Shoulders: The shoulders have rotated about forty-five degrees, or half as far as on the groundstrokes. Note that the shoulders, arm, and racket have moved as a unit.

2. The Hitting Arm: The hitting arm remains in the double bend position, with the elbow in and the wrist slightly laid back. It has rotated in position with the shoulder turn.

3. The Racket: The edge of the racket is even with the *front* edge of the shoulders. The shaft of the racket is forty-five degrees to the court surface. The top of the racket is even with the top of the player's head. The *face* of the racket is vertical to the court.

4. The Legs: Both feet have pivoted sideways. The weight is on the right pivot foot, and the left toes are used for balance. The knees are still flexed.

Start in the Ready Position, and move to the Turn. Establish the position physically using the checkpoints, then create the mental image.

Still Frame 3
The Contact Point

○ ○ ○ ○ ○ ○ ○ ○ ○ ○ ○ ○ ○ ○ ○

Checkpoints:

1. The Shoulders: The shoulders have rotated back toward the net, so that they are almost back to the parallel position, pushing the arm and racket to the contact.

2. The Hitting Arm: There is a slight additional push forward with the hitting arm, following and extending the body rotation. The arm remains in the double bend position, elbow in and wrist back.

3. The Racket: The racket is now about a foot to a foot and a half in front of the body. The shaft is still at a forty-five-degree angle to the court, and the racket face is still vertical.

4. The Legs: The left foot has stepped forward to the ball, with the toes parallel along the edge of a line. The weight is forward on the left front foot. The knees have uncoiled slightly into the ball.

Start in the Ready Position and move through the Turn to the Contact Point. Establish the position physically using the checkpoints, then create the mental image.

3. RACKET

1. SHOULDERS

2. HITTING ARM

4. LEGS

Still Frame 4
The Finish Position

○ ○ ○ ○ ○ ○ ○ ○ ○ ○ ○ ○ ○ ○ ○

Checkpoints:

1. *The Shoulders:* The shoulders have continued to rotate slightly further, until they are again parallel with the net. The upper body is still straight up and down from the waist.

2. *The Hitting Arm:* The hitting arm has pushed the racket through the Contact Point, on the line of the shot. The wrist has not released, and the elbow is still slightly bent.

3. *The Racket:* The racket has moved through the ball, with the shaft still at forty-five degrees and with the face of the racket vertical to the court. The butt of the racket now points at the left, opposite hip.

4. *The Legs:* The weight is now fully forward on the left front foot, and the player has come up on his right toes for balance. The knees are still slightly flexed.

Start in the Ready Position, move through the Turn and the Contact Point to the Finish. Establish the position physically using the checkpoints, then create the mental image.

Putting the Still Frames Together
SIDE VIEW

○ ○ ○ ○ ○ ○ ○ ○ ○ ○ ○ ○ ○ ○ ○ ○ ○ ○ ○

READY POSITION   THE TURN   CONTACT POINT   FINISH POSITION

Executing the Forehand Volley

After you have mastered the four key still frames, put them together into a volley swing pattern as shown above. Start in the Ready Position, move to the Turn, forward to the Contact Point, and then to the Finish Position. Make sure that your checkpoints are correct as you pass through each still frame.

Now you are ready to start building your muscle memory. This is a three-step process. First, practice doing correct swings without actually hitting balls, in front of a mirror if possible. Start with one swing, and build up until you can do ten swings and get the checkpoints correct automatically. The goal is to execute the motion correctly without having to think about it.

The second aspect of building muscle memory is hitting balls in controlled drill. Start in the Ready Position at the net. Initially, you should hit volleys that have low to moderate pace, and which come directly to you at about shoulder level. This will allow you to become familiar with the correct execution of the motion and to build up your confidence. As you work in controlled drill, stop every five to ten balls and do muscle memory corrections. The most common corrections are demonstrated in the next section. As with practice swings, work in controlled drill until you can hit ten strokes with little or no correction. Again, set up the controlled drill situation with a practice partner, by working with your teaching pro, or, if possible, by using a ball machine.

When you can hit ten strokes with precision and good technical form, increase the speed of the balls and the number of repetitions. As you start to feel confident, progress to rallies and then to hitting volleys in matches. The last part of the forehand volley chapter shows you how to develop the stroke keys necessary to execute the shot consistently under game pressure.

The third aspect of developing your muscle memory is to practice visualizing the stroke away from the court. This means practicing seeing yourself hitting perfect forehand volleys. As with the other strokes you can do this by sitting down and allocating practice time, or you can do it in free moments in the course of the day when your mind turns to your tennis. Visualize the stroke, and work up to ten visual repetitions. Experiment with visualizing specific keys, as you develop your own key system for the shot.

Finally, you can work visually on your stroke by watching videos of yourself or other players hitting correct forehand volleys. You should do this by watching existing instructional tapes, professional matches, and also by videoing yourself executing perfect practice swings, or hitting the stroke correctly in controlled drill.

Muscle Memory Corrections

○ ○

Compared with the groundstrokes, there is far less followthrough on the volleys. The key aspect is the early contact point. If the contact is correct, then there is a very good likelihood that the shot will be well executed. Because there is far less emphasis on the role of the followthrough in the volley, there is also less emphasis on correcting the followthrough when learning to hit the shot. However, there are some tendencies in execution of the volley that require muscle memory corrections. These are outlined in detail below.

To do a muscle memory correction on the volley, freeze in the statueman position at the end of the shot. Instead of recovering, compare your actual finish with the checkpoints for the correct Finish Position. Then move directly from wherever you are to the correct position. Your muscles will then feel the difference between what they actually did and the right technical motion. This in turn increases the chance that future volleys will follow the model stroke more closely.

The two most common kinds of errors at the finish on the volley are shown below. These are finishing with the racket head in the wrong position, either by releasing the wrist or by hitting down on the ball too sharply, and finishing the shot with incorrect footwork.

If you have either of these two tendencies, doing corrections will eliminate them from your net game. Do the corrections by working in controlled drill. Stop about every five balls and evaluate your finish according to the checkpoints. Now do the correction. As you work, you will find that your corrections become smaller, until your stroke follows the model automatically. In working on your corrections, you should make regular use of video. By watching videos of your actual stroke production, you will not only see how you are deviating from your model, you will develop a clearer image of the model stroke itself.

Muscle Memory Corrections:
Racket Position

These two sequences demonstrate the two most common errors in racket head position at the finish of the volley.

The first error shows the wrist release, which results from overswinging, and trying to hit the ball too hard. The result is actually the opposite of what the player intends. Releasing the wrist destroys body leverage and early contact. It also causes loss of control of the shot placement, the most crucial aspect of aggressive volleying.

The second error is hitting down on the ball too sharply in an effort to produce underspin. The result is late contact, a loss of pace, and a tendency for the ball to float. The correct method for hitting the forehand volley with underspin is demonstrated at the end of this chapter. To correct both these errors, simply freeze in the statueman position. Using the checkpoints for the correct finish, reposition your racket as shown.

STATUEMAN
Wrist Release
and Correction

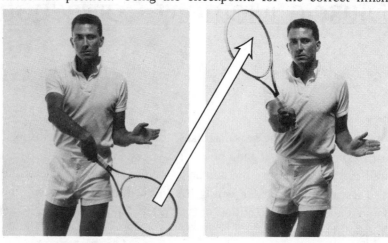

ERROR: WRIST RELEASE   CORRECTED FINISH POSITION

STATUEMAN
Hitting Down (Chop)
and Correction

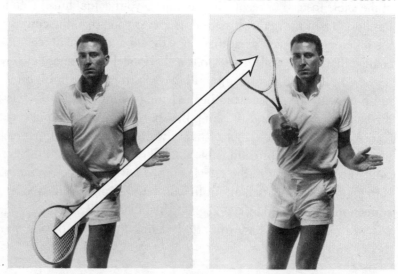

ERROR: HITTING DOWN   CORRECTED FINISH POSITION

Muscle Memory Correction:
Leg Position

This sequence shows the most common error in leg position at the finish of the forehand volley: the player has failed to make the step forward to the ball and has finished the volley with an open stance.

Without this step to close the stance, the shot will lack pace. It will be hit late and without any leverage coming from the legs. The amount of shoulder rotation into the ball will be reduced, and the Contact Point will be behind the plane of the body. To correct this error: freeze in the statueman position. Now adjust the feet by stepping across and forward with the left foot so that the toes are parallel along the edge of the line. This will move the weight forward and make the contact early.

STATUEMAN
Open Stance
and Correction

ERROR: OPEN STANCE AT FINISH

CORRECTED FINISH POSITION

KEYING THE FOREHAND VOLLEY

After you have worked in controlled drill and have developed your muscle memory, the last step in mastering the forehand volley is developing your system of stroke keys. The keys will give you the ability to hit the shot consistently under match play conditions.

Because of the limited stroke pattern, as noted above, the role of the finish in the volley is reduced compared with the groundstrokes. Instead, the most effective key for the volley is usually the image of the Contact Point. If the Contact Point is correct, the finish will take care of itself on the volley, instead of the other way around. Early contact is the key to handling the pace of the oncoming shot, reflecting that pace into your volley, and making precise ball placements. It is what gives a volley that effortless quality characteristic of the great attacking players.

The first key shown is the image of the Contact Point. Again this is shown from the player's perspective, as you will actually visualize the key in your own mind. You may want to visualize the entire key or focus on one aspect of it—the position of the racket head well in front of the body, the double bend position of the arm, etc.

The second key is the rotation of the shoulders. A common error on the volley is simply to take the arm and racket back independently, without rotating the body. This makes early contact impossible, and decimates the velocity of the shot. If you are not using your shoulders to make the Turn, work with this key.

The third key is the step to the Contact Point. This is a more advanced key. As explained, it allows you to produce the entire stroke simply by keying on the step to the ball, with the shoulders, racket and legs working as a single unit.

The learning procedure for creating your stroke keys is identical to that for mastering the still frames. First, establish the position physically, referring to the checkpoints that accompany the image. Next, close your eyes and create an image of the position in your mind's eye, giving it as much detail as possible. Notice how the position feels physically, and make the image and the feeling correspond in your mind. Then test the key in controlled drill. As the ball approaches, hold the image of the key in mind. As you swing, make your racket, hitting arm, shoulders, and legs overlap the image.

If you visualize the key clearly, it should function as a magnet, attracting your racket and body to the correct position. Hit ten to twenty balls in controlled drill. If the key produces consistent strokes, then it is an active key. Progress to rallies and match play and test the key there. You may also find that slight variations of the key are more effective. For example, rather than using the entire still frame, you may want to visualize just one aspect of the Contact Point, such as the position of the racket head in front of your shoulder, or the double bend position of the hitting arm. Experiment with these and other aspects of the images to determine which are best for you.

The keys presented here should be used as a guide in developing your own personal system of forehand volley keys. Your goal is to determine which keys are active. Compile your stroke key chart from the results of this work, and update it as required. As with the groundstrokes, this should include tendency analysis. Correlate your errors with the counteracting keys, and record them on your chart. You can then take the chart with you on the court, and refer to it during your matches, as needed.

As with the groundstrokes, the keys provide a systematic method for creating and sustaining mental focus under the pressure of match play. Particularly at the net, where everything happens twice as fast, a player's anxieties and fears can dominate his mental processes, making concentration impossible. Because a player can visualize key images even at the high speed of net play, the key system allows a player to stay focused, and to achieve consistent execution on his volleys.

Keying the Forehand Volley: The Contact Point from the Player's Perspective

○ ○

Because the Contact Point is the central aspect of a good technical volley, keying on this image is usually the most effective way to produce the shot in match play. This image is shown from the perspective in which you will probably see yourself in your mind's eye—from slightly over your shoulder and behind. Note the various checkpoints: the shaft of the racket is at about forty-five degrees to the court. The face of the racket is perpendicular. The arm is tucked in toward the waist at the elbow, with the wrist laid back. The right shoulder is rotating forward so that it is solidly behind the shot. Finally, the contact itself is roughly a foot ahead of the body. Establish the position physically and create the mental image. Test the key in controlled drill.

Keying the Forehand Volley: Turn the Shoulders

○ ○

READY POSITION   THE TURN   CONTACT POINT

Shoulder rotation is crucial on the forehand volley. Unless the body rotates, there is a tendency to hit the volley with the arm, to overswing, and to lose power. In the sequence at right, we can see that the shoulders, arm, and racket move as a unit. There is no independent motion. Instead, simply by turning the shoulders, the racket will be positioned correctly. Notice that the hitting arm and racket are already in the double bend position in the first photo of the Ready Position.

This position is maintained in the second photo. The shoulders have rotated forty-five degrees to the net, positioning the racket at the front edge of the body. There is no additional arm movement. In the third photo, the shoulders have now rotated back, pushing the arm and racket to the Contact Point. Thus, the entire stroke can be keyed on the rotation of the shoulders. Establish each of the three positions shown above physically, and create a mental image. The key can be any of the three images, or a mini-movie of the entire shoulder motion. Test the key, or keys, in controlled drill.

Keying the Forehand Volley:
The Cross Step to the Ball

○ ○

READY POSITION   **START OF CROSS STEP**   **CONTACT POINT**

Once you have mastered the fundamental elements of the forehand volley, it is possible to key the entire stroke on what is called the cross step to the ball. This is often the most effective key for the high speed of match play. Using this key, the shoulders, the racket, and the feet move as a unit to the Contact Point. As shown above, if the step to the ball is correct, the entire motion will be correct as well.

In the Ready Position, imagine that the butt of the racket and the tip of your left toe are attached to each other by a steel rod, shown by the arrows above. In the second frame, you can see that with the racket and foot attached, the shoulders will start to turn and the racket to move forward automatically as the step begins. At the Contact Point, the right shoulder will rotate forward pushing the racket to early contact, as shown in the third frame.

Practice the cross step to the contact, and as you do, create an image of the motion, and of the steel rod connecting your left foot and the butt of the racket. Now test the key in controlled drill.

Variation:
The Underspin Forehand Volley

○ ○

1
READY POSITION

2
START OF TURN

3
THE TURN

Grip: The primary difference in hitting the forehand volley with underspin is the change from the forehand to the continental grip. The grip should be between the eastern forehand and the eastern backhand grip. This means that part of the heel pad of the racket hand is on the top bevel of the frame. The grip chapter demonstrates how to achieve this correctly.

Generating Underspin: The altered grip itself is the only change that is required to add underspin to the shot. By changing to the continental grip, the face of the racket will automatically be slightly open to the surface of the court at the beginning of the motion. This bevel in the racket face angle is clearly visible at the start of the Turn (Frame 2) and at the completion of the Turn (Frame 3). Once the angle of the racket face is set, it remains unchanged throughout the course of stroke. Thus, the face of the racket remains open at the Step to the Ball (Frame 4), at the Contact Point (Frame 5), all the way through to the Finish Position (Frame 6). By moving through the ball at this angle, the strings will automatically slide underneath the ball creating underspin. Imagine the ball as an orange,

4
STEP TO BALL

5
CONTACT POINT

6
FINISH POSITION

and the racket face as a knife. The knife should slice off the diagonal back third of the ball at contact, as with the underspin backhand groundstroke.

    Developing the Stroke: Because the bio-mechanics of the underspin volley are similar to the flat volley demonstrated above, there is no need to repeat the progression through the still frames and the checkpoints. If you have developed a solid basic volley, you can add underspin simply by changing the grip and the angle of the racket through the swing. Make sure that you allow the face to open (as it will naturally) at the Start of the Turn (Frame 2). Now complete the motion in the same fashion. Step to the ball, keep the arm in the correct double bend position, and make early contact.

    Applications: The underspin volley is necessary for hitting low volleys, and for taking the pace of the ball to make a sharply angled placement or a touch volley. It will also add control on routine volleys at shoulder or waist height. As noted in the Introduction, a major advantage of this shot is that it eliminates the need for grip changes at the net, since the same grip is used for the backhand volley.

Keying the Underspin Forehand Volley: Hitting Through the Ball

○ ○

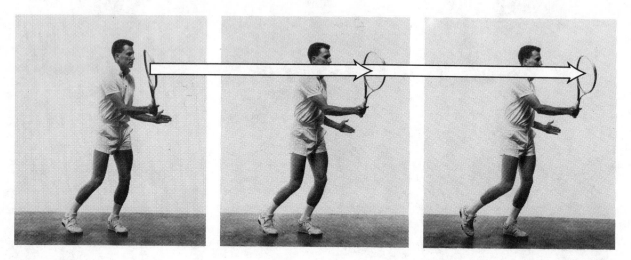

STEP TO BALL   CONTACT POINT   FINISH POSITION

Since the underspin volley shares technical characteristics with the basic, flat forehand volley, most of the keys for the basic shot will apply to the underspin shot as well: these are the image of the early Contact Point, the image of the shoulder turn, and the image of the cross step to the ball.

There is one additional key, however, that is important for the underspin variation. This is the image of hitting through the ball on a straight line. Hitting through the ball is crucial to create body leverage and pace, and for reaching the earliest possible Contact Point. With the racket face open, however, some players will have the tendency to hit down on the ball, believing this is necessary to create spin. The underspin is, in fact, created by the open face moving through the ball. Hitting down will result in late contact and a loss of pace and ball control.

Practice the motion as shown above, moving through the three frames. As you do, create a mental image, or a mini-movie, of the racket face moving through the contact on a straight line. Test the key in controlled drill.

CREATING THE ONE-HANDED BACKHAND VOLLEY SWING PATTERN

In learning the one-handed backhand volley you will follow the familiar visualization progressions, starting with the still frame sequences of the stroke. Using the sequences, you will learn the physical and visual model for the stroke.

The sequences begin by demonstrating the stroke from the front view, and describing the technical characteristics of the shot. The stroke is then shown simultaneously from the front and side, so the four key still frames can be identified. These four frames are:

1. **The Ready Position**
2. **The Turn**
3. **The Contact Point**
4. **The Finish Position**

As is the case with all the strokes, if the motion is correct at these key still frame positions, it will be correct throughout the course of the motion. As with the forehand volley, the backhand volley motion is far more compact than the backhand groundstroke, so there is almost nothing that can go wrong in between if the still frames are correct.

After the still frames are identified, each is individually analyzed and its checkpoints outlined. Using the checkpoints, you will learn how to establish each still frame, and then, to put them together into a smooth stroke. The following sections demonstrate muscle memory corrections and how to create your own system of stroke keys.

1
READY POSITION

2
START OF TURN

3
THE TURN

Characteristics of the One-Handed Backhand Volley FRONT VIEW

○ ○

Ready Position: The Ready Position is the same as for the forehand volley. This means the racket head is up, so that the top of the racket is roughly even with the top of the head (Frame 1). Again this contrasts with the Ready Position for the groundstrokes in which the racket is much lower and points straight at the net.

Grip: The backhand volley is hit with the same grip as the backhand groundstroke. Again, consult the grip chapter if you have a question. In the Ready Position, you should wait with the forehand grip, cradling the throat of your racket with your left hand (Frame 1). The grip change happens as part of the turning motion. This can be clearly seen at the Start of the Turn above (Frame 2). As you start the turn, rotate your right hand toward the top of the frame until you reach your backhand grip position.

4
STEP TO BALL

5
CONTACT POINT

6
FINISH POSITION

Compact Motion: As with the forehand volley, the backhand volley is hit with a very compact motion. There is no real backswing with either the arm or racket. Instead, the shoulders are simply turned sideways to the net (Frame 3). This automatically positions the racket at the front edge of the body. From there the racket moves forward only about two feet. The followthrough never crosses to the opposite side of the body, as on a groundstroke (Frame 6).

Minimum Use of Wrist: As with the forehand volley, the backhand volley is hit with minimal or no wrist. At the Turn (Frame 3), the arm and racket are set in the hitting position. The forearm is horizontal to the court, and the wrist is locked. From this position, the arm and racket move forward together as a unit, pushed to the contact by the right front shoulder.

Role of Shoulders: Again, the entire backhand volley can be keyed on the rotation of the shoulders. If the Turn is correct (Frame 3), the right hitting shoulder is positioned at the front edge of the body. The step to the ball (Frame 4) places the weight squarely behind the shot, providing natural body leverage. The shoulder then moves the arm and racket forward to the Contact Point (Frame 5).

Early Contact Point: As with the forehand volley, the Contact Point on the backhand volley is significantly further in front of the body than on the groundstrokes. The position of the racket at the Turn is approximately the same as the Contact Point on the groundstrokes. However, from this point, the racket moves forward to meet the ball. The Contact Point on the volley is an additional one to two feet further in front of the edge of the body (Frame 5). This early Contact Point, combined with the leverage from the shoulders and legs, is the secret to a consistent, effortless backhand volley.

One-Handed Backhand Volley:
Four Key Still Frames · SIDE VIEW

○○○○○○○○○○○○○○○○○○○○○○○○○○○○

STILL FRAME #1

STILL FRAME #2

READY POSITION

START OF TURN

THE TURN

One-Handed Backhand Volley:
Four Key Still Frames · FRONT VIEW

○○○○○○○○○○○○○○○○○○○○○○○○○○○○○

STILL FRAME #1

STILL FRAME #2

READY POSITION

START OF TURN

THE TURN

140

 STILL FRAME #3

 STILL FRAME #4

STEP TO BALL

CONTACT POINT

FINISH POSITION

 STILL FRAME #3

 STILL FRAME #4

STEP TO BALL

CONTACT POINT

FINISH POSITION

141

Still Frame 1
The Ready Position

○ ○ ○ ○ ○ ○ ○ ○ ○ ○ ○ ○ ○ ○

Checkpoints:

1. The Racket: The tip of the racket is even with the top of the player's head. As with the forehand volley, this higher racket position is a key difference from the Ready Position on the groundstrokes.

2. The Shoulders: The shoulders are parallel with the net. The upper body is straight up and down from the waist. The bend is in the knees, not at the waist.

3. The Hitting Arm: The hitting arm is positioned so the elbow tucks in slightly toward the waist. The hands are slightly above waist level. Wait with the forehand grip.

4. The Legs: The legs are shoulder width apart, or slightly wider. The knees are flexed, and the weight is slightly forward on the balls of the feet.

Establish the Ready Position physically using the checkpoints, then create the mental image.

1. RACKET
2. SHOULDERS
3. HITTING ARM
4. LEGS

Still Frame 2
The Turn Position

○ ○ ○ ○ ○ ○ ○ ○ ○ ○ ○ ○ ○ ○ ○

Checkpoints:

1. The Racket: The edge of the racket is even with the front edge of the shoulders. The top of the racket is still even with the top of the player's head. The shaft of the racket is at about a forty-five-degree angle to the court surface. The *face* of the racket is vertical to the court.

2. The Shoulders: The shoulders have rotated about forty-five degrees, or about half as far as on the groundstrokes. The shoulders, hitting arm, and racket have rotated as a unit.

3. The Hitting Arm: The hitting arm has not moved independently, but has swung into position with the shoulder turn. The player has changed to the backhand grip. The forearm is horizontal to the court and the wrist is locked.

4. The Legs: The feet have pivoted sideways. The weight is on the left pivot foot, and the right toes are used for balance. The knees are still flexed.

Move from the Ready Position to the Turn. Establish the position physically using the checkpoints, then create the mental image.

1. RACKET

2. SHOULDERS

3. HITTING ARM

4. LEGS

Still Frame 3
The Contact Point

○ ○ ○ ○ ○ ○ ○ ○ ○ ○ ○ ○ ○ ○ ○ ○ ○

Checkpoints:

1. RACKET

2. SHOULDERS

3. HITTING ARM

4. LEGS

1. The Racket: The racket has moved forward to the ball, meeting it at least a foot in front of the edge of the right shoulder. The angle of the racket to the court has not changed. The shaft is about forty-five degrees and the face is still vertical.

2. The Shoulders: The shoulders have rotated only slightly. Instead they have stayed basically sideways, keeping the weight behind the ball, while the arm and racket have moved forward.

3. The Hitting Arm: The hitting arm has moved forward to the ball as a *unit*. The forearm is still horizontal to the court and the wrist is still locked.

4. The Legs: The right foot has stepped forward to the ball, so that the toes are parallel along the edge of a line. The weight is forward on the right foot. The knees have uncoiled slightly into the ball.

Move from the Ready Position through the Turn to the Contact Point. Establish the position physically using the checkpoints, then create the mental image.

Still Frame 4
The Finish Position

○ ○ ○ ○ ○ ○ ○ ○ ○ ○ ○ ○ ○ ○ ○

Checkpoints:

1. The Racket: The racket has continued straight out through the line of the shot, about a foot past the Contact Point. The shaft is still forty-five degrees to the court, and the face is still vertical. The butt of the racket now points just off the right hip.

2. The Shoulders: The stroke has finished with a minimum of shoulder rotation. The front right shoulder has rotated back just past perpendicular with the net. The upper body is still straight up and down from the waist.

3. The Hitting Arm: There has been no internal movement in the hitting arm through the course of the stroke. The forearm is still horizontal to the court, and the wrist has not released.

4. The Legs: The weight is now fully forward on the right front foot. The player has come up on his rear toes for balance. The knees are still slightly flexed.

Move from the Ready Position through the Turn and the Contact to the Finish Position. Establish the position physically using the checkpoints, then create the mental image.

Putting the Still Frames Together
FRONT VIEW

○ ○

READY POSITION   THE TURN   CONTACT POINT   FINISH POSITION

Executing the One-Handed Backhand Volley

After you have mastered each of the four key still frames, the next step is to put them together into a backhand volley swing pattern as shown above. Start in the Ready Position, now execute the Turn. Step into the ball and move forward to the Contact Point, and then continue to the Finish Position. Make sure that the checkpoints are correct as you pass through each still frame. Again, if you have mastered the still frames and get them correct, this will virtually guarantee that the entire stroke will be correct.

Now build your muscle memory. Again, there is a three-step process. The first step is to practice doing correct practice swings without hitting balls. Start by doing one perfect backhand volley. Build up to ten or more swings. If possible, do this in front of a full-length mirror. The goal is to be able to do the entire motion correctly without having to think about the checkpoints.

The next aspect of building muscle memory is work in controlled drill. Start at the net in the Ready Position. Initially, hit balls that are low to moderate pace and come directly to you at about shoulder height. This will allow you to get comfortable with the basic motion and to build up your confidence. This should be done either using a ball machine, with a practice partner, or with a teaching pro.

As you work in controlled drill, stop every five or ten balls and do muscle memory corrections, as shown in the next section. As with the practice swings, work until you can hit ten strokes with little or no correction.

When you can hit ten strokes with precision and good technical form, increase the speed of the balls, and the number of repetitions. Next, progress to hitting volleys in a rally. Alternate back and forth between the forehand and backhand volley. Be sure to key on the ball as it leaves the opponent's racket so that you start your motion simultaneously with his hit. The last section of this chapter shows you how to develop the stroke keys for the backhand volley, and how to use them to hit the shot under pressure in match play.

The third aspect of developing your muscle memory is to practice simply visualizing the stroke away from the court. You can do this by setting up regular practice time for visualizations, or do it in free moments in the course of your daily routine. Visualize a perfect one-handed backhand volley. Build up to ten visual repetitions. Experiment with visualizing specific keys, as you develop your key system for the shot.

Finally, work on the shot by watching video of good backhand volleys. Do this by watching instructional tapes, taping professional matches and by making a video of yourself executing perfect practice swings and hitting the ball correctly in controlled drill.

Muscle Memory Corrections

○ ○

As with the forehand volley, the backhand volley has less followthrough than the groundstrokes. Therefore, early contact, rather than the followthrough, is the most important key to good execution. However, there are some tendencies that require muscle memory corrections.

To do a muscle memory correction, freeze in the statueman position at the end of the shot. Do not recover. Instead, hold your position and compare your actual finish with the checkpoints for the correct finish position. Now, move directly to the correct position. Let your muscles feel the difference from what you actually did and what you were trying to do. This will increase the probability that the next shot will follow the model more closely, and over time, will bring the two in line.

The two most common types of errors are outlined below. They are finishing the shot with the racket head in the wrong position and finishing the shot with an open stance. Do the corrections by working in controlled drill. Stop about every five balls and evaluate and correct your finish according to the checkpoints. You will find that your errors become smaller and smaller until your stroke follows the model automatically. In working on your corrections, you should make regular use of video. By watching video of your actual stroke production, you will not only see how you are deviating from your model, you will develop a clearer image of the model stroke itself.

Muscle Memory Corrections:
Racket Position

The two sequences on this page show two common errors in racket head position at the Finish of the backhand volley.

   The first is releasing the wrist. This comes from overswinging in an effort to hit the ball too hard. The result is that the player loses the early Contact Point and natural body leverage, creating the opposite effect—instead of more power, there is usually less, as well as a loss of ball control.

   The second error is hitting straight down on the ball, rather than *through* the ball on the line of the shot. Usually, players who make this error are trying to generate underspin, but instead, this chopping motion causes the ball to float and lose pace. The correct approach for hitting underspin on the backhand volley is demonstrated in a following section. To correct these errors, freeze in the statueman position. Then use the checkpoints to reposition your racket as shown.

STATUEMAN
Wrist Release
and Correction

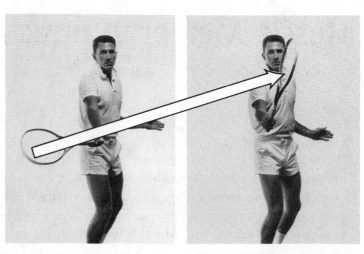

ERROR: WRIST RELEASE   CORRECTED FINISH POSITION

STATUEMAN
Hitting Down (Chop)
and Correction

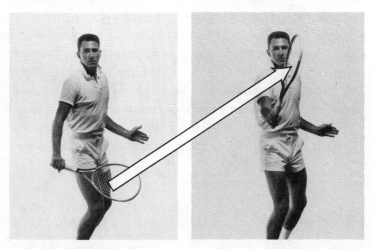

ERROR: HITTING DOWN   CORRECTED FINISH POSITION

Muscle Memory Correction:
Leg Position

This sequence shows the most common error in the footwork on the backhand volley: finishing with an open stance.

The player has failed to step parallel to the ball, as shown in the first photo below. Without this step, the shoulder turn will never be complete, and the body weight cannot be transferred into the shot through the front leg. The result is late contact. The pace of the shot will be reduced, and the swing will tend to be too sharply down instead of out through the ball.

To correct this error, freeze in the statueman position. Now adjust the feet to the correct position by stepping across and forward with the right foot. The toes of the feet should be parallel along the edge of a straight line. The result will be the creation of body leverage, and an early contact.

STATUEMAN
Open Stance
and Correction

ERROR: OPEN STANCE AT FINISH CORRECTED FINISH POSITION

KEYING THE ONE-HANDED BACKHAND VOLLEY

As with the forehand volley, the next step after developing your muscle memory is creating a personal system of stroke keys. The keys are images of basic elements of the stroke. By visualizing them, you activate the entire stroke pattern, and are then able to execute the shot under the pressure of match play.

Because of the reduced role of the followthrough compared with the groundstrokes, the most important key on the backhand volley is usually the image of the Contact Point. Early contact allows you to use the pace of the oncoming ball to create your own power, and to develop precise ball control. Therefore, the image of the Contact Point, and how to use it, is the first key demonstrated in this section.

The second key is the rotation of the shoulders. If a player can achieve the correct shoulder turn on the one-handed backhand volley, he will position the arm and racket automatically, with no additional motion. Many players make the mistake of taking the arm and racket back independently of the shoulders, virtually guaranteeing late ball contact and a loss of power. Often they overcompensate for a poor turn by overswinging, further increasing the chance of error. This key is designed to help you establish the turn, and develop solid contact using body leverage, not the swing, for power.

The third key in this section is the step to the ball. This is an advanced key which allows the player to generate the entire shot by keying on the cross step. As demonstrated, it allows the legs, racket and body to work as a unit. It is the most effective key for many players given the reduced time available to execute a shot at net.

The learning procedure for creating your stroke keys is identical to that for mastering the still frames. First, establish the position physically, referring to the checkpoints that accompany the image. Next, close your eyes and create an image of the position in your mind's eye, giving it as much detail as possible. Notice how the position feels physically, and make the image and the feeling correspond in your mind. Then test the key in controlled drill. As the ball approaches, hold the image of the key in mind. As you swing, make your racket, hitting arm, shoulders, and legs overlap the image.

If you visualize the key clearly, it should function as a magnet, attracting your racket and body to the correct position. Hit ten to twenty balls in controlled drill. If the key produces consistent strokes, then it is an active key. Progress to rallies and match play and test the key there. You may also find that slight variations of the key are more effective. For example, rather than using the entire still frame, you may want to visualize just one aspect of the image. Experiment with these and other aspects of the images to determine which are best for you.

The keys presented here should be used as a guide in developing your own personal system of backhand volley keys. Your goal is to determine which keys are active, and which counteract your own particular tendencies. Correlate your errors with the counteracting keys. Test the keys, and others that you may discover, in controlled drill, rallies, and in match play. Compile your stroke key chart from the results of this work, and update it as required. As with the forehand volley, your stroke key chart provides a reliable method for creating mental focus in match play and avoiding panic at the net, even in the face of the rapid-fire exchanges that are a regular part of net play. By using it, you will develop the ability to execute backhand volleys with routine precision and success.

Keying the One-Handed Backhand Volley: The Contact Point from the Player's Perspective

ooooooooooooooooooo

$\mathbf{A}$s with the forehand volley, the most effective key for the backhand volley is usually the image of the Contact Point. If the contact is early, the shot will have body leverage and natural pace. You will control the placement of the ball, and the stroke will feel effortless.

This image is shown from the perspective you will probably see yourself from in your mind's eye. Note the checkpoints. The shaft of the racket is about forty-five degrees to the court. The face of the racket is perpendicular. The forearm is horizontal, with the elbow slightly bent, and the wrist is locked. Finally, the contact with the ball is at least a foot in front of the right shoulder. Establish the position physically and create the mental image. Test the key in controlled drill.

Keying the One-Handed Backhand Volley: Turning from the Shoulders

ooooooooooooooooooooooooooooooooo

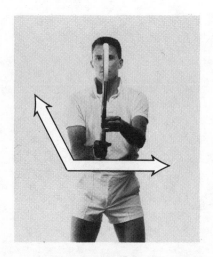  

A common error on the backhand volley is to backswing with the arm and the racket, taking them back without turning. As this sequence shows, the arm and racket stay in virtually the same position throughout the motion.

In the Ready Position, the elbow is in toward the waist, and the forearm is horizontal, or parallel, to the court surface. To make the Turn, the player has rotated his shoulders sideways. The arm and racket will then move as a unit. The elbow is still bent and points in, and the forearm has remained horizontal.

At the Contact Point, this relationship is preserved. The hitting arm and racket have swung forward like a gate on the hinge of the shoulder, with the elbow bent and the forearm still parallel to the court. There are no independent moving parts.

Go through the motion shown above moving the shoulders, hitting the arm, and racket. Create a mental image, or mini-movie, of the motion. Test the key in controlled drill.

Keying the One-Handed Backhand Volley: The Cross Step to the Ball

○ ○

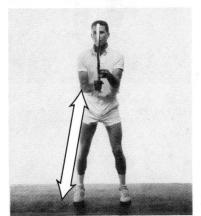  

READY POSITION   START OF CROSS STEP   CONTACT POINT

Once you have mastered the elements of the one-handed backhand volley, you can key the stroke on the cross step to the ball. This is usually an effective key at the high speed of match play, but it also requires that you build up strong muscle memory in controlled drill, so that when you make the cross step, the other elements of the motion remain correct. This allows you to execute the backhand volley with one quick step in match play.

In the Ready Position, imagine that the butt of the racket and the tip of your right toe are attached to each other by a steel rod, shown by the arrows above. In the second frame, you can see that with the racket and foot attached, the shoulders will start to turn and the racket to move forward automatically as the step begins. At the Contact Point, the right shoulder pushes the hitting arm and racket to meet the ball early and in front of the body, as shown in the third frame. Practice the cross step to the contact, and as you do create a mental image of the motion.

Variation:
The Underspin Backhand Volley

○ ○

1
READY POSITION

2
START OF TURN

3
THE TURN

Grip: For the underspin backhand volley use the same continental grip as for the underspin forehand volley. Most players find it easier to produce underspin with this grip than with the more extreme eastern backhand, because it is possible to hit through the line of the shot more easily. This will allow you to hit both volleys with the same grip, and eliminate the grip shift at the net, a major advantage in playing attacking tennis.

Generating Underspin: To create underspin, the key is to set the angle of the racket face correctly at the Start of the Turn (Frame 2). You can see in this frame that the racket face is already slightly open. This is accomplished by rotating the wrist and forearm slightly backward as the motion starts. By the time the Turn is complete (Frame 3), the face of the racket is beveled so that it is at about a thirty-degree angle with the court. Once the angle of the racket face is set, it remains *unchanged* throughout the remaining course of the motion. Thus the racket face remains slightly open at the Step to Ball (Frame 4), at the Contact Point (Frame 5), and at the Finish Position (Frame 6). It has moved straight through the motion on the line of the shot, rather than downward. The angle of the racket face slides under the ball creating underspin automatically, just as on a slice backhand groundstroke.

4
STEP TO BALL

5
CONTACT POINT

6
FINISH POSITION

Developing the Stroke: The basic bio-mechanics of the underspin volley are identical to the flat volley demonstrated earlier, with the exceptions of the change of grip and racket face angle. Therefore, there is no need here to repeat the progression through the still frames and the checkpoints. If you have developed a solid flat volley, you can add the underspin by simply altering the angle of the racket face at the start of the Turn. This is true no matter which volley grip you adopt. The other key elements are the same. The Turn is generated from the shoulders. There is no backswing. The hitting arm and racket stay in the same position throughout the stroke, and the contact is well in front of the right shoulder.

Applications: The underspin backhand volley can be used to make any shot previously made with the flat volley. The underspin gives the player more control of the speed and placement. It is also a necessity for low volleys, sharply angled, or touch volleys. Therefore, with underspin, the player hits all backhand volleys with the same basic bio-mechanics.

Keying the Underspin Backhand Volley: Hitting Through the Ball

○ ○ ○ ○ ○ ○ ○ ○ ○ ○ ○ ○ ○ ○ ○ ○ ○ ○ ○

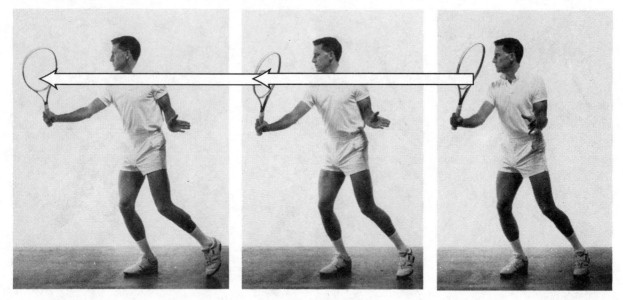

FINISH POSITION   CONTACT POINT   STEP TO BALL

Because it shares the basic technical characteristics of the flat volley, most of the same keys will apply equally well to the underspin variation. These include the image of the early Contact Point, the image of the shoulder turn, and the cross step to the ball.

As with the underspin forehand volley, however, there is one additional key that is important to solid execution. This is the image of hitting through the ball on a line. Because the racket face is open at the turn on the underspin volley, some players will tend to hit *down* rather than *through*. The result is late contact, a loss of body leverage, and, therefore, poor ball control and reduced pace. In reality it is the angle of the racket face that creates the spin, not the downward angle of the swing plane.

Practice the motion as shown above, moving through the three frames. As you do, create a mental image, or a mini-movie, of the open racket face moving through the contact on a straight line. Test the key in controlled drill.

CREATING THE TWO-HANDED BACKHAND VOLLEY SWING PATTERN

The progression for developing the two-handed backhand volley is based on the same still frame photo sequences as the other volleys. These sequences are used, as with the others, to create a physical and visual model of the swing pattern.

The progression begins by showing the two-handed backhand volley from the front view, and explaining the general technical characteristics of the stroke. Next, the stroke is demonstrated simultaneously from the front and the side, and the four key still frames are identified. The four still frames are:

1. **The Ready Position**
2. **The Turn**
3. **The Contact Point**
4. **The Finish Position**

If the player's two-handed backhand volley is correct at each of these four still frames, it will *have* to be correct throughout the course of the motion. Because the motion is so compact, there is virtually nothing that can go wrong between the still frames if they are each correct.

After the four still frames are identified, each one is individually demonstrated, and the checkpoints are outlined. Using the checkpoints you will learn to physically establish the still frames, how to visualize yourself in each still frame position, and then, how to put the frames together into a smooth overall stroke pattern.

The following two sections demonstrate muscle memory corrections for the two-handed backhand volley and the strokes keys that are the basis for the consistent execution of the shot in match play.

1
READY POSITION

2
START OF TURN

3
THE TURN

Characteristics of the Two-Handed Backhand Volley FRONT VIEW

Grip: The two-handed backhand volley is hit with *two* forehand grips, just as with the two-handed backhand groundstroke. The right hand forehand grip is maintained, and a second forehand grip is added with the left hand. The two hands are together, touching, but not overlapping on the racket handle, as can be clearly seen in Frame 2. Again, if you play with two hands, you should wait in the Ready Position with the two-handed grip. The racket head is up, with the top of the frame even with the top of the head, as is the case with either the forehand or the one-handed backhand volley.

Similarity to Two-Handed Groundstroke: The bio-mechanics of the two-handed backhand volley are similar to the two-handed groundstroke in one key respect: the *left*, back arm is the hitting arm. The left arm and the left shoulder generate the motion, almost identically to a left-handed forehand volley. The right arm adds additional, but secondary support. In Frames 4 through 6, you can see the *left* shoulder rotating forward, and the left arm pushing the racket forward to the Contact Point.

4
STEP TO BALL

5
CONTACT POINT

6
FINISH POSITION

Minimum Use of Wrist: The position of the left hitting arm on the two-handed volley is the same as the right arm on the forehand volley. This means the arm is in the double bend position, with the elbow in toward the waist, and the wrist slightly laid back. The forearm is horizontal to the court. The arm and wrist are already in the double bend in the Ready Position (Frame 1). This double bend alignment remains unchanged throughout the motion. The hit is generated from the back left shoulder. The wrist does not release at contact (Frame 5) and is still laid back at the Finish Position (Frame 6).

Compact Motion: As with the other volleys, there is no backswing. The shoulders are turned sideways to the net (Frame 3), and this turn automatically positions the racket at the front edge of the body. From this position, the racket moves forward to the contact and the finish, a total of about two feet. The followthrough never crosses to the opposite side of the body. At the end of the stroke, the butt of the racket points just off the right front hip (Frame 6).

Early Contact Point: Again, the Contact Point is earlier than for the groundstrokes. At the completion of the Turn, the racket is at the front edge of the body, which is the approximate Contact Point on the groundstrokes. From this point the racket moves *forward* to the contact about a foot in front of the body (Frame 5). This early timing generates natural body leverage and shot velocity. It is what gives the volley a solid, effortless feel.

159

Two-Handed Backhand Volley:
Four Key Still Frames · FRONT VIEW

○○○○○○○○○○○○○○○○○○○○○○○○○○○○○○○○○○○○○○○

STILL FRAME #1　　　　　　　　　　　　　　　　　　　　　　　**STILL FRAME #2**

READY POSITION　　　　　　　　**START OF TURN**　　　　　　　　**THE TURN**

Two-Handed Backhand Volley:
Four Key Still Frames · SIDE VIEW

○○○○○○○○○○○○○○○○○○○○○○○○○○○○○○○○○○○○○○○

STILL FRAME #1　　　　　　　　　　　　　　　　　　　　　　　**STILL FRAME #2**

READY POSITION　　　　　　　　**START OF TURN**　　　　　　　　**THE TURN**

160

STILL FRAME #3

STILL FRAME #4

STEP TO BALL

CONTACT POINT

FINISH POSITION

STILL FRAME #3

STILL FRAME #4

STEP TO BALL

CONTACT POINT

FINISH POSITION

161

Still Frame 1
The Ready Position

○ ○ ○ ○ ○ ○ ○ ○ ○ ○ ○ ○ ○ ○

Checkpoints:

1. *The Racket:* The tip of the racket is even with the top of the head. The hands are together in the two-handed backhand grip. Wait with this grip for both the forehand and backhand volley.

2. *The Shoulders:* The shoulders are parallel with the net. The upper body is straight up and down from the waist. The bend is at the knees, not the waist.

3. *The Hitting Arm:* The *left* hitting arm is positioned so that the elbow tucks in toward the waist, with the wrist laid back. The forearms are parallel to the court.

4. *The Legs:* The legs are shoulder width apart, or slightly wider. The knees are flexed, and the weight is forward on the balls of the feet.

Establish the Ready Position physically using the checkpoints, then create the mental image.

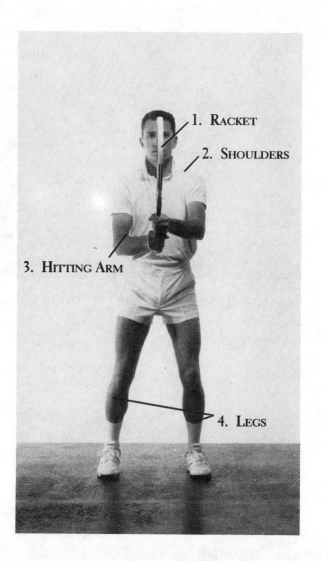

1. RACKET
2. SHOULDERS
3. HITTING ARM
4. LEGS

Still Frame 2
The Turn Position

○ ○ ○ ○ ○ ○ ○ ○ ○ ○ ○ ○ ○

Checkpoints:

*1. **The Racket:*** The top of the racket is still even with the top of the head. The *edge* of the racket is even with the front edge of the shoulders. The shaft of the racket is forty-five degrees to the court. The face of the racket is vertical.

*2. **The Shoulders:*** The shoulders have turned about forty-five degrees or slightly more. The shoulders, hitting arm, and racket have rotated as a unit.

*3. **The Hitting Arm:*** The hitting arm has not moved independently, but has swung into position automatically with the shoulder turn. Both forearms are horizontal to the court. The left wrist is slightly laid back.

*4. **The Legs:*** Both feet have pivoted sideways. The weight is on the left pivot foot, and the right toes are used for balance. The knees are still flexed.

Start in the Ready Position and move to the Turn. Establish the position physically, using the checkpoints, then create the mental image.

1. RACKET

2. SHOULDERS

3. HITTING ARM

4. LEGS

Still Frame 3
The Contact Point

○ ○ ○ ○ ○ ○ ○ ○ ○ ○ ○ ○ ○ ○ ○

Checkpoints:

1. **The Racket:** The left arm has pushed the racket forward to the ball, with contact at least a foot on front of the body. The shaft is forty-five degrees to the court, and the face of the racket is still vertical.

2. **The Shoulders:** The left shoulder has generated the hit by rotating forward and around, pushing the left arm and racket forward to the Contact Point.

3. **The Hitting Arm:** There is a slight additional push forward with the hitting arm to reach the contact. The hitting arm and racket have done this by moving as a unit. The right arm adds only secondary support.

4. **The Legs:** The right foot has stepped forward to the ball, with the toes parallel along a line. The weight is forward on the front foot. The knees have uncoiled slightly into the ball.

Start in the Ready Position and move through the Turn to the Contact. Establish the position physically using the checkpoints, then create the mental image.

1. RACKET

2. SHOULDERS

3. HITTING ARM

4. LEGS

Still Frame 4
The Finish Position

○ ○ ○ ○ ○ ○ ○ ○ ○ ○ ○ ○ ○ ○ ○

Checkpoints:

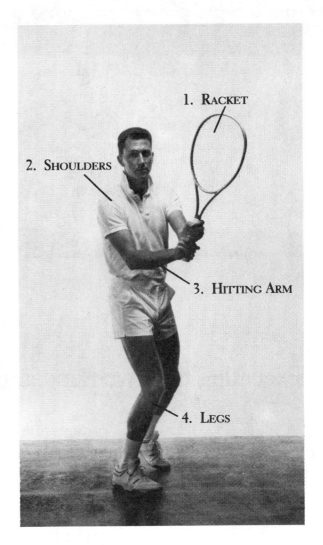

1. RACKET

2. SHOULDERS

3. HITTING ARM

4. LEGS

*1. **The Racket:*** The racket has moved through the Contact Point to the Finish with the shaft still at forty-five degrees, and the face still vertical to the court. The butt of the racket now points at the right hip.

*2. **The Shoulders:*** The shoulders have continued to rotate slightly further past the Contact Point, until they are almost parallel to the net. The upper body is still straight up and down at the waist.

*3. **The Hitting Arm:*** The hitting arm has pushed the racket through the Contact Point to the Finish Position, along the line of the shot. There has been no internal movement of the arm and racket. The elbow is still bent and the wrist laid back.

*4. **The Legs:*** The weight is now fully forward on the right front foot. The player has come up on his right rear toes for balance. The knees are still slightly flexed.

Move from Ready Position through the Turn and the Contact to the Finish. Establish the position physically using the checkpoints, then create the mental image.

Putting the Still Frames Together
SIDE VIEW

○ ○

READY POSITION   **THE TURN**   **CONTACT POINT**   **FINISH POSITION**

Executing the Two-Handed Backhand Volley

After you have mastered the still frames individually, the next step is to put them together into the swing pattern, as shown above.

Start in the Ready Position. Pivot on the balls of the feet, turn the shoulders, and move to the Turn. Now step parallel, increase the knee bend, and with the left shoulder and hitting arm, push the racket forward to the Contact Point. Finally, continue the shoulder rotation, and move the racket to the Finish Position, with the butt of the racket pointing at the right hip.

As you pass through the still frames, make sure each of the checkpoints is correct. If you are unsure of any aspect of the motion, stop and verify the individual checkpoints. If the still frames are correct, it will virtually guarantee that the entire pattern will be correct as well.

Now begin the three-step process to develop your muscle memory on the shot. First, practice executing the swing pattern without hitting balls. This can be done at home, in front of a mirror if possible.

Start by executing one perfect two-handed backhand volley. Make sure the checkpoints are correct. Build up to ten or more swings. Your goal is to execute the motion correctly without having to stop and refer to the checkpoints.

The next aspect of building muscle memory is hitting balls in controlled drill. Start at the net in Ready Position. Initially, you should hit balls that are low to moderate in pace, and that come directly to you at about shoulder height. You can create controlled drill using a ball machine, with a practice partner or your teaching pro. This work will allow you to become comfortable executing the shot, and will build up your confidence.

As you work in the controlled drill stop every five to ten balls and do a muscle memory correction, as demonstrated in the next section. As with the practice swings, work until you can hit ten strokes with little or no correction.

When you can execute ten volleys with consistently correct technique, increase the speed of the balls and the number of repetitions. Alternate back and forth between the backhand and the forehand volleys.

Now you are ready to progress to rallies. Be sure to focus on the ball as it leaves the opponent's racket, so that you start your motion simultaneously with the hit. The last section on the two-handed backhand volley will show you how to develop the stroke keys for this shot, and how to use them to execute under pressure in matches.

The final aspect of developing muscle memory is to practice visualizing the stroke away from the court. You can do this by setting aside regular times to practice your visualizations, or by doing them in free moments in the course of your daily routine. Visualize yourself hitting a perfect two-handed backhand volley. Build up to ten repetitions. Experiment with visualizing specific keys, as you develop your key system for the shot. In addition, you should work visually by watching video of the backhand volley. You can use instructional videos, watch tapes of professional matches, and also make a video of yourself executing perfect practice swings and hitting the shot correctly in controlled drill.

Muscle Memory Corrections

○ ○

As with the other volleys there is minimal followthrough in the two-handed backhand volley. However, using muscle memory corrections at the Finish Position is important to eliminate certain common errors.

The three most frequent errors and their corrections are demonstrated below. These are errors in racket position, and in footwork. To make a muscle memory correction, freeze at the end of the shot in the statueman position. Do not recover. Hold this position, and compare your actual finish with the checkpoints for the correct finish. Now move directly from your actual position to the correct one. This process teaches your muscles to feel the difference between what you were trying to do and what you actually did. As with the groundstrokes and other volleys, doing muscle memory corrections over time will bring your stroke closer to the model, until you are executing it correctly on a consistent basis. Again, in working on your corrections, you should make regular use of video. By watching video of your actual stroke production, you will not only see how you are deviating from your model, you will develop a clear image of the model stroke itself.

Muscle Memory Corrections:
Racket Position

The next two sequences show two common errors in the racket position at the finish of the two-handed backhand volley.

The first is releasing the wrists at the Contact Point. Doing this, in an attempt to hit with more pace, the player actually cuts off his body leverage, creating a loss instead of a gain. Releasing the wrists also causes sudden changes in the direction of the racket head, which results in a lack of control over shot placement.

The second error is releasing the left hand at contact. This error causes the player to lose the primary source of leverage on the shot, which is the body rotation, and the pushing action of the back, left hitting arm. The result is chronically late contact. The player has a difficult time controlling shots hit to him with pace, and again, he loses ball control.

To correct these errors, simply freeze in the statueman position, then, referring to the checkpoints if necessary, reposition the racket to the correct Finish Position as shown.

STATUEMAN
Wrist Release
and Correction

ERROR: WRIST RELEASE   CORRECTED FINISH POSITION

STATUEMAN
Releasing the Left Hand
and Correction

ERROR: RELEASING LEFT HAND   CORRECTED FINISH POSITION

Muscle Memory Correction:
Leg Position

This sequence shows a typical footwork error on the two-handed backhand volley, finishing with an open stance. The player in the first photo has not stepped forward into the ball. Without this step to the ball, the stance will be open at the Finish Position. The shoulder turn will not be complete, limiting the body rotation. In addition, the body weight cannot be transferred into the shot. As a consequence, the swing pattern will often be too sharply down, the contact will be late, and the shot will tend to float. To correct this error, freeze in the statueman position. Now adjust the feet to the correct position by stepping across and forward with the right foot. The toes of the feet should be parallel along the edge of a straight line.

STATUEMAN
Open Stance
and Correction

ERROR: OPEN STANCE AT FINISH   CORRECTED FINISH POSITION

KEYING THE TWO-HANDED BACKHAND VOLLEY

As with the other volleys, the final step in learning to execute the two-handed volley in match play is to develop your stroke key system. Again, the most effective key for most players is the image of the early contact. Early contact is the key to effortless power and good ball control. It is the first key outlined below.

The second key is the shoulder rotation. A fatal error made frequently at the net is to take the arm and racket back independently, rather than allowing the shoulder turn to swing them into position. Working with this key, you can correct this problem, and assure the role of body rotation in the stroke.

The third key, as in the case of the other volleys, is the cross step to the ball. A more advanced key, it allows you to produce the entire stroke pattern by keying on a single step to the ball. With this key, the racket, the shoulders, and the legs move as a unit. It allows the player to execute solid technical volleys in the rapid-fire exchanges of net play.

The learning procedure for creating your stroke keys is identical to that for mastering the still frames. First, establish the position physically, referring to the checkpoints that accompany the image. Next, close your eyes and create an image of the position in your mind's eye, giving it as much detail as possible. Notice how the position feels physically, and make the image and the feeling correspond in your mind. Then test the key in controlled drill. As the ball approaches, hold the image of the key in mind. As you swing, make your racket, hitting arm, shoulders, and legs overlap the image.

If you visualize the key clearly, it should function as a magnet, attracting your racket and body to the correct position. Hit ten to twenty balls in controlled drill. If the key produces consistent strokes, then it is an active key. Progress to rallies and match play and test the key there. You may also find that slight variations of the key are more effective. For example, rather than using the entire still frame, you may want to visualize just one aspect of the image.

The keys presented here should be used as a guide in developing your own personal system of two-handed backhand volley keys. Your goal is to determine which keys are active, and which counteract your own particular tendencies. Correlate your errors with the counteracting keys. Test the keys, and others that you may discover, in controlled drill, rallies, and in match play. Compile your stroke key chart from the results of this work, and update it as required. Your stroke key chart provides a reliable method for creating mental focus in match play and avoiding panic in the face of the rapid-fire exchanges at the net. By using it, you will develop the ability to execute two-handed backhand volleys with routine precision and success.

Keying the Two-Handed Backhand Volley: The Contact Point from the Player's Perspective

○ ○

Early contact is the most powerful key on any volley, and the two-handed backhand is no exception. The image here is shown from the player's perspective from over the shoulder and slightly behind.

Note the position of the various checkpoints. The shaft of the racket is about forty-five degrees to the court. The face of the racket is vertical. The elbow of the left, hitting arm is slightly bent, and the wrist is laid back. The left shoulder has rotated forward, pushing the arm and the racket to the ball, and creating natural body leverage. Finally, the contact is about a foot in front of the body. Establish the Contact Point physically and create a mental image. Test the key in controlled drill.

Keying the Two-Handed Backhand Volley: Turning from the Shoulders

○ ○

READY POSITION   THE TURN   CONTACT POINT

A crucial aspect of the two-handed volley is the use of shoulder rotation. The arm and racket should never go back independently, but move in unison with the shoulders. As the first image above shows, the shoulders start parallel to the net.

In the second image, the shoulders have turned to the ball, so that they are about forty-five degrees to the net. By making this rotation, the player swings the hitting arm and racket into correct position. In the third image, the shoulders have rotated back toward the parallel position, pushing the hitting arm and racket forward to the ball. The result is early contact and natural power. Move through the motion several times as shown above, keying on the role of the shoulders. As you do, create a mental image, or a mini-movie of the movement. Now test the key in controlled drill.

Keying the Two-Handed Backhand Volley: The Cross Step to the Ball

○ ○

READY POSITION   START OF CROSS STEP   CONTACT POINT

As with all volleys, the two-handed backhand volley can be keyed on the cross step to the ball. This key allows the player to execute the shot consistently in high-speed exchanges. With the step, as the sequence shows, the shoulders, arm, and racket all move as a unit to the ball. However, the use of this key requires mastery of the other basic elements and should be used only when the muscle memory for the stroke has been firmly established.

In the Ready Position, imagine that the butt of the racket and the tip of your right toe are attached to each other by a steel rod, shown by the arrows above. In the second frame, you can see that with the racket and foot attached, the shoulders will start to turn and the racket to move forward automatically as the step begins. At the Contact Point, the left rear shoulder pushes the hitting arm and racket forward to meet the ball early, as shown in the third frame.

Practice the cross step to the contact, and as you do create a mental image of the motion, and of the steel rod connecting your right foot and the racket butt. Now test the key in controlled drill.

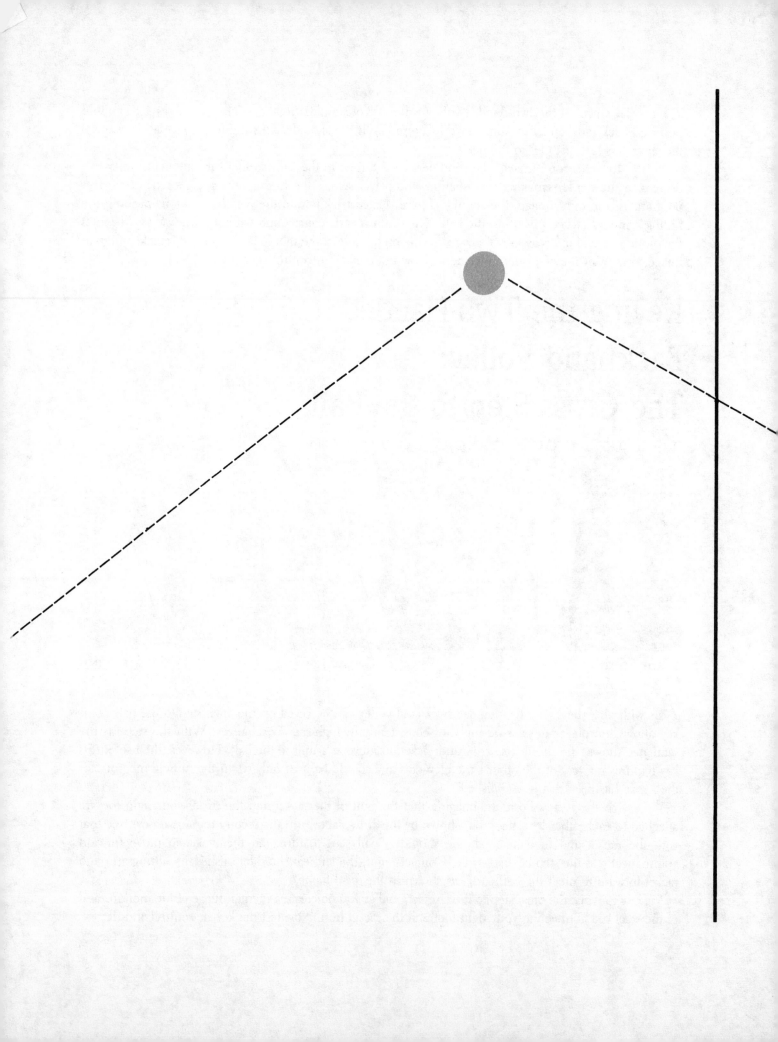

THE SERVE

*T*here is a saying in tennis: you are only as good as your serve. In match play, if you hold your serve, the worst that can happen is that every set will go to a tiebreaker. And, if you hold your serve, with just one service break, you would win every set. All great players have the capacity to win most of their service games as a matter of routine. The ability to hold serve at higher and higher levels of competition is usually what determines how far a player can progress competitively in the game.

Unfortunately, at the recreational level, the opposite is often true: many players are only as bad as their serves. They are unable to hold serve on a consistent basis, and are under continuous pressure to break serve just to stay even in the match. Often they hit the first serve as hard and as flat as possible. But since it rarely goes in, they are reduced to a tentative, pushed second serve. This destroys the advantage of serving. It allows the opponent to take the offensive from the first ball. It turns what should be the most positive aspect of the game into an immediate liability.

There is a certain confidence and sense of rhythm that comes from playing consistent service games. Knowing that he can serve effectively, the player's focus shifts to putting together the necessary shot combinations to break his opponent. Once this is achieved, the remainder of the match can be played almost on automatic pilot.

Most recreational players, and many competitive players as well, never approach this frame of mind. There are many reasons why this is true, but as in the case of the other basic shots in the game, good serving can be boiled down to one factor—consistent technical execution. And of all the strokes in the game, the serve is probably the one which most players execute the most poorly.

175

In one fundamental way, the serve differs from every other shot in tennis. When you serve, you are not hitting an oncoming ball. Rather than reacting to a speeding ball directed at you by an opponent, you are, instead, hitting a ball that has no oncoming velocity—it is virtually hanging in the air in front of you. Since the server starts the point with the ball in his hand, nothing happens until he makes it happen himself.

Most players, however, fail to realize what this absence of oncoming ball velocity means in terms of the bio-mechanics of the motion. In the case of a groundstroke or a volley, the oncoming velocity of the ball means that at contact, there is a significant impact. Even though there should be a feeling of smoothness and relaxation to these strokes, there is a certain level of muscle tension required to withstand the impact. But there is no similar collision between the racket and the ball on the serve. In the other strokes, a large part of the speed of the shot comes from the force already present in the oncoming ball. With the serve, there is no oncoming velocity. The goal, instead, is to generate this initial velocity through the service motion. To do this requires greater racket head acceleration than on the groundstrokes or volleys. And the key to maximizing the racket head acceleration on the serve is a relaxed, full motion.

Unfortunately, few recreational players approach the service motion with these facts in mind. They are used to the level of muscle tension required for groundstrokes, and simply carry this feeling over into the service motion. Or worse, in an attempt to increase the speed of the serve, they tense up and muscle the ball even *more*. The result is a stiff, constricted motion, and an actual reduction in the pace generated.

If you look at the path of the racket on the serve, you will see that it is more than twice as long as the swing on the groundstrokes, and takes at least twice as long to execute. This long, full motion produces maximum racket head acceleration at the contact point, and is the primary power source on the serve. In addition to the swing path, there are two sources of additional power: the rotation of the shoulders and the body into the shot, and the uncoiling action of the legs.

The second power source, body rotation, will happen automatically, provided that the player begins the motion with the shoulders positioned correctly. As the photo sequences will demonstrate, the motion should begin with the shoulders perpendicular to the net. This is analogous to the correct position of the shoulders at the completion of the Turn on the groundstrokes. As with the groundstrokes, the correct shoulder rotation will then occur naturally as a consequence of the swing pattern. Most recreational players, however, unknowingly eliminate this automatic power source from the game by standing incorrectly in the Ready Position.

The full value of shoulder rotation as a power source in the service motion can be seen by examining the delivery of John McEnroe. Though many observers have labeled his serve unorthodox, or at least, idiosyncratic, the truth is it represents a significant advance in the bio-mechanics of the motion. What sets McEnroe's serve apart is his distinctive sideways stance. This stance confuses critics, and is what has led to this misunderstanding of what actually happens during his motion. In fact, if McEnroe were to start his motion from the traditional position, it would appear flawlessly classical. But, by standing with both feet parallel along the edge of the baseline, McEnroe adds a new dimension to the concept of body leverage in the serve. The fact is, with the sideways stance, McEnroe actually doubles the role of the shoulders in the execution of the motion. When McEnroe starts his forward motion to the ball, his back is literally turned to the net. Unlike the standard motion in which the shoulders rotate a maximum of 90 degrees, McEnroe achieves almost twice that, or nearly 180 degrees of shoulder rotation throughout the course of the motion. The result is tremendous additional power, and ball rotation.

Advanced students of the game may want to experiment with the sideways stance after they have developed full control of the other aspects of the service motion. The vast majority of players, however, can learn something from McEnroe simply by developing full shoulder rotation within the context of the classical motion. This means standing with the front foot parallel to the baseline, and the shoulders perpendicular to the net. If you watch pro tennis on television, you will notice how many of the top players known for their serves start in this position.

After the shoulders, the third and final power source in the service motion is the legs. The topic of the correct leg work on the serve is also a debated one, with opinion divided into two primary viewpoints. The older view, a standard in the library of tennis tips, is that, to maximize power on the serve, you should step through the shot with the back, right leg. This was the pattern followed by many of the great Australian champions in the 1960s and early 1970s, and also by a small number of the current top players.

In my opinion, this is the single worst mistake made by recreational players on the serve, because stepping through the ball with the back right foot on the serve destroys the timing of the body rotation. It gets the hips and the shoulders out of sync with the racket. They rotate too soon, so that by the time the racket gets to the ball, a significant amount of the potential body leverage is wasted. In addition, the step and the premature rotation make it impossible to coil the knees fully, the real source of additional power on the serve. Stepping through the shot on the serve would be the equivalent of stepping through the groundstrokes with the back foot. Imagine the loss of timing and body leverage if you stepped to the ball with the back *right* foot on the forehand!

The whole idea behind the step theory is to get the body into the shot. In reality, this can be accomplished only by relying on the legs and knees. The principle is the same as for the groundstrokes: coil the quadriceps by maximizing the knee bend. This allows them to release into the ball as a natural consequence of the swing. A player who uses his knees in this fashion will automatically spring upward into the ball. When the knees are properly coiled, rather than cross stepping with the back foot, the player will land on the front foot, and the back leg will kick away from the body for balance. This footwork pattern is sometimes called the thrust, or the hop. It is easily the dominant technique on the pro tour. Examples of players who use it include most of the great servers in the game: John McEnroe, Ivan Lendl, Stefan Edberg, Martina Navratilova, and Steffi Graf, among others.

Another debated issue in serving theory is ball toss. This subject has also been widely misunderstood, to the great detriment of vast numbers of recreational players. According to the predominant tennis tip theory, the correct toss should be low, so that the player strikes the ball at the top of the toss, or even on the way up. The player usually cited as a model for the perfect toss by this school is Roscoe Tanner, a top American player in the 1970s and early 1980s. Although he never won a Grand Slam title, Tanner was widely known for the tremendous velocity of his serve, clocked on radar at over 140 miles per hour. This velocity was indeed due in part to his extremely low service toss. Because the toss was low, Tanner was forced to execute the service motion very rapidly, and this in turn led to increased racket head speed and his famous ball velocity.

There are, however, many problems with this theory. First, to execute the motion so quickly, it is crucial that the player stay extremely loose and relaxed. As noted above, this is already a major difficulty for any player on the serve. The low toss tends to compound the problem. The average player, in his anxiety to get the racket around, tends to tense up even more, preventing the very effect he is hoping to accomplish. A related problem with the low toss is the need for superior timing, to get the racket head positioned correctly at contact in so brief an interval. Even a slight error in the angle of the racket head at contact can produce an inaccurate delivery, and thus become a fundamental cause of inconsistency. These factors of relaxation and timing plagued Tanner under the pressure of big matches (for example, his Wimbledon final loss to Bjorn Borg in 1979) when his percentage of first serves dropped dramatically.

According to the low toss argument, a higher ball toss is much more difficult to time. This is true, allegedly, because as the ball starts to drop down, it begins to accelerate, and this change in speed makes timing the contact difficult. But this is a ridiculous claim. The speed of the ball during the toss is a fraction of the velocity of an oncoming groundstroke. A player who is struggling with his timing on his serve because of a low toss often has no trouble timing oncoming shots that are traveling with great velocity. On the toss the ball is moving at a fraction of this speed. Any player capable of rallying the ball at even a very low pace has more than enough hand-eye coordination to time the speed of the ball on the service toss.

In reality a high service toss is actually much easier to time. The real problem is having enough time to execute the motion smoothly and with technical precision. Again, the swing path on the serve is more than twice the length of the groundstrokes. To complete the motion correctly takes time, and it is the height of the toss that gives the player the chance to do this. Therefore, a high toss is a primary key to developing an effective serve. If you doubt this, take a quick look at the ball tosses on the tour. The overwhelming majority of professional players have high tosses, and hit the ball somewhere on the way down. There is not a single player on the tour today with a toss as low as Roscoe Tanner's. McEnroe has one of the lower tosses among the top players, but his ball typically drops six inches to a foot before contact. Other players, such as Lendl, Edberg, and Becker, toss the ball much higher than McEnroe, with Lendl about two feet higher than the contact point. If these players need a high toss in order to execute their service motions, how much more so the majority of tournament and recreational players.

A high toss is crucial for a successful serve. The only real issue is *how high* the toss should be. The key to answering this question is the personal rhythm of the individual server. Every player has a slightly different rhythm to his delivery. The trick is to find the toss that suits it best. Some players can move through the motion relatively quickly, stay relaxed, and keep the delivery smooth. Others need more time, and move through the backswing at a significantly slower pace. The slower your natural windup, the higher your toss should be. The correct pace for your serve can be determined only by experimentation and feel. As a rule of thumb, you should start by tossing about a foot above the contact point and evaluate the results. If you feel rushed and tense, give yourself additional time by tossing higher. If you feel you are waiting for the ball, and your racket is lagging, then lower the toss a little until you find the right tempo.

Finally, there is the question of service grip. Although there are occasional exceptions, most players should learn the basic motion for the serve with their forehand grip. This will produce a flat shot, but the player will develop a basic feeling for the motion, for striking the ball solidly, and for controlling the direction of the shot. Initially, the focus should be on establishing the correct technical swing path.

Once the basic swing is consistent, the player can change to a true serving grip and can begin to develop spin. Unfortunately, a great many recreational players never make this step, although hitting with spin is absolutely essential in developing an effective serve. They wind up with a hard, flat first serve that rarely goes in, and a weak second serve that opponents routinely attack. As with the groundstrokes, spin on the serve causes the ball to arc rather than travel in a straight line. This means more net clearance, and a ball that will drop more sharply down into the service box. By hitting with spin, the player is able to hit the ball harder and still have confidence that the serve will be in. On the second serve, this confidence is vital. By increasing the amount of rotation on the ball, the player ensures that he will hit this critical shot with unfailing consistency.

There are two keys to developing spin. The first, as I have noted, is the grip. There are two variations of the serve grip that are widely used. One is the full backhand grip. The second, which is more comfortable and effective for most players, is the continental. These are demonstrated in the grip chapter. By simply changing to a service grip and executing the same basic motion, the player will automatically generate spin. This is because the grip change will alter the angle at which the racket face strikes the ball, causing the strings to brush across the back of the ball.

The second factor in the creation of spin is the angle of the racket head movement when it strikes the ball. Typically, the types of spin on the serve are described as either "slice" or "top-spin." In reality, the type of spin is really a matter of degree. If the racket head is traveling across in more of a horizontal line, the serve will have more sidespin, the ball will move from right to left, and will have a little less kick, and will bounce lower, after it hits the court. Typically, this rotation is described as a slice serve. McEnroe's serve is a good example of this variation. If, on the other hand, the angle of the diagonal is more vertical, so that the racket head is moving more sharply upward at contact, then the ball will travel in a straighter path, but will dip more sharply, and will tend to kick or bounce higher upon contact with the court. This is the topspin serve.

For most players, the topspin variation will probably be the easiest to master, and the most effective. The increased arc makes it a higher percentage stroke. The spin produces more net clearance and the dipping action brings the ball down into the service box. Furthermore, the higher bounce creates problems for opponents on the return. With this spin, the ball can be kicked up to shoulder level or even higher, forcing the returning player to hit a high, weak return. His only effective counterplay is to take the ball on the rise, before it can get up and on top of him. Since this is a difficult return to time consistently, and is also a likely source of errors, it generates free points for the server.

With the basic motion and use of spin described in this chapter, the difference between the first serve and the second serve is primarily a matter of degree. The first ball can be hit slightly flatter, and thus with a little more pace. The second ball should have more rotation—giving the player complete confidence in his ability to place the ball in the box, even under the pressure of big points. As described above, however, most players have a consistent tendency to overhit the first serve. It may be going 100 miles an hour, but that is of little benefit if it never goes into the court. Players who cannot achieve a first serve percentage of 65 to 75 percent should increase the rotation on their first ball to achieve this consistency. They may discover that this delivery leads to winning more service games more easily.

According to one school of thought, every player should develop the ability to hit both a topspin and a slice serve. This school also advocates changing the toss for the different spins. Thus, a slice toss should be more to the right of the server, and possibly lower, making it easier to hit around the side of the ball. The toss for the topspin serve should be further back to the left, slightly over the server's head, so that the player can hit up on the ball more radically for topspin. Again, if we look at the top players, we can see that none of them hit two distinct types of spin, much less have two different ball tosses. In the first place, making such a basic change in the motion from ball to ball is prohibitively difficult. The serve requires the rhythmic coordination of the toss and the motion of the body. It is difficult enough to develop one consistent service delivery, let alone two. In the second place, an experienced player will quickly learn to read changes in the placement of the toss, and will then know what serve you are planning to hit almost as soon as you do yourself. This will drastically reduce, if not completely eliminate, any advantage in alternating between two spins.

Instead of having two different service motions, top players develop variations in the *degree of spin*. These can be hit off the same toss, with the exact same motion. The variation in the amount of spin comes from altering the spot on which the racket makes contact with the ball, and the angle of the diagonal along which the racket head is moving, not by making a fundamental change in the service motion itself. By using the same toss for every serve, the player makes it difficult for an opponent to read his delivery. By following this approach, a player will actually develop *three* service variations, not two. He will be able to hit the first serve fairly flat, and also, with moderate spin. In addition, he will be able to hit the second ball with heavier rotation. This heavier spin can also be mixed with the other two varieties on the first serve, to keep the opponent guessing and off balance, or if the server finds that his opponent has trouble with the higher bounce. This will be the case more often than most players realize. Some players will hit much better returns off flat, hard serves. Unless a server can generate enough velocity to overpower his opponents, hitting flat deliveries may actually be counterproductive. This is particularly true when playing serve and volley tennis, when hard servers frequently find themselves scraping bullet returns off their shoe laces on the first volley. The ball with heavier spin, on the other hand, travels slightly slower, so it allows the net rusher to close to the net faster, as well as forcing higher, floating returns that are much easier to volley.

In this chapter, the process of learning to serve with the proper mix of power, control, and spin is divided into stages. The first is the mastery of the swing pattern. This is presented in the basic serve sequence photos and teaching progressions. The second step is developing the ability to hit moderate spin, staying within the framework of the basic motion. This is presented as a variation on the basic serve sequence. The third step is learning to hit with heavier ball rotation. Finally, the fourth step is adding advanced footwork, the leg thrust described above, and the source of the superior power of the great servers in modern game. This is demonstrated in a second still photo sequence. Following the progressions, it is possible for any player to bring his serve up to the level of the other parts of his game, and learn to win serve on a regular basis in both recreational and tournament play.

CREATING THE SWING PATTERN FOR THE BASIC SERVE

In this chapter, you will use the principles of visualization to learn the swing pattern for the basic serve. As with all the other strokes, you will learn a physical and visual model of the motion, using a combination of sequence photos and text. The model, in turn, will become your personal blueprint for developing a solid and effective serve.

First, the motion is shown from the front view, broken down into its component frames, and its general technical characteristics are outlined. Then the stroke is presented from the front and side views simultaneously, and the key still frames are identified. Because of the longer, more complex swing pattern required, there are six key still frames on the serve, versus four still frames for groundstrokes and volleys. These still frames are:

1. **The Ready Position**
2. **The Toss**
3. **The Backswing**
4. **The Racket Drop**
5. **The Contact Point**
6. **The Finish Position**

The still frames are the basis for mastering the physical and visual models. Note that, as with the groundstrokes and the volleys, if the player passes through each of the still frames correctly, this will guarantee that the entire swing pattern is correct as well.

The next section shows you how to learn each of the six still frames for the serve, by teaching you the checkpoints. The following section shows you how to do muscle memory corrections for the serve. The key section teaches you how to develop your own system of stroke keys for producing the serve consistently in rallies and match play. Finally, the advanced serve, which maximizes the use of the legs for additional power and spin, is presented as a variation, along with the necessary additional keys.

1
READY POSITION

2
ARM DROP

3
TOSS POSITION

4
BACKSWING

5
**START OF
RACKET DROP**

Characteristics of the Basic Serve
FRONT VIEW

○ ○

Grip: To learn the basic motion, start with your forehand grip, unless it is a severe modified eastern grip, in which case it is probably easier to start with a grip closer to the pure eastern. As soon as the player has mastered the basic swing and developed a feel for solid contact with the forehand grip, he should progress to the continental grip to develop spin, as explained later in this chapter. The continental grip is demonstrated in the grip chapter.

Full Motion: Compared with the groundstrokes, the basic swing pattern on the serve is twice as long. It starts with the racket pointing straight at the net (Frame 1). The arms drop down together (Frame 2), and then go up together until the hitting arm is completely straight and pointing directly at the back fence (Frame 3). The racket movement continues upward until it points directly up (Frame 4), and then drops all the way down the back (Frame 6). From there the hitting arm snaps the racket up to the Contact Point at full extension (Frame 8). The followthrough is all the way across the body, ending

6	7	8	9	10	11
RACKET DROP	**START OF HIT**	**CONTACT POINT**	**FOLLOWTHROUGH**		**FINISH POSITION**

when the racket hand touches down on the front of the left leg (Frame 11). This full swing path is the primary power source in the motion.

High Toss: A key aspect to the successful execution of the motion is a high toss. The toss allows the player time to reach full extension at the Contact Point, extending as fully as possible from the tip of the toes to the tip of the racket (Frame 8). It also allows him to develop a smooth, relaxed rhythm, and maximize the acceleration of the racket head. The height should be a minimum of six inches to a foot higher than the actual contact, so that the player hits the ball slightly on the way down. The toss should also be to the right and in front of the body, so that the Contact Point is directly above the right shoulder, and in front of the left front foot. The key to a consistent toss is keeping the tossing arm straight. It is straight in the Ready Position (Frame 1), as it drops down to the leg (Frame 2), and at the ball release (Frame 3). At the completion of the Backswing (Frame 4), it is still straight and fully extended.

Additional Power Sources: After a complete swing path, the second power source is shoulder rotation. If the serve starts with the shoulders in the correct position perpendicular to the net (Frame 1), the rotation is produced automatically in the course of the swing. At the start of the upward hitting motion (Frame 7), the shoulders have already begun to rotate into the shot. This continues through the course of the motion, so that the shoulders are parallel to the net at the finish, and have rotated a full ninety degrees. The final power source is the legs. Note that at the completion of the Backswing (Frame 4), the weight is fully shifted forward to the left, front foot, and the knees are coiled. From this position the legs release into the shot as a natural consequence of hitting motion (Frames 5–7).

Basic Serve:
Six Key Still Frames · SIDE VIEW

○○○○○○○○○○○○○○○○○○○○○○○○○○○○○

STILL FRAME #1   STILL FRAME #2   STILL FRAME #3

READY POSITION ARM DROP   TOSS POSITION   BACKSWING   START OF RACKET DROP

Basic Serve:
Six Key Still Frames · FRONT VIEW

○○○○○○○○○○○○○○○○○○○○○○○○○○○○○

STILL FRAME #1   STILL FRAME #2   STILL FRAME #3

READY POSITION   ARM DROP   TOSS POSITION   BACKSWING   START OF RACKET DROP

STILL FRAME #4   STILL FRAME #5   STILL FRAME #6

RACKET DROP   START OF HIT   CONTACT POINT   FOLLOWTHROUGH   FINISH POSITION

                          STILL FRAME #5

STILL FRAME #4   STILL FRAME #6

RACKET DROP   START OF HIT   CONTACT POINT   FOLLOWTHROUGH   FINISH POSITION

Still Frame 1
The Ready Position

○ ○ ○ ○ ○ ○ ○ ○ ○ ○ ○ ○ ○ ○ ○ ○

Checkpoints:

1. The Shoulders: The shoulders start perpendicular to the net in the Ready Position. The player stands straight up and down from the waist. The knees are slightly flexed.

2. The Hitting Arm: The hitting arm is straight, and hangs down from the shoulder so that it is in line with the front leg. The basic serve can be executed with either the forehand or the continental grip.

3. The Racket: The tip of the racket points straight at net. The shaft of the racket is parallel with the court, and the face is perpendicular. The left, tossing arm is straight, and the ball is on the face of the racket.

4. The Legs: The feet are sideways, parallel to the baseline, with the heels in line. The weight is equally distributed on both feet, and knees are slightly flexed.

Establish the position physically using the checkpoints, then create the mental image.

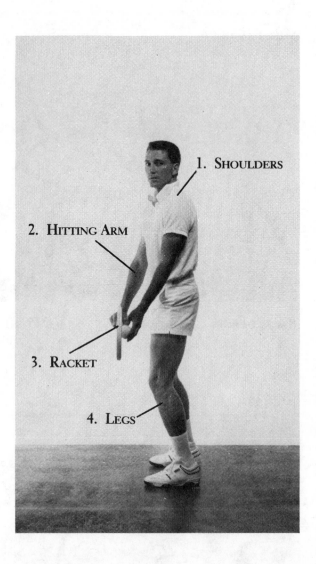

1. SHOULDERS

2. HITTING ARM

3. RACKET

4. LEGS

Still Frame 2
The Toss

○○○○○○○○○○

Checkpoints:

*1. **The Shoulders:*** The shoulders have remained perpendicular to the net. The left tossing arm is straight and has dropped straight down to the front of the left leg on the hinge of the shoulder. From there, the tossing arm moves straight upward releasing the ball at about shoulder height.

*2. **The Hitting Arm:*** The hitting arm has traced a perfect half circle from the Ready Position until it points directly back at the back fence. The arm has not gone back behind the plane of the body, but is still on the right side of the shoulders.

*3. **The Racket:*** The racket now points straight back at the back fence as well. It has traced the circumference of a half circle. The face of the racket has turned over at the bottom of the arm.

*4. **The Legs:*** The weight has started to shift forward to the left front foot. The knee bend has increased, particularly in the front left leg as the weight is transferred.

Start in the Ready Position and move to the Toss. Establish the position physically by using the checkpoints, then create the mental image.

3. RACKET

1. SHOULDERS

2. HITTING ARM

4. LEGS

Still Frame 3
The Backswing

○ ○ ○ ○ ○ ○ ○ ○ ○ ○ ○

Checkpoints:

1. The Shoulders: The shoulders have remained in their original perpendicular position. The body is straight up and down from the waist. The left tossing arm is still straight and fully extended.

2. The Hitting Arm: The upper arm is still pointing back at the back fence, but the elbow has started to bend, so that the forearm points directly up at the sky.

3. The Racket: The shaft of the racket is also pointing directly up, and the face of the racket is still vertical to the court. In effect, the tip of the racket has traced a path that is three fourths of the circumference of a circle.

4. The Legs: The weight has now fully shifted to the left front leg, and the knee bend is maximized. The player has started to come up on his back toes. Note that there has been no stepping motion with the back foot.

Start in the Ready Position. Move through the Toss to the Backswing. Establish the position physically using the checkpoints, then create the mental image.

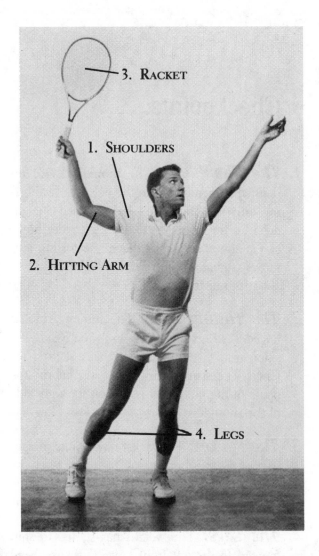

Still Frame 4
The Racket Drop

○ ○ ○ ○ ○ ○ ○ ○ ○ ○ ○ ○ ○

Checkpoints:

1. The Shoulders: At the Racket Drop, the shoulders remain sideways or perpendicular, and the player is still straight up and down from the waist.

2. The Hitting Arm: The hitting arm has relaxed and bent at the elbow, so that the racket can fully drop. The elbow position is high, about thirty degrees above the perpendicular position at the completion of the Backswing.

3. The Racket: The racket has dropped all the way down the back. The edge of the racket is in position to scratch the center of the spine. The tip of the racket is pointing directly down at the court.

4. The Legs: The weight is still forward on the left front foot. The knees have started to release naturally as a consequence of the motion.

Move from the Ready Position through the still frames to the Racket Drop. Establish the position physically using the checkpoints, then create the mental image.

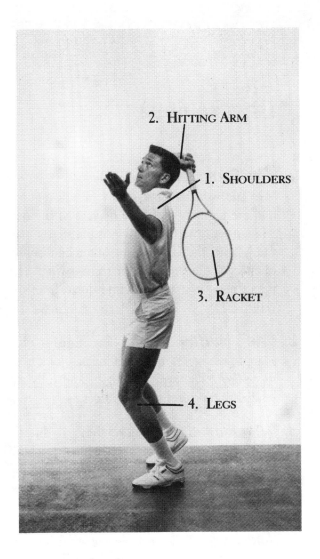

Still Frame 5
The Contact Point

○ ○ ○ ○ ○ ○ ○ ○ ○ ○ ○ ○ ○ ○ ○

Checkpoints:

1. The Shoulders: The shoulders have started to rotate with the start of the hitting motion, and are at about forty-five degrees to the net. The power from the rotation is transferred naturally into the ball, as an automatic consequence of the proper stance and swing. The upper body is straight up and down from the waist.

2. The Hitting Arm: The forearm has snapped the racket up to the Contact Point from the elbow. The arm is straight, and fully extended upward from the shoulder.

3. The Racket: The racket head is directly above the right shoulder and slightly in front of the front foot, so that the contact is over the court and in front of the body. The shaft of the racket is perpendicular to the court.

4. The Legs: The knees have released from their coiled position upward into the ball, but are still slightly flexed. The weight is on the front foot, and the player is starting to come up on the back toes. The player has not stepped through the shot, and remains on balance.

Start in the Ready Position, and move through the still frames to the Contact Point. Establish the position physically using the checkpoints, then create the mental image.

3. RACKET

2. HITTING ARM

1. SHOULDERS

4. LEGS

Still Frame 6
The Finish Position

○ ○ ○ ○ ○ ○ ○ ○ ○ ○ ○ ○ ○ ○ ○

Checkpoints:

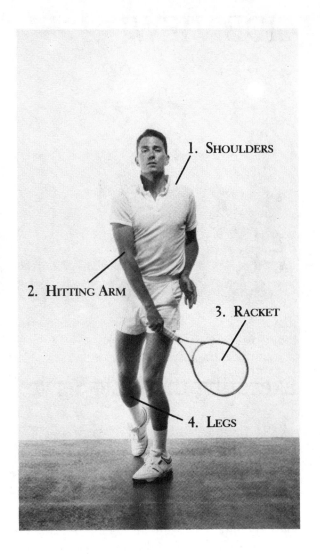

1. The Shoulders: The shoulders have rotated a full ninety degrees from the Ready Position until they are parallel with the net. The upper body has remained straight up and down from the waist.

2. The Hitting Arm: The hitting arm has remained relaxed, carrying the racket all the way through to the finish in a smooth motion. The right racket hand should touch down in the middle of the left front leg.

3. The Racket: The racket has accelerated all the way through the hit. The racket head moves out along the line of the shot, and then down and across the body. At the finish the racket is on the left side of the left front leg.

4. The Legs: The weight is now fully forward on the left front foot, and the player has come up on his right toes for balance. The knees have uncoiled into the ball, but remain slightly flexed.

Start in the Ready Position, and move all the way through the still frames to the Finish Position. Establish the position physically using the checkpoints, then create the mental image.

1. SHOULDERS

2. HITTING ARM

3. RACKET

4. LEGS

Putting the Still Frames Together
SIDE VIEW

○ ○

READY POSITION   **TOSS POSITION**   **BACKSWING**   **RACKET DROP**   **CONTACT POINT**   **FINISH POSITION**

Executing the Basic Serve

After you are comfortable with the six still frames and the checkpoints for the basic serve, the next step is to put them together into a full swing pattern as shown.

Start in the Ready Position. Drop your arms and shift the weight forward to the left, front foot. As the motion starts, the hitting arm drops down and points down at the court, then turns over and moves backward and upward to the Toss Position, along the edge of the circumference of an imaginary circle. Meanwhile, the tossing arm goes straight down to the front of the leg, and then straight up. The ball release is at about shoulder level. Next, move the racket upward to the Backswing position. The tip of the racket points up toward the sky, and the upper arm is still horizontal to the court. The tossing arm is now fully extended. Relax the arm and let it drop all the way down the back. From here the forearm snaps the racket up to full extension. The Contact Point is high, above the shoulder and slightly to the right, and also, slightly in front of the plane of the body. Finally, the motion finishes with the hitting arm and racket following through all the way across the body. The whole motion should be relaxed and executed much more slowly and with less muscle tension than the groundstrokes or volleys.

Start the development of your muscle memory with practice swings—executing the motion without actually hitting balls. As you pass through the individual still frames, make sure that each checkpoint is correct. If you are unsure, stop and verify the checkpoints for the particular still frame. As with the other strokes, if each still frame is correct, this virtually guarantees that the entire motion will be correct as well. Build up to ten swings. If possible, do this work in front of a mirror.

Next, progress to controlled drill. For the serve, this means using as many practice balls as possible. A minimum is about 20, although about 100 balls is ideal. Some clubs and tennis centers will let you use their teaching balls for this purpose. Start serving in the add court. This makes it easier to align the shoulders in the correct perpendicular position in the Ready Position. Initially, it is not important that the ball goes in the court on every serve, rather your goal is to develop a feeling for the correct technical motion. As you become comfortable with the swing, the ball will start to find the service box automatically, and with increasing frequency.

Many beginning players find that executing the complete motion poses problems, at least initially. If this is true for you, you should wind up *before* the ball Toss. Progress through the still frames and stop in the Racket Drop Position. Now toss the ball, and execute the rest of the motion. If you are a more advanced player who has problems making a full Racket Drop, you should follow this procedure as well, and wind up before the Toss. Once your execution is correct using the two-part motion, you can begin to put the serve together into one continuous movement.

Once you can execute the motion consistently in controlled drill, you can serve practice points. The best way to do achieve confidence doing this is to play what are called "no double fault" points with a practice partner. This means that you serve however many balls are required—one, two, twenty, or whatever—to get the ball in the box, with correct technical form. This removes the fear of double faulting, and the tendency to abandon the correct technical motion and push the second serve in the box. Once the server gets a good serve in, the partner returns the ball, and the point is played out. Now the server goes to the other court and the process is repeated. Most players who play these no double fault points quickly find that they regularly get at least one of two serves in the box anyway. This process should give you the confidence to execute the correct motion under the pressure of the double fault. Once the serve is consistent playing practice points, you should progress to match play.

As with the other strokes, the final aspect of developing deep muscle memory on the serve is to practice visualizing the motion away from the court. You can do this by setting aside visual practice time, or simply utilizing spare moments in the course of the day. Visualize the entire stroke pattern, and as you develop your stroke key system as outlined below, practice visualizing the keys that are active for you. Have yourself videotaped executing the serve correctly in controlled drill, and watch this as well as instructional footage of correct serving technique.

As explained in the introduction, most players master the basic elements of the motion more easily by beginning with some version of a forehand grip. As soon as the motion is solid, however, they should add spin to their delivery. The process for doing this is presented in the key section. If the biomechanics are established, this is relatively simple to achieve, requiring only a grip change, and a slight alteration in the racket swing path prior to contact.

The final step in maximizing the potential of the serve is to develop advanced footwork. This allows the player to make use of the legs, adding tremendous additional power and spin. The advanced serve is presented as a variation in the last section of the chapter.

Muscle Memory Corrections

○ ○

As with the volleys, the role of muscle memory correction is less central in developing the serve than the groundstrokes. This is because of the crucial role of the Racket Drop, and of the Contact Point. However, there are several common errors that can be quickly eliminated by the use of muscle memory correction. They are demonstrated below.

The process for doing this is the same as with the other strokes. At the conclusion of the stroke, the player simply freezes in the statueman position. Instead of recovering, he stops and compares his actual position to the checkpoints for the correct finish. Next, he moves directly from wherever he actually is to where he should have been if he had followed the pattern correctly. This process teaches the muscles the difference between an error and the right technical motion, and increases the probability the next serve will follow the pattern more accurately. Over time, the correction process will bring the stroke and the model closely in line. As with the groundstrokes and the volleys, you should make regular use of video. By watching video of your actual stroke production, you will not only see how you are deviating from your model, you will develop the clearest possible image of the model stroke.

The three most common errors at the finish on the basic serve are finishing with a short followthrough, stepping through the ball with the back foot, and bending over at the waist in the course of the motion. All three errors typically result from trying to generate additional pace at the expense of proper technique. They are demonstrated below, along with the corrections to eliminate them from your game. Do these corrections while you are working on your serve in controlled drill. Stop every five balls, evaluate your position, and adjust to the right finish using the checkpoints. Over time the corrections will become smaller and smaller, and your motion will follow the model more precisely and consistently.

Muscle Memory Correction: Followthrough

A common tendency on the serve is to overhit the ball by tightening the arm muscles and stopping short on the followthrough in a misguided effort to generate additional power. In reality, the short followthrough creates a power loss. Real power is generated by racket head speed, and racket head speed is maximized by a full, fluid motion. Also, without a full followthrough, there is a corresponding reduction in spin, which is also dependent on the speed of the racket head as it brushes the ball.

To check the followthrough and correct any errors, freeze in the statueman position at the end of the stroke. Using the checkpoints, reposition your arm and racket as shown. The racket hand should finish fully across the body, touching down on the left, front leg.

STATUEMAN
Short Followthrough
and Correction

ERROR: SHORT FOLLOWTHROUGH   CORRECTED FINISH POSITION

Muscle Memory Correction:
Leg Position

One of the most common errors in club tennis is the tendency to "step through" the serve in the hope that this will get the body into the shot, or start the serve and volley player on his way to the net more quickly. In fact, stepping with the back foot causes the hips and shoulders to rotate through the motion too soon, throwing off the natural release of body leverage. In the extreme case, it can cause the player to get himself ahead of the toss, so that the contact is behind the plane of the body. The correct method for maximizing body leverage is not by stepping through the shot, but by coiling and releasing the knees, as shown in the section on advanced serve. Hitting off a solid base on the basic serve lays the foundation for developing this more advanced footwork.

To correct this error, freeze in the statueman position, and check the position of your legs. If you have stepped through, reposition your feet as shown, using the checkpoints for the Finish Position.

STATUEMAN
Stepping Through
the Serve
and Correction

ERROR: STEPPING THROUGH WITH THE BACK FOOT   **CORRECTED FINISH POSITION**

Muscle Memory Correction:
Body Position

Another common error on the basic motion is the tendency to bend at the waist. Again, this a result of trying to overhit the ball by throwing the shoulders forward in the course of the hitting motion. Instead of additional power, the bend results in a lower Contact Point and less net clearance. The player cuts his body leverage in half, eliminating to a great extent the role of the hips and legs in transferring power into the shot.

To correct this error, freeze in the statueman position, and adjust your body until you are standing straight up and down from the waist. This will allow you to reach full extension at contact, and allow the automatic generation of body leverage.

STATUEMAN
Bending at the Waist
and Correction

ERROR: BEND FROM THE WAIST   **CORRECTED FINISH POSITION**

KEYING
THE BASIC SERVE

As with each of the basic strokes, the final step in mastering the basic serve is to create your own system of stroke keys. By visualizing a key while on the court, the player activates the entire stroke pattern. The keys presented here will provide you with a reliable method for serving well in match play. They also provide the antidote for difficult technical problems that many players have been unable to remedy through traditional lessons.

In this section, six different keys are presented. The first key is for the timing of the motion. Assuming the swing pattern is correct, the biggest problem most players face is developing and maintaining the slower rhythm of the stroke, particularly in the excitement of matches. This key shows you how to key the timing of the motion to a three count that will keep the rhythm smooth. The next three keys are images of the still frames, all shown from the player's perspective: the Racket Drop, the Contact Point, and the Finish Position. These keys are not only effective in producing consistent execution, but can also be used to correct certain technical problems with the swing itself, as explained below.

The fifth key is for the tossing motion. Without a good toss, it is simply impossible to hit the serve correctly, and for many players, the toss is the single most difficult obstacle. Finally, the last key shows you how to generate spin on the basic serve once the fundamental motion is solid. This is the key to serving aggressively in tennis. Spin gives a player the confidence that he can get both his first and second serve in the court, even under pressure, without having to hold back the motion. It allows the player to have confidence that he can hit out on the serve and actually increase his serving percentages and accuracy. The learning procedure for creating your stroke keys is identical to that for mastering the still frames. First, establish the key physically, referring to the checkpoints that accompany the image. Next, close your eyes and create an image of the key in your mind's eye, giving it as much detail as possible. Notice how it feels physically, and make the image and the feeling correspond in your mind. Then test the key in controlled drill. As you start your service motion, hold the image of the key in your mind, and make the motion overlap the image.

If you visualize the key clearly, it should result in the correct execution of the entire service motion. Hit ten or twenty balls in controlled drill. If the key produces consistent serves, then it is an active key. Progress to practice points and match play and test the key there. You may also find that slight variations of the key are more effective. For example, rather than using the entire still frame, you may want to visualize just one aspect of the image.

The keys presented here should be used as a guide in developing your own personal system of serve keys. Your goal is to determine which keys are active, and which counteract your own particular tendencies. Correlate your errors with the counteracting keys. Test the keys, and others that you may discover, in controlled drill, rallies, and in match play. Compile your stroke key chart from the results of this work, and update it as required.

Keying the Basic Serve: The Three Count

○ ○

1   2   3

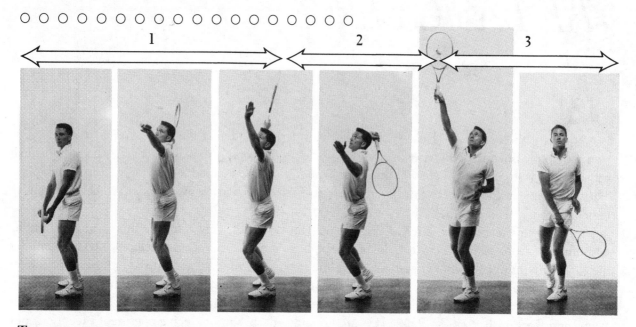

THE COORDINATION OF THE PARTS OF THE SERVICE MOTION WITH THE RHYTHM OF THE THREE COUNT.

The best key for keeping the rhythm of the motion even, and thus keeping the arm relaxed, is the use of the three count. Start in the Ready Position. Now, as you start the motion, count to yourself "one, two, three." The count should be slow and even. "One" should correspond, roughly, with the Arm Drop, and the start of the Backswing. Count "two" as the Backswing continues and the racket drops behind the back. "Three" corresponds with the start of motion upward to the ball, the contact, and the followthrough.

The problem most players face is that, somewhere between two and three, they tense up the arm and try to speed up the motion artificially, rather than allowing it to accelerate naturally. This constricts the flow of the movement and reduces racket head speed. By keeping the rhythm of the count even, you will keep the rhythm of the serve even as well. This will maximize the speed of your swing.

There is an interrelationship between the height of the toss and the rhythm of the service motion. Some players will find that they can move through the motion fairly quickly, stay relaxed, and keep the rhythm even. Other players find that if they move too quickly, they inevitably tense up too much, and rush the motion, particularly between "two" and "three." The slower your own individual rhythm, the higher you need to toss the ball. The exact height and the exact correspondence between the three count and the parts of the motion are something you must determine through experimentation. A rule of thumb is to start by tossing six inches to a foot above your Contact Point, and then to evaluate your rhythm. If you feel rushed, increase the height of the toss. If you feel that you are waiting to hit the ball, then lower the toss slightly. To create this key, start in the Ready Position. Now close your eyes and count to yourself. As you count, visualize yourself executing the serve motion, in synchronization with the count. Now test the key in controlled drill.

Keying the Basic Serve:
The Racket Drop

○ ○ ○ ○ ○ ○ ○ ○ ○ ○ ○ ○ ○ ○ ○ ○ ○ ○

The primary power source on the service motion is the snap of the racket up to the contact from the drop position. However, many players fail to achieve a complete drop, reducing the role of this fundamental factor. As any teaching pro knows, an incomplete drop is one of the most difficult flaws to correct. If this has been your problem, working with this key can eliminate it from your game. This key is also highly effective for players who may tend to shorten the motion under the pressure of match play. The key is shown from the player's perspective, the angle you will actually see it from in your own mind when you construct your mental image.

Note that the edge of the racket is in line with the center of the spine. The tip of the racket points down at the court, and the elbow position is high. Establish the Racket Drop physically. Now create the mental image. Test the key in controlled drill.

Keying the Basic Serve:
The Contact Point
from the Player's
Perspective

○ ○ ○ ○ ○ ○ ○ ○ ○ ○ ○ ○ ○ ○ ○ ○ ○ ○

High contact is crucial to the service motion. It ensures maximum net clearance; it also imparts the correct trajectory so that the ball lands consistently within the service box. High contact also maximizes body leverage, and is a major factor in shot velocity. The great servers are extended at contact from the tip of the toes to the tip of the racket. This key, presented from the player's perspective, is designed to help you achieve this yourself.

Note several key points: the arm is fully extended; it is directly above the shoulder; and the face of the racket is in front of the plane of the body, so that the contact is slightly out over the court. Establish the position physically and create the mental image.

199

Keying the Basic Serve: The Finish Position from the Player's Perspective

○ ○ ○ ○ ○ ○ ○ ○ ○ ○ ○ ○ ○ ○ ○

As with the groundstrokes, the followthrough on the serve is a primary key to maintaining racket head acceleration throughout the course of the stroke. A common tendency is to overhit the ball by tightening up the arm muscles. This leads to a short, constricted followthrough, and a loss of shot velocity, instead of a gain.

If you find that your followthrough is consistently short, this should be a primary key for you. At the end of the motion, your racket hand should touch down on your left front leg, as shown above. This full finish will allow you to keep the arm relaxed and the swing flowing. Establish the position physically and create the mental image. Now test the key in controlled drill. Hold the image at the correct finish, and make your hand and racket overlap this blueprint.

Keying the Basic Serve:
The Tossing Motion

○ ○ ○ ○ ○ ○ ○ ○ ○ ○ ○ ○ ○ ○ ○ ○ ○ ○

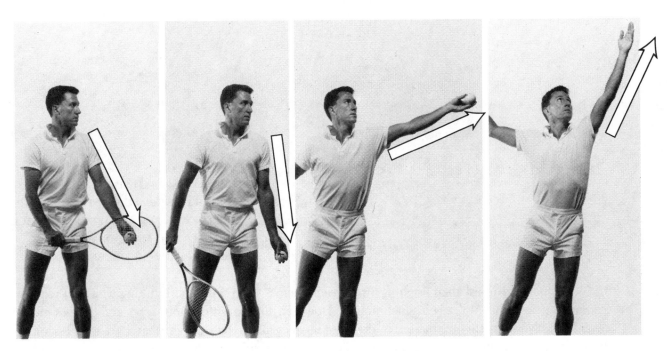

THIS SEQUENCE SHOWS THE STRAIGHT ARM POSITION AT THE READY POSITION, THE DROP OF THE ARMS, THE RELEASE OF THE BALL, AND THE EXTENSION OF THE MOTION.

Even if a player develops consistent muscle memory for the service motion, his delivery will be ineffective without a reliable toss. The key to the toss is to simplify it as much as possible. This means keeping the arm straight throughout the motion. Notice that with the arm locked at the elbow and the wrist there is no internal movement. Instead, the entire arm simply drops straight down from the hinge of the shoulder and then moves straight up to the ball release and full extension. Instead of throwing, or flipping the ball, the player simply opens his hand, allowing the ball to roll off of his fingertips. Thus, the ball toss is really more a ball *release*, rather than a toss or a throw. Typically, it is bending at the elbow or flipping the wrist that causes inconsistency in the toss placement. Execute the tossing motion with the arm straight several times. As you do, create a mental image. Now test the key in controlled drill. As you start the motion, visualize the image of your arm moving straight down and all the way up to the full extension.

Keying the Basic Serve: Developing Spin

○ ○ ○ ○ ○ ○ ○ ○ ○ ○ ○ ○ ○ ○ ○ ○ ○ ○ ○

TO CREATE BALL ROTATION, THE RACKET MUST STRIKE THE BALL AT A POINT TO THE LOWER LEFT OF THE CENTER OF THE FACE OF THE BALL AND MOVE ON A DIAGONAL ACROSS THE FACE OF THE BALL.

Often, students will ask their teaching pro to teach them a "spin serve," as if hitting with spin required learning a new and completely distinct motion. However, hitting with various types and degrees of spin actually involves only slight variations in the basic service pattern. The bio-mechanics remain essentially the same. What is different is the angle at which the racket strikes the ball.

The first step in generating ball rotation is to change to the continental grip. If you bring your racket up to the Contact Point with the continental grip, you will see that the racket face will strike the ball at an angle. Many players who execute their basic service motion with the continental grip produce spin immediately and automatically. Initially, however, you may find that the ball moves too sharply to the left. To straighten it out you must learn to strike the ball at a point to the lower left of the center, with the racket face moving upward and across the face of the ball on a diagonal line, as shown below.

To create this image, close your eyes and imagine the path of the racket and the point of contact on the ball's surface. There are the two elements in the image—the diagonal path of the racket, and the spot to the lower left at which the racket contacts the ball. You may see it in terms of a still frame of the Contact Point, or a mini-movie of the racket as it moves through the swing. Test the image you create in controlled drill.

The additional ball rotation should give the flight of your serve a noticeable arc, and cause it to drop more sharply down into the serving box. This allows you to hit the serve with confidence and pace, knowing that the ball rotation will keep it in the court. Once you feel comfortable with hitting spin in controlled drill, move on to practice points, and then match play.

At this point, you can begin to vary the type and the amount of rotation. Typically, by using the key shown above, a player will produce a ball that moves slightly from right to left, but one that also kicks up at least somewhat after the bounce. Most spin serves fall somewhere between pure slice, or a ball that rotates sideways from right to left, and pure topspin, or a ball that rotates from top to bottom. The ball spins at the angle of the diagonal at which the racket head is moving at contact.

As you develop your own particular serving style, you can experiment with variations on this basic spin. By altering the path of the diagonal line so that it is slightly more horizontal, you can generate more slice. This serve will have less arc, but will move more sharply from right to left. By making the diagonal slightly more vertical, you can generate more topspin. This serve will have more arc, and will travel in a straighter line, but it will also kick up much higher after the bounce.

A final factor influencing the type and amount of ball rotation is the placement of the toss. As described in the tossing key, a player should strive to place the toss directly above the hitting shoulder so that he can achieve maximum extension at contact. However, many players find that varying the toss placement by a few inches to the left or right makes it easier to achieve different spins. A toss slightly to the right of the shoulder increases the tendency to hit around the ball, generating slice. Similarly, a toss slightly back and to the left lends itself to hitting up and over the ball, generating topspin.

The bottom line is that most players gravitate to one type of rotation or the other. It is a question of determining which variation of toss and ball rotation is most natural and effective for you. However, after a period of experimentation, it is important that a player settle on one tossing variation.

The most effective approach, as noted at the beginning of the chapter, is to develop one basic type of ball rotation, and then to develop slight variations on that basic pattern based on the use of a single toss. This is in fact the usual pattern at the highest levels of pro tennis. John McEnroe, for example, hits the ball with a degree of sideways, slicing rotation. This is perfectly suited to his game and helps him move the ball around the service box as widely as possible. His toss, typical for this type of spin, is directly above his shoulder, or slightly to the right. Within this framework, McEnroe hits two additional variations: he can flatten out the delivery on his first serve, and he can increase the amount of spin as well, usually for his second delivery.

In contrast, players such as Ivan Lendl, Stefan Edberg, and Boris Becker serve with more of a topspin, kicking rotation. All three toss the ball more to the left than McEnroe—somewhere between the shoulder and the edge of the head. This tossing position is naturally conducive to hitting up and over the ball. It allows them to hit with more velocity, and is suited to their powerful styles. Like McEnroe, however, they have three basic variations on a single theme: a relatively flat first serve, a first serve hit with moderate rotation, and a second serve hit with increased spin. These three serves are mixed together as part of an overall serving strategy, depending on the opponent, the court surface, and the situation in a particular match.

Variation:
The Advanced Serve

○ ○ ○ ○ ○ ○ ○ ○ ○ ○ ○ ○ ○ ○ ○ ○ ○

1	2	3	4	5
READY POSITION	**ARM DROP**	**START OF KNEE BEND**	**MAXIMUM BEND**	**START OF RELEASE**

Progression to the Advanced Serve: As noted in the introduction to this chapter, most of the great servers in the modern game use the advanced footwork shown here, which is also known as the thrust, or the hop. Every player who wishes to develop his serving ability to the fullest should eventually progress to the advanced serve shown above, but only after the bio-mechanics for the basic service motion are solid. This basic competence should include the ability to hit spin consistently on both the first and second serves.

Differences from Basic Serve: The distinguishing characteristic of the advanced serve is the greatly increased role of the legs in generating additional power and spin. A key element in the basic service motion is the weight shift forward to the front, left foot, and the accompanying knee bend. In the advanced serve, this weight shift and the knee bend are maximized (Frame 4). The result is that, as the motion uncoils, the player is literally propelled upward into the ball (Frame 7). This full use of the legs creates tremendous additional ball leverage, and can increase the velocity and ball rotation of your serve by as much as 25 percent.

Producing the Advanced Serve: The key element in creating the advanced serve is increasing the knee bend at the beginning of the motion, starting when the arms drop (Frame 2), and continuing until the bend is maximized at the completion of the Backswing (Frame 4). By going down in the knees as far as possible, the player guarantees that he will uncoil upward into the ball as an

6	7	8	9	10	11
RACKET DROP	START OF KICK	CONTACT POINT	FOLLOWTHROUGH	LAND ON LEFT FOOT	FINISH POSITION

automatic consequence of the hitting motion (Frames 6 through 8). As the legs release upward into the ball the player simultaneously kicks his rear foot back and away from his body (Frames 8 through 11). The rear foot serves as a counterweight, allowing the player to launch himself upward into the ball, while remaining on balance and straight up and down at the waist. Aside from this greatly increased roll of the legs, the bio-mechanics of the motion are unchanged, and all the stroke keys from the basic serve apply.

Landing on the Front Foot: A central aspect of the advanced footwork is that the player lands on his left, front foot (Frame 10). Thus at the conclusion of the motion, the right foot is still behind, as it has been through the motion. He has not stepped forward and through the shot—in fact, the back leg has actually moved *away* from his body, kicking backward as the motion uncoils. This relationship between the feet is crucial for unlocking the added power of the legs, and retaining the proper sequence of the body rotation into the ball. If a player is proceding to net, he can then take the next step forward with the back leg, or he can simply recover to the Ready Position for baseline play. In developing this motion it is important to be able to stop the motion and retain balance after the hop, with the weight still on the front foot (Frame 11).

Keying the Advanced Serve: Maximizing Knee Bend

○ ○ ○ ○ ○ ○ ○ ○ ○ ○ ○ ○

IMAGE OF MAXIMUM KNEE BEND WITH THE WEIGHT SHIFTED FULLY FORWARD TO THE FRONT FOOT.

The use of the legs in the advanced serve motion preserves and expands upon the bio-mechanics of the basic motion. The basic serve calls for a shift of the weight to the left foot, knee bend, with the right foot finishing up on the tips of the toes. The advanced serve takes this basic leg action to its logical conclusion. By adding this increased knee bend the player can generate significant additional velocity and spin, without any other changes in the motion, and he can continue to use the full range of keys developed for the basic serve in executing the advanced motion. These keys are supplemented by the knee bend key shown above.

The first step in developing the knee bend key is determining physically how far down you are capable of bending. This will depend on your physical strength, and also, your flexibility. Players such as McEnroe go down until the knees are bent almost at a right angle. Most players cannot match this, but this is something you must determine for yourself. The bend shown above is a fairly typical maximum for most players. To do this, let the arm drop and start the knee bend. Shift as much weight as possible to the left front foot and see how far down in the knees you can actually go. Now create the visual image, as shown above. See yourself from the waist down with your weight on the left, front foot, and the maximum possible bend. As you start your service motion, hold the image of your knee bend, and make your legs overlap the image. Visualize yourself staying down as long as possible. As the swing progresses, you will automatically uncoil upward from the legs. You should land on your front foot, with the rear leg kicking backward, as described below. Now test the key in controlled drill.

Keying the Advanced Serve: Kicking Back with the Back Leg

○ ○ ○ ○ ○ ○ ○ ○ ○ ○ ○ ○ ○ ○ ○ ○

THIS IMAGE SHOWS HOW THE BACK RIGHT LEG SERVES AS A COUNTER-WEIGHT, KICKING AWAY FROM THE BODY AS THE MOTION UNCOILS.

As noted in the introduction to this chapter, probably the most common flaw in most service motions is the tendency to step through the motion with the back leg. This throws off the synchronization of the motion, makes the body rotation too early, causes a loss of power, and is responsible for much of the serving inconsistency in the modern game, even at the highest levels of professional tennis.

This key is designed to help you control the back foot properly, and is crucial to the proper use of the legs on the advanced serve. By kicking out and away from the body as the knees uncoil, the back leg serves as a counterweight. It allows the player to retain good balance, remain straight up and down from the waist, and also, achieve full extension at contact. Most important, the leg kick keeps the player's weight behind the ball, so he can take full advantage of the extra body leverage generated by the uncoiling of the legs, and still land on the front foot, as demonstrated in the sequence photos of the advanced serve. If you watch the great serve and volley players you will see that they almost all land on the front foot, before continuing on to the net. This is possible only if the rear leg is used correctly for balance.

To create this key, start in the Ready Position. Now drop the arms and bend the knees, going down to whatever is your maximum amount of bend. Then, without continuing the swing or hitting the ball, release the knees so that you hop upward and forward. As you do this, kick your rear, right leg back and away from your body as shown above. Now, repeat this motion, and create a visual image of the right leg as it moves backward. Test the key in controlled drill. Once the advanced footwork is solid, you can alternate the key for kicking back and for the increased knee bend with the other keys that are active for your particular service motion, such as the Toss, the Racket Drop, etc.

USING YOUR STROKE KEYS ON THE COURT

By following the progressions in the individual chapters, you have developed models and keys for each of the individual strokes. You should now have a clear mental picture of every aspect of your game. If used correctly this system of keys provides a method for achieving superior execution on a regular basis. To do this, however, means having the mental discipline to think about what you are doing when you are actually on the court. Playing consistently excellent tennis requires consistently excellent mental focus. In my opinion, this is rarely achieved below the highest levels of the game. Many, if not most, players allow their minds to wander wildly during match play. Their thoughts are dominated by fears about choking or losing the match, or worse, they drift away to entirely unrelated subjects. The stroke key system is designed to eliminate this tendency, by giving you a clear framework for blocking out fears and other distracting thoughts on the court and creating continuous mental focus. This ability is crucial if you want to achieve your goals in the game of tennis.

It does no good to do the development work in lessons and controlled drill if the player never truly applies what he has learned in his matches. For many players, doing this requires radically changing their mental patterns. From the moment you walk on the court until the completion of match point, you should use the keying process described in the preceding chapters. This means knowing what your active keys are for every stroke, visualizing them beginning with the start of the warm-up, and continuing this process unbroken through the course of the match.

Often, players who are struggling to develop this mental framework do best by actually taking stroke key charts on the court with them. The stroke charts are a physical reminder of how the player intends to think during the match, and they are a reference source that the player can consult on the game change-overs. For example, if your backhand becomes erratic, you can use your backhand stroke key chart to remind yourself what your tendencies are, identify the problem, and apply the counteracting key. A player who truly reshapes his mental approach using the visual system presented here has the tools for reaching whatever goals he sets for himself in tennis.

Following are examples of stroke key charts constructed by two of my students. They can serve as models for creating charts of your own. There is also a blank chart that you can Xerox in order to do this.

The stroke key chart included here allows you to deal with any situation that may occur on the court. It is divided into two parts: keys and tendency analysis. For each stroke you should develop a series of two to four primary keys. When you go to the court, begin the warm-up by consciously visualizing one or more of these keys to activate your stroke. From this point on, the goal is to hold a specific key image on every shot throughout the match.

The second part of the chart is tendency analysis. Typically, when a stroke breaks down, it will be one of a limited number of elements that are incorrect. Every player has his tendencies, the way he happens to deviate from the model strokes. The art is in identifying what your particular tendencies are, and how to manage them on the court. The beauty of doing tendency analysis is that it allows you to correct your errors as they happen. By working in controlled drill, and by doing video and match play analysis with a teaching pro or coach, each player should pinpoint the tendencies in each of his strokes that lead to technical breakdowns and unforced errors. Then each tendency should be paired with one more counteracting key. Because each player will have only a limited number of tendencies, it is easy to identify the source of errors. The player is then pre-

pared to deal with any breakdowns in stroke production that occur in the course of play, and to correct them virtually instantaneously.

For example, against a hard-hitting opponent, a player may tend to feel rushed and fail to achieve complete preparation. The counteracting key is to visualize the image of the correct racket and shoulder position at the Turn. Then as the motion starts, the player simply makes his racket and shoulder position overlap the image, and his preparation problem is eliminated. Or against a weaker opponent, a player may overhit the ball trying to win the points too quickly, shortening the followthrough and hitting long. The counteracting key here should be some variation on the image of the Finish Position. By visualizing the correct position of the racket on the followthrough, and then bringing his racket to this image, the player can eliminate the tendency to constrict the swing and muscle the ball, quickly reestablishing a full, fluid stroke pattern.

The stroke keys provide an almost foolproof system for executing your strokes with consistent technical excellence, and if your stroke execution is consistently excellent, you will play your best tennis on a regular basis, and win more than your share of matches. This will happen because you will eliminate unforced errors from your game, the major problem faced by all players below the professional level. Your matches will then be won or lost by superior shot making. This ability to hit your shots under pressure will take your game to a higher level than you may have thought possible. By using your stroke keys on the big points, you can go for the execution of your shots, and let the chips fall where they may, knowing that more often than not, you will make the shot if your swing simply follows the model stroke.

If you use your personal stroke keys correctly and consistently, you will experience the physical and aesthetic pleasure of playing technically superior, classical tennis. Playing tennis with this level of skill and confidence can be phenomenally satisfying. I think you will find that it is more than worth the effort required.

PERSONAL STROKE KEY CHART

NAME: _Sara Welch_   AGE: _17_

ABILITY LEVEL: _Girl's 18's Ranked Junior_

STROKE: _2-Handed Backhand_

ACTIVE KEYS:
1. _Image of smooth stroke_
2. _Hit up on ball_
3. _Set on front foot_
4. _____

TENDENCIES:

TENDENCY:	KEY:
releasing wrist	wrist back at finish
hitting long	hit up on ball

PERSONAL STROKE KEY CHART

NAME: _CLIFF WEST_ AGE: _41_

ABILITY LEVEL: _A_

STROKE: _FOREHAND GROUNDSTROKE_

ACTIVE KEYS:
1. _IMAGE OF TURN_
2. _WRIST BACK / VERTICAL SWING_
3. _WEIGHT ON FRONT FOOT_
4. _FULL KNEE BEND_

TENDENCIES:

TENDENCY:	KEY:
HIT SHORT	EARLY CONTACT
HIT LONG	HIT UP AT CONTACT

PERSONAL STROKE KEY CHART

NAME:_ AGE:_ _ _ _ _ _ _ _ _ _ _ _ _ _ _ _

ABILITY LEVEL:_ _

STROKE:_ _

ACTIVE KEYS: 1._ _

2._ _

3._ _

4._ _

TENDENCIES:

TENDENCY: KEY:

_ _ _ _ _ _ _ _ _ _ _ _ _ _ _ _ _ _   _ _ _ _ _ _ _ _ _ _ _ _ _ _ _ _ _ _

_ _ _ _ _ _ _ _ _ _ _ _ _ _ _ _ _ _   _ _ _ _ _ _ _ _ _ _ _ _ _ _ _ _ _ _

_ _ _ _ _ _ _ _ _ _ _ _ _ _ _ _ _ _   _ _ _ _ _ _ _ _ _ _ _ _ _ _ _ _ _ _

THE GRIPS

The foundation for developing each of the classical stroke patterns is the correct grip. As previously discussed, most players already have some version of the correct grip on most strokes. However, if you have questions about your grip, or about the possible grip variations on a given stroke, this chapter should answer them.

The terminology used to define the various grip positions has varied over the years. There are many points of confusion, stemming from the way the grips have changed in the evolution of the modern game.[1]

On the forehand, I have outlined two variations—the pure eastern, and the modified eastern. While most authorities agree with my definition of the pure eastern grip, others would call

what I label the modified eastern the "extreme eastern" or even the "semi-western." In my opinion, however, this grip is a relatively slight modification of the pure eastern grip and is central to classical stroke production. Far from being "extreme," it is the grip that the majority of players find most comfortable and effective. Although this grip rotates the palm slightly downward toward the western position, the term "semi-western" is still inappropriate, since this grip is commonly used to produce a classical swing pattern. The term "semi-western" implies that the swing will have some of the characteristics of the western game, which is untrue. Even a player such as Andre Agassi, who pushes the modified eastern grip further toward the western than most players, plays with

[1]*For the best discussion of the grips, using the older terminology, see Paul Metzler,* Tennis Styles and Stylists *(New York: Macmillan, 1969), pp. 201–8.*

what is best described as a classical technical style.

In defining the backhand grips, there is also considerable confusion. Some writers would call the eastern backhand grip described here "continental," since two great champions of the past, Fred Perry and Rod Laver, played with this grip on both the forehand and backhand. According to this viewpoint, a "true" eastern backhand grip would be the more extreme heavy topspin grip discussed below. What I have called the eastern backhand grip is, however, the grip used almost universally by the eastern-style players discussed in this book, and thus, in discussing the modern game, it makes the most sense to label it as such.

What I have called the continental grip is the grip used by most players on both the volley and the serve, falling halfway in between the eastern forehand and the eastern backhand. This grip is sometimes called the "Australian," or the "modified continental." I refer to it as simply the continental, since it is the grip that is most commonly used on the serve and on the volleys by classical players. It is, in fact, the grip used on every stroke by John McEnroe, one of the very few pure continental stylists in the modern era.

Finally, it is important to note that, when it comes to defining the position of the hand on the racket for the various grips, I have abandoned the traditional alignment of the "V" formed by the thumb and forefinger as the main checkpoint. Instead, throughout this chapter, I have used the position of the lower heel pad of the racket hand. This is a change that has been long overdue in the theory of tennis instruction.

Because the shape and proportions of people's hands vary so much, the same "V" alignment can produce different grips with different players, even if the player is using the correct grip size. But more significant still is the change in the shape of racket handles with the introduction of the oversize and mid-size graphite and synthetic frames. Because of the slimness of the new racket shafts, the handles are now much more rectangular than the old wooden frames which were used to devise the "V" checkpoints. For example, on the eastern forehand grip, the traditional checkpoint is to align the "V" in the center of the top racket bevel. As the photos clearly show, however, using a modern frame, the "V" is to the right of center, with the pure eastern grip. And on the most common eastern forehand grip, the modified eastern, it is off the top bevel altogether.

If you have been hitting your forehand with a grip based on the alignment of the "V," you may actually be trying to hit your forehand with some version of a backhand grip. In any case, the alignment of the heel pad gives a much more accurate indication of the position of the palm in relation to the racket head, which is the central factor in achieving a correct grip for any stroke.

THE FOREHAND GRIPS

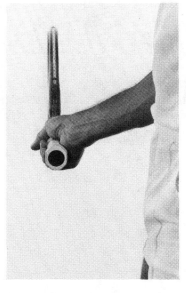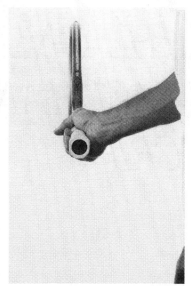

THE PURE EASTERN GRIP. THE HEEL PADS AT THE EDGE OF THE TOP BEVEL OF THE RACKET HANDLE. (LEFT)   THE MODIFIED EASTERN FOREHAND GRIP, THE MORE COMMON AND EFFECTIVE VERSION OF THE CLASSICAL FOREHAND GRIP. NOTE THE SLIGHTLY LOWER HEEL PAD POSITION. (RIGHT)

The central characteristic of the classical or eastern forehand grip is that it places the palm of the hand in line with the face of the racket. This means that when the hand is closed around the racket, most of the palm is on the *back* bevel of the handle. This palm position allows the player to hit through the shot with the wrist slightly laid back, without releasing it at contact. A correct forehand grip, then, is critical to the proper execution of the stroke.

To get the forehand grip, hold the racket by the throat with your *left* hand. Place your *right* palm flat on the face of the strings and simply slide your palm down along the shaft of the racket to the grip. Now close your hand around the grip and shake hands with the racket. The top, index finger should be slightly spread from the rest of the fingers.

The key checkpoint in determining whether the grip is correct is the position of the heel pad of the hand. It should be on either the top or middle side bevel of the handle. If any part of the heel pad is on the *top* bevel of the frame, you no longer have an eastern forehand grip. Instead, you have some version of a backhand or continental grip. To correct this, simply rotate your hand slightly to the right to reposition the heel pad.

Within this general framework, there are two major variations of the forehand grip. They will work equally well in producing the classical stroke. Which you chose is really a matter of comfort and preference. If the heel pad is on the top *side* bevel (see forehand photos), then this is a "pure" eastern forehand grip. The heel pad is as close as possible to the top of the frame, without actually touching the top bevel. This grip is used by players such as Chris Evert and Martina Navratilova.

The second variation is the modified eastern forehand grip. In this grip, the hand has rotated slightly further to the right, so that the heel pad is resting on the center, *back* bevel of the racket handle. This is the grip used by Ivan Lendl, Steffi Graf, and Jimmy Connors, among many others. It is probably the predominant forehand grip in recreational and tournament tennis today, and most players find it more comfortable than the pure eastern version.

THE ONE-HANDED BACKHAND GRIP

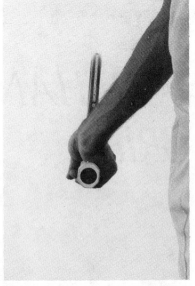

THE EASTERN BACKHAND GRIP.
THE HEEL PAD HAS ROTATED TO
THE LEFT OF THE FOREHAND
AND IS ON THE TOP BEVEL OF
THE FRAME.

To hit the one-handed backhand, it is necessary to change the grip at the beginning of the stroke. To do this, rotate your racket hand to the left, toward the *top* of the frame, until your heel pad is resting squarely on the top bevel. The second, lower knuckle of the index finger should now be in line with the center of the top *right* bevel.

The eastern backhand grip will work equally well for hitting the ball flat, with topspin, or with slice. There are two other possible one-hand backhand grips, although in my opinion, neither one is advisable for developing classical stroke patterns. The first is an extreme eastern backhand grip, in which the hand is rotated even further to the left. This grip will produce heavier topspin on the backhand, but forces the player to make contact much further in front of the body is very difficult to time. Also, it is much tougher to hit a solid slice backhand using this grip, since it is necessary to dip the swing radically under the ball, to make contact with an open racket face. Doing this requires movement in the elbow and the wrist, and is a major source of potential errors. Using this grip, the player simply cannot hit through the ball on a line to produce slice, as demonstrated in the backhand chapter.

The other alternative backhand grip is the continental—the same grip shown in this chapter for use on the serve and volleys. This grip places *part* of the heel pad on the top bevel, but the heel pad does not sit squarely on the top of the frame. Although this grip is probably equal, or even slightly superior, to the eastern backhand for hitting the slice drive, it is more difficult to generate topspin using it. To hit topspin, it is necessary to tilt the wrist downward to get the racket face vertical at contact, and this results in a loss of body leverage, somewhat later contact, and a tendency to have too much internal arm movement. Since a good one-handed player needs to hit both with equal facility, the eastern backhand grip is clearly the best choice for the majority of players.

FOCUS ON HEALTH

FOCUS ON HEALTH

Dale B. Hahn, Ph.D.
Wayne A. Payne, Ed.D.
Both of Ball State University
Muncie, Indiana

with 164 illustrations

WCB
McGraw-Hill

Boston   Burr Ridge, IL   Dubuque, IA   Madison, WI   New York   San Francisco   St. Louis
Bangkok   Bogotá   Caracas   Lisbon   London   Madrid
Mexico City   Milan   New Delhi   Seoul   Singapore   Sydney   Taipei   Toronto

Fourth
Edition

WCB/McGraw-Hill

*A Division of The **McGraw·Hill** Companies*

FOCUS ON HEALTH, FOURTH EDITION

 This book is printed on recycled paper containing 10% postconsumer waste.

1 2 3 4 5 6 7 8 9 0 QPD/QPD 9 3 2 1 0 9 8

ISBN 0–07–303445–2

Publisher: *Edward E. Bartell*
Executive editor: *Vicki Malinee*
Senior developmental editor: *Melissa Martin*
Senior marketing manager: *Pamela S. Cooper*
Project manager: *Sheila M. Frank*
Production supervisor: *Sandy Ludovissy*
Freelance design coordinator: *Mary L. Christianson*
Photo research coordinator: *John C. Leland*
Supplement coordinator: *Sandra M. Schnee*
Compositor: *Shepherd, Inc.*
Typeface: *10/12 Palatino*
Printer: *Quebecor Printing Book Group/Dubuque, IA*

Freelance cover designer: *Kay Fulton*
Cover photograph: *© Steve Satushek/Image Bank*

The credits section for this book begins on page C-1 and is considered an extension of the copyright page.

Library of Congress Cataloging-in-Publication Data

Hahn, Dale B.
    Focus on health / Dale B. Hahn, Wayne A. Payne. — 4th ed.
      p.   cm.
    Includes bibliographical references and index.
    ISBN 0–07–303445–2
    1. Health.   I. Payne, Wayne A. II. Title.
RA776.H142 1999   98–22674
613—dc21   CIP

www.mhhe.com

To all of our students, with the hope that the decisions they make will be healthy ones.

Contents in Brief

PART

1   The Mind

1   Shaping Your Health, 1
2   Achieving Emotional Maturity, 24
3   Managing Stress, 43

2   The Body

4   Becoming Physically Fit, 66
5   Understanding Nutrition and Your Diet, 92
6   Maintaining a Healthy Weight, 127

3   Addictive Substances

7   Choosing a Drug-Free Lifestyle, 154
8   Taking Control of Alcohol Use, 178
9   Rejecting Tobacco Use, 201

4   Diseases

10   Reducing Your Risk of Cardiovascular Disease, 228
11   Living with Cancer and Chronic Conditions, 249
12   Preventing Infectious Diseases, 279

5   Sexuality

13   Understanding Sexuality, 310
14   Managing Your Fertility, 343

6   Consumerism and Environment

15   Making Consumer and Health Care Choices, 378
16   Protecting Your Safety, 402
17   Controlling Environmental Influences, 422

7   The Life Cycle

18   Accepting Dying and Death, 448

Contents

1   Shaping Your Health, 1
    Health Concerns of the Late1990s, 2
    Definitions of Health-Related Terms, 2
        A traditional definition of health, 2
        Holistic health, 3
        Health promotion, 3
        Wellness, 3
        Empowerment, 4
    Developmental Tasks for College Students, 5
        Forming an initial adult identity, 6
        Establishing independence, 6
        Assuming responsibility, 6
        Developing social skills, 6
        Developing intimacy, 7
    Developmental Tasks of Midlife Adults, 7
        Achieving generativity, 7
        Reassessing the plans of young adulthood, 8
    Developmental Tasks of Elderly Adults, 8
        Accepting the decline of aging, 8
        Maintaining a high level of physical function, 8
        Establishing a sense of integrity, 9
    The Role of Health, 9
    The Composition of Health, 9
        Physical dimension, 10
        Emotional dimension, 10
        Social dimension, 10
        Intellectual dimension, 10
        Spiritual dimension, 10
        Occupational dimension, 10
    Our Definition of Health, 11
    Charting a Plan for Behavior Change, 11
    Personal Assessment: A Personal Profile:
    Evaluating Your Health, 12
    Summary, 16
    Focus on the Diversity of Today's College
    Students, 19

PART 1   THE MIND, 23
    2   Achieving Emotional Maturity, 24
        Characteristics of an Emotionally Well Person, 25
        Emotional and Psychological Wellness, 25
            Normal range of emotions, 25
            Self-esteem, 25
        Personal Assessment: How Does My Self-Concept
        Compare with My Idealized Self? 26
            Hardiness, 27
        Emotional Wellness of Midlife and Elderly
        Adults, 27
            An optimistic view of aging, 27
            The joys of midlife, 27
            The midlife crisis, 28
            Quality of life for elderly adults, 28
        Affronts to Emotional Wellness, 28
            Depression, 29
            Loneliness, 29
            Shyness, 30
            Suicide, 30
        Enhancing Emotional Wellness, 31
            Improving communication, 31
            Using humor effectively, 31
            Improving conflict management skills, 32
            Taking a proactive approach to life, 33
        Reflections of Emotional Wellness, 34
            Maslow's hierarchy of needs, 34
            Spiritual or faith development, 35
            Creative expression, 36
        Summary, 38
        Focus on Enhancing Spirituality and Wellness, 40

    3   Managing Stress, 43
        Stress and Stressors, 44
            Variation in response to stressors, 44
            Uncontrolled stress related to disease states, 44

College-Centered Stressors, 45
Personal Assessment: How Stressed Are You? 45
Personal Assessment: How Vulnerable Are You to Stress? 46
Generalized Physiological Response to Stressors, 47
   Alarm reaction stage, 48
   Resistance stage, 48
   Exhaustion stage, 48
The Stress Response, 48
   Stressors, 48
   Sensory modalities, 50
   Cerebral cortex, 50
   Endocrine system involvement, 50
   Epinephrine-influenced responses, 51
   Influences of corticoids and epinephrine on energy release, 52
Stress and Psychoimmunology, 52
   Personality traits, 53
Coping: Reacting to Stressors, 53
   Stress management techniques, 53
   Health practices and stress, 56
   A realistic perspective on stress and life, 57
Summary, 58
Focus on Managing Work-Related Stress, 60

PART 2   THE BODY, 65
  4   Becoming Physically Fit, 66
     Components of Physical Fitness, 67
       Cardiorespiratory endurance, 67
       Muscular strength, 68
       Muscular endurance, 70
       Flexibility, 70
       Body composition, 70
     Aging Physically, 71
       Health concerns of midlife adults, 71
       Health concerns of elderly adults, 73
     Developing a Cardiorespiratory Fitness Program, 73
     Personal Assessment: What Is Your Level of Fitness? 74
       Mode of activity, 76
       Frequency of training, 76
       Intensity of training, 76

       Duration of training, 77
       Resistance training, 78
       Warm-up, workout, cooldown, 78
       Exercise for older adults, 78
       Low back pain, 79
     Fitness Questions and Answers, 79
       Should I see my doctor before I get started? 79
       How important is breast support for female exercisers? 80
       How beneficial is aerobic exercise? 80
       What are low-impact aerobic activities? 81
       What is the most effective means of fluid replacement during exercise? 81
       What effect does alcohol have on sport performance? 82
       Why has bodybuilding become so popular? 82
       Where can I find out about proper equipment? 82
       How worthwhile are commercial health and fitness clubs? 82
       What is crosstraining? 83
       What are steroids and why do some athletes use them? 83
       Are today's children physically fit? 85
       How does sleep contribute to overall fitness? 83
       What exercise danger signs should I watch for? 86
     Summary, 88
     Focus on Staying Fit During Pregnancy, 90

  5   Understanding Nutrition and Your Diet, 92
     Types and Sources of Nutrients, 93
       Carbohydrates, 93
       Fats, 93
     Personal Assessment: Do You Have Fatty Habits? 95
       Proteins, 97
       Vitamins, 99
       Minerals, 102
       Water, 102
       Fiber, 104
     The Food Groups, 107
       Fruits, 107
       Vegetables, 109

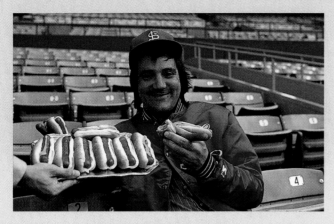

Basal metabolism, 136
Thermic effect of food, 137
Lifetime weight control, 138
Weight Management Techniques, 138
Dietary alterations, 139
Personal Assessment: Should You Consider a
Weight Loss Program? 140
Physical intervention, 142
Surgical measures, 144

Personal Assessment: Seven-Day Diet Study, 110
Milk, yogurt, and cheese, 111
Meat, poultry, fish, dry beans, eggs, and nuts, 111
Bread, cereal, rice, and pasta, 111
Fats, oils, and sweets, 111
Fast Foods, 111
Phytochemicals, 113
Food Additives, 114
Food Labels, 114
Guidelines for Dietary Health, 115
Vegetarian Diets, 116
Ovolactovegetarian diet, 117
Lactovegetarian diet, 118
Vegan vegetarian diet, 119
Dietary (food) supplements, 120
Nutrient Density, 120
Nutrition and the Older Adult, 120
International Nutritional Concerns, 121
Summary, 122
Focus on Following a Semivegetarian Diet, 125

6   Maintaining a Healthy Weight, 127
Body Image and Self-Concept, 128
Overweight and Obesity Defined, 128
Determining Weight and Body Composition, 129
Height-weight tables, 129
Healthy body weight, 129
Body mass index, 130
Electrical impedance, 130
Skinfold measurements, 130
Hydrostatic weighing, 131
Appearance, 132
Origins of Obesity, 132
Genetic basis for obesity, 132
Appetite center, 133
Set point theory, 133
Body type, 134
Infant and adult feeding patterns, 134
Endocrine influence, 134
Pregnancy, 134
Decreasing basal metabolic rate, 134
Family dietary practices, 135
Inactivity, 135
Caloric Balance, 135
Energy Needs of the Body, 136
Activity requirements, 136

Eating Disorders, 145
Anorexia nervosa, 145
Bulimia nervosa, 145
Compulsive exercise and compulsive eating, 146
Treatment for eating disorders, 146
Undernutrition, 147
Summary, 148
Focus on Gaining Weight Healthfully, 151

PART 3   ADDICTIVE SUBSTANCES, 153

7   Choosing a Drug-Free Lifestyle, 154
Addictive Behavior, 155
The process of addiction, 155
Intervention and treatment, 156
Drug Terminology, 156
Dependence, 156
Drug misuse and abuse, 157
Personal Assessment: Recognizing Drug Abuse, 158
Effects of Drugs on the Central Nervous System, 159
Drug Classifications, 159
Stimulants, 159
Cocaine, 163
Depressants, 164
Hallucinogens, 165
Cannabis, 166
Narcotics, 167
Inhalants, 168
Combination Drug Effects, 168
Society's Response to Drug Use, 169
Drug testing, 169
College and Community Support Services for Drug Dependence, 170
Treatment, 170
Personal Assessment: Getting a Drug-Free High, 171
Summary, 173
Focus on Prescription Drug Abuse, 175

8   Taking Control of Alcohol Use, 178
Choosing to Drink, 179
Alcohol Use Patterns, 179
Binge drinking, 180
Personal Assessment: How Do You Use Alcoholic Beverages? 181
The Nature of Alcoholic Beverages, 182
The Physiological Effects of Alcohol, 182
Factors that influence the absorption of alcohol, 182
Blood alcohol concentration, 184
Sobering up, 185
First aid for acute alcohol intoxication, 185
Alcohol-Related Health Problems, 186
Fetal alcohol syndrome and fetal alcohol effects, 186
Alcohol-Related Social Problems, 188
Accidents, 188
Crime and violence, 189
Suicide, 189
Hosting a Responsible Party, 189

Organizations That Support Responsible Drinking, 190
Mothers Against Drunk Driving, 190
Students Against Driving Drunk, 190
Boost Alcohol Consciousness Concerning the Health of University Students, 190
Other approaches, 190
Problem Drinking and Alcoholism, 191
Problem drinking, 191
Alcohol and driving, 192
Alcoholism, 192
Denial and enabling, 193
Alcoholism and the family, 193
Codependence, 194
Helping the alcoholic: rehabilitation and recovery, 194
Drug to treat alcoholism, 194
Current Alcohol Concerns, 195
Adult children of alcoholic parents, 195
Women and alcohol, 195
Alcohol advertising, 196
Summary, 197
Focus on Alcohol and Violence, 199

9   Rejecting Tobacco Use, 201
Tobacco Use in American Society, 202
Use among college students and young adults, 202
The influence of education, 202
Cigarette preferences, 202
Advertising approaches, 202
Pipe and cigar smoking, 203
The Development of Dependence on Tobacco Products, 203
Personal Assessment: How Much Do You Know about Cigarette Smoking? 204
Physiological factors, 205
Nicotine as an addictive drug, 206
Psychosocial factors, 207
Preventing teen smoking, 209
Tobacco: The Source of Physiologically Active Compounds, 209
Nicotine, 210
Carbon monoxide, 210
Illness, Premature Death, and Tobacco Use, 210
Cardiovascular disease, 210
Cancer, 211
Chronic obstructive lung disease, 213
Additional health concerns, 214
Tobacco and Caffeine Use, 214
Smoking and Reproduction, 214
Infertility, 214
Problem pregnancy, 214
Breastfeeding, 215
Health problems among infants, 215
Oral Contraceptives and Tobacco Use, 215
Smokeless Tobacco Use, 216
Involuntary (Passive) Smoking, 216
Stopping What You Started, 217
Tobacco Use: A Question of Rights, 220
Improving Communication between Smokers and Nonsmokers, 220

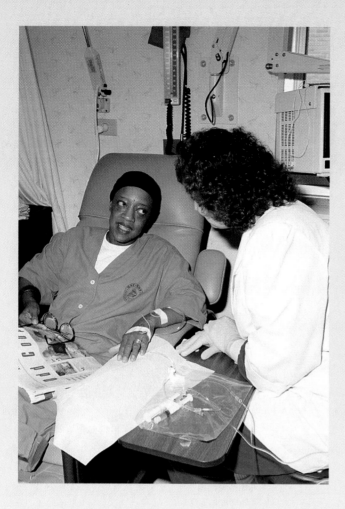

Summary, 221
Focus on Smokers vs. Nonsmokers: A Question of
Rights, 224

PART 4   DISEASES, 227

10   Reducing Your Risk of Cardiovascular
      Disease, 228
      Prevalence of Cardiovascular Disease, 229
      Normal Cardiovascular Function, 229
          The vascular system, 229
          The heart, 230
          Blood, 231
      Cardiovascular Disease Risk Factors, 231
      Personal Assessment: What Is Your Risk for Heart
      Disease? 232
          Risk factors that cannot be changed, 233
          Risk factors that can be changed, 234
          Other risk factors that contribute to heart
          disease, 235
      Forms of Cardiovascular Disease, 236
          Coronary heart disease, 236
          Hypertension, 241
          Stroke, 242

          Congenital heart disease, 242
          Rheumatic heart disease, 243
      Summary, 245
      Focus on Hypertension in African-Americans, 247

11   Living with Cancer and Chronic
      Conditions, 249
      The Status of Cancer Today and Tomorrow, 250
      Cancer: A Problem of Cell Regulation, 250
          Cell regulation, 250
          Oncogene formation, 250
          The cancerous cell, 251
          Benign tumors, 251
          Types of cancer and their locations, 252
      Cancer at Selected Sites in the Body, 253
          Lung, 253
          Breast, 255
      Personal Assessment: Are You at Risk for Skin,
      Breast, or Cervical Cancer? 256
          Uterus, 257
          Vagina, 258
          Ovary, 258
          Prostate, 259
          Testicle, 260
          Colon and rectum, 260
          Pancreas, 261
          Skin, 261
      The Diagnosis of Cancer, 263
          Treatment, 263
      Risk Reduction, 265
      Chronic Health Conditions, 266
          Diabetes mellitus, 266
          Multiple sclerosis, 270
          Asthma, 271
          Systemic lupus erythematosus, 272
      Summary, 272
      Focus on Managing Chronic Pain, 275

12   Preventing Infectious Diseases, 279
      Infectious Diseases in the Late 1990s, 280
      Infectious Disease Transmission, 280
          Pathogens, 280
          Chain of infection, 280
          Stages of infection, 282
      Body Defenses: Mechanical and Cellular Immune
      Systems, 283
          Divisions of the immune system, 283
      Immunizations, 284
      The Immune Response, 285
      Causes and Management of Selected Infectious
      Diseases, 286
          The common cold, 286
          Influenza, 287
          Tuberculosis, 288
          Pneumonia, 289
          Mononucleosis, 289
          Chronic fatigue syndrome, 290
          Measles, 290
          Mumps, 290
          Lyme disease, 291
          Hantavirus pulmonary syndrome, 291

Toxic shock syndrome, 292
Hepatitis, 292
AIDS, 293
Sexually Transmitted Diseases, 296
Chlamydia (nonspecific urethritis), 297
Personal Assessment: What Is Your Risk of
Contracting a Sexually Transmitted Disease? 298
Human papillomavirus, 299
Gonorrhea, 299
Herpes simplex, 299
Syphilis, 301
Pubic lice, 301
Vaginal infections, 301
Cystitis and urethritis, 303
Summary, 303
Focus on Controlling Infectious Disease
Transmission, 306

PART 5   SEXUALITY, 309

13   Understanding Sexuality, 310
Biological Bases of Human Sexuality, 311
Genetic basis, 311
Gonadal basis, 311
Structural development, 311
Biological sexuality and the childhood years, 311
Puberty, 311
Psychosocial Bases of Human Sexuality, 312
Gender identity, 313
Gender preference, 313
Gender adoption, 313
Initial adult gender identification, 313
Transsexualism, 314
Androgyny: Sharing the Pluses, 314

Reproductive Systems, 315
Male reproductive system, 315
Female reproductive system, 317
Human Sexual Response Pattern, 321
Is there a predictable pattern associated
with the sexual responses of males and
females? 321
Is the sexual response pattern stimuli-
specific? 322
What differences occur in the sexual response
pattern? 322
What are the basic physiological mechanisms
underlying the sexual response pattern? 322
What role is played by specific organs and
organ systems within the sexual response
pattern? 325
Patterns of Sexual Behavior, 325
Celibacy, 325
Masturbation, 325
Fantasy and erotic dreams, 325
Personal Assessment: Sexual Attitudes: A Matter
of Feelings, 327
Shared touching, 328
Genital contact, 328
Oral-genital stimulation, 328
Intercourse, 328
Sexuality and Aging, 329
The Dating Process, 329
Love, 330
Recognizing Unhealthy Relationships, 330
Friendship, 330
Personal Assessment: How Compatible Are
You? 331
Intimacy, 332
Marriage, 332
Divorce, 333
Alternatives to Marriage, 334
Singlehood, 334
Cohabitation, 335
Personal Assessment: Are You Enjoying the Single
Life? 335
Single parenthood, 336
Sexual Orientation, 336
Heterosexuality, 336
Homosexuality, 336
Bisexuality, 337
Paraphilias, 337
Summary, 337
Focus on Sex on the Internet, 340

14   Managing Your Fertility, 343
Birth Control vs. Contraception, 344
Reasons for Choosing to Use Birth Control, 344
Theoretical Effectiveness vs. Use Effectiveness, 344
Selecting Your Contraceptive Method, 345
Current Birth Control Methods, 345
Withdrawal, 345
Periodic abstinence, 345

Infertility, 368
Summary, 370
Focus on the Consequences of Unintended
Pregnancy, 373

PART 6   CONSUMERISM AND ENVIRONMENT, 377

15   Making Consumer and Health Care
      Choices, 378
          Health Information, 379
              The informed consumer, 379
              Sources of information, 379
          Personal Assessment: Are You a Skilled Health
          Consumer? 380
          Health Care Providers, 383
              Physicians and their training, 383
              Alternative practitioners, 384
              Restricted-practice health care providers, 385
              Nurse professionals, 387
              Allied health care professionals, 387
          Self-Care, 387

Personal Assessment: Which Birth Control Method
Is Best for You? 348
    Vaginal spermicides, 349
    Condoms, 350
    Diaphragm, 351
    Cervical cap, 352
    Intrauterine device, 352
    Oral contraceptives, 354
    Injectable contraceptives, 357
    Subdermal implants, 357
    Sterilization, 357
    Abortion, 359
Becoming Parents, 361
    Parenting issues for couples, 361
    A parenting prescription for the early years, 362
Pregnancy: An Extension of the Partnership, 362
    Physiological obstacles and aids to
    fertilization, 362
    Signs of pregnancy, 363
    Agents that can damage a fetus, 364
Childbirth: the Labor of Delivery, 365
    Stage one: effacement and dilation of the
    cervix, 365
    Stage two: delivery of the fetus, 367
    Stage three: delivery of the placenta, 367
    Cesarean deliveries, 368

Health Care Costs and Reimbursement, 388
    Health insurance, 388
    Health maintenance organizations, 390
    Government insurance plans, 391
    Medicare supplement policies (Medigap), 392
    Extended care insurance, 392
Health-Related Products, 393
    Prescription drugs, 393
    Over-the-counter drugs, 394
    Cosmetics, 395
Health Care Quackery and Consumer Fraud, 395
Summary, 396
Focus on Separating Fact from Fiction: Using
Health Information on the Internet, 399

16   Protecting Your Safety, 402
Intentional Injuries, 403
    Homicide, 403
Personal Assessment: How Well Do You Protect
Your Safety? 404
    Domestic violence, 405
    Gangs and youth violence, 407
    Gun violence, 408
    Bias and hate crimes, 408
    Stalking, 409
Sexual Victimization, 410
    Rape and sexual assault, 410
    Violence and the commercialization of sex, 413
Unintentional Injuries, 414
    Residential safety, 414
    Recreational safety, 414
    Firearm safety, 414
    Motor vehicle safety, 415
    Home accident prevention for children and the
    elderly, 415
Campus Safety and Violence Prevention, 417
Summary, 417
Focus on Drowsy Driving, 423

17   Controlling Environmental Influences, 422
World Population Growth, 423

Air Pollution, 423
Personal Assessment: Are You Helping the
Environment? 424
    Sources of air pollution, 425
    Temperature inversions, 427
    Indoor air pollution, 428
    Health implications, 429
Water Pollution, 429
    Yesterday's pollution problem, 429
    Today's pollution problem, 429
    Sources of water pollution, 430
    Effects on wetlands, 431
    Health implications, 431
Land Pollution, 432
    Solid waste, 432
    Chemical waste, 434
    Pesticides, 435
    Herbicides, 435
Radiation, 435
    Health effects of radiation exposure, 436
    Electromagnetic radiation, 436
    Nuclear reactor accidents and waste disposal, 437
    Radiation tests, 438
Noise Pollution, 438
    Noise-induced hearing loss, 438
    Noise as a stressor, 438
In Search of Balance, 438
Summary, 440
Focus on Telecommuting, 444

PART 7   THE LIFE CYCLE, 447

18   Accepting Dying and Death, 448
Dying in Today's Society, 449
Definitions of Death, 449
Euthanasia, 449
Advance Medical Directives, 450
Emotional Stages of Dying, 452
Near-Death Experiences, 452
Interacting with Dying People, 453
Talking with Children about Death, 453
Death of a Child, 453
Hospice Care for the Terminally Ill, 454
Grief and the Resolution of Grief, 455
Rituals of Death, 456
    Full funeral services, 456
    Disposition of the body, 457
Personal Assessment: Planning Your Funeral, 458
    Costs, 460
Personal Preparation for Death, 460
Summary, 461
Focus on Death of an Infant or Unborn Child, 464

Appendix 1   Commonly Used Over-the-Counter
              Products, A-1

Appendix 2   First Aid, A-5

Appendix 3   Mental Disorders, A-8

Appendix 4   Body Systems, A-10

Glossary, G-1

Exam Prep, E-1

Credits, C-1

Preface

As a health educator, you already know that the personal health course is one of the most exciting courses a college student will take. Today's media-oriented college students are aware of the critical health issues of the late 1990s. They hear about environmental issues, substance abuse, sexually transmitted diseases, fitness, and nutrition virtually every day. The value of the personal health course is its potential to expand students' knowledge of these and other health topics. Students will then be able to examine their attitudes toward health issues and modify their behavior to improve their health and perhaps even prevent or delay the onset of certain health conditions.

Focus on Health accomplishes this task with a carefully composed, well-documented manuscript written by two health educators who teach the personal health course to nearly 1000 students each year. We understand the teaching issues you face daily in the classroom and have written this text with your concerns in mind.

This book is written for college students in a wide variety of settings, from community colleges to large four-year universities. The content has been carefully constructed to be meaningful to both traditional and nontraditional-age students. We have paid special attention to the increasing numbers of nontraditional students who have decided to pursue a college education. Points in the discussion often address the particular needs of these nontraditional students. *Focus on Health* continues to encourage students of all ages and backgrounds to achieve their goals.

SPECIAL FEATURES
Updated Content

As experienced health educators and authors, we know how important it is to provide students with the most current information available. Throughout each chapter we have included the very latest information and statistics, and the "As we go to press . . ." feature has allowed us to comment on breaking news right up to press time. In addition, we have introduced many timely topics and issues that are sure to pique students' interest and stimulate class discussion.

HealthQuest Activities

Many chapters contain a new activities box to complement the HealthQuest CD-ROM that accompanies the text. These activities allow students to assess their health behavior in each of nine different areas. HealthQuest's exciting graphics and interactive approach will encourage students to learn about topics such as condom use, cancer prevention, and healthy eating behavior as they complete the activities.

Health on the Web Learning Activities

Today's computer-savvy students can find reliable health information at their fingertips when they search the world wide web. New activities, prepared by Jerome E. Kotecki, of Ball State University, direct students to important health websites related to the material in each chapter. For each activity, students explore a website and then complete a quiz or self-assessment offered at the site. These activities help students think critically about valuable health information.

Healthy People: Looking Ahead to 2010

Each chapter begins with an update of how far we've come as a nation in achieving the *Healthy People 2000* objectives established in 1990. These national health care goals are explained and the reasons for progress or lack of improvement explored. The section concludes with projections about the goals to be outlined in the *Healthy People 2010* document, which is now being drafted.

Integrated Presentation of Aging

Topics of interest to midlife and elderly adults no longer appear in the chapter on death and dying, thus sending a more positive message about aging. Instead, the material has been integrated into appropriate chapters according to subject. For example, Alzheimer's disease is now discussed in Chapter 11, Living with Cancer and Chronic Conditions. This organization allows both traditional and nontraditional students to learn about the physical and emotional changes that take place as we age.

Comprehensive Discussion of Sexuality

The biological and psychosocial origins of sexuality, sexual behavior, and intimate relationships are presented in a single, comprehensive chapter. This organization gives the student a better framework for studying these complex topics.

Personal Safety Chapter

With good reason, students are more concerned than ever about issues related to violence and safety both on and off campus. Chapter 16, Protecting Your Safety, delves into critically important current issues such as homicide; domestic violence; hate crimes; sexual victimization; and recreational, residential, and motor vehicle safety.

Wellness and Disease Prevention

Throughout this new edition, you will notice that students are continually urged to be proactive in shaping their future health. For example, Chapter 5, Understanding Nutrition and Your Diet, explains the health benefits of following a semivegetarian or other low-fat diet. Chapter 10, Reducing Your Risk of Cardiovascular Disease, opens with a discussion of the "big four" risk factors for heart disease and emphasizes that prevention must begin early. Even the chapter titles themselves invite students to take control of their own health behavior.

Spirituality

A highly developed sense of spirituality is integral to wellness. Accordingly, we have included a "Focus On . . ." article in Chapter 2 that explores topics such as holistic healing, mind-body disciplines, and enhancement of spirituality through volunteering.

"Focus On . . ." Articles

"Focus On . . ." articles examine current issues that students are hearing about in today's news, such as alcohol and violence, telecommuting, smokers' rights, and even sex on the Internet. These often controversial health-related topics are a perfect starting point for class or group discussions. Because these essays are set at the end of each chapter, they can be covered or not at the instructor's option.

Attractive Design and Updated Illustration Program

The inviting look, bold colors, and exciting graphics in *Focus on Health* will draw students in with every turn of the page. Photographs are sharp and appealing, drawings are attractive and informative, and anatomical illustrations are accurately rendered and appropriately detailed. In addition, the anatomical illustrations in the cardiovascular disease and sexuality chapters have been reproduced at a large size for greater clarity.

"Exam Prep" Guide

A perforated exam preparation section is included in the back of the book. The multiple-choice questions test students' retention of the material they have read. The critical thinking questions allow them to integrate the concepts introduced in the text with the information presented in class lectures and discussions. This built-in study guide is a good value for students.

Vegetarian Food Pyramid

Many students now follow or are considering a vegetarian diet. To help them understand how such a diet meets nutrient needs, we have printed a vegetarian food pyramid with the USDA Food Guide Pyramid inside the back cover of this textbook. For students who want to significantly reduce but not eliminate meat consumption, a "Focus On . . ." article about the health benefits of following a semivegetarian diet is included in Chapter 5.

New or Expanded Topics

We are committed to making *Focus on Health* the most up-to-date health textbook available. Below is a sampling of topics that are either completely new to this edition or covered in greater depth than in the previous edition:

Chapter 1: Shaping Your Health
Updated top 10 causes of death in the U.S.
Updated minority enrollment statistics
The Healthy People 2010 initiative

Chapter 2: Achieving Emotional Maturity
New references
New suggested readings

Chapter 3: Managing Stress
Two new personal assessments
The competitive job search environment
Stress and Gulf War syndrome

Chapter 4: Becoming Physically Fit
New photos of athletic shoes
Choosing a basketball shoe
The latest exercise guidelines

Chapter 5: Understanding Nutrition and Your Diet
New low-fat foods in the marketplace
Folic acid supplementation of food
Food as medicine (chemoprevention)
Fast food nutrition information and flavor ratings
Use of the term "organic" on food labels

Chapter 6: Maintaining a Healthy Weight
Advantages and disadvantages of selected diets
Removal of fen/phen and Redux from market
Portion sizes
Feeding and satiety centers in the brain
Unsafe techniques used by wrestlers to "make weight"

Chapter 7: Choosing a Drug-Free Lifestyle
Updated statistics on college students' drug use
Federal expenditures in the war against drugs
Updated street names for psychoactive drugs
The possible link between caffeine and SIDS

Chapter 8: Taking Control of Alcohol Use
Current alcohol use trends
Binge drinking deaths on campus
Lowering the legal BAC limit
Alcohol advertising on the web

Chapter 9: Rejecting Tobacco Use
Recent changes in tobacco advertising, regulation,
    and liability
Smoking trends among women and minorities
New cigarette marketing ploys
The demise of Joe Camel
Inhalation device for nicotine replacement
Antidepressants to aid smoking cessation

Chapter 10: Reducing Your Risk of Cardiovascular Disease
HRT/ERT
Prevalence of major cardiovascular diseases
Deaths from heart disease

Chapter 11: Living with Cancer and Chronic Conditions
New ACS recommendations for early cancer detection

New guidelines for diabetes screening
New drug to treat Alzheimer's disease

Chapter 12: Preventing Infectious Diseases
Childhood immunization statistics
New vaccine for infant diarrhea
Home HIV/AIDS tests
Protease inhibitor drug "cocktails"
Search for an AIDS vaccine
Infectious agents in biological weapons

Chapter 13: Understanding Sexuality
Recognizing unhealthy relationships
Cohabitation
Single parenthood

Chapter 14: Managing Your Fertility
Pending FDA approval of RU-486
FDA regulation of human cloning
Intact D & E ("partial birth") abortion procedure

Chapter 15: Making Consumer and Health Care Choices
NIH study of alternative medicine
Homeopathy, naturopathy, and herbalism
Choosing an alternative practitioner
Access to health care
Focus On . . . Using Health Information on the Internet

Chapter 16: Protecting Your Safety
Lower homicide rates
Updated violent crime statistics, including
    hate crimes and murder
Marv Albert sexual assault case

Chapter 17: Controlling Environmental Influences
Proposed new air quality standards
El Niño and La Niña
Recycling cars for cash

Chapter 18: Accepting Dying and Death
Physician-assisted suicide
Funeral costs
New postmortem options, such as
    sending ashes to outer space
Karla Fay Tucker execution

SUCCESSFUL FEATURES

Along with its new features, *Focus on Health* has many unique existing features that enhance student learning:

Two Central Themes

As mentioned earlier, two central themes—the multiple dimensions of health and the developmental tasks—are presented in Chapter 1. These give students a foundation for understanding their own health and achieving positive behavior change.

Flexibility of Chapter Organization

The fourth edition of *Focus on Health* has 18 chapters. The first stands alone as an introductory chapter that explains the focus of the book. The arrangement of the remaining chapters follows the recommendations of both the users of previous editions of the book and reviewers of this edition. Of course, professors can choose to cover the chapters in any sequence that suits the needs of their courses.

Health Reference Guide

The Health Reference Guide found at the back of the book lists many of the most commonly used health resources. In this edition, we have included many Internet addresses, as well as phone numbers and mailing addresses of various organizations and government agencies. The guide is perforated and laminated, making it durable enough for students to keep for later use.

Pedagogical Aids

In addition to the new pedagogical features listed previously, the teaching aids described below proved to be successful in the first three editions of this book and have been included in this new edition:

Star Boxes

In each chapter, special material in Star Boxes encourages students to delve into a particular topic or closely examine an important health issue.

Personal Assessment Inventories

Each chapter contains at least one Personal Assessment inventory, beginning with a comprehensive health inventory in Chapter 1. These self-assessment exercises serve three important functions: they capture students' attention, serve as a basis for introspection and behavior change, and provide suggestions for carrying the applications further.

Health Action Guides

These unique boxes provide step-by-step guidelines for achieving health behavior change. They allow students to apply their knowledge in practical and life-enhancing ways.

Definition Boxes

Key terms are set in boldface type and are defined in corresponding boxes. Pronunciation guides are provided where appropriate. Other important terms in the text are set in italics for emphasis. Both approaches facilitate student vocabulary comprehension.

Comprehensive Glossary

At the end of the text, all terms defined in boxes, as well as pertinent italicized terms, are merged into a comprehensive glossary.

Chapter Summaries

Each chapter concludes with a bulleted summary of key concepts and their significance or application. The student can then return to any topic in the chapter for clarification or study.

Review Questions

A set of questions appears at the end of each chapter to aid the student in review and analysis of chapter content.

Think About This . . .

These engaging questions encourage students to apply what they have learned in the chapter by analyzing their own health habits and finding appropriate solutions to the issues raised.

Suggested Readings

Because some students want to know more about a particular topic, a list of annotated readings is given at the end of each chapter. The suggested readings are readily available at bookstores or public libraries. This edition contains more than 60 new annotated readings.

Appendixes

Focus on Health includes four appendixes that are valuable resources for the student:
- **Commonly used over-the-counter products.** Popular categories of over-the-counter drugs are discussed in detail, with recommendations for consumers of these products. Newly available OTC products, such as naproxen, ketoprofen, minoxidil, and nicotine-containing gum, are included.
- **First aid.** This appendix outlines important general first-aid measures, such as what to do when someone is choking, bleeding, or in shock. It includes a special section on recognition and first-aid treatment of epileptic seizures.

- **Mental disorders.** Categories of mental disorders and therapeutic approaches are outlined in this appendix.
- **Body systems.** The systems of the human body have been clearly and accurately rendered in this appendix to make difficult anatomical concepts easier for students to understand.

ANCILLARIES

An extensive ancillary package is available to qualified adopters to enhance the teaching-learning process. We have made a concerted effort to produce supplements of extraordinary utility and quality. This package has been carefully planned and developed to help instructors derive the greatest benefit from the text. We encourage instructors to examine these materials carefully. Beyond the following brief descriptions, additional information about these ancillaries is available from your WCB/McGraw-Hill sales representative.

Instructor's Manual and Test Bank

Prepared by Virginia Lee Mermel, of Wellness Resources, the instructor's manual features chapter overviews, learning objectives, suggested lecture outlines with notes and recommended activities for teaching each chapter, Debating the Issues boxes, individual and community activities sections, suggestions for guest lectures, a list of current media resources, including software and on-line resources, and 60 full-page transparency masters of helpful illustrations and charts. In addition, the Personal Assessment inventories in the textbook and 50 others are combined into a single section of the instructor's manual. These assessments can be easily photocopied and given to each student as a single packet. The test bank, prepared by Dayna Brown, of Morehead State University, contains multiple-choice, true or false, matching, and critical thinking exam questions. It also includes questions to test students' knowledge of the new supplemental "Focus On . . ." boxes that appear at the end of each chapter in the text. The manual is perforated and three-hole punched for convenience of use.

Computerized Test Bank

The test bank software provides a unique combination of user-friendly aids that enables the instructor to select, edit, delete, or add questions, as well as construct and print tests and answer keys. The computerized test bank package is available for IBM Windows and Macintosh computers.

Overhead Transparency Acetates

Sixty key illustrations and graphics are available as transparency acetates. Attractively printed in full color, these useful tools facilitate learning and classroom discussion. They were chosen specifically to help the instructor explain complex concepts.

Video Library

Choose from our WCB/McGraw-Hill videotape library, which contains many quality videotapes, including selected Films for Humanities and all videos from the award-winning series *Healthy Living: Road to Wellness*.

TestWell: Making Wellness Work for You

This is a self-scoring, pencil-and-paper wellness assessment booklet developed by the National Wellness Institute in Stevens Point, Wisconsin, and distributed exclusively by WCB/McGraw-Hill. It adds flexibility to any personal health or wellness course by allowing adopters to offer pre- and post-assessments at the beginning and end of the course, or at any time time during the semester.

Health Net: A Health & Wellness Guide to the Internet

This valuable new booklet is your navigational tool for exploring the vast array of health resources available on the Internet. A helpful introduction provides general information about the Internet. Each of the following sections in the booklet contains an annotated list of websites to supplement those listed in the text.

HealthQuest CD-ROM
by Robert Gold, Nancy Atkinson, Kathleen Mullen, and Robert McDermott

This interactive CD-ROM contains many assessment activities with customized feedback, activities to assess readiness for behavior change, a risk-analysis component, many articles from journals and other sources, and video and animation. An accompanying instructor's manual assists in using this program in your course.

WCB/McGraw-Hill's NutriQuest CD-ROM

This user-friendly nutrition-analysis program can be used in a wide variety of courses. NutriQuest helps your students understand and apply key nutritional concepts. Users enter their food intake and energy expenditure, compare recommended servings, calories, and nutrients, and use this information to implement an appropriate weight loss (or gain) plan. Data can be stored for a specific food group, a meal, or a one- to three-day average.

The AIDS Booklet, Fifth Edition

This booklet, by Frank D. Cox, offers current, accurate information about HIV and AIDS: what it is, how the virus is transmitted, how the disease progresses, its prevalance among various population groups, symptoms of HIV infection, and strategies for prevention. Also included are discussions of the legal, social, medical, and ethical issues related to AIDS and HIV. Updated semiannually, this short booklet makes AIDS and HIV understandable to your students and ensures that they have the most current information possible.

UC–Berkeley Wellness Letter

Available to qualified adopters, this highly regarded health newsletter keeps you informed of the latest developments in the field.

WCB/MCGraw-Hill Personal Health Web Page

Visit our personal health website for the tools you need to personalize your course. Download photos and illustrations, read our online newletters, and print out personal assessments and lab activities. You can also download a helpful PowerPoint presentation that corresponds to each chapter in *Focus on Health*. In addition, our website helps you stay on top of the latest health news with regular updates to HealthNet and *The AIDS Booklet*.
www.mhhe.com/hper/personalhealth

ACKNOWLEDGMENTS

The publisher's reviewers made excellent comments and suggestions that were very useful to us in writing and revising this book. Their contributions are present in every chapter. We would like to express our sincere appreciation for both their critical and comparative readings.

For the fourth edition:

S. Eugene Barnes
University of Southern Alabama

Anne K. Black
Austin Peay State University

Susan Ceriale
University of California–Santa Barbara

Bridget M. Finn
William Paterson University

Marianne Frauenknecht
Western Michigan University

Edna Gillis
Valdosta State University

Joe Goldfarb
University of Missouri–Columbia

Phil Huntsinger
University of Kansas

Gordon B. James
Weber State University

Sylvia M. Kubsch
University of Wisconsin–Green Bay

Frederick M. Randolph
Western Illinois University

Dell Smith
University of Central Arkansas

B. McKinley Thomas
Augusta State University

Chuck Ulrich
Western Illinois University

For the third edition:

Dayna S. Brown
Morehead State University

Diane M. Hamilton
Georgia Southern University

Joe Herzstein
Trenton State College

Rebecca Rutt Leas
Clarion University

Dorinda Maynard
Eastern Kentucky University

Steven Navarro
Cerritos College

Mary Beth Tighe
The Ohio State University

For the second edition:

James D. Aguiar
Ithaca College

Carolyn M. Allred
Central Piedmont Community College

Joan Benson
University of Utah

Daniel E. Berney
California State University–Dominguez Hills

Ronnie Carda
Emporia State University

Barbara Funke
Georgia College

William C. Gross
Western Michigan University

Richard Hurley
Brigham Young University

Raeann Koerner Smith
Ventura College

L. Clark McCammon
Western Illinois University

Dan Neal
Southwestern Oregon Community College

David Quadagno
Florida State University

Leslie Rurey
Community Colleges of Spokane

Scott E. Scobell
West Virginia State College

Karen T. Sullivan
Marymount University

Joan Tudor
Chapman University

Stuart L. Whitney
University of Vermont

For the first edition:

Sandra L. Bonneau
Golden West College

Richard A. Kaye
Kingsborough Community College

Donald Haynes
University of Minnesota–Duluth

J. Dale Wagoner
Chabot College

SPECIAL ACKNOWLEDGMENTS

The fourth edition of *Focus on Health* is the twelfth book we have written since the mid 1980s. We could not have accomplished all of this without the help of many people. Among these are our faculty colleagues at Ball State University who continue to keep us abreast of new information in areas related to personal health. A special thanks goes out to all of you.

Additionally, we want to recognize our administrative colleagues. We are fortunate to have worked with administrators who maintain the vision that (a) textbooks represent important resources for today's college students, and (b) textbooks reflect faculty contributions that shed favorable light on a college community. We very much appreciate the support of Dr. C. Warren Vander Hill, Provost and Vice President for Academic Affairs, and Dr. Ronald L. Johnstone, Dean of the College of Sciences and Humanities at Ball State University.

The list of dedicated people at WCB/McGraw-Hill is quite long. Many have played a direct part in influencing the direction of this writing project. Ed Bartell, Vicki Malinee, and Pam Cooper are exceptional people who have championed this project since its inception. They understand clearly the demands authors face as they juggle family, teaching, and writing schedules. They do their best to provide a supportive environment for WCB/McGraw-Hill authors.

Another key player is our developmental editor, Melissa Martin. This edition of *Focus on Health* is the third project we have completed with Melissa. Her experience as a production editor combines so well with her editorial skills that her finished products continue to be both attractively packaged and technically sound. Melissa has been on top of every detail from the moment we started this revision. We appreciate her talent, effort, and humor very much.

We also wish to acknowledge the contributions of Virginia Lee Mermel and Dayna Brown. Over the years, we have learned the importance of providing professors with a comprehensive, well-written instructor's manual and test bank. Virginia Lee Mermel and Dayna Brown have developed an excellent instructor's manual and test bank that will benefit experienced instructors, as well as new ones.

One of the unique new features of this edition of *Focus on Health* is its "Focus On . . ." articles. Dawn L. Elmore-McCrary, of San Antonio College, and Thomas Neil McCrary combined their teaching experience and health expertise to develop, research, and write these outstanding essays. We are grateful for the considerable time and effort they devoted to making these articles up-to-date, exciting, and informative.

It is difficult for the authors to know the many people who work on the production end of a textbook project. Our principal connection with this part of WCB/McGraw-Hill has been our project manager Sheila Frank. Sheila made certain that every manuscript detail was clear and every production deadline met. In addition, the credit for the book's attractiveness goes to the designer, Mary Christianson.

Finally, we would like to thank our families for the continued support and love they have given us. Perhaps more than others, our families understand the effort and commitment it takes to write books. We truly appreciate their sacrifices.

Dale B. Hahn
Wayne A. Payne

FOCUS ON HEALTH

Shaping Your Health

Healthy People: Looking Ahead to 2010

In 1990 a document titled *Healthy People 2000: National Health Promotion and Disease Prevention* Objectives outlined a strategic plan for promoting the health of the American public. The plan included 300 health objectives in 22 priority areas. Forty-seven of the 300 were identified as "sentinel" objectives—particularly significant goals that could quickly indicate the progress of 1990s health promotion efforts.

Progress toward achieving the objectives was assessed near the middle of the decade and reported in a document titled *Healthy People 2000: Midcourse Review and 1995 Revisions.* Progress was reported in many areas, but little or no headway had been made in others. In particular, few gains were made toward achieving the three broadest objectives: (1) increasing the span of healthy life; (2) reducing health disparities (differences) among Americans; and (3) gaining access to preventive services.

A new plan for improving the health of Americans, called *Healthy People 2010* (see p. 4), is now being formulated and will be completed by January 2000. We will refer to this new plan within each chapter where appropriate.

This chapter focuses on two questions: "What is health?" and "How does health contribute to the process of living a satisfying life?" We help you answer these questions by providing a framework around which to view health, and we encourage you to study your own health as it relates to your growth and development throughout the stages of life.

HEALTH CONCERNS OF THE LATE 1990s

As we move closer to the new century, health concerns such as heart disease, cancer, accidents, drug use, and mental health are important to us, even if we are not directly affected by them (Table 1-1). Environmental pollution, violence, health care costs, and acquired immunodeficiency syndrome (AIDS) and other sexually transmitted diseases are of significant importance as well. World hunger, population control, and the threat of terrorism using nuclear and biological weapons are also concerns for this generation and for those to follow.

The Star Box at right lists the top five health issues college students face in the 1990s. Many of these health conditions can be prevented or managed successfully. As you learn more about health, you will find out how to lower your risk for many of these conditions. Your behavior is within your control, and the choices you make will undoubtedly affect your health. We encourage you to select a plan of healthful living that incorporates a sound diet, proper exercise, adequate rest, periodic medical checkups, and elimination (or moderation) of drug use, including tobacco and alcohol use. One goal of this textbook is to provide you with the information and motivation to help you select the lifestyle that will make you a happy and healthy person.

DEFINITIONS OF HEALTH-RELATED TERMS

A Traditional Definition of Health

One of the most widely recognized and frequently quoted definitions of health is that given by the Geneva-based World Health Organization:[1]

> Health is a state of complete physical, mental, and social well-being and not merely the absence of disease and infirmity.

This multifaceted view of health includes physical, mental, and social dimensions, indicating that health extends beyond the structure and function of your body to include feelings, values, and the ability to rea-

Table 1-1 Top 10 Causes of Death in the United States for 1996–1997*†	
Cause of Death	**Number of Cases**
1. Heart disease	721,480
2. Malignant neoplasms (cancer)	535,190
3. Cerebrovascular disease (stroke)	155,450
4. Chronic obstructive pulmonary disease	105,920
5. Accidents	90,310
6. Pneumonia	83,240
7. Diabetes	61,160
8. Suicide	30,320
9. HIV/AIDS	25,040
10. Homicide and legal intervention (males only)	19,750

*For the 12-month period ending April 1997
†Reference #2.

Key Health Issues Facing College Students in the 1990s

The American College Health Association, a prominent group of health educators, medical professionals, and college residence hall staff professionals identified the following as the most critical health issues faced by college students in the 1990s. The issues are listed in the order of importance:

- *Sexual health concerns,* including topics such as sexually transmitted diseases, relationship issues, unintended pregnancy, and sexual violence
- *Substance abuse,* including a wide range of issues related to the abuse of alcohol, tobacco, and other drugs, and dependency and codependency
- *Mental health concerns,* including stress management, fear of failure, coping skills, complex family relationships, and depression
- *Nutrition issues,* including healthful diets, weight management, chronic disease prevention, and eating disorders
- *Health care services,* including financing and delivering comprehensive, low-cost health services to students and their families

Because these issues have been important in the decade now ending, and because of their relevance to you, all of these health issues are discussed in this text. We also cover many other issues of concern to both traditional and nontraditional-age students.

son. It also includes the nature of your interpersonal relationships. Furthermore, it can be inferred that health can exist in the presence of disease and infirmity; you do not have to be a "picture of health" to be productive and satisfied. Nevertheless, for all the definition's value, one question remains unanswered: "How does health contribute to the process of living a satisfying life?"

Holistic Health

One popular description of health expands the definition supplied by the World Health Organization. **Holistic health** extends the physical, mental, and social aspects of the definition to include intellectual, spiritual, and occupational dimensions. The holistically healthy person functions as a total person. Some experts say that holistically healthy people have reached a "high level of wellness."

Holistic health may be the broadest explanation of health. Through a holistic concept of health, we are better able to understand how a person who has a serious physical illness can also be considered quite healthy.

Health Promotion

The term **health promotion** is frequently linked to disease prevention. Health promoters believe that if you accept scientific opinion regarding health and adopt specific health-enhancing practices, you will become healthy. On the basis of this view of health, if you have enhanced your health, you should live longer and have fewer health problems than the average person and feel better than an unhealthy person.

To promote the health of a person or a group, health professionals use a number of strategies. Health screenings (such as blood pressure or cholesterol measurements), health education activities (such as first aid, human immunodeficiency virus [HIV] education, or cardiopulmonary resuscitation [CPR] training), behavior change strategies (such as the use of specific eating plans or exercise programs), and health maintenance activities (such as the use of regular medical checkups) are examples of approaches used to keep people healthy and alive for many years.

Although these strategies are admirable, this interpretation presents health as an end in itself rather than a means to an end. Living a long time, not being sick, and doing only healthful things are important, but will they assure you of growing and developing to your fullest potential?

Wellness

Whereas *health promotion* is a term used by many in the health field, **wellness** may be the most popular health-related term of the late 1990s. Wellness is a process of periodically assessing risk factors and providing information, behavior change strategies, and individual or group counseling that ultimately leads to the adoption of a *wellness lifestyle.* This lifestyle, which is characterized by low-risk, health-enhancing behavior, should eventually produce a sense of well-being.[3]

Compared with other perceptions of health, wellness practitioners believe that wellness is not driven by concerns about illness or longevity (long life). Rather, they believe that following a wellness lifestyle can help people reach their fullest potential as they interact within the family, classroom, or workplace.

To achieve this human potential, wellness experts believe that individuals must take responsibility for their health behavior.[4] People must understand that they have more control over their health behavior than they might think. A wellness perspective encourages people to focus on the present and future and not on the past, especially when one's past includes negative health behavior. Wellness also discourages blaming others for one's own behavior.

The behavioral intervention that takes place in wellness programs is intended to reduce health risks. Thus we question wellness practitioners' claim that wellness does not focus on preventing illness and extending life, since these goals are the logical outcomes of risk reduction activities.

The college campus is an ideal place to view the concept of wellness in action. College administrators and even casual observers report that today's college

---

holistic health
Broadest view of the composition of health; views health in terms of its physical, emotional, social, intellectual, spiritual, and occupational makeup.

health promotion
A movement in which knowledge, practices, and values are transmitted to people for use in lengthening their lives, reducing the incidence of illness, and feeling better.

wellness
A broadly based term used to describe a highly developed level of health that encourages people to achieve their human potential.

Healthy People 2010

In the introduction to this chapter, we provided a brief review of the federal government's initiatives to promote health: *Healthy People 2000: National Health Promotion and Disease Prevention Objectives* (1990) and *Healthy People 2000: Midcourse Review and 1995 Revisions*. We also introduced the newest set of national health objectives, *Healthy People 2010,*[5] which is now being formulated.

Healthy People 2010 will be a health promotion program intended to complement a global initiative, *Health for All*, being launched by the World Health Organization. Although the goals of the two programs will be similar, *Healthy People 2010* focuses on the projected needs of *this* country as we begin the next century. The *Healthy People 2000* program is becoming outdated because of changing demographics since 1990, such as rapidly growing populations of elderly and nonwhite people. In addition, new preventive therapies, vaccines, and pharmaceuticals and new diagnostic and treatment technologies have changed the face of medical care and health promotion. Global forces, such as emerging infectious diseases, destruction of tropical rainforests, and environmental interdependence, have also influenced Americans' health needs.

Central to the design of *Healthy People 2010* are 20 areas in which health promotion activities are critically important, such as mental disability, chronic disease prevention and treatment, increased physical activity, improved nutrition, and more rigorous food and drug safety requirements. Making progress in these twenty areas of health promotion will allow the nation to reach four "enabling goals": (1) the promotion of healthy behavior; (2) the protection of health; (3) the assurance of access to quality health care; and (4) the strengthening of community prevention. When these goals have been achieved, the American public should anticipate two additional benefits: (1) increased years of healthy life; and (2) the elimination of health disparities between various segments of the population. These latter two accomplishments were also goals of the earlier programs.

The success of *Healthy People 2010* will not be known for many years. However, if we ultimately reach these goals, Americans can expect both an increased quantity and quality of life.

---

students seem to be embracing wellness. Students, faculty, and staff members realize the importance of health and are participating in activities designed to promote wellness, such as health screenings, nutrition awareness seminars, and fitness-focus weeks. Throughout this textbook, we encourage readers to develop the wellness lifestyle with which they feel most comfortable.

With the increased emphasis on wellness programs on many college campuses, it is not surprising to see the influence of wellness extending to many aspects of daily life, including schools and the workplace. Commonly offered wellness programs cover smoking cessation, weight control, cholesterol screening, stress management, exercise, and nutrition. Many major corporations report that employee participation in wellness activities reduces health care costs (insurance premiums) and increases employee satisfaction and productivity.[6] Indeed, you will see wellness extending beyond your college campus.

Empowerment

In the early 1990s, the term *empowerment* began to appear in professional health education and health promotion literature.[7] In the context of health, empowerment refers to a process in which individuals or groups of people gain increasing measures of control over their health. To take control of health matters, people or groups must learn to "liberate themselves" from a variety of barriers that tend to restrict health enhancement, including the complicated and expensive health care system, limited access to health care or fitness facilities, the fear of discovering an illness or serious health condition, and the concern that one might be viewed as a "health nut."

When people empower themselves to overcome these barriers, they begin to take charge of their lives, regardless of the current forces that discourage positive health changes. Empowered people do not blame individuals or environmental realities for health conditions but focus on producing constructive change through dialogue and collaboration.

Empowerment programs have produced positive health consequences for individuals and groups that have been traditionally underserved by the health care system, such as the economically disadvantaged, the elderly, and minority populations. Have you seen empowerment programs working in your community? You probably have if you can identify programs where people have organized a grassroots campaign to prevent neighborhood violence, improve childhood nutrition, promote healthy lifestyles, or prevent drug use among youth. Only when people realize that they can "make a difference" will they become empowered. We believe that your personal health course can help you become empowered in your own life.

DEVELOPMENTAL TASKS FOR COLLEGE STUDENTS

Because *most* of today's undergraduate college students range between 18 and perhaps 40 years of age, we present five developmental tasks that reflect this broad student range (Figure 1-1). The first four tasks (involving identity, responsibility, independence, and social skills) are especially pertinent to the more traditional-age college student. The fifth task (concerning intimacy) is probably more important for students who have moved just beyond the **young adult years.** We hope that the gains you make with each of these tasks will help you move more successfully through your life.

However, keep in mind that many college students, regardless of their age, continue to make gains in all five developmental areas because each person's experience and development are unique. For example, **nontraditional students** remind us that their identity

young adult years
Segment of the life cycle from ages 18 to 24; a transitional period between adolescence and adulthood.

nontraditional students
Administrative term used by colleges and universities to refer to students who, for whatever reason, are pursuing undergraduate work at an age other than that associated with the traditional college years (18 to 24).

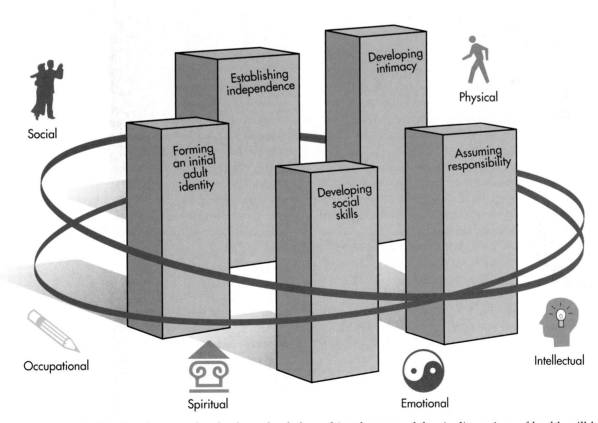

Figure 1-1 Mastery of the developmental tasks through a balanced involvement of the six dimensions of health will lead to your enjoying a more productive and satisfying life.

continues to change as they see themselves progressing through college. They realize that they are not the same people they were when they started back to school. Their identity keeps developing as they learn new concepts and meet new people.

Forming an Initial Adult Identity

For most of your youth, you were seen by adults within your neighborhood or community as someone's son or daughter. That stage has now nearly passed; both you and society are beginning to look at each other in new ways.

As an emerging adult, you probably wish to present a unique identity to society. Internally you are constructing a perception of yourself as the person you wish to be; externally you are forming the behavioral patterns that will project this identity to others.

The completion of this first developmental task is necessary so that you can have a productive and satisfying life. Through your experiences in achieving an adult identity, you will eventually be capable of answering the central question of young adulthood: "Who am I?" Interestingly, many nontraditional students are also asking this question as they progress through college.

Establishing Independence

In contemporary society the primary responsibility for socialization during childhood and adolescence is assigned to the family. For many years, your family was the primary contributor to your knowledge, values, and behavior. By this time, however, you should be demonstrating an interest in moving away from that dependent relationship.

Travel, peer relationships, marriage, military service, and, of course, college have been traditional avenues for disengagement from the family. Generally, your ability and willingness to follow one or more of these paths will help you to establish your independence. Your success in these endeavors will be based on your willingness to use the resources you have. You will need to draw on physical, emotional, social, intellectual, spiritual, and occupational strengths to undertake the new experiences that will bring about your independence. In a sense, your family laid the foundation for the resources and experiences you will now use to draw yourself away from the family.

Assuming Responsibility

The assumption of increasing levels of responsibility is a third developmental task in which you are

HealthQuest Activities

- Use the Wellboard to report your life score (number of years out of 114) and the score percentages for each of the eight health areas.
- Fill out the Wellboard using data from a fictional college student. On the first assessment screen, change the demographics to show how gender, ethnicity, age, marital status, and community affect average life expectancy.

expected to progress. For adults, the opportunity to assume responsibility can come from a variety of sources. You may sometimes accept responsibility voluntarily, such as when you join a campus organization or establish a new friendship. Other responsibilities are placed on you when professors assign term papers, when dating partners exert pressure on you to conform to their expectations, or when employers require that you be consistently productive. In other situations, you may accept responsibility for doing a particular task not for yourself but for the benefit of someone else, such as when you donate a unit of blood during a campus blood drive.

As important and demanding as these areas of responsibility are, a more basic responsibility awaits the adult: that of maintaining and improving your health and the health of others. You will be challenged to be responsible for recognizing, improving, and then using the strengths that constitute your physical, emotional, social, intellectual, spiritual, and occupational makeup. At the same time, you will be equally responsible for recognizing, accepting, and working within your limitations. None of the specific areas of responsibility associated with school, employment, and parenting can be undertaken with maximum effectiveness unless you make a commitment to be responsible for your own health.

Developing Social Skills

A fourth developmental task is developing appropriate and dependable social skills. The college experience has traditionally prepared students very effectively in this regard, but the interactions in friendships, work relationships, or parenting may require that you make an effort to grow and develop beyond levels you might achieve from being a college student. You will probably need to refine a variety of social skills, including communication, listening, and conflict management.

This need to interact socially will at times compromise your health. Examples might be the weekend party that prevents you from doing well on a Monday morning examination or the recreational or intramural activities that sometimes result in serious injury. Generally, however, social interaction contributes to your total health and is an important aid in helping you have a productive and satisfying life.

Developing Intimacy

This developmental task usually presents itself to people between young adulthood and midlife, when it appears important to establish one or more intimate relationships. Indeed, we are looking at intimacy in its broadest sense as a deeply close, sharing relationship. Intimacy may stem from a marriage relationship or other close friendship.

People vary in their number of intimate relationships, with some having many intimate friends, while others have only one or two deep relationships. The number does not matter. What matters is that each person has someone with whom to share intimate thoughts, feelings, and emotions.

After becoming familiar with these developmental tasks, you should see that there is considerable overlap in the accomplishment of each task. For example, your development and refinement of social skills can enhance your independence from your family. Your willingness to accept increasing responsibility may influence your ability to develop an intimate relationship with someone.

DEVELOPMENTAL TASKS OF MIDLIFE ADULTS

If you are a traditional-age student, have you wondered what it would be like to be 20 or 30 years older than you are now? What would you be doing, feeling, and thinking if you were the age of your parents?

One thought that probably recurs all too often for your parents is the reality of their own eventual death. Their awareness that they will not live forever is a subtle but profoundly influential force that can cause them to be restless, to renew their religious faith, and to be more highly motivated to master the developmental tasks of midlife. This motivation and the awareness of the reality of death combine to produce the dynamic concept of being at "the prime of life"—a time when there seems to be a great deal to accomplish and less time in which to accomplish it.

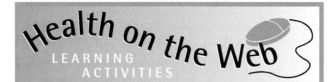

Activity 1

In the context of health, *empowerment* refers to a process in which individuals or groups of people gain increasing control over their health. *Prevention*'s "Healthy Ideas" is especially interested in those who have met a health or fitness goal and maintained it for a year or more. To submit your success story, go to http://www.healthyideas.com and select "Publish your success story." Take a moment to fill out the form shown. The publishers will review your submission and contact you if they are interested in your story.

Activity 2

All behavior change programs should have some form of goal setting. To obtain these goals, knowing who you are and what you can do is important. In health terminology, this is referred to as your *locus of control.* An inventory is available at http://www.psychtests.com/lc.html. Complete the inventory and then click on "score" to receive your score on-line.

Activity 3

Each segment of the life cycle should be approached with the fullest involvement possible. This is still true when one completes the developmental tasks of elderly adulthood. Today, about 40 million Americans are at or close to retirement age. An inventory is available at http://www.mayohealth.org/mayo/9405/htm/conf_tab.htm to evaluate your confidence related to retirement. Score yourself in the following areas: attitudes and lifestyle, health, and financial security.

Achieving Generativity

In a very real sense, midlife people are asked to do something they have not been expected to do previously. As a part of their development as unique people, they are expected to "pay back" society for the support it has given them. Most people in midlife begin to realize that the collective society, through its institutions (families, schools, churches), has been generous in its support of their own growth and development and that it is time to replenish these resources. Younger and older people may have needs that middle-aged people can best meet. By meeting the needs of others, midlife people can fulfill their own needs to grow and develop. *Generativity* reflects this process of contributing to the collective good.[8]

The process of repaying society for its support is structured around familiar types of activities. Developmentally speaking, midlife people are able to select the activities that best use their abilities to contribute to the good of society.[9]

The most traditional way in which midlife people repay society is through parenting. Children, with their potential for becoming valuable members of the next generation, need the support of people who recognize the contribution they can make. By supporting children, either directly through quality parenting or through institutions that function on behalf of children, middle-aged people repay society for the support they have themselves received. As they extend themselves outward on behalf of the next generation, they ensure their own growth and development. In similar fashion, their support of aging parents and institutions that serve the elderly provides another means to express generativity.

For people who possess artistic talent, generativity may be accomplished through the pleasure brought to others. Artists, craftsmen, and musicians have unique opportunities to speak directly to others through their talents. Volunteer work serves as another avenue for generativity. Most midlife people also express generativity through their jobs by providing quality products or services and thus contribute to the well-being of those who desire or need these goods and services.

Reassessing the Plans of Young Adulthood

It is also essential for midlife people to come to terms with the finality of their own deaths. Having done this, they often feel that it is time to think about their goals for adulthood they formulated 25 or more years previously. Their "dreams" must be revisited.[9] This reassessment constitutes a second developmental task of midlife adults.

By carefully reviewing the aspirations they had as young adults, middle-aged people can more clearly study their short- and long-term goals. Specifically, strengths and limitations that were unrecognizable when they were young adults are now more clearly seen. The inexperience of youth is replaced by the insights gained through experience. A commitment to quality often replaces the desire for quantity during the second half of the life cycle. Time is valued more highly because it is now seen in a more realistic perspective. The dream for the future is more sharply focused, and the successes and failures of the past are more fully understood as this developmental task of reassessing earlier plans of young adulthood is accomplished.

DEVELOPMENTAL TASKS OF ELDERLY ADULTS

In this section, we focus on the developmental tasks confronted by elderly people. Accepting the physical decline of aging, maintaining high levels of physical function, and establishing a sense of integrity are tasks of the elderly period.

Accepting the Decline of Aging

The general decline associated with the latter part of the life cycle is particularly serious between the seventh and eighth decades. Physically, emotionally, socially, intellectually, and occupationally, elderly people must accept at least some decline. For example, a person may no longer be physically able to drive a car, which could in turn limit participation in social activities. Even a spiritual loss may be encountered at those times when life seems less ordered or less humane. Clearly, a developmental task to be accomplished by the elderly is to accept the nature and extent of these losses.[10]

Maintaining a High Level of Physical Function

Because each segment of the life cycle should be approached with the fullest level of involvement possible, the second developmental task of the elderly is to maintain the highest level of physical function possible.

For areas of decline in which some measure of reversal is possible, the elderly are afforded an opportunity to seek **rehabilitation.** Whether through an individually designed program or through the aid of a skilled professional, the elderly can bring back some function to a previously high level. For example, the regular use of light weights can improve an older person's ability to rise from a chair or walk more steadily.

The second approach, often used in combination with rehabilitation, is **remediation,** whereby an alternative to the area of loss is introduced. Examples of remediation include the use of hearing aids, audio cassettes, and prescription shoes. By using alternative resources, function can often be returned and may actually be improved.

rehabilitation
Return of function to a previous level.

remediation
Development of alternative forms of function to replace those that have been lost or were poorly developed.

For a growing number of older adults, rehabilitation and remediation are rarely necessary because of the high level of physical fitness that they enjoy. For these older people, physical fitness has been maintained through regular physical conditioning activities (see Chapter 4). For most, only minor modifications are necessary to enjoy injury-free involvement.

Establishing a Sense of Integrity

The third major developmental task that awaits the elderly is to establish a sense of *integrity,* or a sense of wholeness, concerning the journey that may be nearly complete.[8] The elderly must look back over their lives to see the value in what they were able to accomplish. They must address the simple but critical questions, "Would I do it over again?" "Am I satisfied with what I managed to accomplish?" "Can I accept the fact that others will have experiences to which I can never return?"

If the elderly can answer these questions positively, then they will feel a sense of wholeness, personal value, and worth. Having established this sense of integrity, they will believe that their lives have had meaning and fullness and that they have helped society.

Since they have already experienced so much, many elderly people have no fear of death, even though they may fear the process of dying. Their ability to come to terms with death thus reinforces their sense of integrity.

Like all of the other developmental tasks, this critical area of growth and development is a personal experience. The elderly must assume this last developmental task with the same sense of purpose they used for earlier tasks. When elderly people can feel this sense of integrity, their reasons for having lived will be fully understood.[3]

THE ROLE OF HEALTH

Having been introduced to the developmental tasks of college students, as well as those of midlife and elderly adults, you can better answer the question, "What is the *role of health* in my life?" The role of health is to assist you in mastering the developmental tasks that will make your life more satisfying and productive.

Health can be described meaningfully only in conjunction with your developmental tasks. If your health allows you to successfully complete your developmental tasks, then we would say that you have developed a high level of health.

For most of today's college students, the tasks we are identifying as those likely to be accomplished with high-level health are the five already presented. For midlife and elderly students, the continued refinement of these tasks and the mastery of additional tasks just presented will depend on their level of health.

THE COMPOSITION OF HEALTH

Your health is composed of six interacting, *dynamic* dimensions. By becoming familiar with these dimensions, you can more easily recognize what it is about your health that may or may not be helping you to master your developmental tasks. Fortunately, because your health is dynamic, you can modify aspects of its dimensions to make it a better tool to help you live a productive, satisfying life.

Your health is not static; it cannot be stored on a shelf or given to others. The health you had yesterday no longer exists. The health you aspire to have next week or next year is not guaranteed. However, scien-

HEALTH Action Guide

Cultural Diversity at Your Campus

To help you develop some understanding of the ethnically diverse culture at your college or university, try to find the answers to these basic questions:

- What are the minority population figures for the community in which your college is located? Try to include figures for African-Americans, Hispanics, Asians, and Native Americans.
- What are the minority population figures for your college or university?
- Do these figures surprise you?

The following is the resource center for the federal agency whose mission is to improve the health status of minority populations in the United States. To receive information or publications, call the 800 number listed below:

Office of Minority Health (OMH)
Information Resource Center
P.O. Box 37337
Washington, DC 20013-7337
(1-800-444-6472)

For more information about the diversity of today's college students, see the Focus Box on pp. 19–21.

tific evidence suggests that what you do today will help determine the quality of your future health. We now briefly consider each of the six dimensions of health so that you can more clearly see how each forms a part of your total health.

Physical Dimension

A number of physiological and structural characteristics help you accomplish your developmental tasks, including your level of susceptibility to disease, body weight, visual ability, strength, coordination, level of endurance, and powers of recuperation. In certain situations the physical dimension of your health may be the most important. Perhaps this is why many authorities have for so long equated health with the design and operation of the body.

Emotional Dimension

Your emotional characteristics can also aid you as you grow and develop. The emotional dimension of health includes the degree to which you are able to cope with stress, remain flexible, and compromise to resolve conflict. This dimension may be the one that is most closely related to your feelings. How you feel about your family and friends, your life goals and ambitions, and your daily life situations is all tied to the emotional dimension of health.

Your growth and development can be associated with some vulnerability, which may lead to feelings of rejection and failure that could reduce your overall productivity and satisfaction. People who consistently try to improve their emotional health appear to lead lives of greater enjoyment than those who let feelings of vulnerability overwhelm them or block their creativity. Specific techniques for improving your emotional health are presented in Chapter 2.

Social Dimension

Social ability is the third dimension of total health. Whether you call it social graces, skills, or insights, you probably have many strengths in this area. Because most of your growth and development has occurred in the presence of others, you can appreciate how this dimension of your health may be a critically important factor in your life.

The social abilities of many nontraditional students may already be firmly established. Entering college may encourage them to develop new social skills that help them socialize with their traditional-age student colleagues. After being on campus for a while, nontraditional students often interact comfortably with tradi-

tional students in such diverse places as the library, the student center, and the bookstore, which enhances the social dimension of health for both types of students.

Intellectual Dimension

Your ability to process and act on information, clarify values and beliefs, and exercise your decision-making capacity ranks among the most important aspects of total health. Coping skills, flexibility, or the knack of saying the right thing at the right time may not serve you as well as does your ability to use information or understand a new idea. Certainly a refusal to grasp new information or to undertake an analysis of your beliefs could hinder the degree of growth and development that your college experience can provide.

Spiritual Dimension

The fifth dimension of health is the spiritual dimension.[11] Although you certainly could include your religious beliefs and practices in this category, we would extend it to include your relationship to other living things, the role of a spiritual direction in your life, the nature of human behavior, and your willingness to serve others.

Many of today's students appear to be searching for a deeper understanding of the meaning of life. Although you may not feel uneasy about the nature of your spiritual beliefs, many students do feel anxious about the spiritual side of their lives. In fact, one explanation for the renewed interest in the spiritual dimension of health probably stems from its value as a resource during periods of personal stress. The spiritual dimension of health is so significant that some health professionals believe it to be the actual "core of wellness."[11]

Cultivating the spiritual side of your health may help you discover how you "fit" into this universe. You can enhance your spiritual health in a variety of ways, many of which involve opening yourself to new experiences with nature, art, body movement, or music. Taking a walk in the woods, visiting an art museum, listening to classical music, talking with young children, writing poetry, caring for the environment, painting a picture, or pushing your body to its physical limits are just a few ways that you can develop spiritual health.

Occupational Dimension

The sixth dimension of health reflects the fact that employment satisfaction is directly related to many aspects of a person's health. When people feel good about their jobs, they tend to feel good about themselves and are more likely to have a healthier lifestyle. Usually, people have positive feelings about their employment situation if their jobs provide both external rewards (such as adequate salary and benefits) and internal rewards (such as positive social interactions and the opportunity for creative input).

As professors, we encourage our students to consider how closely their future occupations will be linked to their future health status. Fortunately, many colleges have career counseling offices, where students can talk with professionals about career opportunities. Sometimes during career counseling, students undertake a series of psychological tests to help in determining the kinds of jobs that could best fit their personality profiles. Students can also learn about job opportunities in their major areas of study by talking with professors and from volunteer work, student employment or internships, and summer job experiences.

It should also be noted that some health professionals are calling for the inclusion of additional dimensions of health. Although a case can be made for including *environmental* or *consumer* dimensions of health, we believe that too many dimensions can cause confusion because they overlap. For example, consumer health can be seen as a facet of social or intellectual health, and the environmental dimension may involve your initial adult identity and growing sense of responsibility.

OUR DEFINITION OF HEALTH

By combining the role of health with the composition of health, we offer a new definition of health that we believe is unique to this book:

> Health is the blending of physical, emotional, social, intellectual, spiritual, and occupational resources as they assist you in mastering the developmental tasks necessary for a satisfying and productive life.

Remember that this blending of your health resources is a never-ending process. Whether you are a traditional or nontraditional student, your ability to master the tasks that await you hinges on this unique combination of health dimensions.

CHARTING A PLAN FOR BEHAVIOR CHANGE

Students taking a personal health course usually decide to change their health behavior in one or more specific ways. We encourage our students to complete a "health behavior change project" as part of their course requirements. Sometimes, students know

LEARNING from ALL CULTURES

The Important Things in Life

What are the most important things in life for maintaining a happy and healthy existence? If any number of Americans responded to this question, the answers would vary. For some, success and happiness might mean a good job or a satisfying career, whereas for others, contentment with oneself, family, and friends might be the answer.

The same holds true for people of other cultures. There are common experiences, however, that people from different countries consider important to their well-being. Mexico, for example, is a country with a large gap between the rich and the poor; but for the great majority of Mexicans, celebrations or "fiestas" contribute greatly to their joy of living. Religious holidays and civil events are important occasions for fiestas and can be national or local celebrations. They are generally held outdoors and last from 1 to 3 days.[12]

Chile, like Mexico, is a country of the very rich and the very poor. Regardless of economic or social status, however, most Chileans derive pride and happiness from their families, and families typically are very close. Chileans generally are also extremely hospitable and enjoy interacting with strangers or visitors.[13]

Lebanese and other Middle Eastern people are also known for their hospitality and welcome visitors and foreigners into their homes for refreshment. In fact, much of their social life revolves around sharing refreshment, particularly Arabic coffee, with friends.

Although all these countries face many challenges, their people still strive for happiness and continue to participate in things that bring them joy. What things in your life do you find most important for achieving happiness?

exactly which behavior they want to alter. They may have found this behavior while completing the Personal Assessment on p. 12.

Other students browse through various chapters in the textbook to see what topics are of special interest to them. It might be helpful for you to examine the personal assessments in each chapter. For example, if you are interested in behavior change related to alcohol use, you might look at p. 181 and complete the Personal Assessment entitled "How do you use alcoholic beverages?" If you are thinking about a behavior

Text continued on p. 15.

PERSONAL ASSESSMENT

A Personal Profile: Evaluating Your Health

Your health is influenced by behavior in a number of aspects of living. This personal health profile will help you assess this behavior. For each statement, circle the number of the response that best describes your behavior or how you think you will behave when confronted with a particular situation. At the end of each section, add the points received on the statements in that section and record your point total on the appropriate line. At the conclusion of the inventory you will be able to make a broad interpretation of the influence of your behavior on your personal health status.

Stress Management

	Rarely, if ever	Some of the time	Most of the time	Almost always
1. I seek out change and accept its presence with a sense of confidence and anticipation.	1	2	3	4
2. I participate regularly in a physical activity that allows me to expend nervous energy.	1	2	3	4
3. I turn to friends for advice and assistance during periods of disruption in my life.	1	2	3	4
4. I periodically reevaluate my experiences with stressful events in anticipation of future events of the same type.	1	2	3	4
5. I seek the counsel of professional advisors when stress becomes too difficult to manage.	1	2	3	4
6. I seek comfort and support from my faith when faced with a difficult period of adjustment.	1	2	3	4

Points _____

Physical Fitness

1. I participate in vigorous activity for approximately 30 minutes four times per week.	1	2	3	4
2. I am active during the day and prefer a more vigorous approach to work and leisure activity.	1	2	3	4
3. I do exercises specifically designed to condition my muscles and joints.	1	2	3	4
4. I enter into vigorous activity only after I am warmed up, and I cool down after vigorous activity.	1	2	3	4
5. I select properly designed and well-maintained equipment and clothing for each activity.	1	2	3	4
6. I listen to my body regarding injury and fatigue, and I seek appropriate care when injured.	1	2	3	4

Points _____

Social Relationships

1. I feel comfortable and confident when meeting people for the first time.	1	2	3	4
2. I establish social relationships with people of both genders with equal ease and enjoyment.	1	2	3	4
3. I participate in a wide variety of groups, including educational, recreational, religious, and occupational groups.	1	2	3	4
4. I find the roles of leader and subordinate to be equally acceptable.	1	2	3	4
5. I seek out opportunities to become proficient at a variety of social skills.	1	2	3	4
6. I am open and accessible to others in the development of intimate relationships.	1	2	3	4

Points _____

	Rarely, if ever	Some of the time	Most of the time	Almost always

Spiritual Health

1. I find myself searching for spiritual connections in my life. 1 2 3 4
2. I can identify ways I can improve the spiritual dimension of my health. 1 2 3 4

Points _____

Nutrition

1. I select a wide variety of foods in an attempt to eat a balanced diet. 1 2 3 4
2. I select breads, cereals, fresh fruits, and vegetables in preference to pastries, candies, sodas, and fruits canned in heavy syrup. 1 2 3 4
3. I select such foods as peas, beans, and peanut butter as my primary sources of protein while limiting my consumption of red meat and high-fat dairy products. 1 2 3 4
4. I select foods prepared with unsaturated vegetable oils while reducing my consumption of red meats, organ meats, dairy products, and foods prepared with lard or butter. 1 2 3 4
5. I limit snacking, and I select nutritious foods when I do snack. 1 2 3 4
6. I attempt to balance my caloric intake with my activity level. 1 2 3 4

Points _____

Alcohol, Tobacco, and Drug Use

1. I abstain from alcohol use, or I use alcohol infrequently and in very limited amounts. 1 2 3 4
2. I avoid riding with people who are consuming alcohol, and I drive defensively, remaining aware that other drivers may be using alcohol. 1 2 3 4
3. I avoid the use of tobacco products in all forms, including cigarettes, cigars, pipes, and smokeless tobacco products. 1 2 3 4
4. I limit my contact with others who are using tobacco, particularly when in confined spaces or when exposure would be for an extended period. 1 2 3 4
5. I take prescription drugs only in the manner prescribed, and I use over-the-counter drugs in accordance with directions. 1 2 3 4
6. I refrain from using illegal drugs. 1 2 3 4

Points _____

Safety

1. I attempt to identify the sources of risk or potential danger in each new setting or activity. 1 2 3 4
2. I learn procedures and precautions before undertaking new recreational or occupational activities. 1 2 3 4
3. I select appropriate equipment for all activities and maintain equipment in good working order. 1 2 3 4
4. I curtail my participation in activities when I am not feeling well or am distracted by other demands. 1 2 3 4
5. I refrain from using alcohol or drugs when engaged in potentially dangerous recreational or occupational activities. 1 2 3 4
6. I repair or report dangerous conditions to individuals responsible for maintenance. 1 2 3 4

Points _____

Continued

Self-Care

1. I maintain an accurate, updated personal health history.

1	2	3	4
Not at all	To a very limited degree	Almost completely	Completely

2. I routinely monitor my weight and blood pressure, as well as factors related to specific conditions applicable to my health.

1	2	3	4
Rarely, if ever	Some of the time	Most of the time	Almost always

3. I practice home dental health care, including brushing and flossing.

1	2	3	4
Rarely, if ever	Some of the time	Most of the time	Almost always

4. I maintain my immunization status and receive boosters when scheduled or required by specific conditions.

1	2	3	4
Not at all	To a very limited degree	Almost completely	Completely

5. I take prescription medication through the entire course of the prescribed period of use rather than stopping use when symptoms subside.

1	2	3	4
Rarely, if ever	Some of the time	Most of the time	Almost always

6. I consult a reliable home-medical reference book before beginning self-care.

1	2	3	4
Rarely, if ever	Some of the time	Most of the time	Almost always

Points _____

Answer When Applicable

1. I routinely examine my testicles for the presence of small masses or other unusual signs.

1	2	3	4
Rarely, if ever	Some of the time	Most of the time	Almost always

2. I routinely examine my breasts for the presence of masses or other unusual signs.

1	2	3	4
Rarely, if ever	Some of the time	Most of the time	Almost always

3. I routinely receive a Pap smear.

1	2	3	4
Rarely, if ever	Some of the time	Most of the time	Almost always

4. I use my birth control technique in the manner intended to maximize its effectiveness.

1	2	3	4
Rarely, if ever	Some of the time	Most of the time	Almost always

Points _____

Hereditary

1. I can identify members of my family tree for the previous three generations.

1	2	3	4
Not at all	To a limited degree	Almost completely	Completely

2. I can identify the age at death and the cause of death for all family members to whom I am genetically related for the previous three generations.

1	2	3	4
Not for any	For a few but not for most	For most but not for all	For all

3. I receive medical consultation for conditions for which I may have a genetic predisposition (diabetes, hypertension, etc.).

1	2	3	4
Not at all	To a very limited degree	Relatively continuous consultation	Continuous consultation

4. I limit my exposure to radiation and to toxic environmental pollutants.

1	2	3	4
Rarely, if ever	Some of the time	Most of the time	Almost always

5. I will openly share information concerning inheritance abnormalities with potential mates.

1	2	3	4
Not likely	Perhaps	Very likely	Certainly

6. I will seek genetic counseling for known inherited conditions before having children.

1	2	3	4
Not likely	Perhaps	Very likely	Certainly

Points _____

Sleep, Rest, and Relaxation

1. I plan my daily schedule to allow time for leisure activity.

1	2	3	4
Rarely, if ever	Some of the time	Most of the time	Almost always

2. I plan my daily schedule to allow time for contemplation, meditation, or prayer.

1	2	3	4
Rarely, if ever	Some of the time	Most of the time	Almost always

3. I receive between 7 and 8 hours of sleep daily.

1	2	3	4
Rarely, if ever	Some of the time	Most of the time	Almost always

4. I refrain from using sleep-inducing over-the-counter drugs.

1	2	3	4
Rarely, if ever	Some of the time	Most of the time	Almost always

5. I curtail activities when I need to recover from illnesses and injuries.

1	2	3	4
Rarely, if ever	Some of the time	Most of the time	Almost always

6. I attempt to leave the demands of work, school, or parenting outside of my leisure or relaxation time of the day.

1	2	3	4
Rarely, if ever	Some of the time	Most of the time	Almost always

Points _____

Health Consumerism

1. I am skeptical of practitioners and clinics who advertise or offer services at rates substantially lower than those charged by reputable providers.

1	2	3	4
Rarely, if ever	Some of the time	Most of the time	Almost always

2. I have the financial resources necessary to cover the costs associated with a major illness or hospitalization.

1	2	3	4
Not at all	To a limited degree	Almost completely	Completely

3. I am skeptical of claims that "guarantee" the effectiveness of a particular health-care service or product.

1	2	3	4
Rarely, if ever	Some of the time	Most of the time	Almost always

4. I accept information that is deemed valid by the established scientific community.

1	2	3	4
Rarely, if ever	Some of the time	Most of the time	Almost always

5. I pursue my rights in matters of misrepresentation or consumer dissatisfaction.

1	2	3	4
Rarely, if ever	Some of the time	Most of the time	Almost always

6. I seek additional opinions regarding diagnoses indicating a need for surgery or other costly therapies.

1	2	3	4
Rarely, if ever	Some of the time	Most of the time	Almost always

Points _____

YOUR TOTAL POINTS _____

Interpretation

213-264   Behavior is very supportive of high-level health.

164-212   Behavior is relatively supportive of high-level health.

115-163   Behavior is relatively destructive to high-level health.

66-114   Behavior is very destructive to high-level health.

To Carry This Further . . .

Were you surprised at your score? Remember that this assessment provides a brief look at your health behavior. It should help identify areas you may want to pay careful attention to as you read this book. We hope this assessment will serve as a positive motivator for you, regardless of your score. Remember that you can change your health behavior. This health textbook and your instructor can get you started in the right direction. Good luck.

change concerning weight management, you could take the Personal Assessment titled "Should you consider a weight loss program?" on p. 140.

Some of the health behaviors our students typically want to change are the following:

- To gain or lose weight
- To stop smoking
- To stop using smokeless tobacco
- To eliminate or reduce caffeine consumption
- To develop better sleeping patterns
- To reduce levels of stress
- To improve physical fitness
- To reduce alcohol consumption
- To eat more nutritiously
- To develop more friendships
- To enhance the spiritual dimension of health

To change your behavior, the following 10-step program might be helpful:

1. *Establish some baseline data about your behavior. Baseline data* is information about your current health and behavior that you can use later for comparison. This could take many forms, depending on your behavior. For example, you might weigh yourself for 3 consecutive days early in the morning. If you plan to stop smoking, keep track of your smoking patterns for a few days. If you are changing your diet, write down everything you eat for a 3- or 4-day period. We suggest keeping a journal and recording your activities and feelings related to the behavior.

2. *Summarize your baseline data.* Identify any patterns you see. Accept this information as an accurate

indicator of your current health behavior. Use this textbook to find information about your behavior that could help you plan behavior-change strategies.

3. *Establish some specific goals.* Start with increments small enough to be within your grasp. For example, if you plan to lose weight, you might start out with a goal of 1 pound per week for the next 3 weeks. If you plan to stop smoking, you might start out by cutting down on your daily intake by five cigarettes. Think in terms of small, gradual progress toward your goals.

4. *Make a personal contract to accomplish your goals.* In this contract, you will want to indicate both starting and completion dates. Especially useful at this point are the Health Action Guides found in each chapter. These guides, such as the ones on p. 117 (Dietary Recommendations), p. 265 (Eat to Lower Your Cancer Risk), and p. 239 (Monitoring Your Cholesterol Level), will help you focus on specific activities to reach your goals. Identify any milestones along the way. Indicate the time, personal resources, and energy you will need to commit to this project.

5. *Devise a plan of action.* As you develop your strategy, try to control the environment in which you function so that you can replace old cues with new ones. For example, if you are trying to improve your sleep, you may wish to calm yourself before bed by reading rather than by listening to loud music or watching a television drama. If you are trying to improve your eating behavior, make a careful attempt to avoid walking by a place where donuts are available.

6. *Chart your progress in your diary or journal.* As you implement your behavior-change plan, keep a record of how you are doing. Making this chart visible also helps. For instance, posting an eating record on the refrigerator door is a good motivator for some people.

7. *Encourage your family and friends to help you.* Social support is important in any behavior-change attempt. Your friends may want to join you so that they can change their own behavior, and you can support each other. However, some friends or family members might be jealous of or misunderstand your efforts, and their behavior might discourage you. Avoid these people if at all possible . . . at least while your project is under way.

8. *Set up a reward system.* Rewards tend to motivate people and can serve to reinforce your positive changes. If you achieve success at a particular point in your plan, reward yourself with a special meal, new clothes, or a weekend trip. Pat yourself on the back occasionally for your efforts. Relish your success.

9. *Prepare for obstacles along the way.* No one who achieved anything of importance did it without a few setbacks along the way. For example, you might neglect your fitness plan during a long holiday weekend. Prepare yourself mentally for an occasional obstacle. The key is to try to get back on course as soon as possible after a setback. Work through your setbacks with a "forgive and forget" attitude.

10. *Revise your plan as necessary.* Try to remain somewhat flexible in your approach to behavior change. A strategy that works for a while might not work as well after a month or two, so be prepared to reevaluate your goals and try new techniques when necessary.

Summary

- The World Health Organization definition of health states that health is more than the absence of disease.
- Holistic health views health in its multiple dimensions.
- Health promotion, wellness, and empowerment reflect important movements in the health field.
- To move successfully through life, critical developmental tasks must be achieved. Chapter 1 focuses on five tasks that involve identity, independence, responsibility, social skill development, and intimacy.

- One's health is composed of six dimensions: physical, emotional, social, intellectual, spiritual, and occupational.
- Midlife adults have two key developmental tasks: achieving generativity and reassessing the plans of young adulthood.
- Developmental tasks of the elderly include accepting aging, maintaining physical function, and establishing a sense of integrity.
- The authors define the role and composition of health in terms of the six dimensions' ability to help one successfully complete developmental tasks.

Review Questions

1. How does the World Health Organization's definition of health differ from the definition developed in this chapter?
2. Define holistic health, health promotion, wellness, and empowerment.
3. What were the three broad goals of the 1990 *Healthy People 2000* report?
4. What is a developmental task?
5. Identify the five developmental tasks of college students.
6. What developmental tasks exist for midlife and elderly adults?
7. What is the difference between the *role* of health and the *composition* of health?
8. What is meant by "health is dynamic"?
9. Describe the six dimensions of health.

 ## Think About This . . .

- Does your lifestyle reflect a "wellness" approach to living?
- To what degree does your campus reflect a multicultural community?
- How closely related do you think the developmental tasks of independence and responsibility are? Can you have one without the other?
- Which of the six dimensions of health have you developed most fully? Least fully?

References

1. World Health Organization: Constitution of the World Health Organization, *Chronicle of the World Health Organization* 1:29, 1947.
2. U.S. Bureau of the Census, *Statistical Abstract of the United States: 1997*, ed 117, Washington, DC, 1997.
3. Payne W, Hahn D: *Understanding your health*, ed 5, Boston, 1998 WCB/McGraw-Hill. 1998.
4. Anspaugh D, Hamrick M, Rosato F: *Wellness: concepts and applications*, ed 2, St Louis, 1994, Mosby.
5. *Developing Objectives for Healthy People 2010*, U.S. Department of Health and Human Services, Office of Disease Prevention and Health Promotion, September 1997.
6. Anderson K: Cash rewards are made to faithful few, *USA Today*, May 27, 1992, 1B
7. McKenzie J, Smeltzer J: *Planning, implementing, and evaluating health promotion programs*, ed 2, Boston, 1997, Allyn and Bacon.
8. Erikson E: *Childhood and society*, New York, 1963, WW Norton.
9. Levinson D: *The seasons of a man's life*, New York, 1978, Alfred A. Knopf.
10. Cavanaugh J: *Adult development and aging*, ed 3, Pacific Grove, CA, 1997, Brooks-Cole.
11. Myers J, Witmer M, Sweeney T: Spirituality: the core of wellness, *Wellness Connections* 4(2):1, 6-8, 1993.
12. Rummel J: *Mexico*, New York, 1990, Chelsea House.
13. Galvin I: *Chile: land of poets and patriots*, Minneapolis, 1990, Dillon Press.

Suggested Readings

Santrock J, Ninnettt A, Campbell B: The authoritative guide to self-help books, New York: Guilford Press, 1995. (Available only by telephone, 1-800-365-7006)

Over 350 self-help books on 32 different categories were submitted to several hundred experts for review regarding accuracy of information and helpfulness. On the basis of this information, a rating system was developed and each book was assigned a "star" designation ranging from five stars (highest) to one star (lowest). However, some concern exists regarding the limited number of reviewers that responded to any one book.

Micozzi MS: *Fundamentals of complementary and alternative medicine.* New York: Churchill, 1995.

The author, a physician and a former senior investigator at the National Cancer Institute, has written this book in an attempt to bridge the gap between conventional medicine and healing approaches that currently lie outside traditional medicine. Detailed information regarding the background, scope, and application of healing approaches from China, India, Latin America, and other world areas is provided. Consideration of osteopathy, chiropractic, and other specific techniques from this country are also reviewed.

Weil A: *Spontaneous healing,* New York, 1995, Alfred A. Knopf.

Written by a physician who is a leading voice in the practice of alternative medicine, including natural, noninvasive treatments. This book acknowledges that the body has an intrinsic healing system that mends the body and maintains well-being. Weil provides numerous case histories.

AS WE GO TO PRESS . . .

Death rates have fallen for almost all of the top 10 causes of death, listed in Table 1-1. The CDC report that in 1997 there was an impressive 26% decline in the death rate from HIV/AIDS (attributable to the use of protease inhibitors), an 11% decline in homicides, and a 4% decline in both suicides and heart disease.

One of the goals in *Healthy People 2010* is to improve access to mental health care. However, about 50% of primary care physicians recently reported that they were frequently or almost always unsuccessful in obtaining both outpatient and inpatient mental health services for their patients. These unacceptably high failure rates are probably due to patients' lack of health insurance and to insurance companies' willingness to approve mental health coverage for policyholders.

The health care marketplace has demanded that providers become more consumer friendly by offering more convenient services at an affordable cost. Psychotherapists have responded by offering innovative new treatment formats. For example, patients can now schedule evening visits that do not conflict with their work schedules. In addition, "psychoeducation therapy," a short-session format that lasts only 15 minutes, has become increasingly popular. Some therapists are now conducting "therapy checkups" by telephone. In light of these trends, can e-mail therapy be far away? If so, how will clients be assured that their therapists are competent professionals? Stay tuned!

ON...

The Diversity of Today's College Students

It's the fall of 1970, and you're about to meet Joe College, a student in a freshman health class at State University. Joe is an 18-year-old white man who graduated from City High School last summer in the top half of his class. He lives in State U's dormitory, and because his tuition is being paid by his parents, he is able to devote himself to his studies and college life on a full-time basis. When Joe looks around his health class, he sees some women and a few minorities and older students, but most of his fellow students are much like himself. In short, Joe College is a typical college student.

Flash forward to today. When you look around your health classroom, what kinds of students do you see? Undoubtedly, Joe College is still present in today's university; however, he no longer composes the overwhelming majority of the student body. The many changes in American society that have taken place over the past 25 years are reflected in today's colleges and universities. Nowadays, slightly more women than men are graduating from college. As more older people find that they need better skills and more training or a degree to keep their present jobs or to find new ones, the average age of college students has risen. Also, schools are focusing efforts to more actively recruit minority students. Finally, recent laws that affirm the rights of disabled Americans to have access to most public facilities have allowed disabled individuals the opportunity to attend college. As you look at your fellow students, you will probably notice that these changes are reflected in your health class and at your school in general. Because of these changes, schools must adapt to meet the educational needs of all their students.

Enrollment Statistics

College enrollment statistics cited in the *Chronicle of Higher Education* show that enrollment has increased dramatically for certain minority groups in the United States. The numbers of Asian students increased from 390,000 in 1984 to 724,000 in 1993, an increase of over 85%. Hispanic enrollment also increased by 84.9% over that same period. African-American enrollment increased by 31%, and Native American enrollment rose by 45.2%. White enrollment increased by only 8% from 1984 to 1993: enrollment of white men increased by only 1.4% during this span, whereas enrollment of white women increased by 14%.[1]

Even with the huge increases in enrollment within several groups, overall college enrollment only went up 16.9% from 1984 to 1993. This is because whites continue to make up the vast majority of college students, comprising 74.1% of all college students in 1993. Even so, the numbers show a gradual change in college demographics, since 80% of all college enrollees in 1984 were white.[1]

In 1993 a Census Bureau survey showed that over 40% of all students were 25 years of age or older.[1] This suggests that college campuses are no longer dominated by traditional-age students (age 18-24). The influx of older students, coupled with the strong increase in minority enrollment, has greatly increased the diversity on college campuses.

Causes Behind the Changes

So why are these changes occurring? Several factors seem to be affecting enrollment figures in the United States. Clearly the changing climate of the economy has affected enrollment. Corporate trends toward a more streamlined workforce and the gradual shift toward a service-oriented marketplace have caused many workers to seek training for new careers or to seek additional training for their current jobs. And although the nation's economy has been "growing" for the last several years, things do not always look so good to those outside of Wall Street. Many working people are finding that their wages are not enough to make ends meet, and many elderly people are finding that their Social Security benefits are not nearly enough to survive on. As a result, people who never thought they would see the inside of a classroom again are drawn back to school in hope of improving their careers.[2] Colleges have also become

more accessible in recent years. The trend toward open admissions, especially at community colleges, has opened the doors of higher education to those who otherwise would be held back by low high school grades or low test scores. Colleges have attempted to meet the needs of these new students with remedial courses and special programs designed to prepare students whose academic records indicate that they are in need of extra help to meet academic standards.[3]

Social changes have also played an important role in the changing demographics on college campuses. The civil rights movement in the 1950s and 1960s was instrumental in making a college education available to minorities, and minority enrollment continues to increase as overall awareness of civil rights becomes more entrenched in society. Students with various physical disabilities are also finding it easier to obtain a college education. The Americans with Disabilities Act, signed into law in 1990, guarantees that people with disabilities will have access to employment, education, and public services. As a result, people with disabilities are able to pursue careers that were previously inaccessible, and many are heading to college to receive training for those careers.

As higher education has become more accessible, there has been an attitude change toward going to college. There is now a more prevalent feeling in society that everyone should go to college after high school. Population demographics as a whole may also have an effect on college demographics. Populations within minority groups have been increasing at a much higher rate than the white population in the United States, and this may in part account for the rise in minority enrollment.

Practical Implications of Diversity on Campus

With the rise of new populations on campuses, many practical changes have taken place at colleges and universities to reflect the needs and interests of students on today's campuses. San Antonio College, one of the largest community colleges in the United States, is a good example of the types of changes that are occurring nationwide. To meet the needs of students who are not prepared for college work, SAC has a large developmental education program designed to help students develop their skills in reading, writing, and mathematics. For working students, evening and weekend divisions offer courses in many disciplines to accommodate busy schedules. The college also houses the Student Support Services Project, an educational program sponsored by the United States Department of Education that serves the needs of disabled and first-generation college students from low-income families.[4]

Changes are also reflected in SAC's course offerings, student organizations, and facilities. In addition to offering traditional courses in Western and American literature and history, the college also offers courses in African-American literature, Mexican literature, and world literature (including Third World works), and interdisciplinary studies courses that examine community issues, social issues, and the fine arts from a multicultural perspective. Student organizations include the Black Student Alliance, Chicanos in the Arts, and the Mexican American Engineering students, as well as more traditional student government organizations, major interest organizations, and honor societies. The campus learning center has large collections of multicultural literature and history books, and the library recently added a set of computers so that students can access the World Wide Web and use the Internet to make intercultural connections with other students from across the country and around the world.[4] All these changes were implemented (at least in part) to make the campus a more friendly and inviting environment for today's college students.

Changing Campuses and the Study of Health

Many changes have taken place on campus in recent years. Why mention them here in a health text? Because of the increasing diversity on college campuses, students studying health (and most other disciplines) should be made aware not only of issues that affect them personally but also of issues that affect others of different backgrounds as well. For example, many people are unaware of the fact that most pharmaceutical research is performed on men and then generalized to apply to women, a potentially dangerous practice given that women are at greater risk for adverse drug reactions.[5] Another good example of a cultural health issue is the use of alternative medical practitioners. Native Americans view health care as a holistic rather than symptom-based process, and they are more likely to respond to a "medicine man" who looks at both the physical and spiritual person than to a physician who examines only diseased body parts.[6] Similarly, some Mexican Americans will either rely on or supplement traditional health care with *curanderismo,* a medical system that combines Western health care practices with folklore, magic, herbalism, and religion.[7] Knowledge of these and other related cultural health care issues will allow college students to better understand all members of today's culturally diverse American society.

It is no longer possible to accept the traditional version of what health should be as the whole story. To get a complete picture of what health care issues are important today, we must understand health beliefs and health actions of the various segments of our culture.[8] Bringing cultural awareness into the health classroom can introduce students to concepts they might not otherwise be exposed to. During your college career, you will likely encounter students from a variety of backgrounds. They may be young or old, from a rich or poor family, from a rural or urban environment, or from an ethnic group different from yours. Just as your culture has its own unique health concerns, every other culture has its own set of health concerns as well, and you should be aware of them. *Focus on Health* will attempt to address the needs of students from different cultural backgrounds when appropriate.

For Discussion . . .

Consider the following items:

Prosthetics	Scurvy and rickets
Tay-Sachs disease	Cochlear implants
Sickle-cell anemia	Osteoporosis
Hemophilia	Cystic fibrosis
Alzheimer's disease	Breast cancer

For each item, determine which cultural group(s) are more likely to consider the item as a health concern (do a little research if needed). Can you think of other health concerns that are unique to certain cultures or groups? What are the particular health concerns of your culture?

References

1. The nation. *The chronicle of higher education*, Almanac Issue, 42(1), Sept 1, 1995.
2. Troyka LQ: Perspectives on legacies and literacy in the 1980s. In *A sourcebook for basic writing teachers*, New York, 1987, McGraw-Hill.
3. Mutnick D: *Writing in an alien world*, Portsmouth, NH, 1996, Boynton/Cook.
4. *San Antonio College Bulletin, 1995-1996*, San Antonio, Tex, 1995, San Antonio College.
5. Nechas E, Foley D: *Unequal treatment*, New York, 1994, Simon & Schuster.
6. Sorrell MS, Smith BA: Navajo beliefs: implications for health professionals, *Journal of Health Education* 24(6), 1991.
7. Stauber D: Curanderismo in the Mexican-American community, *Journal of Health Education* 25(6), 1994.
8. Airhihenbuwa CO: Culture, health education, and critical consciousness. *Journal of Health Education* 26(5), 1995.

PART 1

THE MIND

Achieving Emotional Maturity

Healthy People: Looking Ahead to 2010

In the area of emotional, mental, and cognitive disorders, an important objective of the *Healthy People 2000* report was to reduce the prevalence of mental disorders within the general population. The Midcourse Review, however, did not address progress in reaching this objective.

Another important objective was to increase the use of community support services in the prevention and treatment of severe, persistent mental disorders. Data reported in the Midcourse Review clearly showed that substantial gains were made in the development of state-level clearinghouses to better identify existing resources. Unfortunately, adult patients of primary care providers, including family physicians, internal medicine specialists, and obstetricians and gynecologists, were unlikely to have received counseling or referral to these resources for treatment.

Healthy People 2010[1] will probably continue the focus on mental health and mental disorders that was established in 1990. Services will be offered to primary care physicians to help them recognize and refer patients with cognitive, emotional, and behavioral problems.

Emotionally healthy people have a high level of self-esteem and find social interaction to be comfortable and rewarding. Having stated that self-esteem is inseparable from emotional health, we must, however, caution that you cannot expect to feel personally fulfilled by everything. There will always be situations in which you must act against your own best interests so that others are best served. Additionally, self-esteem is not always enough to completely offset the health problems that can afflict us.

CHARACTERISTICS OF AN EMOTIONALLY WELL PERSON

We define an emotionally well person as one who is capable of using resources from each of the six dimensions of health mentioned in Chapter 1 to feel good about life and other people. A more specific yardstick for measuring emotional health comes from the National Mental Health Association. This group describes emotionally well people as having three fundamental characteristics:[2]

- They feel comfortable about themselves. They are not overwhelmed by their own feelings, and they can accept many of life's disappointments in stride. They experience the full range of human emotions (for example, fear, anger, love, jealousy, guilt, and joy) but are not overcome by them.
- They interact well with other people. They are comfortable with others and are able to give and receive love. They are concerned about others' well-being and have relationships that are satisfying and lasting.
- They are able to meet the demands of life. Emotionally healthy people respond appropriately to their problems, accept responsibility, plan ahead without fearing the future, and are able to establish reachable goals.

We do not wish to give the impression that emotionally well people are perfect. At times, emotionally healthy people experience stress, frustration, feelings of self-doubt, failure, and rejection. What distinguishes the emotionally well person is resilience—the ability to recapture a sense of emotional wellness within a reasonable period of time after encountering difficult situations.

EMOTIONAL AND PSYCHOLOGICAL WELLNESS

Is there a difference between emotional and psychological wellness? Many people believe that there is little real difference between the terms. Rather, they both reflect the absence of emotional illness and psychopathology. However, some people believe that emotional health refers specifically to the feelings people experience in response to changes in their environment. These feelings, such as anger, jealousy, joy, disappointment, compassion, and sympathy, are familiar, healthy emotions. Responses to change vary from one person to the next and reflect each person's values. Emotionally healthy people feel good about their responses, whereas those who are less emotionally well feel negative about their responses.

In contrast to emotional health, some people think that psychological health refers more broadly to the development and functioning of a wide array of mental abilities, such as language, memory, perception, and awareness. For example, a person who believes he is being followed by government agents has faulty perception, so we would say that he is not psychologically healthy. Those who are psychologically healthy deal rationally with the world, have a fully functional personality, and resolve conflict nondestructively. Finally, the psychophysical (mind-body) interface of the psychologically healthy person is sound.

Normal Range of Emotions

Have you known people who seem to be "up" all the time? These people appear to be confident, happy, and full of good feelings 24 hours a day. Although some people may have these traits, they are truly the exceptions. For most people, emotions are more like a roller coaster ride. There are times when they feel good about themselves and others, and there are times when nothing seems to be going right. This is normal and healthy. Life has its ups and downs, and the concept of the "normal range of emotions" reflects this.

Self-Esteem

Perhaps the key to overall emotional wellness is self-esteem. When people have positive self-esteem, they feel comfortable in social situations and with their own thoughts and feelings. They are able to get along with others, cope in stressful situations, and make contributions when they work with others. Self-esteem may offset self-defeating or self-destructive behavior problems. For example, a young woman who is slightly overweight but has high self-esteem would be unlikely to go on an unhealthy crash diet in an effort to conform to the currently fashionable body image. As you will see when you complete the Personal Assessment on p. 26, people with high levels of

PERSONAL ASSESSMENT

How Does My Self-Concept Compare with My Idealized Self?

Below is a list of 15 personal attributes, each portrayed on a 9-point continuum. Mark with an X where you think you rank on each attribute. Try to be candid and accurate; these marks will collectively describe a portion of your sense of self-concept. When you are finished with the task, go back and circle where you *wish* you could be on each dimension. These marks describe your idealized self. Finally, in the spaces on the right, indicate the difference between your self-concept and your idealized self for each attribute.

Decisive	Indecisive	_____
9 8 7 6 5 4 3 2 1		
Anxious	Relaxed	_____
9 8 7 6 5 4 3 2 1		
Easily influenced	Independent thinker	_____
9 8 7 6 5 4 3 2 1		
Very intelligent	Less intelligent	_____
9 8 7 6 5 4 3 2 1		
In good physical shape	In poor physical shape	_____
9 8 7 6 5 4 3 2 1		
Undependable	Dependable	_____
9 8 7 6 5 4 3 2 1		
Deceitful	Honest	_____
9 8 7 6 5 4 3 2 1		
A leader	A follower	_____
9 8 7 6 5 4 3 2 1		
Unambitious	Ambitious	_____
9 8 7 6 5 4 3 2 1		
Self-confident	Insecure	_____
9 8 7 6 5 4 3 2 1		
Conservative	Adventurous	_____
9 8 7 6 5 4 3 2 1		
Extroverted	Introverted	_____
9 8 7 6 5 4 3 2 1		
Physically attractive	Physically unattractive	_____
9 8 7 6 5 4 3 2 1		
Lazy	Hardworking	_____
9 8 7 6 5 4 3 2 1		
Funny	Little sense of humor	_____
9 8 7 6 5 4 3 2 1		

To Carry This Further . . .

1. Overall, how would you describe the discrepancy between your self-concept and your self-ideal (large, moderate, small, large on a few dimensions)?

2. How do sizable gaps for any of your attributes affect your sense of self-esteem?

3. Do you think that any of the gaps exist because you have had others' ideals imposed on you or because you have thoughtlessly accepted others' ideals?

4. Identify several attributes that you realistically believe can be changed to narrow the gap between your self-concept and your self-ideal and, thus, foster a well-developed sense of self-esteem. ☑

self-esteem find a comfortable balance between their idealized self and where they actually are.

For some people the lack of self-esteem is understandable. Growing up in a dysfunctional household, being overloaded with guilt in conjunction with religious upbringing, and failing in early undertakings can all damage feelings of self-worth.

The foundation of positive self-esteem can be traced back to childhood.[3] There are many ways in which interaction with young children imparts powerful messages about self-worth. Warm and supportive physical contact, verbal exchanges involving talking "with" rather than "to" children, and the gradual loosening of control so that more and more decisions become those of the child inform children that they are competent and valued. Children's emerging self-esteem, then, is strongly influenced by their parents' behavior. Children from less supportive or overly protective home environments will eventually seek positive feedback from other sources.

As important as parents and others, including the peer group, are to the development of self-esteem in children, people eventually become responsible for enhancing their own self-esteem. The extent to which people wish to nurture their own self-esteem varies. However, many want to take an active role in developing a more solid sense of self-worth.

Hardiness

Working in conjunction with a sense of self-esteem to ensure emotional wellness is *hardiness*.[4] Hardiness exists when a person consistently shows three important traits. First, a hardy person possesses a high level of *commitment* to something or someone and in doing so has the basis for a value orientation and a sense of purpose in life. The maintenance of this sense of commitment provides structure and direction even in the face of a wide variety of stressors (see Chapter 3). Second, a sense of *control* characterizes hardy people. By possessing the ability to orchestrate events in life, the hardy person reduces the chance of feeling helpless and vulnerable in the face of change imposed from outside. Third, the hardy person welcomes *challenge*. That is, he or she has the ability to take control of change and shape it in the direction of personal growth and fulfillment.

Hardiness may be more common among some types of people than others. Nevertheless, a high level of hardiness can be developed by focusing on signals from the body, assessing and responding to previous stressors, and engaging in activities that strengthen commitment, control, and challenge.

Health on the Web
LEARNING ACTIVITIES

Activity 1

Perhaps the key to overall emotional wellness is self-esteem. Using the following URL, http://www.queendom.com/selfest.html, take the self-esteem test Do you believe in yourself? Read each of the 30 statements carefully and indicate the degree to which it applies to you, or the degree to which you endorse it. When you finish the inventory, click on the "submit" button to receive your results.

Activity 2

Only a small percentage of depressed people ever seek help. This is unfortunate in light of the high success rate of treatment. The Depression Evaluation and Assessment Research Evaluation survey can be located at http://genesis.psc.sc.edu/~fliu/dear/. By volunteering to participate in this survey, you receive a score on your stress levels. The inventory consists of 20 questions related to your feelings and behavior.

Activity 3

A higher level of emotional health is often achieved by improving certain skills and abilities, such as verbal and nonverbal communication. A helpful inventory called Are you saying what you think you are saying? can be located at http://www.queendom.com/communic.html. The inventory consists of 34 statements related to your interpersonal communication skills. Complete the assessment to determine your communication score.

EMOTIONAL WELLNESS OF MIDLIFE AND ELDERLY ADULTS

An Optimistic View of Aging

It is not uncommon for our students to find the study of the aging process somewhat "uninteresting." However, for the nontraditional-age students, and eventually for the traditional-age students, aging is seen in a much more positive light. Older people report that they are generally happy and satisfied. Many of our midlife (between 45 and 64 years of age) students report that they are starting a "new life." Intelligence, creativity, attractiveness, physical fitness, and sexual intimacy can continue in harmony with the aging process as long as people continue to participate in the activities that enhance these qualities.

The Joys of Midlife

Contrary to some stereotypical views, most midlife adults do not experience a multitude of problems that fill them with melancholy and despair. The lives of these midlife adults are characterized by positive elements. It is a myth that every midlife adult must have a midlife crisis. Most probably do not experience such an ordeal. Midlife adults may frequently find themselves more reflective than when they were young, but to label this behavior damaging is to fail to appreciate the value of careful self-examination. Perhaps midlife adults just have more to think about than they did when they were younger.

From our perspective, much of what midlifers think about is positive. Many see themselves as being in the prime of life. Certain potentially difficult aspects of life have been completed. Many have completed a formal education, become established in an occupation, gained financial security, and raised a family. Midlife adults can find great satisfaction with these accomplishments and can begin planning for future challenges.

By being relatively free from financial problems and no longer responsible for young children, midlife adults can pursue some of their own dreams. For example, it is not surprising to see midlife adults travel more than they did earlier in life. Many midlifers rededicate themselves to a fitness program or a hobby, such as reading or gardening. Some seem to love reliving their own college days vicariously through the lives of their college-aged children. For many midlifers, joyous moments also come with being grandparents. Can you think of other ways midlife adults experience deeply satisfying feelings?

The Midlife Crisis

For some adults, reaching midlife is a milestone that triggers a "midlife crisis," during which they reconsider the paths their lives have taken.[5] They wonder whether they have made the right career and family decisions, and they reevaluate the meaning and value of their own lives. For some people, the midlife crisis can be a precarious period of reassessment because it coincides with a deep sense of vulnerability to time. The years seem to be slipping away, and they sense that personal growth should be occurring. If it is not, the alternatives seem to be limited. Dropping out of their current lives and starting over may seem like an attractive alternative to facing the future.

For most adults who have a midlife crisis, however, this period of questioning enhances emotional wellness because it prompts them to repeat the four-step process of emotional growth described on pp. 33–34.

Quality of Life for Elderly Adults

For the elderly, as for all adults, the quality of life is often judged on the basis of the status of several traits or conditions. We believe that life will be described as being "good" by older people who have not yet shown significant declines in the majority of areas listed below:[6]

- *Health.* As long as the person feels well, has sufficient energy, and is not limited in terms of mobility, health is not a distracting factor to a good life.
- *Social status.* As long as the elderly person continues to participate in social activities that were enjoyed before retirement or the death of the spouse, social status remains unchanged and is not a negative factor in the quality of life.
- *Economic status.* As long as income is sufficient to maintain an acceptable lifestyle, provide the basic necessities, and form a cushion against unexpected major expenses, economic status is not a negative factor in a good life.
- *Marital status.* For most men, marital status remains unchanged. For women, widowhood can prove to be a significant factor detracting from the quality of life. If a support group can fill part of the void left by the spouse's death, the effect of a changed marital status can be minimized.
- *Living conditions.* Only 5% of the elderly are living in nursing homes. As long as residential arrangements are unchanged, or, if changed, undertaken with minimal disruption, living conditions are not significant factors in defining the quality of life.
- *Educational level.* Educational level in general and an active interest in learning and experimenting in particular seem to foster positive experiences during aging. Limited education may inhibit some elderly people from learning more about the changing world around them.
- *Sexual intimacy.* Assuming the availability of a partner, sexual practices closely follow the patterns established during earlier periods of adulthood.[6] As long as both partners are satisfied, adjustment is not adversely influenced. Divergent expectations can cause difficulty for one or both partners.

AFFRONTS TO EMOTIONAL WELLNESS

In spite of their best efforts to be hardy and resilient, many people have a less than optimal level of emotional wellness. Depression is the most common and one of the most treatable of these dysfunctional emotional states. Loneliness, shyness, and, of course, thoughts of suicide are also challenges to high-level emotional wellness. Although this chapter focuses on emotional well-being rather than illness, an examination of these conditions is necessary because most of us at some time during our lives will either have emotional problems ourselves or know someone who is having difficulties.

Depression

Depression is an "emotional state characterized by exaggerated feelings of sadness, melancholy, dejection, worthlessness, emptiness, and hopelessness that are inappropriate and out of proportion to reality."[7] Some of the common symptoms of depression are listed in the accompanying Star Box. One key indicator of depression is the long-term presence of some of these symptoms. Everyone feels "down" or "blue" at times, but depression is characterized by a more chronic state of feeling "low."

In the United States, it is estimated that approximately 25% of the adult population will have some symptoms of major depression during their lifetime.[8] People with depression commonly have a number of compounding problems, including family problems and difficulty with social relationships. Depression is a common factor related to most suicides.[9]

Types of depression

According to mental-health experts, there are two main types of depression. When depression develops after a period of difficulty, such as a divorce or loss of a job, it is called *secondary* or *reactive depression*. However, when depression begins for no apparent reason, it is called *primary depression* and is caused by changes in brain chemistry. People with this type of depres-

Common Symptoms of Depression
Any of the following may be indications of possible depression:
- Persistent sad moods
- Feelings of hopelessness or pessimism
- Loss of interest or pleasure in ordinary activities, including sex
- Sleep and eating disorders
- Restlessness, irritability, or fatigue
- Difficulty concentrating, remembering, or making decisions
- Thoughts of death or suicide
- Persistent physical symptoms or pains that do not respond to treatment

sion are helped most by antidepressant drugs, whereas people with secondary depression often require counseling in addition to medication.

Through a variety of therapies, between 70% and 90% of depressed people can be helped. Types of therapy range from various "talking" strategies (including counseling) to the use of antidepressant drugs. Most antidepressant drugs prescribed today work by influencing neurotransmitters, chemicals released by the nervous system that help transmit impulses (see Chapter 7). Today, four main types of antidepressant medications are in use, including tricyclics, monoamine oxidase inhibitors, selective serotonin uptake inhibitors, and the heterocyclics.[10] When use is monitored carefully, many of today's antidepressant drugs produce few side effects.

Only a small percentage (about 33%) of depressed people ever seek help. This is unfortunate in light of the high rate of successful treatment. The Health Action Guide on p. 30 lists several resources available to help people with depression.

Loneliness

Many depressed people display signs of loneliness, although it is not always associated with depression. People are said to be lonely if they "desire close personal relationships but are unable to establish them."[11] It is possible to feel isolated and friendless even when you are around many people every day. In fact, loneliness is common among college students.

The difference between "being alone" and "feeling lonely" is important. Many people enjoy being alone occasionally to relax, to exercise, to read, to enjoy music, or just to think. These people can appreciate being alone, but they can also interact comfortably with others when they wish. However, when being alone or isolated is not enjoyable and seeking close relationships is very difficult, then feeling lonely can produce serious feelings of rejection.

One unfortunate aspect of loneliness is that it tends to continue in people year after year unless they take an active part in changing it. Chronically lonely people frequently cope with their loneliness by becoming consumed by their occupations or adopting habit-forming behavior that further makes them feel lonely.

Fortunately, there are successful techniques to help most lonely people. Counseling can help change how these people think about themselves when they interact with others. Another technique involves teaching people important social skills, such as starting a conversation, taking social risks, and introducing themselves. Through social skills training, people can also

HEALTH
Action Guide ----->

Resources for Help with Depression

If you or a friend had concerns about depression, would you know where to search for help? Regardless of where you are—large city, suburban community, or a rural area—a variety of resources are available.

- Seek help from your university health center, personal physician, or community health center.
- Try your university mental health counseling and treatment programs.
- Family and social service agencies can identify mental health specialists.
- Check the telephone book for private psychologists or psychiatric clinics.
- Talk with your professor.
- Contact one of the organizations listed.

The Depression/Awareness, Recognition and Treatment Program (operated by the National Institute of Mental Health)
Room 15-C-05, 5600 Fishers Lane
Rockville, MD 20857
(301) 460-3062

The National Foundation for Depressive Illness
P.O. Box 2257
New York, NY 10016-2257
(800) 248-4344
www.depression.org

The National Mental Health Association
1021 Prince St.
Alexandria, VA 22314
(703) 684-7722   <------
www.nmha.org

---

learn how to talk comfortably on the telephone, give and receive compliments, and even enhance their appearance. If you need help in this area, contact your campus counseling center or health center.

Shyness

Is loneliness the result of an inability to interact comfortably with others, something brought about by shyness? If so, why are some people so shy? Some contend that shyness is a genetic component of temperament. Thus shy people do not want to be shy, they have not been conditioned to avoid contact with others, and they have not had unpleasant experiences with others; rather, they are genetically programmed to feel uncomfortable in settings involving other people. Accordingly, they cope by avoiding such situations. Even if shyness *is* a genetic trait, the social skills counseling and training suggested in the discussion of loneliness can help those who are shy.

Suicide

One of the tragedies of our times is the high incidence of suicide. In the last year for which statistics are available (1994), 31,142 people in the United States killed themselves.[12] Among young people (including college students), suicides follow accidents as the second leading cause of death.

What separates the potentially suicidal person from the nonsuicidal person is the degree of despair and depression the person feels and the ability to cope with it. Suicidal people tend to become overwhelmed with a range of destructive emotions, including anxiety, anger, loneliness, loss of self-esteem, and hopelessness. They may believe that death is the only solution to all of their problems.

In fact, college students who commit suicide to resolve academic failure, relationship difficulties, or unemployment leave problems for others that dwarf the original concerns.

Suicide prevention

Many communities now recognize the need to provide suicide prevention services or expand services that are already available. Most suicide prevention centers operate 24-hour hotlines and are staffed through volunteer agencies, mental health centers, public health departments, or hospitals. Staff members have extensive training in the counseling skills required to deal with suicidal people. Phone numbers for these services can be found in the telephone directory.

The Star Box on p. 31 lists the signs and symptoms we should watch for that could indicate that a person might be considering suicide. People need professional help when they show a clustering of these suicide warning signs for more than 2 weeks.

Warning Signs of Suicidal Behavior
- Change in appetite
- Change in sleep pattern
- Decreased concentration
- Decreased interest in activities that were a source of pleasure
- Sudden agitation or sudden slowing down in level of activity
- Social withdrawal
- Feelings of hopelessness, worthlessness, and self-reproach
- Inappropriate or excessive guilt
- Suicidal thoughts and/or talk
- Making a suicide plan
- Writing a suicide note
- Giving away prized possessions
- Recent humiliating life event
- Lack of social support

ENHANCING EMOTIONAL WELLNESS

Most people have the opportunity to function at an enhanced level of emotional well-being. This higher level of emotional health is often achieved by improving certain skills and abilities, including improving verbal and nonverbal communication, learning to use humor effectively, developing better conflict resolution skills, and taking a proactive approach to life. In this section, each of these facets of emotional well-being are explored.

Improving Communication

Communication can be viewed in terms of your role as sender or receiver of spoken language. In regard to sending messages, it may be possible to enhance effectiveness in *verbal* communication by implementing several specific types of behavior.[13] First, you should be willing to take time before speaking to understand what needs to be said. For example, does the audience need information, encouragement, humor, or something else? In addition, try to focus on the most important thoughts and ideas, since not every thought is central to effective communication. Effective speakers also talk with, rather than at, listeners to facilitate comfortable exchanges. Further, verbal exchanges should begin on a positive note so that you can establish and maintain a positive environment with listeners. Also, by seeking frequent feedback

from listeners through the use of "minimal encouragers," such as short questions, and by avoiding slanted language, spoken communication is more constructive. Lastly, you should recognize when other forms of communication, such as written notes, do a better job in transmitting information or ideas.

Effective verbal communication also requires that you function as a skilled listener. Certainly there are skills that can enhance listening abilities, such as the ability to listen attentively to hear everything that is being said. Also, listening selectively to filter out redundant ideas or information unrelated to the central theme allows you to pay greater attention to pertinent points. This technique is often used by adults when listening to young children or when information being shared by others is grossly inaccurate or exaggerated. A final measure can be used to be an effective listener: stopping the speaker from continuing the conversation by suggesting that he or she repeat or rephrase what was previously said. This technique ensures that you are hearing correctly the points the other person is trying to make rather than focusing only on your own responses.

Your ability to strengthen *nonverbal* communication skills may also enhance emotional well-being. For a variety of reasons, it may be necessary or desirable to communicate without speaking, a process that can be accomplished in many different ways.[14] One way is by using facial expressions. For example, a smile may open lines of communication that would have remained closed in the presence of a less friendly face. Eye contact, too, is an important component of positive nonverbal communication, although staring is undesirable. Effective eye contact can actually be practiced by studying facial expressions in the mirror.

Beyond facial expressions and mannerisms, other techniques for enhancing nonverbal communication exist. Touching comfortably, maintaining an appropriate distance from people, and wearing appropriate clothing aid in the silent exchange of information between people. In fact, the overall posture of the body may contribute to your ability to "hear" what others are attempting to communicate.

Using Humor Effectively

Possessing a sense of humor is an important component of high-level emotional health.[15] This means being able to see that life is not meant to be one long, boring exercise. Part of the reason for living is to have fun. You must not, therefore, take yourself or your life situations too seriously. In fact, as seen in the Learning from All Cultures box on p. 32, humor is an important component of life in all cultures.

LEARNING *from* ALL CULTURES

Humor

Humor is universal. In fact, there is no known culture in which humor is not present. People everywhere enjoy the funnier moments of everyday life. Humans all use the same elements of humor: incongruity, surprise, and familiar thinking patterns. Situations, however, differ from country to country, therefore making humor somewhat cultural.[16]

A nation's humor reflects its people's lives. Sexuality is a common topic for humor in Great Britain.[14] In the United States, sexual jokes are also popular, but in China and Israel, they are almost nonexistent. Israeli humor is described as aggressive humor, humor that perhaps reflects the instability of its people's lives because of war and discrimination. This type of humor is evident in American society as we trade jokes about various groups of people, such as jokes about gays or women with blond hair. The French also are known to enjoy aggressive humor, by playfully making fun of others.[16]

A society's history, traditions, and language influence what its people find humorous. Imagine going through life without the ability to see, appreciate, and most importantly, laugh at the incongruities and surprises of our daily existence!

Recognizing the humor in daily situations and occasionally being able to laugh at yourself will make you feel better about yourself. People feel better when they build humor into their daily lives, and others enjoy being around them more. Some researchers have suggested that recovery from an injury or illness is enhanced when patients have a positive attitude that includes a sense of humor.

Improving Conflict Management Skills

In spite of our best efforts to avoid it, conflict regularly occurs when people interact. In fact, it is the presence of conflict, and the change that arises in the course of resolving it, that leads to growth. The ability to meet and resolve conflict reflects a mature state of emotional health. However, some forms of conflict resolution are more effective than others. In the discussion that follows, different approaches to conflict resolution are considered.[17]

Many people believe that a *hostile aggressive* approach to conflict resolution, in which the parties involved attempt to use force to win out, is the least emotionally mature approach to resolving differences. For example, attacking others for simply disagreeing with them shows both hostility and aggression. Regardless of whether the weapon of choice is a loud voice or a physical blow, the outcome of this approach is usually more and deeper conflict.

Although different in character from hostile aggression, the use of *submission* is also an unacceptable technique for resolving conflict. When one person involved in the conflict gives in, the disagreement may at first appear to have been resolved, but the accommodating party generally remains angry, with the conflict merely driven temporarily out of sight and likely to reappear later in a more intense form. Ask yourself, for example, "How long would I be willing to do only what others want, rather than what I would enjoy doing, before I became angry and resentful?"

A third and somewhat emotionally immature approach to conflict resolution is *withdrawal* by one or both parties. Simply walking out of a room to avoid further disagreement with others is an example of this conflict resolution approach. This regressive form of resolution may seem to calm the atmosphere but rarely leads to a true and constructive resolution of the conflict. However, withdrawal can be constructive if it provides time for one or both people to rethink the conflict situation and return to it later, using a more constructive approach.

One of the positive conflict resolution approaches is *persuasion*. In this approach, one or both parties to the conflict use words to explain their reasons for the position they are taking. Pointing out the advantages to pursuing one course of action versus another is an example of persuasion. In the face of a convincing presentation, it is hoped that the other party involved will become motivated to resolve the conflict, most likely by accepting the position being advanced. If all parties involved in the conflict are given an opportunity to "have the floor," this approach to conflict resolution can be considered more constructive than those described previously.

Perhaps the most mature conflict resolution technique is *dialogue*. In this approach, a verbal exchange of facts, opinions, and perceptions takes place to better understand the costs or benefits associated with each of the positions being advanced. The goal of this exchange is to reach an acceptable compromise that all parties involved will feel they had a share in formulating. Of course, this form of resolution frequently characterizes the lengthy negotiations that come before the signing of accords between nations. Often when this form of resolution is used, there are no losers in the traditional sense, but rather the compromise position agreed on allows all parties to contribute to a healthier relationship.

Taking a Proactive Approach to Life

Beyond the several approaches to high-level emotional health already discussed, the plan that follows is intended to give you even greater control of enhancing your feelings of self-esteem. A key to emotional health is the ability to control the outcomes of experiences and thus to learn about your own emotional resources.[18] Figure 2-1 shows a four-step process that continues throughout life: constructing perceptions of yourself, accepting these perceptions, undertaking new experiences, and reframing your perceptions based on new information. With some thought and practice, this process can be undertaken regularly by most people.

Constructing mental pictures

Actively taking charge of emotional growth begins when you construct a mental picture of what you are like. This mental picture or perception should be composed of the most recent and accurate information you have about yourself concerning the knowledge that is important to you, the values that you hold, and the activities in which you are competent.

To construct this mental picture, you will need to set aside a period of uninterrupted quiet time for reflection. Even in the midst of a busy schedule, most people can find several moments to complete a task that is important.

Before continuing to the second step in the plan for emotional development, it is important that you construct, in addition to a mental picture about *yourself*, similar mental pictures about yourself in relation to

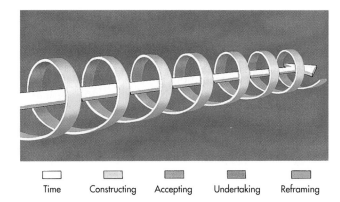

| Time | Constructing | Accepting | Undertaking | Reframing |

Figure 2-1   If you visualize the growth of the emotional dimension of health as a four-step process, you will see that continued emotional growth occurs in cycles throughout your life.

other people and *material objects*, including your residence and college or work environment, to gain a clearer picture of these relationships.

For example, Clara moved to a large city to become a jewelry designer after graduating from college with a degree in fine arts. Two years later, Clara's small business was thriving and she had been able to move to a spacious loft apartment in which one room served as her studio. Nevertheless, Clara felt that something was missing. She constructed a mental picture in which she saw herself as a resourceful, creative, independent person who was comfortable in her new surroundings. However, Clara realized that she wanted a partner with whom to share her success and her life.

Accepting mental pictures

The second step of the plan involves an *acceptance* of these perceptions. Acceptance implies a willingness to honor the truthfulness of the perceptions that you have formed about yourself and other people. For example, Clara should acknowledge her professional success and her artistic ability but must also accept that she has been unable to establish the long-term romantic relationship she desires.

As in the first step of the plan, the second stage requires time and commitment. Controlling emotional development is rarely a passive process. You must be willing to be *introspective* (inwardly reflective) about yourself and the world around you.

Undertaking new experiences

To mature emotionally, you must progress beyond the first two steps of the prescription and test the newly formed perceptions you have constructed. This *testing* is accomplished by *undertaking a new experience* or by reexperiencing something in a different way.

For example, I traveled to London with 31 students, and most of them took advantage of every opportunity out of class to meet new people, see new places, and have new experiences. No part of the United Kingdom (or Europe, for that matter) seemed to be beyond their reach. Over the course of our 15 weeks together, I could see them become more confident and self-assured as the result of being independent and self-directed in taking risks. In retrospect, I realize that no combination of reading assignments, guest lectures, and field trips could have produced the emotionally fulfilling maturation that was accomplished away from our university's London Centre.

New experiences do not necessarily require high levels of risk, foreign travel, or money. They may be no more "new" than deciding to move from the dorm into an apartment, to change from one shift at work to another, or to pursue new friendships. The experience itself is not the end that you should be seeking; rather, it is a means of collecting a new "pool" of information about yourself, others, and the objects that form your material world.

For instance, Clara volunteered to teach art therapy classes to chronically ill patients at a local hospital. This work was enjoyable and fulfilling for Clara, and she formed friendships with a few of the other hospital volunteers. Clara also met and began dating Marcel, a staff physical therapist.

Reframing mental pictures

When you have completed the first three steps in the plan for achieving emotional growth, the new information about yourself, others, and objects

Completing an internship in a career field that interests you could be a challenging new experience.

becomes the most current source of information available. Regardless of the type of new experience you have undertaken and its outcome, you are now in a position to modify the initial perceptions that were constructed during the first step of the plan. Once completed, you have new insights, knowledge, and perspectives.

Clara, whom we described previously, reframed her mental pictures in light of the changes that had taken place in her life. Her volunteer work gave her a new appreciation for art, and she discovered depths of caring in herself that she had not known existed. In addition, she now saw herself as part of a circle of friends and as a partner in a long-term relationship with Marcel. With her proactive approach to life, Clara had created challenges for herself from which she changed and grew.

The Star Box on p. 35 provides suggestions for fostering emotional growth and thus enhancing emotional well-being. Opportunities to participate in these activities exist on or near most college campuses.

REFLECTIONS OF EMOTIONAL WELLNESS

What characterizes people who have most fully developed their emotional wellness? In the discussion that follows, we suggest three areas in which emotional healthfulness can be evident to the observer. These include movement toward fulfilling the highest level of need as defined by Maslow, development of a mature level of faith, and expression of creativity in the context of a world that often restricts creative expression.

Maslow's Hierarchy of Needs

One of the most familiar constructs in the field of developmental psychology is Abraham Maslow's model of need fulfillment. Maslow views emotional growth in terms of inner needs and motivation. He lists motivational requirements in the following order: physiological needs, safety needs, belonging and love needs, esteem needs, and **self-actualization** needs (Figure 2-2).[19] Maslow distinguishes between the lower *deficiency needs* and the higher *being needs*. People do not seek the higher needs until the lower demands have been reasonably satisfied. Accordingly, people who are hungry, feel unsafe, or have few friends will be highly unlikely to have high self-esteem until their lower needs have been met.

Fostering Your Emotional Growth

Emotional growth requires both knowing about yourself and learning from new experiences. The activities listed below can be used in support of these requirements.

- Keep a daily journal. Writing down your thoughts and taking note of experiences are effective tools in fostering greater self-understanding. Once written, the information that these accounts contain can be reprocessed for an even greater awareness of self.
- Join a support group. Sharing experiences and feelings in the presence of people who can "stand in your shoes" creates an environment that will support your efforts to grow as a more interesting and self-directed person. Additionally, being an active participant in a support group also functions as a "new experience" through which new insights into your sense of self-worth can be gained.
- Take an assertiveness course. Learning how to greet others, give and receive compliments, use "I" statements, express spontaneity, and state your feelings of disagreement are important tools in developing self-confidence. Very likely, an assertiveness course is or will be offered on your campus.
- Seek counseling. Nowhere is counseling generally more available and affordable than on a college campus. Clearly, much can be learned about your sense of self and the psychological factors that have shaped it. Furthermore, growth-enhancing skills can be formulated and tested in both individual and group counseling sessions. Contact the campus health center or the psychological services center for referral to an experienced psychologist or counselor.

What additional activities can you think of that would further your self-knowledge or serve as new experiences?

The healthiest and most effective people in society are those whose lives embody *being values* such as truth, beauty, goodness, faith, wholeness, and love. Maslow labels these as "Theory Z" people, or **transcenders.** Self-actualization, the highest level of self-development, is clearly evident in the personality of the transcender. Transcenders are described as follows[19]:

- Transcenders have more peak or creative experiences and naturally speak the language of being values.
- Transcenders are more responsive to beauty, are more holistic in their perceptions of humanity and the cosmos, adjust well to conflict situations, and work more wholeheartedly toward goals and purposes.
- Transcenders are innovators who are attracted to mystery and the unknown and see themselves as people who live according to transcendent values, such as unconditional acceptance, love, honesty, and forgiveness.
- Transcenders tend to fuse work and play. They are less attracted by the rewards of money and objects and more motivated by the satisfaction of being and service values.
- Transcenders are more likely to accept others with an unconditional positive regard, and they tend to be more oriented toward spiritual reality.

Most people will notice the similarity between transcenders and people with positive self-esteem. In following the Health Action Guide to improve self-esteem, you may also find yourself fulfilling Maslow's higher needs.

Spiritual or Faith Development

A fully developed sense of self-esteem most likely requires that you be knowledgeable and accepting of yourself as a person of **faith.** Certainly, many older adults have little difficulty sharing that they believe in something, such as the universal truths of beauty, honesty, and love, or someone greater than themselves and that this belief brings them great comfort and a sense of support. Many report that because of their personal level of faith, they do not fear death because they

self-actualization
The highest level of personality development; self-actualized people recognize their roles in life and use personal strengths to reach their fullest potential.

transcenders
Self-actualized people who have achieved a quality of being ordinarily associated with higher levels of spiritual growth.

faith
The purposes and meaning that underlie an individual's hopes and dreams.

Self-Actualization and Fulfillment
Enrichment, Adaptive flexibility, Life patterns, Creativity, Legacies and transcendence, Recreation and leisure.

Ego-Strength and Self-Esteem
Effective coping, intelligence, Maintaining autonomy and control, Assertiveness, Transitional states, Culture of cohorts

Belonging and Love
Communication, Relationships (intimates, family, friends, groups, communities), Sexuality

Safety and Security
Sensory function, Environmental safety, Legal and economic protection

Basic Physiological Integrity
Body function, Respiration, Circulation, Nutrition, Elimination, Sleep, Activity, Rest, Comfort

Figure 2-2   Maslow's hierarchy of needs.

know that their lives have had meaning within the context of their deeply held beliefs. Further, they would urge younger people to search for both the strength and direction in their lives that faith provides.[20]

As a resource in the spiritual dimension of health, the existence of faith provides a basis on which a belief system can mature and an expanding awareness of life's meaning can be fostered. In addition, the existence of faith gives meaning (or additional meaning) to your vocation and assists you in better understanding the consequences of your vocational efforts. For example, a college student might choose to major in education instead of marketing because he or she would find greater spiritual fulfillment in teaching than in business. Further, faith in something (or someone) influences many of the experiences that you will seek throughout life and tempers the emotional relationships that you have with these experiences.[21] The questions posed in the Star Box on p. 37 will help you consider how your faith affects your own life. The topic of spirituality is considered further in the Focus Box on p. 40–42.

In nearly all cultures, faith and its accompanying belief system provide individuals and groups with rituals and practices that foster a sense of community— "a community of faith." In turn, the community provides the authority and guidance that nurture the emotional stability, confidence, and sense of competence needed for living life fully.[20]

Creative Expression

Emotionally healthy individuals have a free and open approach to life. They think and act positively. They also assess people and situations realistically and constructively. When interacting with emotionally healthy people, others quickly notice their flexibility in solving problems. How did these people become so secure, competent, and constructive? Is it possible that most people will mature in this direction? What resources will you need to grow in a similar fashion?

Assuming that **creativity** is closely related to emotional health, these traits might help describe emotionally healthy people:

- Creative people are intuitive and open to new experiences. They are relatively free from fear

How Does My Faith Affect My Life?

James Fowler[21] describes the nature of faith as a fundamental, universal, but infinitely varied value response within the human experience. Faith can include religious practice but also can be quite distinct. Faith is the most fundamental category in the human quest for the meaning of life. It is a developing focus of the total person that gives purpose and meaning to thoughts.

By the time people reach college age, it is possible that the maturation of their faith has placed them into a series of uncomfortable situations. These include the need to take seriously the burden of responsibility for their own commitments, lifestyles, beliefs, and attitudes. Tension and anxiety can arise because the growth of faith requires them to make personal decisions. It demands objectivity and a certain amount of independence and requires finding a balance between personal aspirations and a developing sense of service to others. Finally, symbols and doctrines must be translated into personalized spiritual concepts that can then be validated on the basis of experience.

- In light of the potential for young adults to grow in their faith, what have been your own experiences?
- Would you consider yourself to be more or less "faithful" than your friends or other family members?
- What school-related experiences have affected most powerfully the spiritual dimension of your health?

Creative expression can occur in a variety of forms.

and are not disturbed by the unknown, the mysterious, or the puzzling.

- Creative people are less interested in detail than in meaning and implications. They tend to be more theoretical than practical in their orientation.
- Creative people are independent, self-accepting, and nonauthoritarian in their attitudes. They tend to resist group work and function best when allowed to work independently.
- Creative people are flexible. They do not use all-or-none thinking but recognize that there are many ways to interpret the same situation.
- Creative people have an internal set of values and are always working toward goals.

Some people may recognize many of these characteristics as being already well developed in their own personalities. Or they may not yet possess some of the traits listed, and these may now appear beyond their reach. Nevertheless, having a high level of health will increase their creativity by giving them the resources to face new challenges.

> **creativity**
> Innovative ability; insightful capacity to solve problems; ability to move beyond analytical or logical approaches to experiences.

Summary

- Emotionally well people feel comfortable about themselves and other people and are able to meet the demands of life.
- Emotional wellness refers specifically to one's feelings in response to change, whereas psychological wellness refers more broadly to the adequate development and proper functioning of mental abilities.
- Emotions are not always constant; people experience a normal range of emotions.
- A sense of self-esteem may be the essence of emotional maturity.
- Hardiness reflects the existence of confidence and commitment and an ability to build on challenge.
- Depression can be recognized by the presence of characteristic symptoms.
- Loneliness results from the absence of adequate human contact.
- Shyness may be a basic component of temperament, yet social skills counseling can help shy people learn to interact more comfortably with others.
- Suicide represents an extreme and ineffective attempt to cope with life-centered problems.
- Effective verbal and nonverbal communication skills can be learned and will enhance emotional well-being.
- Humor can contribute to emotional health and well-being.
- Conflict management skills can include a variety of approaches, some of which are more effective than others.
- A four-step plan can be used to foster greater emotional growth and enhanced emotional wellness.
- The ability to meet basic human needs establishes a basis for pursuing higher emotional needs.
- People who possess a mature faith recognize the existence of guiding values in their lives and live within a community of faith.
- Creative people possess a positive outlook and take a unique approach to life and living.

Review Questions

1. What are the characteristics of an emotionally healthy person?
2. How is psychological health related to but different from emotional health?
3. What is meant by the "normal range of emotions"?
4. Define self-esteem. List strategies that can be used to improve self-esteem.
5. What are three characteristics of hardy people?
6. What is depression, and what are the behavioral patterns of depressed people? How do primary and secondary depression differ?
7. What is the important component missing in the lives of those who are lonely? What skills can be learned by lonely people that might be effective in easing their sense of loneliness?
8. On the basis of current understanding, what is the most likely origin of shyness?
9. What behavioral characteristics indicate a suicidal tendency? How should someone who observes these traits in another person respond?
10. What are several characteristics of effective verbal communication?
11. What nonverbal cues encourage positive communication? What nonverbal cues detract from positive interpersonal communication?
12. What message is given to others by those who allow humor to be a part of their social interaction?
13. Which techniques are the more effective approaches to conflict management? Which are less effective?
14. Identify and explain the four components of the cyclic process that will help you enhance your emotional growth.
15. In what order are human needs encountered as one moves toward self-actualization?
16. What aspects of life are brought into focus as the spiritual dimension of health matures?
17. List several characteristics of creative people.

Think About This . . .

- How close do you come to meeting the characteristics of a mentally healthy person?
- Are you ready to undertake a new experience? What kind of experience will it be?

- Do you take yourself too seriously at times?
- Which traits of creativity have you developed?

References

1. *Developing objectives for healthy people 2010,* U.S. Department of Health and Human Services, Office of Disease Prevention and Health Promotion, September 1997.
2. *Mental health and you,* Alexandria, VA, 1997, National Mental Health Association.
3. Berne P, Savary L: *Building self-esteem in children,* Los Angeles, CA, 1996, Crossroad Publishing Company.
4. Maddi, S Kobasa S: *The hardy executive: health under stress,* Burr Ridge, IL, 1984, Irwin Professional Publishing.
5. Conway J: *Men in midlife crisis* Colorado Springs, CO, 1997, Chariot Victor Publishing.
6. Dychtwald K: *Wellness and health promotion for the elderly,* Rockville, MD, 1986, Aspen Publication.
7. *Mosby's medical, nursing, and allied health directory* (5th ed), St. Louis, MO, 1997, Mosby.
8. Johnson D, Weissman M, Klerman G: Service utilization and social mobility associated with depressive symptoms in the community, *JAMA,* 267(11):1478, 1992.
9. Keltner N, Schwecke L, Bostrom C: *Psychiatric nursing* (2nd ed), St. Louis, 1995, Mosby.
10. Stuart G: *Brightening your days,* Indianapolis, IN, 1997, PCS Healthy Results.
11. Baron R, Byrne D: Social psychology: understanding human interaction (8th ed), Boston, 1996, Allyn & Bacon.
12. U.S. Bureau of the Census, *Statistical abstract of the United States:* 1997 (117th ed). Washington, DC, 1997.
13. Masters W, Johnson V, Kolodny R: *Human sexuality* (5th ed), New York, 1995, HarperCollins.
14. Hass A, Hass K: *Understanding sexuality* (3rd ed), St. Louis, 1993, Mosby.
15. DuPre A: *Humor and the healing arts: a multimethod analysis of humor use in health care,* Mahway, NJ, 1998, L. Erlbaum Associates.
16. Ziv A, editor: *National styles of humor,* New York, 1988, Greenwood Press.
17. Tannen D: *That's not what I mean: how conversational style makes or breaks relationships,* New York, 1987, Ballantine.
18. Sprunger, M: Psychologist, Personal communication, January, 1998.
19. Maslow A: *The farthest reaches of human nature,* Magnolia, MA, 1983, Peter Smith.
20. Hemenway J, editor: *Assessing spiritual needs: a guide for care-givers,* Minneapolis, MN, 1993, Augsburg.
21. Fowler J: *Faith development and pastoral care,* Philadelphia, 1987, Fortress Press.

Suggested Readings

Greene B: *The 50 year dash: The feelings, foibles, and fears of being half-a-century old,* New York, 1997, Doubleday.

Syndicated columnist Bob Greene shares his personal feelings about being in the throes of midlife. Although some would contend that the content is more about the author than about middle age, the book is, nevertheless, a humorous, if not muddled, view of everything from family, career, and money to the importance of the intestate highway system. Traditional-age students might consider this as a gift for their baby-boomer parents.

Sussman MB: *A perilous calling: the hazards of psychotherapy practice.* New York: John Wiley & Sons, 1995.

Although the title may suggest a critical attack on the mental health profession, the book actually offers an empathetic look at the pressures and stresses associated with the profession. A variety of factors that influence these practitioners, ranging from the influence of third-party payers to deeply held personal fears, are discussed.

Caplan PJ: *They say you're crazy: how the world's most powerful psychiatrists decide who's normal.* Reading, MA: Addison-Wesley, 1996.

This book, written by a mental health professional, is a highly critical look at the limitations of the *Diagnostic and Statistical Manual of Mental Disorders,* which is used throughout the field as the basis for diagnosing disorders. Once identified as dysfunctional by the content of the manual, the label often remains for a lifetime. The author is particularly critical of the weakness of the manual in regard to conditions seen in women and the emotional damage that exists until the end of life.

Fancher RT: *Cultures of healing: correcting the image of American mental health care,* New York, 1995, WH Freeman.

This is one of a series of recent books written by mental health professionals who are critical of the profession's use of *DSM (Diagnostic and statistical manual of mental disorders)* in labeling patients. The author sees misuse as a part of professional infighting regarding the effectiveness of various treatment approaches.

FOCUS ON...

Enhancing Spirituality and Wellness

Often our thoughts on the subject of health are confined to the scientific. Indeed, much of the study of health is involved with exploring topics in physical and emotional health from a practical point of view, with conclusions based on sound medical research. But are there other aspects to health and wellness that are not grounded in science? Some health care professionals are now beginning to embrace the concept that a person's spirituality may be an important factor in maintaining both emotional and physical health.[1,2]

Ways to Improve Spiritual Well-Being

The idea of "emotional wellness" may mean different things to different people. A person's emotional well-being can be affected by several components, including family, friends, finances, and occupation. For example, a person employed as a health care worker may gain a high degree of spiritual satisfaction from working. The same person may not be as spiritually fulfilled if he or she were a collections agent. Although a complete career change may not be possible in many cases, there are other things a person can do to increase spiritual well-being.

One simple way to achieve better spiritual health is to find a way to feel better about yourself. Helping others in need through volunteer work is one way to do that. Voluntarism is becoming more popular in the United States.[3] Besides the obvious benefits to the people being helped, the volunteer can also benefit. Charity work can boost self-confidence and make you feel good about what you are doing.[4] If you want to travel, some types of volunteer work can take you to other parts of the country (or even to other nations) and can help broaden your knowledge of other peoples. There are many opportunities close to home as well for those who cannot afford to travel or do not want to be away from home. Many community and neighborhood organizations offer opportunities for volunteer work,[3] and some businesses offer incentives for employees who perform community service.[4] If you cannot volunteer time, giving material goods or money can also help you feel better about your contribution to society. Providing toys, clothes, or used tools or furniture for those who need them can boost your sense of spiritual well-being.[5]

Teens and college students can also benefit by volunteering in a field related to their career interests.[3] Such work can improve skills, provide work experience, and increase the chances of obtaining a job in that field in the future. Such work also allows students to explore career fields they are interested in to determine which positions may be best for a future job. Families who volunteer as a unit can enjoy the benefits of helping others while spending quality time together.[5] Such work can bring families closer together. Children can learn about working with other people and gain an understanding about the community, and teaching kids early about the moral values associated with helping others may make them more likely to continue to volunteer as they grow older.[5]

If volunteer work doesn't interest you, other activities can also help improve your spiritual health. Taking time to do things you enjoy can make your outlook on life more positive. Take up a new hobby, spend more time with your family, listen to music, exercise, or do something that makes you happy. Although most recreational activities do not seem to fall under the classic definition of spirituality, they can improve your emotional well-being by taking your mind off of stressful things in your life.

Religion and Mental Health

The traditional view of "spirituality" involves a person's religious or spiritual beliefs. Such beliefs can be very important in maintaining wellness. In recent years, churches and synagogues have experienced an increase in attendance, reflecting an upsurge in spiritual awareness in America. Money, education, and success might not have provided meaning to people's lives, so some are turning to religion to fill this void.[6] Congregating with people who have similar beliefs and values provides an outlet for sharing spiritual experiences and can make religion more meaningful. Many modern worshipers (especially those who are younger) tend to be very selective about where they attend, however. Often, people will try out several places of worship before settling on one they like. This suggests that people are looking for specific benefits from their place of worship, perhaps to make the experience more meaningful.

Spirituality may play a stronger role in people's health as they become older. Studies have shown that older people are in general more religious than younger people and that belief in God increases with age.[2] Some 50% of adults age 65 and older attend church on a regular basis.[2] Religion and the belief that there is something better than life on Earth may help older people cope with the various afflictions that come with the aging process. Spiritual beliefs may help people adapt to the stress that occurs as they grow older.[2] Spirituality may also help with mental disorders. Religion has been shown to fight the effects of depression. Several studies have suggested that there is an inverse relationship between religious coping and depression.[2] The better a person is able to use religion to cope with life's problems, the less likely he or she is to become depressed.

A person's spiritual well-being can be enhanced without embracing traditional Western religion. Mind-body disciplines, many of which are based in Far Eastern religions, have gained in popularity in the United States.[7] Mind-body disciplines such as yoga or t'ai chi require focused breathing in coordination with controlled body movements. Performing such activities calms the mind and boosts the spirit while toning and strengthening the muscles.[7] Meditation is a component of many of these disciplines, and it may be advantageous to combine meditation with exercise, since some people may not have the discipline to just sit and meditate.[7] Those who use mind-body disciplines regularly say that the exercise and meditation help them tap into unconscious issues and treat emotional or physical injuries.[7]

New age spirituality is also gaining a following. New age spirituality takes on many forms. Among the disciplines included in the new age category are yoga, meditation, and visualization. Other new age activities include the use of psychics, astrology, tarot cards, and crystals.[6] Most mainstream religious groups generally do not approve of such activities. They claim that many of the benefits touted by new age promoters, such as meditation, ordering of daily life, and group care of souls, are already present in traditional religion.[8] Nevertheless, new age publishing and retailing brings in $1 billion a year in sales, and $45 billion is spent yearly on self-development.[6]

The Changing Role of Spirituality in Health Care

If spirituality can play a positive role in emotional wellness, it follows that a person's physical health may benefit from spirituality also. The spiritual aspects of health and well-being have not been studied very extensively, but in recent years more people involved in medicine have been willing to embrace the idea that spirituality can have an effect on physical health. Traditionally, physicians have been unable or unwilling to pay attention to spiritual needs of patients, possibly because some doctors feared being labeled as "quacks" if they pushed the idea of holistic healing too much.[1] Others worried that patients might deny their illnesses.[1] Patients might concentrate solely on holistic methods for healing and ignore conventional medicine, therapy, and methods. And though statistics show that most Americans believe in a supreme being,[2] this may not be the case with certain

groups within the medical community. An American Psychiatric Association survey of psychiatrists showed that only 43% believed in God, and only 1.5% to 2.5% of published studies in four major psychiatric journals had a religious commitment.[2] But there is a growing belief among medical professionals that spirituality, in conjunction with conventional medicine, may help patients with the healing process.

There may be a connection between prayer and healing, and religion may help people cope with ailments. Spirituality has been cited as a positive force in the healing process, and religious beliefs may account for certain cases of spontaneous disease remission. Many patients ask for prayer as a component of their healing regimen, and more doctors of late have been willing to comply with their patients' wishes. The holistic health movement is increasing in popularity among physicians and patients alike.[1] There is some feeling in the medical community that physicians should consider and respect the religious and spiritual beliefs of patients. The American Psychological Association's *Diagnostic and Statistical Manual of Mental Disorders* now includes an entry for "Religious/Spiritual Problem," which may represent an acknowledgment from some medical professionals that faith can play a role in a person's health.[1]

There may be some advantages to looking at the person as a whole rather than as distinct parts. Although conventional exercise and medicine certainly help improve overall physical health, perhaps a spiritual component to healing should be considered as well. In some cases at least, physicians should be open to the idea that a patient's spirituality can be used as an important medical tool.

Thousands of volunteers used sandbags to shore up levees along the Mississippi River and its tributaries during the Great Flood of '93.

For Discussion . . .

In your personal experience, has your spirituality had an effect on your overall wellness? Does getting involved with a group project enhance your spirituality? Have you tried unorthodox methods of spirituality? Do you think that cases of "miracle cures" (spontaneous remission of disease) may be explained through religious or spiritual beliefs? ◉

References

1. Martinez D: Rx: prayer—health care gets a dose of spirituality, *National Catholic Reporter* 30(24), 1994.
2. Marwick C: Should physicians prescribe prayer for health? *JAMA* 273(20), 1993.
3. Taibbi R: Teens who help, *Current Health* 2 21(3), 1994.
4. Caring in the community, *Management Today*, March 1995.
5. Friedman J: Family values, *MPLS-St. Paul Magazine* 21(12), 1993.
6. McDonald M: The new spirituality: mainstream N. America is on a massive search for meaning in life, *Maclean's* 107(41), Oct 10, 1994.
7. Hulet D: Mind over matter (return of spirituality), *Los Angeles Magazine,* 40(1), 1995.
8. Oder TC: Blinded by the 'lite': dying modernity is "into" spirituality, *Christianity Today* 38(10), 1994.

3

Managing Stress

Healthy People: Looking Ahead to 2010

An initial objective of the *Healthy People 2000* report was to reduce the proportion of people with stress-related health conditions. Progress in this area at middecade was most likely related to the development of worksite stress management programs. By 1995, nearly 40% more employees had access to stress management programs than in 1990.

However, the *Midcourse Review* also noted a lack of progress in reducing the number of people who were under stress but were unable to or uninterested in addressing this condition. For some people, community and worksite stress management programs continued to be unavailable. For others, the inability to master coping techniques or use them regularly reduced the effectiveness of the programs in which they enrolled.

Because stress significantly influences the development of illnesses such as cancer, cardiovascular disease, eating disorders, and infectious conditions, *Healthy People 2010* will continue to emphasize the importance of better and more widely available stress management programs. Several focus areas, including mental-health services and community and educational programs, lend themselves to the further development of stress management programs.

Change influences daily living. Each person, institution, and situation in a person's environment holds the potential for change, some of which may be seen as threatening. Being able to control or adjust to this change is often challenging, stimulating, and rewarding, which contributes to a sense of well-being.

When people handle change poorly, however, their responses result in stress that can be disruptive to their health and unpleasant to experience.

STRESS AND STRESSORS

Almost every day on a college campus, people can be heard commenting about how much **stress** they are under. Certainly, for both traditional and nontraditional college students, the demands of school, work, marriage, and parenting can produce feelings of distress that detract from wellness.

Although we have all experienced stress, we may have questions about what it is. Hans Selye, the originator of stress theory, described stress as "the nonspecific response of the body to any demand made on it."[1] Stress can be viewed as a physical and emotional response that occurs when people are exposed to change. The events that produce stress are called **stressors.** Stressors always come before stress. Stressors are the cause; stress is the effect.

Variation in Response to Stressors

Because individuals are unique, a stressor for one person might not be a stressor for another. For example, if the bookstore is out of a textbook or if a babysitter must be found because the local public schools are closed for a teachers' in-service day, some people are more *distressed* than others. This variation results from the unique information that each person applies in making decisions about the seriousness of the situation.[2]

Positive or negative stressors

Stressors produce the same generalized physical response whether an individual views the stressor as good or bad. Poor academic performance, loss of a friend, or being the only minority student on the dorm floor can cause stress, just as giving birth, receiving a promotion, or starting a passionate romance can be stressors. In each case, the effect on the body's physical systems is relatively similar.

Selye coined the word **eustress** for positive stress. Stressors that produce eustress can enhance longevity, productivity, and life satisfaction. Examples include the mild stress that helps you stay alert during a midterm examination, the anticipation felt on the first

day of a new job, and the exhilarating stress you feel while exercising. In fact, some suggest that a personality type, type R (risk takers), may "require" the regular occurrence of high-risk activities.[3] Activities such as sky diving, roller coaster riding, and white-water rafting are undertaken frequently by those with type R personalities to generate a hormonal rush (see p. 50) and thus a sense of well-being. These people in particular demonstrate a strong sense of confidence, self-effectiveness, courage, creativity, and optimism that they use to *plan to be stressed.* Recent research suggests that this risk-taking behavior may be caused by a genetic predisposition.[4]

Selye calls harmful, unpleasant stress **distress.** Distress that is not controlled can result in physical and emotional disruption, illness, and even death.[5] Examples of distress are chronic pain, lack of meaningful relationships, physical confrontation, and anxiety and depression.

Uncontrolled Stress Related to Disease States

If the effect of a stressor is not minimized or resolved, the human body becomes exhausted, producing emotional and physical breakdown. Depending on the strength of the stressor and the resistance of the person, this breakdown may occur quickly or over many years.

Clearly, the effects of unresolved stress can build up until the body begins to break down. This breakdown leads to stress-related diseases and disorders. Among the major diseases that have some origin in unresolved stress are hypertension, stroke, heart disease, kidney disease, depression, alcoholism, and gastrointestinal disorders (including ulcers, irritable bowel syndrome, and diverticulitis).[6] Other stress-related disorders are

College life presents many stressors.

PERSONAL ASSESSMENT

How Stressed Are You?

You must know how much stress you are under and what events are triggering your feelings of stress before you can begin to cope effectively. In the following stress test, developed by researchers at Carnegie Mellon University, you can obtain a rough measure of the level of stress you are under. The questions reflect some of the most familiar perceptions of people who are experiencing distress.

The higher your total score on this test, the higher your level of stress. In the general population, the average score for men was 12 and for women was 14.

Other stress assessments indicate that difficult or unexpected life events, such as the death of a family member, arrest and incarceration, the demands of school or work, a pregnancy (yours or your partner's), a serious illness or injury, and even marriage, are among the greatest sources of stress for most adults. How familiar are you with these events?

In the last month, how often have you felt:	Never	Almost never	Sometimes	Fairly often	Very often
Upset because of something that happened unexpectedly?	0	1	2	3	4
Unable to control the important things in your life?	0	1	2	3	4
Nervous and "stressed"?	0	1	2	3	4
Unable to cope with all the things you had to do?	0	1	2	3	4
Angered because of things that were beyond your control?	0	1	2	3	4
That difficulties were piling up so high that you could not overcome them?	0	1	2	3	4
Confident about your abilities to handle your personal problems?	4	3	2	1	0
That things were going your way?	4	3	2	1	0
Able to control irritations in your life?	4	3	2	1	0
That were on top of things?	4	3	2	1	0

Total score: _____

migraine headaches, allergies, asthma, hay fever, anxiety, insomnia, impotence, and menstrual irregularities. The dependency-related behaviors of cigarette smoking, overeating and undereating, and underactivity relate in part to unresolved stress. Even the immune system, which protects the body from infections and cancer, may be weakened by stress. This is thought to be the result of prolonged exposure to corticoids produced by the adrenal cortex (see p. 50).[7]

COLLEGE-CENTERED STRESSORS

For some people who have not attempted college course work, the idea that college life could be stressful must seem strange. After all, even for nontraditional students, isn't college the good life?

stress
The physiological and psychological state of disruption caused by the presence of an unanticipated, disruptive, or stimulating event.

stressors
Factors or events, real or imagined, that elicit a state of stress.

eustress (yoo stress)
Stress that enhances the quality of life.

distress
Stress that diminishes the quality of life; commonly associated with disease, illness, and maladaptation.

PERSONAL ASSESSMENT

How Vulnerable Are You to Stress?

A wide variety of situations can serve as stressors that challenge us physically and emotionally. This assessment will help you identify potentially stressful situations and determine your overall vulnerability to stress. Use the following scoring system for each situation listed:

1 = Always (yes)
2 = Almost always
3 = Sometimes
4 = Almost never
5 = Never (no)

_____ 1. I eat at least one hot, balanced meal a day.

_____ 2. I sleep seven to eight hours a night at least four nights a week.

_____ 3. I regularly give and receive affection.

_____ 4. I have at least one relative within fifty miles on whom I can rely.

_____ 5. I exercise to the point of perspiration at least twice a week.

_____ 6. I don't smoke.

_____ 7. I drink fewer than five alcoholic drinks a week.

_____ 8. I am an appropriate weight for my height.

_____ 9. I have an income adequate to meet my expenses.

_____ 10. I draw strength from my religious or spiritual beliefs.

_____ 11. I regularly attend club or social activities.

_____ 12. I have a network of friends and acquaintances.

_____ 13. I have one or more friends in whom I confide about personal matters.

_____ 14. I am in good health (including eyesight, hearing, and dental health).

_____ 15. I am able to express my feelings openly when angry or worried.

_____ 16. I talk regularly with my family or roommates about domestic issues, such as chores and financial matters.

_____ 17. I do something fun at least once a week.

_____ 18. I am able to organize my time effectively.

_____ 19. I drink fewer than three cups of coffee (or tea or caffeinated soft drinks) a day.

_____ 20. I take quiet time for myself during the day.

_____ TOTAL

To calculate your score, add up your number of points and subtract 20. A score of more than 30 indicates that you are vulnerable to stress. You are seriously vulnerable if your score is between 50 and 75, and you are extremely vulnerable if it is over 75.

However, for those who study or teach on college campuses, these perceptions are hard to understand. They know all too well that the undergraduate experience is serious because of its role in preparation for life. For the part-time, nontraditional student who comes to campus for course work (often at night) and then returns to work, family, and community responsibilities, college classes can be especially stressful. Complete the Personal Assessment above to determine your level of vulnerability to stress.

In college and university settings, stressors could arise from a variety of areas, including the following:

- School policies that seem to make going to school too complicated, such as the inconvenient scheduling of classes and the restrictions on parking

- Expectations of faculty regarding various course requirements, such as attendance, out-of-class participation, and the type of examinations given by a particular instructor (see the Health Action Guide on p. 47)

- Difficulty in qualifying for loans or other forms of financial assistance, and, of course, the need to work to afford school

- Personal goals that become unachievable, including making an athletic team, earning a desired grade point average, or graduating with honors

HEALTH
Action Guide - - - - - ➤

Coping With Test Anxiety

Examinations have been a major part of student life for decades and will likely continue to be so. Consequently, many students develop an incapacitating anxiety when preparing to take tests. Compare your current test preparation activities with the approach recommended by experts, described below.

- Find a location conducive to study.
- Set a formal schedule for your test preparation.
- Keep complete resources, including class notes, background reading material, and reference texts, available.
- Create learning aids to help you, such as review questions, illustrations, outlines, definitions of technical terms, and sample test items.
- Be your own best friend by going to class, taking notes, joining and contributing to an ongoing study group, asking questions in class, and making appointments to visit your professor to clarify material.
- Be kind to yourself by getting an adequate amount of sleep, eating balanced meals, exercising, taking time to be reflective, and staying sober.

On the basis of your comparisons, do you have any greater insight as to why you might be anxious about examinations? How do your study habits compare? Remember, most colleges and universities have counseling centers that can help you with study skills and test anxiety. ◄- - - - -➤

Interpersonal relationships can be a source of stress.

believe you are capable of giving. Not surprisingly, it is frequently the source of many stressors.

Beyond the college setting, day-to-day living presents stressors that must be confronted and resolved. Although these stressors differ from those associated with college, these life-centered stressors hold the same potential for causing physical and emotional distress and challenges to well-being. Read the Focus Box on p. 60 for advice on coping with stress in the workplace.

GENERALIZED PHYSIOLOGICAL RESPONSE TO STRESSORS

Once under the influence of a stressor, people's bodies respond in remarkably similar, predictable ways. For example, on being asked to stand up in front of a group and talk, a person's heart rate increases, throat becomes dry, palms sweat, and he or she feels dizzy or lightheaded. The person may even become nauseated. Similar feelings would be felt if a person were told that she had lost her job or that her spouse wanted a divorce. It is clear that different stressors are able to elicit these common physical reactions.

Selye described the typical physical response to a stressor in his **general adaptation syndrome** model.

- Uncertainties about previously held beliefs, including those related to religion, sexual abstinence, and politics
- Interpersonal relationships and decisions regarding interracial or interfaith dating, changing roommates, and, perhaps, being older than classmates
- Availability of a job or acceptance into graduate or professional school, and, of course, the rapid approach of "real world" responsibilities
- Family expectations concerning whether school is being taken seriously enough, friends will be made, or money will be used wisely

Education in a college or university setting is never passive. It nearly always demands active participation and effort and at times may demand more than you

general adaptation syndrome
A sequenced physiological response to the presence of a stressor; the alarm, resistance, recovery, and exhaustion stages of the stress response.

Graduation marks a transition from familiar stressors to new ones.

Selye stated that the human body moves through three stages when confronted by stressors, as explained below.

Alarm Reaction Stage

Once exposed to any event that is seen as threatening, the body immediately prepares for difficulty. The involuntary changes described in Figure 3-1 are controlled by hormonal and nervous system functions and quickly prepare the body for the **fight-or-flight response.**[1]

Resistance Stage

The second stage of response to a stressor, the resistance stage, reflects the body's attempt to reestablish internal balance, or a state of *homeostasis.* The high level of energy seen in the initial alarm stage cannot be maintained very long. The body therefore attempts to reduce the intensity of the initial response to a more manageable level. This is accomplished by reducing the production of adrenocorticotropic hormone (ACTH) (see p. 50), thus allowing *specificity of adaptation* to occur. Specific organ systems become the focus of the body's response, such as the cardiovascular and digestive systems.[1]

Because of the ability to move from an alarm stage into a less damaging resistance stage, effective coping or a change in the status of the stressor will probably occur. In fact, as control over the stressful situation is gained, homeostasis is even more completely established and movement toward full recovery is seen. At the completion of the *recovery stage,* the body has returned to its prestressed state and there is minimal evidence of the stressor's existence.[1]

Exhaustion Stage

Body adjustments required as a result of long-term exposure to a stressor often result in an overload. Specific organs and body systems that were called on during the resistance stage may not be able to resist a stressor indefinitely. Exhaustion results, and the stress-producing hormone levels again rise. In extreme or chronic cases, exhaustion can become so pronounced that death can occur.

THE STRESS RESPONSE

Why could something as familiar as a telephone ringing late at night cause a person to feel fear and near-panic? Why is it that the hands sweat, muscles tense, and the appetite leaves as you wait in the hallway outside the classroom in which your final examination is to be held? Is the "cotton-mouth" feeling described by athletes a valuable aid to performance? These answers are simple and based on the body's primitive interpretation of reality. The body is looking for energy because it believes that all change is threatening and can be confronted by running, fighting, scaring the "adversary" away, or engaging it in sexual activity (the flight, fight, fright, or folly response). For these responses, the body simply needs energy for physical activity. In the sections that follow, Figure 3-1 will be explained.

Stressors

For a state of stress to exist, a person must first be confronted by change, real or imagined. Any change

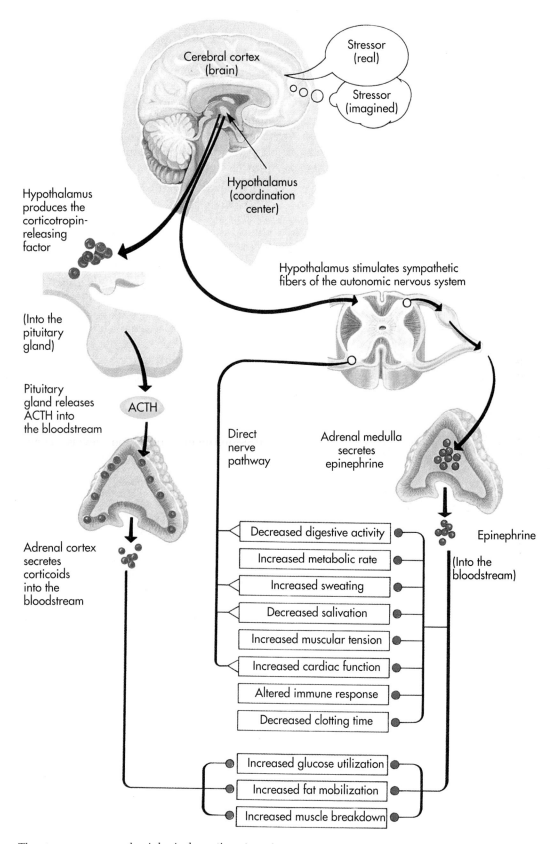

Figure 3-1   The stress response: physiological reactions to a stressor.

holds the potential for becoming a stressor and subsequently stimulating the stress response.

Sensory Modalities

Before a change event can be responded to as a stressor, however, it must first be sensed by the *central nervous system*. With the exception of stressors that are products of the imagination, a person must hear, smell, taste, feel, or see something changing so that they can be transformed into electrical impulses within the nervous system and thus capable of eliciting the stress response.

Cerebral Cortex

Events become stressors when, on entering the *cerebral cortex* of the brain, they are perceived as stressors. By a person's own determination, some, but not all, events are stressors. Remember the phone ringing late at night? Should that very same phone have rung 12 hours earlier (during the afternoon), its ringing would probably not have been interpreted as stressful.

Endocrine System Involvement

The body's response to the presence of a stressor involves not only the brain and nervous system but also the *endocrine system*. The process of interconnecting the nervous system and the endocrine system is the task of the **hypothalamus,** a structure located deep within the brain. The hypothalamus is situated immediately above the gland that plays the most important role in regulating the endocrine system, the **pituitary gland.**[8]

During periods of stress, communication between the hypothalamus and the pituitary gland is accomplished by the release from the hypothalamus of a chemical messenger into the blood flowing directly to the pituitary gland. This chemical stimulates the pituitary gland to produce its own powerful hormone, **adrenocorticotropic hormone (ACTH).** ACTH is then released into the bloodstream, ultimately reaching a pair of glands of the endocrine system called the **adrenal glands.**[8] ACTH stimulates the outer layer *(cortex)* of the adrenal glands to produce chemical substances called **corticoids.** Corticoids support the powerful hormone **epinephrine**

Headaches

An estimated 45 million Americans have frequent, bothersome headaches. If you have chronic headache symptoms or symptoms that are especially painful, you should seek medical help. Headaches can have many causes including stress. The three most common categories are described here:

Tension

Description

A dull, constricting pain centered in the hatband region. Pain may be on both sides of the head and extend down the neck to the shoulders. Produced by stress, eye strain, muscle tension, sinus congestion, TMJ dysfunction, nasal congestion, or caffeine withdrawal.

Treatment

Nonnarcotic pain relievers, muscle relaxants, relaxation exercises, massage.

Prevention

Preventive relaxation exercises, certain antidepressant medications.

Migraine

Description

Throbbing pain on one side of the head, usually preceded by visual disturbances. Sensitivity to lights and sounds; nausea and dizziness. More common in women. Can last from a few hours to 2 days.

Treatment

Three oral prescription medications (Imitrex, Maxalt, and Zomig) are now available. Imitrex will soon be available as a nasal spray. An OTC medication, Excedrin Extra Strength, is effective for many.

Prevention

Avoidance of certain foods, including red wines, other alcoholic beverages, ripened cheeses, chocolate, cured meats, and monosodium glutamate (MSG). In some cases, prescription medications are recommended.

Cluster

Description

Focused, intense pain near one eye, often producing a red and teary eye and a runny nose. Headaches occur daily for weeks or months. They mainly affect men and last up to 2 hours.

Treatment

Oxygen and/or ergot compounds during the headache.

Prevention

Avoidance of alcohol and nitrite-containing foods. Various prescription medications, including antidepressants, steroids, ergotlike compounds, or heart-regulating drugs.

(commonly known as **adrenaline**) in the production of energy.

The hypothalamus also activates the adrenal gland directly through a branch of the nervous system. This direct stimulation of the adrenal gland is responsible for the production of epinephrine. Epinephrine causes most of the changes that occur in the body to produce the rapid, short-term high energy levels required in the stress response.

Epinephrine-Influenced Responses

Once epinephrine has been released by the adrenal gland, many of the following tissue responses can be expected.

Decreased digestive activity

Because the body needs energy when a stressor must be avoided or an adversary must be defeated, it cannot wait for digestion to change food into glucose. Rather, the body must turn to the glucose already circulating in the bloodstream or in a storage form within tissue. As a consequence, the entire digestive system slows down. It is not surprising, then, that many people who are under chronic stress report various forms of gastric distress.

Increased metabolic rate

Epinephrine increases the **metabolic rate.** Glucose already within the system is rushed by blood circulation to the cells, where it is combined with oxygen (cellular respiration) for the release of energy.

Increased sweating

To control the elevated temperature generated by the accelerated energy production, the body sweats. The accumulated fluid forms on the skin surface, where it evaporates, thus lowering the body's temperature. This sweat also contains more organic material and can thus produce an unpleasant body odor during stressful situations.

Decreased salivation

As a result of the overall shutdown of the digestive system, the production of saliva, which contains digestive enzymes, is also reduced. Thus people who are under the influence of any type of stressor may report a "cotton-mouth" sensation.

Increased muscular tension

Twitching and tautness of the arms and legs during times of stress reflect how close to the fully contracted state the body's skeletal muscles have become. By maintaining the muscles in this condition, the body is prepared for the fight-or-flight response. When muscle tension is continued for extended periods, however, headaches (see the Star Box on p. 50), a stiff neck, and temporomandibular joint (TMJ) dysfunction can result.

Increased rate of cardiac and pulmonary function

During periods of stress, the heart and lungs shift into high gear. Epinephrine helps increase the rate of *cardiac* and *pulmonary* function. An overall upsurge in

---

fight-or-flight response
The reaction to a stressor by confrontation or avoidance (sometimes called the fight, fright, flight, or folly [or 4F] response).

hypothalamus (hype oh **thal** a muss)
The portion of the midbrain that connects the cerebral cortex and the pituitary gland.

pituitary gland (puh **too** it tary)
The "master gland" of the endocrine system; the wide variety of hormones produced by the pituitary are sent to structures throughout the body.

adrenocorticotropic hormone (ACTH) (uh **dreen** oh kore tick oh **trope** ick)
A hormone produced in the pituitary gland and transmitted to the cortex of the adrenal glands; stimulates production and release of corticoids.

adrenal glands
Paired triangular endocrine glands located on the top of each kidney; site of epinephrine and corticoid production.

corticoids (**kore** tick oids)
Hormones generated by the adrenal cortex; corticoids influence the body's control of glucose, protein, and fat metabolism.

epinephrine (epp in **eff** rin)
A powerful adrenal hormone whose presence in the bloodstream prepares the body for maximal energy production and skeletal muscle response.

adrenaline
The common name for epinephrine.

metabolic rate (met uh **bol** ick)
The rate or intensity at which the body produces energy.

heart output and blood pressure and the rate and depth of breathing ensure maximal oxygenation of tissue.

Altered immune system response

At the onset of the stress response, immune system cells are mobilized as if in anticipation of bodily injury. However, during periods of prolonged stress, elevated levels of adrenal hormones appear to have a destructive effect on important cells within the immune system.[9] Infectious illnesses contracted during or shortly after long periods of stress may be directly related to the suppression of these cells, which are part of the body's immune system.

Decreased clotting time

The body prepares for injury during the stress response. Blood clotting time decreases during stress. As a consequence, blood tends to clot more easily.

Influences of Corticoids and Epinephrine on Energy Release

Increased glucose use

Because glucose is the body's most basic source of energy, an early feature of the stress response is the release of glycogen (the storage form of glucose) from its deposit sites, particularly the liver.

Increased fat use

If a stressor is not eliminated promptly, the body's supply of glucose may become depleted. The body then turns to its two remaining energy reserves, fat deposits and muscle tissue. Fat breakdown will result in the production of metabolic waste products that will eventually cause the body to use its most protected energy deposits, muscle tissue.

Muscle tissue breakdown and use

If the stressor is unusually powerful, energy demands will continue to the point that muscle tissue becomes involved. Fortunately, most of today's stressors are resolved long before this occurs.

Although in the short term all of the responses shown in Figure 3-1 are valuable when confronting a stressor, long-term exposure to these breakdown processes has a destructive effect on physical health. During the resistance phase of the stress response, the body will shift the efforts of a prolonged "fight" to specific body systems. When this shift occurs, the **psychogenic disorders** and **psychosomatic disorders** associated with chronic stress begin.

STRESS AND PSYCHOIMMUNOLOGY

In an earlier section of the chapter, the relationship of stress to both illness and the function of the immune system is briefly discussed (see p. 51). Additional information seems warranted in light of the growing interest in these topics within the scientific community.[10]

On the basis of clinical observation and laboratory studies, it is recognized that feelings associated with stress (depression and anxiety) and the disruption of social support systems relate to the weakening of the immune response and the development of some illnesses.[10] For example, a study involving self-assessment of stress levels and the occurrence of colds demonstrated that as stress levels increase, colds become more common.[11] In yet another study, immunizations were less effective in producing an immune response in students stressed by upcoming examinations than in those not scheduled to take examinations. What is not known, however, is which mechanisms certain stressors use in altering immune system function (nervous and endocrine systems ver-

HealthQuest Activities

- The *How Stressed Are You?* activity in Module 1 allows you to look at several areas of your life (including money, school, relationships, and health) and identify stress caused by events and daily hassles. You can also rate your perceived stress level for each area. Use this feature to find out which area or areas generate the highest levels of stress for you.
- The *CyberStress* Activity in Module 1 simulates a stress-filled day and can be used to help you assess your reactions to daily stressors. Choose the scenario that most closely matches your own. For example, if you work and go to school, you should check both on the preferences screen. As you are presented with stressful situations, choose the reaction that is closest to how you would react. At the feedback screen, print the screen showing your score. Then evaluate your experience by answering the questions in the *What do you think?* section.

sus nervous system only), whether studies done with immune cells removed from the body are reflective of what occurs in the body, and whether studies done with animals can be applied to humans.

In spite of these limitations, theoretical explanations for a strong relationship between stress and the absence of social support and immune system function can be made. Accordingly, a growing number of studies are under way to further clarify which pathways are involved in the stress–immune system interplay, and the use of social support therapy is becoming a component in the treatment of serious illness, such as breast cancer.

Personality Traits

Can personality play a role in making people more or less prone to stress? If so, what outlook on life is now considered to be the most stress-producing? The answer to the latter question has changed over the past two decades.

The initial, and still widely recognized, theory describing personality's role in fostering stress was that of type A and type B personalities, developed by cardiologists Friedman and Rosenman. In this model, time-dependence (hurry sickness) was related to high levels of stress and, eventually, to heart disease.

Today, the concept of time-dependence as being the most influential personality trait associated with high levels of stress has given way to concern over high levels of *anger* and *cynicism*. Anger is the intense feeling of rage and fury that accompanies unexpected change. For people who for whatever reasons seem to be always angry, the stress put on the body is detrimental to both physical and emotional health.[12] The term *angry heart* describes a condition frequently seen in people who have had a heart attack.

Closely akin to anger is cynicism, the second personality trait that fosters high levels of stress. This trait is associated with deeply held dislike and distrust of others and their ideas. Cynics have nothing good to say about others. They are, perhaps, profoundly angry about their relationships with others and can only express this feeling by being very critical. Regardless, cynicism, like anger, places the body under chronic stress and erodes the physical and emotional well-being of the cynic. Perhaps the only effective treatment for chronically angry or cynical people is either a profoundly moving personal experience that truly changes their outlook on life, such as the birth of a child, or counseling to get in touch with the reasons underlying their negative outlook.

COPING: REACTING TO STRESSORS

It is in some ways more difficult than in the past to develop appropriate and effective coping skills. No longer is it socially acceptable to escape stressors through negative dependency behavior, withdrawal, or aggressiveness. The emphasis now is on lifestyle management techniques, such as time management (see the Health Action Guide on p. 54), that are not only effective but also supportive of overall health, social relationships, and the environment.

Stress Management Techniques

Experts in stress management have proposed several effective techniques for coping with stress. Each of these techniques is described in the material that follows, with specific instructions for use provided for some. You will not know whether a particular coping technique is effective for you until you study the technique and then use it for an adequate period of time.

Self-hypnosis

Techniques for increased awareness, mental relaxation, and enhanced self-directedness are taught by trained professionals to people capable of being hypnotized. These techniques, which can be learned in one lesson, are self-administered in daily sessions lasting 10 to 20 minutes each. Beware of unqualified practitioners, who frequently sell their services through newspaper advertisements. Professional organizations, such as psychological or psychiatric societies, can recommend qualified therapists.

The relaxation response

The "relaxation response" is a relaxation technique developed by Herbert Benson, M.D., through which one learns to quiet the body and mind. Relaxation technique centers on exhalation and allowing the body to relax while sitting in a comfortable position.

psychogenic disorders Illnesses with observable symptoms that are generated by stress but are not associated with tissue change.

psychosomatic disorders (sye cho so **mat** ick) Physical illnesses of the body involving tissue change generated by the effects of stress.

Time Management

Many college students think that the most significant problem about being a student is everything that can interfere with the academic side of school, including campus activities, athletics, work, marriage, parenting, and just having free time for relaxation. Therefore, too often perhaps, choices regarding time are made in ways that cause classroom work to be more stressful than it should be. Ultimately, however, it becomes an issue of priorities and the management of time so that academic demands can be met sufficiently.

Although there is no single best approach to managing time, most experts suggest that the following should be helpful:

1. Keep a log of how you use your time for 1 week. Make an entry about each half hour to see what you are doing.

2. Analyze your records, and eliminate those activities that unnecessarily take too much time.

3. Once the eliminations have been made, divide your time into blocks so that related activities can be scheduled together. There should be a block for each major area of responsibility applicable to you. Examples might include academics, employment, recreation, and social activities.

4. Schedule specific activities within each block of time. Attempt to conclude activities that you have started.

Reassess your time management activities occasionally, and make adjustments when necessary.[13]

◀━━━━━━▶

This technique can be learned in a single session but requires a commitment to making time to practice. Relatively effective for most people, the technique is described in Dr. Benson's book, *The Relaxation Response*.

Progressive muscular relaxation

Pioneered by the work of Edmund Johnson (author of *You Must Relax*), progressive muscle relaxation (PMR) is a procedure in which each of several muscle groups is systematically contracted and relaxed. By learning to recognize the difference between contracted and relaxed muscles, Johnson believed that people would be able to purposely place certain mus-

cles into a controlled state of stress-reducing relaxation.

PMR is based on the appropriate use of positioning, breathing, and concentration. The position of choice is lying on the floor, with the hands at the sides and palms facing upward. Once a comfortable position has been assumed, alternating periods of inhalation and exhalation are begun. As a person inhales, the muscles are contracted, whereas during exhalation, muscle groups are relaxed. Concentration is focused on the "feelings" of relaxation that accompany the release of tension during each exhalation. Once mastered, the basics of participation can be carried out in almost every setting, including a moving car, at work at one's desk, and in a college classroom. Depending on a person's levels of expertise, contractions last from a maximum of 100 seconds, through 50 seconds, to a minimum of 5 seconds. The face, jaw, neck, shoulders, upper chest, hands and forearms, abdomen, lower back, buttocks, thighs, calves, and

Periods of reduced stress are vital for mental health.

Reducing Stress

Many of us are looking for ways to reduce stress in our lives, whether we do it by exercising, reading self-help books, performing relaxation exercises, or seeing a therapist. Is peace of mind illusive, or is it achievable in today's society?

Stress is experienced by all people, regardless of culture. The Lebanese, for example, purchase "worry beads" and handle them for periods of time to help them deal with anger or anxiety. If one were to visit Lebanon, the clicking of beads might be a commonly heard sound.[14]

Perhaps we can learn from the Far Eastern cultures and their ways of dealing with stress. Eastern people seem to understand the concept of inner peace, and they work and practice to develop it. Many Japanese, through self-discipline and training, learn to block out outside disturbances and stressors. This practice is described as achieving tranquility.[15]

Tranquility does not come naturally to the Japanese. It is learned through very specific exercises. The exercises consist of three levels: stillness of the body, breathing, and the center of being. It is not known exactly how these exercises originated, but it has been suggested that they are derived from the practices of Buddhist monks and Shinto priests.[15]

For the Japanese, the idea of tranquility seems to be a way of life and a goal to achieve. Does one have to be from the Eastern culture to understand the concept of tranquility, or is it a practice that those of us from Western society can learn and internalize? 🐜

---

feet are tightened and then relaxed progressively. To the extent possible, each muscle group within the area is included.

Quieting

Quieting involves using a set of specific responses, such as striving for a positive mental state, an "inner smile," and a deep exhalation, with the tongue and the shoulders relaxed, immediately on sensing the onset of stress. This technique can be practiced at any time; it is easily learned and supplies immediate feelings of being "on top of stress." The technique can be learned by reading *QR: The Quieting Reflex,* by Charles Stroebel, M.D., Ph.D.

Yoga

An ancient exercise program for the mind and body, yoga can be learned from a qualified instructor in 1 to 3 months. Yoga is practiced daily in a quiet setting in sessions lasting 15 to 45 minutes. It can alter specific physiological functions, enhance flexibility, and free the mind from worry. Many good yoga books, classes, and videotapes are available.

Diaphragmatic breathing

A coping technique with elements of both relaxation and quieting is diaphragmatic breathing (Figure 3-2). Aspects of this practice are seen in the Lamaze approach to childbirth, yoga, and t'ai chi. Although no single explanation for its effectiveness can be given, when practiced regularly, diaphragmatic breathing produces relaxation that buffers the powerful stress response. A three-component approach to the practice of diaphragmatic breathing is described below:

1. **Assume a comfortable position.** Lie on the floor with arms by your sides, eyes closed, back straight. Begin breathing from the diaphragm, rather than by the normal method of lifting the chest.

2. **Concentrate.** The ability to concentrate is important in diaphragmatic breathing. This can be difficult but is most easily mastered by following the flow of air as it enters the body and flows deeply into the lower levels of the lungs, followed by the rising of the stomach as the air leaves the lungs. Each ventilation can be fragmented into four distinct steps: (1) take air into your lungs through the nose and mouth, (2) pause slightly before exhaling, (3) release the air to flow out via the path from which it entered, and (4) pause slightly after exhalation before repeating step 1.

3. **Visualize.** Diaphragmatic breathing promotes relaxation most fully when it is practiced in conjunction with visualization. What is visualized varies from person to person, but many feel that envisioning the air or even clouds entering the body with each breath, traveling down the path taken by the air, and leaving through the nostrils is very effective. Extending the image of the air flowing through the entire body (energy breathing) rather than only into the lungs is even more effective.

Once mastered, diaphragmatic breathing will quiet the body. Experienced users of this technique can temporarily lower their breathing rate from a typical rate of 14 to 18 breaths per minute to a few as four breaths per minute. In doing so, the entire nervous system is

1. Assume a Comfortable Position
Breathe from the diaphragm rather than by lifting the chest, as a person normally breathes.

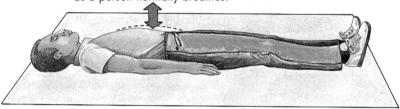

2. Concentrate
Focus on the flow of air as it moves deeply into the lower levels of the lungs, followed by the rising of the stomach as the air leaves.

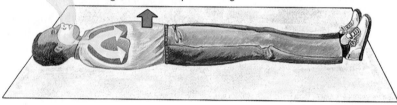

3. Visualize
Visualize the air flowing through the entire body, rather than only into the lungs.

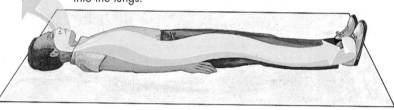

Figure 3-2   Diaphragmatic breathing.

slowed, in direct opposition to its role in the stress response.

Transcendental meditation

Transcendental meditation (TM) allows the mind to transcend thought effortlessly when the person recites a mantra, or a personal word, twice daily for 20 minutes. TM is a seven-step program that is taught by trained professionals. TM centers are listed in the telephone directory under Transcendental Meditation.

Biofeedback

Biofeedback is a system for monitoring and subsequently controlling specific physiological functions, such as heart rate, respiratory rate, and body temperature. Training with an experienced instructor and appropriate monitoring instruments requires weekly sessions that last 1 hour or longer over a period of 12 or more weeks. When used with other tension reduction techniques, biofeedback provides concrete reinforcement of stress-reduction goals. For more infor-

mation, contact the Biofeedback Society of America, 4301 Owens Street, Wheat Ridge, CO 80033.

Exercise

A wide variety of movement activities are intended to reduce stress, expend energy, promote relaxation, provide enjoyment through social contact and, possibly, promote the formation of biological opiates. Running, jogging, lap swimming, walking, rope skipping, biking, stair climbing, and aerobic dancing workouts are all excellent ways to burn the energy produced by the stress response. Equipment needs, facilities, and required skills vary. Three to four sessions per week lasting a half hour per session are sufficient for most people. Health and fitness clubs offer exercise programs.

Health Practices and Stress

Beyond practicing the variety of stress reduction techniques and time management skills described in this chapter, one's health is important in the management of stress. There is little doubt that people who lead a wellness-oriented lifestyle have an advantage in dealing with stress. When people are rested, well conditioned, healthfully nourished, seen regularly by health care professionals, often in the company of friends, and secure in their beliefs, the demands imposed by change are more manageable. In fact, health, in combination with a realistic outlook on life such as that described in the next section, may be the basis on which all successful coping is built.

A Realistic Perspective on Stress and Life

Although we would like our lives to be stress-free, reality dictates otherwise. Therefore it is desirable that we approach life with a tough-minded optimism that provides a sense of hope and anticipation, as well as an understanding that life will never be without stress. The development of this realistic approach to today's fast-paced, demanding lifestyle may best be achieved by fostering many of the perspectives listed below:[16]

- **Do not be surprised by trouble.** Anticipate problems, and see yourself as a problem solver.
- **Search for solutions.** Act on a partial solution, even when a complete solution seems distant.
- **Take control of your own future.** Set out to accomplish all of your goals. Do not view yourself as a victim of circumstances.
- **Move away from negative thought patterns.** Do not extend or generalize difficulties from one area into another.
- **Rehearse success.** Do not disregard the possibility of failure. Rather, focus on the things that are necessary and possible to ensure success.
- **Accept the unchangeable.** The direction your life takes is only in part the result of your own doing. Cope as effectively as possible with the events over which you have no direct control.
- **Live each day well.** Combine activity, contemplation, and a sense of cheerfulness with the many things that must be done each day. Celebrate special occasions.
- **Act on your capacity for growth.** Undertake new experiences, and then extract from them new information about your interests and abilities.
- **Allow for renewal.** Make time for yourself, and take advantage of opportunities to pursue new and fulfilling relationships. Foster growth of your spiritual nature.
- **Tolerate mistakes.** Both you and others will make mistakes. Recognize that these can cause

Activity 1

Almost every day on a college campus, people can be heard commenting about how much stress they are under. Because people are unique, a stressor for one person might not be a stressor for another. Rating your stress requires you to inventory the stressors in your life and determine whether you are susceptible to stress. Go to the Thrive on-line website document at http://cgi.pathfinder.com/cgi-bin/GDML/gdmldb/thrive?stresslife and answer the questions about stress. The quiz consists of two parts: the first part measures your stressors and the second part assesses your level of susceptibility to stress.

Activity 2

The initial and still widely recognized theory describing the role of personality in fostering stress was that of type A and type B personalities, developed by cardiologists Friedman and Rosenman. People who have type A personalities are at higher risk of developing coronary artery disease. Type in the URL http://www.psychtests.com/typea.html to determine whether you have a Type A personality. Answer each of the 17 questions listed and then click on "submit" to receive your on-line score.

Activity 3

In college and university settings, stressors can arise from a variety of areas, including looking for a job, applying for acceptance into graduate or professional school, and, of course, recognizing the rapid approach of "real world" responsibilities. Go to http://www.queendom.com/test_frm.html and scroll down to the "Mental and Emotional Health" category. Select the "Stress Indicator Test" to see how vulnerable you may be to the stress of job hunting. Complete the 20-question test and submit your answers to receive your score on-line.

anger or frustration, and learn to avoid feelings of hostility.

With a realistic and positive outlook on life, you will need less coping time to live a satisfying and productive life. Change in all aspects of life is inevitable. In the presence of good health, change should be anticipated, nurtured, and then incorporated into the maturing sense of well-being.

Summary

- Stress is the physiological and emotional response to the presence of a stressor. Stressors are events that generate the stress response.
- Distress and eustress reflect similar physiological responses but different emotional interpretations.
- Uncontrolled stress can lead to a variety of illnesses. Since the effects of stress are cumulative, stress-related health problems can develop slowly.
- The college experience can generate stressors from several different areas, including finances, classroom requirements, and personal expectations.
- Day-to-day living is routinely the source of many types of stressors.
- The general adaptation syndrome consists of three distinct stages: alarm, resistance, and exhaustion. Hopefully, exhaustion from excessive stress will not occur, and recovery will follow.
- An intricate interplay involving the brain, nervous system, and endocrine system results in a series of physiological changes that prepare the body to respond to stressors.
- The stress response mobilizes energy for the fight-or-flight response.
- Critical to the stress response are the senses, the cerebral cortex, the hypothalamus, the adrenal glands, the hormone ACTH, corticoids, and epinephrine.
- Stress influences the function of the immune system, resulting in susceptibility to illnesses.
- Chronic feelings of anger and cynicism can be central to feelings of stress.
- A variety of coping techniques can be easily learned and may prove to be beneficial in reducing stress.
- An optimistic outlook on life may protect some people from the potentially damaging effects of stressors. Further, a less stressful life enhances health and provides a greater sense of well-being.

Review Questions

1. What is the difference between stress and stressors?
2. How do distress and eustress differ? In what way are they similar?
3. What are several of the more familiar health conditions attributed to chronic unresolved stress? To what extent are the effects of stress cumulative?
4. In what way does the college experience contribute to the stress level of students? What life experience do typical Americans report as being most stressful?
5. In what predictable manner does the stress response unfold? What is the role of the endocrine system? How do the digestive and cardiovascular systems contribute to the fight-or-flight response?
6. What is psychoimmunology? To date, what has research found in regard to immune function and the occurrence of stress?
7. How has the popular type A/type B theory of time-dependence changed in regard to the cause of stress? In what manner do anger and cynicism contribute to stress? How do type R persons use the stress response?
8. What coping techniques have proved helpful when used on a regular basis? How are progressive muscular relaxation and diaphragmatic breathing practiced?
9. What traits characterize the optimistic lifestyle?

🔦 Think About This . . .

- Can you remember a stressful experience you recently had in which your body responses clearly followed the pattern of Selye's general adaptation syndrome? How long did you remain in each of the specific stages?
- If the body's response to stressors is similar for distress and eustress, how do we learn to distinguish between the two?
- Do you have a realistic perception about the potential stressful nature of life?
- Which dimension of your health (physical, emotional, social, occupational, intellectual, or spiritual) do you most frequently rely on when you are confronted with a stressful situation?
- If you believe that the enhancement of your stress management skills will be important to you in the future, which of the suggested approaches to coping with stress could you most comfortably develop? When can you start to develop these skills?

References

1. Selye H: *Stress without distress,* New York, 1975, New American Library.
2. Blonna R: *Stress management,* St. Louis, 1996, Mosby.
3. Seaward BL: *Managing stress: principles and strategies for health and wellbeing,* Boston, 1994, Jones & Bartlett.
4. Benjamin J., et al: Population and familial association between the D4 dopamine receptor gene and measures of novelty seeking. *Nature Genetics,* 12(1):81–84, Jan. 1996.
5. Julius M, et al: Anger-coping types, blood pressure, and all causes of mortality: a follow-up in Tecumseh, Michigan (1971–1983), *Am J Epidemiol,* 124:220–233, 1986.
6. McGinnis J: *Medicine for the layman: behavioral patterns and health,* US Department of Health and Human Services, NIH Pub No 85–2682, Washington, DC, 1986, US Government Printing Office.
7. Van De Graaff, KM: *Human anatomy,* New York, 1998, WCB/McGraw-Hill.
8. Mader S: *Understanding human anatomy & physiology* (3rd ed), New York, 1997, WCB/McGraw-Hill.
9. O'Leary A: Stress, emotion, and human immune function, *Psychol Bull,* 108(3):335–363, 1990.
10. Vitkovic L, Koslow SH, editors: *Neuroimmunology and mental health,* NIH Pub No 94-3274, US Department of Health and Human Services, Public Health Service, National Institute of Health, Rockville, MD, 1994, US Government Printing Office.
11. Cohen S, et al: Psychological stress and susceptibility to the common cold, *N Engl J Med,* 325:606–612, 1991.
12. Almada SJ, et al: Neuroticism and cynicism and risk of death in middle-aged men: the Western Electric study, *Psychosom Med,* 53(2):165–175, 1991.
13. Hedrick LH: *355 ways to save time* (Time Warner Quick Reads), New York, 1995, Warner Books.
14. Cahill MJ: *Lebanon,* New York, 1987, Chelsea House.
15. Durchkeim, K: *The Japanese cult of tranquility,* York Beach, ME, 1991, Samuel Weiser.
16. McGinnis L: *The power of optimism,* New York, 1990, Harper & Row.

Suggested Readings

Eliot RE: *From stress to strength: How to lighten your load and save your life,* New York: Bantam Books, 1994.
NICE factors, derived from new, interesting, challenging experiences, reduce the incipient factors that are responsible for the anger that many people continuously carry around. The author suggests a variety of ways in which "hot reactors" can be gradually "cooled" through controlling anger. An easy-to-use assessment intended to identify sources of stress (and anger) is provided, including directions for quantifying levels of stress.

O'Grady D: *Taking the fear out of change,* Rainier, WA: Adams Publishing, 1995.
Although change can frequently be the source of stress, the absence of change can be equally stressful for many people. The author describes multiple reasons people fear change and the problems these fears create. In addition, techniques for fostering change are discussed, including the need for psychotherapy when the fear of change is incapacitating.

Seymour T: *31 days to increase your stress,* Vancouver, BC, 1997, Adventure Publishing.

Most of us know people who are too stressed to realize how stressed they really are. For these people, being stressed is the rule, rather than the exception. Using sarcastic humor, this book will allow readers to see how they appear to others and to recognize the possibility that they could enjoy a less stressful life.

The book of calm, New York, 1997, Time Life.
As the title implies, the physical, spiritual, and emotional key to effective stress management is calming the mind by calming the body. This informative book explains the role of calming techniques, such as relaxation, aromatherapy, massage, meditation, and yoga, and shows how to apply them. The current increased interest in and understanding of alternative healing practices makes this book very timely.

Hendrie W: *Anger at work: Learning the art of anger management on the job,* New York, 1996, William Morrow & Co.
The author of this book draws on fifteen years' experience with anger management to share usable approaches to dealing with difficult people at work, such as a boss who manages with an iron fist.

 # AS WE GO TO PRESS . . .

Early in 1998, a special White House panel investigating Gulf War syndrome concluded that battlefield stress was almost certainly a contributing factor to the illness, which may affect as many as 50,000 Gulf War veterans. The panel said current scientific evidence does not link the veterans' ailments to any specific environmental contaminant in the Persian Gulf, including pesticides, nerve gas, and oil well fires. However, Gulf War veterans' groups questioned the panel's findings, particularly the suggestion that wartime stress may explain the syndrome. The White House panel and the Pentagon will continue to investigate the causes of the illness.

Managing Work-Related Stress

When someone is introduced to you, the first bit of information you learn is the person's name. More often than not, the next part of the introduction will have some mention of that person's occupation, and at the very least you will have some idea about the person's job within the first few minutes of conversation. Americans often identify people with the jobs they perform, and much of our own self-identity is linked with our occupations. As a result, anything that threatens our jobs or our job performance is also a threat to our sense of personal worth.[1]

Job stress is becoming a part of everyday life. It affects society as a whole in a variety of ways, contributing to rising health care costs, increasing insurance rates, and decreasing national productivity.[2] If left unchecked, work-related stress can have profound effects on the physical and mental health of individuals as well.

Sources of Job Stress

Since we so often attach our jobs to our sense of self-worth, work-related stress can be an important problem in our daily lives. It is therefore important to identify things that can cause stress in the workplace (job stressors), and, when possible, deal with them in a healthy manner. Common job stressors include the following[1-4]:

- Conflicts with colleagues, supervisors, or workers under your supervision
- Changes in work routine
- Deadlines
- Too much (or too little) responsibility
- Lack of control over work methods and planning
- Long working hours
- Repetitive tasks
- Excessive or rhythmic noise
- Poor time management or organization
- Working with hazardous equipment or substances
- Threat of pay reduction or unemployment
- Lack of necessary resources

These are factors that nearly everyone has to deal with at one time or another in the workplace. These stressors may vary from job to job, and individuals react in different ways to these stimuli, but we are all usually affected in some way by job stressors.

Job Stress Among Older Workers

Although workers of any age can succumb to stress in the workplace, older workers in general are hit the hardest by job stress.[5] Technological advances tend to cause more stress for older workers, especially those who have been performing a similar routine for a long time and are suddenly forced to assimilate new technology into their daily work. Older workers are also prime targets for lay-offs. They have worked their way up the pay scale and in general are paid a higher wage than their younger counterparts. As a result, many older workers are leaving the workforce at an earlier age than they normally would because of increased stress.[5]

Stress in the Modern Workplace

Stress in the workplace has increased greatly over the last 15 years. Corporate mergers and buyouts have eliminated entire companies and thousands of jobs, new technology has caused a drastic increase in work pace, and the competitiveness of the modern economy has forced individual employees to take on much heavier workloads.[5]

Technology

Today's worker has to deal with stressors that are unique to the times we live in. The most obvious of these is the drastic increase in workplace technology. Increased mechanical efficiency leads to the need for fewer workers but requires employees to become more knowledgeable concerning the new machines they work with.[2,4] Personal computers and computer networks, although increasing workplace efficiency and speed, are themselves contributors to job stress. Increased work speed is a double-edged sword. Getting more work done within a specified time may mean more profit for a company, but it also leads to the expectation that more work will always be accomplished in less time. Computers drastically reduce the time needed to perform tasks, but the person running the computer may then be asked to perform more tasks within the workday, causing stress. Workers are also asked to know about the many uses of various computer software programs, which are constantly being changed and improved. The constant upgrading of computer programs requires that employees be reeducated continually to keep up. The increased productivity provided by the computer may lead to the elimination of many jobs, since one worker may now be able to do the work of two or more.

The computer itself may also contribute to physical problems. The monitor of the computer may cause eyestrain, headaches, fatigue, and muscle tension.[4] Constant work on a keyboard may place excess stress on fingers, hands, and wrists. This in turn may contribute to arthritic conditions or to the newly recognized affliction known as *carpal tunnel syndrome*. The simple act of sitting at the computer for extended periods with the body in a fixed position can put stress on the muscles and bones of the back, neck, and limbs.[3, 4]

Afflictions such as these, which are caused by repetitive motions, unusual body postures, or holding static joint positions over extended periods, are now referred to as *repetitive strain injuries* (RSIs). The risk of developing RSIs is increased during periods of emotional stress or while trying to beat a deadline.[6] RSIs can also develop because of improper placement of equipment (such as a keyboard) or by certain work practices.[6] Company production goals based on quotas, such as counting workers' keystrokes throughout the day, can force employees to work through needed break periods to meet the expected work output; this in turn can increase the risk of RSI development.

Downsizing
The current corporate trend of eliminating jobs to cut costs—"downsizing"—has contributed greatly to the problem of job stress. This practice affects not only rank-and-file workers but employees in management as well. Often cuts are made with little or no regard to an employee's years of service or experience (or because of this, to save money), so anyone on the payroll may be vulnerable. This lack of job security has been an important contributor to job stress over the last decade.

Although the current popularity of downsizing may be unprecedented, the effects of the fear of unemployment have been studied as early as the 1960s. For example, from 1965 to 1973 the workforce at Cape Canaveral was downsized from 65,000 employees to 32,000.[1] Aerospace workers, highly trained and highly paid, were being laid off in large numbers as the government cut back on the space program. With few skills that could be transferred to other jobs, many found themselves bagging groceries and taking tickets for a living.[1] The fear of being unemployed and the difficult transition after being laid off caused many physical and mental problems for Cape Canaveral workers and their families. Because of the heavy stress, these families suffered from anxiety and depression and led the nation in divorce rates, drinking, drug use, and sudden heart attack deaths.[1] Autopsies on these heart attack victims, some of whom were as young as 29, showed that no significant risk factors were present except for high levels of chemicals (such as epinephrine) that are released in response to stress.[1]

The situation that these aerospace workers were faced with is now happening in workplaces across the nation. Recent layoffs have occurred at many major corporations across the United States, and many of these are a direct result of corporate downsizing. AT&T, the telecommunications giant, is planning to lay off approximately 40,000 employees by the end of 1998, with up to 30,000 of those

cuts coming in 1996.[7] Other major corporations, such as IBM, McDonnell Douglas, and Apple Computer, have had layoffs in recent years as well.

Competition

Although there are more than enough jobs being created to replace those lost through downsizing, these new jobs offer lower pay, fewer benefits, and less desirable working conditions. As a result, competition for good jobs is growing stiffer.[8] A college education, which used to be a can't-miss ticket to a well-paying and rewarding job, is now merely a ticket to enter the fiercely competitive contest that is today's job market. Over 20% of adults hold at least a bachelor's degree, and over 40% of adults have some college experience. The most current statistics available (1994-95 academic year) indicate that over 14 million students are currently enrolled at institutions of higher education.[9] Workers whose jobs are cut are facing competition from new college graduates, who will often work for less money, as well as from others who have been laid off. New graduates, on the other hand, are competing with displaced workers, who usually have a wealth of work experience.

All of this uncertainty in the workplace has led many people to broaden their knowledge to become more competitive within their chosen field, or to change careers altogether. This has meant booming business for colleges and universities. According to the most current data available, over 26% of all college students enrolled in the United States were over the age of 24.[9] Many of these nontraditional students (and a great many traditional-age students) face the challenge of succeeding at school while trying to raise a family or hold down a job at the same time. Job stress is thus compounded with classroom stress. Even though the task seems daunting, more and more students are willing to try. It is not uncommon for students to attend classes either before or after working a full shift at a regular job.

Reducing Work-Related Stress

The changing climate of today's economy, marked by expanding technology, increasing demands on the individual, and decreasing job security, is taking its toll on the American worker. Since work-related stress appears to be increasing in nearly all professions, it is more important than ever to be able to recognize the physical signs of stress and to be able to reduce job stress when possible. Here are a few things you can do to reduce the effects of work-related stress:[1-4]

- Recognize when stress is getting to you. Be able to identify early warning signs that you may be under heavy stress. Emotional signs may include anxiety, lack of interest, and irritability. Mental fatigue, physical exhaustion, and frequent illness may be physical manifestations of stress as well. Not everyone reacts to stressful situations in the same way, so know yourself well enough to recognize when stressors are affecting you.
- Control your environment when you can. Not every work situation can be controlled, but controlling some situations can help reduce stress. Try not to schedule stressful work activities for the same time. Break larger jobs down into smaller parts. If it is safe to do so, rearrange your work area to keep things fresh.
- Know the things you cannot control and deal with them. Not even a CEO is under total control of his or her job. Becoming angry or obsessed over a situation you can't do anything about only increases your stress level. Developing a more flexible attitude toward situations on the job that are not flexible can be a very healthy thing to do.
- Take a break. Schedule some down time to keep yourself refreshed. If your breaks are scheduled for you, don't use them to get extra work done. Your physical and mental health can be helped immensely by taking advantage of your time off. When performing repetitive tasks, step away from the task whenever you can. If you work at a computer terminal, get up occasionally and move around.
- Get some exercise. Physical activity can be healthy for the mind and the body. Exercise can actually increase energy levels and increase physical resistance to stress.
- Make your workplace safe. Stress resulting from hazardous situations can be reduced by taking safety precautions when possible. If safety equipment is available, make use of it. Use a shade screen on your computer monitor if possible to reduce eyestrain and headaches. Staying safe on the job can prevent stressful situations that may occur because of an injury, such as missed work, decreased productivity, and physical pain.

If stress on the job seems to be greatly affecting you physically or mentally, it is important that you see your family doctor or a qualified mental health professional as soon as possible. Although everyone experiences some type of stress as a result of the workplace, this stress does not have to become an overwhelming factor in your life. Managing work-related stressors is an important skill that all employees of today must learn to master, so take some time to assess your problems and devise some strategies to deal with your stressful situations.

References

1. Eliot RS, Breo DL: *Is it worth dying for?* New York, 1984, Bantam Books.

2. Goliszek AG: *Breaking the stress habit,* Winston-Salem, NC, 1987, Carolina Press.

3. Gardell B: Efficiency and health hazards in mechanized work. In Quick et al, editors: *Work stress: health care systems in the workplace,* New York, 1987, Prager.

4. Haynes SG et al: The effect of high job demands and low control on the health of employed women. In Quick et al, editors: *Work stress: health care systems in the workplace,* New York, 1987, Prager.

5. Williams G: Flaming out on the job: How to recognize when it's all too much, *Modern Maturity,* 34(5), 1991.

6. Williamson E: Caught in the grip of RSI: a first-hand account, *Managing Office Technology,* 39(5), 1994.

7. "John Doe." American Telephone and Telegraph employee. Personal interview, January 29, 1996.

8. Church GJ: Are we better off? *Time,* 147(5), Jan 29, 1996.

9. U.S. Bureau of the Census, *Statistical abstract of the United States: 1997* (117th ed), Washington, D.C.

PART 2

THE BODY

4

Becoming Physically Fit

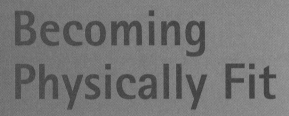

Healthy People: Looking Ahead to 2010

Many of the *Healthy People 2000* objectives
focused on getting Americans to increase their
participation in activities that improve cardiorespiratory fitness. With an estimated 250,000 deaths
per year in the United States attributable to the lack
of physical activity, encouraging our sedentary
society to become more active is clearly important.

The *Midcourse Review* concluded that progress
toward achieving these objectives has been mixed. A
somewhat higher percentage of adults now engage
in moderate to vigorous physical activity. However,
no progress has been made in reducing the percentage of adults who do not participate in leisure-time
physical activity. The objective of increasing the
number of worksite fitness programs has been fully
achieved.

Unfortunately, the nation has lost ground in several areas. For example, since 1990 the percentage of
students in grades 9 through 12 involved in physical
education courses has decreased. The proportion of
time that students are physically active during these
class periods has also dropped. The *Healthy People
2010* document is expected to address these serious
concerns.

When your day begins early in the morning, then you go to class or work or immerse yourself in family activities, and your day does not end until after midnight, you must be physically fit to keep up the pace. Even a highly motivated college student must have a conditioned, rested body to maintain such a schedule.

OK, let's simplify things a bit. The paragraph above reflects how college health professors might view the value of fitness—it helps people function well enough to cope with their hectic lifestyles. But what motivates students to value fitness? Quite simply, students say that overall body fitness helps them look and feel better.

Many college students want to look in the mirror and see the kind of body they see in the media: one with well-toned muscles, a trim waistline, and an absence of flabby tissue, especially on the arms and legs. Students become motivated to start fitness programs because they hope that they can build a better body for themselves. Through their efforts to do so, students usually start to feel better, both physically and mentally. They realize that change is possible, since they see it happening to their bodies with each passing week. "Go for it" and "just do it" then become more than just sports marketing phrases; they become reminders that the activities that lead to fitness are a meaningful part of their lives. Fitness actually becomes *fun*.

Fortunately, you do not have to be a top-notch athlete to receive the health benefits of physical activity. In fact, even a modest increase in your daily activity level can be rewarding. The health benefits of fitness can come from regular participation in moderate exercise, such as brisk walking or dancing.[1]

Your increase in physical activity will not only help you; it can help the nation to achieve its *Healthy People 2000* objectives. Further, although fitness will not guarantee you a longer life, it can help you enjoy the years that you have.

COMPONENTS OF PHYSICAL FITNESS

Physical fitness is achieved when "the organic systems of the body are healthy and function efficiently so as to resist disease, to enable the fit person to engage in vigorous tasks and leisure activities, and to handle situations of emergency."[2] In the following sections, we discuss cardiorespiratory endurance, muscular strength, muscular endurance, flexibility, and body composition.

Cardiorespiratory Endurance

If you were limited to improving only one area of your physical fitness, which would you choose—muscular strength, muscular endurance, or flexibility? Which would a dancer choose? Which would a marathon runner select? Which would an expert recommend?

We think the experts, who are exercise physiologists, would say that another fitness dimension is of even greater importance than those listed above. These research scientists regard improvement of your heart, lung, and blood vessel function as the key focal point of a physical fitness program. **Cardiorespiratory endurance** forms the foundation for whole-body fitness.

Cardiorespiratory endurance increases your capacity to sustain a given level of energy production for a

 # HealthQuest Activities

- The *How Fit Are You?* exercise in Module 2 will help you determine your current level of fitness in four major areas: body composition, cardiorespiratory capacity, muscular strength, and flexibility. Complete the series of questions about how much you exercise, what types of training you do, how intensely you exercise, and body size. After you complete the questions, *HealthQuest* will give you feedback in each of the four areas mentioned above. Then develop an individual plan for improving or maintaining your current fitness level.

- The *Exercise Interest Inventory* in Module 2 allows you to rate your feelings about certain aspects of exercise. *HealthQuest* provides feedback about the activities and exercises you would most enjoy, based on your individual needs and preferences. First, write down the five fitness activities that you like best or in which you most often participate. After each one, indicate your motivation for engaging in that particular activity. For example, you could list "enjoyment," "habit," or "convenience." When you have completed the *Exercise Interest Inventory*, compare the two lists. Are there any surprises? What factors had you not considered to be influential in your choice of exercise?

cardiorespiratory endurance (**car** dee oh **ress** pur uh tory)
The ability of the heart, lungs, and blood vessels to process and transport oxygen required by muscle cells so that they can contract over a period of time.

Cardiorespiratory endurance is produced by physical activity that requires continuous, repetitive movements.

short-duration activities that quickly cause muscle fatigue; they are generally considered anaerobic activities.

Activities that are not generally associated with anaerobic energy production (walking, distance jogging, and bicycle touring) become anaerobic activities when they are either increased in intensity or continued for an extended period.

If you usually work or play at low intensity but for a long duration, you have developed an ability to maintain **aerobic (with oxygen) energy production.** As long as your body can meet its energy demands in this oxygen-rich mode, it will not convert to anaerobic energy production. Thus fatigue will not be an important factor in determining whether you can continue to participate. Marathon runners, serious joggers, distance swimmers, bikers, and aerobic dancers can perform because of their highly developed aerobic fitness. The cardiorespiratory systems of these aerobically fit people take in, transport, and use oxygen in the most efficient manner possible.

Besides allowing you to participate in activities such as those mentioned, aerobic conditioning (cardiorespiratory endurance conditioning) may also provide certain structural and functional benefits that affect other dimensions of your life. These recognized benefits (see the Star Box on p. 69) have received considerable documented support. Some data, for example, strongly suggest that aerobic fitness can increase life expectancy[3] and reduce the risk of developing cancer of the colon, heart, uterus, cervix, and ovaries.[4]

Muscular Strength

Muscular strength is essential for your body to accomplish *work.* Your ability to maintain posture, walk, lift, push, and pull are familiar examples of the constant demands you make on your muscles to maintain or increase their level of *contraction.* The stronger you are, the greater your ability to contract muscles and maintain a level of contraction sufficient to complete tasks.

Muscular strength can best be improved by training activities that use the **overload principle.** By overloading, or gradually increasing the resistance (load, object, or weight) your muscles must move, you can increase your muscular strength. The following three types of training exercises are based on the overload principle.

In **isometric** (meaning "same measure") **exercises,** the resistance is so great that your contracting mus-

prolonged period. Development of cardiorespiratory endurance helps your body to work longer and at greater levels of intensity.

Your body cannot always produce the energy it needs for long-term activity. Certain activities require performance at a level of intensity that will outstrip your cardiorespiratory system's ability to transport oxygen efficiently to contracting muscle fibers. When the oxygen demands of the muscles cannot be met, **oxygen debt** occurs. Any activity that continues beyond the point at which oxygen debt begins requires a form of energy production that does not depend on oxygen.

This oxygen-deprived form of energy production is called **anaerobic (without oxygen) energy production,** the type that fuels many intense, short-duration activities. For example, rope climbing, weight lifting for strength, and sprinting are

Structural and Functional Benefits of Cardiorespiratory (Aerobic) Fitness

Aerobic fitness can help you do the following:
- Complete and enjoy your daily activities
- Strengthen and increase the efficiency of your heart muscle
- Increase the proportion of high-density lipoproteins in your blood
- Increase the capillary network in your body
- Improve **collateral circulation**
- Control your weight
- Stimulate bone growth
- Cope with stressors
- Ward off infections
- Improve the efficiency of your other body systems
- Bolster your self-esteem
- Achieve self-directed fitness goals
- Reduce negative dependence behavior
- Sleep better
- Recover more quickly from common illnesses
- Meet people with similar interests
- Receive reduced insurance premiums

cles cannot move the resistant object at all. Thus your muscles contract against immovable objects, usually with increasingly greater efforts (Figure 4-1). Because of the difficulty of precisely evaluating the training effects, isometric exercises are not usually used as a primary means of developing muscular strength and can be dangerous for people with hypertension.

Progressive resistance exercises, also called *isotonic* or *same-tension* exercises, are currently the most popular type of strength-building exercises. Progressive resistance exercises include the use of traditional free weights (dumbbells and barbells), as well as Universal and Nautilus machines. People who perform progressive resistance exercises use various muscle groups to move (or lift) specific fixed resistances or weights. Although during a given repetitive exercise the weight resistance remains the same, the muscular contraction effort required varies according to the joint angles in the *range of motion.*[2] The greatest effort is required at the start and finish of the movement.

Isokinetic (meaning "same motion") **exercises** use mechanical devices that provide resistances that consistently overload muscles throughout the entire range of motion. The resistance will move only at a preset speed regardless of the force applied to it. For the exercise to be effective, a user must apply maximal force.[2] Isokinetic training requires elaborate, expensive equipment.

Thus the use of isokinetic equipment may be limited to certain athletic teams, diagnostic centers, or rehabilitation clinics. The most common isokinetic machines are Cybex, Orthotron, Mini-Gym, and Exergenie.

oxygen debt
The physical state that occurs when the body can no longer process and transport sufficient amounts of oxygen for continued muscle contraction.

anaerobic energy production
The body's means of energy production when the necessary amount of oxygen is not available.

aerobic energy production
The body's means of energy production when the respiratory and circulatory systems are able to process and transport a sufficient amount of oxygen to muscle cells.

collateral circulation
The ability of nearby blood vessels to enlarge and carry additional blood around a blocked blood vessel.

muscular strength
The ability to contract skeletal muscles to engage in work; the force that a muscle can exert.

overload principle
The principle whereby a person gradually increases the resistance load that must be moved or lifted; this principle also applies to other types of fitness training.

isometric exercises (eye so **met** rick)
Muscular strength training exercises in which the resistance is so great that the object cannot be moved.

progressive resistance exercises
Muscular strength training exercises in which traditional barbells and dumbbells with fixed resistances are used.

isokinetic exercises (**eye** so kin **et** ick)
Muscular strength training exercises in which machines are used to provide variable resistances throughout the full range of motion.

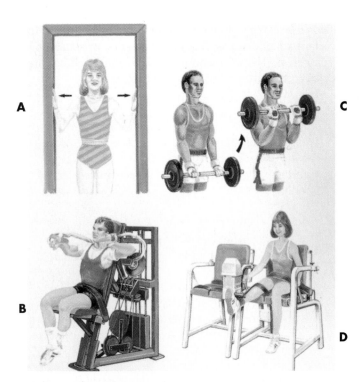

Figure 4-1 Three types of training exercises to improve muscular strength. **A,** Isometric exercise. **B** and **C,** Progressive resistance exercises. **D,** Isokinetic exercise. Exercise is important to the cardiorespiratory system at any age.

Which type of strength-building exercise (machines or free weights) is most effective? Take your choice, since all will help develop muscular strength. Some people prefer machines because they are simple to use, do not require stacking the weights, and are already balanced and less likely to drop and cause injury.

Other people prefer free weights because they encourage the user to work harder to maintain balance during the lift. In addition, free weights can be used in a greater variety of exercises than weight machines.

Muscular Endurance

Muscular endurance is a component of physical fitness associated with strength. When muscles contract and their individual muscle fibers shorten, energy is needed. Energy production requires that oxygen and nutrients be delivered by the circulatory system to the muscles. After these products are transformed into energy by individual muscle cells, the body must remove the potentially toxic waste by-products.

Amateur and professional athletes often wish to increase the endurance of specific muscle groups associated with their sports activities. This can be achieved by using exercises that gradually increase the number of repetitions of a given movement. However, muscular endurance is not the physiological equivalent of cardiorespiratory endurance. For example, a world-ranked distance runner with highly developed cardiorespiratory endurance and extensive muscular endurance of the legs may not have a corresponding level of muscular endurance of the abdominal muscles.

Flexibility

The ability of your joints to move through their natural range of motion is a measure of your **flexibility.** This fitness trait, like so many other aspects of structure and function, differs from point to point within your body and among different people. Not every joint in your body is equally flexible (by design), and over the course of time, use or disuse will alter the flexibility of a given joint. Certainly gender, age, genetically determined body build, and current level of physical fitness will affect your flexibility.

Inability to move easily during physical activity can be a constant reminder that aging and inactivity are the foes of flexibility. Failure to use joints regularly will quickly result in a loss of elasticity in the connective tissue and shortening of muscles associated with the joints. Benefits of flexibility include improved balance, posture, and athletic performance and reduced risk of low back pain.

As seen in young gymnasts, flexibility can be highly developed and maintained with a program of activity that includes regular stretching. Stretching also helps reduce the risk of injury. Athletic trainers generally prefer **static stretching** to **ballistic stretching** for people who wish to improve their range of motion. Guidelines for stretching are given in the Star Box on p. 71.

Body Composition

Body composition is the "makeup of the body in terms of muscle, bone, fat, and other elements."[2] Of particular interest to fitness experts are percentages of body fat and fat-free weight. Health experts are especially concerned about the large number of people in our society who are overweight and obese. Increasingly, cardiorespiratory fitness trainers are recognizing the importance of body composition and are including strength-training exercises to help reduce

Static stretching can develop and maintain flexibility.

body fat. (See Chapter 6 for further information about body composition, health effects of obesity, and weight management.)

AGING PHYSICALLY

With aging, physical decline will occur and the components of physical fitness become more difficult to maintain. From the fourth decade onward, a gradual decline in vigor and resistance eventually gives way to various types of illnesses. In the opinion of many authorities, people do not die of old age. Rather, old age worsens specific conditions responsible for death. However, physical decline can be slowed and the onset of illness delayed by staying physically active. The process of aging can be described on the basis of predictable occurrences:[5]

- *Change is gradual.* In aging, there are gradual changes in body structure or function that occur before specific health problems are identified.
- *Individual differences occur.* When two people of the same age are compared for the type and extent of change that has occurred with age, important differences can be noted. Even within the same person, different systems decline at differing rates and to varying extents.
- *Greatest change is noted in areas of complex function.* In physiological processes involving two or more major body systems, the most profound effects of physiological aging can be noted.

- *Homeostatic decline occurs with age.* Becoming older is associated with a growing difficulty in maintaining homeostasis (the dynamic balance among body systems). In the face of stressors the older adult's system takes longer to respond, does not respond with the same magnitude, and may take longer to return to baseline.

Like growth and development, aging is predictable yet unique for each person.

muscular endurance
The ability of a muscle or muscle group to function over time; supported by the respiratory and circulatory systems.

flexibility
The ability of joints to function through an intended range of motion.

static stretching
The slow lengthening of a muscle group to an extended stretch; followed by holding the extended position for a recommended period.

ballistic stretching
A "bouncing" form of stretching in which a muscle group is lengthened repetitively to produce multiple quick, forceful stretches.

Health Concerns of Midlife Adults

The period between 45 and 64 years of age brings with it a variety of subtle changes in the body's structure and function. When life is busy and the mind is active, these changes are generally not evident. Even when they become evident, they are not usually the source of profound concern. Your parents, older students in your class, and people with whom you will be working are, nevertheless, experiencing these changes:[6]

- Decrease in bone mass and density
- Increase in vertebral compression
- Degenerative changes in joint cartilage
- Increase in adipose tissue—loss of lean body mass
- Decrease in capacity to engage in physical work
- Decrease in visual acuity
- Decrease in basal energy requirements
- Decrease in fertility
- Decrease in sexual function

For some midlife adults these health concerns can be quite threatening, especially for those who view aging with apprehension and fear. Some middle-aged people reject these physical changes and convince themselves they are sick. Indeed, *hypochondriasis* is much more common among midlife people than among young people.

Osteoporosis

Osteoporosis is a condition frequently seen in late middle-aged women. However, it is not fully understood why white menopausal women are so susceptible to the increase in calcium loss that leads to fracture of the hip, wrist, and vertebral column. Well over 90% of all people with osteoporosis are white women.

The endocrine system plays a large role in the development of osteoporosis. At the time of menopause, a woman's ovaries begin a rapid decrease in the production of *estrogen*, one of two main hormones associated with the menstrual cycle. This lower level of estrogen may decrease the conversion of the precursors of vitamin D into the active form of vitamin D, the form necessary for absorbing calcium from the digestive tract. As a result, calcium may be drawn from the bones for use elsewhere in the body.

Additional explanations of osteoporosis focus on two other possibilities—*hyperparathyroidism* (another endocrine dysfunction) and the below-average degree of muscle development seen in osteoporotic women. In this latter explanation the reduced muscle mass is associated with decreased activity that in turn

deprives the body of the mechanical stimulation needed to facilitate bone growth.

Premenopausal women have the opportunity to build and maintain a healthy skeleton through an appropriate intake of calcium. Current recommendations are for an intake of 1200 mg of calcium per day. Three to four daily servings of low-fat dairy products should provide sufficient calcium. Adequate vitamin D must also be in the diet because it aids in the absorption of calcium.

Many women do not take in an adequate amount of calcium. Calcium supplements, again in combination with vitamin D, can be used to achieve recommended calcium levels. It is now known that calcium carbonate, a highly advertised form of calcium, is no more easily absorbed by the body than are other forms of calcium salts. Consumers of calcium supplements should compare brands to determine which, if any, they will buy.

In premenopausal women, calcium deposition in bone is facilitated by exercise, particularly exercise that involves movement of the extremities. Today, women are encouraged to consume at least the recommended servings from the milk group and engage in regular physical activity that involves the weight-bearing muscles of the legs, such as aerobics, jogging, or walking.

Postmenstrual women who are not elderly can markedly slow the resorption of calcium from their bones through the use of estrogen replacement therapy. When combined with a daily intake of 1500 mg of calcium, vitamin D, and regular exercise, estrogen therapy almost eliminates calcium loss. Of course, women will need to work closely with their physicians in monitoring the use of estrogen because of continuing concern over the role of estrogen replacement therapy and the development of breast cancer.

Osteoarthritis

Arthritis is an umbrella term for more than 100 forms of joint inflammation. The most common form is **osteoarthritis.** It is likely that as we age, all of us will develop osteoarthritis to some degree. Often called "wear and tear" arthritis, osteoarthritis occurs primarily in the weight-bearing joints of the knee, hip, and spine. In this form of arthritis, joint damage can occur to bone ends, cartilaginous cushions, and related structures as the years of constant friction and stress accumulate.

The object of current management of osteoarthritis (and other forms) is not to cure the disease but rather to reduce discomfort, limit joint destruction, and maximize joint mobility. Aspirin and nonsteroidal anti-inflammatory agents are the drugs most frequently used to treat osteoarthritis.

It is now believed that osteoarthritis develops most commonly in people with a genetic predisposition for excessive damage to the weight-bearing joints. Thus the condition seems to "run in families." Further, studies comparing the occurrence of osteoarthritis in those who exercise and those who do not demonstrate that regular movement activity may decrease the likelihood of developing this form of arthritis.

Health Concerns of Elderly Adults

In elderly people, it is frequently difficult to distinguish between changes caused by aging and those caused by disease. For virtually every body system, biomedical indexes for the old and young can overlap. In the respiratory system, for example, the oxygen uptake capacity of a man 70 years old may be no different from that of a man 55 years old who has a history of heavy cigarette smoking. Is the level in the elderly man to be considered an indicator of a disease, or should it be considered a reflection of normal old age? In dealing with the elderly, physicians frequently must make this kind of distinction.

In elderly people, as in midlife people, structural and physiological changes are routinely seen. In some cases, these are closely related to disease processes, but in most cases they reflect the gradual decline that is thought to be a result of the normal aging process. The most frequently seen changes include the following:
- Decrease in bone mass
- Changes in the structure of bone
- Decrease in muscle bulk and strength
- Decrease in oxygen uptake
- Loss of nonreproducing cells in the nervous system
- Decrease in hearing and vision abilities
- Decrease in all other sensory modalities, including the sense of body positioning
- Slower reaction time
- Gait and posture changes resulting from a weakening of the muscles of the trunk and legs

In addition to these changes, the most likely change seen in the elderly is the increased sensitivity of the body's homeostatic mechanism. Because of this sensitivity, a minor infection or superficial injury can be traumatic enough to decrease the body's ability to maintain its internal balance. An illness that would be easily controlled in a younger person could even prove fatal to a seemingly healthy 75-year-old person.

Continuing to follow a physical fitness plan throughout midlife and older adulthood is essential to minimizing age-related health problems. The plan should be modified as necessary to accommodate changes in physical functioning.

DEVELOPING A CARDIORESPIRATORY FITNESS PROGRAM

For people of all ages, cardiorespiratory conditioning can be achieved through many activities. As long as the activity you choose places sufficient demand on the heart and lungs, improved fitness is possible. In addition to the familiar activities of swimming, running, cycling, and aerobic dance, many people today are participating in brisk walking, rollerblading, cross-country skiing, swimnastics, skating, rowing, and even weight training (often combined with some form of aerobic activity). Regardless of age or physical limitations, you can select from a variety of enjoyable activities that will condition the cardiorespiratory system. Complete the Personal Assessment on pp. 74-75 to determine your level of fitness.

Many people think that any kind of physical activity will produce cardiorespiratory fitness. Golf, bowling, hunting, fishing, and archery are considered to be forms of exercise. However, these activities would generally fail to produce positive changes in your cardiorespiratory and overall muscular fitness; they may enhance your health, be enjoyable, and produce some fatigue after lengthy participation, but they do not meet the fitness standards recently established by the American College of Sports Medicine (ACSM), the nation's premier professional organization of exercise physiologists and sport physicians.[7]

The ACSM's most recent recommendations for achieving cardiorespiratory fitness were approved in 1990 and include five major areas: (1) mode of activity, (2) frequency of training, (3) intensity of training,

---

osteoporosis
Loss of calcium from the bone, seen primarily in postmenopausal women.

osteoarthritis
Arthritis that develops with age; largely caused by weight bearing and deterioration of the joints.

PERSONAL ASSESSMENT

What Is Your Level of Fitness?

You can determine your level of fitness in 30 minutes or less by completing this short group of tests based on the National Fitness Test developed by the President's Council on Physical Fitness and Sports. If you are over 40 years old or have chronic medical disorders such as diabetes or obesity, check with your physician before taking this or any other fitness test. You will need another person to monitor your test and keep time.

Three-minute step test
Aerobic capacity. Equipment: 12-inch bench, crate, block, or step ladder; stopwatch. Procedure: face bench. Complete 24 full steps (both feet on the bench, both feet on the ground) per minute for 3 minutes. After finishing, sit down, have your partner find your pulse within 5 seconds, and take your pulse for 1 minute. Your score is your pulse rate for 1 full minute.

Scoring standards (heart rate for 1 minute)

Age	18-29		30-39		40-49		50-59		60+	
Gender	F	M	F	M	F	M	F	M	F	M
Excellent	<80	<75	<84	<78	<88	<80	<92	<85	<95	<90
Good	80-110	75-100	84-115	78-109	88-118	80-112	92-123	85-115	95-127	90-118
Average	>110	>100	>115	>109	>118	>112	>123	>115	>127	>118

Sit and reach
Hamstring flexibility. Equipment: yardstick; tape. Between your legs, tape the yardstick to the floor. Sit with legs straight and heels about 5 inches apart, heels even with the 15-inch mark on the yardstick. While in a sitting position, slowly stretch forward as far as possible. Your score is the number of inches reached.

Scoring standards (inches)

Age	18-29		30-39		40-49		50-59		60+	
Gender	F	M	F	M	F	M	F	M	F	M
Excellent	>22	>21	>22	>21	>21	>20	>20	>19	>20	>19
Good	17-22	13-21	17-22	13-21	15-21	13-20	14-20	12-19	14-20	12-19
Average	<17	<13	<17	<13	<15	<13	<14	<12	<14	<12

Arm hang
Upper body strength. Equipment: horizontal bar (high enough to prevent your feet from touching the floor); stopwatch. Procedure: hang with straight arms, palms facing forward. Start watch when subject is in position. Stop when subject lets go. Your score is the number of minutes and seconds spent hanging.

Scoring standards (heart rate for 1 minute)

Age	18-29		30-39		40-49		50-59		60+	
Gender	F	M	F	M	F	M	F	M	F	M
Excellent	>1:30	>2:00	>1:20	>1:50	>1:10	>1:35	>1:00	>1:20	>:50	>1:10
Good	:46-1:30	1:00-2:00	:40-1:20	:50-1:50	:30-1:10	:45-1:35	:30-1:00	:35-1:20	:21-:50	:30-1:10
Average	<:46	<1:00	<:40	<:50	<:30	<:45	<:30	<:35	<:21	<:30

Curl-ups

Abdominal and low back strength. Equipment: stopwatch. Procedure: Lie flat on upper back, knees bent, shoulders touching the floor, arms extended above your thighs or by your sides, palms down. Bend knees so that feet are flat and 12 inches from the buttocks. Curl up by lifting head and shoulders off the floor, sliding hands forward above your thighs or the floor. Curl down and repeat. Your score is the number of curl-ups in 1 minute.

Scoring standards (number in 1 minute)

Age	18-29		30-39		40-49		50-59		60+	
Gender	F	M	F	M	F	M	F	M	F	M
Excellent	>45	>50	>40	>45	>35	>40	>30	>35	>25	>30
Good	25-45	30-50	20-40	22-45	16-35	21-40	12-30	18-35	11-25	15-30
Average	<25	<30	<20	<22	<16	<21	<12	<18	<11	<15

Push-ups (men)

Upper body strength. Equipment: stopwatch. Assume a front-leaning position. Lower your body until chest touches the floor. Raise and repeat for 1 minute. Your score is the number of push-ups completed in 1 minute.

Scoring standards (number in 1 minute)

Age	18-29	30-39	40-49	50-59	60+
Excellent	>50	>45	>40	>35	>30
Good	25-50	22-45	19-40	15-35	10-30
Average	<25	<22	<19	<15	<10

Modified Push-ups (women)

Upper body strength. Equipment: stopwatch. Assume a front-leaning position with knees bent up, hands under shoulders. Lower your chest to the floor, raise, and repeat. Your score is the number of push-ups completed in 1 minute.

Scoring standards (number in 1 minute)

Age	18-29	30-39	40-49	50-59	60+
Excellent	>45	>40	>35	>30	>25
Good	17-45	12-40	8-35	6-30	5-25
Average	<17	<12	<8	<6	<5

To carry this further . . .

Note your areas of strengths and weaknesses. To improve your fitness, become involved in a fitness program that reflects the concepts discussed in this chapter. Talking with fitness experts on your campus might be a good first step.

(4) duration of training, and (5) resistance training. We summarize these recommendations. You may wish to compare your existing fitness program with these standards.

Mode of Activity

The ACSM recommends that the mode of activity be any continuous physical activity that uses large muscle groups and can be rhythmic and aerobic in nature. Among the activities that generally meet this requirement are continuous swimming, cycling, aerobics, basketball, cross-country skiing, rollerblading, step training (bench aerobics), hiking, walking, rowing, stair climbing, dancing, and running. Recently, water exercise (water or aqua aerobics) has become a popular fitness mode, since it is especially effective for pregnant women and elderly, injured, or disabled people.[8] (The Focus Box on p. 90-91 provides more information about exercise during pregnancy.)

Endurance games and activities, such as tennis, racquetball, and handball, are fine as long as you and your partner are skilled enough to keep the ball in play; walking after the ball will do very little for you. Riding a bicycle is a good activity if you keep pedaling. Coasting will do little to improve fitness. Softball and football are generally less than sufficient continuous activities—especially the way they are played by weekend athletes.

Regardless of which continuous activity you select, it should also be enjoyable. Running, for example, is not for everyone—despite what some accomplished runners say! Find an activity you enjoy. If you need others around you to have a good time, corral a group of friends to join you. Vary your activities to keep from becoming bored. You might cycle in the summer, run in the fall, swim in the winter, and play racquetball in the spring. To help you maintain your fitness program, see the suggestions in the Health Action Guide at right.

Frequency of Training

Frequency of training refers to the number of times per week a person should exercise. The ACSM recommends three to five times per week. For most people, participation in fitness activities more than five times each week does not significantly improve their level of conditioning. Likewise, an average of only two workouts each week does not seem to produce a measureable improvement in cardiorespiratory conditioning. Thus, although you may have a lot

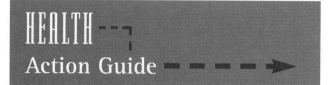

Tips to Help You Stick to Your Exercise Program

Sometimes it seems difficult to continue an exercise program. Here are a few tips to keep you going:

- Fit your program into your daily lifestyle
- Exercise with your friends
- Incorporate music into your activity
- Vary your activities frequently; crosstrain
- Reward yourself when you reach a fitness goal
- Avoid a complicated exercise program; keep it simple
- Measure your improvement by keeping a log or diary
- Take some time off to rest and recuperate
- Keep in mind how important physical activity is to your life and health ◄------

of fun cycling twice each week, do not expect to see a significant improvement in your cardiorespiratory fitness level.

Intensity of Training

How much effort should you put into an activity? Should you run quickly, jog slowly, or swim at a comfortable pace? Must a person sweat profusely to become fit? These questions all refer to **intensity** of effort.

The ACSM recommends that healthy adults exercise at an intensity level of between 60% and 90% of their maximum heart rate (calculated by subtracting your age from 220). This level of intensity is called the **target heart rate (THR).** This rate refers to the minimum number of times your heart needs to contract (beat) each minute to have a positive effect on your heart, lungs, and blood vessels. This improvement is called the *training effect.* Intensity of activity below the THR will be insufficient to make a significant improvement in your fitness level. Although intensity below the THR will still help you expend calories and thus lose weight, it will probably do little to make you more aerobically fit. On the other hand, intensity that is significantly above your THR will probably cause you to become so fatigued that you will be forced to stop the activity before the training effect can be achieved.

Choosing a particular THR between 60% and 90% of your maximum heart rate depends on your initial level of fitness. If you are already in relatively good physical shape, you might want to start exercising at 75% of your maximum heart rate. A well-conditioned person might select a higher THR for his or her intensity level, whereas a person with a low fitness level will still be able to achieve a training effect at the lower THR of 60% of maximum.

In the Star Box at right, the younger person would need to participate in a continuous activity for an extended period while working at a THR of 160 beats per minute. The older person would need to function at a THR of 117 beats per minute to achieve a positive training effect.

Determining your heart rate is not a complicated procedure. Find a location on your body where an artery passes near the surface of the skin. Pulse rates are difficult to determine by touching veins, which are more superficial than arteries. Two easily accessible sites for determining heart rate are the *carotid artery* (one on either side of the windpipe at the front of your neck) and the *radial artery* (on the inside of your wrist, just above the base of the thumb).

You should practice placing the front surface of your index and middle fingertips at either of these locations and feeling for a pulse. Once you have found a regular pulse, look at the second hand of a watch. Count the number of beats you feel in a 10-second period. Multiply this number by 6. This number is your heart rate. With a little practice, you can become very proficient at determining your heart rate.

Duration of Training

The ACSM recommends that the **duration** of training be between 20 and 60 minutes of continuous aerobic activity. Generally speaking, the duration can be on the shorter end of this range for athletic people whose activities use a high intensity of training (80% to 90% of maximum heart rate). Those who choose activities with a low range of intensity (60% to 70% of maximum heart rate) should maintain that activity for a longer time. Thus a fast jog and a moderate walk will require different lengths of time to accomplish the training effect. The fast jog might be maintained for 25 minutes, whereas the brisk walk should be kept up longer—perhaps for 50 minutes. Recently, however, some fitness experts have advocated a modified version of the ACSM's recommendations to accommodate less directed physical activity. See the Star Box on p. 78 for a more detailed discussion.

How to Calculate Your Target Heart Rate
The target heart rate (THR) is the recommended rate for increasing cardiorespiratory endurance. To maintain a training effect, you must sustain activity at your THR. To calculate your THR, subtract your age from 220 (the maximum heart rate) and multiply by .60 to .90. Here are two examples:

For a 20-year-old person who wants a THR of 80% of maximum	**For a 40-year-old person who wants a THR of 65% of maximum**
Maximum heart rate:	Maximum heart rate:
$220 - 20 = 200$	$220 - 40 = 180$
$200 \times .80 = 160$	$180 \times .65 = 117$
THR = 160 beats per minute	THR = 117 beats per minute

Muscular strength is an important component of physical fitness.

frequency
The number of times per week one should exercise to achieve a training effect.

intensity
The level of effort put into an activity.

target heart rate (THR)
The number of times per minute the heart must contract to produce a training effect.

duration
The length of time one needs to exercise at the THR to produce a training effect.

Resistance Training

Recognizing the important fact that overall body fitness includes muscular fitness, the ACSM now recommends resistance training in its current standards. The ACSM suggests participation in strength training of moderate intensity at least two times a week. This training should help develop and maintain a healthy body composition—one with an emphasis on lean body mass. The goal of resistance training is not to improve cardiorespiratory endurance but to improve overall muscle strength and tone. For the average person, resistance training with heavy weights is not recommended because it can induce a sudden and dangerous increase in blood pressure. See the Health Action Guide on p. 79 for safety precautions to observe during strength training.

The resistance training recommended by the ACSM includes one set of 8 to 12 repetitions of 8 to 10 different exercises. These exercises should be geared to the body's major muscle groups (that is, legs, arms, shoulders, trunk, and back) and should not focus on just one or two body areas. Isotonic (progressive resistance) or isokinetic exercises are recommended (see p. 69). For the average person, resistance training activities should be done at a moderate-to-slow speed, use the full range of motion, and not impair normal breathing. With just one set recommended for each exercise, resistance training is not very time consuming.

Warm-up, Workout, Cooldown

Each training session consists of three basic parts: the warm-up, the workout, and the cooldown.[2] The warm-up should last 10 to 15 minutes. During this period, you should begin slow, gradual, comfortable movements related to the upcoming activity, such as walking or slow jogging. All body segments and muscle groups should be exercised as you gradually increase your heart rate. Near the end of the warm-up period, the major muscle groups should be stretched. This preparation helps protect you from muscle strains and joint sprains.

The warm-up is a fine time to socialize. Furthermore, you can mentally prepare yourself for your activity or think about the beauty of the morning sky, the changing colors of the leaves, or the friends you will meet later in the day. Mental warm-ups can be as beneficial for you psychologically as physical warm-ups are physiologically.

The second part of the training session is the workout, the part of the session that involves improving muscular strength and endurance, cardiorespiratory

A Revised Approach to Fitness?

A number of health professionals have recently begun to urge the American public to consider the health benefits of less directed physical activity than that prescribed by the American College of Sports Medicine. These fitness experts believe that people shy away from physical activity because they are afraid that a fitness program requires too much effort and commitment.

One key aspect of this revised approach is the belief that the 20 to 60 minutes of daily physical activity does not have to be accomplished all at once. People can accumulate their minutes in segments over the course of the day. For example, raking leaves for 15 minutes, walking briskly for 10 minutes at lunch, and dancing for 10 minutes can produce health benefits if done on most days.

Opponents of this "kinder, gentler" approach to fitness are concerned that people who already exercise regularly may slack off and actually reduce their current fitness levels. Opponents also believe that, without a prescription for exercise, the public will fool itself into thinking it is much more active than it really is.

Which approach would be better for you? Do you wish to follow prescribed fitness guidelines, such as those given by the ACSM? Or do you believe that a lifestyle that incorporates short-term fitness activities throughout the day is a better approach for you?

endurance, and flexibility. Workouts can be tailor-made, but they should follow the ACSM guidelines discussed previously in this chapter.

The third important part of each fitness session, the cooldown, consists of a 5- to 10-minute session of relaxing exercises, such as slow jogging, walking, and stretching.[9] This activity allows your body to cool and return to a resting state. A cooldown period helps reduce muscle soreness.

Exercise for Older Adults

An exercise program designed for younger adults may be inappropriate for older people, particularly those over age 50. Special attention must be paid to matching the program to the interests and abilities of the participants. The goals of the program should include both social interaction and physical conditioning.

Older adults, especially those with a personal or family history of heart problems, should have a physical examination before starting a fitness program.

Safety Precautions for Strength Training

To avoid injury during strength-training exercises, you should observe the following safety precautions:

- Warm up appropriately
- Use proper lifting techniques
- Always have a spotter if you are using free weights
- Do not hold your breath during a lift
- Avoid single lifts of very heavy weights
- Before using a machine (such as Nautilus, Universal, or Cybex), be certain you know how to use it correctly
- Seek advice for training programs from properly licensed or certified experts
- Work within your limitations; avoid "showing off"

This examination should include a stress cardiogram, a blood pressure check, and an evaluation of joint functioning. Participants should learn how to monitor their own cardiorespiratory status during exercise.

Well-designed fitness programs for older adults will include activities that begin slowly, are monitored frequently, and are geared to the enjoyment of the participants.[10] The professional staff coordinating the program should be familiar with the signs of distress (excessively elevated heart rate, nausea, breathing difficulty, pallor, and pain) and must be able to perform CPR. Warm-up and cooldown periods should be included. Activities to increase flexibility are beneficial in the beginning and ending segments of the program. Participants should wear comfortable clothing and appropriate shoes and should be mentally prepared to enjoy the activities.

A program designed for older adults will largely conform to the ACSM criteria specified previously in this chapter. However, except for certain very fit older adults (such as runners and triathletes), the THR should not exceed 120 beats per minute. Also, because of possible joint, muscular, or skeletal problems, certain activities may have to be done in a sitting position. Pain or discomfort should be reported immediately to the fitness instructor.

Fortunately, properly screened older adults will rarely have health emergencies during a well-monitored fitness program. Of course, for some older adults, individual fitness activities may be more enjoyable than supervised group activities. Either choice offers important benefits.

Low Back Pain

A common occurrence among adults is the sudden onset of low back pain.[11] Each year, 10 million adults develop this condition, which can be so uncomfortable that they miss work, lose sleep, and generally feel incapable of engaging in daily activities. Eighty percent of all adults who have this condition will experience these effects two to three times per year.

Although low back pain can reflect serious health problems, most low back pain is caused by mechanical (postural) problems. As unpleasant as low back pain is, the problem usually corrects itself within a week or two. The services of a physician, physical therapist, or chiropractor are not generally required after an initial visit.

By engaging in regular exercise, such as swimming, walking, and bicycling, and by paying attention to your back during bending, lifting, and sitting, you can minimize the occurrence of this uncomfortable and incapacitating condition.

FITNESS QUESTIONS AND ANSWERS

Along with the five necessary elements to include in your fitness program, you should consider many additional issues when you start a fitness program.

Should I See My Doctor Before I Get Started?

This issue has probably kept thousands of people from ever beginning a fitness program. The hassle and expense of getting a comprehensive physical examination is an excellent alibi for people who are not completely sold on the idea of exercise. A complete examination, including *blood analysis, stress test, cardiogram, serum lipid analysis,* and *body fat analysis,* is a valuable tool for developing some baseline physical data for your medical record.

Is this examination really necessary? Most exercise physiologists do not think so. The value of these measurements as safety predictors is questioned by many professionals. A good rule of thumb to follow is to

Exercise is important to maintain health at any age.

undergo a physical examination if (1) you have an existing medical condition (for example, diabetes, obesity, hypertension, heart abnormalities, or arthritis), (2) you are a man over age 40 or a woman over age 50,[12] or (3) you smoke.

How Important Is Breast Support for Female Exercisers?

Because of the vigorous up-and-down and lateral breast movement that can occur with jumping and running activities, it is important that women wear bras that fully support their breasts. This is especially important for large-breasted women. A good support bra can reduce discomfort and distraction during physical activity. Also, adequate support reduces damage to the Cooper's ligaments. Damage to these ligaments can cause premature sagging of the breasts.

Another problem that female exercisers may face is a condition called *runner's nipples*. This is an abrasion caused by the constant friction from the jogger's shirt. A good bra prevents this, as well as a condition called *bicyclist's nipples,* in which the nipples become painful because of the combination of sweat evaporation and wind chill.[9]

Researchers believe that the characteristics of the ideal sports bra depend on a woman's weight and breast size, her physical activity, and what feels comfortable. Sports bras should be made with (a) a material that is breathable, (b) minimal amounts of elastic, (c) no seams directly over the nipple area, (d) comfortable support under the breasts that prevents the bra from rising during activity, and (e) nonelastic straps that prevent the shoulder straps from slipping off during activity.

How Beneficial Is Aerobic Exercise?

One of the most popular fitness approaches is aerobic exercise, including aerobic dancing. Many organizations sponsor classes in this form of continuous dancing and movement. The rise in popularity of televised and videotaped aerobic exercise programs reflects the enthusiasm for this form of exercise. Because extravagant claims are often made about the value of these programs, the wise consumer should observe at least one session of the activity before enrolling. Discover for yourself whether the program meets the criteria outlined previously in this chapter: mode of activity, frequency, intensity, duration, and resistance training.

Street dancing is fast becoming one of the most popular aerobic exercises. Popularized by rap music, classic funk, and the growth of vigorous "street jam" dancing in music videos, street dancing is an excellent way of having fun and developing cardiorespiratory fitness. Have you experienced the exhilaration that results from an hour or two of dancing?

LEARNING from ALL CULTURES

Staying Fit

It is not uncommon in the United States for men and women to take time out of their day to go to an aerobics class, jog for several miles, or play a few games of racquetball. This practice is not unique to Americans. The people of Japan are also beginning to show a greater interest in fitness and sport, and commercialized sports facilities are rapidly developing. Japanese women, especially, are now participating in fitness activities. Many women who do not work outside the home participate in activities such as aerobic exercise, jazzercise, yoga, and Chinese martial arts; these activities are taught through programs at the sports centers.[16]

In China, commercialized sports centers do not exist, but there is an emphasis on physical fitness and sport. This emphasis comes from the government. For students in primary and secondary school, two physical education classes are required per week, each 50 minutes long. For adult workers, participation in exercise is also encouraged. In offices and factories, employees take 10-minute exercise breaks in the mornings and afternoons. Physical activities may include calisthenics and even eye exercises.[17]

Fitness seems to have gained popularity because many people recognize its benefits. However, one German visitor observed that many Americans get in their cars and drive to their fitness clubs, exercise, and then drive back to work or home. Merely walking to their destinations and forgetting the club seemed to make more sense to him!

Knowing how important fitness is to good health, think about your own daily routine. What kinds of exercise and activities do you participate in to enhance your fitness?

What Are Low-Impact Aerobic Activities?

Because long-term participation in some aerobic activities (for example, jogging, running, aerobic dancing, and rope skipping) may damage the hip, knee, and ankle joints, many fitness experts promote low-impact aerobic activities. Low-impact aerobic dancing, water aerobics, bench aerobics, and brisk walking are examples of this kind of fitness activity. Participants still conform to the principal components of a cardiorespiratory fitness program. THR levels are the same as in high-impact aerobic activities.

The main difference between low-impact and high-impact aerobic activities is the use of the legs. Low-impact aerobics do not require having both feet off the ground at the same time. Thus weight transfer does not occur with the forcefulness seen in traditional, high-impact aerobic activities. In addition, low-impact activities may include exaggerated arm movements and the use of hand or wrist weights. All of these variations are designed to increase the heart rate to the THR without damaging the joints of the lower extremities. Low-impact aerobics are excellent for people of all ages, and they may be especially beneficial to older adults.

In-line skating (rollerblading) is one of the fastest-growing participant fitness activities. This low-impact activity has cardiorespiratory and muscular benefits similar to those of running without the pounding effect that running can produce. Rollerblading requires important safety equipment: sturdy skates, knee and elbow pads, wrist supports, and a helmet.

What Is the Most Effective Means of Fluid Replacement During Exercise?

Despite all the advertising hype associated with commercial fluid replacement products, for an average person involved in typical fitness activities, water is still the best fluid replacement. The availability and cost are unbeatable. However, when activity is prolonged and intense, commercial sport drinks may be preferable to water because they contain electrolytes (which replace lost sodium and potassium) and carbohydrates (which replace depleted energy stores).[13] However, the carbohydrates in sports drinks are actually simple forms of sugar. Thus sports drinks tend to be high in calories just like regular soft drinks. Regardless of the drink you choose, exercise physiologists recommend that you drink fluids before and at frequent intervals throughout the activity.

What Effect Does Alcohol Have on Sport Performance?

It probably comes as no surprise that alcohol use is generally detrimental to sport performance. Alcohol consumption, especially excessive intake the evening before a performance, consistently decreases the level of performance. Many research studies have documented the negative effects of alcohol on activities involving speed, strength, power, and endurance.[14]

Lowered performance appears to be related to a variety of factors, including impaired judgment, reduced coordination, depressed heart function, liver interference, and dehydration. Understandably, sports federations within the International Olympic Committee have banned the use of alcohol in conjunction with sports competition.

Only in the sports of precision shooting (pistol shooting, riflery, and archery) have studies shown that low-level alcohol use may improve performance, by reducing the shooter's anxiety and permitting steady hand movements. However, alcohol use has also been banned from these sports.[14] Weapons and alcohol do not mix.

Why Has Bodybuilding Become So Popular?

It is true that the popularity of *bodybuilding* has increased significantly in recent years. There are many reasons for this growth. Bodybuilders often start lifting weights to get into better shape—to improve muscle tone. They may just want to look healthier and feel stronger. Once they realize that they can alter the shape of their bodies, they find that bodybuilding offers challenges that, through hard work, are attainable. Bodybuilders also report enjoying the physical sensations (the "pump") that result from a good workout. The results of their efforts are clearly visible and measurable. Some bodybuilders become involved in competitive events to test their advancements.

Perhaps we should dispel a few myths about bodybuilding. Are bodybuilders strong? The answer is emphatically—yes! Will muscle cells turn into fat cells if weightlifting programs are discontinued? *No,* muscle cells are physiologically incapable of turning into fat cells. Will women develop bulky muscles through weight training? *No,* they can improve muscle strength and tone, but unless they take steroids, their muscle mass cannot increase like men's muscle mass. Is bodybuilding socially acceptable? *Yes,* for many people. Just observe all the health clubs that cater to weightlifters and bodybuilders. Can strength training improve heart functioning? *Yes,* cardiovascular im-

Bodybuilding improves muscle tone and makes you look healthier and feel stronger.

provement has been seen among people who lift weights, especially those who use light weights repetitively.

Where Can I Find Out about Proper Equipment?

College students are generally in an excellent setting to locate people who have the resources to provide helpful information about sports equipment. Contacting physical education or health education faculty members who have an interest in your chosen activity might be a good start. Most colleges also have a number of clubs that specialize in fitness interests—cycling, hiking, and jogging clubs, for example. Attend one of their upcoming meetings.

Sporting goods and specialty stores (for runners, tennis and racquetball players, and cyclists) are convenient places to obtain information. Employees of these stores are usually knowledgable about sports and equipment (see the Star Box on pp. 85-86).

How Worthwhile Are Commercial Health and Fitness Clubs?

The health and fitness club business is booming. Fitness clubs offer activities ranging from free weights to weight machines to step walking to general aerobics. Some clubs have saunas and whirlpools and lots of frills. Others have course offerings that include wellness, smoking cessation, stress management, time management, dance, and yoga. The atmosphere at most clubs is friendly, and people are encouraged to have a good time while working out.

If your purpose in joining a fitness club is to improve your cardiorespiratory fitness, measure the program offered by the club against the ACSM standards. If your primary purpose in joining is to meet people and have fun, request a trial membership for a month or so to see whether you like the environment.

Before signing a contract at a health club or spa, do some careful questioning. Find out when the business was established, ask about the qualifications of the employees, contact some members for their observations, and request a thorough tour of the facilities. You might even consult your local Better Business Bureau for additional information. Finally, make certain that you read and understand every word of the contract.

What Is Crosstraining?

Crosstraining is the use of more than one aerobic activity to achieve cardiorespiratory fitness. For example, runners may use swimming, cycling, or rowing periodically to replace running in their training routines. Crosstraining allows certain muscle groups to rest and injuries to heal. Also, crosstraining provides a refreshing change of pace for the participant. You will probably enjoy your fitness program more if you vary the activities. Further, your enjoyment will make it more likely that the *Healthy People 2010* objectives can be reached.

What Are Steroids and Why Do Some Athletes Use Them?

Steroids are drugs that can be legally prescribed by physicians for a variety of health conditions, including certain forms of anemia, inadequate growth patterns, and chronic debilitating diseases. Steroids can also be prescribed to aid recovery from surgery or burns. **Anabolic steroids** are drugs that function like the male sex hormone *testosterone*.[15] They can be taken orally or by injection.

Anabolic steroids are used by athletes who hope to gain weight, muscular size and strength, power, endurance, and aggressiveness. Over the last few decades, many bodybuilders, weightlifters, track athletes, and football players have chosen to ignore the serious health risks posed by illegal steroid use.

The use of steroids is highly dangerous because of serious, life-threatening side effects and adverse reactions. These effects include heart problems, certain forms of cancer, liver complications, and even psychological disturbances. The side effects on female steroid users are as dangerous as those on men. Figure 4-2 shows the adverse effects of steroid use.

Steroid users have developed a terminology of their own. Anabolic steroids are called "roids" or "juice." "Roid rage" is an aggressive, psychotic response to chronic steroid use. "Stacking" is a term that describes the use of multiple steroids at the same time.

Many organizations that control athletic competition (for example, the National Collegiate Athletic Association [NCAA], The Athletics Congress, the National Football League, and the International Olympic Committee) have banned steroids and are testing athletes for illegal use. The death of professional football player Lyle Alzado highlighted the serious threat posed by steroid use. Fortunately, athletes finally seem to be getting the message and are steering clear of steroids.

Are Today's Children Physically Fit?

Major research studies published during the last 10 years have indicated that U.S. children and teenagers lead very sedentary lives. Children ages 6 to 17 score extremely poorly in the areas of strength, flexibility, and cardiorespiratory endurance. In many cases, parents are in better shape than their children.

This information presents a challenge to educators and parents to emphasize the need for strenuous play activity. Television watching and parental inactivity were implicated as major reasons in these studies. For students reading this text who are parents or grandparents of young children, what can you do to encourage more physical activity and less sedentary activity?

How Does Sleep Contribute to Overall Fitness?

Although sleep may seem to be the opposite of exercise, it is an important adjunct to a well-planned exercise program. Sleep is so vital to health that people who are unable to sleep sufficiently (those with insomnia) or who are deprived of sleep experience

anabolic steroids (ann uh **bol** ick)
Drugs that function like testosterone to produce increases in weight, strength, endurance, and aggressiveness.

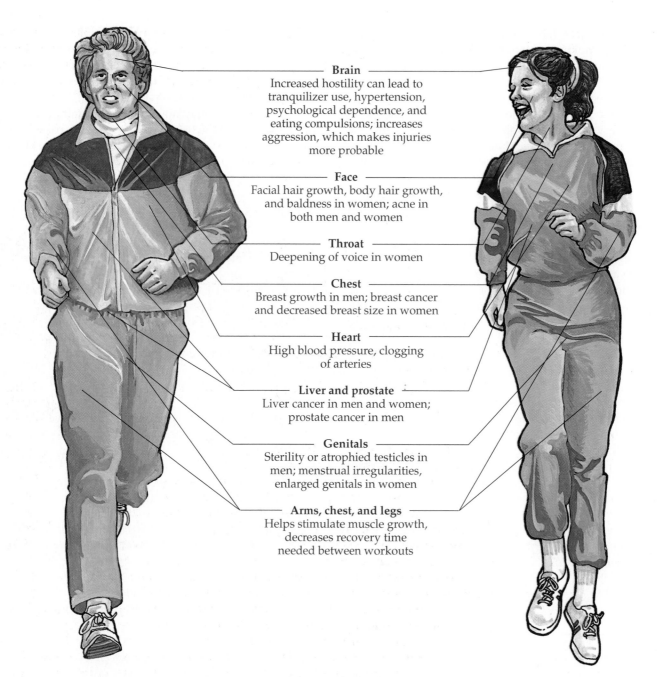

Brain
Increased hostility can lead to tranquilizer use, hypertension, psychological dependence, and eating compulsions; increases aggression, which makes injuries more probable

Face
Facial hair growth, body hair growth, and baldness in women; acne in both men and women

Throat
Deepening of voice in women

Chest
Breast growth in men; breast cancer and decreased breast size in women

Heart
High blood pressure, clogging of arteries

Liver and prostate
Liver cancer in men and women; prostate cancer in men

Genitals
Sterility or atrophied testicles in men; menstrual irregularities, enlarged genitals in women

Arms, chest, and legs
Helps stimulate muscle growth, decreases recovery time needed between workouts

Figure 4-2   Adverse effects of steroids on various parts of the body.

Choosing an Athletic Shoe

Aerobic Shoes

When selecting shoes for aerobic dancing, J. Lynn Reese, president of J. Lynn & Co. Endurance Sports, Washington, DC, advises the following:

- Check the width of the shoe at the widest part of your foot. The bottom of the shoe should be as wide as the bottom of your foot; the uppers shouldn't go over the sides.
- Look for leather or nylon uppers. Leather is durable and gives good support, but it can stretch. Nylon won't stretch and gives support, but it's not as durable. Canvas generally doesn't offer much support.
- Look for rubber rather than polyurethane or black carbon rubber soles. Treads should be fairly flat in the forefoot. If you dance on carpet, you can go with less tread; if you dance on gym floors, you may need more grab.

Basketball Shoes

What's most important when choosing a basketball shoe? John Burleson, of the Sports Authority, offers this advice:

- Cushioning. Cushioning is especially important in the forefoot area. Each shoe manufacturer has its own cushioning "system." For example, Nike offers "Air" and Reebok promotes its "Hexalite" material, composed of hexagonal air chambers.
- Side support. Side support, also called lateral and medial support, is important for making quick directional changes.
- Fit of heel cup. Try on the shoe, and then put your little finger in behind the heel. It should fit snugly.
- Traction. Keep in mind the surface on which you play most often. More traction is needed on asphalt than on hardwood.
- Socks. Socks should be breathable and pull moisture away from the foot.
- Laces. "Rope" laces are more convenient than the traditional flat laces because pulling on the ends will tighten up the laces on the whole shoe at once.

Running Shoes

Need new running shoes? Here's advice from Jeff Galloway, former Olympic runner and founder and president of Phidippides International aerobic sports stores, headquartered in Atlanta.

- Take time to shop, and find a knowledgeable salesperson. Good advice is crucial.
- Check the wear pattern on your old shoes to see whether you have floppy or rigid feet. Floppy-footed runners wear out their soles on the outside and inside edges; rigid-footed runners wear out soles predominantly on the outside edges. Floppy-footed runners can sacrifice cushioning for support; rigid-footed runners can sacrifice support for cushioning.
- Know whether your feet are curved or straight and whether you have high arches or are flatfooted. The shoe should fit the shape of your foot.

Aerobic Shoes

Flexibility:
More at ball of foot than running shoes; less flexible than court shoes or running shoes; sole is firmer than running shoes

Uppers:
Most are leather or leather-reinforced nylon

Heel:
Little or no flare

Soles:
Rubber if you dance on wood floors; polyurethane for other surfaces

Cushioning:
More than court shoes; less than running shoes

Tread:
Should be fairly flat, especially on forefoot; may also have "dot" on the ball of the foot for pivoting

Continued

Basketball and Court Shoes

Soles:
Can be made from rubber for durability, EVA for light-weight cushioning, or polyurethane, which is both light-weight and durable.

Flexibility:
Should be most flexible in the forefoot, for making jump shots or sudden stops.

Cushioning:
Should absorb shock in the ball of the foot, for landing after jump shots.

Heel:
A snug-fitting heel cup is essential to keep the ankle in place; the shoe can be high-, mid-, or low-cut, depending on the amount of ankle support desired.

Tread:
For playing outdoors, the sole should be harder and the tread deeper; a smoother tread works well for playing on a court.

Uppers:
Can be made of leather for durability or nylon or other synthetics for breathability.

Running Shoes

Heel:
Flare gives foot broader, more stable base

Soles:
Usually carbon-based for longer wear

Cushioning:
More than basketball and court shoes, especially at heel

Tread:
"Waffle" or other deep-cut tread for grip on many surfaces

---

deterioration in every dimension of their health. Fortunately, exercise is frequently associated with improvement in sleeping.

The value of sleep is apparent in a variety of positive changes in the body. Dreaming is thought to play an important role in supporting the emotional dimension of health. Problem-solving scenarios that occur during dreams seem to afford some carryover value in actual coping experiences. A variety of changes in physiological functioning, particularly a deceleration of the cardiovascular system, occur while you sleep. The feeling of being well rested is an expression of the mental and physiological rejuvenation you feel after a good night's sleep.

The amount of sleep needed varies among people. In fact, for any person, sleep needs vary according to activity level and overall state of health. As we age, the need for sleep appears to decrease from the 6 to 8 hours young adults require. Elderly people routinely sleep less than they did when they were younger. This decrease may be offset by the short naps older people often take during the day. For all people, however, periods of relaxation, daydreaming, and even an occasional afternoon nap promote electrical activity patterns that help regenerate the mind and body (see the Health Action Guide on p. 87).

What Exercise Danger Signs Should I Watch For?

The human body is an amazing piece of equipment. It functions well whether or not you are conscious of its processes. It also delivers clear signals when something goes wrong.

You should monitor any sign that seems abnormal during or after your exercise. "Listen to your body" is a good rule for self-awareness. The Star Box on p. 87 lists some common warning signs to monitor.

However, such occurrences are extremely unusual. Fear of developing these difficulties should not deter you from starting a fitness program. These risks are minimal—and the benefits far outweigh the risks.

Activity 1

Many college students want to look in the mirror and see the kind of body they see in the media. Students become motivated to start fitness programs because they hope that they can build a better, healthier body for themselves. Do you know what it takes to become fit? Test your fitness and physical activity IQ by taking a short quiz. Go to http://cgi.pathfinder.com/cgi-bin/GDML/gdmldb/thrive?ShapeSmart and answer the fitness questions. Then press the "submit" button to see how you did.

Activity 2

College students are generally in an excellent setting to locate people who can provide helpful information about fitness. An excellent source on the web is the National Federation of Personal Trainers, at http://www.nfpt.com. Go to its website, scroll down, and select "Fitness Quiz." Complete the quiz and then submit your results to see how much you know about fitness.

Activity 3

Should you see your doctor before you begin a fitness program? If you are between the ages of 15 and 69, the PAR-Q can help you decide whether this is necessary. Go to http://www.thriveonline.com/@@HUG40gQAZGhX1qS7/thrive/health/tools.parq.html and answer the seven questions on the questionnaire. Then submit your responses, and you will receive a recommendation based on your individual profile.

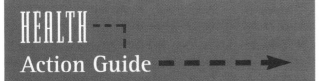

The Power Nap

College students rarely get the amount of sleep they really need. This may be especially true for older students who are the parents of young children and students who are involved in many extracurricular activities, such as student government or athletics. College students should aim for 8 to 10 hours of sleep each night. If this amount of sleep cannot be achieved, students might want to consider the value of afternoon napping to make up the sleep debt. A short nap of about 20 or 30 minutes (a "power nap") can be quite refreshing and valuable to overall performance. Experts recommend that the nap remain short—never longer than an hour or two, since too much afternoon sleep might disrupt or delay one's nighttime sleep.

Exercise Danger Signs
- A delay of over 1 hour in your body's return to a fully relaxed, comfortable state after exercise.
- A change in sleep patterns.
- Any noticeable breathing difficulties or chest pains. Exercise at your THR should not initiate these problems. You should consult a physician.
- Persistent joint or muscle pain. Any lingering joint or muscle pain might signal a problem. Seek the help of an athletic trainer, a physical therapist, or your physician.
- Unusual changes in urine composition or output. Marked color change in your urine could signal possible kidney or bladder difficulties. Drink plenty of water before, during, and after you participate in your activity.
- Anything unusual that you notice after starting your fitness program. Examples are headaches, nosebleeds, fainting, numbness in an extremity, and hemorrhoids.

Summary

- Physical fitness allows one to avoid illness, perform routine activities, and respond to emergencies.
- The health benefits of exercise can be achieved through regular, moderate exercise.
- Fitness is composed of five components: cardiorespiratory endurance, muscular strength, muscular endurance, flexibility, and body composition.
- The American College of Sports Medicine's program for cardiorespiratory fitness has five components: mode of activity, frequency of training, intensity of training, duration of training, and resistance training.

- The *target heart rate* refers to the number of times per minute the heart must contract to produce a training effect.
- Training sessions should take place in three phases: warm-up, workout, and cooldown.
- Fitness experts are concerned about the lack of fitness in today's youth.
- Street dancing, step aerobics, and rollerblading are currently popular aerobic activities.
- College students who are interested in fitness should understand the important topics of steroid use, crosstraining, fluid replacement, bodybuilding, and proper sleep.

Review Questions

1. Identify the five components of fitness described in this chapter. How does each component relate to physical fitness?
2. What is the difference between anaerobic and aerobic energy production? What types of activities are associated with anaerobic energy production? With aerobic energy production?
3. List some of the benefits of aerobic fitness.
4. Describe the various methods used to promote muscular strength.
5. What does the principle of overload mean in regard to fitness training programs?

6. Identify the ACSM's five components of an effective cardiorespiratory fitness program. Explain the important aspects of each component.
7. Under what circumstances should you see a physician before starting a physical fitness program?
8. Identify and describe the three parts of a training session.
9. Describe some of the negative consequences of anabolic steroid use.
10. How can people improve their sleeping habits?

Think About This . . .

- What are your attitudes toward physical fitness? Do you participate in a regular physical fitness program? Why or why not?
- Does your present level of fitness allow you to effectively carry out the activities your schedule demands? Are there things that you would like to do but cannot because of your current level of fitness?
- Describe your level of fitness, taking into consideration cardiorespiratory endurance, strength, and flexibility.
- After determining your own THR, calculate the

THR for a parent or older friend. Talk to these people about starting their own fitness programs. Be ready to help with encouragement and accurate information. They may look to you as a role model for their own health.
- Design a physical fitness plan for yourself, taking into consideration all of the dimensions of body structure and function and the five components of an effective fitness program described in this chapter. What are the chances that you will continue this program after college?

References

1. Blair SN: Exercise and health, *Sports Science Exchange* 3(29):1-6, 1990.
2. Prentice WE: *Fitness for college and life,* ed 4, St Louis, 1994, Mosby.
3. Fit, fitter, fittest, *Harvard Medical School Health Letter* 15(4):2, 1990.
4. Simon HB: Can you run away from cancer? *Harvard Medical School Health Letter* 17(5):5-7, 1992.
5. Cavanaugh J: *Adult development and aging,* Belmont, Calif, 1990, Wadsworth.
6. Ferrini AF, Ferrini RL: *Health in later years,* ed 2, Madison, WI, 1992, Brown & Benchmark.
7. American College of Sports Medicine: Position statement on the recommended quantity and quality of exercise for developing and maintaining fitness in healthy adults, *Med Sci Sports Exerc* 22(2):265-274, 1990.
8. White MD: *Water exercise,* Champaign, IL, 1995, Human Kinetics.
9. Arnheim DD, Prentice WE: *Principles of athletic training,* ed 8, St Louis, 1993, Mosby.
10. An exercise prescription for older people, *Harvard Heart Letter,* 8(10):1-4, January 1998.
11. National Institute of Arthritis and Musculoskeletal and Skin Diseases Clearinghouse, *Low back pain: information package,* National Institutes of Health (Public Health Service), updated September 1997.
12. U.S. Department of Health and Human Services. *Physical activity and health: A report of the Surgeon General:* Centers for Disease Control and Prevention, National Center for Chronic Disease Prevention and Health Promotion, 1996.
13. Maughan RJ, Rehrer NJ: Gastric emptying during exercise, *Sports Science Exchange* 6(5):1-5, 1993.
14. Williams MH: Alcohol and sport performance, *Sports Science Exchange* 4(40):1-4, 1992.
15. Mishra R: Steroids and sports are a losing proposition, *FDA Consumer* 25(7):25-27, 1991.
16. Saeki T: Sport in Japan. In Wagner E, editor: *Sport in Asia and Africa: a comparative handbook,* New York, 1989, Greenwood Press.
17. Rizak G: Sport in the People's Republic of China. In Wagner E, editor: *Sport in Asia and Africa: a comparative handbook,* New York, 1989, Greenwood Press.

Suggested Readings

Burleigh WB: *Fitness lite: a guide for those who have never taken exercise seriously,* Santa Barbara, CA, 1995, Capra Press.
A short, easy-to-read, humorous look at fitness. Disguised in the humor is a solid 16-week fitness program that incorporates important elements, including nutrition, weight management, and aerobic exercise. Fun to read.

Cooper KH: *Antioxidant revolution,* Nashville, TN. 1997, Thomas Nelson Inc.
Written by Dr. Kenneth H. Cooper (the "father of aerobics"), this book examines the benefits of antioxidant supplementation combined with aerobic exercise. Cooper contends that vitamin C, vitamin E, beta-carotene, and other antioxidants strengthen the body's tissues by counteracting the effects of unstable oxygen molecules.

Newby-Fraser P: *Peak fitness for women,* Champaign, IL, 1995, Human Kinetics.
You might think a seven-time Ironman Triathlon champion would aim a fitness book at only swimming, cycling, and running. However, Newby-Fraser elaborates on strength training, nutrition, crosstraining, flexibility training, and competition for women. Sound information, excellent photos, and beneficial workout sheets are included.

Peterson JA, Bryant CX, Peterson SC: *Strength training for women,* Champaign, IL, 1995, Human Kinetics.
This is a comprehensive yet easy-to-read guide to strength training for women. Free weights, weight machines, and non-equipment options are explored. Many illustrations and the pros and cons of various approaches are presented so that the user can tailor a program for herself.

Prentice WE: *Fitness and wellness for life,* ed 5, Dubuque, IA, 1999, WCB/McGraw-Hill.
This highly recommended, comprehensive textbook covers all aspects of fitness and wellness. The book provides particularly well-written coverage of strength training and stretching activities. The author's unique background as a scholar, athletic trainer, and physical therapist increases the credibility of the book.

Prentice WE: *Get fit, stay fit,* St Louis, 1996, Mosby.
This text explains not only how to go about getting fit, but also why it is important to make fitness and exercise a part of your life. It includes specific techniques and guidelines so that you can tailor your fitness program to your individual needs.

White MD: *Water exercise,* Champaign, IL, 1995, Human Kinetics.
Written by a licensed occupational and massage therapist, this book focuses on fitness development and injury rehabilitation through water activities. Nearly 80 exercises are discussed and illustrated. Step-by-step programs are presented from beginner to advanced levels.

Staying Fit During Pregnancy

Like many other attitudes, our thinking on fitness during pregnancy has changed in recent years.[1] No longer is a pregnant woman treated as fragile. A woman needs to be quite careful when carrying a baby, but these days a doctor is more likely to advise against a sedentary lifestyle for a healthy pregnant woman. Exercise during pregnancy can increase a woman's muscle strength, making delivery of the baby easier and faster. Exercise can also help control her weight, making it easier to get back to normal weight after delivery. The baby may benefit from the mother's exercise program as well.

Importance of Exercise for Pregnant Women

Exercise in general is beneficial to the human body, and it is even more important for pregnant women to exercise regularly.[2] During pregnancy a woman's entire body undergoes many physical changes. Muscles are stretched, joints are loosened, and tissues are subjected to stress. If a woman is in good physiological condition, she is more likely to handle these changes with few complications.[3] The baby may also benefit: studies have shown that women who exercise during pregnancy tend to give birth to healthier babies.[2]

Types of Exercise

The types of exercises a woman should perform during pregnancy will vary with the individual and with the stage of pregnancy. General exercises that increase overall fitness and stamina should be practiced, as well as exercises that strengthen specific muscle groups. Muscles of the pelvic floor, for example, should be exercised regularly, since these muscles will be supporting most of the extra weight of the baby. The pelvic floor muscles are involved with control of the bladder and rectum and with controlling increases in pressure within the abdominal cavity resulting from pushing during labor.[3] General exercises for the pelvic floor muscles include Kegel exercises. These exercises involve the contraction of pelvic floor muscles, and they can be performed by squeezing and then relaxing the anal sphincter.[3] These exercises work on the sphincters (rings of muscle) that control the openings of the urethra and anus.

The abdominal muscles are responsible for supporting the load of the growing fetus in the front of the mother's body. They are also used for pushing during delivery. These muscles must be kept in good shape so they can adequately support the increased weight.[3] Muscles involved in maintaining good posture, such as the

back and leg muscles, should also be exercised. Efficient breathing should be practiced as well.

A variety of exercises are available, including walking, swimming, stretching, and strengthening exercises.[2] Yoga and t'ai chi are also good forms of exercise for pregnant women. The muscles of the pelvic floor, abdomen, and back are especially subject to stress and strain during pregnancy and delivery, so certain exercises can also be performed to strengthen these muscles. Exercises can also be performed to speed up recovery after delivery.[4] Such postpartum exercises can be started in some cases within 24 hours after delivery. Exercises can even be started before conception if a pregnancy is anticipated.

Hydrotherapy is becoming a popular option for expectant mothers. Exercising in the water helps reduce stress on joints, since the buoyancy of water reduces body weight by up to 90% of what it is on land.[5] Water also provides more resistance than air, so muscles get a better workout. No special equipment is needed, but various props such as weights or fans can be used to increase resistance. Immersion in water has also been shown to decrease blood pressure, reduce heart rate, and reduce tissue swelling in pregnant women.[2,6] Exercising in water may also reduce the risk for pregnant women of getting overheated or tired.[5] The water must not be too warm, however, since water that is too hot (around 97° F or above) may damage the nervous system and brain of the fetus.[2]

Risks to the Fetus

Although exercise during pregnancy has definite advantages, there are some drawbacks that must be considered as well. Studies suggest that exercise can be harmful to the fetus in some cases. Women who undergo exercise for long periods may experience a prolonged increase in core body temperature (a condition called *hyperthermia*), which may in turn increase the body temperature of the fetus. It is thought that such increases in fetal temperature may in turn put the baby at risk for congenital malformations. It has been shown that fever-induced hyperthermia is related to congenital malformation in many mammals, and recent studies suggest that this may be true for humans as well.[6] If fever from illness can increase the expectant mother's core temperature enough to produce malformations in the fetus, then it is possible that an increase in the mother's core temperature resulting from prolonged exercise may have similar effects. Fortunately, exercise over short periods (15 minutes or less) is not likely to raise the mother's core temperature enough to cause problems.[6]

Water exercise is especially beneficial for pregnant women.

Exercising Safely

If the expectant mother exercised regularly before becoming pregnant, she may have to alter her exercise routine. Intense, high-impact workouts should be avoided in favor of moderate exercise, since very intense workouts may reduce blood flow to the fetus and deprive it of nutrients. Sports that involve sudden stops, such as basketball or tennis, should be avoided,[7] and certain strenuous sports may eventually result in birth complications.[2] Exercises that involve lying on the back should not be performed after the first trimester of pregnancy, since they may reduce blood flow to the mother's heart and the heart of the fetus.[7] Exercises should be chosen that minimize the risk of injury to the fetus and the mother. Because of the changes in the mother's weight distribution during the course of pregnancy, she should be especially aware of balance during workouts. Exercises that may put her at a risk of losing balance and falling should be avoided, especially during the last trimester.[2]

Once safety factors have been accounted for, the healthy pregnant woman still has an array of options to choose from for her exercise routine. As with any workout program, she should consult her physician before beginning. Her obstetrician can tell her which exercises will be most beneficial and can also give tips to reduce potential injury to her and her baby. The obstetrician can give the expectant mother guidelines concerning safe levels of exertion and duration times of exercise as well.

For Discussion . . .

Do you think exercise during pregnancy is a good idea or not? Do the benefits outweigh the risks?

References

1. Kaehler K, Tivers C: *Primetime pregnancy: the proven program for staying in shape before and after your baby is born,* Chicago, IL, 1997, Contemporary Books.
2. Marti J, Hine A: *The alternative health and medicine encyclopedia,* Gale, Cincinnati, 1995, Gale.
3. Noble E: *Essential exercises for the childbearing year,* ed 2, Boston, 1982, Houghton Mifflin.
4. Parr R, Rudnitsky DA: *Rob Parr's post-pregnancy workout,* New York, 1997, Berkeley Publishing Group.
5. Brody JE: For gentler aerobics, just add water, *The Saturday Evening Post* 263(6), Sept-Oct 1991.
6. Cefalo RC, Moos M-K: *Preconceptional health care: a practical guide,* ed 2, St Louis, 1995, Mosby.
7. Good news about exercise and pregnancy, *Parents,* 70(8), August 1995.

Understanding Nutrition and Your Diet

Healthy People: Looking Ahead to 2010

Nutrition and dietary practices are closely related to many aspects of wellness, including fitness, weight management, cardiovascular health, and the prevention of diseases such as cancer, osteoporosis, and diabetes mellitus. Accordingly, several important nutrition-related objectives were included in the *Healthy People 2000* report.

One objective was to reduce the percentage of total calories from fat, especially saturated fat, in Americans' diets. In 1995 the *Midcourse Review* reported that we were about one quarter of the way toward reaching these goals. Two related goals, introducing fat-reduced foods into supermarkets and restaurants and limiting the sale of processed foods in stores and vending machines, had been reached at mid-decade.

The *Healthy People 2010* goals in the area of nutrition will probably focus on two areas. The first is food safety, especially reducing bacterial contamination in processing and preparation. The second area is the refinement and expansion of food labeling, including the use of the term "organic" on food labels. The goals might also focus on countering the fast-food industry's aggressive marketing of super-size food items.

From the prenatal period throughout life, we must follow sound dietary practices to maintain high-level health. Food provides the body with the **nutrients** needed for production of energy, repair of damaged tissue, growth of new tissue, and regulation of physiological processes.

Physiologically, these nutrients—carbohydrates, fat, protein, vitamins, minerals, dietary fiber, and water—are essential in adequate quantity. In addition, the production, preparation, and serving of food enriches our lives in ways not directly related to its physiological value.

TYPES AND SOURCES OF NUTRIENTS

We discuss first the familiar nutrients: carbohydrates, fats, and proteins. These three nutrients provide our bodies with **calories**.* Calories are used quickly by our bodies in energy metabolism or are stored in the form of glycogen or adipose tissue, the tissue composed of fat cells designed to hold liquefied fat. Because the other nutrient groups are not sources of *energy* for the body, we discuss them later.

Carbohydrates

Carbohydrates are various combinations of sugar units, or saccharides. The body uses carbohydrates primarily for energy. Each gram of carbohydrate contains 4 calories. Since the average person requires approximately 2000 calories per day and about 60% of our calories come from carbohydrates, we obtain roughly 1200 calories per day from carbohydrates.[1]

Carbohydrates occur in three forms, depending on the number of saccharide (sugar) units that make up the molecule. Carbohydrates that contain only one saccharide unit are classified as *monosaccharides* (glucose, or blood sugar), those with two units are *disaccharides* (sucrose, or table sugar), and those with more than two units are *polysaccharides* (starches).

In terms of sucrose Americans now consume about 125 pounds of sugar each year—usually in colas, candies, and pastries, which offer few additional nutritional benefits.[2] For years, excess sugar intake was blamed for a number of serious health problems, including obesity, mineral deficiencies, behavioral disorders, dental cavities, diabetes mellitus, and cardiovascular disease. However, with the exception of dental cavities, current scientific data fail to confirm that sugar per se directly causes any of these health problems. This said, however, the inability of some people to digest milk sugar (lactose) is well documented. Lactose-intolerant people lack an enzyme used in the digestion of this simple sugar. The brisk sales of enzyme supplements now available near dairy cases in supermarkets may, however, suggest that the problem is more widespread than experts believe. Regardless, today it is recommended that no more than 10% of our total calories come from simple sugars.

Much of the sugar we consume is hidden—that is, sugar is a principal product we may overlook in many food items. Foods such as ketchup, salad dressings, cured meat products, and canned vegetables and fruits frequently contain much hidden sugar. High-fructose corn syrup, often found in these items, is a very concentrated sugar solution.

Starches are complex carbohydrates composed of long chains of sugar units. However, these starches should not be confused with the adjective *starchy*. When people refer to starchy foods, they are usually referring to bland, bread-filled, or "heavy" foods. True starches are among the most important sources of dietary carbohydrates. Starches are found primarily in vegetables, fruits, and grains. Eating true starches is overall very nutritionally beneficial because most starch sources also contain much-needed vitamins, minerals, protein, and water.

Fats

Fats (lipids) are an important nutrient in our diets. Fats provide a concentrated form of energy (9 calories per gram) and help give our foods high *satiety value*.

---

*The term *calorie* is used here to mean kilocalorie (kcal), which is the accepted scientific expression of the energy value of a food.

---

nutrients
Elements in foods that are required for the energy, growth, and repair of tissues and regulation of body processes.

calories
Units of heat (energy); specifically, one calorie equals the amount of heat required to raise the temperature of 1 kilogram of water by 1° C.

carbohydrates
Chemical compounds composed of sugar units; the body's primary source of energy.

How Much Fat Is Enough?

How advisable is a diet in which fat intake is restricted to less than 30% of total calories? Controversy over this question stems from an article in the *Journal of the American Medical Association*.[3] Researchers reported that men who had high cholesterol levels, a known risk factor for cardiovascular disease, showed an unexpected decline in levels of high-density lipoprotein (HDL) cholesterol, the so-called good cholesterol thought to favor heart health, when fat intake was restricted. The researchers recommended caution in lowering fat intake too much.

Critics of the report content that the researchers failed to consider the improved structural appearance of the arteries of people who restrict fat intake to as little as 10% of total calories. Perhaps the controversy can be laid to rest if the study is repeated and includes an assessment of artery wall changes.

Fat also helps give food its pleasing taste, or *palatability*. Fats carry the fat-soluble vitamins A, D, E, and K. Without fat, these vitamins would quickly pass through the body. Fat insulates our bodies to help us retain heat.

Dietary sources of fat are often difficult to identify. The visible fats in our diet, such as butter, salad oils, and the layer of fat on some cuts of meat, represent only about 40% of the fat we consume. Most of the fat we eat is "hidden" in food.

When shopping, we often notice that the fat content of some foods is reported in terms of a percentage of the product's weight. In selecting the type of milk we drink, for example, we see that milk ranges from skim milk (no fat) to low-fat milk (½%) through reduced-fat milk (1% to 2%) to whole milk (3% to 4%). The labeling term *reduced fat* for 1% and 2% milk was introduced in 1997 to reflect that these types of milk are no longer considered low fat.

Today, it is recommended that no more than 25% to 30% of our calories come from fat. Complete the Personal Assessment on pp. 95-96 to see whether you eat too many fatty foods. If so, the Health Action Guide on p. 97 offers tips for reducing the amount of fat in your diet. Children under 2 years of age, however, need adequate fat in their diets.[4] Check with your doctor before restricting the amount of fat in a young child's diet.

Every type of dietary fat is made up of a combination of three forms of fat: saturated, monounsaturated, and polyunsaturated, based on chemical composition. Consumers should pay attention to the amount of each type of fat in dietary fat because of the role that each form plays in heart disease (see Chapter 10). **Saturated fats,** including those found in animal sources and in vegetable oils to which hydrogen has

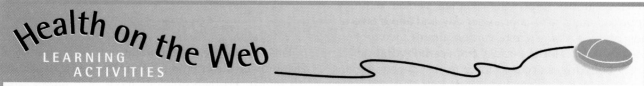

Health on the Web
LEARNING ACTIVITIES

Activity 1

Although the government has issued dietary guidelines of one kind or another on many occasions, the 1995 Dietary Guidelines for Americans are the most current and widely disseminated guidelines. Go to *Prevention*'s Healthy Ideas at http://www.healthyideas.com and select the forum *Are the dietary guidelines too strict?* Read the "Food for Thought" information and then answer "What do you think?" Is there a better way to achieve good health than following the U.S. government's or another group's recommended dietary allowances? Are the dietary guidelines too restrictive? Cast your cyberspace vote and comments with others.

Activity 2

Nutrition and dietary practices are closely related to many aspects of wellness. You have learned the basics of healthy eating from reading this chapter. Type in the URL http://cgi.pathfinder.com/cgi-bin/GDML/gdmldb/thrive?NutriTest and answer the nutrition quiz questions listed. When you are finished, click on the "submit" button to see your nutrition quiz score.

Activity 3

Fast foods are convenience foods prepared in walk-in or drive-through restaurants. In contrast to that of junk foods, the nutritional value of fast foods can vary considerably. With the help of registered dietitian Jennifer K. Nelson, the Mayo Clinic has put together a quiz based on data supplied by the fast-food restaurants themselves. Go to the web document at http://www.mayohealth.org/mayo/9708/htm/fastfood/start.htm and select "Take the quiz." Complete the questions on the fast-food quiz. How well did you do?

PERSONAL ASSESSMENT

Do You Have Fatty Habits?

Fat has earned a bad reputation because of the health problems to which it contributes when we eat too much of it. The questionnaire below will help you think about the amounts and types of fat that you generally eat. For each general type of food or food habit, circle the response category that is most typical for you. If you never or almost never eat any items of a particular food type, just skip that type.

Food Type/Habit	High Fat	Medium Fat	Low Fat
Chicken	Fried with the skin	Baked, broiled, or barbecued with the skin	Baked, broiled, or barbecued without the skin
Fat present on meats	Usually eat	Sometimes eat	Never eat
Fat used in cooking	Butter, lard, bacon grease, chicken fat	Margarine, oil	Nonstick cooking spray or no fat used
Additions to rice, bread, potatoes, vegetables, etc.	Butter, lard, bacon grease, chicken fat, coconut oil, cream cheese	Margarine, oil, peanut butter	Butter-flavored granules or no fat used
Pizza toppings	Sausage, pepperoni, extra cheese, combination	Canadian bacon	Vegetable
Sandwich spreads	Mayonnaise or mayonnaise-type dressing	Light mayonnaise, oil and vinegar	Mustard, fat-free mayonnaise
Milk and milk products (e.g., yogurt)	Whole milk and whole-milk products	Reduced fat and low-fat milk and milk products	Skim milk and milk products
Sandwich side orders	Chips, potato salad, macaroni salad with creamy dressing	Coleslaw, pasta salad with clear dressing	Vegetable sticks, pretzels, pickle
Salad dressings	Blue cheese, ranch, Thousand Island, other creamy type	Oil and vinegar, clear-base dressing	Oil-free dressing, lemon juice, flavored vinegar
Typical meat portion eaten	6-8 ounces or more	4-5 ounces	2-3 ounces
Sandwich fillings	Beef or pork hot dogs, salami, bologna, pepperoni, cheese, tuna or chicken salad	Turkey hot dogs, 85% fat-free lunch meats, corned beef, peanut butter, hummus (chickpea paste)	95% fat-free lunch meats, roast turkey, roast beef, lean ham
Ground meats	Regular ground beef, sausage meat, ground meat, ground pork (about 30% fat)	Lean ground beef, ground chuck, turkey sausage meat (20%-25% fat)	Ground turkey, extra lean ground beef, ground round (about 15% fat)
Deep-fried foods (e.g., french fries, onion rings, fish or chicken patties, egg rolls, tempura)	Eat every day	Eat once a week	Eat once a month or never
Bread for sandwiches	Croissant	Biscuit	Whole wheat, French, tortilla, pita or pocket bread, bagel, sourdough, or English muffin

Continued

Food Type/Habit	High Fat	Medium Fat	Low Fat
Cheeses	Hard cheeses (e.g., cheddar, Swiss, provolone, Jack, American, processed)	Part skim mozzarella, part skim ricotta, low-fat and reduced fat cheeses	Nonfat cheeses, nonfat cottage cheese, no cheese
Frozen desserts	Premium or regular ice cream	Ice milk or low-fat frozen yogurt	Sherbet, Italian water ice, nonfat frozen yogurt, frozen fruit whip
Coffee lighteners	Cream, liquid or powdered creamer	Whole milk	Low-fat or skim milk
Snacks	Chips, pies, cheese and crackers, nuts, donuts, microwave popcorn, chocolate, granola bars	Muffins, toaster pastries, unbuttered commercial popcorn	Pretzels, vegetable sticks, fresh or dried fruit, air-popped popcorn, bread sticks, jelly beans, hard candy
Cookies	Chocolate coated, chocolate chip, peanut butter, filled sandwich type	Oatmeal	Ginger snaps, vanilla wafers, graham crackers, animal crackers, fruit newtons

SCORING: (_____ × 2)   +   (_____ × 1)   +   (_____ × 0)   =

Total Score _____

Once you have completed the questionnaire, count the number of circles in each column and calculate your score as follows: multiply the number of choices in the left-hand (high fat) column by 2 and multiply the number of choices in the middle by 1. Any number of choices in the right-hand column will equal 0.

Less than 10 = Excellent fat habits
10 to 20 = Good fat habits
20 to 30 = Need to trim some fat
Over 30 = Very high fat diet

If your score is 20 or above, try to substitute more foods from the middle (medium fat) column or, better still, the right (low fat) column for foods in the left-hand (high fat) column.

been added (hydrogenated), becoming *trans-fatty acids*, need to be carefully limited in a modern healthy diet. Concern over the presence of trans-fatty acids (an altered form of normal vegetable oil molecule) is associated with changes to the cell membrane, including those cells lining the artery wall. This possibly prevents these vessel wall cells from freeing cholesterol from their surfaces.[5] The amount of trans-fatty acids in the diet can be reduced by using liquefied margarines rather than the solid stick forms. In addition, several products containing low-calorie fat substitutes are now on the market (see the Star Box on p. 97).

Tropical oils

Although all cooking oils (and fats such as butter, lard, margarine, and shortening) have the same number of calories by weight (9 calories per gram), some oils contain high percentages of saturated fats. All oils and fats contain varying percentages of saturated, monounsaturated, and polyunsaturated fats. How-ever, the tropical oils—coconut, palm, and palm kernel—contain much higher percentages of saturated fats than do other cooking oils.[4] Coconut oil, for example, is 92% saturated fat (Figure 5-1). Tropical oils can still be found in some brands of snack foods, crackers, cookies, nondairy creamers, and breakfast cereals, although they have been removed from most national brands. Do you check for tropical oils on the ingredients labels of the foods you select?

Cholesterol

A high blood level of **cholesterol** has also been reported to be a risk factor for the development of cardiovascular disease (see Chapter 10). Cholesterol is necessary in all animal tissue and is manufactured by our bodies. Evidence first reported more than a decade ago suggests that increased intake of saturated fats may increase serum (blood) cholesterol levels.[6] However, the relationship between intake of dietary cholesterol and serum cholesterol levels remains unclear.[7]

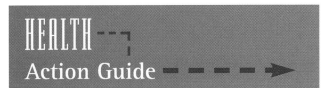

Tips for Reducing the Fat Content of Meals

A combination of the following practices can be used to reduce the fat content of meals. Can you suggest additional ways to reduce fat in your diet?

- Become familiar with today's food labels, and use the information provided to reduce the fat content of meals.
- Cut away and discard skin from meats such as chicken.
- When eating out, do not order foods with cream-based sauces, such as fettuccine alfredo.
- Trim fat from cuts of meat, including both the fat interspersed within the cut and that along the edges.
- Layer vegetables over baked potatoes to reduce the tendency to add butter, margarine, or sour cream.
- Request salad dressing and other condiments on the side so that you can control the amount you use.
- Eat more vegetables, fruits, and breads in place of meats and cheeses.
- Use jelly and apple butter in place of butter and margarine on toast, bread, and bagels.

Nevertheless, most doctors still recommend that people restrict their dietary intake of cholesterol to 300 mg or less per day, reduce total fat and saturated fat intake, and exercise regularly. High-cholesterol foods include whole milk, shellfish, animal fat, and egg yolks. Only foods of animal origin can contain cholesterol. Thus labels that appear on foods such as peanut butter and margarine trumpeting "cholesterol free" are overstating the obvious.

Low-fat foods

Reflecting our growing concern about the role of dietary fats in many health problems has been the explosion of fat-free, low-fat, or reduced-fat food items appearing in stores and restaurants. Nutritionists believe, however, that this trend could soon wane as the fast-food industry moves away from low-fat items. Apparently the public favors good taste over the long-term benefits of weight maintenance and reduced incidence of heart disease.[8] As healthful as these foods might be, however, it is important to remember that they may still be high in calories and, therefore, should not be consumed in large amounts just because of their lower-fat formulation.

Proteins

Proteins are found in every living cell; they are composed of chains of **amino acids.** Of the 20 naturally occurring amino acids, the body can synthesize

Low-Calorie Fat Substitutes
Newly developed products containing fat substitutes such as Simplesse, Simple Pleasures, Olestra, and Trailblazer are now or will soon be available. By combining high-protein sources such as egg whites and milk through a process called *microparticulation*, or by constructing new undigestible molecules, food technologists are able to restructure the configuration of protein to resemble that of fat. These new products contain no cholesterol and have 80% fewer calories than similar products made with fat. When several Olestra food products were test marketed in selected Midwestern communities, some people complained that they could not tolerate the fat substitute. Most of these people reported gastrointestinal upset, including bloating, gas, and diarrhea. A recent study, however, failed to demonstrate a significant level of distress caused by eating products containing Olestra.[9]

saturated fats
Fats that are difficult for the body to use; they are in solid form at room temperature; primarily animal fats.

cholesterol
A primary form of fat found in the blood; lipid material manufactured within the body and derived from dietary sources.

proteins
Compounds composed of chains of amino acids; the primary components of muscle and connective tissue.

amino acids
The chief components of protein; can be manufactured by the body or obtained from dietary sources.

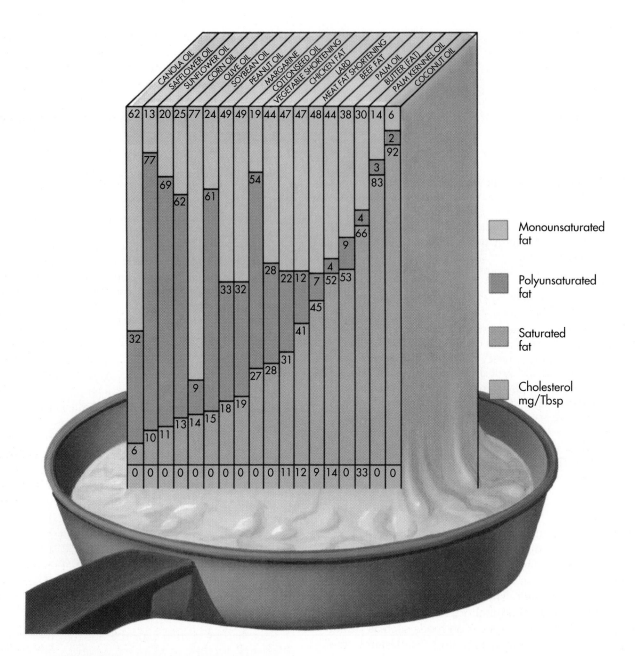

Figure 5-1 Comparison of dietary fats (fatty acid content normalized to 100%). Every fat shown above is a combination of three forms of fat: monounsaturated, polyunsaturated, and saturated.

all but nine *essential amino acids** from the foods we eat. A food that contains all nine essential amino acids is called a *complete protein* food. Sources of complete protein are animal products, including milk, meat, cheese, and eggs. A food source that does not contain all nine essential amino acids is called an *incomplete*

protein food. Vegetables, grains, and *legumes* (peas or beans—including chickpeas, butter beans, soybean curd [tofu], and peanuts) are principal sources of incomplete protein. For some people, including vegan vegetarians (see pp. 117-120 and the Focus Box on p. 125), people with limited access to animal-based food sources, or those who have significantly limited their meat, egg, and dairy product consumption, it is important to understand how essential amino acids can be obtained from incomplete protein sources. This requires the careful selection of plant foods in combi-

---

*Eight additional compounds are sometimes classified as amino acids; thus some nutritionists believe that there are more than 20 amino acids.

A Variety of Diets

Do you eat to live or live to eat? Maybe it depends on what day it is! We do know that to stay healthy we need to eat a variety of good foods.

What we eat reflects our culture. In the United States, we have "American" food, such as hamburgers and corn on the cob. Because of the variety of ethnic groups in this country, we also enjoy many foods from other cultures. In fact, it would be difficult to identify the staple foods of the American diet.

People in other countries often consume those particular foods that are most widely available. Corn, for example, is the main ingredient in food for most Mexicans, and it is eaten in a variety of forms. Beans, or *frijoles,* are another staple food found in the Mexican diet. There are many varieties, and they are commonly eaten with rice and hot peppers. The diet is basically a healthy one, but there is not enough food to feed all the people, especially the poorest peasants.

Seafood is enjoyed by many Canadians. Fishing is an important industry for northern Canadian natives. Some Native Canadian groups have a long history of commercial fishing. Salmon and cod have been caught and sold by the Inuit of Labrador for many years, and fish were sold to the Gold Rush miners by Native Canadians from the Yukon. Fisheries run by Native Canadians are operational today, through government assistance, and provide fish to northern and southern parts of the country.

Can you identify food choices in your own diet that are commonly found in other cultures, such as Asian cuisine?

nations that will provide all of the essential amino acids. The list below shows many usable combinations that include legumes and grains:

- Sunflower seeds/green peas
- Navy beans/barley
- Green peas/corn
- Red beans/rice
- Sesame seeds/soybeans
- Black-eyed peas/rice and peanuts
- Green peas/rice
- Corn/pinto beans

When even one essential amino acid is missing from the diet, deficiency can develop.

Protein primarily promotes growth and maintenance of body tissue. However, when caloric intake falls, protein will be broken down and converted into glucose. This loss of protein can impede growth and repair of tissue. Protein also is a primary component of enzyme and hormone structure, helps maintain the *acid-base balance* of our bodies, and is a source of energy (4 calories per gram consumed). Nutritionists recommend that 12% to 15% of our caloric intake be from protein, particularly that of plant origin.

Vitamins

Vitamins are organic compounds that are required in small amounts for normal growth, reproduction, and maintenance of health. Vitamins differ from carbohydrates, fats, and proteins in that they do not provide calories or serve as structural elements for our bodies. Vitamins are *coenzymes.* By facilitating the action of **enzymes,** vitamins help initiate a wide variety of body responses, including energy production, use of minerals, and growth of healthy tissue.

Vitamins can be classified as *water soluble* (capable of being dissolved in water) or *fat soluble* (capable of being dissolved in fat or lipid tissue). Water-soluble vitamins include the B-complex vitamins and vitamin C. Most of the excess of these water-soluble vitamins will be eliminated from the body in the urine. The fat-soluble vitamins are vitamins A, D, E, and K. Excessive intake of these vitamins causes them to be stored in the body in the adipose (fat) tissue. It is therefore possible to consume and retain too many of these vitamins, particularly vitamins A and D. Because excess fat-soluble vitamins are stored in the body's fat, organs that contain fat, such as the liver, are primary storage sites. (See Tables 5-1 and 5-2 for general properties of fat-soluble and water-soluble vitamins.)

Because water-soluble vitamins dissolve quickly in water, you should be careful not to lose them during the preparation of fresh fruits and vegetables. One precaution is not to overcook fresh vegetables. The longer vegetables are steamed or boiled, the more

> **vitamins**
> Organic compounds that facilitate the action of enzymes.
>
> **enzymes**
> Organic substances that control the rate of physiological reactions but are not themselves altered in the process.

Table 5-1	The Fat-Soluble Vitamins, Their Functions, Deficiency Conditions, and Food Sources					
Vitamin	Major functions	Deficiency symptoms	People most at risk	Dietary sources	RDA	Toxicity symptoms
Vitamin A (retinoids) and provitamin A (carotenoids)	1. Vision, light, and color 2. Promotes growth 3. Prevents drying of skin and eyes 4. Promotes resistance to bacterial infection	1. Night blindness 2. Xerophthalmia 3. Poor growth 4. Dry skin (keratinization)	People in poverty, especially preschool children (still very rare)	Vitamin A Liver Fortified milk Provitamin A Sweet potatoes Spinach Greens Carrots Cantaloupe Apricots Broccoli	Women: 800 RE (4000 IU) Men: 1000 RE (5000 IU)	Fetal malformations, hair loss, skin changes, pain in bones
Vitamin D (cholecalciferol and ergocalciferol)	1. Facilitates absorption of calcium and phosphorus 2. Maintains optimum calcification of bone	1. Rickets 2. Osteomalacia	Breastfed infants, elderly shut-ins	Vitamin D-fortified milk Fish oils Tuna fish Salmon	5-10 micrograms (200-400 IU)	Growth retardation, kidney damage, calcium deposits in soft tissue
Vitamin E (tocopherols, tocotrienols)	1. Antioxidant: prevents breakdown of vitamin A and unsaturated fatty acids	1. Hemolysis of red blood cells 2. Nerve destruction	People with poor fat absorption (still very rare)	Vegetable oils Some greens Some fruits	Women: 8 α-tocopherol equivalents Men: 10 α-tocopherol equivalents	Muscle weakness, headaches, fatigue, nausea, inhibition of vitamin K metabolism
Vitamin K (phylloquinone and menaquinone)	1. Helps form prothrombin and other factors for blood clotting	1. Hemorrhage	People taking antibiotics for months at a time	Green vegetables Liver	60-80 micrograms	Anemia and jaundice

RE, Retinol equivalents; IU, international units.

water-soluble vitamins will be lost. You may wish to drink (or use in cooking) any water in which vegetables were boiled or steamed.

To ensure an adequate vitamin intake, eat a variety of foods. Unless there are special circumstances, such as pregnancy, lactation, infancy, or an existing health problem, nearly everyone who eats a reasonably well-rounded diet consumes enough vitamins to prevent deficiencies.

In spite of the availability of vitamin-rich foods, not all people eat a balanced diet based on a variety of foods. Recent studies suggest that a somewhat higher intake of vitamins A, C, and E for adults might reduce the risk of developing cancer, atherosclerosis, and de-

pressed levels of HDL cholesterol (see Chapter 10).[10,11] In addition, consumption of an adequate amount of folic acid before and during pregnancy has been shown to reduce the incidence of birth defects.[12] To ensure adequate folic acid intake (400 micrograms/day), in 1997 the FDA began to require that bread and cereal products be supplemented with folic acid. The goal of this requirement is for pregnant women and women of childbearing age to receive at least 140 micrograms/day through dietary intake. Taking a daily multivitamin before and during pregnancy would easily provide the remaining amount of folic acid necessary to promote fetal neural tube closure. Unfortunately, less than a quarter of pregnant women do so.[13]

Table 5-2   The Water-Soluble Vitamins, Their Functions, Deficiency Conditions, and Food Sources

Name	Major functions	Deficiency symptoms	People most at risk	Dietary sources	RDA or ESADDI	Toxicity
Thiamin	Coenzyme involved with enzymes in carbohydrate metabolism; nerve function	Beriberi, nervous tingling, poor coordination, edema, heart changes, weakness	People with alcoholism, people in poverty	Sunflower seeds, pork, whole and enriched grains, dried beans, peas, brewer's yeast	1.1-1.5 milligrams	None possible from food
Riboflavin	Coenzyme involved in energy metabolism	Inflammation of mouth and tongue, cracks at corners of the mouth, eye disorders	Possibly people on certain medications if no dairy products consumed	Milk, mushrooms, spinach, liver, enriched grains	1.2-1.7 milligrams	None reported
Niacin	Coenzyme involved in energy metabolism, fat synthesis, fat breakdown	Pellagra, diarrhea, dermatitis, dementia	People in severe poverty where corn is dominant food, people with alcoholism	Mushrooms, bran, tuna, salmon, chicken, beef, liver, peanuts, enriched grains	15-19 milligrams	Flushing of skin at >100 milligrams
Pantothenic acid	Coenzyme involved in energy metabolism, fat synthesis, fat breakdown	Using an antagonist causes tingling in hands, fatigue, headache, nausea	People with alcoholism	Mushrooms, liver, broccoli, eggs; most foods have some	4-7 milligrams	None
Biotin	Coenzyme involved in glucose production, fat synthesis	Dermatitis, tongue soreness, anemia, depression	People with alcoholism	Cheese, egg yolks, cauliflower, peanut butter, liver	30-100 micrograms	Unknown
Vitamin B$_6$, pyridoxine, and other forms	Coenzyme involved in protein metabolism, neurotransmitter synthesis, hemoglobin synthesis, many other functions	Headache, anemia, convulsions, nausea, vomiting, flaky skin, sore tongue	Adolescent and adult women, people on certain medications, people with alcoholism	Animal protein foods, spinach, broccoli, bananas, salmon, sunflower seeds	1.8-2 milligrams	Nerve destruction at doses >100 milligrams

Continued

Table 5-2, cont'd.

Name	Major functions	Deficiency symptoms	People most at risk	Dietary sources	RDA or ESADDI	Toxicity
Folate (folic acid)	Coenzyme involved in DNA synthesis	Megaloblastic anemia, inflammation of tongue, diarrhea, poor growth, mental disorders	People with alcoholism, pregnant women, people taking certain medications	Green leafy vegetables, orange juice, organ meats, sprouts, sunflower seeds	180-200 microgram	None, nonprescription vitamin dosage is controlled by FDA
Vitamin B_{12} (cobalamins)	Coenzyme involved in folate metabolism, nerve function	Macrocytic anemia, poor nerve function	Elderly because of poor absorption, vegans	Animal foods, especially organ meats, oysters, clams (B_{12} not naturally in plant foods)	2 micrograms	None
Vitamin C (ascorbic acid)	Collagen synthesis, hormone synthesis, neurotransmitter synthesis	Scurvy: poor wound healing, pinpoint hemorrhages, bleeding gums, edema	People with alcoholism, elderly men living alone	Citrus fruits, strawberries, broccoli, greens	60 milligrams	Doses >1-2 grams cause diarrhea and can alter some diagnostic tests

At the same time that many health experts are recommending some vitamin supplementation, the FDA has prohibited manufacturers of food supplements, including vitamins, from making *unsubstantiated claims* for the cure and prevention of disease.[14] Supplement manufacturers fought against the implementation of this regulation by trying to make the public think that vitamins might become available only by prescription. This, of course, did not happen. Today, the sale of food supplements (vitamins, minerals, and amino acids) is a huge industry in this country, with 75 million Americans using *dietary aids* at an annual cost of more than $1.5 billion.

Minerals

Nearly 5% of the body is composed of inorganic materials, the *minerals.* Minerals function primarily as structural elements (in teeth, muscles, hemoglobin, and hormones). They are also critical in the regulation of body processes, including muscle contraction, heart function, blood clotting, protein synthesis, and red blood cell formation. Approximately 21 minerals have been recognized as essential for human health.

Major minerals are those that are seen in relatively high amounts in our body tissues. Examples of major minerals are calcium, phosphorus, sulfur, sodium, potassium, and magnesium. Examples of **trace elements,** minerals seen in relatively small amounts in body tissues, include zinc, iron, copper, selenium, and iodine. Trace elements are required only in small quantities; nevertheless, they are essential for good health. (See Tables 5-3 and 5-4 for lists of minerals and their functions.) As with vitamins, the safest, most appropriate way to prevent a mineral deficiency is to eat a balanced diet.

Water

Water may well be our most essential nutrient, since without water most of us would die from **dehydration** effects in less than a week. We could survive for weeks or even years without some of the essential minerals and vitamins, but not without water. More than half our body weight comes from water. Water provides the medium for nutrient and waste transport, controls body temperature, and plays a key role in nearly all of our body's biochemical reactions.

Table 5-3   Key Trace Minerals

Mineral	Major functions	Deficiency symptoms	People most at risk	RDA or ESADDI	Nutrient–dense dietary sources	Results of toxicity
Iron	Part of hemoglobin and other key compounds used in respiration; used for immune function	Low serum iron levels, small, pale red blood cells, low blood hemoglobin values	Infants, preschool children, adolescents, women in childbearing years	Men: 10 milligrams Women: 15 milligrams	Meats, spinach, seafood, broccoli, peas, bran, enriched breads	Toxicity is seen in children who consume 200-400 milligrams in iron pills and in people with hemochromatosis; in this latter case, people overabsorb iron
Zinc	Over 200 enzymes need zinc, including enzymes involved in growth, immunity, alcohol metabolism, sexual development, and reproduction	Skin rash, diarrhea, decreased appetite and sense of taste, hair loss, poor growth and development, poor wound healing	Vegetarians, women in general, the elderly	Men: 15 milligrams Women: 12 milligrams	Seafood, meats, greens, whole grains	Reduces iron and copper absorption; can cause diarrhea, cramps, and depressed immune function
Selenium	Part of antioxidant system	Muscle pain, muscle weakness, heart disease	Unknown	55-70 micrograms	Meats, eggs, fish, seafood, whole grains	Nausea, vomiting, hair loss, weakness, liver disease
Iodide	Part of thyroid hormone	Goiter, poor growth in infancy when mother is deficient in pregnancy	None in America, since salt is usually fortified	150 micrograms	Iodized salt, white bread, saltwater fish, dairy products	Inhibition of function of the thyroid gland
Copper	Aids in iron metabolism; works with many enzymes, such as those involved in protein metabolism and hormone synthesis	Anemia, low white blood cell count, poor growth	Infants recovering from malnutrition, people who use overzealous supplementation of zinc	1.5-3 milligrams	Liver, cocoa, beans, nuts, whole grains, dried fruits	Vomiting, nervous system disorders

Continued

Table 5-3, cont'd

Mineral	Major functions	Deficiency symptoms	People most at risk	RDA or ESADDI	Nutrient-dense dietary sources	Results of toxicity
Fluoride	Increases resistance of tooth enamel to dental caries	Increased risk of dental caries	Areas where water is not fluoridated and dental treatments do not make up for this lack of fluoride	1.5-4 milligrams	Fluoridated water, toothpaste, dental treatments, tea, seaweed	Stomach upset, mottling (staining) of teeth during development
Chromium	Enhances blood glucose control	High blood glucose levels after eating	People on total parenteral nutrition and perhaps elderly people with non–insulin-dependent diabetes mellitus	50-200 micrograms	Egg yolks, whole grains, pork	Caused by industrial contamination, not dietary excess
Manganese	Aids action of some enzymes, such as those involved in carbohydrate metabolism	None in humans	Unknown	2-5 milligrams	Nuts, rice, oats, beans	Unknown in humans
Molybdenum	Aids action of some enzymes	None in humans	Unknown	75-250 micrograms	Beans, grains, nuts	Unknown in humans

Most people seldom think about the importance of an adequate intake of water and fluids. Adults require about six to ten glasses a day, depending on their activity level and environment. People who drink beverages that tend to dehydrate the body (tea, coffee, and alcohol) should increase their water consumption. Of course, we also obtain needed fluids from fruits, vegetables, fruit and vegetable juices, milk, and noncaffeinated soft drinks. However, excessive water consumption by infants can dilute sodium stores in the body to dangerously low levels, possible causing death.[15]

Fiber

Although not considered a nutrient by definition, **fiber** is an important component of sound nutrition. Fiber consists of plant material that is not digested but rather moves through the digestive tract and out of the body. Cereal, fruits, and vegetables all provide us with dietary fiber.

Fiber can be classified into two large groups on the basis of water solubility. *Insoluble* fibers are those that can absorb water from the intestinal tract. By absorbing water, the insoluble fibers give the stool bulk and decrease the time it takes the stool to move through the digestive tract. In contrast, *soluble* fiber turns to a "gel" within the intestinal tract and in so doing binds to liver bile, to which cholesterol is attached. Thus the soluble fibers may be valuable in removing cholesterol, which lowers blood cholesterol levels.[1] Also, since foods high in soluble fiber are generally low in sugar and saturated fats, fiber may indirectly contribute to keeping the blood sugar level low and reducing the risk of colon cancer associated with diets high in saturated fat.[16]

In recent years, attention has been directed toward

Table 5-4   Water and the Major Minerals

Name	Major functions	Deficiency symptoms	People most at risk	RDA or minimum requirement	Nutrient–dense dietary sources	Results of toxicity
Water	Medium for chemical reactions, removal of waste products, perspiration to cool the body	Thirst, muscle weakness, poor endurance	Infants with a fever, elderly in nursing homes	1 milliliter per calorie burned*	As such and in foods	Probably occurs only in mental disorders: headache, blurred vision, convulsions
Sodium	A major ion of the extracellular fluid; nerve impulse transmission	Muscle cramps	People who severely restrict sodium to lower blood pressure (250-500 milligrams/day)	500 milligrams	Table salt, processed foods	High blood pressure in susceptible individuals
Potassium	A major ion of intracellular fluid; nerve impulse transmission	Irregular heartbeat, loss of appetite, muscle cramps	People who use potassium-wasting diuretics or have poor diets, as seen in poverty and with alcoholism	2000 milligrams	Spinach, squash, bananas, orange juice, other vegetables and fruits, milk	Slowing of the heartbeat; seen in kidney failure
Chloride	A major ion of the extracellular fluid; acid production in stomach; nerve transmission	Convulsions in infants	No one, probably, when infant formula manufacturers control product quality adequately	700 milligrams	Table salt, some vegetables	High blood pressure in susceptible people when combined with sodium
Calcium	Bone and tooth strength; blood clotting; nerve impulse transmission; muscle contractions; cell regulation	Poor intake increases the risk for osteoporosis	Women in general, especially those who constantly restrict their energy intake and consume few dairy products	800 milligrams (older than 24 years old)	Dairy products, canned fish, leafy vegetables, tofu, fortified orange juice	Very high intakes may cause kidney stones in susceptible people

Continued

*An approximation; best to keep urine volume greater than 1 liter (4 cups) per day.

Table 5-4, cont'd.

Name	Major functions	Deficiency symptoms	People most at risk	RDA or minimum requirement	Nutrient-dense dietary sources	Results of toxicity
Phosphorus	Bone and tooth strength; part of various metabolic compounds; major ion of intracellular fluid	Probably none; poor bone maintenance possible	Elderly consuming very nutrient-poor diets, possibly total vegetarians and those with alcoholism	800 milligrams (older than 24 years)	Dairy products, processed foods, fish, soft drinks	Hampers bone health in people with kidney failure; poor bone mineralization if calcium intakes are low
Magnesium	Bone strength; enzyme function; nerve and heart function	Weakness, muscle pain, poor heart function	People on thiazide diuretics, women in general	Men: 350 milligrams Women: 280 milligrams	Wheat bran, green vegetables, nuts, chocolate	Causes weakness in people with kidney failure
Sulfur	Part of vitamins and amino acids; drug detoxification; acid-base balance	None	People who do not meet their protein needs	None	Protein food	None likely

Table 5-5A   Adult Recommended Dietary Allowances,[1] Revised 1989

Category	Age (years)	Weight[2] (kg)	Weight[2] (lb)	Height[2] (cm)	Height[2] (in)	Protein (g)	Fat-soluble vitamins Vitamin A (μg RE)[3]	Vitamin D (μg)[4]	Vitamin E (μg α-TE)[5]	Vitamin K (μg)
Males	15-18	66	145	176	69	59	1000	10	10	65
	19-24	72	160	177	70	58	1000	10	10	70
	25-50	79	174	176	70	63	1000	5	10	80
	51+	77	170	173	68	63	1000	5	10	80
Females	15-18	55	120	163	64	44	800	10	8	55
	19-24	58	128	164	65	46	800	10	8	60
	25-50	63	138	163	64	50	800	5	8	65
	51+	65	143	160	63	50	800	5	8	65
Pregnant						60	800	10	10	65
Lactating	1st 6 Months					65	1300	10	12	65
	2nd 6 Months					62	1200	10	11	65

[1]The allowances, expressed as average daily intakes over time, are intended to provide for individual variations among most normal people as they live in the United States under usual environmental stresses. Diets should be based on a variety of common foods to provide other nutrients for which human requirements have been less well defined. See text for detailed discussion of allowances and of nutrients not tabulated.

[2]Weights and heights of reference adults are actual medians for the U.S. population of the designated age, as reported by NHANES II. The use of these figures does not imply that the height-to-weight ratios are ideal.

three forms of soluble fiber—oat bran, psyllium (from the weed plantain), and rice bran—because of their ability to lower blood cholesterol levels. Psyllium can be obtained by using laxatives, such as Metamucil, Konsyl, Fiberall fiber wafers, and Perdiem Fiber.

Although earlier studies were contradictory regarding the effectiveness of soluble fiber in lowering cholesterol levels, today it appears that oat bran can lower cholesterol levels by five to six points in people whose initial cholesterol levels are moderately high.[17] To accomplish this reduction, a daily consumption of oat bran equal to a large bowl of cold oat bran cereal or three or more packs of instant oatmeal would be necessary. Of course, oatmeal can be eaten as a cooked cereal or used in other foods, such as hamburgers, pancakes, or meat loaf.

THE FOOD GROUPS

As is so frequently heard, the most effective way to take in adequate amounts of nutrients is to eat a **balanced diet,** that is, to eat a diet that includes a wide variety of foods from different food groups (Table 5-5, A to C). Over the past several decades, various methods of grouping foods have identified five, seven, four, and now (again) five food groups from which selections are to be made. Today, the United States Department of Agriculture (USDA) Food Guide Pyramid outlines five groups for which recommendations

have been established and an additional group (fats, oils, and sweets) for which no specific recommendations exist (Figure 5-2). Table 5-6 summarizes the major nutrients each food group supplies. To determine whether you are eating a healthful diet balanced with choices from each food group, complete the Personal Assessment on p. 110.

Fruits

Two to four daily servings from the fruit group are recommended for an adult. The important functions

trace elements
Minerals present in very small amounts in the body; micronutrient elements.

dehydration
The abnormal depletion of fluids from the body; severe dehydration can be fatal.

fiber
Plant material that cannot be digested; found in cereal, fruits, and vegetables.

balanced diet
A diet featuring food selections from each of the five basic food groups.

Water-soluble vitamins							Minerals						
Vitamin C	Thia-min	Ribo-flavin	Niacin	Vitamin B$_6$	Folate	Vitamin B$_{12}$	Calcium	Phos-phorus	Mag-nesium	Iron	Zinc	Iodide	Sele-nium
(mg)	(mg)	(mg)	(mg NE)[6]	(mg)	(µg)	(µg)	(mg)	(mg)	(mg)	(mg)	(mg)	(µg)	(µg)
60	1.5	1.8	20	2.0	200	2.0	1200	1200	400	12	15	150	50
60	1.5	1.7	19	2.0	200	2.0	1200	1200	350	10	15	150	70
60	1.5	1.7	19	2.0	200	2.0	800	800	350	10	15	150	70
60	1.2	1.4	15	2.0	200	2.0	800	800	350	10	15	150	70
60	1.1	1.3	15	1.5	180	2.0	1200	1200	300	15	12	150	50
60	1.1	1.3	15	1.6	180	2.0	1200	1200	280	15	12	150	55
60	1.1	1.3	15	1.6	180	2.0	800	800	280	15	12	150	55
60	1.0	1.2	13	1.6	180	2.0	800	800	280	10	12	150	55
70	1.5	1.6	17	2.2	400	2.2	1200	1200	320	30	15	175	65
95	1.6	1.8	20	2.1	280	2.6	1200	1200	355	15	19	200	75
95	1.6	1.7	20	2.1	260	2.6	1200	1200	340	15	16	200	75

[3]Retinol equivalents. 1 retinol = 1 µg retinol or 6 µg ß-carotene.
[4]As cholecalciferol. 10 µg cholecalciferol = 400 IU of vitamin D.
[5]α-Tocopherol equivalents. 1 mg d-α tocopherol = 1 α-TE.
[6]1 NE (niacin equivalent) is equal to 1 mg of niacin or 60 mg of dietary tryptophan.

Table 5-5B   Estimated Safe and Adequate Daily Dietary Intakes (ESADDIs) of Selected Vitamins and Minerals for Adults*

Vitamins		Trace elements†				
Biotin (μg)	Pantothenic acid (mg)	Copper (mg)	Manganese (mg)	Fluoride (mg)	Chromium (mg)	Molybdenum (μg)
30-100	4-7	1.5-3.0	2.0-5.0	1.5-4.0	50-200	75-250

*Because there is less information on which to base allowances, these figures are not given in the main table of RDAs and are provided here in the form of ranges of recommended intakes.
†Because the toxic levels for many trace elements may be only several times the usual intake, the upper levels for the trace elements given in this table should not be habitually exceeded.

Table 5-5C   Estimated Minimum Sodium, Chloride, and Potassium Requirements of Healthy People*

Age	Weight (kg)*	Sodium (mg)*†	Chloride (mg)*†	Potassium (mg)‡
10-18	50.0	500	750	2000
>18§	70.0	500	750	2000

*No allowance has been included for large, prolonged losses from the skin through sweat.
†There is no evidence that higher intakes confer any health benefit.
‡Desirable intakes of potassium considerably exceed these values (~3500 mg for adults).
§No allowance included for growth. Values for those below 18 years assume a growth rate at the 50th percentile reported by the National Center for Health Statistics and averaged for men and women.

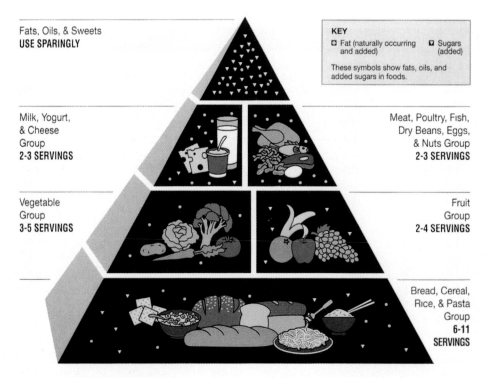

Figure 5-2   The USDA Food Guide Pyramid.

Table 5-6   Guide to Daily Food Choices

Food group	Serving	Major contributions	Foods and serving size*
Milk, yogurt, and cheese	2 (adult†) 3 (children, teens, young adults, and pregnant or lactating women)	Calcium Riboflavin Protein Potassium Zinc	1 cup milk 1½ oz cheese 2 oz processed cheese 1 cup yogurt 2 cups cottage cheese 1 cup custard/pudding 1½ cups ice cream
Meat, poultry, fish, dry beans, eggs, and nuts	2-3	Protein Niacin Iron Vitamin B_6 Zinc Thiamin Vitamin B_{12}‡	2-3 oz cooked meat, poultry, fish 1-1½ cups cooked dry beans 4 T peanut butter 2 eggs ½-1 cup nuts
Fruits	2-4	Vitamin C Fiber	¼ cup dried fruit ½ cup cooked fruit ¾ cup juice 1 whole piece fruit 1 melon wedge
Vegetables	3-5	Vitamin A Vitamin C Folate Magnesium Fiber	½ cup raw or cooked vegetables 1 cup raw leafy vegetables
Bread, cereals, rice, and pasta	6-11	Starch Thiamin Riboflavin§ Iron Niacin Folate Magnesium ‖ Fiber ‖ Zinc ‖	1 slice of bread 1 oz ready-to-eat cereal ½-¾ cup cooked cereal, rice, or pasta
Fats, oils, and sweets		Foods from this group should not replace any from the other groups. Amounts consumed should be determined by individual energy needs.	

This is a practical way to turn the RDA into food choices. You can get all essential nutrients by eating a balanced variety of foods each day from the food groups listed here. Eat a variety of foods in each food group, and adjust serving sizes appropriately to reach and maintain desirable weight.

*May be reduced for children's servings.   ‡Only in animal food choices.   §If enriched.
†≥25 years of age.   ‖Whole grains especially.

of this group are to provide vitamin A, vitamin C, complex carbohydrates, and fiber in our diets. At least one serving high in vitamin C should be eaten daily.

Vegetables

Three to five servings from the vegetable group are recommended for an adult. As with the fruit group, the important functions of this group are to provide vitamin A, vitamin C, complex carbohydrates, and fiber. Foods included in this group are dark green, yellow, and orange vegetables, canned or cooked vegetables, and tossed salads. **Cruciferous vegetables,** such as broccoli, cabbage, brussels sprouts, and cauliflower, may be especially important in the prevention of certain forms of cancer.[18]

PERSONAL ASSESSMENT

Seven-Day Diet Study

A primary requirement for good nutrition is a balanced diet. A variety of food selections from each food group forms the basis of this diet.

For a 7-day period, assign yourself the points indicated when each dietary requirement is met. Record your points in the appropriate column for each day. Total your daily and weekly points. Negative points for junk food consumption should be subtracted from your daily and weekly totals.

Food	Points	Maximum Score	Daily Score						
			M	T	W	T	F	S	S
Milk and milk products		30							
One cup of milk or equivalent	10								
Second cup of milk	10								
Third cup of milk	10								
Protein-rich foods		25							
One serving of egg, meat, fish, poultry, cheese, dried beans, or peas	15								
One or two additional servings of egg, meat, fish, poultry, or cheese	10 each								
Fruits and vegetables		30							
One serving of green or yellow vegetables	10								
One serving of citrus fruit, tomato, or cabbage	10								
Two or more servings of other fruits and vegetables, including potatoes	5 each								
Breads and cereals		15							
Four or more servings of whole-grain or enriched cereals or breads	5 each								
Junk foods (or negative point value foods)									
Sweet rolls	−5								
Fruit pies	−5								
Potato chips, corn chips, or cheese curls	−5								
Candy	−5								
Nondiet sodas	−5								
		100							

Point Record

			Interpretation
Weekly point total	————	600–700	Excellent dietary practices
Negative point total	————	450–599	Adequate dietary practices
Adjusted weekly point total	————	300–449	Marginal dietary practices
		Below 300	Poor dietary practices

Milk, Yogurt, and Cheese

This group contributes two primary nutritional benefits: high-quality protein and calcium (required for bone and tooth development). Foods included in this group are whole milk, low-fat milk, yogurt, cheese, and ice cream. The adult recommendation is 2 to 3 cups of milk or two to three equivalent servings from this group each day. Premenopausal women should consume three to four daily servings from this group to provide maximal protection from osteoporosis.

Because of the general concern about saturated fat, cholesterol, and additional calories, low-fat milk products are recommended in place of high-fat milk products. The Star Box below depicts the differences in calories (per cup), fat content (in grams), and % Daily Value among types of milk now in the marketplace.[19] Of course, aside from differences in fat content, all forms of milk offer similar nutritional benefits.

Meat, Poultry, Fish, Dry Beans, Eggs, and Nuts

Our need for daily selections from the protein-rich group is based on our daily need for protein, iron, and the B vitamins. Meats include all red meat (beef, pork, and game), fish, and poultry. Meat substitutes include eggs, cheese, dried peas and beans (legumes), and peanut butter. Eggs can also be used as meat substitutes; however, using only the separated egg whites provides excellent protein without the accompanying fat, including cholesterol. The current recommendation for adults is 4 ounces total per day, preferably in two to three servings.

The fat content of meat varies considerably. Some forms of meat yield only 1% fat, whereas others may be as high as 40% fat. Poultry and fish are usually significantly lower in overall fat than red meat. Interestingly, the higher the grade of red meat, the more fat will be marbled throughout the muscle fiber and thus the higher will be its caloric value.

Bread, Cereal, Rice, and Pasta

The nutritional benefit from this group lies in its contribution of B-complex vitamins and energy (in the form of calories) to our diets. Some nutritionists believe that the use of foods from this group also promotes protein intake, since many foods in this group are prepared with foods in other groups as complete-protein foods: macaroni and cheese, cereal and milk, and bread and meat sandwiches. Six to eleven servings daily from this group is recommended. Several daily servings of any **enriched** or whole-grain bread or cereal is recommended.

Fats, Oils, and Sweets

Where do such items as butter, candy, colas, cookies, corn chips, and pastries fit into this food group pattern? They are included under the label "fats, oils, and sweets." Most of the items mentioned contribute relatively little to healthful nutrition other than providing additional calories (generally from table sugar) and large amounts of salt and fat. This concern about sugar and high total calories must also be extended to the popular new cookies, crackers, and desserts that are "fat free" or "low fat." It is not surprising that many of these items are referred to collectively as *junk foods*.

FAST FOODS

Fast foods are convenience foods usually prepared in walk-in or drive-through restaurants. In contrast to that of junk foods, the nutritional value of fast foods can vary considerably (see the Star Box on pp. 112-113). As you can see in the "Calories from fat (%)" column, **fat density** is a serious limitation of fast foods. In

Milk's New Names

Old Name	Possible New Names	Total Fat [per 240 mililiters (1 cup)] Grams	%Daily Value	Calories per 240 mL
Milk	Milk	8.0 g	12%	150
Low-fat 2 percent milk	Reduced fat or less-fat milk	4.7 g	7%	122
Not on the market	Light milk	4 g or less	6% or less	116 or less
Low-fat 1 percent milk	Low-fat milk	2.6 g	4%	102
Skim milk	Fat-free, skim, zero-fat, no-fat or nonfat milk	less than 0.5 g	0%	80

cruciferous vegetables (crew **sif** er us)
Vegetables that have flowers with four leaves in the pattern of a cross.

enrichment
The process of returning to foods some of the nutritional elements (B vitamins and iron) removed during processing.

fat density
The percentage of a food's total calories that are derived from fat; above 30% is considered to be a high fat density.

Fast Food Ratings and Recommendations

Overall Ratings *Within types, listed in order of least to most fat*

Menu Item	Price	Weight	Fat TOTAL	Fat SATURATED	Calories from fat	Calories	Sodium	Flavor and texture SCORE
CHICKEN SANDWICHES								
McDonald's Grilled Chicken Deluxe	$2.80	8 oz.	6 g.	1 g.	16%	330	970 mg.	◯
Subway Roasted Chicken	3.20	9	6	1	16	348	978	◐
Wendy's Grilled Chicken	2.75	7	8	1.5	23	310	790	◯
Jack in the Box Grilled Chicken Fillet	3.20	7	19	5	40	430	1070	◯
Burger King BK Broiler	2.90	9	26	5	44	530	1060	◯
Boston Market Boston Carver Chicken	4.30	12	32	11	38	760	1810	◯
ROAST BEEF SANDWICHES								
Subway Roast Beef	2.95	8	5	1	15	303	939	◯
Hardee's Big Roast Beef	2.50	6	24	9	47	460	1230	◯
Arby's Giant Roast Beef	2.90	8	28	11	45	555	1561	◯
CHICKEN NUGGETS/STRIPS/TENDERS *(number of pieces in order)*								
Wendy's Chicken Nuggets (5)	1.00	3	14	3	60	210	460	◯
KFC Colonel's Crispy Strips (3)	2.65	3	16	3.7	54	261	658	◯
McDonald's Chicken Nuggets (6)	1.90	4	17	3.5	53	290	510	◯
Burger King Chicken Tenders (8)	2.50	4	22	7	57	350	940	◯
Popeye's Chicken Tenderloins (5)	4.50	6	35	NA	57	550	800	◐
CHICKEN ENTREES [1]								
Boston Market (roasted)	5.25	5	17	4.5	46	330	530	◯
KFC Tender Roast (roasted)	3.20	7	19	5.1	45	372	1161	◯
Popeye's Louisiana Mild (fried)	3.50	5	27	NA	56	430	950	◐
KFC Original Recipe (fried)	3.25	7	34	8.5	57	540	1530	◯
BURGERS								
Wendy's Single with Everything	2.10	8	20	7	43	420	920	◯
Burger King Whopper Jr.	1.05	6	24	8	51	420	530	◯
McDonald's Big Mac	2.20	8	28	10	48	530	880	◯
Wendy's Big Bacon Classic	2.75	10	30	12	47	580	1460	◐
Hardee's The Works	2.05	8	30	12	51	530	1030	◯
McDonald's Arch Deluxe with Bacon	2.65	9	34	12	50	610	1250	◯
Burger King Double Cheeseburger with Bacon	2.55	8	39	18	55	640	1240	◯
Jack in the Box Jumbo Jack with Cheese	1.50	9	40	14	55	650	1150	◯
Burger King Big King	*1.99	8	43	18	59	660	920	[2]
Burger King Whopper with Cheese	1.85	10	46	16	57	730	1350	◯
MASHED POTATOES WITH GRAVY								
KFC with Gravy	.95	5	6	1	45	120	440	◖
Popeye's with Cajun Gravy	1.30	4	6	NA	54	100	460	◯

[1] *Each item consists of a breast and wing; white meat*

[2] *Tested in only one city, where it scored* ◯.

 Excellent   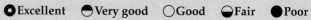 **Very good**   ◯ **Good**   **Fair**   **Poor**

Fast Food Ratings and Recommendations—cont'd.

Menu Item	Price	Weight	Fat TOTAL	Fat SATURATED	Calories from fat	Calories	Sodium	Flavor and texture SCORE
MASHED POTATOES WITH GRAVY *continued*								
Boston Market Homestyle and Gravy	$1.55	7 oz.	9 g.	5 g.	41%	200	560 mg.	◗
FRENCH FRIES *(size)*								
Hardee's (Large)	1.30	6	18	5	38	430	190	○
Jack in the Box (Jumbo)	1.35	4	19	5	43	400	220	○
McDonald's (Large)	1.33	5	22	4	44	450	290	◗
Wendy's (Biggie)	1.05	6	23	3.5	44	470	150	○
Burger King (Large)	1.35	5	25	7	48	470	300	○

comparison with the recommended standard (25% to 30% of total calories from fat), 40% to 50% of the calories in fast foods come from fats. The conversion by many fast-food restaurants from animal fat to vegetable oil for frying (to reduce cholesterol levels) did not lower the fat density of these food items. One fast-food meal supplies over one half the amount of fat needed in a day. In addition, fast foods are often high in sugar and salt.

During the early 1990s, the fast-food industry made an effort to offer alternatives to its fat-dense menu items, such as pasta bars, whole-wheat rolls, and lighter dressing. Unfortunately, this limited effort has nearly disappeared as customers indicated their preference for large serving sizes (at low cost) and fat-dense foods. Today, super-size burgers packing nearly 1,000 calories each and pizza by the foot are popular choices among 18- to 35-year-old customers.[20] The Health Action Guide on p. 114 offers advice for choosing healthful foods when you're eating out.

PHYTOCHEMICALS

In recent years a large group of physiologically active components thought to be able to deactivate carcinogens or function as antioxidants have been identified in a variety of fruits and vegetables. Among these are the carotenoids (from green vegetables), polyphenols (from onions and garlic), indoles (from cruciferous vegetables), and the allyl sulfides (from garlic, chives, and onions). These *phytochemicals* may play an important role in reducing the risk of cancer in people who consume a large quantity of foods (vegetarian or semivegetarian diets) from these two food groups.[21] So important are these several distinct classes of chemicals that they have been called "as essential as vitamins."[22]

In fact, a serious study of foods and food supplements, part of a larger study of alternative medicine, is increasingly changing our view of certain foods. Some foods are now being described as botanical pharmacological agents, or simply as medicines.

Pizza is a fast food popular among college students.

FOOD ADDITIVES

The nostalgia some people have for the "good old days" certainly extends to our current food supply. Today many people believe that the food they consume is unhealthy because of the 2800 generally recognized as safe (GRAS) **food additives** that can be put into food during production, processing, and preparation. But should these additives be banned?

Today's food manufacturers add chemical compounds to the food supply for several reasons that they believe we the consumers support: (1) to maintain the nutritional value of the food; (2) to maintain the food's freshness by preventing changes in its color, flavor, and texture; (3) to contribute to the processing of the food by controlling its texture, acidity, and thickness; and (4) to make the food more appealing to the consumer by enhancing its flavor and standardizing its color. Market research indicates that consumers will continue to accept these alterations regardless of what we might say about our desire that they not be made.

HealthQuest Activities

Apparently we recognize that living in urban areas, working outside the home, and having foods available at all times during the year are worth the price of additives being a part of our once "natural" food supply.

FOOD LABELS

Since 1973, food manufacturers have been required by the FDA to provide nutritional information (labels) on products to which one or more additional nutrients have been added or for which some nutritional claim has been made. Despite the presence of these labels, there was concern about whether the public could understand the labels as they appeared and whether additional information was required. Accordingly, the FDA, in consultation with individual states and public interest groups, developed new labeling regulations. Revised labels began appearing on food packages in May 1993. The newly adopted label is shown in Figure 5-3. Specific types of information contained on the new label are highlighted.

Foods not initially covered by the 1993 food labeling guidelines are gradually being assigned labels. For example, many single-ingredient meats are now being labeled. Processed meat, fish, and poultry products, such as hot dogs and chicken patties, must bear labels. Fresh fruits and vegetables are not required to be labeled, but may stores do so voluntarily.

In addition, some new food labeling initiatives have been proposed. These include the labeling of fruit juices for pasteurization (unpasteurized juices can be a source of *Escherichia coli* [*E. coli*] contamination), the identification of milk from cows whose food has been enhanced with *bovine growth hormone,* and the issuing of specific

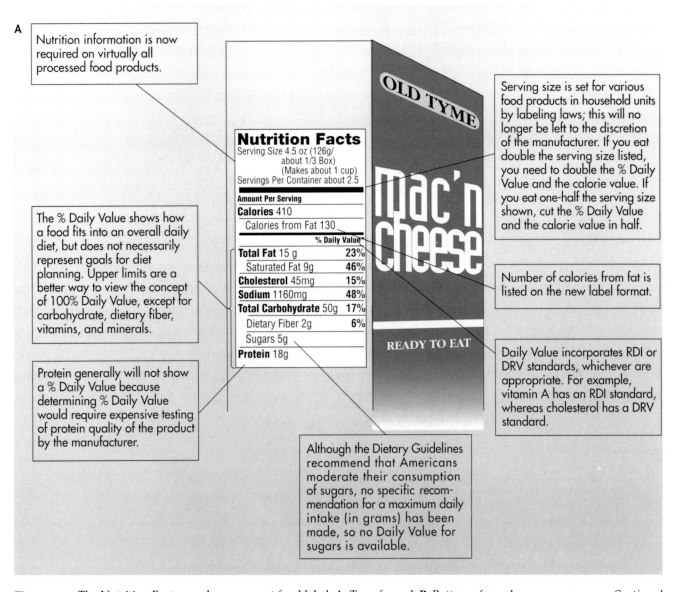

A

Nutrition information is now required on virtually all processed food products.

The % Daily Value shows how a food fits into an overall daily diet, but does not necessarily represent goals for diet planning. Upper limits are a better way to view the concept of 100% Daily Value, except for carbohydrate, dietary fiber, vitamins, and minerals.

Protein generally will not show a % Daily Value because determining % Daily Value would require expensive testing of protein quality of the product by the manufacturer.

Nutrition Facts
Serving Size 4.5 oz (126g/ about 1/3 Box)
(Makes about 1 cup)
Servings Per Container about 2.5

Amount Per Serving

Calories 410

Calories from Fat 130

	% Daily Value*
Total Fat 15 g	23%
Saturated Fat 9g	46%
Cholesterol 45mg	15%
Sodium 1160mg	48%
Total Carbohydrate 50g	17%
Dietary Fiber 2g	6%
Sugars 5g	
Protein 18g	

OLD TYME
mac'n cheese
READY TO EAT

Serving size is set for various food products in household units by labeling laws; this will no longer be left to the discretion of the manufacturer. If you eat double the serving size listed, you need to double the % Daily Value and the calorie value. If you eat one-half the serving size shown, cut the % Daily Value and the calorie value in half.

Number of calories from fat is listed on the new label format.

Daily Value incorporates RDI or DRV standards, whichever are appropriate. For example, vitamin A has an RDI standard, whereas cholesterol has a DRV standard.

Although the Dietary Guidelines recommend that Americans moderate their consumption of sugars, no specific recommendation for a maximum daily intake (in grams) has been made, so no Daily Value for sugars is available.

Figure 5-3   The Nutrition Facts panel on a current food label. **A,** Top of panel. **B,** Bottom of panel.   *Continued*

criteria for legal use of the term "organic." Some supermarkets also label fresh and frozen poultry and seafood with information about how it was prepared and stored. Some restaurant menus now state the nutritional content of some selections and provide cautionary notes regarding the safe cooking. Menu items made with organically grown ingredients are likely to be clearly identified or even highlighted.

GUIDELINES FOR DIETARY HEALTH

Although dietary guidelines of one type or another have been issued on many occasions, the Dietary Guidelines for Americans are the most current and widely disseminated guidelines. The newest version appeared in 1995 as the fourth edition of *Nutrition and Your Health: Dietary Guidelines for Americans*.[23] As presently constructed, these guidelines are directed to healthy Americans 2 years of age and older and to the health professional who can influence public dietary practices. Information contained within these guidelines came from a variety of sources, including the

food additives
Chemical compounds intentionally added to our food supply to change some aspect of the food, such as its color or texture.

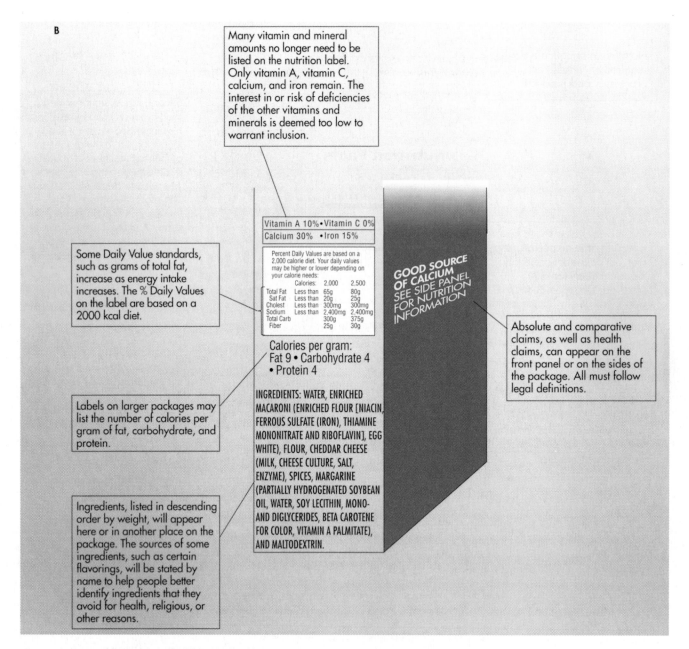

B

Many vitamin and mineral amounts no longer need to be listed on the nutrition label. Only vitamin A, vitamin C, calcium, and iron remain. The interest in or risk of deficiencies of the other vitamins and minerals is deemed too low to warrant inclusion.

Vitamin A 10% • Vitamin C 0%
Calcium 30% • Iron 15%

Percent Daily Values are based on a 2,000 calorie diet. Your daily values may be higher or lower depending on your calorie needs:

		Calories:	2,000	2,500
Total Fat	Less than		65g	80g
Sat Fat	Less than		20g	25g
Cholest	Less than		300mg	300mg
Sodium	Less than		2,400mg	2,400mg
Total Carb			300g	375g
Fiber			25g	30g

Some Daily Value standards, such as grams of total fat, increase as energy intake increases. The % Daily Values on the label are based on a 2000 kcal diet.

Calories per gram:
Fat 9 • Carbohydrate 4 • Protein 4

Labels on larger packages may list the number of calories per gram of fat, carbohydrate, and protein.

INGREDIENTS: WATER, ENRICHED MACARONI (ENRICHED FLOUR [NIACIN, FERROUS SULFATE (IRON), THIAMINE MONONITRATE AND RIBOFLAVIN], EGG WHITE), FLOUR, CHEDDAR CHEESE (MILK, CHEESE CULTURE, SALT, ENZYME), SPICES, MARGARINE (PARTIALLY HYDROGENATED SOYBEAN OIL, WATER, SOY LECITHIN, MONO- AND DIGLYCERIDES, BETA CAROTENE FOR COLOR, VITAMIN A PALMITATE), AND MALTODEXTRIN.

GOOD SOURCE OF CALCIUM SEE SIDE PANEL FOR NUTRITION INFORMATION

Absolute and comparative claims, as well as health claims, can appear on the front panel or on the sides of the package. All must follow legal definitions.

Ingredients, listed in descending order by weight, will appear here or in another place on the package. The sources of some ingredients, such as certain flavorings, will be stated by name to help people better identify ingredients that they avoid for health, religious, or other reasons.

Figure 5-3 *cont'd.* For legend see previous page.

Surgeon General's Report on Nutrition and Health. The most recent dietary guidelines are shown in Figure 5-4 and in the Star Box on p. 117.

Table 5-7 shows how healthful dietary changes can lead to reduced chances of developing certain major diseases. Notice that a reduction in fat and better control of caloric intake are important factors in reducing the likelihood of chronic illness.

Whether the newest Dietary Guidelines for Americans will be more fully implemented than their predecessors remains to be seen. Regardless, almost all Americans could move much closer to meeting these

guidelines. The Health Action Guide on p. 117 presents recommendations for making healthful food choices.

VEGETARIAN DIETS

It is not uncommon during the college years to follow some kind of nontraditional diet. Vegetarian diets, weight-reduction diets, and overreliance on fast foods represent some of these nontraditional diet approaches. Most nutritionists believe that these diets

HEALTH
Action Guide - - - - ➤

Dietary Recommendations

Issues for Most People

Your nutritional health could probably be improved by implementing the practices described below.

- **Fats and cholesterol:** Reduce consumption of fat (especially saturated fat) and cholesterol. Choose foods relatively low in fat and cholesterol, such as vegetables, fruits, whole-grain foods, fish, poultry, lean meat, and low-fat dairy products. Use food preparation methods that add little or no fat.
- **Energy and weight control:** Achieve and maintain a desirable body weight. To do so, choose a dietary pattern in which energy (caloric) intake is consistent with energy expenditure. To reduce energy intake, limit consumption of foods relatively high in calories, fat, and sugar and minimize alcohol consumption. Increase energy expenditure through regular and sustained physical activity.
- **Complex carbohydrates and fiber:** Increase consumption of whole-grain foods and cereal products, vegetables (including dried beans and peas), and fruits.
- **Sodium:** Reduce sodium intake by choosing foods relatively low in sodium and limiting the amount of salt added in food preparation and at the table.
- **Alcohol:** To reduce the risk of chronic disease, drink alcohol only in moderation (no more than two drinks a day), if at all. Avoid drinking any alcohol before or while driving, operating machinery, taking medications, or engaging in any other activity requiring judgment. Avoid drinking alcohol while pregnant.

Issues for Some People

The following recommendations are for people with special nutritional needs:

- **Fluoride:** Community water systems should contain fluoride at optimal levels for prevention of tooth decay. If such water is not available, use other appropriate sources of fluoride.
- **Sugars:** Those who are particularly vulnerable to dental caries (cavities), especially children, should limit their consumption and frequency of use of foods high in sugar.
- **Calcium:** Adolescent girls and adult women should increase consumption of foods high in calcium, including low-fat dairy products.
- **Iron:** Children, adolescents, and women of childbearing age should consume foods that are good sources of iron, such as lean red meat, fish, certain beans, and iron-enriched cereals and whole-grain products. This issue is of special concern for low-income families, since iron-rich foods, particularly lean meat, may be too expensive to consume on a regular basis.

◄ - - - - - ◗

---

need not be discontinued or avoided, but that they should be undertaken with care and insight because of potential nutritional limitations.

Dietary Guidelines for Americans—1995
- Eat a variety of foods.
- Balance the food you eat with physical activity—maintain or improve your weight.
- Choose a diet with plenty of grain products, vegetables, and fruits.
- Choose a diet low in fat, saturated fat, and cholesterol.
- Choose a diet moderate in sugars.
- Choose a diet moderate in salt and sodium.
- If you drink alcoholic beverages, do so in moderation.

A *vegetarian diet* relies on plant sources for all or most of the nutrients needed by the body. Vegetarian diets encompass a continuum from diets that allow some animal sources of nutrients to those that not only exclude animal sources but also are restrictive in terms of the plant sources of nutrients permitted. We briefly describe three types of vegetarian diets, beginning with the least restrictive.

Ovolactovegetarian Diet

Depending on the particular pattern of consuming eggs *(ovo)* and milk *(lacto)* or using one but not the other, **ovolactovegetarianism** can be an extremely sound approach to healthful eating during the adult years. Ovolactovegetarian diets provide the body with the essential amino acids and limit the high intake of fats seen in more conventional diets. The exclusion of meat as a protein source lowers the total

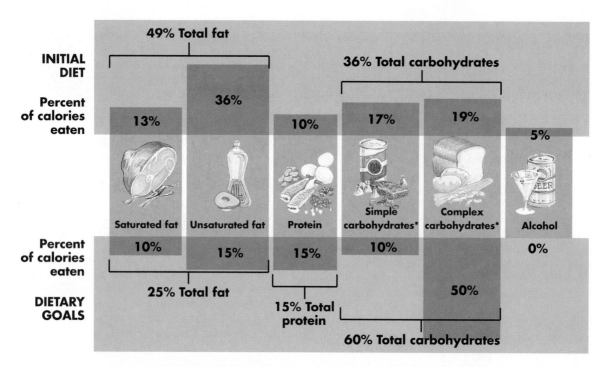

*Estimates based on Senate Select Subcommittee on Nutrition and Health data (circa 1970).
**Some versions of the Dietary Goals use ranges rather than specific values:
Fats   25%-30%
Protein   12%-15%
Carbohydrate   58%-60%

Figure 5-4   Where do your calories come from? This figure compares the sources of calories in the U.S. diet near 1970 with the sources that are currently recommended by nutritionists. How close are you to obtaining your calories from these sources in the recommended percentages? Some experts express each goal as a range: 25% to 30% of calories should come from fat, 12% to 15% from protein, and 58% to 60% from carbohydrates.

fat intake, and the consumption of milk or eggs allows an adequate amount of saturated fat to remain in the diet. The consistent use of vegetable products as the primary source of nutrients complies with the current dietary recommendations for an increase in overall carbohydrates, complex carbohydrates, and fiber.

Lactovegetarian Diet

People who include dairy products in their diet but no other animal products, including eggs, are *lactovegetarians*. As with the ovolactovegetarian diet, there is little risk associated with this dietary pattern.

Table 5-7   Recommended Dietary Changes to Reduce the Risk of Diseases and Their Complications

Change in Diet:	Reduce Fats	Control Calories	Increase Starch* and Fiber	Reduce Sodium	Control Alcohol
Reduce risk of:					
Heart disease	√	√		√	
Cancer	√	√	√		√
Stroke	√	√		√	√
Diabetes	√	√	√		
Gastrointestinal disease†	√	√	√		√

*Starch refers to complex carbohydrates provided by fruits, vegetables, and whole grain products.
†Primarily gallbladder disease (fat), diverticular disease (fiber), and cirrhosis (alcohol).

HEALTH
Action Guide → - - - - →

Making Healthful Food Choices

It is very likely that you can improve your dietary health and reduce the risk of developing heart disease and cancer by implementing the following practices.

Eat More High-Fiber Foods
- Choose dried beans, peas, and lentils more often.
- Eat whole-grain breads, cereals, and crackers.
- Eat more vegetables—raw and cooked.
- Eat whole fruit in place of drinking fruit juice.
- Try other high-fiber foods, such as oat bran, barley, brown rice, or wild rice.

Eat Less Sugar
- Avoid regular soft drinks. One 12-ounce can has nine teaspoons of sugar!
- Avoid eating table sugar, honey, syrup, jam, jelly, candy, sweet rolls, fruit canned in syrup, regular gelatin desserts, cake with icing, pie, or other sweets.
- Choose fresh fruit or fruit canned in natural juice or water.
- If desired, use sweeteners that don't have any calories, such as saccharin or aspartame, instead of sugar.

Use Less Salt
- Reduce the amount of salt you use in cooking.
- Try not to salt your food at the table.
- Eat fewer high-salt foods, such as canned soups, ham, sauerkraut, hot dogs, pickles, and foods that taste salty.
- Eat fewer convenience and fast foods.

Eat Less Fat
- Eat smaller servings of meat. Eat fish and poultry more often. Choose lean cuts of red meat.
- Prepare all meats by roasting, baking, or broiling. Trim off all fat. Be careful of added sauces or gravy. Remove skin from poultry.
- Avoid fried foods. Avoid adding fat when cooking.
- Eat fewer high-fat foods, such as cold cuts, bacon, sausage, hot dogs, butter, margarine, nuts, salad dressing, lard, and solid shortening.
- Drink skim or low-fat milk.
- Eat less ice cream, cheese, sour cream, cream, whole milk, and other high-fat dairy products. ← - - - - - - →

Vegan Vegetarian Diet

A **vegan vegetarian diet** is one in which not only meat but also other animal products, including milk, cheese, and eggs, are not part of the diet. When compared with the ovolactovegetarian diet, the vegan diet requires greater nutritional understanding to avoid malnourishment.

When plants are the body's only source of nutrients, some difficulties can arise. The novice vegan will need to be particularly alert for these difficulties. One potential difficulty is obtaining all the essential amino acids. Since a single plant source does not contain all the essential amino acids, the vegan must learn to consistently use a complementary diet. By carefully combining various grains, seeds, and legumes, amino acid deficiency can be prevented. This diet probably should not be used by children, pregnant women, and **lactating** mothers.

In addition to the potential difficulty with amino acid deficiency, the vegan could have some difficulty in maintaining the necessary intake of vitamin B_{12}.

Vegans often have trouble maintaining adequate intakes of iron, zinc, and calcium. In addition, vitamin D deficiencies can occur.

Because of its nutritional limitations, many nutritionists do not recommend the vegan vegetarian diet. This diet should be followed only for reasons related to ecological, philosophical, or animal rights beliefs, since the total exclusion of animal products seems

---

ovolactovegetarian diet (oh voe **lack** toe vegetarian)
A diet that excludes all meat but does include the consumption of eggs and dairy products.

vegan vegetarian diet (**vay** gan *or* **vee** gan)
A vegetarian diet that excludes all animal products, including eggs and dairy products.

lactating
Breastfeeding, nursing.

to accomplish little from a nutritional point of view that cannot be accomplished through ovolactovegetarianism. Clearly, the ovolactovegetarian diet is much less likely to lead to malnutrition than is the vegan diet. Many people have now adopted *semivegetarian diets,* in which meat consumption is significantly reduced but not eliminated. We take a closer look at this type of diet in the article on pp. 125-126.

Dietary (Food) Supplements

Supermarkets, drug stores, and health food stores across American stock a wide array of products containing biologically active ingredients derived largely from plants. Vitamins, herbal preparations, various amino acids, botanicals such as fungi, and homeopathic medications are among the more familiar of these nonprescription products. By law, these products, in the form of capsules, tablets, and liquids, are marketed to supplement the diet. They are not defined by the federal government as pharmaceutical agents intended to treat or prevent illness and thus are not required to demonstrate the safety and effectiveness of prescription and over-the-counter (OTC) medications.[24]

A number of these dietary supplements are now undergoing their first carefully controlled study to asses their legitimate role in preventing disease and illness. Two dietary supplements, calcium and folic acid, have been proved to be safe and effective in **chemoprevention.** As research is completed, it is likely that more dietary supplements will be recognized as safe and effective chemopreventive agents. Until then, the public must remain wary about the claims made by manufacturers of these products.

NUTRIENT DENSITY

For many college students, the consideration of nutrient density may prompt certain dietary adjustments. The *nutrient density* of a food item relates to its ability to supply proportionally more of the RDA for select vitamins and minerals than it does daily calorie requirements. Foods with a high nutrient density are better choices than those that supply only *empty calories* (Figure 5-5). For example, a bag of potato chips or a bottle of beer has a much lower nutrient density than either a serving of lightly steamed mixed vegetables or a 3-oz. serving of broiled skinless chicken breast. Choosing to eat foods with high nutrient density is especially important for people who are trying to limit caloric intake.

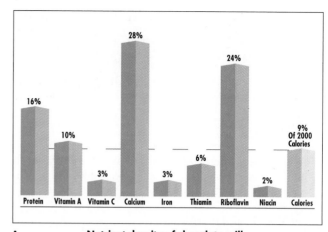

A   **Nutrient density of chocolate milk**

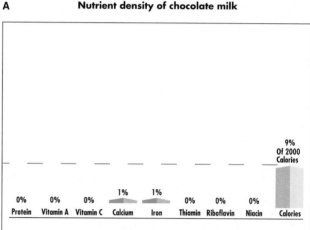

B   **Nutrient density of soda**

Figure 5-5   A comparison of the nutrient density of chocolate milk with that of soda. **A,** The bars that represent protein, vitamin A, calcium, and riboflavin are all taller than the calorie bar, showing that chocolate milk is nutrient dense for these nutrients. **B,** All of the nutrient bars are shorter than the calorie bar, illustrating that soda has a low nutrient density relative to the number of calories it supplies.

NUTRITION AND THE OLDER ADULT

Nutritional needs change as adults age. Age-related changes to the structure and function of the body are primarily responsible for altered nutritional requirements. These age-related changes can involve the teeth, salivary glands, taste buds, oral muscles, gastric acid production, and peristaltic action. In addition, chronic constipation resulting from changes in gastrointestinal tract function can decrease interest in eating.

The progressive lowering of the body's basal metabolism is another factor that will eventually influence the dietary patterns of older adults. As energy requirements fall, the body gradually senses the need for less food. Because of this decreased need for calories, nutrient density—the nutritional value of food relative to calories supplied—is an important consideration for the elderly.

In addition to the physiological factors that influence dietary patterns among the elderly, psychosocial factors alter the role of food in the lives of many older adults. Social isolation, depression, chronic alcohol consumption, loss of income, transportation limitations, and housing are lifestyle factors that can alter the ease and enjoyment associated with the preparation and consumption of food. Consequently, a person's food intake might decrease.

INTERNATIONAL NUTRITIONAL CONCERNS

Whereas nutritional concerns in this country are centered on overnutrition, including fat density and excessive caloric intake, the main concern in many areas of the world is the limited quantity and quality of food. Reasons for these problems are many, including the limitations imposed by weather, the availability of arable land, religious practices, political unrest, war, social infrastructure, and material and technical shortages. Underlying nearly all of these factors, however, is unabated population growth.

In an attempt to increase the availability of food to countries whose demand for food outweighs their ability to produce it, a number of steps have been suggested, including the following:

- Increase the yield of land currently under cultivation.
- Increase the amount of land under cultivation.
- Increase animal production on land not suitable for cultivation.
- Use water (seas, lakes, and ponds) more efficiently for the production of food.
- Develop unconventional foods through the application of technology.
- Improve nutritional practices through education.

Little progress is being made despite impressive technological breakthroughs in agriculture and food technology (such as "miracle" rice, disease-resistant high-yield corn, and soybean-enhanced infant foods), the efforts of governmental programs, and the support of the Food and Agricultural Organization of the United Nations and the USDA. Particularly in Third World countries, where fertility rates are two to four times higher than those of the United States, annual food production would have to increase between 2.7% and 3.9%. If population growth and food production are not altered in these countries, basic needs will continue to be unmet.

LEARNING from ALL CULTURES

A Comparison of Dietary Practices

Dietary practices differ among various areas of the world. This simple concept is clearly demonstrated when comparing dietary patterns in China with those in the West. These differing patterns then influence the prevalence of health problems. Notice in the data presented below that the average cholesterol difference could be explained on the basis of dietary practices. It is likely that the limited consumption of meat and the heavy consumption of vegetables gives China an advantage in "heart health."

Dietary Intake	China	West
Total protein	64.1 g	91.0 g
Plant protein	60.0 g	27.0 g
Complex carbohydrates	371.0 g	120.0 g
Fat as a percent of total calories	14.5%	38.8%
Cholesterol	127 mg/100 mg	212 mg/100 mg

chemoprevention
The safe and effective use of dietary supplements in the prevention of illness and disease.

Summary

- Carbohydrates, fat, and protein supply the body with calories.
- Carbohydrates differ on the basis of their molecular makeup, with sugars being the least complex and starches the most complex.
- Fat plays important roles in nutritional health beyond serving as the body's primary means of storage of excess calories.
- Saturated fats, including trans-fatty acids, should be carefully limited because of their association with chronic diseases.
- Dietary intake of cholesterol should be limited through careful monitoring of food choices.
- Protein supplies the body with amino acids needed to construct its own protein.
- When few foods of animal origin are consumed, incomplete protein sources must be carefully balanced to provide complete protein in the diet.
- Vitamins serve as catalysts for body responses and are found in water-soluble and fat-soluble forms.
- The use of vitamin supplements is desirable for some people, but extensive use of food supplements can be dangerous.
- Minerals are incorporated into various tissues of the body and participate in regulatory functions within the body.
- An adequate amount of water and other fluids is required by the body daily and is obtained from a variety of food sources, including beverages.
- Fiber is undigestible plant material and has two forms, water-soluble and water-insoluble.
- Foods are currently classified into six groups, although recommendations regarding the needed number of daily servings have been given for only five of them.
- Fat-free or low-fat foods can be more calorie dense than anticipated.
- Fast foods should play only a limited role in daily food intake because of their high fat density and their high levels of sugar and sodium.
- Phytochemicals, capable of protecting the body from carcinogens or free radicals, are now being identified in many types of vegetables.
- Food additives enhance the overall quality and convenient use of our food supply.
- New food labels provide considerably more information for the consumer than did labels used previously.
- Current dietary recommendations focus on the role of fat, saturated fat, starch, and sodium in health and disease.
- Ovolactovegetarianism, lactovegetarianism, and vegan vegetarianism are different forms of vegetarianism. Semivegetarianism is similar in some important ways to other forms of vegetarianism.
- Some dietary supplements may play a role as safe and effective agents in the chemoprevention of illness and disease.
- Nutrient density plays an important role in the management of caloric intake for people of all ages, particularly older adults.
- A variety of factors contribute to malnourishment in many areas of the world.

Review Questions

1. Which nutrients supply the body with calories?
2. How do sugars differ structurally from starches?
3. What roles does fat play in nutritional health besides serving as the body's primary means of storage for excess calories? What is the basis of our current concern about saturated fats, cholesterol, and trans-fatty acids?
4. What is the principal role of protein in the body? How can complete protein be obtained by people who eat few or no animal products?
5. Which vitamins are water soluble and which are fat soluble? What is the current perception regarding the need for vitamin supplementation? Which vitamins are regarded as antioxidants?
6. What functions do minerals have in the body? What is a trace element?
7. What are the two principal forms of fiber, and how does each of them contribute to health?
8. How many glasses of water daily are currently recommended?
9. What method of grouping foods is now used?
10. What are the current dietary recommendations regarding fat, saturated fat, starch, and sodium intake?
11. How can fat-free or low-fat foods be both low in nutritional density and high in caloric density?
12. What are phytochemicals? What are their principal dietary sources?
13. What information can be obtained from our current food labels?
14. If additives were eliminated from our food, what lifestyle adjustments would the public be forced to make?

15. What are an ovolactovegetarian diet and semivegetarianism, and how do they differ from a vegan diet?

16. What is the legally defined role of dietary supplements? What is chemoprevention?

17. What is nutrient density, and how does it relate to the aging process?

 Think About This . . .

- Is it more economical to buy a generic brand of cereal and take a generic multivitamin than to buy a highly supplemented but more expensive brand-name cereal?
- What nutrients are missing from your diet?
- Do your roles in parenting, employment, school, or home management compromise your ability to eat healthfully?
- Analyze your diet in terms of the recommendations made by *Nutrition and Your Health: Dietary Guidelines for Americans.*

- Consider your own dietary practices and those of your friends. Are sound nutritional guidelines being followed?
- Would you say that you live to eat or eat to live?
- What are the most immediate changes that need to be made in your diet?
- In your opinion, what is the role of diet in both the cause and prevention of chronic disease? Are we currently too concerned about the role of food in preventing disease and enhancing health?

References

1. Wardlaw GM, Insel PM: *Perspective in nutrition,* St. Louis, MO, 1996, Mosby.

2. Wardlaw GM: *Contemporary nutrition: issues and insights.* New York, 1997, WCB/McGraw-Hill.

3. Noop RH et al: Long-term cholesterol-lowering effects of 4 fat-restricted diets in hypercholesterolemic and combined hyperlipidemic men. The dietary alternatives study, *JAMA,* 278(18):1509-1515, 1997.

4. U.S. Department of Health and Human Services: *Report on the expert panel on population strategies for blood cholesterol lowering,* NIH Pub No 90-3046, Washington, DC, 1990, US Government Printing Office.

5. Hu FB et al: Dietary fat intake and the risk of coronary disease in women, *N Engl J Med,* 337(21):491-494, 1997.

6. United States Department of Health and Human Services: *The Surgeon General's report on nutrition and health,* DHHS Pub No 88-50210. Washington, DC, 1988. US Government Printing Office.

7. Addis P: Coronary heart disease: an update with emphasis on dietary lipid oxidation products, *Food & Nutrition News,* 52(2):7-14, 1990.

8. Hogan EH: American Dietetic Association, as reported in, Waning concern over nutrition, *USA Today,* Oct 28, 1997, 10D.

9. Cheskin LJ et al: Gastrointestinal symptoms following consumption of Olestra or regular triglyceride potato chips score, *JAMA,* 279(2):150-152, 1998.

10. Rimm EB et al: Vitamin E consumption and the risk of coronary heart disease in men, *N Engl J Med,* 328(20):1450-1456, 1993.

11. Leary WE: Vitamins cut cancer in China study, *The New York Times,* Sept 15, 1993.

12. Czeizel AE, Dudas I: Prevention of the first occurrence of neural-tube defects by periconceptional vitamin supplementation, *N Engl J Med,* 327(26):1832-1835, 1992.

13. Johnston RJ (director), March of Dimes Birth Defects Foundation, as reported in, Few women take folic acid to prepare for pregnancy, *USA Today,* June 10, 1996, 4D.

14. Food labeling: Health claims and labeling statements: antioxidant vitamins and cancer, *Federal Register,* 58(2)3:2622-2660, Washington, DC, Jan 6, 1993, US Government Printing Office.

15. Scariati PD et al: Water supplementation of infants in the first month of life, *Arch Pediatr Adolesc Med,* 151(8):830-832, 1997.

16. Fiber: essential to a healthy diet, *Worldview,* 3(3):1-5, 1991.

17. Ripsin CM et al: Oat products and lipid lowering: a metaanalysis, *JAMA,* 276(24):3317-3325, 1992.

18. American Cancer Society: *Cancer facts and figures—1997,* Atlanta, 1997, The Association.

19. Kurtzweil P: Skimming the milk label: fat-reduced milk products join the food labeling fold, *FDA Consumer,* 32(1), Jan-Feb, 1998.

20. Horovitz B: Fast-food chains bank on bigger-is-better mentality, *USA Today,* Sep 12, 1997, 1B.

21. Phytochemicals in disease prevention, *Nutri-News,* St. Louis, 1995, Mosby.

22. Schardt D: Phytochemical: plants against cancer, *Nutritional Action Health Letter,* April, 1994.

23. US Department of Agriculture, US Department of Health and Human Services: *Nutrition and your health: dietary guidelines for Americans,* ed 4, Home & Garden Bulletin No. 323, Washington, DC, 1995, US Government Printing Office.

24. Pinger RR et al. *Drugs: issues for today.* New York, 1998, WCB/McGraw-Hill.

Suggested Readings

Havala S: *Being vegetarian* (The American Dietetic Association Nutrition Now Series), Minnetonka, MN, 1996, Chronimed.

This book is an excellent guide for anyone interested in beginning a vegetarian diet. Not only does it describe the various kinds of vegetarianism, but it provides important tips for incorporating vegetarianism into one's lifestyle.

Doyle W: *Healthy eating for pregnancy*, Rochester, NY, 1997, Teach Yourself.

This guide is an excellent primer for women and their partners before and during pregnancy to ensure the best nutrition possible for mother and baby. Topic areas include "A Healthy Diet," "Assessing Your Diet," "A General Health Check," and many others. Several appendices provide additional information, including specific dietary requirements and addresses to write to for additional information about pregnancy.

Ornish D: *Everyday cooking with Dr. Dean Ornish: 150 easy, low-fat, high-flavor recipes.* New York, 1997, HarperCollins.

Dr. Ornish is a widely recognized clinician whose research has shown that some forms of heart disease can be reversed through dietary modification. Accordingly, this book adds to a long list of others that describe the lifestyle adjustments needed to achieve this reversal. As the title suggests, this is a recipe book that would be most useful to readers who are familiar with the author's larger plan.

The American Dietetic Association, Duyff RL. *Complete food & nutrition guide.* Minnetonka, MN, 1996, Chronimed.

This very sizable book is literally packed with information concerning every aspect of eating and food safety. Sections range from calculating healthy weight, shopping for fresh produce, and eating while traveling to recommendations from a variety of organizations associated with sound dietary practices. Highly recommended for those who desire the fullest understanding of heathful eating.

Fonda J. *Cooking for healthy living.* Atlanta, 1996, Turner Publishing.

Jane Fonda shares more than a hundred recipes for food items that she and her husband, Ted Turner, include in their long-standing commitment to healthy living. Nutritionists reviewing the book report that it is "easy to use" and that its content is excellent in regard to nutritionally healthy menu planning. The book features a wide variety of food items, using foods found in every community, and is supported by photographs depicting preparation and the finished product.

Following a Semivegetarian Diet

People become vegetarians for many reasons. Some shun meat and animal products for ethical reasons. Others may choose vegetarianism for health reasons. Often it seems that vegetarians are placed in opposition to those who eat meat, and that the two lifestyles are not compatible. In recent years, however, some people are choosing a "middle ground" between the two eating styles. These so-called "semivegetarians" are increasing their intake of vegetables and cutting back greatly on meat consumption but not necessarily eliminating meat entirely.

There are several types of vegetarians. *Vegans* are the most restrictive with their diets, eating only fruits, grains, and vegetables.[1] *Lactovegetarians* consume milk products along with fruits, vegetables, and grains, and *ovolactovegetarians* include both eggs and milk products in their diets.[1] *Semivegetarians* add occasional servings of fish and poultry to the ovolactovegetarian diet,[1] and some even eat red meat on occasion.[2,3]

Benefits of Vegetarianism

Semivegetarianism is the most popular option among the 12 million Americans who consider themselves to be vegetarians.[3] Whereas most vegetarians seem to embrace this lifestyle for health reasons,[3] some people become vegetarians for ethical reasons. These people cite the inhumane conditions in which factory farm animals are raised and processed as reasons to boycott the eating of animal products.[4] The convictions of these people suggest that they are more likely to be vegans, lactovegetarians, or ovolactovegetarians than semivegetarians.

The health benefits of vegetarianism are many. Six of the ten leading causes of death in the United States are linked to red meat consumption.[5] Cutting meat consumption can decrease the risk of heart attacks,[3] and eating more vegetables in place of meat may decrease the risk of some types of cancer.[1,6] In addition, animals raised in factory farms are often given antibiotics to keep them healthy until they get to market; however, constant exposure to antibiotics may cause some bacteria to become resistant, and these bacteria may therefore be present in meat at the store.[7] A vegetarian diet can also aid in weight loss and prevention of obesity.[1]

There are risks associated with following a purely vegetarian diet, however. Protein in plants is generally of lower quality than protein found in animal products,[1] so those on a vegetarian diet must be careful to eat a variety of plant foods to get all of the essential amino acids. Eliminating meat altogether may also lead to a deficiency of vitamin B_{12}, which can lead to brain and nerve damage.[1] Eating foods (such as cereals) fortified with this vitamin or taking vitamin supplements can ward off B_{12} deficiency.[1] Vitamin D, which is needed for bone and tooth development, may be lacking in vegetarian diets.[1] Vegans must make sure they get enough vitamin D by eating fortified foods or getting enough sunlight exposure to promote vitamin D production in the body. Vegetarians should eat plant foods high in iron to prevent deficiency, and calcium supplements may also be necessary, since vegan diets may make calcium difficult to absorb.[1]

Is Semivegetarianism Really Vegetarian?

There is some controversy over whether the semivegetarian diet truly qualifies as "vegetarian." Many people on a strict vegetarian diet do not consider the semivegetarian diet to be vegetarian. To them, any consumption of meat products is considered a compromise to vegetarian principles.[4] Likewise, there are debates over the appropriate use of dairy products and eggs among the various vegetarian groups. Some semivegetarians even acknowledge that they are not "real" vegetarians.[8]

The use of the term "semivegetarian" may not be acceptable to some vegetarians, but there is little doubt that the semivegetarian diet is much healthier than the typical meat-laden Western diet. Interest in the semivegetarian diet came about as a result of recommendations from several groups in the 1980s. The American Cancer Society, the American Heart Association, and the National Academy of Scientists all recommended dietary changes that were closely related to the typical semivege-

tarian diet.[7] The health benefits of such a diet are well documented. The debate over whether semivegetarians should be categorized as vegetarians seems to revolve around ethical questions concerning treatment of animals. Many vegans especially denounce the eating of any meat or animal products, since animals must be exploited to obtain these foods,[4] and they are thus morally opposed to semivegetarianism. Cutting back, however, may at least cause a decrease in demand for meat and animal products, and some semivegetarians may see this as a moral justification for their dietary changes. Although the semivegetarian diet may not effectively address the ethical questions raised by animal rights activists, it has become an acceptable way of eating for many people who are looking for a way to eat more healthfully.

Becoming Semivegetarian

The semivegetarian diet may be desirable to some people because the limited consumption of meat products may help ward off some nutrient deficiencies,[3] and such a diet can be healthier than that of the typical American. A person who wishes to adopt the semivegetarian diet should not make the change overnight.[2] A sudden elimination of most meat and other animal products can be too drastic of a change to adhere to, so it is best to cut back on them gradually. Such a change should also be discussed first with a doctor, since dietary alterations can cause difficulty for people who are pregnant, nursing, or have health problems.[3]

A gradual cutback in meat consumption can be accomplished by keeping track of how much meat you consume per day. Reduce meat consumption slowly until you have tapered off to about 4 ounces a day.[9] Meat can be used as a condiment (such as chicken strips on a salad) instead of as a main course, and fish can be substituted for red meat.[9] Try new vegetarian foods at each meal, and keep track of your likes and dislikes.[2] Adding more fruit to your meals can increase the variety of your diet as well.[2]

Arlene Spark, a nutrition expert from New York Medical College, has developed a vegetarian food pyramid to help non–meat eaters and semivegetarians to follow a healthful diet (see the inside back cover of this textbook). This pyramid is similar to the USDA Food Guide Pyramid (see Figure 5-2), but it replaces the meat, poultry, fish, dry beans, eggs, and nuts group with a meat/fish substitutes group. It also includes special recommendations for vegans. The pyramid advises vegetarians of all types to eat 6 to 11 servings of grains or starchy vegetables, at least 3 servings of other vegetables, 2 to 4 servings of fruit, and 2 to 4 servings of milk or milk substitutes per day.[10] Legumes can be used as a substitute for

meats for obtaining iron, calcium, protein, and zinc, but keep in mind that vitamin B_{12} is not found in plant foods.[9] Semivegetarians can obtain some B_{12} from the limited meats they consume, but should be careful not to decrease B_{12} intake too much. Also, the occasional fast-food meal is not forbidden. Fast food can provide a change of pace,[2] and many healthy fast-food meals are available.[5]

Children can also be involved in the change of diet (but consult your pediatrician first to be safe). Making dietary changes a "family affair" can make the adjustment easier. Getting kids involved in meal planning, cooking, and label reading can make things more interesting for them.[5] Dietary changes can be a difficult adjustment for kids, however, so don't hold them to the same restrictions as the adults.[2] This may help parents and children avoid arguments over meals and can make meals more enjoyable for the kids.

A semivegetarian diet may be an acceptable alternative for people who want to cut back significantly on meat consumption but who do not want to give up meat altogther. Reducing the amount of meat in the diet can have definite health benefits. Check with your doctor to see if such a diet could have advantages for you.

For Discussion . . .

Is semivegetarianism more ethically sound than the typical Western diet, or is there no difference between eating meat occasionally and eating it often? Should semivegetarians be considered vegetarians? Is the ethical treatment of animals a consideration for you in the food choices you make? Is health a concern for you in your diet? ◎

References

1. *Macmillan health encyclopedia, Vol 4*, New York, 1993, Macmillan.
2. Monroe C, Fuller K: Hooked on good health, *Better Homes and Gardens* 73(3), March 1995.
3. Springer I: Are you ready to go vegetarian? *Cosmopolitan* 219(4), October 1995.
4. Singer P: *Animal liberation*, New York, 1975, Avon.
5. Dinwiddie-Boyd E: Raising vegetarians, *Essence* 23(1), May 1992.
6. Eat your vegetables, *Harvard Health Letter* 20(1), Nov 1994.
7. Null G: *The vegetarian handbook*, New York, 1987, St Martin's Press.
8. Lee K: *The occasional vegetarian*, New York, 1995, Warner.
9. Nash J: The transition diet: from meat eater to vegetarian, *Essence* 25(9), Jan 1995.
10. Vegetarian pyramid, *Better Homes and Gardens*, October 1994.

Maintaining a Healthy Weight

Healthy People: Looking Ahead to 2010

In the area of weight management, the *Healthy People 2000 Midcourse Review* indicated almost no progress. Obesity increased by over 100% among all adults ages 18 to 74. The lack of success in controlling weight among those under age 18 was particularly distressing. This failure was perhaps related to the demise of physical education classes in many school systems and to an increasingly sedentary lifestyle that revolves around watching television and playing electronic games.

Nevertheless, some positive programs were initiated during the 1990s. These included an increase in worksite physical fitness programs and nutrition programs that feature a weight management component. In addition, the percentage of adults who reported exercising regularly increased slightly.

Weight management goals will continue to receive significant attention in the *Healthy People 2010* objectives now being formulated. At least three of the target areas—chronic disease prevention, nutrition, and physical fitness—are clearly related to weight management. Reaching objectives in these areas will help to meet the broader goal of increasing years of healthy life among all Americans.

You are probably aware that obesity is a serious health concern. Still, most people are above their healthy weight, and a large percentage of adults (25% to 30%) are classified as obese.[1] In a society that has an abundance of high-quality food and a wide variety of labor-saving devices, being overweight is almost the rule rather than the exception.

When the body is supplied with more energy than it can use, a predictable response is seen—the storage of excess energy (or a **positive caloric balance**) in the form of fat. This continuous buildup of fat can eventually result in obesity. The prevailing feeling has been that in terms of medical risk, being only mildly overweight is not dangerous. Today, however, some information suggests otherwise. In fact, in a large study of thousands of nurses, it was found that being average to slightly below average weight relates positively with lower levels of premature death.[2]

Regardless of whether slight to moderate overweight is unhealthy, few experts question the real dangers to health and wellness from obesity.[3] Among the health problems caused by or complicated by obesity are increased surgical risk, hypertension, various forms of heart disease, stroke, type II diabetes mellitus, several forms of cancer, deterioration of joints, complications during pregnancy, gallbladder disease, and an overall increased risk of mortality (see the Star Box at right). Obesity is so closely associated with these chronic conditions that medical experts now recommend that obesity itself be defined and treated as a chronic disease.[4]

BODY IMAGE AND SELF-CONCEPT

In spite of the fact that physicians focus on obesity, for our image-conscious general population there is little debate about overweight also being a problem. All too often, the media tell people that being overweight is undesirable, particularly when it interferes with their ability to conform to certain ideal body images (such as being tall, thin, and "cut" with muscular definition). To cite a case in point, the average actress and model is thinner than 95% of the female population and weighs 23% less than the average woman. Today's lean but muscular version of perfection is a very demanding standard for both women and men to meet.

In light of this challenge, people may become dissatisfied and concerned about their inability to resemble these ideals. The scope of this dissatisfaction is evident in a study of over 800 women, which revealed that nearly half were unhappy with their weight, muscle tone, hips, thighs, buttocks, and legs (men may not be very different in this regard).[5] Not surpris-

Health Risks of Obesity
Each of the diseases listed below is followed by the percentage of cases that are caused by obesity:

Colon cancer	10%
Breast cancer	11%
Hypertension	33%
Heart disease	70%
Diabetes (type II, non–insulin-dependent)	90%

As these statistics show, being obese greatly increases your risk of many serious and even life-threatening chronic conditions.

ingly, when this dissatisfaction exists, people can begin to question their own attractiveness, and eventually, for some, their self-concept changes and self-esteem declines. Only growing older lessens, but does not eliminate, this dissatisfaction.

In comparison with being overweight, there has traditionally been little media attention paid to being underweight (see pp. 147-148). However, the body image problems experienced by some extremely thin people can be equally distressing.

OVERWEIGHT AND OBESITY DEFINED

How can we tell the difference between overweight and obesity? Nutritionists have traditionally said that obesity is present when fat accumulation produces a body weight that is more than 20% above an ideal or **desirable weight.** People are said to be overweight if their weight is between 1% and 19% above their desirable weight. As weight increases above the 20% level, the label *obese* is routinely applied. Of course, an exception to this relationship between overweight and obesity is excessive weight caused by extreme muscularity, such as that seen in many football players.

The term *obesity* requires further refinement. When people are between 20% and 40% above desirable weight, their obesity is described as *mild* (about 90% of all obese people), whereas excessive weight in the range of 41% to 99% above desirable weight is defined as *moderate obesity* (9%) and weight of 100% or more above desirable weight is defined as *severe, gross,* or *morbid obesity* (< 1%).

Being most familiar with the weight guidelines

used in the past, most clinicians and the general public continue to use standard height-weight tables to determine the extent to which scale weight exceeds desirable weight and thus the existence of mild, moderate, or severe obesity. At this time, however, other, more precise techniques are available that can be used to determine body composition. In the following section, several of those techniques, including waist-to-hip ratio (*healthy body weight*), body mass index, hydrostatic weighing, skinfold measurements, and electrical impedance, are described.

DETERMINING WEIGHT AND BODY COMPOSITION

As mentioned previously, a variety of techniques can be used to determine the existence of overweight and obesity. Some techniques are common and routinely used by the general public, whereas others are expensive and of limited availability.

Height-Weight Tables

Over the last 50 years a number of height and weight tables have been developed to assist people in determining the relationship between their weight and desirable standards. Criticisms of one kind or another have been made against nearly every version of these tables, including the absence of consideration of variables such as gender, age, frame size, and body composition. Further, some versions were thought to be too rigorous in establishing cutoff points for desirable or ideal weight, and others were deemed too generous in allowing people to weigh too much. Accordingly, these tables are being gradually replaced by other assessment techniques. Regardless, height and weight tables remain available. Table 6–1 shows the widely used 1983 Metropolitan Life Insurance Company height-weight table.

Healthy Body Weight

You can determine your **healthy body weight** by using the weight guidelines (Table 6-2) that are found in the *Dietary Guidelines for Americans*.[6] This assessment involves converting two body measurements, the waist and the hip circumferences, into a waist-to-hip ratio (WHR) that can then be applied to weight ranges for people of particular ages and heights. Among people who have an acceptable WHR, female "healthy weight" is near the lower end of each weight range, whereas male "healthy weight" is at the higher end of each weight range.

Table 6-1   1983 Metropolitan Life Insurance Height and Weight Table

Height	Small Frame	Medium Frame	Large Frame
	Weight in pounds		
Men*			
5'2"	128-134	131-141	138-150
5'3"	130-136	133-143	140-153
5'4"	132-138	135-145	142-156
5'5"	134-140	137-148	144-160
5'6"	136-142	139-151	146-164
5'7"	138-145	142-154	149-168
5'8"	140-148	145-157	152-172
5'9"	142-151	148-160	155-176
5'10"	144-154	151-163	158-180
5'11"	146-157	154-166	161-184
6'0"	149-160	157-170	164-188
6'1"	152-164	160-174	168-192
6'2"	155-168	164-178	172-197
6'3"	158-172	167-182	176-202
6'4"	162-176	171-187	181-207
Women†			
4'10"	102-111	109-121	118-131
4'11"	103-113	111-123	120-134
5'0"	104-115	113-126	122-137
5'1"	106-118	115-129	125-140
5'2"	108-121	118-132	128-143
5'3"	111-124	121-135	131-147
5'4"	114-127	124-138	134-151
5'5"	117-130	127-141	137-155
5'6"	120-133	130-144	140-159
5'7"	123-136	133-147	143-163
5'8"	126-139	136-150	146-167
5'9"	129-142	139-153	149-170
5'10"	132-145	142-156	152-173
5'11"	135-148	145-159	155-176
6'0"	138-151	148-162	158-179

*Weights at ages 25 to 59, based on lowest mortality. Weight in pounds according to frame (in indoor clothing weighing 5 lb, shoes with 1" heels).
†Weights at ages 25 to 59, based on lowest mortality. Weight in pounds according to frame (in indoor clothing weighing 3 lb, shoes with 1" heels).

positive caloric balance
Caloric intake greater than caloric expenditure.

desirable weight
The weight range deemed appropriate for people of a specific gender, age, and frame size.

healthy body weight
Body weight within a weight range appropriate for a person with an acceptable waist-to-hip ratio.

Table 6-2 Healthy Weight: Recommended Guidelines

Height without shoes	Weight without clothes	
	19-34 years	35 years and over
5'	97-128	108-138
5'1"	101-132	111-143
5'2"	104-137	115-148
5'3"	107-141	119-152
5'4"	111-146	122-157
5'5"	114-150	126-162
5'6"	118-155	130-167
5'7"	121-160	134-172
5'8"	125-164	138-178
5'9"	129-169	142-183
5'10"	132-174	146-188
5'11"	136-179	151-194
6'	140-184	155-199
6'1"	144-189	159-205
6'2"	148-195	164-210
6'3"	152-200	168-216
6'4"	156-205	173-222
6'5"	160-211	177-228
6'6"	164-216	182-234

To use these new weight ranges, the following procedure must be performed:

1. Measure around your waist near your navel while you stand relaxed, not pulling in your stomach.
2. Measure around your hips, over the buttocks where hips are the largest.
3. Divide the waist measurement by the hip measurement.

For example, a woman with a 25-inch waist and 36-inch hips has a WHR of .69, which is well within the healthful range. Women with a WHR of less than .85 generally have a body weight that falls within the healthy range for their age and height; men with a WHR of less than 1.00 will also probably fall within the range that is considered healthy for their age and height. Any person whose WHR is equal to or greater than the recommended ratio should attempt to lose weight. Weight loss should occur no faster than ½ to 1 pound per week.

This new system was developed because of the growing concern over the relationship between the amount of fat that is around the waist (the spare tire) and the development of several serious health problems. In addition to an unacceptably high WHR, a bulging stomach or high blood pressure indicates a need to lose weight. Certainly people who exhibit all three of these signs are most in need of weight loss.

Body Mass Index

Another procedure for assessing healthy body weight is the **body mass index (BMI)**. The BMI indicates the relationship of body weight (expressed in kilograms) to height (expressed in meters) for both men and women.[7] The BMI does not reflect body composition (fat versus lean tissue) or consider the degree of fat accumulated within the central body cavity, nor is it adjusted for age. It is, nevertheless, widely used in determining obesity. A BMI greater than 27.8 for men or 27.3 for women indicates obesity.

An alternative method of determining the BMI is to use a **nomogram** such as that in Figure 6-1. Like the BMI, the nomogram requires information about both weight and height.

Once the BMI has been obtained, its relationship to a desirable BMI can be determined using Table 6-3.

Electrical Impedance

Electrical impedance is a relatively new method used to determine body composition. This computerized assessment procedure measures the electrical impedance (resistance) to a weak electrical flow directed through the body. Electrodes are attached to the arm and leg. Because adipose tissue resists the passage of the electrical current more than muscle tissue does, electrical impedance can be used to accurately calculate the percentage of body fat. Fortunately, electrical impedance measurements are painless. Additional techniques in which highly accurate but expensive technology is used to determine body composition, including *computerized axial tomography (CAT) scans, magnetic resonance imaging (MRI), infrared light transmission,* and *neutron activation,* may become common ways of measuring body composition in the future.

Skinfold Measurements

Skinfold measurements are a relatively precise and inexpensive indicator of body composition. In this assessment procedure, constant-pressure **calipers** are used to measure the thickness of the layer of fat beneath the skin's surface, the *subcutaneous fat layer.* Skinfold measurements of subcutaneous fat are taken at key places on the body (Figure 6-2). Through the use of specific formulas, skinfold measurements can be used to calculate the percentage of body fat. Additionally, the percent body fat value can be used in determining desirable weight.

Young adult men normally have a body fat percentage of 10% to 15%. The normal range for young adult women is 20% to 25%.[8] When a man's body fat percentage is higher than 20% and a woman's body

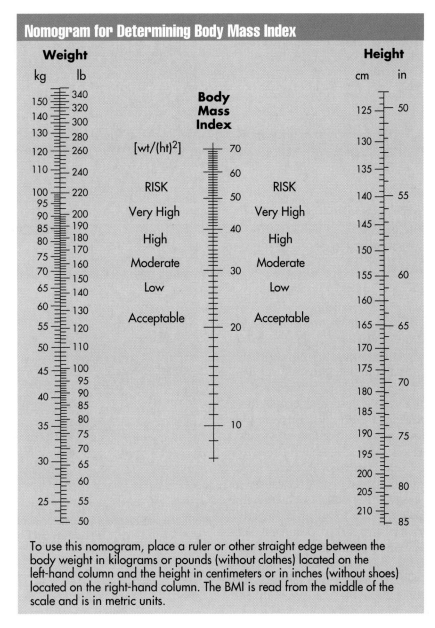

Nomogram for Determining Body Mass Index

To use this nomogram, place a ruler or other straight edge between the body weight in kilograms or pounds (without clothes) located on the left-hand column and the height in centimeters or in inches (without shoes) located on the right-hand column. The BMI is read from the middle of the scale and is in metric units.

Figure 6-1

fat percentage is above 30%, they are considered to be obese. The higher percentage of fat typically found in women is related to preparation for pregnancy and breastfeeding.

Hydrostatic Weighing

Hydrostatic (underwater) *weighing* is yet another precise method for determining the relative amounts of fat and lean body mass that make up body weight. A person's percentage of body fat is determined by comparing the underwater weight with the body weight out of water. The need for expensive facilities (a tank or pool) and experienced technicians make the

body mass index (BMI)
A numerical expression of body weight based on height and weight.

nomogram
Graphic means for finding an unknown value.

electrical impedance
Method to test for the percentage of body fat using resistance to the flow of electrical current.

calipers
A device used to measure the thickness of a skinfold, from which percent body fat can be calculated.

Table 6-3 Desirable Body Mass Index in Relation to Age	
Age Group (years)	BMI (kg/m²)
19-24	19-24
25-34	20-25
35-44	21-26
45-54	22-27
55-65	23-28
>65	24-29

availability and cost of this procedure limited to small-scale application, usually at a large research university or teaching hospital.

Appearance

Despite the many ways to determine obesity, the simplest method may be to look in the mirror. The old saying "mirrors don't lie" speaks for itself. For most people, this method is fairly accurate and certainly inexpensive. Unless a person is very muscular or has retained an excessive amount of water, the reflection in the mirror should be a good indicator of whether one's weight is appropriate. Although this simple method does not allow a person to pinpoint a body fat percentage, the person should be able to visually determine whether he or she is excessively fat.

For some overweight and obese people, however, it can be difficult to be objective. They may not accurately judge their bodies. Their imagined (or desired) **body image** and their actual image are markedly different. For these people, disappointment and frustration are likely.

Many people believe it is important to appear physically attractive. Unfortunately, the body image they desire may not be compatible with their inherited body type or their ability to lose or gain weight.

ORIGINS OF OBESITY

Experts continue to investigate the origins of obesity. Many theories focus on factors within the individual and from the environment. If the definitive cause of obesity is ever identified, it will probably have a complex basis that includes strong genetic and **neurophysiological** factors.

Genetic Basis for Obesity

Based on studies involving identical and nonidentical twins, some raised together and others separately, researchers have concluded that both environ-

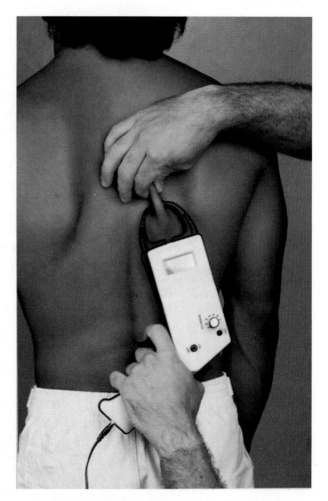

Figure 6-2   Subscapular body fat determination using skinfold calipers. Skinfold measurements are used in equations that calculate body fat density and percent body fat.

ment and genetics influence obesity. In some cases an inherited tendency toward excessive weight appears to be almost solely responsible for the amount and distribution of body fat,[9] whereas in other cases the role of genetics is clearly limited.

Within the last 5 years, the role of a genetic contribution has been clarified somewhat by the discovery of "fat" genes in mice and, subsequently, an "obese" gene in humans.[10] Speculation regarding the influence of these (or additional) genes centers on flawed genetic receipt of a protein that normally signals the body to terminate food consumption.[11] Research, in fact, found this protein, *leptin*, in low levels in overweight mice. Researchers suspected that leptin would be found in lower levels in obese humans compared with those of average weight. Their results demonstrated, however, that obese humans actually have higher levels of leptin than those of average weight.[12]

In addition, a genetic basis for an altered form of metabolism in people whose adipose tissue tends to accumulate in the midline may now be known. The "spare tire," associated unhealthy body weight, severe obesity, and type II diabetes mellitus (see p. 266), is now thought to reflect yet another abnormal gene.[13]

Appetite Center

Building on information about the neurophysiological basis of obesity, researchers have identified centers for the control of eating within the central nervous system (CNS). These centers, the *feeding center* for hunger and the *satiety center* for fullness, tell the body when eating should begin and end. These centers are believed to monitor continuously a variety of factors related to food intake, including olfactory and visual cues, the body's stores of glucose, amino acids, free fatty acids, the degree of stomach distention, basal metabolic rate, gastrointestinal hormone levels,[14] and GLP-1, a satiety-influencing hormone. Certain drugs, including amphetamines, phentermine and fenfluramine, dexfenfluramine (Redux), and fluoxetine (Prozac), can influence hunger or satiety, at least temporarily. This fact supports the idea that the CNS has a role in controlling food intake.

Set Point Theory

Traditional theory has suggested that the energy expenditure and energy storage centers of the body possess a genetically programmed awareness of the body's most physiologically desirable weight. To "honor" this so-called **set point** for desirable weight, the body adjusts its baseline use of energy, the basal metabolic rate (see pp. 137-138), upward or downward to accommodate an excessive intake of calories or an inadequate intake of calories, as the case may be. Thus by burning more energy or storing more energy, the body maintains its "best" weight through the process of **adaptive thermogenesis.**

Using the set point theory to explain the difficulty of losing weight, it has been suggested that in the case of a person with a genetically conditioned tendency to store excessive energy (to gain weight easily), the body prevents planned weight loss from occurring easily by adjusting the set point to a lower level. In addition, according to the set point theory, to prevent further episodes of "starvation" from occurring, a new, higher set point is established and lost weight is regained to a level above that of the initial set point. Every time the dieter again attempts to lose weight, he or she will **yo-yo** between weight loss and subsequent weight gain.

Today, a body of evidence suggests that the yo-yo dieting model, explained on the basis of set point readjustment, may not be accurate. Perhaps the weight gain that follows a period of dieting occurs merely because of the tendency for most people to gain fat and weight as they age. Perhaps, however, it is a reflection of the difficulty of losing weight only through caloric restriction, without increasing caloric expenditure.[15]

Related somewhat to set point and adaptive thermogenesis is the renewed interest in whether the small stores of brown fat (most fat is white fat) found in humans are involved in weight control. Located in small amounts in the upper back between the shoulder blades, this fat has the physiological ability to expend calories solely as heat without generating the high-energy units that are capable of being stored in fat cells.[16] Researchers recently discovered an "uncoupling" protein produced by a gene, called the uncoupling protein 2 gene (*UCP2*), that may somehow relate to the functioning of brown fat.[17]

Although considered dangerous by health experts, some have experimented with the use of an enzyme, 2,4 Dinitrophenol (DNP), that is capable of "uncoupling" high-energy units in a manner similar to that done naturally by brown fat, thus preventing energy storage and weight gain.

---

body image
A person's subjective perception of how his or her body appears.

neurophysiological
Pertaining to nervous system functioning; processes through which the body senses and responds to its internal and external environments.

set point
A genetically programmed range of body weight beyond which a person finds it difficult to gain or lose additional weight.

adaptive thermogenesis
Physiological response of the body to adjust its metabolic rate to the presence of food.

yo-yo syndrome
The repeated weight loss followed by weight gain experienced by many dieters.

Body Type

An inheritance basis for obesity could involve the interplay of *somatotype* (body build) and other unique energy processing characteristics passed on from parents to their children.

The classic work of Sheldon is credited with establishing the now-familiar body types: *ectomorph, mesomorph,* and *endomorph.* In the case of the ectomorphic body type, a tall slender body seems to virtually protect individuals from difficulty with excessive weight. Ectomorphs usually have difficulty maintaining normal weight for their height.

The somewhat shorter, more heavily muscled, athletic body of the mesomorph represents a genetic middle ground in inherited body types. During childhood, adolescence, and adulthood, as long as activity levels are maintained, mesomorphic people will appear to be "solid" without appearing to be obese. For well-conditioned mesomorphs, scale weight may suggest obesity, but the excessive weight is more likely the result of heavy muscularity. Mesomorphs have their greatest difficulty with obesity during adulthood when eating patterns fail to adjust to a decline in physical activity.

Endomorphs have body types that tend to be round and soft. Many endomorphs have excessively large abdomens and report having had weight problems since childhood.

Sheldon was interested in the personality traits and temperament of people with each body type. The relationship of body type to inheritance, body weight, and weight management cannot, however, go unnoticed. Sheldon's work simply gives us labels with which to discuss our observations.

Infant and Adult Feeding Patterns

Obesity can be categorized according to the way in which feeding patterns seem to produce it. Two general feeding patterns are related to two forms of obesity: hypercellular obesity and hypertrophic obesity.

The first of these patterns involves infant feeding. Many researchers believe that the number of fat cells a person has will be initially determined during the first 2 years of life. Babies who are overfed will develop a greater number of fat cells than babies who receive a balanced diet of appropriate, infant-sized portions. Overfed babies, especially those with a family history of obesity, will tend to develop **hypercellular obesity.** When these children reach adulthood, they will have more fat cells.

Late childhood and adolescence are also times during which excessive weight gain may result in the formation of addition fat cells. For adults, substantial weight gain can also stimulate an increase in the number of fat cells and thus move them toward hypercellular obesity.

A second type of obesity that has its origins in an eating pattern is called **hypertrophic obesity.** This form of obesity is related to a long-term positive caloric balance during adulthood. Over a period of years, existing fat cells increase in size to accommodate excess food intake.

Hypertrophic obesity is generally associated with excessive fat around the waist and is thought to contribute to conditions such as diabetes mellitus (type II, non–insulin-dependent diabetes), high levels of fat in the blood, high blood pressure, and heart disease. In our society, hypertrophic obesity shows itself during middle age—a time when our physical activity generally declines while our food intake remains the same.

Endocrine Influence

For a number of years, people believed that obesity was the result of "glandular" problems. Often the thyroid gland was said to be underactive, thus preventing the person from "burning up" food. Today, it is known that only a few obese people have an endocrine dysfunction of the type that would cause obesity.

Pregnancy

During a normal pregnancy, approximately 75,000 additional calories are required to support the development of the fetus and the formation of *maternal supportive tissues* and to fuel the mother's basal metabolic rate. In addition, the woman will develop approximately 9 extra pounds of fat tissue, which will be used as an energy source during breastfeeding. In total, the typical woman gives birth having gained approximately 28 pounds over her prepregnancy weight.[18]

After the birth of the baby, the mother will ideally have a weight gain of only 2 to 3 pounds over her prepregnancy weight. This small amount of additional weight will normally be lost by the end of the sixth to eighth month after birth. Of course, in the absence of the sound diet and exercise components stressed in the prenatal period, weight gain could be considerably greater.

Decreasing Basal Metabolic Rate

The body's requirement for energy to maintain basic physiological processes falls steadily with age. This change reflects the loss of muscle tissue with age in both men and women. Although on a short-term basis little adjustment needs to be made to maintain

Satisfying Our Appetites

All people satisfy hunger by eating, but because of cultural differences, when and how our appetites are satisfied vary. All people usually eat at least one meal in a 24-hour period. Some African tribes and other developing societies are accustomed to eating only one meal per day, as a result of occasional or continual food shortages. Other substances are known to be used by some of these societies to suppress hunger, such as coca leaves (which contain cocaine), peyote (a hallucinogen derived from a cactus), tobacco, coffee, and tea.[19] Appetite suppressants in the form of diet aids in the United States serve the same purpose but for different reasons.

Typically in North America, three meals a day is the custom, although skipping regular meals and snacking are common. The British usually eat four times a day, whereas continental European people may eat five or six times. Of course, these practices vary according to changing lifestyles.[19]

For most, eating is a pleasurable experience, but not just for the sake of nourishment. Business deals are made over lunch, agreements between countries are discussed over a meal, relationships are begun during a romantic dinner, and events are celebrated by the sharing of food.

Think about your own eating habits. Why and when do you eat? How do your eating habits reflect your culture and lifestyle?

---

weight, weight gain can become a problem over time if adjustments are not made. A gradual decrease in food intake or an effort to exercise more can be effective in preventing the gradual onset of obesity.

Family Dietary Practices

Food preferences and eating practices are among the many areas of instruction for which the family assumes responsibility. In some families the lessons are taught as though they were outlined from a nutrition textbook, whereas for others the lessons taught are destined to lead to a lifetime of malnourishment, including obesity. For example, between-meal snacking involving highly sugared or high-fat foods, large serving sizes, multiple servings, and high-calorie meals are poor lessons taught by some families.

Inactivity

When weight management experts are asked to identify the single most important reason there is so much obesity in today's society, they are almost certain to point to inactivity. People of all ages tend to do less and therefore burn fewer calories than did their ancestors only a few generations ago. Automation in the workplace, labor-saving devices in the home, the inactivity associated with watching television, and a general dislike of exercise are a few of the reasons that account for this inactivity.

CALORIC BALANCE

As previously mentioned, any calories consumed in excess of those that are used by the body are converted to fat. We gain weight when our energy input is greater than our energy output. On the other hand, we lose weight when our energy output is greater than our energy input (Figure 6-3). Weight remains constant when caloric input and output are identical. In such situations, our bodies are said to be in *caloric balance.*

ENERGY NEEDS OF THE BODY

What are our energy needs? How many calories should we consume (or burn) to achieve a healthy weight? Although there are some ballpark estimates for college-aged men (2500 to 3300 calories daily) and women (approximately 2500 calories daily), we all

---

hypercellular obesity
A form of obesity seen in people who possess an abnormally large number of fat cells.

hypertrophic obesity (high per **troh** fick)
A form of obesity in which fat cells are enlarged but not excessive in number.

vary in our specific energy needs.[20] These needs are based on three factors: (1) activity requirements, (2) basal metabolic rate, and (3) the thermic effect of food.

We often ignore opportunities to become more active.

Activity Requirements

Each person's caloric *activity requirements* vary directly according to the amount of daily physical work completed. For example, sedentary office workers will require a smaller daily caloric intake than will construction workers, lumberjacks, or farm workers.

Physical activity that occurs outside the workplace also increases caloric needs. Sedentary office workers may be quite active in their recreational pursuits. Active employees may spend their off hours lounging in front of the television. You must closely examine the total amount of work or activity an individual engages in to accurately estimate that person's caloric requirements. Physical activity uses 20% to 40% of caloric intake. See Table 6-4 for a breakdown of caloric expenditures for various recreational pursuits.

Basal Metabolism

Of the three factors that determine energy needs, basal metabolism uses the highest proportion (50%

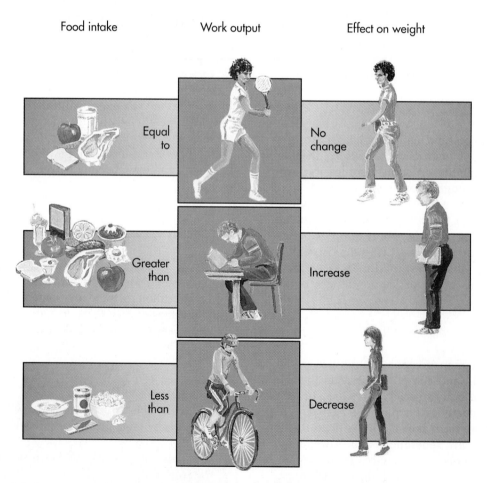

Figure 6-3   Caloric balance: energy input equals energy output, some of which comes from physical activity.

to 70%) of the total calories required by each person. Expressed as a **basal metabolic rate (BMR),** basal metabolism reflects the minimum amount of energy the body requires to carry on all vital functions, such as blood circulation and glandular activity. Even when a person is totally relaxed or sleeping, these vital body functions continue to expend calories.

Basal metabolism changes as people age. For both males and females, the BMR is relatively high at birth and continues to increase until the age of 2. Except for a slight rise at puberty, their BMR will then gradually decline throughout life.[16] If people fail to recognize that their BMR decreases as they grow older (2% per decade), they might also fail to adjust their food intake and activity level accordingly. Thus they will gradually put on unwanted pounds as they move through the life cycle. Use the formula given in the Star Box on p. 138 to determine your BMR.

Thermic Effect of Food

Formerly called the *specific dynamic action* of food, or *dietary thermogenesis,* the thermic effect of food represents the energy our bodies require for the diges-

Table 6-4   Calories Expended During Physical Activity

To determine the number of calories you have spent in an hour of activity, simply multiply the *calories per hour per pound* column by your weight (in pounds). For example, after an hour of archery, a 120-pound person will have expended 209 calories; a 160-pound person, 278 calories; and a 220-pound person, 383 calories.

Activity	Calories/hour/pound	Activity	Calories/hour/pound
Archery	1.74	Marching (rapid)	3.84
Basketball	3.78	Painting (outside)	2.10
Baseball	1.86	Playing music (sitting)	1.08
Boxing (sparring)	3.78	Racquetball	3.90
Canoeing (leisure)	1.20	Running (cross-country)	4.44
Climbing hills (no load)	3.30	Running	
Cleaning	1.62	11 min 30 sec per mile	3.66
Cooking	1.20	9 min per mile	5.28
Cycling		8 min per mile	5.64
5.5 mph	1.74	7 min per mile	6.24
9.4 mph	2.70	6 min per mile	6.84
Racing	4.62	5 min 30 sec per mile	7.86
Dance (modern)	2.28	Scrubbing floors	3.00
Eating (sitting)	0.60	Sailing	1.20
Field hockey	3.66	Skiing	
Fishing	1.68	Cross-country	4.43
Football	3.60	Snow, downhill	3.84
Gardening		Water	3.12
Digging	3.42	Skating (moderate)	2.28
Mowing	3.06	Soccer	3.54
Raking	1.44	Squash	5.76
Golf	2.34	Swimming	
Gymnastics	1.80	Backstroke	4.62
Handball	3.78	Breaststroke	4.44
Hiking	2.52	Free, fast	4.26
Horseback riding		Free, slow	3.48
Galloping	3.72	Butterfly	4.68
Trotting	3.00	Table tennis	1.86
Walking	1.14	Tennis	3.00
Ice hockey	5.70	Volleyball	1.32
Jogging	4.15	Walking (normal pace)	2.16
Judo	5.34	Weight training	1.90
Knitting (sewing)	0.60	Wrestling	5.10
Lacrosse	5.70	Writing (sitting)	0.78

tion, absorption, and transportation of food. This energy breaks the electrochemical bonds that hold complex food molecules together, resulting in smaller nutrient units that can be distributed throughout the body. This energy need is in addition to activity needs and basal metabolic needs. The thermic effect of food is estimated to represent about 10% of total energy needs.[7] Some nutritionists now consider the thermic effect of food merely a component of overall basal metabolism.

Lifetime Weight Control

Obesity and frequent fluctuation in weight are thought to be associated with higher levels of morbidity and mortality. Therefore the maintenance of weight and body composition at or near optimum levels is highly desirable. Although people may believe that this is a difficult goal to achieve, it is not unrealistic when begun early in life and from a starting point at or near optimum levels. The following are some keys to success:

- *Exercise:* Caloric expenditure through regular exercise, including cardiovascular exercise and strength training, is a key to maintaining optimum weight and body composition (see Chapter 4).
- *Dietary modification:* Meals planned around foods low in total fat and saturated fat and high in complex carbohydrates also play an important role in maintaining optimum weight and body composition (see Chapter 5).
- *Lifestyle support:* Not only must people be committed to a lifestyle featuring regular physical activity and careful food choices, they must also build a support system that will encourage them in these endeavors. People should inform family, friends, classmates, and co-workers about their intent to rely on them for support and encouragement.
- *Problem solving:* People should reevaluate their current approaches to dealing with stressors. They must replace any reliance on food as a coping mechanism with nonfood options, such as exercise or talking with friends or family members.
- *Redefinition of health:* People must develop the ability to think about health and wellness in a manner that recognizes the importance of proactivity (see Chapter 2) and involvement, rather than simply focusing on not becoming sick or incapacitated.

Assuming that a person has an acceptable weight and body composition at this time, the lifestyle choices just suggested will make a significant contribution to avoiding a weight problem during the adult years.

WEIGHT MANAGEMENT TECHNIQUES

For those who are already overweight, the need to reduce weight to attain their optimum weight and body composition will require intervention that may

Calculating Basal Metabolic Rate

The basal metabolic rate (BMR) reflects the amount of energy in calories (C) that your body requires to sustain basic functions. The formula below can be used to calculate your approximate basal metabolic rate.

$$\text{BMR per day} = 1\,C \times \frac{\text{body weight (lb)}}{2.2} \times 24$$

EXAMPLE: 150-lb person

$$\text{BMR per day} = 1\,C \times \frac{150}{2.2} \times 24$$

$$= 1\,C \times 68.2 \times 24$$

$$= 1636.8\,C$$

This person would need approximately 1637 calories to sustain the body at rest for an entire day. Activity of any kind, of course, elevates the requirement for calories.

NOTE: A woman's BMR would be approximately 5% lower than that of a man of the same age.

 HealthQuest Activities

- The *Stages of Change* activity in Module 3 assesses your readiness to follow a diet containing appropriate levels of fats, carbohydrates, and proteins. It outlines concrete steps you can take to maintain healthy intake levels of these nutrients. The feedback for this activity is provided separately for each of these three dietary areas. You may address all three areas or choose among them. Develop a strategy for overcoming unhealthful eating habits, and keep an ongoing account of your progress. Record your mood, activity level, schedule, and any other factors that may affect your eating behavior. Then write down several ways to lessen the effects of such events on your eating behavior.

be different from the total lifestyle approach just described. However, on reaching a more healthful weight and body composition, maintenance of that status will depend on adopting the lifestyle changes described on p. 138.

Weight loss occurs when the amount of energy taken into the body is less than that demanded by the body for physiological maintenance and voluntary activity. A number of approaches to weight loss can be pursued. Complete the Personal Assessment on p. 140 to determine whether you are a candidate for weight loss.

Dietary Alterations

A diet that reduces caloric intake is the most common approach to what seems to be a national obsession with weight loss. The choice of foods included in the diet and the amount of food that can be consumed are the two factors that distinguish the wide range of diets currently available. Unfortunately, dieting alone usually does not result in long-term weight loss. In fact, whether managing their diets by themselves or following the advice of one of the widely recognized weight loss programs, most dieters regain at least two thirds of the weight they lost within 2 years after their initial loss.[21] A study of successful dieters, conducted by the National Weight Control Registry, demonstrated that people in this select group relied on balanced diets and exercise, rather than medication, to lose weight and maintain that loss.[22]

Balanced diets supported by portion control

For nutritional health, a logical approach to weight loss and subsequent weight maintenance is to establish a nutritionally sound balanced diet (low in fat, especially saturated fat, and high in complex carbohydrates) that controls portions. A working understanding of portion size can be achieved using diet scales or through a nutrition education program in which realistic models of food servings are used. Most people have difficulty controlling portion sizes. The labels of many packaged foods provide nutrition information for a single serving, yet the package often contains two servings of the food. In addition, restaurants rarely serve standard portion sizes, preferring to heap food on the plate to justify high menu prices.[23] Nevertheless, a balanced diet, portion control approach to weight loss is a nutritionally sound program with which there is some probability of success.

Fad diets

People use a variety of fad diets in an attempt to lose weight within a short time. These popular diets are often promoted in best-selling books written by

Modifying your eating behavior requires making thoughtful food choices.

people who claim to be nutrition "experts" (see the Health Action Guide on p. 141, right). With few exceptions, these approaches are both ineffective and potentially unhealthful. In addition, some require far greater expense than would be associated with weight loss or management techniques using portion control and regular physical activity. The pros and cons of a variety of popular diet plans are presented in Table 6-5.

Low-calorie or low-fat foods and controlled serving sizes

Recently a variety of familiar foods have been developed in a reduced-calorie form. By lowering the carbohydrate content with the use of nonnutritive sweeteners, reducing the portion size, or reducing the

basal metabolic rate (BMR) (**bay** sal)
The amount of energy (in calories) your body requires to maintain basic functions.

PERSONAL ASSESSMENT

Should You Consider a Weight Loss Program?

Before undertaking a program, it is important to look at your past experiences and feelings about weight loss. Perhaps in doing so, you might decide that you would do better with other alternatives besides dieting.

Answer each of the following items with a "True" or "False" as it applies to you.

_____ 1. I am frustrated about my inability to stick to a diet.

_____ 2. I have less self-control than most dieters.

_____ 3. Most of the times I try to lose weight, I lose control and go off my diet.

_____ 4. When I try to develop a habit of regular exercise, something always interferes and I stop.

_____ 5. Exercise seems to be an ordeal to me.

_____ 6. I often feel tired during the day.

_____ 7. My weight has gone up and down several times when I go on and off diets.

_____ 8. My body seems to be getting thicker in the middle over the years.

_____ 9. My weight seems to be increasing over the years.

_____ 10. I find myself thinking about food more than I should.

_____ 11. I find myself thinking about my weight all through the day.

_____ 12. I feel there is probably no hope for my weight problem.

_____ 13. Sometimes I lose control and really binge on food.

_____ 14. I use food to make myself feel better when I am angry, nervous, or depressed.

_____ 15. Some people reject me as a friend because I am too heavy.

_____ 16. My social life is limited because of my weight.

_____ 17. My sex life is limited because of my weight.

_____ 18. Other people think I am unattractive because of my weight.

_____ 19. I put a lot of effort into choosing clothes that tend to cover up my weight problem.

To Carry This Further . . .

For those items that you answered as true, consider these recommendations:

Items 1, 2, and 3: Rather than going on a diet, why not try to reduce your fat intake by avoiding fried food and foods with added fat. Eat more low-fat foods, and make certain that your dairy products are low-fat and your meats are lean.

Items 4, 5, and 6: You need a gradual but regular exercise program. Check around your community, and identify a reputable program that has a proven success rate in helping others who have had a weight problem.

Items 7, 8, and 9: These items indicate the development of a weight problem that could truly be damaging your health. These are reasons for being serious about weight loss that go beyond appearance.

Items 10, 11, 12, 13, and 14: You may be into "living to eat" rather than "eating to live." Now is the time to give serious thought on what is important in your life, other than appearance-related needs.

Items 15, 16, and 17: Work at forming new relationships. Seek out people who are capable of looking beyond your physical appearance for those attributes that they will find to be attractive in you.

Items 18 and 19: As for 15 to 17, assess your current relationships. Put your efforts into relationships with people who seem capable of looking "into" you, rather than only "at" you.

---

fat content of the original formulations, manufacturers have produced "lite" versions of many food products. For example, numerous frozen entrees, such as Healthy Choice Oriental Beef with Vegetables (290 calories), Weight Watchers Lasagna Florentine (210 calories), and Healthy Choice Fettucine with Turkey and Vegetables (350 calories), are attractively low in calories. An additional aid to selecting lower-calorie and lower-fat foods is the newly required food label, described in Chapter 5.

Controlled fasting

In cases of extreme obesity, physicians place some patients on a complete fast in a hospital setting. The patient is maintained on only water, electrolytes, and vitamins. Weight loss is profound because the body is quickly forced to begin **catabolizing** its fat and muscle tissues. Sodium loss, a negative nitrogen balance, and potassium loss are particular concerns.

Today, some people regularly practice unsupervised, short periods of modified fasting. Solid foods

Changing Your Eating Patterns

Following the tips listed below will help you achieve your weight loss goals:
- Keep a log of the times, settings, reasons, and feelings associated with your eating.
- Set realistic long-term goals (for example, loss of a pound per week instead of 5 lb per week).
- Do not completely deprive yourself of enjoyable foods (occasionally reward yourself with a small treat).
- Realize that the sacrifices you are making are what *you* feel are important for *your* health and happiness.
- Eat slowly. It takes about 20 minutes for your brain to recognize satiety signals from your body.
- Put more physical activity into your daily routine (taking stairs instead of elevators or parking in the distant part of a parking lot, for example).
- Reward yourself when you reach your goals (with new clothes, sporting equipment, a vacation trip).
- Share your commitment to weight loss with your family and friends so that they can support your efforts.
- Keep careful records of daily food consumption and weekly weight change.
- Be prepared to deal with occasional plateaus and setbacks in your quest for weight loss.
- Remember that low-fat, low–saturated fat, and high–complex carbohydrate meals in combination with regular physical activity is the basis on which these strategies are applied. ◄------►

Choosing A Diet Book

- Make sure the program described in the book incorporates a balanced diet, an exercise program, and behavior modification.
- Beware of inflexible plans, such as those that require you to eat certain foods on certain days.
- Avoid plans that allow fewer than 1200 calories a day, the minimum needed to get essential nutrients.
- Make sure the recommended rate of weight loss does not exceed 2 lb per week.
- Steer clear of books that promote vitamins, pills, shots, gimmicks, gadgets, or brand-name diet foods.
- Read reviews to see if the book received approval from a reputable nutrition expert, institution, or journal.
- Check the author's credentials. He or she should have a degree in nutrition from an accredited university or should use reliable sources for the information.
- Make sure the book is based on up-to-date scientific research.
- Beware of diets that promise fast, easy, or effortless weight loss or "a new secret formula."
- Choose a plan that teaches how to keep the weight off once you've lost it. ◄------

are removed from the diet for a number of days. Fruit juice, water, supplements, and vitamins are used to minimize the risks described in association with total fasting. However, too frequent unsupervised short-term fasting can be dangerous and is not generally recommended.

Commercial weight reduction programs

In virtually every area of the country, at least one version of the popular commercial weight reduction programs, such as TOPS (Take Off Pounds Sensibly), Jenny Craig, and Nutri-Systems Weight Loss Centers, can be found. Popularized by Weight Watchers, these programs generally feature a format consisting of (1) a well-balanced diet emphasizing portion control and low-fat, low–saturated fat, and high–complex carbohydrate foods, (2) realistic weight loss goals to be attained over a reasonable period of time, (3) encouragement from supportive leaders and fellow group members, (4) emphasis on regular physical activity, and (5) a weight management program (follow-up program). The Star Box on p. 144 presents some guidelines for choosing a commercial weight loss program.

Although in theory these programs offer an opportunity to lose weight for people who cannot or will not

catabolism
The metabolic process of breaking down tissue for the purpose of converting it into energy.

Table 6-5   Advantages and Disadvantages of Selected Diets

Type of diet	Advantages	Disadvantages	Examples
Limited food choice diets	Reduce the number of food choices made by the users Limited opportunity to make mistakes Almost certainly low in calories after the first few days	Deficient in many nutrients, depending on the foods allowed Monotonous—difficult to adhere to Eating out and eating socially are difficult Do not retrain dieters in acceptable eating habits Low long-term success rates No scientific basis for these diets	Banana and milk diet Fitonics for Life Diet Kempner rice diet Lecithin, vinegar, kelp, and vitamin B_6 diet The New Beverly Hills Diet Fit for Life
Restricted-calorie, balanced food plans	Sufficiently low in calories to permit steady weight loss Nutritionally balanced Palatable Include readily available foods Reasonable in cost Can be adapted from family meals Permit eating out and social eating Promote a new set of eating habits	Do not appeal to people who want a "unique" diet Do not produce immediate and large weight losses	Weight Watchers Diet Prudent Diet (American Heart Association) Eating Thin for Life Lou Arrone's Weigh Less, Live Longer Take Off Pounds Sensibly (TOPS) Overeaters Anonymous
Fasting starvation diet	Rapid initial loss	Nutrient deficient Danger of ketosis >60% loss is muscle <40% loss is fat Low long-term success rate	ZIP Diet 5-Day Miracle Diet
High-carbohydrate diet	Emphasizes grains, fruits, and vegetables High in bulk Low in cholesterol	Limits milk, meat Nutritionally very inadequate for calcium, iron, and protein	Quick Weight Loss Diet Pritikin Diet Hilton Head Metabolism Diet

participate in an activity program, their effectiveness is very limited. In fact, the limited success of these programs and the difficulty that working women have in attending meetings has resulted in falling enrollment and the development of home-based programs, such as those developed by hospital-based wellness programs, many YMCAs and YWCAs, and even Weight Watchers. Further, these programs are costly when compared with self-directed approaches, especially when the program markets its own food products.

Physical Intervention

A second approach to weight loss involves techniques and products designed to alter basic eating patterns. These techniques range from those that are

Type of diet	Advantages	Disadvantages	Examples
High-protein, low-carbohydrate diets Usually include all the meat, fish, poultry, and eggs you can eat Occasionally permit milk and cheese in limited amounts Prohibit fruits, vegetables, and any bread or cereal products	Rapid initial weight loss because of diuretic effect Very little hunger	Too low in carbohydrates Deficient in many nutrients— vitamin C, vitamin A (unless eggs are included), calcium, and several trace elements High in saturated fat, choles- terol, and total fat Extreme diets of this type could cause death Impossible to adhere to these diets long enough to lose any appreciable amount of weight Dangerous for people with kid- ney disease Weight lost, which is largely water, is rapidly regained Expensive Unpalatable after first few days Difficult for dieter to eat out	Dr. Stillman's Quick Weight Loss Diet Calories Don't Count by Dr. Taller Dr. Atkin's New Diet Revolution Scarsdale Diet Air Force Diet The Carbohydrate Addict's Life Span Program Mastering the Zone Diet
Low-calorie, high-protein supplement diets Usually a premea- sured powder to be reconstituted with water or a prepared liquid formula	Rapid initial weight loss Easy to prepare—already mea- sured Palatable for first few days Usually fortified to provide rec- ommended amount of micronutrients Must be labeled if >50% protein	Usually prescribed at danger- ously low calorie intake of 300 to 500 Cal Overpriced Low in fiber and bulk—consti- pating in short amount of time	Metracal Diet Cambridge Diet Liquid Protein Diet Last Chance Diet Oxford Diet
High-fiber, low-calorie diets	High satiety value Provide bulk	Irritating to the lower colon Decreases absorption of trace elements, especially iron Nutritionally deficient Low in protein	Pritikin Diet F Diet Zen Macrobiotic Diet
Protein-sparing modified fats <50% protein: 400 Cal	Safe under supervision High-quality protein Minimize loss of lean body mass	Decreases BMR Monotonous Expensive	Optifast Medifast
Premeasured food plans	Provide prescribed portion sizes—little chance of too small or too large a portion Total food programs Some provide adequate calories (1200) Nutritionally balanced or sup- plemented	Expensive Do not retrain dieters in accept- able eating habits Preclude eating out or social eating Often low in bulk Monotonous Low long-term success rates	Nutri-System Carnation Plan

Choosing a Reputable Weight Loss Program

When checking out commercial weight loss programs, keep the following criteria in mind. Steer clear of any program that:

- Is not led by qualified specialists, including a registered dietitian
- Promises or encourages quick weight loss
- Does not require a preenrollment physical examination
- Does not warn clients of the risk of developing health problems related to weight loss, such as ketosis and diabetes-related complications
- Claims that an unusually high percentage of its clients are successful in achieving and maintaining weight loss
- Requires you to buy its products, such as foods or nutritional supplements
- Does not encourage lifestyle changes, including an exercise program
- Does not provide follow-up support after you reach your weight loss goal

self-selected and self-applied to those that must be administered within an institutional setting by highly trained professionals.

Hunger- and satiety-influencing products

One of the fondest wishes of overweight people is to lose the desire to eat or to feel that they have eaten enough. Today, many dieters are confused about the safety of pharmaceutical approaches to weight loss, including both OTC and prescription drugs.

Some OTC appetite suppressants containing **phenylpropanolamine (PPA)** may still be sold in drugstores and supermarkets. People with high blood pressure, thyroid conditions, diabetes, depression, or glaucoma should not use these products.

The FDA also continues to voice concern about OTC weight loss and energy-promotion products containing ephedrine (*ma huong* and Chinese ephedra). Ephedrine has been linked to heart attacks and strokes and should be used with caution.

Some prescription medications have been shown to have serious side effects. Two prescription medications, *phentermine* and *fenfluramine*, were prescribed for patients who wanted to lose weight. Both of the drugs affect levels of serotonin, the neurotransmitter associated with satiety. This popular combination, widely referred to as *phen-fen*, gradually raised concern among health experts because of side effects in people with angina, glaucoma, and high blood pressure. In addition, reports began to surface that some patients had developed a rare but lethal condition

called *pulmonary hypertension.* Nevertheless, use of the drugs continued unabated.

During the mid-1990s a new serotonin-specific weight loss drug, *dexfenfluramine* (Redux), was approved for use in the United States. Results among patients who used the drug, in combination with dietary modification and exercise, seemed impressive during the initial months of its widespread use. However, with tragic results, some patients began to take dexfenfluramine with phentermine in an attempt to find a new combination that would be even more effective than phen-fen or Redux when used alone. Thus, two combinations of three serotonin-specific drugs were in vogue in early 1997. In May 1997, however, the Mayo Clinic and a clinic in Fargo, North Dakota, reported that they were seeing an increasing number of patients with damage to their heart valves. Several of these patients' lives could be saved only through valve replacement surgery.[24] All of these people had taken phen-fen or phen-dexfenfluramine for weight loss. In August 1997 the FDA banned the use of phentermine, fenfluramine, and dexfenfluramine, alone and in combination.

A non-serotonin-influencing drug, *orlistat* (Xenical), has recently been approved. Unlike the serotonin-specific drugs, orlistat reduces fat absorption in the small intestine by about 30%. The drug is intended for use among people who are 20% or more above ideal weight. It could cause a 10% loss of body weight without significant dietary restriction. Some concern exists about the lack of absorption of fat-soluble vitamins among people taking the drug.

Surgical Measures

When weight loss is imperative and a person is morbidly obese, surgical intervention may be considered. A *gastric resection* is a major operation in which a portion of the small intestine is bypassed in an attempt to decrease the body's ability to absorb nutrients. Although the procedure can produce a major loss of body weight, it is associated with many unpleasant side effects (including diarrhea and liver damage) and various nutritional deficiencies.

Gastroplasty (stomach stapling) is a surgical procedure that involves sealing off about half of the stomach with surgical staples. Once the procedure has been completed, the reduced capacity of the stomach decreases the amount of food that can be processed at any one time. As a result, patients feel full more quickly after eating a small meal. This procedure is reversible but carries the risks associated with surgery and the costs of a major surgical procedure.

Liposuction

Another form of surgical weight loss management is *liposuction*, or *lipoplasty*. During this procedure, a physician inserts a small tube through the skin and vacuum aspirates away fat cells. This procedure is generally used for stubborn, localized pockets of fat and is usually appropriate for people under the age of 40.

Liposuction is more a cosmetic procedure than a general approach to weight loss. Along with unrealistic expectations, the risks of infection, pain and discomfort, bruising, swelling, discoloration, abscesses, and unattractive changes in body contours are possible outcomes of liposuction. Therefore people considering this procedure should carefully investigate all aspects of it, including the training and experience of the surgeon, to determine whether it is appropriate.

EATING DISORDERS

Perhaps it is not surprising that some people have medically identifiable, potentially serious difficulties with body image, body weight, and food selection. Among these disorders are two that are frequently seen among college students, anorexia nervosa and bulimia. In addition, compulsive exercising, compulsive eating, and disorders involving various combinations of anorexic and bulimic practices are also found in college populations. We have included these topics in the chapter on weight management because most eating disorders begin with dieting. However, most eating disorders also involve inappropriate food choices, as well as deep emotional needs. Those issues are discussed in Chapters 2 and 5.

Anorexia Nervosa

A young woman, competitive and perfectionistic by nature, determines that her weight (and appearance) is unacceptable. She begins to disregard her appetite, and her food consumption virtually ceases.

The young woman in this description may be seen by her friends or roommates as active and intelligent and simply dieting and exercising with an unusual degree of commitment. Eventually, however, they observe that her food consumption has nearly stopped. Her weight loss has continued beyond the point that is pleasing—at least to others. Nevertheless, her activity level remains high. When questioned about her weight loss, she says that she still needs to lose more weight.

This person is suffering from a medical condition called **anorexia nervosa** (see the Star Box on p. 146). This self-induced starvation is life-threatening in 5% to 20% of cases. The stunning amount of weight that some anorexic people lose—up to 50% of their body weight—eventually leads to failure of the heart, lungs, and kidneys.

As weight loss–oriented as this condition seems, experts believe that the anorexic person is attempting to meet a much deeper need for control. Specifically, in a family setting in which much is expected of the individual but little opportunity for self-directed behavior is provided, control over the body becomes a need-fulfilling tool.[25] Eventually, however, a normal body image is lost and the condition progresses in the manner described above. Fortunately, psychological intervention in combination with medical and dietary support can return the anorexic person to a more life-sustaining pattern of eating. Thus the anorexic person needs to seek professional help. Your obligation when you observe this condition in a friend is to secure immediate assistance for this person.

Bulimia Nervosa

Bulimia nervosa is an eating disorder in which people gorge themselves with food. When people practice a pattern of massive eating followed by **purging,** they are said to suffer from *bulimarexia*, or *bulimia nervosa* (see the Star Box on p. 146). Most often, however, the term *bulimia* is used to describe this binge-purge pattern. As with anorexic people, most people with bulimia are young women, although the incidence in men is growing.

People with bulimia lose or maintain weight not because they stop eating but because they eat and then purge their digestive system by vomiting, using laxatives, or taking syrup of ipecac, a dangerous drug used to stimulate vomiting after an accidental poisoning. People with bulimia may gorge themselves with food (up to 10,000 calories in a sitting) and then disappear, only to return later seemingly unaffected by the

phenylpropanolamine (PPA)
The active chemical compound found in most over-the-counter diet products.

anorexia nervosa
A disorder of emotional origin in which appetite and hunger are suppressed and marked weight loss occurs.

bulimia nervosa
A disorder of emotional origin in which binge eating patterns are established; usually accompanied by purging.

purging
Using vomiting or laxatives to remove undigested food from the body.

Recognizing Anorexia Nervosa and Bulimia

The American Psychological Association uses the following diagnostic criteria to identify anorexia nervosa and bulimia:

Anorexia

- 15% or more below desirable weight
- Fear of weight gain
- Altered body image
- Three or more missed menstrual periods; in young adolescents, no onset of menstruation

Bulimia

- Binge eating two or more times a week for 3 months
- A lack of control over bingeing
- Purging
- Concern about body image

Characteristic symptoms include the following. However, it is unlikely that all the symptoms will be evident in any one individual.

Anorexia

- Looks thin and keeps getting thinner
- Skips meals, cuts food into small pieces, moves food around plate to appear to have eaten
- Loss of menstrual periods
- Wears "layered look" in an attempt to disguise weight loss
- Loss of hair from the head
- Growth of fine hair (lanugo) on face, arms, and chest
- Extreme sensitivity to cold

Bulimia

- Bathroom use immediately after eating
- Inconspicuous eating
- Excessive time (and money) spent food shopping
- Shopping for food at several stores rather than one store
- Menstrual irregularities
- Excessive constipation
- Swollen and/or infected salivary glands, sore throat
- Bursting blood vessels in the eyes
- Damaged teeth and gums
- Dehydration and kidney dysfunction

amount of food they ate. In all likelihood, they have quickly and quietly regurgitated the food. In the mid-1980s, medical experts estimated that as many as 19% of 18- to 22-year-old women developed all the principal symptoms of bulimia. However, when all of the criteria mentioned in the Star Box are applied rather than simply reporting "experience" with bulimia-associated behavior, the percentage drops to less than 2%.

In addition to the binge-purge disorder, people who binge but do not purge also suffer from an eating disorder. Whether called *bulimia*, "eating disorder not otherwise specified," or *binge-eating disorder*, this practice also requires intervention and effective treatment.

Compulsive Exercise and Compulsive Eating

The compulsive nature of some people's exercising or eating patterns suggests a slightly different version of the two principal eating disorders. More than likely, a wide array of causes can account for both of these behavior patterns. In the case of compulsive exercise, a desire for control may exist, as in anorexia nervosa, whereas with compulsive eating the role of food in reducing feelings of insecurity and stress may explain the inability to resist food whenever it is present. Again, dieting may be the starting point for both of these behavior patterns. As in the more classic eating disorders, family members and friends should not fail to identify and respond to these conditions.

Treatment for Eating Disorders

The treatment of eating disorders is complex and demanding. The initial physical care for a person with anorexia most often begins with hospitalization to stabilize the physical deterioration associated with starvation. Stomach tubes and intravenous feedings are sometimes necessary, particularly when the patient will not (or cannot) eat. In addition, drugs used to treat depression, obsessive-compulsive disorder, and anxiety are often prescribed. Behavior modification, including eating contracts, is used, as is psychotherapy in both individual and group formats. Nutritional and family counseling complete the therapy.[26]

Treatment for bulimia involves individual, family, and nutritional counseling. Unlike treatment for anorexia, however, bulimia treatment does not as frequently involve hospitalization. The Star Box on p. 147 lists resources for people with eating disorders.

Resources for Anorexia and Bulimia Treatment

Local Resources
- College or university health centers
- College or university counseling centers
- Comprehensive mental health centers
- Crisis intervention centers
- Mental health associations

Organizations and Self-Help Groups
American Anorexia/Bulimia Association, Inc.
165 W. 46th St., Suite 1108, New York, NY 10036
http://members.aol.com/amanbu

Anorexia Nervosa and Associated Disorders, Inc.
P.O. Box 7, Highland Park, IL 60035
(847) 831-3438

Anorexia Nervosa and Related Eating Disorders, Inc.
P.O. Box 5102, Eugene, OR 97405
(541) 344-1144

Bulimia Anorexia Nervosa Association
300 Cabana Rd. East,
Windsor, Ontario, Canada N9G 1A3
(519) 969–2112

National Eating Disorders Association (NEDO) at Laureate
Psychiatric Hospital
P.O. Box 470207, Tulsa, OK 74147
(918) 481-4092
www.laureate.org

Mental Health Net
Eating Disorders: Anorexia Nervosa
www.cmhc.com/factsfam/anorexia.htm

National Institute of Mental Health
Eating Disorders Information Page
www.nimh.nih.gov/publicat/eatdis.htm

UNDERNUTRITION

For some young adults, the lack of adequate body weight is a serious concern. Particularly for those who have inherited an ectomorphic body build (tall, narrow shoulders and hips, tendency to thinness), attempts to gain weight are routinely undertaken, often with limited success. If these people are to be successful in gaining weight, they must discover an effective way to take in more calories than they burn (see the article on pp. 151-152).

Nutritionists believe that the healthiest way to gain weight is to increase the intake of calorie-dense food.

Health on the Web
LEARNING ACTIVITIES

Activity 1

After reading this chapter, you are aware that obesity is a serious health concern. If you have attempted to shed some pounds, you are familiar with the challenge that this goal requires. A number of important factors can help you stay motivated. Go to the URL http://cgi.pathfinder.com/cgi-bin/thrive/cg/gdm12x/game/thrive/shape_weight98 and take the *Ready to lose weight?* quiz. The instructions encourage you to click on the statement that best describes your feelings. Press the "submit" button, and your attitude results will appear below.

Activity 2

All too often, the media tell people that being even slightly overweight is undesirable. This may lead people to become dissatisfied and concerned about their ability to resemble an ideal body image that is unrealistic. You can take a quiz to find out how close you are to your ideal weight and learn ways to make peace with your body. Type in the URL http://cgi.pathfinder.com/cgi-bin/thrive/cg/gdm12x/game/thrive/hungup and choose an answer you prefer for each of the 16 questions listed. Then submit your answers to find out your results.

Activity 3

A variety of techniques can be used to determine whether a person is overweight or obese. One reliable indicator for assessing weight is the body mass index (BMI). The BMI is based on the relationship of body weight (expressed in kilograms) to height (expressed in meters) for both men and women. Go to the web document at http://www.mayohealth.org/mayo/9707/htm/weight.htm to calculate your BMI. Fill in the boxes for your height and weight and then select "calculate." How does your BMI compare with the suggested ranges?

These foods are characterized by high fat density resulting from high levels of vegetable fats (polyunsaturated fats). Particularly good foods in this regard are dried fruits, bananas, nuts, granola, and cheeses made from low-fat milk. It is important, however, to consume these foods later in a meal so that the onset of satiety that quickly follows eating fat-rich foods does not occur.

A second component of weight gain for those who are underweight is the curtailment of excessive physical activity. By carefully reducing their activity level, they can prevent the "burning up" of calories and thus use them for development of body fat. Of course, activity should not be restricted to the point that cardiovascular conditioning declines or enjoyable activities are no longer available.

For those who cannot gain weight in spite of having tried the above approaches, a medical evaluation could supply an explanation for being underweight. If no medical explanation can be found, the person must begin to accept the reality of his or her unique body type. The article on pp. 151-152 explores further the problems of being underweight.

Summary

- Overweight and obesity are the most common forms of malnutrition in the United States.
- Obesity results from an abnormal accumulation of fat.
- Little question exists regarding the health implications of moderate to severe obesity, but the seriousness of mildly obese or overweight is questioned by some.
- Body image and self-concept can be adversely influenced by obesity.
- Obesity and overweight can be defined in a variety of ways and determined using any of several methods.
- Maintaining a healthy body weight is desirable because central body cavity obesity relates to a variety of serious health problems.
- Theories regarding the cause of obesity focus on factors from within the individual and from the environment.
- Many complex theories exist regarding the role of inheritance, set point, body type, feeding patterns, pregnancy, aging, inactivity, and family eating patterns.
- Caloric balance influences weight gain, loss, and maintenance.
- The body's energy needs arise from three areas: activity, BMR, and the thermic effect of food.

- Weight loss can be attempted through dieting, which is the restriction of food intake.
- Drugs, behavior modification, and other techniques, including surgery, can be used to achieve weight loss.
- A combination approach involving low-fat, low–saturated fat, high–complex carbohydrate food, portion-controlled dieting, and exercise may be the most effective way to lose weight.
- Although many people can lose some weight through dieting, very few who do are able to maintain that weight loss.
- The use of certain prescription medications in various combinations caused serious heart valve damage and other dangerous side effects, leading to the drugs' removal from the market.
- The weight loss industry is facing declining participation as people become more aware of information regarding limited success rates.
- Serious eating disorders usually begin with dieting but are often sustained in an attempt to meet deeper needs.
- Underweight is a condition of concern to many that may be resolved through the use of calorie-dense foods and restricted caloric expenditure.

Review Questions

1. Why are obesity and overweight considered to be forms of malnutrition and potentially serious health problems?
2. How are obesity and overweight defined? Why is it possible to be overweight without being overfat? What is the set point?
3. In what ways can obesity be determined? What is desirable weight? What is body mass index? What is waist-to-hip ratio? Why is central body cavity obesity of concern to physicians?
4. Describe the role that each of the following could play in causing obesity: heredity, set point, body type, infant feeding patterns, pregnancy, aging, inactivity, and family eating patterns.

5. What is caloric balance? What are the body's three areas of energy needs? How does aging influence caloric balance? What role exists for exercise in both weight loss and long-term weight maintenance?

6. What is the role of surgery, fasting, and fad diets? What advances are being made in the development of drugs that are effective in weight management?

7. How effective is dieting in terms of both immediate success and later weight maintenance? Why has participation in some commercial weight loss programs fallen in recent years?

8. What two techniques are used in a combination approach to weight loss? How should this program be structured to ensure the highest level of success? What is now known about the use of certain medications prescribed in combination to treat obesity?

9. What are the two principal eating disorders within the college community? In what ways do they differ? What is *binge-eating disorder*? What are compulsive exercise and compulsive eating? How are eating disorders treated?

 ## Think About This . . .

- What methods have you used to determine whether you are underweight, overweight, or obese?
- What are your attitudes toward people with weight control problems? Why do you feel this way?
- Do you believe that being underweight is as psychologically traumatic as being overweight?
- If you have ever attempted to lose weight, what methods have you used? Were any of these methods potentially dangerous?

- Regardless of your weight, which of your personality traits do others find positive? How can you present these attributes to others?
- If you have a weight problem, do you agree or disagree that you have a responsibility to yourself and to other people to reduce your weight?
- What do you see as your responsibility in dealing with a friend or family member who is displaying signs of an eating disorder?

References

1. Morgan K, Morgan S, Quitno N, editors: *Health care state ranking 1998: health care in the 50 United States,* Lawrence, KA, Morgan Quitno Press, 1998.

2. Manson J, et al: Body weight and mortality among women, *N Engl J Med,* 333(11):677-685, 1995.

3. Crowley LV: *Introduction to human disease,* ed 4, Boston, 1996, Jones & Bartlett.

4. Physician advocates treating obesity as chronic disease. Knight-Ridder Newspapers. January 19, 1997.

5. Cash T, Henry P: Women's body images: the results of a national survey in the U.S.A., *Sex Roles: A Journal of Research,* 33(1-2):19-29, 1995.

6. United States Department of Agriculture/United States Department of Health and Human Services: *Nutrition and your health: dietary guidelines for Americans,* 1995, Home and Garden Bulletin 232.

7. Wardlaw GB: *Contemporary nutrition: issues and insights,* New York, 1997, WCB/McGraw-Hill.

8. Prentice WE: *Fitness for college and life,* ed 5, New York, 1997, WCB/McGraw-Hill.

9. Montague CT et al: Congenital leptin deficiency is associated with severe early-onset obesity in humans, *Nature,* 387(6636):903-908, 1997.

10. Clement K et al: Genetic variation in the B3-androgenic receptors and an increased capacity to gain weight in patients with morbid obesity, *N Engl J Med,* 333(6):353-354, 1995.

11. Halass J et al: Weight-inducing effects on the plasma protein encoded by the obese gene, *Science,* 269(5223):543-546, 1995.

12. Considine R et al: Serum immunoreactive-leptin concentration in normal-weight and obese humans, *N Engl J Med,* 333(6):348-351, 1995.

13. Widen E et al: Association of a polymorphism in the B3-andrenergic receptor gene with features of the insulin resistance syndrome in Finns, *N Engl J Med,* 333(6):348-351, 1995.

14. Moffett D, Moffett S, Schauf C: *Human physiology: foundations and frontiers,* ed 2, St. Louis, 1993, Mosby.

15. National Task Force on the Prevention and Treatment of Obesity: weight cycling, *JAMA,* 272(15):1196-1202, 1994.

16. Ganong WF: *Review of medical physiology,* ed 18, Norwalk, CT, 1997, Appleton & Lange.

17. Fleury C, Neverova M, Collins S: Uncoupling protein 2 gene, *Nat Genet,* 15:269-272, 1997.

18. Schauberger CW, Rooney BL, Brimer LM: Factors that influence weight loss in the puerperium, *Obstet Gynecol,* 79(3):424-429, 1992.
19. Fieldhouse P: *Food and nutrition: customs and culture,* London, 1986, Cromm Helm.
20. Food and Nutrition Board: *Recommended dietary allowances,* Washington, DC, 1989, National Academy of Sciences, National Research Council.
21. Losing weight: what works and what doesn't work, *Consumer Reports,* 58(6):347-352, 1993.
22. What it takes to take off weight (and keep it off), Tufts University Health & Nutrition Letter, 15(4):4-5, January, 1998.
23. Mowma P: What will customers want in 1996 and beyond, *Restaurants USA,* December, 1995.
24. Connolly HM et al: Valvular heart disease associated with fenfluramine-phentermine, *N Engl J Med,* 337(9):581-588, 1997.
25. Zerbe K: *The body betrayed,* Carlsbad, CA, 1995, Gurse Books.
26. Costin C: *The eating disorder sourcebook: a comprehensive guide to the causes, treatments, and prevention of eating disorders,* Los Angeles, 1996, Lowell House.

Suggested Readings

Daum M and Lemley A: *The can-do eating plan for overweight kids and teens: helping kids control weight, look better, and feel great,* New York, 1997, Avon Books.

Michelle Daum, a respected pediatric nutritionist, joins Amy Lemley to describe how three well-balanced meals, plus attractive treats, can be planned and incorporated into the lives of busy children and parents. If undertaken carefully, this approach to weight loss should be successful and will make mealtimes more pleasant for every member of the family.

Nash JD: *The new maximize your body potential: Lifetime skills for successful weight management,* Menlo Park, CA, 1997, Bull Publishing Company.

Do you have a history of failure in achieving weight loss? If so, the self-tests, checklists, and activities in this book will help you set realistic goals, modify your diet, and design an exercise program. If followed over the long term, the plan can help you lose and manage your weight and reduce your risk of chronic illness.

Price D: *Healing the hungry self: the diet-free solution to lifelong weight management,* New York, 1998, Plume.

Can you control your weight without extensive reliance on marginal diets and risky medications? Deirdra Price provides a variety of aids, including checklists and charts, that will allow you to modify each dimension of your health to establish a lifestyle that promotes weight maintenance and high-level wellness.

Costin C: *The eating disorders sourcebook: A comprehensive guide to the causes, treatments, and prevention of eating disorders,* Los Angeles, 1996, Lowell House.

Using a multidimensional approach that includes nutritional, psychological, and biochemical aspects, the author provides insights and guidance about potentially fatal eating disorders. Leading experts in the field have written each chapter of this highly regarded sourcebook.

Claude-Pierre P: *The secret language of eating disorders,* New York, 1997, Random House.

Both patients and professionals consider this book to be a radical departure from the traditional perception of how eating disorders arise and how they should be treated. Rather than treating the symptoms, this author advocates resolving the situations that generate the negative thoughts that drive the patient toward developing an eating disorder.

 # AS WE GO TO PRESS . . .

Concern is mounting about the techniques used by collegiate and interscholastic wrestlers to "make weight." A University of Michigan wrestler died during the fall of 1997, leading to the suspension of the sport at that university and to a call for the restructuring of weight categories at all levels of competition. In addition, researchers are studying the specific techniques wrestlers use to rapidly lose large amounts of scale weight. The findings of these studies may help both scientists and athletes to understand the dangers of this risky practice. In 1998 the use of rubber suits was prohibited.

ON...

Gaining Weight Healthfully

"I can't believe how thin you are! It must be so great to eat whatever you want. I wish I had your problem. Of course, it wouldn't hurt you to put on a few pounds. You sure would look healthier!"

"Hey, stick! Do you have anorexia or what? Don't you ever eat?"

These excerpts from real-life exchanges are just two examples of how cruel people can be to the underweight. Some observers think that naturally thin people must have an eating disorder because of their appearance; others are envious because they wish they could indulge in high-fat foods without a second thought. Even in a society where thin is in, being too thin can be just as emotionally and physically devastating as being too heavy. Our society has little understanding or sympathy for people who can eat all they want and never gain a pound.

Causes of Being Underweight

A person is considered to be underweight when he or she is 10% to 15% or more under the ideal weight as indicated on a standard height and weight chart.[1,2] Such a condition can be caused by heredity, poor eating habits, or disease.[2,3] Hereditary causes of being underweight center on high metabolism. Being underweight can be caused by a tendency to burn more calories than are taken in.[3] Many researchers believe that people have a natural "set point" for their metabolic rate[4] that determines how quickly and efficiently calories are used in the body. Metabolism also may prevent people from reaching unrealistic goals with regard to weight gain.[4]

Poor eating habits may also play a role in being underweight. The same concept applies to eating as to metabolism; not consuming enough calories can lead to a person burning more calories than are taken in.[3] High-calorie foods may be lacking in the diets of some underweight people. Other underweight people may include high-calorie foods in their diets but simply do not consume enough total calories to gain weight.[3] Weight control disorders resulting from anorexia, bulimia, or other diseases should be treated by a doctor and are not considered here.

Effects of Being Underweight

Being underweight can cause a variety of physical problems. Women who are underweight are at increased risk of amenorrhea, a reproductive system disorder characterized by a complete absence of menstruation.[5] Underweight people tend to have lower bone mass than people of normal weight, which may place underweight people at risk for bone fractures and osteoporosis.[6-8] Being female, over 65, and underweight can increase the risk for hip fractures.[6] Being too thin can also shorten the life expectancy for men and women.[1,7]

The dangers of being underweight are gradually being discovered. Some studies have shown that being underweight may be as dangerous as being overweight. Government weight guidelines now include data showing that being too thin is as dangerous as being too heavy, and people who are obese by government standards are living longer than those who are underweight.[7]

Being underweight can cause psychological problems in addition to physical problems. Anna, a young woman who spent her youth, teenage years, and early twenties as an underweight person, recalls what life was like for her during that time. "It was like a never-ending nightmare. I hated to go to school because the kids made fun of me all the time. They called me names like 'concentration camp victim' and 'twig.' Many nights I would cry myself to sleep because I hated the way I looked so much. I tried everything I could think of to gain weight: eating as much high-calorie food as I could, using commercial weight-gain products, even not exercising in hopes that I'd get fatter. Nothing worked. When I graduated from high school, I was five feet eight inches tall and still weighed 98 lbs. So many people had told me that I was ugly that I believed it must be true. I spent 6 years in therapy trying to get my self-esteem back. Thank God I finally began to gain weight when I graduated from college. I'm actually a little overweight now. If I had to choose between being this way or being the way I was, there's no question in my mind that I'd choose to be like I am now. People say and do things to underweight people that they'd never dream of saying or doing to people who are overweight."[9]

Gaining Weight Safely

If you are underweight, gaining weight safely is not just a matter of continuously gorging on food. Gaining fat pounds will increase a person's actual weight but will not make him or her any healthier. Diet and exercise plans are available for those who wish to gain weight safely. You should first consult a physician to determine the cause of being underweight. If it has been determined that the underweight condition is not due to disease, a combination of diet and exercise can be prescribed to gain lean body mass. Such a weight-gain plan should include a diet that is high in complex carbohydrates and low in fat. About 60% of the caloric intake should consist of complex carbohydrates,[10] which can be obtained from foods such as pastas. Fat intake should be low (about 10% of total caloric intake), since gaining weight in the form of fat is not healthy.[4,10] Protein should make up about 30% of the caloric intake, but protein supplements are not recommended,[4,10] since their use could damage the kidneys.

An underweight person must exercise to gain muscle mass. The exercise program should be a combination of weight training and endurance training.[4,10] About 80% of the exercise program should consist of weight training, with the other 20% consisting of endurance exercises such as aerobics.[10] Fairly heavy weights should be used with fewer repetitions to gain lean body mass,[10] since more repetitions with lighter weights will not increase lean body mass as effectively. Stretching and calisthenics can be incorporated into the weight training as well.[4] Weight training can help underweight people (and women in particular) gain upper body strength that may be lacking.[4] Exercise is also important because it improves cardiovascular fitness and may deter osteoporosis.[4]

The important thing to remember about such changes in diet and lifestyle is that they must be continued on a long-term basis. It may take 6 to 12 months to see results,[4] and if the program is halted, any weight gained may be lost again.[10] A person must maintain a lifetime commitment to gaining the weight and keeping it on. As always, consult your physician before starting any exercise or diet program.

For Discussion . . .
Why might being underweight be just as dangerous as being overweight? Is it easier to chastise underweight people than overweight people? What are the similarities and differences between people who are thin resulting from metabolism and those who are thin resulting from disease (such as anorexia)?

References
1. Weight control, *Grolier wellness encyclopedia, vol 15*, Guilford, Conn, 1992, Dushkin.
2. Nutrition and fitness ("Underweight"), *Macmillan health encyclopedia, vol 4*, New York, 1993, Macmillan.
3. Nutrition and fitness ("weight gain strategy"), *Macmillan health encyclopedia, vol 4*, New York, 1993, Macmillan.
4. Blackburn GL: Gaining weight without "getting fat," *Prevention* 40(10), 1988.
5. Amenhorrea: What your body is trying to tell you, *Cosmopolitan* 25(4), 1993.
6. Cooper C, Barker JP: Risk factors for hip fracture, *N Engl J Med* 332(2), 1995.
7. Good news for heavyweights, *USA Today Magazine*, 122(2585), Feb 1994.
8. Who is at risk? *USA Today Magazine*, 122(2585), Feb 1994.
9. "Anna," Personal interview, 1996.
10. Bishop D, MD, Personal interview, 1996.
11. Schrieber B: Living and learning, *Shape* 14(12), Aug 1995.

PART 3

ADDICTIVE SUBSTANCES

Choosing a Drug-Free Lifestyle

Healthy People: Looking Ahead to 2010

Achieving the *Healthy People 2000* objectives in the area of drug abuse is critically important for the nation. Substance abuse is directly responsible for 120,000 deaths each year in the United States, 100,000 of which are related to alcohol abuse and 20,000 to other drug use. In addition, substance abuse harms the emotional health of individuals, destroys families, and devastates communities.

For the first time in years, some headway was made in 1997 in preventing drug-related deaths and in reducing the number of drug-related hospital emergency room visits.[1] However, there remains a group of hard-core drug users who are difficult to reach with anti-drug abuse messages. In addition, no progress appears to have been made in raising the age of first use of cigarettes, alcohol, or marijuana by children.[2]

The 1997 Monitoring the Future[3] study indicated that for the first time in the decade of the 1990s, marijuana and other drug use among 8th graders was declining. While 10th and 12th graders' marijuana use was still rising, the use of other drugs among these groups was leveling off. Preventing initial and repeat drug abuse and providing adequate treatment for addicts will remain a high priority in the *Healthy People 2010* objectives now being drafted.

The use of psychoactive drugs can be tremendously disruptive in many people's lives, from tragic deaths to the loss of employment opportunities (most Fortune 500 companies use preemployment drug testing) to the deterioration of personal relationships. Perhaps realizing this, college students have generally moved away from using the most dangerous illegal drugs.[4]

Since the early 1980s, college students' illegal drug use has consistently dropped. However, a 1993 major survey of college students' drug use reported that this decline may have bottomed out (Figure 7-1).[5] For the first time in years, there was a slight increase in the percentage of students who reported using an illegal drug within the past year. Slightly less than one third of college students reported using an illegal drug during the past year. The good news, of course, is that more than two thirds of college students *did not* use illegal drugs. Overall, drug use remained steady or actually dropped in all drug categories except hallucinogens and marijuana.

It is safe to say that in the late 1990s, drug use remains a significant problem for both college students and the general population. Alcohol is the most important problem drug for most college students (see Chapter 8), but other drugs pose risks for certain students. Some of these drugs are specified in the Healthy People 2000 objectives. Additionally, many nontraditional students see the destructive effects of drug use on their neighborhoods and worry about their children being exploited by those who deal drugs.

ADDICTIVE BEHAVIOR

This chapter explores the health consequences of drug use, misuse, and abuse. Before talking about specific drugs, however, drug use should be put in the broader context of addictive behavior. Experts in human behavior view drug use and abuse as just one of the many forms of addictive behavior. Addictive behavior includes addictions to shopping, eating, gambling, sex, television, video games, and work, as well as addictions to alcohol or other drugs.

The Process of Addiction

The process of developing an addiction has been a much-studied topic. There seem to be three common aspects of addictive behavior.

Exposure

An addiction can begin after a person is exposed to a drug (such as alcohol) or a behavior (such as gambling) that he or she finds pleasurable. Perhaps this drug or behavior temporarily replaces an unpleasant feeling or sensation. This initial pleasure gradually (or in some cases quickly) becomes a focal point in the person's life.

Compulsion

Increasingly more energy, time, and money are spent pursuing the drug use or behavior. At this point

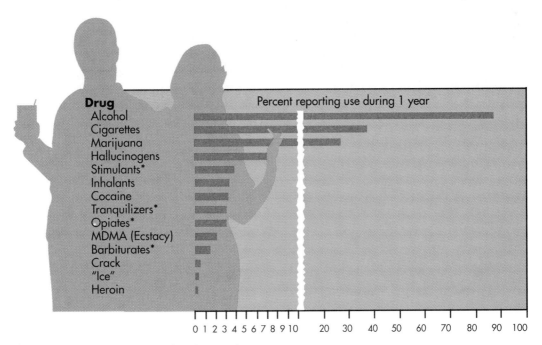

Drug   Percent reporting use during 1 year

Alcohol
Cigarettes
Marijuana
Hallucinogens
Stimulants*
Inhalants
Cocaine
Tranquilizers*
Opiates*
MDMA (Ecstacy)
Barbiturates*
Crack
"Ice"
Heroin

0 1 2 3 4 5 6 7 8 9 10   20   30   40   50   60   70   80   90   100

* Drug use was not under a doctor's orders.

Figure 7-1   Alcohol, cigarettes, marijuana, and hallucinogens are the four most common substances used by college students.

in the addictive process, the person can be said to have a compulsion for the drug or behavior. Frequently, repeated exposure to the drug or behavior continues despite negative consequences, such as the gradual loss of family and friends, unpleasant physical symptoms after taking the drug, and problems at work.

During the compulsion phase of the addictive behavior, a person's "normal" life is likely to degenerate while she or he searches for increased pleasures from the drug or the behavior. An addicted person's family life, circle of friends, work, or study patterns become less important than the search for more and better "highs." The development of tolerance and withdrawal are distinct possibilities. (These terms are discussed later in the chapter.)

Why some people develop compulsions and others do not is difficult to pinpoint, but addiction might be influenced by genetic makeup, family dynamics, physiological processes, personality type, peer groups, and available resources for help.

Loss of control

Over time, the search for highs changes to a search to avoid the effects of withdrawal from the drug or behavior. Addicted people lose their ability to control their behavior. Despite overwhelming negative consequences (for example, deterioration of health, alienation of family and friends, or loss of all financial resources), addicted people continue to behave in ways that make their lives worse. The person addicted to alcohol continues to drink heavily, the person addicted to shopping continues to run up heavy debts, and the person addicted to food continues to eat indiscriminately. This behavior reflects a loss of control over one's life. Frequently, a person has addictions to more than one drug or behavior.

Intervention and Treatment

The good news for people with addictions is that help is available. Within the last two decades, much attention has been focused on intervention and treatment for addictive behavior. Many people can be helped through programs such as those described at the end of this chapter (see p. 170). These programs often include inpatient or outpatient treatment, family counseling, and long-term aftercare counseling.

It is common for people in aftercare treatment for addictive behavior to belong to a self-help support group, such as Alcoholics Anonymous, Gamblers Anonymous, or Sex Addicts Anonymous. These groups are often listed in the phone book or in the classified section of the newspaper.

DRUG TERMINOLOGY

Before discussing drug actions or drug behavior, you must first be familiar with some basic terminology. Much of this terminology originates from the field of *pharmacology,* or the study of the interaction of chemical agents with living material.

What does the word *drug* mean? Each of us may have different ideas about what a drug is. Although a number of definitions are available, we will consider a drug to be "any substance, other than food, that by its chemical or physical nature alters structure or function in the living organism."[6] Included in this broad definition is a variety of psychoactive drugs, medicines, and substances that many people do not usually consider to be drugs.

Psychoactive drugs alter the user's feelings, behavior, perceptions, or moods. Psychoactive drugs include stimulants, depressants, hallucinogens, opiates, and inhalants. *Medicines* function to heal unhealthy tissue. Medicines are also used to ease pain, prevent illness, and diagnose health conditions. Although some psychoactive drugs are used for medical reasons, as in the case of tranquilizers and some narcotics, the most commonly prescribed medicines are antibiotics, sulfa drugs, diuretics, oral contraceptives, and antihypertensive drugs. Legal substances not usually considered to be drugs (but which certainly are drugs) include caffeine, tobacco, alcohol, aspirin, and other over-the-counter (OTC) preparations. These common substances are used so frequently in our society that they are rarely perceived as true drugs.

For organizational reasons, this chapter primarily deals with psychoactive drugs. Alcohol is covered in Chapter 8. The effects of tobacco are delineated in Chapter 9. Prescription and OTC drugs and medicines are discussed at length in Chapter 15. Environmental pollutants are covered in Chapter 17. Anabolic steroids, drugs used primarily for increasing muscle growth, are discussed in Chapter 4.

Dependence

Psychoactive drugs have a strong potential for the development of **dependence.** When users take a psychoactive drug, the patterns of nervous system function are altered. If these altered functions provide perceived benefits for the user, drug use may continue, perhaps at increasingly larger dosages. If persistent use continues, the user can develop a dependence on the drug. Pharmacologists have identified two types of dependences—physical and psychological.

A person can be said to have developed a *physical dependence* when the body cells have become reliant on a drug. Continued use of the drug is then required because body tissues have adapted to its presence.[7] The person's body needs the drug to maintain homeostasis, or dynamic balance. If the drug is not taken or is suddenly withdrawn, the user develops a characteristic **withdrawal illness.** The symptoms of withdrawal reflect the attempt by the body's cells to regain normality without the drug. Withdrawal symptoms are always unpleasant (ranging from mild to severe irritability, depression, nervousness, digestive difficulties, and abdominal pain) and can be life threatening, as in the case of abrupt withdrawal from barbiturates or alcohol. In this chapter the term *addiction* is used interchangeably with physical dependence.

Continued use of most drugs can lead to **tolerance.** Tolerance is an acquired reaction to a drug in which continued intake of the same dose has diminishing effects.[7] The user needs larger doses of the drug to receive previously felt sensations. The continued use of depressants, including alcohol, and opiates can cause users to quickly develop a tolerance to the drug.

For example, college seniors who have engaged in 4 years of beer drinking usually recognize that their bodies have developed a degree of tolerance. Many such students can vividly recall the initial and subsequent sensations they felt after drinking. For example, five beers consumed during a freshman social gathering might well have resulted in inebriation, but if these same students continued to drink beer regularly for 4 years, five beers would probably fail to produce the response they experienced as freshmen. Perhaps seven or eight beers would be needed to produce such a response. Clearly, they have developed a tolerance to alcohol.

Furthermore, tolerance developed for one drug may carry over to another drug within the same general category. This phenomenon is known as **cross-tolerance.** The heavy abuser of alcohol, for example, might require a larger dose of a preoperative sedative to become relaxed before surgery than the average person. The tolerance to alcohol "crosses over" to the other depressant drug.

A person who possesses a strong desire to continue using a particular drug is said to have developed *psychological dependence* (see the Star Box on p. 158, top). People who are psychologically dependent on a drug believe that they need to consume the drug to maintain a sense of well-being. They crave the drug for emotional reasons in spite of having persistent or recurrent physical, social, psychological, or occupational problems that are caused or worsened by the drug use. Abrupt withdrawal from a drug by such a person

would not trigger the fully expressed withdrawal illness, although some unpleasant symptoms of withdrawal might be felt. The term *habituation* is often used interchangeably with psychological dependence.

Drugs whose continued use can quickly lead to both physical and psychological dependence are the depressants (barbiturates, tranquilizers, and alcohol), narcotics (the opiates, which are derivatives of the Oriental poppy: heroin, morphine, and codeine), and synthetic narcotics (Demerol and methadone). Drugs whose continued use can lead to various degrees of psychological dependence and occasionally to significant (but not life-threatening) physical dependence in some users are the stimulants (amphetamines, caffeine, and cocaine), hallucinogens (LSD, peyote, mescaline, and marijuana), and inhalants (glues, gases, and petroleum products).

Drug Misuse and Abuse

So far in this chapter we have used the term *use* (or *user*) in association with the taking of psychoactive drugs. At this point, however, it is important to define *use* and to introduce the terms *misuse* and *abuse*.[6] By doing so, we can more accurately describe the ways in which drugs are used.

The term *use* is all-encompassing and describes drug-taking in the most general way. For example,

psychoactive drug
Any substance capable of altering feelings, moods, or perceptions.

dependence
General term that refers to the need to continue using a drug for psychological and/or physical reasons.

withdrawal illness
Uncomfortable, perhaps toxic response of the body as it attempts to maintain homeostasis in the absence of a drug; also called *abstinence syndrome*.

tolerance
An acquired reaction to a drug; continued intake of the same dose has diminished results.

cross-tolerance
Transfer of tolerance from one drug to another within the same general category.

Why People Use Drugs
- To medicate themselves
- To get high (a buzz)
- To be cool
- To ease pain
- To experiment
- Peer pressure
- Family problems
- To calm nerves
- To get down
- To escape
- To commit suicide
- Because it feels good
- Because they are addicted
- To work better
- To be alert
- Because they are bored
- To hurt themselves
- To hurt someone else
- To get in a good mood
- For a dare
- Fear of stopping

Americans use drugs of many types. The term *use* can also refer more narrowly to misuse and abuse. We most often use the word in this latter regard.

The term **misuse** refers to the inappropriate use of legal drugs intended to be medications. Misuse may occur when a patient misunderstands the directions for use of a prescription or OTC drug or when a patient shares a prescription with a friend or family member for whom the drug was not prescribed. Misuse also occurs when a patient takes the prescription or OTC drug for a purpose or condition other than that for which it was intended or at a dosage other than that recommended.

The term **abuse** applies to any use of an illegal drug or any use of a legal drug when it is detrimental to health and well-being. The costs of drug abuse to the individual are extensive and include absenteeism and underachievement, loss of job, marital instability, loss of self-esteem, serious illnesses, and even death. Complete the Personal Assessment below to determine whether you or someone you know may be abusing drugs.

PERSONAL ASSESSMENT

Recognizing Drug Abuse

To assess whether you or someone you know may be abusing drugs circle **Y** for yes and **N** for no.

1. A sudden increase in or loss of appetite   Y   N
    or sudden weight loss or gain
2. Moodiness, depression, irritability, or   Y   N
    withdrawal
3. Disorientation, lack of concentration, or   Y   N
    forgetfulness
4. Frequent use of eye drops or inappropri-   Y   N
    ate wearing of sunglasses
5. Disruption or change in sleep patterns or   Y   N
    a lack of energy
6. Borrowing money more and more, work-   Y   N
    ing excessive hours, selling personal
    items, or stealing or shoplifting
7. Persistent and frequent nosebleeds, snif-   Y   N
    fles, coughs, and other signs of upper
    respiratory infection

8. Change in speech patterns or vocabu-   Y   N
    lary or a deterioration in academic per-
    formance
9. Feeling ill at ease with family members   Y   N
    and other adults
10. Neglect of personal appearance   Y   N

Interpretation:
A yes response to more than three questions indicates that there may be drug dependence, and professional help should be obtained.

To Carry This Further . . .
See the Star Box on p. 171 and the Health Reference Guide at the back of this text for information about national groups and hot lines for drug use. They will help you find additional information about drug dependence and how to combat it.

EFFECTS OF DRUGS ON THE CENTRAL NERVOUS SYSTEM

To better understand the disruption caused by the actions of psychoactive drugs, a general knowledge of the normal functioning of the nervous system's basic unit, the **neuron,** is required.

First, stimuli from the internal or external environment are received by the appropriate sensory receptor, perhaps an organ such as an eye or an ear. Once sensed, these stimuli are converted into electrical impulses. These impulses are then directed along the neuron's **dendrite,** through the cell body, and along the **axon** toward the *synaptic junction* near an adjacent neuron. On arrival at the **synapse,** the electrical impulses stimulate the production and release of chemical messengers called *neurotransmitters.*[8] These neurotransmitters transmit the electrical impulses from one neuron to the dendrites of adjoining neurons. Thus neurons function in a coordinated fashion to send information to the brain for interpretation and to relay appropriate response commands outward to the tissues of the body.

The role of neurotransmitters is critically important to the relay of information within the system. A substance that has the ability to alter some aspect of transmitter function has the potential to seriously disrupt the otherwise normally functioning system. Psychoactive drugs are capable of exerting these disruptive influences on the neurotransmitters. Drugs "work" by changing the way neurotransmitters work, often by blocking the production of a neurotransmitter or forcing the continued release of a neurotransmitter (see the Star Box on p. 160).

DRUG CLASSIFICATIONS

Drugs can be categorized according to the nature of their physiological effects. Most psychoactive drugs fall into one of six general categories: stimulants, depressants, hallucinogens, cannabis, narcotics, and inhalants (Table 7-1).

Stimulants

In general, **stimulants** excite or increase the activity of the CNS. Also called "uppers," stimulants alert the CNS by increasing heart rate, blood pressure, and the rate of brain function. Users feel uplifted and less fatigued. Examples of stimulant drugs include caffeine, amphetamines, and cocaine. Most stimulants produce psychological dependence and tolerance relatively quickly, but they are unlikely to produce significant physical dependence when judged by life-threatening withdrawal symptoms. The important exception is cocaine, which seems to be capable of producing psychological dependence and withdrawal so powerful that continued use of the drug is inevitable in some users.

Caffeine

Caffeine, the tasteless drug found in chocolate, some soft drinks, coffee, tea, some aspirin products, and OTC "stay-awake" pills, is a relatively harmless stimulant when consumed in moderate amounts (Table 7-2). Many coffee drinkers believe that they cannot start the day successfully without the benefit of a cup or two of coffee in the morning.

Pregnant women are advised to consume caffeine sparingly.[9] For the average healthy adult, moderate consumption of caffeine is unlikely to pose any serious health threat. However, excessive consumption (equivalent to 10 or more cups of coffee daily) could lead to anxiety, diarrhea, restlessness, delayed onset of sleep or frequent awakening, headache, and heart palpitations.

Amphetamines

Amphetamines produce increased activity and mood elevation in almost all users. The amphetamines include several closely related compounds:

---

misuse
Inappropriate use of legal drugs intended to be medications.

abuse
Any use of a legal or illegal drug in a way that is detrimental to health.

neuron (noor on)
A nerve cell.

dendrite (den drite)
The portion of a neuron that receives electrical stimuli from adjacent neurons; neurons typically have several such branches or extensions.

axon
The portion of a neuron that conducts electrical impulses to the dendrites of adjacent neurons; neurons typically have one axon.

synapse (sinn aps)
The location at which an electrical impulse from one neuron is transmitted to an adjacent neuron; also referred to as a *synaptic junction.*

stimulants
Psychoactive drugs that stimulate the function of the central nervous system.

Effect of Drugs on the Central Nervous System

This illustration depicts the disruption caused by the action of psychoactive drugs on the central nervous system. Neurotransmitters are chemical messengers that transfer electrical impulses across the synapses between nerve cells.[6] Psychoactive drugs interrupt this process, thus disrupting the coordinated functioning of the nervous system.

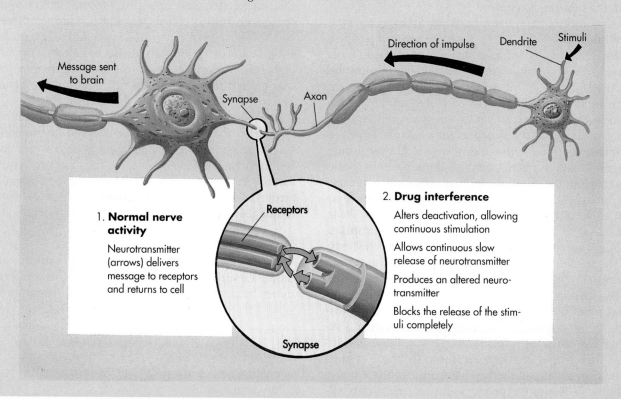

Table 7-1   Psychoactive Drug Categories

Drugs	Trade or Common Names	Medical Uses	Possible Effects
Stimulants			
Cocaine*	Coke, crack, gin, girlfriend, girl, double bubble, California cornflakes, caballo, bouncing powder, flake, snow	Local anesthetic	Increased alertness, excitation, euphoria, increased pulse rate and blood pressure, insomnia, loss of appetite
Amphetamines	Biphetamine, Delcobese, Desoxyn, Dexedrine, mediatic, methamphetamine (ice), black Mollies, aimies, amps, bam, beans, benz	Hyperactivity, narcolepsy, weight control	
Phendimetrazine	Prelu-2		
Methylphenidate	Ritalin, Methidate		
Other stimulants	Adipex, Bacarate, Cylert, Didrex, Ionamin, Plegine, PreSate, Sanorex, Tenuate, Tepanil, Voranil		
Depressants			
Chloral hydrate	Noctec, Somnos	Hypnotic	Slurred speech, disorientation, drunken behavior without odor of alcohol
Barbiturates	Amobarbital, Butisol, phenobarbital, phenoxbarbital, secobarbital, Tuinal, blockbusters, black bombers, blue devils, blue dogs, blue tips, tombica	Anesthetic, anticonvulsant, sedative, hypnotic	
Glutethimide	Doriden	Sedative, hypnotic	

Table 7-1, cont'd

Drugs	Trade or Common Names	Medical Uses	Possible Effects
Methaqualone	Optimil, Parest, Quaalude, Somnafec, Sopor	Sedative, hypnotic	
Benzodiazepines	Ativan, Azene, Clonopin, Dalmane, diazepam, Librium, Serax, Tranxene, Valium, Verstran	Antianxiety, anticonvulsant, sedative, hypnotic	
Other depressants	Equanil, Miltown, Noludar, Placidyl, Valmid	Antianxiety, sedative, hypnotic	
Hallucinogens			
LSD	Acid, microdot, brown dot, cap, California sunshine, brown bomber	None	Delusions and hallucinations, poor perception of time and distance
Mescaline and peyote	Mesc, buttons, cactus, chief	None	
Amphetamine variants (designer drugs)	2,5-DMA, DOM, DOP, MDA, MDMA, PMA, STP, TMA, clarity, chocolate, chips, booty juice	None	
Phencyclidine	Angel dust, hog, PCP, AD, boat, black whack, amoeba, angel hair, angel smoke	Veterinary anesthetic	
Phencyclidine analogs	PCE, PCPy, TCP	None	Euphoria, relaxed inhibitions, increased appetite, disorientation
Other hallucinogens	Bufotenin, DMT, DET, ibogaine, psilocybin, psilocyn	None	
Cannabis			
Marijuana	Acapulco gold, black Bart, black mote, blue sage, bobo, butterflowers, cannabis-T, cess, cheeba, grass, pot, sinsemilla, Thai sticks	Under investigation	Euphoria, relaxed inhibitions, increased appetite, disoriented behavior
Tetrahydrocannabinol	THC	Under investigation	
Hashish	Hash	None	
Hashish oil	Hash oil	None	
Narcotics			
Opium	Dover's powder, paregoric, Parapectolin, cruz, Chinese tobacco, China	Analgesic, antidiarrheal	Euphoria, drowsiness, respiratory depression, constricted pupils, nausea
Morphine	Morphine, Pectoal syrup, emsel, first line	Analgesic, antitussive	
Codeine	Codeine, Empirin compound with codeine, Robitussin A-C	Analgesic, antitussive	
Heroin	Diacetylmorphine, horse, smack, courage pills, dead on arrival (DOA)	Under investigation	
Hydromorphone	Dilaudid	Analgesic	Intoxication, excitation, disorientation, aggression, hallucination
Meperidine (pethidine)	Demerol, Pethadol	Analgesic	
Methadone	Dolophine, Methadone, Methadose	Analgesic, heroin substitute	
Other narcotics	Darvon,† Dromoran, Fentanyl, LAAM, Leitine, Levo-Dromoran, Percodan, Tussionex, Talwin,† Lomotil	Analgesic, antidiarrheal, antitussive	
Inhalants			
Anesthetic gases	Aerosols, petroleum products, solvents	Surgical anesthesia	Intoxication, excitation, disorientation, aggression, hallucination, variable effects
Vasodilators (amyl nitrite, butyl nitrite)	Aerosols, petroleum products, solvents	None	

*Designated a narcotic under the Controlled Substances Act.
†Not designated a narcotic under the Controlled Substances Act.

Table 7-2 Caffeine Content of Beverages, Food, and Drug Preparations

Coffee (5 oz cup)	Caffeine (mg)	Soft Drinks (12 oz)	Caffeine (mg)	Pain Relievers	Caffeine (mg)
Drip method	110-150	Mountain Dew	54	Anacin	32
Percolated	64-124	Mello Yello	52	Excedrin	65
Instant	40-108	TAB	46	Midol	32
Decaffeinated	2-5	Coca-Cola	46	Plain aspirin	0
		Diet Coke	46	Vanquish	33
Tea (5 oz cup)		Shasta Cola	44		
		Mr. Pibb	40	**Diuretics**	
1-min brew	9-33	Dr. Pepper	40		
3-min brew	20-46	Diet Dr. Pepper	40	Aqua Ban	100
5-min brew	20-50	Pepsi Cola	38		
Instant tea	12-28	Diet Pepsi	36	**Cold Remedies**	
Iced tea (12 oz)	22-36				
				Coryban-D	30
Cocoa		**Stimulants**		Dristan	0
				Triaminicin	30
Made from mix	6	NoDoz tablets	100		
Milk chocolate (1 oz)	6	Vivarin tablets	200	**Weight-Control Aids**	
Baking chocolate	35				
				Dexatrim	200
				Prolamine	140
				Prescription Pain Relievers	
				Cafergot	100
				Darvon compound	32
				Fiorinal	40
				Migralam	100

amphetamine, dextroamphetamine, and methamphetamine. These compounds do not have any natural sources and are completely manufactured in the laboratory. Medical use of amphetamines is limited primarily to the treatment of obesity, **narcolepsy,** and **attention deficit disorder (ADD).**

Amphetamines can be ingested, injected, or snorted (inhaled). At low-to-moderate doses, amphetamines elevate mood and increase alertness and feelings of energy by stimulating receptor sites for two naturally occurring neurotransmitters. They also slow the activity of the stomach and intestine and decrease hunger. In the 1960s and 1970s, in fact, amphetamines were commonly prescribed for dieters, but when it was discovered that the appetite suppression effect of amphetamines lasted only a few weeks, most physicians stopped prescribing them. At high doses, amphetamines can increase heart rate and blood pressure to dangerous levels. As amphetamines are eliminated from the body, the user becomes tired.

When chronically abused, amphetamines produce rapid tolerance and strong psychological dependence.

Other effects of chronic use include impotence and episodes of psychosis. When use is discontinued, periods of depression may develop.

Today the abuse of amphetamines is a more pressing concern than it has been in the recent past. Underlying this sharp increase in abuse is methamphetamine. Known by a variety of names and forms, including "crank," "ice," "crystal," "meth," "speed," "crystal meth," and "zip," methamphetamine is produced in illegal home laboratories.

Ice

Crystal meth or ice is among the most recent and dangerous forms of methamphetamine. Ice is a very pure form of methamphetamine that looks like rock candy. When smoked, the effects of ice are felt in about 7 seconds as a wave of intense physical and psychological exhilaration. This effect lasts for several hours (much longer than the effects of *crack*) until the user becomes physically exhausted. Chronic use leads to nutritional difficulties, weight loss, reduced resistance to infection, and damage to the liver, lungs, and kidneys. Psychological dependence is quickly estab-

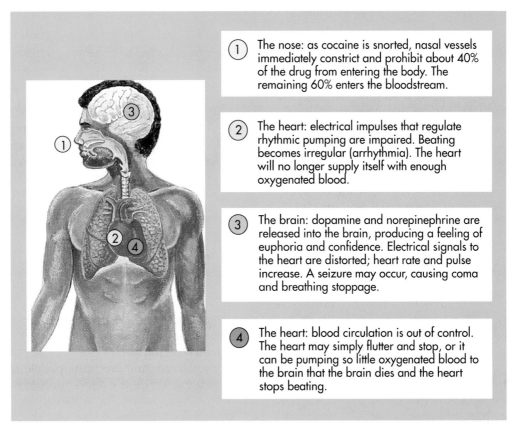

(1) The nose: as cocaine is snorted, nasal vessels immediately constrict and prohibit about 40% of the drug from entering the body. The remaining 60% enters the bloodstream.

(2) The heart: electrical impulses that regulate rhythmic pumping are impaired. Beating becomes irregular (arrhythmia). The heart will no longer supply itself with enough oxygenated blood.

(3) The brain: dopamine and norepinephrine are released into the brain, producing a feeling of euphoria and confidence. Electrical signals to the heart are distorted; heart rate and pulse increase. A seizure may occur, causing coma and breathing stoppage.

(4) The heart: blood circulation is out of control. The heart may simply flutter and stop, or it can be pumping so little oxygenated blood to the brain that the brain dies and the heart stops beating.

Figure 7-2   Cocaine's effects on the body.

HealthQuest Activities

- Drug abuse can occur with illegal drugs or with over-the-counter or prescription drugs. Complete the assessment activity *Drugs: Are You at Risk?* in Module 9 to raise your awareness of the many decisions you make about drugs. What is your overall risk score? Do you think the score is accurate? Do you think your score reflects campuswide drug use? What are the causes of drug abuse and what can be done to prevent it?

lished. Withdrawal causes acute depression and fatigue but not significant physical discomfort.

Cocaine

Cocaine, perhaps the strongest of the stimulant drugs, has received much media attention. Cocaine is the primary psychoactive substance found in the leaves of the South American coca plant. The effects of cocaine are brief—from 5 to 30 minutes (Figure 7-2). Regardless of the form in which it is consumed, cocaine produces an immediate, near-orgasmic "rush," or feeling of exhilaration. This euphoria is quickly followed by a period of marked depression. Used only occasionally as a topical anesthetic, cocaine is usually inhaled (snorted), injected, or smoked (as *freebase* or crack). There is overwhelming scientific evidence that users quickly develop a strong psychologi-

narcolepsy (**nar** co lep see)
A sleep-related disorder in which a person has a recurrent, overwhelming, and uncontrollable desire to sleep.

attention deficit disorder (ADD)
Above-normal rate of physical movement; often accompanied by an inability to concentrate well on a specified task; also called *hyperactivity*.

cal dependence to cocaine. There is considerable evidence that physical dependence also rapidly develops. However, physical dependence on cocaine does not lead to death on withdrawal.

The status of cocaine as a substitute for amphetamines (during the 1960s), as a recreational drug for the wealthy (during the 1970s), and as a widely abused drug by many segments of society (during the 1980s) is well documented. During the 1990s, overall cocaine use has decreased, although heavy use has increased. Today, freebasing and the use of crack have replaced the inhalation of "lines" of cocaine, which was the primary route of administration in the 1980s.

Freebasing

Freebasing and the use of crack cocaine are the most recent techniques for maximizing the psychoactive effects of the drug. Freebasing first requires that the common form of powdered cocaine (cocaine hydrochloride) be chemically altered (alkalized). This altered form is then dissolved in a solvent, such as ether or benzene. This liquid solution is heated to evaporate the solvent. The heating process leaves the freebase cocaine in a powder form that can then be smoked, often through a water pipe. Because of the large surface area of the lungs, smoking cocaine facilitates fast absorption into the bloodstream.

One danger of freebasing cocaine is the risk related to the solvents used. Ether is a highly volatile solvent capable of exploding and causing serious burns. Benzene is a known carcinogen associated with the development of leukemia. Clearly, neither solvent can be used without increasing the level of risk normally associated with cocaine use. This method of making smokeable cocaine led to a new epidemic of cocaine use, smoking crack.

Crack

In contrast to freebase cocaine, crack is made by combining cocaine hydrochloride with common baking soda. When this pastelike mixture is allowed to dry, a small rocklike crystalline material remains. This crack is heated in the bowl of a small pipe, and the vapors are inhaled into the lungs. A single dose of crack currently sells for $20 to $30. Some crack users spend hundreds of dollars a day to maintain their habit.

The effect of crack is almost instantaneous. Within 10 seconds after inhalation, cocaine reaches the CNS and influences the action of several neurotransmitters at specific sites in the brain. As with the use of other forms of cocaine, convulsions, seizures, respiratory distress, and cardiac failure have been reported with this sudden, extensive stimulation of the nervous system.

Within about 6 minutes, the stimulating effect of crack has been completely expended, and users frequently become depressed. Dependence develops within a few weeks, since users consume more crack in response to the short duration of stimulation and rapid onset of depression.

Intravenous administration has been the preferred route for cocaine users who are also regular users of heroin and other injectable drugs. Intravenous injection results in an almost immediate high, which lasts about 10 minutes. A "smoother ride" is said to be obtained from a "speedball," the injectable mixture of heroin and cocaine (or methamphetamine).[7]

Cocaine and society

It is beyond the scope of this book to chronicle the way in which cocaine use has profoundly damaged our nation. However, we encourage students to watch or read the daily media reports about this topic. A few of the central reasons why civic and government leaders have declared war on the use of illicit drugs, especially cocaine, follow.

Although cocaine use hurts people from all walks of life, it most critically affects people from inner-city minority groups and the urban poor.[10] Cocaine use provides an instant temporary escape from an unpromising future. For many inner-city youths, selling cocaine or crack is the easiest way to escape poverty. However, drug dealing also brings with it an escalation of involvement in street gangs, crime, and violence.[11] Crack houses are also notorious for promoting the spread of HIV infection and other serious diseases. Tragically, a high percentage of babies born in large city hospitals are addicted to cocaine and have both physical and neurological difficulties. Some are born with an HIV infection that soon leads to AIDS. Indeed, the personal and social cost of cocaine use is enormous.

Depressants

Depressants (or sedatives) sedate the user, slowing down CNS function. Drugs included in this category are alcohol (see Chapter 8), barbiturates, and tranquilizers. Depressants produce tolerance in abusers, as well as strong psychological and physical dependence.

Barbiturates

Barbiturates are the so-called sleeping compounds that function by enhancing the effect of inhibitory neurotransmitters. They depress the CNS to the point where the user drops off to sleep or, as is the case with surgical anesthetics, the patient becomes anesthetized. Medically, barbiturates are used in widely varied dosages as anesthetics and for treatment of anxiety, insomnia, and epilepsy.[6] Regular use of a barbiturate quickly produces tolerance—eventually such a high dose is required that the user still feels the effects of the drug throughout the next morning. Some abusers then begin to alternate barbiturates with stimulants, producing a vicious circle of dependence. Other misusers combine alcohol and barbiturates or tranquilizers, inadvertently producing toxic or even lethal results. Abrupt withdrawal from barbiturate use frequently produces a withdrawal syndrome that can involve seizures, delusions, hallucinations, and even death.

Methaqualone (Quaalude, "ludes," Sopor) was developed as a sedative that would not have the dependence properties of other barbiturates.[6] Although this did not happen, Quaaludes were occasionally prescribed for anxious patients. Today, compounds resembling Quaaludes are manufactured in home laboratories and sold illegally so that they can be combined with small amounts of alcohol for an inexpensive, drunklike effect.

Tranquilizers

Tranquilizers are depressants that are intended to reduce anxiety and to relax people who are having problems managing stress. They are not specifically designed to produce sleep but rather to help people cope during their waking hours. Such tranquilizers are termed *minor tranquilizers,* of which diazepam (Valium) and chlordiazepoxide (Librium) may be the most commonly prescribed examples. Unfortunately, some people become addicted to these and other prescription drugs (see the article on pp. 175-176).

Some tranquilizers are further designed to control hospitalized psychotic patients who may be suicidal or who are potential threats to others. These *major tranquilizers* subdue people physically but permit them to remain conscious. Their use is generally limited to institutional settings. All tranquilizers can produce physical and psychological dependence and tolerance.

Hallucinogens

As the name suggests, hallucinogenic drugs produce hallucinations—perceived distortions of reality. Also known as *psychedelic* drugs or *phantasticants,* **hallucinogens** reached their height of popularity during the 1960s (see the Learning from All Cultures box at right). At that time, young people were encouraged to use hallucinogenic drugs to "expand the mind," "reach an altered state," or "discover reality." Not all of the reality distortions, or "trips," were pleasant. Many users reported "bummers," or trips during which they perceived negative, frightening distortions.

LEARNING from ALL CULTURES

Hallucinogens and Religious Ceremonies

Hallucinogens became very popular in the United States in the 1960s, and they are still used today. Some of these substances have been fairly recently discovered, whereas others have been used for hundreds of years by certain societies. Some forms have been and continue to be used by Native Americans as part of their religious ceremonies.

Mescaline is a hallucinogen derived from the peyote cactus. Native American tribes in Mexico used peyote in religious ceremonies many years ago to enhance the spiritual experience. The practice then spread to Native American tribes in the United States. Today, the Native American Church of North America still uses peyote in religious ceremonies.[17]

Some tribes have had to change their practices of peyote use because of state laws. The legality of using peyote for religious ceremonies is a state decision. A Supreme Court ruling in favor of the state of Oregon, prohibiting the use of peyote, stated that Native American tribes must comply with the state laws concerning the use of peyote in religious rituals. However, 23 other states allow ceremonial peyote use by the Native American Church.[17]

Other religious practices, such as the sacrifice of animals, have been questioned by some state governments. How much authority should the government have in regulating the ceremonial rituals of religious groups?

Hallucinogenic drugs include laboratory-produced lysergic acid diethylamide (LSD), mescaline (from the peyote cactus plant), and psilocybin (from a particular genus of mushroom). Consumption of hallucinogens seems to produce not physical dependence but mild levels of psychological dependence. The development of tolerance is questionable. *Synesthesia,* a sensation in which users report hearing a color, smelling music, or touching a taste, is sometimes produced with hallucinogen use.

The long-term effects of hallucinogenic drug use are not fully understood. Questions about genetic

hallucinogens
Psychoactive drugs capable of producing hallucinations (distortions of reality).

abnormalities in offspring, fertility, sex drive and performance, and the development of personality disorders have not been fully answered. One phenomenon that has been identified and documented is the development of *flashbacks*—the unpredictable return to a psychedelic trip that occurred months or even years earlier. Flashbacks are thought to result from the accumulation of a drug within body cells.

LSD

The most well-known hallucinogen is lysergic acid diethylamide. LSD is a drug that helped define the counterculture movement of the 1960s. During the 1970s and the 1980s, this drug lost considerable popularity. However, in the 1990s, LSD is making a comeback, with some studies showing that about 1 in 10 high school students and 1 in 20 college students has experimented with LSD. Fear of cocaine and other powerful drugs, boredom, low cost, and an attempt to revisit the culture of the '60s are thought to have increased LSD's attractiveness to today's young people.

LSD is manufactured in home laboratories and frequently distributed in blotter paper decorated with cartoon characters. Users place the paper on their tongue or chew the paper to ingest the drug. LSD can produce a psychedelic (mind-viewing) effect that includes altered perception of shapes, images, time, sound, and body form. Synesthesia is common to LSD users. Ingested in doses known as "hits," LSD produces a 6- to 9-hour experience. Hits range in price from $3 to $5.[12]

Although the hits today are about half as powerful as those in the 1960s, users still tend to develop high tolerance to LSD. Physical dependence does not occur. Not all LSD trips are pleasant. Hallucinations produced from LSD can be frightening and dangerous. Users can injure or kill themselves accidentally during a bad trip. Dangerous side effects include panic attacks, flashbacks, and occasional prolonged psychosis.

Designer drugs

In recent years, chemists who produce many of the illicit drugs in home laboratories have designed versions of drugs listed on **FDA Schedule 1.** These *designer drugs* are similar to the controlled drugs on the FDA Schedule 1 but are sufficiently different so that they escape governmental control. The designer drugs are either newly synthesized products that are similar to already outlawed drugs but against which no law yet exists, or they are reconstituted or renamed illegal substances. Designer drugs are said to produce effects similar to their controlled drug counterparts.

People who use designer drugs do so at great risk because the manufacturing of these drugs is unregulated. The neurophysiological effect of these home-made drugs can be quite dangerous. So far, a synthetic heroin product (MPPP) and several amphetamine derivatives with hallucinogenic properties have been designed for the unwary drug consumer.

DOM (STP), MDA (the "love drug"), and MDMA ("ecstasy" or "XTC") are examples of amphetamine-derivative, hallucinogenic designer drugs. These drugs produce mild LSD-like hallucinogenic experiences, positive feelings, and enhanced alertness. They also have a number of potentially dangerous effects. Experts are particularly concerned that MDMA can produce strong psychological dependence and can deplete serotonin, an important excitatory neurotransmitter associated with a state of alertness. Permanent brain damage is possible.[6]

Phencyclidine

Phencyclidine (PCP, "angel dust") has been classified variously as a hallucinogen, a stimulant, a depressant, and an anesthetic. PCP was studied for years during the 1950s and 1960s and was found to be an unsuitable animal and human anesthetic. PCP is an extremely unpredictable drug. Easily manufactured in home laboratories in tablet or powder form, PCP can be injected, inhaled, taken orally, or smoked. The effects vary. Some users report mild euphoria, although most report bizarre perceptions, paranoid feelings, and aggressive behavior. PCP overdose may cause convulsions, cardiovascular collapse, and damage to the brain's respiratory center.

In a number of cases the aggressive behavior caused by PCP has led users to commit brutal crimes against both friends and innocent strangers. PCP accumulates in cells and may stimulate bizarre behavior months after initial use.

Cannabis

Cannabis (marijuana) has been labeled a mild hallucinogen for a number of years. However, most experts now consider it to be a drug category in itself. Marijuana produces mild effects like those of stimulants and depressants. The recent implication of marijuana in a large number of traffic fatalities makes this drug one whose consumption should be carefully considered. Marijuana is actually a wild plant *(Cannabis sativa)* whose fibers were once used in the manufacture of hemp rope. When the leafy material and small stems are dried and crushed, users can smoke the mixture in rolled cigarettes ("joints") or pipes. The resins collected from scraping the flowering tops of the plant yield a mari-

Smoking pot.

juana product called *hashish,* or *hash,* commonly smoked in a pipe.

The potency of marijuana's hallucinogenic effect is determined by the percentage of the active ingredient tetrahydrocannabinol (THC) present in the product. Based on the analysis of samples from drug seizures and street buys in the United States, the concentration of THC averages about 3.5% for marijuana, 7% to 9% for higher-quality marijuana (sinsemilla), 8% to 14% for hashish, and as high as 50% for hash oil.

THC is a fat-soluble substance and thus is absorbed and retained in fat tissues within the body. Before being excreted, THC can remain in the body for up to a month. With the sophistication of today's drug tests, trace amounts of THC can be detected for up to 3 weeks after consumption.[6] It is possible that the THC that comes from passive inhalation (for example, during an indoor rock concert) can also be detected for a short time after exposure.

Once marijuana is consumed, its effects vary from person to person. Being "high" or "stoned" or "wrecked" means different things to different people. Many people report heightened sensitivity to music, cravings for particular foods, and a relaxed mood. There is widespread consensus that marijuana's behavioral effects includes four probabilities: (1) users must learn to recognize what a marijuana high is like, (2) marijuana impairs short-term memory, (3) users overestimate the passage of time, and (4) users lose the ability to maintain attention to a task.[6]

The long-term effects of marijuana use are still being studied. Chronic abuse may lead to an *amotivational syndrome* in some people. The irritating effects of marijuana smoke on lung tissue are more pronounced than those of cigarette smoke, and some of the over 400 chemicals in marijuana are now linked to lung cancer development. In fact, one of the most potent carcinogens, benzopyrene, is found in higher levels in marijuana smoke than in tobacco smoke. Marijuana smokers tend to inhale deeply and hold the smoke in the lungs for long periods. It is likely that at some point the lungs of chronic marijuana smokers will be damaged.

Long-term marijuana use is also associated with damage to the immune system and to the male and female reproductive systems and with an increase in birth defects in babies born to mothers who smoke marijuana. Chronic marijuana use lowers testosterone levels in men, but the effect of this change is not known. The effect of long-term marijuana use on a variety of types of sexual behavior is also not fully understood.

Because the drug can distort perceptions and thus perceptual ability (especially when combined with alcohol), its use by automobile drivers clearly jeopardizes the lives of many innocent people.

The only medical uses for marijuana are to relieve the nausea caused by chemotherapy, to improve appetites in AIDS patients, and to ease the pressure that builds up in the eyes of glaucoma patients. However, a variety of other drugs, many of which are nearly as effective, are also used for these purposes.

One particularly alarming statistic concerning marijuana use emerged in late 1995 with the release of the 1994 National Household Survey on Drug Abuse.[13] This national report indicated that marijuana use among 12- to 17-year-olds had nearly doubled in a 2-year period. In 1992, 4% of this age group reported monthly marijuana use, yet by 1994, 7.3% indicated monthly marijuana use.

Along with this increase in marijuana use was the finding that fewer American youths perceived great risk of harm in using marijuana occasionally.[13] Why do you think that today's young people believe that marijuana use is not dangerous?

Narcotics

The **narcotics** are among the most dependence-producing drugs. Medically, narcotics are used to relieve pain and induce sleep. On the basis of origin,

---

FDA Schedule 1
A list of drugs that have a high potential for abuse but no medical use.

narcotics
Opiates; psychoactive drugs derived from the Oriental poppy plant; narcotics relieve pain and induce sleep.

narcotics can be subgrouped into the natural, quasi-synthetic, and synthetic narcotics.

Natural narcotics

Naturally occurring substances derived from the Oriental poppy plant include opium (the primary psychoactive substance extracted from the Oriental poppy), morphine (the primary active ingredient in opium), and thebaine (a compound not used as a drug). Morphine and related compounds have medical use as analgesics in the treatment of mild to severe pain.

Quasisynthetic narcotics

Quasisynthetic narcotics are compounds created by chemically altering morphine. These laboratory-produced drugs are intended to be used as analgesics, but their benefits are largely outweighed by a high dependence rate and a great risk of toxicity. The best known of the quasisynthetic narcotics is heroin. Although heroin is a fast-acting and very effective analgesic, it is extremely addictive. Once injected into a vein or "skin-popped" (injected beneath the skin surface), heroin produces dreamlike euphoria and, like all narcotics, strong physical and psychological dependence and tolerance.

As with the use of all other injectable illegal drugs, the practice of sharing needles increases the likelihood of transmission of various communicable diseases, including HIV (see Chapter 12). Abrupt withdrawal from heroin use is rarely fatal, but the discomfort during **cold turkey** withdrawal is reported to be overwhelming. The use of heroin has increased during the last decade. The purity of heroin has improved while the price has dropped. Cocaine abusers may use heroin to "come down" from the high associated with cocaine.

Synthetic narcotics

Meperidine (Demerol) and propoxyphene (Darvon), common postsurgical painkillers, and methadone, the drug prescribed during the rehabilitation of heroin addicts, are *synthetic narcotics*. These opiate-like drugs are manufactured in medical laboratories. They are not natural narcotics or quasisynthetic narcotics because they do not originate from the Oriental poppy plant. Like true narcotics, however, these drugs can rapidly induce physical dependence. One important criticism of methadone rehabilitation programs is that they merely shift the addiction from heroin to methadone.

Inhalants

Inhalants are a class of drugs that includes a variety of volatile (quickly evaporating) compounds that generally produce unpredictable, drunklike effects in users. Users of inhalants may also have some delusions and hallucinations. Some users may become quite aggressive. Drugs in this category include anesthetic gases (chloroform, nitrous oxide, and ether), vasodilators (amyl nitrite and butyl nitrite), petroleum products and commercial solvents (gasoline, kerosene, plastic cement, glue, typewriter correction fluid, paint, and paint thinner), and certain aerosols (found in some propelled spray products, fertilizers, and insecticides).

Most of the danger in using inhalants lies in the damaging, sometimes fatal effects on the respiratory system. Furthermore, users may unknowingly place themselves in dangerous situations because of the drunklike hallucinogenic effects. Aggressive behavior might also make users a threat to themselves and others.

COMBINATION DRUG EFFECTS

Drugs taken in various combinations and dosages can alter and perhaps intensify effects.

A **synergistic drug effect** is a dangerous consequence of taking different drugs in the same general category at the same time. The combination exaggerates each individual drug's effects. For example, the combined use of alcohol and tranquilizers produces a synergistic effect greater than the total effect of each of the two drugs taken separately. In this instance a much-amplified, perhaps fatal sedation will occur. In a simplistic sense, "one plus one equals four or five."

When taken at or near the same time, drug combinations produce a variety of effects. Drug combinations have additive, potentiating, or antagonistic effects. When two or more drugs are taken and the result is merely a combined total effect of each drug, the result is an **additive effect.** The sum of the effects is not exaggerated. In a sense, "one plus one plus one equals three."

When one drug intensifies the action of a second drug, the first drug is said to have a **potentiated effect** on the second drug. One popular drug-taking practice during the 1970s was the consumption of Quaaludes and beer. Quaaludes potentiated the inhibition-releasing, sedative effects of alcohol. This particular drug combination produced an inexpensive but potentially fatal drunklike euphoria in the user.

An **antagonistic effect** is an opposite effect one drug has on another drug. One drug may be able to reduce another drug's influence on the body. Knowledge of this principle has been useful in the medical treatment of certain drug overdoses, as in the use of tranquilizers to relieve the effects of LSD or other hallucinogenic drugs.

SOCIETY'S RESPONSE TO DRUG USE

During the last 20 years, society has responded to illegal drug use with growing concern. Most adults see drug abuse as a clear danger to society. This position has been supported by the development of community, school, state, and national organizations interested in the reduction of illegal drug use. These organizations have included such diverse groups as Parents Against Drugs, Parents for a Drug-Free Youth, Mothers Against Drunk Driving (MADD), Narcotics Anonymous, and the federal Drug Enforcement Administration. Certain groups have concentrated their efforts on education, others on enforcement, and still others on the development of laws and public policy.

The personal and social issues related to drug abuse are very complex. Innovative solutions continue to be devised. Some believe that only through early childhood education will people learn alternatives to drug use. Starting drug education in the preschool years may have a more positive effect than waiting until the upper elementary or junior high school years. Recently, the focus on reducing young people's exposure to so-called **gateway drugs** (especially tobacco, alcohol, and marijuana) may help slow down the move to other addictive drugs. Some people advocate much harsher penalties for drug use and drug trafficking, including extreme measures such as public executions.

Others support legalizing all drugs and making governmental agencies responsible for drug regulation and control, as is the case with alcohol. Advocates of this position believe that drug-related crime and violence would virtually cease once the demand for illegal products is reduced. Sound arguments can be made on both sides of this issue. What is your opinion?

Unless significant changes in society's response to drug use take place soon, the disastrous effects of virtually uncontrolled drug abuse will continue to be felt. Families and communities will continue to be plagued by drug-related tragedies. Law enforcement officials will be pressed to the limits of their resources in their attempts to reduce drug flow. Our judicial system will be heavily burdened by thousands of court cases. Health care facilities could face overwhelming numbers of patients.

In comparison with other federally funded programs, the "war on drugs" is less expensive than farm support, food stamps, Medicare, and national defense. However, it remains to be seen whether any amount of money spent on enforcement, without adequate support for education, treatment, and poverty reduction, can reduce the illegal drug demand and supply. The United States now spends nearly $15 billion annually to fight the drug war. About two thirds is spent on law enforcement and one third on education, prevention, and treatment.

Drug Testing

Society's response to concern over drug use includes the development and growing use of drug tests. At present, the five largest drug-testing laboratories in the United States process over 1 million urine specimens per month combined.[14] Most of the specimens come from corporations that screen employees for commonly abused drugs. Among these are amphetamines, barbiturates, benzodiazepines (the chemical bases for prescription tranquilizers such as Valium and Librium), cannabinoids (THC, hashish, and marijuana), methaqualone, opiates (heroin,

cold turkey
Immediate, total discontinuation of use of a drug; associated withdrawal discomfort.

inhalants
Psychoactive drugs that enter the body through inhalation.

synergistic drug effect (sin er **jist** ick)
Heightened, exaggerated effect produced by the concurrent use of two or more drugs.

additive effect
The combined (but not exaggerated) effect produced by the concurrent use of two or more drugs.

potentiated effect (poe **ten** she ay ted)
Phenomenon whereby the use of one drug intensifies the effect of a second drug.

antagonistic effect
Effect produced when one drug reduces or offsets the effects of a second drug.

gateway drug
An easily obtainable legal or illegal drug that represents a user's first experience with a mind-altering drug.

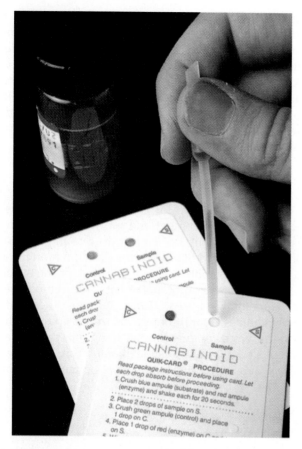

A drug test.

codeine, and morphine), and PCP. With the exception of marijuana, most traces of these drugs are eliminated by the body within a few days after use. Marijuana can remain detectable for weeks after use.

How accurate are the results of drug testing? At typical cutoff standards, drug tests will likely identify 90% of recent drug users. This means that about 10% of recent users will pass undetected. (These 10% are considered false negatives.) Nonusers whose drug tests indicate drug use (false positives) are quite rare. (Follow-up tests on these false positives would nearly always show negative results.) Human errors are probably more responsible than technical errors for inaccuracies in drug tests.[14]

Recently, scientists have been refining procedures that use hair samples to detect the presence of drugs.[15] These procedures seem to hold much promise, although certain technical obstacles remain. Watch for refinements in hair-sample drug testing in the near future.

Most Fortune 500 companies, the armed forces, various government agencies, and nearly all athletic organizations have already implemented mandatory drug testing. Corporate substance abuse policies are being developed, with careful attention to legal and ethical issues.[16]

Do you think that the possibility of having to take a drug test would have any effect on college students' use of drugs?

COLLEGE AND COMMUNITY SUPPORT SERVICES FOR DRUG DEPENDENCE

Students who have drug problems and realize they need assistance might select assistance based on the services available on campus or in the surrounding community and the costs they are willing to pay for treatment services.

One recently developed approach to convince drug-dependent people to enter treatment programs is the use of *confrontation.* People who live or work with chemically dependent people are being encouraged to confront them directly about their addiction. Direct confrontation helps chemically dependent people realize the effect their behavior has on others. Once chemically dependent people realize that others will no longer tolerate their behavior, the likelihood of their entering treatment programs is increased significantly. Although effective, this approach is very stressful for family members and friends and requires the assistance of professionals in the field of chemical dependence. These professionals can be contacted at a drug treatment center in your area.

Treatment

Comprehensive drug treatment programs are available in very few college or university health centers. College settings for drug dependence programs are more commonly found in the university counseling center. At such a center the emphasis will probably be not on the medical management of dependence but on the behavioral dimensions of drug abuse. Trained counselors and psychologists who specialize in chemical dependence counseling will work with students to (1) analyze their particular concerns, (2) establish constructive ways to cope with stress, and (3) search for alternative ways to achieve new "highs" (see the Personal Assessment on p. 171).

Medical treatment for the management of drug problems may need to be obtained through the services of a community treatment facility administered by a local health department, community mental health center, private clinic, or local hospital. Treatment may be on an inpatient or outpatient basis. Medical management

PERSONAL ASSESSMENT

Getting a Drug-Free High

Experts agree that drug use provides only short-term, ineffective, and often destructive solutions to problems. We hope that you have found (or will find) innovative, invigorating drug-free experiences that make your life more exciting. Circle the number for each activity that reflects your intention to try that activity. Use the following guide:

1   No intention of trying this activity
2   Intend to try this within 2 years
3   Intend to try this within 6 months
4   Already tried this activity
5   Regularly engage in this activity

1.	Learn to juggle	1 2 3 4 5
2.	Go backpacking	1 2 3 4 5
3.	Complete a marathon race	1 2 3 4 5
4.	Start a vegetable garden	1 2 3 4 5
5.	Ride in a hot air balloon	1 2 3 4 5
6.	Snow ski or water ski	1 2 3 4 5
7.	Donate blood	1 2 3 4 5
8.	Go river rafting	1 2 3 4 5
9.	Learn to play a musical instrument	1 2 3 4 5
10.	Cycle 100 miles	1 2 3 4 5
11.	Go skydiving	1 2 3 4 5
12.	Go rockclimbing	1 2 3 4 5
13.	Play a role in a theater production	1 2 3 4 5
14.	Build a piece of furniture	1 2 3 4 5
15.	Solicit funds for a worthy cause	1 2 3 4 5
16.	Learn to swim	1 2 3 4 5
17.	Overhaul a car engine	1 2 3 4 5
18.	Compose a song	1 2 3 4 5
19.	Travel to a foreign country	1 2 3 4 5
20.	Write the first chapter of a book	1 2 3 4 5

Your total points _____

Interpretation

61-100   You participate in many challenging experiences

41-60   You are willing to try some challenging new experiences

20-40   You take few of the challenging risks described here

To Carry This Further . . .

Looking at your point total, were you surprised at the degree to which you are aware of alternative activities? What are the top five activities, and can you understand their importance? What activities would you add to this list?

National Anti–Drug Abuse Groups: Hot Lines and Web Pages

National Groups
- PRIDE (Parent's Resource Institute for Drug Education)
  (800) 853-7867
  www.prideusa.org
- National Health Information Center
  (800) 336-4798
- National Clearinghouse for Alcohol and Drug Information
  (800) 729-6686
- National Institute on Drug Abuse Home Page
  www.nida.hih.gov
- Narcotics Anonymous
  (818) 773-9999
  www.wsoinc.com
- Toughlove
  (800) 333-1069
  http://members.aol.com/tljax/tufluv/htm
- Alcoholics Anonymous
  (888) 255-5440
  www.alcoholics-anonymous.org

Hot Lines
- National Institute on Alcohol and Drug Abuse Hot Line
  (800) 662-HELP
- National Cocaine Hot Line
  (800) COCAINE
- National Alcohol Hot Line
  (800) ALCOHOL
- Cocaine Abuse Hot Line
  (800) 888-9383; (800) 234-0420

Cocaine Anonymous
- Cocaine Anonymous
  (800) 347-8998
  www.ca.org

Health on the Web

LEARNING
ACTIVITIES

Activity 1

During the last 20 years, society has responded to drug abuse with growing concern. The National Center on Addiction and Substance Abuse (CASA), at Columbia University, takes an interdisciplinary approach (including health policy, medicine and nursing, communications, economics, sociology, and anthropology, law and law enforcement, business, religion, and education) to studying all forms of substance abuse. CASA's mission is to inform the American people of the cost of abuse of all substances. Visit the CASA web site at http://www.casacolumbia.org and take the *New National Substance Abuse IQ Quiz*.

Activity 2

Chronic cocaine abuse results in tolerance. More and more cocaine is needed with each successive use to achieve the same level of euphoria achieved by the previous dose. Visit the Cocaine Anonymous web site at http://www.ca.org and complete the *Self-Test for Cocaine Addiction*.

Activity 3

Students who realize that they need help for a drug problem might select assistance based on the services available on campus or in the surrounding community and on the costs they are able to pay for treatment services. The decision to get treatment for a child or adolescent is important. Parents, family members, and friends must be encouraged to consult professionals when making decisions about substance abuse treatment for minors. When properly informed, close friends and relatives can be partners in the treatment process. But it is vital that they ask the right questions. Go to the web site at http://www.aacap.org/factsFam/subabuse.htm and read through the list of 12 questions that are recommended by the American Academy of Child and Adolescent Psychiatry. Which questions would be most difficult to ask? Which are most important?

This is your brain.

this is drugs.

this is your brain on drugs.

Partnership For A Drug-Free America   N.Y., NY 10017

Will this approach reduce the rate of drug abuse?

might include detoxification, treatment of secondary health complications and nutritional deficiencies, and therapeutic counseling related to chemical dependence.

Some communities have voluntary health agencies that deliver services and treatment programs for drug-dependent people. Check your telephone book for listings of drug-treatment facilities. Some communities have drug hot lines that offer advice for people with questions about drugs (see the Star Box on p. 171 for a list of anti–drug abuse organizations and hot line numbers).

Costs of treatment for dependence

Drug-treatment programs that are administered by colleges and universities for faculty and students usually require no fees. Local agencies may provide either free services or services based on a **sliding scale.** Private hospitals, physicians, and clinics are the most expensive forms of treatment. Inpatient treatment at a private facility may cost as much as $1000 per day. Since the length of inpatient treatment averages 3 to 4 weeks, a patient can quickly accumulate a very large bill. However, with many types of health insurance policies now providing coverage for alcohol and other drug dependences, even these services may not require additional out-of-pocket expenses.

> **sliding scale**
> A method of payment by which patient fees are scaled according to income.

Summary

- Drug abuse has a devastating effect on society.
- Drug use, drug abuse, tolerance, and dependence are important terms to understand.
- A drug affects the CNS by altering neurotransmitter activity on the neuron.
- Drugs can be placed into six categories: stimulants, depressants, hallucinogens, cannabis, narcotics, and inhalants.

- Combination drug effects include synergistic, additive, potentiated, and antagonistic effects.
- Society's response to drug abuse has been widely varied and has included education, enforcement, treatment, testing, and the search for drug-free ways to achieve highs.
- Drug testing is becoming increasingly common in our society.

Review Questions

1. How is the term *drug* defined in this chapter? What are psychoactive drugs? How do medicines differ from drugs?
2. Explain what *dependence* means. Identify and explain the two types of dependence.
3. Define the word *tolerance*. What does *cross-tolerance* mean? Give an example of cross-tolerance.
4. Differentiate between drug misuse and drug abuse.
5. Identify some reasons commonly given for why people use psychoactive drugs.
6. Describe how neurotransmitters work.
7. List the six general categories of drugs. For each category, give several examples of drugs and explain the effects they would have on the user. What are designer drugs?
8. What is the active ingredient in marijuana? What are its common effects on the user? What are the long-term effects of marijuana use?
9. Explain the terms *synergistic effect*, *additive effect*, *potentiated effect*, and *antagonistic effect*.
10. How accurate is drug testing?

Think About This . . .

- Are there any drugs on which you may have developed either a physical or psychological dependence?
- Do you find that you now require a larger dose of a particular drug to reach a high or low that you once felt with a smaller dose?

- Evaluate your own use of drugs, including caffeine, tobacco, and OTC pain medication. Do you consider your drug use to be a problem?
- Think about your own life experiences. What things have you done that have produced drug-free highs?

References

1. Levy D: Drug-caused emergency room visits drop, *USA Today*, December 31, 1997, p. 3-A.
2. Manning A: Teens starting substance abuse at younger ages, *USA Today*, August 14, p. 8-D.
3. *Drug use among American teens shows some signs of leveling after a long rise*. Monitoring the Future press release, University of Michigan News and Information Services, December 20, 1997.
4. Office of the National Drug Control Policy: *1992 national drug control strategy: a nation responds to drug use*, January 1992, U.S. Government Printing Office.
5. U.S. Department of Health and Human Services: *Smoking, drinking, and illicit drug use among American secondary school students, college students, and young adults 1975-1992*, vol 2, NIH Pub No BKD-124, Washington DC, U.S. Government Printing Office.
6. Ray O, Ksir C: *Drugs, society, and human behavior*, ed 7, St Louis, 1996, Mosby.
7. Pinger RR, Payne WA, Hahn DB, Hahn EJ: *Drugs: issues for today*, ed 3, New York, 1998, WCB/McGraw-Hill.
8. Thibodeau GA, Patton KT: *Structure and function of the body*, ed 10, St Louis, 1996, Mosby.
9. Armstrong BG, McDonald AD, Sloan M: Cigarette, alcohol, and caffeine consumption and spontaneous abortion, *Am J Public Health* 82(1):85-87, 1991.
10. Cocaine: the first decade, 1992, *Rand Drug Policy Research Center Issue Paper*, 1(1):1-4.
11. U.S. Department of Justice (Bureau of Justice Statistics): *Drugs and crime facts, 1994*, Washington DC, U.S. Government Printing Office.
12. Urban J: Thirty years later, LSD again becoming the drug of choice, *The Muncie Star*, March 21, 1993, p. 6B.
13. U.S. Department of Health and Human Services (Substance Abuse and Mental Health Services Administration): *National drug survey results released with new youth public education materials* (press release), September 12, 1995, pp. 1-3.
14. Ackerman S: Drug testing: the state of the art, *Am Sci* 77:19-23, 1989.
15. Mieczkowski T: New approaches in drug testing: a review of hair analysis, *Ann Am Acad Pol Soc Sci* 521:132-150, 1992.
16. *Comprehensive procedures for drug testing in the workplace*, National Institute on Drug Abuse, 1991, DHHS Publication No. (ADM)91-1731.
17. Religious liberties, *Time*, April 30, 1990. p. 85.

Suggested Readings

Reinarman C, Levine HG (editors): *Crack in America: demon drugs and social justice*, Berkeley, CA, 1997, University of California Press.
This is a collection of essays written by veteran drug researchers in medicine, law, and the social sciences. The book examines the myths and realities of crack cocaine and how government policies toward crack may reflect racism and classism. The failure of drug prohibition to work effectively is also explored.

West JW: *The Betty Ford Center book of answers: help for those struggling with substance abuse and the people who love them*, New York, 1997, Pocket Books.
This book is written by the former director of the Betty Ford Center, one of the leading alcohol and drug treatment centers in the United States. This authoritative source provides answers to many of the most frequently asked questions about treatment and recovery. The book provides comprehensive coverage of drug abuse issues for addicts and their families.

James WH, Johnson SL: *Doin' drugs: patterns of African-American addiction*. Austin, TX, 1997, University of Texas Press.
This is a scholarly work for whose who want to learn about historical and current patterns of drug use in the African-American community. The book begins with a solid historical overview, followed by chapters that focus on specific drugs, such as alcohol and cocaine. Separate chapters discuss gains and the role of the church in dealing with drug-related problems.

Twerski AJ: *Addictive thinking: understanding self-deception*. Central City, MN, 1997, Hazelden.
This book focuses on overcoming the denial that usually accompanies addiction. This revised edition features expanded coverage of depression and affective disorders. The author, a physician, writes in an authoritative yet accessible style.

 AS WE GO TO PRESS . . .

The drug-related death of popular comedian Chris Farley has had an effect on the marketing of drug prevention messages. In early 1998, a newspaper ad in Farley's hometown of Madison, Wisconsin, portrayed a healthy Farley with the message, "Drugs and alcohol can kill the laughter in anybody." Farley died in December 1997 of an overdose of cocaine and morphine. He died at age 33—the same age as his comedic idol, John Belushi, who also died of a drug overdose.

A new study reported in the journal *Archives of Disease in Childhood* indicates that caffeine intake by pregnant women may be linked to sudden infant death syndrome (SIDS). The study showed that drinking four or more cups of coffee a day throughout pregnancy almost doubles the chance of SIDS. Researchers hypothesize that a high caffeine intake may damage the fetus's respiratory system. More studies are needed to confirm the findings; until then, doctors advise pregnant women to avoid caffeinated beverages or drink no more than the equivalent of one cup of coffee a day.

ON...

Prescription Drug Abuse

Lucy, a 35-year-old mother of two, seems like a typical suburban homemaker. She attends church regularly, belongs to the PTA, and volunteers at the local battered women's shelter. Her husband is a well-respected businessman and her children are honor students at the local high school. In short, life seems perfect for Lucy and her family, at least on the outside. However, Lucy has a secret that few outside her family know about.

Lucy's children and husband regularly come home to a disheveled household, finding Lucy passed out somewhere in the house or sometimes even on the back porch. Lucy's mood swings are unpredictable. One day, she will be a loving, devoted wife and mother; the next, she will talk rapidly and endlessly to whomever she can get to listen; still later, her speech will slur and she will seem incoherent. All this usually occurs whenever a stressful or unpleasant situation comes up in her life with which she cannot cope. Lucy's family never knows what to expect from one day to the next. The children have moved in and out of the home to live with their grandparents dozens of times over the past several years, and Lucy's husband has threatened her with divorce. Lucy has been to inpatient detoxification programs three times, only to "fall off the wagon" whenever a stressful event occurs.

You would probably guess that Lucy is an alcoholic or an illegal drug addict; however, Lucy's drugs of choice are all legal and all readily available to her from any one of a number of reputable physicians she visits. She uses a combination of drugs that range from sedatives to tranquilizers to antidepressants. Lucy is a prescription drug addict. Her suppliers are unwitting physicians who have no idea that she is seeing other doctors.

The reported numbers on the abuse of prescription drugs are alarming. In 1993 there were an estimated 7.9 million prescription drug abusers in the United States, with 125,000 deaths per year attributed to prescription drug abuse.[1] Over 100,000 prescription drug overdoses were reported in 1993, compared with fewer than 62,000 reported heroin overdoses.[2] Approximately 245,000 senior citizens are hospitalized each year for abuse of prescription drugs.[2] It is estimated that up to 50% of all prescriptions are used incorrectly.[1,2]

Most people would be surprised to learn that according to the Drug Enforcement Administration, 12 of the top 20 most abused controlled substances are prescription drugs.[1] These drugs fall into the following categories:

- *Opioids*. These drugs are narcotics typically prescribed to relieve acute or chronic pain. Common prescription drugs include Demerol, Darvocet, Vicodin, and drugs with codeine.
- *Stimulants*. These drugs affect the central nervous system and increase mental alertness, decrease fatigue, and produce a sense of well-being. They are usually prescribed for appetite suppression, attention deficit disorder, and narcolepsy. Common prescription drugs include Dexedrine, Ritalin, Fastin, and Cyclert.
- *Sedatives*. These drugs depress the central nervous system and are frequently used to treat anxiety, panic disorder, and insomnia. They may be dispensed for either daytime or nighttime use. Common prescription drugs include Xanax, Valium, Ativan, Dalmane, and Halcion.

Under certain conditions, nearly anybody could wind up abusing a prescription drug, but there are particular groups of people who are at high risk for prescription drug abuse. People with a family history of depression, smokers, and excessive drinkers are more likely to become addicted to prescription drugs, as are those with a history of abusing illegal drugs. Stress from traumatic experiences can also make a person more likely to abuse prescription drugs, and people who are hyperactive, obese, or who suffer from chronic pain are also at risk. Health care professionals are considered to be a high-risk group,[2,3,4] and older people have a greater tendency to abuse prescription drugs.[5]

A patient can become physiologically dependent on a drug, which is considered to be a more manageable condition than addiction. Physiological dependence, which involves the body's adaptation to a drug over time, is considered a temporary, benign condition. Physiological dependence is usually treated by gradual reductions in use of the drug, and although there may be withdrawal symptoms during this period, there is not normally a relapse afterward. The gradual reduction in dosage can be handled with medical supervision, and the patient does not normally need to enter a substance abuse program. Addiction involves a continued need to use a drug for psychological effects or mood alteration, and the patient goes to great lengths to obtain the drug even if its effects become harmful to him or her. Addiction is considered a chronic, complex problem and is usually handled with specific chemical dependence treatment.[1]

Abuse is often caused or continued because of deliberate deception on the part of the patient, but misuse of a prescription drug can start innocently enough. A patient may be receiving several prescriptions that have the same effect, or a patient may have several doctors prescribing the same medication. Prescription drugs may react with each other and cause different effects than intended. Sometimes communication problems between patient and physician cause errors in prescription dispensation. The patient may unintentionally use the prescription incorrectly. One of these situations or a combination of factors can start prescription drug abuse.[5] Often a single prescription drug, such as a painkiller or sedative, is enough to start the process of dependence.

Older people are considered at high risk for prescription drug abuse for several reasons. The process of aging or the transition to retirement can leave a person with symptoms of depression or anxiety, and illnesses can also increase as a person gets older. Many people see multiple doctors as they get older and thus may wind up getting several prescriptions for the same drug under different brand names without realizing it. Sometimes physicians give older patients the same dosages as younger patients. Body functions slow and change with age, and when this occurs, the duration and intensity of drug effects can change as well.[5] Such conditions can increase the risk of drug abuse among the elderly.

If addiction starts, older people may then resort to the same tactics as any prescription drug addict. They may begin to "doctor-hop" (moving from one doctor to the next without informing the doctors) to get multiple prescriptions, or they may go to an emergency room to get a quick fix of a particular drug. Patients may also hoard pills or swap pills with friends to cut costs and ensure availability of their drug of choice. In the United States, it is estimated that 2 million older adults are at risk of addiction or are addicted to tranquilizers or sleeping pills.[5]

Health care professionals are also at high risk for prescription drug abuse. Physicians are five times more likely than the general population to take sedatives or tranquilizers without another doctor's supervision. The high stress of the job and the availability of drugs are both believed to be contributing factors to abuse among health care professionals. However, studies suggest that those physicians who are psychologically sound had little problem handling the stress of their jobs and generally resisted the temptation of readily available drugs. Those physicians considered to have psychological problems were more likely to be abusers.[3]

Effects of Abuse

As abuse of a drug continues, the tolerance of the body to that drug increases, which can lead to stronger self-dosing. As use increases, the detoxification process can become more difficult. In some cases, people refuse to believe they are addicted, and older people who are isolated from others do not even realize they are hooked.[5] Physicians may inadvertently promote the abuse by failing or refusing to acknowledge the signs of addiction in a patient.

If a person admits he or she has a problem with a drug, the recovery process can begin, but trying to kick the habit without professional help may only make things worse. If the person tries to cut back or stop use of the drug, withdrawal symptoms may occur. These symptoms include pain, nausea, sleeplessness, nervousness, irritability, hallucinations, and confusion, and can be quite severe. Sometimes other underlying psychological problems (for example, depression) must also be dealt with to prevent a relapse.[5] In short, recovery from prescription drug abuse becomes as difficult as recovery from abuse of illegal drugs. For these reasons, professional help is usually necessary for a full recovery from prescription drug abuse.

If you or someone you know is abusing prescription drugs, help is available. Many hospitals that sponsor detoxification programs for alcoholics and illegal drug addicts also have programs for individuals who are addicted to prescription drugs. Often, insurance will cover the costs of these programs. After detoxification the individual will need to continue recovery through a program such as Alcoholics Anonymous (the principles used for recovery from alcoholism are also applicable to recovery from drug addiction), Narcotics Anonymous, or Benzodiazepine Anonymous. These organizations can be found in the white pages of any local telephone directory. If the addicted person has family or close friends who are being seriously affected by addiction issues, they may want to try Al-Anon, Alateen, or Adult Children of Alcoholics support groups. Finally, individual or family counseling may be of value in helping to sort out emotional issues that lie behind the addiction. A certified addictions counselor may be the most helpful person to an addict, or the family may choose a psychiatrist, psychologist, or social worker who has knowledge of addiction issues.

Although prescription drug addicts will always be "recovering" rather than "recovered," they can still lead relatively normal lives with proper physical and psychological treatment. However, there are no quick fixes or easy answers. Recovery is an ongoing process for both the addict and his or her family.

For Discussion . . .
Do you know of anyone who has intentionally abused prescription drugs? Have you ever taken a prescription drug in a different way than it was prescribed? Have you ever taken someone else's prescription drug, and if so, why did you do it? Can you think of a case where use of another person's prescription drug can be justified?

References
1. Colvin R: *Prescription drug abuse: the hidden epidemic*, Omaha, NE, 1995, Addicus Books.
2. Colvin R: I tried to be my brother's keeper: one family's battle with prescription drug abuse, *Family Circle*, 108(13), Sep 19, 1995.
3. Vaillant GE: Physician, cherish thyself: the hazards of self prescribing, *JAMA* 267(17), 1992.
4. Dabney D, Heffington TR: The pharmacy profession's reaction to substance abuse among pharmacists: the process and consequences of medicalization, *Journal of Drug Issues* 26(4), Fall 1996.
5. Chastain S: The accidental addict: are you hooked on your prescriptions? *Modern Maturity*, 35(1), Feb-Mar 1992.

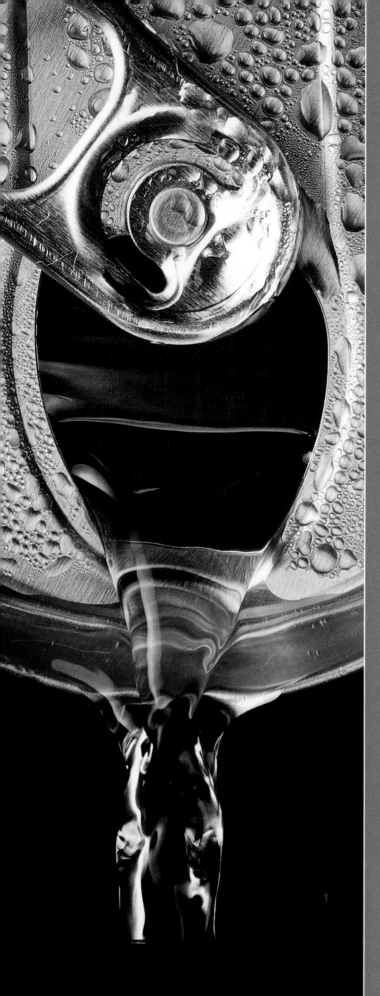

Taking Control of Alcohol Use

Healthy People: Looking Ahead to 2010

The *Healthy People 2000 Midcourse Review* highlighted significant progress toward achieving several important alcohol-related objectives. The most notable and encouraging change was the reduction in the number of alcohol-related traffic fatalities. The original 1990 goal was easily surpassed in this area. This success was largely attributable to the passage of state laws that revoked drunk drivers' licenses and lowered the legal limit for blood alcohol concentration (BAC) from .10% to .08%.

At mid-decade, the number of deaths caused by cirrhosis (alcohol-related liver disease) had declined, and per capital alcohol consumption had dropped. When the Midcourse Review was issued, the nation was about halfway toward reaching the specific targets for these two objectives.

The *Healthy People 2010* document will probably contain objectives aimed at reducing binge drinking (measured by the number of people who report heavy drinking during the past two weeks) among youth and college-age students. These objectives will be critical ones, especially in light of the 1997 Monitoring the Future Study, which indicated that binge drinking was still on the rise among America's youth.[1]

The push for zero tolerance laws, the tightening of standards for determining legal intoxication, and the growing influence of national groups concerned with alcohol misuse indicate that our society is more sensitive than ever to the growing misuse of alcohol.

People are concerned about the consequences of drunk driving, alcohol-related crime, and lowered job productivity. National data indicate that per capita alcohol consumption has gradually dropped in the United States.[2] Alcohol use remains the preferred form of drug use for most adults (including college students), but as a society, we are increasingly uncomfortable with the ease with which alcohol can be misused.

CHOOSING TO DRINK

Clearly, people drink for many different reasons (see the Star Box at right). We believe that most people drink because alcohol is an effective, affordable, and legal substance for altering the brain's chemistry. As **inhibitions** are removed by the influence of alcohol, behavior that is generally held in check is expressed. At least temporarily, drinkers become a different version of themselves—more outgoing, relaxed, and adventuresome. If alcohol did not make

Why Do I Choose an Alcoholic Beverage?
- I think alcoholic beverages are more thirst quenching than nonalcoholic alternatives.
- Alcoholic beverages taste better—their flavor is unique and satisfying.
- My friends always choose alcoholic beverages—I've learned to do the same.
- Alcoholic drinks are an important part of the larger statement I am making about myself. They reflect that I am an adult.
- Drinking alcoholic beverages makes me feel different—I like the changes that come about when I drink.

these changes in people, it would not be consumed as much. Do you agree or disagree?

ALCOHOL USE PATTERNS

From magazines to billboards to television, alcohol is one of the most heavily advertised consumer products in the country.[3] You cannot watch television,

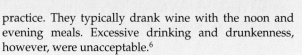

LEARNING from ALL CULTURES

Alcohol Use

Whether or not people use alcohol is often a reflection of attitudes developed through the culture in which they live. How much they drink, what they drink, when they drink, and why they drink are all habits derived from their particular environments. Attitudes that a particular culture develops also influence rates of alcoholism. Times change, however, and countries are less isolated than they once were. Those cultural attitudes of a generation ago probably had more influence on behavior, such as drinking alcohol, than they do today. Still, culture does play a role in developing attitudes and behavior concerning alcohol consumption.

Italy is the second largest wine-producing country in the world, and Italians have historically enjoyed drinking wine. Yet a generation ago, Italy's rates of alcoholism were low. Most Italians drank wine and approved of the

practice. They typically drank wine with the noon and evening meals. Excessive drinking and drunkenness, however, were unacceptable.[6]

Jews, like Italians, have had low rates of alcoholism. Their attitudes toward drinking and drinking habits have been very similar to those of Italians.[6]

Attitudes continue to change in different cultures, but there are a few factors that seem to affect the rate of alcoholism. In societies in which alcohol is introduced to children in small amounts on special occasions and within a sound family structure, the rates of alcoholism are low. This is also true when drinking is not the main focus of entertainment but accompanies another activity. Conversely, high rates of alcoholism are common in cultures that seem to have no standards about how to drink and how much to drink.[6]

Consider the attitudes toward drinking within your culture and family. How do these attitudes and practices influence your own opinions toward alcohol use?

Do you see this kind of behavior frequently on your campus?

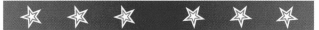

Moderate Drinking Redefined

Alcohol Alert, a publication of the National Institute on Alcohol Abuse and Alcoholism (NIAAA), indicates that moderate drinking can be defined as no more than two drinks each day for most men and one drink each day for women.[13] These cutoff levels are based on the amount of alcohol that can be consumed without causing problems, either for the drinker or society. (The gender difference is due primarily to the higher percentage of body fat in women and to the lower amount of an essential stomach enzyme in women.) Elderly people are limited to no more than one drink each day, again due to a higher percentage of body fat.

These consumption levels are applicable to most people. Indeed, people who plan to drive, women who are pregnant, people recovering from alcohol addiction, people under age 21, people taking medications, and those with existing medical concerns should not consume alcohol. Additionally, although some studies have shown that low levels of alcohol consumption may have minor psychological and cardiovascular benefits, the NIAAA does not advise nondrinkers to start drinking.

listen to the radio, or read a newspaper without being encouraged to buy a particular brand of beer, wine, or liquor. The advertisements create a warm aura about the nature of alcohol use. The implications are clear: alcohol use will bring you good times, handsome men or seductive women, exotic settings, and a chance to forget the hassles of hard work and study.

Perhaps as a consequence of the many pressures to drink, it is not surprising that most adults drink alcoholic beverages. Two thirds of all American adults are classified as drinkers. Yet one in three adults does not drink. In the college environment, where surveys indicate that 85% to 90% of all students drink, it is difficult for many students to imagine that every third adult is an abstainer. Complete the Personal Assessment on p. 181 to rate your own alcohol use.

Alcohol consumption figures are reported in many different ways, depending on the researchers' criteria. Figures from various sources support the contention that about one third of adults 18 years of age and older are abstainers, about one third are light drinkers, and one third are moderate-to-heavy drinkers (see the Star Box at right). As a single category, heavy drinkers make up about 10% of the adult drinking population. Students who drink in college tend to classify themselves as light-to-moderate drinkers. It comes as a shock to students, though, when they read the criteria for each drinking classification. According to the combination of quantity of alcohol consumed per occasion and the frequency of drinking, these criteria are established as shown in Table 8-1.

In a recent unpublished survey of our undergraduate health science classes, we found that 37% of the 200 students met the criteria for heavy drinking, 26%

met the criteria for moderate drinking, 13% met the criteria for light drinking, 11% were infrequent drinkers, and 13% were abstainers.[4] It is not surprising that many students, faculty, and administrators believe that alcohol abuse is a serious problem on their campuses.

Binge Drinking

Alcohol abuse by college students usually takes place through a drinking pattern called *binge drinking.* Binge drinking refers to the consumption of five drinks in a row, at least once during the previous 2-week period.[5] College students who fit the category of "heavy drinkers" rarely consume small amounts of alcohol each day but instead binge on 1 or 2 nights a week. Some students in our classes openly admit that they plan to "get really drunk" on the weekend. They plan to binge drink.

By its very nature, binge drinking can be dangerous. Drunk driving, physical violence, property destruction, date rape, police arrest, and lowered academic performance are all highly associated with binge drinking. Reducing binge drinking is one of the Healthy People 2000 objectives. The direct correlation between the amount of alcohol consumed and lowered academic performance is crystal clear (Figure 8-1). Frequently,

PERSONAL ASSESSMENT

How Do You Use Alcoholic Beverages?

Answer the following questions about your own alcohol use. Record your number of "yes" and "no" responses in the box at the end of the questionnaire.

Do you: Yes   No

1. Drink more often than you did a year ago?

2. Drink more heavily than you did a year ago?

3. Plan to drink, sometimes days in advance?

4. Gulp or "chug" your drinks, perhaps in a contest?

5. Set personal limits on the amount you plan to drink but then consistently disregard these limits?

6. Drink at a rate greater than two drinks per hour?

7. Encourage or even pressure others to drink with you?

8. Frequently want a nonalcoholic beverage but then end up drinking an alcoholic drink?

9. Drive your car while under the influence of alcohol or ride with another person who has been drinking?

10. Use alcoholic beverages while taking prescription or OTC medications?

11. Forget what happened while you were drinking?

12. Have a tendency to disregard information about the effects of drinking?

13. Find your reputation fading because of alcohol use?

TOTAL

Interpretation

If you answered "yes" to any of these questions, you may be using alcohol irresponsibly. Two or more "yes" responses indicate an unacceptable pattern of alcohol use and may reflect problem drinking behavior.

To Carry This Further . . .

Ask your friends or roommates to take this assessment. Are they willing to take this assessment and then talk about their results with you? Be prepared to discuss any follow-up questions they might have about their (or your) alcohol consumption patterns. Your willingness to talk about drinking behavior might help someone realize that this topic can and should be discussed openly. Finally, be aware of how people in your area can get professional help with drinking or other drug concerns.

---

the social costs of binge drinking can be very high, especially when intoxicated people demonstrate their level of immaturity. How common is binge drinking on your campus?

For large numbers of students who drink, the college years are a time when they will drink more heavily than at any other period during their lifetime. Some will suffer serious consequences as a result

(Figure 8-2). These years will also mark the entry into a lifetime of problem drinking for some.

inhibitions
Inner controls that prevent a person from engaging in certain types of behavior.

Table 8-1 Criteria for Drinking Classifications	
Classification	Alcohol-Related Behavior
Abstainers	Do not drink or drink less often than once a year
Infrequent drinkers	Drink once a month at most and drink small amounts per typical drinking occasion
Light drinkers	Drink once a month at most and drink medium amounts per typical drinking occasion, or drink no more than three to four times a month and drink small amounts per typical drinking occasion
Moderate drinkers	Drink at least once a week and small amounts per typical drinking occasion or three to four times a month and medium amounts per typical drinking occasion or no more than once a month and large amounts per typical drinking occasion
Moderate/heavy drinkers	Drink at least once a week and medium amounts per typical drinking occasion or three to four times a month and large amounts per typical drinking occasion
Heavy drinkers	Drink at least once a week and large amounts per typical drinking occasion

NOTE: Small amounts = One drink or less per drinking occasion

Medium amounts = Two to four drinks per drinking occasion

Large amounts = Five or more drinks per drinking occasion (binge drinking)

Drink = 12 fluid oz of beer, 4 fluid oz of wine, or 1 fluid oz of distilled spirits

THE NATURE OF ALCOHOLIC BEVERAGES

Alcohol (also known as *ethyl alcohol* or *ethanol*) is the principal product of **fermentation**. In this process, yeast cells act on the sugar content of fruits and grains to produce alcohol and carbon dioxide.

The alcohol concentration in distilled beverages (such as whiskey, gin, rum, and vodka) is expressed by the term *proof,* a number that is twice the percentage of alcohol by volume in a beverage. Thus 70% of the fluid in a bottle of 140 proof gin is pure alcohol.

Most proofs in distilled beverages range from 80 to 160. The familiar, pure *grain alcohol* that is often added to fruit punches and similar beverages has a proof of almost 200 (see Table 8-2).

The nutritional value of alcohol is extremely limited. Alcoholic beverages produced today through modern processing methods contain nothing but empty calories—about 100 calories per fluid ounce of 100-proof distilled spirits and about 150 calories per each 12-ounce bottle or can of beer.[6] Clearly, alcohol consumption is a significant contributor to the additional pounds of fat that many college students accumulate. Pure alcohol contains only simple carbohydrates; it has no vitamins and minerals, and no fats or protein.

"Lite" beer and low-calorie wines have been introduced in response to concerns about the number of calories that alcoholic beverages provide. These "lite" beverages are not low-alcohol beverages but merely low-calorie beverages. Only beverages marked "low alcohol" contain a lower concentration of alcohol than the usual beverages of that type. In fact, the popular new ice beers actually contain a higher percentage of alcohol than other types of beer.

THE PHYSIOLOGICAL EFFECTS OF ALCOHOL

First and foremost, alcohol is classified as a drug—a very strong CNS depressant. The primary depressant effect of alcohol is seen in the brain and spinal cord. Many people think of alcohol as a stimulant because of the way most users feel after consuming a serving or two of their favorite drink. Any temporary sensations of jubilation, boldness, or relief are attributable to alcohol's ability as a depressant drug to release personal inhibitions and provide temporary relief from tension.

Factors That Influence the Absorption of Alcohol

The **absorption** of alcohol is influenced by several factors, most of which can be controlled by the individual. These factors include the following:

- *Strength of the beverage.* The stronger the beverage, the greater the amount of alcohol that will accumulate within the digestive tract.
- *Number of drinks consumed.* As more drinks are consumed, more alcohol is absorbed.
- *Speed of consumption.* If consumed rapidly, even relatively few drinks will result in a large con-

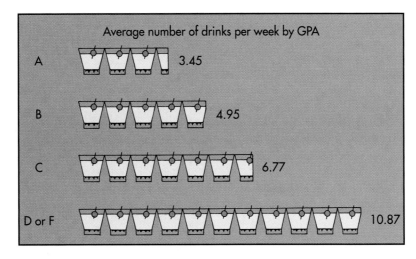

Figure 8-1   Average number of drinks consumed per week by grade point average.

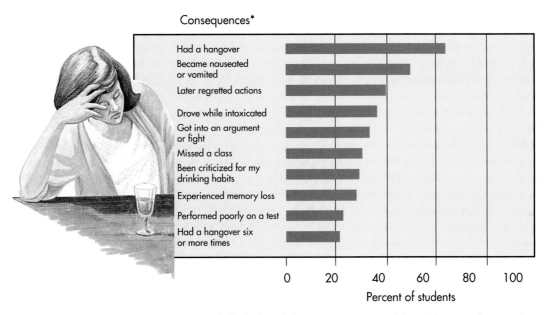

Figure 8-2   Negative consequences of alcohol and drug use as reported by college students. (*Occurred at least once in the past year.)

centration gradient that will lead to high blood alcohol concentration.

- *Presence of food.* Food can compete with alcohol for absorption into the bloodstream, thus slowing the absorption of alcohol. By slowing alcohol absorption, removal of the alcohol already in the bloodstream can occur. Slow absorption favors better control of blood alcohol concentration.
- *Body chemistry.* Each person has an individual pattern of physiological functioning that may affect the ability to process alcohol. For example, in some conditions, such as that marked by "dumping syndrome," the stomach empties more rapidly than is normal, and alcohol seems

fermentation
A chemical process whereby plant products are converted into alcohol by the action of yeast cells on carbohydrate materials.

absorption
The passage of nutrients or alcohol through the walls of the stomach or intestinal tract into the bloodstream.

Table 8-2   Categories of Alcohol Beverages*

Alcohol Beverage	Alcohol Content (%)†	Normal Measure
Beer		
Ale	5	12-oz bottle
Ice beer	5.5	12-oz bottle
Malt liquor	7	12-oz bottle
Lite beer	4	12-oz bottle
Regular beer	4	12-oz bottle
Low-alcohol beer	1.5	12-oz bottle
Wine		
Fortified: port, sherry, muscatel, etc.	18	3-oz glass
Natural: red/white	12	3-oz glass
Champagne	12	4-oz glass
Wine cooler	6	12-oz bottle
Cider (Hard)	10	6-oz glass
Liqueurs		
Strong: sweet, syrupy	40	1-oz glass
Medium: fruit brandies	25	2-oz glass
Distilled Spirits		
Brandy, cognac, rum, scotch, vodka, whiskey	45	1-oz glass
Mixed Drinks and Cocktails		
Strong martini, manhattan	30	3½-oz glass
Medium: old-fashioned, daiquiri, Alexander	15	4-oz glass
Light: highball, sweet and sour mixes, tonics	7	8-oz glass

*In all major alcohol beverages—beer, table wines, cocktail and dessert wines, liqueurs and cordials, and distilled spirits—the significant ingredient is identical: alcohol. The typical drink, half an ounce of pure alcohol, is provided by a shot of spirits, a glass of fortified wine, a larger glass of table wine, or a bottle of beer.

†In addition, these beverages contain other chemical constituents. Some come from the original grains, grapes, or other fruits; others are produced during the chemical processes of fermentation, distillation, and storage. Some are added as flavoring or coloring. These nonalcohol substances contribute to the effects of certain beverages either by directly affecting the body or by affecting the rates at which alcohol is absorbed into the blood.

to be absorbed more quickly. The emptying time may be either slowed or quickened by anger, fear, stress, nausea, and the condition of the stomach tissues.

- *Gender.* A significant study published in the *New England Journal of Medicine* reported that women produce much less alcohol dehydrogenase than men do.[7] This enzyme is responsible for breaking down alcohol in the stomach. With

HealthQuest Activities

- The alcohol self-assessment activity in Module 8 will help you understand your current drinking behavior and determine how that behavior may affect your health. You can assess your beliefs about alcohol and take a critical look at your ideas about whether alcohol use harms various aspects of your life, such as your friendships, family relationships, and appearance. *HealthQuest* will help you estimate your risk of becoming a problem drinker or alcoholic. After completing the assessment activity, briefly record your answers to the following questions: Do your beliefs about alcohol reflect your own drinking behavior? What factors might cause a person's beliefs and behaviors to be incompatible? What life experiences or influences, such as family, religion, and advertising, have helped form your own beliefs about alcohol? Do you think your beliefs and behavior patterns are fixed, or will they change over time?

- The *Alcohol Decision Maze*, found in Module 8, simulates an evening out with a friend. The activity prompts you to make a variety of choices throughout the evening that may influence whether or how much you drink. First you will choose among several companions for the evening. Then you must decide where to go. At each location, such as a restaurant or sporting event, you can choose from a list of activities in which to participate. The choice to buy or drink alcohol surfaces often. *HealthQuest* will then provide feedback on the outcome of the evening and estimate your blood alcohol content. Complete this activity several times, making different decisions each time. Does the outcome of the evening reflect the drinking behavior you entered? Why or why not?

less alcohol dehydrogenase action, women absorb about 30% more alcohol into the bloodstream than men, despite an identical number of drinks and equal body weight.

Three other reasons help explain why women tend to absorb alcohol more quickly than men of the same body weight: (1) Women have proportionately more body fat than men. Since alcohol is not very fat soluble, it enters the bloodstream relatively quickly. (2) Women's bodies have proportionately less water than men's bodies of equal weight. Thus alcohol consumed does not become as diluted as in men. (3) Alcohol absorption is influenced by a woman's menstrual cycle. Alcohol is more quickly absorbed during the premenstrual phase of a woman's cycle. Also, there is evidence that women using birth control pills absorb alcohol faster than usual.[6]

With the exception of a person's body chemistry and gender, all factors that influence absorption can be moderated by the alcohol user.

Binge-Drinking Deaths on Campus

Two highly publicized college binge-drinking deaths occurred during the fall semester of 1997. The first death took place in August on the campus of Louisiana State University, where an underage student died of acute alcohol intoxication after a 7-hour drinking binge with other fraternity pledges. This student had a blood alcohol concentration nearly six times the legal limit.

The second death occurred in September at the Massachusetts Institute of Technology (MIT), where an 18-year-old student was found unconscious following a fraternity party and died a short time later. These tragedies came on the heels of deaths the previous academic year at Frostburg State University, in Maryland, and Radford University, in Virginia.

In an effort to prevent alcohol-related injuries and deaths, two national fraternities, Sigma Nu and Phi Delta Theta, have banned alcoholic beverages in their chapter houses across the country. Do you support such a policy? Do any fraternities or sororities on your campus have a no-alcohol policy?

Blood Alcohol Concentration

A person's **blood alcohol concentration (BAC)** rises when alcohol is consumed faster than it can be removed (oxidized) by the liver. A fairly predictable sequence of events takes place when a person drinks alcohol at a rate faster than one drink every hour. When the BAC reaches 0.05%, initial measurable changes in mood and behavior take place. Inhibitions and everyday tensions appear to be released, while judgment and critical thinking are somewhat impaired. This BAC would be achieved by a 160-pound person taking about two drinks in an hour.

At a level of 0.10% (one part alcohol to 1000 parts blood), the drinker typically loses significant motor coordination. Voluntary motor function becomes quite clumsy. At this BAC, most states consider a drinker legally intoxicated and thus incapable of safely operating a vehicle. Although physiological changes associated with this BAC do occur, certain users do not feel intoxicated or do not outwardly appear to be impaired.

As a person continues to elevate the BAC from 0.20% to 0.50%, the health risk of acute alcohol intoxication increases rapidly. A BAC of 0.20% is characterized by the loud, boisterous, obnoxious drunk person who staggers. A 0.30% BAC produces further depression and stuporous behavior, during which time the drinker becomes so confused that he or she may not be capable of understanding anything. The 0.40% or 0.50% BAC produces unconsciousness. At this BAC a person can die, since brain centers that control body temperature, heartbeat, and respiration may be virtually shut down.

An important factor influencing the BAC is the individual's blood volume. The larger the person, the greater the amount of blood into which alcohol can be distributed. Conversely, the smaller person has less blood into which alcohol can be distributed, and as a result, a higher BAC will develop.

Sobering Up

Alcohol is removed from the bloodstream principally through the process of **oxidation.** Oxidation occurs at a constant rate (about ¼ to ⅓ oz of pure alcohol per hour) that cannot be appreciably altered. Since each typical drink of beer, wine, or distilled spirits contains about ½ oz of pure alcohol, it takes about 2 hours for the body to fully oxidize one typical alcoholic drink.[8]

Although people have attempted to sober up by drinking hot coffee, taking cold showers, or exercising, the oxidation rate of alcohol is unaffected. Thus far the FDA has not approved any commercial product that can help people achieve sobriety. Passage of time remains the only effective remedy for diminishing alcohol's effects.

First Aid for Acute Alcohol Intoxication

Not everyone who goes to sleep, passes out, or even becomes unconscious after drinking has a high BAC. People who are already sleepy, have not eaten well, are sick, or are bored may drink a little alcohol and quickly fall asleep. However, people who drink heavily in a rather short time may be setting themselves up for an extremely unpleasant, toxic, potentially life-threatening experience because of their high BAC.

Although responsible drinking would prevent **acute alcohol intoxication** (poisoning), such responsi-

blood alcohol concentration (BAC)
The percentage of alcohol in a measured quantity of blood; BACs can be determined directly through the analysis of a blood sample or indirectly, through the analysis of exhaled air.

oxidation
The process that removes alcohol from the bloodstream.

acute alcohol intoxication
A potentially fatal elevation of the BAC, often resulting from heavy, rapid consumption of alcohol.

ble drinking will never be a reality for everyone. As caring adults, what should we know about this health emergency that may help us save a life—perhaps even a friend's life?

The first real danger sign we need to recognize are the typical signs of **shock.** By the time these signs are evident, a drinker will already have become unconscious. He or she cannot be aroused from a deep stupor. The person will probably have a weak, rapid pulse (over 100 beats per minute). Skin will be cool and damp, and breathing will be increased to once every 3 or 4 seconds. These breaths may be shallow or deep but will certainly occur in an irregular pattern. Skin will be pale or bluish. (In the case of a person with dark skin, these color changes will be more evident in the fingernail beds or in the mucous membranes inside the mouth or under the eyelids.) Whenever any of these signs is present, seek emergency medical help immediately (see the Health Action Guide below for a summary of these signs).

Involuntary regurgitation (vomiting) can be another potentially life-threatening emergency for a person who has drunk too much alcohol. When a drinker has consumed more alcohol than the liver can oxidize, the pyloric valve at the base of the stomach tends to close. Additional alcohol remains in the stomach. This alcohol irritates the lining of the stomach so much that involuntary muscle contractions force the stomach contents to flow back through the esophagus. By removing alcohol from the stomach, vomiting may be a life-saving mechanism for conscious drinkers.

An unconscious drinker who vomits may be lying in such a position that the airway becomes obstructed with the vomitus from the stomach. This person is in great risk of dying from **asphyxiation.** As a first-aid measure, unconscious drinkers should always be rolled onto their sides to minimize the chance of airway obstruction. If you are with a person who is vomiting, make certain that his or her head is positioned lower than the rest of the body. This position minimizes the chance that vomitus will obstruct the air passages.

It is also important to keep a close watch on anyone who passes out from heavy drinking. Unfortunately, party goers sometimes make the mistake of carrying these people to bed and then forgetting about them. We should do our best to monitor the physical condition of anyone who becomes unconscious from heavy drinking because of the risks of death. If you really care about these people, you will observe them at regular intervals until they appear to be clearly out of danger. Although this may mean an evening of interrupted sleep for you, you might save a friend's life.

ALCOHOL-RELATED HEALTH PROBLEMS

The relationship of chronic alcohol use to the structure and function of the body is reasonably well understood. Heavy alcohol use causes a variety of changes to the body that lead to an increase in morbidity and mortality. Figure 8-3 describes these changes. Some of these health problems are specifically addressed in the *Healthy People 2000* objectives.

Research clearly shows that chronic alcohol use also damages the immune system and the nervous system. Thus chronic users are at high risk for a variety of infections and neurological complications.[2]

Fetal Alcohol Syndrome and Fetal Alcohol Effects

A growing body of scientific evidence indicates that alcohol use by pregnant women can result in birth defects in unborn children. When alcohol crosses the **placenta,** it enters the fetal bloodstream in a concentration equal to that in the mother's bloodstream. Because of the underdeveloped nature of the fetal liver, this alcohol is oxidized much more slowly than the alcohol in the mother. During this time of slow detoxification, the developing fetus is certain to be

HEALTH ---┐

Action Guide - - - - →

Alcohol Intoxication

You should seek emergency help for acute alcohol intoxication when you find that a person drinking heavily:
- Cannot be aroused
- Has a weak, rapid pulse
- Has an unusual or irregular breathing pattern
- Has cool (possibly damp), pale, or bluish skin

◄ - - - - - -

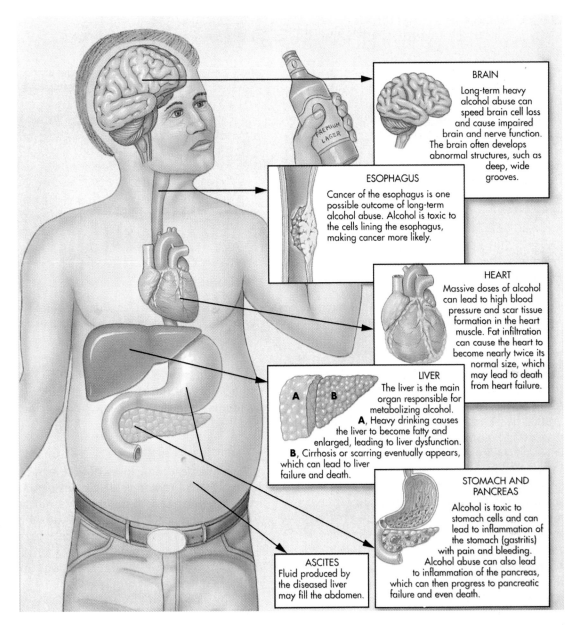

BRAIN
Long-term heavy alcohol abuse can speed brain cell loss and cause impaired brain and nerve function. The brain often develops abnormal structures, such as deep, wide grooves.

ESOPHAGUS
Cancer of the esophagus is one possible outcome of long-term alcohol abuse. Alcohol is toxic to the cells lining the esophagus, making cancer more likely.

HEART
Massive doses of alcohol can lead to high blood pressure and scar tissue formation in the heart muscle. Fat infiltration can cause the heart to become nearly twice its normal size, which may lead to death from heart failure.

LIVER
The liver is the main organ responsible for metabolizing alcohol. **A**, Heavy drinking causes the liver to become fatty and enlarged, leading to liver dysfunction. **B**, Cirrhosis or scarring eventually appears, which can lead to liver failure and death.

STOMACH AND PANCREAS
Alcohol is toxic to stomach cells and can lead to inflammation of the stomach (gastritis) with pain and bleeding. Alcohol abuse can also lead to inflammation of the pancreas, which can then progress to pancreatic failure and even death.

ASCITES
Fluid produced by the diseased liver may fill the abdomen.

Figure 8-3   Effects of alcohol use on the body. The mind-altering effects of alcohol begin soon after it enters the bloodstream. Within minutes, alcohol numbs nerve cells in the brain. The heart muscle strains to cope with alcohol's depressive action. If drinking continues, the rising BAC causes impaired speech, vision, balance, and judgment. With an extremely high BAC, respiratory failure is possible. Over time, alcohol abuse increases the risk for certain forms of heart disease and cancer and makes liver and pancreas failure more likely.

overexposed to the toxic effects of alcohol. Mental retardation frequently develops.

This exposure has additional disastrous consequences for the developing fetus. Low birth weight, facial abnormalities (e.g., small head, widely spaced eyes), and heart problems are often seen in such infants (Figure 8-4). This combination of effects is called **fetal alcohol syndrome.** Recent estimates indi-

cirrhosis (sir **oh** sis)
Pathological changes to the liver resulting from chronic, heavy alcohol consumption; a frequent cause of death among heavy alcohol users (see Figure 8-3).

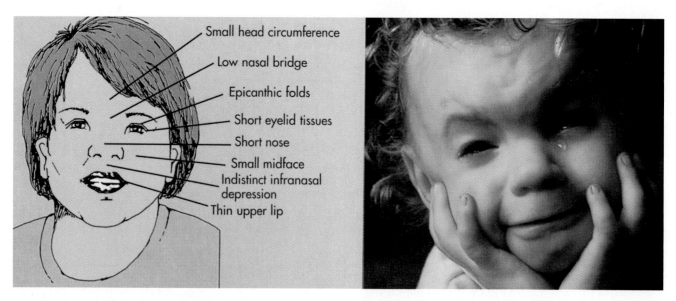

Small head circumference
Low nasal bridge
Epicanthic folds
Short eyelid tissues
Short nose
Small midface
Indistinct infranasal depression
Thin upper lip

Figure 8-4   Fetal alcohol syndrome. The facial features shown are characteristic of affected children. Additional abnormalities in the brain and other internal organs accompany fetal alcohol syndrome but are not obvious from simply looking at the child.

cate that the full expression of this syndrome occurs at a rate of between 1 and 3 per 1000 births. Partial expression (fetal alcohol effects [FAE]) can be seen in 3 to 9 per 1000 live births.[2] In addition, it is likely that many cases of FAE go undetected.

Is there a safe limit to the number of drinks a woman can consume during pregnancy? Since no one can accurately predict the effect of drinking even small amounts of alcohol during pregnancy, the wisest plan is to avoid alcohol altogether.

Because of the critical growth and development that occur during the first months of fetal life, women who have any reason to suspect they are pregnant should stop all alcohol consumption. Furthermore, women who are planning to become pregnant and women who are not practicing effective contraception must also consider keeping their alcohol use to a minimum.

ALCOHOL-RELATED SOCIAL PROBLEMS

Beyond personal health problems, alcohol abuse is related to a variety of social problems. These problems affect the quality of interpersonal relationships, employment stability, and the financial security of both the individual and family. Clearly, alcohol's negative social consequences lower our quality of life. In financial terms the cost of alcohol abuse and dependence has been estimated at more than $150 billion.

The effect of alcohol consumption on several problems was summarized in the *7th Special Report to the U.S. Congress on Alcohol and Health.*[2] This important publication documented reported findings related to accidents, crime and violence, and suicide.

Accidents

The four leading causes of accidental death in the United States (motor vehicle collisions, falls, drownings, and fires and burns) have significant statistical connections to alcohol use. Approximately 40% of all fatal traffic crashes are alcohol related. Further, the likelihood of being involved in a fatal collision is about eight times higher for a drunk driver (0.10% BAC) than for a sober one.

Many people are surprised to learn that falls are the second leading cause of accidental death in the United States, with about 13,000 deaths per year. Alcohol use increases the risk for falls. Various studies suggest that alcohol is involved in between 17% and 53% of deadly falls and between 21% and 77% of nonfatal falls.

Drownings are the third leading cause of accidental death in the United States. Studies have shown that alcohol use is implicated in approximately 38% of these deaths. Over one third of boaters have been found to drink alcohol while boating.

Fires and burns are responsible for an estimated 6000 deaths each year in the United States, the fourth leading cause of accidental death. This cause is also connected to alcohol use: studies indicate that nearly half of burn victims have BACs above the legal limit.

Crime and Violence

You may have noticed at your college that most of the violent behavior and vandalism on campus is related to alcohol use. Indeed, the connection of alcohol to crime has a long history. Prison populations have large percentages of alcohol abusers and alcoholics: People who commit crimes are more likely to have alcohol problems than people in the general population. This is especially true for young criminals. Furthermore, alcohol use has been reported in 67% of all homicides, with either the victim, the perpetrator, or both found to have been drinking. In rape situations, rapists are intoxicated 50% of the time and victims 30% of the time.[6]

Because of research methodological problems, pinpointing alcohol's connection to family violence is difficult.[2] However, it seems clear that among a large number of families, alcohol is associated with violence and other harmful behavior, including physical abuse, child abuse, psychological abuse, and abandonment.[6] The article on pp. 199-200 explores the link between alcohol and violence.

Suicide

The *7th Special Report to the U.S. Congress on Alcohol and Health* points out alcohol's relationship to suicide. Between 20% and 36% of suicide victims have a history of alcohol abuse or were drinking shortly before their suicides. Also, alcohol use is associated with impulsive suicides rather than with premeditated ones. Drinking is also connected with more violent and lethal means of suicide, such as the use of firearms.[2]

For many of these social problems, alcohol use impairs critical judgment and allows a person's behavior to quickly become reckless, antisocial, and deadly. Because most of us wish to minimize problems associated with alcohol use, acting responsibly when we host a party is a first step in this direction.

HOSTING A RESPONSIBLE PARTY

Some people might say that no party is totally safe when alcohol is served. These people are probably right, considering the possibility of unexpected **drug synergism,** overconsumption, and the consequences of released inhibitions. Fortunately, an increasing awareness of the value of responsible party hosting seems to be spreading among college communities. The impetus for this awareness has come from various sources, including respect for an individual's right to choose not to drink alcohol, the growing recognition that many automobile accidents are alcohol related, and the legal threats posed by **host negligence.**

For whatever reasons, responsibly hosting parties at which alcohol is served is becoming a trend, especially among college-educated young adults. The Education Commission of the States' Task Force on Responsible Decisions about Alcohol has generated a list of guidelines for hosting a social event at which alcoholic beverages are served. The list includes the recommendations shown in the Star Box on p. 190.

In addition to these suggestions, the use of a **designated driver** is an important component of responsible alcohol use. By planning to abstain from alcohol or to carefully limit their own alcohol consumption, designated drivers are able to safely transport friends who have been drinking. Have you noticed an increased use of designated drivers in your community? Would you be willing to be a designated driver?

shock
Profound collapse of many vital body functions; evident during acute alcohol intoxication and other serious health emergencies.

asphyxiation
Death resulting from lack of oxygen to the brain.

placenta
The structure through which nutrients, metabolic wastes, and drugs (including alcohol) pass from the bloodstream of the mother into the bloodstream of the developing fetus.

fetal alcohol syndrome
Characteristic birth defects noted in the children of some women who consume alcohol during their pregnancies.

drug synergism (sin er jism**)**
Enhancement of a drug's effect as a result of the presence of additional drugs within the system.

host negligence
A legal term that reflects the failure of a host to provide reasonable care and safety for people visiting the host's residence or business.

designated driver
A person who abstains from or carefully limits alcohol consumption to be able to safely transport other people who have been drinking.

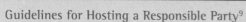

Guidelines for Hosting a Responsible Party[9]

- Provide other social activities as a primary focus when alcohol is served.
- Respect an individual's decision about alcohol if that decision is either to abstain or to drink responsibly.
- Recognize the decision not to drink and the respect it warrants by providing equally attractive and accessible nonalcohol drinks when alcohol is served.
- Recognize that drunkenness is neither healthy nor safe. One should not excuse otherwise unacceptable behavior solely because of "too much to drink."
- Provide food when alcohol is served.
- Serve diluted drinks, and do not urge that glasses be constantly full.

- Keep the cocktail hour before dinner to a reasonable time and consumption limit.
- Recognize your responsibility for the health, safety, and pleasure of both the drinker and the nondrinker by avoiding intoxication and helping others do the same.
- Make contingency plans for intoxication. If it occurs in spite of efforts to prevent it, assume responsibility for the health and safety of guests—for example, by providing transportation home or overnight accommodations.
- Serve or use alcohol only in environments conducive to pleasant and relaxing behavior.

ORGANIZATIONS THAT SUPPORT RESPONSIBLE DRINKING

The serious consequences of the irresponsible use of alcohol have led to the formation of a number of concerned-citizen groups. Although each organization has a unique approach, all attempt to deal objectively with two indisputable facts: Alcohol use is part of our society, and irresponsible alcohol use can be deadly.

Mothers Against Drunk Driving

Mothers Against Drunk Driving (MADD) is a national network of over 400 local chapters in the United States and Canada. MADD attempts to educate people about alcohol's effects on driving and to influence legislation and enforcement of laws related to drunk drivers. MADD clearly had a strong influence on the passage of a federal law requiring states to raise the drinking age to 21 or risk the loss of federal highway funds.

Students Against Driving Drunk

Students Against Driving Drunk (SADD) is an organization composed primarily of high school students whose goal is to reduce alcohol-related deaths among teenagers. Founded in 1981, SADD now has approximately 15,000 chapters and about 4 million members. In this organization, students help educate other students about the consequences of combining drinking and driving. One interesting practice of this organization's effort is to encourage students and their parents to sign a "contract" to provide transportation for each other if either is unable to drive

safely after consuming alcohol. This pact also stipulates that no consequences are to be discussed until the following day.

Boost Alcohol Consciousness Concerning the Health of University Students

BACCHUS is an acronym for Boost Alcohol Consciousness Concerning the Health of University Students. Run by student volunteers, this college-based organization promotes responsible drinking among university students who choose to drink. BACCHUS supports responsible party hosting, including providing quantities of food and nonalcoholic beverages. The individual chapters of BACCHUS (which now total well over 200) are encouraged to use a number of innovative educational approaches to promote alcohol awareness.

Other Approaches

Other responsible approaches to alcohol use are surfacing nearly every day. Even among college fraternity organizations, attitudes toward the indiscriminate use of alcohol are changing. Most fraternity rush functions are now conducted without the use of alcohol.

Another encouraging sign seen on college campuses is the increasing number of alcohol use task forces. Although each of these study committees has its own focus and title, many of these groups are meeting to discuss alcohol-related concerns on their particular campus. These task forces often attempt to formulate detailed, comprehensive policies for alcohol use across the entire campus community.

Membership on these committees often includes students (on-campus and off-campus, graduate and undergraduate), faculty and staff members, academic administrators, residence hall advisors, university police, health center personnel, alumni, and local citizens. Does your college have such a committee?

PROBLEM DRINKING AND ALCOHOLISM

Problem Drinking

At times the line separating **problem drinking** from alcoholism is difficult to distinguish (see the Star Box below). There may be no true line, with the exception that an alcoholic is unable to stop drinking. Problem drinking is a pattern of alcohol use in which a drinker's behavior creates personal difficulties or difficulties for other people. What are some of these behaviors? Examples might be drinking to avoid life stressors, going to work intoxicated, drinking and driving, becoming injured or injuring others while drinking, solitary drinking, morning drinking, an occasional **blackout,** and being told by others that you drink too much. For college students, two clear indications of problem drinking are missing classes and lowered academic performance caused by alcohol involvement. The Health Action Guide at right offers suggestions that can help you keep drinking under control.

Problem drinkers are not always heavy drinkers; they might not be daily or even weekly drinkers. Unlike alcoholics, problem drinkers do not need to drink to maintain "normal" body functions. However, when they do drink, they (and others around them) experience problems . . . sometimes with tragic conse-

HEALTH Action Guide

Tips to Help You Keep Drinking Under Control

- Do not drink before a party.
- Avoid drinking when you are anxious, angry, or depressed.
- Measure the liquor you put in mixed drinks (use only 1-1½ oz).
- Eat ample amounts of food and drink lots of water before and during the time you are drinking.
- Avoid salty foods that may make you drink more than you had planned.
- Drink slowly.
- Do not participate in drinking games.
- Do not drive after drinking; use a designated non-drinking driver.
- Consume only a predetermined number of drinks.
- Stop alcohol consumption at a predetermined hour.

problem drinking
An alcohol use pattern in which a drinker's behavior creates personal difficulties or difficulties for other people.

blackout
A temporary state of amnesia experienced by an alcoholic; an inability to remember events that occurred during a period of alcohol use.

Progressive Stages of Alcohol Dependence

Early	**Middle**	**Late**
• Escape drinking	• Loss of control	• Prolonged binges
• Binge drinking	• Self-hate	• Alcohol used to control withdrawal symptoms
• Guilt feelings	• Impaired social relationships	• Alcohol psychosis
• Sneaking drinks	• Changes in drinking patterns (more frequent binge drinking)	• Nutritional disease
• Difficulty stopping once drinking has begun	• Temporary sobriety	• Frequent blackouts
• Increased tolerance	• Morning drinking	
• Preoccupation with drinking	• Dietary neglect	
• Occasional blackouts	• Increased blackouts	

quences. It is not surprising that problem drinkers are more likely than other drinkers to eventually develop alcoholism. Are there people around you that you believe show signs of problem drinking?

Alcohol and Driving

Reports indicate that the percentage of traffic deaths resulting from alcohol use has dropped to well below 50%. However, the 20,000 deaths attributed annually to drunk driving remains an unacceptably high number, and the additional number of serious injuries is great. All states have raised the legal drinking age to 21 years. Most states have set 0.10% as the BAC at which drivers are considered to be legally drunk (Figure 8-5). However, by December 1997, 15 states had lowered this standard to 0.08%, and legislative efforts are being made in many other states to follow this lead. Many states had also enacted **zero tolerance laws** to help prevent underage drinking and driving.[10] These laws may help the United States achieve some of its major health objectives for the year 2000.

Other programs and policies are being implemented that are designed to prevent intoxicated people from driving. Included are efforts to educate bartenders to recognize intoxicated customers, to encourage people to establish designated drivers, to use off-duty police officers as observers in bars, to use police roadblocks, and to develop mechanical devices that prevent intoxicated drivers from starting their cars.

Alcoholism

In the early 1990s a revised definition of **alcoholism** was established by a joint committee of experts on alco-

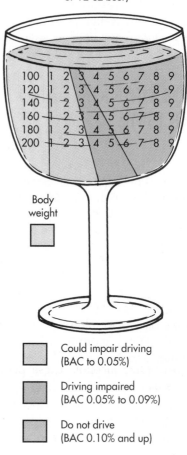

Number of drinks
in 2-hour period
(1½-oz 86-proof liquor
or 12-oz beer)

Body weight

Could impair driving
(BAC to 0.05%)

Driving impaired
(BAC 0.05% to 0.09%)

Do not drive
(BAC 0.10% and up)

Figure 8-5 For most states, a BAC of 0.10% constitutes legal intoxication. However, a BAC as low as 0.05% can impair functioning enough to cause a serious accident.

hol dependence.[11] This committee defined alcoholism as follows:

> Alcoholism is a primary, chronic disease with genetic, psychosocial, and environmental factors influencing its development and manifestations. The disease is often progressive and fatal. It is characterized by impaired control over drinking, preoccupation with the drug alcohol, use of alcohol despite adverse consequences, and distortions in thinking, most notably denial. Each of these symptoms may be continuous or periodic.

This definition incorporates much of the knowledge gained from addiction research during the last two decades. It is well recognized that alcoholics do not drink for the pleasurable effects of alcohol but to escape being sober. For alcoholics, being sober is stressful.

Unlike problem drinking, alcoholism involves a physical addiction to alcohol. For the true alcoholic,

Drinking drivers often hurt themselves and others.

when the body is deprived of alcohol, physical and mental withdrawal symptoms become evident. These withdrawal symptoms can be life threatening. Uncontrollable shaking can progress to nausea, vomiting, hallucinations, shock, and cardiac and pulmonary arrest. Uncontrollable shaking combined with irrational hallucinations is called *delirium tremens* (DT), an occasional manifestation of alcohol withdrawal.

The complex reasons for the physical and emotional dependence of alcoholism have not been fully explained. Why, when more than 100 million adults use alcohol without becoming dependent on it, do 10 million or more others become unable to control its use?

Could alcoholism be an inherited disease? Studies in humans and animals have provided strong evidence that genetics plays a role in some cases of alcoholism. Two forms of alcoholism are thought to be inherited: type I and type II. Type I is thought to take years to develop and may not surface until midlife. Type II is a more severe form and appears to be passed primarily from fathers to sons. This form of alcoholism frequently begins earlier in a person's life and may even start in adolescence.

Genetics may also help protect some Asians from developing alcoholism. About half of all Far East Asians produce low levels of an important enzyme that helps metabolize alcohol. These people cannot tolerate even small amounts of alcohol. Genetic factors pertaining to the absorption rates of alcohol in the intestinal tract have been hypothesized to predispose some Native Americans to alcoholism. It is likely that more research will be undertaken concerning the role of genetic factors in all forms of chemical dependence.

The role of personality traits as conditioning factors in the development of alcoholism has received considerable attention. Factors ranging from unusually low self-esteem to an antisocial personality have been implicated. Additional factors making people susceptible to alcoholism may include excessive reliance on denial, hypervigilance, compulsiveness, and chronic levels of anxiety. Always complicating the study of personality traits is the uncertainty of whether the personality profile is a predisposing factor (perhaps from inheritance) or is caused by alcoholism.

Denial and Enabling

Problem drinkers and alcoholics frequently use the psychological defense mechanism of *denial* to maintain their drinking behavior. By convincing themselves that their lives are not affected by their drinking, problem drinkers and alcoholics are able to maintain their drinking patterns. A person's denial is an unconscious process that is apparent only to rational observers.

Formerly, it was up to alcoholics to admit that their denial was no longer effective before they could be admitted to a treatment program. This is not the case today. Currently, family members, friends, or co-workers of alcohol-dependent people are encouraged to intervene and force an alcohol-dependent person into treatment.

During treatment, it is important for chemically dependent people to break through the security of denial and to admit that alcohol controls their lives. This process will be demanding and often time consuming, but no alternative exists if they are to recover.

For family and friends of chemically dependent people, denial is part of a process known as *enabling*. In this process, people close to the problem drinker or alcoholic inadvertently support drinking behavior by denying that a problem really exists. Enablers unconsciously make excuses for the drinker, try to keep the drinker's work and family life intact, and in effect make the continued abuse of alcohol possible. For example, college students enable problem drinkers when they clean up a drinker's messy room, lie to professors about a student's class absences, and provide class notes or other assistance to a drinker who cannot keep up academically. In fact, even the use of designated drivers has been criticized as enabling behavior (see the Star Box on p. 194).

Alcohol counselors contend that enablers are an alcoholic's worst enemy because they can significantly delay the onset of effective therapy. Do you know of a situation in which you or others have enabled a person with alcohol problems?

Alcoholism and the Family

There is considerable disruption in the families of alcoholics, not only by the consequences of the drinking behavior (such as violence, illness, and unemployment), but also by the uncertainty of the family's role

zero tolerance laws
Laws that severely restrict the right to operate motor vehicles for underage drinkers who have been convicted of driving under any influence.

alcoholism
A primary, chronic disease with genetic, psychosocial, and environmental factors influencing its development and manifestations.

in causing and prolonging the situation. Family members often begin to adopt a variety of new roles that will allow them to cope with the presence of the alcoholic in the family. Among the more commonly seen roles are the family hero, the lost child, the family mascot, and the scapegoat.[6] Unless family members receive appropriate counseling, these roles may remain intact for a lifetime.

Once an alcoholic's therapy has begun, family members are encouraged to participate in many aspects of the recovery. This participation will also help them understand the ways in which they are affected by alcoholism. If therapy and aftercare include participation in Alcoholics Anonymous (AA), family members will be encouraged to become affiliated with related support groups.

Codependence

Within the last decade, a new term has been used to describe the relationship between drug-dependent people and those around them—*codependence.* This term implies a kind of dual addiction. The alcoholic and the person close to the alcoholic are both addicted, one to alcohol and the other to the alcoholic. People who are codependent often find themselves denying the addiction and enabling the alcohol-dependent person.

Unfortunately, this kind of behavior damages both the alcoholic and the codependent. The alcoholic's intervention and treatment may be delayed for a considerable time. Codependent people often pay a heavy price as well. They often become drug or alcohol dependent themselves, or they may suffer a variety of psychological consequences related to guilt, loss of self-esteem, depression, and anxiety. Codependents may be at increased risk for physical and sexual abuse.

Fortunately, researchers continue to explore this dimension of alcoholism. Many students have found some of the sources listed on p. 196 and at the end of this chapter to be especially helpful.

Helping the Alcoholic: Rehabilitation and Recovery

Once an alcoholic realizes that alcoholism is not a form of moral weakness but rather a clearly defined illness, the chances for recovery are remarkably good. It is estimated that as many as two thirds of alcoholics can recover. Recovery is especially enhanced when the addicted person has a good emotional support system, including concerned family members, friends, and employer. When this support system is not well

Are Designated Drivers "Enablers"?
In recent years the number of deaths resulting from drunk driving has declined. This decline can be partially attributed to the use of designated drivers. This is the good news.

However, there may be a down side. Some health professionals are concerned that the use of designated drivers allows the nondrivers to drink more heavily than they might otherwise. In effect, designated drivers "enable" drinkers to be less responsible for their own behavior. The concern is that this freedom from responsibility might eventually lead to further problems for the drinkers. What do you think?

established, the alcoholic's chances for recovery are considerably lower.

AA is a voluntary support group of recovering alcoholics who meet regularly to help each other get and stay sober. Over 19,000 groups exist in the United States. AA encourages alcoholics to admit their lack of power over alcohol and to turn their lives over to a higher power (although the organization is nonsectarian). Members of AA are encouraged not to be judgmental about the behavior of other members. They support anyone with a problem caused by alcohol.

Al-Anon and Alateen are parallel organizations that give support to people who live with alcoholics. Al-Anon is geared toward spouses and other relatives, whereas Alateen focuses on children of alcoholics. Both organizations help members realize that they are not alone and that successful adjustments can be made to nearly every alcoholic-related situation. AA, Al-Anon, and Alateen chapter organizations are usually listed in the telephone book or in the classified sections of local newspapers.

For people who feel uncomfortable with the concept that their lives are controlled by a higher power, *secular recovery programs* are becoming popular. These programs maintain that sobriety comes from within the alcoholic. Secular programs strongly emphasize self-reliance, self-determination, and rational thinking about one's drinking. Secular Organizations for Sobriety (SOS) and Rational Recovery are examples of secular recovery programs.

New Drug to Treat Alcoholism

Could there be a medical cure for alcoholism? For nearly 50 years, the only prescription drug physicians could use to help drinkers stop drinking was

Health on the Web
LEARNING ACTIVITIES

Activity 1

Blood alcohol concentration (BAC) is the ratio of alcohol to total blood volume. The world's leading manufacturer of alcohol breath testing instruments, Intoximeters, Inc., has a web site (http://www.intox.com) where you can instantly estimate your BAC. Go to the site, select *Drink Wheel*, and complete the form listed. When you have submitted the data, your estimated BAC will be instantly computed. Try entering different amounts of alcohol consumed over various time periods. Were you surprised that so few drinks could raise your BAC above the legal limit? What strategies might you use to keep your BAC at a lower level the next time you drink alcohol?

Activity 2

Alateen is for young people whose lives have been affected by someone else's drinking. Visit their web site at http://www.al-anon.org and scroll down to *Alateen: Young People Helping Young People* and click.

Answer the 20 questions listed to decide whether Alateen is for you.

Activity 3

Many students will drink more heavily during college than at any other time in their lives. Assessing your drinking behavior may help you avoid serious alcohol-related problems, such as alcoholism, violence, and drunk driving. Go to the web site at http://www.mayohealth.org/mayo/9707/htm/q.htm and use the educational tool called *Assess Yourself*, provided by Mayo Clinic to help you evaluate your drinking patterns. No record of your individual responses will be kept, and no attempt will be made to identify the person filling out the questionnaire. If the results of the assessment indicate that you should be concerned about your alcohol use, seek advice from your campus counseling center or one of the organizations listed on the Health Reference Guide at the back of this book.

Antabuse. Antabuse would cause drinkers to become extremely nauseated whenever they used alcohol.

In 1995 the Food and Drug Administration approved a drug (naltrexone) that works by reducing the craving for alcohol and the pleasurable sensations felt when drinking. Combining naltrexone with conventional behavior modification has been shown to reduce alcohol relapse significantly. It will be interesting to see how effective this drug will be on a long-term basis.

CURRENT ALCOHOL CONCERNS
Adult Children of Alcoholic Parents

In recent years a new dimension of alcoholism has been identified—the unusually high prevalence of alcoholism among adult children of alcoholics (ACOAs). It is estimated that these children are about four times more likely to develop alcoholism than children whose parents are not alcoholics. Even the ACOAs who do

not become alcoholics may have a difficult time adjusting to everyday living. Janet Geringer Woititz, author of the best-selling book *Adult Children of Alcoholics*,[12] describes 13 traits that, to some degree, most ACOAs exhibit (see the Star Box on p. 196).

In response to this concern, support groups have been formed to prevent the adult sons and daughters of alcoholics from developing the condition that afflicted their parents (see the Star Box on p. 196). If a stronger link for an inherited genetic predisposition to alcoholism is found, these groups may play an even greater role in the prevention of alcoholism.

Women and Alcohol

For decades, women have consumed less alcohol and had fewer alcohol-related problems than men. As we move through the 1990s, evidence is mounting that a greater percentage of women are choosing to drink and that some subgroups of women, especially young women, are drinking more heavily. An increased number of admissions of women to treat-

Common Traits of ACOAs

Adult children of alcoholics may:

- Have difficulty identifying normal behavior
- Have difficulty following a project from beginning to end
- Lie when it would be just as easy to tell the truth
- Judge themselves without mercy
- Have difficulty having fun
- Take themselves very seriously
- Have difficulty with intimate relationships
- Overreact to changes over which they have no control
- Constantly seek approval and affirmation
- Feel that they are different from other people
- Be super-responsible or super-irresponsible
- Be extremely loyal, even in the face of evidence that the loyalty is undeserved
- Tend to lock themselves into a course of action without considering the consequences

ment centers may also reflect that alcohol consumption among women is on the rise.[2]

Studies indicate that there are now almost as many female as male alcoholics. However, there appear to be differences between men and women when it comes to alcohol abuse:[6] (1) More women than men can point to a specific triggering event (such as a divorce, death of a spouse, a career change, or children leaving home) that started them drinking heav-

ily. (2) Alcoholism among women often starts later and progresses more quickly than alcoholism among men. (3) Women tend to be prescribed more mood-altering drugs than men. Thus women face greater risk of drug interaction or cross-tolerance. (4) Nonalcoholic men tend to divorce their alcoholic spouses nine times more often than nonalcoholic women divorce their alcoholic spouses. Thus alcoholic women are not as likely to have a family support system to aid them in their recovery attempts. (5) Female alcoholics do not tend to receive as much social support as men in their treatment and recovery. (6) Unmarried, divorced, or single-parent women tend to have significant economic problems that may make entry into a treatment program especially difficult.[6] In light of the generally recognized educational, occupational, and social gains made by women during the last two decades, it will be interesting to see whether these male-female differences continue. What's your best guess?

Alcohol Advertising

Every few years, careful observers can see subtle changes in the ways the alcoholic beverage industry markets its products (see the Star Box on p. 197).

Recently, the marketing push appears to be directed toward minorities (through advertisements for malt liquor and fortified wines), women (through wine and wine cooler ads), and youth (through trendy, young adult–oriented commercials).

Resources for Adult Children of Alcoholics

Experts agree that adult children of alcoholics who believe they have come to terms with their feelings sometimes face lingering problems. It can prove worthwhile to seek help if you experience the following:

- Difficulty in identifying your needs
- Persistent anger or sadness
- Inability to enjoy your successes
- Willingness to tolerate inappropriate behavior
- Continual fear of losing control

Support groups to contact for more information are listed below:

Al-Anon Adult Family Groups
P.O. Box 862 Midtown Station
New York, NY 10018-0862
(212) 302-7240

Al-Anon Adult Children Groups
One Park Avenue
New York, NY 10016
(212) 302-7240

Children of Alcoholics Foundation, Inc.
200 Park Avenue, 31st Floor
New York, NY 10010
(212) 351-2680

National Council on Alcoholism and Drug Dependence
12 West 21st Street
New York, NY 10010
(212) 206-6770
(800) NCA-CALL (800-622-2255)

On the college campus, aggressive alcohol campaigns have used rock stars, beach party scenes, athletic event sponsorships, and colorful newspaper supplements as vehicles to encourage the purchase of alcohol. Critics claim that most of the collegiate advertising is directed at the "below age 21" crowd and that the prevention messages are not strong enough to offset the potential health damage to this population. As a college student, how do you feel about alcohol advertising on your campus? If you are a nontraditional student, do you find the advertising campaigns amusing or potentially dangerous?

Alcohol Ads on the Web

Public health experts and children's advocates are becoming increasingly concerned about the way alcohol products are marketed in cyberspace. More than 35 alcohol brands maintain colorful, slick websites that use games, on-line chats, and cartoon characters to promote messages that advocate drinking. For example, a cartoonish rodent called J. C. Roadhog on the Cuervo website makes his way through the desert strewn with empty tequila bottles. At the Anheuser-Busch website, young Internet surfers can visit "The Pad" to meet the three frogs from the famous series of television commercials.[14]

Representatives from Cuervo, Anheuser-Busch, and Seagram deny that the web advertisements are intended to attract underage drinkers. Nevertheless, the Center for Media Education issues a report urging liquor and beer companies to make their websites less appealing to children. Do you think messages on these Internet sites should be regulated?

Summary

- Alcohol is the drug of choice among college students and the rest of American society.
- Many factors affect the rate of absorption of alcohol into the bloodstream.
- As BAC rises, predictable depressant effects take place.
- People with acute alcohol intoxication must receive first-aid care immediately.
- The health effects of chronic alcohol abuse are quite serious.
- Problem drinking reflects an alcohol use pattern in which a drinker's behavior creates personal difficulties or problems for others.
- Alcoholism is a primary, chronic disease with a variety of possible causes and characteristics.
- Denial, enabling, codependence, ACOAs, and alcohol advertising are current issues related to alcohol abuse in the United States.
- Recovery and rehabilitation programs can be effective in helping alcoholics become sober.
- Antabuse and naltrexone are drugs prescribed by physicians to help alcoholics stop drinking.

Review Questions

1. What percentage of American adults consume alcohol? Approximately what percentage of adults are classified as abstainers? What percentage of college students drink?
2. What is binge drinking?
3. What is meant by the term *proof*?
4. What is the nutritional value of alcohol? How do "lite" and low-alcohol beverages compare?
5. Identify and explain the various factors that influence the absorption of alcohol. Why is it important to be aware of these factors?
6. What is BAC? Describe the general sequence of physiological events that takes place when a person drinks alcohol at a rate faster than the liver can oxidize it.
7. What are the signs and symptoms of acute alcohol intoxication? What are the first-aid steps you should take to help a person with this problem?
8. Describe the characteristics of fetal alcohol syndrome and fetal alcohol effects.
9. Explain the differences between problem drinking and alcoholism.
10. What roles do denial and enabling play in alcoholism? What is codependence?
11. What are some common traits of ACOAs?
12. What unique alcohol-related problems exist for women?

Think About This . . .

- How much is your decision to drink or not drink influenced by those around you?
- Did you know that drinking alcohol in cold weather actually causes heat loss? The feeling of warmth results from the loss of body heat caused by the dilation of blood vessels under the skin. In effect, you may feel warmer but are actually getting colder.
- This chapter refers to data indicating that about one third of college drinkers can be considered heavy drinkers. Do you think this is true at your college?
- What role should men play in the prevention of fetal alcohol syndrome?
- How can you tell whether you and your friends are drinking responsibly?
- Do you believe it is your responsibility to make sure friends do not drink and drive?
- Do you think your drinking pattern will change when you are out of college?

References

1. Drug use among American teens shows some signs of leveling off after a long rise, Monitoring the Future press release, University of Michigan News and Information Services, December 20, 1997.
2. U.S. Department of Health and Human Services: *Alcohol and health: Seventh special report to the U.S. Congress,* DHHS Pub No (ADM) 90-1656, Washington, DC, 1990, U.S. Government Printing Office.
3. U.S. Bureau of the Census: *Statistical abstract of the United States, 1994,* annual, ed 114, Washington, DC, 1995, U.S. Government Printing Office.
4. Payne WA, Hahn DB: Alcohol consumption of students in the personal health class, 1997, unpublished research.
5. Presley CA, Meilman PW: *Alcohol and drugs on American college campuses: a report to college presidents, June 1992,* U.S. Department of Education, Drug Prevention in Higher Education Program (FIPSE Grant), Southern Illinois University Student Health Program Wellness Center.
6. Kinney J, Leaton G: *Loosening the grip: a handbook of alcohol information,* ed 6. St. Louis, 1998, WCB/McGraw-Hill.
7. Frezza M et al: High blood alcohol levels in women: role of decreased gastric alcohol dehydrogenase activity and first-pass metabolism, *N Engl J Med* 322:(4) 95-99, 1990.
8. Ray O, Ksir C: *Drugs, society, and human behavior,* ed 7, St. Louis, 1996, Mosby.
9. Task Force on Responsible Decisions about Alcohol: *Interim report no 2,* Denver, Education Commission of the States.
10. Marshall S: Zero tolerance sobering for teen drivers, *USA Today,* p. 1-A, June 19, 1995.
11. Morse RM et al: The definition of alcoholism, *JAMA,* 268(8):1012-1014, 1992.
12. Woititz JG: *Adult children of alcoholics,* Pompano Beach, FL, 1990, Health Communications, Inc.
13. U.S. Department of Health and Human Services: *NIAAA Alcohol Alert,* No 13 (PH 297), Washington, DC, July 1991, US Government Printing Office.
14. Schiesel S: On web, new threats to young are seen, *New York Times Cyber Times* (online edition), March 7, 1997.

Suggested Readings

Makela K (editor): *Alcoholics Anonymous as a mutual-help movement: a study in eight societies,* Madison, WI, 1996, University of Wisconsin Press.
This book is one of the first comprehensive studies of Alcoholics Anonymous as a social movement and a model for small-group interaction. Experts collaborated to examine the history of an organization that was founded in the 1930s and now has nearly 2 million members worldwide. The book describes what happens at AA meetings, how AA is organized, and how it serves as a professional health care provider across many cultures.

Schaefer D: *Choices and consequences: what to do when a teenager uses alcohol or drugs.* Minneapolis, MN, 1996, The Johnson Institute.
This paperback book, published by the highly regarded Johnson Institute, is a useful guide that can help parents, teachers, youth leaders, and other adults recognize and better understand all types of drinking behavior or drug use by teenagers. Schaefer helps adults recognize the role that intervention can play in working against a teenager's denial and resistance.

ON...

Alcohol and Violence

In recent years, there has been an increase in public service messages to raise awareness about driving under the influence of alcohol. In fact, the massive campaign against drinking and driving has been quite successful in reducing the number of drunk-driving accidents and fatalities. However, people may think that as long as a person doesn't get behind the wheel, it's okay to drink. But there are other potential dangers to the abuse of alcohol. One particular problem that perhaps has not been stressed enough in the media is the link between alcohol use and violent crime.[1]

The Link Between Alcohol and Violence

The first question that arises when discussing the relationship between alcohol use and violence is whether there is a link at all. Obviously, not everyone who drinks becomes violent, but in many violent crimes at least one person involved has been drinking. The answer is perhaps that alcohol by itself is not enough to cause violence, but use of alcohol may be one of several factors that act in combination to cause violent behavior in some instances.[2]

Who is most likely to be involved in an alcohol-related violent crime? A 9-year study of over 4000 Los Angeles homicide victims suggests that men are much more likely to be involved than women. In the study, 51.3% of the male victims had detectable blood alcohol concentrations compared with 25.8% of the female victims.[2] Other studies have shown that young people under age 30 are more likely than older people to be involved in both sexual and nonsexual assault when alcohol is a factor. Data on race and ethnicity are inconclusive; some studies show that whites are more likely to be involved in alcohol-related homicides, whereas others show that African-Americans are. In the Los Angeles study, 38.2% of Hispanic homicide victims had detectable blood alcohol concentrations; this places them between the percentage figures for male victims and female victims and thus shows no tendency for or against involvement in alcohol-related violence. Alcohol-related homicides and assaults are more likely to occur on weekends than weekdays in part because more people tend to drink on weekends.[2]

Alcohol and Types of Violent Crime

The risk of a person's perpetrating a violent event is higher among heavy drinkers than light drinkers. Heavy drinkers are also at higher risk of being victims of violent crime and are also more likely to inflict and to receive violent injuries.[3] A Johns Hopkins University study shows that being a victim of sexual abuse or assault is also linked to high rates of alcohol use.[4] An environment where alcohol is prevalent is a risk factor associated with gun injuries, particularly deaths among youths.[5] Alcohol-related violence tends to be more prevalent in urban environments. It is estimated that eliminating the glut of inner city alcohol outlets could cut the U.S. homicide rate by 10% and could save 2000 lives annually.[6]

Alcohol plays a significant role in various types of violent crime. Substantial numbers of sexual-assault victims and offenders were drinking before their crime occurred. Alcohol use is present in over half of all domestic violence cases, and frequency of drunkenness for husbands appears to be associated with spouse abuse.[2] One study estimated that incidence of spouse abuse were almost 15 times higher for households where husbands were described as often drunk as opposed to never drunk. And drinking may also increase the risk of becoming a robbery victim.[2]

Campus Crime and the Effects of Alcohol

Of particular interest to college students are the data linking campus crimes to alcohol use. A USA Today study of 13,000 students suggests that as many as 4 out of 5 campus crimes committed by students are related to alcohol or drug use or both. The attitudes of college students may be a contributing factor to alcohol abuse on campus; 85% of freshmen in the survey condoned binge drinking (defined in this study as over 5 drinks in a continuous period). Victims of violent crime on campus generally reported heavier drinking habits than nonvictims,[7] and this parallels data from the general population.[2] When sexual assaults and rapes were reported, both the perpetrator and the victim had typically been drinking.[7]

So why is alcohol a contributing factor in violent crime? Alcohol acts as a depressant, which can reduce reaction time, impair coordination, and cloud judgment. Such impairment could decrease the chances of avoiding personal injury once a physical altercation begins. Alcohol also decreases inhibitions and may increase aggressive behavior. It also may increase the likelihood of inflicting or receiving a severe injury during a violent act and has been shown to increase the severity of injuries obtained in violent acts. Alcohol impairs cognitive abilities and may increase the chances for miscommunication or misinterpretation during verbal conflicts.[2,3]

What You Can Do

Although alcohol alone may not cause violence, when alcohol is introduced into a situation that has the potential to become violent, it can increase the chances that violence will occur. As the number of drunk drivers on the road has decreased, so has the number of drunk-driving accidents and fatalities. It seems logical to assume that if alcohol is kept out of the hands of people who are predisposed to violence, the number of alcohol-related crimes may also decrease. This is not always possible, but it is possible for you to use good common sense when you are drinking or if you are with people who are drinking. Try to avoid potentially violent situations, and avoid people drinking around you who are acting in a reckless or violent manner. Drink in moderation, and help your companions recognize when they have had too much. Perhaps you or one of your companions can remain sober (a "designated thinker") to help avoid potentially dangerous situations and stay safe while partying.

For Discussion . . .

Have you ever encountered an angry drinker? Is there a safe way to handle a person who is drunk and intending to do harm to someone? If you have ever been drunk, do you feel that you could have controlled your actions in a confrontation while you were drunk?

References

1. Jamiolkowski RM: *Drugs and domestic violence*. Minneapolis, MN, 1997, Hazelden.
2. Messerschmidt PM: Epidemiology of alcohol related violence, *Alcohol Health and Research World*, 17(2), 1993.
3. Cherpitel CJ: What emergency room studies reveal about alcohol involvement in violence-related injuries, *Alcohol Health and Research World*, 17(2), 1993.
4. Violence, drugs, alcohol spur decline of youth health across U.S., study says, *Jet*, 88(7), June 26, 1995.
5. Voelker R: Taking aim at handgun violence, *JAMA* 273(22), 1995.
6. Abramson H: Quick fix for violence: cut back on liquor stores, *Nation's Cities Weekly*, 18(3), 1995.
7. Siegel D: What is behind the growth of violence on college campuses? *USA Today Magazine*, 122(2588), May 1994.

Rejecting Tobacco Use

Healthy People: Looking Ahead to 2010

Several of the original *Healthy People 2000* objectives were aimed at reducing the use of tobacco products, especially cigarettes, to prevent heart disease, stroke, and lung cancer and to promote physical activity, fitness, and oral health.

Although the 1995 *Midcourse Review* did not assess progress in these areas, other sources of information indicated that neither lung cancer nor chronic obstructive lung disease rates had declined at mid-decade. Smoking rates had leveled off for men and nearly leveled off for women but had increased among adolescents. Accordingly, no progress was expected toward preventing the other tobacco-related diseases.

Healthy People 2010 will focus on several areas related to tobacco use, such as reducing the incidence of chronic disease, increasing levels of physical activity, improving environmental health, reducing the incidence of oral disease, and improving maternal and child health. A principal goal of *Healthy People 2010* is to increase years of healthy life among Americans; therefore, decreasing tobacco use and reducing exposure to secondhand smoke are absolute necessities.

Today the evidence linking tobacco use to impaired health is beyond any serious challenge.[1] The regular user of tobacco products, particularly cigarettes, is more likely to become sick, remain sick for extended periods, and die prematurely than a nonuser. It is estimated that tobacco use, and cigarette smoking in particular, will result in 2 million deaths between 1986 and the year 2000, with nearly 419,000 deaths occurring annually.[1] Consequently, any contention made by the tobacco industry suggesting that tobacco use is not dangerous is little more than a groundless statement that ignores the growing weight of scientific evidence.

TOBACCO USE IN AMERICAN SOCIETY

In 1995 the Centers for Disease Control and Prevention and the Institute for Social Research, at the University of Michigan, indicated that 25.5% of adults 18 and older were smokers. Men are slightly more likely to smoke than women. Smoking rates among men have fallen steadily since 1964, while rates among women increased until the early 1990s, when they began to level off.

Use among College Students and Young Adults

Smoking rates among college students and young adults dropped significantly between 1964 and 1987 and then remained fairly constant until 1991, when smoking rates increased in both groups. Young adults age 19 to 28 who were not students had higher smoking rates (21.7%) than college students (13.8%).[2] Most of these smokers began smoking as teenagers.

Today, late adolescents and early young adults are much more likely to smoke than they were in 1991. Among 18- to 25-year-olds, 35.5% are smokers, with men being more likely to smoke than women.[3]

The Influence of Education

The more formal education an adult has completed, the less likely he or she is to smoke. Education helps people understand the risks of cigarette smoking. In contrast to the general population, in which a higher percentage of men than women smoke, college women are more likely to smoke than college men, perhaps because they want to control their weight. In 1990 16% of college women smoked, whereas only 12% of college men smoked.[4] African-American men enrolled in predominantly black colleges are the

group of college students least likely to smoke. Unfortunately, data being analyzed at the present time indicate that smoking has increased significantly among college students.

How much do you know about cigarette smoking? Find out by completing the Personal Assessment on pp. 204-205.

Cigarette Preferences

Today only a small percentage of smokers prefer the small, unfiltered cigarettes that were popular until the 1950s. Even the king-size filtered cigarettes in vogue during the 1960s have lost popularity. These high-tar, high-nicotine cigarettes have been replaced by low-tar, low-nicotine (15 mg tar or less) and ultralow-tar, ultralow-nicotine (4 mg tar or less) brands, which have a major share of the market. However, tobacco industry documents indicate that these tar levels may be understated because of the method of testing used by the Federal Trade Commission.[5]

Advertising Approaches

The change in the American public's preference in cigarettes is a reflection of the strength of the tobacco industry in shaping demand for their products. Through continuous product development, skilled marketing, aggressive political lobbying, and diversification, the industry has managed to remain viable in the face of overwhelming evidence that their products are life threatening. Several of their survival techniques are:

- Shrink-wrapping three packs of brand-name cigarettes and selling them for the price of two, or offering mail-in rebate coupons, making the products more affordable to young and low-income buyers
- Continued marketing of generic brands under the label of "value brands"
- Lowering the price of brand-name cigarettes to compete with value brands
- Carefully targeted advertising, particularly to women, minorities, and less-educated young adults
- Youth-oriented advertisements (while simultaneously supporting public policy statements to control minors' access to cigarettes)
- Increased marketing of tobacco products overseas where health restrictions are less forceful (see the Learning from All Cultures box on p. 206)
- Acquiring non–tobacco-related companies (corporate diversification) to minimize the loss of revenues from decreased sales of tobacco products

Fighting Big Tobacco: Is a Settlement in Sight?

In 1997, the attorneys general of 41 states filed a massive class action suit against the tobacco industry. The states' aim is to recoup 350 billion dollars of state and federal money spent by Medicaid to treat ill and dying smokers. Tobacco-related illnesses tend to be chronic and severe, and the cost of their treatment often depletes the financial resources of uninsured smokers and their families. Medicaid must then step in to pick up the hefty tab for treatment. In Minnesota, Blue Cross/Blue Shield joined that state's class action suit to recover excessive losses associated with what it termed "unnecessary illnesses."

After decades of failed lawsuits brought by private citizens, what prompted the attorneys general to confront the tobacco industry? In the mid-1990s, a disgruntled employee of Brown & Williamson, the nation's third largest tobacco company, left his employer with nearly 4,000 documents from the company's archives. These historic "tobacco papers" included memos in which tobacco company executives admitted their knowledge that cigarette smoking is addictive and causes cancer. The papers also described the tobacco industry's attempts to cover up this knowledge and detailed the companies' plans for recruiting new smokers to replace those who had died prematurely of smoking-related causes. The subsequent court-ordered release of almost 400,000 additional documents, including letters, memos, reports, research records, and position papers, has established beyond question that the tobacco industry engaged in a large-scale cover-up of its activities.

In an effort to avoid the expense of facing each state individually in court (five of the 41 states have now settled separately), the industry has encouraged Congress to draft a settlement that will satisfy all parties involved in the class action suit. In addition to a monetary settlement, the states and various public health advocacy groups want the plan to increase federal taxes on tobacco products, to call for stricter regulation of the advertising and sale of tobacco products to young people, and to grant the FDA authority to regulate the nicotine content of tobacco products. In return, the tobacco industry expects the plan to offer protection from future lawsuits in which plaintiffs seek compensation for tobacco-related illnesses and deaths.

A settlement acceptable to both the states and the tobacco industry has not yet been reached. Congress's efforts to draft such a settlement have been continually hampered by the political relationship between Congress and Big Tobacco, by disagreements between Republicans and Democrats, and by the conflicting interests of the executive and legislative branches of government. Tobacco industry representatives say that if Congress does not propose a reasonable settlement soon, the industry will withdraw its cooperation with the federal government and begin to fight the class action suits in state courts. As you read this chapter, the outcome of the dispute has probably been decided. Do you know whether a settlement was reached? If so, what were its consequences for the states, for the tobacco industry, and for the American public health?

- Marshalling tobacco users into a "grass roots" effort to counter the growing political power of antismoking groups

Clearly, the tobacco industry remains healthy and their products remain life threatening to smokers and nonsmokers alike.

Pipe and Cigar Smoking

Many people believe that pipe or cigar smoking is a safe alternative to cigarette smoking. Unfortunately, this is not the case. All forms of tobacco present users with a series of health threats.

When compared with cigarette smokers, pipe and cigar smokers have cancer of the mouth, throat, larynx (voice box), and esophagus at the same frequency. Cigarette smokers are more likely than pipe and cigar smokers to have lung cancer, chronic obstructive lung disease (COLD), and heart disease. However, the incidence of respiratory disease and heart disease in pipe and cigar smokers is still greater than that among nonusers of tobacco.

THE DEVELOPMENT OF DEPENDENCE ON TOBACCO PRODUCTS

Dependence can imply both a physical and psychological relationship. Particularly with cigarettes, *physical dependence* or *addiction,* with its associated *tolerance, withdrawal,* and **titration,** is strongly developed by nearly one half of all smokers. Most of the remaining population of smokers will experience lesser degrees of physical dependence.[6] *Psychological dependence* or

---

titration (tie **tray** shun)
Particular level of a drug within the body; adjusting the level of nicotine by adjusting the rate of smoking.

PERSONAL ASSESSMENT

How Much Do You Know about Cigarette Smoking?

Assumption

1. There are now safe cigarettes on the market.

2. A small number of cigarettes can be smoked without risk.
3. Most early changes in the body resulting from cigarette smoking are temporary.
4. Filters provide a measure of safety to cigarette smokers.
5. Low-tar, low-nicotine cigarettes are safer than high-tar, high-nicotine brands.

6. Mentholated cigarettes are better for the smoker than are nonmentholated brands.

7. It has been scientifically proven that cigarette smoking causes cancer.
8. No specific agent capable of causing cancer has ever been identified in the tobacco used in smokeless tobacco.
9. The cure rate for lung cancer is so good that no one should fear developing this form of cancer.

10. Smoking is not harmful as long as the smoke is not inhaled.

11. The "smoker's cough" reflects underlying damage to the tissue of the airways.

12. Cigarette smoking does not appear to be associated with damage to the heart and blood vessels.

13. Because of the design of the placenta, smoking does not present a major risk to the developing fetus.

14. Women who smoke cigarettes and use an oral contraceptive should decide which they wish to continue because there is a risk in using both.

15. Air pollution is a greater risk to our respiratory health than is cigarette smoking.

16. Addiction, in the sense of physical addiction, is found in conjunction with cigarette smoking.

Discussion

F   Depending on the brand, some cigarettes contain less tar and nicotine; none are safe, however.

F   Even a low level of smoking exposes the body to harmful substances in tobacco smoke.
T   Some changes, however, cannot be reversed—particularly changes associated with emphysema.
T   However, the protection is far from adequate.

T   Many people, however, smoke low-tar, low-nicotine cigarettes in a manner that makes them just as dangerous as stronger cigarettes.
F   Menthol simply makes cigarette smoke feel cooler. The smoke contains all of the harmful agents found in the smoke from regular cigarettes.
T   Particularly lung cancer and cancers of the larynx, esophagus, oral cavity, and urinary bladder.
F   Unfortunately, smokeless tobacco is no safer than the tobacco that is burned. The user of smokeless tobacco swallows much of what the smoker inhales.
F   Approximately 14% of people who have lung cancer will live the 5 years required to meet the medical definition of "cured."
F   Because of the toxic material in smoke, even its contact with the tissue of the oral cavity introduces a measure of risk in this form of cigarette use.
T   The "cough" occurs in response to an inability to clear the airway of mucus as a result of changes in the cells that normally keep the air passages clear.
F   Cigarette smoking is in fact the single most important risk factor in the development of cardiovascular disease.
F   Children born to women who smoked during pregnancy show a variety of health impairments, including smaller birth size, premature birth, and more illnesses during the first year of life. Smoking women also have more stillbirths than nonsmokers.
T   Women over 35 years of age, in particular, are at risk of experiencing serious heart disease should they continue using both cigarettes and an oral contraceptive.
F   Although air pollution does expose the body to potentially serious problems, the risk is considerably less than that associated with smoking.
T   Dependence, including true physical addiction, is widely recognized in cigarette smokers.

17. Among the best "teachers" a young smoker has are his or her parents.

T   There is a strong correlation between cigarette smoking of parents and the subsequent smoking of their children. Parents who do not want their children to smoke should not smoke.

18. Nonsmoking and higher levels of education are directly related.

T   The higher one's level of education, the less likely one is to smoke.

19. About as many women smoke cigarettes as do men.

T   Although in the past, more men smoked than did women, the gap is narrowing.

20. Fortunately, for those who now smoke, stopping is relatively easy.

F   Unfortunately, relatively few smokers can quit. The best advice is never to begin smoking.

To Carry This Further . . .
Were you surprised at the number of items that you answered correctly? In what areas did you hold misconceptions regarding cigarette smoking? Do you think that most university students are as knowledgeable as you?

Where do you see the general public in terms of its understanding of cigarette smoking? How can the health care community do a better job in educating the public about tobacco use?

---

habituation, with its accompanying psychological *compulsion* and *indulgence,* is frequently seen.

Compulsion is a strong emotional desire to continue tobacco use despite restrictions on smoking and the awareness of health risks. Very likely, the user is "compelled" to engage in uninterrupted tobacco use in fear of the unpleasant physical, emotional, and social effects that result from discontinuing use. In compulsion, indulgence is seen as "rewarding" oneself for aligning with a particular group or behavior pattern. Indulgence is made possible by the existence of various reward systems built around the use of tobacco.

Much to the benefit of the tobacco industry, dependence on tobacco is easily established. Many experts believe that physical dependence on tobacco is far more easily established than is dependence on alcohol, cocaine (other than crack), or heroin. Of all people who experiment with cigarettes, 85% develop various aspects of a dependent relationship. This potential for causing dependence, including addiction, has prompted the FDA to request that tobacco products be defined as drug-delivery systems, which would allow the FDA to regulate their availability.

A small percentage of smokers, known as "chippers," can smoke a few cigarettes on a daily basis without becoming dependent. Experts believe that they are less likely to use cigarettes to influence their mood and thus do not "require" cigarettes to feel a sense of pleasure. Unfortunately, many inexperienced smokers feel that they too are only "social smokers"; however, a few additional months of this type of occasional smoking could be a transitional period into a dependence pattern of tobacco use.

Physiological Factors

In the brain, **nicotine** stimulates the production of excitatory neurotransmitters, including norepinephrine, dopamine, acetylcholine, and serotonin, that generate a pleasurable sensation of arousal. Wanting to maintain this feeling of arousal, the smoker inhales again and again. Several hundred puffs per day quickly establish the schedule necessary to maintain the desired effect.

Beyond the action described above, nicotine may also stimulate the release of adrenocorticotropic hormone (ACTH) from the pituitary gland (see Chapter 3). In response to ACTH, beta endorphins (naturally occurring opiate-like chemicals) are produced in specific areas of the brain, leading to mild feelings of euphoria. Perhaps this stresslike response mechanism involving ACTH may also account for the increased energy expenditure seen in smokers and thus their tendency to maintain lower body weight than nonsmokers.

When these physiological responses are viewed collectively, nicotine may be seen as biochemically influencing brain activity by enhancing the extent and strength of various forms of "communication" between different brain areas. If this is the case, it is apparent why once addicted, the functioning of the

nicotine
Physiologically active, dependence-producing drug found in tobacco.

LEARNING *from* ALL CULTURES

Tobacco Use

American cigarette companies are coping with the declining U.S. cigarette consumption by increasing their sales abroad, especially in developing nations. In the industrialized world, smoking is decreasing about 1% each year. However, in Asia and Latin America the incidence of smoking is growing 7% faster than the population. In Africa, it is growing 18% faster.

The 1,836 cigarettes smoked per capita in the United States annually pales in comparison with the 4,153 and 2,793 cigarettes smoked per person in South Korea and Japan, respectively. Per capita consumption exceeds 2,100 in many European countries, including Hungary, Greece, Poland, and Romania.[7]

Even with the availability of low- and ultralow-tar and low- and ultralow-nicotine cigarettes, given enough time, the health effects of cigarette smoking will begin to be seen in these countries. Who will take responsibility for the sickness and death that will occur?

Although the tobacco industry continues to advertise in developing countries, some governments of the Latin American countries are passing legislation restricting advertising and promotion of tobacco products. Fifteen Latin American countries have enacted legislation to discourage the use of cigarettes by adolescents and children, and 13 of those countries have restricted the kind of advertising that targets young people. In six Latin American countries, it is illegal to sell tobacco products to minors.

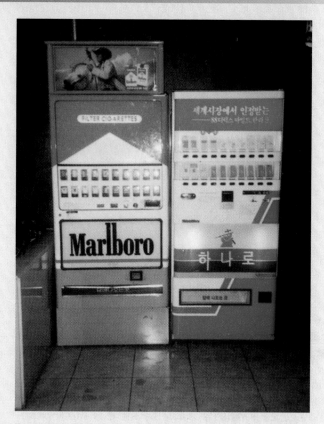

smoker's nervous system is much altered in comparison with that of nonsmokers.

Yet another explanation, called *self-medication*, suggests that nicotine, through the effects of mood-enhancing neurotransmitters, may allow smokers to "treat" feelings of tiredness and lack of motivation. In other words, a "smoke" lifts the spirits, if only briefly. Eventually, however, smokers become dependent on tobacco as a "medication" to make them feel better. Because tobacco is a legal drug, it becomes "preferred" over equally effective illegal drugs such as cocaine and stimulants.

Eventually for almost all smokers to some degree, smoking behavior is adjusted to maintain titration and prevent the uncomfortableness of withdrawal. Thus for most smokers, the desire to not experience withdrawal is as important as the arousal produced by nicotine.

Nicotine as an Addictive Drug

A great deal of interest and controversy now exists regarding information contained in documents released by people once inside the tobacco industry pertaining to the addictive nature of nicotine. Included among these issues are the extent to which the tobacco industry was aware of the addictive nature of nicotine and the appropriateness of studies conducted by the tobacco industry to determine whether young children would become future smokers. Further issues include allegations that the tobacco industry adjusted the pH levels of smokeless tobacco brands to alter nicotine levels and that research was conducted by the industry regarding nicotine enhancement of tobacco products.[8] Many people believe that if tobacco companies knew of the dangers of smoking and nevertheless encouraged nicotine addiction, they should compensate smokers or their families for losses resulting from smoking-related illnesses. This topic is discussed in the Star Box below.

Although these issues are far from resolved and a lawsuit has been won by the tobacco industry against the American Broadcasting Corporation for publicizing aspects of these documents, the FDA and various other health organizations remain convinced that tobacco products are, in fact, drug delivery systems intended to deliver a powerfully addictive drug, nicotine. If this latter contention is supported by the U.S. Congress, the FDA could be given the power to regulate the availability of tobacco products.

Psychosocial Factors

In the view of behavioral scientists, dependence on tobacco can also be explained on the basis of psychosocial factors. Both research and general observation support many of the powerful influences these factors have on the beginning smoker.

Modeling

Because tobacco use is a learned behavior, it is reasonable to accept that *modeling* acts as a stimulus to experimental smoking. Modeling suggests that susceptible people smoke to emulate, or model their behavior after, smokers whom they admire or with whom they share other types of social or emotional bonds. Particularly for young adolescents (ages 14 to 17), smoking behavior correlates with the smoking behavior of slightly older peers and very young adults (ages 18 to 22), older siblings, and to some degree, parents. Is it possible that the very young and attractive models used in tobacco (and beer) advertisements may be seen by young adolescents as being closer to their own age than they really are?

Modeling is particularly evident when smoking is a central factor in peer group formation and peer

Tobacco Industry Liability

For years, ill and dying smokers (and their survivors) have been suing, without success, tobacco companies for damages resulting from tobacco-induced illnesses. The success for the industry in countering these suits has been built around the contention that before 1964, they were unaware of any suspected dangers, and since 1966, they have warned smokers of the dangers they faced when using cigarettes. Accordingly, smokers were found to be responsible for their own poor judgment and the tobacco companies free of liability because of their compliance with mandates to warn smokers.

For the first time, in a Supreme Court ruling on June 24, 1992, the door was opened for smokers (or their families) to attempt to prove that the smoking-induced illness resulted because smokers were enticed into smoking by the tobacco industry in spite of its compliance with governmental mandates to warn smokers of the risk of cigarette smoking. In other words, the court began allowing plaintiffs to attempt to prove that the tobacco companies said one thing (our products are potentially dangerous) and did another (make smoking appear safe and attractive). As recently as October 1997, these suits have continued to be unsuccessful.[9]

Does smoking make young people appear older?

group association and can lead to a shared behavioral pattern, which differentiates the group from others and from adults. Further, when risk-taking behavior and disregard for authority are common to the group, smoking becomes the behavioral pattern that most consistently identifies and bonds the group. Particularly for those young people who lack self-directedness or the ability to resist peer pressure, initial membership in a tobacco-using peer group may become inescapable.[10]

Further, when adolescents have lower levels of self-esteem and are searching for an avenue to improve self-image, a role model who smokes is often seen as tough, sociable, and sexually attractive. The latter two traits have been played up by the tobacco industry in their carefully crafted advertisements.

Manipulation

In addition to tobacco use's psychosocial link with modeling, tobacco use may meet the beginning smoker's need to physically manipulate something and at the same time provide the manipulative "tool" necessary to offset boredom, feelings of depression, or social immaturity. The ability to take out a cigarette or fill a pipe adds a measure of structure and control to situations in which they might otherwise feel somewhat ill at ease. The cigarette becomes a readily available and dependable "friend" to turn to during stressful moments.

Susceptibility to advertising

The images of the smoker's world portrayed in tobacco advertisements can be attractive. For adolescents, women, minorities, and other carefully targeted groups of adults, the tobacco industry has associated the suggestion of a better life with the use of their products (see the Star Box below). Young and potential users are told that using tobacco products is associated with a sense of power, liberation, affluence, sophistication, and adult status. The message they are told (or sold) is that smoking will allow them to achieve things for which most people must work a long time.

A second aspect of the tobacco advertising strategy is giving away "free" products by the tobacco companies. Clearly in terms of college students, the readily

Cigarette Advertising Approaches

As the incidence of smoking declines within the general population, the tobacco industry has altered its advertising approaches to attract new markets and solidify their position in other markets. One tobacco company has attempted to target two groups: minorities from inner cities and undereducated "virile females," a term used to describe 18- to 20-year old women who have limited formal education and traditionally male occupations and interests. The R.J. Reynolds company unsuccessfully tried to test market a brand called Uptown. This cigarette was aimed principally at urban minorities. Test marketing of this brand was discontinued. Reynolds also introduced a cigarette called Dakota. The group targeted for this cigarette was "virile females."

Philip Morris Tobacco Company targeted a different group with its super-thin, low-smoke cigarette Superslims. Apparently, marketing of Superslims has been aimed at a more sophisticated woman who is so concerned about her weight that she is willing to disregard the health risks of smoking in an attempt to remain thin.

Misty is a value-brand (lower-cost) cigarette being marketed to young women who are just beginning their professional careers. By producing this "fashionably inexpensive" cigarette, American Tobacco is offering a more affordable alternative to Virginia Slims and Slims. Of course, the model, Misty, appearing in the brand's initial advertisements, is thin. Although these brands are advertised to mature young women, their appeal has been primarily to female adolescents.

Macho men are not being spared the attention of tobacco companies either. Brands including Magna, Bucks, and a new version of Bull Durham appeared in 1990. As more highly educated men continue to move away from tobacco use, these brands are designed to appeal to younger, less highly educated men.

Cartoon characters make seductive models. R.J. Reynolds' Joe Camel campaign was so successful that Joe was a familiar face to American youngsters, rivaling Mickey Mouse. Some health experts even suggest that Joe was largely responsible for adding 3000 new (adolescent age) smokers into the pipeline every day—the number needed by the tobacco industry to replace smokers who die or give up smoking. Regardless of whether they were new smokers or crossovers, preference for the Camel brand among younger smokers has increased from 2% to nearly 30%—five times the market share of the adult population. Despite Joe's success, however, R.J. Reynolds retired him in June 1997 in response to increasing criticism of the tobacco industry's targeting of children.[11]

Reynolds, along with Philip Morris, the makers of Marlboro, uses another marketing ploy to appeal to youth: the sale of promotional items such as magazines, calculators, T-shirts, caps, can holders, and posters. "Camel Cash" and other promotional coupons may soon become worthless, however, if Congress approves the settlement negotiated between the tobacco industry and the federal government.

available cap, T-shirt, beverage can carrier, or light-weight jacket, all with logos, indicate social affiliation and serve as "a little reward" for doing nothing more than smoking a particular brand. However, these promotional items may soon be discontinued, as part of the tobacco industry's settlement with the federal government.

In spite of the psychological needs that are met through continuing to use tobacco, approximately 90% of adult smokers have, on at least one occasion, expressed a desire to quit, and 80% have actually attempted to become nonsmokers.

Preventing Teen Smoking

Even before the tobacco industry released documents in 1997 confirming that it had targeted adolescents (ages 11 to 14), the federal government stated its intention to curb cigarette advertisements directed at this group. In August 1995 the FDA outlined the specific steps that it wanted to be given authority to implement.[12] These actions, listed below, were intended to discourage cigarette smoking among American teens, resulting in 50% fewer adolescents beginning to smoke in 2002 than in 1995.

1. Limit tobacco advertising in publications that appeal to teens; restrict billboard advertisements to no closer than 1,000 feet of schools and playgrounds.

2. Restrict the use of tobacco company logos and other images on nontobacco products, such as towels, T-shirts, and caps.

3. Bar certain sources of access to tobacco products, such as mail-order sales, the distribution of free samples, and vending machines.

4. Prohibit sponsorship of high-visibility sporting events, such as auto racing, in which brand names appear on highly televised surfaces, including hoods, fenders, and uniforms.

5. Require merchants to obtain proof of age when selling tobacco products. (This provision became law in 1997. Merchants are required to validate the age of people whom they suspect to be younger than 27 before selling cigarettes to adults 18 years or older. If found in violation, the salesperson and the store owner will be fined $500 each.)

The tobacco industry initially responded to these proposed restrictions on the promotion and sale of its products by promising to challenge in the courts any attempt to restrict its right to engage in fair trade. However, since the 1997 release of the "tobacco papers," the industry appears willing to accept these restrictions in return for protection from future lawsuits.

A recent study suggests that the law prohibiting cigarette sales to minors is routinely violated by clerks

Activity 1

Education helps people understand the risks of cigarette smoking. How much do you know about cigarette smoking? Go to Wellness Web document at http://www.wellweb.com/smoking/SMOKIQ.HTM and take the *Smoking I.Q. Quiz* developed by the National Heart, Lung, and Blood Institute. Just answer "true" or "false" to the 10 statements listed. The answers that follow include excellent information about the effects of smoking.

Activity 2

Smoking cessation programs come in a variety of formats. Quitting smoking is not easy. An excellent interactive source is available at http://beta.quit-net.org. This site offers several methods to make the quitting process go more smoothly. Select "Quitting help" and then select "Interactive tools." You may then choose from a number of inventories that can assist you in the quitting process.

Activity 3

As encouraging as it is that adults have moved away from smoking in recent decades, the most current data about smoking by adolescents are discouraging. How much do you know about teenage smoking? Go to http://www.mayohealth.org/mayo/9710/htm/smokjava.htm to take a knowledge quiz. Answer the eight questions listed. How well did you do?

and store owners. Various studies indicate that 58% to 63% of teen smokers report that they rarely have trouble purchasing cigarettes.[13]

TOBACCO: THE SOURCE OF PHYSIOLOGICALLY ACTIVE COMPOUNDS

When burned, the tobacco in cigarettes, cigars, and pipe mixtures is a source of an array of physiologically active chemicals, many of which are closely linked to significant changes in normal body structure and function. With each puff of smoke the body is exposed to over 4000 chemical compounds, hundreds of which are known to be physiologically active, toxic, and carcinogenic. An annual 50,000 puffs taken in by the one-pack-a-day cigarette smoker results in a regularly occurring environment that makes the most polluted urban environment seem clean in comparison.

Cigarette, cigar, and pipe smoke can be described on the basis of two phases or components: the particulate phase and the gaseous phase. The **particulate phase** includes nicotine, water, and a variety of powerful chemical compounds known collectively as *tar*. Tar includes phenol, cresol, pyrene, DDT, and a benzene-ring group of compounds that includes benzo[a]pyrene. A person who smokes one pack of cigarettes per day will cause the collection of 4 oz of tar in the lungs in one year.[10] As tar is drawn down the airway, the larger particles settle along its length, while the smaller particles reach the alveoli, or small saclike ends of the airway, where air comes in close association with the bloodstream. Most carcinogenic (cancer-causing) compounds are found within the tar.

The **gaseous phase** of tobacco smoke, like the particulate phase, is composed of a variety of physiologically active compounds, including carbon monoxide, carbon dioxide, ammonia, hydrogen cyanide, isoprene, acetaldehyde, and acetone. At least 43 of these compounds have been determined to be carcinogenic.[14] *Carbon monoxide* is the most damaging compound found in this component of tobacco smoke. Its effects are discussed shortly.

Nicotine

Nicotine is a powerful psychotropic (psychoactive) chemical agent found in the particulate phase of tobacco smoke. When drawn into the lungs, about one fourth of the nicotine in the inhaled smoke passes into the circulation and into the brain within 10 seconds of inhalation. *Nicotine receptors* within the brain are activated and produce a variety of responses, most of which are stimulating (see the discussion of nicotine addiction on pp. 205-207). High levels of nicotine, however, depress the CNS and result in the relaxation associated with heavy smoking.

The remaining nicotine absorbed into the blood travels throughout the body to nicotinic receptors located in a variety of tissues. Among the presently understood additional effects of nicotine are the reduction of intestinal activity, the release of epinephrine from the adrenal glands, the release of **norepinephrine** from peripheral nerves, an increase in heart rate, the constriction of peripheral blood vessels, and the dilation of airways within the respiratory system.

Nicotine that enters the body by routes other than inhalation produces similar effects but at a much slower rate. Smokeless tobacco, for example, reaches its fullest physiological effect by the end of 20 minutes, nicotine-containing gum within 30 minutes, and transdermal nicotine patches within several hours.

Carbon Monoxide

Burning tobacco forms **carbon monoxide (CO)** gas. Carbon monoxide is one of the most harmful components of tobacco smoke.

Carbon monoxide is a colorless, odorless, tasteless gas that possesses a very strong physiological attraction for hemoglobin, the oxygen-carrying component of each red blood cell. When carbon monoxide is inhaled, it quickly bonds with hemoglobin and forms a new compound, *carboxyhemoglobin*. In this form, hemoglobin is unable to transport oxygen to the tissues and cells where it is needed.

The presence of excessive levels of carboxyhemoglobin in the blood of smokers leads to shortness of breath and lowered endurance. Brain function may be reduced, reactions and judgment are dulled, and, of course, cardiovascular function is impaired. Fetuses are especially at risk for this oxygen deprivation because fetal development is so critically dependent on a sufficient oxygen supply from the mother.

ILLNESS, PREMATURE DEATH, AND TOBACCO USE

For people who begin tobacco use as adolescents or young adults, smoke heavily, and continue to smoke, the likelihood of premature death is virtually ensured. Two-pack-a-day cigarette smokers can expect to die 7 to 8 years earlier than their nonsmoking counterparts. Only nonsmoking-related deaths that can afflict both smokers and nonsmokers alike, such as automobile accidents, keep the difference at this level rather than much higher. Not only will these people die sooner, but they also will probably be plagued with painful, debilitating illnesses for an extended time.

Cardiovascular Disease

Cardiovascular disease is the leading cause of death among all adults, accounting for 945,000 deaths annually in the United States.[15] Tobacco use, and cigarette smoking in particular, is clearly one of the major factors contributing to this cause. So important is tobacco use as a contributing factor in deaths from heart disease that cigarette smokers double the risk of experiencing a **myocardial infarction** and increase their risk of **sudden cardiac death** by two to four times. Fully one third of all cardiovascular disease can be traced to cigarette smoking. The relationship between tobacco use and cardiovascular disease is centered on two major components of tobacco smoke: nicotine and carbon monoxide.

Nicotine and cardiovascular disease

The influence of nicotine on the cardiovascular system occurs when it stimulates the nervous system to release norepinephrine. This powerful stimulant increases the rate at which the heart contracts. The extent to which this is dangerous depends in part on the ability of the heart's own blood supply system to provide blood to the working heart muscle.

In addition to its influence on heart rate, nicotine is also a powerful constrictor of blood vessels throughout the body. As vessels constrict, the pressure within them goes up. Recent research shows that nonreversible atherosclerotic damage to major arteries also occurs with smoking.[16]

Nicotine also increases blood **platelet adhesiveness**. *Platelets* are the components of blood that causes it to clot, or coagulate, after an injury. Nicotine makes these platelets more likely to adhere to one another, or "clump," which can cause blood clots to develop in the arteries. Heart attacks occur when clots form within the coronary arteries (see Chapter 10) or are transported to the heart from other areas of the body.

In addition to other influences on the cardiovascular system, nicotine possesses the ability to decrease the proportion of high-density lipoproteins (HDLs) and to increase the proportion of low-density lipoproteins (LDLs) and very-low-density lipoproteins that make up the body's blood cholesterol. (See Chapter 10 for further information about cholesterol's role in cardiovascular disease.)

Carbon monoxide and cardiovascular disease

Carbon monoxide, a second substance contributed by tobacco, influences the type and extent of cardiovascular disease found among tobacco users. Carbon monoxide interferes with oxygen transport within the circulatory system.

As described previously, carbon monoxide is a component of the gaseous phase of tobacco smoke and readily attaches to the hemoglobin of the red blood cells. Once attached, carbon monoxide makes the red blood cell permanently weaker in its ability to transport oxygen. These red blood cells remain relatively useless during the remainder of their 120-day life. Levels of carboxyhemoglobin in heavy smokers are associated with significant increases in the incidence of heart attack.

When a person has impaired oxygen-transporting abilities, physical exertion becomes increasingly demanding on both the heart and the lungs. The cardiovascular system will attempt to respond to the body's demand for oxygen, but these responses are themselves impaired as a result of the influence of nicotine on the cardiovascular system. If tobacco does create the good life, as advertisers claim, it also unfortunately lowers ability to participate actively in that life.

Cancer

Data supplied by the American Cancer Society (ACS) indicate that during 1997 an estimated 1,382,400 Americans were diagnosed with cancer.* These cases were nearly equally divided between the genders and will eventually result in approximately 560,000 deaths.[1] In the opinion of the ACS, 30% of all cancer cases are heavily influenced by tobacco use. Lung cancer alone accounted for about 178,100 of the new cancer cases and 160,400 deaths in 1997. Fully 87% of male lung cancer victims were cigarette smokers. Cancer of the respiratory system, including lung cancer and cancers of the mouth and throat, accounted for

*Excluding about 800,000 cases of nonmelanoma skin cancer.

particulate phase
Portion of the tobacco smoke composed of small suspended particles.

gaseous phase
Portion of the tobacco smoke containing carbon monoxide and many other physiologically active gaseous compounds.

norepinephrine (nor epp in **eff** rin)
Adrenaline-like chemical produced within the nervous system.

carbon monoxide (CO)
Chemical compound that can "inactivate" red blood cells.

myocardial infarction
Heart attack; the death of heart muscle as a result of a blockage in one of the coronary arteries.

sudden cardiac death
Immediate death resulting from a sudden change in the rhythm of the heart.

platelet adhesiveness
Tendency of platelets to clump together, thus enhancing the speed at which the blood clots.

about 194,600 new cases of cancer and 165,920 deaths.[1] Despite these high figures, not all smokers develop cancer. Perhaps the extent to which the body's cancer suppressor genes are influenced by carcinogenic substances in tobacco smoke makes some smokers at greater risk for tobacco-related cancer than others.[17]

Recall that tobacco smoke has both a gaseous phase and a particulate phase. The particulate phase contains the tar fragment of tobacco smoke. This rich chemical environment contains over 4000 known chemical compounds, hundreds of which are known as possible carcinogens.

In the normally functioning respiratory system, particulate matter suspended in the inhaled air settles on the tissues lining the airways and is trapped in **mucus** produced by specialized *goblet cells* (Figure 9-1). This mucus, with its trapped impurities, is continuously swept upward by the beating action of hairlike **cilia** of the cells lining the air passages. On reaching the throat, this mucus is swallowed and eventually removed through the digestive system.

When tobacco smoke is drawn into the respiratory system, however, its rapidly dropping temperature allows the particulate matter to accumulate. This brown, sticky tar contains compounds known to harm the ciliated cells, goblet cells, and the *basal cells* of the respiratory lining. As the damage from smoking increases, the cilia becomes less effective in sweeping mucus upward to the throat. When cilia can no longer clean the airway, tar accumulates on the surfaces and brings carcinogenic compounds into direct contact with the tissues of the airway.

At the same time that the sweeping action of the lining cells is being slowed, substances in the tar are stimulating the goblet cells to increase the amount of mucus they normally produce. The "smoker's cough" is an attempt to remove this excess mucus.

With prolonged exposure to the carcinogenic materials in tar, predictable changes will begin to occur within the respiratory system's *basal cell layer* (see Figure 9-1). The basal cells begin to display changes characteristic of all cancer cells (Figure 9-2). When a person stops smoking, these cells do not repair themselves as quickly as once thought.[18]

By the time lung cancer is usually diagnosed, its development is so advanced that the chance for recovery is very poor. Only 14% of all lung cancer victims survive for 5 years or more after diagnosis.[1] Most die in a very agonizing, painful way.

Cancerous activity in other areas of the respiratory system, including the *larynx,* and within the oral cavity (mouth) follows a similar course. In the case of oral cavity cancer, carcinogens found within the smoke and within the saliva are involved in the can-

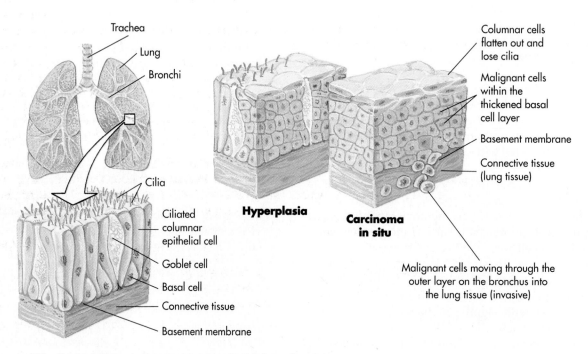

Figure 9-1 Histological (tissue) changes associated with bronchogenic carcinoma.

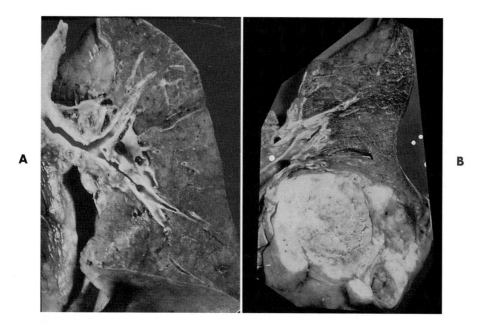

Figure 9-2   **A,** Normal lung. **B,** Cancerous lung.

cerous changes. Tobacco users, such as pipe smokers, cigar smokers, and the users of smokeless tobacco, have a very high rate of cancer of the mouth, tongue, and voice box.

In addition to drawing smoke into the lungs, tobacco users swallow saliva that contains an array of chemical compounds from tobacco. As this saliva is swallowed, carcinogens are absorbed into the circulatory system and transported to all areas of the body. The filtering of the blood by the liver, kidneys, and bladder may account for the higher than normal levels of cancer in these organs among smokers.

Chronic Obstructive Lung Disease

Chronic obstructive lung disease (COLD) is a chronic disorder in which air flow in and out of the lungs becomes progressively limited. COLD is a disease state that is made up of two separate but related diseases: **chronic bronchitis** and **pulmonary emphysema.**

With chronic bronchitis, excess mucus is produced in response to the effects of smoking on airway tissue, and the walls of the bronchi become inflamed and infected. This produces a characteristic narrowing of the air passages. Breathing becomes difficult, and activity can be severely restricted. People who stop smoking can reverse chronic bronchitis.

For college students who have only recently begun smoking, the chronic nature of bronchitis may not yet be in place. Be forewarned, however, that the now occasional episodes of airway inflammation and congestion will occur on a more regular basis, and eventually the foundation on which COLD is built will be in place.

Pulmonary emphysema causes damage to the tiny

mucus
Clear, sticky material produced by specialized cells within the mucous membranes of the body; mucus traps much of the suspended particulate matter within tobacco smoke.

cilia (sill ee uh)
Small, hairlike structures that extend from cells that line the air passages.

chronic bronchitis
Persistent inflammation and infection of the smaller airways within the lung.

pulmonary emphysema
Irreversible disease process in which the alveoli are destroyed.

air sacs of the lungs, the **alveoli,** that cannot be reversed. Chest pressure builds when air becomes trapped by narrowed air passages (chronic bronchitis), and the thin-walled sacs rupture. Emphysema patients often develop a "barrel chest" as they lose the ability to exhale fully. You have most likely seen people with this condition in shopping malls and other locations as they walk slowly by, carrying or pulling behind them their portable oxygen tanks.

More than 10 million Americans have COLD. It is responsible for a greater limitation of physical activity than any other disease, including heart disease.[19] COLD patients tend to die a very unpleasant, prolonged death, often from a general collapse of normal cardiorespiratory function that results in *congestive heart failure* (see Chapter 10).

Additional Health Concerns

In addition to the serious health problems stemming from tobacco use already described, other health-related changes that are routinely seen include a generally poor state of nutrition, the gradual loss of the sense of smell, and premature wrinkling of the skin. Tobacco users are also more likely to experience strokes (a potentially fatal condition), lose bone mass leading to osteoporosis, experience more back pain and muscle injury, and find that fractures heal more slowly. Further, smokers who have surgery spend more time in the recovery room. Although not perceived as a "health problem" by people who continue smoking to control weight, smoking does appear to minimize weight gain. In studies using male identical twins, the siblings who smoked were 6 to 8 pounds lighter than their nonsmoking siblings.[20]

TOBACCO AND CAFFEINE USE

As discussed in Chapter 7, caffeine is the psychotropic drug in coffee, tea, cocoa, many soft drinks, and several nonprescription drugs, and it produces a stimulatory effect on the CNS. Because of caffeine's presence in such widely used and legal products, it may be the most used (and potentially misused) drug in this country. Refer back to Table 7-2, which depicts the amount of caffeine in various soft drinks, the major sources of caffeine for children and for many adults.

Think about how often you see someone light up a cigarette while enjoying a cup of coffee. The exact action of caffeine on the body is not fully understood, but its stimulatory effects are widespread. In low doses, consumption results in increased mental awareness, alertness, and a quickening of thought processes. At higher doses, restlessness, agitation, tremors, and cardiac dysrhythmia occur. Dependence on caffeine, including addiction and habituation, develops rapidly (some studies suggest within a matter of a few days). Unpleasant withdrawal symptoms develop within several hours after the end of consumption. For those who smoke, this becomes a second dependence added to their nicotine addiction.

Chronic heavy consumption of caffeine is called *caffeinism* and is associated with a number of physiological indicators including nervousness, irritability, tremors, insomnia, heart palpitation, and gastrointestinal disturbances.[21] Efforts have been made to link caffeine consumption to coronary heart disease, pancreatic cancer, fibrocystic breast disease, and most recently, bone loss. To date, there has been little conclusive evidence relating serious health problems and caffeine consumption. However, caffeine does appear to be associated with a risk for miscarriage during pregnancy and should not, therefore, be consumed by women during pregnancy.[22] Regardless, for other adults, caffeine should most likely be consumed in moderation, particularly in light of its widespread presence in foods and products.

SMOKING AND REPRODUCTION

In all of its dimensions the reproductive process is impaired by the use of tobacco, particularly cigarette smoking. Problems can be found in association with infertility, problem pregnancy, breastfeeding, and the health of the newborn.

Infertility

Recent research indicates that cigarette smoking by both men and women can reduce levels of fertility. Among men, smoking adversely affects sperm motility and sperm shape and can inhibit sperm production. Among women, lower levels of estrogen (a hormone necessary for uterine wall development), a reduced ability to conceive, and a somewhat earlier onset of menopause appear to be related to cigarette smoking.

Problem Pregnancy

The harmful effects of tobacco smoke on the course of pregnancy are principally the result of the carbon monoxide and nicotine to which the mother and her fetus are exposed. Carbon monoxide is carried to the placenta, where it "locks up" fetal hemoglobin. As a

Tobacco use during pregnancy is harmful to the fetus.

result of this exposure to carbon monoxide, the fetus is deprived of normal oxygen transport and in effect suffocates.

Nicotine also exerts its influence on the developing fetus. Thermographs of the placenta and fetus show signs of marked constriction of blood vessels within a few seconds after inhalation by the mother. This constriction further reduces oxygen supplies. In addition, nicotine stimulates the mother's stress response, placing the mother and fetus under the potentially harmful influence of elevated epinephrine and corticoid levels (see Chapter 3). Any fetus exposed to all of these agents is more likely to be *miscarried* or *stillborn.* Children born to mothers who smoked during pregnancy often have low birth weights and may show other signs of having had a stressful life in the uterus.

Breastfeeding

Women who smoke while they breastfeed their infants will continue to expose their children to the harmful effects of tobacco smoke. Mothers who stop smoking during pregnancy should be encouraged to continue to refrain from smoking while they are breastfeeding.

Health Problems among Infants

Babies born to women who smoked during pregnancy will, on average, be shorter and have a lower birth weight than children born to nonsmoking mothers. During the earliest months of life, babies born to mothers who smoke experience an elevated rate of death caused by *sudden infant death syndrome* (SIDS). Statistics also show that these infants are more likely to develop chronic respiratory problems, be hospitalized, and have poorer overall health during their early years of life. Additionally, children exposed to the influences of tobacco prenatally may hold a greater chance of developing *attention deficit disorder* (ADD). Studies suggest that babies whose mothers were exposed to passive smoke during pregnancy may be harmed as much as babies whose mothers smoked during pregnancy.[23]

Parenting, in the sense of assuming responsibility for the well-being of a child, begins before birth, especially in the case of smoking. A pregnant woman who continues to smoke is disregarding the well-being of the child she is carrying. Other family members, friends, and co-workers who subject pregnant women to cigarette, pipe, or cigar smoke are, in a sense, contributing a measure of their own disregard for the health of the next generation.

ORAL CONTRACEPTIVES AND TOBACCO USE

Women who smoke and use oral contraceptives are placing themselves at a much greater risk of experiencing a fatal cardiovascular accident (heart attack, stroke, or **embolism**) than oral contraceptive users who do not smoke. This risk of cardiovascular complications is further increased for oral contraceptive

alveoli (al **vee** oh lie)
Thin, saclike terminal ends of the airways; the site at which gases are exchanged between the blood and inhaled air.

embolism (**em** boe liz um)
Potentially fatal condition in which a circulating blood clot lodges itself in a smaller vessel.

users 25 years of age or older. Women who both smoke and use oral contraceptives are four times more likely to die from myocardial infarction (heart attack) than women who only smoke.[24] Because of this adverse relationship, *it is strongly recommended that women who smoke not use oral contraceptives.*

SMOKELESS TOBACCO USE

As the term implies, smokeless tobacco is not burned; rather, it is placed into the mouth. Once in place, the physiologically active nicotine and other soluble compounds are absorbed through the mucous membranes and into the blood. Within a few minutes, chewing tobacco and snuff generate blood levels of nicotine in amounts equivalent to those seen in cigarette smokers.

Chewing tobacco is taken from its foil pouch, formed into a small ball (called a "wad," "chaw," or "chew"), and placed into the mouth. Once in place, the ball of tobacco is sucked and occasionally chewed but not swallowed. Some users develop great skill at spitting the copious dark brown liquid residue into an empty coffee can, out a car window, or on the sidewalk.

Snuff, a more finely shredded smokeless tobacco product, is marketed in small, round cans. Snuff is formed into a small mass (or "quid"). The quid is "dipped," or placed between the jaw and the cheek; the user sucks the quid and spits out the brown liquid.

Although smokeless tobacco would seem to free the tobacco user from many of the risks associated with smoking, chewing and dipping are not without their own substantial risks. The presence of *leukoplakia* (white spots) and *erythroplakia* (red spots) on the tissues of the mouth indicate precancerous changes (see the Health Action Guide at right). In addition, an increase in **periodontal disease** (with the pulling away of the gum from the teeth and later tooth loss), the abrasive damage to the enamel of the teeth, and the high concentration of sugar in processed tobacco all contribute to health problems seen among users of smokeless tobacco.

In addition to the damage done to the tissues of the mouth, the need to process the inadvertently swallowed saliva that contains dissolved carcinogens places both the digestive and urinary systems at risk of cancer.

In the opinion of health experts the use of smokeless tobacco and its potential for life-threatening disease is presently at the place cigarette smoking was 40 years ago. Consequently, television advertisement has been banned, and one of the following warnings appears on every package of smokeless tobacco:

WARNING: THIS PRODUCT MAY CAUSE MOUTH CANCER.

WARNING: THIS PRODUCT MAY CAUSE GUM DISEASE AND TOOTH LOSS.

WARNING: THIS PRODUCT IS NOT A SAFE ALTERNATIVE TO CIGARETTE SMOKING.

Clearly, smokeless tobacco is a dangerous product. There is little doubt that continued use of tobacco in this form is a serious problem to health in all of its dimensions.

INVOLUNTARY (PASSIVE) SMOKING

The smoke generated by the burning of tobacco can be classified as either **mainstream smoke** (the smoke inhaled and then exhaled by the smoker) or **sidestream smoke** (the smoke that comes from the burning end of the cigarette, pipe, or cigar). When either form of tobacco smoke is diluted and stays within a common source of air, it is referred to as **environmental tobacco smoke.** All three forms of tobacco smoke lead to *involuntary smoking* and can present health problems for both nonsmokers and smokers.

Surprisingly, mainstream smoke makes up only 15% of our exposure to involuntary smoking. This is because much of the nicotine, carbon monoxide, and particulate matter are retained within the active smokers.

HEALTH Action Guide

Smokeless Tobacco Use

If you use smokeless tobacco, you are at risk for serious health problems. If you have any of the following signs, see your dentist or physician immediately:
- Lumps in the jaw or neck area
- Color changes or lumps inside the lips
- White, smooth, or scaly patches in the mouth or on the neck, lips, or tongue
- A red spot or sore on the lips or gums or inside the mouth that does not heal in 2 weeks
- Repeated bleeding in the mouth
- Difficulty or abnormality in speaking or swallowing

Sidestream smoke is responsible for 85% of our involuntary smoke exposure. Because it is not filtered by the tobacco, the filter, or the smoker's lungs, sidestream smoke contains more free nicotine and produces higher yields of both carbon dioxide and carbon monoxide. Much to the detriment of nonsmokers, sidestream smoke has 20 to 100 times the quantity of highly carcinogenic substances (N-nitrosamines) that mainstream smoke has.

Current scientific opinion suggests that smokers and nonsmokers are exposed to very much the same smoke when tobacco is used within a common airspace. The important difference is the quantity of smoke inhaled by smokers and nonsmokers. It is likely that for each pack of cigarettes smoked by a smoker, nonsmokers who must share a common air supply with the smokers will involuntarily smoke the equivalent of three to five cigarettes per day. Because of the small size of the particles produced by burning tobacco, environmental tobacco smoke cannot be completely removed from an indoor site by even the most effective ventilation system.

On the basis of recently reported research, involuntary smoke exposure may be responsible for between 10,000 and 20,000 premature deaths per year among nonsmokers in the United States (other estimates range upward to 53,000 premature deaths).[25] In addition, environmental tobacco smoke is associated with lung cancer, asthma, low birth weight babies, ear infections, eye irritation, headaches, and coughs in nonsmokers.[26]

For these reasons, state, local, and private-sector initiatives to restrict smoking have been introduced. Most buildings in which people work, study, play, reside, eat, or shop now have some smoking restrictions. Some have complete smoking bans. The most highly visible of these bans occurred in 1994 when McDonald's announced that all 1400 company-owned restaurants were smoke-free. Franchised-owned stores began the movement to smoke-free environments in the belief that such an environment is in the best interest of children and is preferred by adults. Arby's and Wendy's have banned smoking in some stores as well. Nowhere is smoking more noticeably prohibited than in the U.S. airline industry. Currently, smoking is banned on all domestic plane flights. American Airlines has extended the ban on smoking to selected international flights as well.

Involuntary smoking poses serious threats to nonsmokers within residential settings.[27] Spouses and children of smokers are at greatest risk from involuntary smoking. Scientific studies suggest that nonsmokers married to smokers are three times more likely to experience heart attacks than nonsmoking

spouses of nonsmokers, and they have a 30% greater risk of lung cancer than nonsmoking spouses of nonsmokers.

The children of parents who smoke are twice as likely as children of nonsmoking parents to experience bronchitis or pneumonia during the first year of life. In addition, throughout childhood, these children will experience more wheezing, coughing, and sputum production than children whose parents do not smoke.[27] Of course, the impact on children who have two parents who smoke is greater than on children who have only one parent who smokes.

STOPPING WHAT YOU STARTED

As in the case of weight reduction, there are several ways to attempt to stop smoking. Among these are the *cold turkey* approach, a gradual reduction in cigarette use, organized smoking cessation programs, and the use of medically prescribed and OTC drug treatment. For those who fear the discomfort of going cold turkey, a more gradual approach can be attempted. The Health Action Guide on p. 218 provides several suggestions for quitting smoking or cutting down on tobacco consumption until stopping totally is possible.

Although it is far from easy to stop smoking, most of the 1.3 million people who quit smoking each year do so by throwing their cigarettes away and going cold turkey. After days, weeks, or even months of discomfort, the body will eventually function more effectively. Respiratory capacity will return, the ability to taste will return, and, if undertaken soon enough, tissues of the airways will begin returning to a more normal appearance. On a less pleasant note, it may take years before the mental pictures of

periodontal disease (pare ee oh **don** tal)
Destruction to soft tissue and bone that surround the teeth.

mainstream smoke
Smoke inhaled and then exhaled by a smoker.

sidestream smoke
Smoke that comes from the burning end of a cigarette, pipe, or cigar.

environmental tobacco smoke
Tobacco smoke that is diluted and stays within a common source of air.

"smoking pleasures" have faded. For most, some weight will be gained (about 6 to 8 pounds), but this represents a minimal health risk in comparison with the benefits of not smoking. The Health Action Guide on p. 219 offers tips for avoiding weight gain when you quit smoking.

As mentioned above, many group-based smoking cessation programs exist. These programs are usually operated by hospitals, universities, health departments, voluntary health agencies, private physicians, and even local churches. Perhaps the best that can be said is that the better programs will have limited success—a 20% to 50% success rate as measured over 1 year—whereas the remainder will have even poorer levels of success.

Two approaches for weaning smokers from cigarettes to a nontobacco source of nicotine dependency are nicotine-containing chewing gum (Nicorette) and the transdermal nicotine patches (Nicoderm, Habitrol, Prostep) that allow nicotine to slowly diffuse through the skin surface into the body. The chewing gum has been on the market for a number of years and, when used correctly along with smoking cessation counseling, has demonstrated a success rate of 40% or more. Correct use of nicotine-containing chewing gum requires an immediate cessation of smoking, a determination of the initial dosage (4 mg or 2 mg of nicotine per piece), the manner of chewing each piece (rate of chewing and the avoidance of certain foods or beverages), the number of pieces to be chewed each day (usually 9 to 12), and the individual manner of withdrawal from chewing the gum after 2 to 3 months of its use. In 1996 a nonprescription version of Nicorette became available.

In comparison with nicotine-containing chewing gum, the more recently developed transdermal nico-

HEALTH
Action Guide

Quitting or Reducing Smoking

Instead of reaching for a cigarette, reach out for life and health. The suggestions below, many of which are recommended by the American Cancer Society, will help you make a concerted effort to stop smoking. Are you ready to try?

- Get mad at yourself for having become less fully self-directed than you could be. Few smokers can contend that they are fully self-directed when they can barely function in the absence of their cigarettes.
- Think of one sentence that expresses your personal reason for wanting to quit smoking. Repeat the sentence to yourself often.
- Observe nonsmokers. Note that nonsmokers are not missing out on anything as the result of not smoking. Recognize that the price you will pay for no longer smoking is not as high as it might have first appeared.
- Pick a quit day, sometime within the next 2 weeks. Plan either to stop cold turkey or to cut down gradually.
- Plan ahead for how you will handle tough times in your first few days off cigarettes.
- Stock up on low- or no-calorie snacks.
- On your quit day, drink a lot of water and keep busy.
- Limit your contact with other cigarette smokers. Keep in mind that once you quit, smokers won't go out of their way to assist you in your efforts.

- Stay clear, as much as possible, of the locations and activities that are now associated with your smoking. Old habits will be hard to break, but at least you do not have to be constantly reminded by their presence.
- Establish a series of rewards that you will give yourself as you progress through your smoking cessation program.
- Call the American Cancer Society for more information about quitting: self-help, how-to's, and group sessions in your community.

An alternative to total cessation is, of course, to reduce exposure to tobacco. This reduction can be accomplished through one or more of the following approaches:

- Reduce the consumption of your present high-tar and high-nicotine brand by smoking fewer cigarettes, inhaling less often and less deeply, and by smoking the cigarette only halfway down.
- Switch to a low-tar and low-nicotine brand of cigarette. However, you must not compensate for this change by smoking more cigarettes or by inhaling more deeply and frequently. Instead, try to reduce the number of cigarettes smoked and the depth and number of inhalations, and smoke only a limited portion of each cigarette.
- Switch to a smokeless form of tobacco, but be prepared for the potential problems that were discussed earlier in this chapter.

HEALTH
Action Guide →

Avoiding Weight Gain When You Stop Smoking

For many smokers, particularly women, an important "plus" for smoking is weight management. In their minds the risks associated with tobacco use are more than offset by the cigarette's ability to curb appetite and thus serve as an aid in restricting caloric intake. Accordingly, the fear of weight gain frequently prevents any serious attempts at stopping smoking or permits easy relapse back into cigarette use.

The fear described above is in fact true. Most people who quit smoking do gain weight during the 10 years after cessation and in amounts greater than that seen in people who continue smoking or who have never smoked. It is also true, however, that this weight gain is relatively small (2.4 pounds for women and 3.8 pounds for men) and only slightly greater than that experienced by age-mates who smoke or have never smoked. Certainly, the weight gained is a minimal health risk compared with the risks associated with continued smoking.

The keys to minimizing weight gain after smoking ces-

sation are centered in two areas: (1) the ability to manage the "smoking urges" associated with the first several months of being a former smoker without resorting to eating and (2) the willingness to adopt healthy eating and exercise behaviors.

In regard to the management of smoking urges, people who are attempting to quit smoking should recognize that these powerful urges are very temporary, usually lasting only about 2 minutes. During these periods of intense desire for a cigarette, coping activities such as taking a short walk, drinking water or a diet beverage, or talking with a co-worker or family member will distract the mind from a cigarette until the urge has passed. If one "must" eat during these times, then healthy low-calorie snacks, such as apple slices, should be selected.

To minimize weight gain (or actually achieve a lower weight than when smoking) in the years after stopping smoking, a serious wellness-oriented lifestyle change involving both exercise and diet should be implemented. Specific information regarding adult fitness and sound nutrition can be found in Chapters 4 and 5, respectively. ←-----

---

tine patches appear to be somewhat less effective than the chewing gum but easier to use. The transdermal nicotine patches, such as Nicoderm, can now be obtained in OTC versions. Because transdermal patches come in three dosages, a determination must be made as to the appropriate initial dosage, the length of time at that dosage and lower dosages, and the manner of withdrawal after the usual 8 to 12

weeks of patch wearing. In 1997 a nicotine replacement therapy using inhalation was approved by the FDA. This new delivery technique uses a nicotine cartridge inserted into a device that resembles a cigarette holder, through which the user inhales. This system, available by prescription, should prove very effective because of the large surface area of the lungs, which allows rapid absorption of nicotine into the blood.

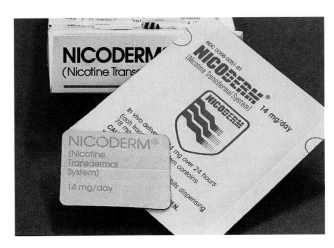
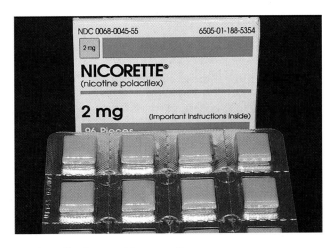

A transdermal nicotine patch or nicotine-containing gum can be part of an effective smoking cessation program.

To aid smoking cessation efforts, nicotine replacement products can be used alone or with other therapies. Zyban and Wellbutrin are antidepressant medications that increase the production of dopamine, a neurotransmitter. Dopamine production declines when a smoker quits, creating the craving to smoke. Prozac, a serotonin-specific antidepressant, has also shown promise in boosting success rates of smokers who try to quit.

Most health insurance will not cover the costs of smoking cessation therapies, particularly if the treatment is not directly supervised by a physician.

TOBACCO USE: A QUESTION OF RIGHTS

Let us offer two simple questions concerning the issues of smokers' vs. nonsmokers' rights:

- To what extent should smokers be allowed to pollute the air and endanger the health of nonsmokers?
- To what extent should nonsmokers be allowed to restrict the personal freedom of smokers, particularly since tobacco products are sold legally?

At this time, answers to these questions are only partially available, but one trend is developing: the tobacco user is being forced to give ground to the nonsmoker. Today, in fact, it is becoming more a matter of when the smoker will be allowed to smoke rather than a matter of when smoking will be restricted. Increasingly, smoking is tolerated less and less. The health concerns of the majority are prevailing over the dependence needs of the minority. See article on pp. 224-226 for a fuller explanation of this topic.

IMPROVING COMMUNICATION BETWEEN SMOKERS AND NONSMOKERS

Exchanges between smokers and nonsmokers are sometimes strained, and in many cases, friendships are damaged beyond the point of repair. As you have more than likely observed, roommates are changed, dates are refused, and memberships in groups are withheld or rejected because of the opposing rights of these two groups.

Recognizing that social skill development is an important task for young adults, the following simple considerations or approaches for smokers can reduce some conflict presently associated with smoking.

- Ask whether smoking would bother others near you.

- When in a neutral setting, seek physical space in which you will be able to smoke and in a reasonable way not interfere with nonsmokers' comfort.
- Accept the validity of the nonsmoker's statement that your smoke causes everything and everyone to smell.
- Respect stated prohibitions against smoking.
- If a nonsmoker requests that you refrain from smoking, respond with courtesy, regardless of whether you intend to comply.
- Practice "civil smoking" by applying a measure of restraint when you recognize that smoking is offensive to others. Particularly, respect the aesthetics that should accompany any act of smoking—ashes on dinner plates and cigarette butts in flower pots are hardly popular with others.

The suggestions above can become skills for the social dimension of your health that can be applied to other social conflicts. Remember that as a smoker, you are part of a statistical minority living in a society that often makes decisions and resolves conflict based on majority rule.

For those of you who are nonsmokers, we would suggest several approaches we believe will make you more sensitive and skilled in dealing with smoking behavior:

- Attempt to develop a feeling for or a sensitivity to the power of the dependence that smokers have on their cigarettes.
- Accept the reality of the smoker's sensory insensitivity—an insensitivity that is so profound that the odors you complain about are not even recognized by the smoker.
- When in a neutral setting, allow smokers their fair share of physical space in which to smoke. As long as the host does not object to smoking, you as a guest do not have the right to infringe on a person's right to smoke.
- When asking a person to not smoke, use a manner that reflects social consideration and skill. State your request clearly, and accept a refusal gracefully.
- Respond with honesty to inquiries from the smoker as to whether the smoke is bothering you.

For those who are contemplating smoking, we ask you to explore closely whether the social isolation that appears to be more and more common for smokers will be offset by the benefits you might receive from cigarettes. The ability to find satisfaction through social contact may be one of the most important dimensions in a productive and satisfying adult life.

Summary

- The percentage of American adults who smoke is continuing to decline.
- The incidence of adolescent and young-adult smoking is increasing.
- The federal government has proposed a broadly based program intended to reduce the use of cigarettes by adolescents.
- In spite of initial denials by the tobacco industry, tobacco-related marketing was directed to adolescents and very young adults.
- Dependence, including addiction and habituation, is established quickly through tobacco use.
- Nicotine is the addictive agent in tobacco whose level in tobacco products can be modified.
- Modeling, self-reward, and self-medication play important roles in the development of tobacco dependence.
- The tobacco industry is constantly targeting new markets, such as women, minorities, and adolescents, through a variety of techniques, including the sale of logo-bearing products and an appealing, although no longer used cartoon character, Joe Camel.
- Tobacco smoke can be divided into gaseous and particulate phases. Each phase has its unique chemical composition.
- Nicotine, carbon monoxide, and phenol have damaging effects on various body tissues. Several hundred carcinogenic agents are found in tobacco smoke.
- Nicotine has predictable effects on the function of the cardiovascular system when used at relatively low doses.

- Most forms of cancer are worsened by tobacco use. Lung cancer progresses in a predictable fashion.
- Chronic obstructive lung disease (COLD) is a likely consequence of long-term cigarette smoking, with early symptoms appearing shortly after beginning regular smoking.
- Caffeine consumption produces predictable changes in nervous system function, but its long-term effect on health is uncertain.
- Smoking alters normal structure and function of the body, as seen in premature wrinkling, diminished ability to smell, and bone loss leading to osteoporosis.
- Several areas of reproductive health are negatively influenced by tobacco use. Cigarette smoking and long-term use of oral contraceptives are not compatible.
- Smokeless tobacco carries its own health risks, including oral cancer.
- Involuntary smoke carries with it a wide variety of threats to the spouse, children, and co-workers of the smoker.
- Stopping smoking can be undertaken in any one of several ways, including going cold turkey.
- Smoking cessation therapies are available in a variety of forms, including nicotine gum, trans dermal patches, nicotine inhalation devices, and oral medications that affect neurotransmitters.
- Both smokers and nonsmokers have certain rights regarding the use of tobacco. Effective communication can be established between smokers and nonsmokers.

Review Questions

1. What percentage of the American adult population smokes? In what direction has change been occurring? What is the current direction that adolescent smoking is taking? What factors may account for this newly observed trend?
2. In what way do modeling and advertising explain the development of emotional dependency on tobacco? How do self-esteem, self-image, and self-directedness relate to tobacco use?
3. How is the federal government attempting to limit the exposure that children and adolescents currently have to tobacco products and tobacco advertisements? What techniques have been developed by the tobacco industry to market their

products to children and adolescents, in spite of their initial contentions to the contrary?
4. What are the principal components of the gaseous and particulate phases of tobacco smoke?
5. What are the specific influences of nicotine, carbon monoxide, and phenol on the normal function of the body?
6. In what ways does cigarette smoking contribute to cardiovascular disease? What effect does nicotine have on the cardiovascular system?
7. To what extent is tobacco use a factor in cancer? What specific airway tissues are involved in lung cancer?
8. What is the traditional progression of chronic

obstructive lung disease? In what ways does tobacco use impair reproductive health?

9. In what ways is smokeless tobacco equal to smoking in the development of serious health concerns?

10. What is our current understanding about chronic caffeine consumption as a health problem?

11. What is involuntary smoking? Why is there growing concern about the effects of passive smoke on spouses and children?

12. What is the most effective way to stop smoking? What is the average weight gain after stopping smoking? How effective are other approaches to stopping smoking? What are the principal nicotine replacement systems in use today? What role do antidepressants play in smoking cessation?

13. What rights do smokers and nonsmokers have in public places? How can communication be enhanced between smokers and nonsmokers?

 ## Think About This . . .

- Why do proportionally more highly educated women than highly educated men smoke cigarettes?
- If you saw a minor being sold cigarettes, would you feel comfortable mentioning your concern to the merchant?

- If you are a smoker, do you understand why you are more "winded" than nonsmokers with whom you try to compete athletically?
- If you are a smoker, have you ever been asked to extinguish your cigarette? How did you react? How did you feel about this?

References

1. *Cancer facts & figures—1997*, Atlanta, GA, 1997, American Cancer Society.
2. Johnston LS, O'Malley PM, Bachman JG: *Smoking, drinking, and illicit drug use among American secondary school students, college students, and young adults, 1975-1991*, vol 2. *College students and young adults*, NIH Pub No. 93-3481. Rockville, MD, 1992, National Institute on Drug Abuse, USDHHS, USPHS.
3. Substance Abuse and Mental Health Services Administration Office of Applied Studies. *National household survey on drug abuse: population estimates 1995*. U.S. Department of Health and Human Services, DHHS Pub No. (SMA) 96-3095, 1996.
4. National survey results on drug use. From *The monitoring the future study*, 1975-1992, vol 11, NIH Pub No. 93-3598, Washington, DC, 1993, National Institute on Drug Abuse.
5. Levy D: Firm knew cigarette tar tested low. *USA Today*, p. 1D, Aug 2, 1995.
6. Personal interview, Art Uline, MD, NBC News, New York, Nov 6, 1995.
7. Carey AR, Mullins ME: World's heavy smokers (as reported by *Euromonitor*), *USA Today*, p. 1A, Oct 28, 1998.
8. Henningfield JE, Radzius A, Cone EJ: Estimation of available nicotine content of six smokeless tobacco products, *Tobacco Control*, 4:57-61. 1995.
9. Judge throws out major class-action tobacco suit, *USA Today*, Oct 20, 1997.
10. Pinger RR, Payne WA, Hahn DB, Hahn EJ: *Drugs: issues for today*, ed 3, Dubuque, IA, 1998, WCB/McGraw-Hill.
11. Thompson C: Joe Camel dies, victim of his own success, *USA Today*, p. 1A, July 11, 1977.
12. Regulations restricting the sale and distribution of cigarettes and smokeless tobacco products to protect children and adolescents, *Federal Register* 60(156):41314-41451, Washington, DC, Aug 11, 1995.
13. Rigotti NA et al: The effect of enforcing tobacco-sales laws on adolescents' access to and smoking behavior, *N Engl J Med* 337(15):1044-1051, 1997.
14. Centers for Disease Control: The Surgeon General's 1998 report on reducing the health consequences of smoking: 25 years of progress (executive summary), *MMWR* 38 (suppl 5) 2:1, 1989.
15. American Heart Association: *1997 heart and stroke facts: 1997 statistical supplement*, Dallas, 1996, The Association.
16. Howard G et al: Cigarette smoking and progression of atherosclerosis, *JAMA* 279(2):119-124, 1998.
17. Brennhan J et al: Association between cigarette smoking and mutation of the p53 gene in squamous-cell carcinoma of the head and neck, *N Engl J Med* 332:712-717, 1995.
18. Wistuba I et al: Molecular damage in the bronchial epithelium of smokers, *J Natl Cancer Inst* 89(18):1366-1373, 1997.
19. Crowley LV: *Introduction to human disease*, ed 4, Boston, 1996, Jones & Bartlett.
20. Eisen S, Lyon M, Goldberg J, True W: The impact of cigarette and alcohol consumption on weight and obesity: an analysis of 1911 monozygotic male twin pairs, *Arch Intern Med* 153(21):2457-2463, 1993.
21. Julien RM: *A primer of drug action*, ed 7, New York, 1995, W.H. Freeman.

22. Caffeine during pregnancy: grounds for concern? *JAMA* 270(24):2973, 1993 (editorial).

23. Eliopoulos C et al: Hair concentrations of nicotine in women and their newborn infants, *JAMA* 271(8):621-623, 1994.

24. Hatcher RA et al: Contraceptive technology, ed 18, New York, 1994, Irvington Publishers.

25. Glantz S, Parmely WW: Passive smoking and heart disease, epidemiology, physiology, and biochemistry, *Circulation* 83(1):1-12, 1991.

26. Robinson JP, Switzer P, Ott W: Daily exposure to environmental tobacco smoke: Smokers vs nonsmokers in California, *AJPH* 86(9):1303-1305, 1996.

27. Overpeck MD, Moss AJ: Children's exposure to environmental cigarette smoke before and after birth: United States, 1998, *Advanced data from vital and health statistics, no 202*, Hyattsville, MD, 1991, National Center for Health Statistics.

28. Glantz SA, Smith LR: The effect of ordinances requiring smoke-free restaurants and bars on revenue: a follow-up, *Am J Pub Health* 87(10):1687-1693, 1997.

Suggested Readings

Rustin TA: *Keep quit: a motivation guide to a life without smoking,* Sherman Oaks, CA, 1996, Hazelden.

For people trying to quit smoking, temptation to smoke often occurs at certain times or places or around certain people. This book offers 365 exercises to help the quitter deal with these triggers, thus improving his or her likelihood of success.

Libbon RP, Izenberg N: *How to raise non-smoking kids,* New York, 1997, Pocket Books.

When the next Great American Smokeout occurs, parents may want to use the occasion to encourage their children to remain smoke-free as they grow up. This book describes a variety of activities designed to explore the effects of smoking on health.

Katahn M: *How to quit smoking without gaining weight,* New York, 1996, W.W. Norton.

Although most people who quit smoking do gain weight, the author of this book contends that putting on pounds is avoidable. Using information about metabolism and biochemical pathways, the author proposes a simple program to prevent weight gain after smoking cessation, without going on a diet.

Glantz S (editor): *The cigarette papers,* Berkeley, CA, 1996, University of California Press.

Staton Glantz, a professor of medicine at the University of California-San Francisco, is a true thorn in the side of the tobacco industry. His book gives readers an array of information obtained from 4000 recently released tobacco industry documents. He and a panel of experts tell the inside story of how the industry manipulated the product, the government, and the public in order to retain smokers and disclaim the dangers of tobacco.

Whelan EM (editor): *Cigarettes: what the warning label doesn't tell you,* Amherst, NY, 1997, Prometheus Books.

Drawing on the expertise of clinicians and researchers in many areas, this 20-chapter book investigates virtually every area of human structure and function harmed by smoking. The information in the book would be of interest to both health care providers and laypeople.

Fahs J: *Cigarette confidential: the unfiltered truth about the ultimate American addiction,* New York, 1996, Berkeley Publishing Group.

As the title suggests, this book is an informative and entertaining assessment of the tobacco industry's attempts to profit at the expense of Americans' health. Using historical accounts and other sources, the author exposes the industry's methods of concealment and influence buying to sustain their deadly business.

 AS WE GO TO PRESS . . .

On January 1, 1998, a law passed by the California State Assembly took effect prohibiting smoking in bars, casinos, and clubs. This law, similar to an earlier one prohibiting smoking in restaurants, was enacted to protect employees of these businesses from being exposed to high levels of environmental tobacco smoke. Business owners who opposed the legislation contended that their profits would suffer from the loss of smokers as patrons, and smokers claimed they had a right to smoke while enjoying gaming, food, and alcoholic beverages.

A study demonstrated that the law did not lower the profits of bars, casinos, and clubs. Nevertheless, the California State Assembly voted to rescind the law, effective January 1, 1999. Widespread violation of the law convinced the legislature that the law was unenforceable. One comment on a radio talk show summed up the view this way: "I guess no one really goes into those type of places to do anything healthy anyway."[28]

Smokers vs. Nonsmokers: A Question of Rights

A quiet battle is being waged in the United States over smoking, an activity that was once universally accepted. Within the last decade, regulations restricting the act of smoking have affected stores, restaurants, offices, and public buildings. It is difficult these days to find a place of business in the United States where smoking is totally unrestricted. Some of these restrictions are put in place by law or municipal ordinances; some are placed voluntarily by business management. However, it is clear that the voices of nonsmokers, long silent and largely ignored by society, are finally being heard and are behind the recent increase in restrictions on smoking.

As antismokers have made progress in cutting back on unwanted environmental smoke, smokers have begun to fight back. As restrictions have mounted, they have united and mobilized to prevent themselves from being pushed to the fringes of society. The two sides have sparked a debate that goes to the heart of the American value system and is questioning the way we think about the rights of the individual.

Changing attitudes

For decades, there was no debate or controversy. People smoked whenever and wherever they wished. Smoking was glamorized in the movies, on television, and in print throughout most of the twentieth century. Famous athletes and movie stars could be found in cigarette advertisements. Some ads even promoted the "health benefits" of smoking. Although there were a few people who felt that smoking was dangerous, their voices had little effect on society's acceptance of tobacco use. Gradually, however, attitudes began to change. As data from medical studies began to accumulate on the dangers of tobacco, antismoking advocates started to achieve some victories in society and in public policy.

Restrictions on tobacco use

In the 1980s, restrictions on smoking greatly increased. In 1987, smoking was banned on all domestic airplane flights of less than 2 hours; in 1990, this ban was later increased to all domestic flights of less than 6 hours.[1] A growing number of state and local laws curtailing or banning smoking in places of business have been enacted. For example, Maryland has banned smoking in all workplaces except those with a sealed, separately ventilated room for smokers,[2] and in the state of Washington, smoking is prohibited in all enclosed public and private offices.[2] Many businesses that were not forced by law to restrict smoking did so anyway, citing public sentiment in favor of such regulations. Smoking is prohibited on over 80% of Amtrak trains, and 1400 company-owned McDonald's restaurants are now smoke free.[2]

As a result of these restrictions, smoking areas in places of business are shrinking in size or are being eliminated. Congregations of smokers outside of office buildings have become a common sight. Some smokers have taken the changes in stride. Others have cut back on smoking or have quit smoking altogether. Many, however, are not happy about having to step outside in all kinds of weather to smoke. They feel ostracized and are speaking out against what they perceive as an outright attack on their personal freedoms.

The prosmoker defense

In response to these perceived attacks, smokers have started to become organized on a worldwide level and within individual communities and workplaces. They are clearly worried that this trend of restricting tobacco use will not stop until smoking is eliminated everywhere and the use of tobacco becomes illegal.

Groups such as the British-based Freedom Organisation for the Right to Enjoy Smoking Tobacco (FOREST) have actively pushed smokers' rights and have espoused the "benefits" of smoking.[3] They cite controversial scientific studies demonstrating that smokers are less likely to develop Alzheimer's disease and Parkinson's disease and that teen acne is "almost exclusively" a nonsmokers' affliction.[3]

Smokers are also worried about how their smoking activities are perceived by employers and insurers. Companies are growing less tolerant of unhealthy activities by their employees, since they have to pay increased insurance costs for treatment. Many fear that insurance companies will begin to refuse treatment to smokers who continue to smoke. They cite cases such as one from the United Kingdom in which a cardiac patient was refused treatment because he continued to smoke and had a poor prognosis for recovery.[4] Talk of changing the U.S. health care system to a more European-style system has smoking activists worried that such treatment refusals could become commonplace here.

Some companies in the United States have gone as far as to conduct breath tests to determine if employees have been smoking away from the workplace.[3] Smoking activists feel that what employees do in the privacy of their own home is their own business and that these tests are akin to urine tests for illegal drugs. Some fear that restrictions will continue to reach into the home setting.

As a result, smoking activists have teamed up with the tobacco industry and the American Civil Liberties Union to convince states to adopt laws prohibiting companies from discriminating against smokers. These lobbying activities have been successful in 28 states.[5]

The worst-case scenario for smokers is that their smoking will be restricted even at home. "What if the government starts keeping us from having kids because we smoke?" worries "Earl," a two-pack-a-day smoker. "I've heard tell that we could have our kids taken away because we smoke at home. Do we have to step outside of our own homes to smoke?"[6]

Fighting for clean air

Many nonsmokers are just as adamant about defending their side, saying that smokers have been subjecting them to cancer-causing agents for decades and that the restrictions are long overdue. They are tired of having smoke blown in their faces in public. Antismoking activists find the "individual freedom" argument of smokers objectionable. "What about my right to breathe?" asks "Stan," an office worker who is subjected to smoke from nearby cubicles. "The management, most of whom smoke, have decided that since we don't deal directly with the public, smoking is okay," he complains.[7]

Many nonsmoking activists feel that it is in the public's best interest to restrict exposure to tobacco smoke and to cut back on tobacco use as a whole. They are angered not only that they have to be exposed to it, but that a good chunk of their insurance premiums is going toward health care costs from smoking. It is estimated that $65 billion a year goes to treat tobacco-related diseases, roughly one fourth of all money spent on health care in the United States each year.[8] The groundswell of support for tobacco regulations may be happening in response to the growing number of medical studies that show the dangers of tobacco use. The Centers for Disease Control and Prevention estimate that 418,000 deaths per year can be attributed to tobacco smoke, and approximately 3000 nonsmokers die yearly from lung cancer caused by exposure to tobacco smoke.[2] As the data accumulate on the hazards of smoking, many nonsmokers are becoming concerned about their exposure to secondhand smoke. They are also worried about the addictive properties of nicotine and are concerned that their children may get hooked.

Though they have had much success in getting restrictions adopted, antismoking activists have also faced defeat in the legislatures as well. Municipalities in North Carolina can no longer pass local laws restricting smoking, thanks to a preemptive state law passed on July 15, 1993.[9] HB 957 allows local regulations adopted before October 15, 1993, to remain in effect, but it bans any future regulations from being adopted. The 3-month period between passage of the bill and the regulation deadline left a very short window of time for local bodies to organize, debate, and vote on smoking restrictions. As a result, 59% of workers in North Carolina have no legal protection at all from exposure to tobacco smoke.[9]

Even without the health problems posed by tobacco smoke, many nonsmokers feel that it should be curtailed simply because of its unpleasant smell. Since smoking is not a self-contained activity, smoke diffuses far away from the smoker, often offending people many feet away. "What good does it do to seat a nonsmoker next to the smoking section in a restaurant?" notes "Irina," an avid antismoking activist.[10] "The smoke just drifts over anyway. It stinks, and not just during the meal. It gets into your clothes and hair and stays with you all day. Why must we tolerate smoke?"

What the future may hold

Such arguments may open the door to more restrictions on smoking, a possibility that has smokers' rights advocates angry. Many are convinced that antismoking forces want nothing less than a total ban on tobacco use. Although this scenario is highly unlikely, more regulations may be on the way. Former FDA head David Kessler considered a proposal that would eliminate cigarette vending machines (an easy tobacco source for juveniles) and restrict tobacco advertisements near schools.[2] The group Action on Smoking and Health has petitioned the Occupational Safety and Health Administration to ban all workplace smoking.[11] The EPA has labeled secondhand smoke as a Class A carcinogen.[11] The restrictions reach into the home as well, since some child custody cases are being decided (at least in part) by the smoking habits of the adults involved,[11] and some physicians now consider exposure to smoke in the home a form of child endangerment.

Antismoking advocates do not see these regulations as restrictions on individual freedom. Instead, they see these regulations as a means of liberation from decades of exposure to smoke with little or no means of legal recourse. Many nonsmokers feel that they should not be forced to breathe in smoke simply because someone wants to light up. Advocates for these regulations claim that tobacco-related illnesses increase health care costs for everyone. They also complain that their tax dollars are being used to subsidize the tobacco industry, so that in effect they are paying to be exposed to the smoke of others. Restrictions on smoking are a welcome means of relief for those nonsmokers with lung diseases or allergies to tobacco as well.

Since smoking by its very nature is not a self-contained

activity, conflicts are bound to happen, but perhaps some acceptable middle ground can be reached between smokers and nonsmokers both in law and in society.

For Discussion . . .

Have you ever asked someone not to smoke near you or been asked not to smoke around someone? Should taxpayers be responsible for taking on the burden of those being treated for smoking-related diseases? Are the individual freedoms of smokers being infringed on by smoking regulations? Are the individual freedoms of nonsmokers being violated by smokers? Is smoking at home around your children a form of child endangerment?

References

1. The tyranny of the majority, *The Economist* 313(7626), Oct 28, 1989.
2. Farley CJ, Toufexis A: The butt stops here, 143(16), *Time* Apr 18, 1994.
3. Platt S: Ashes to ashes, *New Statesman and Society* 7(289), Feb 11, 1994.
4. McNulty K: A smoky issue, *Science World* 50(11), Mar 11, 1994.
5. A get-tough approach can pose pitfalls, *Nation's Business* 83(9), Sept 1995.
6. Anonymous, personal communication, January 1996.
7. Anonymous, personal communication, June 1994.
8. What are they smoking? *FW* 161(5), Mar 3, 1992.
9. Conlisk E et al: The status of local smoking regulations in North Carolina following a state preemption bill, *JAMA* 273(10), 1995.
10. Anonymous, personal communication, March 1996.
11. Holt TH: Pests' attacks on smoking threaten individual freedoms, *Insight, vol. 42*, Oct 18, 1993.

PART 4

DISEASES

Reducing Your Risk of Cardiovascular Disease

Healthy People: Looking Ahead to 2010

The *Midcourse Review* reported that we have successfully moved toward achieving 15 of the 17 *Healthy People 2000* objectives in the priority area of cardiovascular disease. This was not surprising, since widespread public education programs have been developed and implemented during the last 25 years. Measures to identify high-risk groups have been initiated and refined. The ability to control high blood pressure and blood cholesterol levels has improved markedly. A great deal of evidence now indicates that heart disease can indeed be prevented through lifestyle changes.

Nevertheless, cardiovascular disease remains the nation's number one cause of death and disability, considerably outdistancing the number two cause. The *Midcourse Review* reminded us that premature morbidity (sickness) is devastating for many heart disease patients. Affected people often cannot participate fully in daily activities, and many become unable to function independently. The annual economic impact of heart disease is estimated to be $259 billion, which includes health care expenses, medications, and lost work productivity resulting from disability and death.[1] Heart disease will certainly be among the most important chronic conditions addressed in the *Healthy People 2010* objectives now being drafted.

This section of the book contains three chapters that deal with diseases. It is not surprising that diseases and adverse health conditions can be major obstacles to a healthy life. Although uninformed people claim that "there is nothing you can do to avoid disease," there is ample evidence that positive personal health choices can help reduce the chances of developing many diseases, from cardiovascular disease to cancer to sexually transmitted diseases, including HIV and AIDS.

Look at the progress made with respect to **cardiovascular** disease (CVD), the focus of this chapter. Although heart disease continues to be the number one killer of Americans, between 1984 and 1994 the death rates from CVD declined 22.4%.[1] The American Heart Association, in its *1997 Heart and Stroke Statistical Update*, credits this reduction to a combination of (1) changing American lifestyles and (2) medical advances in the diagnosis and treatment of CVD.[1]

This chapter provides you with material to help you understand how the heart works. Beyond this, it will help you identify your CVD risk factors and suggest ways you can alter certain lifestyle behaviors to reduce the risk of developing heart disease.

PREVALENCE OF CARDIOVASCULAR DISEASE

Cardiovascular diseases are directly related to over 40% of deaths in the United States and indirectly related to a large percentage of additional deaths.[1]

Heart disease, stroke, and related blood vessel disorders combined to kill nearly 1 million Americans in 1994 (Figure 10-1). This figure represents more deaths than were caused by cancer, accidents, pneumonia, influenza, lung diseases, diabetes, and AIDS combined. Indeed, cardiovascular disease is our nation's number one "killer" (see the Star Box on p. 230).

NORMAL CARDIOVASCULAR FUNCTION

The cardiovascular or circulatory system uses a muscular pump to send a complex fluid on a continuous trip through a closed system of tubes. The pump is the heart, the fluid is blood, and the closed system of tubes is the network of blood vessels.

The Vascular System

The term *vascular system* refers to the body's blood vessels. Although we might be familiar with the arteries (vessels that carry blood away from the heart) and the veins (vessels that carry blood toward the heart), arterioles, capillaries, and venules are also included in

> cardiovascular
> Pertaining to the heart (cardio) and blood vessels (vascular).

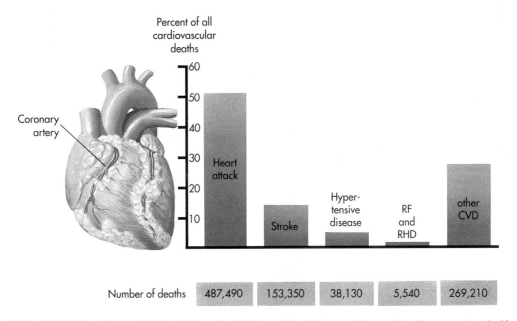

| Number of deaths | 487,490 | 153,350 | 38,130 | 5,540 | 269,210 |

Figure 10-1   Of the 954,720 deaths in the United States in 1994 resulting from cardiovascular diseases, over half were attributable to heart attack.[1]

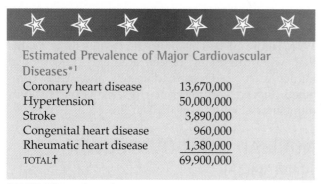

Estimated Prevalence of Major Cardiovascular Diseases*[1]	
Coronary heart disease	13,670,000
Hypertension	50,000,000
Stroke	3,890,000
Congenital heart disease	960,000
Rheumatic heart disease	1,380,000
TOTAL†	69,900,000

*57,490,000 people total.

†The sum of the individual estimates exceeds 57,490,000 because many people have more than one cardiovascular disorder.

the vascular system. Arterioles are the farther, smaller-diameter extensions of arteries. These arterioles lead eventually to capillaries, the smallest extensions of the vascular system. At the capillary level, exchanges of oxygen, food, and waste occur between cells and the blood.

Once the blood leaves the capillaries and begins its return to the heart, it drains into small veins, or venules. The blood in the venules flows into increasingly larger vessels called *veins*. Blood pressure is highest in arteries and lowest in veins, especially the largest veins, which empty into the right atrium of the heart.

The Heart

The heart is a four-chambered pump designed to create the pressure required to circulate blood throughout the body. Usually considered to be about the size of a person's clenched fist, this organ lies slightly tilted between the lungs in the central portion of the **thorax.** The heart does not lie completely in the center of the chest. Rather, approximately two thirds of the heart is to the left of the body midline and one third is to the right.[2]

Two upper chambers, called *atria,* and two lower chambers, called *ventricles,* form the heart. The thin-walled atrial chambers are considered collecting chambers, whereas the thick-walled muscular ventricles are considered the pumping chambers. The right and left sides of the heart are divided by a partition called the *septum.* Study Figure 10-2 and follow the flow of blood through the heart's four chambers.

For the heart muscle to function well, it must be supplied with adequate amounts of oxygen. The two main **coronary arteries** (and their numerous branches) accomplish this. These arteries are located outside of the heart (see Figure 10-1). If the coronary arteries are diseased and not functioning well, a heart attack is possible.

Heart stimulation

The heart contracts and relaxes through the delicate interplay of **cardiac muscle** tissue and cardiac electrical centers called *nodes.* Nodal tissue generates the electrical impulses necessary to contract heart

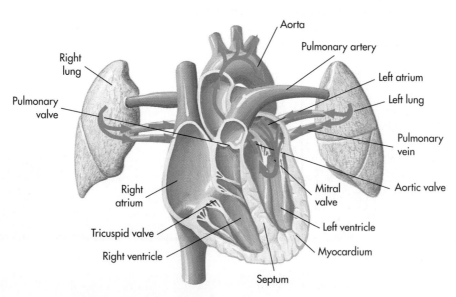

Figure 10-2   The heart functions like a complex double pump. The right side of the heart pumps deoxygenated blood to the lungs. The left side of the heart pumps oxygenated blood through the aorta to all parts of the body. Note the thickness of the walls of the ventricles. These are the primary pumping chambers.

muscle.[3] The heart's electrical activity is measured by an instrument called an *electrocardiograph* (ECG or EKG), which provides a printout called an electrocardiogram that can be evaluated to determine cardiac electrical functioning.

Blood

The average-sized adult has approximately 6 quarts of blood in his or her circulatory system. Blood's functions, which are performed continuously, are quite similar to the overall functions of the circulatory system and include the following:

- Transportation of nutrients, oxygen, wastes, hormones, and enzymes
- Regulation of water content of body cells and fluids
- Buffering to help maintain appropriate pH balance of body fluids
- Regulation of body temperature; the water component in the blood absorbs heat and transfers it
- Prevention of blood loss; by coagulating or clotting, the blood can alter its form to prevent blood loss through injured vessels
- Protection against toxins and microorganisms, accomplished by chemical substances called *antibodies* and specialized cellular elements circulating in the bloodstream

CARDIOVASCULAR DISEASE RISK FACTORS

As you have just read, the heart and blood vessels are among the most important structures in the human body. By protecting your cardiovascular system, you lay the groundwork for a more exciting, productive, and energetic life. The best time to start protecting and improving your cardiovascular system is early in life, when lifestyle patterns are developed and reinforced (see the Star Box at right). Of course, it is difficult to move backward through time, so the second best time to start protecting your heart is *today.* Improvements in certain lifestyle activities can pay significant dividends as your life unfolds. Complete the Personal Assessment on pp. 232-233 to determine your risk for heart disease.

The American Heart Association encourages people to protect and enhance their heart health by examining the 10 cardiovascular risk factors that are related to various forms of heart disease.[4] A *cardiovascular risk factor* is an attribute that a person has or is exposed to that increases the likelihood that he or she will

Prevention of Heart Disease Begins in Childhood

For many aspects of wellness, preventive behaviors are often best learned in childhood, where they can be repeated and reinforced by family members and caregivers. This is especially true for preventive actions concerning heart disease. Although many problems related to heart disease are seen most frequently at midlife and beyond, the roots of heart disease start early in life.

The most serious childhood health behaviors associated with heart disease are poor dietary practices, lack of physical activity, and cigarette smoking. Sadly, the present state of health for America's youth shows severe deficiencies in these three areas. Children's diets lack nutrient density and remain alarmingly high in overall fat. Teenaged children are becoming increasingly overweight and obese. Studies consistently show a deterioration in the amount of physical activity by today's youth, as television and video games have become the after-school companions for large numbers of children. Sadly, cigarette smoking continues to rise among schoolchildren, especially teenagers.

These unhealthy behaviors are laying the foundation for coronary artery disease, hypertension, and stroke in the future. Rather than trying to repair sick people in their older years, increased efforts on childhood prevention should be a focus for today's adults. Those of us who are parents must make better efforts to encourage our children to eat more nutritiously and be physically active. We can discourage cigarette use. Perhaps the best thing all adults can do for our youth is to set a good example by adopting our own heart-healthy behaviors. Following the Food Guide Pyramid (p. 108) and exercising regularly are excellent strategies that can be started early in life.

thorax
The chest; portion of the torso above the diaphragm and within the rib cage.

coronary arteries
Vessels that supply oxygenated blood to heart muscle tissues.

cardiac muscle
Specialized smooth muscle tissue that forms the middle (muscular) layer of the heart wall.

PERSONAL ASSESSMENT

What Is Your Risk for Heart Disease?

Cholesterol

Your serum cholesterol level is:

0	190 or below
+ 2	191 to 230
+ 6	231 to 289
+12	290 to 319
+16	Over 320

Your HDL cholesterol is:

− 2	Over 60
0	45 to 60
+ 2	35 to 44
+ 6	29 to 34
+12	23 to 28
+16	Below 23

Smoking

You smoke now or have in the past:

0	Never smoked, or quit more than 5 years ago
+1	Quit 2 to 4 years ago
+3	Quit about 1 year ago
+6	Quit during the past year

You now smoke:

+ 9	½ to 1 pack a day
+12	1 to 2 packs a day
+15	More than 2 packs a day

The quality of the air you breathe is:

0	Unpolluted by smoke, exhaust, or industry at home **and** at work
+2	Live **or** work with smokers in unpolluted area
+4	Live **and** work with smokers in unpolluted area
+6	Live **or** work with smokers **and** live or work in air-polluted area
+8	Live **and** work with smokers **and** live and work in air-polluted area

Blood Pressure

Your blood pressure is:

0	120/75 or below
+ 2	120/75 to 140/85
+ 6	140/85 to 150/90
+ 8	150/90 to 175/100
+10	175/100 to 190/110
+12	190/110 or above

Exercise

Your exercise habits are:

0	Exercise vigorously 4 or 5 times a week
+2	Exercise moderately 4 or 5 times a week
+4	Exercise only on weekends
+6	Exercise occasionally
+8	Little or no exercise

Weight

Your weight is:

0	Always at or near ideal weight
+1	Now 10% overweight
+2	Now 20% overweight
+3	Now 30% or more overweight
+4	Now 20% or more overweight and have been since before age 30

Stress

You feel overstressed:

0	Rarely at work or at home
+ 3	Somewhat at home but not at work
+ 5	Somewhat at work but not at home
+ 7	Somewhat at work **and** at home
+ 9	Usually at work **or** at home
+12	Usually at work **and** at home

Diabetes

Your diabetic history is:

0	Blood sugar always normal
+2	Blood glucose slightly high (prediabetic) or slightly low (hypoglycemic)
+4	Diabetic beginning after age 40 requiring strict dietary or insulin control
+5	Diabetic beginning before age 30 requiring strict dietary or insulin control

Alcohol

You drink alcoholic beverages:

0	Never or only socially, about once or twice a month, or only one 5-ounce glass of wine or 12-ounce glass of beer or 1½ ounces of hard liquor about 5 times a week
+2	Two to three 5-ounce glasses of wine or 12-ounce glasses of beer or 1½-ounce cocktails about 5 times a week
+4	More than three 1½-ounce cocktails or more than three 5-ounce glasses of wine or 12-ounce glasses of beer almost every day

Continued

Interpretation
Add all sources and check below
0 to 20: Low risk. Excellent family history and lifestyle habits.
21 to 50: Moderate risk. Family history or lifestyle habits put you at some risk. You might lower your risks and minimize your genetic predisposition if you change any poor habits.
51 to 74: High risk. Habits and family history indicate high risk of heart disease. Change your habits now.

Above 75: Very high risk. Family history and a lifetime of poor habits put you at very high risk of heart disease. Eliminate as many of the risk factors as you can.

To Carry This Further . . .
Were you surprised with your score on this assessment? What were your most significant risk factors? Do you plan to make any changes in your lifestyle to reduce your cardiovascular risks? Why or why not?

develop some form of heart disease. Three risk factors are ones you will be unable to change. An additional four risk factors are ones you can clearly change. Three final risk factors are ones that are thought to be contributing factors to heart disease.

Risk Factors That Cannot Be Changed

The three risk factors that you cannot change are increasing age, male gender, and heredity.[4] Despite the fact that these risk factors cannot be changed, your knowledge that they might be an influence in your life should encourage you to make a more serious commitment to the risk factors you *can* change.

Increasing age

Heart diseases tend to develop gradually over the course of one's life. Although we may know of a person or two who experienced a heart attack in their thirties or forties, most of the serious consequences of heart disease are evident in older ages. For example, approximately 80% of people who die from heart attack are age 65 and older.

Male gender

Young women have lower rates of heart disease than young men. Yet when women move through menopause (typically in their fifties), their rates of heart disease are similar to men's rates (see the Star Box on p. 234). It is thought that women are somewhat more protected from heart disease than men because of their natural production of the hormone estrogen during their fertile years.

Heredity

Like increasing age and male gender, this risk factor cannot be changed. By the luck of the draw, some people are born into families where heart disease has never been a serious problem, whereas others are born into families where heart disease is quite prevalent. In this latter case, children are said to have a genetic pre-

disposition (tendency) to develop heart disease as they grow and develop throughout their lives. These people have every reason to be highly motivated to reduce the risk factors they can control.

Race is also a consideration related to heart disease. African-Americans have moderately high blood pressure at rates twice that of whites and severe hypertension at rates three times higher than whites (for a detailed discussion of this topic, see "Focus on . . . Hypertension among African-Americans," pp. 247-248). Hypertension significantly increases the risk of both heart disease and stroke. Fortunately, as you will soon read, hypertension can be controlled through a variety of methods. It is especially impor-

HealthQuest Activities

- The *Heart Attack Risk* and *Cardiovascular Exploration* activities in Module 5 allow you to assess your risk for cardiovascular disease. In the first of these activities, *Heart Attack Risk,* answer the questions about your health history, behavioral practices, and knowledge about heart disease. *HealthQuest* will then provide the correct answers and point out any health risks indicated by your responses. In the *Cardiovascular Exploration* section, fill out all of the items, and then click on the "Show Me!" button to find out your overall risk. You can get more specific feedback on each risk factor by clicking on the underlined words.

- Many traditional-age college students have difficulty understanding how cardiovascular disease affects quality of life. Heart disease seems only a distant possibility, but for many, it can become all too real. To learn more, read about heart disease among women and minority groups in the *Social Perspectives* section. List several health choices that can increase the likelihood of developing cardiovascular disease, and explain how one's family history can affect the risk. Finally, describe what you would do if you observed someone having a heart attack.

Women and Heart Disease

Do you think heart disease is a problem just for men? You might be surprised to discover that data from the American Heart Association indicate that 52% of all cardiovascular disease deaths are in women. 20,800 women under the age of 65 die from heart attack each year and 29% of women who die from coronary artery disease are under age 55. Also, 44% of women who have a heart attack will die within 1 year, compared with 27% of men. A total of 60% of the deaths from stroke and high blood pressure are in women, compared with 40% in men. Women who smoke and also take oral contraceptives are 39 times more likely to have a heart attack and 22 times more likely to have a stroke than women who neither smoke nor use oral contraceptives.[5]

For many years, it was thought that men were at much greater risk than women for the development of cardiovascular problems. It is now known that younger men are more prone to heart disease than young women, yet once women reach menopause (usually in their early to middle 50s), their rates of heart-related problems quickly equal those of men.

The protective mechanism for young women seems to be the female hormone estrogen. Estrogen appears to help women maintain a beneficial profile of blood fats. When the production of estrogen is severely reduced at menopause, this protective factor no longer exists. This is one of the reasons that increasing numbers of physicians are prescribing estrogen replacement therapy (ERT) for many postmenopausal women. ERT (also called HRT, or hormone replacement therapy) may not be helpful for all women. Women should discuss this option with their physicians.[6]

Of course, young women should not rely solely on naturally-produced estrogen to prevent heart disease. The general recommendations for maintaining heart health through a good diet, adequate physical activity, monitoring blood pressure and cholesterol levels, controlling weight, avoiding smoking, and managing stress will benefit women at every stage of life.

---

tant for African-Americans to take advantage of every opportunity to have their blood pressure measured so that preventive actions can be started immediately if necessary.

Risk Factors That Can Be Changed

There are four cardiovascular risk factors that are influenced, in large part, by our lifestyle choices. These risk factors are cigarette/tobacco smoke, physical inactivity, high blood pressure, and high blood cholesterol level. Healthful behavior changes you make concerning these "big four" risk factors can help you protect and enhance your cardiovascular system.

Cigarette or tobacco smoke

Although the other three controllable risk factors are important, this one may be the most critical risk factor. Smokers have a heart attack risk that is over twice that of nonsmokers. Smoking cigarettes is *the* major risk factor associated with sudden cardiac death. In fact, smokers have two to four times the risk of dying from sudden cardiac arrest than nonsmokers.

Cigarette or tobacco smoke also adversely affects nonsmokers who are exposed to environmental tobacco smoke. Studies suggest that the risk of death caused by heart disease is increased about 30 percent in people exposed to secondhand smoke in the home.[5] Because of the health threat to nonsmokers, restrictions on indoor smoking in public areas and business settings are increasing tremendously in every part of the country.

For years the notion was that if you had smoked for many years, it was pointless to try to quit; the damage to one's health could never be reversed. However, the American Heart Association now indicates that by quitting smoking, regardless of how long or how much you have smoked, your risk of heart disease declines rapidly. For people who have smoked a pack or less of cigarettes per day, within 3 years after quitting smoking, their heart disease risk is virtually the same as those who never smoked.

This news is exciting and should encourage people to quit smoking, regardless of how long they have smoked. Of course, if you have started to smoke, the healthy approach would be to *quit now* . . . before the nicotine controls your life and damages your heart. (For additional information about the health effects of tobacco, see Chapter 9.)

Physical inactivity

Lack of exercise is a significant risk factor for heart disease. Regular aerobic exercise (discussed in Chapter 4) helps strengthen the heart muscle, maintain healthy blood vessels, and improve the ability of the vascular system to transfer blood and oxygen to all parts of the body. Additionally, physical activity helps lower overall blood cholesterol levels for most people, encourages weight loss and retention of lean muscle

Regular aerobic exercise helps maintain cardiovascular health.

mass, and allows people to moderate the stress in their lives.

With all the benefits that come with physical activity, it amazes health professionals that so many Americans refuse to participate in regular exercise. Perhaps people feel that they do not have enough time or that they must work out strenuously. However, you will recall from Chapter 4 that only 20 to 60 minutes of moderate aerobic activity three to five times each week is recommended. This is not a large price to pay for a lifetime of cardiovascular health. Find a partner and get started!

If you are middle-aged or older and have been inactive, you should consult with a physician before starting an exercise program. Also, if you have any known health condition that could be aggravated by physical activity, check with a physician first.

High blood cholesterol level

The third controllable risk factor for heart disease is high blood cholesterol level. Generally speaking, the higher the blood cholesterol level, the greater the risk for heart disease. When high blood cholesterol levels are combined with other important risk factors, the risks become much greater.

Fortunately, blood cholesterol levels are relatively easy to measure. Many campus health and wellness centers provide cholesterol screenings for employees and students. These screenings help identify people whose cholesterol levels (or profiles) may be potentially dangerous. Medical professionals have been able to determine the link between a person's diet and his or her cholesterol levels. People with high blood cholesterol levels are encouraged to consume a heart-healthy diet (see Chapter 5) and to become physically active. In recent years a variety of cholesterol-lowering drugs have also been developed that are very effective at lowering cholesterol levels. In an upcoming section in this chapter, you will read more about cholesterol.

High blood pressure

The fourth of the "big four" cardiovascular risk factors is high blood pressure, or hypertension. You will soon be reading more about hypertension, but for now, suffice it say that high blood pressure can seriously damage a person's heart and blood vessels. High blood pressure causes the heart to work much harder, eventually causing the heart to enlarge and weaken. High blood pressure increases the chances for stroke, heart attack, congestive heart failure, and kidney disease.

When high blood pressure is seen with other risk factors, the risk for stroke or heart attack is increased tremendously. As you will soon see, this "silent killer" is easy to monitor and can be effectively controlled using a variety of approaches. This is the positive message about high blood pressure.

Other Risk Factors That Contribute to Heart Disease

The American Heart Association identifies three other risk factors that are associated with an increased risk of heart disease. These risk factors are diabetes, obesity, and stress.

Diabetes

Diabetes mellitus (discussed in detail on pp. 266-269) is a debilitating chronic disease that has a significant effect on the human body. In addition to increasing the risks of developing kidney disease, blindness, and nerve damage, diabetes increases the likelihood of developing heart and blood vessel diseases. Over 80% of people with diabetes die of some type of heart or blood vessel disease. The cardiovascular damage is thought to occur when diabetes begins to alter normal cholesterol and blood fat levels. With weight management, exercise, dietary changes, and drug therapy, diabetes can be relatively well controlled in most people. Despite

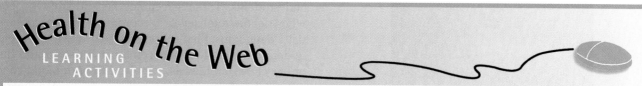

Health on the Web
LEARNING ACTIVITIES

Activity 1

The American Heart Association (AHA) comprises over 4 million volunteers in all 50 states and in Washington, D.C., and Puerto Rico. These men and women are working to fight the nation's number one killer—cardiovascular disease and stroke. The AHA spent more than $251 million during fiscal year 1995–96 for research support, public and professional education, and community programs. With more than 4 million volunteers, the AHA is the largest voluntary health organization dedicated to fighting heart disease and stroke, diseases that kill more than 950,000 Americans every year. Visit the AHA website at http:www.amhrt.org. Click on *What's Your Risk of Heart Disease?* and calculate your risk of coronary heart disease by completing the risk assessment profile.

Activity 2

This chapter presents material to help you understand the risks of cardiovascular disease. To test your heart IQ, go to http://www.wellweb.com/heart/htquiz.htm#heartiq and take the quiz developed by the National Heart, Lung, and Blood Institute. Answer true or false to each of the statements listed, and then check your answers. What did you learn?

Activity 3

A great deal of evidence now indicates that some types of heart disease can indeed be prevented through lifestyle changes. Nevertheless, cardiovascular disease remains the nation's leading cause of death and disability. Affected people often cannot participate fully in daily activities. Go to http://www.mayohealth.org/cgibin/apps/quiz.cgi/mayo/expert/htm/9510quiz.txt?/mayo/common/htm/top.txt,/mayo/common/htm/bottom.txt to take the quiz *Heart Disease: Who Gets It and How to Avoid It*. Answer the 10 questions listed. How well did you do?

---

careful management of this disease, diabetic patients remain quite susceptible to eventual heart and blood vessel damage.

Obesity

Even if they have no other risk factors, obese people are more likely than nonobese people to develop heart disease and stroke. Obesity places considerable strain on the heart, and it tends to influence both blood pressure and blood cholesterol levels. Also, obesity tends to trigger diabetes in predisposed people. The importance of maintaining body weight within a desirable range minimizes the chances of obesity ever happening. To accomplish this, you can elect to make a commitment to a reasonably sound diet and an active lifestyle.

Individual response to stress

Unresolved stress over a long period may be a contributing factor to the development of heart disease. Certainly, people who are unable to cope with stressful life experiences are more likely to develop negative dependence behaviors (for example, smoking, underactivity, poor dietary practices), which can then lead to cardiovascular problems through changes in blood fat profiles, blood pressure, and heart workload. To discover ways of coping with stress, you might wish to return to the discussion in Chapter 3.

FORMS OF CARDIOVASCULAR DISEASE

The American Heart Association describes the five major forms of CVD as coronary heart disease, hypertension, stroke, congenital heart disease, and rheumatic heart disease.[1] A person may have just one of these five diseases or a combination of forms at the same time. Each form exists in varying degrees of severity. All forms are capable of causing secondary damage to other body organs and body systems.

Coronary Heart Disease

This form of CVD, also known as *coronary artery disease*, involves damage to the vessels that supply blood to the heart muscle. The bulk of this blood is supplied by the coronary arteries. Any damage to these important vessels can cause a reduction of blood (and its vital oxygen and nutrients) to specific areas of heart muscle. The ultimate result of inadequate blood supply is a heart attack.

Atherosclerosis

The principal cause for the development of coronary heart disease is atherosclerosis (Figure 10-3). **Atherosclerosis** produces a narrowing of the coronary arteries. This narrowing stems from the long-

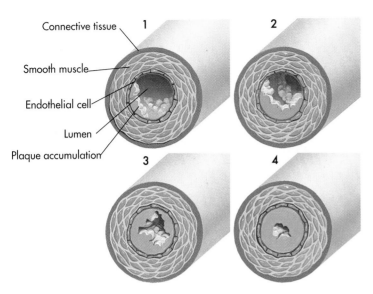

Connective tissue

Smooth muscle

Endothelial cell

Lumen

Plaque accumulation

Figure 10-3 Progression of atherosclerosis. This diagram shows how plaque deposits gradually accumulate to narrow the lumen (interior space) of an artery. Although enlarged here, coronary arteries are only as wide as a pencil lead.

term buildup of fatty deposits, called *plaque,* on the inner walls of the arteries. This buildup reduces the blood supply to specific portions of the heart. Some arteries of the heart can become so blocked (occluded) that all blood supply is stopped. Heart muscle tissue begins to die when it is deprived of oxygen and nutrients. This damage is known as **myocardial infarction.** In lay terms, this event is called a *heart attack.* The Health Action Guide on p. 238 explains how to recognize the signs of a heart attack and what to do next.

Cholesterol and lipoproteins. For many years, scientists have known that atherosclerosis is a complicated disease that has many causes. Some of these causes are not well understood, but others are clearly understood. *Cholesterol,* a soft, fatlike material, is manufactured in the liver and small intestine and is necessary in the formation of sex hormones, cell membranes, bile salts, and nerve fibers. Elevated levels of serum cholesterol (200 mg/dl or more for adults age 20 and older, and 170 mg/dl or more for young people below age 20) are associated with an increased risk for developing atherosclerosis[1] (see the Health Action Guide on p. 239).

Some 52% of American adults age 20 and older exceed the "borderline high" 200 mg/dl cholesterol level. It is estimated that nearly 40% of American youth age 19 and below have "borderline high" cholesterol levels of 170 mg/dl and above. About one out of five American adults has a "high" blood cholesterol level, that is, 240 mg/dl or greater.[1]

Initially, most people can help lower their serum cholesterol level by adopting three dietary changes:

lowering the intake of saturated fats, lowering the intake of dietary cholesterol, and lowering caloric intake to a level that does not exceed body requirements. The aim is to reduce excess fat, cholesterol, and calories in our diet while promoting sound nutrition. By carefully following such a diet plan, people with elevated serum cholesterol levels typically are able to reduce their cholesterol levels by 30 to 55 mg/dl. However, dietary changes do not affect people equally; some will experience greater reductions than others. Some will not respond at all to dietary changes and may need to take cholesterol-lowering medications and increase physical activity.

Cholesterol is attached to structures called *lipoproteins.* Lipoproteins are particles that circulate in the blood and transport lipids (including cholesterol).[4] Two major classes of lipoproteins exist: **low-density lipoproteins (LDLs)** and **high-density lipoproteins (HDLs).** A person's total cholesterol level is mostly determined by the amount of the LDLs and HDLs in a measured sample of blood. (For example, a person's total cholesterol level of 200 mg/dl could be represented by an LDL level of 160 and an HDL level of 40, or an LDL level of 140 and an HDL level of 60.)

After much scientific study, it has been determined that high levels of LDL are a significant cause of atherosclerosis. This makes sense because LDLs carry the greatest percentage of cholesterol in the bloodstream. LDLs are more likely to deposit excess cholesterol into the artery walls. This contributes to plaque formation.

atherosclerosis
Buildup of plaque on the inner walls of arteries.

myocardial infarction
Heart attack; the death of part of the heart muscle as a result of a blockage in one of the coronary arteries.

low-density lipoprotein (LDL)
The type of lipoprotein that transports the largest amount of cholesterol in the bloodstream; high levels of LDL are related to heart disease.

high-density lipoprotein (HDL)
The type of lipoprotein that transports cholesterol from the bloodstream to the liver, where it is eventually removed from the body; high levels of HDL are related to a reduction in heart disease.

HEALTH
Action Guide

Recognizing Signs of a Heart Attack and Taking Action

Warning Signs of a Heart Attack
- Uncomfortable pressure, fullness, squeezing, or pain in the center of your chest lasting 2 minutes or longer
- Pain spreading to your shoulders, neck, or arms
- Severe pain, dizziness, fainting, sweating, nausea, or shortness of breath

Not all of these warning signs occur with every heart attack. If some start to occur, don't wait. Get help immediately!

What to Do in an Emergency
- Find out which hospitals in your area have 24-hour emergency cardiac care.
- Determine (in advance) the hospital or medical facility that is nearest your home and office, and tell your family and friends to call this facility in an emergency.
- Keep a list of emergency rescue service numbers next to your telephone and in your pocket, wallet, or purse.
- If you have chest discomfort that lasts for 2 minutes or more, call the emergency rescue service.
- If you can get to a hospital faster by going yourself and not waiting for an ambulance, have someone drive you there.

Be a Heart Saver
- If you are with someone experiencing the signs of a heart attack and the warning signs last for 2 minutes or longer, act immediately.
- Expect a "denial." It is normal for someone with chest discomfort to deny the possibility of something as serious as a heart attack. Don't take "no" for an answer. Insist on taking prompt action.
- Call the rescue service (911), or get to the nearest hospital emergency room that offers 24-hour emergency cardiac care.
- Give CPR (mouth-to-mouth breathing and chest compression) if it is necessary and if you are properly trained.

For this reason, LDLs are often called the "bad cholesterol."[7] High LDL levels are determined partially by inheritance, but they are also clearly associated with smoking, poor dietary patterns, obesity, and lack of exercise.

On the other hand, high levels of HDLs are related to a decrease in the development of atherosclerosis. HDLs are thought to transport cholesterol out of the bloodstream. Thus HDLs have been called the "good cholesterol." Certain lifestyle alterations, such as quitting smoking, reducing obesity, increasing physical activity, and decreasing dietary fats, help many people increase their level of HDLs.

Reducing total serum cholesterol levels is a significant step in reducing the risk of death from coronary heart disease. For people with elevated cholesterol levels, a 1% reduction in serum cholesterol level yields about a 2% reduction in the risk of death from heart disease. Thus a 10% to 15% cholesterol reduction can reduce risk by 20% to 30%.[8] Study Table 10-1 for cholesterol classifications and current recommended follow-up.

Angina pectoris. When coronary arteries become narrowed, chest pain, or *angina pectoris,* is often felt. This pain results from a reduced supply of oxygen to heart muscle tissue. Usually, angina is felt when the patient becomes stressed or exercises too strenuously. Angina reportedly can range from a feeling of mild indigestion to a severe viselike pressure in the chest. The pain may extend from the center of the chest to the arms and even up to the jaw. Generally, the more severe the blockage, the more pain is felt.

Table 10-1	Classification and Recommended Follow-up Based on Total Cholesterol Level	
Total Cholesterol Level	**Classification**	**Recommended Follow-up**
<200 mg/dl	Desirable blood cholesterol level	Repeat test within 5 years
200-239 mg/dl	Borderline-high blood cholesterol level	*Without* definite CHD or two other CHD risk factors (one of which may be male gender): dietary modification and annual retesting *With* definite CHD or two other CHD risk factors: lipoprotein analysis; further action based on LDL-cholesterol level
≤240 mg/dl	High blood cholesterol level	Lipoprotein analysis; further action based on LDL-cholesterol level

Some cardiac patients relieve angina with the drug *nitroglycerin*, a powerful blood vessel dilator. This prescription drug, available in slow-release transdermal patches or small pills that are placed under the patient's tongue, causes the coronary arteries to dilate and allow a greater flow of blood into heart muscle tissue. Other cardiac patients may be prescribed drugs such as **calcium channel blockers** or **beta blockers.**

Emergency response to heart crises

Heart attacks are not always fatal. The consequences of any heart attack depend on the location of the damage to the heart, the extent to which heart muscle is damaged, and the speed with which adequate circulation is restored. Injury to the ventricles may very well prove fatal unless medical countermeasures are immediately undertaken. The recognition of heart attack is critically important (see the Health Action Guide on p. 238).

Cardiopulmonary resuscitation (CPR) is one of the most important immediate countermeasures that trained people can use when confronted with a victim of heart attack. Public education programs sponsored by the American Red Cross and the American Heart Association teach people how to recognize, evaluate, and manage heart attack emergencies. CPR trainees are taught how to restore breathing (through mouth-to-mouth resuscitation) and circulation (through external chest compression) in people who require such emergency countermeasures. Frequently, colleges offer CPR classes through health science or physical education departments. We encourage each student to enroll in a CPR course.

Diagnosis and coronary repair

Once a person's vital signs have stabilized, further diagnostic examinations can reveal the type and extent of damage to heart muscle. Initially an ECG might be taken. This test analyzes the electrical activity of the heart. *Heart catheterization*, also called *coronary arteriography*, is a minor surgical procedure that starts by placing a thin plastic tube into an arm or leg

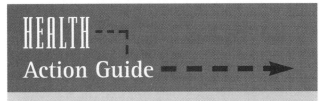

HEALTH
Action Guide ----→

Monitoring Your Cholesterol Level

The next time you get your blood cholesterol level checked, try to find out more than just your total cholesterol level. Ask for the following three measurements, and compare them with the desirable measurements for adults, listed below.

Readings for	Your measurement	Desirable measurement
HDL level:	_____	Above 45 mg/dl
LDL level:	_____	Below 130 mg/dl
Total level:	_____	Below 200 mg/dl

How do your measurements compare with the desirable measurements? If they are not satisfactory, refer to Table 10-1 and the discussion on pp. 237-238 to improve your levels. ◄------

calcium channel blockers
Drugs that prevent arterial spasms; used in the long-term management of angina pectoris.

beta blockers
Drugs that prevent overactivity of the heart, which results in angina pectoris.

artery. This tube, called a *catheter,* is guided through the artery until it reaches the coronary circulation, where a *radiopaque dye* is then released. X-ray pictures called *angiograms* then record the progress of the dye through the coronary arteries. Areas of blockage are relatively easily identified.

Once the extent of damage is identified, a physician or team of physicians can decide on a medical course of action. Currently popular is an extensive form of surgery called **coronary artery bypass surgery.** An estimated 501,000 bypass surgeries were performed in 1994.[1] The purpose of such surgery is to detour (bypass) areas of coronary artery obstruction by using a section of a vein from the patient's leg (often the saphenous vein) or an artery from the patient's chest (the internal mammary artery) and grafting it from the aorta to a location just beyond the area of obstruction. Multiple areas of obstruction result in double, triple, or quadruple bypasses.

Angioplasty. *Angioplasty,* an alternative to bypass surgery, involves the surgical insertion of a dough-nut-shaped "balloon" directly into the narrowed coronary artery (Figure 10-4). When this balloon is inflated, plaque and fatty deposits are compressed against the artery walls, widening the space through which blood flows. These balloons usually remain within the artery for less than 1 hour. Renarrowing of the artery will occur in about one quarter of angioplasty patients. Nearly 405,000 angioplasty procedures were performed in 1994.[1] Balloon angioplasty can be used for blockages in the heart, kidneys, arms, and legs. The decision whether to have angioplasty or bypass surgery can be a difficult one to make.

In 1990 the FDA approved a new device for clearing heart and leg arteries. This device is called a *motorized scraper.*[9] Inserted through a leg artery and held in place by a tiny inflated balloon, this motor-driven cutter shaves off plaque deposits from inside the artery. A nose cone in the scraper unit stores the plaque until the device is removed.

The use of laser beams to dissolve plaque that blocks arteries has been slowly evolving. The FDA has approved three laser devices for use in clogged leg arteries. In February 1992 the FDA approved the use of an excimer laser for use in coronary arteries.

Aspirin. Studies released in the late 1980s highlighted the role of aspirin in reducing the risk of heart attack in men who had no history of previous attacks. Specifically, the studies concluded that for men with hypertension, elevated cholesterol levels, or both, taking one aspirin per day was a significant factor in reducing their risk of heart attack. Aspirin works by making the blood less able to clot. This reduces the likelihood of blood vessel blockages. Presently, there is differing opinion regarding the age at which this preventive action should begin. The safest advice is to check with your physician before starting aspirin therapy. Recent research now indicates that aspirin therapy is also beneficial for women.[10]

Alcohol. For years, scientists have been uncertain about the extent to which alcohol consumption is related to a reduced risk for heart disease. The current thinking is that moderate drinking (defined as no more than two drinks per day for men and one drink per day for women) is related to a lower heart disease risk. However, the benefit is much smaller than proven risk reduction behavior such as stopping smoking, reducing cholesterol level, lowering blood pressure, and increasing physical activity. Experts caution that heavy drinking increases cardiovascular risks and that nondrinkers should not start to drink just to reduce heart disease risk.

Heart transplants and artificial hearts. For approximately 30 years, surgeons have been able to surgically replace a person's damaged heart with that of another human being. Although very risky, these transplant operations have added years to the lives of a number of patients who otherwise would have lived only a short time. In 1995, 2360 heart transplants were performed in the United States.[1]

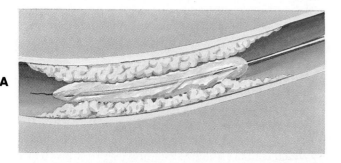 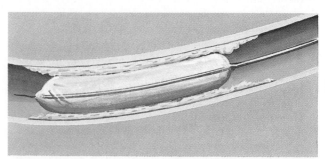

A   B

Figure 10-4 Angioplasty. **A,** A "balloon" is surgically inserted into the narrowed coronary artery. **B,** The balloon is inflated, compressing plaque and fatty deposits against the artery walls.

Artificial hearts have also been developed and implanted in humans. These mechanical devices have extended the lives of patients and have also served as temporary hearts while patients are waiting for a suitable donor heart. One of the important difficulties with artificial heart implantation has been the control of blood clots that may form, especially around the artificial valves.

Hypertension

Just as your car's water pump recirculates water and maintains water pressure, your heart recirculates blood and maintains blood pressure. When the heart contracts, blood is forced through your arteries and veins. Your blood pressure is a measure of the force that your circulating blood exerts against the interior walls of your arteries and veins.

Blood pressure is measured with a *sphygmomanometer*. A sphygmomanometer is attached to an arm-cuff device that can be inflated to stop the flow of blood temporarily in the brachial artery. This artery is a major supplier of blood to the lower arm. It is located on the inside of the upper arm, between the biceps and triceps muscles.

A physician, nurse, or technician using a stethoscope will listen for blood flow while the pressure in the cuff is released. Two pressure measurements will be recorded: the **systolic pressure** is the blood pressure against the vessel walls when the heart contracts, and the **diastolic pressure** is the blood pressure against the vessel walls when the heart relaxes (between heartbeats). Expressed in millimeters of mercury displaced on the sphygmomanometer, blood pressure is recorded in the form of a fraction, for example, 115/82. Because blood pressure drops when the heart relaxes, the diastolic pressure is always lower than the systolic pressure.

Although many people still consider 120/80 as a "normal" or safe blood pressure for a young adult, variations from this figure do not necessarily indicate a medical problem. In fact, many young college women of average weight will indicate blood pressures that seem to be relatively low (100/60, for example), yet these lowered blood pressures are quite "normal" for them. Any wide deviation from 120/80 in your blood pressure should be discussed with a physician.

Hypertension refers to a consistently elevated blood pressure. Generally, concern about a young adult's high blood pressure begins when he or she has a systolic reading of 140 or above or a diastolic reading of 90 or above. Approximately 50 million American adults and children have hypertension. The American Heart Association reports that African-Americans, Puerto Ricans, Cuban-Americans, and Mexican-Americans have significantly higher rates of high blood pressure than white Americans.[1] Asian-Americans and Pacific Islanders have significantly lower rates of hypertension, however.[1]

Although the reasons for 90% to 95% of the cases of hypertension are not known, the health risks produced by uncontrolled hypertension are clearly understood. Throughout the body, hypertension makes arteries and arterioles become less elastic and thus incapable of dilating under a heavy workload. Brittle, calcified blood vessels can burst unexpectedly and produce serious strokes (brain accidents), kidney failure (renal accidents), or eye damage **(retinal hemorrhage)**. Furthermore, it appears that blood and fat clots are more easily formed and dislodged in a vascular system affected by hypertension. Thus hypertension can be a cause of heart attacks. Clearly, hypertension is a potential killer.

Ironically, despite its deadly nature, hypertension is referred to as "the silent killer" because people with hypertension often are not aware that they have the condition. People with this disorder cannot feel the sensation of high blood pressure. The condition does not produce dizziness, headaches, or memory loss unless one is experiencing a medical crisis. Because it is a silent killer, it is estimated that nearly 35% of the people who have hypertension do not realize they have it.[5] Many who are aware of their hypertension do little to control it. Only a small percentage (21%) of people who have hypertension control it adequately, generally through dietary control, supervised fitness, relaxation training, and drug therapy.

Hypertension is not thought of as a curable disease; rather, it is a controllable disease. Once therapy is stopped, the condition returns. As a responsible adult, use every opportunity you can to measure your blood pressure on a regular basis.

coronary artery bypass surgery
Surgical procedure designed to improve blood flow to the heart by providing alternative routes for blood to take around points of blockage.

systolic pressure (sis **tol** ick)
Blood pressure against blood vessel walls when the heart contracts.

diastolic pressure (dye uh **stol** ick)
Blood pressure against blood vessel walls when the heart relaxes.

retinal hemorrhage
Uncontrolled bleeding from arteries within the eye's retina.

Prevention and treatment. Weight reduction, physical activity, moderation in alcohol use, and sodium restriction are often used to reduce hypertension. For overweight or obese people, a reduction in body weight may produce a significant drop in blood pressure. Physical activity helps lower blood pressure by expending calories (which leads to weight loss) and improving overall circulation. Reducing alcohol consumption to less than 2 ounces daily helps reduce blood pressure in some people.

The restriction of sodium (salt) in the diet also helps some people reduce hypertension. Interestingly, this strategy is effective only for those who are **salt sensitive**—estimated to be about 25% of the population. Reducing salt intake would have little effect on the blood pressure of the rest of the population. Nevertheless, since our daily intake of salt vastly exceeds our need for salt, the general recommendation to curb salt intake still makes good sense.

Many of the stress reduction activities we discuss in Chapter 3 are receiving increased attention in the struggle to reduce hypertension. In recent years, behavioral scientists have reported the success of meditation, biofeedback, controlled breathing, and muscle relaxation exercises in reducing hypertension. Look for further research findings in these areas in the years to come.

In the late 1990s, there are literally dozens of drugs that are available for use by people with hypertension. Unfortunately, many patients refuse to take their medication on a consistent basis, probably because of the mistaken notion that "you must feel sick to be sick." Nutritional supplements, such as calcium, magnesium, potassium, and fish oil, are not effective in lowering blood pressure.[11]

Stroke

Stroke is a general term for a wide variety of crises (sometimes called *cerebrovascular accidents* [CVAs]) that result from blood vessel damage in the brain. African-Americans have a 60% greater risk of stroke than white Americans do, probably because African-Americans have a greater likelihood of having hypertension than white Americans. Data for 1994 indicate that 154,350 deaths and half a million new cases of stroke occurred.[1] Just as the heart muscle needs an adequate blood supply, so does the brain. Any disturbance in the proper supply of oxygen and nutrients to the brain can pose a threat.

Perhaps the most common form of stroke results from the blockage of a cerebral (brain) artery. Similar to coronary occlusions, **cerebrovascular occlusions** can be started by a clot that forms within an artery, called a *thrombus*, or by a clot that travels from another part of the body to the brain, called an *embolus* (Figure 10-5, *A* and *B*). The resultant accidents (*cerebral thrombosis* or *cerebral embolism*) cause between 70% and 80% of all strokes. The portion of the brain deprived of oxygen and nutrients can literally die.

A third type of stroke can result from an artery that bursts to produce a crisis called *cerebral hemorrhage* (Figure 10-5, *C*). Damaged, brittle arteries can be especially susceptible to bursting when a person has hypertension.

A fourth form of stroke is a *cerebral aneurysm*. An aneurysm is a ballooning or outpouching on a weakened area of an artery (Figure 10-5, *D*). Aneurysms may occur in various locations of the body and are not always life threatening. The development of aneurysms is not fully understood, although there seems to be a relationship between aneurysms and hypertension. It is quite possible that many aneurysms are congenital defects. In any case, when a cerebral aneurysm bursts, a stroke results. See the Health Action Guide on p. 244 to learn the warning signs of stroke.

A person who reports any warning signs of stroke or any small stroke, called a **transient ischemic attack (TIA),** will undergo a battery of diagnostic tests, which could include a physical examination, a search for possible brain tumors, tests to identify areas of the brain affected, use of the electroencephalogram, cerebral arteriography, and the use of the **CAT** (computerized axial tomography) **scan** or **MRI** (magnetic resonance imaging) **scan.** Many additional tests are also available.

Treatment of stroke patients depends on the nature and extent of the damage. Some patients require surgery (to repair vessels and relieve pressure) and acute care in the hospital. Others undergo drug treatment, especially the use of anticoagulant drugs, including aspirin and TPA (the "clot buster" drug).

The advancements made in the rehabilitation of stroke patients are amazing. Although some severely affected patients have little hope of improvement, our increasing advancements in the application of computer technology to such disciplines as speech and physical therapy offer encouraging signs for stroke patients and their families.

Congenital Heart Disease

A congenital defect is one that is present at birth. The American Heart Association estimates that each year about 32,000 babies are born with a congenital heart defect. In 1993, 5388 children (mostly infants) died of congenital heart disease.[1]

A variety of abnormalities may be produced by congenital heart disease, including valve damage, holes in the walls of the septum, blood vessel transpo-

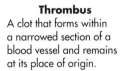
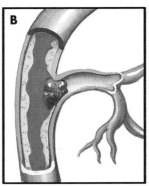
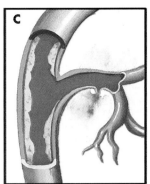
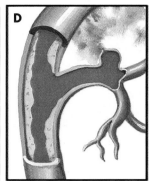

Thrombus
A clot that forms within a narrowed section of a blood vessel and remains at its place of origin.

Embolus
A clot that moves through the circulatory system and becomes lodged at a narrowed point within a vessel.

Hemorrhage
The sudden bursting of a blood vessel.

Aneurysm
A sac formed when a section of a blood vessel thins and balloons; the weakened wall of the sac can burst, or rupture, as shown here.

Figure 10-5   Causes of stroke.

sition, and an underdevelopment of the left side of the heart. All of these problems ultimately prevent a newborn baby from adequately oxygenating tissues throughout the body. A bluish skin color (cyanosis) is seen in some infants with such congenital heart defects. These infants are sometimes referred to as *blue babies.*

The cause of congenital heart defects is not clearly understood, although one cause, *rubella,* has been identified. The fetuses of mothers who contract the rubella virus during the first 3 months of pregnancy are at great risk of developing *congenital rubella syndrome (CRS),* a catchall term for a wide variety of congenital defects, including heart defects, deafness, cataracts, and mental retardation. Other hypotheses about the development of congenital heart disease implicate environmental pollutants; maternal use of drugs, including alcohol, during pregnancy; and unknown genetic factors (see the Star Box on p. 244).

Treatment of congenital defects usually requires surgery, although some conditions may respond well to drug therapy. Defective blood vessels and certain malformations of the heart can be surgically repaired. This surgery is so successful that many children respond quite quickly to the increased circulation and oxygenation. Many are able to lead normal, active lives.

Rheumatic Heart Disease

Rheumatic heart disease is the final stage in a series of complications started by a streptococcal infection of the throat (strep throat). The Star Box at

salt sensitive
Term used to describe people whose bodies overreact to the presence of sodium by retaining fluid and thus experience an increase in blood pressure.

cerebrovascular occlusion
(ser **ee** bro **vas** kyou lar)
Blockages to arteries supplying blood to the cerebral cortex of the brain; strokes.

transient ischemic attack (TIA) (**tran** see ent iss **key** mick)
Strokelike symptoms caused by temporary spasm of cerebral blood vessels.

CAT scan
Computerized axial tomography scan; an x-ray procedure that is designed to visualize structures within the body that would not normally be seen through conventional x-ray procedures.

MRI scan
Magnetic resonance imaging scan; an imaging procedure that uses a giant magnet to generate an image of body tissue.

rheumatic heart disease
Chronic damage to the heart (especially heart valves) resulting from a streptococcal infection within the heart; a complication associated with rheumatic fever.

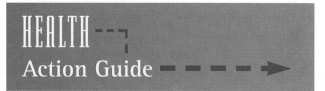

HEALTH
Action Guide ----→

Recognizing Warning Signs of Stroke

Although many stroke victims have little advance warning of an impending crisis, there are some warning signals of stroke that should be recognized. The American Heart Association encourages everyone to be aware of the following signs:

- Sudden, temporary weakness or numbness of the face, arm, and leg on one side of the body
- Temporary loss of speech or trouble in speaking or understanding speech
- Temporary dimness or loss of vision, particularly in one eye
- Unexplained dizziness, unsteadiness, or sudden falls

Many severe strokes are preceded by "little strokes," warning signals like the above, experienced days, weeks, or months before the more severe event. Prompt medical or surgical attention to these symptoms may prevent a fatal or disabling stroke from occurring. ◀------•

right lists common symtoms of strep throat. This bacterial infection, if untreated, can result in an inflammatory disease called *rheumatic fever* (and a related condition, scarlet fever). Rheumatic fever is a whole-body (systemic) reaction that can produce fever, joint pain, skin rashes, and possible brain and heart damage. A person who has had rheumatic fever is more susceptible to subsequent attacks. Rheumatic fever tends to run in families. Approximately 5540 Americans died from rheumatic fever and rheumatic heart disease in 1994.[1]

Damage from rheumatic fever centers on the heart's valves. For some reason the bacteria tend to proliferate in the heart valves. Defective heart valves may fail either to open fully (*stenosis*) or to close fully (*insufficiency*). Diagnosis of valve damage might initially come when a physician hears a backwashing or backflow of blood (a **murmur**). Further tests—including chest x-rays, cardiac catheterization, and echocardiography—can reveal the extent of valve damage.[4] Once identified, a faulty valve can be replaced surgically with a metal or plastic artificial valve or a valve taken from an animal's heart.

Related cardiovascular conditions

Besides the cardiovascular diseases already discussed, the heart and blood vessels are also subject to other pathological conditions. Tumors of the heart, although rare, occur. Infectious conditions involving the pericardial sac that surrounds the heart (*pericarditis*) and the innermost layer of the heart (*endocarditis*) are more commonly seen. In addition, inflammation of the veins (*phlebitis*) is troublesome to some people.

Peripheral artery disease. Peripheral artery disease (PAD), also called *peripheral vascular disease (PVD),* is a blood vessel disease characterized by pathological changes to the arteries and arterioles in the extremities (primarily the legs and feet but sometimes the hands). These changes result from years of damage to the peripheral blood vessels. Important causes of PAD are cigarette smoking, a high-fat diet, obesity, and sedentary occupations. In some cases, PAD is aggravated by blood vessel changes resulting from diabetes.

PAD severely restricts blood flow to the extremities. The reduction in blood flow is responsible for leg pain or cramping during exercise, numbness, tingling, coldness, and loss of hair in the affected limb. The most serious consequence of PAD is the increased likelihood of developing ulcerations and tissue death. These conditions can lead to gangrene and may eventually necessitate amputation.

The treatment of PAD consists of multiple approaches and may include efforts to improve blood lipid levels (through diet, exercise, or drug therapy), reduce hypertension, reduce body weight, and

Risk Factors for Congenital and Rheumatic Heart Disease

Risk Factors for Congenital Heart Disease
Fetal exposure to rubella, other viral infections, pollutants, alcohol, or tobacco smoke during pregnancy

Risk Factors for Rheumatic Heart Disease
Streptococcal infection

Common Symptoms of Strep Throat
Sudden onset of sore throat, particularly with pain when swallowing

Fever
Swollen, tender glands under the angle of the jaw
Headache
Nausea and vomiting
Tonsils covered with a yellow or white pus or discharge

eliminate smoking. Blood vessel surgery may be a possibility.

Congestive heart failure. Congestive heart failure is a condition in which the heart lacks the strength to continue to circulate blood normally throughout the body. During congestive heart failure, the heart continues to work, but it cannot function well enough to maintain appropriate circulation. Venous blood flow starts to "back up." Swelling occurs, especially in the legs and ankles. Fluid can collect in the lungs and cause breathing difficulties and shortness of breath, and kidney function may be damaged.[4]

Congestive heart failure can result from heart damage caused by congenital heart defects, lung disease, rheumatic fever, heart attack, atherosclerosis, or high blood pressure. Generally, congestive heart failure is treatable through a combined program of rest, proper diet, modified daily activities, and the use of appropriate drugs. Without medical care, congestive heart failure can be fatal.

murmur
An atypical heart sound that suggests a back-washing of blood into a chamber of the heart from which it has just left.

peripheral artery disease (PAD)
Damage resulting from restricted blood flow to the extremities, especially the legs and feet.

congestive heart failure
Inability of the heart to pump out all the blood that returns to it; can lead to dangerous fluid accumulations in veins, lungs, and kidneys.

Summary

- Cardiovascular disorders are responsible for more disabilities and deaths than any other disease.
- The cardiovascular system consists of the heart, blood, and blood vessels. This system performs many functions.
- Our overall health depends on the health of the cardiovascular system.
- A cardiovascular risk factor is an attribute that a person has or is exposed to that increases the likelihood of heart disease.
- The "big four" risk factors are cigarette smoking, high blood pressure, high blood cholesterol level, and physical inactivity. These are controllable risk factors.
- Heredity, male gender, and increasing age are risk factors that cannot be controlled.
- Contributing risk factors are diabetes, obesity, and individual response to stress.
- The major forms of cardiovascular disease include coronary artery disease, high blood pressure, stroke, congenital heart disease, and rheumatic heart disease. Each disease develops in a specific way and may require a highly specialized form of treatment.

Review Questions

1. Identify the principal components of the cardiovascular system. Trace the path of blood through the heart and cardiovascular system.
2. How much blood does the average adult have? What are some of the important functions of blood?
3. Define cardiovascular risk factor. What relationship do risk factors have to cardiovascular disease?
4. Identify those risk factors for cardiovascular disease that cannot be changed. Identify those risk factors that can be changed. Identify those risk factors that are contributing factors.
5. What are the major forms of cardiovascular disease? For each of these diseases, describe what the disease is, its cause (if known), and its treatment.
6. Describe how high-density lipoproteins differ from low-density lipoproteins.
7. What problems does atherosclerosis produce?
8. Why is hypertension referred to as "the silent killer"?
9. What are the warning signals of stroke?

Think About This . . .

- Have you ever considered your potential for developing heart disease?
- In the last week, what have you done to improve your cardiovascular system?
- Do you know your total cholesterol reading? Do you know your levels of LDLs and HDLs?

- When was the last time you had your blood pressure checked? What were the readings?
- What role should men play in reducing the threats of congenital heart disease?
- Are you comfortable talking with your relatives about their possible risk factors?

References

1. American Heart Association: *1997 Heart and Stroke statistical update,* Dallas, 1997, The Association.
2. Thibodeau GA: *Structure and function of the body,* ed 10, St Louis, 1996, Mosby.
3. Thibodeau GA, Patton KT: *The human body in health and disease,* ed 2, St Louis, 1996, Mosby.
4. American Heart Association: *Heart and stroke facts,* Dallas, 1996, The Association.
5. American Heart Association: *Heart and stroke facts: 1995 statistical supplement,* Dallas, 1995, The Association.
6. Hormone replacement therapy: weighing the risks and benefits, *Harvard Health Letter* 22:12, October 1997, 1-3.
7. HDL: the good (but complex) cholesterol, *Harvard Heart Letter* 8:1, September 1997, 1-4.
8. Cholesterol: up with the good, *Harvard Heart Letter,* 5:11, July 1995, 3-4.
9. Farley D: Help for hearts and blood vessels: balloons, lasers and scrapers, *FDA Consumer* (25:3):22-27, 1991.
10. Aspirin for coronary disease: beneficial in women, too, *Harvard Heart Letter* (7:7), March 1997, 8.
11. Trials of Hypertension Prevention Collaborative Research Group: The effects of nonpharmacologic interventions on blood pressure of persons with high normal levels: results of the trials of hypertension prevention, Phase 1, *JAMA* 267(9):1213-1220, 1992.

Suggested Readings

American Heart Associaton: *Around the world cookbook: healthy recipes with an international flavor,* New York, 1996, Time Books.

This cookbook, by the American Heart Association, includes 200 healthy recipes for great-tasting dishes from ethnic cuisines around the world. The chefs who developed the recipes altered the ingredients from traditional (often unhealthy) versions of well-known ethnic foods to create healthier fare. Nutritional analysis is given for each dish.

Castelli WP, Griffin GC: *Good fat, bad fat: how to lower your cholesterol and reduce the risks of a heart attack,* Tucson, AZ, 1997, Fisher Books.

This is a 300-page handbook you can use to reduce fat and cholesterol in your diet. Castelli, a renowned cardiovascular specialist and researcher, and Griffin explain how to lower your blood cholesterol and keep it under control. The authors discuss today's cholesterol-lowering drugs, and more than 200 healthy recipes are included.

Klein T: *A user's guide to bypass surgery,* Athens, OH, 1996, Ohio University Press.

This is a personal guidebook for anyone facing the possibility of coronary bypass surgery. Klein provides interesting insights about all aspects of heart surgery, including diagnostic tests, physician diagnosis, preparation for surgery, the surgery itself, recovery, and convalescence. Klein shares the experience of his own quadruple-bypass surgery, in 1989.

ON...

Hypertension in African-Americans

Development of disease is an area in which each societal group is disadvantaged in one way or another. Practically every group has a tendency to develop one or more afflictions at a higher rate than the general population. For the African-American community, one particular problem is hypertension.

The existing data show that hypertension is more common in African-Americans[1,2] and is more aggressive and less well managed in African-Americans than in whites. African-Americans also have higher rates of morbidity and mortality from diseases related to high blood pressure, such as stroke and renal failure. The natural nocturnal fall in blood pressure is less pronounced in African-Americans, and their systolic blood pressure while awake is higher than in people of other races.[1]

The exact causes of these differences have not been pinpointed, but research seems to be focused in two general areas. Some research suggests that certain physical and genetic factors contribute to increased incidence of hypertension in African-Americans, whereas other studies have shown that hypertension in African-Americans is related to environmental stress. This debate involves not just medical data but socioeconomic factors as well. In short, it is a nature vs. nurture debate, and there are supporting data for both arguments.

Nature vs. nurture

Studies have shown that environmental stress may contribute to increased hypertension in African-Americans. A study conducted by Dr. Norman Anderson of Duke University[3] shows that chronic stress may lead to an increase in the release of the hormone norepinephrine to the bloodstream. Norepinephrine reduces the amount of salt eliminated from the kidneys, and the resulting increase in blood salt content can lead to increased blood pressure. This chain reaction has been shown to occur in animal studies. The high rate of chronic exposure to stress in many African-American communities has been well documented.[3] If these studies hold true for humans, it would lend credence to the idea that certain stressful factors found in some African-American communities could cause hypertension. Stressors such as poverty, unemployment, the threat of violence, and racial discrimination could be shown to cause kidneys to reduce elimination of salt and thus may also increase the risk of hypertension.[3]

Anger in response to racism may be a significant contributing factor in increased hypertension in African-Americans. A study conducted jointly at the University of Tennessee and Saint Louis University showed that blood pressure in African-Americans increased significantly when they were shown film clips of racially motivated violence.[4] The responses of African-Americans to these scenes of racial discrimination were more pronounced than their responses to viewing scenes that were anger-provoking but had no racial component. The increases in blood pressure were not into the hypertension range, but researchers believe that over time, such continued elevation of blood pressure could become dangerous.

Such conclusions seem to suggest that socioeconomic factors are the main cause of hypertension among African-Americans. A study performed on 26 African-American women on strict low-fat diets seems to support this. The data showed that women of higher socioeconomic status had more excretion of salt than those of lower status.[3] Since proportionately more African-Americans are in lower socioeconomic classes than whites, increased stress from lower status could be the main factor behind the inflated rate of hypertension among the African-American population.

But is it all due to environment? Perhaps not. Other groups of traditionally lower socioeconomic status, such as Hispanics, Asians, and Native Americans, have been found to have the same incidence of hypertension as whites.[1] African-American children have been found to have higher blood pressure in general than white children;[1] it is not known whether stress plays a significant role in affecting the blood pressure of these children so early in life.

There is also evidence that African-Americans may be predisposed to hypertension at the cellular level. Microscopic studies of blood vessels in African-Americans with severe hypertension revealed that renal arterioles were thickened and had reduced flow. This thickening, not found in the renal arterioles of hypertensive whites, was caused by hypertrophy (excess growth) of smooth muscle cells in the muscle walls of the arterioles. This thickening reduced the size of the lumen (inside opening) of the vessels, and the resulting reduced blood flow may have caused increased blood pressure. The smooth muscle cells were thought to be responding abnormally to growth factors, which caused the hypertrophy to occur.[2] The reason behind this abnormal reaction was not determined, however.

The best explanation of why African-Americans are more prone to develop hypertension may not involve environment or genetics alone, but a combination of the two. Stress factors unique to the African-American community may serve to aggravate or intensify an existing physical predisposition toward hypertension. It has already been shown that the tendency toward developing hypertension can be passed from parents to their children. Add several unique stress factors to a population already predisposed to high blood pressure, and the potential exists for high numbers of people to develop hypertension. Commenting on the UT-SLU study, Dr. Elijah Saunders agreed that "racism and Black rage are emotional stressors that could worsen a physiological tendency toward hypertension."[4]

Treatment for hypertension in African-Americans

The good news is that African-Americans respond to medical treatment in a similar manner to whites. The treatment regimen for African-Americans may have to be altered somewhat, however, since they do not respond as well to some hypertension medications as people of other races. For unknown reasons, drugs such as beta-blockers and ACE (angiotensin converting enzyme) inhibitors do not work as well in African-Americans and may need to be supplemented by other medications, such as diuretics.[1]

Lifestyle changes may also be needed and may be a more effective tool in lowering blood pressure in African-Americans than in people of other races.[1] Effort should be made to exercise and lose weight if needed, since excess weight can be a contributing factor in hypertension. Hypertensive African-Americans tend to have lower intakes of potassium and calcium, so diet changes should be made that ensure that these minerals are in adequate supply. A reduction in sodium may also be desirable, since research suggests that African-Americans may be more sensitive to the effects of sodium on the cardiovascular system.[1]

Although African-Americans are more likely to develop high blood pressure, prevention and treatment can help keep hypertension from becoming a deadly affliction. Proper diagnosis is essential, so people at risk should see their doctors to determine whether they have hypertension or are at risk for developing it. Through recommending lifestyle modifications, prescribing medications, or both, a physician can help manage this condition or help prevent its onset.[5]

For Discussion . . .

Do you feel that people in lower (or higher) socioeconomic groups suffer more from everyday stress? Do you believe physiological or genetic differences may exist between different ethnic or racial groups?

References

1. Kaplan NM: Ethnic aspects of hypertension, *Lancet* 344(8920), 1994.
2. Dustan HP: Growth factors and racial differences in severity of hypertension and renal diseases, *Lancet* 339(8805), 1992.
3. Haywood RL: Why Black Americans suffer with more high blood pressure than Whites, *Jet* Dec 5, 1994, 87(5).
4. Study reveals anger over racism causes high blood pressure in Blacks, *Jet* May 14, 1990, 78(5).
5. Too little attention paid to high blood pressure, *Tufts University Health and Nutrition Letter*, (15:11), January 1998, p. 1.

Living with Cancer and Chronic Conditions

Healthy People: Looking Ahead to 2010

Reversing the rise in the incidence of cancer-related deaths was a key objective of *Healthy People 2000.* The *Midcourse Review* reported encouraging success in reducing the death rate of some cancers, but overall mortality remained near the same level.

Since the *Midcourse Review* was issued, other sources have indicated encouraging progress.[1] In men, the incidence of deaths from lung cancer, colorectal cancer, and prostate cancer has declined, particularly among African-American men. In women, the death rate from breast cancer, colorectal cancer, and some types of gynecologic cancer has also declined. This modest progress is encouraging.

Healthy People 2010 will set goals for the nation of increasing years of healthy life and eliminating disparities in health care. For these goals to be accomplished, more attention must be focused on all types of cancer. This effort will require a broad-based approach that includes education, early detection, research, and treatment.

Most people can attest to the disruptive influence an illness can have on their ability to participate in day-to-day activities. When we are ill, school, employment, and leisure activities are replaced by periods of lessened activity and even periods of bed rest or hospitalization. When an illness is **chronic,** the effect of being ill may extend over long periods, perhaps even an entire life. People with chronic illness must eventually find a balance between day-to-day function and the continuous presence of their condition. Cancer is usually an illness that is chronic in nature.

THE STATUS OF CANCER TODAY AND TOMORROW

In spite of our understanding of its relationship to human health and our ceaseless attempts to prevent and cure it, progress in cancer prevention is at best limited. Cancer is clearly expensive, both in terms of its human toll and its monetary costs. It is estimated that 1,382,000 new cases of cancer were diagnosed and 560,000 Americans died of the disease in 1996.[2] It is impossible to give a simple explanation for our lack of overall progress in the war against cancer. It could, however, be a combination of factors, including the aging of the population, our failure to curb tobacco use, the high fat content of the typical American diet, the continuing urbanization and pollution of our environment, the presence of millions of people without health insurance to pay for early diagnosis and proper treatment, or, simply, our ability to recognize its true role in deaths ascribed to other causes. Regardless, we are still challenged to bring under control the abnormal cellular activity that we call cancer.

CANCER: A PROBLEM OF CELL REGULATION

In much the same manner that a corporation depends on competent individuals to staff its various departments, the body depends on its basic units of function—the cells. Cells band together as tissues, such as muscle tissue, to perform a prescribed function. Tissues in turn join to form organs, such as the heart, and organs are assembled into the body's several organ systems, such as the cardiovascular system. Such is the "corporate structure" of the body.

If individuals and cells are the basic units of function for their respective organizations, the failure of either to perform in a prescribed, dependable manner can erode the overall organization to the extent that it might not be able to continue. Cancer, the second leading cause of death among adults, is a condition reflecting cell dysfunction in its most extreme form.[3] In cancer the normal behavior of cells ceases.

Cell Regulation

Most of the tissues of the body lose cells over time. This continual loss requires that replacement cells be brought forward from areas of young and less specialized cells. The process of *specialization* required to turn the less specialized cells into mature cells is carefully controlled by genes within the cells. On becoming specialized, these newest cells copy, or *replicate*, themselves. These two processes are carefully monitored by the cells' **regulatory genes.** Failure to regulate specialization and replication results in abnormal, or cancerous, cells.[3]

In addition to genes that regulate specialization and replication, cells also have genes designed to repair mistakes in the copying of genetic material (the basis of replication) and genes to suppress the growth of abnormal cells should they occur. Thus *repair genes* and *suppressor genes,* such as the p53 gene, join regulatory genes to prevent the development of abnormal cells.[3] Should these genes fail to function properly, resulting in the development of malignant (cancerous) cells, the immune system (see Chapter 12) will ideally recognize their presence and remove them before a clinical (diagnosable) case of cancer can develop.

Because specialization, replication, repair, and suppressor genes can become cancer-causing genes, or **oncogenes,** when not working properly, these four types of genes could also be referred to as **protooncogenes,** or potential oncogenes.[3] The failure of tumor suppressor genes to regulate the formation of abnormal cells is now thought to be a critical factor in the development of cancer. In addition to the p53 gene, other specific genes have been associated with certain types of breast cancer, ovarian cancer, colon cancer, and prostate cancer.[3]

Oncogene Formation

Recognizing that all cells have protooncogenes, what events alter otherwise normal cancer-preventing genes so that they become cancer-causing genes? Three mechanisms, genetic mutations, viral infections, and carcinogens, have received much attention.

Genetic mutations develop when dividing cells miscopy genetic information. If the gene that is miscopied is a protooncogene, the oncogene that results will stimulate the formation of cancerous cells. A variety of factors, including aging, free radical formation, radiation, and an array of carcinogens, are associated with the miscopying of the complex genetic information that comprises the genes found within the cell, including those intended to prevent cancer.

In both animals and humans, *cancer-producing viruses,* such as the feline leukemia virus in cats and the HIV virus, herpes virus, and human papillomavirus (HPV) in humans (see Chapter 12), have been identified. These viruses seek out cells of a particular type, such as cells of the immune system, and alter their genetic material to convert these cells into virus-producing cells. In so doing, however, they change the makeup of one or more of the regulatory genes, converting the protooncogenes into oncogenes. Once converted into oncogenes, the altered genes are passed on through cell division.

A third possible explanation for the conversion of protooncogenes into oncogenes involves the presence of environmental agents known as *carcinogens.* Over an extended period, carcinogens, such as chemicals found in tobacco smoke, polluted air and water, toxic wastes, and even the high fat content of foods, may convert protooncogenes into oncogenes. These carcinogens may work alone or in combination (*co-carcinogens*). Thus people might develop lung cancer only if they are exposed to the right combination of carcinogens over an extended period.

Our understanding of the role of genes in the development of cancer is expanding rapidly. In conjunction with the **Human Genome Project,** the scientific community has now identified dozens of genes that function as oncogenes in a variety of human cancers. Among these are genes involved in the development of lung cancer (p16), breast cancer (BRCA1 and BRCA2), colon cancer (MSH2 and MSH1), and a form of leukemia (ALL-1 and AF-9).[4-6] As geneticists continue to discover additional genetic links to cancer, the possibility of some form of "gene-repair" technology or a "gene chip" to aid screening becomes a possibility in the war against cancer.

The Cancerous Cell

In comparison with their noncancerous cousins, cancer cells are both similar and dissimilar in terms of how they function. It is the dissimilar aspects that in most cases make them unpredictable and more difficult to manage.

Perhaps the most different aspect of cancerous cells is their infinite life expectancy. Specifically, it appears that cancerous cells can produce an enzyme, *telomerase,* that blocks the biological clock that informs normal cells that it is time to die.[7] In spite of this ability to live forever, cancer cells do not necessarily divide more quickly than normal cells. In fact, they can divide at the same rate or even at a slower rate.[3]

Because cancerous cells do not possess the *contact inhibition* (a control mechanism that influences the

number of cells that can occupy a particular space) of normal cells, they can accumulate and eventually alter the structure of a body organ or break through its wall into neighboring areas (invasion). Additionally, the absence of *cellular cohesiveness* (a property seen in normal cells that "keeps them at home") allows cancer cells to spread through the circulatory or lymphatic system to distant points via **metastasis** (Figure 11-1). A final unique characteristic of cancerous cells is their ability to command additional blood supply to meet their metabolic needs and to provide additional routes for metastasis. This *angiogenesis potential* of cancer cells makes them extremely hardy in comparison with noncancerous cells, although progress against this capability is being made.[8] Two anti-angiogenesis proteins (angiostatin and endostatin) have been tested in animals and are moving toward human trials.

Benign Tumors

Noncancerous, or **benign,** tumors can also form in the body. These tumors are usually enclosed by a

chronic
Develops slowly and persists for a long period of time.

regulatory genes
Genes within the cell that control cellular replication or doubling.

oncogenes
Genes that are believed to activate the development of cancer.

protooncogenes (**pro** toe **on** co genes)
Normal regulatory genes that may become oncogenes.

Human Genome Project
International quest by geneticists to identify the location and composition of every gene within the human cell.

metastasis (muh **tas** ta sis)
The spread of cancerous cells from their site of origin to other areas of the body.

benign
Noncancerous; tumors that do not spread.

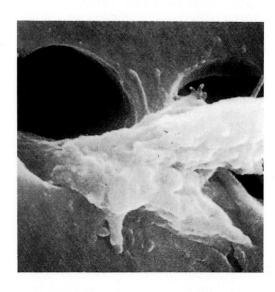

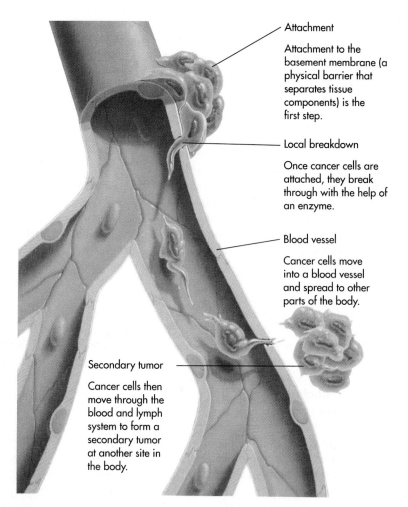

Attachment

Attachment to the basement membrane (a physical barrier that separates tissue components) is the first step.

Local breakdown

Once cancer cells are attached, they break through with the help of an enzyme.

Blood vessel

Cancer cells move into a blood vessel and spread to other parts of the body.

Secondary tumor

Cancer cells then move through the blood and lymph system to form a secondary tumor at another site in the body.

Figure 11-1   How cancer spreads. Locomotion is integral to the process of metastasis. Scientists have identified a protein that causes cancer cells to grow arms, or pseudopodia, enabling them to move to other parts of the body.

fibrous membrane and do not spread from their point of origin as cancerous tumors can. Benign tumors are dangerous, however, when they crowd out normal tissue within a confined space.

Types of Cancer and Their Locations

Cancers are named on the basis of the type of tissues in which they occur. The classifications below are used by physicians to describe malignancies to the layperson:

carcinoma   Found most frequently in the skin, nose, mouth, throat, stomach, intestinal tract, glands, nerves, breasts, urinary and genital structures, lungs, kidneys, and liver; approximately 85% of all malignant tumors are classified as carcinomas

sarcoma   Formed in the connective tissues of the body; bone, cartilage, and tendons are the sites of sarcoma development; only 2% of all malignancies are of this type

melanoma   Arises from the melanin-containing cells of skin; found most often in individuals who have had extensive sun exposure, particularly a deep, penetrating sunburn; although once rare, the amount of this cancer has increased markedly in recent years; remains among the most deadly forms of cancer

neuroblastoma   Originates in the immature cells found within the central nervous system; neuroblastomas are rare; usually found in children

adenocarcinoma   Derived from cells of the endocrine glands

hepatoma   Originates in cells of the liver; although not thought to be directly caused by alcohol use, hepatomas are more frequently seen in individuals who have experienced **sclerotic changes** in the liver

leukemia   Found in cells of the blood and blood-forming tissues; characterized by abnormal, immature white blood cell formation; multiple forms found in children and adults

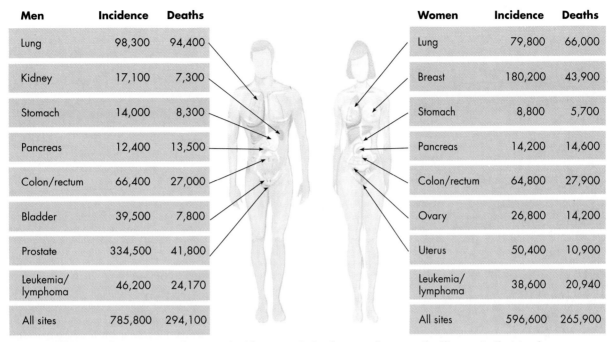

Men	Incidence	Deaths
Lung	98,300	94,400
Kidney	17,100	7,300
Stomach	14,000	8,300
Pancreas	12,400	13,500
Colon/rectum	66,400	27,000
Bladder	39,500	7,800
Prostate	334,500	41,800
Leukemia/lymphoma	46,200	24,170
All sites	785,800	294,100

Women	Incidence	Deaths
Lung	79,800	66,000
Breast	180,200	43,900
Stomach	8,800	5,700
Pancreas	14,200	14,600
Colon/rectum	64,800	27,900
Ovary	26,800	14,200
Uterus	50,400	10,900
Leukemia/lymphoma	38,600	20,940
All sites	596,600	265,900

Figure 11-2   These 1997 estimates of cancer incidence and deaths reveal some significant similarities between men and women. Note that lung cancer is the leading cause of cancer deaths for both genders.

lymphoma   Arises in cells of the lymphatic tissues or other immune system tissues; includes lymphosarcomas and Hodgkin's disease, characterized by abnormal white cell production and decreased resistance

Figure 11-2 presents information about the incidence of cancer and the deaths from cancer at various sites in both men and women.[2]

CANCER AT SELECTED SITES IN THE BODY

A second and more familiar way to describe cancer is on the basis of the organ (or tissue) site at which it occurs.[2] The following discussion relates to some of these more familiar sites. Regular screening procedures can lead to early identification of cancer at these sites (see the Health Action Guide on p. 254).

Lung

Lung cancer is one of the most lethal forms of cancer that is frequently diagnosed. Primarily because of the advanced stage at the time symptoms first appear, only 14% of all lung cancer victims survive 5 years beyond diagnosis.[2] By the time victims are sufficiently concerned about their persistent cough, blood-streaked sputum, and chest pain, it is often too late for treatment to be effective.

Today it is known that a genetic predisposition is important in the development of lung cancer. Perhaps as many as 70% of the people who develop this form of cancer have an inherited "headstart."[9] When people who are genetically at risk also smoke, their level of risk for developing lung cancer is hundreds of times greater than it is for nonsmokers. About 30% of lung cancer cases appear in people who smoke but are not genetically predisposed. Smokers account for 87% of all reported cases of lung cancer, and lung cancer causes 30% of all cancer deaths. Environmental agents, such as radon, asbestos, and air pollutants, contribute to a lesser degree in the development of lung cancer.

According to the World Health Organization, the incidence of lung cancer has risen 200% for women, paralleling their increased smoking. Currently, lung cancer exceeds breast cancer as the leading cause of cancer deaths in women. The incidence of lung cancer has shown an encouraging decline in men while their use of tobacco drops.

sclerotic changes (skluh **rot** ick)
Thickening or hardening of tissues.

HEALTH
Action Guide ----->

Summary of American Cancer Society Recommendations for the Early Detection of Cancer in Asymptomatic People

Text	Population Sex	Age	Frequency
Sigmoidoscopy, preferably flexible	M & F	50 and over	Every 3–5 years
Fecal Occult Blood Test	M & F	50 and over	Every year
Digital Rectal Exam	M & F	40 and over	Every year
Prostate Exam*	M	50 and over	Every year
Pap Test	F	All women who are, or who have been, sexually active, or have reached age 18, should have an annual Pap test and pelvic examination. After a woman has had three or more consecutive satisfactory normal annual examinations, the Pap test may be performed less frequently at the discretion of her physician.	
Breast Self-examination	F	20 and over	Every month
Breast clinical examination	F	20–40 Over 40	Every 3 years Every year
Mammography†	F	40–49 50 and over	Every 1–2 years Every year

*Annual digital rectal examination and prostate-specific antigen should be performed on men 50 years and older. If either result is abnormal, further evaluation should be considered.
†Screening mammography should begin at age 40.
©1997, American Cancer Society, Inc.

HealthQuest Activities

- The self-assessment activity *Cancer: What's Your Risk?*, found in Module 6, allows you to examine how your family history, personal health history, occupation, environment, and behavior affect your risk of developing cancer. *HealthQuest* will estimate whether you are at decreased, average, or above average risk of developing several kinds of cancer. Complete the self-assessment and then gather more information about the cancers for which you are at increased risk. Use the "Cancer Info" feature in the "Connections" section to help you.

- Like other chronic diseases that occur more frequently as people age, cancer may appear to be an unlikely possibility to young adults. Review the *Cancer Info* feature to learn how cancer affects quality of life. Then read the "Connections" article on social support for people with cancer. Finally, increase your awareness of skin cancer prevention by using the *Skin Cancer Exploration*. List the factors that put a person at highest and at lowest risk for skin cancer. Then determine which factors are modifiable and which are not.

Breast

Surpassed only by lung cancer, breast cancer is the second leading cause of death from cancer in women. Now, nearly 1 in 8 women will develop breast cancer.[2] As they age, women are increasingly at risk for developing breast cancer. Regardless of age, however, waiting to learn whether a suspicious lump is benign or is a fluid-filled cyst will be stressful. Early detection is the key to complete recovery. In fact, 97% of women who discover their breast cancer before it has spread will survive more than 5 years.[2]

Although all women and men are at some risk for developing breast cancer, women whose menstrual periods began when they were young and for whom menopause was late (longer exposure to higher estrogen levels), women who had no children (high risk seen later in life) or had their first child later in life (nursing helps lower risk, however), and women with a family history of breast cancer are at greater risk.[9] Also, women whose diets are high in saturated fats and who have excessive fat in the waist-hip area are more likely to develop breast cancer,[10] although the exact role of dietary fats remains contested. Alcohol consumption, use of an oral contraceptive, and use of ERT still foster controversy regarding their roles in women's risk for developing breast cancer. Most recently, the role of environmental pollutants and regional influences were introduced as causative factors in the development of breast cancer.[11] In the latter case, lifestyle differences may account for different breast cancer rates from region to region of the country. The incidence of breast cancer among various people and groups is discussed in the Learning from All Cultures box at right. In addition, the Personal Assessment on pp. 256-257 will help you evaluate your own risk for developing breast cancer.

Breast self-examination is recommended for women 20 years of age and older (see the Health Action Guide on p. 258). *Mammograms* are recommended every year for women 50 years and older if they have no symptoms. Mammography is recommended every 1 to 2 years for women 40 to 49 years old if they have no established risk factors.[2]

Regardless of age, each woman is unique in terms of her risk profile, and therefore the recommendation of her physician should be given careful consideration. Additionally, it is strongly advised that the procedure be performed in a facility that does a large number of mammography studies on a regular basis (with the most recent equipment, more skilled technicians, and more experienced radiologists reading the films).

In addition to breast self-examination and mammography, new techniques for detection are being

LEARNING from ALL CULTURES

Breast Cancer

Research on breast cancer has identified a number of risk factors, which are discussed in this text. Some of these factors can be changed or controlled, but others cannot. The following is additional information about the incidence of breast cancer. In demographic terms, breast cancer is likely to occur in the following people or groups:

1. Women much more often than men; it is 100 times more common in women.

2. Whites more often than blacks; however, one factor may be greater awareness and better access to medical resources by the white population.

3. Women over 50 more frequently than in younger women.

4. Women who are obese rather than thin.

5. Smokers rather than nonsmokers.

6. Women of Western cultures; Japanese women living in Japan seem to have a low rate of incidence. However, for those Japanese women who move to Western cultures, the rate of incidence increases. Women in the Netherlands are reported as having the highest rates of all countries.

Consider this last risk factor. What can you hypothesize about the Western culture and the increased incidence of breast cancer?

considered. For example, MRI can see through dense tissue areas and collected breast fluid more effectively than x-rays.

Women who have the BRCA1 or BRCA2 genetic mutation will be monitored closely;[12] they may elect to undergo a *prophylactic mastectomy*.[13] This inheritance pattern, however, may affect only 5% of all women.

Regardless of the method of detection, if a lump is found, a breast biopsy can determine what the lump is. If the lump is cancerous, treatment is highly effective if the cancer is found in an early stage. Since many choices exist about the type of surgery required to remove the cancer, women should seek a second opinion. The least extensive surgery, the lumpectomy, in combination with drug therapy, has proved highly effective.[14,15] However, for some women, even when their cancer is in an early stage, radical mastectomy may be the preferred route of treatment. Today, breast

PERSONAL ASSESSMENT

Are You at Risk for Skin, Breast, or Cervical Cancer?

Some people may have more than an average risk of developing particular types of cancer. These people can be identified by certain risk factors.

This simple self-testing method is designed by the American Cancer Society to help you assess your risk factors for three common types of cancer. These are the major risk factors but by no means represent the only ones that might be involved.

Check your response to each risk factor. Add the numbers in the parentheses to arrive at a total score for each cancer type. Find out what your score means by reading the information in the "Interpretation" section. You are advised to discuss the information with your physician if you are at a higher risk.

Skin Cancer

1. Frequent work or play in the sun
   a. Yes (10)   b. No (1)

2. Work in mines, around coal tars, or around radio activity
   a. Yes (10)   b. No (1)

3. Complexion—fair skin or light skin
   a. Yes (10)   b. No (1)

Your total points _____

Explanation

Excessive ultraviolet light causes skin cancer. Protect yourself with a sunscreen.

These materials can cause skin cancer.

Light complexions need more protection than others.

Interpretation

Numerical risks for skin cancer are difficult to state. For instance, a person with a dark complexion can work longer in the sun and be less likely to develop cancer than a light-complected person. Furthermore, a person wearing a long-sleeved shirt and a wide-brimmed hat may work in the sun and be less at risk than a person who wears a bathing suit and stays in the sun for only a short period. The risk increases greatly with age.

The key here is if you answered "yes" to any question, you need to realize that you have above-average risk.

Breast Cancer

1. Age group
   a. 20-34 (10)   b. 35-49 (40)   c. 50 and over (90)
2. Race/nationality
   a. Asian (5)   c. White (25)
   b. Black (20)   d. Mexican American (10)
3. Family history of breast cancer
   a. Mother, sister, or grandmother (30)
   b. None (10)

4. Your history
   a. No breast disease (10)
   b. Previous noncancerous lumps or cysts (25)
   c. Previous breast cancer (100)
5. Maternity
   a. First pregnancy before age 25 (10)
   b. First pregnancy after age 25 (15)
   c. No pregnancies (20)

Your total points _____

Interpretation

Under 100	Low-risk women should practice monthly breast self-examination (BSE) and have their breasts examined by a doctor as part of a cancer-related checkup.
100-199	Moderate-risk women should practice monthly BSE and have their breasts examined by a doctor as part of a cancer-related checkup. Periodic mammograms should be included as your doctor may advise.
200 or more	High-risk women should practice monthly BSE and have the examinations and mammograms described earlier.

Cervical Cancer*

1. Age group
   a. Less than 25 (10)   c. 40-54 (30)
   b. 25-39 (20)   d. 55 and over (30)

2. Race/nationality
   a. Asian (10)   d. White (10)
   b. Puerto Rican (20)   e. Mexican American (20)
   c. Black (20)

3. Number of pregnancies
   a. 0 (10)   c. 4 and over (30)
   b. 1 to 3 (20)

4. Viral infections
   a. Herpes and other viral infections or ulcer formations on the vagina (10)
   b. Never (1)

5. Age at first intercourse
   a. Before 15 (40)   c. 20-24 (20)
   b. 15-19 (30)   d. 25 and over (10)

6. Bleeding between periods or after intercourse
   a. Yes (40)   b. No (1)

Your total points _____

Explanation

The highest occurrence is in the 40-and-over age group. The numbers represent the relative rates of cancer for different age groups. A 45-year-old woman has a risk three times higher than a 20 year old.

Puerto Ricans, Blacks, and Mexican Americans have higher rates of cervical cancer.

Women who have delivered more children have a higher occurrence.

Viral infections of the cervix and vagina are associated with cervical cancer.

Women with earlier intercourse and with more sexual partners are at a higher risk.

Irregular bleeding may be a sign of uterine cancer.

Interpretation/To Carry This Further . . .

40-69   This is a low-risk group. Ask your doctor for a Pap test. You will be advised how often you should be tested after your first test.

70-99   In this moderate-risk group, more frequent Pap tests may be required.

100 or higher   You are in a high-risk group and should have a Pap test (and pelvic examination) as advised by your doctor. ☑

*Lower portion of uterus. These questions would not apply to a woman who has had a complete hysterectomy.

reconstruction is often possible after more radical surgery (see the Star Box on p. 259).

Uterus

In 1997, approximately 49,400 new cases of cancer of the uterus were anticipated in the United States.[2] Included in this figure were 34,900 cases of cancer of the uterine lining (endometrial cancer) and 14,500 cases of cancer of the uterine neck (cervical cancer). Fortunately, the death rate from uterine cancer has dropped greatly since 1950, largely because of the use of the **Pap test.** This test looks for precancerous changes in the cells taken from the cervix.

The importance of women having a Pap test for cervical cancer done on a routine basis cannot be overemphasized. Without screening, a 20-year-old of average risk has a 250 in 10,000 chance of getting cervical cancer and a 118 in 10,000 chance of dying from it. With screening, a 20-year-old of average risk has a 35 in 10,000 chance of getting this form of cancer and only an 11 in 10,000 chance of dying from it.[16] The Pap test is not perfect, however; about 7% of the tests will miss finding abnormal changes.[17] Further, not all women whose test results are abnormal receive adequate follow-up care, nor do they have subsequent Pap tests on a regular enough basis.[17] On a more positive note, potentially more effective computerized tests are currently awaiting FDA approval.

In addition to changes discovered by a Pap test, symptoms suggesting cancer of the uterus include abnormal bleeding between periods. Risk factors associated with developing this form of cancer include early age of first intercourse, number of sexual partners, history of infertility, human papillomavirus (HPV) infections (see p. 299 in Chapter 12), and excessive fat tissue around the waist. Women who have received ERT (see p. 72) may also have a

Pap test
A cancer screening procedure in which cells are removed from the cervix and examined for precancerous changes.

HEALTH
Action Guide ----->

Breast Self-Examination

The following explains how to do a breast self-examination:

1. *In the shower:* Examine your breasts during a bath or shower; hands glide more easily over wet skin. With your fingers flat, move gently over every part of each breast. Use right hand to examine left breast, left hand for right breast. Check for any lump, hard knot, or thickening. This self-examination should be done monthly, preferably a day or two after the end of the menstrual period.

2. *Before a mirror:* Inspect your breasts with arms at your sides. Next, raise your arms high overhead. Look for any changes in contour of each breast, a swelling, dimpling of skin, changes in the nipple. Then rest palms on hips, and press down firmly to flex your chest muscles. Left and right breast will not exactly match—few women's breasts do.

3. *Lying down:* To examine your right breast, put a pillow or folded towel under your right shoulder. Place right hand behind your head—this distributes breast tissue more evenly on the chest. With left hand, fingers flat, press gently in small circular motions around an imaginary clock face. Begin at outermost top of your right breast for 12 o'clock, then move to 1 o'clock, and so on around the circle back to 12 o'clock. A ridge of firm tissue in the lower curve of each breast is normal. Then move in an inch toward the nipple; keep circling to examine *every part of your breast,* including the nipple. This requires at least three more circles. Now slowly repeat the procedure on your left breast with a pillow under your left shoulder and left hand behind head. Notice how your breast structure feels. Finally, squeeze the nipple of each breast gently between thumb and index finger. Any discharge, clear or bloody, should be reported to your doctor immediately.

Breast cancer can occur in men too. Therefore this examination should be performed monthly by men. Regular inspection shows what is normal for you and will give you confidence in your examination.. <-----

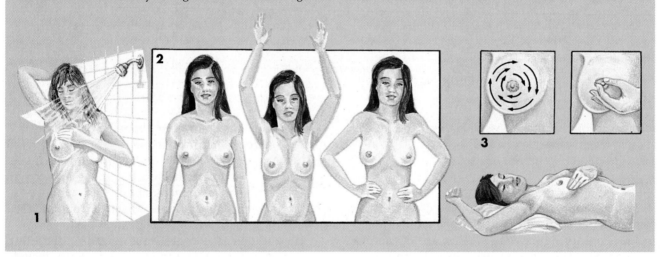

higher risk. A lower level of risk for uterine cancer is seen in women who have used barrier contraceptives (condoms, diaphragms, and spermicides). The Personal Assessment on pp. 256-257 will help you evaluate your risk of developing cervical cancer.

Vagina

Although rare, cancer of the vagina (the passage leading to the uterus) is of concern to a particular group of women: the daughters of over 3 million mothers who were given the drug DES (diethylstilbestrol) to prevent miscarriages. Because of the effects of DES on the fetal development of the reproductive system, these daughters now face the risk of developing a form of vaginal (and cervical) cancer called *clear cell cancer.* Since the risk was identified 30 years ago, the medical community has been following large groups of daughters to better assess their level of risk. To date, 1 in every 1000 exposed daughters has developed this form of cancer, some as early as 15 years of age.

Health on the Web
LEARNING ACTIVITIES

Activity 1

It has been said that "fear paralyzes and understanding facilitates." The American Cancer Society is a nationwide, community-based, voluntary health organization dedicated to preventing cancer, saving lives, and diminishing suffering from cancer, through research, education, advocacy, and service. Visit the American Cancer Society website at http://www.cancer.org/frames. Scroll down and click on "Cancer Info" and then select "Specific Cancers." Choose a cancer on the basis of its site and learn more about it. Describe how this type of cancer is prevented, detected, and treated.

Activity 2

A familiar way to describe cancer is on the basis of the organ or tissue site at which it occurs. Regular screening procedures can lead to early identification of cancer. Go to http://www.mayohealth.org/mayo/9702/htm/cancquiz/start.htm and take the *Cancer Incidence Quiz*. The quiz provides questions related to some of the more familiar cancer sites. How well did you do?

Activity 3

According to the American Diabetes Association, more than 16 million Americans have diabetes and many more are at risk for developing the condition. The American Diabetes Association is the nation's leading nonprofit health organization providing diabetes research, information, and advocacy. The mission of the organization is to prevent and cure diabetes and to improve the lives of all people affected by diabetes. You can estimate your risk of developing diabetes by going to the ADA's website at http://www.diabetes.org/default.htm. Scroll down and click on "Diabetes Info" and then choose "Take the *Diabetes Risk* test." Complete the inventory and then click on the "calculate" button to find out your estimated risk of developing diabetes.

Ovary

Since the death of actress Gilda Radner in 1989, public awareness of ovarian cancer has increased in this country. In 1997, it was estimated that 26,800 new cases would be identified and 14,200 women would die.[2] Most cases develop in women who are older than 40 years of age and who have not had children or began menstruation at an early age. The highest rate is in women over the age of 60. The incidence of ovarian cancer is greatest among women who have had a relatively longer exposure to hormones during their menstrual cycles.[18, 19]

Because of its vague symptoms, ovarian cancer has been referred to as a *silent* cancer. Digestive disturbances, gas, and stomach distention are often its only symptoms. Today, diagnosis of this highly lethal cancer is made using transvaginal ultrasound and surgery. A new three-drug combination, which includes Taxol, has extended average remission by nearly two years. This is the first significant progress in the treatment of ovarian cancer.

Prostate

The prostate gland is a walnut-size gland located near the base of the penis. It surrounds the neck of the bladder and the urethra. Cancer of the prostate is the third most common form of cancer in men and a leading cause of death from cancer in older men. On the basis of current statistics, approximately 1 out of 6 men will develop this form of cancer.[2] Men with a family history of prostate cancer are at greater risk of developing this form of cancer than men without this family history. Additionally, a link between prostate cancer and dietary patterns, such as excessive red meat and dairy product consumption, has been suggested.[20] A genetic link also appears to be a factor in the development of this form of cancer.

The symptoms of prostate disease, including prostate cancer, are listed in the Star Box on p. 260. Should these symptoms appear, particularly in men 50 years of age and older, a physician should be consulted. Screening for prostate cancer should begin by age 50 and involves an annual rectal examination and

mastectomy
Removal of breast tissue.

Symptoms of Prostate Disease
- Difficulty in urinating
- Frequent urination, particularly at night
- Continued wetness for a short time after urination
- Blood in the urine
- Low back pain
- Ache in upper thighs

the prostate-specific antigen (PSA) blood test. This test has been joined by a more sensitive version that can identify the "free" antigen most closely associated with prostate cancer, thus cutting down on the false positives and extensive use of biopsies. In addition, an ultrasound rectal examination will be used in men whose PSA scores are abnormally high.

Traditionally, prostate cancer has been treated through surgery or the use of radiation and chemotherapy, with a survival rate of 99% when diagnosed early and 87% overall.[2] Because this type of cancer grows slowly, it is increasingly likely that men whose cancer is very localized and whose life expectancy is less than 10 years at the time of diagnosis will not receive treatment but rather will be closely monitored for any progression in the cancer.

Testicle

Cancer of the testicle is among the least common forms of cancer; however, it represents the most common solid tumor in men between the ages of 20 and 34 years. Testicular cancer has a tendency to run in families and is more common in men whose testicles were undescended during childhood. The incidence of this cancer has been increasing in recent years. However, no single explanation can be given for this increase. Factors such as a difficult pregnancy, elevated temperature in the groin, or mumps may be involved. The incidence of this cancer has increased by 100% since 1930, while a corresponding drop in sperm count has been seen. Agricultural pesticide toxicity may be involved in both of these changes. In 1997, 7200 new cases were diagnosed and 350 deaths occurred.[2]

Symptoms of cancer of the testicles include a small, painless lump on the side of the testicle, a swollen or enlarged testicle, or heaviness or a dragging sensation in the groin or scrotum. Risk factors include confirmed injury, mumps, and hormonal treatments given to the mother before the child's birth. The importance of testicular self-examination, as well as early diagnosis and prompt treatment, cannot be overemphasized for men in the at-risk age-group of 20 to 34 years. The Health

Action Guide below explains how to perform a testicular self-examination.

Colon and Rectum

Cancer of the colon and rectum (colorectal cancer) has a combined incidence and death rate second only to that of lung cancer. Two types of tumors, carcinoma and lymphoma, can be found in both the colon and rectum. Fortunately, when diagnosed in a localized state, colorectal cancer has a relatively high survival rate of 90% through the first 5 years.[2] Genes have

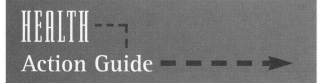

HEALTH
Action Guide

Testicular Self-Examination

Your best hope for early detection of testicular cancer is a simple 3-minute monthly self-examination. The following explains how to do a testicular self-examination. The best time is after a warm bath or shower, when the scrotal skin is most relaxed.

1. Roll each testicle gently between the thumb and fingers of both hands.

2. If you find any hard lumps or nodules, you should see your doctor promptly. They may not be malignant, but only your doctor can make the diagnosis.

After a thorough physical examination, your doctor may perform certain x-ray studies to make the most accurate diagnosis possible.

Testicular self-examinations are as important for men as breast self-examinations are for women.

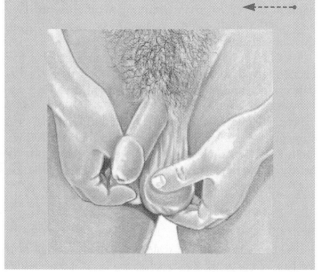

recently been discovered that lead to familial colon cancer and familial polyposis (abnormal tissue growth that occurs before formation of cancer) that are believed to be responsible for the tendency for colon and rectal cancer to run in families.[21] These forms of cancer are also seen in people whose diets are both high in saturated fat from red meat and low in fruits and vegetables, which contain antioxidant vitamins and fiber. Additionally, an association between colorectal cancer and smoking has been identified, suggesting that carcinogens may be ingested or pass into the digestive system from the bloodstream.

Symptoms associated with colon and rectal cancers include bleeding from the rectum, blood in the stool, or a change in bowel habits. Also, a family history of inflammatory bowel disease, polyp formation, or colorectal cancer should make one more alert to symptoms. In people over 50 years of age, any sudden change in bowel habits that lasts 10 days or longer should be evaluated by a physician. The American Cancer Society recommends preventive health care that includes digital (manual) rectal examination after age 40, a stool blood test after age 50, and a flexible sigmoidoscopy examination every 3 to 5 years after age 50. Prompt removal of polyps has been shown to be effective in lowering the risk of developing colorectal cancer. Further, there is evidence that the development of colorectal cancer may be prevented or slowed through regular exercise and through the regular use of aspirin.[22]

The treatment of colorectal cancer involves surgery combined with the use of chemotherapy drugs. A *colostomy* is required in 15% of the cases of colon and rectal cancer.

Pancreas

Pancreatic cancer is one of the most lethal forms of cancer, with a survival rate of only 4% at 5 years after diagnosis.[2] In light of the organ's important roles in both digestion and metabolic processes (see the discussion of diabetes mellitus on pp. 266-269), its destruction leaves the body in a state incompatible with living.

In 1997, 27,600 new cases of pancreatic cancer were diagnosed.[2] The disease is more common in men than women and occurs most frequently in African-American men. Early detection of this cancer is difficult because of the absence of symptoms until late in its course. Risk of developing this form of cancer increases with age; with diabetes mellitus, pancreatitis (inflammation of the pancreas), or cirrhosis (see Chapter 8); and with diets high in fat. To date, little in the way of effective treatment has been found.

Skin

Thanks in large part to our desire for a fashionable tan, too many teens and adults are spending more time in the sun (and in tanning booths) than their skin can tolerate. As a result, skin cancer, once common only among those people who had to work in the sun, is occurring with alarming frequency. In 1997, more than 900,000 Americans developed basal or squamous cell skin cancer and 40,300 cases of highly dangerous malignant melanoma were diagnosed.[2] Severe sunburning during childhood and chronic sun exposure during adolescence and younger adulthood are responsible for these increases in skin cancer.

Although many doctors do not emphasize this point enough, the key to the successful treatment of skin cancer lies in early detection. In the case of basal cell or squamous cell cancer, the development of a pale, waxlike, pearly nodule or red, scaly patch may be the first symptom. For others, skin cancer may be noticed as a gradual change in the appearance of an already existing skin mole. If such a change is noted, a physician should be contacted. Melanoma usually

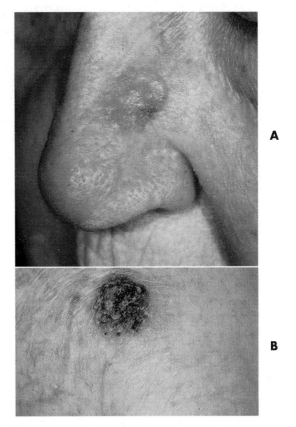

Figure 11-3 **A,** Basal cell carcinoma. Note the typical raised, rolled edge. **B,** Squamous cell carcinoma.

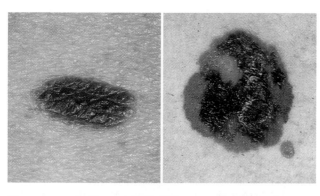

Figure 11-4   **A,** Normal mole. This type of lesion is often seen in large numbers on the skin of young adults and may affect any body site. Note its symmetrical shape, regular borders, uniform color, and relatively small size (about 6 millimeters). **B,** Malignant melanoma. Note its asymmetrical shape, irregular borders, uneven color, and relatively large size (about 2 centimeters).

begins as a small, molelike growth that increases progressively in size, changes color, ulcerates, and bleeds easily. For use in detecting melanoma, the American Cancer Society recommends using the guidelines below:

A   is for asymmetry
B   is for border irregularity
C   is for color (change)
D   is for a diameter greater than 6 mm

Figure 11-4 shows a mole that would be considered harmless and one that clearly demonstrates the ABCD characteristics described above. Again, it is important to be observant and not fail to recognize the changing status of a mole or other skin lesion. The Health Action Guide below depicts the steps to be taken in making a regular inspection of the skin.

When nonmelanoma skin cancer is found, an almost 100% cure rate can be expected. Treatment of these skin

HEALTH
Action Guide ━ ━ ━ ━ ➤

How to look for melanoma

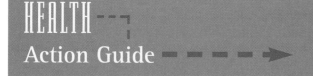

1. Examine your body front and back in the mirror, then right and left sides with arms raised.

2. Bend your elbows and carefully look at your palms, forearms and under your upper arms.

3. Look at the backs of your legs and feet, the spaces between your toes and the soles of your feet.

4. Examine the back of your neck and scalp with a hand mirror. Part your hair for a closer look.

5. Finally, check your back and buttocks with a hand mirror.

What to look for
Potential signs of malignancy in moles or pigmented spots:

Asymmetry
One half unlike the other half

Irregularity
Border irregular— or poorly circumscribed

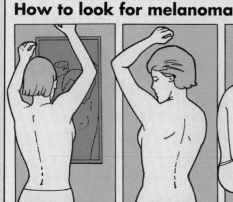

Color
Color varies from one area to another; shades of tan brown or black

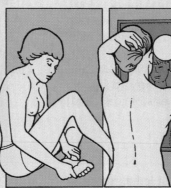

Size
Diameter larger than 6 mm as a rule (diameter of a pencil eraser)

cancers can involve surgical removal, destruction through burning or freezing, or the use of x-ray therapy. When the more serious melanomas are found in an early stage, a high cure rate is accomplished using the same techniques. However, when malignant melanomas are more advanced, extensive surgery and chemotherapy will be necessary, and, unfortunately, recovery is rare.

Prevention of skin cancer should be a high priority for people who enjoy the sun or must work outdoors. The use of sunscreen is of great importance. Table 11-1 provides guidance in selecting the sunscreen that is appropriate for your skin. In addition, parents can help their children prevent skin cancer later in life by restricting their outdoor play from 11:00 AM to 2:00 PM, requiring them to wear hats that shade their faces, and applying a sunscreen with SPF 15 on their children regardless of skin tone.

A relationship between the presence of certain abnormal moles, called *dysplastic nevi,* and the risk of developing malignant melanoma has recently been established. By counting these "indicator moles," physicians can estimate a patient's risk of developing this serious form of skin cancer before it appears.[23] The Personal Assessment on pp. 256-257 will help you determine your own risk of developing this kind of cancer.

THE DIAGNOSIS OF CANCER

Is cancer survivable? The answer is, of course, yes. The chances for survival (defined as living at least 5 years after diagnosis) depend greatly on the promptness of identification, diagnosis, and treatment.

Thus the chances for recovery from cancer are best when cancer is detected early. The familiar "cancer's seven warning signals" can serve as a basis for early

Cancer's Seven Warning Signs

Listed below are the seven warning signs of cancer, which the acronym **CAUTION** will help you remember:

1. Change in bowel or bladder habits
2. A sore that does not heal
3. Unusual bleeding or discharge
4. Thickening or lump in breast or elsewhere
5. Indigestion or difficulty in swallowing
6. Obvious change in a wart or mole
7. Nagging cough or hoarseness

If you have a warning sign that persists for more than 5 days, see your doctor!

detection (see the Star Box above). Also, unexplained weight loss can be a signal for the presence of a malignancy. Weight loss, however, is not usually an early indicator of cancer. Persistent headaches and vision changes should be evaluated by a physician.

In addition to the recognition of danger signals, undergoing regularly scheduled screening for malignancy-related changes is important. Note that monthly breast self-examination for all women over the age of 20 is recommended. Further, we strongly recommend testicular self-examination for men. Step-by-step procedures for both of these self-examinations are provided in the Star Boxes on pp. 258 and 260. The remaining screening procedures require the services of a medical practitioner.

Treatment

In today's approach to cancer treatment, proven therapies and promising new experimental approaches are often combined. The traditional therapies

Skin Type	Pigmentation	Sunburn/Tanning History	Sun Protection Factor (SPF)
I	Very fair skin; freckling; blond, red, or brown hair	Always burns easily; never tans	15-30
II	Fair skin; blond, red, or brown hair	Always burns easily, tans minimally	15-20
III	Brown hair and eyes, darker skin (light brown)	Burns moderately, tans gradually and uniformly	8-15
IV	Light brown skin; dark hair and eyes (moderate brown)	Burns minimally; always tans well	8-15
V	Brown skin; dark hair and eyes	Rarely burns, tans profusely (dark brown)	Recommended same as skin type IV
VI	Brown-black skin; dark hair and eyes	Never burns, deeply pigmented (black)	Recommended same as skin type IV

Table 11-1   Sunscreen Guide

NOTE: Although formulas as high as 60 are available, an SPF of 30 is usually appropriate for use, perhaps requiring more frequent applications. *As deterioration of the ozone layer continues, it may be necessary to use an even more protective sunscreen.*

are surgery, radiation, and chemotherapy. Used independently or in combination, they form the backbone of our increasingly successful efforts in treating cancer. Newer, more experimental therapies are also being used on a limited basis. One or more experimental approaches may be combined with surgery, radiation, and chemotherapy as a basis for treatment.

In the sections that follow, a brief description of each treatment is given.

Surgery

Surgical removal of tissue suspected to contain cancerous cells is the oldest approach to cancer therapy. When undertaken early in the course of the disease, surgery is particularly suited for cancers of the skin, gastrointestinal tract, breast, uterus, cervix, prostate gland, and testicle. Minimal procedures are undertaken whenever possible, and radiation or chemotherapy is often used with surgery to ensure maximum effectiveness.

Radiation

Radiation is capable of killing cancer cells by altering their genetic material while it is in an exposed state during cell division. Of course, since neighboring cells also divide, they are exposed to the damaging effects of radiation as well. However, by carefully planning the length of exposure and time of treatment, and by focusing of the radiation with precision, damage to noncancerous cells can be held to a minimum.

Chemotherapy

The important advances in successful treatment of cancer can be attributed to advances in chemotherapy, both in terms of new drugs and the more effective combination of new drugs and familiar chemotherapeutic agents. Most often, these drugs work by destroying cancer cells' ability to use important materials or carry out cell division in a normal manner. Because chemotherapy influences cell division, it will influence noncancerous cells that divide frequently. Among the cells most susceptible to this influence are those that make up bone marrow, the lining of the intestinal tract, and the hair follicles. People who are undergoing chemotherapy often have side effects directly related to these changes—immune system suppression, diarrhea, and hair loss.

Immunotherapy

Immunotherapy refers to the use of a variety of substances to trigger a person's own immune system to attack cancer cells or prevent cancer cells from becoming activated. Among these new forms of immunotherapy are the use of interferon, monoclonal antibodies, interleukin-2, tumor necrosis factor (TNF), and certain bone

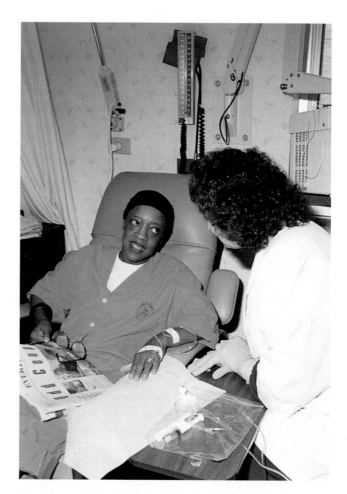

The effects of chemotherapy are carefully monitored.

marrow growth regulators. These products are being manufactured using genetic engineering technology.

Alternative (complementary) cancer therapies

In spite of advances made in the diagnosis and treatment of cancer during this century, cancer rates are climbing as we move toward the next century. In response to climbing rates and to requests made by cancer victims and many clinicians to expand the range of treatments, the National Institutes of Health has begun an in-depth study of alternative or nonconventional cancer treatments. Through the use of new and carefully controlled studies and the reassessment of research and records already available, an attempt will be made by the NIH to better understand the benefits to be derived from alternative or complementary therapies.

Among the treatments to be given closer and more careful consideration are chiropractic (the manipulation of the spine), acupressure (finger and thumb pressure to relieve pain), and acupuncture (needles inserted to relieve pain and promote the flow of energy within the body). Additional areas of investigation will include ayurveda (a traditional Indian lifestyle that involves the use of herbs and a particular diet), biofeedback (monitoring of body functions to control body processes), homeopathy (use of minuscule doses of toxic substances), and naturopathy (use of natural remedies, including sunshine and vitamins). Further focus will be directed toward oxidizing agents (substances believed to kill viruses), reflexology (the massaging of points on the feet), therapeutic touch (redirecting of "life forces" through touching areas of the body), and visualization (learning to "see" a cure occurring).

Time and study will answer many questions about the effectiveness of these methods of treating cancer. Should these areas prove to be more effective than traditional medical science now believes, their incorporation will probably be very gradual.

RISK REDUCTION

Because cancer will probably continue to be the second most common disease among adults, it is important that you explore ways to reduce your risk of developing cancer. The following factors, which could make you vulnerable to cancer, can be controlled or at least recognized.

- *Know your family history.* You are the recipient of the genetic strengths and weaknesses of your biological parents and your more distant relatives. If cancer is prevalent in your family medical history, you cannot afford to disregard this fact. It may be appropriate for you to be screened for certain types of cancer more often or at a young age.
- *Select your occupation carefully.* Because of recently discovered relationships between cancer and occupations that bring employees into contact with carcinogenic agents, you must be aware of risks with certain job selections and assignments. Worksites associated with frequent contact with pesticides, strong solvents, volatile hydocarbons, and airborne fibers could pay well but also shorten life.
- *Do not use tobacco products.* You may want to review Chapter 9 on the overwhelming evidence linking all forms of tobacco use (including smokeless tobacco) to the development of cancer. Smoking is so detrimental to health that it is considered the number one preventable cause of death.
- *Follow a sound diet.* The Health Action Guide above provides general guidelines on eating to reduce your cancer risk. In addition, review

HEALTH Action Guide

Eat to Lower Your Cancer Risk

The American Cancer Society recommends the following dietary precautions to help reduce the risk of getting cancer:
- Avoid obesity.
- Reduce total fat intake.
- Eat more high-fiber foods.
- Include foods rich in vitamins A and C in your daily diet.
- Include cruciferous vegetables in your diet.
- Avoid smoked, salt-cured, and nitrate-cured foods.
- Limit alcohol consumption.

Chapter 5 for information regarding dietary practices and the incidence of various diseases, including cancer. In that chapter the role of fruits and vegetables known to be sources of cancer-preventing phytochemicals is introduced. Table 11-2 provides a detailed listing of the phytochemicals found in a variety of foods that may play a constructive role in cancer prevention. Notice that a wide variety of fruits and vegetables, particularly the cruciferous vegetables, including cauliflower, broccoli, and brussels sprouts, and the fruits that are high in beta-carotene, vitamin C, and fiber, are listed. Should research demonstrate an even clearer role for nutrients, *chemoprevention* may become an even more widely practiced component of cancer prevention.

- *Control your body weight.* Particularly for women, obesity is related to a higher incidence of cancer of the uterus, ovary, and breast. Maintaining a desirable body weight could improve overall health and lead to more successful management of cancer should it develop.
- *Exercise regularly.* Chapter 4 discusses in detail the importance of regular moderate exercise to all aspects of health, including reducing the risk of chronic illnesses. Moderate exercise increases the body's ability to deliver oxygen to its tissues and thus to reduce the formation of cancer-enhancing free radicals formed during incomplete oxidation of nutrients. Moderate exercise

Table 11-2   Phytochemicals Involved in Cancer Prevention

Phytochemical Class	Food Source
Allium compounds	Garlic, onions, chives, leeks
Carotenoids	Yellow and orange vegetables and fruits, dark green leafy vegetables
Coumarins	Vegetables and citrus fruits
Dithiolthiones	Cruciferous vegetables
Flavonoids	Most fruits and vegetables
Glucosinolates, indoles	Cruciferous vegetables, especially brussels sprouts, rutabaga, mustard greens, dried horseradish
Inositol hexaphosphate	Plant foods, especially soybeans and cereals
Isoflavones	Soybeans
Isothiocyanates	Cruciferous vegetables
Limonene	Citrus fruits
Phenols	Nearly all fruits and vegetables
Protease inhibitors	Plant foods, especially seeds and legumes, including soybeans

also stimulates the production of enzymes that remove free radicals. Some concern exists, however, that extensive exercise might actually reduce the body's ability to produce the enzymes mentioned above and thus contribute to the development of free-radical–based cellular changes, including cancer.

- *Limit your exposure to sun.* It is important to heed this message, even if you enjoy many outdoor activities. Particularly for people with light complexions, the radiation received through chronic exposure to the sun may foster the development of skin cancer.

- *Consume alcohol in moderation if at all.* Heavier users of alcohol experience an increased prevalence of several types of cancer, including cancer of the oral cavity, larynx, and esophagus. Whether this results directly from the presence of carcinogens in alcohol or is more closely related to the alcohol user's tendency to smoke has not yet been established.

When the suggestions made above are given careful consideration, it should be obvious that much can be done by individuals to prevent or at least minimize the development of cancer. A wellness-oriented lifestyle is the best weapon in your "personal war against cancer." Having said this, however, all risk factor reduction is, in the final analysis, relative in nature. Observation and experience indicate that life cannot be totally struc-tured around the desire to achieve maximum longevity or reduce morbidity at all costs. Most people need a balance between life that is emo-tionally, socially, and spiritually satisfying and life that is structured solely for the purpose of living a long time and minimizing exposure to illness. Regardless of our personal

lifestyle, we can, however, educate others, give comfort and support to those who are living with cancer, and support the funding of continuing and innovative new cancer research. Resources available for people with cancer and their families are listed in the Star Box on p. 267.

CHRONIC HEALTH CONDITIONS

In addition to the two most widely recognized chronic health problems of adulthood—cardiovascular disease and cancer—aging increases the probability that the incidence of other conditions will increase as we grow older. In this section of the chapter, we examine four noncancerous, noncardiovascular chronic health conditions: diabetes mellitus, multiple sclerosis, asthma, and systemic lupus erythematosus. Of course, many additional chronic conditions are discussed in other chapters of this textbook. See the Star Box on p. 268 for information about Alzheimer's disease, a chronic illness that affects many elderly adults. See the Star Box on p. 269 for an explanation of sickle cell trait and sickle cell disease, disorders that can affect African-Americans.

Diabetes Mellitus

Diabetes mellitus is not a single condition but rather two metabolic disorders with important similarities and differences.

Non–insulin-dependent diabetes mellitus (Type II)

In people who do not have diabetes mellitus the body's need for energy is met through the "burning" of glucose (blood sugar) within the cells. Glucose is

absorbed from the digestive tract and carried to the cells by the blood system. Passage of glucose into the cell is achieved through a transport system that moves the glucose molecule across the cell's membrane. Activation of this glucose transport mechanism requires the presence of the hormone insulin (Figure 11-5). Specific receptor sites for **insulin** can be found on the cell membrane. In addition to its role in the transport of glucose into sensitive cells, insulin is also required for the conversion of glucose into glycogen in the liver and the formation of fatty acids in adipose cells. Insulin is produced in the cells of the islets of Langerhans within the pancreas. The release of insulin from the pancreas corresponds to the changing levels of glucose within the blood.[24]

In adults with a **genetic predisposition** for developing non–insulin-dependent diabetes mellitus a trigger mechanism (most likely obesity) begins a process through which the body cells become increasingly less sensitive to the presence of insulin, although a normal (or slightly greater than normal) amount of insulin is produced by the pancreas. The growing ineffectiveness of insulin in getting glucose into cells results in the buildup of glucose in the blood. Elevated levels of glucose give rise to *hyperglycemia,* a hallmark symptom of non–insulin-dependent diabetes mellitus.

In response to this buildup the kidneys begin the process of filtering glucose from the blood. Excess glucose then spills over into the urine. This removal of glucose in the urine demands large amounts of water, a process called *diuresis,* a second important symptom of adult-onset diabetes. Increased *thirst,* a third symptom of developing diabetes, results in response to the

movement of fluid from extracellular spaces into the circulatory system to maintain homeostasis.[25]

For many adults with diabetes, dietary modification (with an emphasis on monitoring total carbohydrate intake, not just sugar) and regular exercise is the only treatment required to maintain an acceptable level of glucose use.[26] Weight loss will improve the condition by "releasing" more insulin receptors, and exercise increases the actual number of receptor sites. With better insulin recognition, the person can return to a more normal state of functioning.

For people whose condition is more advanced, dietary modification and weight loss alone will not accomplish the level of management required, and oral drugs, including sulfonylureas and metformin, or even insulin may be necessary. For those who require insulin, management of the condition becomes much more demanding.

In addition to genetic predisposition and obesity as important factors in non–insulin-dependent diabetes mellitus, unresolved stress appears to play a role in the development of hyperglycemic states. Although stress alone probably cannot produce a diabetic condition, it

insulin
A pancreatic hormone required by the body for the effective metabolism of glucose (blood sugar).

genetic predisposition
An inherited tendency to develop a disease process if necessary environmental factors exist.

Alzheimer's Disease

Although it affects fewer than 1% to 2% of elderly people, organic brain syndrome, in either its acute or chronic form, is an incapacitating, heart-rending, and costly affliction. **Alzheimer's disease** represents the best known of the presenile dementia disorders affecting between 2 and 4 million adults. Today, more than ever before, it is *the* disease associated with those individuals who have lived a long time.

The initial indication of Alzheimer's disease is often subtle and may be confused with mild depression. At this stage of the disease process, however, the person might experience some difficulty answering questions like these:

- Where are we now?
- What month is it?
- What is today's date?
- When is your birthday?
- Who is the President?

During the ensuing months, victims experience greater memory loss, confusion, and *dementia* (or loss of reasoning). In the most advanced stage, Alzheimer's victims experience incontinence, infantile behavior, and finally total incapacitation resulting from the destruction of brain tissue. Institutionalization of people with advanced Alzheimer's disease is certain.

The precise diagnosis of Alzheimer's disease and other, similar disorders remains difficult to make before the death of the victim. At that time the characteristic *neurofibrillary tangles, neuritic plaques,* and loss of neurons can be identified. Before death, all other conditions capable of leading to dementia are individually ruled out. The initial diagnosis of Alzheimer's disease is made based on a process of elimination.

Several theories exist concerning the cause of Alzheimer's disease. Growing research indicates that genetic mutations in chromosomes 14, 19, or 21 may encourage the development of the disease. Additional theories suggest possible links between Alzheimer's disease and abnormal protein development, deficiencies in acetylcholine (a neurotransmitter) production, abnormal blood flow, or exposure to infectious agents or toxins.

Drugs to treat Alzheimer's disease effectively have not yet been developed. One drug, tacrine (Cognex), shows minor improvements, as does donepezil (Aricept), a new drug with a simular mechanism, with Alzheimer's patients when used early in the disease process.

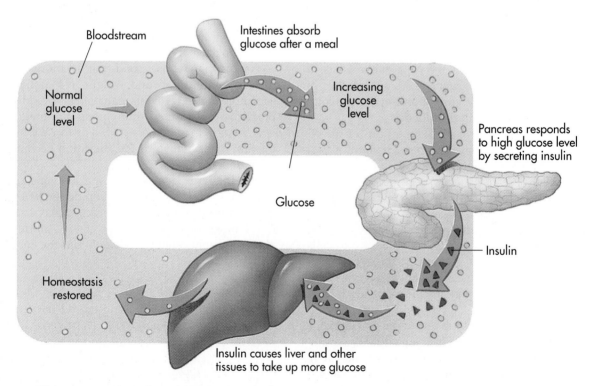

Figure 11-5   The secretion of insulin is regulated by a mechanism that tends to reverse any deviation from normal. Thus an increase in blood glucose level triggers secretion of insulin. Since insulin promotes glucose uptake by cells, blood glucose level is restored to its lower, normal level.

Sickle Cell Trait and Sickle Cell Disease

Of all the chemical compounds found within the body, few occur in as many forms as hemoglobin, which helps bind oxygen to the red blood cell. Two forms of hemoglobin are associated with sickle cell trait and sickle cell disease. African-Americans can be the recipients of either form of this abnormal hemoglobin. Those who inherit the trait-form do not develop the disease but are capable of transmitting the gene for abnormal hemoglobin to their offspring. Those people who inherit the disease-form face a shortened life characterized by periods of pain and impairment.

Approximately 8% of all African-Americans have the gene for sickle cell trait; they experience little impairment, and they can transmit the gene to their children.

For approximately 1.5% of African-Americans, sickle cell disease is a painful, incapacitating, and life-shortening disease. Red blood cells are elongated, crescent-shaped (or sickled), and unable to pass through the body's minute capillaries. The body responds to the presence of these abnormal red blood cells by removing them very quickly. This sets the stage for anemia—thus the condition is often called *sickle cell anemia*. In addition to anemia, this form of the condition is associated with many serious medical problems, including impaired lung function, congestive heart failure, gallbladder infections, bone changes, and possible abnormalities of the eye and skin. Today, a bone marrow transplant can save the lives of about 1% to 2% of people with sickle cell disease.[27]

If a key exists for preventing the occurrence of sickle cell trait and disease, it lies in the area of genetic counseling to help in making decisions regarding reproduction, including pregnancy termination. The decision to have children and perhaps risk passing on the gene for defective hemoglobin to the next generation is one that must be carefully made.

is likely that stress can create a series of endocrine changes that can lead to a state of hyperglycemia.

Diabetes can cause serious damage to several important structures within the body. The rate and extent to which people with diabetes develop these pathological changes can be markedly influenced by the nature of their particular condition and the type of management with which they comply. For those who already have diabetes, an understanding of the condition and a commitment to management are important elements in living with diabetes mellitus.

Insulin–dependent diabetes mellitus (Type I)

A second type of diabetes mellitus is insulin-dependent diabetes mellitus, or Type I diabetes. The onset of this type of diabetes generally occurs before the age of 35, most often during childhood. In contrast to Type II diabetes, in which insulin is produced but is ineffective because of insensitivity, in Type I diabetes the body does not produce insulin at all. Destruction of the insulin-producing cells of the pancreas by the person's immune system (possibly in search of a viral infection

within the islet cells of the pancreas) accounts for this sudden and irreversible loss of insulin production.[28]

In most ways the two forms of diabetes are similar, with the important exception that insulin-dependent diabetes mellitus requires the use of insulin from an outside source (see the Star Box on p. 270, top). Today this insulin is obtained either from animals or through genetically engineered bacteria and is taken by injection (one to four times per day) or through the use of an insulin pump that provides a constant supply of insulin to the body. Development of the glucometer, a highly accurate device for measuring the amount of glucose in the blood, allows for sound management of this condition and a life expectancy that is essentially

Alzheimer's disease
Gradual development of memory loss, confusion, and loss of reasoning; will eventually lead to total intellectual incapacitation, brain degeneration, and death.

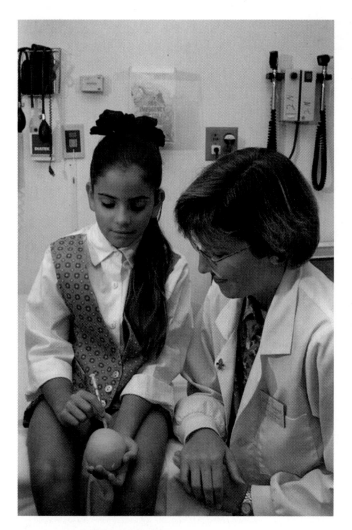

Learning to self-inject insulin.

normal. Of course, with both forms of diabetes mellitus, sound dietary practice, planned activity, and control of stress are important for keeping blood glucose levels within normal ranges. In the absence of good management of diabetes mellitus, several serious problems can result, including blindness, gangrene of the extremities, kidney disease, and heart attack. These and other common complications of diabetes are listed in the Star Box at the right. People who cannot establish good control are likely to live a shorter life than those who can.

Multiple Sclerosis

For proper nerve conduction to occur within portions of the brain and spinal cord, an insulating sheath of *myelin* must surround *neurons*. In the progressive disease multiple sclerosis (MS), the cells that produce myelin are destroyed and myelin production ceases. This disruption of normal neurological functioning eventually reaches an extent to which vital functions of the body can no longer be carried out.

Differences between Types of Diabetes Mellitus

Insulin-Dependent (Type I)
(These symptoms usually develop rapidly.)
- Extreme hunger
- Extreme thirst
- Frequent urination
- Extreme weight loss
- Irritability
- Weakness and fatigue
- Nausea and vomiting

Non–Insulin-Dependent (Type II)
(These symptoms usually develop gradually.)
- Any of the symptoms for insulin-dependent diabetes
- Blurred vision or a change in sight
- Itchy skin
- Tingling or numbness in the limbs

If you notice these symptoms occurring, bring them to the attention of your physician.

The cause of MS is not fully understood. Research continues to focus on virus-induced **autoimmune** mechanisms in which T cells attack viral-infected myelin-producing cells.[26]

Multiple sclerosis is a disease that most often appears for the first time during the young adult years—the traditional college years. After its onset, the disease progresses off and on over the next 20 to 25 years. The initial symptoms of the condition are often visual impairment, prickling and burning in the extremities, or an altered **gait.** Deterioration of nervous system function occurs in various forms during the course of MS. In the disease's most advanced stages, movement is greatly impaired, and mental deterioration may be present.

Common Complications of Diabetes
- Cataract formation
- Glaucoma
- Blindness
- Dental caries
- Stillbirths/miscarriages
- Neonatal deaths
- Congenital defects
- Cardiovascular disease
- Kidney disease
- Gangrene
- Impotence

Treatment for MS involves attempts to reduce the severity of the symptoms and extend the periods of remission. Today a variety of therapies are used, including immune system–targeted drugs, steroid drugs, drugs to relieve muscle spasms, injections of nerve blockers, and physical therapy.

The development of immune system–related agents is very much at the center of the fight against MS. Betaseron, a genetically engineered form of interferon, is a drug that effectively reduces the symptoms of MS but may not slow the progression of the disease. Betaseron is currently used by 40,000 people. Most recently, Avonex and Copolymer 1, drugs that slow the development of lesions and delay periods of relapse, have been given approval by FDA advisory panels. These drugs too are modified forms of interferon.

In addition to drug therapy, psychotherapy is an important adjunct to the treatment of MS. Profound periods of depression often accompany the initial diagnosis of this condition. Emotional support is helpful in dealing with the progressive impairment associated with the condition.

Asthma

Bronchial asthma is a chronic respiratory disease characterized by acute attacks of breathlessness and wheezing caused by narrowing of the bronchioles.

Two main types of the asthma have been identified: *extrinsic* and *intrinsic.* In extrinsic asthma, allergens such as pollen, house dust, house-dust mites, animal fur, and feathers produce sudden and extensive bronchoconstriction that narrows the airways. Increased sputum production further narrows the bronchioles and restricts the passage of air. This narrowing fosters the development of chronic inflammation of the airways, which is the most damaging aspect of asthma. Wheezing is most pronounced when the victim attempts to exhale air through the narrowed air passages. For many asthmatic people, exercise, cigarette smoke, and particular foods or drugs can cause an asthma attack.

Intrinsic asthma, the least common form, displays similar symptoms but is caused by stress or is a consequence of frequent respiratory tract infections. Allergens as such are not involved in this form of asthma.

Prevention and effective management of asthma is often possible through the use of a combination of approaches. Most basic, of course, is the maintenance of high-level wellness through a healthful lifestyle that includes sound diet, exercise, and stress management. In this approach, exercises that are well tolerated, such as swimming, have proved beneficial in maintaining a more normal level of respiratory function. Secondly, *immunotherapy,* in which the patient is desensitized through injections of weakened aller-

gens, is a frequently attempted form of prevention. In addition, the careful use of corticosteroid drugs several times per day reduces inflammation and thus minimizes the likelihood of attacks occurring.

Once an attack has started, people with asthma now use low-dose steroids delivered through an inhaler.[29] After inhalation, normal breathing is restored within several minutes. Each year in this country, however, several thousand people die as the result of asthma attacks. Some experts believe that this number could be reduced if physicians were more aggressive in their treatment of the bronchial inflammation component of the condition.

For people with exercise-induced asthma (EIA), one of the more frequently seen forms, several important steps should be taken when attempting to exercise (see the Health Action Guide below).

Regardless of the potential seriousness of asthma, however, many people who experience asthma during childhood can manage well with the proper use of exercise and medication and may experience less asthma, or none at all, as they reach adulthood.

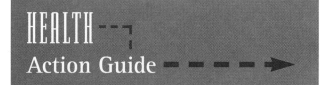

HEALTH
Action Guide

Tips for Controlling Exercise-Induced Asthma

- Obtain a treatment and prevention plan from your physician.
- Alert instructors and coaches about the existence of any treatment plan.
- Medicate before exercising according to your physician's instruction.
- Warm up slowly to increase heart rate gradually and cool down slowly after exercise.
- Carry your bronchodilator with you at all times if one was prescribed.
- Wear a scarf or mask over your mouth and nose during cold weather to warm and moisten the air you breathe.
- Wear an allergy mask over the mouth and nose when exercising during pollen season.

autoimmune
An immune response against the cells of a person's own body.

gait
Pattern of walking.

Systemic Lupus Erythematosus

Systemic lupus erythematosus (SLE), or simply *lupus,* is perhaps the most familiar of a class of chronic conditions known as autoimmune disorders, or *connective tissue disorders.* Collectively, these conditions reflect an extensive and inappropriate attack by the body's immune system on its own tissues, which then serve as *self-antigens* (see Chapter 12 for a discussion of the immune response).

The name *systemic lupus erythematosus* reflects the widespread (systemic) destruction of fibrous connective tissue and other tissues and the appearance of a reddish rash (erythematosus) that imparts a characteristic "mask" to the face. SLE is most often seen in women who developed the condition during young adulthood. The course of the condition is gradual, with intermittent periods of inflammation, stiffness, fatigue, pleurisy (chest pain), and discomfort over wide areas of the body, including muscles, joints, and skin. Similar changes may also occur with tissue of the nervous system, kidneys, and heart. Diagnosis is made on the bases of a number of laboratory tests, including the identification of SLE factor in the blood.

The reason the immune system turns on the body in such a widely based and aggressive manner is not fully understood. It is likely, however, that a combination of genetic predisposition and an earlier viral infection may be involved in its development. Episodes (called *flares*) of lupus often follow exposure to the sun, periods of fatigue, or an infectious disease; all these should be avoided to the fullest extent possible. Management of the condition generally involves the long-term (and low-dose) use of prednisone (a corticosteroid) to suppress the adrenal gland's cortisone. In some cases the immune system itself may be medically suppressed as well. These treatments must be managed carefully because they carry serious side effects.[30]

Summary

- The "war on cancer" has made gains in many areas, but it is far from being won, with overall death rates having climbed since 1971.
- Cancer is a condition reflecting the body's inability to control the growth and specialization of cells.
- Genes that control replication, specialization, repair, and suppression of abnormal activity hold the potential of becoming oncogenes and thus can be considered protooncogenes.
- A variety of agents, including genetic mutations, viruses, and carcinogens (and co-carginogens) stimulate the conversion of regulatory genes (protooncogenes) into oncogenes. The identification of oncogenes continues at a rapid pace in conjunction with the Human Genome Project.
- Cancer cells demonstrate a variety of interesting characteristics in comparison with normal cells of the same type. Benign tumors, made up of noncancerous cells, can present serious health problems.
- Cancer can be described on the basis of the type of tissue in which it has its origin—carcinoma, sarcoma, melanoma, etc.
- Cancer can be described on the basis of its location within the body—lung, breast, prostate, etc.
- Cigarette smoking and having a genetic predisposition are both related to the development of lung cancer.
- Breast cancer demonstrates clear familial patterns that suggest a genetic predisposition. Mammograms are recommended as an important component of breast cancer identification. Important options should be considered before the treatment of breast cancer.
- Regular use of Pap tests is related to the early detection of uterine (cervical) cancer. A group of middle-aged women who are the daughters of mothers given the drug DES during pregnancy have high levels of vaginal cancer. Ovarian cancer is often "silent" in its presentation of symptoms.
- The PSA test improves the ability to diagnose prostate cancer. A more sensitive PSA test will soon be available.
- Regular self-examination of the testicles leads to early detection of testicular cancer.
- Colon and rectal cancers have strong familial links and are seen in populations that consume diets high in fat and low in fruits and vegetables.
- Pancreatic cancer is very difficult to survive, in part because of the absence of symptoms early in the disease's course.
- Skin cancer prevention requires protection from excessive sun exposure.
- Early detection based on self-examination and screening is the basis for the identification and successful treatment of many cancers. Conventional and alternative treatment methods can be used to treat cancer.
- Cancer risk reduction techniques should be practiced on a regular basis.
- Diabetes mellitus, in both of its forms, is a chronic condition reflecting the body's inability to use glucose in a normal manner.
- Multiple sclerosis involves the autoimmune destruction of the insulating cover of neurons.
- Asthma may be a response to extrinsic factors such as pollen, dust, or exercise. Factors such as stress or chronic respiratory infections are the basis of a less commonly seen form of asthma called *intrinsic asthma.*
- Autoimmune disorders, such as SLE, reflect the immune system's failure to recognize the body's own tissue as being "self." Flares involving episodes of inflammation, swelling, pain, and discomfort occur periodically in conjunction with the disease.

Review Questions

1. What is the relationship between regulatory genes and tumor suppressor genes in the development of cancer? Why are regulatory genes called both *protooncogenes* and *oncogenes*?
2. What are some of the major types of cancer, based on the tissue in which they have their origin?
3. What are the principal factors that contribute to the development of lung cancer? Of breast cancer?
4. When should regular use of mammography begin, and which women should begin using it earliest?
5. How does the PSA test contribute to the early detection of prostate cancer?
6. What signs indicate the possibility that a skin lesion has become cancerous?
7. What important information can be obtained with the use of Pap tests?
8. What are the steps for effective self-examination of the breasts and testicles?
9. Why is ovarian cancer described as a "silent" cancer?
10. What are the conventional and alternative cancer treatments most often used in the treatment of cancer?
11. What are the risk reduction activities identified in this chapter?
12. How do non–insulin-dependent and insulin-dependent diabetes mellitus differ? How are they similar?
13. What is the role of the immune system in multiple sclerosis?
14. How do chronic respiratory tract inflammation and airway constriction relate to asthma? What is the role of exercise in both the cause and the prevention of asthma?
15. What is the role of the immune system is connective tissue disorders such as SLE? What factors are associated with the development of the disorder? Why does treatment involving immune system depression carry risks for people with SLE?

 ## Think About This . . .

- Do you believe you could cope with a significant health problem at this time in your life?
- Do you know anyone who has or has had cancer? How did cancer affect that person's life?
- How regularly do you perform either breast or testicular self-examination?

- If you were diagnosed as having a terminal illness, how willing would you be to serve as a subject in a research project that tested a potentially toxic experimental drug?
- Which conditions in this chapter are you likely to develop, and which are you not likely to develop?

References

1. Cancer mortality starts to decline, finally, *Cancer Smart,* 3(1):5, March 1997.
2. American Cancer Society, *Cancer facts and figures: 1997,* Atlanta, 1997, The Society.
3. Songer J, oncologist, personal interview, February 1998.
4. Marx J: New tumor suppressor may rival p53 (Research News), *Science* 264(5157):334-345, 1994.
5. Wooster R et al: Identification of the breast cancer susceptibility gene BRCA2, *Nature* 378(6559):789-792, 1995.
6. Eastman P: The cancer genetics revolution: science and ethics at the crossroads, *Oncology Times* 16(8), August 1994.
7. Kim NW et al: Specific association of human telomerase activity with immortal cells and cancer, *Science* 266(5193):2011-2015, 1994.
8. Antiangiogenesis: depriving cancer of life support, *Cancer Smart* 3(2)11, June 1997.
9. Sidransky D, Stix G: Advances in cancer detection, *Scientific American* 275(3):104-106, 1996.
10. Ballard, Barbash R et al: Body fat distribution and breast cancer in the Framingham study, *J Natl Cancer Inst* 82(24):1943-1944, 1990.
11. Blat WJ, McLaughlin JK: Geographic patterns of breast cancer among American women, *J Natl Cancer Inst* 87(24):1819-1820, 1995.
12. Struewing JP, Hartge P, Wacholder S: The risk of cancer associated with specific mutations of BRCAS1 and BRCA2 among Ashkenazi Jews, *N Engl J Med* 336(20):1401-1408, 1997.
13. Prophylactic cancer surgeries offer no guarantees, uncertain outcomes, *J Natl Cancer Inst (News)* 20(8):1-3, 1996.
14. Jacbson JA et al: Ten-year results of a comparison of conservation with mastectomy in the treatment of stage I and II breast cancer, *N Engl J Med* 332(14):907-911, 1995.
15. Fisher BF et al: Reanalysis and results after 12 years follow-up in a randomized clinical trail comparing total mastectomy with lumpectomy with or without irradiation in the treatment of breast cancer, *N Engl J Med* 333(22):1456-1461, 1995.
16. Eddy DM et al: Screening for cervical cancer, *Ann Intern Med* 113(7):560-561, 1990.
17. Janerich DT et al: The screening histories of women with invasive cervical cancer, Connecticut, *Am J Public Health* 85(6):791-794, 1995.
18. Familial breast cancer (editorial), *The Cancer Journal* 9(3):1-4, May-June 1996.
19. Schildkraut JM, Berchuck A: Relationship between lifetime ovulatory cycles and overexpression of mutant p53 in epithelial ovarian cancer, *J Natl Cancer Inst* 89(13):932-938, 1997.

20. Gann PH et al: Prospective study of plasma fatty acids and risk of prostate cancer (Reports), *J Natl Cancer Inst* 86(4):281-286, 1994.
21. Peterson SK et al: Familial colorectal cancer in Ashkenazim due to a hypermutable tract in APC, *Nat Genet* 17(1):79-83, 1997.
22. Giovannucci E et al: Aspirin and the risk of colorectal cancer in women, *N Engl J Med* 332(14):609-614, 1995.
23. Tucker MA et al: Clinically recognized dysplastic nevi: a central risk factor for cutaneous melanoma, *JAMA* 277(18):1439-1444, 1997.
24. Mader SS: *Understanding human anatomy and physiology,* ed 3, Dubuque, IA. 1997, Wm C. Brown.
25. Thibodeau G, Patton K: *Human body in health and disease,* ed 2, St. Louis, 1996, Mosby.
26. Crowley LV: *Introduction to human diseases,* ed 2, Boston, 1996, Jones & Bartlett.
27. Walters MC et al: Bone marrow transplantation for sickle cell disease, *N Engl J Med* 335(6):369-376, 1996.
28. Conrad B et al: Evidence of superantigen involvement in insulin-dependent diabetes mellitus aetiology, *Nature* 371(6495):351-354, 1994.
29. Pauwels RA et al: Effect of inhaled formoterol and budesonide on exacerbations of asthma. Formoterol and corticosteroids establishing therapy (FACET) international study group, *N Engl J Med* 13(337):1405-1411, 1997.
30. Price SA, Wilson L: Pathophysiology: clinical concepts of disease processes, ed 5, St. Louis, 1996, Mosby.
31. Sternberg S: Universal diabetes test urged, *USA Today,* p. 1A, June 24, 1997.

Suggested Readings

Krentz AJ: *Diabetes* (colour guide), New York, 1997, Churchill Livingstone.
This book is intended for adolescents who have recently been diagnosed with insulin-dependent diabetes mellitus. The topic is introduced by recounting the stories of several young people with the disease and describing the demands it places on their lives. The author presents information about the disease's causes, symptoms, diagnosis, and management and directs young readers and their parents to helpful resources. The book can be found in many school and public libraries.

Mairs N: *Waist-high in the world: a life among the disabled,* Boston, 1998, Beacon Press.
Author Nancy Mairs shares her perspective on life from the vantage point of a woman with multiple sclerosis who must use a wheelchair. Drawing on two decades of being eye-to-navel with the world, Mairs's 10 essays are upbeat, witty, funny, touching, and honest. This is a must-read for people at all levels above the pavement.

Korda M: *Man to man: surviving prostate cancer,* New York, 1997, Vintage Books.
Michael Korda, a highly regarded editor for a major publisher, first began to have prostate problems when he was 60. Shortly afterward he was diagnosed with prostate cancer. Korda uses his experience to talk about a disease that most men are sheltered from. The author's personal approach presents the condition in an informative and positive way.

Shockney L: *Breast cancer survivors' club: a nurse's experience,* Port Saint Lucie, FL, 1997, Windsor House.
Breast cancer has always been a part of the author's life—as the daughter of a mother whose best friend had the disease, as a nurse who cared for women with breast cancer, and finally as a "member of the club" herself. This encompassing relationship with the disease is apparent as Shockney shares usable medical information and describes her sources of interpersonal strength during treatment and recovery.

Oesterling JE, Moyad MA: *The ABCs of prostate cancer: the book that could save your life,* Lanham, MD, 1997, Madison Books.
This book combines solid medical information with inspirational testimonials by 50 well-known men who have had prostate cancer. Chapters cover the prostate checkup, the biopsy, forms of treatment, questions to ask your doctor, and the experiences of famous men who have had the disease, including General Norman Schwarzkopf, Richard Petty, and Senator Jesse Helms.

 ## AS WE GO TO PRESS . . .

In May 1998, every major American newspaper ran headlines announcing the development of a pair of new drugs that held the promise of curing cancer. Many consumers, including thousands of cancer patients and their families, demanded that human trials begin immediately. Investors clamored to buy shares of EntreMed, the small pharmaceutical company that is supporting the drugs' development. But do these drugs offer hope, or just hype?

In the last 20 years, other drugs have been hailed as breakthroughs in cancer treatment, including interferon, interleukin-2, various monoclonal antibodies, vaccines made from cancer cells, and new botanical drugs such as Taxol, obtained from the bark of the Pacific yew tree. Although these agents have been helpful in the battle against cancer, none has been a "magic bullet."

The latest drugs to receive the public's attention are angiostatin and endostatin. These agents have been found effective in shrinking certain types of tumors in mice, but they have not yet been tested on humans. Angiostatin and endostatin inhibit *angiogenesis* (*angio-* means "vessel" and *-genesis* means "formation"), the tumor's ability to develop vessels that supply it with blood. This blood vessel system allows the tumor to grow by providing oxygen and nutrients and removing wastes. In addition, malignant cells in the tumor's blood supply can enter the general circulation, where they may be carried to another site to form a secondary tumor (this process is called *metastasis*). Angiostatin and endostatin "starve" the tumor and block its routes for metastasis.

These drugs are just beginning to be tested in humans and are months away from large-scale clinical trials, making claims about their effectiveness premature at best. Clearly, however, the national news media, stock market investors, and thousands of cancer patients believe that the drug's eventual FDA approval will bring victory in the war against cancer.

Managing Chronic Pain

Carlotta loved to spend her spare time puttering around in her flower garden. Every weekend, she would work outside for hours tilling soil, putting in new plants, pruning, and landscaping. One Saturday afternoon as she was lifting some railroad ties to provide a new border for her plant paradise, she heard a loud popping noise and felt a sharp pain in her lower back. She tried aspirin, bed rest, massage, and heat, but the pain was still excruciating even after 2 weeks. She went to see her doctor, who prescribed pain medication and a brief course of physical therapy, but the pain persisted. Finally, after nearly a year passed with no relief, her doctor recommended back surgery. Carlotta spent almost 3 months recovering from the surgery, after which she hoped to be able to lead a normal, pain-free life.

Unfortunately, Carlotta's pain persists even today, almost 2 years since her initial injury. Carlotta suffers from chronic pain, a type of pain that persists beyond the expected healing time of an injury or illness. Chronic pain differs from most ordinary encounters with pain, such as pain resulting from a headache, a fall, or surgery. According to the American Pain Society, chronic pain is difficult to treat because it does not respond to normal pain treatments. Also, some of the usual signs that accompany acute pain, such as sweating, increased heart rate, and dilated pupils, are not present in individuals with chronic pain.[1] Because physicians have difficulty in diagnosing the source of chronic pain, they have a tendency to think a patient's suffering is "all in her head." As a result, many of the 130 million chronic pain sufferers do not get the types of treatment they so desperately need.[2,3]

Causes of Chronic Pain

Chronic pain occurs as the result of one of three primary causes. In some patients, chronic pain may be linked to injuries to the central or peripheral nervous systems, according to John D. Loeser, M.D., director of the Multidisciplinary Pain Center at the University of Washington School of Medicine.[1] In these patients, no tissue damage ever occurred in the part of their body that hurts. Whenever the nervous system heals itself, the functions of the nerve cells lost in the injury are not restored during the healing process.[2] As a result, the patient's neurological functions are impaired. This type of pain can occur as a result of limb amputation, shingles, diabetes, or surgery.[1]

A second cause of chronic pain is linked to degenerative changes in joints. In these cases, tissue damage that has occurred may not heal properly. Patients have both inflammation of the joints and chronic degenerative problems.[1] This cause of pain usually accompanies diseases such as arthritis and lupus.

The third "cause" of pain is the catchall category: "no known pathological mechanism."[1] Doctors are unsure why these patients are having pain. The one criterion used to place a patient in this category is whether the patient's pain complaints exceed the physician's expectations based on the illness or injury the patient has suffered.

Conditions Associated with Chronic Pain

Several types of conditions are commonly associated with sufferers of chronic pain, the most common being the headache. Up to 57% of men and 76% of women in the adolescent and young adult age-groups experience recurrent headaches. The National Headache Foundation estimates that 45 million Americans suffer from chronic headaches. Of these sufferers, 86% are women. Although doctors have identified 55 types of headaches, the four most commonly associated with chronic pain are tension headaches, migraines, cluster headaches, and sinus headaches.[3]

Like Carlotta in our previous example, four out of five Americans experience back pain at some point in their lives. The problem usually resolves itself for most people; however, it is estimated that more than 11 million Americans have enough back pain to cause impairment. This cause of chronic pain is particularly troublesome because of its economic impact on society. Attorney's costs for pursuing back injuries as a result of worker's compensation and other accidents approached $5 billion in 1990. The indirect costs for lost wages and homemakers' potential lost earnings are near $3.6 billion. Based on all analyses of possible cost factors, back pain costs society anywhere from $75 billion to $100 billion annually.[1]

Another debilitating condition commonly associated with chronic pain is arthritis. More than 35 million Americans have a form of this disease. Two types of arthritis exist. *Osteoarthritis* is the breaking down of the cartilage found at the ends of the long bones. Weight-bearing and frequently used joints are the areas most commonly affected. *Rheumatoid arthritis* is an autoimmune disorder in which the patient's own immune system produces antibodies that attack the tissues in the joints of the body.[1] Symptoms of both types include stiffness and swelling of the joints.

Cancer and Chronic Pain

Although cancer is one of the conditions often associated with chronic pain, pain experts put it into a class by itself because of its special circumstances. Chronic cancer pain is complex because the pain can occur as a result of bone invasion, tumors compressing nerves, tumors affecting internal organs, obstruction of blood vessels, surgery, chemotherapy, or radiation treatment.[1]

Effects of Chronic Pain

Because chronic pain is such a disruptive, ongoing phenomenon, it can affect almost every aspect of an individual's life. Richard Linchitz, M.D., a pain specialist and chronic pain sufferer, describes what his life was like after a disk in his lower back became herniated: "As bad as the pain was, the worst aspect for me was the growing and quite depressing sense that my days of vigorous exercise were over. My doctor began ruling out, one by one, the very activities—running, bicycling, weightlifting—that had become a part of my identity . . ."[4] Veronica, one of Dr. Norman J. Marcus's patients, found it difficult not only to pursue hobbies but even to complete simple everyday tasks such as washing the dishes.[3]

The devastation of losing a job is another potential effect of suffering with chronic pain. Because the pain is so invasive and persistent, it affects a person's ability to concentrate, perform essential job duties, or even go to work. Toni, another of Dr. Marcus's patients, had been the manager of a high-pressure department of a busy store. She had always been conscientious and hard working until she began having pain in her hip. Because of the pain, she had difficulty performing her job, and she also had to take time off from work frequently either because of doctor's appointments or because her pain was too severe. As a result, Toni was fired.[3]

Sleep disorders are a third potential effect of chronic pain. Sleep disorders can come about in two ways. Either a patient is unable to sleep because of the pain, or the individual becomes dependent on a pain or sleep medication that disrupts the sleep cycle. Toni, who was described in the previous paragraph, was on many medications, including both painkillers and sleeping pills, yet she "never slept." On being admitted to a pain management center, Toni was taken off all her medications and given a mild antidepressant instead. She slept for 10 hours that night, "the first good night's sleep I'd had in four years."[3]

Serious psychological problems can also result from chronic pain. Depression is one of the most common ailments. Henry, another patient at Dr. Marcus's pain clinic and a former construction worker, had always been a calm, easygoing person who got along well with others and served as the chief provider for his family. One day

at work, Henry was struck in the back of the neck by a steel beam. He suffered pain not just in his neck but also throughout his body. As time went on and the pain did not improve, Henry's entire personality began to change. He went from being easygoing to being a chronic worrier because he was concerned about the family's financial security. He isolated himself from his family and friends, and he began to snap at anyone who asked him questions about his condition. The more Henry hurt, the more he worried about hurting; the more he worried about hurting, the more he hurt. Henry was caught in a downward spiral of depression that set him apart from his family and friends.[3]

The final significant side effect of chronic pain is the potential damage it can do to the immune system. This effect can be particularly troublesome in patients whose chronic pain is the result of cancer. Studies have shown that pain can suppress the immune system, thus causing cancer patients to have difficulty recovering.[5] Because of this potentially fatal problem, it is especially important for cancer patients to have their pain treated promptly and effectively.

Methods of Managing Chronic Pain

Although chronic pain has several negative side effects, many of these effects can be controlled through proper pain management methods. Most pain specialists recommend that sufferers be treated through a multidisciplinary approach that uses a combination of methods to achieve maximal relief.

One of the most common and effective methods of achieving relief of chronic pain is the use of opioid drugs, also known as *Schedule II drugs*. These drugs have been proven to provide quick relief of pain, particularly among cancer patients and headache sufferers.[5,6] However, physicians are often reluctant to prescribe these drugs for several reasons. First, doctors are afraid that if they are perceived as prescribing too many opioids, they could be reported to the medical board and ultimately lose their licenses. Second, American society in general disapproves of prescribing narcotics because of the fear of addiction and the idea that all narcotics are bad, despite their potential for providing pain relief. Finally, medical personnel tend to underestimate the amount of pain that patients suffer. Most people who suffer severe pain and request narcotics will not become addicts, but some medical personnel who work with pain sufferers have the mindset that people with chronic pain do not hurt as badly as they claim to.[5]

For chronic headache sufferers, several other types of drugs offer hope as well. Small doses of tricyclic antidepressants taken at bedtime seem to help headache sufferers sleep better and have some preventive effect during the day. Other drugs that provide relief include beta-blockers, calcium channel blockers, and anticonvulsants. Doctors may try several combinations of these drugs to see which will most effectively relieve headache symptoms, with the eventual goal of removing as many medications as possible from the patient's daily regimen.[6]

For patients with arthritis, two classes of drugs appear to offer the most relief. The first type is known as *nonsteroidal antiinflammatory drugs*, or *NSAIDs*. The most well-known types of these drugs are Advil, Nuprin, Naprosyn, and Anaprox. They provide relief within 2 hours. A second type of antiarthritic medicine is known as *slow-acting antirheumatic drugs*, or *SAARDs*. These drugs provide time-released, long-lasting relief. Other treatments that may be used in conjunction with these two types of drugs include injectable gold and corticosteroids.[7]

Surgery is another option in the array of choices for managing chronic pain. This option is most effective in helping patients with cancer. Removing diseased cells or tumors often removes the source that is causing pain for the patient.[5] Surgery may also become necessary for the arthritis pain sufferer. Replacement of cartilage or an affected joint will often help a sufferer lead a more normal, less painful life.[6] Surprisingly, however, surgery is rarely a good option for back pain sufferers. Studies of hospital records show that back surgery often does more harm than good.[2,4]

Because the mind is such a powerful instrument of healing, pain specialists often recommend that patients undertake psychological methods of pain relief in conjunction with traditional methods. For example, many headache specialists recommend biofeedback techniques so that patients can learn to control their responses to pain.[6] Pain specialists at a pain clinic in Dallas teach their patients to do deep-breathing exercises and then advance them to meditation techniques to promote relaxation.[2] Also, positive thinking about one's situation and prospects for recovery can help patients need fewer medications, according to a recent British study.[7]

Physical methods of managing pain can add another dimension to chronic pain management. One time-tested method of relief is massage.[3] Other helpful treatments include nerve blocks to the affected area, physical therapy, and exercises as prescribed by a physical therapist or physician.[2-4] Finally, a patient can make some lifestyle changes to lessen the pain. Eating regularly, getting plenty of rest, and reducing caffeine intake have all been found to be particularly helpful to headache sufferers but may also help others afflicted with chronic pain.[6]

The Future of Chronic Pain Management

Although they were virtually unheard of just a few years ago, pain clinics, or pain centers, are becoming more prevalent in the medical community.[8] These centers feature physicians and other health care professionals who use the multidisciplinary approach to pain management. Personnel on site might include physicians, physical therapists, exercise physiologists, psychologists, and psychiatrists.[3] Pain centers are also at the forefront of pain research. A pain center in Dallas is currently studying the possibility of using gene therapy to conquer chronic pain. The new genes would enable patients to grow new, undamaged nerves, which would also enhance endorphin production.[2] Whether through medication, therapy, or research, the goal of all pain centers is the same: to improve the patient's condition so that on leaving the center, the person will be able to resume normal activities, need a minimal amount of medication, and maintain a positive attitude.[3]

An additional hope for better chronic pain management comes in the form of training of tomorrow's doctors. The American Medical Association (AMA) has called for better education about pain and pain management in both undergraduate and postgraduate medical training.[8,9] In particular, the AMA hopes to make the use of opioid drugs more acceptable to health care personnel as an option for relieving pain.[8] Hospitals are also instituting quality assurance programs so that patients can be more empowered to demand and receive the pain relief they need.[9]

An option for terminal cancer patients who are in need of relief from chronic pain is the hospice movement. Hospices put into practice a philosophy that allows medical personnel to focus on the patients rather than their diseases. The main goals of hospices are to provide pain relief and to give psychological support to both the patient and his or her family. Hospices also use a multidisciplinary approach that includes physicians, nurses, social workers, physical therapists, and members of the clergy.[1] The hospice can provide the care and support that cancer sufferers and their families need as the patient nears the end of life.

Although there is not yet a cure for chronic pain, it can be managed successfully with the help of trained personnel from a variety of fields. Unfortunately, chronic pain sufferers must be vocal and persistent to get the help they desperately need. Doctors and patients alike must realize that chronic pain is not "all in the patient's head" but a real, treatable condition.

For Discussion . . .

Have you ever known someone who suffered (or still suffers) from chronic pain? What were your feelings about this person and his or her pain? If you suffered from chronic pain, what treatments do you think would be the best for you? Would you be willing to try nonconventional therapies like the ones described in this article, or would you be more comfortable with traditional methods of therapy? Why?

References

1. Cowles J: *Pain relief*, New York, 1993, Mastermedia.
2. Atkinson J: Nerve center, *Texas Monthly* p 6, June 1994.
3. Marcus NJ: *Freedom from chronic pain*, New York, 1994, Simon & Schuster.
4. Linchitz RM: *Life without pain*, New York, 1987, Addison-Wesley.
5. Buterbaugh L: Breaking through cancer pain barriers, *Medical World* p 10, Oct 15, 1993.
6. Brooks PM: Clinical management of rheumatoid arthritis, *Lancet* (341)8840, 1993.
7. Meinson M: Brain against pain, *Prevention* p 48, Jan 1, 1996.
8. Goldsmith MF: Pain speaking—and anesthesiologists answer, *JAMA* (267)12, 1992.
9. Hill CS Jr: When will adequate pain treatment be the norm? *JAMA* (274)23, 1995.

Preventing Infectious Diseases

Healthy People: Looking Ahead to 2010

Progress was uneven in achieving the *Healthy People 2000* objectives in the area of infectious disease prevention. On the positive side, the nation has moved steadily toward reducing the incidence of vaccine-preventable infectious diseases in people under 25. In addition, the *Midcourse Review* reported an increase in condom use, an important aspect of controlling transmission of HIV/AIDS.

Healthy People 2010 will, of course, continue to recommend federally supported efforts to control infectious diseases. The objectives related to infectious conditions will focus on several important areas, including substance abuse, sexual health, food safety, maternal-child health, delivery of health services, and improvement of public health care. Education and community health promotion will probably be emphasized. The new initiative will also continue to support basic research in infectious diseases.

INFECTIOUS DISEASES IN THE LATE 1990s

Before the turn of the twentieth century, infectious diseases were the leading cause of death. These deaths came after exposure to the organisms that produced such diseases as smallpox, tuberculosis (TB), influenza, whooping cough (pertussis), typhoid, diphtheria, and tetanus. However, by midcentury, improvements in public sanitation, the widespread use of antibiotic drugs as a treatment method, and vaccinations as preventive therapy had considerably reduced the numbers of people dying from infectious diseases. People are now more likely to die from chronic, long-term disease processes.

Today, however, we have a new respect for infectious diseases. We have learned that AIDS continues to threaten millions of people in many areas of the world. We are witnessing the resurgence of TB. We recognize the role of pelvic infections in infertility. We also know that failure to fully immunize children has laid the groundwork for a return of whooping cough, polio, and other serious childhood diseases.

New dimensions of infectious disease have recently arisen. These include the appearance of extremely virulent viruses, such as the Ebola virus in Zaire, which is fatal to 75% of those who contract it and for which there is neither an immunization nor an understanding of its transmission; the increasing resistance of bacteria such as *Staphylococcus aureus*, *Enterococcus*, and *Mycobacterium* (which causes tuberculosis) to antibiotics as the result of overuse, improper use, and biological "redesign" of the organisms themselves; the role of a bacterium (*Helicobacter pylori*) in the development of gastric ulcers; and, finally, the growing concern over transmission of infectious organisms through contaminated food, improper preparation of food, and contamination of water. However, more restrictive use of a popular antibiotic, erythromycin, caused a decline in the numbers of antibiotic-resistant organisms.[1] New antibiotics and more cautious use of current ones should allow this encouraging trend to continue.

INFECTIOUS DISEASE TRANSMISSION

Infectious diseases can generally be transferred from person to person, although there is not always a direct transfer from one person to another. Infectious diseases can be especially dangerous because of their ability to spread to large numbers of people, producing *epidemics* or *pandemics*.

The sections that follow explain the process of disease transmission and the stages of infection. For a discussion of preventing infectious disease transmission, turn to the article on pp. 306-307.

Pathogens

For a disease to be transferred, a person must come into contact with the disease-producing agent, or **pathogen,** such as a virus, bacterium, or fungus. When pathogens enter our bodies, they are sometimes able to resist body defense systems, flourish, and produce an illness. We commonly call this an *infection*. Because of their small size, pathogens are sometimes referred to as *microorganisms, microbes,* or *germs*. Table 12-1 describes the more familiar infectious disease agents and some of the illnesses they produce.

Chain of Infection

The transmission of a pathogenic agent through the various links in the chain of infection (Figure 12-1) forms the basis for an understanding of how diseases spread.[2] Not every pathogenic agent will move all the way through the chain of infection because various links in the chain can be broken. Therefore the presence of a pathogen creates only the potential for a disease.

Agent

The first link in the chain of infection is the disease-causing **agent.** Whereas some agents are very **virulent** and cause serious infectious illnesses such as HIV, which causes AIDS, others produce far less serious infections, as in the common cold. Through mutation, some pathogenic agents, particularly viruses, become more virulent than they once were.

Reservoir

Infectious agents must have the support and protection of a favorable environment to survive. This environment forms the second link in the chain of infection and is referred to as the *reservoir* in which the agent resides. In many of the most common infectious diseases, the reservoirs in which the pathogenic organisms live are the bodies of already infected people. Here the agents thrive before being spread to others. These infected people are, accordingly, the hosts for particular disease agents.

For other infectious diseases, however, the reservoirs in which the agents are maintained are the bodies of animals. Rabies is among the most familiar of the animal-reservoir diseases. Not in all cases will the animals be sick or show symptoms similar to those seen in infected persons.

The third type of reservoir in which disease-causing agents can reside is on or in nonliving environ-

Table 12-1   Pathogens and Common Infectious Diseases

Pathogen	Description	Representative Disease Processes
Viruses	Smallest common pathogens; nonliving particles of genetic material (DNA) surrounded by a protein coat	Rubeola, mumps, chickenpox, rubella, influenza, warts, colds, oral and genital herpes, shingles, AIDS, genital warts
Bacteria	One-celled microorganisms with sturdy, well-defined cell walls; three distinctive forms: spherical (cocci), rod shaped (bacilli), and spiral shaped (spirilla)	Tetanus, strep throat, scarlet fever, gonorrhea, syphilis, chlamydia, toxic shock syndrome, Legionnaires' disease, bacterial pneumonia, meningitis, diphtheria, food poisoning, Lyme disease
Fungi	Plantlike microorganisms; molds and yeasts	Athlete's foot, ringworm, histoplasmosis, San Joaquin Valley fever, candidiasis
Protozoa	Simplest animal form, generally one-celled organisms	Malaria, amebic dysentery, trichomoniasis, vaginitis
Rickettsia	Viruslike organisms that require a host's living cells for growth and replication	Typhus, Rocky Mountain spotted fever, rickettsialpox
Parasitic worms	Many-celled organisms; represented by tapeworms, leeches, and roundworms	Dirofilariasis (dog heartworm), elephantiasis, onchocerciasis

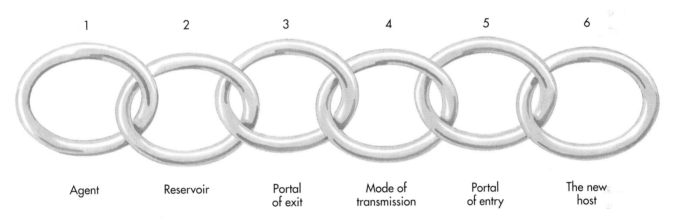

1	2	3	4	5	6
Agent	Reservoir	Portal of exit	Mode of transmission	Portal of entry	The new host

Figure 12-1   The six links in the chain of infection.

ments, such as the soil. (The spores of the tetanus bacterium can survive in soil for up to 50 years, entering the human body in a puncture wound.) Warm and moist locker-room floors are another example of this environment because the fungi that cause ringworm and jock itch can survive there.

Portal of exit

For pathogenic agents to cause diseases and illnesses in others, it is necessary that they leave their reservoirs. The third link in the chain of infection is the portal of exit, or the point at which agents leave their reservoirs.

Particularly in terms of infectious diseases that involve human reservoirs, the principal portals of exit are familiar—the digestive system, urinary system, respiratory system, reproductive system, and the blood.

Mode of transmission

The fourth link in the chain of infection is the mode of transmission, or the way that pathogens are passed from reservoirs to susceptible hosts. Two principal methods are *direct transmission* and *indirect transmission*.

pathogen
Disease-causing agent.

agent
Causal pathogen of a particular disease.

virulent (**veer** yuh lent)
Capable of causing disease.

Three types of direct transmission are observed in human-to-human transmission. These include *contact* between body surfaces (such as kissing, touching, and sexual intercourse), *droplet spread* (inhalation of contaminated air droplets), and *fecal-oral spread* (feces on the hands are brought into contact with the mouth).

Indirect transmission occurs between infected and uninfected people when infectious agents travel by means of nonhuman materials. Vehicles of transmission include *inanimate objects,* such as water, food items, soil, towels, items of clothing, and eating utensils.

A second method of indirect transmission of infectious agents occurs in conjunction with vectors. The term *vector* is related to living things, such as insects, birds, and other animals that carry diseases from human to human. An example of a vector is the deer tick that transmits Lyme disease.

Airborne indirect transmission involves the *inhalation* of infected particles that have been suspended in an air source for an extended period. Unlike droplet transmission, in which both infected and uninfected people must be in close physical proximity, noninfected people can become infected through airborne transmission by sharing air with infected people who were in the same room hours earlier. Viral infections such as German measles may be spread in this manner.

Portal of entry

The fifth link in the chain of infection is the portal of entry. As with the portals of exit, there are three primary portals of entry for pathogenic agents to enter the bodies of uninfected people. These are through the digestive system, respiratory system, and reproductive system. In addition, a break in the skin provides another portal of entry. In most infectious conditions the portals of entry prove to be within the same systems as the portals of exit were for the infected people. In the case of HIV, however, cross-system transmission is observed. Oral and anal sex allow for infectious agents to pass between the warm, moist tissues of the reproductive and digestive systems.

The new host

All people are in theory at risk for contracting infectious diseases and thus could be identified as susceptible hosts. In practice, however, factors such as overall health, acquired immunity, health care services, and health-related behavior can influence susceptibility to infectious diseases.

Stages of Infection

When a new host is assaulted by a pathogenic agent, a reasonably predictable sequence of events takes place. That is, the disease moves through five rather distinctive stages.[3] You may be able to recognize these stages of infection each time you catch a cold.

1. *The incubation stage.* This stage lasts from the time a pathogen enters the body until it multiplies enough to produce signs and symptoms of the disease. The length of this stage can vary from a few hours to many months, depending on the virulence of the organisms, the concentration of organisms, the host's level of immune responsiveness, and other health problems. This stage has been called a *silent stage.* Transmission of the pathogen to a new host is possible but not probable during this stage: a host may be infected during this stage but not infectious. HIV infection is an exception to this rule.

2. *The prodromal stage.* The incubation stage is followed by a short period during which the host may experience a variety of general signs and symptoms, including watery eyes, runny nose, slight fever, and overall tiredness. These symptoms are nonspecific in nature and may not be overwhelming enough to force the host to rest. During this stage the pathogenic agent continues to multiply. Now the host is capable of transferring pathogens to a new host. Self-imposed isolation should be practiced during this stage to protect others. Again, HIV infection is different in regard to this stage.

3. *The clinical stage.* This stage, also called the *acme* or *acute stage*, is often the most unpleasant stage for the host. At this time the disease reaches its highest point of development. All of the clinical (observable) signs and symptoms for the particular disease can be seen or analyzed by appropriate laboratory tests. The likelihood of transmitting the disease to others is highest during this peak stage; all of our available defense mechanisms are in the process of resisting further damage from the pathogen.

4. *The decline stage.* During this stage the first signs of recovery occur. The infection is ending or, in some cases, being reduced to a subclinical level. Relapse may occur if people overextend themselves. In HIV and AIDS, this is almost always the last stage before death.

5. *The recovery stage.* Also called the *convalescence stage*, this stage is characterized by apparent recovery from the invading agent. Disease transmission during this stage is possible but not probable. Until the host's overall health has been strengthened, he or she may be especially susceptible to another (perhaps different) disease pathogen. Fortunately, after the recovery stage, further susceptibility to the pathogenic agent should be reduced because of the body's buildup of immunity. This buildup of immunity is not always permanent; for example, many sexually transmitted diseases can be contracted repeatedly.

BODY DEFENSES: MECHANICAL AND CELLULAR IMMUNE SYSTEMS

Much as a military installation is protected by a series of defensive alignments, so too is the body. These defenses can be classified as being either mechanical or cellular (Figure 12-2). *Mechanical* defenses are first-line defenses, since they physically separate the internal body from the external environment. Included among these are the skin, the mucous membranes that line the respiratory and gastrointestinal tracts, earwax, the tiny hairs and cilia that filter incoming air, and even tears. These defenses serve primarily as a shield against foreign materials that may contain pathogenic agents. These defenses can, however, be disarmed, as is done when tobacco smoke kills the cilia that protect the airway, resulting in chronic bronchitis, or when contact lenses decrease tearing, leading to irritation and eye infection.

The second component of the body's protective defenses is the *cellular* system or, more commonly, the **immune system.** The cellular component is, in comparison with the mechanical defenses, far more specific, with the elimination of microorganisms, foreign proteins, and cells foreign to the body as its primary mission. A wellness-oriented lifestyle, including sound nutrition, effective stress management, and regular exercise, undergirds this important division of the immune system. The microorganism, foreign proteins, or abnormal cells whose presence activates this cellular component are identified collectively as *antigens.*[4]

Divisions of the Immune System

Closer examination of the immune system, or cellular defenses, reveals two separate but highly cooperative groups of cells. One group of cells has its origins in the fetal thymus gland and thus has become known as *T cell–mediated immunity,* or simply cell-mediated immunity. The second group of cells that make up cellular immunity are the B cells (**b**ursa of Fabricius) that are the working units of *humoral immunity.*[5] Cellular elements of both cell-mediated and humoral immunity can be found within the bloodstream, the lymphatic tissues of the body, and the fluid that surrounds body cells.

Although we are born with the structural elements of both cell-mediated and humoral immunity, the development of an immune response requires that components of these cellular systems encounter and successfully defend against specific antigens. Once this has occurred, the immune system is primed to respond quickly and effectively should the same antigens be encountered again. This confrontation results in the development of a state of **acquired immunity (AI).** As seen in Figure 12-2, the development of AI can occur in different ways.

- **Naturally acquired immunity (NAI)** occurs when the body is exposed to infectious agents.

immune system
System of cellular elements that protects the body from invading pathogens and foreign materials.

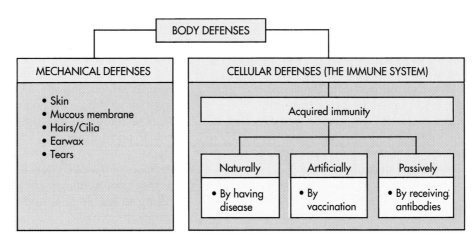

Figure 12-2 The body has a variety of defenses against invading organisms. Mechanical defenses are the first means of protection, since they separate the internal body from the external environment. Cellular defenses include chemicals and specialized cells that provide immunity to subsequent infections.

Table 12-2   Recommended Immunization Schedule*,†

	Months							Years
	Birth	1-2	2	4	6	6-18	12-15	6
Diphtheria/pertussis/ tetanus (DPT)			X	X	X		X‡	X
Polio (OPV)			X	X	X			X
Measles/mumps/ rubella (MMR)						X		X
Haemophilus influenzae (Hib)			X	X	X§		X	
Hepatitis B ‖ (Hep B)	X	X				X		
or:		X		X		X		

*Foreign travelers: renew immunizations for diseases prevalent in the countries of travel.
†Influenza: yearly for elderly adults, workers in occupations (such as health care workers and teachers) exposed to infected persons, and for all adults with chronic respiratory and heart disease.
‡As early as 12 months, as long as at least 6 months since last DTP dose.
§May not be required, depending on which Hib vaccine is used.
‖Anyone exposed to infected individuals or contaminated food and water, and foreign travelers and health care workers.
For referral to an immunization clinic or for other information, contact the Centers for Disease Control and Prevention National Immunization Program: (800) 232-2522 in English or TDD; (800) 232-0233 in Spanish.

Thus when we catch an infectious disease, we fight the infection and in the process become immune (protected) from developing that illness again should reinfection occur.

- **Artificially acquired immunity (AAI)** occurs when the body is exposed to weakened or killed infectious agents introduced through vaccination or immunization. As in NAI, the body engages the infectious agents and produces a record of how to fight the same battle again. Young children, older adults, and adults in high-risk occupations should consult their physicians about immunizations. Table 12-2 shows a schedule for immunization.

- **Passively acquired immunity (PAI)**, a third form of immunity, results when antibodies are introduced into the body. These antibodies are for a variety of specific infections and are produced outside the body (either in animals or by the genetic manipulation of microorganisms). When introduced into the human body, they provide immediate protection until a more natural form of immunity can be developed.

Collectively, these forms of immunity can provide important protection against infectious disease.

IMMUNIZATIONS

Although the incidence of several childhood communicable diseases is at or near the lowest level ever,

the risk of a resurgence of diseases such as measles, polio, diphtheria, and rubella is very real. This possible upturn in childhood infectious diseases could be prevented if parents ensured that their children were fully immunized. Overall, about 90% of children receive all necessary immunizations. The CDC reports, for example, that the level of immunization against polio is about 90% for black children, 96% for Asian children, and 89% for Hispanic children and Native American children.[6]

On the basis of current technology, vaccinations against several potentially serious infectious conditions are available and, of course, should be given. These include the following:

- *Diphtheria:* a potentially fatal illness that leads to inflammation of the membranes that line the throat, to swollen lymph nodes, and to heart and kidney failure

- *Whooping cough:* a bacterial infection of the airways and lungs that results in deep, noisy breathing and coughing

- *Hepatitis B:* a viral infection that can be transmitted sexually or through the exchange of blood or body fluids and causes serious liver damage

- *Haemophilus influenzae type B:* a bacterial infection that can damage the heart and brain, resulting in meningitis, and can produce profound hearing loss

- *Tetanus:* a fatal infection caused by bacteria found in the soil that damages the central nervous system

- *Rubella (German measles):* a viral infection of the upper respiratory tract that can cause damage to a developing fetus when the mother contracts the infection during the first trimester of pregnancy
- *Measles (red measles):* a highly contagious viral infection leading to a rash, high fever, and other upper respiratory tract symptoms
- *Polio:* a viral infection capable of causing paralysis of the large muscles of the extremities
- *Mumps:* a viral infection of the salivary glands
- *Chickenpox:* a varicella zoster virus spread by airborne droplets leading to a sore throat, rash, and fluid-filled blisters

Parents of newborns should take their infants to their family care physicians, pediatricians, or well-baby clinics operated by county health departments to begin the immunization schedule. The schedule shown in Table 12-2 is recommended by the Centers for Disease Control and Prevention (CDC). It is hoped that a single immunization to protect children against all of the infectious childhood illnesses will soon be available, perhaps only 10 years away. The newest vaccine, VariVax, a vaccine against chickenpox, is now available but has not yet been well accepted by physicians or parents. In addition, a new vaccine against infant diarrhea caused by rotaviruses has been found safe and effective, and its approval has been recommended.[7] More than 50,000 children are hospitalized annually for dehydration following severe diarrhea, and 125 deaths occur.

THE IMMUNE RESPONSE

To fully understand the function of the immune system requires a substantial understanding of human biology and is beyond the scope of this text. Figure 12-3 provides a simplified view of the immune response.

When antigens (whether microorganisms, foreign substances, or abnormal cells) are discovered within the body, some antigens are confronted by various types of white blood cells and their number is initially reduced by the destructive action of these blood cells. At the same time, macrophages (a very large white blood cell) encounter other antigens and signal components of cell-mediated immunity called *helper T cells* to assist in the immune response.

Once activated by the presence of the macrophage/antigens complex, helper T cells notify a second component of cellular immunity, the killer T cells, and a component of humoral immunity, B cells. Killer T cells produce powerful chemical messengers that activate specific white blood cells that are capable of destroying antigens. At the same time, B cells are transformed into specialized cells (plasma cells) capable of producing **antibodies** and into memory cells that record information pertaining to the antigen and the appropriate immune system response.

At the same time that helper T cells and killer T cells are engaged in destroying invading antigens, two additional components of cellular immunity are formed: memory T cells and suppressor T cells. As the name suggests, the memory T cells remember additional aspects of the immune system's responses so that reinfections can be encountered even more quickly and decisively. Suppressor T cells are specialized T cells that moderate B cell activity by offsetting the action of helper T cells. Their action allows the production of antibodies to be reduced once it is apparent that the immune system has won its battle.

Clearly, without a normal immune system involving both cellular and humoral elements, we would quickly become the victims of serious and life-shortening infections and malignancies. As you will see later, this is exactly what occurs in virtually all people infected with HIV.

acquired immunity (AI)
The "arming" of the immune system through the intial exposure of the immune system to an antigen.

naturally acquired immunity (NAI)
Type of acquired immunity resulting from the body's response to naturally occurring pathogens.

artificially acquired immunity (AAI)
Type of acquired immunity resulting from the body's response to pathogens introduced into the body through immunizations.

passively acquired immunity (PAI)
Temporary immunity achieved by providing antibodies to a person exposed to a particular pathogen.

antibodies
Chemical compounds produced by the body's immune system to destroy antigens and their toxins.

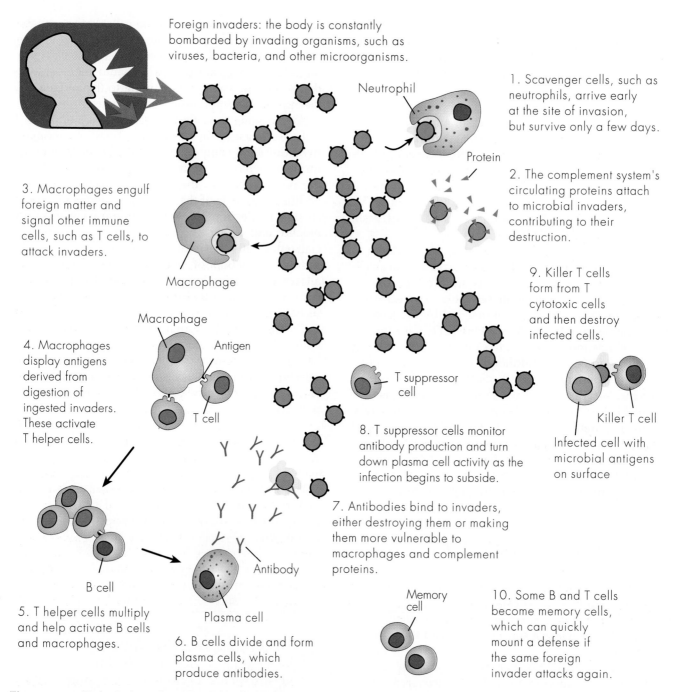

Foreign invaders: the body is constantly bombarded by invading organisms, such as viruses, bacteria, and other microorganisms.

Neutrophil

1. Scavenger cells, such as neutrophils, arrive early at the site of invasion, but survive only a few days.

Protein

2. The complement system's circulating proteins attach to microbial invaders, contributing to their destruction.

3. Macrophages engulf foreign matter and signal other immune cells, such as T cells, to attack invaders.

Macrophage

9. Killer T cells form from T cytotoxic cells and then destroy infected cells.

Macrophage

Antigen

T cell

4. Macrophages display antigens derived from digestion of ingested invaders. These activate T helper cells.

T suppressor cell

8. T suppressor cells monitor antibody production and turn down plasma cell activity as the infection begins to subside.

Killer T cell

Infected cell with microbial antigens on surface

B cell

Antibody

Plasma cell

5. T helper cells multiply and help activate B cells and macrophages.

6. B cells divide and form plasma cells, which produce antibodies.

7. Antibodies bind to invaders, either destroying them or making them more vulnerable to macrophages and complement proteins.

Memory cell

10. Some B and T cells become memory cells, which can quickly mount a defense if the same foreign invader attacks again.

Figure 12-3   Biological warfare. The body commands an army of defenders to reduce the danger of infection and guard against repeat infections. Antigens are the ultimate targets of all immune responses.

CAUSES AND MANAGEMENT OF SELECTED INFECTIOUS DISEASES

This section focuses on some of the common infectious diseases and some that, although less common, are serious when contracted. We hope this informa-tion provides some reference points you can use to judge your own disease susceptibility.

The Common Cold

The common cold, an acute upper respiratory tract infection, must reign as humankind's supreme infec-

Activity 1

The successful prevention and treatment of sexually transmitted diseases is a primary health objective for the nation. Important components of prevention are knowing about STDs and understanding what places you at risk for contracting them. The Pfizer corporation has developed two web documents to allow you to evaluate these two components. Go to the Pfizer website, at http://www.unspeakable.com/std-index.html. Click on "here" to learn "the naked truth" about your risk of contracting sexually transmitted diseases. For the first activity, click on *STD Quiz.* This 10-question quiz is an anonymous service provided solely for educational purposes. Absolutely no information about you is collected when you answer the questions. You are the only person who can view the results, which are deleted forever when your browser session ends.

Activity 2

Using the same website as in Activity 1, calculate your risk of contracting an STD. Select "Risk Profiler." This features accepts your answers to questions about your age, gender, sexual history, and behavior and describes how these factors create your own personal risk profile. After each question, the meter shows you the relative risk based on your answer. When you have finished answering all the questions, click on the "Generate Report" button. This makes a report of your answers that you may use for future reference.

Activity 3

The common cold, an acute upper respiratory tract infection, is a highly contagious infection that can be caused by any of the nearly 200 known rhinoviruses. Go to http://www.mayohealth.org/mayo/9511/htm/coldquiz.htm to take the *Cold Quiz.* Answer the nine questions listed. How much did you know about colds?

tious disease. Also known as **acute rhinitis,** this highly contagious viral infection can be caused by any of the nearly 200 known rhinoviruses.[5] Colds are particularly common during periods in which people spend time in crowded indoor environments, such as classrooms.

The signs and symptoms of a cold are fairly predictable. Runny nose, watery eyes, general aches and pains, a listless feeling, and a slight fever may all accompany a cold in its early stages. Eventually the nasal passages swell and the inflammation may spread to the throat. Stuffy nose, sore throat, and coughing may follow. The senses of taste and smell are blocked, and appetite declines.

With the onset of symptoms, management of a cold should begin promptly. After a few days, most of the cold's symptoms subside. In the meantime, people should isolate themselves from others, drink plenty of fluids, eat moderately, and rest. Keep in mind that antibiotics are effective only against bacterial infections—not viral infections like colds.

Management of a cold can be aided by using some of the many OTC cold remedies. These remedies will not cure your cold but may lessen the discomfort associated with it. Nasal decongestants, expectorants, cough syrups, and aspirin or acetaminophen can all provide some temporary relief. Use of some of these products for more than a few days is not recommended, however, since a rebound effect may occur.

If a cold appears to become more persistent, as evidenced by prolonged chills, noticeable fever above 103° F, chest heaviness or aches, shortness of breath, coughing up rust-colored mucus, or persistent sore throat or hoarseness, a physician should be contacted.

Unfortunately, it appears to be nearly impossible to prevent colds. Since colds are now thought to be transmitted most readily by hand contact, frequent handwashing and the use of tissues are recommended.

Influenza

Influenza is also an acute, contagious disease caused by viruses. Some influenza outbreaks have produced widespread death, as seen in the influenza pandemics of 1889 to 1890, 1918 to 1919, and 1957. The viral strains that produce this infectious disease have the potential for more severe complications than the viral strains that produce the common cold. The

acute rhinitis
The common cold; the sudden onset of nasal inflammation.

viral strain for a particular form of influenza enters the body through the respiratory tract. After brief incubation and prodromal stages, the host develops signs and symptoms not just in the upper respiratory tract but throughout the entire body. These symptoms include fever, chills, cough, sore throat, headache, gastrointestinal disturbances, and muscular pain.

Physicians may recommend only aspirin, fluids, and rest. Of course, parents are reminded not to give aspirin to children. Two prescription medications, amantadine and rimantadine, can alleviate symptoms of influenza A. A third medication, zanamivir, is now being studied in clinical trials. It is an inhaled powder for use against both influenza A and B.[8] (See Table 12-3 for a comparison of influenza with the common cold.)

Most young adults can cope with the milder strains of influenza that are prevalent each winter or spring. However, pregnant women and older people—especially older people with additional health complications—are not so capable of handling this viral attack. They may quickly develop secondary bacterial complications, especially pneumonia, which can prove fatal. Flu vaccinations are routinely recommended for older people, but they have also proved effective for younger adults.[9]

Tuberculosis

Until the mid-1980s, TB, a bacterial infection of the lungs resulting in chronic coughing, weight loss, and even death, was considered to be under control in this country. Then, however, an upsurge in cases occurred, with a peak of 26,283 cases in 1992. Since that time, a decline has been noted, with 7% fewer cases between 1995 (22,860) and 1996 (21,327).[10] However, immigration of people from areas of the world in which TB is considerably higher and the emergence of drug-resistant strains of the bacterium require that continuing attention be paid to this infectious disease.

Because TB is spread through coughing, the disease thrives in crowded places where infected people are in constant contact with others. Prisons, hospitals, public housing units, and even college residence halls are places where close day-to-day contact occurs. In such settings a single infected person can spread the TB agents to many others.

When healthy people are exposed to TB agents, their immune systems generally are able to contain the bacteria in a way that both prevents the development of symptoms and reduces the likelihood of infecting others. However, when the immune system may be damaged, such as in the elderly, the malnourished, and those who are infected with HIV, the dis-

Table 12-3   Is It a Cold or the Flu?

	Cold	Flu
Symptoms		
Fever	Rare	Characteristic, high (102°-104°+ F); lasts 3-4 days
Headache	Rare	Prominent
General aches, pains	Slight	Usual; often severe
Fatigue, weakness	Quite mild	Can last up to 2-3 weeks
Extreme exhaustion	Never	Early and prominent
Stuffy nose	Common	Sometimes
Sneezing	Usual	Sometimes
Sore throat	Common	Sometimes
Chest discomfort, cough	Mild to moderate; hacking cough	Common; can become severe
Complications	Sinus congestion, earache	Pneumonia, bronchitis; can be life threatening
Prevention	Avoidance of infected people	Annual vaccination; amantadine or rimantadine (antiviral drugs)
Treatment	Temporary relief	Amantadine or rimantadine within 24-48 hours after onset of symptoms

ease can become established and eventually be transmitted to other people at risk.

As previously mentioned, multiple drug–resistant (MDR) TB has been reported (2% of all TB cases). Increasingly prevalent in this country, MDR TB is the result of patients' inability to follow their physicians' instructions when initially treated (for whatever reason), inadequate treatment by physicians, and increased exposure of HIV-infected people to TB. Only 50% of people with this form of TB can be cured.

Health officials are again requesting that TB testing programs be implemented and that those infected, once found, be isolated and closely supervised during the entire 6 to 8 months of treatment required for a complete recovery. New diagnostic tests have been developed and should result in more prompt treatment and effective control of the transmission of the disease.

Pneumonia

Pneumonia is a general term under which a variety of infectious respiratory conditions can be placed. Bacterial, viral, fungal, rickettsial, mycoplasmal, and parasitic forms of pneumonia exist.[11] However, bacterial pneumonia is the most common form and is often seen in conjunction with other illnesses that weaken the body's immune system. This is why even healthy young people should consider colds and flu as potentially serious and treat them properly. In fact, pneumonia is so common in the frail elderly that it is often the specific condition causing death. *Pneumocystis carinii* pneumonia, a parasitic form, is of great importance today, since it is a principal opportunistic infection associated with the diagnosis of AIDS in HIV-infected people.

Among older adults with a history of chronic obstructive lung disease, cardiovascular disease, diabetes, or alcoholism, a midwinter form of pneumonia known as *acute community-acquired pneumonia* is often a serious health problem.[11] The sudden onset of chills, chest pain, and a cough producing sputum are characteristics of this condition. Additionally, a symptom-free form of pneumonia known as *walking pneumonia* is also commonly seen in adults and can become serious without warning. Individuals with the illnesses listed above should be watched carefully during the high-risk season of the year and provided with effective treatment should symptoms develop.

Mononucleosis

Of all the common infectious diseases that a college student can contract, **mononucleosis ("mono")** can

force a lengthy period of bed rest during a semester or quarter when it can least be afforded. Other common diseases that can attack you can be managed with minimal amounts of disruption. However, the overall weakness and fatigue seen in many people with mono sometimes require a month or two of rest and recuperation.

Mono is a viral infection in which the body produces an excess number of mononuclear leukocytes (a type of white blood cell). After uncertain, perhaps lengthy, incubation and prodromal stages, the acute symptoms of mono can appear, including weakness, headache, low-grade fever, swollen lymph glands (especially in the neck), and sore throat (Figure 12-4). Mental fatigue and depression are sometimes reported as side effects of mononucleosis. Usually after the acute symptoms disappear, the weakness and fatigue remain—perhaps for a few months. Mono is diagnosed on the basis of characteristic symptoms. Also, the Monospot blood smear can be used to determine the prevalence of abnormal white blood cells. In addition, an antibody test can detect activity of the immune system that is characteristic of the illness.

Since this disease is caused by a virus (Epstein-Barr virus), antibiotic therapy is not recommended. Treatment most often includes bed rest and the use of OTC remedies for fever (aspirin or acetaminophen) and sore throat (lozenges). In extreme cases, corticosteroid drugs can be used. Appropriate fluid intake and a well-balanced diet are also important in the recovery stages of mono. Fortunately, the body tends to develop NAI to the mono virus, so subsequent infections of mono are unusual.

For years, mono has been labeled the "kissing disease"; however, mono is not highly contagious and is known to be spread by direct transmission in ways other than kissing. No vaccine has been developed to confer AAI for mononucleosis. The best preventive measures include the steps that you can take to increase your resistance to most infectious diseases: (1) eat a well-balanced diet, (2) exercise regularly, (3) sleep sufficiently, (4) use health care services appropriately, (5) live in a reasonably healthful environment, and (6) avoid direct contact with infected people.

mononucleosis ("mono")
Viral infection characterized by weakness, fatigue, swollen glands, sore throat, and low-grade fever.

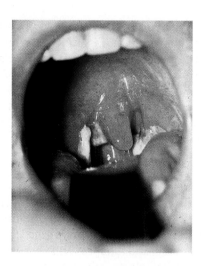

Figure 12-4   The throat of a person with mononucleosis. The tonsils are enlarged, and each is covered with a white membrane.

Chronic Fatigue Syndrome

Perhaps the most perplexing "infectious" condition seen by physicians is **chronic fatigue syndrome (CFS).** First identified in 1985, this mononucleosis-like condition is most commonly seen in women in their thirties and forties. People with CFS, many of whom are busy professional people, report flu-like symptoms, including severe exhaustion, fatigue, headaches, muscle aches, fever, inability to concentrate, allergies, intolerance to exercise, and depression. Examinations done on the first people with CFS revealed antibodies to the Epstein-Barr virus. Thus it was assumed to be an infectious viral disease (and initially called *chronic Epstein-Barr syndrome*).

In the two decades since its first appearance the condition has received a great deal of attention regarding its exact nature. Today, opinions vary widely as to whether the condition is a specific viral infection, a condition involving both viral infections and nonviral components, or some other disorder. An association has been suggested between CFS and neurally mediated hypotension, a condition in which blood pressure drops suddenly and substantially after long periods of standing, physical activity, or exposure to high temperatures.[12] Some physicians even view CFS as a psychological disorder. On an encouraging note, a recent study reported improvement in persons with CFS following enrollment in an aerobic conditioning program.[13]

Regardless of its cause or causes, CFS is extremely unpleasant for its victims. Certainly, those experiencing the symptoms over an extended time need to be seen by a physician experienced in dealing with CFS.

Measles

Previously thought to be only a childhood disease, *red measles* (also called **rubeola** or *common measles*) has recently been seen in large numbers on some American college campuses. Red measles is the highly contagious type of measles characterized by a short-lived, relatively high fever (103° to 104° F) and a whole-body red spotty rash that lasts about a week. The other type of measles, *German measles* (**rubella,** or 3-day measles), is a much milder form of measles that has serious implications for newborn babies of mothers who contracted this disease during pregnancy.[14] Highly successful vaccines are now available for both varieties of measles and are usually given in the same injection. Women should receive these vaccinations before they become pregnant.

The outbreak of red measles among college students during each of the last several school years points to the fact that our society mistakenly believes that most infectious diseases have now been eliminated. Public health experts now realize that those who contracted the disease either had never been vaccinated or had been vaccinated with a killed variety vaccine used before 1969. Only students who had already had red measles as children or who had been vaccinated with a live virus were guaranteed full immunity against the red measles virus. Nontraditional college students in particular should attempt to determine whether their immunization status is based on use of the older, less effective vaccine.

Today, most public school systems are requiring documented proof of immunization from a physician or clinic before children can attend classes. As educated parents, you should be conscientious about adhering to immunization schedules for your children. In fact, measles immunization efforts have increased so effectively because of school and public health department involvement that the number of measles cases fell from 55,000 cases between 1989 and 1991 to 488 cases in 1996.[15]

Mumps

Mumps is one of the more familiar childhood infectious diseases. A viral illness, mumps is characterized by inflammation and swelling in one or both salivary glands at the angle of the jaw. Fever, pain, and difficulty swallowing are common symptoms associated with mumps. Treatment involves fluids, bed rest, painkillers, and, in children, a few days' absence from school.

When mumps occurs in older male children, adolescents, and adults, the likelihood of infection to the testicles increases. A less common condition is inflammation of the pancreas, with abdominal pain and vomiting.

Today, protection against mumps is available with the standard childhood immunization series, measles-mumps-rubella (MMR). Those who contract mumps will develop NAI to the disease.

Lyme Disease

An infectious disease that is becoming increasingly common in Eastern, Southeastern, upper Midwestern, and West Coast states is **Lyme disease,** with 16,461 cases in 1996. This bacterial disease results when infected deer ticks, usually in the nymph (immature) state, attach to the skin and inject the infectious agent as they feed on a host's blood. Deer ticks become infected by feeding on infected white-tailed deer or white-footed mice.[2]

The symptoms of Lyme disease are variable but generally first appear within 30 days as small red bumps surrounded by a circular red rash at the site of bites. In conjunction with this phase I stage, flulike symptoms may appear, including chills, headaches, muscle and joint aches, and low-grade fever. For approximately 20% of infected people, a phase II stage develops in which nervous system or heart disorders may occur. For those who remain untreated even to this stage, a phase III stage can develop in which chronic arthritis, lasting up to 2 years, can occur. Fortunately, Lyme disease can be treated with antibiotics. Unfortunately, however, no immunity develops, so subsequent infections can occur.[2] The ability to diagnose the presence of Lyme disease in children may be more difficult than for adults.[16] Although not yet available, a three-stage Lyme disease vaccine has been recently completed.

For people living in susceptible areas, outdoor activities can expose them to the nearly invisible tick nymphs that have fallen from deer into the grass. Thus people who are active outdoors should check themselves frequently to be sure that they are tick free. Shirts should be tucked into pants, pants tucked into socks, and gloves and hats worn when possible. It is also helpful to shower after coming in from outdoors and to check clothing for evidence of ticks. Pets can carry infected ticks into the house. If ticks are found, they should be carefully removed from the skin with tweezers and the affected area washed. A physician should be consulted if symptoms appear or you are concerned that you might have been exposed.

During 1995, it was discovered that the tick that carries Lyme disease has also been responsible for a potentially fatal bacterial infection, *human granulocytic ehrlichiosis* (HGE). This disease is associated with high fever, headache, muscle aches, and chills. Fortunately, HGE is successfully treated with doxycycline, an antibiotic that can also be used in the treatment of Lyme disease. Certainly, people with these symptoms, particularly when they are "outdoor people" and living in areas of the country in which Lyme disease is reported, should make certain that HGE is also considered in the diagnosis and treatment of their symptoms.

Hantavirus Pulmonary Syndrome

Since 1993 a small but rapidly expanding number of people have died of extreme pulmonary distress caused by the leakage of plasma into the lungs. In all of the initial cases, the people lived in the Southwest, had been well until they began developing flulike symptoms over 1 or 2 days, then quickly experienced difficulty breathing, and died only hours later. Epidemiologists quickly suspected a viral agent such as the hantavirus known to exist in Asia and, to a lesser degree, in Europe. Exhaustive laboratory work led to the culturing of the virus and confirmed that all of the victims had been infected with an American version of the hantavirus. The latest infectious condition, *hantavirus pulmonary syndrome,* was identified.

Today the hantavirus disease described above has been reported in areas beyond the Southwest, including most of the Western states and in some of the Eastern states. The common denominator in all areas in which the hantavirus infection has occurred is the presence of deer mice. It is now known that this common rodent serves as the reservoir for the virus.

The mode of transmission of the virus from deer mice to humans involves the inhalation of dust contaminated with dried virus-rich rodent urine or saliva-contaminated materials, such as nests. In areas with deer mouse populations (most of the United States), health experts are now warning people to be extremely careful when cleaning houses and barns in

---

chronic fatigue syndrome
Illness that causes severe exhaustion, fatigue, aches, and depression; mostly affects women in their thirties and forties.

rubeola (roo **be** oh luh)
Red or common measles.

rubella
German or 3-day measles.

Lyme disease
Bacterial infection transmitted by deer ticks.

which deer mouse droppings are likely to be found. Should it be necessary to remove rodent nests, wear rubber gloves, pour Lysol or bleach on the nests and soak them thoroughly, and finally, pick up nests with shovels and burn or bury them in holes that are several feet deep.[17]

The first case of human-to-human transmission of hantavirus has been reported in Argentina. Eighteen people were infected, including physicians who were caring for patients, and nine of them died.[18]

There is no vaccine for hantavirus pulmonary syndrome, although the illness is now more quickly recognized. As a result of awareness of the importance of early evaluation of flulike symptoms, the death rate has begun to fall.

Toxic Shock Syndrome

Toxic shock syndrome (TSS), first reported in 1978, made front-page headlines in 1980, when it was reported by the CDC that there was a connection between TSS and the presence of a specific bacterial agent (*Staphylococcus aureus*) in the vagina associated with the use of tampons.

TSS presents the signs and symptoms listed in the Star Box below. Superabsorbent varieties of tampons apparently can irritate the vaginal lining three times more quickly than regular tampons. This vaginal irritation is enhanced when the tampons remain in the vagina for a long time (over 5 hours). Once this irritation has begun, the staphylococcal bacteria (which are commonly present in the vagina) have relatively easy access to the bloodstream. Proliferation of these bacteria in the circulatory system and their resultant toxins produce toxic shock syndrome. Left untreated, the victim can die—usually as a result of cardiovascular failure. Fortunately, less than 10% of women diagnosed as having TSS actually die.

Although the extent of this disease is still quite limited (only about 3 to 6 cases per 100,000 women per year) and the mortality figures are low (comparable with those in women who use oral contraceptives), each woman should still exercise reasonable caution in the use of tampons. Recommendations are that (1) tampons should not be the sole form of sanitary protection used, and (2) tampons should not be in place for too long. Accordingly, women should change tampons every few hours and intermittently use sanitary napkins. Tampons should not be used during sleep.

The incidence of TSS has dropped significantly since the early 1980s. Possible reasons for this decrease are the removal of some superabsorbent tampons from the market and the standardization of the labels for junior, super, and super-plus tampons that began in 1990.

Hepatitis

Hepatitis is an inflammatory process in the liver and can be caused by several viruses. Types A, B, C (once called non-A and non-B), and D have been recognized. Additionally, hepatitis can result indirectly from abuse of alcohol and other drugs. General symptoms of hepatitis include fever, nausea, loss of appetite, abdominal pain, and jaundice (yellowing of the skin and eyes).[2]

Type A hepatitis is often associated with eating fecal contaminated food, such as raw shellfish, or water. Poor sanitation, particularly with the handling of food, has led to outbreaks associated with restaurants, while diaper-changing activities have resulted in outbreaks in child care centers. It is estimated that up to 200,000 people per year experience this infection, although many fewer cases are reported. In 1995 a vaccine, Harvix, was given FDA approval.

Type B hepatitis (HBV) is spread in various ways, including sexual contact, intravenous drug use, tattooing, and through medical and dental practice. Once spread principally through blood transfusions, this route no longer exists because of the use of effective screening tests. Chronic HBV infection has been associated with liver cirrhosis and liver cancer. The problem of HBV infection is discussed in the Learning from All Cultures box on p. 293.

Type C hepatitis is contracted in similar ways as HBV (sexual contact, tainted blood, and shared needles). Before 1992, tests to screen blood for hepatitis C were either inadequate or unavailable. Therefore, it is now recommended that anyone who received a blood transfusion before 1992 be tested for this virus.[19] As many of 290,000 people might be infected with this slow-acting virus, which eventually causes serious or even fatal liver disease.

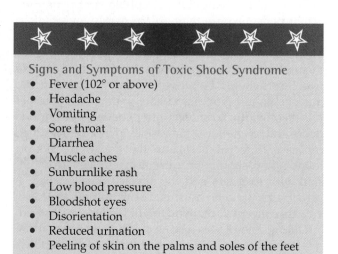

Signs and Symptoms of Toxic Shock Syndrome
- Fever (102° or above)
- Headache
- Vomiting
- Sore throat
- Diarrhea
- Muscle aches
- Sunburnlike rash
- Low blood pressure
- Bloodshot eyes
- Disorientation
- Reduced urination
- Peeling of skin on the palms and soles of the feet

LEARNING *from* ALL CULTURES

Hepatitis B

Because of the AIDS epidemic, some serious diseases get little attention from the media. Hepatitis B is one of these potentially dangerous diseases. It is estimated that 200 million people in the world are chronic carriers and can therefore infect others. The virus is transmitted through blood, sexual contact, and from mother to infant.

Some people who contract hepatitis B develop chronic health problems, such as cirrhosis of the liver or liver cancer. In Asia and Africa the hepatitis B virus is believed to be a significant cause of liver cancer. The chronic effects of this virus are considered a serious world health problem. A vaccine to prevent the virus is available, but for people in developing countries, it is not widely administered.

Treatment for limiting liver damage caused by hepatitis B is currently being researched. Some folk medicines, such as the extracts of tropical weeds, are being tested. In some parts of the world these extracts are used to treat jaundice caused by some type of illness involving the liver. At the present time, treatments like this are being used on patients in India.

Considering that hepatitis B is potentially preventable, why does it remain such a worldwide health concern? What do you think the focus of research should be on hepatitis B: prevention, treatment, or cure?

The newly identified *type D (delta) hepatitis* has proven very difficult to treat but is found almost exclusively in people already suffering from type B hepatitis. Transmission of this virus, along with type B hepatitis and HIV, makes unprotected sexual contact, including anal and oral sex, very risky.[2]

AIDS

AIDS is rapidly becoming the most devastating infectious disease to have occurred in modern times. On the basis of current data, since the initial reporting of the disease in 1981, through June 1997, 612,078 Americans have been diagnosed with AIDS and 379,258 (62% of all cases) have died from the disease.[20] The Star Box on p. 294 shows the extent to which various groups of people have been affected by the disease. The monetary cost of caring for people with HIV/AIDS is also considerable. The most recent data available (1995) indicate that combined annual health care and out-of-pocket costs for HIV/AIDS care were between $36,000 and $50,700 per patient.[21] Because of new drugs that extend life expectancy, current costs are undoubtedly much higher.

Cause of AIDS

AIDS is caused by HIV, a virus that attacks the helper T cells of the immune system (see pp. 285-286). When HIV attacks helper T cells, people lose the ability to fight off a variety of infections that normally would be easily controlled. Thus because these infections develop during a period in which people are vulnerable, they are collectively called *opportunistic infections.* HIV-infected patients become vulnerable to infection by bacteria, protozoa, fungi, and a number of viruses. Although not infections, a variety of malignancies (see Chapter 11) also develop during this period of immune system vulnerability.

During the initial years of the AIDS epidemic the presence of specific diagnosable conditions formed the basis of receiving the clinical label of HIV with AIDS. Among these were *Pneumocystis carinii* pneumonia and Kaposi's sarcoma, a rare but deadly form of skin cancer. Gradually, additional conditions were recognized as being associated with advancing deterioration of the immune system and thus were added to the list of AIDS conditions. Eventually this list contained over 25 definitive conditions, with more conditions being added as they become apparent. Among the conditions found on the current version of the list are toxoplasmosis within the brain, cytomegalovirus retinitis with loss of

toxic shock syndrome (TSS)
Potentially fatal condition resulting from the proliferation of certain bacteria in the vagina that enter the general blood circulation.

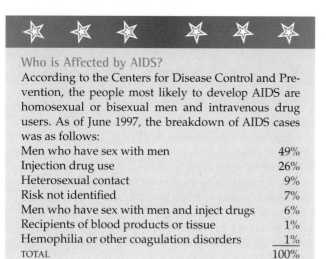

Who is Affected by AIDS?

According to the Centers for Disease Control and Prevention, the people most likely to develop AIDS are homosexual or bisexual men and intravenous drug users. As of June 1997, the breakdown of AIDS cases was as follows:

Men who have sex with men	49%
Injection drug use	26%
Heterosexual contact	9%
Risk not identified	7%
Men who have sex with men and inject drugs	6%
Recipients of blood products or tissue	1%
Hemophilia or other coagulation disorders	1%
TOTAL	100%

vision, lymphoma involving the brain, recurrent salmonella septicemia, and a wasting syndrome that includes invasive cervical cancer in women, recurrent pneumonia, and recurrent tuberculosis. Today, however, there is a growing tendency to assign the label of HIV with AIDS to HIV-infected people when their level of helper T cells drops below 200 cells per cubic millimeter, regardless of whether specific conditions are present.

Spread of HIV

HIV cannot be contracted easily. The chances of contracting HIV through casual contact with HIV-infected people at work, school, or at home are extremely rare or nonexistent. HIV is known to be spread only by direct sexual contact involving the exchange of body fluids (including blood, semen, and vaginal secretions), the sharing of hypodermic needles, transfusion of infected blood or blood products, and perinatal transmission (from an infected mother to a fetus or newborn baby). For HIV to be transmitted, it must enter the bloodstream of the noninfected person, which is done through contaminated blood or needles and tears in body tissues lining the rectum, mouth, and reproductive system. Current research also indicates that HIV is not transmitted by sweat, saliva, or tears, although the virus may be found in very low concentrations in these fluids. Oral transmission of HIV should also be considered a possibility because of gingivitis and bleeding gums. However, the presence of enzymes within the remainder of the digestive tract makes transmission via ingestion impossible.

Women are at much greater risk (12 times the risk) than men for the heterosexual transmission of HIV because of the higher concentration of HIV in semen than in vaginal secretions.

Signs and symptoms of HIV infection

Most people infected with HIV initially feel well and have no symptoms (that is, they are asymptomatic). The incubation period for HIV infection is generally considered to be from 6 months to 10 or more years, with the average being approximately 6 years. Despite the lengthy period between infection and the first clinical

Signing of the AIDS quilt in Washington, D.C., develops community support for AIDS education.

observation of damage to the immune system, antibodies to HIV may appear within several weeks to 3 months of contracting the virus. This short period before the appearance of antibodies is the small "window of opportunity" that exists even to this day in terms of the blood supply. Of course, relatively few people are tested for HIV infection *at any time* during the incubation period. Thus infected people could remain in the asymptomatic state (more currently referred to as HIV+ without symptoms) and be carriers of HIV for years before they would experience signs of illness sufficient enough to warrant a physical examination.

In the absence of symptoms of immune system deterioration and of AIDS testing results, sexually active people need to redefine the meaning of *monogamous*. Today it is very possible that two people need to account for the sexual partners that they both have had over a 10-year period before it is completely safe to assume that there have been no other partners involved in their special relationship. Unfortunately, this is done, or even considered, so infrequently that some are labeling today's late adolescents and young adults as "a generation in jeopardy."

Virtually all people infected with HIV eventually develop signs and symptoms of a more advanced stage of the disease. These signs and symptoms include tiredness, fever, loss of appetite and weight, diarrhea, night sweats, and swollen glands (usually in the neck, armpits, and groin). At this point, they are said to have HIV+ with symptoms. Table 12-4 indicates that these people are infectious and have damage to the immune system.

It is estimated that given sufficient time, perhaps as long as 15 years, the vast majority (95%) of infected people will move beyond HIV with symptoms to develop one or more of the nearly 30 conditions whose presence leads to the label HIV with AIDS or AIDS being applied, with death following within 2 to 5 years. Although not fully understood (perhaps a suppressor compound formed by specific immune system cells), a small percentage of infected people (5%) possess an ability to hold the infection in check and have survived for two decades without developing AIDS.

As mentioned earlier, in addition to being labeled AIDS on the basis of being HIV positive and having one or more of the conditions, the label is also applied to those people whose helper T cell count falls below 200 per cubic millimeter. A normal helper T cell range is 800 to 1000. Therefore, even in the absence of specific conditions, some people will qualify for the label AIDS because of the degree of damage already done to their immune systems.

Diagnosis of HIV infection

The CDC has established specific criteria that physicians and researchers use to define HIV infection. In addition to a clinical examination and laboratory tests for accompanying infections, HIV infection is diagnosed by the use of an initial screening test, the enzyme-linked immunosorbent assay (ELISA). If antibodies to HIV are identified, a confirming test, the western blot, can be performed. Home tests, such as Home Access and Confide, provide accurate, confidential, anonymous results within 24 hours, using a blood droplet test that is mailed to the company for analysis. It is estimated that 1.5 to 3 million people in this country have been infected with HIV.

Table 12-4   The Spectrum of HIV Infection

	HIV+ Without Symptoms (Asymptomatic)	HIV+ With Symptoms	HIV+ With AIDS
External signs	No symptoms Looks well	Fever Night sweats Swollen lymph glands Weight loss Diarrhea Minor infections Fatigue	Kaposi's sarcoma *Pneumocystis carinii* pneumonia and/or other predetermined illnesses Neurological disorders One or more of an additional 25 + diagnosable conditions or a T4 helper cell count below 200 per cubic milliliter
Incubation	Invasion of virus to 10 years	Several months to 10 or more years	Several months to 10-12 or more years
Internal level of infection	Antibodies are produced Immune system remains intact Positive antibody test	Antibodies are produced Immune system weakened Positive antibody test	Immune system deficient Positive antibody test
Infectious?	Yes	Yes	Yes

Treatment of HIV and AIDS

There is no cure for HIV and AIDS. The most effective treatment seems to be a "drug cocktail" in which one *protease inhibitor* is combined with two reverse transcriptase inhibitors. The protease inhibitor (such as indinavir, ritonavir, and saquinavir) blocks the action of an enzyme that the virus needs to uncouple polypeptides into smaller fragments for use in reproducing itself within the host's cells. The reverse transcriptase inhibitors (such as AZT, DDI, ddC, and 3TC) block the copying of RNA into a form that can enter a host cell's nucleus, a process known as *reverse transcription*. The combined effect of the protease inhibitors and reverse transcriptase inhibitors is to inhibit the ability of HIV to reproduce. These agents can reduce the viral load to a level at which the virus can no longer be detected in the blood.

The introduction of the protease inhibitors has revolutionized HIV/AIDS care, reducing the virus to undetectable levels in thousands of people.[22] The number of deaths from AIDS fell in 1996 for the first time since the virus was identified.[20] However, these drugs can have serious side effects and can cause viral resistance. In addition, the agents have no effect on viral particles that have taken shelter in other immune cells and within neurons.[23]

A "cure" for HIV/AIDS remains elusive. A study reported at the Interscience Conference on Antimicrobial Agents and Chemotherapy indicated that, in a group of AIDS patients taking protease inhibitors in combination with other drugs, 53% of patients were unable to suppress the virus to undetectable levels.

Experts agree that developing a vaccine is the only way to stop the spread of HIV infection. In June 1998 a California company received permission from the FDA to begin the first large-scale test of an AIDS vaccine. Although the trial is not expected to be successful, it may help researchers learn how to design a safe, affordable, effective vaccine.

This ability of the virus to change its appearance is so prolific that dozens of strains of HIV exist at all times in the United States. There may even be more than one version of HIV within a single individual. To date, over 20 killed-virus vaccines have been developed, but none has proven effective against this rapidly changing virus. A live-virus vaccine, although effective in animal studies, is still considered too dangerous for trials involving uninfected humans. However, a group of American physicians disagrees. They want to inject themselves with an attenuated live-virus vaccine because they believe it is safe for uninfected humans.

Prevention of HIV infection

Can HIV infection be prevented? The answer is a definite yes. Although HIV infection rates on college campuses are thought to be low (approximately 0.2%), students can be at risk. There are a number of steps an individual can take to reduce the risk of contracting and transmitting HIV. All of these steps involve understanding one's behavior and the methods by which HIV can be transmitted. Particularly applicable for college-aged people are *abstinence, safer sex, sobriety,* and *communication* with potential sexual partners. Excluding the recommendation to abstain from sexual activity if you desire the highest level of protection from HIV, the Health Action Guide on p. 297 lists specific points that relate to safer sex, sobriety, and the exchange of honest, accurate information regarding sexual histories.

To carry protection further, the U.S. Public Health Service has provided recommendations for the following groups: (1) the general public, (2) people at increased risk of infection (including health care workers), and (3) people with a positive HIV antibody test. The Public Health Service has a toll-free AIDS telephone hot line (1-800-342-AIDS), and local or state hot lines may exist. Keep informed about HIV infection and AIDS!

SEXUALLY TRANSMITTED DISEASES

Sexually transmitted diseases (STDs) were once referred to as venereal diseases (for Venus, the Roman goddess of love). Today the term *venereal disease* has been superseded by the broader term *sexually transmitted disease*. The current emphasis is on the successful prevention and treatment of STDs rather than on the ethics of sexuality. In conjunction with this, the following points should be remembered: (1) more than one STD can exist in a person at a given point in time; (2) the symptoms of STDs can vary over time and from person to person; (3) little immunity is developed for STDs; and (4) STDs can predispose people to additional health problems, including infertility, birth defects in their children, cancer, and long-term disability. Additionally, the risk of HIV infection is higher when sexual partners are also infected with STDs.

This section focuses on the STDs most frequently diagnosed among college students (chlamydia, gonorrhea, human papillomavirus infection, herpes simplex, syphilis, and pubic lice). A short section follows, covering common vaginal infections, some of which may occur without sexual contact. Completing the

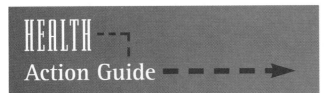

Reducing Your Risk of Contracting HIV

It is important to keep in mind that sexual partners may not reveal their true sexual history or drug habits. If you are sexually active, you can lower your risk of infection with HIV, as well as other STDs, by adopting the following safer sex practices.

- Learn the sexual history and HIV status of your sex partner.
- Limit your sex partners.
- Always use condoms correctly and consistently.
- Avoid contact with body fluids, feces, and semen.
- Curtail use of drugs that impair good judgment.
- Never share hypodermic needles.
- Refrain from sex with known injectable drug abusers.*
- Avoid sex with HIV-infected patients, those with signs and symptoms of AIDS, and the partners of high-risk individuals.*
- Get regular tests for STD infections.
- Do not engage in unprotected anal intercourse.

How easy will it be to adopt these behaviors? How real is your risk of becoming HIV positive?

---

*Current studies indicate that the elimination of high-risk people as sexual partners is the single most effective safer sex practice that can be implemented.

Personal Assessment on p. 298 will help you determine your own risk of contracting an STD. Also, refer to the Health Action Guide above for safer sex practices.

Chlamydia (Nonspecific Urethritis)

Chlamydia is considered the most prevalent STD in the United States today. Chlamydia infections occur an estimated 5 times more frequently than gonorrhea and up to 10 times more frequently than syphilis. This gap is expected to widen, since new cases of syphilis are at their lowest level in 40 years.

Chlamydia trachomatis is the bacterial agent that causes the chlamydia infection. Chlamydia is the most common cause of nonspecific urethritis (NSU).[24] NSU refers to infections of the **urethra** and surrounding tissues that are not caused by the bacterium responsible for gonorrhea. Only when a culture for suspected gonorrhea proves negative do clinicians diagnose NSU, usually by calling it *chlamydia*. Although not as accurate, new diagnostic tests, such as Test Pack, should allow a diagnosis to be made more quickly. About 80% of men with chlamydia indicate gonorrhea-like signs and symptoms, including painful urination and a whitish pus discharge from the penis. As in gonorrheal infections and many other STDs, most women report no overt signs or symptoms. A few women might exhibit a mild urethral discharge, painful urination, and swelling of vulval tissues. Whereas oral forms of penicillin are used in the treatment of gonococcal infections, oral tetracycline or doxycycline is prescribed for chlamydia and other NSUs.

As with all STDs, both sexual partners should receive treatment to avoid the ping-pong effect: the back-and-forth reinfection that occurs among couples when only one partner receives treatment. Furthermore, as with other STDs, having chlamydia does not effectively confer immunity.

Unresolved chlamydia can lead to the same negative health consequences that result from untreated gonorrheal infections. In men the pathogens can invade and damage the deeper reproductive structures (the prostate gland, the seminal vesicles, and Cowper's glands). Sterility can result. The pathogens can spread further and produce joint problems (arthritis) and heart complications (damaged heart valves, blood vessels, and heart muscle tissue).

In women the pathogens enter the body through the urethra or the cervical area. If not properly treated, the invasion can reach the deeper pelvic

---

sexually transmitted diseases (STDs)
Infectious diseases that are spread primarily through intimate sexual contact.

chlamydia
The most prevalent sexually transmitted disease. Caused by a nongonococcal bacterium.

urethra (yoo **ree** thra)
Passageway through which urine leaves the urinary bladder.

PERSONAL ASSESSMENT

What Is Your Risk of Contracting a Sexually Transmitted Disease?

A variety of factors interact to determine your risk of contracting a sexually transmitted disease (STD). This inventory is intended to provide you with an estimate of your level of risk.

Circle the number of each row that best characterizes you. Enter that number on the line at the end of the row (points). After assigning yourself a number in each row, total the number appearing in the points column. Your total points will allow you to interpret your risk for contracting an STD.

Age

1	3	4	5	3	2	Points
0-9	10-14	15-19	20-29	30-34	35+	_____

Sexual Practices

0	1	2	4	6	8	
Never engage in sex	One sex partner	More than one sex partner but never more than one at a time	Two to five sex partners	Five to ten sex partners	Ten or more sex partners	_____

Sexual Attitudes

0	1	8	1	7	8	
Will not engage in nonmarital sex	Premarital sex is okay if it is with future spouse	Any kind of premarital sex is okay	Extramarital sex is not for me	Extramarital sex is okay	Believe in complete sexual freedom	_____

Attitudes toward Contraception

1	1	6	5	4	8	
Would use condom to prevent pregnancy	Would use condom to prevent STDs	Would never use a condom	Would use the birth control pill	Would use other contraceptive measure	Would not use any- thing	_____

Attitudes toward STD

3	3	4	6	6	6	
Am not sexually active so I do not worry	Would be able to talk about STD with my partner	Would check an infection to be sure	Would be afraid to check out an infection	Can't even talk about an infection	STDs are no problem— easily cured	_____

YOUR TOTAL POINTS _____

Interpretation

5-8	Your risk is well below average
9-13	Your risk is below average
14-17	Your risk is at or near average
18-21	Your risk is moderately high
22+	Your risk is high

To Carry This Further . . .

Having taken this Personal Assessment, were you surprised at your level of risk? What is the primary reason for this level? How concerned are you and your classmates and friends about contracting an STD?

structures, producing a syndrome called **pelvic inflammatory disease (PID).** The inner uterine wall (endometrium), the fallopian tubes, and any surrounding structures may be attacked to produce this painful syndrome. A variety of further complications can result, including sterility and **peritonitis.** Infected women can transmit a chlamydia infection to the eyes and lungs of newborns during a vaginal birth. For both men and women the early detection of chlamydia and other NSUs is of paramount concern.

Human Papillomavirus

With all of the concern about HIV and other STDs, the presence of an additional STD is unwanted news. Nevertheless, such is the case with **human papillomavirus (HPV).** Because HPV infections are generally asymptomatic, the exact extent of the disease is unknown. However, because the HPV virus is sexually transmitted, about 15% to 20% of American young adults may be infected.[25] College students' patterns of sexual activity may have exposed 60% of the college population to the risk of infection. It is currently believed that for women, risk factors for HPV infection include: (1) sexual activity before age 20, (2) intercourse with three or more partners before age 35, and (3) intercourse with a partner who has three or more partners.[26] The extent of HPV infection in men is even less clearly known, but it is likely widespread.

The concern about HPV infections is centered on the ability of some of the more than 50 forms of the virus to foster precancerous changes in the cervix. In addition, HPV is associated with the development of genital warts (condyloma acuminata). These pinkish-white lesions may be found in raised clusters that resemble tiny heads of cauliflower. Found most commonly on the penis, scrotum, labia, cervix, and around the anus, genital warts are the most common symptomatic viral STD in this country. Although most genital wart colonies are small, they may become very large and block the anus or birth canal during pregnancy.

Treatment for HPV, including genital warts, may include burning, freezing, removal with a CO_2 laser, or the use of various medications. Regardless of treatment, however, return of the viral colonies will most likely occur. Condom use should be encouraged in an attempt to prevent transmission of HPV.

Gonorrhea

Another extremely common STD, gonorrhea is caused by a bacterium (*Neisseria gonorrhoea*). In men this bacterial agent can produce a milky-white discharge from the penis, accompanied by painful urina-

tion. About 80% of men who contract gonorrhea report varying degrees of these symptoms. This figure is approximately reversed for women: only about 20% of women are symptomatic and thus report varying degrees of frequent, painful urination, with a slimy yellow-green discharge from the vagina or urethra. Oral sex with an infected partner can produce a gonorrheal infection of the throat (pharyngeal gonorrhea). Gonorrhea can also be transmitted to the rectal areas of both men and women.

Diagnosis of gonorrhea is made by culturing the bacteria. Antibiotic treatment regimens include use of penicillin, tetracycline, ampicillin, or other drugs. Some strains of gonorrhea (penicillin-resistant strains) are much more difficult to treat than others.

Testing for gonorrhea is included as a part of prenatal care so that infections in mothers can be treated before birth. If the birth canal is infected, newborns could easily contract the infection in the mucous membranes of the eye. Most states still require that drops be placed in the eyes of all newborns to prevent this infection.

Herpes Simplex

Public health officials think that the sexually transmitted genital herpes virus infection rivals chlamydia as the most prevalent STD. Recent studies show that about 20% of the adult population is infected with genital herpes virus, although most people are asymptomatic for genital herpes.[27] Herpes is really a family of over 50 viruses, some of which produce recognized diseases in humans (chickenpox, **shingles,**

---

pelvic inflammatory disease (PID)
Acute or chronic infection of the peritoneum or lining of the abdominopelvic cavity; associated with a variety of symptoms and a potential cause of sterility.

peritonitis (pare it ton **eye** tis)
Inflammation of the peritoneum or lining of the abdominopelvic cavity.

human papillomavirus (HPV)
Sexually transmitted virus capable of causing precancerous changes in the cervix; causative agent for genital warts.

shingles
Viral infection affecting the nerve endings of the skin.

mononucleosis, and others). One subgroup called *herpes simplex 1 virus* (HSV-1) produces an infection called *labial herpes* (oral or lip herpes). Labial herpes produces common fever blisters or cold sores seen around the lips and oral cavity. Herpes simplex 2 virus (HSV-2) is a different strain that produces similar clumps of blisterlike lesions in the genital region (Figure 12-5). Laypeople have referred to this second type of herpes as the STD type, although both types produce identical clinical pictures. Both forms can exist at either site. Oral-genital sexual practices have resulted in genital herpes cases now being caused by HSV-1.

Herpes appears as a single sore or as a small cluster of blisterlike sores. These sores burn, itch, and (for some) become quite painful. The infected person might also report swollen lymph glands, muscular aches and pains, and fever. Some patients feel weak and sleepy when blisters are present. The lesions may last from a few days to a few weeks. A week is the average time for active viral shedding; then the blisters begin scabbing, and new skin is formed.

Herpes is an interesting virus for several reasons. It can lie dormant for extended periods. However, for reasons not well understood but perhaps related to stress, diet, or overall health, the viral particles can be stimulated to travel along the nerve pathways to the skin and then create an active infection. Thus herpes can be considered a recurrent infection. Fortunately for most people, recurrent infections are less severe than the initial episode and do not last as long. Herpes is also interesting because, unlike most STDs, no

treatment method has been successful at killing the virus. Acyclovir (Zovirax), in oral, ointment, and intravenous forms, has been used successfully in reducing the number and length of genital herpes infections in certain groups of patients. An FDA advisory panel recently recommended that this medication be made available as an OTC product. There are also some medications that may provide symptomatic relief. Diagnosis of genital herpes is almost always made by a clinical examination.

The best prevention against ever getting a herpes infection is to avoid all direct contact with a person who has an active infection. Do not kiss someone with a fever blister—or let them kiss you (or your children) if they have an active lesion. Do not share drinking glasses or eating utensils. Check your partner's genitals. Do not have intimate sexual contact with someone who displays the blisterlike clusters or rash. (Condoms are only marginally helpful and cannot protect against lesions on the female vulva or the lower abdominal area of men). Be careful not to infect yourself by touching a blister and then touching any other part of your body. The Health Action Guide on p. 301 provides helpful advice for talking to your partner if you have genital herpes.

Newborn babies are especially susceptible to the virus should they come into contact with an active lesion during the birth process. Newborns have not developed the defense capabilities to resist the invasion. They can quickly develop a systemic, general infection (neonatal herpes) that is often fatal or local infections that produce permanent brain damage or

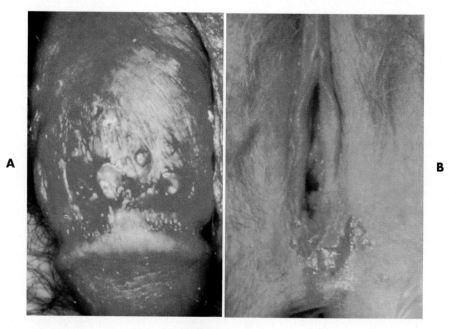

Figure 12-5   Herpes infections of the male **(A)** and female **(B)** genitals.

blindness. Fortunately, most of these possible problems can be prevented through proper prenatal care. If there is any chance that the viral particles may be present at birth, a cesarean delivery can be performed, although this is less commonly done today than in the past.

Syphilis

Like gonorrhea, syphilis is caused by a bacterium (*Treponema pallidum*) and is transmitted almost exclusively by sexual intercourse. The incidence of syphilis, a CDC-reportable disease, is far lower than that of gonorrhea. In 1950 a record 217,558 cases of syphilis were reported in this country. The number of cases then fell steadily to less than 80,000 cases in 1980. From 1980 through 1990 the incidence climbed, reaching nearly 140,000 cases in 1990. A subsequent decline then began, and in 1994 the number of cases dropped to 82,000.[28] In spite of a downward trend, an alarming number of today's cases have also been associated with HIV infections. More information on this once nearly defeated disease is presented in the Star Box on p. 302. An alarming increase in infant syphilis has been noted in children born to mothers who use drugs and support their habit through sexual activity.

Pubic Lice

Three types of lice infect humans: the head louse, the body louse, and the pubic louse all feed on the blood of the host. Except for the relatively uncommon body louse, these tiny insects do not carry diseases. They are, however, quite annoying.

Pubic lice, also called *crabs*, attach themselves to the base of the pubic hairs, where they live and attach their eggs (nits). These eggs move into a larval stage after 1 week; after 2 more weeks, they develop into mature adult crab lice (Figure 12-6).

People usually notice they have a pubic lice infestation when they are confronted with intense itching in the genital region. Fortunately, both prescription and OTC creams, lotions, and shampoos are extremely effective in killing both the lice and their eggs.

Lice are not transmitted exclusively through sexual contact, but also by contact with bedsheets and clothes that may be contaminated. If you develop a pubic lice infestation, you will have to treat yourself, your clothes, your sheets, and your furniture.

Vaginal Infections

Two common pathogens produce uncomfortable vaginal infections in women. The first is the yeast or

HEALTH Action Guide

Talking with Your Partner about Herpes

Although herpes rarely has serious consequences, the lesions are infectious and tend to reappear. It is important to talk openly with your partner about this sexually transmitted disease. Here are some tips to make things easier:

- *Educate yourself.*
Be aware that herpes is rarely dangerous.
Learn when the disease is most contagious (during the eruption and blister stage) and when sex is safest.
- *Choose the right time to talk.*
Discuss herpes with your partner only after you have gotten to know each other.
- *Listen to your partner.*
Be prepared to answer any questions that he or she may have.
- *Together, put things in perspective.*
Keep a positive outlook.
Remember that you are not alone.
Be aware that using a condom and abstaining from coitus during the most infectious period can prevent transmission of the disease.
Although there is no known cure, research continues on an antiviral drug.
Join a local support group together.

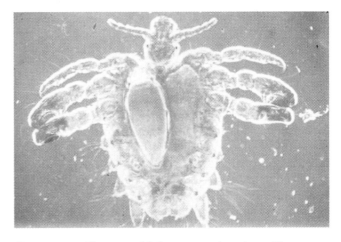

Figure 12-6   Human pubic louse, greatly enlarged by magnification.

Syphilis

Although we may think less often of syphilis than other sexually transmitted diseases, it remains a serious disease that if left untreated is capable of causing death. The chance of contracting syphilis during a single sexual encounter with an infected partner is now about 30%. The course taken by syphilis is well established once it is contracted.

Infection

The bacterium of syphilis, *Treponema pallidum*, a spirochete, is transmitted from an infected person to a new host through intimate contact. Moist, warm tissue, such as that lining the reproductive, urinary, and digestive systems, offers an ideal environment for the agent.

Incubation

After infection, an asymptomatic incubation period of 10 to 90 days gives way to the characteristic primary stage of the disease.

Primary Stage

Lasting 1 to 5 weeks, the primary stage of syphilis is associated with the formation of a small, raised, painless sore called a *chancre*. In 90% of women and 50% of men this highly infectious lesion is not easily identified; thus treatment is generally not sought. The chancre heals in 4 to 8 weeks.

Secondary Stage

The extremely contagious secondary stage of the disease is seen 6 to 12 weeks after initial infection. Because the infectious agents are now systemic, symptoms may include a generalized body rash, a sore throat, or a patchy loss of hair. A blood test (VDRL) will be positive, and treatment can be effectively administered. If untreated, the second stage will subside within 2 to 6 weeks. This is a stage during which syphilis can easily be transmitted by a pregnant woman to her fetus. Congenital syphilis often results in stillbirth or an infant born with a variety of life-threatening complications. Early treatment of infected pregnant women can prevent congenital syphilis.

Latent Stage

After the secondary stage subsides, an extended period of noninfectiousness is seen. The infectious agents remain dormant within the body cells, and few clinical signs exist during this stage.

Late Stage

Syphilis can recur for a third time 15 to 25 years after initial contact. In late-stage syphilis, tissue damage will be profound and irreversible. Damage to the cardiovascular system, central nervous system, eyes, and skin occurs, and death from the effects of the disease is likely.

Treatment

Syphilis is treated with penicillin, tetracycline, or erythromycin. Such treatment can kill the pathogen at any stage of the infection, but it cannot reverse the physical damage caused during the late stage of syphilis.

---

fungus pathogen *Candida (Monilia) albicans,* which produces the yeast infection often called *thrush.* These organisms, commonly found in the vagina, seem to multiply rapidly when some unusual stressor (pregnancy, use of birth control pills, diabetes, use of antibiotics) affects a woman's body. This infection, called *candidiasis,* is easily noticed by a white or cream-colored vaginal discharge that resembles cottage cheese. Vaginal itching and swelling are also commonly reported. Treatment often consists of an oral antibiotic or antibiotic douche to reduce the organisms to a normal level. Recently introduced nonprescription drugs for vaginal yeast infections allow for effective home treatment. Initial consultation with a physician is recommended before using these new products for the first time. (Men rarely report this monilial infection, although some may report mildly painful urination or a mild discharge at the urethral opening or beneath the foreskin of the penis.)

A second common agent that produces a vaginal infection is the protozoan *Trichomonas vaginalis.* This parasite can be transmitted through sexual intercourse or by contact with contaminated (often damp) objects, such as towels, clothing, or toilet seats that may contain some vaginal discharge. In women, this infection, called *trichomoniasis,* or "trich," produces a foamy, yellow-green, foul-smelling discharge that may be accompanied by itching, swelling, and painful urination. Treatment consists of a 2-week course of oral medication that helps kill the parasite. Men infrequently contract trichomoniasis but may harbor the organisms without realizing it.

Since the vagina is warm, dark, and moist, it is an ideal breeding environment for a variety of organisms. Normal hygienic measures help keep vaginal infections at a minimum. Unfortunately, use of some highly promoted commercial products seem to lead to increased incidences of vaginal infections. Among these are tight panty hose (without cotton panels), which tend to increase the vaginal temperature, and commercial vaginal douches, which can alter the acidic level of the vagina. Use of both of these products might promote infections. Women are advised to wipe from front to back after every bowel movement to reduce the opportunity for direct transmission of pathogenic agents from the rectum to the vagina. Avoiding public bath facilities is also a good suggestion. Of course, if you notice any unusual discharge from the vagina, you should report this to your physician.

Cystitis and Urethritis

Cystitis, an infection of the urinary bladder, and *urethritis,* an infection of the urethra, are conditions that can be caused by a sexually transmitted organism. Other modes of transmission are also associated with cystitis and urethritis, including infection with the organisms that cause vaginitis and organisms found in the intestinal tract. A culture is required to determine the specific pathogen associated with a particular case of cystitis or urethritis. The symptoms include pain when urinating, the need to urinate frequently, a dull aching pain above the pubic bone, and the passing of blood-streaked urine.

Cystitis and urethritis can be easily treated with antibiotics when the specific organism has been identified. Few complications result from infections that are treated promptly. If cystitis and urethritis are left untreated, the infectious agents could move upward in the urinary system and produce an infection of the ureters and kidneys. These upper urinary tract infections are more serious and require more extensive evaluation and aggressive treatment. It is therefore very important to obtain medical care on noticing symptoms.

Prevention of cystitis and urethritis depends to some degree on the source of the infectious agent. In a general sense, however, the incidence of infection can be lowered by urinating completely (to fully empty the urinary bladder) and by drinking ample quantities of fluids to flush the urinary tract. Whether the drinking of cranberry juice helps reduce urinary tract infections is a debatable issue.

Summary

- Progress has been made in reducing the incidence of some forms of infectious disease, but other infectious conditions are becoming more prevalent.
- A variety of pathogenic agents are responsible for infectious conditions.
- A chain of infection with six links characterizes every infectious condition.
- Infectious conditions progress through five distinct stages.
- Immunity can be acquired through both natural and artificial means. Immunization should be received on a regularly scheduled basis.
- The immune system's response to infection relies on cellular and humoral elements.
- The common cold and influenza display many similar symptoms but differ in terms of infectious agents, incubation period, prevention, and treatment.
- Tuberculosis and pneumonia are potentially fatal infections of the respiratory system.
- Mononucleosis and chronic fatigue syndrome are infections that result in chronic tiredness.
- Measles and mumps are childhood infections that can be harmful when contracted during adulthood.
- Lyme disease is a bacterial infection contracted in conjunction with outdoor activities.
- Hantavirus pulmonary syndrome is caused by a virus carried by deer mice.
- Hepatitis B (serum hepatitis) is a bloodborne infectious condition that can lead to serious liver damage. Hepatitis A, C, and D also exist.
- HIV/AIDS is a widespread, incurable viral disease transmitted through sexual activity, intravenous drug use, the use of infected blood products, or across the placenta during pregnancy.
- The definitive definition of AIDS can be based on the presence of specific conditions or the diminished number of helper T cells.
- Effective treatment of HIV and AIDS is limited, and prevention through the use of an effective vaccine is nonexistent.
- A variety of sexually transmitted conditions exists, many of which do not produce symptoms in most infected women and many infected men.
- Safer sex practices can reduce the risk of contracting STDs.

Review Questions

1. What are the agents responsible for the most familiar infectious conditions?
2. What are the six links that form the chain of infection?
3. What are the five stages that characterize the progression of infectious conditions?
4. What are the two principal components of the immune system, and how do they cooperate to protect the body from infectious agents and abnormal cells?
5. How are the common cold and influenza similar? How do they differ in terms of causative agents, incubation period, prevention, and treatment?
6. What symptoms make mononucleosis and chronic fatigue syndrome similar? What aspects of each are different?
7. Why are mumps and measles more serious conditions when they develop in adults?
8. Why is outdoor activity a risk factor in contracting Lyme disease?
9. How is hepatitis B transmitted, and which occupational group is at greatest risk of contracting this infection? How do forms A, C, and D compare with hepatitis B?
10. How is HIV transmitted? To what extent is the treatment of HIV/AIDS effective? What is meant by the term *safer sex*?
11. What specific infectious diseases could be classified as being STDs?
12. Why are women more often asymptomatic for STDs than men?
13. To what extent and in what manner can STD transmission be prevented?

 ## Think About This . . .

- How do you feel when a classmate or co-worker comes to class or work ill? Is it fair to expose you to his or her illness?
- Which infectious disease have you had in the recent past? What impact did this infection have on your day-to-day activities?
- What diseases have you been immunized against?
- How do you feel about parents who do not have their children immunized?
- What would your initial reaction be if you found out that someone close to you had a sexually transmitted disease?

References

1. Swartz MN: Use of antimicrobial agents and drug resistance, *N Engl J Med* 337(7):491-497, 1997.
2. Crowley L: *Introduction to human disease,* ed 4, Boston, 1996, Jones & Bartlett.
3. Hamann B: *Disease: identification, prevention and control,* Dubuque, IA, 1994, WCB/McGraw-Hill.
4. Saladin KS: *Anatomy & physiology: unity of form and function,* (ed 1) Dubuque, IA, 1998, WCB/McGraw-Hill.
5. Moffett D, Moffett S, Schauf C: Human physiology: foundations and frontiers, ed 2, St. Louis, 1993, Mosby.
6. Vaccinations among minorities at a peak, *USA Today,* p. 4D, October 20, 1997.
7. Santosham M et al: Efficacy and safety of high-dose rhesus-human reassortant rotavirus vaccine in Native American populations, *J Pediatr* 131(4):632-638, 1997.
8. Crouch RB: A new antiviral agent for influenza—is there a clinical niche? *N Engl J Med* 337(13):927-928, 1997.
9. Nichol KI et al: The effectiveness of vaccination against influenza in healthy, working adults, *N Engl J Med* 333(14):889-893, 1995.
10. Centers for Disease Control: Tuberculosis morbidity—United States, 1996, *MMWR* 46(30):695-699.
11. Mandell D, Bennett JE, Dolin R: *Principles and practice of infectious disease,* ed 4, New York, 1995, Churchill Livingston.
12. New treatment for chronic fatigue syndrome, *Tufts University Diet and Nutrition Newsletter,* 13:12, 1996.
13. Fulcher K, White P: How might chronic fatigue syndrome be treated? *Br Med J* 314:1647-1652, 1997.
14. Lee S et al: Resurgence of congenital rubella syndrome in the 1990s: report on missing opportunities and failed prevention policies among women of childbearing age, *JAMA* 267(19):2616, 1992.
15. Centers for Disease Control, as reported in, Prevention strikes have beaten back many diseases, *USA Today,* p. 8D, Oct 2, 1997.

16. Feber HM, Hunt MS: Pitfalls in the diagnosis and treatment of Lyme disease in children (Brief Report), *JAMA* 274(1):66-68, 1995.

17. Update: Hantavirus infections—United States, 1993, *MMWR* 42:517-519, 1993, as reported in *JAMA* 270(4):429-432, 1993.

18. Wells RM et al: An unusual hantavirus outbreak in southern Argentina: person-to-person transmission? *J Emerging Infectious Diseases* 3(2):171-174, 1997.

19. United States Public Health Service Advisory Council, as reported in, Widespread testing for hepatitis C recommended, *USA Today*, p. 8D, August 13, 1997.

20. Centers for Disease Control and Prevention: *HIV/AIDS Surveillance Report* 9(1), 1997.

21. Epstein AM et al: Costs of medical care and out-of-pocket expenditures for persons with AIDS in the Boston Health Study, *Inquiry* 32(2):211-221, 1995.

22. Living with AIDS, *The Economist* 348(8016):79, 1997.

23. Balter M: HIV survives drug onslaught by hiding out in T cells (Research News), *Science* 278:1227, 1997.

24. Atlas RM: *Principles of microbiology*, ed 2, Dubuque, IA, 1996, WCB/McGraw-Hill.

25. Alvey J: *Genital warts and contagious cancers: The coming epidemic*, Jefferson, NC, 1990, McFarland & Company.

26. Hatcher R et al: *Contraceptive technology: 17th* ed, New York, 1998, Irvington.

27. Flemming DT et al: Herpes simplex virus type 2 in the United States, 1976 to 1994, *N Engl J Med* 337(16):1105-1111, 1997.

28. U.S. Bureau of the Census, *Statistical abstract of the United States, 1997*, ed 117, Washington, DC.

29. U.S. Army Medical Research Institute of Infectious Diseases, *JAMA*, Aug 6, 1997.

Suggested Readings

Wyatt-Morley C: *AIDS memoir: journal of an HIV-positive mother*, West Hartford, CT, 1997, Kumarian Press.

In 1994, following a hysterectomy, the author learned that she was HIV-positive, having been infected by her alcoholic husband. Wyatt-Morley shares the day-to-day trials of physical decline, demanding medical care, and the reluctance of her pastor to provide spiritual support. She offers her story in support of other women, especially minority women, who are facing this illness.

Jussim D: *AIDS & HIV: risky business*, Springfield, NJ, 1997, Enslow Publishers.

This factual account of HIV/AIDS for adolescent readers may make parents and librarians uncomfortable because of its approach, but it does tell the story of the disease in a straightforward way. Information about transmission, treatment, and most important, prevention (including abstinence) is up-to-date and told from a perspective that will appeal to adolescents and teens.

Bond GC, Kreniske J, and Susser I: *AIDS in Africa and the Caribbean*, Boulder, CO, 1997, Westview Press.

This book examines the effect of HIV/AIDS on the economic, social, political, and historical fabric of developing countries. Readers will see how aspects of the disease either mirror or contrast with those that we are familiar with in our own country.

Hurster MH: *Communicable and non-communicable disease basics: a primer*, Westport, CT, 1997, Bergin & Garvey.

Less clinical than the title might suggest, this book describes a variety of diseases. The book focuses in particular on the relationships that exist among individuals, communities, and governments in their efforts to prevent, detect, control, and manage diseases.

Lehmann RH: *Cooking for life: a guide to nutrition and food safety for the HIV-positive community*, New York, 1997, Dell Publishing Company.

People with HIV/AIDS must pay careful attention to their diets, both because their illness might cause weight loss and because the effectiveness of their medications might depend in part on what they eat. The author, a professional chef, translates the advice of medical personnel into dietary advice designed to maintain both the body and spirit of patients, their friends, and their families.

 AS WE GO TO PRESS . . .

The potential to create or release biological weapons is in the hands of a growing number of countries and groups. Dispersal of the infectious agents in these weapons could cause illness or death for millions of people. The agent could cause *anthrax* (a spore-borne infection that causes death within a few days of exposure), *brucellosis* (a bacterial infection that causes long periods of debilitating illness), *plague* (a respiratory infection that is fatal if untreated), and *Q fever* (a livestock infection that can cause months of fatigue in humans).[29]

ON...

Controlling Infectious Disease Transmission

Ever since it was determined that microorganisms were the primary cause of communicable diseases, scientists have looked for ways to eradicate them. In the early part of the twentieth century, scientists searched for a "magic bullet" drug that would kill any organism that produced disease. Research, however, showed that disease-causing bacteria, viruses, protozoa, and other organisms were much too diverse to be wiped out with a single chemical. Still, research efforts continued to find cures for individual diseases. Slowly the significant scourges of humankind were conquered: polio, small-pox, measles, tetanus, and diphtheria. These and other killers were brought under control by the creation of various antibiotics and vaccines.[1] Starting in the 1950s, a massive campaign to immunize the world's population began, and the incidence of these diseases decreased sharply. A disease-free world seemed a real possibility.

However, that has not occurred. We underestimated the ability of these microbes to survive and adapt. Now we are continually facing the comeback of diseases we once thought were firmly under control. Outbreaks of measles, tuberculosis, and other "conquered" diseases are occurring with more frequency. To make matters worse, new disease-causing organisms that have the potential to kill on a grand scale are constantly being discovered. Why is this happening? Also, just as importantly, what can we do to bring it under control?

The Immunization Problem

Part of the problem has been our inability to continue the great strides in disease prevention made in earlier decades. Vaccination programs that were so effective in the 1960s and 1970s have not been as effective in recent years. As many as 4 million of the nation's 7.8 million 2-year-olds may not be fully immunized.[2] Failure to immunize children against childhood disease is an important cause of the increase in cases of these diseases. Measles once caused up to 400,000 infections per year in the United States, but by 1983 a successful immunization campaign had reduced the number to under 1500.[3] Despite an upsurge in the late 1980s caused by ineffective vaccines and failure to immunize 2-year-old children, improved vaccines and greater parental cooperation led to a drop to 1000 cases in 1994.[4] The incidence of diseases such as polio and influenza is also on the rise even though there are vaccines available for them.

So why the decline in the number of immunizations? The answer is complex. Part of the reason may be the lack of accessible health care, especially for the economi-

cally disadvantaged.[5] Many families are not able to afford routine health care, and health care clinics have had to resort to extreme measures to get vaccines to children. Some clinics have vehicles that bring the vaccines to the public. Others use various means to encourage families to bring their children in for vaccinations. Cuts in funding have made such enticements impractical for most clinics, however.[5]

Some parents have become fearful of the vaccines themselves. Many worry about the risk of side effects from vaccinations, even though the chances of problems occurring are remote. The pertussis (whooping cough) vaccine, for example, carries a slight risk of causing brain damage (about 1 in 300,000). Since the DPT (diphtheria-pertussis-tetanus) vaccine is given in several doses, the pertussis portion can be eliminated if the child shows signs of side effects.[5] Yet some parents think the risk is too great and therefore reject the entire series of vaccines. Thus their children miss out on the diphtheria and tetanus vaccines as well.

Children are not the only ones who suffer without proper immunizations. Adults, especially the elderly and those in high-risk groups, also need to be immunized against certain diseases. Older adults are at risk for influenza and pneumococcal disease, as are those with underlying diseases, such as heart disease or asthma.[6] Yet only about one fourth of people in these high-risk groups get immunized against influenza each year, and even fewer get immunized against pneumococcal infections.[6] Only 30% of those at risk for hepatitis B (including health care workers, homosexual men, heterosexuals with multiple partners, and IV drug users) obtain vaccinations, even though 300,000 new cases of the disease occur each year.[4]

New diseases have also caused some people to neglect vaccinations. Human immunodeficiency virus (HIV) is the most highly publicized, but others are also problematic. Before they were identified and treatments were devised, such afflictions as Lyme disease and Legionnaires' disease caused panics. Lyme disease is difficult to diagnose, and it is spread by tiny parasites known as deer ticks, which are sometimes difficult to detect on the body. Medical personnel and the general public are now more knowledgeable about ticks and the signs of the disease. The bacterium that causes Legionnaires' disease was found to thrive in places such as water from air cooling systems, so the air-handling system of a large building (such as a hotel or hospital) contaminated with this organism could potentially spread the disease to dozens of people. Managers of such facilities need to be aware of the danger from these and other organisms and need to learn how to prevent contamination.

More resistant viruses and bacteria are also causing problems. A dangerous resistant strain of pertussis broke out in Cincinnati in 1993. Many of the children who contracted the disease had already been vaccinated against the most common strain.[1] A deadly strain of the common bacterium *E. coli* wound up in the meat supply of a large fast-food restaurant chain, killing at least one child and making several other people violently ill.

Some of these new diseases are extremely frightening. For example, the Ebola virus, which kills most of those it infects, has been highly publicized in recent years.[7] This particular virus causes devastating symptoms, including severe abdominal pain, fever, muscle aches, and hemorrhaging. Outbreaks of viruses such as Ebola have been contained successfully in fairly remote regions, but the efficiency of air travel creates the potential for an outbreak to spread quickly from one continent to another. Strains of Ebola have already been found in the United States, carried by infected primates used for research.

Staying healthy and avoiding infection is largely a matter of common sense. For an infection to occur, a disease-causing agent must be present, there must be enough of the organism to cause disease, the person must be susceptible to the disease, and the organism must have an appropriate portal of entry.[8] If one or more of these factors are eliminated, infection can be prevented. Here are a few things you can do to prevent disease:

Wash your hands. Frequent hand washing, especially with antimicrobial soap, can prevent many germs from being transmitted to you and from you to others.

Keep your vaccinations up to date. Check to make sure you and any children in your care have had all of your vaccinations, and be sure that all of your booster doses (such as tetanus vaccine) are current. Also, if you are in an at-risk group, you may want to take advantage of seasonal vaccines for diseases such as influenza. People who travel abroad in underdeveloped areas also need to be immunized against diseases they may encounter.

Cut off potential routes of transmission. Avoid making contact with any substances that may harbor bacteria. These include (but are not limited to) soiled food plates, utensils, and facial tissues and body fluids. This is espe-

cially important for those people in occupations where such contact is common (such as health care workers).

Clean and cook your food properly. Wash fresh vegetables to rid them of dirt. Be sure to cook all food thoroughly, especially foods such as meats, fish, and poultry, which are very likely to harbor harmful organisms.

Exercise and eat nutritious foods. Keeping yourself in shape and obtaining proper nutrients can help keep your immune system functioning properly and make you less susceptible to disease.

Take all of your medicine. When you do get sick, take your medicine exactly as prescribed. This is especially important when taking antibiotics. Not finishing the medication may contribute to a recurrence of the infection.

Practice safer sex. You cannot tell if a person has a bloodborne disease (such as AIDS or hepatitis B) or a sexually transmitted disease by looking at him or her. Safer sex practices can help prevent transmission of such diseases.

For Discussion . . .

Are you familiar with your immunization record? Have you ever failed to finish antibiotics that were prescribed for you? Do you feel that viruses such as Ebola are a real threat to Americans?

References

1. Lemonick MD: The killers all around: new viruses and drug-resistant bacteria are reversing human victories over infectious disease, *Time*, p11, Sept 12, 1994.
2. Standards for pediatric immunization practices (Ad Hoc Working Group for the Development of Standards for Pediatric Immunization Practices), *JAMA* 269(14), 1993.
3. Fisher LL, Douglas RG: Infectious diseases, *JAMA* 265(23), 1991 (Contempo 1991 Special Issue).
4. U.S. Bureau of the Census, *Statistical abstract of the United States: 1997*, ed 117, Washington, DC.
5. Levine A: Return of the old childhood scourges, *US News and World Report*, p1, June 4, 1988.
6. Eickhoff TC, Strikas, RA, Williams, WW: Update on adult immunization, *Patient Care* 26(15), 1992.
7. Preston R: *The hot zone*, New York, 1994, Random House.
8. American Red Cross: *Preventing disease transmission*, St Louis, 1993, Mosby Lifeline.

PART 5

SEXUALITY

Understanding Sexuality

Healthy People: Looking Ahead to 2010

Key indicators of progress in areas related to sexuality include reducing the number of unintended pregnancies, increasing the age of initial sexual intercourse, increasing the rate of abstinence among young people who have already had sexual and increasing the use of effective contraception (including the use of methods that also reduce the risk of various sexually transmitted diseases) among sexually active young people.

Progress toward achieving the target goals in these areas has been mixed. Despite intensive efforts to curb early sexual exploration, the age of initial sexual intercourse continues to drop. However, some small gains have been made in promoting abstinence among girls who have already been sexually active. In addition, there has been a slight increase in the percentage of teenagers who use effective contraception.

As we near the turn of the century, college students have become especially interested in developing meaningful, safe relationships. Like generations of students in the past, many of today's college students are sexually active. With sexual health as one of the main focus areas of the *Healthy People 2010* framework, we can expect a variety of health objectives aimed at college students and other young adults.

As we approach the year 2000, we have reached an understanding of both the biological and psychosocial factors that contribute to the complex expression of our **sexuality.** As a society, we are now inclined to view human behavior in terms of a complex script written on the basis of both biology and conditioning.

Reflecting this understanding is the way in which we use the words "male" or "female" to refer to the biological roots of our sexuality and the words "man" or "woman" to refer to the psychosocial roots of our sexuality. In this chapter, we explore human sexuality as it relates to the dynamic interplay of the biological and psychosocial bases that form your **masculinity** or **femininity.**

BIOLOGICAL BASES OF HUMAN SEXUALITY

Within a few seconds after the birth of a baby, someone (a doctor, nurse, or parent) emphatically labels the child: "It's a boy," or "It's a girl." For the parents and society as a whole, the child's **biological sexuality** is being displayed and identified. Another female or male enters the world.

Genetic Basis

At the moment of conception, a Y-bearing or an X-bearing sperm cell joins with the X-bearing ovum to establish the true basis of biological sexuality.[1] A fertilized ovum with sex chromosomes XX is biologically female, whereas fertilized ovum bearing the XY sex chromosomes is biologically male. Genetics forms the most basic level of an individual's biological sexuality.

Gonadal Basis

The gonadal basis for biological sexuality refers to the growing embryo's development of **gonads.** Male embryos develop testes about the seventh week after conception, and female embryos develop ovaries about the twelfth week after conception.

Structural Development

The development of male or female reproductive structures is initially determined by the presence or absence of hormones produced by the developing testes—androgens and müllerian inhibiting substance (MIS). With these hormones present, the male embryo starts to develop male reproductive structures (penis, scrotum, vas deferens, seminal vesicles, prostate gland, and Cowper's glands).

Because the female embryo is not exposed to these male hormones, it develops the characteristic female reproductive structures: the uterus, fallopian tubes, vagina, labia, and clitoris.

Biological Sexuality and the Childhood Years

The growth and development of the child in terms of reproductive organs and physiological processes have traditionally been thought to be "latent" during the childhood years. However, a gradual degree of growth occurs in both girls and boys. The reproductive organs, however, will undergo more greatly accelerated growth at the onset of **puberty** and will achieve their adult size and capabilities shortly.

Puberty

The entry into puberty is a gradual maturing process for young girls and boys. For young girls, the onset of menstruation, called **menarche,** occurs around age 13 but may come somewhat earlier or later.[2] Early menstrual cycles tend to be **anovulatory.** Menarche is usually preceded by a growth spurt that includes the budding of breasts and the growth of pubic and underarm hair.[3]

---

sexuality
The quality of being sexual; can be viewed from many biological and psychosocial perspectives.

masculinity
Behavioral expressions traditionally observed in males.

femininity
Behavioral expressions traditionally observed in females.

biological sexuality
Male and female aspects of sexuality.

gonads
Male or female sex glands; testes produce sperm and ovaries produce eggs.

puberty
Achievement of reproductive ability.

menarche (muh **nar** key)
Time of a female's first menstrual cycle.

anovulatory (an **oh** vyu luh tory)
Not ovulating.

Young males follow a similar pattern of maturation, including a growth spurt followed by a gradual sexual maturity. However, this process takes place about 2 years later than in young females. Genital enlargement, underarm and pubic hair growth, and a lowering of the voice commonly occur. The male's first ejaculation is generally experienced by the age of 14, most commonly through **nocturnal emission** or masturbation. For many young boys, fully mature sperm do not develop until about age 15.

Reproductive capability only gradually declines over the course of the adult years. In the woman, however, the onset of **menopause** signals a more direct turning off of the reproductive system than is the case for the male adult. By the early to mid-fifties, virtually all women have entered a postmenopausal period, but for men, relatively high-level **spermatogenesis** may continue for a decade or two.

The story of sexual maturation and reproductive maturity cannot, however, be solely focused on the changes that take place in the body. Now we discuss the psychosocial processes that accompany the biological changes.

PSYCHOSOCIAL BASES OF HUMAN SEXUALITY

If growth and development of our sexuality were to be visualized as a step ladder (Figure 13-1), one vertical rail of the ladder would represent our biological sexuality. Arising at various points along this rail would be rungs representing the sequential unfolding of the genetic, gonadal, and structural components.

Because humans, more so than any other life form, can rise above a life centered on reproduction, a second dimension or rail to our sexuality exists—our **psychosocial sexuality.** The reason we possess the ability to be more than reproductive beings is a question for the theologian or philosopher. We are considerably more complex than the functions determined by biology. The process that transforms a male into a

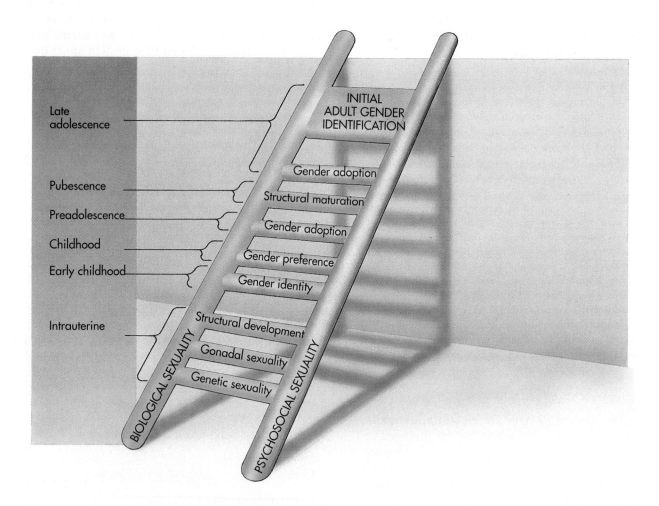

Figure 13-1   Our sexuality develops through biological and psychosocial stages.

man and a female into a woman begins at birth and continues to influence us through the course of our lives.

Gender Identity

Although expectant parents may prefer to have a child of one **gender** over the other, they frequently must wait until the birth of the baby to have their question answered. External genitals "cast the die," and femininity or masculinity begins to receive its traditional reinforcement by the parents and society in general. By the eighteenth month, typical children have both the language and the insight to correctly identify their gender. They have established a **gender identity.**[4] The first rung rising from the psychosocial rail of the ladder has been climbed.

Gender Preference

During the preschool years, children receive the second component of the *scripting* required for the full development of psychosocial sexuality—the preference for the gender to which they have been assigned. The process whereby **gender preference** is transmitted to the child is more than likely a less subtle form of the practices observed during the gender identity period (the first 18 months). Many parents begin to control the child's exposure to experiences traditionally reserved for children of the opposite gender. This is particularly true for boys; parents will stop play activities they perceive as being too feminine.

With the recent acceleration in the importance of competitive sports for women, many of the skills and experiences once reserved for boys are now being fostered in young girls. What effect, if any, this movement will have on the speed at which gender preference is reached will be a topic or further research.*

Gender Adoption

The process of reaching an initial adult gender identification requires a considerable period of time. The specific knowledge, attitudes, and behavior characteristic of adults must be observed, analyzed, and practiced. The process of acquiring and personalizing these "insights" about how men and women think, feel, and act is reflected by the term **gender adoption,**

---

*If you want to test the existence of gender preference, ask a group of first- or second-grade boys or girls if they would be happier being a member of the opposite gender. Be prepared for some frank replies.

the first and third rungs below the initial adult gender identification rail of the ladder in Figure 13-1.

In addition to the construction of a personalized version of an adult sexual identity, it is important that the child and particularly the adolescent construct a *gender schema* for a member of the opposite gender. Clearly, the world of adulthood, with its involvement with intimacy, parenting, and employment, will require that men know women and women know men. Gender adoption provides an opportunity to begin to assemble this equally valuable "picture" of what the other gender is like.

Initial Adult Gender Identification

By the time young people have climbed all of the rungs of the sexuality ladder, they have arrived at the chronological point in the life cycle when they need to construct an initial adult **gender identification.** You

---

nocturnal emission
Ejaculation that occurs during sleep; "wet dream."

menopause
Decline and eventual cessation of hormone production by the female reproductive system.

spermatogenesis (sper mat oh **jen** uh sis)
Process of sperm production.

psychosocial sexuality
Masculine and feminine aspects of sexuality.

gender
General term reflecting a biological basis of sexuality; the male gender *or* the female gender.

gender identity
Recognition of one's gender.

gender preference
Emotional and intellectual acceptance of one's own gender.

gender adoption
Lengthy process of learning the behavior that is traditional for one's gender.

gender identification
Achievement of a personally satisfying interpretation of one's masculinity or femininity.

might notice that this label seems remarkably similar to the terminology used to describe one of the developmental tasks being used in this textbook. In fact, the task of forming an initial adult identity is closely related to developing an initial adult image of oneself as a man or a woman. Although most of us currently support the concept of "person" in many gender-neutral contexts (for some very valid reasons), we still must identify ourselves as either a man or a woman.

Transsexualism

Students are often intrigued by a sexual variance that is first noticed during one or two of the psychosocial stages just discussed. Transsexualism is a sexual variance of the most profound nature because it represents a complete rejection by an individual of his or her biological sexuality. The male transsexual believes that he is female and thus desires to be the woman that he knows he is. The female transsexual believes that she is male and thus desires to become the man that she knows she should be. It should be noted that psychiatrists and sex therapists do not view transsexuals as homosexual in their sexual orientation.

For transsexuals, the periods of gender preference and gender adoption are perplexing as they attempt, with limited success, to resolve the conflict between what their mind tells them is true and what their body displays. Adolescent and young adult transsexuals often cross-dress, undertake homosexual relationships (which they view as being heterosexual relationships), experiment with hormone replacement therapy, and in some cases actively pursue a **sex reassignment operation.** Several thousand of these operations have been performed at some of the leading medical centers in the United States.

ANDROGYNY: SHARING THE PLUSES

Over the last 20 years our society has increasingly accepted an image of a person who possesses both masculine and feminine qualities. This accepted image has taken years to develop because our society traditionally has reinforced rigid masculine roles for men and rigid feminine roles for women.

In the past, from the time a child was born, we assigned and reinforced only those roles and traits that were thought to be directly related to his or her biological gender. Boys were not allowed to cry, play with dolls, or help in the kitchen. Girls were not encouraged to become involved in sports; they were told to learn to sew, cook, and baby-sit. Men were encouraged to be strong, expressive, dominant, aggressive, and career oriented, whereas women were encouraged to be weak, shy, submissive, passive, and home oriented.

These traditional biases have resulted in some interesting phenomena related to career opportunities. Women were denied jobs requiring above-average physical strength, admittance into professional schools requiring high intellectual capacities, such as law, medicine, and business, and entry into most levels of military participation. Likewise, men were not encouraged to enter traditionally feminine careers, such as nursing, clerical work, and elementary school teaching.

For a variety of reasons, the traditional picture has changed. **Androgyny,** or the blending of both feminine and masculine qualities, is more clearly evident in our society now than ever before. Today it is more acceptable to see men involved in raising children (including changing diapers) and doing routine housework. On the other hand, it is also more acceptable to see women entering the workplace in jobs traditionally managed by men and participating in sports traditionally played by men. Men are not scoffed at when they are seen crying after a touching movie. Women are not laughed at when they choose to assert themselves. The disposal of numerous sexual stereotypes has probably benefited our society immensely by relieving people of the pressure to be 100% "womanly" or 100% "macho."

Many women are now entering traditionally male professions, such as law, medicine, and business.

Research data suggest that androgynous people are more flexible, have greater self-esteem, and show more social skills and motivation to achieve.[4] This should encourage you to be unafraid to break the gender role stereotype.

REPRODUCTIVE SYSTEMS

The most familiar aspects of biological sexuality are the structures that compose the reproductive systems. Each structure contributes in unique ways to the reproductive process. Thus with these structures, males have the ability to impregnate. Females have the ability to become pregnant, give birth, and nourish infants through breastfeeding. In addition, many of these structures are associated with nonreproductive sexual behavior.

Male Reproductive System

The male reproductive system consists of external structures of genitals (the penis and scrotum) and internal structures (the testes, various passageways or ducts, seminal vesicles, the prostate gland, and the Cowper's glands) (Figure 13-2, *A*). The *testes* (also called *gonads* or *testicles*) are two egg-shaped bodies that lie within a saclike structure called the *scrotum*. During most of fetal development, the testes lie within the abdominal cavity. They descend into the scrotum during the last 2 months of fetal life. The testes are housed in the scrotum because a temperature lower than the body core temperature is required for adequate sperm development. The walls of the scrotum are composed of contractile tissue and can draw the testes closer to the body during cold temperatures (and sexual arousal) and relax during warm temperatures. Scrotal contraction and relaxation allow a constant, productive temperature to be maintained in the testes.

A cross-sectional view of a single testis reveals an intricate network of structures called *seminiferous tubules* (Figure 13-2, *B*). Within these 300 or so seminiferous tubules, the process of sperm production (spermatogenesis) takes place. Sperm cell development starts at about age 11 in boys and is influenced by the release of the hormone **ICSH (interstitial cell-stimulating hormone)** from the pituitary gland. ICSH does primarily what its name suggests: it stimulates specific cells (called *interstitial cells*) within the testes to begin producing the male sex hormone *testosterone*. Testosterone in turn is primarily responsible for the gradual development of the male secondary sex characteristics at the onset of puberty. By the time a boy is

approximately 15 years old, sufficient levels of testosterone exist so that the testes become capable of full spermatogenesis.

Before the age of about 15, most of the sperm cells produced in the testes are incapable of fertilization. The production of fully mature sperm (*spermatozoa*) is triggered by another hormone secreted by the brain's pituitary gland—**FSH (follicle-stimulating hormone)**. FSH influences the seminiferous tubules to begin producing spermatozoa that are capable of fertilization.

Spermatogenesis takes place around the clock, with hundreds of millions of sperm cells produced daily. The sperm cells do not stay in the seminiferous tubules but rather are transferred through a system of ducts that lead into the *epididymis*. The epididymis is a tubular coil that attaches to the back side of each testicle. These collecting structures house the maturing sperm cells for 2 to 3 weeks. During this period the sperm finally become capable of motion, but they remain inactive until they mix with the secretions from the accessory glands (the seminal vesicles, prostate gland, and Cowper's glands).

Each epididymis leads into an 18-inch passageway known as the *vas deferens*. Sperm, moved along by the action of hairlike projections called *cilia*, can also remain in the vas deferens for an extended time without losing their ability to fertilize an egg.

The two vasa deferens extend into the abdominal cavity, where each meets with a *seminal vesicle*—the first of the three accessory structures or glands. Each seminal vesicle contributes a clear, alkaline fluid that

---

sex reassignment operation
Surgical procedure designed to remove the external genitalia and replace them with genitalia appropriate to the opposite gender.

androgyny (an **droj** en ee)
The blending of both masculine and feminine qualities.

ICSH (interstitial cell-stimulating hormone)
(in ter **stish** ul)
A gonadotropic hormone of the male required for the production of testosterone.

FSH (follicle-stimulating hormone)
A gonadotropic hormone required for initial development of ova (in the female) and sperm (in the male).

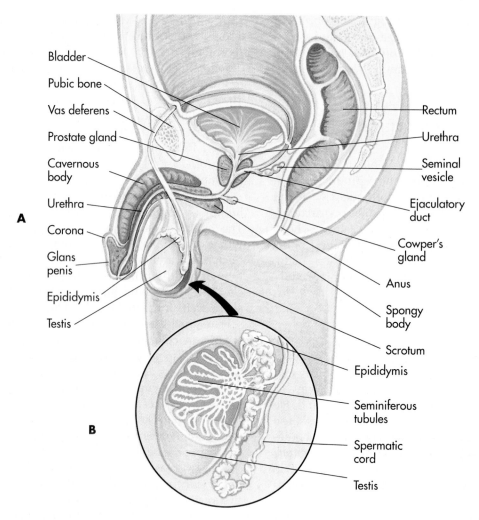

Bladder
Pubic bone
Vas deferens
Prostate gland
Cavernous body
Urethra
Corona
Glans penis
Epididymis
Testis

A

Rectum
Urethra
Seminal vesicle
Ejaculatory duct
Cowper's gland
Anus
Spongy body
Scrotum
Epididymis
Seminiferous tubules
Spermatic cord
Testis

B

Figure 13-2   **A,** Male reproductive structures, side view. The production and delivery of sperm, as well as the production of the sex hormone testosterone, is accomplished by the male reproductive structures. **B,** Cross section of a testis.

nourishes the sperm cells with fructose and permits the sperm cells to be suspended in a movable medium. The fusion of a vas deferens with the seminal vesicle results in the formation of a passageway called the *ejaculatory duct.* Each ejaculatory duct is only about 1 inch long and empties into the final passageway for the sperm—the urethra.

This juncture takes place in an area surrounded by the second accessory gland—the *prostate gland.* The prostate gland secretes a milky fluid containing a variety of substances, including proteins, cholesterol, citric acid, calcium, buffering salts, and various enzymes. The prostate secretions further nourish the sperm cells and also raise the pH level, making the mixture quite alkaline. This alkalinity permits the sperm to have greater longevity as they are transported during ejaculation through the urethra, out of the penis, and into the highly acidic vagina.

The third accessory glands, the Cowper's glands, serve primarily to lubricate the urethra with a clear, viscous mucus. These paired glands empty their small amounts of preejaculatory fluid during the arousal stage of the sexual response cycle. Alkaline in nature, this fluid also neutralizes the acidic level of the urethra. It is hypothesized that viable sperm cells can be suspended in this fluid and can enter the female reproductive tract before full ejaculation by the male.[3] This may account for many of the failures of the "withdrawal" method of contraception.

The sperm cells, when combined with secretions from the seminal vesicles and the prostate gland, form a sticky substance called **semen.** Interestingly, the microscopic sperm actually makes up less than 5% of the seminal fluid discharged at ejaculation. Contrary to popular belief, the paired seminal vesicles contribute about 60% of the semen volume, and the prostate gland adds about 30%.[5] Thus the fear of some men that a **vasectomy** will destroy their ability to ejaculate is completely unfounded (see Chapter 14).

During *emission* (the gathering of semen in the upper part of the urethra), a sphincter muscle at the base of the bladder contracts and inhibits semen from being pushed into the bladder and urine from being deposited into the urethra.[3] Thus semen and urine rarely intermingle, even though they leave the body through the same passageway.

Ejaculation takes place when the semen is forced out of the penis through the urethral opening. The involuntary, rhythmic muscle contractions that control ejaculation result in a series of pleasurable sensations known as *orgasm.*

The urethra lies on the underside of the penis and extends through one of three cylindrical chambers of erectile tissue (two cavernous bodies and one spongy body). Each of these three chambers provides the vascular space required for sufficient erection of the penis. When a male becomes sexually aroused, these areas become congested with blood (*vasocongestion*). After ejaculation or when a male is no longer sexually stimulated, these chambers release the blood into the general circulation and the penis returns to a **flaccid** state.

The *shaft* of the penis is covered by a thin layer of skin that is an extension of the skin that covers the scrotum. This loose layer of skin is sensitive to sexual stimulation and extends over the head of the penis, except in males who have been circumcised. The *glans* (or head) of the penis is the most sexually sensitive (to tactile stimulation) part of the male body. Nerve receptor sites are especially prominent along the *corona* (the ridge of the glans) and the *frenulum* (the thin tissue at the base of the glans).

Female Reproductive System

The external structures (genitals) of the female reproductive system consist of the mons pubis, labia majora, labia minora, clitoris, and vestibule (Figure 13-3). Collectively these structures form the *vulva* or vulval area. The *mons pubis* is the fatty covering over the pubic bone. The mons pubis (or mons veneris, "mound of Venus") is covered by pubic hair and is quite sensitive to sexual stimulation. The *labia majora* are large longitudinal folds of skin that cover the entrance to the vagina, whereas the *labia minora* are the smaller longitudinal skin folds that lie within the labia majora. These hairless skin folds of the labia minora join at the top to form the *prepuce.* The prepuce covers the glans of the *clitoris*, which is the most sexually sensitive part of the female body.

A rather direct analogy can be made between the penis and the clitoris. In terms of the tactile sensitivity, both structures are the most sensitive parts of the male and female genitals. Both contain a glans and a shaft (although the clitoral shaft is beneath the skin surface). Both organs are composed of erectile tissue that can become engorged with blood. Both are covered by skin folds (the clitoral prepuce of the female and the foreskin of the male), and both structures can collect **smegma** beneath these tissue folds.[4]

The *vestibule* is the region enclosed by the labia minora. Evident here are the urethral opening and the entrance to the vagina (or vaginal orifice). Also located at the vaginal opening are the *Bartholin's glands*, which secrete a minute amount of lubricating fluid during sexual excitement.

The *hymen* is a thin layer of tissue that stretches across the opening of the vagina. Once thought to be the only indication of virginity, the intact hymen rarely covers the vaginal opening entirely. Openings in the hymen are necessary for the discharge of menstrual fluid and vaginal secretions. Many hymens are stretched or torn to full opening by adolescent physical activity or by the insertion of tampons. In women whose hymens are not fully ruptured, the first act of sexual intercourse will generally accomplish this. Pain may accompany first intercourse in females with relatively intact hymens.

The internal reproductive structures of the female include the vagina, uterus, fallopian tubes, and ovaries. The *vagina* is the structure that accepts the penis during sexual intercourse. Normally the walls of the vagina are collapsed, except during sexual stim-

---

semen
Secretion containing sperm and nutrients discharged from the urethra at ejaculation.

vasectomy
Surgical procedure in which the vasa deferens are cut to prevent the passage of sperm from the testicles; the most common form of male sterilization.

flaccid (**fla** sid)
Nonerect; the state of erectile tissue when vasocongestion is not occurring.

smegma
Cellular discharge that can accumulate beneath the clitoral hood and the foreskin of an uncircumcised penis.

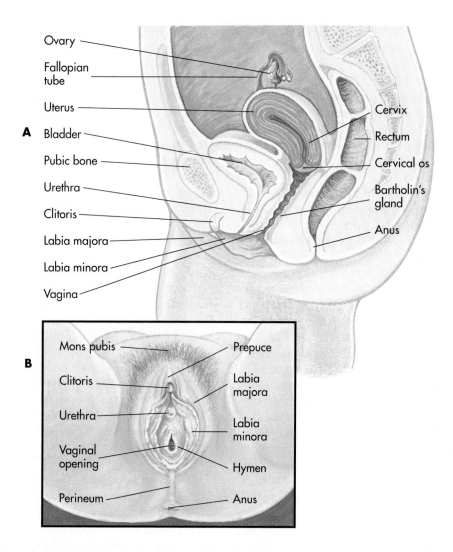

Figure 13-3 **A,** Female reproductive structures, side view. The formation of ova, production of the sex hormones estrogen and progesterone, and support for the developing fetus are functions of the structures of the female reproductive system. **B,** External view of the female genitals.

ulation, when the vaginal walls widen and elongate to accommodate the erect penis. Only the outer third of the vagina is especially sensitive to sexual stimulation. In this location, vaginal tissues swell considerably to form the **orgasmic platform.** This platform constricts the vaginal opening and in effect "grips" the penis (or other inserted object)—regardless of its size.[4] Thus the belief that a woman receives considerably more sexual pleasure from men with large penises is not supported from an anatomical standpoint.

The *uterus* (or *womb*) is approximately the size and shape of a small pear. This highly muscular organ is capable of undergoing a wide range of physical changes, as evidenced by its enlargement during pregnancy, its contraction during menstruation and labor, and its movement during the orgasmic phase of the female sexual response cycle. The primary func-

tion of the uterus is to provide a suitable environment for the possible implantation of a fertilized ovum, or egg. This implantation, should it occur, will take place in the innermost lining of the uterus—the *endometrium.* In the mature female, the endometrium undergoes cyclic changes as it prepares a new lining on a near-monthly basis.

The lower third of the uterus is called the *cervix.* The cervix extends slightly into the vagina. Sperm can enter the uterus through the cervical opening, or *cervical os.* Mucous glands in the cervix secrete a fluid that is thin and watery near the time of ovulation. Mucus of this consistency apparently facilitates sperm passage into the uterus and deeper structures. However, cervical mucus is much thicker during portions of the menstrual cycle when pregnancy is improbable, and during pregnancy, to protect against bacterial agents and other substances that are especially dangerous to the developing fetus.

The upper two thirds of the uterus is called the *corpus* or *body*. This is where implantation of the fertilized ovum generally takes place. The upper portion of the uterus opens into two *fallopian tubes,* or *oviducts,* each about 4 inches long. The fallopian tubes are each directed toward an *ovary.* They serve as a passageway for the ovum in its week-long voyage toward the uterus. In most cases, conception takes place in the upper third of the fallopian tubes.

The ovaries are analogous to the testes in the male. Their function is to produce the ovum, or egg. Usually, one ovary produces and releases just one egg each month. Approximately the size and shape of an unshelled almond, an ovary produces viable ova in the process known as *oogenesis.* The ovaries also produce the female sex hormones through the efforts of specific structures within the ovaries. These hormones play multiple roles in the development of female secondary sex characteristics, but their primary function is to prepare the endometrium of the uterus for possible implantation of a fertilized ovum. In the average healthy female, this preparation takes place about 13 times a year for a period of about 35 years. At menopause, the ovaries shrink considerably and stop nearly all hormonal production.

Menstrual cycle

Each month or so, the inner wall of the uterus prepares for a possible pregnancy. When a pregnancy does not occur (as is the case throughout most months of a woman's fertile years), this lining must be released and a new one prepared. The breakdown of this endometrial wall and the resultant discharge of blood and endometrial tissue is known as *menstruation* (or *menses*) (Figure 13-4). The cyclic timing of menstruation is governed by hormones released from two sources: the pituitary gland and the ovaries.

Girls generally have their first menstrual cycle, the onset of which is called *menarche,* sometime between 12 and 14 years of age. Body weight, nutrition, heredity, and overall health are factors related to menarche. Interestingly, after a girl first menstruates, she may be anovulatory for a year or longer before she releases a viable ovum during her cycle. She will then continue this cyclic activity until about age 45 to 55.

This text refers to a menstrual cycle that lasts 28 days. Be assured that few women display absolutely perfect 28-day cycles. Most women fluctuate by a few days to a week around this 28-day pattern, and some women vary extremely from this cycle.

Your knowledge about the menstrual cycle is critical for your understanding of pregnancy, contraception,

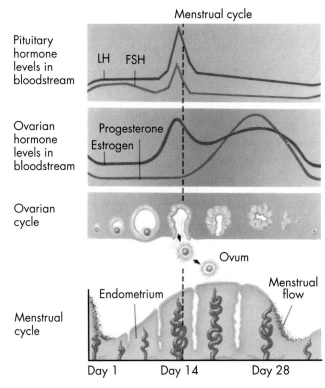

Figure 13-4   The menstrual cycle involves the development and release of an ovum, supported by hormones from the pituitary, and the buildup of the endometrium, supported by hormones from the ovary, for the purpose of establishing a pregnancy.

menopause, and issues related to the overall health and comfort of women (see the Star Box on p. 320 for a discussion of endometriosis). Although at first it may sound like a complicated process, each segment of the cycle can be studied separately for better understanding.

The menstrual cycle can be thought of as occurring in three segments or phases: the menstrual phase (lasting about 1 week), the proliferative phase (also lasting about 1 week), and the secretory phase (lasting about 2 weeks). Day 1 of this cycle starts with the first day of bleeding, or menstrual flow.

The *menstrual phase* signals the woman that a pregnancy has not taken place and that her uterine lining is being sloughed off. During a 5- to 7-day period, a woman will discharge about ¼ to ½ cup of blood and tissue. (Only about 1 ounce of the menstrual flow is actual blood.) The menstrual flow is heaviest during

orgasmic platform
Expanded outer third of the vagina that grips the penis during the plateau phase of the sexual response pattern.

Endometriosis

Endometriosis is a condition in which endometrial tissue that normally lines the uterus is found growing within the pelvic cavity. Because the tissue remains sensitive to circulating hormones, it is the source of pain and discomfort during the latter half of the menstrual cycle. Endometriosis is most commonly found in younger women and is frequently related to infertility.

In addition to discomfort before menstruation, the symptoms of endometriosis include low back pain, pain during intercourse, and a variety of lower digestive tract symptoms, such as diarrhea and constipation. As with the general pain and discomfort of endometriosis, these symptoms are also more noticeable during the latter weeks of the cycle.

Treatment of endometriosis largely depends on its extent. Drugs to suppress ovulation, including birth control pills, may be helpful in mild cases. For more severe cases, surgical removal of the tissue or a hysterectomy may be necessary. For some women, endometriosis is suppressed during pregnancy and does not return after pregnancy.

the first days of this phase. Since the muscular uterus must contract to accomplish this tissue removal, some women have uncomfortable cramping during menstruation. Most women, however, report more pain and discomfort during the few days before the first day of bleeding. (See the discussion of premenstrual syndrome [PMS] at right.)

Modern methods of absorbing menstrual flow include the use of internal tampons and external pads. Caution must be exercised by the users of tampons to prevent the possibility of toxic shock syndrome (TSS) (see Chapter 12). Since menstrual flow is a positive sign of good health, women are encouraged to be normally active during menstruation.

The *proliferative phase* of the menstrual cycle starts about the time menstruation stops. Lasting about 1 week, this phase is first influenced by the release of FSH from the pituitary gland. FSH circulates in the bloodstream and directs the ovaries to start the process of maturing approximately 20 primary ovarian *follicles.* Thousands of primary egg follicles are present in each ovary at birth. These follicles resemble shells that house immature ova. As these follicles ripen under FSH influence, they release the hormone estrogen. Estrogen's primary function is to direct the endometrium to start the development of a thick, highly vascular wall. As the estrogen levels increase, the pituitary gland's secretion of FSH is reduced. Now the pituitary gland prepares for the surge of the

luteinizing hormone (LH) required to accomplish ovulation.[6]

In the days immediately preceding ovulation, one of the primary follicles (called the *graafian follicle*) matures fully. The other primary follicles degenerate and are absorbed by the body. The graafian follicle moves toward the surface of the ovary. When LH is released in massive quantities on about day 14, the graafian follicle bursts to release the fully mature ovum. The release of the ovum is ovulation. Regardless of the overall length of a woman's cycle, ovulation occurs 14 days before her first day of menstrual flow.

The ovum is quickly captured by the fingerlike projections (*fimbriae*) of the fallopian tubes. In the upper third of the fallopian tubes, the ovum is capable of being fertilized in a 24- to 36-hour period. If the ovum is not fertilized by a sperm cell, it will begin to degenerate and eventually be absorbed by the body.

After ovulation, the *secretory phase* of the menstrual cycle starts when the remnants of the graafian follicle restructure themselves into a corpus luteum. The corpus luteum remains inside the ovary, secreting estrogen and a fourth hormone called *progesterone.* Progesterone, which literally means "for pregnancy," continues to direct the endometrial buildup. If pregnancy occurs, the corpus luteum monitors progesterone and estrogen levels throughout the pregnancy. If pregnancy does not occur, high levels of progesterone signal the pituitary to stop the release of LH and the corpus luteum starts to degenerate on about day 24. When estrogen and progesterone levels diminish significantly by day 28, the endometrium is discharged from the uterus and out the vagina. The secretory phase ends, and the menstrual phase begins. The cycle is complete.

PMS. PMS is characterized by psychological symptoms, such as depression, lethargy, irritability, and aggressiveness, or somatic symptoms, such as headache, backache, asthma, acne, and epilepsy, that recur in the same phase of each menstrual cycle, followed by a symptom-free phase in each cycle. Some of the more frequently reported symptoms of PMS include tension, tender breasts, fainting, fatigue, abdominal cramps, and weight gain.

The cause of PMS appears to be hormonal. Perhaps a woman's body is insensitive to a normal level of progesterone, or her ovaries fail to produce a normal amount of progesterone. These reasons seem plausible because PMS types of symptoms do not occur during pregnancy, during which natural progesterone levels are very high, and because women with PMS seem to feel much better after receiving high doses of natural progesterone in suppository form. When using oral contraceptives that supply synthetic progesterone at normal levels, many women report relief from some symptoms of PMS. However, the effectiveness of the most frequently used form of treatment, progesterone suppositories, is now being questioned.

Until the effectiveness of progesterone has been fully researched, it is unlikely that the medical community will deal with PMS through any approach other than a relatively conservative treatment of symptoms through the use of *analgesic drugs* (including *prostaglandin inhibitors*), diuretic drugs, dietary modifications (including restriction of caffeine and salt), vitamin B_6 therapy, exercise, and stress-reduction exercises. The exact nature of PMS has been further complicated by the classification of severe PMS as a mental disturbance by some segments of the American Psychiatric Association.

Fibrocystic breast condition. In some women, particularly those who have never been pregnant, stimulation of the breast tissues by estrogen and progesterone during the menstrual cycle results in an unusually high degree of secretory activity by the cells lining the ducts. The fluid released by the secretory lining finds its way into the fibrous connective tissue areas in the lower half of the breast, where in pocketlike cysts the fluid presses against neighboring tissues. Excessive secretory activity produces in many women a fibrocystic breast condition characterized by swollen, firm or hardened, tender breast tissue before menstruation.

Women who experience a more extensive fibrocystic condition can be treated with drugs that have a "calming" effect on progesterone production. In addition, occasional draining of the fluid-filled cysts can bring relief.

Menopause

For the vast majority of women in their late forties through their mid-fifties, a gradual decline in reproductive system function, called *menopause,* occurs. Menopause is a normal physiological process, not a disease process. It can, however, become a health concern for some middle-aged women who have unpleasant side effects resulting from this natural stoppage of ovum production and menstruation.

As ovarian function and hormone production diminish, a period of adjustment must be made by the hypothalamus, ovaries, uterus, and other estrogen-sensitive tissues. The extent of menopause as a health problem is determined by the degree to which **hot flashes,** vaginal wall dryness, depression and melancholy, breast changes, and the uncertainty of fertility are seen as problems.

In comparison with past generations, today's mid-life women are much less likely to find menopause to be a negative experience. The end of fertility, com-bined with children leaving the home, makes the middle years a period of personal rediscovery for many women.

For women who are troubled by the changes brought about by menopause, physicians may prescribe **estrogen replacement therapy** (ERT). This can relieve many symptoms and offer benefits to help reduce the incidence of osteoporosis (see Chapters 5 and 11) and heart disease.

HUMAN SEXUAL RESPONSE PATTERN

Although history has many written and visual accounts of the human's ability to be sexually aroused, it was not until the pioneering work of Masters and Johnson[7] that the events associated with arousal were clinically documented. Five questions posed by these researchers gave direction to a series of studies involving the scientific evaluation of human sexual response:

Is There a Predictable Pattern Associated with the Sexual Responses of Males and Females?

The answer to the first question posed by the researchers was an emphatic yes. A predictable sexual response pattern was identified;[7] it consists of an

---

luteinizing hormone (LH) (loo ten eye zing)
A gonadotropic hormone of the female required for fullest development and release of ova; ovulating hormone.

ovulation
The release of a mature egg from the ovary.

corpus luteum (kore pus loo **tee** um)
Cellular remnant of the graafian follicle after the release of an ovum.

hot flashes
Temporary feelings of warmth experienced by women during and after menopause, caused by blood vessel dilation.

estrogen replacement therapy
Medically administered estrogen to replace estrogen lost as the result of menopause.

initial **excitement stage,** a **plateau stage,** an **orgasmic stage,** and a **resolution stage.** Each stage involves predictable changes in the structural characteristics and physiological function of reproductive and nonreproductive organs in both the male and female. These changes are shown in the Star Box on pp. 323-324.

Is the Sexual Response Pattern Stimuli-Specific?

The research of Masters and Johnson[7] clearly established a no answer to the second question concerning stimuli specificity. Their findings demonstrated that numerous senses can supply the stimuli necessary for initiating the sexual response pattern. Although touching activities might initiate arousal in most people and maximize it for the vast majority of people, in both males and females, sight, smell, sound, and *vicariously formed stimuli* can also stimulate the same sexual arousal patterns.

What Differences Occur in the Sexual Response Pattern?

Differences between males and females

In response to the third question, several differences are observable when comparing the sexual response patterns of males and females:

- With the exception of some later adolescent males, the vast majority of males are not multiorgasmic. The **refractory phase** of the resolution stage prevents most males from experiencing more than one orgasm in a short time period, even though sufficient stimulation is available.
- Females possess a **multiorgasmic capacity.** Masters and Johnson[7] found that as many as 10% to 30% of all female adults routinely experience multiple orgasms.
- Although they possess multiorgasmic potential, some 10% of all female adults are *anorgasmic*— that is, they never experience an orgasm.[7] For many anorgasmic females, orgasms can be experienced when masturbation, rather than **coitus,** provides the stimulation.
- When measured during coitus, males reach orgasm far more quickly than do females. However, when masturbation is the source of stimulation, females reach orgasm as quickly as do males.[7]

More important than any of the differences pointed out is the finding that the sexual response patterns of males and females are far more alike than they are different. Not only do males and females experience the four basic stages of the response pattern, but they also have similar responses in specific areas, including the **erection** and *tumescence* of sexual structures; the appearance of a **sex flush;** the increase in cardiac output, blood pressure, and respiratory rate; and the occurrence of *rhythmic pelvic thrusting.*[7]

Differences among subjects within a same-gender group

When a group of subjects of the same gender was studied in an attempt to answer questions about similarities and differences in the sexual response pattern, Masters and Johnson noted considerable variation. Even when variables such as age, race, education, and general health were held constant, the extent and duration of virtually every stage of the response pattern varied.

Differences within the same individual

For a given person the nature of the sexual response pattern does not remain constant, even when observed over a relatively short period. A variety of internal and external factors can alter this pattern. The aging process, changes in general health status, levels of stress, altered environmental settings, use of alcohol and other drugs, and behavioral changes in a sexual partner can cause one's own sexual response pattern to change from one sexual experience to another.[3] Sexual performance difficulties and therapies are discussed in the Star Box on p. 326.

What Are the Basic Physiological Mechanisms Underlying the Sexual Response Pattern?

The basic mechanisms in the fourth question posed by Masters and Johnson are now well recognized. One factor, *vasocongestion,* or the retention of blood or fluid within a particular tissue, is critically important in the development of physiological changes that promote the sexual response pattern.[7] The presence of erectile tissue underlies the changes that can be noted in the penis, breasts, and scrotum of the male and the clitoris, breasts, and labia minora of the female.

A second mechanism now recognized as necessary for the development of the sexual response pattern is that of *myotonia,* or the buildup of *neuromuscular tonus* within a variety of body structures.[7] At the end of the plateau stage of the response pattern, a sudden release of the accumulated neuromuscular tension gives rise to the rhythmic muscular contractions and pleasurable muscular spasms that constitute orgasm, as well as ejaculation in the male.

Sexual Response Pattern

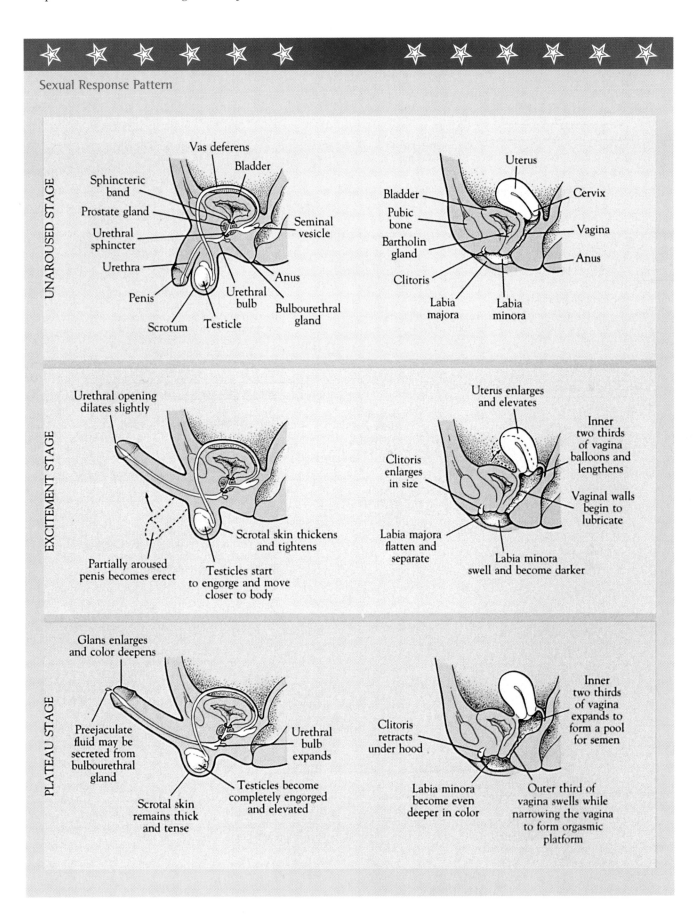

Sexual Response Pattern—cont'd

ORGASMIC STAGE

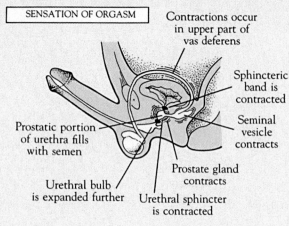

SENSATION OF ORGASM

Contractions occur in upper part of vas deferens

Sphincteric band is contracted

Seminal vesicle contracts

Prostatic portion of urethra fills with semen

Prostate gland contracts

Urethral bulb is expanded further

Urethral sphincter is contracted

Uterine contractions occur

Clitoris remains under hood

Contractions occur in anal sphincter

Contractions in outer third of the vagina occur rhythmically 3 to 15 times; the first of these contractions are spread at 0.8-second intervals; latter contractions are weaker and occur more slowly

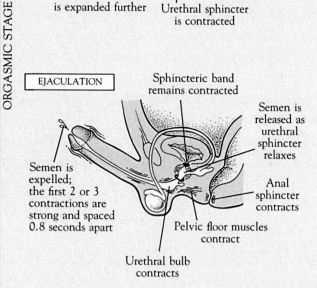

EJACULATION

Sphincteric band remains contracted

Semen is released as urethral sphincter relaxes

Semen is expelled; the first 2 or 3 contractions are strong and spaced 0.8 seconds apart

Anal sphincter contracts

Pelvic floor muscles contract

Urethral bulb contracts

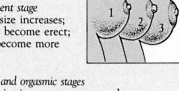

BREAST CHANGES

1 *Unaroused stage*

2 *Excitement stage* Breast size increases; nipples become erect; veins become more visible

3 *Plateau and orgasmic stages* Breast size increases more; areola increases in size (making nipples appear less erect); skin color may become flushed from vasocongestion

RESOLUTION STAGE

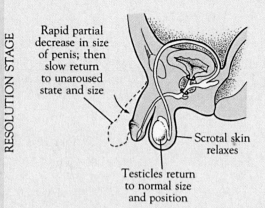

Rapid partial decrease in size of penis; then slow return to unaroused state and size

Scrotal skin relaxes

Testicles return to normal size and position

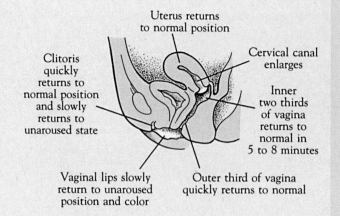

Uterus returns to normal position

Cervical canal enlarges

Clitoris quickly returns to normal position and slowly returns to unaroused state

Inner two thirds of vagina returns to normal in 5 to 8 minutes

Vaginal lips slowly return to unaroused position and color

Outer third of vagina quickly returns to normal

What Role Is Played by Specific Organs and Organ Systems within the Sexual Response Pattern?

The fifth question posed by Masters and Johnson, which concerns the role played by specific organs and organ systems during each stage of the response pattern, can be readily answered by referring to the material presented in the preceding Star Box. As you study this box, remember that direct stimulation of the penis and either direct or indirect stimulation of the clitoris are the principal avenues toward orgasm. Also, intercourse represents only one activity that can lead to orgasmic pleasure.[4]

PATTERNS OF SEXUAL BEHAVIOR

Although sex researchers may see sexual behavior in terms of the human sexual response pattern just described, most people are more interested in the observable dimensions of sexual behavior. Complete the Personal Assessment on p. 327 to determine whether your own attitudes toward sexuality are traditional or nontraditional.

Celibacy

Celibacy can be defined as the self-imposed avoidance of sexual intimacy. Celibacy is synonymous with sexual abstinence. There are many reasons people could choose not to have a sexually intimate relationship. For some, celibacy is part of a religious doctrine. Others might be afraid of sexually transmitted diseases. For most, however, celibacy is preferred simply because it seems appropriate for them. Celibate people can certainly have deep, intimate relationships with other people—just not sexual relationships. Celibacy may be short-term or last a lifetime, and no identified physical or psychological complications appear to result from a celibate lifestyle.

Masturbation

Throughout recorded history, **masturbation** has been a primary method of achieving sexual pleasure. Through masturbation, people can explore their sexual response patterns. Traditionally, some societies and religious groups have condemned this behavior based on the belief that intercourse is the only "right" sexual behavior. With sufficient lubrication, masturbation cannot do physical harm. Today masturbation is considered by most sex therapists and researchers to be a normal source of self-pleasure.

Fantasy and Erotic Dreams

The brain is the most sensual organ in the body. In fact, many sexuality experts classify **sexual fantasies** and **erotic dreams** as forms of sexual behavior. Particularly for people whose verbal ability is highly developed, the ability to create imaginary scenes enriches other forms of sexual behavior.

excitement stage
Initial arousal stage of the sexual response pattern.

plateau stage
Second stage of the sexual response pattern; a leveling off of arousal immediately before orgasm.

orgasmic stage
Third stage of the sexual response pattern; the stage during which neuromuscular tension is released.

resolution stage
Fourth stage of the sexual response pattern; the return of the body to a preexcitement state.

refractory phase
That portion of the male's resolution stage during which sexual arousal cannot occur.

multiorgasmic capacity
Potential to have several orgasms within a single period of sexual arousal.

coitus (co ih tus)
Penile-vaginal intercourse.

erection
The engorgement of erectile tissue with blood; characteristic of the penis, clitoris, nipples, labia minora, and scrotum.

sex flush
The reddish skin response that results from increasing sexual arousal.

masturbation
Self-stimulation of the genitals.

sexual fantasies
Fantasies with sexual themes; sexual daydreams or imaginary events.

erotic dreams
Dreams whose content elicits a sexual response.

Sexual Performance Difficulties and Therapies

For all of the predictability of the human sexual response pattern, many people find that at some point in their lives, they are no longer capable of responding sexually. The inability of a person to perform adequately is identified as a sexual difficulty or dysfunction. Sexual difficul-

ties can have a negative influence on a person's sense of sexual satisfaction and on a partner's satisfaction. Fortunately, most sexual difficulties can be resolved through strategies that use individual, couple, or group counseling. Most sexual performance difficulties stem from psychogenic factors.

Difficulty	Possible Causes	Therapeutic Approaches
Women		
Orgasmic Difficulties Inability to have orgasm	Anxiety, fear, guilt, anger, poor self-concept; lack of knowledge about female responsiveness; inadequate sexual arousal; interpersonal problems with partner	Counseling to improve a couple's communication; educating a woman and her partner about female responsiveness; teaching a woman how to experience orgasm through masturbation
Vaginismus Painful, involuntary contractions of the vaginal muscles	Previous traumatic experiences with intercourse (rape, incest, uncaring partners); fear of pregnancy; religious prohibitions; anxiety about vaginal penetration of any kind (including tampons)	Counseling to alleviate psychogenic causes; gradual dilation of the vagina with woman's fingers or dilators; systematic desensitization exercises; relaxation training
Dyspareunia Painful intercourse	Insufficient sexual arousal; communication problems with partner; infections, inflammations; structural abnormalities; insufficient lubrication	Individual and couple counseling with a focus on relaxation and communication; medical strategies to reduce infections and structural abnormalities
Men		
Erectile Dysfunction Inability to achieve an erection (impotence)	Chronic diseases (including diabetes, vascular problems, and chemical dependencies); trauma; numerous psychogenic factors (including anxiety, guilt, fear, poor self-concept)	Drug therapy (Viagra), medical intervention (including possible vascular surgery or the use of penile implants), couple counseling using sensate focusing, pleasuring, and relaxation strategies
Rapid Ejaculation Ejaculating too quickly after penile penetration; premature ejaculation	Predominately psychogenic in origin; a man's need to prove his sexual prowess; anxiety associated with previous sexual experiences	Counseling to free the man from the anxiety associated with rapid ejaculation; altering coital position, masturbation before intimacy; use of the squeeze technique as orgasm approaches
Dyspareunia Painful intercourse	Primarily physical in origin; inability of the penile foreskin to retract fully; urogenital tract infections; scar tissue in seminal passageways; insufficient lubrication	Medical care to reduce infection or repair damaged or abnormal tissue; additional lubrication

PERSONAL ASSESSMENT

Sexual Attitudes: A Matter of Feelings

Respond to each of the following statements by selecting a numbered response (1-5) that most accurately reflects your feelings. Circle the number of your selection. At the end of the questionnaire, total these numbers for use in interpreting your responses.

1   Agree strongly
2   Agree moderately
3   Uncertain
4   Disagree moderately
5   Disagree strongly

Men and women have greater differences than they have similarities.	1	2	3	4	5
Homosexuality and bisexuality are immoral and unnatural.	1	2	3	4	5
Our society is too sexually oriented.	1	2	3	4	5
Pornography encourages sexual promiscuity.	1	2	3	4	5
Children know far too much about sex.	1	2	3	4	5
Education about sexuality is solely the responsibility of the family.	1	2	3	4	5
Dating begins far too early in our society.	1	2	3	4	5
Sexual intimacy before marriage leads to emotional stress and damage to one's reputation.	1	2	3	4	5
Sexual availability is far too frequently the reason that people marry.	1	2	3	4	5
Reproduction is the most important reason for sexual intimacy during marriage.	1	2	3	4	5
Modern families are too small.	1	2	3	4	5
Family planning clinics should not receive public funds.	1	2	3	4	5
Contraception is the woman's responsibility.	1	2	3	4	5
Abortion is the murder of an innocent child.	1	2	3	4	5
Marriage has been weakened by the changing role of women in society.	1	2	3	4	5
Divorce is an unacceptable means of resolving marital difficulties.	1	2	3	4	5
Extramarital sexual intimacy will destroy a marriage.	1	2	3	4	5
Sexual abuse of a child does not generally occur unless the child encourages the adult.	1	2	3	4	5
Provocative behavior by the woman is a factor in almost every case of rape.	1	2	3	4	5
Reproduction is not a right but a privilege.	1	2	3	4	5

YOUR TOTAL POINTS _____

Interpretation

20-34 points	A very traditional attitude toward sexuality
35-54 points	A moderately traditional attitude toward sexuality
55-65 points	A rather ambivalent attitude toward sexuality
66-85 points	A moderately nontraditional attitude toward sexuality
86-100 points	A very nontraditional attitude toward sexuality

To Carry This Further . . .

Were you surprised at your results? Compare your results with those of a roommate or close friend. How do you think your parents would score on this assessment?

Sexual fantasies are generally found in association with some second type of sexual behavior. When occurring before intercourse or masturbation, fantasies prepare a person for the behavior that will follow. As an example, fantasies experienced while reading a book may focus your attention on sexual activity that will occur later in the day.

When fantasies occur in conjunction with another form of sexual behavior, the second behavior may be greatly enhanced by the supportive fantasy. Both women and men fantasize during foreplay and intercourse. Masturbation and fantasizing are inseparable activities.

Erotic dreams occur during sleep in both men and women. The association between these dreams and ejaculation resulting in a nocturnal emission (wet dream) is readily recognized in males. In females, erotic dreams can lead not only to vaginal lubrication but to orgasm as well.

Shared Touching

Virtually the entire body can be an erogenous zone when sensual contact between partners is involved. A soft, light touch, a slight application of pressure, the brushing back of a partner's hair, and gentle massage are all forms of communication that heighten sexual arousal.

Genital Contact

Two important uses can be identified for the practice of stimulating a partner's genitals. The first is that of being the tactile component of **foreplay.** Genital contact, in the form of holding, rubbing, stroking, or caressing, heightens arousal to a level that allows for progression into intercourse.

The second role of genital contact is that of *mutual masturbation to orgasm.* Stimulation of the genitals so that both partners have orgasm is a form of sexual behavior practiced by many people, as well as couples during the late stage of a pregnancy. For couples not desiring pregnancy, the risk of conception is virtually eliminated when this becomes the form of sexual intimacy practiced.

As is the case of other aspects of intimacy, genital stimulation is best enhanced when partners can talk about their needs, expectations, and reservations. Practice and communication can shape this form of contact into a pleasure-giving approach to sexual intimacy.

Oral-Genital Stimulation

Oral-genital stimulation brings together two of the body's most erogenous areas: the genitalia and the mouth. Couples who engage in oral sex consistently report that this form of intimacy is highly satisfactory. Some people have experimented with oral sex and found it unacceptable, and some have never experienced this form of sexual intimacy. Some couples prefer not to participate in oral sex because they consider it immoral (according to religious doctrine), illegal (which it is in some states), or unhygienic (because of a partner's unclean genitals). Some couples may refrain because of the mistaken belief that oral sex is a homosexual practice. Regardless of the reason, a person who does not consider oral sex to be pleasurable should not be coerced into this behavior.

Because oral-genital stimulation can involve an exchange of body fluids, the risk of disease transmission is real. Small tears of mouth or genital tissue may allow transmission of disease-causing pathogens. Only couples who are absolutely certain that they are free from all sexually transmitted diseases (including HIV infection) can practice unprotected oral sex. Couples in doubt should refrain from oral-genital sex or carefully use a condom (on the male) or a latex square to cover the female's vulval area. Increasingly, latex squares (dental dams) can be obtained from drug stores or pharmacies. (Dentists may also provide you with dental dams, or you can make your own latex square by cutting a condom into an appropriate shape.)

Three basic forms of oral-genital stimulation are practiced by both heterosexual and homosexual couples.[8] **Fellatio,** in which the penis is sucked, licked, or kissed by the partner, is the most common of the three. **Cunnilingus,** in which the vulva of the female is kissed, licked, or penetrated by the partner's tongue, is only slightly less frequently practiced.

Mutual oral-genital stimulation, the third form of oral-genital stimulation, combines both fellatio and cunnilingus. When practiced by a heterosexual couple, the female partner performs fellatio on her partner while her male partner performs cunnilingus on her. Homosexual couples can practice mutual fellatio or cunnilingus.

Intercourse

Sexual intercourse (coitus) refers to the act of inserting the penis into the vagina. Intercourse is the sexual behavior that is most directly associated with **procreation.** For some, intercourse is the only natural and appropriate form of sexual intimacy.

The incidence and frequency of sexual intercourse is a much-studied topic. Information concerning the percentages of people who have engaged in intercourse is readily available in textbooks used in sexuality courses. Data concerning sexual intercourse among college students may be changing somewhat because of concerns about HIV infection and other STDs, but a reasonable estimate of the percentage of college students reporting sexual intercourse is between 65% and 80%.

These percentages reflect two important concepts about the sexual activity of college students. The first is that a large majority of college students is having intercourse. The second concept is that a sizeable percentage (20% to 35%) of students is choosing to refrain from intercourse. Indeed, the belief that "everyone is doing it" may be a bit shortsighted. From a public health standpoint, we believe it is important to provide accurate health information to protect those who choose to have intercourse and to actively support a person's right to choose not to have intercourse.

Couples need to share their expectations concerning techniques and the desired frequency of intercourse. Even the "performance" factors, such as depth of penetration, nature of body movements, tempo of activity, and timing of orgasm are of increasing importance to many couples. Issues concerning sexually transmitted diseases (including HIV infection) are also critically important for couples who are contemplating intercourse. These factors also need to be explored through open communication.

There are a variety of books (including textbooks) that provide written and visually explicit information on intercourse positions. Four basic positions for intercourse—*male above, female above, side by side,* and *rear entry*—each offer relative advantages and disadvantages.

SEXUALITY AND AGING

Students are often curious about how aging affects sexuality. This is understandable because we live in a society that idolizes youth and demands performance. Many younger people become anxious about growing older because of what they think will happen to their ability to express their sexuality. Interestingly, young adults are willing to accept other physical changes of aging (such as the slowing down of basal metabolism, reduced lung capacity, and even wrinkles) but not those changes related to sexuality.

Most of the research in this area suggests that older people are quite capable of performing sexually. As with other aspects of aging, certain anatomical and physiological changes will be evident, but these changes do not necessarily reduce the ability to enjoy sexual activity.[3] Most experts in sexuality report that many older people remain interested in sexual activity. Furthermore, those who are exposed to regular sexual activity throughout a lifetime report being most satisfied with their sex lives as older adults.

As people age, the likelihood of alterations in the male and female sexual response cycles increases. In the postmenopausal woman, vaginal lubrication commonly begins more slowly, and the amount of lubrication usually diminishes. However, clitoral sensitivity and nipple erection remain the same as in earlier years. The female capacity for multiple orgasms remains the same, although the number of contractions that occur at orgasm typically is reduced.

In the older man, physical changes are also evident. This is thought to be caused by the decrease in the production of testosterone between the ages of 20 and 60 years. After age 60 or so, testosterone levels remain relatively steady. Thus many men, despite a decrease in sperm production, remain fertile into their eighties. Older men typically take longer to achieve an erection (however, they are able to maintain their erection longer before ejaculation), have fewer muscular contractions at orgasm, and ejaculate less forcefully than they once did. The volume of seminal fluid ejaculated is typically less than in earlier years, and its consistency is somewhat thinner. The resolution phase is usually longer in older men. In spite of these gradual changes, some elderly men engage in sexual intercourse with the same frequency as do much younger men.

THE DATING PROCESS

A half-century ago, the events involved in a dating relationship were somewhat predictable. People met each other through their daily activities or groups of friends, and a formal "date request" was made. Ninety-nine times out of a hundred, the requestor was male and the invitee was female. After a period of formal and informal dates, a commitment to steady dating was made or the couple decided to "date around." If the relationship progressed, further commitments were made (for example, class rings, letter

foreplay
Activities, often involving touching and caressing, that prepare individuals for sexual intercourse.

fellatio (feh **lay** she oh)
Oral stimulation of the penis.

cunnilingus (cun uh **ling** gus)
Oral stimulation of the vulva or clitoris.

procreation
Reproduction.

jackets, or other jewelry items were exchanged). After months or years of a committed relationship, the couple decided to get married. The man invariably "asked for the woman's hand" (after first receiving permission from her parents), and plans for a wedding ceremony were made.

Does this form of dating and mate selection exist as we approach the year 2000? For some couples, yes. The traditional way of dating and selecting a marriage partner works well for them. However, many young and midlife adults prefer a more flexible, less predictable format for dating and finding a person they might choose to marry. For example, more than ever, women are playing a more assertive role when it comes to initiating and establishing the ground rules for a relationship. Interestingly, a large number of our students do not even like to use the word "dating" because of its connotation to a formalized pattern of behavior used by their parents and grandparents.

What do you think? Have you recognized this more flexible dating format? Has this less traditional pattern been beneficial to couples as they make critical decisions that will influence the rest of their lives?

LOVE

Love may be one of the most elusive yet widely recognized concepts that describe some level of emotional attachment to another. Haas and Haas[3] describe five forms of love, including erotic, friendship, devotional, parental, and altruistic love. Other behavioral scientists[4] have focused primarily on two types of love most closely associated with dating and mate selection: *passionate love* and *companionate love*.

Passionate love, also described as romantic love or **infatuation,** is a "state of extreme absorption in another. It is characterized by intense feelings of tenderness, elation, anxiety, sexual desire, and ecstasy."[4] Often appearing early in a relationship, passionate love typically does not last very long. Passionate love is driven by the excitement of being closely involved with a person whose character is not fully known.

If a relationship progresses, passionate love is gradually replaced by companionate love. This type of love is "a less intense emotion than passionate love. It is characterized by friendly affection and a deep attachment that is based on extensive familiarity with the loved one."[4] This love is enduring and capable of sustaining long-term, mutual growth. Central to companionate love are feelings of empathy for, support of, and tolerance of the partner. Complete the Personal Assessment on p. 331 to determine whether you and your partner are truly compatible.

RECOGNIZING UNHEALTHY RELATIONSHIPS

Clearly, not all dating relationships will continue. Many couples recognize when a partnership is nearing an end, and they reach a mutual decision to break off the relationship. This is a traditional, natural way for people to learn about their interactions with others. They simply decide to split up and move on.

However, sometimes people do not recognize or heed warning signs of an unstable relationship and stay involved long after the risks outweigh the benefits. These warning signs include *abusive behavior,* including both emotional and physical abuse (see Chapter 16). Another red flag is *excessive jealousy* about your interactions with others. Sometimes excessive jealousy evolves into *controlling behavior,* in which your partner attempts to manage your daily activities. By definition, controlling behavior limits your creativity and freedom.

Other warning signs are *dishonesty, irresponsibility, lack of patience,* and any kind of *drug abuse.* Understandably, we do not want to see these qualities in those we have initially judged to be "nice people," even though these unappealing characteristics may be obvious to others. If you suspect that one or more of these problems may be undermining your relationship, talk about your concerns with one or two trusted friends, and seek the advice of a professional counselor at your college or university. Try to realize that ending your relationship might be the best thing you could do for yourself.

FRIENDSHIP

One of the exciting aspects of college life is that you will probably meet many new people. Some of these people will become your best friends. Because of your common experiences, it is likely that you will keep in contact with a few of these friends for a lifetime. Close attachments to other people can have an important influence on all of the dimensions of your health.

What is it that draws friends together? With the exception of physical intimacy, many of the same growth experiences seen in dating and mate selection are also seen in the development of friendships. Think about how you and your best friend developed the relationship you now have. You probably became friends when you shared similar interests and experiences. Your friendship progressed (and even faltered at times) through personal gains or losses. In all likelihood, you cared about each other and learned to

PERSONAL ASSESSMENT

How Compatible Are You?

This quiz will help test how compatible you and your partner's personalities are. You should each rate the truth of these 20 statements based on the following scale. Circle the number that reflects your feelings. Total your scores and check the interpretation following the quiz.

1 Never true
2 Sometimes true
3 Frequently true
4 Always true

	1	2	3	4
We can communicate our innermost thoughts effectively.	1	2	3	4
We trust each other.	1	2	3	4
We agree on whose needs come first.	1	2	3	4
We have realistic expectations of each other and of ourselves.	1	2	3	4
Individual growth is important within our relationship.	1	2	3	4
We will go on as a couple even if our partner doesn't change.	1	2	3	4
Our personal problems are discussed with each other first.	1	2	3	4
We both do our best to compromise.	1	2	3	4
We usually fight fairly.	1	2	3	4
We try not to be rigid or unyielding.	1	2	3	4
We keep any needs to be "perfect" in proper perspective.	1	2	3	4
We can balance desires to be sociable and the need to be alone.	1	2	3	4
We both make friends and keep them.	1	2	3	4
Neither of us stays down or up for long periods.	1	2	3	4
We can tolerate the other's mood without being affected by it.	1	2	3	4
We can deal with disappointment and disillusionment.	1	2	3	4
Both of us can tolerate failure.	1	2	3	4
We can both express anger appropriately.	1	2	3	4
We are both assertive when necessary.	1	2	3	4
We agree on how our personal surroundings are kept.	1	2	3	4

YOUR TOTAL POINTS _____

Interpretation

20-35 points   You and your partner seem quite incompatible. Professional help may open your lines of communication.

36-55 points   You probably need more awareness and compromise.

56-70 points   You are highly compatible. However, be aware of the areas where you can improve.

71-80 points   Your relationship is very fulfilling.

To Carry This Further . . .

Ask your partner to take this test too. You may have a one-sided view of a "perfect" relationship. Even if you scored high on this assessment, be aware of areas where you can still improve.

---

share your deepest beliefs and feelings. Lastly, you cemented your friendship by transferring your beliefs into behavior.

Throughout development of a deep friendship, the qualities of trust, tolerance, empathy, and support must be demonstrated. Otherwise the friendship can fall apart. You may have noticed that the qualities seen in a friendship are very similar to the qualities noted in the description of companionate love. In both cases, people develop deep attachments through extensive familiarity and understanding.

infatuation
A relatively temporary, intensely romantic attraction to another person.

INTIMACY

When most people hear the word **intimacy,** they immediately think about physical intimacy. They think about shared touching, kissing, and even intercourse. However, sexuality experts and family therapists prefer to view intimacy more broadly, as any close, mutual, verbal or nonverbal behavior within a relationship. In this sense, intimate behavior can range from sharing deep feelings and experiences with a partner to sharing profound physical pleasures with a partner.

Intimacy is present in both love and friendship. You have likely shared intimate feelings with your closest friends, as well as with those you love. Intimacy helps us feel connected to others and allows us to feel the full measure of our own self-worth.

MARRIAGE

Just as there is no single best way for two people to move through dating and mate selection, marriage is an equally variable undertaking. In marriage, two people join their lives in a way that affirms each as an individual and both as a legal pair. They are able to resolve conflict constructively (see the Health Action Guide at right). However, for a large percentage of couples, the demands of marriage are too rigorous, confining, and demanding. They will find resolution for their dissatisfaction through divorce or extramarital affairs. For most, though, marriage will be an experience that alternates periods of happiness, productivity, and admiration with periods of frustration, unhappiness, and disillusionment with the partner.

HEALTH Action Guide

Resolving Conflict

Here are some successful ways to manage conflict:

- Show mutual respect.
- Identify and resolve the real issue.
- Seek areas of agreement.
- Mutually participate in decision making.
- Be cooperative and specific.
- Focus on the present and future—not the past.
- Don't try to assign blame.
- Say what you are thinking and feeling.
- When talking, use sentences that begin with "I."
- Avoid using sentences that start with "You" or "Why."
- Set a time limit for discussing problems.
- Accept responsibility.
- Schedule time together.   ◄------

Each of you who marries will find the experience unique in every regard. The Star Box below presents some advice for improving marriage.

As we move through the 1990s, certain trends regarding marriage are evident. The most obvious of these is the age at first marriage. Today men are waiting longer than ever to marry. Now the average age at first marriage for men is 26 years.[9] In addition, these new

---

Improving Marriage

Few marital relationships are "perfect." All marriages are faced with occasional periods of strain or turmoil. Even marriages that do not exhibit major signs of distress can be improved, mostly through better communication. Marriage experts suggest that implementing some of these patterns can strengthen marriages:

- Problems that exist within the marriage should be brought into the open so that both partners are aware of the difficulties.
- Balance should exist between the needs and expectations of each partner. Decisions should be made jointly. Partners should support each other as best as they can. When a partner's goals cannot be actively supported, he or she should at least receive moral support and encouragement.

- Realistic expectations should be established. Partners should negotiate areas in which disagreement exists. They should work together to determine the manner in which resources should be shared.
- Participating in marriage counseling and marriage encounter groups can be helpful.

Beyond the patterns listed above, a sense of permanence helps sustain a marriage over the course of time. If the partners are convinced that their relationship can withstand difficult times, then they are more likely to take the time to make needed changes. Couples can develop a sense of permanence by implementing some of the patterns described above.

LEARNING *from* ALL CULTURES

Marriage Customs

The institution of marriage is found in many societies, although the rules, practices, and laws can be very different. In the United States and other Western nations, marriage is a reflection of the Judeo-Christian heritage. Monogamy is practiced, fidelity is emphasized, and the permanence of marriage is stressed.[13]

In primitive societies, marriage practices greatly vary. Some accepted forms are arranged marriages, bride abductions, and bride payments. Polygyny (having two or more wives) is common, although monogamy is also practiced, especially when economic conditions make it difficult for a man to have more than one wife.[13]

In nations in which the Islamic faith is practiced, polygyny is accepted. In countries such as India and China, parents choose marriage partners for their children or the unions are arranged. The practice of choosing one's own mate, however, is becoming more acceptable in those countries.[13]

In view of the high divorce rate in the United States, are arranged marriages any less successful than our own practices? How can men and women make wise choices in deciding on a marriage partner?

husbands are better educated than in the past and are more likely to be established in their careers. Women are also waiting longer to get married and tend to be more educated and career oriented. Recent statistics indicate that the average age at first marriage is 24 years.[9]

Marriage still appeals to most adults. Currently, 77% of adults age 18 and older are either married, widowed, or divorced.[9] Thus only about one fifth of today's adults have not married. Within the last decade, the percentage of adults who have decided not to marry has nearly doubled. Singlehood and other alternatives to marriage are discussed later in this chapter. See the Learning from All Cultures box above for a discussion of marriage customs in other cultures.

DIVORCE

Marriages, like many other kinds of interpersonal relationships, can end. Today, marriages—relationships begun with the intent of permanence "until death do us part"—end through divorce nearly as frequently as not ending.

Why should approximately half of marital relationships be so likely to end? Unfortunately, marriage experts cannot provide one clear answer to this question. Rather, they suggest that divorce is a reflection of unfulfilled expectations for marriage on the part of one or both partners, including the following:

* The belief that marriage will ease your need to deal with your own faults and that your failures can be shared by your partner

intimacy
Any close, mutual, verbal or nonverbal behavior within a relationship.

- The belief that marriage will change faults that you know exist in your partner
- The belief that the high level of romance of your dating and courtship period will be continued through marriage
- The belief that marriage can provide you with an arena for the development of your personal power, and that once married, you will not need to compromise with your partner
- The belief that your marital partner will be successful in meeting all of your needs

If these expectations seem to be ones you anticipate through marriage, then you may find that disappointments will abound. To varying degrees, marriage is a partnership that requires much cooperation and compromise. Marriage can be complicated. Because of the high expectations that many people hold for marriage, the termination of marriage can be an emotionally difficult process to undertake (see the Health Action Guide below).

Concern is frequently voiced over the well-being of children whose parents divorce. Different factors, however, influence the extent to which divorce affects children. Included among these factors are the gender and age of the children, custody arrangements, financial support, and the remarriage of one or both parents. For many children, adjustments must be made to accept their new status as a member of a blended family.

ALTERNATIVES TO MARRIAGE

Although the great majority of you have experienced or will experience marriage, alternatives to marriage certainly exist. This section briefly explores singlehood, cohabitation, and single parenthood.

Singlehood

An alternative to marriage for adults is *singlehood*. For many people, being single is a lifestyle that affords the potential for pursuing intimacy, if desired, and provides an uncluttered path for independence and self-directedness. Other people, however, are single because of divorce, separation, death, or the absence of an opportunity to establish a partnership. The U.S. Bureau of the Census indicates that 41% of women and 37% of men over the age of 18 are currently single.[9]

HEALTH
Action Guide

Coping With a Breakup

The end of a marriage or other long-term relationship is always a wrenching and painful experience. The following tips suggest both alternatives to breakup and ways to cope with it.

- *Talk first.* Try to deal effectively and directly with the conflicts. The old theory said that it was good for a couple to fight. However, anger can cause more anger and even lead to violence. Freely venting anger is as likely to damage a relationship as to improve it. Therefore cool off first, then discuss issues fully and freely.
- *Trial separation.* Sometimes only a few weeks apart can convince a couple that it is far better to work together than to go it totally alone. It is generally better to establish the rules of such a trial quite firmly. Will the individuals see others? What are the responsibilities if children are involved? There should also

be a time limit, perhaps a month or two, after which the partners reunite and discuss their situation again.
- *Obtain help.* The services of a *qualified* counselor, psychologist, or psychiatrist may help a couple resolve their problems. Notice the emphasis on the word *qualified.* Some people who have little training or competence represent themselves as counselors. For this reason a couple should insist on verifying the counselor's training and licensing.
- *Allow time for grief and healing.* When a relationship ends, people are often tempted to immediately become as socially and sexually active as possible. This can be a way to express anger and relieve pain. But it can also cause frustration and despair. A better solution for many is to acknowledge the grief the breakup has caused and allow time for healing. Up to a year of continuing one's life and solidifying friendships typically helps the rejected partner establish a new equilibrium.

Health on the Web
LEARNING ACTIVITIES

Activity 1

Our relationships with others are an essential aspect of our health. Relationships offer us the opportunity to fulfill our need to love and be loved. Type in the URL http://www.psychtests.com/rel_sat.html and complete the *Relationship Satisfaction Test.* This inventory is designed to evaluate various aspects of your interaction with another person. This relationship/love test is not based on value judgments about how a relationship is supposed to work. Complete the inventory and then click on the "submit" button to receive your on-line results.

Activity 2

The more we understand the biological and psychological factors that contribute to the complex expression of our sexuality, the better our health will be. Dr. Britton provides new questions on a weekly basis to test your understanding of a number of factors related to your sexuality. Visit the Sex Clinic website at http://www.sexclinic.com/main.html and select "Playroom-test your sex savvy." Then take this week's quiz. The Sex Clinic site is developed for educational purposes. It does not substitute for medical treatment or clinical care.

Activity 3

What qualities do you look for in a romantic partner? Honesty? Kindness? A great smile? Most of us have some idea of what characteristics are important to us. To learn more about what you're looking for in your perfect match, go to http://cgi.pathfinder.com/cgi-bin/thrive/cg/gdml2x/game/thrive/sexquiz1 to take the fun quiz *What Type of Mate Turns Your Head—and Turns You On?*

Many different living arrangements are seen among singles. Some single people live alone and choose not to share a household. Other arrangements for singles include cohabitation, periodic cohabitation, singlehood during the week and cohabitation on the weekends or during vacations, or the *platonic* sharing of a household with others. For young adults, large percentages of single men and women live with their parents (see Table 13-1).

Like habitation arrangements, the sexual intimacy patterns of singles are individually tailored. Some singles practice celibacy, others pursue heterosexual or homosexual intimate relationships in a **monogamous** pattern, and others may have multiple partners. As in all interpersonal relationships, including marriage, the levels of commitment are as variable as the people involved.

Cohabitation

Cohabitation, or the sharing of living quarters by unmarried people, represents yet another alternative to marriage. According to the U.S. Bureau of the Census, the number of unmarried, opposite-gender

Table 13-1 Percentage of Young Adults Living with Their Parents: 1970 and 1994[9]*				
	Age 18–24		Age 25–34	
	1970	1994	1970	1994
Male	54	60	10	16
Female	41	46	7	9
TOTAL	47	53	8	12

*Includes unmarried college students living in dormitories.

monogamous (mo **nog** a mus)
Paired relationship with one partner.

cohabitation
Sharing of a residence by two unrelated, unmarried people; living together.

couples living together doubled between 1980 and 1995, from 1.6 million couples to over 3.7 million couples.[9]

Although cohabitation may seem to imply a vision of sexual intimacy between male and female roommates, several forms of shared living arrangements can be viewed as cohabitation. For some couples, cohabitation is only a part-time arrangement for weekends, during summer vacation, or on a variable schedule. In addition, **platonic** cohabitation can exist when a couple shares living quarters but does so without establishing an intimate relationship. Close friends and people of retirement age might be included in a group called *cohabitants*.

The archetype of a cohabitation arrangement is the couple who has drifted into cohabitation as the result of a dating relationship in which sexual intimacy and occasional "overnighting" have already occurred. In the living arrangement that follows, both material possessions and emotional support are generally shared. A contractual relationship is only occasionally established. Monogamy will usually exist. Approximately half of cohabitation relationships will disband, and the people involved will depart with the feeling that they would cohabit again if it appears desirable. Finally, cohabitation is neither more nor less likely to lead to marriage than is a more traditional dating relationship. It is, in fact, only an alternative to marriage.

Single Parenthood

Unmarried young women becoming pregnant and then becoming single parents is a continuing reality in this country. A new and significantly different form of single parenthood is, however, also a reality in this country: the planned entry into a single parenthood by older, better educated people, the vast majority of whom are women.

In contrast to the teenaged girl who becomes a single parent through an unwed pregnancy, the more mature woman who desires single parenting has usually planned carefully for the experience. She has explored several important concerns, including questions regarding how she will become pregnant (with or without the knowledge of a male partner or through artificial insemination), the need for a father figure for the child, the effect of single parenting on her social life, and, of course, its effect on her career development. Once these questions have been resolved, no legal barriers stand in the way of her becoming a single parent.

A very large number of women and a growing number of men are actively participating in single parenthood in conjunction with a divorce settlement or separation agreement involving sole or joint custody of children. In 1995, single women headed up 7.6 million households with children under age 18. In contrast, single men headed up 1.4 million households in 1995 with children under age 18.[9]

A few single parents have been awarded children through adoption. The likelihood of a single person's receiving a child is small, but more people have been successful recently in single-parent adoptions.

SEXUAL ORIENTATION

Sexual orientation refers to the direction in which people focus their sexual interests. People can focus their attention on opposite-gender partners, same-gender partners, or partners of both genders.

Heterosexuality

Heterosexuality (or heterosexual orientation) refers to an attraction to opposite-gender partners. (*Heteros* is a Greek word that means "the other.") Throughout the world, this is the most common sexual orientation. For reasons related to species survival, heterosexuality has its most basic roots in the biological dimension of human sexuality. Beyond its biological roots, heterosexuality has significant cultural and religious support in virtually every country in the world. Most societies expect men to be attracted to women and women to be attracted to men. Worldwide, laws related to marriage, living arrangements, health benefits, child rearing, financial matters, sexual behavior, and inheritance generally support relationships that are heterosexual in nature.

Homosexuality

Homosexuality (or homosexual orientation) refers to an attraction to same-gender partners. The term *homosexuality* comes from the Greek word *homos*, meaning "same." The word *homosexuality* may be used with regard to males or females. Thus we use the terms *homosexual males* and *homosexual females*. Frequently the word *gay* is used to refer to homosexual orientation in both males and females. *Lesbianism* is also used to refer to the sexual attraction between females.

The distinctions among the three categories of sexual orientation are much less clear than their definitions might suggest. Most people probably fall somewhere along a continuum between exclusive heterosexuality and exclusive homosexuality. Kinsey in 1948 presented just such a continuum.[10]

Why does a given individual have a particular orientation? There is no simple answer to this question. (College human sexuality textbooks devote entire chapters to this topic.) In the mid-1990s, some research pointed to differences in the sizes of certain brain structures as a possible biological basis for homosexuality.[11] However, for sexual orientation in general, no one theory has emerged that fully explains this developmental process. Regardless of the cause, however, reversal to heterosexuality generally does not occur. Furthermore, most homosexuals report that no one event "triggered" their homosexuality. Many homosexuals also indicate that they knew their orientations were "different" from other children as far back as their prepuberty years.

The extent of homosexuality in our society is a debatable issue. Clearly, gathering valid information of this kind is difficult. The extent of homosexual orientation is probably much greater than many heterosexuals realize. Furthermore, many people refuse to reveal their homosexuality and thus prefer to remain "in the closet."

Although operational definitions of homosexuality may vary from researcher to researcher, Kinsey estimated that about 2% of American females and 4% of American males were exclusively homosexual.[10,12] More recent estimates place the overall combined figure of homosexuals at about 10% of the population.[4] Clearly the expression of same-gender attraction is not uncommon.

Bisexuality

People whose preference for sexual partners includes both genders are referred to as *bisexuals.* Bisexuals may fall into one of three groups: those who are (1) genuinely attracted to both genders, (2) homosexual but also feel the need to behave heterosexually, or (3) aroused physically by the same gender but attracted emotionally to the opposite gender. Some people participate in a bisexual lifestyle for extended periods, whereas others move quickly to a more exclusive orientation. Little research has been conducted on bisexuality, and thus the size of the bisexual population is not accurately known.

A particularly pressing reason for learning more about the bisexual lifestyle is its relationship to the transmission of HIV infection. Next to intravenous drug users, bisexuals hold the greatest potential for extending HIV infection into the heterosexual population. Since the prevalence of bisexuality is unknown, the consistent use of safer sex practices becomes more important than ever.

PARAPHILIAS

A **paraphilia** is a "preference for unusual sexual practices."[3] A paraphilia involves special erotic activities, some of which have the potential to harm nonconsenting individuals. In the interest of brevity the following lists a variety of paraphilias:

- Zoophilia: sexual excitement through contact with animals; also called *bestiality*
- Pedophilia: sexual contact with children
- Incest: marriage or sexual contact with a close relative
- Fetishism: an obsession with a body part or inanimate object as the primary focus of sexual excitement
- Transvestism: sexual excitement gained from cross-dressing, or wearing the clothes of another gender
- Exhibitionism: displaying one's genitals to an involuntary observer
- Voyeurism: observing unsuspecting people removing their clothes or engaging in sexual activity
- Masochism: obtaining sexual excitement from receiving pain
- Sadism: obtaining sexual excitement from causing pain to another person
- Sadomasochism: obtaining sexual excitement by both causing and receiving pain

platonic (pluh **ton** ick)
Close association between two people that does not include a sexual relationship.

paraphilia
A preference for unusual sexual practices.

Summary

- Biological and psychosocial factors contribute to the complex expression of our sexuality.
- The structural basis of sexuality begins as the male and female reproductive structures develop in the growing embryo and fetus. Structural sexuality changes as one moves through adolescence and later life.
- The psychosocial processes of gender identity, gender preference, and gender adoption form the basis for an initial adult gender identification.

- The male and female reproductive structures are external and internal. The complex functioning of these structures is controlled by hormones.
- The menstrual cycle's primary functions are to produce ova and to develop a supportive environment for the fetus in the uterus.
- The sexual response pattern consists of four stages: excitement, plateau, orgasm, and resolution.
- Many older people remain interested and active in sexual activities. Physiological changes may alter the way in which some older people perform sexually.
- Although most individuals marry at some time in their lives, alternatives to marriage exist, including singlehood, cohabitation, and single parenthood.
- Three sexual orientations are heterosexuality, homosexuality, and bisexuality.

Review Questions

1. Describe the following foundations of our biological sexuality: the genetic basis, the gonadal basis, and structural development.
2. Define and explain the following terms: gender identity, gender preference, gender adoption, initial adult gender identification, and transsexualism.
3. Identify the major components of the male and female reproductive systems. Trace the passageways for sperm and ova.
4. Explain the menstrual cycle. Identify and describe the four main hormones that control the menstrual cycle.
5. What similarities and differences exist between the sexual response patterns of males and females?
6. Approximately what percentage of today's college students report having had sexual intercourse?
7. Explain the differences between heterosexuality, homosexuality, and bisexuality. How common are each of these sexual orientations in our society?

Think About This . . .

- How would you summarize your feelings about the changes in your body that took place during puberty?
- To what extent do you think that knowledge about the menstrual cycle will be pertinent to you as you move through adulthood? (This question is for BOTH men and women.)
- Do you think a celibate lifestyle is possible or practical in the late 1990s? Why or why not?
- What are your estimates of the percentages of men and women at your college or university who have had sexual intercourse?
- In comparison with a decade ago, are heterosexuals generally more comfortable or less comfortable with homosexuals in our society? Support your answer with specific examples.

References

1. Thibodeau GA, Patton KT: *The human body in health and disease*, ed 2, St Louis, 1996, Mosby.
2. Hyde JS, DeLamater J: *Understanding human sexuality*, ed 6, New York, 1997, McGraw-Hill.
3. Haas K, Haas A: *Understanding sexuality*, ed 3, St Louis, 1993, Mosby.
4. Crooks R. Baur K: *Our sexuality*, ed 6, Pacific Grove, CA, 1995, Brooks/Cole.
5. Thibodeau GA: *Structure and function of the body*, ed 10, St Louis, 1996, Mosby.
6. Hatcher RA et al: *Contraceptive technology*, ed 16, New York, 1994, Irvington Publishers.
7. Masters W, Johnson V: *Human sexual response*, Boston, 1996, Little, Brown.
8. Rathus SA, Nevid JS, Fichner-Rathus L: *Human sexuality in the world of discovery*, ed 3, Needham Heights, MA, 1997, Allyn and Bacon.
9. U.S. Bureau of the Census: *Statistical abstract of the United States: 1996*, ed 116, Washington, DC, 1996, U.S. Government Printing Office.

10. Kinsey A, Pomeroy W, Martin C: *Sexual behavior in the human male*, Philadelphia, 1948, WB Saunders.
11. Allen LS, Gorski RA: Sexual orientation and the size of the anterior commissure in the human brain, *Proc Nat Acad Sci USA* 89(15):7199–7202, 1992.
12. Kinsey A et al: *Sexual behavior in the human female*, Philadelphia, 1953, WB Saunders.
13. Fletcher R: Mating, the family, and marriage: a sociological view. In Reynolds V, Kellet J, editors: *Mating and marriage*, Oxford, 1991, Oxford University Press.

Suggested Readings

Berzon B: *The intimacy dance: a guide to long-term success in gay and lesbian relationships,* New York, 1997, Plume.

Betty Berzon, the author of the successful book Permanent Partners, uses her own 22-year relationship as an important backdrop in this guide for gay and lesbian couples. Berzon points out many of the common problems that occur in long-term relationships, such as merging identities, lack of communication, lessening of sexual activity, and nonmonogamous relationships.

Copelan R: *100 ways to make sex sensational and 100% safe: enjoy monogamy without monotony,* ed 2, Portland, Oregon, 1997, Lifetime Books.

This book is for couples who want to have enjoyable sex and a great relationship. It provides solid information about improving communication and developing a sensitive relationship. The author believes that romance is the key to unlocking greater sexual intimacy.

Naylor S: *100 reasons to keep him, 100 reasons to dump him,* New York, 1997, Random House.

Written by the author of the bestseller The Rules, this book suggests a plan for rationally judging whether to keep a relationship going. Sharon Naylor, a journalist, writes primarily for women, but the book also gives men some interesting insights into how women view relationships.

Page S: *The 8 essential traits of couples that thrive,* New York, 1997, Delta Trade Paperbacks.

Therapist Susan Page describes the eight traits commonly seen in couples who have healthy relationships. These traits can be developed by couples who are willing to do the day-to-day things that contribute to successful interaction. Page focuses on maintaining a positive, optimistic attitude and establishing realistic expectations.

White B: *The 100 best ways to meet people,* New York, 1998, Dell Publishing Company.

Ben White offers some practical strategies to help people find interesting partners. The book encourages people to stop making excuses for "not being able to find the right person." White places the responsibility on the reader to take the positive steps that are most likely to be successful.

 AS WE GO TO PRESS . . .

In late spring 1998, the FDA approved Viagra, a drug used to treat impotence (the inability to achieve an erection when sexually stimulated). Viagra, a prescription pill taken orally, is the first nonsurgical treatment for impotence that does not require injecting or inserting a needle or other object directly into the penis.

Users of Viagra take the pill about one hour before intercourse and are instructed to use no more than one pill a day. The drug appears to enhance the effects of nitric oxide, a chemical produced when a man is sexually aroused. Nitric oxide induces relaxation of smooth muscle tissue in the penis, thereby increasing blood flow into its erectile chambers. Pfizer Pharmaceuticals, Viagra's developer and manufacturer, has tested the drug only on men, so its effects on women are unknown. Recent reports of possible drug interactions have raised questions about the drug's safety in men.

Viagra costs about $10 per dose, although some discount drug chains are now advertising a reduced price. In its first week on the market, more than 36,000 prescriptions were written for Viagra, setting a record for first-week sales of a prescription drug. Faced with this great demand, health insurance companies are scrambling to decide whether to cover the drug and, if so, what constitutes a typical number of sexual episodes per month.

Sex on the Internet

It's like a singles bar without the loud music. If you have a computer and a modem, you can gain access to the world's largest "meet market." From the comfort of your home, you can browse the Internet and meet people for conversation, friendship, romance, and even "sex" (such as it is in cyberspace). There is a cover charge, but you won't have to buy drinks to start up a conversation or get your toes smashed on the dance floor. You won't even have to worry about getting diseases (save for the occasional computer virus).

However, there are drawbacks when you enter this hangout. Can you be sure the person you're chatting with is all he or she seems to be? How can you be certain of a person's personality, age, or even his or her gender? And is there a safe way to meet a "cyberfriend" face-to-face? The Internet way of meeting people has its own built-in set of advantages—but inviting the world into your home has its dangers as well.

Today's Internet user can find a variety of potential conversation topics using a Web browser and typing in various keywords. As the Internet grows, so do its various websites and USENET discussion groups. Some people see this expansion as a source of entertainment. They think that the Internet is a fun and interesting way to meet people who share their interests. Others think that the Internet allows pornographers, pedophiles, and other deviants to perpetuate their behavior and prey on innocent children. Both groups are attempting to use the law either to keep the Internet as a haven for free speech or to clean it up and make it safer for children. This clash of ideals is creating a continual battle over the nature and character of the Internet.

Fun and games on the Internet

The Internet is a large group of computer networks, both public and private, that connects millions of computer users in an estimated 150 countries. Over 70,000 private computer bulletin boards exist in the United States alone, and private commercial networks such as Prodigy, America Online, and CompuServe provide nearly 6 million subscribers worldwide with access to the Internet.[1] Although the Internet contains information about all facets of life, the sexually oriented sites are proving to be the most popular areas among the general public. For example, alt.sex, a USENET discussion group where people can chat in real time with other users, is the most often visited site on the Internet.[2] Brian Reid, director of the Network Systems Laboratory at Digital Equipment

Corporation, reports that between 180,000 and 500,000 users drop into this discussion group on a monthly basis.[3]

At websites, computer bulletin boards that usually include photographs, interested parties can find almost anything that conforms to their sexual desires. Many pictures of nude men and women that can be found at most adult-oriented video stores and booksellers can be downloaded (placed on a user's computer disk or printed on his or her own printer).[1] However, other types of less common sexual images are also available at websites, including explicit images that many people find objectionable.

The positive side of the Internet

Despite the potentially offensive graphic images available on-line, the Internet does have several good points. One positive aspect is that people who are interested in meeting others can use the Internet as a sort of virtual pick-up bar without many of the unpleasant consequences. It gives people the freedom either to be themselves without fear of repercussions or to adopt a totally new persona. Best of all, cybersex participants don't have to worry about looking their best during a virtual date.[4] Who you are (or who you pretend to be) becomes more important than what you look like in cyberspace chat rooms.

Sexually oriented Internet sites can also be positive in the sense that they sometimes inspire creative impulses and prevent people from engaging in destructive behavior. Some sites house participatory novels in which users

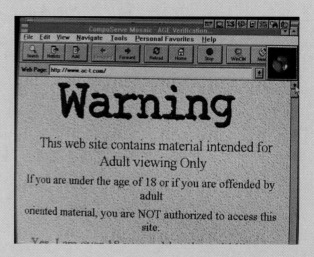

340

can immerse themselves and create new realities for themselves and other participants.[5] In this respect, these sites are similar to fantasy game pages that house activities such as Dungeons & Dragons. People are able to cast off their old identities and create exciting new personas that are able to engage in sexual practices that the users themselves would never attempt in real life. Thus the Internet becomes a harmless outlet for sexual fantasies: the ultimate safe sex.

A third plus to using the Internet to meet people is that occasionally, people who use it do fall in "virtual love," choose to meet face to face, and end up developing a relationship or even getting married.[4] Although this is a rare occurrence, the chance that it could happen is enough to keep some people involved with on-line romances in the hope of finding a perfect cybermate who will be as good in person.

Pitfalls of on-line sex

Although virtual sex has many good points in its favor, there are also several negative aspects. One of the worst possible scenarios of on-line sex is discovering that the person with whom you have been pursuing a virtual relationship is not who he or she claims to be. This pitfall is particularly dangerous when one of the parties in the relationship is a minor. In response to a recent on-line query, 130 female teenagers stated that they had posted erotic stories on a sexually oriented bulletin board and corresponded with adult men. In the stories, the teenagers pretended to be adults. Several of the teenagers also admitted that they had scheduled face-to-face meetings with these adult men without telling anyone.[6] Although none of the teenagers reported any negative consequences as a result of these meetings, the potential for danger was most certainly present. A recent case in which a female 13-year-old from Kentucky ended up in Los Angeles after being lured there by her adult male Internet correspondent provides evidence to prove this point.[3] Additionally, several cases exist in which pedophiles have used computer bulletin boards to contact children, learned their names and addresses, and set up meetings with them. Several rapes have occurred as a result of this.[7]

A second drawback to on-line sex is the considerable cost. Although chat rooms are sometimes free and websites have "visitor's passes" that allow sneak previews, most of the hard-core sexual activity can be very expensive. Some chat rooms charge as much as $12 an hour for a conversation.[4] To get to the more explicit photographs and participatory novels on the Internet, a member's fee is required, which ranges anywhere from $19.95 for 6 months to $129.95 for a year. These fees are generally paid by credit card on-line. A digital video camera, which is necessary to create real-time pictures to transmit through a personal computer, costs at least $100.[8] Upgrades to computer memory and equipment to handle more technologically advanced transmissions such as video clips can also be costly, running into the thousands of dollars.

A third potential problem is cybersex addiction. Some people become so involved with virtual reality that they find themselves uninterested in the real world. A librarian at a large college recently reported that many college students have to be asked to log off the library's computers that have Internet connections. These students ignore library policy that limits their Internet use to 30 minutes. One student had to be threatened by campus police; he was logged onto a sexually oriented chat room for almost 4 hours. In another case at the same college a library employee was disciplined after he was caught downloading sexually explicit material.[9] As a result of these incidents the college now blocks many sexually explicit sites and has disabled its computers' ability to download any material.

Avoiding sex on the Internet

With all the publicity and notoriety surrounding sexually oriented Internet sites, many concerned parents want to ensure that their children do not have access to sexual material through their personal computers. Other people are offended by cybersex and do not want it coming into their homes for religious or moral reasons. For these people, several options exist. Parents can subscribe to an on-line service that blocks potentially offensive sites. CompuServe, one of the largest on-line providers, recently suspended 200 sex discussion groups in response to German authorities' contention that the groups violated German obscenity laws.[10] Also, America Online and Prodigy have mechanisms available on their services to block access to areas that most parents would consider inappropriate for their children.[3] These mechanisms are available free of charge with subscription to the services.

A second option is to purchase a program that will block out undesirable material. One such program, Surfwatch, will automatically block access to 1000 sites and let you screen all user groups, websites, and other electronic avenues. The cost of this program is $49.95 plus a $5.95 monthly service fee. Other types of blocker programs include NetNanny, which lets parents monitor everything that passes through their computer, and Time's Up, which lets parents set up time limits and appropriate times for their children to use the computer.[8]

A third, decidedly low-tech option is the most obvious and also the most overlooked. Parents should watch what their children are doing while they are on-line and monitor all activities, perhaps by making computer use a family activity.[3] As columnist Michael J. Miller points out, much of the fear that children will accidentally stumble onto a sexually oriented site is unfounded. Unlike broadcast media, on the Internet, you must enter a specific address or follow a specific link to reach a sexually oriented site. Parents who watch their kids will know exactly where the kids go during an on-line jaunt. Additionally, parents should teach their children some basic safety information such as never to give out their real name, address, or telephone number to people they meet on-line. Children should understand that even though they may have on-line friends, these people are really strangers that they know little about.[3-8]

The Telecommunications Competition and Deregulation Act

In February 1996, President Clinton signed into law the Telecommunications Competition and Deregulation Act, a law that contains a provision called the Telecommunications Decency Act to block indecency on-line. Anyone caught transmitting obscene, lewd, or indecent communications by any electronic means could be fined as much as $100,000 and sent to prison for as long as 2 years.[1,10,11] Civil libertarians and users of sexually oriented Internet sites oppose this law, stating that the First Amendment guarantees freedom of speech and that this freedom should include the Internet. They also believe that the law as written is too broad and confusing; it could be interpreted as banning any use of profanity or nudity on-line, including news reports, legal documents, literature, and even the Bible.[11]

Some parents and religious groups, on the other hand, are applauding this new act. They feel it gives them more control over what kinds of material are coming into their homes. They believe that this legislation is necessary to protect children from being exposed to pornography on-line. They also believe the law is good because it specifically targets material that is patently offensive and depicts graphic sexual activity.[11]

A line has been drawn in the sand regarding sex on the Internet. Supporters of the new law are joining organizations such as Enough is Enough, the National Coalition against Pornography, and the American Family Association Law Center.[7] These groups work to defend traditional values and fight against increased pornography. Meanwhile, web search engines such as Yahoo protested the legislation by turning their Web pages to black with white lettering for 48 hours to demonstrate "virtual mourning," and the American Civil Liberties Union filed a federal court complaint to block enforcement of the law.[11]

Using the Internet for sexual purposes can have both positive and negative consequences; therefore people who do so should weigh all factors involved before they decide to enter the world of cybersex. Parents should be especially careful about what they allow to come into their homes via the personal computer. Although blocking methods and the new federal laws provide some protection from sexually oriented material, it is ultimately the individual's responsibility to choose and to monitor what type of information comes up while surfing the Internet.

For Discussion . . .

Have you or someone you know ever explored sexually oriented Websites on the Internet? If so, was it a positive or a negative experience? Would you be willing to meet a virtual friend face to face? Why or why not? Do you support the new Telecommunications Indecency Act? Why or why not?

References

1. Lewis PH: Despite a new plan for cooling it off, cybersex stays hot, *New York Times*, p A1, March 26, 1995.
2. Nashawatz C: Where the wild things are: anonymous sex is back, *Entertainment Weekly*, September 23, 1994.
3. Levy S, Stone B: No place for kids: a parents' guide to sex on the Net, *Newsweek*, July 3, 1995.
4. Van der Leur G: Twilight zone of the id, *Time*, (45)2, 1995.
5. Machure B: MUDs and MUSHes and MOOs, *PC Magazine*, p10, April 30, 1995.
6. Bennahan DS: Lolitas on-line, *Harper's Bazaar*, p 3406, Sept 1995.
7. Zipperer J: The naked city, *Christianity Today*, Sept 12, 1994.
8. Miller MJ: Cybersex shock, *PC Magazine*, Oct 10, 1995.
9. Anonymous: Personal communication, March 23, 1996.
10. Mezer M: A bad dream comes true in cyberspace, *Newsweek*, p 2, Jan 8, 1996.
11. Wagner M: Tempers flare over web censorship, *Computerworld*, Feb 12, 1996.

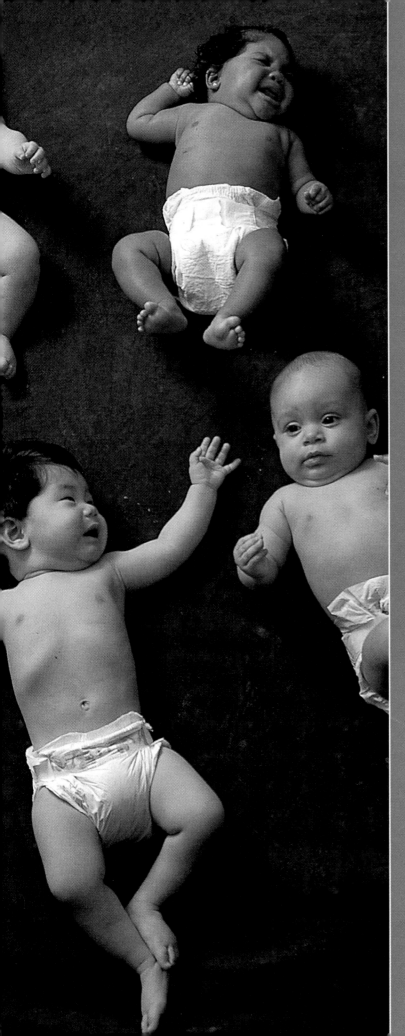

Managing Your Fertility

Healthy People: Looking Ahead to 2010

The *Healthy People 2010* objectives will undoubtedly include many important goals in the areas of family planning, fertility control, pregnancy, and childbirth. Data indicating our progress to date in these areas focus mainly on adolescents and teenagers, not college students. The *Healthy People 2000* objectives for these age groups included reducing pregnancy rates among adolescents, reducing the proportion of young people who have sexual intercourse, increasing the rate of abstinence among those who have already had intercourse, and increasing contraceptive use by sexually active adolescents and teens.

Progress toward achieving these objectives was mixed. The proportion of young people initiating sexual activity by age 15 and by age 17 had increased. Some headway was made in promoting abstinence among girls who had already engaged in sexual intercourse. The only objective for which significant gains were reported was the increased use of contraceptives among teenagers.

The picture is more encouraging in the areas of pregnancy and childbirth. Data concerning pregnancy complications, infant mortality, prenatal care, breastfeeding, and cesarean delivery rates all indicated improvement by the late 1990s. We expect continued gains in these important areas as the specific objectives for *Healthy People 2010* are established.

How you decide to control your **fertility** will have an important effect on your future. Your understanding of information and issues related to fertility control will help you make responsible decisions in this complex area.

For traditional-age students, these decisions may be fast approaching. Frequently, nontraditional students are parents who have had experiences that make them useful resources for other students in the class.

BIRTH CONTROL VS. CONTRACEPTION

Any discussion about the control of your fertility should start with an explanation of the subtle differences between the terms **birth control** and **contraception.** Although many people use the words interchangeably, they reflect different perspectives about fertility control. *Birth control* is an umbrella term that refers to all of the procedures you might use to prevent the birth of a child. Birth control includes all available contraceptive measures, as well as sterilization, use of the intrauterine device (IUD), and abortion procedures.

Contraception is a much more specific term for any procedure used to prevent the fertilization of an ovum. Contraceptive measures vary widely in the mechanisms they use to accomplish this task. They also vary considerably in their method of use and their rate of success in preventing conception. A few examples of contraceptive methods are the use of condoms, oral contraceptives, spermicides, and diaphragms.

Beyond the numerous methods mentioned, certain forms of sexual behavior not involving intercourse could be considered forms of contraception. For example, mutual masturbation by couples eliminates the possibility of pregnancy. This practice, as well as additional forms of sexual expression other than intercourse (such as kissing, touching, and massage), have been given the generic term **outercourse.** Not only does outercourse protect against unplanned pregnancy, it may also significantly reduce the transmission of sexually transmitted diseases, including HIV infection.

REASONS FOR CHOOSING TO USE BIRTH CONTROL

People choose to use birth control for many reasons. Many career-minded individuals carefully plan the timing and spacing of children so that they can best provide for their children's financial support without sacrificing their job status. Others choose methods of birth control to ensure that they will never have children. Some use birth control methods to permit safe participation in a wide variety of sexual behaviors. Fear of contracting a sexually transmitted disease prompts some people to use specific forms of birth control.

Financial and legal considerations can be significant factors in the choice of certain birth control methods. Many people must by necessity take the cost of a method into account when selecting appropriate birth control. The cost of sterilization and abortion can prohibit some low-income people from choosing these alternatives, especially since federal funds do not support such procedures. A number of states have established statutes and policies that make contraceptive information and medical services relatively difficult to obtain.

Another important consideration in the use of birth control methods is the availability of professional services. An example of the effect of this factor may be the selection of birth control methods by college students. Some colleges and universities provide contraceptive services through their student health centers. Students enrolled in these schools have easy access to low-cost, comprehensive contraceptive services. Students enrolled in colleges that do not provide such complete services may find that access to accurate information and clinical services is difficult to obtain and that private professional services are expensive.

For many people, religious doctrine will be a factor in their selection of a birth control method. This influence can be seen in the Roman Catholic Church's ban on the use of all forms of contraception other than natural family planning and in the condemnation of abortion by certain religious groups.

THEORETICAL EFFECTIVENESS VS. USE EFFECTIVENESS

People considering the use of a contraceptive method need to understand the difference between the two effectiveness rates given for each form of contraception. *Theoretical effectiveness* is a measure of a contraceptive method's ability to prevent a pregnancy when the method is used precisely as directed during every act of intercourse. *Use effectiveness,* however, refers to the effectiveness of a method in preventing conception when used by the general public. Use effectiveness rates take into account factors that lower effectiveness below that based on "perfect" use. Failure to follow proper instructions, illness of the user, forgetfulness, physician (or pharmacist) error, and a subconscious desire to experience risk or even pregnancy are a few of the factors that can lower the effectiveness of even the most theoretically effective contraceptive technique.

Effectiveness rates are often expressed in terms of the percentage of women users of childbearing age who do not become pregnant while using the method for 1 year. For some methods the theoretical- and use-effectiveness rates are vastly different; the theoretical rate is always higher than the use rate. Table 14-1 presents data concerning effectiveness rates, advantages, and disadvantages of many birth control methods.

SELECTING YOUR CONTRACEPTIVE METHOD

In this section, we discuss some of the many factors that should be important to you as you consider selecting a contraceptive method. Remember that no method possesses equally high marks in all of the following areas. It is important that you and your partner select a contraceptive method that is both acceptable and effective, as determined by your unique needs and expectations. Completing the Personal Assessment on p. 348 will help you make this decision.

For a contraceptive method to be acceptable to those who wish to exercise a large measure of control over their fertility, the following should be given careful consideration:

- *It should be safe.* The contraceptive approach you select should not pose a significant health risk for you or your partner.
- *It should be effective.* Your approach must have a high success rate in preventing pregnancy.
- *It should be reliable.* The form you select must be able to be used over and over again with consistent success.
- *It should be reversible.* Couples who eventually want to have a family should select a method that can be reversed.
- *It should be affordable.* The cost of a particular method must fit comfortably into a couple's budget.
- *It should be easy to use.* Complicated instructions or procedures can make a method difficult to use effectively.
- *It should not interfere with sexual expression.* An ideal contraceptive fits in comfortably with a couple's intimate sexual behavior.

CURRENT BIRTH CONTROL METHODS
Withdrawal

Withdrawal, or **coitus interruptus,** is the contraceptive practice in which the erect penis is removed from the vagina just before ejaculation of semen. Theoretically this procedure prevents sperm from entering the deeper structures of the female reproductive system. The use effectiveness of this method, however, reflects how unsuccessful this method is in practice (see Table 14-1).

There is strong evidence to suggest that the clear preejaculate fluid that helps neutralize and lubricate the male urethra can contain *viable* (capable of fertilization) sperm.[1] This sperm can be deposited near the cervical opening before withdrawal of the penis. This phenomenon may in part explain the relatively low effectiveness of this method. Furthermore, withdrawal does not protect users from the transmission of STDs.

Periodic Abstinence

There are four approaches included in the birth control strategy called **periodic abstinence:** (1) the

---

fertility
The ability to reproduce.

birth control
All of the methods and procedures that can prevent the birth of a child.

contraception
Any method or procedure that prevents fertilization.

outercourse
Sexual activity that does not involve intercourse.

coitus interruptus (withdrawal) (co ih tus in ter **rup** tus)
A contraceptive practice in which the erect penis is removed from the vagina before ejaculation.

periodic abstinence
Birth control methods that rely on a couple's avoidance of intercourse during the ovulatory phase of a woman's menstrual cycle; also called *fertility awareness* or *natural family planning.*

Table 14-1   Effectiveness Rates of Birth Control for 100 Women during 1 Year of Use

Method	Estimated Effectiveness		Advantages	Disadvantages
	Theoretical	Use		
No method (chance)	15%	15%	Inexpensive	Totally ineffective
Withdrawal	85%	75%-80%	No supplies or advance preparation needed; no side effects; men share responsibility for family planning	Interferes with coitus; may be difficult to use effectively; women must trust men to withdraw as orgasm approaches
Periodic abstinence Calendar Basal body temperature Cervical mucus method Symptothermal	90%-98%	75%-85%	No supplies needed; no side effects; men share responsibility for family planning; women learn about their bodies	Difficult to use, especially if menstrual cycles are irregular, as is common in young women; abstinence may be necessary for long periods; lengthy instruction and ongoing counseling may be needed
Cervical cap	94%	82%	No health risks; helps protect against some STDs and cervical cancer	Limited availability
Spermicide	97%-98%	75%-85%	No health risks; helps protect against some STDs; can be used with condoms to increase effectiveness considerably	Must be inserted 5 to 30 minutes before coitus; effective for only 30 to 60 minutes; some women may find them awkward or embarrassing to use
Diaphragm with spermicide	97%-98%	80%-90%	No health risks; helps protect against some STDs and cervical cancer	Must be inserted with jelly or foam before every act of coitus and left in place for at least 6 hours after coitus; must be fitted by health care personnel; some women may find it awkward or embarrassing to use; may be inconvenient to clean, store, and carry
Male condom and male condom with spermicide	98% 99%	80%-90% 95%	Easy to use; inexpensive and easy to obtain; no health risks; very effective protection against some STDs; men share responsibility for family planning	Must be put on just before coitus; some men and women complain of decreased sensation
Female condom	90%+	74%-79%	Relatively easy to use; no prescription required; polyurethane is stronger than latex; provides some STD protection; silicone-based lubrication provided; useful when male will not use a condom	Contraceptive effectiveness and STD protection not as high as with male condom; couples may be unfamiliar with a device that extends outside the vagina; more expensive than male condoms
IUD	99%	95%-98%	Easy to use; highly effective in preventing pregnancy; does not interfere with coitus; repeated action not needed	May increase risk of pelvic inflammatory disease (PID) and infertility in women with more than one sexual partner; not usually recommended for women who have never had a child; must be inserted by health care personnel; may cause heavy bleeding and pain in some women

Table 14-1, cont'd

| Method | Estimated Effectiveness | | Advantages | Disadvantages |
	Theoretical	Use		
Combined pill (Estrogen-progestin) Triphasic pill	99%	97%-98%	Easy to use; highly effective in preventing pregnancy; does not interfere with coitus; regulates menstrual cycle; reduces heavy bleeding and menstrual pain; helps protect against ovarian and endometrial cancer	Must be taken every day; requires medical examination and prescription; minor side effects such as nausea or menstrual spotting; possibility of circulatory problems, such as blood clotting, strokes, and hypertension, in a small percentage of users
Minipill (progestin only)	99%	96%-97%		
Depo-Provera	99%+	99%+	Easy to use; highly effective for 3-month period; continued use prevents menstruation	Requires supervision by a physician; administered by injection; some women experience irregular menstrual spotting in early months of use
Subdermal implants (progestin only)	99%+	99%+	Highly effective for 5-year period; helps prevent anemia and regulates menstrual cycle	Requires minor surgery; some women experience irregular menstrual spotting
Tubal ligation	99%+	99%+	Permanent; removes fear of pregnancy	Surgery-related risks; generally considered irreversible
Vasectomy	99%+	99%+	Permanent; removes fear of pregnancy	Generally considered irreversible

calendar method, (2) the basal body temperature (BBT) method, (3) the Billings cervical mucus method, and (4) the symptothermal method.[2] All four methods attempt to determine the time a woman ovulates. Figure 14-1 (p. 349) shows a day-to-day fertility calendar used to calculate fertile periods. Most research indicates that an ovum is viable for only about 24 to 36 hours after its release from the ovary. (Once inside the female reproductive tract, some sperm can survive up to a week.) When a woman can accurately determine when she ovulates, she must refrain from intercourse long enough for the ovum to begin to disintegrate. Fertility awareness, rhythm, natural birth control, and natural family planning are terms interchangeable with periodic abstinence. Remember that periodic abstinence methods *do not* provide protection against the spread of sexually transmitted diseases, including HIV infection.

Periodic abstinence is the only acceptable method endorsed by the Roman Catholic Church. For some people who have deep concerns for the spiritual dimensions of their health, the selection of a contraceptive method other than periodic abstinence may indicate a serious compromise of beliefs.

The **calendar method** requires close examination of a woman's menstrual cycle for at least eight cycles. Records are kept of the length (in days) of each cycle.

A *cycle* is defined as the number of days from the first day of bleeding of one cycle to the first day of bleeding of the next cycle.

To determine the days she should abstain from intercourse, a woman should subtract 18 from her shortest cycle; this is the first day she should abstain from intercourse. Then she should subtract 11 from her longest cycle; this is the last day she must abstain from intercourse (see the Health Action Guide on p. 350).[2]

The *basal body temperature method* requires a woman (for about 3 or 4 successive months) to take her body temperature every morning before she rises from bed. A finely calibrated thermometer, available in many drugstores, is used for this purpose. The theory behind this method is that a distinct correlation exists between body temperature and the process of ovulation. Just before ovulation, the body temperature supposedly dips and then rises about 0.5° to 1.0° F for the

calendar method
A form of periodic abstinence in which the variable lengths of a woman's menstrual cycle are used to calculate her fertile period.

PERSONAL ASSESSMENT

Which Birth Control Method Is Best for You?

To assess which birth control method would be best for you, answer the following questions, and check the interpretation below.

Do I:

	Yes	No
1. Need a contraceptive right away?	____	____
2. Want a contraceptive that can be used completely independent of sexual relations?	____	____
3. Need a contraceptive only once in a great while?	____	____
4. Want something with no harmful side effects?	____	____
5. Want to avoid going to the doctor?	____	____
6. Want something that will help protect against sexually transmitted diseases?	____	____
7. Have to be concerned about affordability?	____	____
8. Need to be virtually certain that pregnancy will not result?	____	____
9. Want to avoid pregnancy now but want to have a child sometime in the future?	____	____
10. Have any medical condition or lifestyle that may rule out some form of contraception?	____	____

Interpretation

If you have checked *Yes* to number:

1. Condoms and spermicides may be easily purchased without prescription in any pharmacy.
2. Sterilization, oral contraceptives, hormone implants or injections, cervical caps, and periodic abstinence techniques do not require that anything be done just before sexual relations.
3. Diaphragms, condoms, or spermicides can be used by people who have coitus only once in a while. Peri-

odic abstinence techniques may also be appropriate but require a high degree of skill and motivation.
4. IUDs should be carefully discussed with your physician. Sometimes the use of oral contraceptives or hormone products results in some minor discomfort and may have harmful side effects.
5. Condoms and spermicides do not require a prescription from a physician.
6. Condoms and, to a lesser extent, spermicides and the other barrier methods may help protect against some sexually transmitted diseases. No method (except abstinence) can guarantee complete protection.
7. Be a wise consumer: check prices, ask pharmacists and physicians. The cost of sterilization is high, but there is no additional expense for a lifetime.
8. Sterilization provides near certainty. Oral contraceptives, hormone implants or injections, or a diaphragm-condom-spermicide combination also give a high measure of reliable protection. Periodic abstinence, withdrawal, and douche methods should be avoided. Outercourse may be a good alternative.
9. Although it is sometimes possible to reverse sterilization, it requires surgery and is more complex than simply stopping use of any of the other methods.
10. Smokers and people with a history of blood clots should probably not use oral contraceptives or other hormone approaches. Some people have an allergic reaction to a specific spermicide and should experiment with another brand. Some women cannot be fitted with a diaphragm or cervical cap because of the position of the uterus. The woman and her health care provider will then need to select another suitable means of contraception.

To Carry This Further . . .

There may be more than one method of birth control suitable for you. Always consider how a method you select can also help you avoid an STD. Study the methods suggested above, and consult Table 14-1 to determine what techniques may be most appropriate.

---

rest of the cycle. The woman is instructed to refrain from intercourse during the interval when the temperature change takes place.

Drawbacks of this procedure include the need for consistent, accurate readings and the realization that all women's bodies are different. Some women may not fit the temperature pattern projection because of biochemical differences in their bodies. Also, body

temperatures can fluctuate because of a wide variety of illnesses and physical stressors.

The *Billings cervical mucus method* is another periodic abstinence technique. Generally used with other periodic abstinence techniques, this method requires a woman to evaluate the daily mucous discharge from her cervix. Users of this method become familiar with the changes in both appearance (from clear to cloudy)

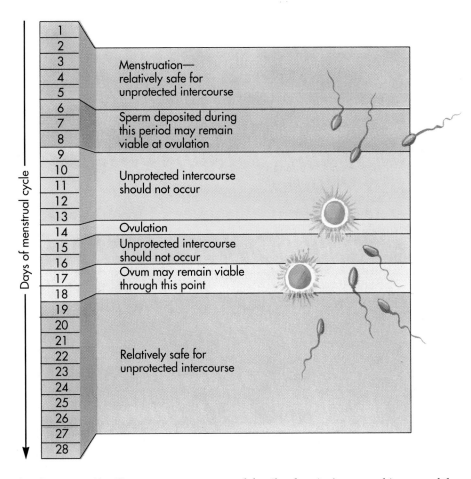

Figure 14-1   Periodic abstinence (fertility awareness or natural family planning) can combine use of the calendar, basal body temperature measurements, and Billings mucus techniques to identify the fertile period. Remember that most women's cycles are not consistently perfect 28-day cycles as shown in most illustrations.

and consistency (from watery to thick) of their cervical mucus throughout their cycles. Women are taught that the unsafe days are when the mucus becomes clear and is the consistency of raw egg whites. Such a technique of ovulation determination must be learned from a physician or family planning professional.

The *symptothermal method* of periodic abstinence combines the use of the BBT method and the cervical mucus method.[2] Of course, couples using the symptothermal method are already using a calendar to chart the woman's body changes. Thus some family planning professionals consider the symptothermal method a combination of all of the periodic abstinence approaches.

Vaginal Spermicides

Although they are not recommended as the primary form of fertility control, spermicidal agents are often recommended to be used with other forms of birth control. Alone, **spermicides** offer a reasonable amount of contraceptive protection for the woman

who is sexually active on an *infrequent* basis. Spermicides containing nonoxynol 9 provide some protection (but *not full* protection) against STDs and HIV infection.

Vaginal spermicide.

spermicides
Chemicals capable of killing sperm.

Determining Your Cycle

Even if you are not sexually active or are not planning to use periodic abstinence, you will find it helpful to use the calendar method of calculations to find the days in your cycle on which you are most fertile. (Hopefully, you are already keeping a record of your cycles on a calendar. This is a good addition to your health history.)

- Subtract 18 from your shortest cycle. Subtract 11 from your longest cycle. The days in between are your unsafe days. Record your results.
- What is your first unsafe day? What is your last unsafe day?
- Can you identify the approximate time during your unsafe days that ovulation actually takes place? ◄------►

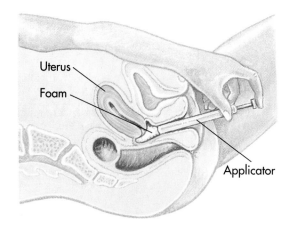

Figure 14-2 Spermicidal foams and suppositories are placed deep into the vagina in the region of the cervix no longer than 30 minutes before intercourse.

Vaginal Contraceptive Film

A unique spermicide delivery system developed in England is vaginal contraceptive film (VCF). Vaginal contraceptive film is a sheet containing nonoxynol 9 that is inserted over the cervical opening. Shortly after insertion of the VCF, it dissolves into a gel-like material that clings to the cervical opening. The VCF can be inserted up to an hour before intercourse. Over the course of several hours, the material will be washed from the vagina in the normal vaginal secretions.

This spermicide is a nonprescription form of contraception that is as effective as other spermicidal foams and jellies. A box of 12 sheets costs about $9. Like other spermicidal agents, VCF may also help in minimizing the risk of some STDs and PID.

Modern spermicides are safe, reasonably effective, reversible forms of contraception that can be obtained without a physician's prescription; they can be purchased in most drugstores and in many supermarkets. Like condoms, spermicides are relatively inexpensive. When used together, spermicides and condoms provide a high degree of contraceptive protection and disease prevention.

Spermicides, which are available in foam, cream, paste, or film form, are made of water-soluble bases with a spermicidal chemical incorporated in the base. The base material is designed to liquefy at body temperature and distribute the spermicidal component in an even layer over the tissues of the upper vagina (Figure 14-2). The Star Box at right describes a unique film type of spermicide.

Spermicides are not specific to sperm cells; they also attack other cells and thus may provide the woman with some additional protection against many sexually transmitted diseases and **pelvic inflammatory disease (PID).** However, when used alone, spermicides do not provide sufficient protection against most pathogens, including the virus that causes AIDS.

Condoms

Colored or natural, smooth or textured, straight or shaped, plain or reservoir-tipped, dry or lubricated—

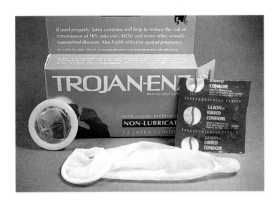

Condoms.

Diaphragm and contraceptive jelly.

the condom is approaching an art form. This is perhaps an exaggeration. Nevertheless, the familiar **condom** remains a safe, effective, reversible contraceptive device. All condoms manufactured in the United States must be approved by the FDA.

For couples who are highly motivated in their desire to prevent a pregnancy, the effectiveness of a condom can approach that of an oral contraceptive—especially if condom use is combined with a spermicide. (Some lubricated condoms now also contain a spermicide.) For couples who are less motivated or who use condoms on an irregular basis, the condom can be considerably less effective. This readily available and inexpensive method of contraception requires responsible use if it is to achieve a high level of effectiveness (see the Health Action Guide on p. 352).

The condom offers a measure of protection against sexually transmitted diseases. For both the man and the woman, chlamydial infections, gonorrhea, HIV infection, and other STDs are less likely to be acquired when the condom is used. When combined with a spermicide containing nonoxynol 9, condoms may become even more effective against the spread of STDs. Although advertisements suggest that condoms provide protection against the transmission of genital herpes, users of condoms must remember that this protection is limited to the penis and vagina—not to the surrounding genital region, where significant numbers of lesions are found. Like other barrier methods of contraception, the condom is a reasonable choice for couples who are motivated in their desire to prevent a pregnancy and who are willing to assume the level of responsibility required. See the Star Box on p. 353 for a discussion of the female condom.

Diaphragm

The **diaphragm** is a soft rubber cup with a spring-like metal rim that, when properly fitted and properly inserted by the user, rests in the top of the vagina. In its proper position the diaphragm covers the cervical opening (Figure 14-4 on p. 354). During intercourse the diaphragm stays in place quite well and cannot usually be felt by either the man or the woman.

The diaphragm is always used with a spermicidal cream or jelly. The diaphragm should be covered with an adequate amount of spermicide inside the cup and around the rim. When used properly with a spermicide, the diaphragm is a relatively effective contraceptive, and when combined with the man's use of a condom, its effectiveness is even greater.

Diaphragms must always be fitted and prescribed by a physician. The cost of obtaining a diaphragm and keeping a supply of spermicide may be higher than that of other methods. Also, a high level of motivation to follow the instructions *exactly* is important.

Diaphragms and other vaginal barrier methods (such as the cervical cap) provide some protection against sexually transmitted diseases, including gonorrhea and chlamydia, PID, and cervical cancer. However, the ability of diaphragms and other vaginal barrier

---

pelvic inflammatory disease (PID)
A generalized infection of the pelvic cavity that results from the spread of an infection through a woman's reproductive structures.

condom
A latex shield designed to cover the erect penis and retain semen on ejaculation; "rubber."

diaphragm
A soft rubber cup designed to cover the cervix.

HEALTH
Action Guide ----->

Maximizing the Effectiveness of Condoms

These simple directions for using condoms correctly, in combination with your motivation and commitment to regular use, should provide you with reasonable protection:

- Keep a supply of condoms at hand. Condoms should be stored in a cool, dry place so that they are readily available at the time of intercourse. Condoms that are stored in wallets or automobile glove compartments may not be in satisfactory condition when they are used. Temperature extremes are to be avoided. Check the condom package for the expiration date.
- Do not test a condom by inflating or stretching it. Handle it gently, and keep it away from sharp fingernails.
- For maximum effectiveness, put the condom on before genital contact. Either the man or the woman can put the condom in place. Early application is particularly important in the prevention of STDs. Early application also lessens the possibility of the release of preejaculate fluid into the vagina.
- Unroll the condom on the erect penis. For those using a condom without a reservoir tip, a $\frac{1}{2}$-inch space should be left to catch the ejaculate. To leave this space, pinch the tip of the condom as you roll it on the erect penis. Do not leave any air in the tip of the condom (Figure 14-3).
- Lubricate the condom if this has not already been done by the manufacturer. When doing this, be certain to use a water-soluble lubricant and not a petroleum-based product such as petroleum jelly. Petroleum can deteriorate the latex material. Other oil-based lubricants, such as mineral oil, baby oil, vegetable oil, shortening, and certain hand lotions, can quickly damage a condom. Use water-based lubricants only!
- After ejaculation, be certain that the condom does

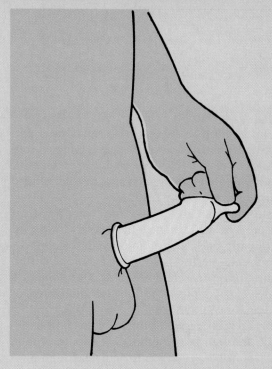

Figure 14-3   Pinch the end of the condom to leave $\frac{1}{2}$ inch of space at the tip.

not become dislodged from the penis. Hold the rim of the condom firmly against the base of the penis during withdrawal. Do not allow the penis to become flaccid (soft) while still in the vagina.
- Inspect the condom for tears before throwing it away. If the condom is damaged in some way, immediately insert a spermicidal agent into the vagina.

<-----

methods to provide protection against HIV infection for either partner is not known. If you are concerned about possible HIV infection, either avoid sexual activity or use a latex condom and spermicide in combination.[3]

Cervical Cap

The **cervical cap** is a small, thimble-shaped device that fits over the entire cervix. Resembling a small diaphragm, the cervical cap is placed deeper than the diaphragm. The cap is held in place by suction rather than by pushing against anatomical structures (Figure 14-5 on p. 355). As with the diaphragm, a spermicide is used with the cervical cap. Thus it requires many of the same skills for insertion and care as does the diaphragm. The use effectiveness of the cervical cap appears to be approximately equal to that of the diaphragm. These devices are distributed in the United States through physician prescription.

Intrauterine Device

The **intrauterine device (IUD)** is a method of birth control that works by reducing the chances that a fertilized ovum will be able to implant itself into the uterus. Most health professionals believe that the IUD

REALITY—the Female Condom

In April 1993, the Wisconsin Pharmacal Company finally gained approval to market a female condom called REALITY. This device consists of a soft, loose-fitting polyurethane sheath and two flexible rings (see photo). REALITY is inserted like a tampon and lines the inner contours of the vagina. The device extends outside the vagina and covers the labia. REALITY will sell in three-packs for about $9.

REALITY does not require a physician's prescription. This device is prelubricated and is intended for one-time use. Manufacturer's studies have shown that female condoms have fewer leaks and less slippage and dislodgement and provide less risk of exposure to semen than do male condoms. The polyurethane used is stronger and more resistant to oils than the latex membrane used for male condoms. Despite these claims, the FDA contends that male latex condoms provide greater contraceptive protection and protection from STDs than female condoms.[3]

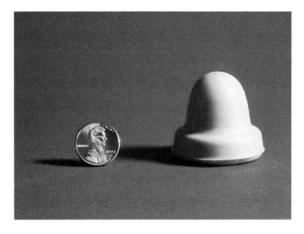

Cervical cap.

Progestasert IUD.

does not prevent conception; thus in a technical sense, the IUD is not a contraceptive device but rather a birth control device.

Two types of IUDs are available in the United States: the Progestasert (a T-shaped IUD containing progestin) and the Copper T 380-A (ParaGard), a T-shaped IUD wrapped with copper wire. The Progestasert must be replaced every year, but the Copper T 380-A can remain in place for up to 4 years. Only a skilled physician can prescribe and insert an IUD. As with many other forms of contraception, IUDs do not offer protection against STDs, including the AIDS virus.

As Table 14-1 indicates, IUDs are very effective birth control devices, surpassed in effectiveness only by abstinence, sterilization, and oral (or implanted, or injected) contraceptives. Some women using IUDs experience increased menstrual bleeding and cramping. Two un-

common but potentially serious side effects of IUD use are uterine perforation (in which the IUD imbeds itself into the uterine wall) and PID (which is a life-threatening infection of the abdominal cavity). However, a study by the World Health Organization indicates that today's IUDs do not increase the risk of pelvic infection except in the early weeks after insertion.[4]

cervical cap
A small, thimble-shaped device designed to fit over the cervix.

intrauterine device (IUD)
A small, plastic, medicated or unmedicated device that prevents continued pregnancy when inserted in the uterus.

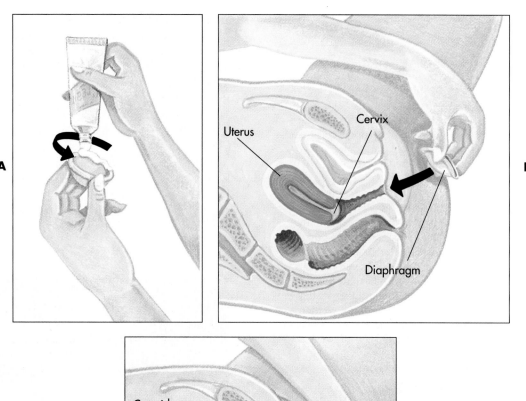

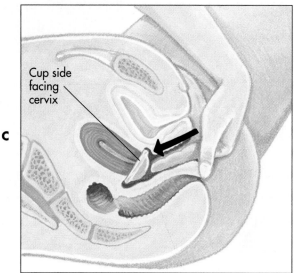

Figure 14-4   A, Spermicidal cream or jelly is placed into the diaphragm. **B,** The diaphragm is folded lengthwise and inserted into the vagina. **C,** The diaphragm is then placed against the cervix so that the cup portion with the spermicide is facing the cervix. The outline of the cervix should be felt through the central part of the diaphragm.

A woman deciding whether to use an IUD must discuss any concerns openly with her physician. The IUD can be a very acceptable form of contraception, especially for women who are in their middle to late reproductive years, unable to take birth control pills, in a stable monogamous relationship, and not at risk for STDs.

Oral Contraceptives

Developed in the 1950s, the **oral contraceptive pill** provides the highest effectiveness rate of any single reversible contraceptive method used today. "The pill" is the method of choice for nearly 17 million users in the United States.[5]

Use of the pill requires a physician's examination and prescription. Since oral contraceptives are available in a wide range of formulas, follow-up examinations are important to ensure that a woman is receiving an effective dosage with as few side effects as possible. Matching the right prescription with the woman may require a few consultations.

All oral contraceptives contain synthetic (laboratory-made) hormones. The *combined pill* uses both

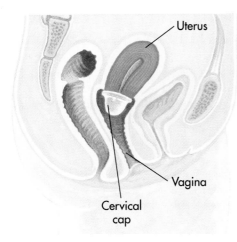

Figure 14-5   After the spermicidal cream or jelly is placed in the cervical cap, the cap is inserted into the vagina and placed against the cervix.

synthetic estrogen and synthetic progesterone in each of 21 pills. In 1984, *triphasic pills* were introduced in the United States. In these pills the level of synthetic progesterone varies every 7 days during the cycle.[2] Estrogen levels remain constant during the cycle. As with many forms of contraception, it must be emphatically stated that *oral contraceptives do not provide protection from the transmission of STDs, including HIV infection.* Furthermore, the use of antibiotics lowers the pill's contraceptive effectiveness.

Oral contraceptives function in several ways. The estrogen in the pill tends to reduce ova development and ovulation. The progesterone in the pill helps reduce ovulation (by lowering the release of luteinizing hormone). The progesterone in the pill also causes the uterine wall to develop inadequately and helps thicken cervical mucus, thus making it difficult for sperm to enter the uterus. (For a discussion of the "morning-after" pill, see the Star Box on p. 356.)

The physical changes produced by the oral contraceptive provide some beneficial side effects in women. Since the synthetic hormones are taken for 21 days and then are followed by **placebo pills** or no pills for 7 days, the menstrual cycle becomes regulated. Even women who have irregular cycles immediately become "regular." Since the uterine lining is not developed to the extent seen in a non–pill-taking woman, the uterus is not forced to contract with the same amount of vigor. Thus menstrual cramping is reduced, and the resultant menstrual flow is diminished. Research indicates that oral contraceptive use may provide protection against anemia, PID, non-cancerous breast tumors, recurrent ovarian cysts, ectopic pregnancy, endometrial cancer, and cancer of the ovaries.[2] No conclusive evidence has been found that links oral contraceptive use to breast cancer. However, oral contraceptive use may be linked to a slight increase in cervical cancer risk.[2]

The negative side effects of the oral contraceptive pill can be divided into two general categories: (1) unpleasant and (2) potentially dangerous. The unpleasant side effects generally subside within 2 or 3 months for most women. A number of women report some or many of the following symptoms:
- Tenderness in breast tissue
- Nausea
- Mild headaches
- Slight, irregular spotting
- Weight gain
- Fluctuations in sex drive
- Mild depression
- More frequent vaginal infections

The potentially dangerous side effects of the oral contraceptive pill are most often seen in the cardiovascular system. Blood clotting, strokes, hypertension, and heart attack all seem to be associated with the estrogen component of the combined pill. When compared with nonusers, the risk of dying from cardiovascular complications is only slightly increased among healthy young oral contraceptive users. Nevertheless, the risks associated with pregnancy and childbirth are still much greater than those associated with oral contraceptive use (see the Learning from All Cultures box on p. 356).

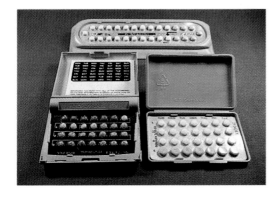

Oral contraceptives.

oral contraceptive pill
A pill taken orally, composed of synthetic female hormones that prevent ovulation or implantation; "the pill."

placebo pills (pla **see** bo)
Pills that contain no active ingredients.

The Morning-After Pill

A "morning-after pill" is an oral contraceptive a woman can take to reduce the possibility of pregnancy after unprotected intercourse. The FDA has not officially approved any oral contraceptive that could be used in this fashion. Formerly, the drug DES (diethylstilbestrol) was used as a type of morning-after pill, although it was primarily for women who were victims of rape. Because of its potentially dangerous side effects, DES was removed from the market. A relatively high-dose combined oral contraceptive (Ovral) is now unofficially the drug of choice as a morning-after pill.

Physicians, who have the right to prescribe drugs for purposes other than those specifically indicated by the FDA, are now prescribing Ovral for patients who have unprotected midcycle intercourse. Some physicians prefer not to use Ovral in this fashion. In taking this drug a woman must take two Ovral pills within 3 days of unprotected intercourse (preferably within 12 to 24 hours). Then she must take two more Ovral pills 12 hours after her first dose of pills. The use of Ovral will start menstrual flow within a few weeks.[2]

The use of a morning-after pill in cases of rape or contraceptive failure is understandable. However, frequent use in cases of unprotected intercourse seems to many people to be a reflection of irresponsibility. What do you think?

There are some **contraindications** for the use of oral contraceptives. If you have a history of blood clotting, migraine headaches, liver disease, a heart condition, high blood pressure, obesity, diabetes, epilepsy, or anemia, or if you have not established regular menstrual cycles, the pill probably should not be your contraceptive choice. A thorough health history is important before a woman starts to take the pill.

Two additional contraindications are receiving considerable attention by the medical community. Cigarette smoking and advancing age are highly associated with an increased risk of potentially serious side effects. Increasing numbers of physicians are not prescribing oral contraceptives for their patients who smoke. The risk of cardiovascular-related deaths is greatly enhanced in women over age 35. The risk is even higher in female smokers over 35. The data are quite convincing.[2]

For the vast majority of women, however, the pill, when properly prescribed, is safe and effective. Careful scrutiny of one's health history and careful follow-

LEARNING from ALL CULTURES

Maternal Deaths during Pregnancy and Childbirth

Throughout the world, one woman dies every minute because of pregnancy-related complications. Most of these deaths take place in developing countries among poor women who have little access to health care services. In developing countries, pregnancy-related complications account for one fourth to one half of the deaths among women of reproductive age. Worldwide, approximately 500,000 women die each year because of pregnancy or childbirth complications.[10]

With the exception of women in China, a typical woman in the developing world has a 1 in 33 chance of dying from pregnancy or childbirth. In contrast, typical women in the developed world have only a 1 in 1500 chance of dying during pregnancy or childbirth.[10]

What makes pregnancy and childbirth so risky in developing countries? The most significant direct causes of death are (1) hemorrhage (severe bleeding after childbirth, abortion, prolonged labor, or ectopic pregnancy), (2) infection (after childbirth or abortion, or related to STDs and resultant PID), and (3) eclampsia (high blood pressure during pregnancy).

What do you think are some of the obstacles that women face in developing countries that make them so vulnerable to this tragedy? Among these, consider issues such as the status of women, the health care delivery system, the age of marriage, prenatal care, and nutrition and health education efforts in developing countries. Do we face some of these same issues in North America?

up examinations when a problem is suspected are essential elements that can provide a margin of safety. The ease of administration, the relatively low cost, and the effectiveness of the pill make it a sound choice for many women.

Minipills

Some women prefer not to use the combined oral contraceptive pill. Thus to avoid some of the potentially serious side effects of the combined pill, some physicians are prescribing **minipills.** These oral contraceptives contain no estrogen—only low-dose progesterone. The minipill seems to work by making an unsuitable environment for the transportation and implantation of the fertilized ovum. The effectiveness of the minipill is slightly lower than that of the combined pill. *Breakthrough bleeding* and **ectopic pregnancy** are more common in minipill users than in combined-pill users.

Injectable Contraceptives

In late 1992 the FDA approved a form of synthetic progesterone called *Depo-Provera.* This contraceptive is injectable and provides an extremely high degree of effectiveness for a 3-month period. The success rate for Depo-Provera is higher than 99%. For women who prefer not to take daily birth control pills or use the Norplant implants described below, Depo-Provera may be a good alternative.

New users of Depo-Provera report occasional breakthrough bleeding as the most common unpleasant side effect.[2] Once the woman's body becomes adjusted to the presence of this drug, breakthrough bleeding is reduced considerably. After this time, the most commonly reported side effect is amenorrhea (the absence of periods), which is understandable, since the drug inhibits ovulation. Many women consider amenorrhea to be a desirable effect of Depo-Provera use. Unlike users of oral contraceptives and subdermal implants, who return to fertility a few months after stopping their use, women who stop using Depo-Provera may experience infertility for a period of up to 1 year.[2]

Subdermal Implants

In late 1990, subdermal implants (Norplant) were approved for use in the United States. This form of contraception uses six silicone rods filled with synthetic progesterone. Using a local anesthetic, the physician implants these rods just beneath the skin of the woman's upper or lower arm. The rods release low levels of the hormone for 5 years. An extremely

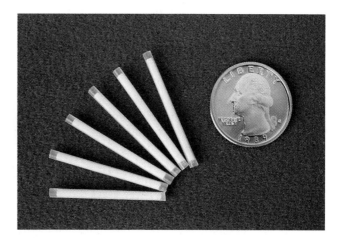

The Norplant subdermal implant.

effective contraceptive, subdermal implants appear to produce minimal side effects. Irregular patterns of menstrual bleeding are the most common side effect. Norplant implants cost approximately $600 to $800 for a 5-year supply.

Sterilization

All of the contraceptive mechanisms or methods already discussed have one quality in common: they are reversible. Although microsurgical techniques are providing medical breakthroughs, **sterilization** should still be considered an irreversible procedure.[6] When you decide to use sterilization, you no longer control your own fertility because you no longer will be able to produce offspring. For this reason, couples considering sterilization procedures usually must undergo extensive discussions with a physician or

contraindications
Factors that make the use of a drug inappropriate or dangerous for a particular person.

minipills
Low-dose progesterone oral contraceptives.

ectopic pregnancy
A pregnancy in which the fertilized ovum implants at a site other than the uterus, typically in the fallopian tubes.

sterilization
Generally permanent birth control techniques that surgically disrupt the normal passage of ova or sperm.

family planning counselor to identify their true feelings about this finality. People must be aware of the possible changes in self-concept they might have after sterilization. If you are a man who equates fertility with masculinity, you may have trouble accepting your new status as a sterile man. If you are a woman who equates motherhood with femininity, you might have adjustment problems after sterilization.

The male sterilization procedure is called a *vasectomy.* Accomplished with a local anesthetic in a physician's office, this 20- to 30-minute procedure consists of the surgical removal of a section of each vas deferens. After a small incision is made through the scrotum, the vas deferens is located and a small section removed. The remaining ends are either tied or *cauterized* (Figure 14-6, *A*).

Immediately after a vasectomy, sperm may still be present in the vas deferens. A backup contraceptive is recommended until a physician microscopically examines a semen specimen. This examination usually occurs about 6 weeks after the surgery. After a vasectomy, men can still produce male sex hormones, get erections, have orgasms, and ejaculate. (Recall that sperm account for only a small portion of the semen.)

Some men even report increased interest in sexual activity, since their chances of impregnating a woman are virtually nonexistent.

What happens to the process of spermatogenesis within each testicle? Sperm cells are still being produced, but they are destroyed by specialized white blood cells called *phagocytic leukocytes.*

The most common method of female sterilization is *tubal ligation.* During this procedure, the fallopian tubes are cut and the ends tied back. Some physicians cauterize the tube ends to ensure complete sealing (Figure 14-6, *B*). The fallopian tubes are usually reached through the abdominal wall. In a *minilaparotomy,* a small incision is made through the abdominal wall just below the navel. The resultant scar is quite small and is the basis for the term *band-aid surgery.*

Female sterilization requires about 20 to 30 minutes, with the patient under a local or general anesthetic. The use of a *laparoscope* has made female sterilization much simpler than in the past. The laparoscope is a small tube equipped with mirrors and lights. Inserted through a single incision, the laparoscope locates the fallopian tubes before they are cut, tied, or cauterized. When a laparoscope is used

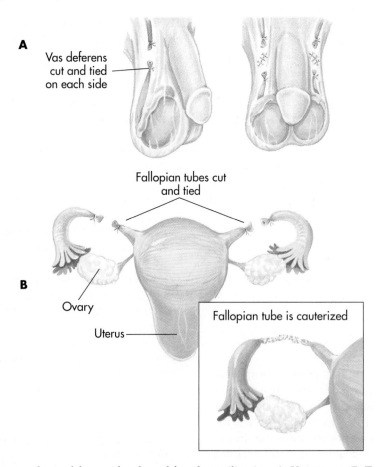

Figure 14-6   The most frequently used forms of male and female sterilization. **A,** Vasectomy. **B,** Tubal ligation.

through an abdominal incision, the procedure is called a *laparoscopy*.

Women who are sterilized still produce female hormones, ovulate, and menstruate. However, the ovum cannot move down the fallopian tube. Within a day of its release, the ovum will start to disintegrate and be absorbed by the body. Freed of the possibility of becoming pregnant, many sterilized women report an increase in sex drive and activity.

Two other procedures produce sterilization in women. *Ovariectomy* (the surgical removal of the ovaries) and *hysterectomy* (the surgical removal of the uterus) accomplish sterilization. However, these procedures are used to remove diseased (cancerous, cystic, or hemorrhaging) organs and are not primarily considered sterilization techniques.

Abortion

Regardless of the circumstances under which pregnancy occurs, women may now choose to terminate their pregnancies. No longer must women who do not want to be pregnant seek potentially dangerous, illegal abortions. On the basis of current technology and legality, women need never experience childbirth. The decision will be theirs to make.

Abortion should never be considered a first-line, preferred form of fertility control. Rather, abortion is a final, last-chance undertaking. It should be used only when responsible control of one's fertility could not be achieved. The decision to abort a fetus is a highly controversial, personal one—one that needs serious consideration by each woman.

On the basis of the landmark 1973 U.S. Supreme Court case *Roe v. Wade,* the United States joined many of the world's most populated countries in legalizing abortions within the following guidelines:

1. For the first 3 months of pregnancy (first trimester), the decision to abort lies with the woman and her doctor.
2. For the next 3 months of pregnancy (second trimester), state law may regulate the abortion procedure in ways that are reasonably related to maternal health.
3. For the last weeks of pregnancy (third trimester) when the fetus is judged capable of surviving if born, any state may regulate or even prohibit abortion except where abortion is necessary to preserve the life or health of the mother. If a pregnancy is terminated during the third trimester, a viable fetus would be considered a live birth and would not be allowed to die.

Each year, approximately 1.5 million women make the decision to terminate a pregnancy in the United States.[5] Thousands of additional women probably consider abortion but elect to continue their pregnancies.

Clearly, abortion is a political issue. It will be interesting to see how future abortion-related decisions will unfold. Special interest groups on both sides of the issues, the Supreme Court, state legislatures, federal agencies (such as the FDA and the Department of Health and Human Services), the Congress, and the President all have a say in the abortion debate in this country. Regardless of the eventual outcomes of this debate, here are the present abortion procedures available in the United States.

First-trimester abortion procedures

Menstrual extraction. Also referred to as *menstrual regulation, menstrual induction,* and *preemptive abortion,* menstrual extraction is a process carried out between the fourth and sixth week after the last menstrual period (or in the days immediately after the first missed menstrual period). Generally performed in a physician's office under a local anesthetic or *paracervical anesthetic,* a small plastic *cannula* is inserted through the undilated cervical canal into the cavity of the uterus. Once the cannula is in position, a small amount of suction is applied by a hand-held syringe. By rotating and moving the cannula across the uterine wall, the physician can withdraw the endometrial tissue.

Vacuum aspiration. Induced abortions undertaken during the sixth through ninth weeks of pregnancy are generally done through *vacuum aspiration* of the uterine contents. Vacuum aspiration is the most commonly performed abortion procedure. This procedure is similar in nature to menstrual extraction. Unlike menstrual extraction, however, vacuum aspiration may require **dilation** of the cervical canal and the use of a local anesthetic. In this more advanced stage of pregnancy, a larger cannula must be inserted into the uterine cavity. This process can be accomplished by using metal dilators of increasingly larger sizes to open the canal. After aspiration by an electric vacuum pump, the uterine wall may also be scraped to confirm complete removal of the uterine contents.

abortion
Induced premature termination of a pregnancy.

dilation
Gradual expansion of an opening or passageway, such as the cervix.

Dilation and curettage (D & C). When a pregnancy is to be terminated during the ninth through fourteenth weeks, vacuum aspiration gives way to a somewhat similar procedure labeled **dilation and curettage,** or more familiarly, **D & C.** D & C usually requires a general anesthetic, not a local anesthetic.[2]

Like vacuum aspiration, the D & C involves the gradual enlargement of the cervical canal through the insertion of increasingly larger metal dilators. When the cervix has been dilated to a size sufficient to allow for the passage of a *curette,* the removal of the endometrial tissue can begin. The curette is a metal instrument resembling a spoon, with a cup-shaped cutting surface on its end. As the curette is drawn across the uterine wall, the soft endometrial tissue and fetal parts are scraped from the wall of the uterus. (The D & C is also used in the medical management of certain health conditions of the uterine wall, such as irregular bleeding or the buildup of endometrial tissue.)

As in the case of menstrual extraction, both vacuum aspiration and D & C are very safe procedures for the woman. The need to dilate the cervix more fully in a D & C increases the risk of cervical trauma and the possibility of perforation, but these risks are reported to be low. Bleeding, cramping, spotting, and infections present minimal controllable risks when procedures are done by experienced clinicians under clinical conditions.

The abortion pill. The Roussel-Uclaf company in Paris, France, has produced a very controversial form of birth control, RU 486 (mifepristone). RU 486 is controversial because it is designed to produce an abortion. This drug is a pill that blocks the action of progesterone. When three 200-mg RU 486 pills are taken and followed 48 hours later by an injection (or vaginal suppository) of prostaglandin, menstruation begins, usually within 5 hours. In May 1994, Roussel-Uclaf agreed to give its patent rights to RU 486 to the Population Council, a New York–based international, nonprofit contraceptive research organization. This action paved the way for the Population Council to test this drug on U.S. women begining in the fall of 1994. After two years of testing, the Food and Drug Administration determined RU 486 to be safe and effective. Final approval of RU 486 as a prescription drug is expected in 1998.[1]

Second-trimester abortion procedures

When a woman's pregnancy continues beyond the fourteenth week of gestation, termination becomes a more difficult matter. The procedures at this stage become more complicated and take longer to be completed, and complications become more common.

Dilation and evacuation. Vacuum aspiration and D & C can be combined in a procedure called *dilation and evacuation (D & E)* during the earliest weeks of the second trimester (Figure 14-7). The use of D & E increases the likelihood of trauma and postprocedural complications, since larger instruments and greater dilation are required. After about 16 weeks, more intensive procedures will be required to terminate the late second trimester pregnancy.

Hypertonic saline procedure. From the sixteenth week of gestation to the end of the second trimester, intrauterine injection of a strong salt solution into the amniotic sac is the procedure most frequently used. The administration of intrauterine **hypertonic saline solution** requires a skilled operator so that the needle used to introduce the salt solution enters the amniotic sac. Once the needle is in place, some amniotic fluid is withdrawn, allowing the saline solution to be injected.

Some physicians support the saline procedure by dilating the cervix with *laminaria* or another dilatory product and administering the hormone oxytocin to stimulate uterine contractions. The onset of uterine contractions will expel the dehydrated uterine contents within 24 to 36 hours.

Prostaglandin procedure. The use of prostaglandin is the third type of abortion procedure used during the second trimester. Prostaglandins are hormonelike chemicals that have a variety of useful effects on human tissue. Produced naturally within the body, these substances influence the contractions of smooth

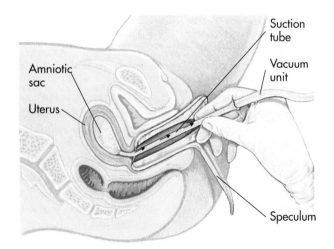

Figure 14-7   During dilation and evacuation, the cervix is dilated and the contents of the uterus are aspirated. This procedure is used to perform abortions up to 16 weeks' gestation.

muscle. Since the uterine wall is composed entirely of smooth muscle, it is particularly sensitive to the presence of prostaglandins. When prostaglandin is administered in sufficient quantity (through either a uterine intramuscular injection or a vaginal suppository), uterine contractions become strong enough to expel the fetal contents.

Third-trimester abortion procedures

Should termination of a pregnancy be required in the latter weeks of the gestational period, a surgical procedure in which the fetus will be removed *(hysterotomy)* or a procedure in which the entire uterus is removed *(hysterectomy)* can be undertaken. As you can imagine, these procedures are more complicated and involve longer hospitalization, major abdominal surgery, and an extended period of recovery.

The U.S. House of Representatives and the U.S. Senate recently voted to ban a rarely used third trimester abortion procedure referred to as *dilation and extraction.* Lawmakers felt this procedure, also called *partial-birth abortion,* was too gruesome to be permitted. President Clinton vetoed this ban, and because the Senate failed to override his veto, the ban on partial-birth abortion did not become law.

BECOMING PARENTS

Although birth control is especially important for many young couples, most couples eventually want to have children and raise a family. In the past, couples had their children very quickly after either high school or college. Now the trend seems to be to wait longer before having children. Most likely, educational, economic, contraceptive, and occupational factors have laid the groundwork for this trend. To the relief of many people, medical research indicates that women above the age of 30 or 35 are quite capable of having healthy babies.

Parenting Issues for Couples

Before deciding to have children, couples should have frank discussions about the effect that pregnancy and a newborn child will have on their lives. For those students contemplating single parenthood, we ask that you consider these issues as they relate to your particular situation and to excuse our consistent use of plural pronouns. In any event, some or all of the following basic considerations should be discussed:

- What effect will pregnancy have on us individually and collectively?
- Why do we want to have a child?
- What effect will a child have on the images we have constructed for ourselves as adults?
- Can we afford to have a child and provide for its needs?
- How will the responsibilities related to raising a child be divided?
- How will our professional careers be affected by the addition of a child?
- Are we ready now to accept the extended responsibilities that can come with a new child?
- How will we rear our child in terms of religious training, discipline, and participation in activities?
- Are we ready to part with much of the freedom associated with late adolescence and the early young adult years?
- How will we handle the possibility of being awakened by 6 AM each morning for the next few years?
- What plans have been made if we discover that our baby (or fetus) has a serious birth defect?
- Are we capable of handling the additional responsibilities associated with having a disabled child?
- Are we comfortable with the thought of bringing another child into an already overcrowded, violent, bigoted, and polluted world?

If these questions seem strikingly negative in tone, there is indeed a reason for this. We believe that all too frequently the "nuts and bolts" issues related to childbearing and parenting are ignored or at least are placed on the back burner. Although it is important for future parents to consider how cute and cuddly a new baby will be, how holidays will be enhanced with a new child, and how pleased the grandparents will be, we consider these issues secondary to the serious realities of having a child enter your lives. For a more detailed discussion of this topic, see "Focus on . . . The Consequences of Unintended Pregnancy" at the end of this chapter.

---

dilation and curettage (D & C) (kyoo re tahzh)
A surgical procedure in which the cervical canal is dilated to allow the uterine wall to be scraped.

hypertonic saline solution
A salt solution with a concentration higher than that found in human fluids.

A Parenting Prescription for the Early Years

Dr. T. Berry Brazelton, internationally known pediatrician and child development specialist, realizes how difficult it is to raise children in the 1990s. Brazelton knows that trying to juggle employment, college work, and family life is especially difficult and can at times seem overwhelming. Firm in his belief that parents can be successful at coping with busy schedules and raising well-adjusted children, Brazelton has identified 14 key parenting points for families with young children.[7]

1. *Separate your home and work environments.* Try to keep the two separate as much as possible.
2. *Plan your daily separation from your children.* Don't just separate without a warm exchange.
3. *Realize that it is okay to feel sad about leaving your child.* This will encourage you to get the best child care available.
4. *Allow yourself to feel a measure of guilt.* In this case, guilt can be a powerful source for solving problems.
5. *Share your stress with friends or support groups.* Interacting with others can provide much-needed support.
6. *Always include your spouse in family activities.* Let him or her have a significant role in important decisions.
7. *Do not feel that you must be a "superparent" or that you must raise "superkids."* Don't hold yourself up to standards that are virtually impossible to reach. It's not fair to you or your kids.
8. *While at work, conserve some energy for your home life.* Plan your day so that you are ready to do more than collapse in front of the television when you get home.
9. *Be sure you understand all the parenting options available at your workplace.* Know the policies related to day care, flexible time schedules, job-sharing possibilities, and sick leave if your child becomes ill.
10. *Prepare yourself for a bit of chaos when you return home after work.* Children often save some of their energy and feelings until they are back with their family.
11. *Hug or hold your young children for at least a few moments when you return from work.* Don't just come home and start your chores or housework without first making close contact with your children.
12. *Encourage your children to help you with your chores.* Most young children want to help. Be patient; encourage and praise their efforts.
13. *Make sure each child has some special time alone with each parent at least once every week.* This shows children that each child is important and deserves attention.
14. *Learn that stress is normal and that you can cope.* Solving problems together as a family can build warm and lasting relationships.

PREGNANCY: AN EXTENSION OF THE PARTNERSHIP

Pregnancy is a condition that requires a series of complex yet coordinated changes to occur in the female body. This chapter follows pregnancy from its beginning, at fertilization, to its conclusion, with labor and childbirth.

Physiological Obstacles and Aids to Fertilization

Many sexually active young people believe that they will become pregnant (or impregnate someone) only when they want to, despite their haphazard contraceptive practices. Because of this mistaken belief, many young people are not sold on the use of contraceptives. It is important for young adults to remember that from a species survival standpoint, our bodies were designed to promote pregnancy. It is estimated that about 85% of sexually active women of childbearing age will become pregnant within 1 year if they do not use some form of contraception.[2]

With regard to pregnancy, each act of intercourse can be considered a game of physiological odds. There are obstacles that may reduce a couple's chance of pregnancy, including the following:

Obstacles to fertilization

1. *The acidic level of the vagina is destructive to sperm.* The low pH of the vagina will kill sperm that fail to enter the uterus quickly.
2. *The cervical mucus is thick during most of the menstrual cycle.* Sperm movement into the uterus is more difficult, except during the few days surrounding ovulation.
3. *The sperm must locate the cervical opening.* The cervical opening is small compared with the rest of the surface area where sperm are deposited.
4. *Half of the sperm travel through the wrong fallopian tube.* Most commonly, only one ovum is released at ovulation. The two ovaries generally "take turns" each month. The sperm have no way of "knowing" which tube they should enter. Thus

it is probable that half will travel through the wrong tube.

5. *The distance sperm must travel is relatively long compared with the tiny size of the sperm cells.* Microscopic sperm must travel about 7 or 8 inches once they are inside the female.

6. *The sperm's travel is relatively "upstream."* The anatomical positioning of the female reproductive structures necessitates an "uphill" movement by the sperm.

7. *The contoured folds of the tubal walls trap many sperm.* These folds make it difficult for sperm to locate the egg. Many sperm are trapped in this maze.

There are also a variety of aids that tend to help sperm and egg cells join. Some of these are listed below.

Aids to fertilization

1. *An astounding number of sperm are deposited during ejaculation.* Each ejaculation contains about a teaspoon of semen.[8] Within this quantity are between 200 and 500 million sperm cells. Even with large numbers of sperm killed in the vagina, millions are able to move to the deeper structures.

2. *Sperm are deposited near the cervical opening.* Penetration into the vagina by the penis allows for the sperm to be placed near the cervical opening.

3. *The male accessory glands help make the semen nonacidic.* The seminal vesicles, prostate gland, and Cowper's glands secrete fluids that pro-

vide an alkaline environment for the sperm. This environment helps sperm be better protected in the vagina until they can move into the deeper, more alkaline uterus and fallopian tubes.

4. *Uterine contractions aid sperm movement.* The rhythmic muscular contractions of the uterus tend to cause the sperm to move in the direction of the fallopian tubes.

5. *Sperm cells move rather quickly.* Despite their tiny size, sperm cells can move relatively quickly—just about 1 inch per hour. Powered by sugar solutions from the male accessory glands and the whiplike movements of their tails, sperm can reach the distant third of the fallopian tubes in less than 8 hours as they swim in the direction of the descending ovum.

6. *Once inside the fallopian tubes, sperm can live for days.* Some sperm may be viable for up to a week after reaching the comfortable, nonacidic environment of the fallopian tubes. Most sperm, however, will survive an average of 48 to 72 hours. Thus they can "wait in the wings" for the moment an ovum is released from the ovary (Figure 14-8).

7. *The cervical mucus is thin and watery at the time of ovulation.* This mucus allows for better passage of sperm through the cervical opening when the ovum is most capable of being fertilized.

Signs of Pregnancy

Aside from pregnancy tests done in a professional laboratory, a woman can sometimes recognize early signs and symptoms. The signs of pregnancy have been divided into three categories:

Presumptive signs of pregnancy

Missed period after unprotected intercourse the previous month

Nausea on awakening (morning sickness)

Increase in size and tenderness of breasts

Darkening of the areolar tissue surrounding the nipples

Probable signs of pregnancy

Increase in the frequency of urination (the growing uterus presses against the bladder)

Increase in the size of the abdomen

Cervix becomes softer by the sixth week (detected by a pelvic examination by clinician)

Positive pregnancy test (see the Star Box on p. 364)

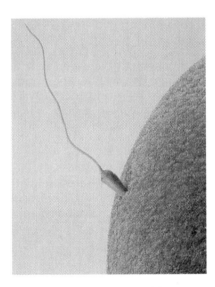

The surface of an ovum is penetrated by sperm at fertilization.

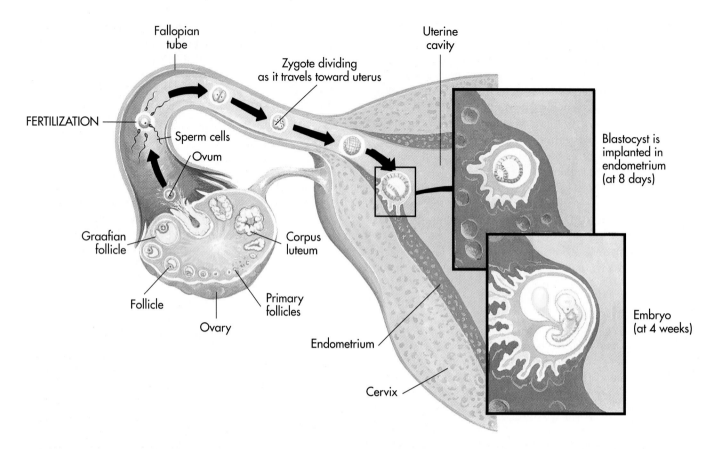

Fallopian tube

Zygote dividing as it travels toward uterus

Uterine cavity

FERTILIZATION

Sperm cells

Ovum

Blastocyst is implanted in endometrium (at 8 days)

Graafian follicle

Corpus luteum

Follicle

Primary follicles

Ovary

Endometrium

Embryo (at 4 weeks)

Cervix

Figure 14-8   After its release from the follicle, the ovum begins its week-long journey down the fallopian tube. Fertilization generally occurs in the outermost third of the tube. Now fertilized, the ovum progresses toward the uterus, where it embeds itself in the endometrium. A pregnancy is established.

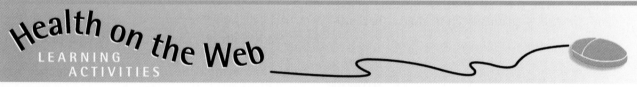

Health on the Web
LEARNING ACTIVITIES

Activity 1

This chapter has addressed a number of birth control methods. You can find more information about birth control on the web. An excellent resource is the Planned Parenthood website at www.igc.apc.org/ppfa/contraception/choices_main.html. Planned Parenthood believes in the right of each individual to manage his or her fertility, regardless of the individual's income, marital status, race, ethnicity, sexual orientation, age, national origin, or residence. To assist people in making reproductive decisions, they provide information on contraceptive choices throughout one's life. Take time to read about the different methods available and consider how well each would work for you if you are sexually active. In addition, consider Planned Parenthood's position on reproductive rights. Do you agree or disagree with this position? Explain your answer.

Activity 2

Healthwise is an interactive question and answer service offered by the Health Education and Wellness Program of the Columbia University Health Service. The service was established to help students make choices that will enhance their health and happiness and the well-being of others. Go to their website, www.columbia.edu/cu/healthwise/index.html, and select the Q & A interactive service. From there, select "Sexual Health." Now select from the list of questions other college students have asked about birth control, or submit your own question.

Activity 3

During pregnancy, a series of complex yet coordinated changes occur in the female body. Go to www.mayohealth.org/mayo/common/htm/duedate/duedate.htm to obtain an interactive due date calculator and a list of other important dates during pregnancy. Use the calculator at this site to determine the milestones during a pregnancy.

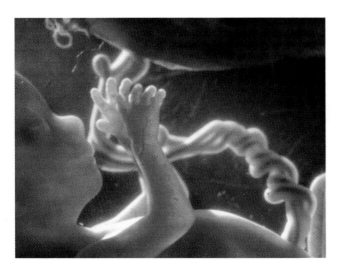

The fetus at 16 weeks' gestation within the amniotic sac.

Positive signs of pregnancy

Determination of a fetal heartbeat

Feeling of the fetus moving (quickening)

Observation of fetus by ultrasound or optical viewers

Agents That Can Damage a Fetus

A large number of agents that come into contact with a pregnant woman can affect fetal development (see the Star Box above). Many of these (rubella and herpes viruses, tobacco smoke, alcohol, and virtually all other drugs) are discussed in other chapters of this text. The best advice for a pregnant woman is to maintain close contact with her obstetrician during pregnancy and to consider carefully the ingestion of any OTC drug (including aspirin, caffeine, and antacids) that could harm the fetus.

It is also important for any woman to avoid exposure to radiation during the pregnancy. Such exposure, most commonly through excessive x-rays or radiation fallout from nuclear testing, can irreversibly damage fetal genetic structures.

CHILDBIRTH: THE LABOR OF DELIVERY

Childbirth, or *parturition,* is one of the true peak life experiences for both men and women. Most of the time, childbirth is a wonderfully exciting venture into the unknown. For the parents, this intriguing experience can provide a stage for personal growth, maturity, and insight into a dynamic, complex world.

During the last few weeks of the third **trimester,** most fetuses will move deeper into the pelvic cavity in a process called *lightening.* During this movement, the fetus's body will rotate and the head will begin to engage more deeply into the mother's pelvic girdle. Many women will report that their babies have "dropped."

Warning: Acne, Accutane, and Birth Defects

Accutane, manufactured by Roche Laboratories, may be the most effective prescription drug for severe cystic acne, a type of acne that often causes deep scarring. In the spring of 1988 the FDA reissued an earlier warning that pregnant women should not use this drug, since it is capable of causing severe birth defects such as brain, skull, facial, and cardiac abnormalities. Women who use Accutane and are planning a pregnancy are encouraged to stop using the drug for two menstrual cycles before becoming pregnant. This gives the body time to clear Accutane from its system before conception. Some physicians recommend that women take a pregnancy test before beginning use of Accutane because of its severe effects on fetuses.

Another indication that parturition may be relatively near is the increased reporting of *Braxton Hicks contractions.* These uterine contractions, which are of mild intensity and often occur at irregular intervals, may be felt throughout a pregnancy. During the last few weeks of pregnancy *(gestation),* these mild contractions can occur more frequently and cause a woman to feel as if she is going into labor **(false labor).**

Labor begins when uterine contractions become more intense and occur at regular intervals. The birth of a child can be divided into three stages: (1) *effacement* and dilation of the cervix, (2) delivery of the fetus, and (3) expulsion of the placenta (Figure 14-9). For a woman having her first child, the birth process lasts an average of 12 to 16 hours. The average length of labor for subsequent births is much shorter—from 4 to 10 hours on the average. Labor is very unpredictable: labors that last between 1 and 24 hours occur daily at most hospitals.

Stage One: Effacement and Dilation of the Cervix

In the first stage of labor the uterine contractions attempt to thin (efface) the normally thick cervical walls and to enlarge (dilate) the cervical opening. These contractions are directed by the release of

trimester
A 3-month period; human pregnancies encompass three trimesters.

false labor
Conditions that resemble the start of true labor; may include irregular uterine contractions, pressure, and discomfort in the lower abdomen.

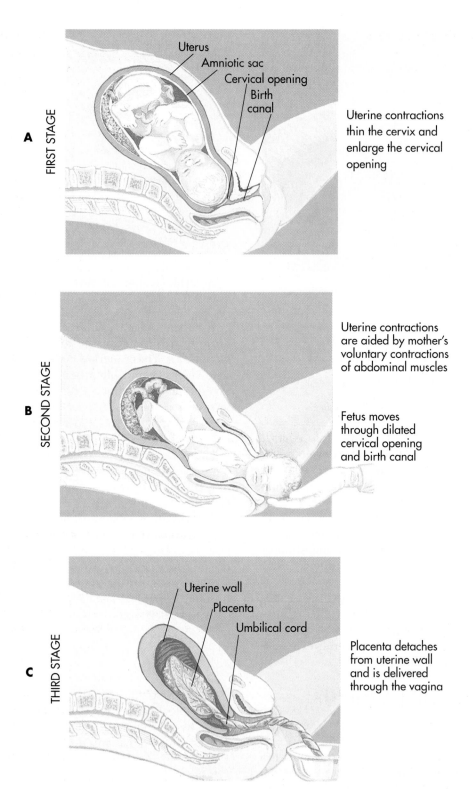

A FIRST STAGE

Uterus
Amniotic sac
Cervical opening
Birth canal

Uterine contractions thin the cervix and enlarge the cervical opening

B SECOND STAGE

Uterine contractions are aided by mother's voluntary contractions of abdominal muscles

Fetus moves through dilated cervical opening and birth canal

C THIRD STAGE

Uterine wall
Placenta
Umbilical cord

Placenta detaches from uterine wall and is delivered through the vagina

Figure 14-9   Labor, or childbirth, is a three-stage process. During effacement and dilation, the first stage, the cervical canal is gradually opened by contractions of the uterine wall. The second stage, delivery of the baby, encompasses the actual delivery of the fetus from the uterus and through the birth canal. The delivery of the placenta, the third stage, empties the uterus, thus completing the process of childbirth.

prostaglandins and the hormone oxytocin into the circulating bloodstream. In women delivering their first babies, effacement will occur before dilation. In subsequent deliveries, effacement and dilation usually occur at the same time.

The first stage of labor is often the longest.[6] The cervical opening must thin and dilate to a diameter of 10 cm before the first stage of labor is considered complete. Often this stage begins with the dislodging of the cervical mucous plug. The subsequent *bloody show* (mucous plug and a small amount of blood) at the vaginal opening may indicate that effacement and dilation have begun. Another indication of labor's onset may be the bursting or tearing of the fetal amniotic sac. "Breaking the bag of waters" refers to this phenomenon, which happens in various measures in expectant women.

The pain of the uterine contractions becomes more intense as the woman moves through this first stage of labor. As the cervical opening effaces and dilates from 0 to 3 cm, many women report feeling happy, exhilarated, and confident. In the early phase of the first stage of labor, the contractions are relatively short (lasting from 15 to 60 seconds) and the intervals between contractions range from 20 minutes to 5 minutes as labor progresses. However, these rest intervals will become shorter and the contractions more forceful when the woman's uterus contracts to dilate 4 to 7 cm.

In this second phase of the first stage of labor, the contractions usually last about 1 minute each and the rest intervals drop from about 5 minutes to 1 minute over a period of 5 to 9 hours.

The third phase of the first stage of labor is called *transition*. During transition, the uterus contracts to dilate the cervical opening to the full 10 cm required for safe passage of the fetus out of the uterus and into the vagina (birth canal). This period of labor is often the most painful part of the entire birth process. Fortunately, it is also the shortest phase of most labors. Lasting between 15 and 30 minutes, transition contractions often last 60 to 90 seconds each. The rest intervals between contractions are short and vary from 30 to 60 seconds.

An examination of the cervix by a nurse or physician will reveal whether full dilation of 10 cm has occurred. Until the full 10-cm dilation, women are cautioned not to "push" the fetus during the contractions. Special breathing and concentration techniques help many women cope with the first stage of labor.

Stage Two: Delivery of the Fetus

Once the mother's cervix is fully dilated, she enters the second stage of labor, the delivery of the fetus through the birth canal. Now the mother is encouraged to help push the baby out (with her abdominal muscles) during each contraction. In this second stage the uterine contractions are less forceful than during the transition phase of the first stage and may last 60 seconds each, with a 1- to 3-minute rest interval.

This second stage may last up to 2 hours in first births.[8] For subsequent births, this stage will usually be much shorter. When the baby's head is first seen at the vaginal opening, *crowning* is said to have taken place. Generally the back of the baby's head appears first. (Infants whose feet or buttocks are presented first are said to be delivered in a *breech position*.) Once the head is delivered, the baby's body rotates upward to let the shoulders come through. The rest of the body follows quite quickly. The second stage of labor ends when the fetus is fully expelled from the vagina.

Newly delivered babies often look far different from the babies seen on television commercials. Their heads are often cone-shaped as a result of the compression of cranial bones that occurs during the delivery through the birth canal. Within a few days after birth, the newborn's head will assume a much more normal shape. Most babies (of all races) appear bluish at first until they begin regular breathing. All babies are covered with a coating of *vernix*, a white, cheeselike substance that protects the skin.

Stage Three: Delivery of the Placenta

Usually within 30 minutes after the fetus is delivered, the uterus will again initiate a series of contractions to expel the placenta (or *afterbirth*). The placenta is examined by the attending physician to ensure that it was completely expelled. Torn remnants of the placenta could lead to dangerous *hemorrhaging* by the mother. Often the physician will perform a manual examination of the uterus after the placenta has been delivered.

Once the placenta has been delivered, the uterus will continue with mild contractions to help control bleeding and start the gradual reduction of the uterus to its normal, nonpregnant size. This final aspect of the birth process is called **postpartum.** External abdominal massage of the lower abdomen seems to help the uterus contract, as does an infant's nursing at the mother's breast.

postpartum
The period after the birth of a baby during which the uterus returns to its prepregnancy size.

Cesarean Deliveries

A **cesarean delivery** (cesarean birth, C-section) is a procedure in which the fetus is surgically removed from the mother's uterus through the abdominal wall. This type of delivery, which is completed in up to an hour, can be performed with the mother having a regional or a general anesthetic.

Currently, 23% of all deliveries are by cesarean section.[5] The use of cesarean deliveries is questioned by some medical experts, although others point to the need for this kind of delivery when one or more of the following factors are present:

- The fetus is improperly positioned.
- The mother's pelvis is too small.
- The fetus is especially large.
- The fetus shows signs of respiratory or cardiac distress.
- The umbilical cord is compressed.
- The placenta is being delivered before the fetus.
- The mother's health is at risk.

Although a cesarean delivery is considered major surgery, most mothers cope well with the delivery and postsurgical and postpartum discomfort. The hospital stay is usually a few days longer than for a vaginal delivery. The mother can still nurse her child and may still be able to have vaginal deliveries with later children. More and more hospitals are allowing the father to be in the operating room during cesarean deliveries. Fortunately, research indicates that early **bonding** between child, mother, and father can still occur with cesarean deliveries. Cesarean deliveries are much more expensive than vaginal deliveries.

INFERTILITY

Most traditional-age college students are interested in preventing pregnancy. However, increasing numbers of other people are trying to do just the opposite: they are trying to become pregnant. It is estimated that about one in six couples has a problem with *infertility*. These couples wish to become pregnant but are unsuccessful.

Why are couples infertile? These reasons are about evenly balanced between men and women. About 10% of infertility cases have no detectable cause. The most frequent male complication is insufficient sperm production and delivery. A number of approaches can be used to increase sperm counts. Among the simple approaches are the application of periodic cold packs on the scrotum and the replacement of tight underwear with boxer shorts. When a structural problem reduces sperm production, surgery can be helpful. Opinion is divided concerning whether increased fre-

quency of intercourse improves fertility. Most experts (fertility endocrinologists) suggest that couples have intercourse at least a couple of times in the week preceding ovulation.

Men can also collect (through masturbation) and save samples of their sperm to use in a procedure called *artificial insemination by partner*. Near the time of ovulation, the collected samples of sperm are then deposited near the woman's cervical opening. In the related procedure called *artificial insemination by donor*, the sperm of a donor are used. Donor semen is screened for the presence of pathogens, including the AIDS virus.

Causes of infertility in women center mostly on obstructions in the reproductive tract and the inability to ovulate. The obstructions frequently result from tissue damage (scarring) caused by infections. Chlamydial and gonorrheal infections often produce fertility problems. In certain women the use of IUDs has produced infections and PID; both of these increase the chances of infertility. Other possible causes of structural abnormalities include scar tissue from previous surgery, fibroid tumors, polyps, and endometriosis. A variety of microsurgical techniques may correct some of these complications.

One of the most recent innovative procedures involves the use of **transcervical balloon tuboplasty.** In this procedure a series of balloon-tipped catheters are inserted through the uterus into the blocked fallopian tubes. Once inflated, these balloon catheters help open the scarred passageways.

When a woman has ovulation difficulties, pinpointing the specific cause can be very difficult. Increasing age produces hormone fluctuations associated with lack of ovulation. Being significantly overweight or underweight also has a serious effect on fertility. However, in women of normal weight who are not approaching menopause, it appears that ovulation difficulties are caused by failure of synchronization between the hormones governing the menstrual cycle. Fertility drugs can help alter the menstrual cycle to produce ovulation. Clomiphene citrate (Clomid), in oral pill form, and injections of a mixture of LH and FSH taken from the urine of menopausal women (Pergonal) are the most common fertility drugs available. Both are capable of producing multiple ova at ovulation.

For couples who are unable to conceive after drug therapy, surgery, and artificial insemination, the use of *in vitro fertilization and embryo transfer (IVF-ET)* is another option. This method is sometimes referred to as the "test tube" procedure. Costing up to $10,000 per attempt, IVF-ET consists of surgically retrieving fertilizable ova from the woman and combining them in a glass dish with sperm. After several days, the fertilized ova are transferred into the uterus. The pregnancy success rate for a single treatment cycle is 19%.[9]

A newer test tube procedure is called *gamete intrafallopian transfer (GIFT)*. Similar to IVF-ET, this procedure deposits a mixture of retrieved eggs and sperm directly into the fallopian tubes. The pregnancy success rate for a single treatment cycle is 29%.[9]

Fertilized ova (zygotes) can also be transferred from a laboratory dish into the fallopian tubes in a procedure called *zygote intrafallopian transfer (ZIFT)*. One advantage of this procedure is that the clinicians are certain that ova have been fertilized before the transfer to the fallopian tubes.

Surrogate parenting is another option that has been explored in the last decade, although the legal and ethical issues surrounding this method of conception have not been fully resolved. Surrogate parenting exists in a number of forms. Typically, an infertile couple will make a contract with a woman (the surrogate parent), who will then be artificially inseminated with semen from the expectant father. In some instances the surrogate will receive an embryo from the donor parents. In some cases, women have served as surrogates for their close relatives. The surrogate will carry the fetus to term and return the newborn to the parents. Because of the concerns about true "ownership" of the baby, surrogate parenting may not be a particularly viable or legal option for many couples. The Star Box at right points out some serious questions raised by surrogate parenting.

The process of coping with infertility problems can be an emotionally stressful experience for a couple. Hours of waiting in physicians' offices, having numerous examinations, scheduling intercourse, producing sperm samples, and undergoing surgical or drug treatments place multiple burdens on a couple. Knowing that other couples are able to conceive so effortlessly adds to the mental strain. Fortunately, support groups exist to assist couples with infertility problems. Some of these groups are listed in the Star Box on p. 370.

What can you do to reduce the chances of developing infertility problems? Certainly avoiding infections of the reproductive organs is one crucial factor. Barrier methods of contraception (condom, diaphragm) with a spermicide reportedly cut the risk of developing infertility in half. The use of an IUD should be carefully considered, and the risk from multiple partners should encourage responsible sexual activity. Men and women should be aware of the dangers from

Surrogate Parenting: Unresolved Questions

Many important questions regarding surrogate parenting have been raised during the last 5 years. Among these are the following:

- Does the surrogate mother sell a service or a product?
- If a surrogate mother charges and is paid a fee, is this different from giving her service free of charge? Do her rights to the baby change?
- Do the people who receive the services of a surrogate mother have the right to reject the baby if it is handicapped or otherwise unacceptable?
- Does the surrogate mother have a right to keep the child?
- Does the surrogate mother have visitation rights to the child?
- Can the infertile couple require the surrogate mother not to consume alcohol, tobacco, or other dangerous products during the pregnancy?
- How can the infertile couple monitor the pregnancy?
- Who pays for long-term health care if the surrogate mother's health status is harmed by the pregnancy or delivery?

working around hazardous chemicals or consuming psychoactive drugs. Maintaining overall good health and having regular medical (and, for women, gynecological) checkups are also good ideas. Finally, since infertility is linked with advancing age, couples may not want to indefinitely delay having children.

cesarean delivery (si **zare** ee an)
Surgical removal of a fetus through the abdominal wall.

bonding
Important initial recognition established between the newborn and those adults on whom the newborn will be dependent.

transcervical balloon tuboplasty
The use of inflatable balloon catheters to open blocked fallopian tubes; a procedure used for some women with fertility problems.

✯ ✯ ✯ ✯ ✯ ✯   ✯ ✯ ✯ ✯ ✯ ✯

Where to Find Help for Infertility

These agencies can provide you with information about infertility and give referrals to specialists in your area:

American Society for Reproductive Medicine
1209 Montgomery Highway
Birmingham, AL 35216-2809
(205) 978-5000
www.asrm.com

Planned Parenthood Federation of America
810 Seventh Avenue
New York, NY 10019
(800) 829-7732
www.plannedparenthood.org

These agencies can provide help to prospective adoptive parents:
The National Adoption Center
1500 Walnut Street
Suite 701
Philadelphia, PA 19102
(215) 735-9988
www.adopt.org

The National Council for Adoption
1930 17th Street, N.W.
Washington, DC 20009
(202) 328-8072
www.ncfa-usa.org

The North American Council on Adoptable Children
970 Raymond Ave.
Suite 106
St. Paul, MN 55114-1149
(612) 644-3036
members.aol.com/nacac

Adoptive Families of America, Inc.
2309 Como Ave.
St. Paul, MN 55108
(800) 372-3300
www.adoptivefam.org
Publishes *OURS* Magazine (Organization for United Response)

Summary

- *Birth control* refers to all of the procedures that can prevent the birth of a child.
- *Contraception* refers to any procedure that prevents fertilization.
- Each birth control method has both a theoretical effectiveness rate and a use effectiveness rate. For some contraceptive approaches, these rates are similar (such as hormonal methods), and for others the rates are very different (such as condoms, diaphragms, and periodic abstinence).
- Many factors should be considered when deciding which contraceptive is best for you.
- Sterilization (vasectomy and tubal ligation) is usually considered an irreversible procedure.

- Currently, abortion remains a woman's choice under the guidelines of the 1973 *Roe v. Wade* decision and various state restrictions.
- Abortion procedures vary according to the stage of the pregnancy.
- There are many important issues for couples to discuss before deciding to have children.
- Childbirth takes place in three distinct stages: effacement and dilation of the cervix, delivery of the fetus, and delivery of the placenta.
- Infertility is an important concern for some couples. Various technologies are improving infertile couples' chances of having children.

Review Questions

1. Explain the difference between the terms *birth control* and *contraception*. Give examples of each.
2. Explain the difference between theoretical and use effectiveness rates. Which one is always higher? Why is it important to know the difference between these two rates?

3. Identify some of the factors that should be given careful consideration when selecting a contraceptive method. Explain each factor.
4. For each of the methods of birth control, explain how it works and its advantages and disadvantages.

5. How do minipills differ from the combined oral contraceptive? What is a morning-after pill? How do subdermal implants (Norplant) differ from Depo-Provera?
6. Identify and describe the different abortion procedures that are used during each trimester of pregnancy. When is the safest time for an abortion?
7. What are some obstacles and aids to fertilization presented in this chapter? Can you think of others?
8. Identify and describe the events that occur during each of the three stages of childbirth. Approximately how long is each stage?
9. What can be done to reduce chances of infertility? Explain IVF-ET, GIFT, and ZIFT procedures.

 Think About This . . .

- What factors would be most important to you in selecting an appropriate contraceptive method?
- How well do you think college students understand that oral contraceptives do not protect against STDs, including HIV infection?
- Under what circumstances, if any, do you believe abortion is acceptable? Unacceptable?
- Will you or your partner someday undergo sterilization? If so, which of you will have the surgery?
- Can you identify locations at or near your college where professional family-planning services are available?

- What effects do you think starting parenthood at a later age has on the parent and on the child?
- How do you feel about a couple's choice not to have children?
- If a woman should not smoke, drink, or use other drugs during pregnancy, should these limitations also be placed on the father? Why or why not?
- To what extent should fathers participate in the birth experience?
- Do you plan to become a parent? If so, when?

References

1. Allgeier EA, Allgeier AR: *Sexual interactions: basic understandings,* Boston, 1998, Houghton Mifflin.
2. Hatcher RA et al: *Contraceptive technology,* ed 16, New York, 1994, Irvington.
3. Goldberg MS: Choosing a contraceptive, *FDA Consumer* 27(7):18-25, 1993.
4. Farley TMM et al: Intrauterine devices and pelvic inflammatory disease: an international study, *Lancet* 339(8796):785-788, 1992.
5. U.S. Bureau of the Census: *Statistical abstract of the United States, 1996,* ed 116, Washington, DC, 1996, U.S. Government Printing Office.
6. Strong B, DeVault C: *Human sexuality: diversity in contemporary America,* ed 2, Mountain View, CA, 1997, Mayfield.
7. Brazelton TB: Bringing up baby: a doctor's prescription for busy parents, *Newsweek,* p. 68, Feb 13, 1989.
8. Hyde JS, Delamater JD: *Understanding human sexuality,* ed 6, New York, 1997, McGraw-Hill.
9. Medical Research International, Society for Assisted Reproductive Technology, The American Fertility Society: In-vitro fertilization-embryo transfer (IVF-ET) in the United States: 1990 results from the IVF-ET registry, *Fertil Steril* (57)1:15, 1992.
10. Population Information Program: Mothers' lives matter: maternal health in the community, *Population Reports* 16:2, 1988; Series L: No. 7, Center for Communications Programs, Johns Hopkins University.

Suggested Readings

Bullough VL, Bullough B: *Contraception: a guide to birth control methods,* ed 2, Amherst, NY, 1997, Prometheus Books.

This book is written not for health professionals, but for general readers interested in knowing about a wide range of contraceptive options. The book contains information about the history of contraception, and probable future developments in contraception.

Mason D, Ingersol D: *Breastfeeding and the working mother,* New York, 1997, St. Martin's Press.

In addition to tips and anecdotes about breastfeeding, this guide discusses issues especially important to professional mothers, such as business travel, meetings, and legal rights. The book helps mothers choose the most appropriate clothing and equipment for nursing. The photos and drawings used throughout the book are helpful in illustrating proper nursing techniques.

Stern DN: *The birth of a mother: how the motherhood experience changes you forever,* New York, 1998, Basic Books.

Written by a well-known psychiatrist, this book describes the tremendous psychological transformation that takes place in many women when they become mothers. The book focuses on the positive, powerful psychological growth that occurs for women who choose motherhood.

Stewart J: *1001 African names: first and last names from the Africa continent,* Secausus, NJ, 1996, Citadel Press.

Julia Stewart identifies names for African-Americans who want to give their children African names or who want to change their own Western names. The book describes the origins of African naming practice and explains the meanings behind the names.

Wisot A, Meldrum D: *Conceptions and misconceptions: a guide through the maze of in vitro fertilization and other assisted reproductive techniques,* Point Roberts, WA, 1997, Hartley and Marks.

Written by two reproductive physicians, this book will be valuable to couples with infertility and anyone else who wants to understand the variety of assisted reproductive technologies. One of the authors is the father of quadruplets who were conceived by *in vitro* fertilization. The reader will learn about the cost and time involved in treating infertility, safety issues, legal concerns, and scams and schemes targeted at people with fertility problems.

 ## AS WE GO TO PRESS . . .

- In early 1998, the U.S. Food and Drug Administration expressed concern when Richard Seed, a Chicago physicist, claimed that he was proceeding with a human cloning. The FDA declared that it would shut down any laboratory that began human cloning experiments without its permission. At the time, state and federal legislators were scrambling to write laws banning this type of cloning. The FDA announcement gave lawmakers more time to proceed carefully to develop legislation that bans cloning, but not at the expense of lifesaving medical research.

- In late January 1998, a large explosion outside a Birmingham, Alabama abortion clinic killed an off-duty police officer and critically injured a nurse at the facility. This was the first fatal bombing at an abortion clinic. The explosion occurred just a week after the 25th anniversary of the Supreme Court's *Roe v. Wade* decision which legalized abortion. As this book went to press, federal agents were trying to determine whether this bombing was related to two bombings that occurred a year earlier at an Atlanta abortion clinic.

ON...

The Consequences of Unintended Pregnancy

"It can't happen to me."

This thought is often used to justify risky actions. Sometimes we even get away with it. We write a bad check but manage to get money to the bank in time to cover it. We leave the seat belt off for a short trip down the block. Sometimes we have sex without protection. It's not the right time in the cycle to get pregnant. Only one pill was missed. Nothing will happen, we tell ourselves. It can't happen to me.

Each day, thousands of single women receive the news that they are pregnant.[1] For those who have been trying to have a child, this news is welcomed. For others, however, the news may not be so joyous. Even in ideal situations, an unintended pregnancy can cause emotional and financial strain for the woman, the potential father, and their families.

Important People in the Decision-Making Process

If the father-to-be or the potential grandparents were not there to hear the news with her, the woman faces the task of telling them she's pregnant. This is often a time of fear and uncertainty for the woman, and the way these people ultimately handle the news can be of critical importance to her.[2] A supportive family and father-to-be make later decision processes easier to deal with, whereas lack of support is sure to cause problems down the road.

The decisions of the potential father concerning the woman and an unplanned pregnancy are extremely important. He may abandon the woman altogether, which will make support from the woman's family even more critical. If he chooses to stay, more decisions must be made. He may want to marry her. He may not want marriage but may still want to play an active role in supporting and rearing the child. He may want to play only a limited role. Whatever his decision, his role is a determining factor for decisions to be made later.

The families of both parents-to-be also play an important role in determining the outcome of the situation, especially when the potential parents are young. In many situations the families may be the primary source of financial support, and lack of this support may prove devastating. The type of emotional support that the potential grandparents provide to the young couple may also be crucial to their decisions regarding the unexpected pregnancy.

Marriage

Traditionally, marriage has been the most socially acceptable alternative for pregnant women and their partners.

In recent years, however, unwed motherhood has become more common and less stigmatized. Currently 30% of births in the United States are to unmarried women, and only 33% of teenage mothers are married.[1,3] Economic factors may play a role in determining whether or not a couple should get married when an unexpected pregnancy occurs. If the woman is financially secure or is receiving financial support from her family, she may find that single parenthood is the most desirable option. If income from both parents is necessary to support the child, marriage may prove to be the logical choice.

Cultural norms may also be considered in the marriage decision. In some segments of American culture, marriage is not considered a necessary consequence of an unplanned pregnancy. Common-law marriages (a relationship where both partners consent to live as a married couple without the formal exchange of vows) are more accepted in Hispanic-American culture.[3] In African-American culture the family is often more matriarchal (female-centered) in structure, reducing the role of the father.[4] In white culture, marriage is more often considered to be the most acceptable choice, but marriage is not always an inevitable step after pregnancy. The belief systems within different cultures are often very strong determining factors in the decisions made by potential parents.

Abortion

Eventually a decision must be reached concerning the fate of the child. The woman must decide to become a parent, put the child up for adoption, or terminate her pregnancy. Some women may consider abortion as an option. This decision is often a complicated and difficult one. The viability of choosing abortion may strongly depend on where a woman lives, her financial situation, and who is involved in the decision-making process with her. A woman is also faced with moral, religious, and legal questions when making such a decision. If her religious and moral beliefs are not compatible with those of her family or the father-to-be, these relationships may become greatly strained. The woman may also struggle with her own belief system and religious upbringing when making such a decision. For younger girls, the decision may be further complicated by the law. Many states require parental consent before an abortion is performed for girls below a certain age. This may eliminate the abortion option for those girls who do not want their parents to know about their pregnancies or for girls whose parents refuse to give consent.[5]

Although an abortion eliminates many long-term financial obligations, this option can be quite expensive in the short term. Because of restricted federal funding for abortion providers, the procedure usually costs several hundred dollars, and the price can run into the thousands for late-term abortions. Elective abortion is not normally covered by insurance, so the cost is strictly out-of-pocket. In many states the low availability of abortion providers is also an obstacle; a day's drive or an overnight stay is sometimes needed. The time involved may make a "secret" trip to a clinic difficult to pull off without deception of family, friends, or employers.[5]

Adoption

Putting the baby up for adoption may be an acceptable alternative for those women who reject abortion but do not wish to take on the responsibilities of childbearing. Many women may choose this option if they are not able to financially support a baby but also cannot consider aborting the child because of moral convictions. This option may eliminate the lifetime financial commitment but may be very difficult to deal with emotionally. The act of giving up a baby after carrying it to term can be heart-rending. The mother may have misgivings about the adoption for many years afterward. Many women who initially choose adoption for their child wind up changing their minds along the way, sometimes even after the baby is born. In recent years, several bitter court battles have been waged over such situations.

Parenthood

If the mother chooses the parenthood option, carrying the baby to term requires selfless devotion to its care. This often requires budgeting for the baby's needs well before it is born.[6] Most first-time parents do not realize the enormous costs that having a baby entails. The cost of giving birth varies widely among states. In 1993 the average total cost of hospital and physician charges for an uncomplicated vaginal delivery was $8840 in New York, but less than half that amount in Arkansas. New York was the most expensive state in which to have a cesarean delivery, with an average cost of $13,700, whereas a cesarean birth in Oklahoma cost about $7730.[7] Pediatrician bills during the first year of a child's life average $600 (assuming the child is healthy), and other necessities for the baby are even more expensive. For example, diapers can run between $500 and $700 a year during the pre–potty training days.[8] Clothes can cost as much as $1000 the first year because the child grows so quickly. Feeding can cost as much as $2000, depending on whether the mother is willing or able to breastfeed.[8]

Because of the large amount of money involved, immediate gratification must be put on hold to save money for later use. For many new parents, this is a problem, especially if they are suddenly being forced to take care of their own finances with little or no help from family. The mother may have to make major changes in lifestyle as well to keep the unborn child healthy. Drinking and smoking should be avoided, which may be quite difficult for those women who are used to participating in these activities. Abstaining from tobacco and alcohol use while out with friends may be difficult for some, and staying home from such outings may strain relationships with friends. As with family, the support of friends can go a long way toward easing the strain of an unintended pregnancy.[6]

Prenatal Care, Day Care, and Insurance

Prenatal care is necessary but can be costly and difficult to find. For a typical, uncomplicated pregnancy, the average cost for adequate prenatal care is $500.[8] Finding a doctor who will supervise care of the baby through birth is becoming more difficult because of the increasing number of lawsuits filed against doctors for malpractice. Such suits have driven many physicians out of obstetrics and caused others to raise prices. To lessen the risk of such suits, doctors who are willing to provide prenatal care are often requiring that expectant women stick to a strict set of behavioral guidelines. A woman is often asked to reveal and document intimate details about her sexual activity, menstrual history, and personal habits. Free clinics are available in some areas for those who cannot afford care otherwise, but the same behavioral restrictions and intense questioning can be expected there as well.[6]

Women who decide to become parents must take steps to ensure that the baby will be taken care of after it is born. The mother must arrange for day care if she hopes to work or continue with school. This can be a problem if there is no spouse or family member able or willing to take care of the baby during times when the mother is gone. Many day care facilities do not take care of newborns, and some require that the child be potty-trained before enrolling. Day care facilities can be quite expensive and often have waiting lists for admission. U.S. Census Bureau data place the average cost of day care for a family with a preschool child and working mother at $79 per week in 1993.[9] These costs tend to be higher in the West and Northeast and in urban environments.[9,10] Preschool day care in urban areas averaged about $400 per month in 1992, care in the urban Northeast averaged $500 per month, and the average for the rural South was $300 per month.[10] More workplaces and schools are now offering free or inexpensive day care services, but such programs are not found everywhere, and waiting lists cause delays as well. Some women are forced to take time off from school because of unintended pregnancy, and some leave altogether resulting from the financial hardships and physical strain of balancing school and parenthood. About half of all teenage mothers drop out of school.[1] Recent legislation has made it easier for new parents to take leave from work without penalty, but the law does not apply to all employers. As a result, some women are forced to leave jobs to care for their children.

Insurance can also be difficult to obtain for the baby. Some providers have waiting periods before insuring an individual.[6] A woman covered under her parents' policies may find that her own child cannot be covered, requiring the woman to obtain a separate policy for the baby. Some companies may not offer coverage of individuals.[6] Obtaining a new policy for mother and unborn child may be difficult as well. Some companies may treat pregnancy as a preexisting condition that may not be covered.[6] Making a budget and sticking to it is therefore crucial to cover medical costs until insurance can be obtained.

In the heat of passion, people often fail to think rationally about the potential outcomes of unprotected sex. Therefore the time to prepare for the romantic moment is *before* you are in a position where you don't want to think about the possibility of an unintended result. If you choose to be sexually active, find a form of contraception that works for you and use it consistently.

For Discussion . . .
What would you do if you (or your partner) became pregnant unintentionally? What decisions would you make regarding the pregnancy? If you are a parent, how would you react if one of your children was involved in an unintended pregnancy? Would your personal decisions be different?

References
1. Book bags and baby bottles, *Scholastic Update* 127(11), March 1995.
2. Bezduch-Moore SL: I was pregnant at sixteen, *Teen Magazine* 39(3), March 1995.
3. Russell C: Why teen births boom, *American Demographics* September 1995.
4. Freeman EW, Rickels K: *Early childbearing: perspectives of black adolescents on pregnancy, abortion, and contraception*, Newbury Park, CA, 1993, Sage Publications.
5. Thompson S: *Going all the way: teenage girls' tales of sex, romance and pregnancy*, New York, 1995, Hill and Wang.
6. Foglino A: Single, pregnant, and struggling to stay in college, *Glamour* November 1995.
7. Winthrop A: How much does it cost to give birth? *American Baby*, p 14, May 1995.
8. What price parenthood, *Town and Country Monthly* 148(5169), June 1994.
9. Census data on child care, *Children Today* 23(4), Fall/Winter 1995.
10. Mitchell A: Day care in the '90s, *Good Housekeeping* 215(3), September 1992.

PART 6

CONSUMERISM AND ENVIRONMENT

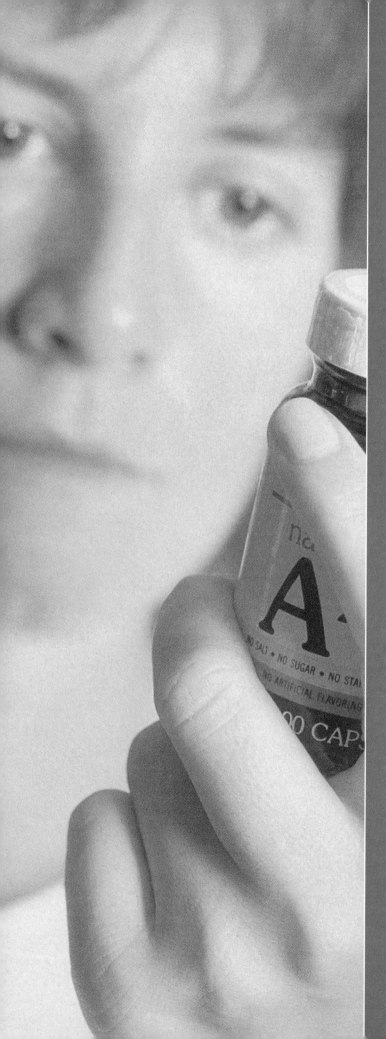

Making Consumer and Health Care Choices

Healthy People: Looking Ahead to 2010

Access to primary medical services by virtually every member of the community is a cornerstone of health consumerism and was an important *Healthy People 2000* objective. The *Midcourse Review* reported that only limited progress had been made toward achieving this goal, and that it probably would not be met by 2000. The lack of agreement among federal legislators regarding a new national health care system, changes in financing the present system, and the growing percentage of the population without health insurance were often cited as obstacles to achieving this objective.

As we move into the new century, *Healthy People 2010* will continue to advance health care delivery goals. The elimination of health disparities is one of two main goals for the nation. Thus it is likely that access to primary care physicians, mental health services, maternal and child services, and a variety of community health promotion programs will take center stage.

Health care providers often evaluate you by criteria pertaining to their area of expertise. The nutritionist knows you by the food you eat. The physical fitness professional knows you by your body type and activity level. In the eyes of the expert in health-related consumerism, you are the product of the health information you believe, the health-influencing services you use, and the products you consume. When your decisions about health information, services, and products are made after careful study and consideration, your health will probably be improved. However, when your decisions lack insight, your health, as well as your pocketbook, may suffer.

HEALTH INFORMATION
The Informed Consumer

To be an informed consumer, people must learn about services and products that can influence health. Practitioners, manufacturers, advertisers, and sales personnel use a variety of approaches in an attempt to get individuals to buy these products or use these services. Because health is potentially at stake when people "buy" into these messages, informed consumerism is important. Complete the Personal Assessment on p. 380 to rate your own skills as a health care consumer.

Sources of Information

The sources of information on a particular health topic to which you have access are as diverse as the number of people you know, the number of publications you read, and the number of experts you see or hear. At present, no single agency or profession regulates the quantity or quality of the health-related information you receive. In the section that follows, we look at many different sources of information. Readers will quickly recognize that all are familiar sources and that some provide more accurate and honest information than others.

Family and friends
From a health consumerism point of view, the accuracy of information provided by a friend or family member may be questionable. Too often the information provided by family and friends is based on common knowledge that is wrong. In addition, family members or friends may provide information they believe is in your best interests rather than providing factual information that may have a more negative effect on you.

Today more than ever, family and friends may provide health-related information as a part of their involvement in the pyramid sales of health products. Strong encouragement toward the use of a particular line of food supplements or vitamins could lead to a forceful sales pitch or even the offer of an opportunity to be a part of their sales team. In a 1996 survey of women, only 5% of the respondents said that friends and relatives were their primary source of health information.[1]

Advertisements and commercials
Many people spend a good portion of every day watching television, listening to the radio, and reading newspapers or magazines. Since many advertisements are health oriented, you should not be surprised to learn that these are significant sources of information. You should also remember that the primary purpose of advertising is to sell products or services. Perhaps no single combination of these factors is more evident than in the currently popular "infomercials" in which a compensated studio audience watches a skillfully produced program designed to inform them about the benefits of a particular product or service.

Labels and directions
Federal law requires that many consumer product labels, including many kinds of food (see Chapter 5) and all medications, contain specific information. For example, when a prescription medication is dispensed by a pharmacist, a detailed information sheet describing the drug should be given along with the medication (Figure 15-1).

Many health care providers and agencies provide consumers with detailed directions about their health problem. Generally, information from these sources is accurate, current, and provided with the health of the consumer in mind.

Folklore
Because it is often passed down from generation to generation, folklore about health is the primary source of health-related information for some people.

The truthfulness of health-related information obtained from family members, neighbors, and co-workers is difficult to evaluate. As a general rule, however, we would recommend caution concerning its scientific soundness. A blanket criticism is not warranted, however, since folk wisdom is on occasion supported by scientific evidence. Also, the emotional support provided by the suppliers of this information could be the best medicine some people need.

PERSONAL ASSESSMENT

Are You a Skilled Health Consumer?

Circle the selection that best describes your practice. Then total your points for an interpretation of your health consumer skills.

1 Never
2 Occasionally
3 Most of the time
4 All of the time

1. I read all warranties and then file them for safekeeping. 1 2 3 4
2. I read labels for information pertaining to the nutritional quality of food. 1 2 3 4
3. I practice comparative shopping and use unit pricing, when available. 1 2 3 4
4. I read health-related advertisements in a critical and careful manner. 1 2 3 4
5. I challenge all claims pertaining to secret cures or revolutionary new health devices. 1 2 3 4
6. I engage in appropriate medical self-care screening procedures. 1 2 3 4
7. I maintain a patient-provider relationship with a variety of health care providers. 1 2 3 4
8. I inquire about the fees charged before using a health care provider's services. 1 2 3 4
9. I maintain adequate health insurance coverage. 1 2 3 4
10. I consult reputable medical self-care books before seeing a physician. 1 2 3 4
11. I ask pertinent questions of health care providers when I am uncertain about the information I have received. 1 2 3 4
12. I seek second opinions when the diagnosis of a condition or the recommended treatment seems questionable. 1 2 3 4
13. I follow directions pertaining to the use of prescription drugs, including continuing their use for the entire period prescribed. 1 2 3 4
14. I buy generic drugs when they are available. 1 2 3 4
15. I follow directions pertaining to the use of OTC drugs. 1 2 3 4
16. I maintain a well-supplied medicine cabinet. 1 2 3 4

YOUR TOTAL POINTS _____

Interpretation

16-24 points	A very poorly skilled health consumer
25-40 points	An inadequately skilled health consumer
41-56 points	An adequately skilled health consumer
57-64 points	A highly skilled health consumer

To Carry This Further...
Could you ever have been the victim of consumer fraud? What will you need to do to be a skilled consumer?

Testimonials

People feel strongly about sharing information that has been beneficial to them. The recommendations made by other people concerning a particular practitioner or health-related product may at first appear to be nothing more than testimonials. Since they are frequently the basis for decision making by others, we assign a small measure of importance to them as sources of health-related information. However, the exaggerated testimonials that accompany the sales pitches of the medical quack or the "satisfied" customers appearing in advertisements and on commercials and infomercials should never be interpreted as valid endorsements.

Mass media

Health programming on cable television stations, lifestyle sections in newspapers, health care correspondents appearing on national network news shows, and a growing number of health-oriented magazines are four examples of health-related information in the mass media.

Although in general, health-related information is presented well, it is sometimes presented with such

Prozac 20 Mg Pulvule
Fluoxetine—Oral

USES: This medication is used to treat mental depression, obsessive-compulsive symptoms associated with Tourette's disorder, and in the treatments of obesity and bulimia nervosa.

This medication has also been used to treat PMS (premenstrual syndrome).

HOW TO TAKE THIS MEDICATION: May be taken with food to prevent stomach upset.

Take this as prescribed. Try to take each dose at the same time(s) each day so you remember to routinely take it.

SIDE EFFECTS: May cause drowsiness or dizziness. Use caution performing tasks that require alertness.

Other side effects include heartburn, loss of appetite, headache, anxiety, flushing or sweating, change in sexual desire or ability. If these symptoms persist or become bothersome, inform your doctor.

Notify your doctor if you develop a rapid heart rate., difficulty breathing, difficulty urinating, a rash or hives while taking this medication.

PRECAUTIONS: Tell doctor if you had a recent heart attack or if you have a history of seizures; heart, liver, or kidney disease; or diabetes.

Fluoxetine may affect the amount of glucose (sugar) in your blood, so your dosage of diabetes medication may need to be adjusted when fluoxetine is started or discontinued.

Women who are pregnant, plan to become pregnant, or are breast-feeding should inform their doctors.

Avoid alcohol while taking this medication.

DRUG INTERACTIONS: Before taking fluoxetine, tell your doctor what prescription and nonprescription medications you are taking (or have taken in the last two weeks), especially tranquilizers, antidepressants (Buspar), MAO inhibitors (isocarboxazid or Marplan, phenelzine or Nardil, tranylcypromine or Parnate), lithium, tryptophan, medication for anxiety (tranquilizers like Valium), and medication for diabetes.

Do not take any nonprescription medication without consulting your doctor.

NOTES: Do not allow anyone else to take this medication.

MISSED DOSE: It is not necessary to make up the missed dose. Skip the missed dose and resume your usual dosing shedule. Do not "double up " the dose to catch up.

STORAGE: Store at room temperature between 59 and 86 degrees F (between 15 and 30 degrees C) away from moisture and sunlight. Do not store in the bathroom.

The information in this leaflet may be used as an educational aid. This information does not cover all possible uses, actions, precautions, side effects, or interactions of this medicine. This information is not intended as medical advice for individual problems.

Copyright First Databank—The Hearst Corporation

Figure 15-1 Prozac, a serotonin-specific antidepressant, is one of today's most frequently prescribed medications. Note that it has uses beyond depression. It may also have "off-label" uses such as smoking abatement or cessation. Pharmacies provide patient information sheets like this one with each prescription dispensed.

quickness or superficiality that it is of limited use. However, the consumer who desires more complete coverage of a health-related topic can obtain it by combining sources. Thirty-one percent of women surveyed about their sources of health information named the media as their primary source.[1]

Practitioners

The health care consumer also receives much information from individual health practitioners and their professional associations. In fact, patient education is so clearly provided by today's health care practitioner that finding one who does not exchange some information with a patient would be unusual. Education enhances patient **compliance** with health care directives, which is important to the practitioner and the consumer.

An important development in the area of practitioner-provided information and patient education has been the evolution of the hospital as an educational institution. Wellness centers, chemical dependence programs, sports medicine centers, and community-based outreach centers have become more common. In fact, 50% of women in a survey reported that health practitioners and other health professionals were their primary source of health information.[1]

On-line computer services

With the expansion of computer technology in the last decade, new avenues for accessing health-related information have developed. Today over 50 million personal computer users can access the Internet for health-related websites, listservs, and chat rooms.[2] In addition, computer-based access to expanded health-related sources of information is available. Telnet and Gopher services, as well as World Wide Web pages, open expansive collections of information, including text and video, to people interested in health-related information.

compliance
Willingness to follow the directions provided by another person.

Health reference publications

It is now believed that a substantial portion of all households own or subscribe to a health reference publication, such as the *The Johns Hopkins Medical Handbook*[3] or the *Physicians' Desk Reference (PDR)*,[4] or a newsletter such as *The Harvard Medical School Health Letter* or *The Harvard Women's Health Watch*.[5]

Personal computer programs and videocassettes featuring health-related information are important sources of information for some consumers.

Reference libraries

Even though a large percentage of households possess health-related reference material and health care professionals are dispensing more and more information to the consumer, public and university libraries continue to be much-used sources of health-related information. Reference librarians can be consulted, and audiovisual collections and printed materials can be checked out. With increasing frequency, more and more of these holdings are becoming available through home computer–based on-line services.

Consumer advocacy groups

A variety of nonprofit consumer advocacy groups patrol the health care marketplace, particularly in relation to services and products (see the Star Box below). These groups produce and send out information designed to aid the consumer in recognizing questionable services and products. Large, well-organized groups, such as The National Consumers' League and Consumers' Union, and smaller groups at the state and local levels champion the right of the consumer to receive valid and reliable information about health care products and services.

Voluntary health agencies

Volunteerism and the traditional approach to health care and health promotion are virtually inseparable. Few countries besides the United States boast so many national voluntary organizations, with state and local affiliates, dedicated to the enhancement of health through research, service, and public education. The American Cancer Society, the American Red Cross, and the American Heart Association are all vol-

---

Consumer Protection Agencies and Organizations

Federal Agencies
Office of Consumer Affairs, Food and Drug Administration
U.S. Department of Health and Human Services
5600 Fishers Lane
Rockville, MD 20857
(301) 827-5006

Federal Trade Commission
Consumer Inquiries
Public Reference Branch
6th Street and Pennsylvania Avenue
Washington, DC 20580
(202) 326-2222
www.ftc.gov

Fraud Division
Chief Postal Inspector
U.S. Postal Inspection Service
475 L'Enfant Plaza
Washington, DC 20260-2166
(202) 268-4299

Consumer Information Center
Pueblo, CO 81009
(719) 948-3334
www.pueblo.gsa.gov

U.S. Consumer Product Safety Commission Hotline
(800) 638-CPSC

Consumer Organizations
Consumers Union of the U.S., Inc.
101 Truman Avenue
Yonkers, NY 10703
(914) 378-2000
www.consumerreports.org

Professional Organizations
American Medical Association
515 N. State St.
Chicago, IL 60610
(312) 464-5000
www.ama-assn.org

American Hospital Association
1 N. Franklin St.
Chicago, IL 60606
(312) 422-3000
www.aha.org

American Pharmaceutical Association
2215 Constitution Avenue, NW
Washington, DC 20037
(202) 628-4410
www.aphanet.org

untary (not-for-profit) health agencies. Consumers can, in fact, anticipate finding a voluntary health agency for virtually every health problem.

Government agencies

Government agencies are effective providers of information to the public. Through meetings and the release of information to the media, agencies such as the Food and Drug Administration, Federal Trade Commission, United States Postal Service, and Environmental Protection Agency contribute to public awareness of health issues. Particularly in terms of labeling, advertising, and the distribution of information through the mail, government agencies also control the quality of information sent out to the buying public. The various divisions of the National Institutes of Health regularly release research findings and recommendations pertaining to clinical practices, which in turn reach the consumer through clinical practitioners.

Despite their best intentions, federal health agencies are often less effective than what the public deserves. A variety of factors, including inadequate staff, poor administration, and lobbying by special interest groups, prevent these federal agencies from enforcing the consumer protection legislation that exists. As a result, the public is left with a sense of false confidence regarding the consumer protection provided by the federal government.

State government also provides the public with health-related information. State agencies are primary sources of information, particularly in the areas of public health and environmental protection.

Qualified health educators

Health educators work in a variety of settings and provide their services to diverse groups of individuals. Community health educators work with virtually all of the agencies mentioned above; patient educators function in primary care settings; and school health educators are found at all educational levels. Increasingly, health educators are being employed in a wide range of wellness-based programs in community, hospital, corporate, and school settings.

HEALTH CARE PROVIDERS

The types and sources of health information just discussed can contribute greatly to the decisions we make as informed consumers. The choices we make about physicians, health services, and medical payment plans will reflect our commitment to remain healthy and our trust in specific people who are trained in keeping us healthy. Refer to the Health Action Guide on p. 384 for tips on choosing a physician.

Physicians and Their Training

In every city and many smaller communities, the local telephone directory will attest to the many types of physicians engaged in the practice of medicine. These health care providers hold the academic degree of Doctor of Medicine (MD) or Doctor of Osteopathy (DO).

At one time, **allopathy** and **osteopathy** were clearly different health care professions in terms of their healing philosophies and modes of practice. Today, however, MDs and DOs receive similar educations and engage in very similar forms of practice. Both can function as **primary care physicians** or as board-certified specialists. The differences that exist are in terms of the osteopathic physician's greater tendency to use manipulation in treating health problems. Additionally, DOs perceive themselves as being more holistically oriented than MDs.

The training of medical and osteopathic physicians is a long process. Usually, 4 years of initial undergraduate preparation is required. There is heavy emphasis on the sciences—biology, chemistry, mathematics, anatomy, and physiology. Most undergraduate schools have preprofessional courses of study for students interested in medical or osteopathic schools.

Once accepted into professional schools, students generally spend 4 or more years in intensive training that includes advanced study in the preclinical medical sciences and clinical practice. On completion of this phase of training, the students are awarded the MD or DO degree and then take the state medical license examination. Most newly licensed physicians complete a residency at a hospital. During this period,

allopathy (ah **lop** ah thee)
System of medical practice in which specific remedies (often pharmaceutical agents) are used to produce effects different from those produced by a disease or injury.

osteopathy (os tee **op** ah thee)
System of medical practice that combines allopathic principles with specific attention to postural mechanics of the body.

primary care physician
The physician who sees a patient on a regular basis, rather than a specialist who sees the patient only for a specific condition or procedure.

HEALTH
Action Guide - - - - - ➔

Choosing a Physician

When choosing a physician, plan to obtain answers to the following questions *during* your initial visit:

- Obtain a description of the physician's medical background, such as education, residencies, and specialty areas.
- How does the physician keep up with new developments in the medical profession? Does the physician attend seminars and conferences, take courses, read medical journals, write articles, participate in professional organizations, or teach at a medical school?
- What are the normal office hours? What should be done if help is needed outside of normal office hours?
- What is included in a comprehensive physical examination?
- How does the physician feel about second and third opinions?
- Which hospitals is the physician affiliated with in your area?
- With which specialists is the physician associated?
- What is the physician's fee schedule?

Ask yourself the following questions *after* your visit:

- Was I comfortable with the physician's age, gender, race, and national origin?
- Was I comfortable with the physician's demeanor?

- Did I find communication with the physician to be understandable and reassuring? Were all my questions answered?
- Did the physician seem interested in having me as a patient?
- Are the physician's training and practice speciality in an area most closely associated with my present needs and concerns?
- Does the physician have staff privileges at a hospital of my preference?
- Does the physician's fee-for-service policy in any way exclude or limit my ability to receive necessary services?
- Did the physician take a complete medical history as a part of my initial visit? Was prevention, health promotion, or wellness addressed by the physician at any point during my visit?
- Did I at any point during my visit sense that the physician was unusually reluctant or anxious to try new medical procedures or medications?
- When the physician is unavailable, are any colleagues on call for 24 hours? Did I feel that telephone calls from me would be welcomed and responded to in a reasonable period?

If you have answered yes to most of these questions, you have found a physician with whom you should feel comfortable. If you have been using the services of a particular physician but are becoming dissatisfied, how could you resolve this dissatisfaction? ◄ - - - - - -

physicians gain experience in various clinical areas and begin specialized programs. Residency programs vary in length from 3 to 4 years. At the conclusion of residency programs, board-eligible or board-certified status is granted. Some believe that an excess of physicians exists, and residency programs are now accepting fewer applicants.

Alternative Practitioners

Several forms of health care offer alternatives within the large health care market. Included within this group are chiropractic, acupuncture, homeopathy, naturopathy, herbalism, reflexology, and ayurveda. Although the traditional medical community has long scoffed at these alternatives as ineffective and unscientific, many people use these forms of health care and believe strongly that they are as effective as (or more effective than) allopathic and osteopathic medicine.

Chiropractic

This system is based on manual manipulation of the spine to correct misalignments. Recent studies have shown that **chiropractic** treatment of some types of low-back pain can be more effective than conventional care. With about 50,000 practitioners in the United States, chiropractic is the third-largest health profession, used by 15 to 20 million people.

Acupuncture

Acupuncture is, for Americans, the most familiar component of the 3,000-year-old Chinese medical system. This system is based on balancing the active and passive forces with the patient's body to strengthen the chi ("chee"), or life force. Acupuncturists place hair-thin needles at certain points in the body to stimulate the patient's chi.

Of all the Chinese therapies, acupuncture is the most widely accepted in the West. Researchers have produced persuasive evidence of acupuncture's effectiveness as an anesthetic and as an antidote to chronic pain, migraines, dysmenorrhea, and osteoarthritis.[6] In addition, some studies have found that acupuncture can help patients overcome addictions to alcohol, drugs, and tobacco. Other studies have shown that acupuncture is far more than a placebo and actually stimulates the body's opioid system.[7]

Reflexology

Reflexology uses principles similar to those of acupuncture but focuses on treating certain disorders through massage of the soles of the feet.

Homeopathy

Homeopathy uses infinitesimal doses of herbs, minerals, or even poisons to stimulate the body's curative powers. The theory on which homeopathy is based, called the *Law of Similars,* is that if large doses of a substance can cause a problem, tiny doses can trigger healing of that same problem. A few small studies have shown homeopathy to be at least somewhat effective in treating hay fever, diarrhea, and flu symptoms, but researchers in the scientific community call the studies flawed or preliminary.[8]

Naturopathy

Proponents of **naturopathy** believe that when the mind and the body are in balance and receiving proper care, with a healthy diet, adequate rest, and minimal stress, the body's own vital forces are sufficient to fight off disease. Getting rid of an ailment is only the first step toward correcting the underlying imbalance that allowed the ailment to take hold, naturists believe. Correcting the imbalance might be as simple as rectifying a shortage of a particular nutrient, or as complex as reducing overlong work hours, strengthening a weakened immune system, and identifying an inability to digest certain foods.[8]

Herbalism

Herbalism may be the world's oldest and most widely used healing form. Herbalists make herbal brews for treating a variety of ills, such as depression, anxiety, and hypertension. In some cases, scientific research supports the herbalists' beliefs. For example, several studies have found St. John's wort to be more effective than a placebo in alleviating mild depression.[9]

Ayurveda

Even older than Chinese medicine, India's **ayurveda** takes a preventive approach and focuses on the whole person. This system employs diet, tailored to the patient's constitutional type, or dosha; herbs; yoga and breathing exercises; meditation; massages; and purges, enemas, and aromatherapy. Research has

shown ayurveda to be effective in treating rheumatoid arthritis, headaches, and chronic sinusitis.

If you would like to consult a practitioner in one of the alternative disciplines but you don't know where to start, see the Health Action Guide on page 386 for some tips on choosing a provider in alternative medicine.

At the urging of many people in both the medical and alternative health care fields, the National Institutes of Health agreed to fund an initial study of the effectiveness of alternative health care procedures. The first fruits of this study, a 1994 report titled *Alternative Medicine: Expanding Medical Horizons,*[10] gathers our current understanding of alternative approaches and provides a framework for well-controlled research

chiropractic
Manipulation of the vertebral column to relieve pressure and cure illness.

acupuncture
Insertion of fine needles into the body to alter electroenergy fields and cure disease.

reflexology
Massage applied to specific areas of the feet to treat illness and disease in other areas of the body.

homeopathy
The use of minute doses of herbs or minerals to stimulate healing.

naturopathy
A system of treatment that avoids drugs and surgery and emphasizes the use of natural agents to correct underlying imbalances.

herbalism
An ancient form of healing in which herbal preparations are used to treat illness and disease.

ayurveda (ai yur **vey** da)
Traditional Indian medicine based on herbal remedies.

orthodontics
Dental specialty that focuses on the proper alignment of the teeth.

prosthodontics
Dental specialty that focuses on the construction and fitting of artificial appliances to replace missing teeth.

HEALTH
Action Guide - - - - - ➡

Choosing the Best Alternative Practitioner for You

Perhaps you are one of the millions of people who feel that their doctors don't encourage them to ask questions, don't seek their opinion about their medical condition, or don't take a thorough medical history. Perhaps you want advice on improving your health rather than just a quick diagnosis and prescription.

For whatever reasons, millions of Americans are turning to alternative medical practitioners, such as doctors of naturopathy, Chinese medicine, or ayurveda. Unfortunately, the patient looking for these alternatives faces other problems: practitioners' training may be weak, they might not be licensed or covered by insurance, they are hard to find, and they usually are not permitted to prescribe drugs unless they also happen to be medical doctors. This means that you must do some legwork to find a good provider who can meet your needs.

Consider the following tips for finding the practitioner who is right for you.

- *Don't forget the family doctor.* Family-practice medicine is enjoying a surge in the United States and many of these doctors tend to think holistically.
- *Find a doctor who believes in alternative therapies.* Your doctor's attitude toward the treatment can be just as important as your own.
- *Give the treatment time.* Alternative therapies encourage the body to do its own healing. This often takes time. Seek a doctor who is confident in your self-healing ability, so you won't become discouraged if it takes some time.

- *Request natural healing.* Natural healing tends to change the internal conditions so that pathogens are less likely to gain a foothold; conventional medicine seeks to destroy the pathogen. Natural healing searches for the causes of symptoms, while conventional medicine treats symptoms.
- *Know your disease.* Find books that describe your conditions and offer alternatives as well as conventional treatments. This way you can discuss your treatment with your doctor and create an effective treatment plan.
- *Treat yourself.* Don't overuse your health care provider, whether conventional or alternative. For many conditions, you can be your own best doctor; of course, persistent or severe symptoms should send you to the doctor.
- *Learn whether the treatment is covered by insurance.* Coverage of alternative treatment differs sharply by state. Some insurance groups are beginning to pay for more alternative medicine, and HMOs are hiring some alternative specialists.
- *Talk to professional associations.* Most of the more established alternative fields have associations that can give you a list of providers. Use it as a start.
- *Get a brochure.* The doctor's literature can tell you a lot about his or her outlook and experience.
- *Interview the doctor.* Before making an appointment, talk with the doctor over the telephone. Then, in the doctor's office, take notes, even use a tape recorder, to make certain you understand. Watch for a doctor who is a good listener, a good communicator, and open-minded. ◀ - - - - - ➡

into the effectiveness of each approach. The NIH's Office of Alternative Medicine is now funding 42 studies, on topics such as using acupuncture to treat depression and using hypnosis to heal fractures.

Restricted-Practice Health Care Providers

We receive much of our health care from medical physicians. However, most of us also use the services of various health care specialists who also have advanced graduate level training. Among these professionals are dentists, psychologists, podiatrists, and optometrists.

Dentists (Doctor of Dental Surgery, DDS) are trained to deal with a wide range of diseases and impairments of the teeth and oral cavity. Dentists undergo under-

graduate predental programs that emphasize the sciences, followed by 4 additional years of graduate study in dental school and, with increasing frequency, an internship program. State licensure examinations are required. As with medical physicians, dentists can also specialize by completing a postdoctoral master's degree in fields such as oral surgery, **orthodontics,** and **prosthodontics.** Dentists are also permitted to prescribe therapy programs (such as appliances for the treatment of temporomandibular joint dysfunction) and drugs that pertain to their practices (primarily analgesics and antibiotics).

Psychologists provide services related to an understanding of behavior patterns or perceptions. Over 40 states have certification or licensing laws that prohibit unqualified people from using the term *psychologist.*

The consumer should examine the credentials of a psychologist. Legitimate psychologists have received advanced graduate training (often leading to a PhD or EdD degree) in clinical, counseling, industrial, or educational psychology. Furthermore, these practitioners will have passed state certification examinations and, in many states, will have met further requirements that allow them to offer health services to the public. Psychologists may have special interests and credentials from professional societies in individual, group, family, or marriage counseling. Some are certified as sex therapists.

Unlike *psychiatrists,* who are medical physicians, psychologists cannot prescribe or dispense drugs. They may refer to or consult with medical physicians about clients who might benefit from drug therapy.

Podiatrists are highly trained clinicians who practice podiatric medicine, or care of the feet (and ankles). Although not MDs or DOs, doctors of podiatric medicine (DPM) treat a wide variety of conditions related to the feet, including corns, bunions, warts, bone spurs, hammertoes, fractures, diabetes-related conditions, athletic injuries, and structural abnormalities. Podiatrists perform surgery, prescribe medications, and apply orthotics (supports or braces), splints, and corrective shoes for structural abnormalities of the feet.

Doctors of podiatric medicine follow an educational path similar to that taken by MDs and DOs, consisting of a 4-year undergraduate preprofessional curriculum, 4 additional years of study in a podiatric medical school, and an optional residency of 1 or 2 years. Board-certified areas of specialization include surgery, orthopedics, and podiatric sports medicine. Hospital affiliation generally requires board certification in a specialized area.

Optometrists are eye specialists who deal primarily with vision problems associated with **refractory errors.** They examine the eyes and prescribe glasses or contact lenses to correct visual disorders. Sometimes optometrists also attempt to correct certain ocular muscle imbalances with specific exercise regimens. Optometrists must complete undergraduate training and additional years of coursework at one of 16 accredited colleges of optometry in the United States, one of two in Canada, or one in Puerto Rico before taking a state licensing examination.[11]

Opticians are technicians who manufacture and fit eyeglasses or contact lenses. Although they are rarely licensed by a state agency, they perform the important function of grinding lenses to the precise prescription designated by an optometrist or *ophthalmologist* (physicians who have specialized in vision care). To save money and time, many consumers take an optometrist's or ophthalmologist's prescription for glasses or contact lenses to optician-staffed retail stores that deal exclusively with eyewear products.

Nurse Professionals

Nurses constitute a large group of health professionals who practice in a variety of settings. Frequently, the responsibilities of nurses vary according to their academic preparation. Registered nurses (RNs) are academically prepared at two levels: (1) the technical nurse, and (2) the professional nurse. The technical nurse is educated in a 2-year associate degree program. The professional nurse receives 4 years of education and earns a bachelor's degree. Both technical and professional nurses must successfully complete state licensing examinations before they can practice as RNs.

Many professional nurses continue their education and earn master's and doctoral degrees in nursing or other health-related fields. Some professional nurses specialize in a clinical area (such as pediatrics, gerontology, public health, or school health) and become certified as *nurse practitioners.* Working under the supervision of physicians, nurse practitioners perform many of the diagnostic and treatment procedures performed by physicians. The ability of these highly trained nurses to function at this level provides communities with additional primary care providers, as well as freeing physicians to deal with more complex cases. Many college health centers employ nurse practitioners because of their ability to deliver high-quality care at a low cost to the institution.

Licensed practical nurses (LPNs) are trained in hospital-based programs ranging from 12 to 18 months. Because of their brief training, LPNs' scope of practice is limited. Most LPN training programs are gradually being phased out.

Allied Health Care Professionals

Our primary health care providers are supported by a large group of allied health care professionals,

refractory errors
Incorrect patterns of light wave transmissions through the structures of the eye.

self-care movement
Trend toward individuals taking increased responsibility for prevention or management of certain health conditions.

who often take the responsibility for highly technical services and procedures. Such professionals include respiratory and inhalation therapists, radiological technologists, nuclear medicine technologists, pathology technicians, general medical technologists, operating room technicians, emergency medical technicians, registered nurse midwives, physical therapists, occupational therapists, cardiac rehabilitation therapists, dental technicians, physician assistants, and dental hygienists. Depending on the particular field, the training for these specialty support areas can take from 1 to 5 years of post–high school study. Programs include hospital-based training leading to a diploma through associate, bachelor's, and master's degrees. Most allied health care professionals must also pass state or national licensing examinations.

SELF–CARE

The emergence of the **self-care movement** suggests that many people are becoming more responsible for the maintenance of their health. They are developing the expertise to prevent or manage numerous types of illness, injuries, and conditions. They are learning to assess their health status and treat, monitor, and rehabilitate themselves in a manner that was once thought possible only with the direct help of a physician or some other health care specialist.

The benefits of this movement are that self-care can (1) lower health care costs, (2) be effective care for particular conditions, (3) free physicians and other health care specialists to spend time with other patients, and (4) enhance interest in health-related activities.

Self-care is an appropriate alternative to professional care in three areas. First, self-care may be appropriate for certain acute conditions that have familiar symptoms and are of limited duration and seriousness. Common colds and flu, many home injuries, sore throats, and nonallergic insect bites are often easily managed with self-care.

A second area in which self-care might be appropriate is therapy. For example, many people are now administering injections for allergies and migraine headaches and continuing physical therapy programs in their homes. Asthma, diabetes, and hypertension are also conditions that can be managed or monitored with self-care.

A third area in which self-care has appropriate application is health promotion. Weight loss programs, physical conditioning activities, and stress reduction programs are particularly well suited to self-care.

People interested in practicing more self-care must be skilled consumers. The self-care marketplace is growing very rapidly and is expected to be a multibillion-dollar industry by the end of the decade. Equipment such as blood pressure–measuring instruments, stethoscopes, and screening kits for cholesterol, HIV, and pregnancy, as well as OTC drugs, can represent significant investments. Clearly, your money, time, and willingness to develop expertise are important components in this growing area of health care consumerism.

HEALTH CARE COSTS AND REIMBURSEMENT

As depicted in Figure 15-2, there are many avenues for receiving health care. However, being able to afford quality health care is among the most important concerns of the American public. Today over 41 million Americans lack health insurance to pay health care costs, including over 10 million dependent children. Furthermore, Americans are less optimistic today about their ability to have adequate health insurance coverage, find reasonably priced health care, and afford long-term home-bound or nursing home care than ever before.[12] Unfortunately, the word *crisis* is appropriate to use when talking about our ability to continue to afford high-quality health care today.

Central to our concern with health care is its cost. As a nation, Americans are now spending over $1 trillion a year on health care,[13] and by the year 2000 the amount is expected to exceed $1.5 trillion.[14] At today's rates, annual health care costs per person will approach $5500 by the year 2000.[14] For the country as a whole, 13.3% of our gross domestic product was devoted to health care costs in 1993.[15] Table 15-1 provides a breakdown of annual health care expenditures in the United States.

In light of factors such as the high cost of modern medical technology, an emphasis on long life at any cost, the growing number of older people with chronic conditions that require expensive extended care, and the AIDS epidemic, controlling the cost of medical care is one of the most complex problems facing the nation. Nevertheless, well over 40 different plans have been advanced since 1990 in response to this problem. These range from only modest changes to the current system to tax credit strategies and mandatory employment-based insurance to a federally controlled national health plan. However, no single plan has yet caught the favor of the American public or their policy makers in Washington.

Health Insurance

Health insurance is a financial agreement between an insurance company and an individual or group for the payment of health costs. After paying a premium to an insurance company, the policyholder is covered

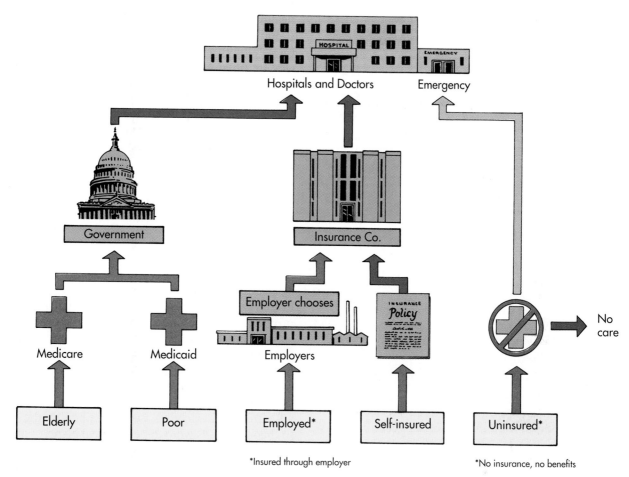

Figure 15-2   In the current U.S. health care system, many layers of bureaucracy lie between people and their doctors.

for specific benefits. The Star Box on p. 390, left, summarizes the types of policies that are available. Each policy is different in terms of coverage for illnesses and injuries. Merely having an insurance policy does not mean that all health care expenses will be covered. Most health insurance policies require various forms of payments on the part of the policyholder, which include provisions for deductible amounts, fixed indemnity benefits, coinsurance, and exclusions. For most Americans, participation in the health care system is possible if they have adequate health insur-

ance. Recall, however, that 41 million Americans have no health insurance.[16]

A *deductible* amount is an established amount that the insuree must pay before the insurer reimburses for services. For example, many policies require that a family pays the first $200 or $400 of expense for that year before it begins to reimburse its percentage (coinsurance) of subsequent expenses. Usually, the lower the deductible amount is, the higher the premium will be.

A policy with *fixed indemnity* benefits will pay only a specified amount for a particular procedure or service. If the policy pays only $1000 for an appendectomy and the actual cost of the appendectomy was $1500, then the policy owner will owe the health care provider $500. A policy with *full-service* benefits, which pays the entire cost of a particular procedure or service, may be worth the extra cost.

Policies that have *coinsurance* features require that the policy owner and the insurance company share the costs of certain covered services, usually on a percentage basis. One standard coinsurance plan requires that the policyholder pay 20% of the costs above a

Table 15-1 Household Health Care Expenditures	
Commodity	Amount (in billions)
Hospitals	$256.0
Physicians	$125.7
Nursing homes	$ 53.1
Drugs/supplies	$ 54.6
Dental care	$ 34.0
Other	$120.0

deductible amount, and the company pays the remaining 80%.

An *exclusion* refers to a service or expense that is not covered by the policy. Elective or cosmetic surgery procedures, unusual treatment protocols, prescription drugs, and certain kinds of consultations are common exclusions in many policies. Illness and injuries that already exist at the time of purchase (preexisting conditions) are often excluded. Also, injuries incurred during high-risk activities (ice hockey, hang gliding, mountain climbing, intramural sports) might not be covered by a policy.

Health insurance can be obtained through individual policies or group plans. Group health insurance plans usually offer the widest range of coverage at the least expensive price and are often purchased cooperatively by companies and their employees. In 1996 the average employer's portion of an employee's health insurance plan was $3,700.[17] Fortunately, no employee is refused entry into a group insurance program. A federal law allows health insurance to be transferred when a person changes employment, without losing coverage because of a preexisting condition. Today, as many large American companies downsize, tens of thousands of employees can lose this important group

health insurance, virtually without warning.

Individual policies can be purchased by one person (or a family) from an insurance company. These policies are often much more expensive than group plans and may provide much less coverage. People who do not have access to a group plan should still attempt to secure individual policies, since the financial burdens resulting from a severe accident or illness that is not covered by some form of health insurance can be devastating. Many colleges and universities offer annually renewable health insurance policies that students can purchase (see the Star Box below). The Health Action Guide on p. 391 gives the consumer some questions to consider before purchasing a health insurance policy.

Health Maintenance Organizations

Health maintenance organizations (HMOs) are health care delivery plans under which health care providers agree to meet the covered medical needs of subscribers for a prepaid amount of money. For a fixed monthly fee, enrollees are given comprehensive health care with an emphasis on preventive health care. Enrollees receive their care from physicians, specialists, allied health professionals, and educators who are hired or contractually retained by the HMO. In theory, HMOs were to be the ideal blend of medical care and health promotion, offering the advantages described later. Today, however, there is growing concern that too many HMOs are being too tightly controlled by a profit motive in which physicians are being paid to not refer patients to specialists or are prevented (gag rules) from discussing certain treat-

HEALTH
Action Guide ━ ━ ━ ━ ➤

Selecting a Health Insurance Policy

Before you purchase a health insurance policy, ask yourself the following questions. The more questions you can answer with a "yes," the better you should feel that the policy you select is right for you.

General Questions
- Do I really need an individual insurance policy?
- Am I already covered by a group insurance policy?
- Is the insurance company I'm considering rated favorably by *Best's Insurance Reports* or my state insurance department?
- Have I compared health insurance policies from at least two other companies?
- Does this company have a "return rate" of 50% or more?
- Can I afford this insurance policy?

- Do I understand the factors that might raise the cost of this policy?

Specific Questions
- Do I clearly understand which health conditions are covered and which are not?
- Do I clearly understand whether I have fixed indemnity benefits or full-service benefits?
- Do I clearly understand the deductible amounts of this policy?
- Do I clearly understand when the major medical portion of this policy starts?
- Do I clearly understand all information in this policy that refers to exclusions and preexisting conditions?
- Do I clearly understand any disability provisions of this policy?
- Do I clearly understand all information concerning both cancellation and renewal of this policy?

◀ ━ ━ ━ ━ ●

ment options with patients because of their costs to the HMOs. In 1997, 70 million Americans were enrolled in HMOs.[18] Premiums are generally 8% to 10% lower than traditional plans, with no deductibles and small ($5 to $10) copayments for office visits.[19]

When operated in the manner consistent with how most members believe they should be operated, one of the potential advantages offered by HMOs is cost containment. Since most of the medical services with an HMO are centralized, there is little duplication of facilities, equipment, or support staff. Central filing of records allows several HMO physicians to have access to a single client's record file. This saves time, administrative costs, and the overlapping of care. HMOs also routinely use health promotion activities to encourage clients to practice illness prevention. All of these approaches could help lower health care costs.

Additional new approaches to *managed health care* involve the formation of *independent practice associations* (IPAs), *preferred provider organizations* (PPOs), and *point of service* (POS) plans. An IPA is a modified form of an HMO that uses a group of doctors who offer prepaid services out of their own offices and not in a central HMO facility. IPAs are viewed as "HMOs without walls." A PPO is a group of private practitioners who sell their services at reduced rates to insurance companies. When policyholders choose a physician who is in that company's PPO, the insurance company will pay the entire physician's fee. A POS plan allows enrollees to see health care providers outside their prepaid group, but they must pay an additional annual premium and a copayment for each visit to a nonnetwork provider. The copayment may be as high as 30% of the fee charged.[19]

Government Insurance Plans

Created in 1965 by amendments to the Social Security Act, **Medicare** represents a governmental form of health insurance. Medicare provides health care reimbursements primarily for people aged 65 years or older. Medicare is a contributory program—that is, through their working years, all employed citizens contribute a portion of their salaries (through Social Security taxes) to the Medicare fund. At present, that

Medicare
Contributory governmental health insurance, primarily for people 65 years of age or older.

Medicaid
Noncontributory governmental health insurance for people receiving other types of public assistance.

amount is 1.45% of the Social Security taxes (FICA) paid on annual earnings.[20] When they reach age 65, some of their health care expenses are covered by Medicare. Regardless of their age, people who require kidney dialysis or transplants are covered by Medicare.

Medicare is actually composed of two parts. Medicare A is essentially a hospital insurance program. Part A will pay for necessary hospital care (semiprivate room) after payment of the required deductible, for medically necessary inpatient care in a nursing home (skilled level care), and hospice care. In addition, it will pay 80% of the cost of approved durable medical equipment, such as walkers, and for all units of blood used by an inpatient, after the first three units.[20] Medicare B is a voluntary program (for which the subscriber must pay a monthly fee, currently $43.80 that supplements Medicare A. Medicare B provides regular medical insurance that covers a broad range of physicians' fees and other health care services. Physicians who "accept assignment" from Medicare agree to charge their elderly patients only the amount that Medicare will cover. Those who do not accept assignment may charge an amount up to 115% of the Medicare amount. However, by doing so, they will be asking their elderly patients not only to pay the 20% copayment but an additional 15% as well. Consequently, many elderly will go only to physicians who accept assignment. Both Medicare plans are subject to yearly changes in coverages and administrative procedures.

One of the most recent attempts by Medicare at cost containment in the area of health care is the prospective pricing system established in 1984 by the federal government. Under this system, Medicare reimbursements to hospitals are based on 467 *diagnosis-related groups* (DRGs) rather than on the costs accrued by the hospitals. Each hospital stay is now assigned a DRG classification, and reimbursement to the hospital is based on that classification. This system encourages hospitals to deliver services at or below the DRG payment schedule.

Currently, a principal focus of American political thought is to balance the federal budget before or only shortly after the end of the decade. Regardless of the particular plan advanced, changes in various aspects of Medicare are a certainty. Regardless of the specific agenda advanced by one group or another, it is hoped that the "new Medicare" will offer older Americans a broader range of choices of health care providers, reduce the amount of fraud and waste associated with current operations, and stimulate greater cooperation among physicians, hospitals, drug manufacturers, and recipients in cost containment.[21]

Medicaid is a noncontributory program for citizens who are receiving other types of public welfare assistance. It is designed to provide both a variety of types of health-related coverage, including hospital, nursing home, physicians, and home care, and Medicare deductibles. Unlike Medicare, Medicaid has no age requirements and is administered cooperatively through federal and state agencies. Medicaid is particularly important to older adults, since it will cover nursing home care once eligibility has been established. In 1995, 20% of the entire Medicaid budget of $155 billion ($31 billion) was spent for nursing home care, principally for the elderly.[22]

Because of the bureaucracy currently surrounding these two governmental insurance programs, a number of private physicians and voluntary hospitals are reluctant to accept Medicaid and Medicare clients. An important concern now seems to be how the United States can provide proper health care for all of its citizens, including the aged, economically disadvantaged, and those whose life savings can be quickly depleted by a catastrophic illness (see the Learning from All Cultures box on p. 393).

Medicare Supplement Policies (Medigap)

Because Medicare A and Medicare B require deductibles and copayment to be made by patients before they will begin payment, insurance to cover these gaps in coverage has been developed. In the most basic "medigap" policies (policy version A), often sold via television, reimbursement is made to the patient for the deductible and copayment portions of the approved charges, as determined by the DRG (Medicare A) and approved physician fee (Medicare B). More expensive and more comprehensive Medicare supplement policies (policy versions B through J) are also available that pay for hospital care and equipment not covered by Medicare A and for physician fees that exceed the approved amount of coverage for Medicare B. The difference in costs between the basic medigap policies and the more comprehensive policies that literally pay for everything that is not covered by Medicare is substantial.

Extended Care Insurance

With the aging of the population and the greater likelihood that nursing home care will be required (at about $34,000 per year), extended care policies have been developed and are being sold. When purchased at an early age (by mid-50s), these policies are much more affordable than if purchased when it is apparent that a spouse or family member will require institu-

LEARNING *from* ALL CULTURES

Health Care in the United States and Canada

Approximately 14% of the United States population does not have access to health care. This amounts to approximately 37 million people, primarily among the poor. A substantial number of people lacking medical coverage are people who work full time at very low-paying jobs without health care benefits. This population may suffer more than the very poor or unemployed because they may not be poor enough to qualify for Medicaid.

Usually people who need emergency or immediate care will not be turned away at a hospital. However, people without health coverage lack primary care—preventive measures like checkups, screenings, and prenatal care. Because of this lack of preventive attention, they eventually may need more extensive and costly care.

Other countries, such as Canada, have addressed the issue of universal health care. Since 1972, Canadian residents have been guaranteed health insurance coverage through a system funded by the federal government and the ten provincial and two territorial governments. Of the total health care cost, 30% to 40% is paid by the federal government, about 25% comes from private sources, and the rest is contributed by the provinces, usually through taxes.

Each individual is guaranteed health care in Canada, but the system is not socialized medicine. Physicians do not work for the government but are independent providers. Providers must, however, accept the provincial plan's reimbursement as total payment if a province is to continue to receive federal support.

Would the Canadian system work in the United States? From where in the federal and state budgets would the funding come? Some argue that there are too many groups of people who would not benefit from a system like the Canadian one. Why would certain groups oppose such a system?

---

tional care. However, not all older adults will need extensive nursing home care, so an extended care policy could be an unnecessary expenditure.

HEALTH-RELATED PRODUCTS

As you might imagine, prescription and OTC drugs constitute an important part of any discussion of health-related products.

Prescription Drugs

Caution: Federal law prohibits dispensing without prescription.

This FDA warning appears on the labels of approximately three fourths of all medications. Prescription drugs must be ordered for patients by a licensed practitioner. Because these compounds are legally controlled and may require special skills in their administration, our access to these drugs is limited.

Although over 2500 compounds listed in the current edition of the *PDR* represent the drugs that can be prescribed by a physician, only 200 drugs make up the bulk of the 2,140,799 new prescriptions and refills dispensed by 34,000 pharmacies in 1994.[23] The most frequently prescribed drugs in 1996, by units dispensed, were Premarin (hormone replacement therapy), Trimox (antibiotic), Synthroid (thyroid), Amoxil (antibiotic), and Zantac (ulcers). Working through physicians and pharmacists, pharmaceutical companies contribute to the improvement of health while generating sales in excess of $25.6 billion per year.[24] Health care dollars spent for prescription drugs account for 13% of the total health care costs accrued by Americans.

Research and development of new drugs

As consumers of prescription drugs, you may be curious about the process by which drugs gain FDA approval for marketing. The rigor of this process may be why fewer than 100 new drugs are added to the list of approved drugs each year.

On a continuous basis, the nation's pharmaceutical companies are exploring the molecular structure of various chemical compounds in an attempt to discover important new compounds with desired types and levels of biological activity. Once these new compounds are identified, extensive in-house research with computer simulations and animal testing is required to determine whether clinical trials with humans are warranted. Of the 125,000 or more compounds under study each year, only a few thousand receive such extensive preclinical evaluation. Even fewer of these are then taken to the FDA to begin the evaluation process necessary to gain approval for further research with humans. Once a drug is approved for clinical trials, the pharmaceutical companies can secure a patent, which prevents the drug from being manufactured by other companies for the next 17 years.

The $400 million price tag for bringing a new drug into the marketplace reflects this slow, careful process.[25] If this 7-year process goes well, a pharmaceutical company will enjoy 10 years of legally protected retail sales before generic versions of the drug can be offered by other companies.

Generic versus brand name drugs

When a new drug comes into the marketplace, it carries with it three names: its **chemical name,** its **generic name,** and its **brand name.** During the time the 17-year patent is in effect, no other drug with the same formulation can be sold. When the patent expires, other companies can manufacture a drug of chemical and therapeutic equivalence and market it under the brand name drug's original generic name. Because extensive research and development are not necessary at this point, the production of generic drugs is far less costly than the initial development of the brand name drug. Nearly all states allow pharmacists to substitute generic drugs for brand name drugs, as long as the prescribing physician approves.

Today the consumer can consult the *Physicians' Desk Reference—Generics* to learn more about generic medications.[26] This publication, introduced in 1995, was well received by both clinicians and the public.

Over-the-Counter Drugs

When people are asked when they last took some form of medication, for many the answer might be, "I took aspirin, or a cold pill, or a laxative this morning." In making this decision, people engaged in self-diagnosis, determined a course for their own treatment, self-administered their treatment, and freed a physician to serve people whose illnesses are more serious than theirs. None of this would have been possible without readily available, inexpensive, and effective OTC drugs.

Health on the Web
LEARNING ACTIVITIES

Activity 1

A new interactive medical information service is available at http://www.healthconsult.com. Created by practicing physicians, this service offers confidential answers to your medical questions as well as your health issues and concerns. This website is patient supported and was developed to educate the general public about various medical issues and allow anyone to ask questions covering all medical specialties. Scroll down to the section on "Patient information in question and answer format and clinical self-examination modules" and click. Choose a topic of interest to you and read the information. What did you learn about the topic you chose?

Activity 2

Group health and life insurance are considered American inventions of the early twentieth century. Health and life insurance, like all other types of insurance, are ways of sharing risk and cost. As someone once said, "If I knew I was going to live this long, I would have taken better care of myself." How long can you expect to live? You can estimate your life expectancy by completing the inventory at the Northwestern Mutual Life website, http://www.northwesternmutual.com. Scroll down to "Games" and click. Then select "Longevity game." The longevity game calculates how long you can expect to live based on life insurance industry research. Everyone starts with the average life expectancy of 73 years and adds or subtracts years from their score as they respond to a number of questions about personal characteristics, such as gender, and health behaviors, such as activity level. What is your estimated life expectancy? How much would it increase if you improved one aspect of your health behavior, such as smoking or diet?

Activity 3

The emergence of the self-care movement suggests that many people are taking more responsibility for maintaining their own health. They are developing the expertise to prevent or manage many types of illness, injuries, and conditions. They are learning to assess their health status and treat, monitor, and rehabilitate themselves in a way that was once thought possible only with the direct help of a physician or some other health care specialist. Go to http://www.mayohealth.org/mayo/9603/htm/quiz.htm and select "Test your knowledge of six symptoms that may spell trouble." How well did you score?

Categories of Over-the-Counter (OTC) Products
- Antacids
- Antimicrobials
- Sedatives and sleep aids
- Analgesics
- Cold remedies and antitussives
- Antihistamines and allergy products
- Mouthwashes
- Topical analgesics
- Antirheumatics
- Hematinics
- Vitamins and minerals
- Antiperspirants
- Laxatives
- Dentrifices and dental products
- Sunburn treatments and preventives
- Contraceptive and vaginal products
- Stimulants
- Hemorrhoidals
- Antidiarrheals
- Dandruff and athlete's foot preparations

In comparison with the 2500 prescription drugs available, there are perhaps as many as 300,000 different OTC products, routinely classified into 26 different families (see the Star Box above). Like prescription drugs, nonprescription drugs are regulated by the FDA. However, for OTC drugs the marketplace is a more powerful determinant of success.

The regulation of OTC drugs is based on a provision in a 1972 amendment to the 1938 Food, Drug, and Cosmetic Act. As a result of that action, OTC drugs were placed in three categories (I, II, and III) on the basis of the safety and effectiveness of their active ingredient(s). Today, only category I OTC drugs that are safe, effective, and truthfully labeled are to be sold. The FDA's drug classification process also allows some OTC drugs to be made stronger and some prescription drugs to become nonprescription drugs by reducing their strength through reformulation. Today more than 600 products (containing over 56 active ingredients) that were once available only by prescription have been approved by the FDA for OTC sale. As many as 25 additional products reach the market each year. For example, some recently reassigned products are nicotine chewing gum (Nicorette), transdermal nicotine patches (Nicotrol and Nicoderm CQ), hydrogen ion inhibitors (Zantac 75, Axid AR, and Pepcid AC), and an agent to promote hair growth (Rogaine).

The current labeling of OTC drugs also reflects the regulatory process described. The labels must clearly state the type and quantity of active ingredients, alcohol content, side effects, instructions for appropriate use, warnings against inappropriate use, and the risks of using the product with other drugs (polydrug use). Unsubstantiated claims must be carefully avoided in advertisements for these products.

Cosmetics

Concern over the safety of cosmetics has existed for more than 50 years. Hyperallergic reactions, bacterial infections, and the presence of carcinogens (agents that cause cancer) and teratogens (agents that cause birth defects) remain at the center of this concern. Because cosmetics are not generally classified as drugs, their regulation is limited in terms of FDA involvement. Legislation is regularly proposed that would increase the ability of the FDA to better control this important segment of the personal care retail trade.

HEALTH CARE QUACKERY AND CONSUMER FRAUD

A person who earns money by marketing inaccurate health information, unreliable health care, or ineffective health products is called a fraud, quack, or charlatan. **Consumer fraud** flourished with the old-fashioned medicine shows of the late 1880s. Unfortunately, consumer fraud still flourishes (see the article on health information on the Internet at the end of this chapter). You need look no further than large city newspapers to see questionable advertisements for disease cures and weight loss products. Quacks have found in health and illness the perfect avenues to realize maximum gain with minimum effort.

chemical name
Name used to describe the molecular structure of a drug.

generic name
Common or nonproprietary name of a drug.

brand name
Specific patented name assigned to a drug by its manufacturer.

consumer fraud
Marketing of unreliable and ineffective services, products, or information under the guise of curing disease or improving health; quackery.

HEALTH
Action Guide

Recognizing Quackery

"Duck" when you encounter these!

- Makes promises of quick, dramatic, simple, painless, or drugless treatment or cures
- Uses anecdotes, case histories, or testimonials to support claims
- Displays credentials or uses titles that might be confused with those of the scientific or medical community, such as Stan Smith, Ph.D. (in result)
- Claims a product or service provides treatment or cure for multiple or all illnesses and conditions
- States that this treatment or cure is either secret or not yet available in the United States

- States that medical doctors should not be trusted because they do more harm than good with their approaches to diagnosis and treatment
- Reports that most disease is due to a faulty diet and can be treated with nutritional supplements
- Promotes the use of hair analysis to diagnose illnesses or deficiencies
- Claims that "natural" products are superior to those sold in drugstores or dispensed by physicians
- Supports the "freedom of choice" concept that should allow you to try something even though it has not been proved safe and effective

When people are in poor health, they may be afraid of dying. So powerful are their desires to live and be free of suffering that people are vulnerable to promises of health improvement and life extension. Even though many people have great faith in their physicians, they also would like to have access to experimental treatments or products touted as being superior to currently available therapies. When tempted with the promise of real help, people are sometimes willing to set aside traditional medical care. Of course, quacks recognize this vulnerability and present a variety of "reasons" to move in their direction (see the Health Action Guide above).[27] Gullibility, blind faith, impatience, superstition, ignorance, or hostility toward professional expertise eventually carry the day. In spite of the best efforts of agencies at all levels, no branch of government can protect consumers from their own errors of judgment that so easily play into the hands of quacks and charlatans.

Regardless of the specific motivation that leads people into consumer fraud, the outcome is frequently the same. First, the consumer suffers financial loss. The services or products provided are grossly overpriced, and the consumers have little recourse to help them recover their money. Second, the consumers often feel disappointed, guilty, and angered by their own carelessness as consumers. Far too frequently, consumer fraud may lead to unnecessary suffering.

Summary

- Sources of health information include family, friends, commercials, labels, and information supplied by health professionals.
- Physicians can be either Doctors of Medicine (MDs) or Doctors of Osteopathy (DOs). They receive similar training and engage in similar forms of practice.
- Although alternative health care providers, including chiropractors, naturopaths, and acupuncturists, meet the health care needs of many people,

- systematic study of these forms of health care is only now under way.
- Restricted-practice health care providers play important roles in meeting the health and wellness needs of the public.
- Nursing at all levels is a critical health care profession.
- Self-care is often a viable approach to preventing illness and reducing the use of health care providers.

- Our growing inability to afford health care services has reached crisis proportions in this country.
- Health insurance is critical in our ability to afford modern health care services.
- Managed health care plans provide alternative ways to receive health care services, although there is concern about the influence of the profit motive in their operation.
- Medicare and Medicaid are governmental plans for paying for health care services that could be significantly altered in our current quest for a balanced budget.
- The development of prescription medication is a long and expensive process for pharmaceutical manufacturers.
- Critical health consumerism, including the avoidance of health quackery, requires careful use of health-related information, products, and services.

Review Questions

1. Determine how you would test the accuracy of the health-related information you have received in your lifetime.
2. Identify and describe some sources of health-related information presented in this chapter. What factors should you consider when using these sources?
3. Point out the similarities between allopathic and osteopathic physicians. What is an alternative health care practitioner? Give examples of each type of alternative practitioner.
4. Describe the services that are provided by the following limited health care providers: dentists, psychologists, podiatrists, optometrists, and opticians. Identify several allied health care professionals.
5. In what ways is the trend toward self-care evident? What are some reasons for the popularity of this movement?

6. What is health insurance? Explain the following terms relating to health insurance: deductible amount, fixed indemnity benefits, full-service benefits, coinsurance, exclusion, and preexisting illness.
7. What is a health maintenance organization? How do HMO plans reduce the costs of health care? What are IPAs, PPOs, and POSs?
8. What do the chemical name, brand name, and generic name of a prescription drug represent? OTC drugs are categorized according to what two factors?
9. What is health care quackery? What responsibilities have been given to the FDA? What can a consumer do to avoid consumer fraud?

Think About This . . .

- How do you rate yourself as an informed consumer of health information, services, and products?
- Are there any types of providers mentioned in this chapter whom you would not choose to consult? Explain your answer.
- To what extent and in what ways have you engaged in self-care?
- Many insurance companies exclude certain kinds of illness (such as AIDS) from coverage and will not pay for the needed drugs. Who then should cover the cost? Under what circumstances do you think that expensive medications should be prescribed for terminally ill patients?
- Is life insurance more important than health insurance for young adults? Explain your answer.
- Why do you think it is difficult to get people to seek help for preventive care even though it is usually less expensive than treatment services?
- When you read a newspaper or magazine, do some health-rated advertisements seem questionable to you?

References

1. *Femstat 3 Report:* American women and self-care, as reported in *USA Today*, p. 10, Aug 12, 1996.
2. Adam Yoder, Ontario Systems, personal correspondence, Feb 10, 1998.
3. Margolis S, Moses H (editors): *The Johns Hopkins medical handbook: The 100 major medical disorders of people over the age of 50,* New York, 1997, Random House.

4. *Physicians' desk reference 1998,* ed 52, Oradel, NJ, Medical Economics Data Production.
5. *Harvard Women's Health Watch,* Boston, 1998, Harvard Medical School Health Publications Group.
6. *NIH consensus development statement: Acupuncture,* (Online), Nov 6, 1997.
7. Schulte E: Acupuncture: where east meets west, *RN* 59(10):55, 1996.
8. Griffin K, Butter K: The new doctors of natural medicine, *Health* 10(6):60, 1996.
9. Verbach EU et al: Efficacy and tolerability of St. John's wort extract LI 160 versus imipramine in patients with severe depression episodes according to ICD-20, *Pharmacopsychiatry* 30(supp.2):81-85, 1997.
10. *Alternative medicine. Expanding medical horizons—a report to the National Institute of Health on alternative medical systems in the United States.* NIH Pub No. 94-066, 1994.
11. American Optometric Association Student Association, Jan 29, 1998, aosa@earthlink.net.
12. Carlson E: AARP submits health-care reform proposal to members for their review, AARP Bulletin 33(3):1, 1992.
13. Levit KR, Lazenby HC, Braden BR: National health spending in 1996, *Health affairs* 17(1):35–51, 1998.
14. Federal budget estimates for 1991-1996, Department of Commerce estimates for 1991-1996, *USA Today,* p. 3B, May 6, 1991.
15. Human development report 1994 (United Nations), *USA Today,* p. 1A, Jan 16, 1994.
16. Anderson GF: In search of value: an international comparison of costs, access, and outcomes, *Health Affairs* 16(6):163-171, 1997.
17. Higgins F: National survey of employer-sponsored health plans, *USA Today,* p. 1B, April 16, 1997.
18. *Special focus: public health and managed care, 1996 projection from HMO & PPO Trend Survey,* AAHP, 1996.
19. New options alter health choices for older Americans, *AARP Bulletin* (special report), p. 10, November 1996.
20. Medicare (1998 Medicare Rates Supplement), Social Security Administration, SSA Publication No. 05-10043, June 1995. ICW 46000.
21. Medicare under attack in Congress, *AARP Voter* 9(1):1-2, Spring 1995.
22. Health Care Financing Administration, *USA Today,* p. 6A, Sept 25, 1995.
23. Top 200 drugs, *American Druggist,* Feb 4, 1996.
24. Annual Rx review: Nicotine patches lead Rx activity to new heights, *Drug Topics* 137(7):72, 1993.
25. Drug development costs, *PhRMA* Facts, February 1996.
26. *Physicians' Desk Reference—Generics,* ed 4, Oradel, NJ, 1998, Medical Economics Data Production.
27. Cornacchia HJ, Barrett S: *Consumer health: a guide to intelligent decisions,* ed 6, St. Louis, 1997, Mosby.

Suggested Readings

Brown TM, Stoudemire A: *Psychiatric side effects of prescription and over-the-counter medications,* Washington, DC, 1998, American Psychiatric Press.

This important book is unique in two respects. First, the authors investigate a wide range of medications and drug interactions that produce psychiatric side effects and explain why these side effects occur. Second, the authors invite readers to share their own experiences or ask questions by e-mail.

Dilulio JJ, Nathan RP, Thompson FJ (editors): *Medicaid and the states: issues and prospects,* Washington, DC, 1998, Brookings Institute.

Medicaid programs are directed by the states and designed to meet the health care needs of the poor, regardless of their age. Each state's funding and criteria for eligibility are different. This book explores the states' ability to and interest in meeting the health care needs of more and more people as the federal government places increasing responsibility on the states. This book is a comprehensive study of a serious situation.

Schissel MJ, Dodes JE: *The whole tooth: how to find a good dentist, keep healthy teeth, and avoid the incompetents, quacks, and frauds,* New York, 1997, St. Martin's Press.

In the authors' opinion, not all dentists are created equal. In fact, as they see it, many dentists perform poorly, while some are nothing more than quacks. In the latter case, the procedures they recommend are often unnecessary and the work they do actually endangers their patients. The book explains how cost cutting, leading to a hurry-up approach to modern dentistry, can make even a good dentist less competent than he or she should be.

Dearborn Financial Publishing: *Long-term care,* Chicago, IL, 1997, Dearborn Financial Publishing.

Many of today's baby boomers will have to face the need to place a frail parent into a nursing home. This book presents an overview of the role of Medicare, Medicaid, and the health insurance industry in making long-term care affordable, which it rarely is. Long-term facilities and the types of care they offer are described for a generation soon to be testing the market, both for their parents and for their own future care.

Reischauer RD (editor): *Medicare: preparing for the challenges of the 21st century,* Washington, DC, 1998, Brookings Institute.

Drawing on the expertise of authorities from various agencies, institutes, and academic disciplines, this book explores the nature of the past, present, and future contracts between Medicare and the American public. The effects that changing demographics, the women's movement, and managed care have had on Medicare are explored and proposals for restructuring are advanced.

ON...

Separating Fact from Fiction: Using Health Information on the Internet

So you want to find some information on health. Maybe you have a paper due in this class. Maybe you need more information on a condition that you or a loved one has. Or maybe you simply want to take advantage of the latest information on fitness and nutrition to make healthful decisions. No matter what information you're looking for, you can probably find it on the Internet. But be wary as you search—a great deal of misinformation is also available, and it may be hard for the average consumer to separate health fact from health fiction.

You can be relatively certain that government sites and links contain reliable information. In fact, the U.S. Department of Health and Human Services has established a new site to provide consumer information. It can be accessed under Health/General Health or directly at www.healthfinder.gov. This site was launched in April 1997 by the U.S. Secretary of Health and Human Services. Donna Shalala, in response to a request by Vice President Al Gore to improve consumer access to federal health information on-line. As Healthfinder points out in its introductory paragraph, information alone can't take the place of health care you may need. But it can make you an informed partner in your own health care. This site leads you to selected on-line publications, databases, websites, support and self-help groups, government agencies, not-for-profit organizations, and universities that provide reliable health information to the public.[1]

Unfortunately, the government does not have the resources to filter out all false and misleading health care information. Many people mistakenly believe that advertising claims must be true or advertisers would not be allowed to continue making them.[2] Not enough time, money, and regulators are available to assess the validity of each and every health claim. However, health care professionals and consumer advocates can give us the tools we need to determine the reliability of health information for ourselves.

What Is Quackery and How Can You Spot It?

One prominent consumer advocate is Stephen Barrett, a retired physician and nationally renowned author (with 42 books to his credit).[3] In 1969 he founded the Lehigh Valley Committee against Health Fraud, which recently changed its name to Quackwatch.[4] Investigation of questionable claims, answering of inquiries, distribution of reliable publications, reporting of illegal marketing, and

Using health information from reliable Internet sites can help you become an active participant in your own health care.

improvement of the overall quality of health information on the Internet are all tasks that this group takes on.

Quackery is more difficult to spot than most people think.[5] Whereas fraud is deliberate deception and more easily recognized and corrected, quackery involves the use of methods that are not scientifically valid.[6] Information purveyed by quacks cannot be scientifically confirmed or denied, and this is where the problem arises. There is no way to separate the good from the bad or the harmful from the benign or helpful.

Anecdotes and Testimonials

Some alternative health care methods have been accepted by the scientific community, having met reliable criteria for safety and effectiveness. Other methods are in the experimental stages. These methods are unproven but are based on plausible, rational principles and are undergoing responsible testing. But many other alternative health remedies are groundless and completely lack scientific rationale.[7] Instead of scientific tests, people who promote these methods rely on anecdotes and testimonials to "prove" the effectiveness of their products. Much of the "success" of these products is due to the placebo effect; no cause and effect relationship has been established between use of the product and abatement of symptoms. People who use the remedies either get better coincidentally or think that their condition has improved simply because they're taking something for it.

Intelligent Consumer Behavior

Americans waste $50 million to $150 million per year on bogus mail-order health remedies.[2] Many of these products are now available on the Internet. You can avoid wasting your money in this way by not buying any of these products without medical advice from your physician or other health care professional. And don't be fooled by money back guarantees; they're usually as phoney as the products that they back.[2]

Be wary of characteristic quackery ploys.[8] Purveyors of quackery may say that they care about you, but their care, even if it were sincere, cannot make useless medicine work. These products are commonly touted as having no side effects. If this is true, then the product is too weak to have any effect at all. Quacks will encourage you to jump on the bandwagon of their time-tested remedy, as if popularity and market longevity are surrogates for effectiveness. When they do claim that their products are backed by scientific studies, these studies turn out to be untraceable, misinterpreted, irrelevant, nonexistent, or based on poorly designed research.[8]

The costs of buying into health-care quackery are more than financial. The psychological effects of disillusionment and the physical harm caused by the method itself or by abandoning more effective care are much worse.

HONcode Principles

Any reputable health information site on the Internet subscribes to the HONcode Principles. These principles are put forth and monitored by the Geneva-based Health On the Net Foundation and have arisen from input from webmasters and medical professionals in several countries.[9] According to these principles, any medical advice appearing at a site must meet the following requirements:

- It must be given by medically trained and qualified professionals unless a clear statement is made that the information comes from a non-medically-qualified individual or organization.
- The information must be intended to support, not replace, the physician-patient relationship.
- Data relating to individual patients and visitors to a medical website are confidential.

- Site information must have clear references to source data and, where possible, specific links to that data.
- Claims related to the benefit or performance of a treatment, product, or service must be supported by appropriate, balanced evidence.
- The webmaster's e-mail address should be clearly displayed throughout the website.
- Commercial and noncommercial support and funding for the site should be clearly revealed.
- There must be a clear differentiation between advertising at the site and the original material created by the institution operating the site.

Be skeptical about any health information you find on the Internet that does not meet these criteria. Ask your physician whether the information is accurate, or move on to a more reliable site.

Assessing Health Care Information

The Internet is a valuable health care tool. Reliable information is supplied by government health agencies, research universities, hospitals, disease foundations, and other experts. However, not all health sites are reputable. As the saying goes, you can't believe everything you read, even if it's on the Internet. Anyone can create an on-line resource that looks professional. Ordinary people who believe they've been helped by a product, companies trying to sell products and services, and even cheats and quacks are all out there spouting their information. To protect yourself, you must be an informed consumer of information. To evaluate the credibility of an on-line source, ask yourself the following questions:

1. Who maintains the information?
2. Is it linked to other reputable sources of mefical information?
3. When was it last updated?
4. Is it selling a product?

While the Internet cannot and should not replace visits with a physician, reliable information obtained on the net can make us more active partners in our own health care. It can give us information we can use to stay healthy and prevent disease. It can help us to ask our doctors the right questions and educate us so that we're not afraid to ask them. It can connect us to people who are experiencing the same things as we are. It can help us learn about our health, receive support from others, and make sound health-care decisions based on fact—not fiction.

For Discussion . . .

Which health-related sites have you visited on the Internet? Did you find them informative? reliable? fun? What could be done to improve the status of health information on the Internet?

References

1. U.S. Department of Health and Human Services. 1997. Healthfinder. http://www.healthfinder.gov

2. Barrett S. Mail-order quackery. 1996. http://www.quackwatch.com/01QuackeryRelatedTopics/mailquack.html

3. Barrett S. About Dr. Barrett. 1997. http://www.quackwatch.com/bio.html

4. Barrett S. Mission statement. 1997. http://www.quackwatch.com/00AboutQuackwatch/mission.html

5. Barrett S. Common misconceptions. 1997. http://www.quackwatch.com/01QuackeryRelatedTopics/miscon.html

6. Barrett S. Quackery: how should it be defined. 1997. http://www.quackwatch.com/quackdof.html

7. Barrett S. Be wary of "alternative" health methods. 1997. http://www.quackwatch.com/01QuackeryRelatedTopics/altwary.html

8. Barrett S, Herbert V. More ploys that may fool you. 1997. http://www.quackwatch.com/01QuackeryRelatedTopics/ploys.html

9. Health On the Net Foundation. HONcode principles. 1997. http://www.quackwatch.com/00AboutQuackwatch/honcode.html

16

Protecting Your Safety

Healthy People: Looking Ahead to 2010

Like the *Healthy People 2000* objectives, the *Healthy People 2010* document will target goals in the two broad focus areas of violent and abusive behavior and unintentional injuries, the topics of this chapter. The mid-1990s assessment of progress in the area of violence indicated that the nation had moved closer to reaching only 3 of 18 objectives. First, suicide rates remained stable for the population as a whole, although suicide rates for young men were on the rise. Second, the incidence of rape and reported rape had declined. Third, fewer adolescents ages 14 to 17 were carrying weapons.

At mid-decade, the nation had lost ground in the areas of homicide, firearm-related deaths, assault injuries, and suicide attempts by adolescents. Public health officials predicted that if the mid-1990s murder trends continued, the rate of firearm deaths would exceed the rate of traffic fatalities by 2003. Fortunately, it appears that homicide and firearm death rates have leveled off.

The data concerning national health objectives in the area of safety were much more positive. Reports issued in the mid-1990s indicated progress toward achieving 14 of 16 objectives in the area of unintentional injuries. However, no gains had been made in reducing hip fractures among older adults and increasing the use of smoke detectors. We can expect continued progress toward achieving the safety objectives now being formulated for the *Healthy People 2010* document.

As recently as two decades ago, the suspicious disappearance of a school-aged child or the death of a bystander during a drive-by shooting was virtually unheard of. As the decade draws to a close, however, violent crimes are committed so frequently in the United States that it is difficult to watch a television news report or read a newspaper without seeing headlines announcing some heinous murder or other senseless act of violence. The Oklahoma City bombing trials, the au pair trial, the Unabomber case, and the still-unsolved murder of JonBenet Ramsey remind us that we live in a violent society.

Domestic violence directed at women and children seems to be increasing, and many people fear being a random victim of a homicide, robbery, or carjacking. Law enforcement officials contend that gang activities and hard-core drug involvement are significant factors that have increased violent behavior in our society.

Although violence may seem to be focused in urban areas, no community is completely safe. Even people who live in small towns and rural areas now must lock their doors and remain vigilant about protecting their safety. Crime on college campuses remains a threat for all students.

For some students the content in this chapter may be the most important information in this textbook. Becoming a victim of violent behavior or sustaining an unintentional injury can harm your health as much (or more) than any of your own unhealthy behavior. The goal of this chapter is to help you understand the scope of violence in our society and learn what you can do to avoid becoming a victim. Complete the Personal Assessment on p. 404 to see whether you are adequately protecting your own safety.

INTENTIONAL INJURIES

Intentional injuries are injuries that are committed on purpose. With the exception of suicide (which is self-directed), intentional injuries reflect violence committed by one person acting against another person. Categories of intentional injuries include homicide, robbery, rape, suicide, assault, child abuse, spouse abuse, and elder abuse. Each year in the United States, intentional injuries cause about 50,000 deaths and another 2 million nonfatal injuries.[1]

In 1996, nearly 37 million crimes were committed against U.S. residents age 12 and older, according to data collected by the National Crime Victimization Survey. Crime rates for 1996 indicate 42 violent crimes per 1000 people. This rate shows a decline from 1995 figures and is the lowest rate recorded since the first such survey was conducted, in 1973.[2]

Homicide

Homicide, or murder, is the intentional killing of one person by another. Sadly, the United States leads the industrialized world in homicide rates. The 1996 murder rate was 7.4 per 100,000 inhabitants. This rate amounted to 19,645 murders, reflecting a 10% decline from the 1995 rate. This decrease was the largest in 4 years.

Criminal justice experts are trying to pinpoint why U.S. homicide rates are dropping. No one answer has emerged, but speculation centers on better community policing efforts; the 1994 passage of the sweeping Federal Crime Bill; recent legislation, such as the Brady law; and a variety of tough state laws, such as the "three strikes and you're out" provisions that mandate life sentences without parole for repeat violent offenders.

There are some clear trends when it comes to the people involved in homicides. The most vulnerable group of homicide victims are African-Americans, especially young male African-Americans. Homicide is the leading cause of death for male African-American ages 15 to 44. African-American men have a 1 in 21 lifetime chance of becoming a victim of homicide.[3]

Another clear trend related to homicide is the extent to which illegal drug activity is related to homicide. A variety of research studies from large cities indicate that 25% to 50% of all homicides are drug related.[4] Most of these murders are related to activities involved in drug trafficking, including disputed drug transactions. Additionally, high percentages of both homicide assailants and victims have drugs in their systems at the time of the homicide.[4]

Finally, another clear trend is that handguns are the weapon of choice for homicides. In 1994, handguns were used in 58% of the homicides in the United States.[5] This is not surprising because handgun use among most categories of violent crime reached record levels in 1992. In 1992, 13% of all violent crimes were committed with offenders using handguns.[6] The proliferation of handguns and their use in violent crimes led to the passage of the so-called Brady law.

intentional injuries
Injuries that are purposely committed by a person.

homicide
The intentional killing of one person by another person.

PERSONAL ASSESSMENT

How Well Do You Protect Your Safety?

This quiz will help you measure how well you manage your personal safety. For each item below, circle the number that reflects the frequency with which you do the safety activity. Then, add up your individual scores and check the interpretation at the end.

3　I regularly do this
2　I sometimes do this
1　I rarely do this

1. I am aware of my surroundings and do not get lost.　3　2　1
2. I avoid locations in which my personal safety could be compromised.　3　2　1
3. I intentionally vary my daily routine (such as walking patterns to and from class, parking places, and jogging or biking routes) so that my whereabouts are not always predictable.　3　2　1
4. I walk across campus at night with other people.　3　2　1
5. I am careful about disclosing personal information (address, phone number, social security number, my daily schedule, etc.) to people I do not know.　3　2　1
6. I carefully monitor my alcohol intake at parties.　3　2　1
7. I watch carefully for dangerous weather conditions and know how to respond if necessary.　3　2　1
8. I do not keep a loaded gun in my home.　3　2　1
9. I know how I would handle myself if I were to be assaulted.　3　2　1
10. I maintain adequate insurance for my health and my property.　3　2　1
11. I keep emergency information numbers near my phone.　3　2　1
12. I keep my first aid skills up-to-date.　3　2　1
13. I use deadbolt locks on the doors of my home.　3　2　1
14. I use the safety locks on the windows at home.　3　2　1
15. I check the batteries used in my home smoke detector.　3　2　1
16. I have installed a carbon monoxide detector in my home.　3　2　1
17. I use adequate lighting in areas around my home and garage.　3　2　1
18. I have the electrical, heating, and cooling equipment in my home inspected regularly for safety and efficiency.　3　2　1
19. I use my car seat belt.　3　2　1
20. I drive my car safely and defensively.　3　2　1
21. I keep my car in good mechanical order.　3　2　1
22. I keep my car doors locked.　3　2　1
23. I have a plan of action if my car should break down while I am driving it.　3　2　1
24. I use appropriate safety equipment, such as flotation devices, helmets, and elbow pads, in my recreational activities.　3　2　1
25. I can swim well enough to save myself in most situations.　3　2　1
26. I use suggestions for personal safety each day.　3　2　1

TOTAL POINTS ＿＿＿＿＿＿

Interpretation

Your total may mean that:

72–78 points	You appear to carefully protect your personal safety.
65–71 points	You adequately protect many aspects of your personal safety.
58–64 points	You should consider improving some of your safety-related behaviors.
Below 58 points	You must consider improving some of your safety-related behaviors.

To Carry This Further . . .

Although no one can be completely safe from personal injury or possible random violence, there are ways to minimize the risks to your safety. Scoring high on this assessment will not guarantee your safety, but your likelihood for injury should remain relatively low. Scoring low on this assessment should encourage you to consider ways to make your life more safe. Refer to the text and this assessment to provide you with useful suggestions to enhance your personal safety. Which safety tips will you use today?

The Marv Albert Case

In October 1997, NBC sports announcer Marv Albert, 54, pleaded guilty to assault and battery charges in a case involving 42-year-old Vanessa Perhach, who had accused Albert of biting her repeatedly on the back before forcing her to perform oral sex. Albert, whose defense team was headed by well-known attorney Roy Black, agreed to a plea bargain in which felony charges of forcible sodomy were dropped in return for his pleading guilty of two other charges. The assault and battery charges were punishable by a maximum of one year in jail and a $2500 fine. A forcible sodomy conviction could have resulted in a prison sentence of 20 years to life.

NBC promptly fired Albert, and he quit his job as the play-by-play announcer for the New York Knicks. Two weeks after the trial, Arlington County, Virginia, Circuit Court Judge Benjamin Kendrick deferred sentencing Albert, a first-time offender, and ruled that charges against him would be dismissed if he stayed out of trouble for a year and if his mental health therapist continued to send regular progress reports to the court.

Domestic Violence

Family life in the 1990s is a far cry from that portrayed in the popular 1950s and 1960s television shows like the *Donna Reed Show, Father Knows Best,* and *Ozzie and Harriet.* The composition of families has changed considerably. In the 1950s a common family pattern included children being raised by both parents. Generally, the father was the income earner and the mother stayed at home and managed the growing family.

Today, family patterns are much more complex. Children are more frequently being raised in blended families or in families headed by single parents. In fact, since 1970, single-parent households have increased 112%, from 4 to 8.9 million homes.[5] A much higher percentage of women are employed outside the home. Because of pressing family economic concerns, many children take care of themselves during after-school hours. Sociologists indicate that families, and the individuals in those families, are under more stress than ever.

Add to this precarious nature of the American family the additional factors of increased societal drug use, increased presence of handguns, and increased crime and violence. What emerges is no surprise—increased domestic violence.

Partner abuse

Partner abuse refers to violence committed against a domestic partner. Most often the victims are women, and a significant percentage of these women are spouses or former spouses of the assailant. Figures from the U.S. Department of Justice[7] are frightening and reflect the magnitude of the problem of violence against women in the United States. More than 2.5 million women are victims of some form of violence every year. Nearly two in three female victims of violent crimes are related to or know their attacker. About three out of four female victims resist the actions of their offenders either physically or verbally.

The most vulnerable female victims are African-American and Hispanic, live in large cities, are young and unmarried, and are from lower socioeconomic groups.[7] However, these trends do not mean that only women from these classifications are vulnerable to violent behavior. Women across all economic, racial, and age categories are potential victims. For example, in the aftermath of the tragic murder of Nicole Brown Simpson, the picture of an affluent woman who had been a victim of domestic violence emerged.

One of the real difficulties related to domestic violence is the vast underreporting of this crime to law enforcement authorities. The U.S. Department of Justice estimates that about half of the victims of domestic violence do not report the crime to police. Too many victims view their violent situations as private or personal matters and not actual crimes. Despite painful injuries, many victims view the offenses against them as minor.[7]

Of course, it is easy to criticize the victims of domestic violence for not reporting the crimes committed against them, but this may be unfair. Why do women stay in these relationships? Many women who are injured may fear being killed if they report the crime. Women may also fear for the safety of their children. Women who receive economic support from an abuser may fear being left with no financial resources.

However, help is available for victims of partner abuse. Most communities have family support or domestic violence hot lines that abused people can call for help. Communities are establishing shelters where abused women and their children can seek safety

---

partner abuse
Violence committed against a domestic partner.

Denise Brown speaks out against domestic violence.

while their cases are being handled by the police or court officials. If you are being abused or know of someone who is the victim of domestic violence, do not hesitate to use the services of these local hot lines or shelters. Also, check the resources listed in the Health Reference Guide at the back of this text.

Child abuse

Like many cases of partner abuse, **child abuse** tends to be a silent crime. It is estimated that about 1 million children are victims of child abuse and neglect each year. Of course, some children are victims of repeated crimes, and since many victims do not report their crimes, the actual incidence of child abuse is difficult to determine.

Children are abused in various ways.[8] Physical abuse reflects physical injury, such as bruises, burns, abrasions, cuts, and fractures of the bones and skull. Sexual abuse includes acts that lead to sexual gratification of the abuser. Examples include fondling,

touching, and various acts involved in rape, sodomy, and incest. Child neglect is also a form of child abuse and includes an extreme failure to provide children with adequate clothing, food, shelter, and medical attention. A strong case can also be made for psychological abuse as a form of child abuse. Certainly, children are scarred by family members and others who routinely damage their psychological development. Unfortunately, this form of abuse is especially difficult to identify and measure.

The most frequent form of child abuse is neglect.[8] The incidence of child neglect is approximately three times the incidence of physical abuse and about seven times the incidence of child sexual abuse. Each form of abuse can have devastating short- and long-term consequences for the child.

Research studies in the various areas of child abuse reveal some interesting trends. Abused children are much more likely than nonabused children to grow up to be child abusers themselves. It is also now understood that abused children are more likely to suffer from poor educational performance, increased health problems, and low levels of overall achievement. Recent research also points out that abused children are significantly more likely than nonabused children to become involved in adult crime and violent criminal behavior.[8]

It is beyond the scope of this book to discuss in detail how to reduce child abuse. However, the violence directed against children can likely be lessened through a combination of early identification measures and violence prevention programs. Teachers, friends, relatives, social workers, counselors, psychologists, police, and the court system must not hesitate to intervene early in cases of suspected child abuse. The later the intervention, the more likely that the abuse will have worsened. Once abuse has occurred, it is likely to happen again.

Violence prevention programs can help parents and caregivers learn how to resolve conflicts, improve communication, cope with anger, improve parenting skills, and challenge the view of violence presented in movies and television. In these programs, it may be possible to stop violence before it begins to damage the lives of young children. Figure 16-1 provides simple alternatives parents can choose to avoid hitting a child.[9]

Elder abuse

Among the nation's 31 million elderly people, 1.5 million are the victims of neglect and abuse. Particularly vulnerable are elderly women over the age of 75 years. More often than not, the abusers are the adult children of the victims.

12 alternatives to lashing out at your child.

The next time everyday pressures build up to the point where you feel like lashing out—STOP! And try any of these simple alternatives.

You'll feel better . . . and so will your child.

1. Take a deep breath. And another. Then remember <u>you</u> are the adult . . .

2. Close your eyes and imagine you're hearing what your child is about to hear.

3. Press your lips together and count to 10. Or better yet, to 20.

4. Put your child in a time-out chair. (Remember the rule: one time-out minute for each year of age.)

5. Put yourself in a time-out chair. Think about why you are angry: is it your child, or is your child simply a convenient target for your anger?

6. Phone a friend.

7. If someone can watch the children, go outside and take a walk.

8. Take a hot bath or splash cold water on your face.

9. Hug a pillow.

10. Turn on some music. Maybe even sing along.

11. Pick up a pencil and write down as many helpful words as you can think of. Save the list.

12. Write for parenting information: Parenting, Box 2866, Chicago, IL 60690.

Take Time Out. Don't Take It Out On Your Child.

National Committee for Prevention of Child Abuse   Ad Council

Figure 16-1   Alternatives to abusing your child.

Many elderly people are hit, kicked, attacked with knives, denied food and medical care, and have their Social Security checks and automobiles stolen. It is likely that this reflects a combination of factors, particularly the stress of caring for failing older people by middle-aged children who are also faced with the additional demands of dependent children and careers. In many cases, the middle-aged children were themselves abused, or there may be a chemical dependence problem. The alternative, institutionalization, is so expensive that it is often not an option for either the abused or the abusers.

Although protective services are available in most communities through welfare departments, elder abuse is frequently unseen and unreported. In many cases, the elderly people themselves are afraid to report their children's behavior because of the fear of embarrassment that they were not good parents to their children. Regardless of the cause, however, elder abuse must be reported to the appropriate protective service so that intervention can occur.

Gangs and Youth Violence

In the last 20 years, gangs and gang activities have been increasingly responsible for escalating violence and criminal activity. Before that time, gangs used fists, tire irons, and occasionally, cheap handguns ("Saturday night specials") as tools of enforcement. Now, gang members do not hesitate to use AK-47s (semiautomatic military assault weapons) that have the potential to kill large groups of people in a few seconds.

Most, but not all, gangs arise from big city environments where many socially alienated, economically disadvantaged young people live. Convinced that society has no significant role for them, gang members can receive support from an association of peers that has well-defined lines of authority. Rituals and membership initiation rites are important in gang socialization. Gangs often control particular territories within a city. Frequently, gangs are involved in criminal activities, the most common of which are illicit drug trafficking and robberies. In the mid-1990s, gang-related murders and drive-by shootings contributed to the rising death toll among young people.

It is not only older male teenagers and young adults who are members of today's gangs. Increasingly, law enforcement officials see younger people (ages 12, 13, and 14) joining gangs. Some gangs have recently included young women as members, and some cities report a growing number of all-female gangs. Some female gangs are reported to be every bit as ruthless as the male gangs.[10]

Youth violence is also spreading from the inner cities to the suburbs. Public health officials and law enforcement personnel claim that youth violence is growing in epidemic proportions. Attorney General Janet Reno[11] has stated that youth violence is "the greatest single crime problem in America today."

Attempting to control gang and youth violence is particularly expensive for communities. When you consider that for every gang-related homicide, there are about 100 nonfatal gang-related intentional injuries, it becomes obvious that gang violence is an

child abuse
Harm that is committed against a child; usually referring to physical abuse, sexual abuse, or child neglect.

expensive health care proposition. Furthermore, gang and youth violence takes an enormous financial and human toll on law enforcement, judicial, and corrections departments. Reducing gang and youth violence will be a daunting task for the nation as it approaches the year 2000.

Gun Violence

The tragic effect of gun violence has already been touched on in a few sections of this chapter. Guns are being used more than ever in our society and in other parts of the world. In 1992, people armed with handguns committed a record 931,000 violent crimes.[6] More than 60% of the homicides and 55% of the suicides committed each year in the United States involve the use of guns. As previously mentioned, gun violence is a leading killer of teenagers and young men, especially African-American men, and the use of semiautomatic assault weapons by individuals and gang members is increasing. Accidental deaths of toddlers and young children from loaded handguns is another dimension of the violence attributable to guns in our society. In addition, guns are often used in **carjackings** (see the Health Action Guide on p. 409).

The proliferation of firearm use has prompted serious discussions concerning the enactment of gun control laws. For years, gun control activists have been in direct battle with the National Rifle Association (NRA) and its congressional supporters. Gun control activists want fewer guns manufactured and greater controls over the sale and possession of handguns. Gun supporters believe that such controls are not necessary and that people (the criminals) are responsible for gun deaths, not simply the guns. This debate will certainly continue.

Bias and Hate Crimes

One sad aspect of any society is how some segments of the majority treat certain people in the minority. Nowhere is this more violently pronounced than in **bias and hate crimes.** These crimes are directed at individuals or groups of people solely because of a racial, ethnic, religious, or other difference attributed to the victims. Victims are often verbally and physically attacked, their houses are spray painted with various slurs, and many are forced to move from one neighborhood or community to another. According to Federal Bureau of Investigation

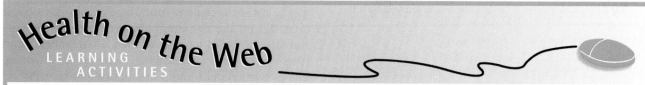

Activity 1

In this chapter you learned about the recent increase in domestic violence. The Family Violence Prevention Fund is a national nonprofit organization that focuses on domestic violence education, prevention, and public policy reform. Go to their website at http://www.igc.org/fund to learn more about domestic violence. Test your knowledge about domestic violence by taking the quiz posted at the site. How well did you do?

Activity 2

Most accidental deaths in the United States take place on our highways and streets. About 40% of fatal traffic crashes are alcohol related. Further, the likelihood of being involved in a fatal collision is about eight times higher for a drunk driver than for a sober one. Go to the California Drunk Driving website at http://www.dui.com/index.shtml to find

information on what you need to know about drinking and driving. Scroll down and select "Frequently asked questions" and then click on *DUI Test—How well are you informed?* Answer the questions to find out how well you know the law.

Activity 3

Unintentional injuries are very expensive for our society, both from a financial standpoint and from the perspective of personal and family loss. Knowing basic first aid procedures may help save the life of someone who has suffered an unintentional injury. We encourage you to take a first aid course from the American Red Cross. To test your knowledge of first aid, go to the Mayo Clinic website at http://www.mayohealth.org/mayo/9704/htm/faidquiz/start.htm and answer the questions listed. How much did you know about first aid?

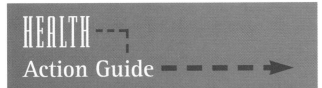

Preventing Carjacking

In the last 10 years a new form of violence has reached the streets of America. This crime is commonly called *carjacking*. Unlike auto theft, in which a car thief attempts to steal an unattended parked car, carjacking involves a thief's attempt to steal a car with a driver still behind the wheel.

Most carjacking attempts begin when a car is stopped at an intersection, usually at a traffic light. A carjacker will approach the driver and force him or her to give up the car. Resisting an armed carjacker can be extremely dangerous. Law enforcement officials offer the following tips to prevent carjacking:

- Drive only on well-lit and well-traveled streets, if possible.
- Always keep your doors locked when driving your car.
- Observe traffic that may be following you. If you think that something suspicious is happening, try to locate a police officer or a busy, populated area to seek help.
- If someone approaches your car and you cannot safely drive away, roll the window down only slightly and leave the car running and in gear. If the situation turns bad, use your wits and quickly flee the scene, either in the car or on foot. Remember: your life is worth more than your car.
- If another car taps the rear bumper of your car (a common carjacking maneuver to get you to exit your car) and you feel uncomfortable about getting out of your car, tell the other driver that you are driving to the police station to complete the accident report.

(FBI) statistics, there are about 7500 hate crime incidents in the United States each year.

Typically, the offenders in bias or hate crimes are fringe elements of the larger society who believe that the mere presence of someone with a racial, ethnic, or religious difference is inherently bad for the community, state, or country. Examples of groups commonly known to commit bias and hate crimes in the United States are skinheads, the Ku Klux Klan, and other white supremacist groups. Increasingly, state and federal laws have been enacted to make bias and hate crimes serious offenses.

With a small but growing presence of neo-Nazi groups in Europe and clear evidence of ethnic cleansing in Bosnia, Serbia, Croatia, and the former Soviet Union, bias and hate crimes are a worldwide problem. It is hoped that the recent push on college campuses to promote multicultural education and the celebration of diversity will make today's generation of college graduates well aware of the importance of tolerance and inclusion rather than bigotry and exclusion.

Stalking

In recent years the crime of stalking has received considerable attention. **Stalking** refers to an assailant's planned efforts at pursuing an intended victim. Most stalkers are male. (One notable exception is the convicted female stalker of talk show host David Letterman.) Many of these stalkers are excessively possessive or jealous and pursue people with whom they formerly had a relationship. Some stalkers pursue people with whom they have had only an imaginary relationship.

Some stalkers have served time in prison and have waited for years to "get back" at their victims. In some cases, stalkers go to great lengths to locate their intended victims and frequently know their daily whereabouts. Although not all stalkers plan to batter or kill their victims, their presence and potential for violence are enough to create an extremely frightening environment for the intended victim and family.

Fortunately, since 1990, virtually all states have enacted or tightened their laws related to stalking and have created stiff penalties for stalkers (see the Star

carjacking
A crime that involves a thief's attempt to steal a car while the owner is behind the wheel; carjackings are usually random, unpredictable, and frequently involve handguns.

bias and hate crimes
Criminal acts directed at a person or group solely because of a specific characteristic, such as race, religion, ethnic background, or political belief.

stalking
A crime involving an assailant's planned efforts to pursue an intended victim.

Box below). In many areas the criminal justice system is proactive in letting possible victims of stalking know, for example, when a particular prison inmate is going to be released. In other areas, citizens are banding together to provide support and protection for people who may be victims of stalkers.

If you think you are or someone you know is being stalked, contact the police (or a local crisis intervention hot line number) to report your case and use their guidance. You might sense that you are a potential stalking victim either through the circumstances of a past relationship or through the unusual behavior of someone who seems to be irrationally jealous of you or overly obsessed with you. Report a person who continues to pester or intimidate you with phone calls, written notes or letters, or unwanted gifts. Report people who make persistent efforts to be with you after you have told them you do not want to see them. Until the situation is resolved, be alert for potentially threatening situations and keep in close touch with friends.

SEXUAL VICTIMIZATION

Ideally, sexual intimacy is a mutual, enjoyable form of communication between two people. Far too often, however, relationships are approached in an aggressive, hostile manner. These sexual aggressors always

Must Victims Face Their Stalkers?
U.S. constitutional law dictates that criminals have the right to face their accusers in court. In early 1996, this court procedure came under attack from stalking victims and their attorneys. One celebrated case involved rock star and actress Madonna and a man accused of trespassing on her property in a purported attempt to establish a relationship with her.

Madonna did not want to face this man directly in court. Such a face-to-face meeting in court would have accomplished exactly what her accused may have wanted in the first place: an opportunity to be near his victim.

However, the judge in the case mandated that Madonna appear in court to face the accused rather than to testify on videotape. (In some cases, child abuse victims are permitted to testify on videotape because of the psychological trauma that could result from face-to-face confrontations with alleged perpetrators.) What do you think? Should this courtesy be extended to adult victims of stalking crimes? Are there cases in which the rights of the victim supersede the rights of the accused?

have a victim—someone who is physically or psychologically traumatized. *Sexual victimization* occurs in many forms and in a variety of settings. In this section we briefly look at sexual victimization as it occurs in rape and sexual assault, sexual abuse of children, sexual harassment, and the commercialization of sex.

Rape and Sexual Assault

As violence in our society increases, the incidence of *rape* and *sexual assault* correspondingly rises. The victims of these crimes fall into no single category. Victims of rape and sexual assault include young and old, male and female. They can be the mentally retarded, prisoners, hospital patients, and college students. We all are potential victims, and self-protection is critical. Read the Star Box below concerning myths about rape.

Sometimes a personal assault begins as a physical assault that may turn into a rape situation. Rape is generally considered a crime of sexual aggression in which the victim is forced to have sexual intercourse.

Myths about Rape
Despite the fact that we are all potential victims, many of us do not fully understand how vulnerable we are. Rape in particular has associated with it a number of myths (false assumptions), including the following:

- *Women are raped by strangers.* In approximately half of all reported rapes, the victim has some prior acquaintance with the rapist. Increasingly, women are being raped by husbands, dating partners, and relatives.
- *Rapes almost always occur in dark alleys or deserted places.* The opposite is true. Most rapes occur in or very near the victim's residence.
- *Rapists are easily identified by their demeanor or psychological profile.* Most experts indicate that rapists do not differ significantly from nonrapists.
- *The incidence of rape is overreported.* Estimates are that only one in five rapes is reported.
- *Rape happens only to people in low socioeconomic classes.* Rape occurs in all socioeconomic classes. Each person, male or female, young or old, is a potential victim.
- *There is a standard way to escape from a potential rape situation.* Each rape situation is different. No one method to avoid rape can work in every potential rape situation. Because of this, we encourage personal health classes to invite speakers from a local rape prevention services bureau to discuss approaches to rape prevention.

Current thought concerning rape characterizes this behavior as a violent act that happens to be carried out through sexual contact. (See the Health Action Guides on rape prevention guidelines and help for the rape victim.)

Acquaintance and date rape

In recent years, closer attention has been paid to the sexual victimization that occurs during relationships. *Acquaintance rape* refers to forced sexual intercourse between individuals who know each other. *Date rape* is a form of acquaintance rape that involves forced sexual intercourse by a dating partner. Studies on a number of campuses suggest that about 20% of college women reported having experienced date rape. An even higher percentage of women report being kissed and touched against their will. Alcohol is frequently a significant contributing factor in these rape situations. (See Chapter 8 concerning alcohol's role in campus crime.) Some men have reported being psychologically coerced into intercourse by their female dating partners. In many cases the aggressive partner will display certain behaviors that can be categorized (see the Health Action Guide on p. 413).

Psychologists believe that aside from the physical harm of date rape, a greater amount of emotional damage may occur. Such damage stems from the concept of broken trust. Date rape victims feel particularly violated because the perpetrator was not a stranger: it was someone they initially trusted, at least to some degree. Once that trust is broken, developing new relationships with other people becomes much more difficult for the date rape victim.

Nearly all victims of date rape seem to suffer from *posttraumatic stress syndrome.* They can have anxiety, sleeplessness, eating disorders, and nightmares. Guilt concerning their own behavior, self-esteem, and judgment of other people can be overwhelming, and the individual may require professional counseling. Because of the seriousness of these consequences, all students should be aware of the existence of date rape.

Sexual abuse of children

One of the most tragic forms of sexual victimization is the sexual abuse of children. Children are especially vulnerable to sexual abuse because of their dependent relationships with parents, relatives, and caregivers (such as babysitters, teachers, and neighbors). Often, children are unable to readily understand the difference between appropriate and inappropriate physical contact. Abuse may range from blatant physical manipulation, including fondling, to oral sex, sodomy, and intercourse.

HEALTH
Action Guide ----->

Rape Prevention Guidelines

To prevent rape from occurring:

- Never forget that you could be a candidate for personal assault.
- Use approved campus security or escort services, especially at night.
- Think carefully about your patterns of movement to and from class or work. Alter your routes frequently.
- Walk briskly with a sense of purpose. Try not to walk alone at night.
- Dress so that the clothes you wear do not unnecessarily restrict your movement or make you more vulnerable.
- Always be aware of your surroundings. Look over your shoulder occasionally. Know where you are so that you won't get lost.
- Avoid getting into a car if you do not know the driver well.
- If you think you are being followed, look for a safe retreat. This might be a store, a fire or police station, or a group of people.
- Be especially cautious of first dates, blind dates, or people you meet at a party or bar who push to be alone with you.
- Let trusted friends know where you are and when you plan to return.
- Keep your car in good working order. Think beforehand how you would handle the situation should your car break down.
- Limit, and even avoid, alcohol to minimize the risk of rape.
- Trust your best instincts if you are assaulted. Each situation is different. Do what you can to protect your life. <------

Because of the subordinate role of children in relationships involving adults, sexually abusive practices often go unreported. Sexual abuse can leave emotional scars that make it difficult to establish meaningful relationships later in life. For this reason, it is especially important for people to pay close attention to any information shared by children that could indicate a potentially abusive situation. Most states require that information concerning child abuse be reported to law enforcement officials.

HEALTH
Action Guide — — — — →

Help for the Rape Victim

If you have been raped, seek help as soon as possible. The following procedures may be helpful.

- *Call the police immediately to report the assault.* Police can take you to the hospital and start gathering information that may help them apprehend the rapist. Fortunately, many police departments now use specially trained officers (many of whom are female) to work closely with rape victims during all stages of the investigation.

- If you would rather not contact the police immediately, *call a local rape crisis center.* Operated generally on a 24-hour hot line basis, these centers have trained counselors to help you evaluate your options, contact

the police, escort you to the hospital, and provide aftercare counseling.

- *Do not alter any potential evidence related to the rape.* Do not change your clothes, douche, take a bath, or rearrange the scene of the crime. Wait until all the evidence has been gathered.

- *Report all bruises, cuts, and scratches, even if they seem insignificant.* Report any information about the attack as completely and accurately as possible.

- *You will probably be given a thorough pelvic examination.* You may have to ask for STD tests and pregnancy tests.

- Although it is unusual for a rape victim's name to appear in the media, you might *request that the police withhold your name* as long as is legally possible.

← — — — —

Sexual harassment

Sexual harassment consists of unwanted attention of a sexual nature that creates embarrassment or stress. Examples of sexual harassment include unwanted physical contact, excessive pressure for dates, sexually explicit humor, sexual innuendos or remarks, offers of job advancement based on sexual favors, and overt sexual assault. Unlike more overt forms of sexual victimization, sexual harassment may be applied in a subtle manner and can, in some cases, go unnoticed by co-workers and fellow students. Nevertheless, sexual harassment produces stress that cannot be resolved until the harasser is identified and forced to

stop. Both men and women can be victims of sexual harassment.

Sexual harassment can occur in many settings, including employment and academic settings. On the college campus, harassment may be primarily in terms of the offer of sex for grades. If this occurs to you, think carefully about the situation and document the specific times, events, and places where the harassment took place. Consult your college's policy concerning harassment. Next, you could report these events to the appropriate administrative officer (perhaps the affirmative action officer, dean of academic affairs, or dean of students). You may also want to

HEALTH Action Guide

Avoiding Date Rape

The first step in avoiding date rape is to consider your partner's behaviors. Many, but not all, date rapists show one or more of the following behaviors: a disrespectful attitude toward you and others, lack of concern for your feelings, violence and hostility, obsessive jealousy, extreme competitiveness, a desire to dominate, and unnecessary physical roughness. Consider these behaviors as warning signs for possible problems in the future. Reevaluate your participation in the relationship.

Below are some specific ways both men and women can avoid a date rape situation:

Men

- *Know your sexual desires and limits.* Communicate them clearly. Be aware of social pressures. It's OK not to score.
- *Being turned down when you ask for sex is not a rejection of you personally.* Women who say no to sex are not rejecting the person; they are expressing their desire not to participate in a single act. Your desires may be beyond control, but your actions are within your control.
- *Accept the woman's decision.* "No" means "No." Don't read other meanings into the answer. Don't continue after you are told "No!"
- *Don't assume that just because a woman dresses in a sexy manner and flirts that she wants to have sexual intercourse.*
- *Don't assume that previous permission for sexual contact applies to the current situation.*
- *Avoid excessive use of alcohol and drugs.* Alcohol and other drugs interfere with clear thinking and effective communication.

Women

- *Know your sexual desires and limits.* Believe in your right to set those limits. If you are not sure, STOP and talk about it.
- *Communicate your limits clearly.* If someone starts to offend you, tell him so firmly and immediately. Polite approaches may be misunderstood or ignored. Say "No" when you mean "No."
- *Be assertive.* Often men interpret passivity as permission. Be direct and firm with someone who is sexually pressuring you.
- *Be aware that your nonverbal actions send a message.* If you dress in a sexy manner and flirt, some men may assume you want to have sex. This does not make your dress or behavior wrong, but it is important to be aware of a possible misunderstanding.
- *Pay attention to what is happening around you.* Watch the nonverbal clues. Do not put yourself into vulnerable situations.
- *Trust your intuitions.* If you feel you are being pressured into unwanted sex, you probably are.
- *Avoid excessive use of alcohol and drugs.* Alcohol and other drugs interfere with clear thinking and effective communication.

---

discuss the situation with a staff member of the university counseling center.

If harassment occurs in the work environment, the victim should document the occurrences and report them to the appropriate management or personnel official. Reporting procedures will vary from setting to setting. Sexual harassment is a form of illegal sex discrimination and violates Title VII of the Civil Rights Act of 1964.

In 1986 the U.S. Supreme Court ruled that the creation of a "hostile environment" in a work setting was sufficient evidence to support the claim of sexual harassment. This action served as an impetus for thousands of women to step forward with sexual harassment allegations. Additionally, some men are also filing sexual harassment lawsuits against female supervisors.

Not surprisingly, this rising number of complaints

has served as a wake-up call for employers. From university settings to factory production lines to corporate board rooms, employers are scrambling to make certain that employees are fully aware of actions that could lead to a sexual harassment lawsuit. Sexual harassment workshops and educational seminars on harassment are now common and serve to educate both men and women about this complex problem.

Violence and the Commercialization of Sex

It is beyond the scope of this book to explore whether sexual violence can be related to society's exploitation or commercialization of sex. However, sexually related products and messages are intentionally placed before the public to try to sway consumer decisions. Do you believe that there could be a connection between commercial products, such as violent pornography in films and magazines, and violence against women? Does prostitution lead directly to violence? Do sexually explicit "900" phone numbers or Internet pornography cause an increase in violent acts? Can the sexual messages in beer commercials lead to acquaintance rape? What do you think?

UNINTENTIONAL INJURIES

Unintentional injuries are injuries that have occurred without anyone intending that any harm be done. Common examples include injuries resulting from car crashes, falls, fires, drownings, firearm accidents, recreational accidents, and residential accidents. Each year, unintentional injuries account for over 150,000 deaths and millions of nonfatal injuries.

Unintentional injuries are very expensive for our society, both from a financial standpoint and from a personal and family standpoint. Fortunately, to a large extent it is possible to avoid becoming a victim of an unintentional injury. By carefully considering the tips presented in the safety categories that follow, you will be protecting yourself from many preventable injuries.

Since this section of the chapter focuses on a selected number of safety categories, we encourage readers to consider some additional, related activities. For further information in the area of safety, consult a safety textbook (one of which is listed in the references for this chapter).[12] To review important points in the area of first aid skills, consult Appendix 2 in this text. Finally, we encourage you to take a first aid course from the American Red Cross. American Red Cross first aid courses incorporate a significant amount of safety prevention information along with the teaching of specific first aid skills.

Residential Safety

Many serious accidents and personal assaults occur in dorm rooms, apartments, and houses. As a responsible adult, you should make every reasonable effort to prevent these tragedies from happening. One good idea is to discuss some of the following points with your family or roommates and see what cooperative strategies you can implement:
- Fireproof your residence. Are all electrical appliances and heating and cooling systems in safe working order? Are flammable materials safely stored?
- Prepare a fire escape plan. Install smoke or heat detectors.
- Do not give personal information over the phone to a stranger.
- Use initials for first names on mailboxes and in phone books.
- Install a peephole and deadbolt locks on outside doors.
- If possible, avoid living in first floor apartments. Change locks when moving to a new apartment or home.
- Put locks on all windows.
- Require repair people or delivery people to show valid identification.
- Do not use an elevator if it is occupied by someone who makes you feel uneasy.
- Be cautious around garages, laundry rooms, and driveways (especially at night). Use lighting for prevention of assault.

Recreational Safety

The thrills we get from risk-taking are an essential part of our recreational endeavors. Sometimes we can get into serious accidents because we fail to consider important recreational safety information. Do some of the following recommendations apply to you?
- Seek appropriate instruction for your intended activity. Few skill activities are as easy as they look.
- Always wear your automobile seat belt.
- Make certain that your equipment is in excellent working order.
- Involve yourself gradually in an activity before attempting more complicated, dangerous skills.
- Enroll in an American Red Cross first aid course to enable you to cope with unexpected injuries.
- Remember that alcohol use greatly increases the likelihood that people will get hurt.
- Protect your eyes from serious injury.
- Learn to swim. Drowning occurs most frequently to people who never intended to be in the water.
- Obey the laws related to your recreational pursuits. Many laws are directly related to the safety of the participants.
- Be aware of weather conditions. Many outdoor activities turn to tragedy with sudden shifts in the weather. Always prepare yourself for the worst possible weather.

Firearm Safety

Each year about 13,000 Americans are murdered with guns and another 2000 die in gun-related accidents. Most murders are committed with handguns. (Shotguns and rifles tend to be more cumbersome than handguns and thus are not as frequently used in murders, accidents, or suicides.) Over half of all murders result from quarrels and arguments between acquaintances or relatives. With many homeowners arming themselves with handguns for protection against intruders, it is not surprising that over half of all gun accidents occur in the home. Children are frequently involved in gun accidents, often after they discover a gun they think is unloaded. Handgun owners are reminded to adhere to the following safety reminders:

* Make certain that you follow the gun possession laws in your state. Special permits may be required to carry a handgun.
* Make certain that your gun is in good mechanical order.
* If you are a novice, enroll in a gun safety course.
* Consider every gun to be a loaded gun, even if someone tells you it is unloaded.
* Never point a gun at an unintended target.
* Keep your finger off the trigger until you are ready to shoot.
* When moving with a handgun, keep the barrel pointed down.
* Load and unload your gun carefully.
* Store your gun and ammunition safely in a locked container. Use a trigger lock on your gun when not in use.
* Take target practice only at approved ranges.
* Never play with guns at parties. Never handle a gun when intoxicated.
* Educate children about gun safety and the potential dangers of gun use. Children must never believe that a gun is a toy.

Motor Vehicle Safety

The greatest number of accidental deaths in the United States take place on highways and streets. Young people are most likely to die from a motor vehicle accident. According to Bever,[12] the following is a description of a prime candidate for such a death:

> a male, 15 to 24 years of age, driving on a two-lane, rural road between the hours of 10 pm and 2 am on a Saturday night. If he has been drinking and is driving a subcompact car or motorcycle, the likelihood that he and his passengers will have a fatal accident is even more pronounced.

Motor vehicle accidents also cause disabling injuries. With nearly 2 million such injuries each year, concern for the prevention of motor vehicle accidents should be important for all college students, regardless of age. With this thought in mind, we offer some important safety tips for motor vehicle operators:

* Make certain that you are familiar with the traffic laws in your state.
* Do not operate an automobile or motorcycle unless it is in good mechanical order. Regularly inspect your brakes, lights, and exhaust system.
* Do not exceed the speed limit. Observe all traffic signs.
* Always wear safety belts, even on short trips. Require your passengers to buckle up. Always keep small children in child restraints.
* Never drink and drive. Avoid horseplay inside a car.
* Be certain that you can hear the traffic outside your car. Keep the car's music system at a reasonable decibel level.
* Give pedestrians the right-of-way.
* Drive defensively at all times. Do not challenge other drivers. Refrain from drag racing.
* Look carefully before changing lanes.
* Be especially careful at intersections and railroad crossings.
* Carry a well-maintained first aid kit that includes flares or other signal devices.
* Alter your driving behavior during bad weather.
* Do not drive when you have not had enough sleep (see "Focus on Drowsy Driving," pp. 420-421).

Home Accident Prevention for Children and the Elderly

Approximately 1 person in 10 is injured each year in a home accident. Children and the elderly spend significantly more hours each day in a home setting than do young adults and midlife people. It is especially important that accident prevention be given primary consideration for these groups (see the Health Action Guide on p. 416). Here are some important tips to remember. Can you think of others?

For everyone

* Be certain that you have adequate insurance protection.
* Install smoke detectors appropriately.
* Keep stairways clear of toys and debris. Install railings.
* Maintain electrical and heating equipment.
* Make certain that inhabitants know how to get emergency help.

unintentional injuries
Injuries that have occurred without anyone intending that harm be done.

HEALTH
Action Guide ----→

Making Your Home Safe, Comfortable, and Secure

Entry

- Install a deadbolt lock on the front door and locks or bars on the windows.
- Add a peephole or small window in the front door.
- Trim bushes so burglars have no place to hide.
- Add lighting to the walkway and next to the front door.
- Get a large dog.

Bedroom and nursery

- Install a smoke alarm and a carbon monoxide detector.
- Remove high threshold at doorway to avoid tripping.
- Humidifiers can be breeding grounds for bacteria; use them sparingly and follow the manufacturer's cleaning instructions.
- In the nursery, install pull-down shades or curtains instead of blinds with strings that could strangle a child.

Living room

- Secure loose throw rugs or use ones with nonskid backing.
- Remove trailing wires where people walk.
- Cover unused electrical outlets if there are small children in the home.
- Provide additional lighting for reading, and install adjustable blinds to regulate glare.

Kitchen

- To avoid burns, move objects stored above the stove to another location.
- Install ceiling lighting and additional task lighting where food is prepared.
- Keep heavy objects on bottom shelves or countertops; store lightweight or seldom-used objects on top shelves.
- Promptly clean and store knives.
- Keep hot liquids such as coffee out of children's reach, and provide close supervision when the stove or other appliances are in use.
- To avoid food-borne illness, thoroughly clean surfaces that have come into contact with raw meat.

Bathroom

- A child can drown in standing water; keep the toilet lid down and the tub empty.
- Clean the shower, tub, sink, and toilet regularly to remove mold, mildew, and bacteria that can contribute to illness.
- Store medications in their original containers in a cool, dry place out of the reach of children.
- Add a bath mat or nonskid strips to the bottom of the tub.
- Add grab bars near the tub or shower and toilet, especially if there are elderly adults in the home.
- Keep a first-aid kit stocked with bandages, first-aid ointment, gauze, pain relievers, syrup of Ipecac, and isotonic eyewash; include your physician's and a nearby emergency center's phone numbers.

Stairway

- Add a handrail for support.
- Remove all obstacles or stored items from stairs and landing.
- Repair or replace flooring material that is in poor condition.
- Add a light switch at the top of the stairs.
- If there is an elderly person in the home, add a contrasting color strip to the first and last steps to identify the change of level.

Fire prevention tips

- Install smoke detectors on every level of your home.
- Keep fire extinguishers handy in the kitchen, basement, and bedrooms.
- Have the chimney and fireplace cleaned by a professional when there is more than ¼ inch of soot accumulation.
- Place space heaters at least 3 feet from beds, curtains, and other flammable objects.
- Don't overload electrical outlets, and position drapes so that they don't touch cords or outlets.
- Recycle or toss combustibles, such as newspapers, rags, old furniture, and chemicals.
- If you smoke, use caution with cigarettes and matches; never light up in bed.
- Plan escape routes and practice using them with your family. ◄------•

For children

- Know all the ways to prevent accidental poisoning.
- Use toys that are appropriate for the age of the child.
- Never leave young children unattended, especially infants.
- Keep any hazardous items (guns, poisons, etc.) locked up.
- Keep small children away from kitchen stoves.

For the elderly

- Protect from falls.
- Be certain that elderly people have a good understanding of the medications they may be taking. Know the side effects.
- Encourage elderly people to seek assistance when it comes to home repairs.
- Make certain that all door locks, lights, and safety equipment are in good working order.

Refer to pp. 406-407 for additional information related to the protection of older adults.

CAMPUS SAFETY AND VIOLENCE PREVENTION

Although many of the topics in this chapter are quite unsettling, students and faculty must continue to lead normal lives in the campus environment despite potential threats to our health. The first step in being able to function adequately is knowing about these potential threats. You have read about these threats in this chapter; now you must think about how this information applies to your campus situation.

The campus environment is no longer immune to many of the social ills that plague our society. At one time the university campus was thought to be a safe haven from the real world. Now there is plenty of evidence to indicate that significant intentional and unintentional injuries can happen to anyone at any time on the college campus.

For this reason, you must make it a habit to think constructively about protecting your safety. In addition to the personal safety tips presented earlier in this chapter, remember to use the safety assistance resources available on your campus. One of these might be your use of university-approved escort services, especially in the evenings as you move from one campus location to another. Another resource is the campus security department (campus police). Typically, campus police have a 24-hour emergency phone number. If you think you need help, do not hesitate to call this number. Campus security departments frequently offer short seminars on safety topics to student organizations or residence hall groups. Your counseling center on campus might also offer programs on rape prevention and personal protection.

If you are motivated to make your campus environment safer, you might wish to contact an organization that focuses on campus crime. Safe Campuses Now is a nonprofit student group that tracks legislation, provides educational seminars, and monitors community incidents involving students. For information about Safe Campuses Now, including how to start a chapter on your campus, call (706) 354-1115, or see their web page at www.uga.edu\~safe-campus. We encourage you to become active in making your campus a safer place to live.

Summary

- Everyone is a potential victim of violent crime.
- Each year in the United States, intentional injuries cause about 50,000 deaths and another 2 million nonfatal injuries.
- Homicide is the leading cause of death for young male African-Americans. Handguns are the weapon of choice for homicides.
- Because of factors related to family structure, increased drug use and crime, and the inability of people to resolve conflicts peacefully, domestic violence is on the rise.
- Forms of child abuse include physical abuse, sexual abuse, and child neglect. Child neglect is the most common form.
- Youth violence is skyrocketing, and much of the violence is related to gang activities.
- Bias and hate crimes, as well as the crime of stalking, are increasingly recognized as serious violent acts.
- Rape and sexual assault, acquaintance rape, date rape, and sexual harassment are forms of sexual victimization in which victims often are both physically and psychologically traumatized.
- Unintentional injuries are injuries that occur accidentally. The numbers of fatal and nonfatal unintentional injuries are exceedingly high.

Review Questions

1. Identify some of the categories of intentional injuries. How many people are affected each year by intentional injuries?
2. What are some of the most important facts concerning homicide in the United States? How are most homicides committed?
3. Identify changes in the traditional family structure that may be related to increased family stress and domestic violence. What additional factors also may be related to increased domestic violence?
4. What reasons might explain why so many women do not report domestic violence?
5. Aside from the immediate consequences of child abuse, what additional problems do many abused children face in the future?
6. Explain why gangs and gang activities have increased tremendously over the last 20 years. What effect do gangs have on a community?
7. List some examples of groups that are known to have committed bias or hate crimes.
8. Identify some general characteristics of a typical stalker.
9. Explain some of the myths associated with rape. How can date rape be prevented?
10. Identify some examples of behaviors that could be considered sexual harassment. Why are employers especially concerned about educating their employees about sexual harassment?
11. Identify some common examples of unintentional injuries. Point out three safety tips from each of the safety areas listed at the end of this chapter.

Think About This . . .

- To what extent are you concerned about your personal safety? Are you comfortable with your level of concern? Or do you think you should be more or less concerned?
- Has there been any gun violence at your college? Are you aware of any students carrying guns or other concealed weapons on your campus?
- Do you know of educational programs on your campus that have dealt with rape prevention or sexual harassment? Where can you go on your campus to seek help for crises related to these issues?
- Is there a particular place on your campus where you believe that your personal safety is threatened? If so, how do you cope with this threat?

References

1. Bureau of Justice Statistics: *Injuries from crime: special report,* U.S. Department of Justice, Washington, DC, 1989, U.S. Government Printing Office.
2. Bureau of Justice Statistics: *National crime victimization survey: Criminal victimization 1996: Changes 1995-96 with trends 1993-1996,* U.S. Department of Justice, Washington, DC, November 1997, NCJ-165821.
3. Swanson JM, Albrecht M: *Community health nursing: promoting the health of aggregates,* Philadelphia, 1993, WB Saunders.
4. Bureau of Justice Statistics: *Drugs, crime, and the justice system: a national report,* U.S. Department of Justice, Washington, DC, December 1992, U.S. Government Printing Office.
5. U.S. Bureau of the Census: *Statistical abstract of the United States: 1996,* ed 116, Washington, DC, 1996, U.S. Government Printing Office.
6. Bureau of Justice Statistics: *Guns and crime: handgun victimization, firearm self-defense, and firearm theft,* U.S. Department of Justice, Washington, DC, April 1994, U.S. Government Printing Office.
7. Bachman R: *Violence against women: a national crime victimization survey report,* U.S. Department of Justice, Washington, DC, January 1994, U.S. Government Printing Office.
8. Widom CS: The cycle of violence, *Research in Brief,* National Institute of Justice, U.S. Department of Justice, Washington, DC, 1992, U.S. Government Printing Office.
9. National Committee for Prevention of Child Abuse: *12 alternatives to whacking your kid,* Chicago, undated pamphlet.
10. Leslie C et al: Girls will be girls, *Newsweek,* p. 40, Aug 2, 1993.
11. Kantrowitz B: Wild in the streets, *Newsweek,* p. 40, Aug 2, 1993.
12. Bever DL: *Safety: a personal focus,* ed 4, St. Louis, 1996, Mosby.

Suggested Readings

American Red Cross: *First aid: responding to emergencies,* St. Louis, 1996, Mosby Lifeline.

A comprehensive guide for handling first aid emergencies and a workbook used by many colleges and universities in their introductory first aid courses. Well illustrated and easy to follow; a considerable amount of safety and prevention information is included.

Rutter P: *Understanding and preventing sexual harassment: the complete guide,* New York, 1997, Bantam Books.

This guide gives the reader a comprehensive look at sexual harassment. The book explains power games, sexual psychology, and acceptable and unacceptable behavior. Using many examples and case studies, the author helps the reader understand why people act as they do in the workplace.

Brandenburg, JB: *Confronting sexual harassment: what schools and colleges can do,* New York, 1997, Teachers College Press.

This book explains the origins and scope of the problem of sexual harassment on campus, describes ways to develop policies and grievance procedures, examines legal issues, and suggests useful education programs and strategies.

Giggans PO, Levy B: *50 ways to a safer world: everyday actions you can take to prevent violence in neighborhoods, schools, and communities,* Seattle, 1997, Seal Press Feminist Publications.

This handbook provides practical advice in an easy-to-read format. It suggests simple, logical ways to prevent violence in the home, on the streets, and in schools. Each of the 50 actions is clearly explained in this short (144-page) publication.

 # AS WE GO TO PRESS . . .

Within a single 2-week period, the lives of two prominent Americans were tragically cut short in separate skiing accidents. In early January 1998, Michael Kennedy, 1 of 11 children of the late Senator Robert F. Kennedy, died in Aspen, Colorado, while playing a game of ski football with 18 friends and family members. Ski football, a risky game played while skiing down a mountain, has been described as a cross between touch football and the ultimate frisbee game. Apparently, 39-year-old Kennedy was distracted and skied directly into a fir tree, causing a severe skull fracture and a severed spinal cord. He died instantly.

Later that month, Sonny Bono, a U.S. Congressman and former entertainer, also died in a skiing accident. Bono, who became famous in the late 1960s and the early 1970s with his then-wife Cher, was killed in Steamboat Springs, Colorado, during a late afternoon ski run. It was not clear what caused Bono, an experienced skier, to ski directly into a tree. Perhaps he was blinded by the late afternoon glare off the slopes, or perhaps a visual disturbance was caused by moving shadows and a localized weather condition. Maybe Bono was simply tired and not paying careful attention when he veered off course.

After these tragic accidents occurred in such a short span of time, some recreational safety experts began calling for all skiers to wear safety helmets. (It is doubtful whether Kennedy or Bono would have survived their accidents even if they had been wearing helmets.) Although increasing numbers of skiers are wearing helmets, most recreational skiers prefer not to use them. The skiing industry generally encourages the use of helmets but also points out that the death rate from bicycling accidents far exceeds that of skiing accidents.

Drowsy Driving

Dean was driving home from college late on a moonlit Friday night. His on-campus job kept him working until 9 PM after a day of classes. He had stopped to shoot pool with some friends after work and started his hour-long trek home at about 11:30. Just after midnight, Dean turned onto a 15-mile stretch of perfectly straight highway that cut through pastures and fields. The summer night was crystal clear. The radio was playing loudly, there were few oncoming cars, and visibility was good.

"I felt fine," Dean recalled later. "I was a little run down, but I wasn't sleepy at all. I was cruising along listening to tunes, and the next thing I knew I was surrounded by corn. The sound of the stalks hitting the car must have woken me up. It scared the hell out of me. I guess I fell asleep for a few seconds, but I don't know how it could have happened."

The Danger of Driving While Sleepy

Dean experienced a phenomenon that is too often ignored. Falling asleep at the wheel is something that no one thinks will happen to them, yet drowsy driving is estimated to cause up to 200,000 accidents per year on American roads.[1,2] Dean was lucky. His car veered right where a dirt tractor path connected with the road, and he missed a deep ditch by only a few feet. He avoided power poles, trees, and oncoming traffic as well. "Since then, I've put off several late-night trips when I thought I might be too tired. I even took a nap once on an overnight drive when I felt myself drifting," Dean said. "If I hadn't fallen asleep at the wheel before, I probably would have kept driving."

Sleepiness is a significant cause of traffic fatalities. Up to 3% of all yearly vehicular deaths in the United States can be attributed to driving while drowsy, yet Americans remain woefully uneducated to this problem.[1]

Sleepiness undermines a person's ability to make sound decisions and reduces attention span considerably.[2] Any condition that impairs the judgment of drivers should be taken seriously. It has been estimated that 100 million Americans fail to get enough sleep and that up to 50% of *all* accident-related fatalities (not just driving fatalities) can be attributed to sleep deprivation.[3]

Early Warning Signs

Drivers are often not aware that they are in need of sleep until after they get behind the wheel, or they ignore the signs of sleep deprivation and drive anyway. When drowsiness sets in, drivers are often caught by surprise, and they can fall asleep without realizing it. Being able to recognize the signs of sleep deprivation before we fall victim to it is therefore important. Some of the symptoms of sleep deprivation you should watch out for are:[1,2]

- Struggling against fatigue throughout the day
- Needing caffeine to stay alert, especially on a daily basis
- Falling asleep quickly (within 5 minutes) after stopping to rest
- Having an irritable or argumentative attitude without knowing why
- Needing an alarm clock to wake up in the morning (well-rested people wake up on time naturally)

Tips to Avoid Drowsy Driving

Because of the stealthy manner in which sleep can overtake you, it is important to evaluate your condition before getting behind the wheel and also while you are on the road. It is also important to prevent regular sleep deprivation. We must reduce the risk of falling asleep while driving by using common sense. The following suggestions should help reduce your chances of driving while drowsy:[1]

- Get plenty of sleep. About 8 hours of sleep per night is desirable. If this is not practical, try to catch up on sleep when possible (take naps, sleep more on weekends, etc.).
- Take breaks while driving. Stop at least every 2 hours on long trips. If possible, avoid driving alone so the driving duties can be split. Don't eat heavy meals, and avoid too much caffeine.
- Stay alert. Talk, listen to the radio, sing, or do whatever you can to keep from drifting off. Don't let all of the passengers in the car sleep; having someone to converse with can help keep the driver alert.
- Don't get too comfortable. Getting too relaxed can promote dozing off. Avoid using cruise control. Reduce use of the heater, and keep the windows open when possible.
- Don't drink and drive. This is true anytime, but even a small amount of alcohol in the system can intensify the effects of fatigue on the body.
- If you feel yourself drifting off or you think you may be in danger of falling asleep, stop driving. Dozing off for a few seconds (a phenomenon known as *microsleep*) is a significant warning sign of fatigue. Don't try to fight through fatigue while driving. Pull off the road at a safe place and take a nap if you need to.

Take time to heed the warning signs of fatigue. Remember that dozing off at the wheel creates a potentially dangerous situation for both yourself and others on or near the road. Being able to recognize when you are at risk of falling asleep and taking steps to avoid driving while drowsy are more than just common sense; they're a necessity for your own and others' personal safety. Getting a few extra winks of sleep and taking the time to ensure you are alert before you get into the driver's seat could save lives.

For Discussion . . .

How much sleep do you get each night on average? Do you regularly experience any of the signs of fatigue men-tioned in this article? Do you experience fatigue more often during certain times of the day or week? If so, can you think of ways to increase the amount of sleep you get? What would you have to give up to accomplish this goal?

References

1. Matson M: Forgotten menace on our highways, *Reader's Digest*, 144(86), June 1994.
2. Toufexis A: Drowsy America, *Time*, 136(26), Dec 17, 1990.
3. Bennett G: Why you must get more sleep, *McCall's*, 122(3), Dec 1994.

17

Controlling Environmental Influences

Healthy People: Looking Ahead to 2010

Progress was inconsistent in meeting the environmental objectives set forth in the *Healthy People 2000* document. However, substantial headway was made in promoting cleaner air. Few counties in the United States now exceed air pollution limits, although this could change if proposed new standards are approved.

Another environmental objective was to reduce human exposure to solid waste contamination of water, air, and soil. Progress toward this goal was limited because of increased production of solid waste by American households. Some gains were made in establishing recycling programs and reducing levels of environmental carcinogens.

Healthy People 2010 will continue our national effort to improve the environment. One change being proposed for the new objectives is to redefine the home and workplace as "environments." Thus some maternal and child health goals and occupational health goals could be considered environmental health objectives.

Throughout this book we have read about areas of health over which people have significant control. For example, people select the foods they eat, how much alcohol they consume, and how they manage the stressors in their lives.

The study of the environment and its effect on health provides an interesting contrast to the daily control people have over their own health. Perhaps because of the natural processes of life and death and the vital function of the environment, we are inclined to think that we cannot make personal decisions concerning it. This is, however, changing.

In comparison with the 1980s, when concerns about the environment focused on problems over which we had little direct responsibility or control (such as the ozone layer and nuclear accidents), the 1990s have been characterized by a focus on the individual and the home. Issues such as the disposal of municipal waste, the recycling of glass, plastic, and aluminum, the venting of radon gas from basements, and the reduction of water use reflect the fact that people can act to support the environment (see the Star Box at right).

Environmental concerns also extend to developing countries as well. With the world population at 6 billion in 1998 and moving toward 10.8 billion in 2060 (with the greatest rate of increase in Third World countries), the demands made on the environment are already substantial. As the continuing destruction of the tropical rain forests shows, the search for living space and natural resources continues unabated despite our knowing the experiences of those who damaged the environment in earlier decades. Complete the Personal Assessment on p. 424 to see how well you are helping protect the environment.

WORLD POPULATION GROWTH

Population growth affects the environment beyond our own homes and communities to include the entire planet. Each year the population of the world grows by 90 million people. By the middle of the next century, there could be 50% more people than there are today (Figure 17-1 on p. 425). By the year 2060, it is projected that 10.8 billion people will be alive. By the year 2000, more than half of the developing countries in the world may not be able to feed their populations from food grown on their own land.[1] As seen in Somalia, the consequences of overpopulation, combined with nonenvironmental factors such as limited agriculture and governmental instability, can lead to human suffering of the highest magnitude. However, as the Earth's population increases by 1 million peo-

10 Things You Can Do to Improve the Environment

1. Visit and help support our national parks.
2. Recycle newspapers, glass, plastic, and aluminum.
3. Conserve energy and use energy-efficient lighting.
4. Keep tires properly inflated to improve gas mileage and extend tire life.
5. Plant trees.
6. Organize a Christmas tree recycling program in your community.
7. Find an alternative to chemical pesticides for your lawn.
8. Purchase only those brands of tuna marked "dolphin safe."
9. Organize a community group to clean up a local stream, highway, park, or beach.
10. Become a member of an environmental action group, such as the Environmental Defense Fund, the Nature Conservancy, or the Sierra Club.

ple every 4 years, we struggle to make family planning available to everyone, to encourage later marriage and childbearing, to encourage breastfeeding not only for the health of infants but also to lengthen the interval between pregnancies, and to improve the status and well-being of women so that they have new roles for themselves and their families. Failing to control population growth, crowding, water pollution and scarcity, hazardous waste accumulation, and air pollution will move us closer yet to ecological disaster.

AIR POLLUTION

If you think that air pollution is a modern concern reflecting technology that has gone astray, keep in mind that the air is routinely polluted by nature. Sea salt, soil particles, ash, dust, soot, microbes, assorted trace elements, and plant pollens are consistently found in the air.

Pollution caused in part by humans also has a long history. From the fires that filled our ancestors' caves with choking smoke, through the "killer fogs" of nineteenth-century London, to the dust storms of the Great Depression, humans have contributed to air pollution. Today, its effects can be seen in countries throughout the world. The five countries that produce the most airborne gases that contribute to global

PERSONAL ASSESSMENT

Are You Helping the Environment?

How many ways can you help the environment? Give yourself two points for each of the following that you do on a regular basis, one point for each that you do occasionally, and a zero for those that you do not do. Total your points and compare your score with those that follow the assessment.

_____ 1. Promptly repair leaky faucets.
_____ 2. Use the microwave as often as possible rather than the stove or the oven.
_____ 3. Buy brands that come in minimal amounts of packaging.
_____ 4. Do not run excess water while washing dishes.
_____ 5. Use paper bags rather than plastic.
_____ 6. Use sponges or dishcloths for spills rather than paper towels.
_____ 7. Recycle newspapers rather than throw them out.
_____ 8. Snip six-pack rings.
_____ 9. Walk or bicycle rather than drive.
_____ 10. Purchase products in the larger sizes.
_____ 11. Preheat your oven for the minimal amount of time necessary.
_____ 12. Turn off water while brushing your teeth.
_____ 13. Do not use a trash compactor.
_____ 14. Serve fresh fruits and vegetables rather than processed foods.
_____ 15. Pull weeds by hand rather than spraying.
_____ 16. Carpool to work.
_____ 17. Limit garbage disposal use as much as possible.
_____ 18. Use canvas or cloth bags for shopping.
_____ 19. Sweep driveways and sidewalks rather than use a hose.
_____ 20. Recycle bottles and jars.
_____ 21. Pick up litter when you see it.
_____ 22. Make note pads out of used office stationery and paper.
_____ 23. Wear clothing that is right for the weather.
_____ 24. Use rechargeable batteries.
_____ 25. Clean the lint screen in the dryer after each load.
_____ 26. Put trash in only one bag (or the fewest needed).
_____ 27. Use refillable containers for household products (such as liquid hand soap).
_____ 28. Keep the water heater at the lowest level needed.

_____ 29. Open blinds and curtains during daylight periods during winter months.
_____ 30. Close blinds and curtains during periods of bright sunshine during summer months.
_____ 31. Turn off lights when you leave a room.
_____ 32. Take quick showers rather than leisurely baths.
_____ 33. Turn off stereos, radios, and televisions when leaving the house.
_____ 34. Turn off the water when washing the car and use a bucket when possible.
_____ 35. Place a brick or a plastic bottle of water inside the toilet storage tank.
_____ 36. Buy laundry detergents that are phosphate-free when there are other options available.
_____ 37. Drink "ice water" from the refrigerator rather than run tap water to get it cooler.
_____ 38. Run the dishwasher only when full.
_____ 39. Use hairspray in nonaerosol bottles.
_____ 40. Clean and change filters on the furnace and air conditioner on a regular basis.
_____ 41. Keep a reusable mug or cup at home or the office.
_____ 42. Purchase clothing that can be washed rather than only dry cleaned.
_____ 43. Wash clothing only when dirty.
_____ 44. Close the refrigerator door promptly.
_____ 45. Keep the car properly tuned.
_____ 46. Collect rain water for use in plants and gardens.
_____ 47. Donate outgrown clothing to nonprofit organizations.
_____ 48. Participate in organized cleanup days when they are held in your community.
_____ 49. Replace conventional shower head with a water-conserving model.
_____ 50. Write elected officials to support environmental legislation.

_____   YOUR TOTAL POINTS

Interpretation

90-100 points: Your conservation efforts are in the superior range. Keep up the excellent work!

80-89 points: You are clearly above average and should also be congratulated!

70-79 points: Although your score is average, your efforts at conserving the environment are important contributions to the total effort. Keep up the good work and look for additional ways to conserve.

60-69 points: Your score is passing but below average. Try to find more ways to help the environment. You have room for improvement.

59 and below: Time has not run out! You can still earn a passing grade but you need to follow the suggestions in this assessment and chapter to help the environment.

To Carry This Further...

Share these suggestions, or any others that you find useful, with family, friends, classmates, and other associates as a means of further helping our environment.

warming (the United States, the former USSR, Japan, China, and Brazil) are located in North America, Europe, Asia, and South America (see pp. 426-427). These countries recently met with 161 other nations in Kyoto, Japan, to formulate a global strategy for reducing greenhouse gases.[2]

Sources of Air Pollution

The sources of modern air pollutants should be familiar. A leading source is the internal combustion engine. Cars, trucks, and buses contribute a variety of materials to the air, including carbon monoxide, carbon dioxide, and hydrocarbons. Industrial processes,

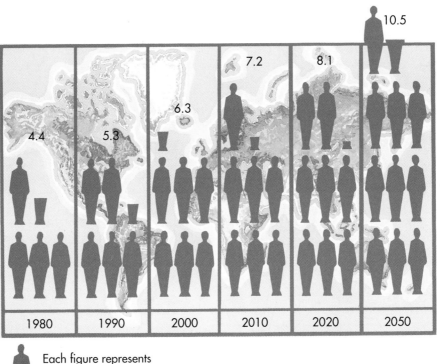

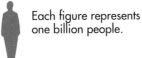

Each figure represents one billion people.

Figure 17-1   At its current rate of growth, the world's population will reach 10 billion about 25 years sooner than predicted a decade ago.

Clearing the Air in Our National Wilderness Areas

The Office of Air and Radiation of the U.S. Environmental Protection Agency (EPA) recently proposed new air quality standards related to ozone levels, particulate matter size, and haze regulations. These stringent new standards were based on air quality studies of 150 national wilderness areas. The EPA contends that implementation of the standards would protect the health of 40 million children and save the lives of 15,000 elderly or frail Americans. In addition, says the EPA, adults and children with asthma and other respiratory disorders would experience improvement, particularly during periods of activity and exercise. In addition, the views of our most-visited national parks would be clearer for those enjoying the sights.

Congressional opposition to these changes has centered on cost factors, especially costs to small businesses, who would be required to install expensive air cleaning technology to reduce their emissions to meet the required standards. Environmentalists and health advocates now fear that the recently enacted Small Business Regulatory Environment and Fairness Act standards may force the proposed guidelines to be watered down.

domestic heating, refuse burning, and the use of pesticides and herbicides also contribute to our air pollution problem. In recent years the massive deforestation of the tropical rain forest in the Amazon River basin of South America has contributed significant amounts of gaseous and particulate pollutants to the air.

Gaseous pollutants

The pollutants dispersed into the air by the sources just identified are generally in the form of gases, including carbon dioxide and carbon monoxide. Carbon dioxide is the natural by-product of combustion and is produced whenever fuels are burned. Electricity production, car and truck emissions, and industry are the principal producers of carbon dioxide.

As first predicted a decade ago, the progressive increase in carbon dioxide appears to have resulted in a **greenhouse effect** (Figure 17-2). This effect has

greenhouse effect
Warming of the Earth's surface that is produced when solar heat becomes trapped by layers of carbon dioxide and other gases.

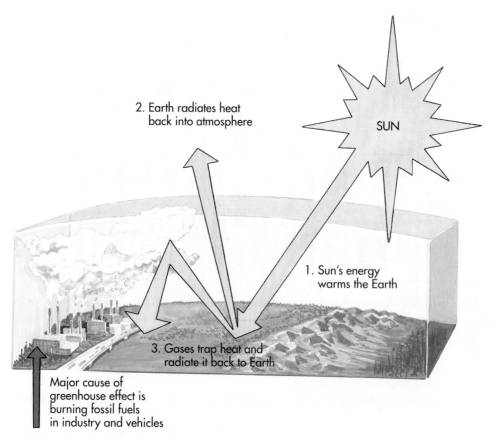

Figure 17-2   The greenhouse effect.

caused a slight but progressive warming of the earth's surface. An increase of only 1.5 degrees since 1860, resulting from increased trapping of industrial gases, has resulted in a shift of the world's hydrologic cycles.[3] Today the atmosphere is more laden with moisture, and air circulation patterns have shifted, leading to greater extremes in all aspects of weather. Weather events in late 1997 and early 1998 offered clear examples of these extremes, including:

- Torrential rains along the entire California coast, which caused flooding and mudslides
- Ice storms in New England and neighboring parts of Canada
- Record snow depths in the Ohio River Valley
- Uncontrolled forest fires in Indonesia caused by the absence of monsoon rains
- Drought in Australia, which nearly devastated the wheat crop
- Flooding in Peru

See the Star Box on p. 440 for an explanation of *El Niño* and *La Niña* and their role in creating these unusual weather conditions.

Whether these trends will continue into the next century is, of course, uncertain. Current attempts to reduce hydrocarbon emissions could be effective enough to begin moderating the temperature increase noted during this century.

Carbon monoxide, the colorless and odorless gas produced when fuels are burned incompletely, has already been discussed in conjunction with cardiovascular disease (see Chapter 10). Also occurring in gaseous form are methane, from decaying vegetation; the terpenes, produced by trees; and benzene and benzo[a]pyrene, which may cause cancer when taken into the respiratory system.[4]

Nitrogen and sulfur compounds are pollutants produced by a variety of industrial processes, including the burning of high–sulfur content fuels, especially coal. When nitrogen and sulfur oxides combine with moisture in the atmosphere, they are converted to nitric and sulfuric acid. The resulting **acid rain,** acid snow, and acid fog are responsible, for example, for the destruction of aquatic life and vegetation in the eastern United States and Canada.[5]

In urban areas located in cooler climates (or other cities during the winter months), sulfur oxides and particulate matter (from heating systems) combine with moisture to form a grayish haze, or **smog.** This *gray-air smog* contributes to respiratory problems that are common in these areas during the winter months. In warmer areas, or during the summer months in other areas, brown-air smog develops when hydrocarbons and particulate matter from automobile exhaust interact in the presence of sunlight.[5] This photochemical smog produces ozone. Ozone is highly reactive to the human respiratory system, plants, and materials such as rubber.

An environmental concern currently being studied is the destruction of the ultraviolet light-absorbing **ozone layer.**[6] Nitrous oxides and materials containing **chlorofluorocarbons (CFCs)** can destroy this protective ozone layer within the stratosphere. Nitrous oxides come from the burning of fossil fuels like coal and gasoline. CFCs are used in air conditioners, many fast-food containers, insulation materials, and solvents.

Although changes in the ozone layer have been recognized for over 15 years, the progress of deterioration is advancing in spite of international efforts to slow its place. Annual satellite images taken over both poles show the seasonal widening of the ozone hole, while data accumulated over a number of years confirm that the Earth's ozone layer is gradually thinning. If deterioration of the ozone layer continues, health dangers such as skin cancer, cataracts, snow-blindness, and premature wrinkling of skin will continue to increase.

Particulate pollutants

There are many particulate pollutants, including both naturally occurring materials and particles derived from industrial processes, mining, agriculture, and, of course, tobacco smoke. Inhalation of particulate matter can cause potentially fatal respiratory diseases, including those caused by quartz dust, asbestos fibers, and cotton fibers. Because of its widespread presence, asbestos is of particular concern. In 1989 the **Environmental Protection Agency (EPA)** ordered asbestos use to be stopped and current sources of asbestos to be removed from public buildings. In the latter regard, some people questioned whether the expense involved ($10 billion in school removal alone) was justified on the basis of the less than clearly defined asbestos safety standards.

Trace mineral elements, including lead, nickel, iron, zinc, copper, and magnesium, are also among the particles polluting the air. Chronic **lead toxicity** is among the most serious health problems associated with this form of air pollution, although significant progress has been made because of legislation requiring the use of nonleaded gasoline. However, even today, lead toxicity is disproportionately seen in children of low-income families, principally because of the lead-based paints found in older houses, heavy motor vehicle traffic on city streets, and the use of lead soldering in older plumbing systems. For these children, lower IQS, learning disabilities, attention deficit disorder, delinquency,[7] and hypertension[8] may result.

Temperature Inversions

On a normal sunny day, radiant energy from the sun warms the ground and the air immediately above it. As this warmed air rises, it carries pollutants upward and disperses them into a larger, cooler air mass above. Cool air sinking to replace the rising warmed air minimizes the concentration of pollutants.

On those occasions when high pressure settles over an area, warm air can be trapped immediately above the ground. Unable to rise, this trapped, warm, polluted air layer stagnates and produces a potentially health-threatening *subsidence inversion*.[5] (This is the inversion layer that meteorologists talk about on the evening news.)

A second form of thermal inversion, *radiation inversion*, is frequently seen during winter.[5] At this time of year, late afternoon cooling of the ground causes a layer of cool air to develop under a higher, warmer layer of air. With the inability of the cool layer of air to rise, pollutants begin to accumulate near the ground and remain there until the next morning. Warming of the ground later in the morning restores the heating of the lower-level air and reestablishes the normal dispersal of pollutants.

Indoor Air Pollution

Not all air pollution occurs outside. Concern is growing over the health risks associated with indoor air pollution. Toxic materials, including cigarette smoke (see Chapter 9), asbestos, radon, formaldehyde, vinyl chloride, and cooking gases, can be found in buildings ranging from houses and apartments to huge office complexes and manufacturing plants.

Of all of the indoor air pollutants, none is of greater concern than *tobacco smoke*. In December 1992 the EPA identified environmental tobacco smoke to be a Group A (known human) carcinogen.[9] It now is believed that 3000 lung cancer deaths occur annually because of this pollutant. Between 150,000 and 300,000 illnesses in infants and young children occur annually as a result of exposure to environmental tobacco smoke.[9]

Radon gas is a form of indoor air pollution whose role as a serious health risk is currently under investigation.[10] This radioactive gas enters buildings through a variety of routes (the water supply, block walls, slab joints, drains, even cracks in the floor) from underlying rock formations and stone building materials where it is found. Because radon gas can concentrate when air is stagnant, energy-efficient airtight homes, schoolrooms, and buildings are most affected. Tests conducted on homes in various areas of the country suggest that 20% of all homes have higher than normal levels and 10% have dangerously high levels. Radon buildup is a concern because of the relationship of radon exposure to the development of lung cancer.

Those who are concerned about the level of radon gas in their homes can purchase test kits (manufactured by some 200 companies at a cost of $10 to $50) or have their homes tested by radon testing laboratories. Opponents of the "radon myth," however, suggest that these tests may generate false-positive rates in excess of 90%.[10] Further, the repair of homes with high radon levels can be expensive, with some costing as much as $30,000. One form of repair, the installation of a home ventilation system, may cost from $300 to $500.

Environmental tobacco smoke and radon gas join formaldehyde (from building material), vinyl chloride (from PVC plumbing), and other pollutants (including asbestos from insulation) to form the basis of the *sick building syndrome*.[11] For people with respiratory illnesses and immune system hypersensitivities, as well as the elderly, home or work sites could be less

acid rain
Rain that has a lower pH (more acidic) than that normally associated with rain.

smog
Air pollution made up of a combination of smoke, photochemical compounds, and fog.

ozone layer
Layer of triatomic oxygen that surrounds the Earth and filters much of the sun's radiation before it can reach the Earth's surface.

chlorofluorocarbons (CFCs)
Gaseous chemical compounds that contain chlorine and fluorine.

Environmental Protection Agency (EPA)
Federal agency charged with the protection of natural resources and the quality of the environment.

lead toxicity
Blood lead level above 25 micrograms/deciliter. (If adopted, the new standard will be 10 micrograms/deciliter.)

radon gas
A naturally occurring radioactive gas produced by the decay of uranium.

healthy than was once thought. The Health Action Guide below describes ways of preventing indoor air pollution.

Health Implications

Because of the complex nature of many health problems, it is difficult to clearly assess the effects of air pollution on health. Age, gender, genetic predisposition, occupation, residency, and personal health practices complicate this assessment. Nevertheless, air pollution may severely affect health problems for elderly people, people who smoke or have respiratory conditions such as asthma, and people who must work in polluted air.

WATER POLLUTION

Although water is the most abundant chemical compound on the Earth's surface, we are finding it increasingly difficult to maintain a plentiful and usable supply. Pollution, excessive use, and misuse are depriving people of the water they need to meet their typical needs (see Table 17-1). As recently as 1994, it was estimated that fully 40% of the freshwater in the United States was unusable.[12]

Yesterday's Pollution Problem

Like air pollution, water pollution is not solely a phenomenon of twentieth century overpopulation or

Table 17-1 Home Water Use	
Use	Gallons
Washing car	100
Taking a bath	36
Washing clothes	35 to 60
Washing dishes	10 to 30
Brushing teeth	10 to 20
Shaving	10 to 20
Watering lawn	8/min
Taking a shower	7/min
Flushing toilet	5 to 7
Leaky faucet	2/day

unchecked technology. Nature has, in fact, routinely polluted our surface and ground water with minerals leached from the soil, acids produced by decaying vegetation, and the decay of animal products. Also, people have polluted their own water supplies. As recently as one generation ago, people living in rural areas occasionally found that their feed lots, chicken coops, and septic tank systems polluted their water supplies.

Today's Pollution Problem

Today, water sources are most often damaged by pollutants from agricultural, urban, and industrial sources. Most of these pollutants are either biological or chemical products, and many can be either removed from the water or brought within acceptable

HEALTH
Action Guide

Preventing Indoor Air Pollution

To minimize the level of indoor pollution in your home, follow these simple steps. How easy or difficult would it be to improve your current level of prevention?

- Hang dry-cleaned clothing outside to air out before hanging it in the closet.
- Clean humidifiers, and replace belts and filters on a regular basis.
- Limit use of aerosol personal care products to the bare minimum.
- Store fuel for mowers, snow blowers, trimmers, and other gasoline-powered tools in an approved container in a well-ventilated area.

- Do not run the engine of a car in an attached garage or closed carport.
- Properly close containers of household cleaning products that are capable of emitting toxic fumes.
- Ventilate rooms in which new carpet and drapes have been installed as often as possible.
- Have fireplaces cleaned and inspected regularly.
- Eliminate smoking of cigarettes within the home.
- Discard unused paint, hobby supplies, herbicides, and pesticides on a regular basis.
- Inspect gas appliances for proper ventilation.
- Use products that are as free as possible from asbestos and formaldehyde when remodeling.

safety limits. For some pollutants, however, management technology has been only partially successful or is still being developed.

Sources of Water Pollution

Water pollution is not the result of only one type of pollutant. In fact, many sources of water pollution exist.

Pathogens

Pathogenic agents, in the form of bacteria, viruses, and protozoa, enter the water supply through human and animal wastes. Communities with sewage treatment systems designed around a combined sanitary and storm system can, during heavy rain or snow melt, allow untreated sewage to rush through the processing plant. In addition, pathogenic organisms can enter the water supply when sewage is flushed from boats. Pathogenic agents are also introduced into the water supply from animal wastes at feed lots and at meat processing facilities.

Sewage treatment plants and public health laboratories routinely test for the presence of pathogenic agents. Unfortunately, however, *undertreated* water is consumed by nearly one fifth of the U.S. population (50 million people). The presence of **coliform bacteria** indicates human or animal feces.

Biological imbalances

Aquatic plants tend to thrive in water rich in nitrates and phosphates. This overabundance leads to **eutrophication,** which can render a stream, pond, or lake unusable.[13]

During hot, dry summers, aquatic plants die in large numbers. Since the decay of vegetation requires aerobic bacterial action, the biochemical oxygen demand will be high.[13] To satisfy the biochemical oxygen demand, much of the water's oxygen is used. When such a condition exits, fish may be killed in great numbers. **Putrefaction** of the dead fish not only further pollutes the water but also fouls the air.

Toxic substances

Of the pollutants found in today's surface water and groundwater supply, perhaps none are of greater concern than toxic chemical substances. These chemical toxins, including metals and hydrocarbons, are dangerous because when in the surface water, they have the ability to enter the food chain. When they do, their concentration per unit of weight increases with each life form in the chain. By the time humans consume the fish that have fed on the contaminated lower forms of aquatic life, the toxic chemicals have been concentrated to dangerous levels.[14] In groundwater supplies, of course, toxic substances are consumed directly by humans in drinking water.

Among the important toxic substances is mercury in the form of methyl mercury. Derived from industrial wastes, methyl mercury is ingested and concentrated by shellfish and other fish. When humans eat these fish regularly, mercury levels increase to the point that hemoglobin and central nervous system function can be seriously impaired.

A variety of other metals have also been found in North American rivers, lakes, and groundwater sources. In the surface water, arsenic, cadmium, copper, lead, and silver are all capable of entering the food chain. In many cases, only very low levels of these metals need to be taken into the body before damage to health becomes evident.

Of the wide variety of agricultural products currently used on American and Canadian farms, *pesticides* and *herbicides* are among the most toxic. Containing more than 1800 different chemical compounds, these agricultural products deliver a diverse array of chemicals to our water supplies, as well as directly on or in the food that people eat. The level of herbicides in the water supply rises particularly rapidly during the summer months.

Today there is mounting concern regarding pesticides and herbicides and the development of testicular cancer and drop in sperm production in men, leukemia in children, and breast cancer in women.[15] Currently the FDA has more than 85 of these agricultural products under study and has proposed new guidelines regarding their appropriate use and disposal.

Among the most serious of the toxic chemicals found in our water are the chlorinated hydrocarbons, including *DDT* (dichlorodiphenyltrichloroethane), *chlordane,* and *Kepone* (chlordecone). The **mutagenic, carcinogenic,** and **teratogenic** effects of these hydrocarbon products continue to receive careful study.

PCBs (polychlorinated biphenyls) are another group of hydrocarbons causing a great deal of concern because of their presence in the water supply.[14] PCBs are, on the basis of their chemical structure, very stable, heat-resistant compounds that have been used extensively in transformers and electrical capacitors. In many areas of the country, discarded electrical equipment has broken open and released PCBs into the surrounding water supply. Tests are now being conducted at these dump sites to determine the extent of contamination of the underground water supply. In laboratory animals, PCBs produce liver and kidney damage, gastric and reproductive disorders, skin lesions, and tumors.[14] Studies on people who have been exposed to high levels of PCBs in drinking water have been ongoing for several years. It is now known that PCBs can concentrate in the fat that comprises breast tissue and that they have been found in women with breast cancer. Since 1990 the use of PCBs in electrical equipment has been banned.

As suggested on page 430, *chlorine,* one of the most extensively used chemicals in industry, is now recognized as a prevalent pollutant of the country's water supply, particularly for the Great Lakes. Experts believe that elevated levels of chlorine from chlorine-containing chemicals inflict damage on animals and could result in a variety of health problems, including cancer, in humans.[16]

The Clear Water Act (1994) mandated changes in the plastics, organic chemicals, pulp and paper processing, and wastewater management industries to replace chlorine with an acceptable substitute. Progress in meeting various requirements will be closely monitored.

Other sources

Three additional types of pollution that affect our water are important, although their effect on human health is not fully understood. The pollution from these sources is detrimental to aquatic life; alters the aesthetic value of our waterways; and reduces recreational use of our rivers, lakes, and shores.

Oil spills include not only the severe spills resulting from tanker accidents but also spills that occur on inland waters and those that result from the seeping of crude oil from the ground. Any kind of oil spill can foul our water. Fish, aquatic plants, seabirds, and beaches can be damaged by both surface-oil film and tar masses that float below the surface or roll along the ocean bottom. Less noticeable but potentially harmful to human health is the contamination of groundwater by inappropriately disposed of oil-based products or by gasoline leaking from underground storage tanks.

Power plants that use water from lakes and rivers to cool their stream turbines cause *thermal pollution.* When this heated water is returned to its source, temperatures in the water may rise significantly. As temperatures increase, the oxygen-carrying capacity of the water decreases and the balance of aquatic life forms is altered. In water that is raised only 10° C (18° F), entire species of fish can disappear and aquatic plants can proliferate out of control.[5]

Finally, *sediments* in the form of sand, clay, and other soil constituents regularly reach waterway channels. Rivers, lakes, reservoirs, and oceans serve as settling basins for these sediments. If cleared land areas cannot be returned to vegetative cover, then dredging may be required to keep the waterway usable, although this is an expensive and relatively ineffective response.

Oceanic oil spills destroy the habitat of hundreds of wildlife species, such as the sea otter, and remain in the ocean for decades.

Effects on Wetlands

The progressive loss of wetlands resulting from drainage and the dumping of debris is of great concern. With the loss of wetlands, the natural habitat for countless species of fish, shellfish, birds, and marine mammals is lost. By the end of this century, over half of the country's wetlands will have vanished.[17] On a more positive note, concerted efforts to reestablish wetlands are occurring throughout the country. Unfortunately, at the same time, continued loss occurs in other areas.

Health Implications

When water becomes polluted, its quality falls below acceptable standards for its intended use, and

coliform bacteria
Intestinal tract bacteria whose presence in a water supply suggests contamination by human or animal waste.

eutrophication
Enrichment of a body of water with nutrients, which causes overabundant growth of plants.

putrefaction
Decomposition of organic matter.

mutagenic
Capable of promoting genetic alterations in cells.

some aspects of our health will be harmed (see the Health Action Guide at right). Polluted water is associated with disease and illness, but it also distresses us emotionally, limits our social activities, and challenges us intellectually and spiritually to become more active stewards of our environment.

LAND POLLUTION

Since we live, work, and play on land, it may be difficult to believe that land constitutes only about 30% of the earth's surface. The rest is, of course, water. When we consider the rivers, streams, marshes, and lakes found on our land surfaces, our land surface seems even smaller. Uninhabitable land areas, such as swamps, deserts, and mountain ranges, further reduce the available land on which humans can live. Our land is a precious commodity—one that we have taken for granted.

The effects of our growing population on our limited land resources are becoming more evident. However, the greatest effect on our land comes from the products our society discards: *solid waste* products and *chemical waste* products.

Solid Waste

The trash that is collected from our homes is composed of a wide variety of familiar materials. Each year, Americans dispose of paper, newspaper, cardboard, clothing, yard waste, wood pallets, food waste, cafeteria waste, glass, metal, disposable tableware, plastics, and an endless variety of other types of *municipal solid waste* (MSW). Each individual American produces over 4.3 pounds of MSW each year.[18] Collectively, we have produced over 200 million tons of solid waste.

Although it is important, MSW makes up only a small amount of the solid waste discarded in this country. Agricultural, mining, and industrial wastes contribute much more to our solid waste problems. Regardless of the source, solid waste requires some form of disposal. Traditionally, these forms have been taken:

- *Open dumping.* Solid waste is compacted and dumped on a dump site. Open dumps are discouraged or illegal in many urban areas.
- *Sanitary landfill.* Solid waste is compacted and buried in huge open pits. Each day, a layer of soil is pushed over the most recently dumped material to encourage decomposition, reduce unpleasant odors, and contain the material to keep it from being scattered.
- *Incineration.* Solid waste can be incinerated. A

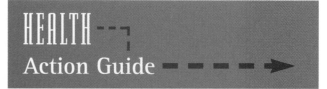

variety of types of incinerators exist, including cement kilns, boilers and furnaces, and commercial incinerators.
- *Ocean dumping.* When near enough to the ocean, solid waste can also be collected, loaded into barges, and taken to offshore dump sites.

Our ability to solve our solid waste disposal problems may depend on **recycling,** or the ability to convert many of our disposable items into reusable materials (see the Star Box on p. 435). It has been difficult to convince manufacturers and the public that many of our solid waste products should be recycled. Efforts to recycle glass, aluminum, paper, and plastic

carcinogenic
Related to the production of cancerous changes; property of environmental agents, including drugs, that may stimulate the development of cancerous changes within cells.

teratogenic
Capable of promoting birth defects.

recycling
The ability to convert disposable items into reusable materials.

LEARNING *from* ALL CULTURES

Cash for Cars: Recycling, European Style

Most of us who recycle our newspapers, glass, and aluminum do so simply to make our own small contribution to a cleaner environment. Money doesn't usually enter the picture—we just like the good feeling we get from making our weekly trip to the local recycling center.

But how would you feel if the government and your favorite automaker asked you to recycle your car—and offered to pay you handsomely for doing so?

That's exactly what's been happening in Italy and some other European countries, and it's been causing quite a stir. After several years of declining sales, car dealers in Italy were buoyed in the early part of 1997 by a surge of new-car purchases. The reason was simple: lust for money. In January of that year, the Italian government offered to pay up to 4,000 lire ($2,550) to each person who traded in a car that was more than 10 years old for a new one. Half the money was put up by the state and the remainder by car manufacturers themselves, who paid their share in part through price increases. The result: automakers expected to sell some 2 million new cars in 1997, the highest number in five years.

Italy isn't the only country to have seized on this idea. In the spring of 1997 Spain introduced another in its series of incentives, worth 80,000 pesetas ($565) to people who exchanged old cars for new. Until the autumn of 1996 France offered up to 7,000 francs ($1,400) in exchange for a car that was at least 8 years old. Under a program that ran in Denmark for 18 months until the summer of 1996, at least 8.5 percent of all the country's cars were traded in—a move that cost the government 780,000 kroner ($130 million).

The auto industry's appeals to prospective buyers have been carefully packaged. Old vehicles are dangerous and polluting, says Italy's National Association for the Automobile Industry. Spain claims that the incentives are needed to phase out leaded gas early in the next century. Not all of the industry's motives are so altruistic, however; another aim of the incentives it to stimulate demand. ✦

Thousands of sanitary landfills like this one are found throughout the United States. Each of us should ask, "Is this really the best way to dispose of solid waste?" "How much of this garbage am I responsible for?" "How can I reduce the amount I contribute?"

Recycling

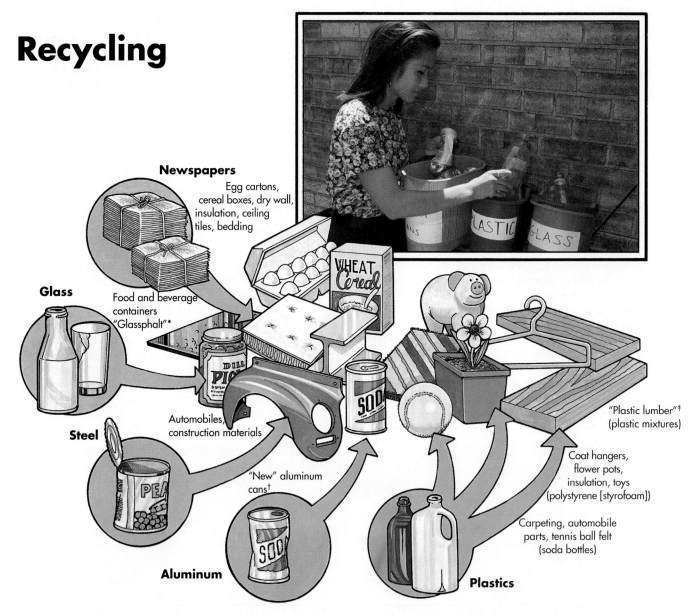

Newspapers
Egg cartons, cereal boxes, dry wall, insulation, ceiling tiles, bedding

Glass
Food and beverage containers "Glassphalt"*

Automobiles, construction materials

Steel

"New" aluminum cans†

Aluminum

Plastics

"Plastic lumber"‡ (plastic mixtures)

Coat hangers, flower pots, insulation, toys (polystyrene [styrofoam])

Carpeting, automobile parts, tennis ball felt (soda bottles)

*A combination of glass and asphalt that makes an attractive roadway.
†20 recycled aluminum cans can be made for the same amount of energy required to make one new can from ore.
‡A durable construction material similar to wood that can be made into fence posts, decks, or park benches.

Figure 17-3   Many useful products can be made from recycled materials. The amount of material that is recycled depends on consumer demand for these products. Would you be willing to use an alternative product made from recycled components, such as a deck made of plastic lumber?

have not been fully adopted by society. Cost of recycling and a lack of markets for reclaimed materials often discourage municipalities and industries from practicing more recycling. Lack of time and interest, failure to understand how to recycle, messiness, and the lack of curbside pickup are also frequently mentioned as reasons for not recycling in the home.

Chemical Waste

According to many environmental consumer group leaders, the quality of our lives is deteriorating, in part because of the unsafe disposal of hazardous chemicals from industrial and agricultural sources. In 1993 alone, according to the EPA, 33.5 billion pounds of potentially toxic chemicals were released into the

The Three R's of Controlling Solid Waste Disposal

As consumers and environmentally concerned citizens, we need to do more than control the disposal of solid waste so that it does not adversely influence our health and the health of our environment. We must prevent this waste from occurring in increasing quantities. To accomplish this goal, a commitment to reduce, reuse, and recycle must be made.

The first step in dealing with the problem of solid waste disposal is to find ways to *reduce* the use of materials that eventually pollute our environment. A concerned public willing to make do with less, such as the amount of packaging material used with small consumer products, is a positive step. As concerned citizens, we must all learn to *reuse* as much as possible. Glass milk bottles that can be used again by the dairy, as well as cloth diapers rather than the nondegradable disposable diapers, are examples of reuse at its best.

Finally, we must *recycle* as much material as possible. Recent experience has taught us that Americans will recycle when a system for collecting material is in place. However, recycling will go only as far as the demand and a market for recycled materials exists.

When combined, the three R's of reduction, reuse, and recycling could significantly reduce our need to engage in the more expensive disposal of toxic wastes.

air, water, land, sewers, and into toxic waste dump sites. Currently, it is estimated that there are over 31,500 toxic waste dump sites sprinkled across the country.[14] Because it costs much more money to detoxify, recycle, and reuse toxic chemical products than to dump them, too many chemical companies have been more than willing to secretly and unlawfully bury their chemical wastes.

Pesticides

Since Rachel Carson wrote her now-classic book *Silent Spring* in 1962, the public has been aware of the potential dangers associated with the use of some **pesticides.** Although Carson's primary concern was with the pesticide DDT, a number of other hazardous pesticides have since been removed from the marketplace. Tighter controls established by the EPA have restricted the availability of other, less hazardous pesticides. Farmers contend they need to use effective poisons to save their crops from insect destruction. However, equal concern seems to be focused now on the effects of pesticides on food and water supplies,

soil quality, animals, other insects, and humans.[19] Harmful agents such as pesticides can enter an **ecosystem** and affect the entire food chain. The Star Box on p. 437 suggests nontoxic ways to garden and control home insects, thus reducing the need to use pesticides.

Herbicides

Herbicides also contribute to the growing problem of water and soil pollution and to the contamination of the food chain. These weed-killing chemicals are sprayed on plants and incorporated into the soil with plowing but are not totally taken up by the plant tissues they are intended to kill. The extent to which herbicides causes illness in humans is not fully known, although the potential appears to be real.

RADIATION

We have lived in the nuclear age since the end of World War II. Today the hopes for nuclear energy primarily lie in its enormous potential to reduce our dependence on fossil fuels as energy sources. Also, nuclear energy can (and already does) improve our industrial and medical technology, as evidenced by an expanding use of radioactive materials in the diagnosis and treatment of various health disorders.

The two greatest concerns over nuclear energy are (1) the harmful health effects that come from day-to-day exposure to radiation and (2) the potential for a nuclear accident of regional or global consequences. In the opinion of some, a third concern, that of nuclear terrorism, also exists.

Fission, the decay of radioactive materials, produces not only a great amount of energy but also **ionizing radiation** in the form of radioactive particles. We are exposed to various forms of ionizing radiation daily through natural radiation, including ultraviolet

pesticide
Agent used to destroy insects and other pests.

ecosystem
An ecological unit made up of both animal and plant life that interact to produce a stable system.

ionizing radiation
Form of radiation capable of releasing electrons from atoms.

Health on the Web

LEARNING ACTIVITIES

Activity 1

You can discover dangerous contaminants in your home by using various safety devices. Enzone's Home Safety Institute describes a number of hazardous contaminants from which to protect yourself and your family. Go to Enzone's Home Safety Institute website at http://www.enzoneusa.com/index.htm. Select one contaminant that could be hazardous to your health. Then read about the recommended tests required to determine whether the contaminant is present. Why is this contaminant dangerous? How difficult and expensive is it to detect and remove?

Activity 2

The effect of overpopulation on the environment extends well beyond our own homes and communities to include the entire planet. Go to the Social Statistics Briefing Room of the White House at http://www.whitehouse.gov/fsbr/demography.html to receive up-to-the-second population counts for the United States and the world. What was the world population when you logged on? Go back to the site a day later. What was the population then?

Activity 3

Topics related to European recycling and the environment are covered at http://www.tecweb.com/recycle/sample.htm. This site consists of more than 100 pages devoted to commercial recycling and materials reconstitution. Recycling topics discussed include aluminum and steel drinks cans, composting, household waste recovery, recovered paper markets, packaging recycling targets, plastic container recovery, scrap metal reprocessing, environmental legislation, motor vehicle dismantling, and construction waste. Go to this site to register for a free sample issue of *Recycling World* magazine.

---

radiation from the sun and natural radioactive mineral deposits, and synthetic radiation, including waste from nuclear reactors, industrial products, and x-ray examinations. Most of the exposures we get on a daily basis produce negligible health risks. Although it is clear that no kind of radiation exposure is good for you, safe levels of exposure are difficult to determine.

Health Effects of Radiation Exposure

The health effects of radiation exposure depend on many factors, including the duration, type, dose of exposure, and individual sensitivity. Clearly, heavy exposure (as in a severe nuclear accident) can produce **radiation sickness** or immediate death. Lesser exposure can be quite harmful as well. Of particular concern are the effects of radiation on egg and sperm production, embryonic development, and dangerous or irreversible changes to the eyes and skin. Cancer, particularly of the blood-forming tissue, is also a concern. From a health perspective, the message is clear: avoid any unnecessary exposure to radioactive materials. Make it a point to question the value of diagnostic x-ray examinations, especially routine dental and chest x-ray studies and mammograms. Routine x-ray stud-

ies have been discouraged by professional societies and consumer groups. Recent studies suggest that the risk is minimal for most people.[20]

Electromagnetic Radiation

What do water bed heaters, electric razors, electric blankets, high-tension electrical transmission lines, and cellular telephones have in common? They all produce electromagnetic fields or electromagnetic waves, even more specifically, electromagnetic fields that come in close proximity to the body or pass very near your home, as in the case of transmission lines.

In recent years, concern has been voiced as to whether the electromagnetic fields generated by these familiar devices could cause cancer. Research using laboratory animals and studies comparing the incidence of cancer in people using these devices with those who do not have been far from conclusive. A recent study of 138,905 utility workers whose exposure to electromagnetic fields was in conjunction with power line sources did, however, show a higher than expected rate of death from brain cancer.[21] Therefore, in light of this study and until more research has been done regarding non–employment-

Nontoxic Home Pest Control

Try the following organic solutions to pest control problems:

- **Ants**—boric acid, which is available in a number of different formulations. Use it in a trap.
- **Roaches**—dry things out with a hair dryer. Roaches are attracted to moisture, so seal cracks, fix leaks. Other ideas: Mix equal parts of oatmeal or flour with plaster of Paris—or equal parts of baking soda and sugar—and spread around infested area.
- **Fleas**—before bed, put a light over a shallow pan of soapy water. Turn out all other lights. Empty water every morning and continue for one month. Fleas go for heat and light, and they can't swim.
- **Lawn weeds**—raise the cutting level on your lawn mower so the grass can grow three to four inches tall, giving it a strong root system that will block weeds. Other methods: Pull weeds, spray with soap solution, or douse with fresh human urine (it's very high in nitrogen and will burn the weed).
- **Garden pests**—suck them up with a hand-held vacuum cleaner.
- **Flies, mosquitoes**—fix screens. Vacuum them up. For flies, hang clusters of cloves; make flypaper by spreading honey on yellow (flies' favorite color) paper; scratch an orange peel and leave it out—the citrus oil repels flies.

related exposure, some care should be exercised in the use of appliances that generate radiation fields. For example, heaters for water beds should be turned on early to allow the bed to warm and then turned off once in the bed, cellular telephone calls should be kept short, and a morning shave should not last more than a few minutes.

Nuclear Reactor Accidents and Waste Disposal

To generate the nuclear energy to produce electrical energy, more than 100 nuclear power plants have been constructed in North America. Built mostly by utility companies, these nuclear power plants were designed to produce electrical energy in an efficient, economical, and safe manner. Much public criticism has been directed at these power plants, claiming that their safety and efficiency have not been documented.

Concern over the safety of nuclear power plants was heightened in this country and around the world when, on April 26, 1986, a **meltdown** occurred at the Chernobyl nuclear power plant in the Soviet Union. Human error was responsible for creating a situation in which excessive heat was allowed to build up in the core of the nuclear reactor. The resultant explosion killed two people, hospitalized hundreds, and exposed hundreds of thousands of people to nuclear radiation. As a result of the Chernobyl accident, the Russian government had to resettle 200,000 people at an estimated cost of $26 billion. Furthermore, a leading Soviet scientist estimated that 10,000 miners and soldiers died as a result of exposure to radiation received during cleanup operations after the accident.

The safe disposal of nuclear waste is an additional serious problem that also has not been fully solved. The by-products of nuclear fission remain radioactive for many years. Although the current method of disposing of these wastes is to bury them, eventual leakage into our environment is a serious risk.

Proponents of nuclear power maintain that not one person in the United States has died as the result of a power plant accident. They point to a spotless safety record and reiterate that our fossil fuel supply is limited. Supporters of the nuclear industry feel that a public commitment to establishing more nuclear reactors is important for the future of our country. Currently, nearly 20% of our electrical energy is generated by nuclear power.

radiation sickness
Illness characterized by fatigue, nausea, weight loss, fever, bleeding from mouth and gums, hair loss, and immune deficiencies, resulting from overexposure to ionizing radiation.

meltdown
The overheating and eventual melting of the uranium fuel rods in the core of a nuclear reactor.

Radiation Tests

Attention was recently called to a potentially dark page in American medical history—the purposeful exposure, between World War II and 1970, of 16,000 American citizens (prisoners, children, mentally retarded people, pregnant women, and patients in public hospitals) to nuclear radiation. In late 1997, the National Cancer Institute released information about the exposure of American children to radiation from atomic bomb testing.[22] In 1952, 55 million children younger than age 14 absorbed an average of 2 rads of radiation in the milk they drank. This milk was produced by cows who had grazed on vegetation contaminated by radioactive fallout. This exposure will result in an estimated 12,000 to 208,000 additional cases of thyroid cancer, half of which have not yet been diagnosed. If identified early, this type of cancer is highly curable.

NOISE POLLUTION

In much the same fashion that a weed is an unwanted plant and can ruin a lawn, noise is an unwanted sound that can be detrimental to our overall health. In some cases a sound that is desirable, such as music, can function like a true noise because of the intensity of the presentation. Regardless, today's world is characterized by sounds whose loudness and unrelenting presence are dangerous to our health. These intense sounds can reduce our hearing acuity, disrupt our emotional tranquility, infringe on our social interactiveness, and interrupt our concentration.

Noise-Induced Hearing Loss

Sound, or a wave of compressed air molecules moving in response to a pressure change, is characterized by two qualities—*frequency* and *intensity*. High intensity is primarily responsible for the loss of hearing experienced by many people living in noise-polluted environments. Intensity of sound exceeding 80 to 85 decibels (1200 to 4800 cycles-per-second frequency range) can cause hearing damage. The Star Box on p. 439 shows sound intensity associated with several common environmental sound sources.

The interpretation of a sound (hearing) is a sophisticated and sensitive physiological process involving the progressive conversion of acoustical energy to mechanical energy, then to hydraulic energy, and, finally, to electrochemical energy. Electrochemical energy is then transmitted by the acoustic nerve to the brain for interpretation. The destructive influence of exposure to sounds of high intensity lies in the destruction of special hair cells in the inner ear that are responsible for converting hydraulic energy into electrochemical energy. Loud music, jet engine noise, vehicular traffic, and a wide range of industrial noises can collapse these sensitive cells. Ironically, the cells that are damaged are those responsible for hearing the high-frequency sounds associated with normal conversation, not those that hear the damaging sound itself. Thus the environmental sources of noise rob you of your ability to hear sound of a far greater value—the sound of the unamplified human voice.

The damage just described is initially reversible. However, with continued exposure, the changes in the sensitive cells of the inner ear become permanent. The Health Action Guide on p. 439 suggests ways to reduce noise pollution.

Noise As a Stressor

In addition to the damaging effects of noise on hearing, the role of noise as a stressor has long been recognized. Indeed, the absence of noise (silence) and prolonged noise are both proven techniques to break the will of prisoners during war. Recently, however, attention has shifted to the role of noise in terms of the stress response, presented in Chapter 3. In people stressed by unrelenting noise, the elevated epinephrine levels contribute to hypertension and other stress-related health problems.

IN SEARCH OF BALANCE

How often have you heard people yearn for a return to the "good old days"? They reminisce about times when people moved more slowly, cared more for their neighbors, and appreciated their natural resources. After listening to these nostalgic impressions, you could believe that our society was once almost idyllic—with little or no pollution, population concerns, or threats of nuclear accidents.

Certainly it is nice to dream, but it is doubtful that our advancing technology and exploding worldwide population will permit us to find such an ideal world. Instead, we need to focus on finding the appropriate balance between technological growth and environmental deterioration.

We must learn to think beyond the present. Each decision we make for the future should be considered in light of its influence on our environmental systems (see the Star Box on p. 441). If our decisions are based solely on financial gain or personal convenience, we will be committing a monumental disservice to our children and future generations.

Noise Pollution and Its Effects on Hearing

The loudness of sounds is measured in decibels (dB). Sound intensity is determined logarithmically, not arithmetically. Each increase of 10 dB produces a tenfold increase in sound intensity. Thus 30 dB has 10 times the intensity of 20 dB, 40 dB has 100 times the intensity of 20 dB, and 110 dB sounds 10 times as loud as 100 dB. Hearing damage depends on the dB level and the length of exposure. Presented below are dB ranges, common sources, and effects on hearing.

Decibel	Common sources	Effect on hearing
0	Lowest sound audible to human ear	—
30	Quiet library, soft whisper	—
40	Quiet office, study lounge, bedroom away from traffic	—
50	Light traffic at a distance, refrigerator, quiet conversation, gentle breeze	—
60	Air conditioner at 20 feet, normal conversation, sewing machine	—
70	Busy traffic, noisy office or cafeteria	Annoying, and may start to affect hearing if constant
80	Heavy city traffic, alarm clock at 2 feet, typical factory	Starts to affect hearing if exposed more than 8 hours
90	Truck traffic, noisy home appliances, shop tools, lawn mower	Temporary hearing loss can occur in less than 8 hours
100	Chain saw, pneumatic drill (jackhammer), loud motorcycle, or farm equipment	Unprotected exposure for 2 hours can produce serious damage to hearing
120	Rock band concert in front of speakers, sand blasting, loud thunderclap	Immediate danger threat
140	Shotgun blast, jet plane from 50 feet	Immediate pain threat; any length of exposure is dangerous
180	Rocket pad area during launch (without ear protection)	Immediate, irreversible, and inevitable hearing loss

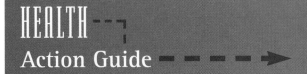

HEALTH
Action Guide

Reducing Noise Pollution

Beyond giving your political support to legislation and enforcement policies designed to reduce environmental noise pollution, what can you do to lessen the degree of noise pollution in your life? The following suggestions are only a few of the recommended approaches:

- Limit your exposure to highly amplified music. The damage from occasional exposure to sound intensity between 110 and 120 decibels can be reversible. Daily exposure, however, will result in permanent hearing loss.
- Reduce the volume on your portable headsets. When others can hear the music coming through your headset while you are wearing it, you should probably turn down the volume.

- Wear ear plugs (wax or soft plastic) and sound-absorbing ear muffs when using firearms or operating loud machinery.
- Maintain your automobile, motorcycle, or lawn mower exhaust systems in good working order.
- Furnish your room, apartment, home, and office with sound-absorbing materials. Drapes, carpeting, and cork wall tiles are excellent for reducing both interior and exterior noises.
- Establish noise reduction as a criterion in selecting a site for your residence. An apartment complex near a freeway or airport or property near an interstate highway may prove to be less than desirable.

Since you are a person with a lifetime of hearing ahead, noise pollution reduction deserves your participation and your support.

El Niño and La Niña: Weather Siblings with a Stormy Disposition

During January and February 1998, many areas of the United States experienced unusual weather, including some of unprecedented severity. Ice storms struck in New England and adjacent parts of Canada, leaving millions of households without electricity for weeks. Torrential rains fell along the California coast, causing devastating floods and mudslides. In the Midwest and Northern Plains states, winter temperatures were often springlike, climbing well into the 50-degree range. Elsewhere in the world, floods ravaged Peru, drought nearly destroyed the wheat crop in Australia, and forest fires burned out of control over wide areas of Indonesia when monsoon rains would normally have been falling. These unusual weather events were caused by a global weather phenomenon known as El Niño.

El Niño is a massive weather pattern that develops in the midlatitudes of the Pacific Ocean when high pressure in the eastern Pacific sends strong trade winds blowing westward. These winds in turn push a ridge of water toward the Asian coast. When the high pressure dissipates, the mass of water now in the western Pacific begins flowing eastward, forcing a layer of cool water (called a *thermocline*) downward, which increases the surface temperature of the ocean. As this surface layer of warm water reaches the continental shelf along the western edge of the Americas, warm currents are deflected northward, toward Alaska, and southward, toward Chile. Warmed by the El Niño effect, eastward-blowing

Storms intensified by El Niño have caused flooding and mudslides in many parts of the country.

winds change the weather patterns across wide areas of North and South America.

La Niña, the sister of El Niño, is a rebound effect that pushes the once–eastward moving ridge of water back toward the western Pacific, where a subsequent reversal will occur, resulting in a second El Niño.

The El Niño phenomenon has occurred periodically for thousands of years. However, the increasing frequency of this weather pattern suggests the influence of global warming. How has El Niño affected the weather in your part of the country?

Summary

- World population is increasing at an alarming rate and with adverse effects on the environment.
- Gases and solid pollutants contribute to air pollution and its associated health concerns.
- Worldwide increases in carbon dioxide production could result in a greenhouse effect, leading to climatic warming and extreme weather conditions.
- Acid rain, acid fog, and acid snow, as well as smog, result from the release of gaseous and particulate pollutants into the air.
- Deterioration of the ozone layer could result in exposure to high levels of ultraviolet radiation and serious health problems.
- Particulate matter, including fibers and trace mineral elements, are found in the air.
- Temperature inversions increase the seriousness of air pollution.
- Indoor air pollution is now recognized as a serious threat to health, particularly from radon gas that can easily accumulate in modern houses.
- Water pollution results from a variety of causative agents, including toxic chemicals and pathogens from human and animal wastes.
- Increased levels of pesticides and herbicides can be found in both surface water and groundwater sources.

Your Role in Creating a Sustainable Environment

As we search for solutions to complex environmental problems, we may have to make some difficult decisions. For example, will Third World populations be forced to use contraception or sterilization? Will we attempt to feed the world's hungry people? Will we continue to protect endangered species of plants and animals? Will we strive more forcefully for nuclear disarmament? Can we commit ourselves to cleaning up all of our toxic waste sites? Answers to these complex questions about *stewardship* will probably be based not only on our knowledge but also on our moral predispositions.

Answers to these sorts of complex questions can come from recognizing the value of a *sustainable environment*. This environment will be developed only when individuals and groups are willing to do the following:

- Evaluate their environment
- Become environmentally educated
- Choose a simpler, less consumption-oriented lifestyle
- Recognize the limitations of technology in solving problems
- Become involved in environmental protection activities
- Work with people on all sides of environmental issues

These suggestions might sound abstract for a person confronted with a local environmental problem. However, each of these steps can be applied to a local situation with only limited modifications. The PCB soil contamination in Indiana, the nerve gas weapons storage in Kentucky, the toxic waste site cleanup in Missouri, and the transportation of nuclear waste materials in California and other states represent local issues to which these steps can be applied. Are you committed enough to a sustainable environment to practice these steps?

- Chlorine from a variety of sources, including PCBs, can also be found in both surface water and groundwater sources.
- Municipal solid waste is a small but important component of all solid waste.
- Solid wastes are traditionally buried, dumped, or incinerated.
- Reduction, reuse, and recycling are important aspects of the prevention of environmental pollution.
- Toxic wastes from both industry and agriculture are serious sources of land pollution.
- As with water pollution, pesticides and herbicides have been found to pollute land.
- Radiation, including ultraviolet and ionizing radiation from nuclear power plants, could result in serious health problems.
- Electromagnetic radiation may be associated with severe health problems, including brain cancer.
- Noise pollution can lead to hearing loss, particularly the ability to hear the human voice.
- We must seek a balance between lifestyle and the health of the environment, not only for our generations but for those who will follow.

Review Questions

1. In what direction is the world population changing? What could be the consequences of this change on the environment? How can the rate of this change be moderated?
2. What is the greenhouse effect? How does deforestation influence this process? What is the anticipated consequence of the greenhouse effect?
3. How are acid rain, acid fog, and acid snow produced? What and where is the damage attributed to them?
4. What is causing the deterioration of the ozone layer? What step has been taken to slow this process? What are the consequences of ozone layer deterioration?

5. What are the major particulate pollutants in our air? What is the principal risk associated with lead as a pollutant? What specific diseases are associated with particulate material in our air?

6. How are gray-air smog and brown-air smog formed? When and where is one form more likely to be seen than the other?

7. What air pollutant has recently been classified as a Group A carcinogen? What other pollutants contribute to indoor air pollution? What risks are associated with radon gas?

8. What toxic chemicals are most often the sources of water pollution? What is the consequence of having too little oxygen dissolved in water? What is thermal pollution? How do pesticides and herbicides enter both our water supply and soil? What is the principal source of the chlorine found in water?

9. What are several forms of municipal solid waste? How much municipal solid waste does the typical person produce per year? How much do Americans produce in a year?

10. How are solid wastes most often disposed of? Why are these techniques less than fully acceptable?

11. What are the three R's of better solid waste prevention?

12. What are the principal sources of radiation that are of concern today? Which are natural sources of radiation, and which are the result of human intervention? What familiar appliances may be sources of electromagnetic fields?

13. How does noise pollution result in hearing loss? What are the most common sources of noise pollution?

14. For whom is a balance between a modern lifestyle and a healthful environment important?

 Think About This . . .

- To what extent do your driving habits contribute to air pollution?
- In what ways do your recreational activities contribute to water pollution?
- If land were very affordable, would you build a new house on land reclaimed from a toxic waste dump site?
- How close to a nuclear power plant would you feel comfortable living?
- Is your home protected from the possibility of radon gas?

- The environmental focus of the 1990s has shifted from global concerns, such as the ozone layer, deforestation, and world population, to local concerns, such as recycling and indoor air pollution. Will it now be possible to "think globally while acting locally"?
- Would you be willing to spend more for a light-bulb designed to last 20,000 hours, use little energy, and last several years rather than a much less expensive incandescent bulb to reduce energy costs?

References

1. *The environment and population growth: decade for action,* Population Reports Series M(10):2-3, 1992.
2. The Kyoto agreement: what now?, *Scientific American Forum,* Dec 6, 1997.
3. Climatic Research Unit, University of East Anglia (England), as reported in *Newsweek,* Jan 22, 1996.
4. Arms K: *Environmental science,* ed 2, Fort Worth, TX, 1994, Saunders College Publishing.
5. Chiras D: *Environmental science: action for a sustainable future,* ed 4, Redwood City, CA, 1994, Benjamin-Cummings.
6. Kerr JB, McElroy CT: Evidence for large upward trends of ultraviolet-B radiation linked to ozone depletion, *Science* 262:1032-1034, 1993.
7. Needleman HL et al: Bone lead levels and delinquent behavior, *JAMA* 275(3):363-369, 1996.
8. Kim R et al: A longitudinal study of low-level lead exposure and impairment of renal function. The Normative Aging Study, *JAMA* 275(15):1177-1181, 1996.
9. Respiratory health effects of passive smoking: lung cancer and other diseases, Office of Health and Environment, Office of Research and Development, U.S. Environmental Protection Agency, December 1992.
10. Cole L: *Element of risk: the politics of radon,* New York, 1994, Oxford University Press.
11. Menzie R et al: The effect of varying levels of outdoor air supply on the symptoms of sick building syndrome, *N Engl J Med* 328(12):821-827, 1993.

12. Kanamine L: EPA: 40% of freshwater is unusable, *USA Today*, p. 1A, April 21, 1994.

13. Cunningham WP, Saigo B: *Environmental science: a global concern*, ed 4, Dubuque, IA 1997, WCB/McGraw-Hill.

14. Miller GT: *Living in the environment: an introduction to environmental science*, ed 7, Belmont, CA, 1992, International Thompson.

15. Leiss JK, Savitz DA: Home pesticide use and childhood cancer: a case-control study, *Am J Public Health* 85(2): 249–252, 1995.

16. Komulainen H et al: Carcinogenicity of the drinking water mutagen 3-chloro-4-(dichloromethyl)-5-hydroxy-2(5H)-furanone in the rat, *J Natl Cancer Inst* 89(12): 848-856, 1997.

17. Cunningham WP: *Understanding our environment*, Dubuque, IA, 1994, WCB/McGraw-Hill.

18. Franklin W, Franklin M: Putting the crusade into perspective: recycling and waste generation both are on the rise, *EPA Journal* 18(3):7, 1992.

19. Kelce WR et al: Persistent DDT Metabolite p,p'=DDE is a potent androgen receptor antagonist, *Nature* 357(6532): 581-585, 1995.

20. Boice J et al: Diagnostic x-ray procedures and risk of leukemia, lymphoma, and multiple myelona, *JAMA* 265(10):1290, 1991.

21. Savitz DA, Loomis DP: Magnetic field exposure in relation to leukemia and brain cancer mortality among electric utility workers, *Am J Epidemiol* 141(2):123-128, 1995.

22. National Cancer Institute, Office of Cancer Communications: *Study to estimate iodine (I-131) doses from nuclear fallout* (press release), Oct 1, 1997.

Suggested Readings

Somerville RC: *The forgiving air: Understanding environmental change*, Berkeley, CA, 1996, University of California Press.
The ozone hole, acid rain, and the greenhouse effect are among the many phenomena caused by human activities. Using authoritative, up-to-date scientific information, the author set forth to educate his readers so that they can participate in important decisions that affect the environment. This reader-friendly book uses historical anecdotes to illustrate contemporary environmental issues.

Mabey N (editor): *Argument in the greenhouse: the international economics of controlling global warming*, New York, 1997, Routledge.
This book is for readers who are interested in the international causes of global warming. It examines the problem of using past and current models and evaluates abatement strategies designed to reduce the economic, political, and cultural need to burn fossil fuels.

Cooper A, Elerling D (illustrator): *Along the seashore*, Boulder, CO, 1997, Roberts Rinehart Publishing.

This is the perfect book for parents who want to introduce their 4- to 8-year-old children to nature's ecosystem. Informative text and beautiful illustrations take them to a tidal pool filled with plants and animals. The book was produced in cooperation with the Denver Museum of Natural History.

Quintana D: *100 jobs in the environment*, Indianapolis, IN, 1997, Macmillan.
You may care about the environment so much that you want to dedicate your life to the cause, yet you also need to earn a living. The jobs described in this book offer the perfect solution. You may have already thought of becoming a wildlife biologist, a nature preserve manager, or a water pollution investigator, but have you considered becoming a windfarmer, an exotic animal nutritionist, or a nature photojournalist? These and many other exciting job opportunities are presented in this book.

 AS WE GO TO PRESS . . .

Hearing loss caused by chronic exposure to loud noise is considered to be irreversible. However, some initial success in restoring hearing damaged by environmental noise was reported at a recent Inner Ear Biology meeting. Using a new drug, R-IPA, that stimulates the natural production of antioxidants, scientists noted signs of structural improvement in the noise-damaged ears of chinchillas. Much more research, including human trials, must be undertaken before the drug can be considered safe and effective for restoring hearing.

Telecommuting

Technological advances continue to astound and amaze. In recent years, many of the most promising advances have been made in the areas of computer technology and communications technonogy. Computers have improved to the point where processes that used to take hours now can be performed in seconds. Communications now allow contact to be established with virtually anyplace in the world within seconds. Such advances have allowed companies and individual employees to save money and valuable environmental resources by taking advantage of telecommuting.

Loosely defined, telecommuting means working at home by logging into your office computer system from your home computer. This growing trend could transform the way business is performed. Companies and employees could save millions of dollars in transportation costs, and the potential environmental benefits from energy conservation and pollution reduction are very appealing to society as a whole. Plane flights, cab rides, and twice-daily commutes could be replaced by a walk to the computer. But will the environmental benefits of telecommuting outweigh the potential costs? And could changes in the traditional office environment prove to be unmanageable for employees and employers?

How Telecommuting Can Change Everyday Life

Debbie is a stock trader, working for a Wall Street firm. She is on top of the daily trends of the stock market and gets market price updates as they happen. She stays in contact with her clients and buys and sells stock for them on a daily basis.

But you won't find Debbie on the trading floor.

She's in Albuquerque.

Debbie is one of a growing number of employees who have opted to telecommute to work. Debbie's situation demonstrates what is possible with telecommuting using today's technology. It also illustrates the savings that are possible when conventional travel is eliminated from the daily schedule, and it shows the potential social advantages that come from working at home.[1]

When her husband's job required a move to Albuquerque, New Mexico, Debbie tried the traditional commuting route, keeping a regular work-week schedule in New York City and flying to Albuquerque on the weekends. The commute took its toll, and she eventually left her job. Then she got an offer from a Wall Street firm that was willing to help accommodate her in this unusual sit-uation. She now has separate phone lines for a fax machine, voice mail, and a direct link to her New York office. She also obtains up-to-the-minute stock quotes through a real-time stock market quote service. This technology has enabled Debbie to avoid the hassles of commuting and the stress of the trading floor and has allowed her to enjoy life with her family while working.

This all sounds too good to be true. Telecommuting has been hailed as the wave of the future in business, and its potential benefits have been touted in the popular press for several years. However, although it may have its advantages, there are some problems that may occur if telecommuting gains widespread acceptance.

Environmental Advantages and Problems

Telecommuting may have advantages with regard to conservation of natural resources. A 1990 study by the Arthur D. Little environmental consulting firm showed that significant benefits could result if telecommuting and videoconferencing could be substituted for conventional transportation. If such substitutions accounted for 10% to 20% of the time spent working, shopping, conducting meetings, and sending data, a net yearly savings of up to $23 billion could result. We could also conserve 3.5 million gallons of gasoline per year and reduce yearly pollution production by 1.8 million tons.[2]

Telecommuting also reduces vehicular wear and tear and lowers energy requirements and costs incurred by driving.[3] It may also reduce traffic on the roads in general. In an effort to reduce vehicular traffic problems, the Environmental Protection Agency may force California and other heavily populated states to require more telecommuting. California businesses have already been trying to find ways to reduce the number of cars coming to and from work on a weekly basis. Carpooling is already encouraged in California, where multiple-passenger cars are allowed sole access to "carpool only" lanes. But telecommuting has the potential to eliminate many cars altogether from the daily commuting process, which can be painfully slow and time consuming in large metropolitan areas. Businesses in California may also be required to install more fiber-optic networks and advanced teleconferencing equipment to reduce both local and long-range travel by employees.[4]

Home-based employees will also have the ability to make their home offices more environmentally sound than the typical office. Using a personal computer that saves energy (look for the "Energy Star" label) is a start.[5] Plain-paper fax machines eliminate the need to make photocopies of faxed documents, and all waste paper, foam packing materials, and toner cartridges can be recycled as well. Home-based employees can also get an energy audit for their home office to help make it as waste-free as possible.[5]

Although there appear to be many environmental advantages to telecommuting, many potential drawbacks to widespread telecommuting have been noted. As workers find that they do not need to live near urban workplaces, many of these workers may move to more rural areas to enhance their quality of life. This trend is not new, but those people who have moved out of the inner city have at least moved to communities within a moderate drive from the city. Telecommuting allows an employee to live virtually anywhere, and some experts fear that many workers may flee not just the city but the suburbs as well. These rural areas may not have the infrastructure to handle a massive influx of new residents.[6] Urban areas may face decay as citizens (and possibly businesses) leave cities.[3] Forests and open land may be destroyed as population expands in rural areas.[6]

The Social Aspects of Telecommuting

The potential advantages of telecommuting are very appealing for the individual worker. The most obvious advantage is that the employee is freed from the stress of physically commuting to the office, thus being spared the aggravation and wasted time of driving or riding to and from work.[7] Up to 3.1 billion hours of personal time could be gained by substituting telecommuting for general work activities 10% to 20% of the time.[2] Staying at home can also give workers more free time and allow employees (in some cases) to adjust their work schedules to fit their lifestyles.[7] Schedules can be more easily altered to adjust to unexpected occurrences, such as illness of a family member.[8] More time at home can allow workers more quality time with their families and may help employees develop deeper emotional relationships with their families and friends. Having more people at or near home may foster greater community stability as well.[3]

The individual telecommuter may face some problems, however. Being at home more often (and being expected to work in a home setting) may place stress on family relationships.[3] Being away from an office setting may cause workers to feel isolated from other company employees,[3,7] and their social skills may suffer as a result of lack of contact with others. The loss of the office as a community and the sense of support from co-workers

may also be felt. Employees may not be able to judge the importance of their work in relation to the goals of the company.[7-9]

Supervisors may also have difficulty in evaluating the work of their employees. A loss of company loyalty may also develop if workers spend more time networking with other telecommuters than with company people.[9] Because of the increase in technology, employees may find themselves on call at all hours instead of working a normal daily schedule. Employers may begin to expect workers to be available to work anytime and anywhere[7] through the use of pagers, cellular phones, and portable computers.

The Future Is Now

Ready or not, this new era of office employment is here. It is estimated that roughly half of all workers could be telecommuting in some form by the year 2000. Technological advances are also paving the way for increased telecommuting. The advent and growth of fiber-optic systems allow information to be transmitted much more quickly and efficiently than before. Thus high-powered personal computers can communicate with large mainframe computers at high speed with few problems. Differences between computer brands and data types are being overcome as well. The Integrated Services Digital Network can interface with other computers regardless of the type of computer used or the data transmitted.[3] For those employees who do not want to stay tied down to the house, portable laptop computers and fax transmission equipment now make it possible to send and receive information from nearly anywhere.

And, as Debbie will tell you, that includes her back porch.

For Discussion . . .

After weighing the pros and cons, do you think telecommuting is beneficial to the environment? Why? Do you think that you would enjoy a job where telecommuting is a mandatory part of your work schedule? What personal benefits could you get from telecommuting? What are the potential drawbacks?

References

1. Young J: Sand, sun, mutual fund, *Forbes* 152(10), Oct 25, 1993.
2. Raven PH, Berg LR, Johnson GB: Telecommuting: good for the planet (Envirobrief), *Environment*, Philadelphia, 1995, Saunders.
3. Cunningham S: Communication networks: a dozen ways they'll change our lives, *The Futurist* 26(1), Jan-Feb 1992.

4. Keaver M: Technology sows some seeds for environmental protection, *PC Week* 6(17), May 1, 1989.

5. Townsend AK: Setting up your green home office, *E* 5(4), Aug 1994.

6. Information superhighway: an environmental menace, *USA Today Magazine* 124(2604), Sept 1995.

7. Lundquist E: A Labor Day look at PCs; home work, *PC Week* 12(35), Sept 4, 1995.

8. Sullivan N: Double whammy, *Home Office Computing* 12(5), May 1994.

9. Connelly J: Let's hear it for the office, *Fortune* 131, Mar 6, 1995.

PART 7

THE LIFE CYCLE

Accepting Dying and Death

Healthy People: Looking Ahead to 2010

In the last decade, national health objectives have focused on increasing the life span and years of healthy life for Americans, reducing death rates from various diseases, and reducing infant mortality rates. With few exceptions, the nation has made steady progress toward reaching target goals for many of these objectives.

For the American population as a whole, life expectancy has increased rapidly, with the average life span now at nearly 76 years. However, among racial and ethnic minorities, these estimates of years of healthy life have been less encouraging. Despite the increase in life expectancy, declines in health-related quality of life measures have been troubling.

Real progress has been made in reducing death rates in other areas. For example, the number of deaths caused by unintentional injuries has declined. A reduction in traffic fatalities, especially among young people, has been the most important factor in meeting this goal. The number of deaths caused by work-related injuries has also been reduced significantly.

With continual advances that preserve life and health, we expect the *Healthy People 2010* objectives to focus on additional ways the nation can reduce death rates and increase longevity. These objectives will be found in the target areas of chronic diseases, unintentional injuries, occupational health, and health services. Special efforts aimed at racial and ethnic minority populations will be an important priority.

The primary goal of this chapter is to help people realize that the reality of death can serve as a focal point for a more enjoyable, productive, and contributive life. Each day in our lives becomes especially meaningful only after we have fully accepted the reality that someday we are going to die. We can then live each day to its fullest, as if it were our last day.

Our mortality provides us with a framework from which to appreciate and conduct our lives. It should help us prioritize our activities so that we can accomplish our goals (in our academic work, our relationships with others, and our recreation) before we die. Quite simply, death gives us our only absolute reason for living.

DYING IN TODAY'S SOCIETY

Since shortly after the turn of the century, the manner in which people experience death in this society has changed significantly. Formerly, most people died in their own homes, surrounded by family and friends. Young children frequently lived in the same home with their aging grandparents and saw them grow older and eventually die. Death was seen as a natural extension of life. Children grew up with a keen sense of what death meant, both to the dying person and to the grieving survivors.

Times have indeed changed. Today approximately 70% of people die in hospitals, nursing homes, and extended care facilities, not in their own homes. The extended family is seldom at the bedside of the dying person.[1] Frequently, frantic efforts are made to keep a dying person from death. Although medical technology has improved our lives, some people believe that it has reduced our ability to die with dignity. Many are convinced that our way of dying has become more artificial and less civilized than it used to be. The trend toward hospice care may be a positive response to this high-tech manner of dying (see p. 454).

DEFINITIONS OF DEATH

Before many of the scientific advancements of the past 30 years, death was relatively easy to define. People were considered dead when a heartbeat could no longer be detected and when breathing ceased. Now, with the technological advancements made in medicine, especially emergency medicine, some patients who give every indication of being dead can be resuscitated. Critically ill people, even those in comas, can now be kept alive for years with many of their bodily functions maintained by medical devices, including feeding tubes and respirators.

Thus death can be a very difficult concept to define.[2] Numerous professional associations and ad hoc interdisciplinary committees have struggled with this problem and have developed criteria by which to establish death. Some of these criteria have been adopted by state legislatures, although there is certainly no consensus definition of death that all states embrace.

Clinical determinants of death refer to measures of bodily functions. Often judged by a physician, who can then sign a legal document called a *medical death certificate,* these clinical criteria include the following:

1. Lack of heartbeat and breathing.
2. Lack of central nervous system function, including all reflex activity and environmental responsiveness. Often this can be confirmed by an **electroencephalograph** reading. If there is no brain wave activity after an initial measurement and a second measurement after 24 hours, the person is said to have undergone *brain death.*
3. The presence of **rigor mortis,** indicating that body tissues and organs are no longer functioning at the cellular level. This is sometimes referred to as *cellular death.*

The *legal determinants* used by government officials are established by state law and often adhere closely to the clinical determinants already listed. A person is not legally dead until a death certificate has been signed by a physician, **coroner,** or health department officer.

EUTHANASIA

There are two types of euthanasia for desperately ill people: they are either intentionally put to death **(direct [active] euthanasia)** or allowed to die without

---

electroencephalograph
An instrument that measures the electrical activity of the brain.

rigor mortis
Rigidity of the body that occurs after death.

coroner
An elected legal official empowered to pronounce death and to determine the official cause of a suspicious or violent death.

direct (active) euthanasia
The process of inducing death, often through the injection of lethal drugs.

being subjected to heroic lifesaving efforts **(indirect [passive] euthanasia).** Direct euthanasia usually involves the administration of large amounts of depressant drugs, which eventually causes all central nervous system functions to stop. Although direct euthanasia is commonly practiced on housepets and laboratory animals, it is illegal for humans in the United States, Canada, and other developed countries. However, in February 1992, the Netherlands became the first developed country to enact legislation that permits euthanasia under strict guidelines. See the Star Box below, which discusses physician-assisted suicide.

Indirect euthanasia is increasingly occurring in a number of hospitals, nursing homes, and medical centers. Physicians who withhold heroic lifesaving techniques or drug therapy treatments or who disconnect life support systems from terminally ill patients are practicing indirect euthanasia. Although some people still consider this form of euthanasia a type of murder, indirect euthanasia seems to be gaining legal and public acceptance for people with certain terminal illnesses—near-death cancer patients, brain-dead acci-

dent victims, and hopelessly ill newborn babies. Physicians' orders of *do not resuscitate* (DNR) and *comfort measures only* (CMO) are examples of passive euthanasia that are familiar to hospital personnel.

ADVANCE MEDICAL DIRECTIVES

Because some physicians and families find it difficult to support indirect euthanasia, many people are starting to use legal documents called *advance medical directives*.[3] One of these medical directives is the living will (see the Star Box on p. 451). This is a document that confirms a dying person's desire to be allowed to die peacefully and with a measure of dignity if a time should arise when there is little hope for recovery from a terminal illness or severe injury. Living will statutes exist in all 50 states and the District of Columbia. The living will requires that physicians or family members carry out a person's wishes to die naturally, without receiving life-sustaining treatments.[4] About 25% to 30% of U.S. citizens have signed living wills.[4]

A second important document that can assist ter-

Physician-Assisted Suicide

Physician-assisted suicide has been at the center of two recent national news stories. The first focuses on Dr. Jack Kevorkian, who has helped nearly 50 people commit suicide since 1990.[5] In February 1998, Dr. Kevorkian had just delivered the body of a 52-year-old cancer patient to an Oakland County hospital. According to the medical examiner's office, the patient had died from a lethal injection.[6]

Kevorkian's supporters say he is fighting for our right not to suffer and our freedom to die as we see fit. Since Kevorkian attended his first suicide in June 1990, he has been called a freedom fighter, a pioneer in the right to die.

His opponents argue that we already have a right not to suffer, by refusing medical treatment, and a right to die, by committing suicide. Further, they contend that many of Kevorkian's patients have not been terminally ill. A few have been severely depressed, and autopsies showed that some had no detectable ailment.[5] Do you believe physicians should be allowed to assist people who wish to die?

The U.S. Supreme Court gave its opinion on this issue in the summer of 1997. In a unanimous decision, the court said that dying people have no fundamental right to physician-assisted suicide.[7] This ruling in effect reinstated two state laws that banned the practice. In their written opinions, the justices emphasized the need for

effective palliative care (pain management) for terminally ill patients. However, for now it appears that states will remain battlegrounds where physician-assisted suicide will continue to be debated.

The Living Will

The living will is a legally binding document in all 50 states and the District of Columbia. This document allows individuals to express their wishes concerning dying with dignity. When such a document has been drawn, families and physicians are better able to deal with the wishes of people who are near death from conditions from which there is no reasonable expectation of recovery. The following is a sample living will for the state of Florida. However, people should use a living will that is specific for the state in which they live. For additional information and materials, contact the Choice in Dying organization by using the toll-free number 1 (800) 989-WILL or by visiting the Choice in Dying website, at http://www.choices.org. For a small fee, you can download state-specific packages.

INSTRUCTIONS	**Florida Living Will**
PRINT THE DATE PRINT YOUR NAME	Declaration made this _____ day of _____, 19 ____ I, _____, willfully and voluntarily make known my desire that my dying not be artificially prolonged under the circumstances set forth below, and I do hereby declare: If at any time I have a terminal condition and if my attending or treating physician and another consulting physician have determined that there is no medical probability of my recovery from such condition, I direct that life-prolonging procedures be withheld and withdrawn when the application of such procedures would serve only to prolong artificially the process of dying, and that I be permitted to die naturally with only the administration of medication or the performance of any medical procedure deemed necessary to provide me with comfort care or to alleviate pain. It is my intention that this declaration be honored by my family and physician as the final expression of my legal right to refuse medical or surgical treatment and to allow the consequences for such refusal. In the event that I have been determined to be unable to provide express and informed consent regarding the withholding, withdrawal, or continuation of life-prolonging procedures, I wish to designate, as my surrogate to carry out the provisions of this declaration:
PRINT THE NAME, HOME ADDRESS, AND TELEPHONE NUMBER OF YOUR SURROGATE	Name: _____ Address: _____ _____ Zip Code: _____ Phone: _____
© 1996 CHOICE IN DYING, INC.	

	I wish to designate the following person as my alternate surrogate, to carry out the provisions of this declaration should my surrogate be unwilling or unable to act on my behalf:
PRINT NAME, HOME ADDRESS, AND TELEPHONE NUMBER OF YOUR ALTERNATE SURROGATE	Name: _____ Address: _____ _____ Zip Code: _____ Phone: _____
ADD PERSONAL INSTRUCTIONS (IF ANY)	Additional instructions (optional):
SIGN THE DOCUMENT	I understand the full importance of this declaration, and I am emotionally and mentally competent to make this declaration. Signed: _____

WITNESSING
PROCEDURE
	Witness 1:
	   Signed: _____
	   Address: _____

TWO WITNESSES
MUST SIGN AND
PRINT THEIR
ADDRESSES
	Witness 2:
	   Signed: _____
	   Address: _____

© 1996 CHOICE IN DYING, INC.	Courtesy of Choice In Dying, Inc. 6/96 1036 80th Street, NW Washington, DC 20007 800-989-9455 PAGE 2

---

minally ill or incapacitated patients is the **medical power of attorney for health care** document. This legal document authorizes another person to make specific health care decisions about treatment and care under specified circumstances, most commonly when patients are in long-term vegetative states and cannot communicate their medical wishes. This document helps inform hospitals and physicians which person will help make the critical medical decisions. Usually this person is a loving relative. It is recommended that people complete both a living will and a medical power of attorney for health care document.

indirect (passive) euthanasia
The process of allowing a person to die by disconnecting life support systems or withholding lifesaving techniques.

medical power of attorney for health care
A legal document that designates who will make health care decisions for people unable to do so for themselves.

EMOTIONAL STAGES OF DYING

A process of self-adjustment has been observed in people who have a terminal illness. The stages in this process have helped form the basis for the modern movement of death education. An awareness of these stages may help you understand how people adjust to other important losses in their lives.

Perhaps the most widely recognized name in the area of death education is Dr. Elisabeth Kübler-Ross. As a psychiatrist working closely with terminally ill patients at the University of Chicago's Billings Hospital, Kübler-Ross was able to observe the emotional reactions of dying people. In her classic book *On Death and Dying*, Kübler-Ross summarized the psychological stages that dying people often experience.[8]

- *Denial.* This is the stage of disbelief. Patients refuse to believe that they actually will die. Denial can serve as a temporary defense mechanism and can allow patients the time to accept their prognosis on their own terms.
- *Anger.* A common emotional reaction after denial is anger. Patients can feel as if they have been cheated. By expressing anger, patients are able to vent some of their fears, jealousies, anxieties, and frustrations. Patients often direct their anger at relatives, physicians and nurses, religious symbols, and normally healthy people.
- *Bargaining.* Terminally ill people follow the anger stage with a stage characterized by bargaining. Patients who desperately want to avoid their inevitable deaths attempt to strike bargains—often with God or a church leader. Some people undergo religious conversions. The goal is to buy time by promising to repent for past sins, to restructure and rededicate their lives, or to make a large financial contribution to a religious cause.
- *Depression.* When patients realize that, at best, bargaining can only postpone their fate, they may begin an unpredictable period of depression. In a sense, terminally ill people are grieving for their own anticipated death. They may become quite withdrawn and refuse to visit with close relatives and friends. Prolonged periods of silence or crying are normal components of this stage and should not be discouraged.
- *Acceptance.* During the acceptance stage, patients fully realize that they are going to die. Acceptance ensures a relative sense of peace for most dying people. Anger, resentment, and depression are usually gone. Kübler-Ross describes this stage as one without much feeling. Patients feel neither happy nor sad. Many are calm and introspective

and prefer to be left either alone or with a few close relatives or friends.

One or two additional points should be made about the psychological stages of dying. Just as each person's life is totally unique, so is each person's death. Unfolding deaths vary as much as do unfolding lives. Some people move through Kübler-Ross's stages of dying very predictably, but others do not. It is not uncommon for some dying people to avoid one or more of these stages entirely.

The second important point to be made about Kübler-Ross's stages of dying is that the family members or friends of dying people often pass through similar stages as they observe their loved ones dying. When informed that a close friend or relative is dying, many people will also experience varying degrees of denial, anger, bargaining, depression, and acceptance. Because of this, as caring people we need to recognize that the emotional needs of the living must be fulfilled in ways that do not differ appreciably from those of the dying.[9]

NEAR-DEATH EXPERIENCES

As Bob lay on the gymnasium floor in apparent cardiac arrest, he watched from above as the team trainer and coaches performed CPR. After observing his own attempted resuscitation, he began walking in the direction of his uncle's voice. The last time he had heard his uncle's voice was a few days before his death 4 years earlier. Suddenly, his uncle instructed Bob to stop and turn back because Bob was not yet ready to join him. Over 24 hours later, Bob regained consciousness in the cardiac intensive care unit of The Ohio State University Hospital.

Death brings an end to our physical existence. Perhaps this is the ultimate connection between death and our physical dimension of health. Many people believe that, in a positive sense, death brings with it a sense of relief and comfort—two qualities that may be most needed when one is dying. The classic work of Raymond Moody,[10] who examined reports of people who had near-death experiences, suggests that we may have less to fear about dying than we have generally thought.

In a comprehensive study of more than 100 people who had near-death experiences, Kenneth Ring[11] reported that these people shared a core experience. This experience was composed of some or all of the following stages:

1. A sense of well-being and peace
2. An out-of-body experience in which the dying person floats above his or her body and is able to witness the activities that are occurring

3. A movement into extreme blackness or darkness
4. A shaft of intense light that generally leads upward or lies in the distance
5. A decision to enter into the light

Central to this experience is the need to make a decision to move toward death or to return to the body that has been temporarily vacated.

Experts are not in agreement as to whether near-death experiences are truly associated with death or more closely associated with the depersonalization that is experienced by some people during particularly frightening situations. In a scientific sense, near-death experiences are impossible to prove. Science can neither verify nor deny the existence of out-of-body experiences.[1]

Regardless, for those who have had near-death experiences, simply knowing that death might not be such an unpleasant experience appears to be comforting. Most seem to have formed a new orientation toward living.[1, 12]

INTERACTING WITH DYING PEOPLE

Facing the impending death of a friend, relative, or loved one is a difficult experience. If you have yet to go through this situation, be assured that, as you grow older, your opportunities will increase. This is part of the reality of living.

Most counselors, physicians, nurses, and ministers who spend time with terminally ill people suggest that you display one quality when interacting with dying people: honesty. Just the thought of talking with a dying person may make you feel uncomfortable. (Most of us have had no training in this sort of thing.) Sometimes, to make ourselves feel less anxious or depressed, we may tend to deny that the person we are with is dying. Our words and nonverbal behavior indicate that we prefer not to face the truth. Our words become stilted as we gloss over the facts and merely attempt to cheer up both our dying friend and ourselves. This behavior is rarely beneficial or supportive—for either party.

As much as possible, we should attempt to be genuine and honest. We should not try to avoid crying if we feel the need to cry. At the same time, we can provide emotional support for dying people by allowing them to express their feelings openly. We should resist the temptation of trying to pull someone out of the denial, anger, or depression. We should not feel obliged to talk constantly and to fill long pauses with idle talk. Sometimes nonverbal communication, including touching, may be much more appreciated than mere talk. Since our interactions with dying people help fulfill our needs, we too should express our emotions and concerns as openly as possible.

TALKING WITH CHILDREN ABOUT DEATH

Because most children are curious about everything, it is not surprising that they are also fascinated about death. From very young ages, children are exposed to death through mass media (cartoons, pictures in newspapers and magazines, and news reports), adult conversations ("Aunt Emily died today," "Uncle George is terminally ill"), and their discoveries (a dead bird, a crushed bug, a dead flower). The manner in which children learn about death will have an important effect on their ability to recognize and accept their own mortality and to cope with the deaths of others.

Psychologists encourage parents and older friends to avoid shielding children from or misleading children about the reality of death. Young children need to realize that death is not temporary and it is not like sleeping. Parents should make certain they understand children's questions about death before they give an answer. Most children want simple, direct answers to their questions, not long, detailed dissertations, which often confuse the issues. For example, when a 4-year-old asks her father, "Why is Tommy's dog dead?" an appropriate answer might be, "Because he got very, very sick and his heart stopped beating." Getting involved in a lengthy discussion about "doggy heaven" or the causes of specific canine diseases may not be necessary or appropriate.

Parents should answer questions when they arise and always respond with openness and honesty. In this way, young children can learn that death is a real part of life and that sad feelings are a normal part of accepting the death of a loved one.

DEATH OF A CHILD

Adults face not only the death of their parents and friends but perhaps also the death of a child. Whether because of sudden infant death syndrome (SIDS), chronic illness, accident, or suicide, children die and adults are forced to grieve the loss of someone who was "too young to die" (see "Focus on . . . Death of an Infant or Unborn Child" at the end of this chapter).

Coping with the death of a child presents adults with a difficult period of adjustment, particularly

Children need support from adults during times of grief.

when the death was unexpected. Experts agree that grieving adults, particularly the parents, should express their grief fully and proceed cautiously on their return to normal routines. Many pitfalls can be avoided. Adults who are grieving for dead children should do the following:

- *Avoid trying to cope by using alcohol or drugs.*
- *Make no important life changes.* Moving to a different home, relocating, or changing jobs usually doesn't help parents deal any better with the grief they are experiencing.
- *Share their feelings with others.* Grieving adults should share their feelings particularly with other adults who have experienced a similar loss. Group support is available in many communities.
- *Avoid trying to erase the death.* Giving away clothing and possessions that belonged to the child cannot erase the memories the adult has of the child.
- *Give themselves the time and space to grieve.* On the anniversary of the child's death or on the child's birthday, grievers should give themselves special time just for grieving.
- *Don't attempt to replace the child.* Do not quickly have another child or use the deceased child's name for another child.

For most adults, grief over the death of a child will require an extended period. Eventually, however, life can return to normal.

HOSPICE CARE FOR THE TERMINALLY ILL

The thought of dying in a hospital ward, with spotless floors, pay television, and strict visiting hours, leaves many people with a cold feeling. Perhaps this thought alone has helped encourage the concept of **hospice care.** Hospice care provides an alternative approach to dying for terminally ill patients and their families. The goal of hospice care is to maximize the quality of life for dying people and their family members. Popularized in England during the 1960s, yet derived from a concept developed during the Middle Ages (where *hospitable lodges* took care of weary travelers), the hospice helps people die comfortably and with dignity by using one or more of the following strategies:

- *Pain control.* Dying people are not usually treated for their terminal disease; they are provided with appropriate drugs to keep them free from pain, alert, and in control of their faculties. Drug dependence is of little concern, and patients can receive pain medication when they feel they need it.
- *Family involvement.* Family members and friends are trained and encouraged to interact with the dying person and with each other. Family members often care for the dying person at home. If the hospice arrangement includes a hospice ward in a hospital or a separate building (also called a hospice), the family members have no restrictions on visitation.
- *Multidisciplinary approach.* The hospice concept promotes a team approach.[13] Specially trained physicians, nurses, social workers, counselors, and volunteers work with the patient and family to fulfill important needs. The needs of the family receive nearly the same priority as those of the patient.
- *Patient decisions.* Contrary to most hospital approaches, hospice programs encourage patients to make their own decisions. The patient decides when to eat, sleep, go for a walk, and just be alone. By maintaining a personal schedule, the patient is more apt to feel in control of his or her life, even as that life is slipping away.

Another way in which the hospice differs from the hospital approach concerns the care given to the survivors. Even after the death of the patient, the family receives a significant amount of follow-up counseling. Helping families with their grief is an important role for the hospice team.

The number of hospices in the United States has climbed quickly to well over 2000.[2] People seem to be convinced that the hospice system does work effectively. Part of this approval may be the cost factor. The cost of caring for a dying person in a hospice is usually less than the cost of full (inpatient) services provided by a hospital. Although insurance companies are delighted to see the lower cost for hospice care, many are still uncertain as to how to define hospice care. Thus not all insurance companies are fully reimbursing patients for their hospice care. Before discussing the possibility of hospice care for members of your family, you should consider the extent of hospice coverage in your health insurance policy.

GRIEF AND THE RESOLUTION OF GRIEF

The emotional feelings that people experience after the death of a friend or relative are collectively called *grief. Mourning* is the process of experiencing these emotional feelings in a culturally defined manner. See the Star Box at right for more information about the grieving process. The expression of grief is seen as a valuable process that gradually permits people to detach themselves from the deceased. Expressing grief, then, is a sign of good health.

Although people experience grief in remarkably different ways, most people have some of the following sensations and emotions:

- *Physical discomfort.* Shortly after the death of a loved one, grieving people display a rather similar pattern of physical discomfort. This discomfort is characterized by "sensations of somatic distress occurring in waves lasting from 20 minutes to an hour at a time, a feeling of tightness in the throat, choking with shortness of breath, need for sighing, and an empty feeling in the abdomen, lack of muscular power, and an intense subjective distress described as a tension or mental pain. The patient soon learns that these waves of discomfort can be precipitated by visits, by mentioning the deceased, and by receiving sympathy."[14]
- *Sense of numbness.* Grieving people may feel as if they are numb or in a state of shock. They may deny the death of their loved one.
- *Feelings of detachment from others.* Grieving people see other people as being distant from them, per-

The Grieving Process

The grieving process consists of four phases, each of which is variable in length and unique in form to the individual. These phases are composed of the following:

1. *Internalization of the deceased person's image.* By forming an idealized mental picture of the dead person, the grieving person is freed from dealing too quickly with the reality of the death.
2. *Intellectualization of the death.* Mental processing of the death and the events leading up to its occurrence move the grieving person to a clear understanding that death has occurred.
3. *Emotional reconciliation.* During this third and often delayed phase, the grieving person allows conflicting feelings and thoughts to be expressed and eventually reconciled with the reality of the death.
4. *Behavioral reconciliation.* Finally, the grieving person is able to comfortably return to a life in which the death has been fully reconciled. Old routines are reestablished and new patterns of living are adopted where necessary. The grieving person has largely recovered.

A mistake that might be made by the friends of a grieving person is encouraging a return to normal behavior too quickly. When friends urge the grieving person to return to work right away, make new friends, or become involved in time-consuming projects, they may be preventing necessary grieving from occurring. It is not easy or desirable to forget about the fact that a spouse, friend, or child has recently died.

haps because the others cannot feel the loss. A person in grief can feel very lonely. This is a common response.

- *Preoccupation with the image of the deceased.* The grieving person may not be able to complete daily tasks without constantly thinking about the deceased.
- *Guilt.* The survivor may be overwhelmed with guilt. Thoughts may center on how the deceased was neglected or ignored. Sensitive survivors feel guilt merely because they are still alive. Indeed, guilt is a common emotion.
- *Hostility.* Survivors may express feelings of loss and remorse through hostility, which they direct

hospice care (**hos** pis)
An approach to caring for terminally ill patients that maximizes the quality of life and allows death with dignity.

at other family members, physicians, lawyers, and others.

- *Disruption in daily schedule.* Grieving people often find it difficult to complete daily routines. They can suffer from an anxious type of depression. Seemingly easy tasks take a great deal of effort. Initiation of new activities and relationships can be difficult. Social interaction skills can be lost.
- *Delayed grief.* In some people, the typical pattern of grief can be delayed for weeks, months, and even years.

The grief process will continue until the bereaved person can establish new relationships, feel comfortable with others, and look back on the life of the deceased person with positive feelings (see the Health Action Guide below). Although the duration of the grief resolution process will vary with the emotional attachments one has to a deceased person, grief usually lasts from a few months to a year. Professional help should be sought when grieving is characterized by unresolved guilt, extreme hostility, physical illness, significant depression, and a lack of other meaningful relationships. Trained counselors, physicians, and hospice workers can all play significant roles in helping people through grief.

RITUALS OF DEATH

Our society has established a number of rituals associated with death that help the survivors accept the reality of death, ease the pain associated with the grief process, and provide a safe disposal of the body (see the Learning from All Cultures box on p. 457). Our rituals give us the chance to formalize our good-byes to a person and to receive emotional support and strength from family members and friends. In recent years, more of our rituals seem to be celebrating the life of the deceased. In doing this, our rituals also reaffirm the value of our own lives.

Most of our funeral rituals take place in funeral homes, churches, and cemeteries. *Funeral homes* (or *mortuaries*) are business establishments that provide a variety of services to the families of dead people. The services are carried out by funeral directors, who are licensed by the state in which they operate. Most funeral directors are responsible for preparing the bodies for viewing, filing death certificates, preparing obituary notices, establishing calling hours, assisting in the preparation and details of the funeral, casket selection, transportation to and from the cemetery, and family counseling. Although licensing procedures vary from state to state, most new funeral directors must complete 1 year of college, 1 year of mortuary school, and 1 year of internship with a funeral home before taking a state licensing examination.

Full Funeral Services

An ethical funeral director will attempt to follow the wishes of the deceased's family and provide only the services requested by the family. Most families want traditional, **full funeral services.** Three signifi-

HEALTH
Action Guide ----►

Helping the Bereaved

Leming and Dickinson[1] point out that the peak time of grief begins in the week after a loved one's funeral. Realizing that there is no one guaranteed formula for helping the bereaved, friends and caregivers can help by performing some or all of the following:

- Make few demands on the bereaved; allow him or her to grieve.
- Help with the household tasks.
- Recognize that the bereaved person may vent anguish and anger and that some of it may be directed at you.
- Recognize that the bereaved person has painful and difficult tasks to complete; mourning cannot be rushed or avoided.
- Do not be afraid to talk about the deceased person; this lets the bereaved know that you care for the deceased.
- Express your own genuine feelings of sadness, but avoid pity. Speak from the heart.
- Reassure bereaved people that the intensity of their emotions is very natural.
- Advise the bereaved to get additional help if you suspect continuing severe emotional or physical distress.
- Keep in regular contact with the bereaved; let him or her know you continue to care about them.

◄------

LEARNING *from* ALL CULTURES

Funeral and Burial Rituals

Funeral rituals typically reflect people's religious beliefs and practices. In North America, most people are buried according to Protestant traditions. People pay their respects to the deceased, a minister conducts a service, and in 75% of the cases, the body is buried after a graveside ceremony.

The rest of the human population, however, bury their dead in a variety of ways. The Parsis, a group of people in India, follow an ancient religion called Zoroastrianism. They perform their burial rituals at the seven Towers of Silence, outside of Bombay. The corpse is brought to one of the towers by six individuals dressed in white. The body is left on a tower for vultures to devour, leaving only the skeleton. A few days later the bones are put into a pit. The Parsis believe this method keeps the air, soil, and water from becoming contaminated.[17]

Hindus believe that the physical body must be gone

for the soul to continue on to reincarnation. Their ritual consists of washing the dead body and dressing it in a shroud adorned with flowers. The body is carried to a funeral pyre, and the closest male relative lights the fire, walks around the burning body three times, and recites Hindu verses.[17]

Buddhists, who live mostly in China, Japan, Sri Lanka, Myanmar, Vietnam, and Cambodia, also cremate their dead. They believe cremation was favored by Buddha.

Unlike Hindus and Buddhists, Muslims do not believe in cremation. Their ritual is to wash the dead body, dress it in three pieces of white cloth, and put it in a wooden coffin. Burial is within 24 hours of death, since there is no embalming unless dictated by law. The body is taken out of the coffin and buried with the head turned toward Mecca.[17]

Most people do not like to think about their own death or plan for it, but there are some individuals who plan their funerals to to the last detail. What would be your wishes concerning your own funeral and burial?

---

cant components of the full funeral services are as follows.

Embalming

Embalming is the process of using formaldehyde-based fluids to replace the blood components. Embalming helps preserve the body and return it to a natural look. Embalming permits friends and family members to view the body without being subjected to the odors associated with tissue decomposition. Embalming is often an optional procedure, except when death results from specific communicable diseases or when body *disposition* (disposal) is delayed.

Calling hours

Sometimes called a *wake,* this is an established time when friends and family members can gather in a room to share their emotions and common experiences about the dead person. Generally in the same room, the body will be in a casket, with the lid open or closed. Open caskets assist some people to confirm that death truly did occur. Some families prefer not to have any calling hours, sometimes called *visiting hours.*

Funeral service

Funeral services vary according to religious preference and the emotional needs of the survivors.

Although some services are held in a church, most funeral services today take place in a funeral home, where a special room might serve as a chapel. Some services are held at the graveside. Families may also choose to have a simple *memorial service* within a few days after the funeral. Completing the Personal Assessment on p. 458 will help you think about what kind of funeral arrangements you would prefer for yourself.

Disposition of the Body

Bodies are disposed of in one of four ways. *Ground burial* is the most common method. About 75% of all bodies are placed in ground burial. The casket is almost always placed in a metal or concrete vault before being buried. The vault serves to further protect the body (a need only of the survivors) and to prevent collapse of ground because of the decaying of caskets. Use of a vault is required by most cemeteries.

> **full funeral services**
> All of the professional services provided by funeral directors.

PERSONAL ASSESSMENT

Planning Your Funeral

In line with this chapter's positive theme of the value of personal death awareness, here is a funeral service assessment that we frequently give to our health classes.

This inventory can help you assess your reactions and thoughts about the funeral arrangements you would prefer for yourself.

After answering each of the following questions, you might wish to discuss your responses with a friend or close relative.

1. Have you ever considered how you would like your body to be handled after your death?
   _____ Yes   _____ No

2. Have you already made funeral prearrangements for yourself?
   _____ Yes   _____ No

3. Have you considered a specific funeral home or mortuary to handle your arrangements?
   _____ Yes   _____ No

4. If you were to die today, which of the following would you prefer?
   _____ Embalming   _____ Ground burial
   _____ Cremation   _____ Entombment
   _____ Donation to medical science

5. If you prefer to be cremated, what would you want done with your ashes?
   _____ Buried   _____ Entombed
   _____ Scattered
   _____ Other; please specify _____

6. If your funeral plans involve a casket, which of the following ones would you prefer?
   _____ Plywood (cloth covered)
   _____ Hardwood (oak, cherry, mahogany, maple, etc.)
   _____ Steel (sealer or nonsealer type)
   _____ Stainless steel
   _____ Copper or bronze
   _____ Other; please specify _____

7. How important would a funeral service be for you?
   _____ Very important
   _____ Somewhat important
   _____ Somewhat unimportant
   _____ Very unimportant
   _____ No opinion

8. What kind of funeral service would you want for yourself?
   _____ No service at all
   _____ Visitation (calling hours) the day before the funeral service; funeral held at church or funeral home

   _____ Graveside service only (no visitation)
   _____ Memorial service (after body disposition)
   _____ Other; please specify _____

9. How many people would you want to attend your funeral service or memorial service?
   _____ I do not want a funeral or memorial service
   _____ 1-10 people
   _____ 11-25 people
   _____ 26-50 people
   _____ Over 51 people
   _____ I do not care how many people attend

10. What format would you prefer at your funeral service or memorial service? Select any of the following that you would like.

	Yes	No
Religious music	_____	_____
Nonreligious music	_____	_____
Clergy present	_____	_____
Flower arrangements	_____	_____
Family member eulogy	_____	_____
Eulogy by friend(s)	_____	_____
Open casket	_____	_____
Religious format	_____	_____
Other; please specify		

11. Using today's prices, how much would you expect to pay for your total funeral arrangements, including cemetery expenses (if applicable)?
    _____ Less than $4500
    _____ Between $4501 and $6000
    _____ Between $6001 and $7500
    _____ Between $7501 and $9000
    _____ Above $9000

To Carry This Further . . .
Which items had you not thought about before? Were you surprised at the arrangements you selected? Will you share your responses with anyone else? If so, whom?

Health on the Web

LEARNING ACTIVITIES

Activity 1

You have read in this chapter about two types of euthanasia, active and passive, for desperately ill people. Some people think that passive euthanasia constitutes murder; however, this form of euthanasia seems to be gaining legal and public acceptance. How do you feel about this issue? Go to the Death and Dying website at http://www.death-dying.com and select "Surveys." Then scroll down and select "Euthanasia." Read the section on "Rights of Euthanasia" and then complete the list of questions on your beliefs about this controversial practice.

Activity 2

The emotional feelings that people experience after the death of a friend or relative are collectively called *grief.* The expression of grief is a valuable process that gradually permits people to detach themselves from the deceased. You can find more information about grieving at GriefNet, at http://rivendell.org, spon-sored by Rivendell Resources. The site provides a collection of resources valuable to those who are experiencing loss and grief. Select from the resources available and reflect back to a time when you have gone through the grieving process.

Activity 3

The living will is a legally binding document in all 50 states and the District of Columbia. This document allows people to express their wishes about dying with dignity. When such a document has been drawn, families and physicians are better able to accommodate the wishes of people who are near death from conditions from which there is no reasonable expectation of recovery. Go the website at http://wwwl.mhv.net/~teahan/willfaq.htm#1, which offers over 40 questions and answers related to wills. Take a few minutes to read the questions that interest you and about which you know little. What did you learn about living wills?

A second type of disposition is *entombment.* Entombment refers to nonground burial, most often in structures called **mausoleums.** A mausoleum has a series of shelves where caskets can be sealed in vault-like areas called *niches.* Entombment can also occur in the basements of buildings, especially in old, large churches. The bodies of famous church leaders are sometimes entombed in vaultlike spaces called **crypts.**

Cremation is a third type of body disposition. In the United States, 21% of all bodies are cremated.[15] This practice is increasing. Generally both the body and casket (or cardboard cremation box) are incinerated so that only the bone ash from the body remains. The body of an average adult produces about 5 to 7 pounds of bone ash. These ashes can then be placed in containers called *urns,* and then buried, entombed, or scattered, if permitted by state law. The cost of cremation (from $200 to $500) is much less than ground burial. Some families choose to cremate after having full funeral services.[16]

A fourth method of body disposition is *anatomical donation.* Separate organs (such as corneal tissue, kidneys, or the heart) can be donated to a medical school, research facility, or organ donor network. Certain states permit people to indicate on their driver's licenses that they wish to donate their organs. However, family consent (by next of kin) is also required at the time of death for organ or tissue donation to occur. Recently, hospitals have been required by federal law to inform the family of a deceased person about organ donation at the time of his or her death. The need for donor organs is far greater than the current supply. For some, the decision to donate body tissue and organs is rewarding and comforting. Organ donors understand that their small sacrifice can help give life or improve the quality of life for another person. In this sense, their death can mean life for others. To become an organ donor, you must fill out a uniform organ donor card like the one in Figure 18-1.

Some people choose to donate their entire body to medical science. Often this is done through prior arrangements with medical schools. Bodies still require embalming. After they are studied, the remains are often cremated and returned to the family, if requested.

mausoleum (moz oh **lee** um)
An above-ground structure, which frequently resembles a small stone house, into which caskets can be placed for disposition.

crypts
Burial locations generally underneath churches.

UNIFORM DONOR CARD

of _____
            (print or type name of donor)
In the hope that I may help others, I hereby make this anatomical gift, if medically acceptable, to take effect upon my death. The words and marks below indicate my wishes:
I give: (a) _____ any needed organs or parts
        (b) _____ only the following organs or parts

        _____
            (specify the organ(s), tissue(s), or part(s)
for the purposes of transplantation, therapy, medical research or education;
        (c) _____ my body for anatomical study if needed.

Limitations or special wishes, if any: _____

Signed by the donor and the following two witnesses in the presence of each other:

_____   _____
Signature of Donor   Date of Birth of Donor

_____   _____
Date Signed   City and State

_____   _____
Witness   Witness

This is a legal document under the Anatomical Gift Act or similar laws.
☐ Yes, I have discussed my wishes with my family.
For further information consult your physician or

THE NATIONAL KIDNEY FOUNDATION
30 East 33rd Street   New York, NY 10016

08-21

Figure 18-1   Signing a uniform organ donor card allows you to donate your organs to a research facility, medical school, or organ donor network.

Costs

The full funeral services offered by a funeral home average from $2000 to $2500, and other expenses must be added to this price. Casket prices vary significantly, with the average cost between $1500 and $2500. If the family chooses an especially fancy casket, then the costs could spiral up to $10,000 or more. Costs that extend beyond these expenses include (should one choose them) those shown in the Star Box at right. When all of the expenses associated with a typical funeral are added up, the average cost is between $5500 and $7000.

Regardless of the rituals you select for the handling of your body (or the body of someone in your care), most educators are encouraging people to prearrange their plans. Before you die, you can save your survivors a lot of misery by putting your wishes in writing. *Funeral prearrangements* relieve the survivors of many of the details that must be handled at the time of your death. You can gather much of the information for your obituary notice and your wishes for the disposition of your body. Prearrangements can be made with a funeral director, family member, or attorney. Many individuals also prepay the costs of their funeral. By making arrangements in advance of need, you can enhance your own peace of mind. Currently about 30% to 40% of funerals are preplanned or prepaid or both. Interestingly, in the 1960s, nearly all funerals were planned by relatives at the time of a person's death.

PERSONAL PREPARATION FOR DEATH

We hope that this chapter helps you discover some new perspectives about death and develop your own personal death awareness. Remember that the ultimate goal of death education is a positive one—to help you best use and enjoy your life. Becoming aware of the reality of your own mortality is a step in the right direction. Reading about the process of dying, grief resolution, and the rituals surrounding death can also help you imagine that someday you too will die.

There are some additional ways in which you can prepare for the reality of your own death. Preparing a will, purchasing a life insurance policy, making funeral prearrangements, preparing a living will, and considering an anatomical or organ donation are measures that help you prepare for your own death (see the Health Action Guide on p. 461). At the appropriate time, you might also wish to talk with family and friends about your own death. You may discover that an upbeat, positive discussion about death can help relieve some of your apprehensions and those of others around you.

Another suggestion to help you emotionally prepare for your own death is to prepare an *obituary*

Estimated Funeral Costs	
Cemetery lot	$400-$1200
Opening and closing of grave	$300-$800
Vault	$350-$1000
Mausoleum space	$1500-$5000
Honorarium for minister	$75-$100
Organist and vocalists	$50-$75 each
Flowers over casket	$100+
Grave marker	$500-$1500+
Beautician services	$75+

HEALTH Action Guide

Organ Donation

Making an organ donation is one of the most compassionate, responsible acts a person can do. Only a few simple steps are required:

1. You must complete a uniform donor card. Obtain a card from a physician, a local hospital, or the nearest regional transplant or organ bank.
2. Print or type your name on the card.
3. Indicate which organs you wish to donate. You may also indicate your desire to donate all organs and tissues.
4. Sign your name in the presence of two witnesses, preferably your next of kin.
5. Fill in any additional information (for example, date of birth, city and state in which the card is completed, and date the card is signed).
6. Tell others about your decision to donate. Some donor cards have detachable portions to give to your family.
7. Always carry your card with you.
8. If you have any questions, you can call the United Network for Organ Sharing (UNOS) at (800) 24-DONOR, or call (613) 727-1380 in Canada.

the current direction your life seems to be taking. Are you doing the kinds of activities for which you want to be known? If so, great! If not, perhaps you will want to consider why your current direction does not reflect how you would like to be remembered. Should you make some changes to restructure your life's agenda in a more personally meaningful fashion?

Another suggestion to help make you aware of your own eventual death is to write your own **epitaph.** Before doing this, you might want to visit a cemetery. (Unfortunately, most of us visit cemeteries only when we are forced to.) Reading the epitaphs of others may help you develop your own epitaph.

Further awareness of your own death might come from attempting to answer these questions in writing (since this pushes you beyond mere thinking): (1) If I had only one day to live, how would I spend it? (2) What one accomplishment would I like to make before I die? (3) Once I am dead, what two or three things will people miss most about me? By answering these questions and accomplishing a few of the tasks suggested in this section, you will have a good start on accepting your own death and the value of life itself.

eulogy
A composition or speech that praises someone; often delivered at a funeral or memorial service.

epitaph
An inscription on a grave marker or monument.

notice or **eulogy** for yourself. Include all the things you would like to have said about you and your life. Now compare your obituary notice and eulogy with

Summary

- Personal death awareness encourages you to live a meaningful life.
- Death denial tends to breed feelings of helplessness and vulnerability.
- Death is determined primarily by clinical and legal factors.
- Euthanasia can be undertaken with either direct or indirect measures.
- The most current advance medical directives are the living will and the medical power of attorney for health care. Both documents permit critically ill people (especially those who cannot communicate) to die with dignity.

- Denial, anger, bargaining, depression, and acceptance are the five classic psychological stages that dying people commonly experience, according to Kübler-Ross. Hospice care provides an alternative approach to dying for terminally ill people and their families.
- The expression of grief is a common experience that can be expected when a friend or relative dies. The grief process can vary in intensity and duration.
- Death in our society is associated with a number of rituals to help survivors cope with the loss of a loved one and to ensure proper disposal of the body.

Review Questions

1. How does the experience of dying today differ from that in the early 1900s?
2. Identify and explain the clinical and legal determinants of death and indicate who establishes each of them.
3. Explain the difference between direct and indirect euthanasia.
4. How does a living will differ from a medical power of attorney for health care document? Why are these advance medical directives becoming increasingly popular?
5. Identify the five psychological stages that dying people tend to experience. Explain each stage.
6. Identify and explain the four strategies that form the basis of hospice care. What are the advantages of hospice care for the patient and the family?
7. Explain what is meant by the term *grief*. Identify and explain the sensations and emotions most people have when they experience grief. When does the grieving process end? How can adults cope with the death of a child? How can we assist grieving people?
8. What purposes do the rituals of death serve? What are the significant components of the full funeral service? What are the four ways in which bodies are disposed?
9. What activities can we undertake to become better aware of our own mortality?

 ## Think About This . . .

- How were issues related to death handled in your family when you were growing up?
- Will hospice care be an option you might choose someday?
- Have you or any of your relatives prepared a living will or a medical power of attorney for health care document?
- At your death, would you want your organs or body tissue donated to help another person? Are there any organs you would prefer not to donate?
- If you found out you were going to die tomorrow, what would you do today?
- If it were determined that you were in a persistent vegetative state, would you want your life support to be disconnected?

References

1. Leming MR, Dickinson GE: *Understanding dying, death, and bereavement*, ed 3, Ft. Worth, TX, 1994, Holt, Rinehart & Winston.
2. Kastenbaum RJ: *Death, society, and human experience*, ed 6, Boston, 1998, Allyn and Bacon.
3. Baer K: Death and dying: the final chapter, *Harvard Health Letter* 20(4):1-3, 1995.
4. Choice in Dying, personal correspondence, Feb 10, 1998.
5. Betzold M. The selling of doctor death. *The New Republic* 1997 May 26:22.
6. Assisted suicide, *USA Today*, p. 3A, Feb 5, 1998.
7. Cooperman J: Community leaders respond to the U.S. Supreme Court decision, *Choices: The newsletter of Choice in Dying* 6(3):1-4, 1997.
8. Kübler-Ross E: *On death and dying*, reprint ed, New York, 1997, Collier Books.
9. Kübler-Ross E: *To live until we say goodbye*, reprint ed, Paramus, NJ, 1997, Prentice-Hall.
10. Moody RA: *Life after life*, New York, 1975, Bantam Books.
11. Ring K: *Life at death; a scientific investigation of the near-death experience*, New York, 1980, Coward, McCann & Geoghegan.
12. Kübler-Ross E: *The wheel of life: a memoir of living and dying*, Old Tappan, NJ, 1997, Scribner.
13. DeSpelder LA, Strickland AL: *The last dance: encouraging death and dying*, ed 4, Mountain View, CA, 1996, Mayfield.
14. Lindemann E: *Symptomology and management of acute grief*. In Fulton et al, editors: *Death and dying: challenge and change*, Reading, MA, 1978. Addison-Wesley.
15. Raether H: Deaths and cremations: 1995, 1996, and beyond, *The Director* (National Funeral Directors Association) 69(11):77-81, 1997.
16. Bowman J, (Licensed Funeral Director), personal correspondence, February 11, 1998.
17. Whalen WJ: How different religions pay their funeral respects. In Dickinson G, Leming M, Mermann M, editors: *Dying, death, and bereavement*, Guilford, CT, 1993, Dushkin Publishing.

Suggested Readings

Jowell BT, Schwisow D: *After he's gone: a guide for widowed and divorced women,* Secaucus, NJ, 1997, Birch Lane Press.

This is a useful guide for women who are facing difficult times after becoming widowed or divorced. Written by two women who have experienced these situations themselves, the book uses humor and practical advice to help women recover their balance after a spouse's death or a divorce. The book includes helpful worksheets, lists, and reminders.

Lundahl CR, Widdison HA: *The eternal journey: how near-death experiences illuminate our earthly lives,* New York, 1997, Warner Books.

This book tries to show life and death from the perspective of an eternal journey. Lundahl and Widdison draw on case studies of near-death experiences to help readers bridge the gap between life on earth and the afterlife. The book includes a good description of the scientific view of near-death experiences. It is written in a way that is easily understood by the general reader but also provocative for the academic reader.

Angel MD: *The orphaned adult: confronting the death of a parent,* Northvale, NJ, 1997, Jason Aronson.

Rabbi Marc Angel writes for the adult who has experienced (or will soon experience) the death of a parent. Although almost everyone will have to confront this event, a parent's death is rarely easy to cope with. Angel shows the reader how to handle a parent's imminent death and the grieving process that follows, and he helps the reader learn ultimately to accept the loss.

Loving C: *My son, my sorrow: a mother's plea to Dr. Kevorkian,* Carrollton, TX, 1998, New Horizon Press.

Carol Living's 27-year-old son begged her to help him die as he developed more and more serious complications from Lou Gehrig's disease. Confronting this dilemma, Loving turned to Dr. Kevorkian for assistance. This book illuminates one side of the debate about physician-assisted suicide.

 # AS WE GO TO PRESS . . .

- Even when they are convicted of unthinkable crimes, women are rarely put to death in America. The debate about executing women took center stage in national newscasts and talk shows during February 1998, when the state of Texas executed a woman for the first time since the Civil War era. Karla Faye Tucker, the so-called "pickax murderer," was executed for her part in the gruesome deaths of two people in the early 1980s. She became the first woman in America to be put to death since 1984, when North Carolina executed a triple murderer. Tucker became a celebrity of sorts during the final months of her life because of her attractive demeanor and her profession of having become a born-again Christian. Tucker was administered a lethal injection on the evening of February 3, after the U.S. Supreme Court and Texas Governor George W. Bush refused final appeals for a stay of execution.

- Two interesting (and to some people, amusing) postmortem options have become available to those who want to connect with the cosmos. The first is the naming of distant celestial stars for people who have died. For a designated fee, ranging from about $100 to $500, a person or his or her loved ones can purchase the rights to name a star. The extent to which this naming is a legally binding arrangement between the payee and the "owner" of the star is subject to debate. However, this process seems to give some measure of comfort to the living.

- The second new adventure in postmortem arrangements is the rocketing of ashes into outer space. For a fee approaching $5000, Celestis, Inc., of Houston, Texas, will launch a cremated person's remains into orbit. However, only a small portion of the person's ashes—enough to fill a lipstick-size vial—will make the voyage. The ashes will be sent with about 100 other vials in a single launch. The Celestis company (www.celestis.com or 1–800–ORBIT–11) believes that these ash vials will orbit the Earth for 18 months to 10 years, when they will vaporize on reentry into the atmosphere.

    Would you consider one of these two unusual options for yourself or a family member?

Death of an Infant or Unborn Child

Life is fragile at all stages but especially so during the prenatal and early formative years. Indeed, from conception through development, birth, infancy and childhood, humans require an amazing amount of parental care and nurturing. Few other organisms are so dependent on others for their safety and well-being during the early months of life. Thus parents and children are tied together by a physical and emotional bond like no other. When that bond is severed by the tragic death of a young child, the pain and anguish the parents feel can be too much to bear. Getting through such a traumatic experience can be one of life's toughest challenges.

Most pregnancies progress to full term and result in the birth of a healthy child. However, researchers now believe that about one third of pregnancies end in miscarriage. Since the development of accurate home-pregnancy tests, many women are finding out early in the first trimester that they are pregnant. Thus, rather than mistaking the miscarriage for a late heavy menstrual period, more women are now aware that their pregnancy has ended. Most then go through the grieving process discussed here. In addition, other complications occur in a small number of cases. These problems can sometimes cause termination of the pregnancy (miscarriage or elective abortion), death of the baby during birth, or death during infancy. Though most people know that such things can happen, many feel that such tragedies happen only to others. When faced with the death or potential loss of a child, parents often find their belief system shaken and their faith tested.[1]

The Mourning Process
The process of grieving is different for each family. There are no set rules for getting over the loss of a child. There is no right way to mourn and no time limit for the mourning process. The first days, months, and years may seem meaningless, and parents may find themselves living day to day with no real purpose or focus.[2]

Despite the pain each individual in the family feels, care must be taken to preserve family unity. Each person must realize that other family members may grieve in different ways. Wives and husbands may grieve differently, and this can cause strain in their marriage. If one parent seems quiet or preoccupied, the other should not mistake this behavior for a lack of emotion. Parents should also make sure that they do not ignore the feelings of other children in the family. Sometimes the mourning parents become wrapped up in their own grief and forget that the tragedy affects their other children as well. Siblings should be encouraged to discuss their feelings to help with their own grief and to reaffirm their importance within the family.[2]

The way a baby dies can affect the mourning process. Whether the child is lost before birth (miscarriage, abortion), during birth (stillbirth, trauma), or in infancy (sudden infant death syndrome [SIDS], accident, birth defect) can affect how the parents deal with the loss. It can also have an effect on how family and friends provide support for the parents.

Death of an Unborn Child
Miscarriage can be especially difficult to deal with for the woman involved. The baby has been lost within the mother's womb, and she may blame herself for the loss as a result. She may think that something she did (or did not do) has caused the miscarriage.[1,3] "One night just before I found out I was pregnant, I went out with friends and had a few beers," recalls Gabrielle, who had a miscarriage when she was 26.[4] "I didn't know I was pregnant. I was late with my period but didn't suspect I was pregnant until later. I can't help but wonder if the alcohol caused it (the miscarriage)." Consumption of alcohol or over-the-counter medications before a woman knows she is pregnant is a common cause of guilt after a miscarriage. An exact cause of a miscarriage may never be determined, and the woman needs to be reassured that she did not cause any abnormalities in the fetus.[1]

A miscarriage can be painful, embarrassing, and stressful for the woman. Physical symptoms may not occur when the baby dies but may be delayed for some time. Rosalinda became pregnant in the first month after she stopped taking her birth control pills. About 3 weeks into the pregnancy, "I found myself crying uncontrollably while driving home from work," she recalls. "Although I had no visible signs of miscarriage, I was sure something was wrong." Rosalinda had always been successful in other endeavors, but she started to fear that she would fail in her attempts to bring a baby into the world. "At 11 weeks my fears came true. We were on a much-needed vacation in Las Vegas. Two days of cramping turned into uncontrollable hemorrhaging." She and her husband wound up in the hotel lobby trying to get a cab to the hospital. "You can imagine my utter embarrassment as I'm holding a towel in front of me to hide the blood as my husband is haggling with the bellman to let us go to the front of the line."[5]

Sometimes parents find out about a potentially fatal or severely debilitating problem with the fetus before the child is born. In these situations the parents are faced with the choice of continuing the pregnancy or terminating it. Hearing such a diagnosis, taking in all available information, and reaching a decision can be a traumatic experience. Parents must weigh many factors when making this decision, including their spiritual beliefs, potential suffering of the baby (if the long-term prognosis is poor), effects on the family of having a child with special needs, and financial considerations. If a decision is made to terminate the pregnancy (or if a continued pregnancy may result in miscarriage or stillbirth), the couple must be prepared for the sadness and trauma of parting with their baby.[3]

Death during the Birthing Process

In some instances, the parents know beforehand that the baby has a poor chance of surviving through birth, so they have a chance to prepare for this occurrence. For others, however, the baby's death is totally unexpected. Parents who thought they would be bringing home a healthy baby end up dealing with the devastation of losing their child. "The worst part was returning home," recalls Marcus, whose wife delivered a stillborn child after complications during birth. "The nursery was all set up . . . that brought back all of the feelings we had initially experienced after the birth."[6]

In the past, babies with lethal birth defects were often quickly taken away from their mothers, but today many parents are being given the option of spending time holding and saying good-bye to their baby, and medical personnel are encouraged to accommodate the parents and support their wishes in this regard.[3]

Losing a Baby after It Is Born

Even after a baby is delivered, there are health risks. After her miscarriage, Gabrielle gave birth to a seemingly healthy daughter, only to lose her 5 months later. "She just stopped breathing," Gabrielle recalls. "We had all been asleep, and when we went in to check on her she wasn't moving or breathing. We tried to wake her . . . she wasn't face down or anything like that. The doctors had no reason for it. They said it was SIDS."

The loss of a second child was devastating for Gabrielle, and it nearly ruined her marriage. "We were both very tense. We thought about trying again, but we felt jinxed. We fought a lot in the weeks after it happened." Gabrielle and her husband received counseling and eventually began to realize that they were not at fault for their tragic losses. They now have a healthy 3-year-old daughter. "We got up the courage to try one more time, thank God," she says.[4]

Dealing with the Loss of a Baby

Support of family and friends is especially important when trying to recover from the death of a child. Friends and co-workers can help by acknowledging the death of the child and offering support.[2] Often people will not mention the baby because they feel that the parents will become upset by bringing up the subject, but not talking about the baby can cause pain for the parents.[2] Showing up in person (as opposed to just calling or sending a card) to offer support can also help.[7]

While the mother is still in the hospital, medical personnel should be made aware of what the mother has been through. Sometimes a mother who has lost her baby will remain in the maternity wing of the hospital. A discreet notice posted on the door of her room will alert personnel that the room's occupant has lost her child, thus preventing any unfortunate assumptions.[1]

Tactful language can also help prevent unpleasant feelings for the parents. If an unhealthy fetus were miscarried or had to be aborted, sometimes people would try to rationalize the loss for the parents by saying it was "nature's way" of preventing the birth of an imperfect child.[7] Such comments are not only insensitive, but they imply that the parents should be grateful that they lost the baby. Even seemingly innocent comments can cause pain in the wrong context. Rosalinda wondered why she had continued to gain weight for 2 months even though the doctor said the baby had probably died only 3 or 4 weeks into her pregnancy. " 'It's probably just pizza,' my husband said. The doctor laughed and agreed." Rosalinda felt that her husband's attempt to lighten the situation was "probably the most insensitive statement I've ever heard him make . . . my opinion of the doctor also dropped dramatically at that point."[5] She later underwent a D & C (dilation and curettage) but was asked to sign a form giving her permission for an abortion even though she had already miscarried. She was "deeply humiliated to have to sign this. Didn't they realize how much I had already been through?"

Often parents will want to hold on to the memory of the child. Such feelings are quite normal and do not mean that the parents are holding on to their grief or are neurotic.[2] Remembering the child can give a sense of meaning to parents' lives. Often parents will do something constructive to help them remember their baby and get over the death. Putting together a scrapbook, donating the baby's clothes and toys to charity, writing memoirs, or setting up a place for remembrance can help the family keep memories of the baby.[2,7,8]

Eventually the grief should lose its intensity. It may flare up again around "anniversaries" (the baby's due date or birthday, the day of the baby's death), but gradually things should become bearable. The family will be forever changed by the experience. The death of a child can cause the value system of the parents to change, and their spiritual beliefs may be shaken as well.[2] But if the parents receive support from medical staff, family, and friends, ultimately the devastation can be overcome. It is hoped that such tragedies, while terribly unfortunate, can make these families stronger and bring them closer together.

For Discussion . . .
What are the differences in dealing with losing a child before, during, or after it is born? If you were faced with the choice of giving birth to a child with severe birth defects or terminating the pregnancy, which would you choose? If you lost a baby, would you try again to have one?

References
1. Hitchcock Pappas DJ, McCoy MC: Grief counseling. In Kuller JA et al, editors: *Prenatal diagnosis and reproductive genetics,* St. Louis, 1995, Mosby.
2. Cole D: When a child dies, *Parents' Magazine,* p. 3 March 1994.
3. Salmon DK: Coping with miscarriage, *Parents' Magazine,* p. 5 May 1991.
4. Anonymous: Personal communication, April 1996.
5. Anonymous: Personal communication, March 1996.
6. Anonymous: Personal communication, Dec 1995.
7. Allison C: For Felicity, *Reader's Digest,* p. 199, Jan 1993.
8. Robb DB: Moving on, *Reader's Digest,* p. 223, Jan 1995.

Commonly Used Over–the–Counter Products

Pain Relievers

Product	Physiological Function*	Potential Side Effect	Product	Physiological Function	Potential Side Effect
Aspirin (only) Aspirin (with caffeine)	Analgesic (pain relief) Antipyretic (fever reduction) Antirheumatic (inflammation reduction) Anticoagulant (slowed clotting time)	Hypersensitivity Gastrointestinal disturbance Internal bleeding Ototoxicity (toxic action on the ear) Prothrombin depression Overdose potential Reye's syndrome	Acetaminophen (with caffeine) Acetaminophen (with aspirin and caffeine) Ibuprofen	Analgesic (pain relief) Antirheumatic (inflammation reduction)	Gastrointestinal disturbance Headache Nervousness Vision distortion Fluid retention Rash
Acetaminophen (only)	Analgesic (pain relief)	Liver damage	Naproxen	Nonsteroidal anti-inflammatory	Stomach irritation Drowsiness
Acetaminophen (with aspirin)	Antipyretic (fever reduction)	Gastric erosion Kidney failure Irregular heartbeat	Ketoprofen	Nonsteroidal anti-inflammatory	Stomach irritation Drowsiness

*Physiological functions for each form of a product are the same (e.g., for aspirin [only] and aspirin [with caffeine]).

Cold and Cough Products

Active Ingredient*†	Physiological Function	Potential Side Effect	Active Ingredient*†	Physiological Function	Potential Side Effect
Decongestant (sympathomimetic amine)			Cough suppressant		
Phenylephrine hydrochloride	Vasoconstriction, which decreases blood flow into nasal tissues, thus decreasing fluid loss	Nervousness, sweating	Dextromethorphan hydrobromide Codeine	Suppression of sensitivity of the brain's cough control center and reduced CNS activity, thus reducing coughing and facilitating sleep	Mild sedation
Antihistamine					
Chlorpheniramine maleate	Blockage of histamine's vasodilating effect on capillaries within nasal tissue, thus reducing fluid loss (runny nose)	Drowsiness, drying of the mouth	Alcohol 20% to 25% per unit volume	CNS depression	Reduction in inhibitions when taken in quantity
Analgesic					
Acetaminophen	Pain relief and fever reduction	Generally few side effects with the amounts found in cold and cough preparations—see p. A1 for additional information on side effects			

*Popular cold and cough medications generally contain an ingredient from each of the five categories listed.
†*Expectorants,* which stimulate respiratory tract secretions, and *bronchodilators,* which increase the diameter of air passages, have also been used in the formulations of cold and cough medications. Their roles are to some degree controversial and are currently under study.

Deodorant and Antiperspirant Products

Two avenues exist for controlling odor resulting from the action of microbes on the organic matter in the perspiration of the apocrine sweat glands.

Function/Product	Active Agents	Adverse Side Effects	Function/Product	Active Agents	Adverse Side Effects
Control or Mask Odor			**Reduce Release of Perspiration**		
Mild deodorant soaps	Hexachlorophene (0.75% or less) Triclocarban (TCC) Tribromosalicylanilide (TBS)	Swelling; blistering on exposure to sun	Antiperspirants	Aluminum chloride Aluminum chlorohydrate Aluminum sulfate	Allergic reactions Should not be used for excessive, offensive, or colored perspiration
Deodorant (toilet water, colognes, perfumes, deodorants)	Alcohol Essential oils Vitamin E	Allergic reactions			

Sun Tanning Products

Sun Protection Factors and Classifications
2	Dark tan for skin that tans easily; minimal protection from sunburn
4	Dark tan for normal skin; minimal to moderate protection from sunburn
6	Golden tan for normal skin; moderate protection from sunburn
8	Gradual tan for normal skin; extra protection from sunburn
15	Gradual tan for sun-sensitive skin; maximal protection from sunburn
25	Protection for sun-sensitive skin; ultraprotection from sunburn
30	Protection for sun-sensitive skin for prolonged exposure

Products with sun protection factors above 30 are available; however, more frequent application of SPF 30 products may be as effective.

Safe and Effective Sunscreens

Aminobenzoic acid

Cinoxate

Diethanolamine p-methoxycinnamate

Digalloyl trioleate

Dioxybenzone

Ethyl 4-bis (hydroxypropyl) aminobenzoate

2-Ethylhexyl 2-cyano-3,3 diphylacrylate

Ethylhexyl p-methoxycinnamate

2-Ethylhexyl salicylate

Glyceryl aminobenzoate

Homosalate

Lawsone with dihydroxyacetone

Menthyl anthranilate

Oxybenzone

Padimate A

Padimate O

2-Phenylbenzimidazole-5-sulfonic acid

Red petrolatum

Sulisobenzone

Titanium dioxide

Triethanolamine salicylate

Adverse Reactions to Excessive Sun Tanning

Skin cancer   Photosensitivity

Skin aging   Allergies

Dental Hygiene Products

Product	Recommendations for Selection or Use	Product	Recommendations for Selection or Use
Toothbrush	Round, soft bristles in four rows; use 3 to 4 minutes with a proven technique; replace brush every 2 to 3 months, weekly when ill	Dental irrigator	Device using a pressurized stream of water to "pick" food debris lodged between teeth; model with a self-contained pump is considered more effective than one using household water pressure
Disclosing solution	Use periodically to familiarize yourself with the locations in which plaque accumulates and to assess the effectiveness of your brushing and flossing technique; sequence: disclose-brush-inspect-brush-redisclose	Mouthwash	Freshens the breath; capable of effecting some plaque reduction only when used in combination with regular brushing and flossing; fluoridated dental rinses can contribute to the prevention of dental caries when used in combination with brushing and flossing
Dental floss	Waxed or unwaxed cotton fiber thread for use in removing food debris from areas not generally reached by brushing alone; pull thread through adjoining tooth surfaces, gently elevating gingival tissues		
		Antiplaque dental rinse	Solution whose effervescent action dislodges plaque from dental surfaces; vigorous swishing of the solution should be followed by regular brushing, then a second application of the anti-plaque rinse should follow
Toothpaste	Tartar-control toothpaste is recommended; select a fluoridated product in the midrange of abrasiveness; products designed to "brighten" or "whiten" teeth are generally too abrasive for general use; dentifrice intended for use with the false teeth should not be used on natural teeth		

Acne Products

Active Ingredient	Representative Brands	Effectiveness
Benzoyl peroxide medications	PanOxyl bar Oxy-5 and Oxy-10 Clearasil cream Noxzema Acne 12	The most effective OTC active ingredient, benzoyl peroxide aids in the prevention of new lesion formation
Salicylic acid cleaners	Clearasil Medicated Cleanser Stri-Dex Maximum Strength Pads PROPA pH Cleaning Pads and Lotion	Salicylic acid aids in unseating blackheads; alcohol base helps remove surface oils; no suppression of lesion formation is associated with these products
Sulfur-based medications	Acnomel Cream Fostril Lotion	Does not prevent lesion formation; active ingredient does help dry areas associated with lesions
Alcohol-based cleansers	Sea Breeze Antiseptic for the Skin Noxema Antiseptic Skin Cleanser	Noneffective
Scrubs	Epi-Clear Scrub Cleanser Komix Cleanser	Too abrasive
Medicated soaps	Clearasil Antibacterial Soap Fostex Medicated Cleansing Bar	No more effective than ordinary soap and water

Hair Regrowth Treatment

Product	Physiological Function	Potential Side Effects
Minoxidil (Rogaine)	Vasodilator	Itching, skin irritation; hair loss will recur if use is discontinued

Smoking Cessation

Product	Physiological Function	Potential Side Effects
Nicorette Nicotrol, Nicoderm, Habitrol, and Prostep transdermal patch	Nicotine replacement Same as Nicorette	Jaw ache, difficult breathing, flushing, dry mouth, cough, drug interactions Rare (report to your doctor): hives, itching, rash, redness or swelling, irregular heartbeat; more common: rapid heartbeat, mild headache, increased appetite, burning at the site of application

Acid Reducers

Product	Physiological Function	Potential Side Effects
Tagamet HB	Hydrogen ion inhibitor	Drug interactions, mental confusion in the elderly
Pepcid AC	Hydrogen ion inhibitor	Same as Tagamet HB
Zantac 75	Hydrogen ion inhibitor	Same as Tagamet HB
Axid AR	Hydrogen ion inhibitor	Same as Tagamet HB

First Aid

Accidents are the leading cause of death for people ages 1 to 37. Injuries sustained in accidents can often be tragic. They are grim reminders of our need to learn first aid skills and to practice preventive safety habits.

First aid knowledge and skills allow you to help people who are in need of immediate emergency care. They also can help you save yourself if you should become injured. We recommend that our students enroll in American Red Cross first aid and safety courses, which are available in local communities or through colleges or universities. In this appendix, we briefly present some information about common first

aid emergencies. (Please note that our information is *not* a substitute for comprehensive American Red Cross first aid instruction.)

FIRST AID

- Keep a list of important phone numbers near your phone (your doctor, ambulance service, hospital, poison control center, police and fire departments).
- In case of serious injury or illness, call the appropriate emergency service immediately for help (if uncertain, call "911" or "0").

Specific Problem	What To Do
Asphyxiation Victim stops breathing and skin, lips, tongue, and fingernail beds turn bluish or gray.	Adult: Tip head back with one hand on forehead and other lifting the lower jaw near the chin. Look, listen, and feel for breathing. If not breathing, place your mouth over victim's mouth, pinch the nose, get a tight seal, and give 2 slow breaths. Recheck the breathing; if still not breathing, give breaths once every 5 seconds for an adult, once every 3 seconds for a child, once every 3 seconds for infants (do not exaggerate head tilt for babies).
Bleeding Victim bleeding severely can quickly go into shock and die within 1 or 2 minutes.	With the palm of your hand, apply firm, direct pressure to the wound with a clean dressing or pad. Elevate the body part if possible. Do not remove blood-soaked dressings; use additional layers, continue to apply pressure, and elevate the site. *Continued*

Specific Problem	What To Do
Choking	
Accidental ingestion or inhalation of food or other objects causes suffocation that can quickly lead to death. There are over 3000 deaths annually, mostly of infants, small children, and the elderly.	The procedure is easy to learn; however, the Heimlich maneuver must be learned from a qualified instructor. The procedure varies somewhat for infants, children, adults, pregnant women, and obese people.
Hyperventilation	
A situation in which a person breathes too rapidly; often the result of fear or anxiety; may cause confusion, shortness of breath, dizziness, or fainting. Intentional hyperventilation before an underwater swim is especially dangerous, since it may cause a swimmer to pass out in the water and drown.	Have the person relax and rest for a few minutes. Provide reassurance and a calming influence. Having the victim take a few breaths in a paper bag (not plastic) may be helpful. Do not permit swimmers to practice hyperventilation before attempting to swim.
Bee Stings	
Not especially dangerous except for people who have developed an allergic hypersensitivity to a particular venom. Those who are not hypersensitive will experience swelling, redness, and pain. Hypersensitive people may develop extreme swelling, chest constriction, breathing difficulties, hives, and shock signs.	For nonsensitive people: Scrape stinger from skin and apply cold compresses or over-the-counter topical preparation for insect bites. For sensitive people: Get professional help immediately. Scrape the stinger from skin; position the person so that the stung body part is below the level of the heart; help administer prescribed medication (if available); apply cold compresses.
Poisoning	
Often poisoning can be prevented with adequate safety awareness. Children are frequent victims.	Call the poison control center immediately; follow the instructions provided. Keep syrup of ipecac on hand.
Shock	
A life-threatening depression of circulation, respiration, and temperature control, recognizable by a victim's cool, clammy, pale skin; weak and rapid pulse; shallow breathing; weakness; nausea; or unconsciousness.	Provide psychological reassurance. Keep victim calm and in a comfortable, reclining position; loosen tight clothing. Prevent loss of body heat; cover if necessary. Elevate legs 8 to 12 inches (if there are no head, neck, or back injuries, or possible broken bones involving the hips or legs). Do not give food or fluids. Seek further emergency assistance.
Burns	
Burns can cause severe tissue damage and lead to serious infection and shock.	Minor burns: immerse in cold water and then cover with sterile dressings; do not apply butter or grease to burns. Major burns: seek help immediately; cover affected area with large quantities of clean dressings or bandages; do not try to clean the burn area or break blisters. Chemical burns: flood the area with running water.
Broken Bones	
Fractures are a common result of car accidents, falls, and recreational accidents.	Do not move the victim unless absolutely necessary to prevent further injury. Immobilize the affected area. Give care for shock while waiting for further emergency assistance.

Epilepsy: Recognition and First Aid

Seizure Type	What It Looks Like	Often Mistaken For	What To Do	What Not To Do
Convulsive Generalized tonic-clonic (also called grand mal)	Sudden cry, fall, rigidity, followed by muscle jerks, frothy saliva on lips, shallow breathing or temporarily suspended breathing, bluish skin, possible loss of bladder or bowel control, usually lasts 2-5 minutes; normal breathing then starts again; there may be some confusion and/or fatigue, followed by return to full consciousness	Heart attack Stroke Unknown but life-threatening emergency	Look for medical identification Protect from nearby hazards Loosen ties or shirt collars Place folded jacket under head Turn on side to keep airway clear; reassure when consciousness returns If single seizure lasted less than 10 minutes, ask if hospital evaluation wanted If multiple seizures, or if one seizure lasts longer than 10 minutes, take to emergency room	Don't put any hard implement in the mouth Don't try to hold tongue; it can't be swallowed Don't try to give liquids during or just after seizure Don't use oxygen unless there are symptoms of heart attack Don't use artificial respiration unless breathing is absent after muscle jerks subside, or unless water has been inhaled Don't restrain
Nonconvulsive	This category includes many different forms of seizures, ranging from temporary unawareness (petit mal) to brief, sudden, massive muscle jerks (myoclonic seizures)	Daydreaming, acting out, clumsiness, poor coordination, intoxication, random activity, mental illness, and many others	Usually no first aid necessary other than to provide reassurance and emotional support. Any nonconvulsive seizure that becomes convulsive should be managed as a convulsive seizure. Medical evaluation is recommended.	Do not shout at, restrain, expect verbal instructions to be obeyed, or grab a person having a nonconvulsive seizure (unless danger threatens)

Mental Disorders

CATEGORIES OF MENTAL DISORDERS

Anxiety Disorders

Anxiety disorders are characterized by a fear that leads to overarousal of heartbeat, muscle tension, and shakiness.

- *Phobic disorder.* Excessive irrational fears. Examples are agoraphobia (fear of open places), claustrophobia (fear of enclosed places), and acrophobia (fear of heights).
- *Panic disorder.* Overwhelming fear of losing control or going crazy. Panic attacks can last from a minute to an hour or more. No clear reason exists as to why panic attacks occur.
- *Generalized anxiety disorder.* Continued, free-floating anxiety that lasts for at least 1 month.
- *Obsessive-compulsive disorder.* Obsessive behavior is characterized by recurring irrational thoughts that remain out of control. Compulsive behavior reflects an irresistible urge to act repeatedly.

Dissociative Disorders

Dissociative disorders are those in which there is a sudden, temporary change in consciousness or self-identity.

- *Psychogenic amnesia.* Inability to recall a stressful event.
- *Psychogenic fugue.* Disorder in which a person loses memory of his or her past, moves to another locale, and takes on a new identity.

- *Multiple personality.* Disorder characterized by several distinct personalities occupying the same person.

Somatoform Disorders

People with somatoform disorders complain of a physical ailment, yet no physical abnormality can be found.

- *Conversion disorder.* Severe, unexplained loss of some physical ability (such as eyesight or use of the legs).
- *Hypochondriasis.* The belief that one is sick, although no medical evidence can be found.

Affective Disorders

In affective disorders a disturbance exists in a person's ability to express emotions.

- *Dysthymic disorder.* Persistent feelings (lasting for at least 2 years) characterized by lack of energy, loss of self-esteem, pessimistic outlook, inability to enjoy other people or pleasurable activities, and thoughts about suicide. The disorder is likely the most common psychological problem in humans.
- *Major depressive disorder.* Depression more severe than dysthymic disorder. Evidenced by poor appetite and significant weight loss, psychomotor symptoms, impaired reality testing, and recurrent thoughts of suicide.

- *Bipolar disorder.* Mood swings from elation to depression (formerly known as manic-depression).

Schizophrenic Disorders

Schizophrenic disorders are largely recognized by a person's verbal behavior. These disorders are characterized by disturbances in thought, perception, and attention. Schizophrenic patients may speak in a meaningless fashion, switch from topic to topic, and convey little important information. They may have delusions of grandeur or persecution, hallucinations, or excited or slowed motor activity. Usually schizophrenic patients do not think that their thoughts and actions are abnormal.

- *Disorganized type.* Characterized by disorganized delusions and frequent hallucinations that may be sexual or religious in nature. Exaggerated social impairment is common.
- *Catatonic type.* Characterized by a marked impairment in motor activity. May hold one body position for hours and not respond to the speech of others.
- *Paranoid type.* Characterized by delusions of persecution, often ones that are complex and systemized. Paranoid schizophrenic patients may experience vivid hallucinations that support their delusions.

THERAPEUTIC APPROACHES TO MENTAL DISORDERS

A variety of approaches can be used to help people who have mental disorders. These approaches involve psychotherapy or the use of biological therapies. A brief outline of the more widely known strategies follows, since a comprehensive presentation on this topic is beyond the scope of this appendix.

Insight-Oriented Therapies

Underlying this category of therapeutic approaches is the belief that the client must gain insight into the experiences that led up to his or her problem or mal-adaptive behavior. By being able to recognize the underlying motives for one's behavior, a client will be better able to objectively view his or her beliefs, feelings, and thinking patterns. These underlying motives often are beneath the person's level of consciousness. Insight-oriented forms of psychotherapy include cognitive therapy, psychoanalysis, person-centered therapy, transactional analysis, and gestalt therapy.

Behavior Therapy

Discussed briefly in Chapter 6, behavior therapy (also called *behavior modification*) attempts to produce behavior change in a client by using scientifically tested principles of classical and operant conditioning and observational learning. Techniques of behavior therapy include operant conditioning (behavior reinforcement), aversive conditioning, systematic desensitization, assertiveness training, and self-control techniques.

Group Therapy

This form of therapy involves a therapist and several clients who have similar problems. Examples might be group therapy for people with eating disorders, smoking concerns, sexual problems, family problems, or relationship concerns. By meeting together and working to resolve their similar concerns, clients often receive support from other group members. With multiple members, a larger volume of pertinent information exists for clients to share. In a practical sense, group therapy is usually less expensive than individual therapy and the therapist can reach more clients at once.

Biological Therapies

Psychiatrists and other physicians are qualified to approach mental disorders from a medical framework. They are able to use chemotherapy (tranquilizers, antidepressants, lithium), electroconvulsive therapy (ECT or shock therapy), and even psychosurgery (brain surgery). Often these approaches are used with clients who have especially serious psychiatric disorders or who do not respond well to psychotherapy.

Body Systems

THE CIRCULATORY SYSTEM

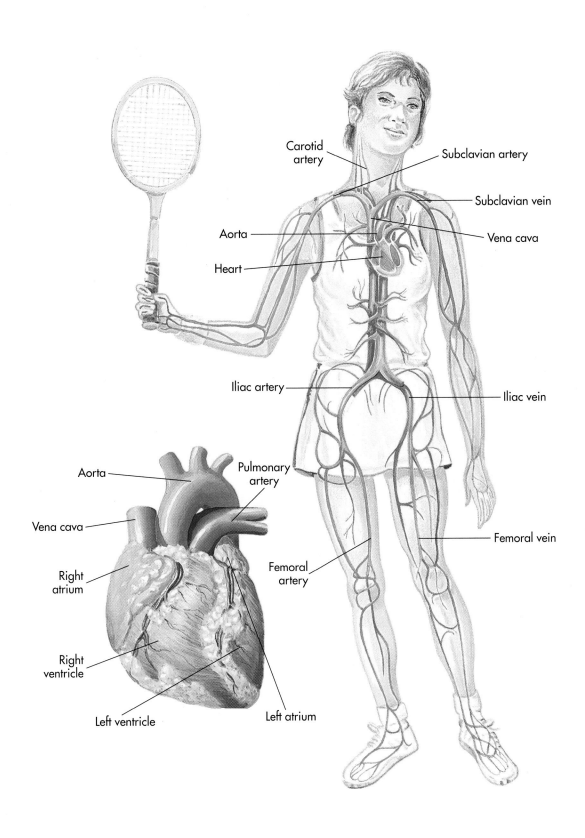

Carotid artery

Subclavian artery

Subclavian vein

Aorta

Vena cava

Heart

Iliac artery

Iliac vein

Aorta

Pulmonary artery

Vena cava

Right atrium

Femoral vein

Right ventricle

Femoral artery

Left ventricle

Left atrium

THE RESPIRATORY SYSTEM

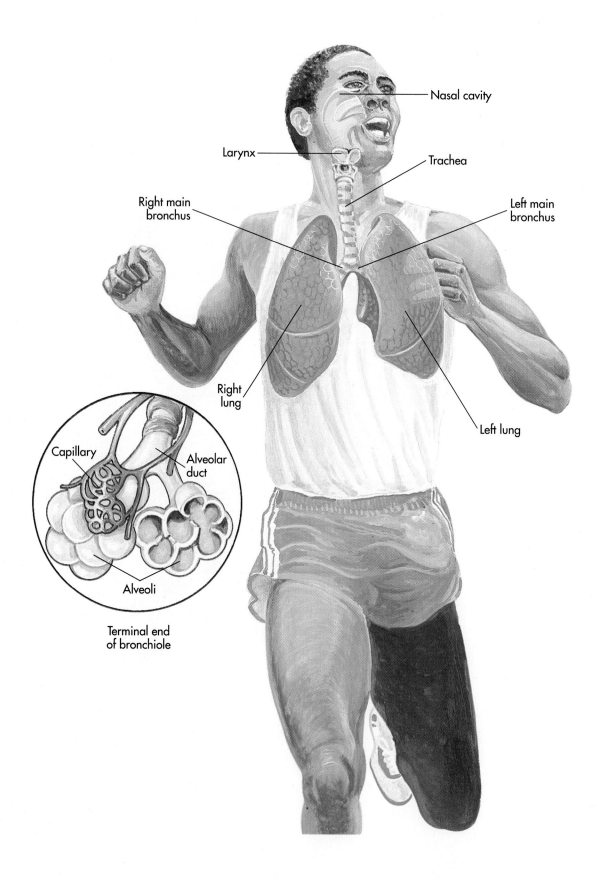

Nasal cavity

Larynx

Trachea

Right main
bronchus

Left main
bronchus

Right
lung

Left lung

Capillary

Alveolar
duct

Alveoli

Terminal end
of bronchiole

THE MUSCULAR SYSTEM

Sternocleidomastoid

Trapezius

Deltoid

Pectoralis major

Biceps

Triceps

Rectus abdominis

Rectus femoris

Sartorius

Gastrocnemius

Ligaments

THE SKELETAL SYSTEM

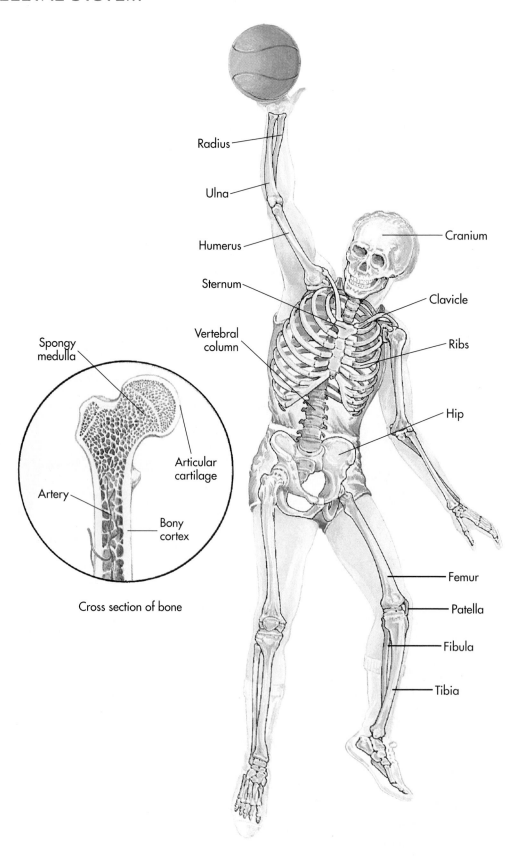

Radius

Ulna

Humerus

Sternum

Vertebral
column

Cranium

Clavicle

Ribs

Hip

Femur

Patella

Fibula

Tibia

Spongy
medulla

Articular
cartilage

Artery

Bony
cortex

Cross section of bone

THE NERVOUS SYSTEM

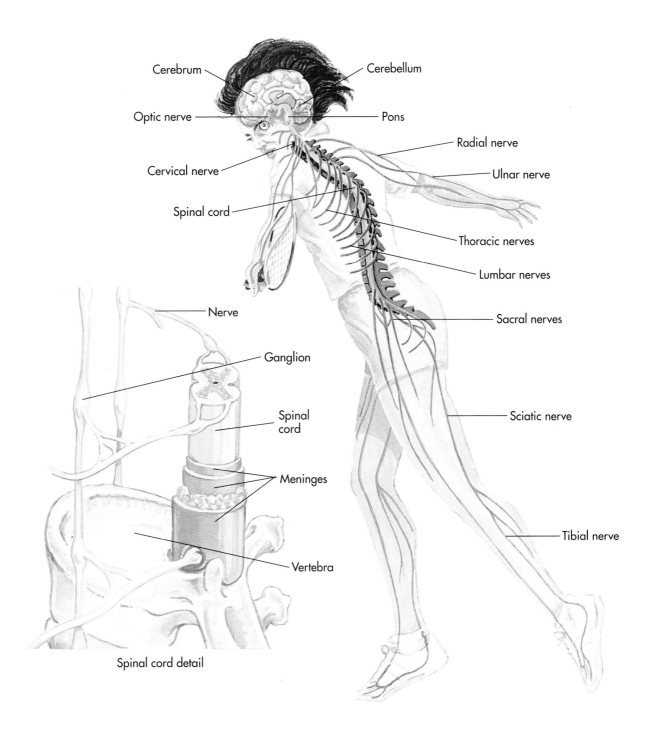

Cerebrum

Cerebellum

Optic nerve

Pons

Radial nerve

Cervical nerve

Ulnar nerve

Spinal cord

Thoracic nerves

Lumbar nerves

Nerve

Sacral nerves

Ganglion

Spinal cord

Meninges

Sciatic nerve

Vertebra

Tibial nerve

Spinal cord detail

THE DIGESTIVE SYSTEM

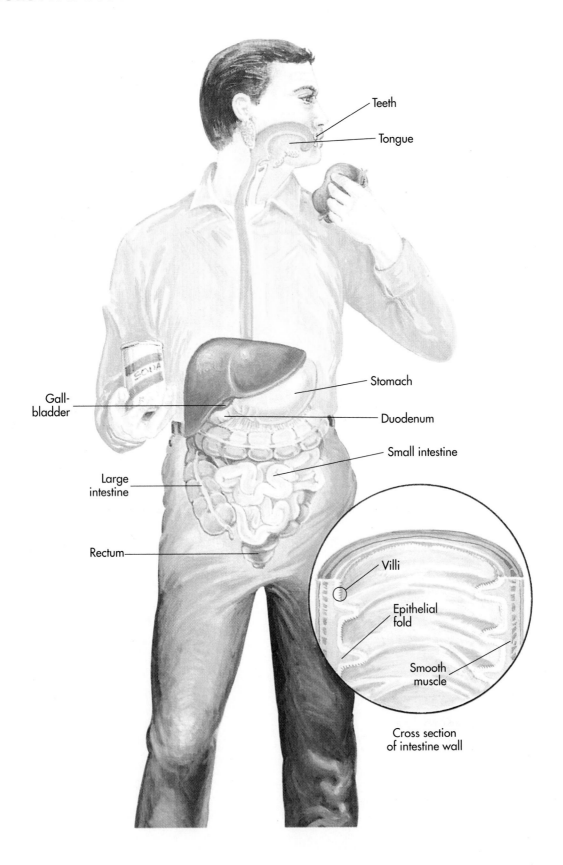

Teeth

Tongue

Stomach

Gall-
bladder

Duodenum

Small intestine

Large
intestine

Rectum

Villi

Epithelial
fold

Smooth
muscle

Cross section
of intestine wall

THE URINARY SYSTEM

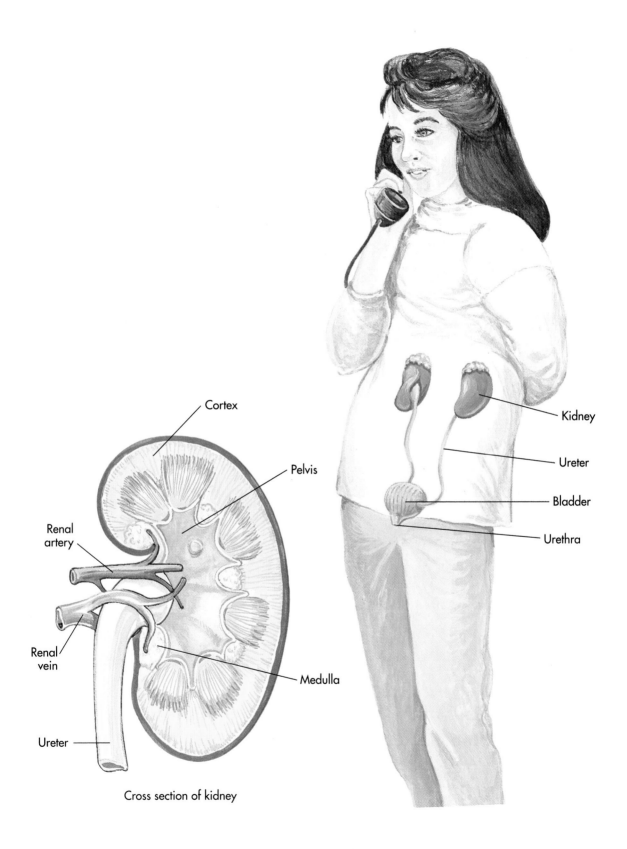

Cortex

Pelvis

Renal
artery

Renal
vein

Medulla

Ureter

Cross section of kidney

Kidney

Ureter

Bladder

Urethra

THE ENDOCRINE SYSTEM

NOTE: Refer to Figures 13-2 and 13-3 for detailed anatomical illustrations of the reproductive systems.

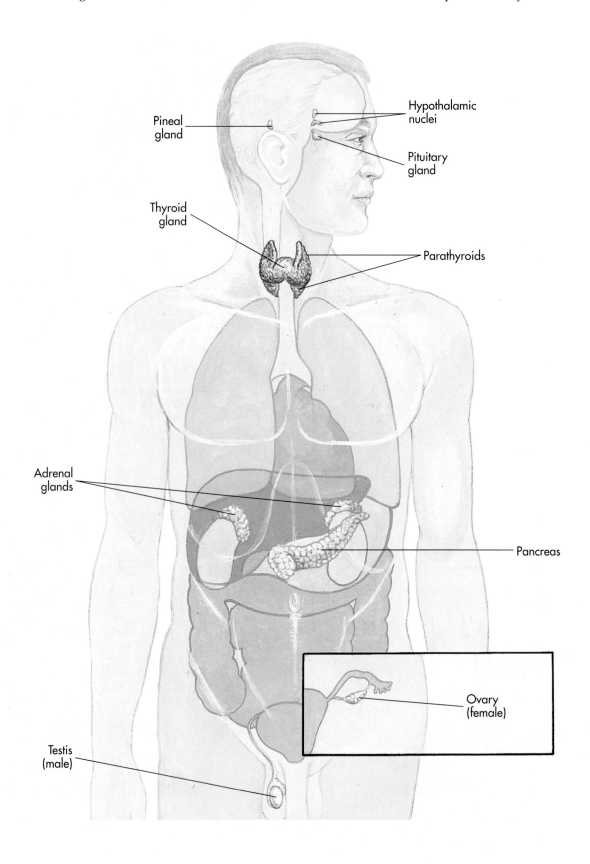

Pineal gland

Hypothalamic nuclei

Pituitary gland

Thyroid gland

Parathyroids

Adrenal glands

Pancreas

Ovary (female)

Testis (male)

Glossary

A

abortion induced premature termination of a pregnancy

absorption passage of nutrients or alcohol through the walls of the stomach or intestinal tract into the bloodstream

abuse any use of a legal or illegal drug that is detrimental to health

acid-base balance acidity-alkalinity of body fluids

acid rain rain that has a lower pH (more acidic) than that normally associated with rain

acquaintance rape forced sexual intercourse between individuals who know each other

acquired immunity significant component of the immune system associated with the formation of antibodies and specialized blood cells that are capable of destroying pathogens

ACTH (adrenocorticotropic hormone) hormone produced in the pituitary gland and transmitted to the cortex of the adrenal glands; stimulates production and release of corticoids

activity requirement calories required for daily physical work

acupuncture insertion of fine needles into the body to alter electroenergy fields and cure disease

acute alcohol intoxication potentially fatal elevation of the blood alcohol concentration, often resulting from rapid consumption of large amounts of alcohol

acute rhinitis the common cold; the sudden onset of nasal inflammation

adaptive thermogenesis physiological response of the body to adjust its metabolic rate to the presence or absence of calories

addiction term used interchangeably with physical dependence

additive effect combined (but not exaggerated) effect produced by the concurrent use of two or more drugs

adrenal cortex outer cell layers of the adrenal glands; cells of the cortex, on stimulation by ACTH, produce corticoid.

adrenal glands paired triangular endocrine glands situated above each kidney; site of epinephrine and corticoid production

adrenaline powerful stress response hormone (*see* epinephrine)

adrenocorticotropic hormone (ACTH) hormone produced in the pituitary gland and transmitted to the cortex of the adrenal glands; stimulates production and release of corticoids

aerobic energy production body's production of energy when the respiratory and circulatory systems are able to process and transport a sufficient amount of oxygen to muscle cells

agent causal pathogen of a particular disease

AIDS acquired immunodeficiency syndrome; viral-based destruction of the immune system, leading to illness and death from opportunistic infections

alcoholism pattern of alcohol use characterized by emotional and physical dependence, as well as a general loss of control over the use of alcohol

allergens environmental substances to which people may be hypersensitive; allergens function as antigens

allopathy system of medical practice in which specific remedies (often pharmaceutical agents) are used to produce effects different from those produced by a disease or injury

alveoli thin, saclike terminal ends of the airways; the sites at which gases are exchanged between the blood and inhaled air

Alzheimer's disease gradual development of memory loss, confusion, and loss of reasoning; will eventually lead to total intellectual incapacitation, brain degeneration, and death

amino acids chief components of protein; synthesized by the body or obtained from dietary sources

amotivational syndrome behavioral pattern characterized by widespread apathy toward productive activities

anabolic steroids drugs that function like testosterone to produce increases in weight and strength

anaerobic energy production body's production of energy when needed amounts of oxygen are not readily available

analgesic drugs drugs that reduce the sensation of pain

anaphylactic shock life-threatening congestion of the airways resulting from hypersensitivity to a foreign protein

androgyny the blending of both masculine and feminine characteristics

anemia condition reflecting abnormally low levels of hemoglobin

aneurysm a ballooning or outpouching on a weakened area of an artery

angina pectoris chest pain that results from impaired blood supply to the heart muscle

angioplasty surgical insertion of a balloon-tipped catheter into the coronary artery to open areas of narrowing

anorexia nervosa emotional disorder in which appetite and hunger are suppressed and marked weight loss occurs

anovulatory not ovulating

antagonistic effect effect produced when one drug nullifies (reduces, offsets) the effects of a second drug

antibodies chemical compounds produced by the immune system to destroy antigens and their toxins

antigens disease-producing microorganisms or foreign substances that on entering the body trigger an immune response

antioncogenes genes whose function is to prevent the activation of oncogenes

ARC AIDS-related complex; condition suggesting some deterioration of the immune system as a result of infection by the HIV agent

arrhythmias irregularities of the heart's normal rhythm or beating pattern

arteriosclerosis calcification of an artery's wall that makes the vessel less elastic, more brittle, and more susceptible to bursting; hardening of the arteries

artificial insemination depositing of sperm in the female reproductive tract in an attempt to impregnate; sperm may be those of the partner or of a donor

artificially acquired immunity type of acquired immunity resulting from the body's response to pathogens introduced into the body through immunizations

asbestos fibrous material found in insulation and many other building materials; causes asbestosis

asphyxiation death resulting from lack of oxygen to the brain

atherosclerosis the buildup of plaque on the inner walls of arteries

attention deficit disorder inability to concentrate well on a specified task; often accompanied by above-normal physical movement; also called *hyperactivity*

audiologists health care professionals trained to assess auditory function

autoimmune immune response against the cells of a person's own body

axon portion of a neuron that conducts electrical impulses to the dendrites of adjacent neurons; neurons typically have one axon

ayurveda traditional Indian medicine based on herbal remedies

AZT (azidothymidine) the first drug approved for use in the treatment of AIDS; capable of reducing symptoms and possibly extending life of a person with AIDS

B

balanced diet diet featuring food selections from each of the five food groups

ballistic stretching a "bouncing" form of stretching in which a muscle group is lengthened repetitively to produce multiply quick, forceful stretches

basal cells foundation cells that underlie the epithelial cells

basal metabolic rate (BMR) the amount of energy (in calories) your body requires to maintain basic functions

behavior modification behavioral therapy designed to change the learned behavior of an individual

benign noncancerous; tumors that do not spread

bestiality alternative term for *zoophilia*

beta blockers drugs that prevent overactivity of the heart, which results in angina pectoris

bias and hate crimes criminal acts directed at a person or group solely because of a specific characteristic, such as race, religion, ethnic background, or political beliefs

binge drinking alcohol use characterized by periods of intense alcohol consumption; for example, drinking heavily on the weekend

bioavailability speed and extent to which a drug becomes biologically active within the body; bioavailability for a drug varies among individuals and within a given individual over time

biochemical oxygen demand index of water pollution based on the rate and extent that organic matter uses dissolved oxygen from a sample of water

biofeedback self-monitoring of physiological processes as they occur within the body

biological sexuality male and female aspects of sexuality

birth control all of the procedures that can prevent the birth of a child

bisexual choosing members of both genders as one's sexual preference

blackout temporary state of amnesia experienced by an alcoholic; an inability to remember events that occur during a period of alcohol use

blood alcohol concentration (BAC) percentage of alcohol in a measured quantity of blood

blood analysis chemical analysis of various substances in the blood; helps determine changes and possible disturbances in the body

body fat analysis determination of the percentage of body tissue composed of fat

body image subjective perception of how one's body appears

bodybuilding sports activity in which the participants train their bodies to reach desired goals of muscular size, symmetry, and proportion

body mass index (BMI) numerical expression of body weight based on height and weight

bonding important initial sense of recognition established between the newborn and those adults on whom the newborn will depend

brain death the absence of brain wave activity after an initial measurement followed by a second measurement 24 hours later

brand name specific name assigned to a patented drug or product by its manufacturer

Braxton Hicks contractions false labor contractions; mild and of irregular spacing

breakthrough bleeding midcycle uterine bleeding; spotting

breech position birth position in which the baby's feet or buttocks are presented first

bulimarexia binge eating followed by purging the body of the food

bulimia emotional disorder in which binge eating patterns are established; usually accompanied by purging

C

calcium channel blockers drugs that prevent arterial spasms; used in the long-term management of angina pectoris

calendar method form of natural family planning in which the variable lengths of a woman's menstrual cycle are used to calculate her fertile period

calipers device to measure the thickness of a skinfold from which percent body fat can be calculated

caloric balance caloric input equals caloric output; weight remains constant

calories units of heat (energy); specifically, 1 calorie equals the heat required to raise 1 kilogram of water $1° C$

cannula hollow metal or plastic tube through which materials can be aspirated

carbohydrates chemical compounds comprising sugar or saccharide units; the body's primary source of energy

carbon monoxide chemical compound (CO) that can inactivate red blood cells

carcinogenic related to the production of cancerous changes; property of environmental agents, including drugs, that may stimulate the development of cancerous changes within cells

carcinoma in situ cancer at its site of origin

cardiac pertaining to the heart

cardiac muscle specialized smooth muscle tissue that forms the middle (muscular) layer of the heart wall

cardiogram reading of heart and lung function from a cardiograph machine

cardiovascular pertaining to the heart (cardio) and blood vessels (vascular)

cardiorespiratory endurance ability of the body to process and transport oxygen required by muscle cells so that these cells can continue to contract

carjacking a crime that involves a thief's attempt to steal a car while the owner is behind the wheel; carjackings are usually random and unpredictable and often involve handguns

CAT scan computerized axial tomography; x-ray procedure designed to visualize structures within the body that would not normally be seen through conventional x-ray procedures

catabolism metabolic process of breaking down tissue for the purpose of converting it to energy

cauterize to apply a small electrical current and permanently close a tube or vessel; to burn

celibacy self-imposed avoidance of sexual intimacy

cell-mediated immunity form of acquired immunity that uses specialized white blood cells to destroy specific antigens that enter the body

central nervous system the brain and spinal cord

cereal germ highly nutritious portions of the cereal grain, often removed during milling

cerebral cortex outer covering of the brain; site of intellect, memory, thought processes, and rationalization

cerebral hemorrhage bleeding from the cerebral arteries within the brain

cerebrovascular accident stroke; brain tissue damage resulting from impaired circulation of blood vessels in the brain

cerebrovascular occlusion blockage to arteries supplying blood to the cerebral cortex of the brain; stroke

cervical cap small, thimble-shaped contraceptive device designed to fit over the cervix

cesarean delivery surgical removal of a fetus through the abdominal wall

chemical name name used to describe the molecular structure of a drug

chemoprevention the safe and effective use of dietary supplements in the prevention of illness and disease

child abuse harm committed against a child; usually refers to physical abuse, sexual abuse, or child neglect

chiropractic manipulation of the vertebral column to relieve pressure and cure illness

chlamydia the most prevalent sexually transmitted disease; caused by a nongonococcal bacterium

chlorofluorocarbons (CFCs) gaseous chemical compounds that contain chlorine and fluorine

cholesterol a primary form of fat found in the blood; lipid material manufactured within the body, as well as derived through dietary sources

chronic develops slowly and persists for a long period of time

chronic bronchitis persistent inflammation and infection of the smaller airways within the lungs

chronic fatigue syndrome (CFS) illness that causes severe exhaustion, fatigue, aches, and depression; mostly affects women in their thirties and forties

cilia small, hairlike structures that extend from cells that line the air passage

cirrhosis condition characterized by pathological changes to the liver resulting from chronic heavy alcohol consumption; a frequent cause of death among heavy alcohol users

clitoris small shaft of erectile tissue located in front of the vaginal opening; the female homolog of the male penis

cochlea small, snail-shaped organ of the inner ear in which the energy of sound is converted into electrical energy for transmission to the brain

coenzyme vitamin-based organic compound that assists a particular enzyme in performing its role in regulating biochemical reactions

cohabitation sharing of a residence by two unrelated, unmarried people; living together

coitus penile-vaginal intercourse

coitus interruptus (withdrawal) a contraceptive practice in which the erect penis is removed from the vagina before ejaculation

cold turkey immediate, total discontinuation of use of tobacco or other addictive substances

coliform bacteria intestinal tract bacteria whose presence in a water supply suggests contamination by human or animal waste

collateral circulation ability of nearby blood vessels to enlarge and carry additional blood around a blocked blood vessel

companionate love friendly affection and deep attachment, based on extensive familiarity with another person

compliance willingness to follow the directions provided by another person

condom latex shield designed to cover the erect penis and retain semen on ejaculation

confrontation an approach to convince drug-dependent people to enter treatment

congestive heart failure inability of the heart to pump out all the blood that returns to it; can lead to dangerous fluid accumulations in veins, lungs, and kidneys

consumer fraud marketing of unreliable and ineffective services, products, or information under the guise of curing disease or improving health; quackery

contact inhibition ability of a tissue, on reaching its mature size, to suppress additional growth

contraception any procedure that prevents fertilization

contraindications factors that make the use of a drug inappropriate or dangerous for a particular person

cooldown stretching and walking after exercise

coronary arteries vessels that supply oxygenated blood to heart muscle tissues

coronary artery bypass surgery surgical procedure designed to improve blood flow to the heart by providing alternative routes for blood around points of blockage

coroner an elected legal official empowered to pronounce death and to determine the official cause of a suspicious or violent death

corpus luteum cellular remnant of the graafian follicle after the release of an ovum

corticoids hormones generated by the adrenal cortex; corticoids influence the body's control of glucose, protein, and fat metabolism

CPR cardiopulmonary resuscitation; first aid procedure designed to restore breathing and heart function

crack a crystalline form of cocaine that is smoked; has an instantaneous effect and is highly dependence-producing

creativity innovative ability; insightful capacity to solve problems; ability to move beyond analytical or logical approaches to experiences

cross-tolerance transfer of tolerance from one drug to another within the same general category

crosstraining use of more than one aerobic activity to achieve cardiovascular fitness

crowning first appearance of the fetal head at the vaginal opening

cruciferous vegetables vegetables that have flowers with four leaves in the pattern of a cross

crypts burial locations generally located beneath churches

cunnilingus oral stimulation of the vulva or clitoris

cystitis infection of the urinary bladder

D

date rape a form of acquaintance rape that involves forced sexual intercourse by a dating partner

dehydration abnormal depletion of fluids from the body; severe dehydration can lead to death

delirium tremens (DTs) uncontrollable shaking associated with withdrawal from heavy chronic alcohol use

dendrite portion of a neuron that receives electrical stimuli from adjacent neurons; neurons typically have several such branches or extensions

denial in this case, the failure to acknowledge that alcohol or drug use seriously affects one's life

dependence general term that reflects the need to keep consuming a drug for psychological or physical reasons, or both

depressants the psychoactive drugs that reduce the function of the central nervous system

designated driver a person who abstains from or carefully limits alcohol use to drive others safely

designer drugs drugs that chemically resemble drugs on the FDA Schedule 1

desirable weight weight range deemed appropriate for people of a specific gender, age, and frame size

diaphragm soft rubber vaginal cup designed to cover the cervix

diastolic pressure blood pressure against blood vessel walls when the heart relaxes

dilation gradual expansion of an opening or passageway

dilation and curettage (D & C) surgical procedure in which the cervical canal is dilated to allow the uterine wall to be scraped

dilation and evacuation (D & E) surgical procedure using cervical dilation and vacuum aspiration to remove uterine wall material and fetal parts

direct (active) euthanasia process of inducing death, often through the injection of a lethal drug

distress stress that diminishes the quality of life; commonly associated with disease, illness, and maladaptation

diuresis increased discharge of fluid from the body; frequent urination

diuretic drugs drugs that aid the body in removing excess fluid

drug synergism enhancement of a drug's effect as a result of the presence of additional drugs within the system

duration length of time one needs to exercise at the target heart rate to produce the training effect

dynamic in a state of change; health is dynamic in the sense that it is influenced by factors from both within and outside the individual

E

ECG electrocardiograph; an instrument to measure and record the electrical activity within the heart

echocardiography procedure that uses high-frequency sound waves to visualize the structure and function of the heart

ecosystem an ecological unit made up of both animal and plant life that interact to produce a stable system

ectopic pregnancy a pregnancy wherein the fertilized ovum implants at a site other than the uterus, typically in the fallopian tube

effacement a thinning and pulling back of the cervical opening to allow movement of the fetus from the uterus

electrical impedance method of testing the percentage of body fat using an electrical current

electroencephalograph instrument that measures the electrical activity of the brain

embolism potentially fatal situation in which a circulating blood clot lodges itself in a smaller vessel

enabling in this case, the inadvertent support that some people provide to alcohol or drug abusers

endometrium innermost lining of the uterus, broken down and discharged during menstruation

enrichment process of returning to foods some of the nutritional elements (B vitamins and iron) removed during processing

Environmental Protection Agency (EPA) federal agency charged with the protection of natural resources and the quality of the environment

environmental tobacco smoke tobacco smoke that is diluted and stays within a common source of air

enzymes organic substances that control the rate of physiological reactions but are not themselves altered in the process

epinephrine powerful adrenal hormone whose presence in the bloodstream prepares the body for maximal energy production and skeletal muscle response

epitaph inscription on a grave marker or monument

erection the engorgement of erectile tissue with blood; characteristic of the penis, clitoris, nipple, labia minora, and scrotum

erotic dreams dreams whose content elicits a sexual response

essential amino acids nine amino acids that can be obtained only from dietary sources

essential hypertension hypertension (high blood pressure) resulting from chronic widespread constriction of arterioles

estrogen ovarian hormone that initiates the development of the uterine wall

estrogen replacement therapy medically administered estrogen to replace estrogen lost as the result of menopause

eulogy a composition or speech that praises someone; often delivered at a funeral or memorial service

eustress stress that enhances the quality of life

eutrophication enrichment of a body of water with nutrients, which allows for overabundant growth of plants

excitement stage initial arousal stage of the sexual response pattern

exhibitionism exposure of one's genitals for the purpose of shocking other people

F

faith the purposes and meaning that underlie an individual's hopes and dreams

fallopian tubes paired tubes that allow passage of ova from the ovaries to the uterus; the oviducts

false labor conditions that tend to resemble the start of true labor; may include irregular uterine contractions, pressure, and discomfort in the lower abdomen

fast foods convenience foods; foods featured in a variety of restaurants, including hamburgers, pizza, and tacos

fat density percent of the total calories in a food item derived from fat

FDA Schedule 1 list comprising drugs that hold a high potential for abuse but have no medical use

fecundity the ability to produce offspring

fellatio oral stimulation of the penis

femininity behavioral expressions traditionally observed in females

fermentation chemical process whereby plant products are converted into alcohol by the action of yeast cells on carbohydrates

fertility ability to reproduce

fetal alcohol effects developmental impairment in a child linked to a mother's use of alcohol during pregnancy

fetal alcohol syndrome characteristic birth defects noted in the children of some women who consume alcohol during their pregnancies

fetishism choice of a body part or inanimate object as a source of sexual excitement

fiber plant material that cannot be digested; found in cereal, fruits, and vegetables

fight-or-flight response the reaction to a stressor by confrontation or avoidance (sometimes called the fight, fright, flight, or folly [or 4F] response)

flaccid nonerect; the state of erectile tissue when vasocongestion is not occurring

flashback unpredictable return of a psychedelic trip

flexibility ability of joints to function through an intended range of motion

follicle-stimulating hormone (FSH) gonadotropic hormone required for initial development of ova (in the female) and sperm (in the male)

food additives chemical compounds that are intentionally or unintentionally added to our food supply that change some property of the food such as color or texture

foreplay activities, often involving touching and caressing, that prepare individuals for sexual intercourse

freebase altered form of cocaine that can be smoked

frequency number of times per week one should exercise to achieve a training effect

full funeral services all of the professional services provided by funeral directors

G

gait pattern of walking

gamete intrafallopian transfer (GIFT) retrieved ovum and partner's sperm are positioned in the fallopian tube for fertilization and subsequent movement into the uterus for implantation

gaseous phase portion of tobacco smoke containing carbon monoxide and many other physiologically active gaseous compounds

gateway drugs easily obtained legal or illegal drugs (alcohol, tobacco, marijuana) whose use may precede the use of less common illegal drugs

gender general term reflecting a biological basis of sexuality; the male gender or the female gender

gender adoption lengthy process of learning the behaviors that are traditional for one's gender

gender identification achievement of a personally satisfying interpretation of one's masculinity or feminity

gender identity recognition of one's gender

gender preference emotional and intellectual acceptance of one's gender

gender schema mental image of the cognitive, affective, and performance characteristics appropriate to a particular gender; a mental picture of being a man or a woman

general adaptation syndrome sequenced physiological response to the presence of a stressor; the alarm, resistance, and exhaustion stages of the stress response

generativity midlife developmental task; repaying society for its support through contributions associated with parenting, creativity, and occupation

generic name common or nonproprietary name of a drug

genetic counseling medical counseling regarding the transmission and management of inherited conditions

genetic predisposition inherited tendency to develop a disease process if necessary environmental factors exist

glucose blood sugar; the body's primary source of energy

goblet cells cells within the epithelial lining of the airways that produce the mucus required for cleaning the airways

gonads male or female sex glands; testes produce sperm and ovaries produce eggs

greenhouse effect warming of the Earth's surface that is produced when solar heat becomes trapped by layers of carbon dioxide and other gases

H

habituation term used interchangeably with *psychological dependence*

hallucinogens psychoactive drugs capable of producing hallucinations (distortions of reality)

hashish resins collected from the flowering tops of marijuana plants

health maintenance organizations (HMOs) groups that supply prepaid comprehensive health care with an emphasis on prevention

health promotion movement in which knowledge, practices, and values are transmitted to people for their use in lengthening their lives, reducing the incidence of illness, and feeling better

healthy body weight body weight within a weight range appropriate for a person with an acceptable weight-to-height ratio

heart catheterization procedure wherein a thin catheter is introduced through an arm or leg artery into the coronary circulation to visualize areas of blockage

heart-lung machine device that oxygenates and circulates blood during bypass surgery

hemorrhaging bleeding; often implies profuse bleeding

herbalism an ancient form of healing in which herbal preparations are used to treat illness and disease

heterosexual having a sexual preference for a member of the opposite gender

high-density lipoprotein (HDL) the type of lipoprotein that transports cholesterol from the bloodstream to the liver where it is eventually removed from the body; high levels of HDL are related to a reduction in heart disease

HIV human immunodeficiency virus

holistic health broadest view of the composition of health; views health in terms of its physical, emotional, social, intellectual, spiritual, and occupational makeup

homeopathy the use of minute doses of herbs or minerals to stimulate healing

homicide the intentional killing of one person by another

homosexual choosing a member of one's own gender as one's sexual preference

hospice care approach to caring for terminally ill patients that maximizes the quality of life and allows death with dignity

host negligence a legal term that reflects the failure of a host to provide reasonable care and safety for people visiting the host's residence or business

hot flashes temporary feelings of warmth experienced by women during and after menopause; caused by blood vessel dilation

Human Genome Project international quest by geneticists to identify the location and composition of every gene within the human cell

human papillomavirus sexually transmitted virus capable of causing precancerous changes in the cervix; causative agent for genital warts

humoral immunity form of acquired immunity that uses antibodies to counter specific antigens that enter the body

hypercellular obesity form of obesity seen in individuals who possess an abnormally large number of fat cells

hyperglycemia elevated blood glucose levels; an important indicator of diabetes mellitus

hyperparathyroidism condition reflecting the overactive production of parathyroid hormone by the parathyroid glands

hypertonic saline solution salt solution with a concentration higher than that found in human fluids

hypertrophic obesity form of obesity in which fat cells are enlarged, but not excessive in number

hypochondriasis neurotic conviction that one is ill or afflicted with a particular disease

hypothalamus portion of the midbrain that connects the cerebral cortex and pituitary gland

hysterectomy surgical removal of the uterus

I

immune system system of biochemical and cellular elements that protect the body from invading pathogens and foreign materials

immunizations laboratory-prepared pathogens that are introduced into the body for the purpose of stimulating the body's immune system

incest marriage or coitus (sexual intercourse) between closely related individuals

incomplete protein food that lacks one or more of the essential amino acids

incubation stage time required for a pathogen to multiply significantly enough for signs and symptoms to appear

independent practice association (IPA) a modified HMO in which a group of physicians provides prepaid health care but not from a central location within an HMO

indirect (passive) euthanasia process of allowing a person to die by disconnecting life support systems or withholding lifesaving techniques

infatuation a relatively temporary, intensely romantic attraction to another person

infertility inability of a male to impregnate or of a female to become pregnant

inhalants psychoactive drugs that enter the body through inhalation

inhibitions inner controls that prevent a person's engaging in certain types of behavior

insulin pancreatic hormone required by the body for the effective metabolism of glucose (blood sugar)

insulin-dependent (type 1) diabetes mellitus form of diabetes generally seen for the first time in childhood or adolescence; juvenile onset diabetes

intensity level of effort one puts into an activity

intentional injuries injuries that are purposely inflicted on one person by another person

interstitial cell stimulating hormone (ICSH) a gonadotropic hormone of the male required for the production of testosterone

interstitial cells specialized cells within the testicles that on stimulation by ICSH produce the male sex hormone testosterone

intimacy any close, mutual verbal or nonverbal behavior within a relationship

intrauterine device (IUD) small plastic medicated or unmedicated device that when inserted in the uterus prevents continued pregnancy

introspective looking inward to examine one's feelings and beliefs

in vitro fertilization and embryo transfer (IVF-ET) laboratory fertilization of an ovum taken from the woman with subsequent return of the developing embryo into the woman's uterus

ionizing radiation form of radiation capable of releasing electrons from atoms

isokinetic exercises muscular strength training exercises that use machines to provide variable resistances throughout the full range of motion

isometric exercises muscular strength training exercises that use a resistance so great that the resistance object cannot be moved

L

labia majora larger, more external skin folds that surround the vaginal opening

labia minora small, liplike folds of skin immediately adjacent to the vaginal opening

lactating breastfeeding; nursing

lactovegetarian diet vegetarian diet that allows for the consumption of milk and dairy products

laminaria plugs made of seaweed that on exposure to moisture expand and dilate the canal into which they have been placed

lead toxicity blood lead level above 25 micrograms/deciliter (if adopted, the new standard will be 10 micrograms/deciliter)

legumes peas and beans; plant sources high in the essential amino acids

lesbianism female homosexuality

lightening movement of fetus deeper into the pelvic cavity before the onset of the birth process

lipoprotein proteinlike structure in the bloodstream to which circulating fatty materials attach; associated with cardiovascular disease

living will document confirming a person's desire to be allowed to die peacefully and with a measure of dignity in case of terminal illness or major injury

low-density lipoprotein (LDL) the type of lipoprotein that transports the largest amount of cholesterol in the bloodstream; high levels of LDL are related to heart disease

luteinizing hormone (LH) female gonadotropic hormone required for fullest development and release of ova; ovulating hormone

Lyme disease systemic bacterial infection transmitted by deer ticks

M

macrobiotic diet vegetarian diet composed almost entirely of brown rice

mainstream smoke the smoke inhaled and then exhaled by a smoker

mammogram x-ray examination of the breast

masculinity behavioral expressions traditionally observed in males

masochism sexual excitement while being injured or humiliated

mastectomy removal of breast tissue

masturbation self-stimulation of the genitals

maternal supportive tissues general term referring to the development of the placenta and other tissues specifically associated with pregnancy

mausoleum above-ground structure into which caskets can be placed for disposition and that frequently resembles a small stone house

maximum heart rate maximum number of times the heart can beat per minute

Medicaid noncontributory governmental health insurance for people receiving other types of public assistance

medical power of attorney for health care a legal document that designates who will make health care decisions for people unable to do so for themselves

Medicare contributory governmental health insurance, primarily for people 65 years of age or older

meltdown the overheating and eventual melting of the uranium fuel rods in the core of a nuclear reactor

menarche time of a female's first menstrual cycle

menopause decline and eventual cessation of hormone production by the reproductive system

menstrual extraction procedure using vacuum aspiration to remove uterine wall material within 2 weeks after a missed menstrual period

menstrual phase phase of the menstrual cycle during which the broken-down lining of the uterus (endometrium) is discharged from the body

menstruation the cyclic buildup and destruction of the uterine wall

metabolic rate rate or intensity at which the body uses energy

metastasis spread of cancerous cells from their site of origin to other areas of the body

midlife period between 45 and 64 years of age

midlife crisis period of emotional upheaval noted among some midlife people as they struggle with the finality of death and the nature of their past and future accomplishments

migraine headaches severe, recurrent headaches, usually affecting one side of the head

minerals chemical elements that serve as structural elements within body tissue or participate in physiological processes

minipills low-dose progesterone oral contraceptives

misuse inappropriate use of legal drugs intended to be medications

monogamous paired relationship with one partner

mononuclear leukocytes large white blood cells that have only one nucleus

mononucleosis ("mono") viral infection characterized by weakness, fatigue, swollen glands, and low-grade fever

monounsaturated fats fats made of compounds in which one hydrogen-bonding position remains to be filled; semisolid at room temperature; derived primarily from peanut and olive oils

morning-after pill high-dose combination oral contraceptive used to terminate a possible pregnancy

motorized scraper a motor-driven cutter that shaves off plaque deposits from inside artery walls

MRI scan magnetic resonance imaging; an imaging procedure that uses a giant magnet to generate an image of body tissue

mucus clear, sticky material produced by specialized cells within the mucous membranes of the body; mucus traps much of the suspended particulate matter from tobacco smoke

multiorgasmic capacity potential to have several orgasms within a single period of sexual arousal

murmur an atypical heart sound that suggests a backwashing of blood into a chamber of the heart from which it has just left

muscular endurance ability of a muscle or muscle group to function over time; depends on well-developed respiratory and circulatory systems

muscular strength ability to contract skeletal muscles to engage in work

mutagenic capable of promoting genetic alterations in cells

myelin white, fatty insulating material that surrounds the axons of many nerve cells

myocardial infarction heart attack; the death of heart muscle as a result of a blockage in one of the coronary arteries

myotonia buildup of neuromuscular tonus within a particular tissue

N

narcolepsy sleep-related disorder in which a person has a recurrent, overwhelming, and uncontrollable desire to sleep

narcotics psychoactive drugs derived from the oriental poppy plant; narcotics relieve pain and induce sleep

naturally acquired immunity (NAI) type of acquired immunity resulting from the body's response to naturally occurring pathogens

naturopathy a system of treatment that avoids drugs and surgery and emphasizes the use of natural agents to correct underlying imbalances

nerve blockers drugs that can stop the flow of electrical impulses through the nerves into which they have been injected

neuromuscular tonus level of nervous tension within the muscle

neuron nerve cell; the structural unit of the nervous system

neurophysiological nervous system function; processes through which the body senses and responds to its internal and external environments

neurotransmitters chemical messengers released by neurons that permit electrical impulses to be transferred from one nerve cell to another

nicotine physiologically active, dependence-producing drug found in tobacco

nitroglycerin a blood vessel dilator used by some cardiac patients to relieve angina

nocturnal emission ejaculation that occurs during sleep; "wet dream"

nodes in this case, the electrical centers found in cardiac muscle

nomogram graphic means of finding an unknown value

non–insulin-dependent (type 2) diabetes mellitus form of diabetes generally seen for the first time in people 35 years of age and older; adult-onset diabetes

nonoxynol 9 a spermicide commonly used with contraceptive devices

nontraditional students administrative term used by colleges and universities for students who, for whatever reason, are pursuing undergraduate work at an age other than that associated with traditional college years (18-24)

norepinephrine adrenaline-like neurotransmitter produced within the nervous system

nurse practitioners registered nurses who have taken specialized training in one or more clinical areas and are able to engage in limited diagnosis and treatment of illnesses

nutrients elements in foods that are required for the growth, repair, and regulation of body processes

O

obesity condition in which overweight is the result of excess body fat

oncogenes genes that are believed to activate the development of cancer

oogenesis production of ova in a biologically mature female

oral contraceptive pill pill taken orally, composed of synthetic female hormones that prevent ovulation or implantation; "the pill"

orgasmic platform expanded outer third of the vagina that during the plateau phase of the sexual response grips the penis

orgasmic stage third stage of the sexual response pattern; the stage during which neuromuscular tension is released

orthodontics dental specialty that focuses on the proper alignment of the teeth

osteoarthritis arthritis that develops with age

osteopathy system of medical practice that combines allopathic principles with specific attention to postural mechanics of the body

osteoporosis resorption of calcium from the bone caused by the inability of the body to use dietary calcium; seen primarily in postmenopausal women

outercourse sexual activity that does not involve intercourse

ovary female reproductive structure that produces ova and the female gonadal sex hormones estrogen and progesterone

overload principle principle whereby a person gradually increases the resistance load that must be moved or lifted

overweight condition in which body weight is above desirable weight

ovolactovegetarian diet diet that excludes the use of all meat but does allow the consumption of eggs and dairy products

ovulation the release of a mature egg from the ovary

oxidation in this case, the process that removes alcohol from the bloodstream

oxygen debt physical state that occurs when the body can no longer process and transport sufficient amounts of oxygen for continued muscle contraction

ozone layer layer of triatomic oxygen that surrounds the Earth and filters much of the sun's radiation before it can reach the Earth's surface

P

pacemaker sinoatrial or SA node; an area of cells within the heart that controls its electrical activity

Pap test a cancer screening procedure in which cells are removed from the cervix and examined for precancerous changes

paracervical anesthetic anesthetic injected into tissues surrounding the cervical opening

paraphilia a preference for unusual sexual practices

particulate phase portion of tobacco smoke composed of small suspended particles

particulate pollutants class of air pollutants composed of small solid particles and liquid droplets

partner abuse violence committed against a domestic partner

parturition childbirth

passionate love state of extreme absorption in another; tenderness, elation, anxiety, sexual desire, and ecstasy

passive smoking inhalation of air that is heavily contaminated with tobacco smoke

passively acquired immunity temporary immunity achieved by providing antibodies to a person exposed to a particular pathogen

pathogen disease-causing agent

peak stage stage of an infectious disease at which symptoms are most fully expressed; acute stage

pedophilia sexual contact with children as a source of sexual excitement

pelvic inflammatory disease (PID) acute or chronic infections of the peritoneum or lining of the abdominopelvic cavity; associated with a variety of symptoms and a potential cause of sterility

periodic abstinence birth control methods that rely on a couple's avoidance of intercourse during the ovulatory phase of a woman's menstrual cycle; also called *fertility awareness* or *natural family planning*

periodontal disease destruction of soft tissue and bone that surround the teeth

peripheral artery disease (PAD) damage resulting from restricted blood flow to the extremities, especially the legs and feet

peritonitis inflammation of the pertoneum or lining of the abdominopelvic cavity

pesticide agent used to destroy insects and other pests

phenylpropanolamine (PPA) active chemical compound found in most over-the-counter diet products

physical dependence need to continue using a drug to maintain normal body function and to avoid withdrawal illness; also called *addiction*

pituitary gland "master gland" of the endocrine system; the wide variety of hormones produced by the pituitary are sent to structures throughout the body

placebo pills pills that contain no active ingredients

placenta structure through which nutrients, metabolic wastes, and drugs (including alcohol) pass from the bloodstream of the mother into the bloodstream of the developing fetus

plateau stage second stage of the sexual response pattern; a leveling off of arousal immediately before orgasm

platelet adhesiveness tendency of platelets to clump together, thus enhancing speed at which the blood clots

platonic close association between two people that does not include a sexual relationship

podiatrists specialists who treat a variety of ailments of the feet

polychlorinated biphenyls (PCBs) class of chlorinated organic compounds similar to the herbicide DDT

polyunsaturated fats fats composed of compounds in which multiple hydrogen-bonding positions remain open; these fats are liquids at room temperature; derived from a variety of vegetable sources

positive caloric balance caloric intake greater than caloric expenditure

postpartum period of time after the birth of a baby during which the uterus returns to its prepregnancy size

potentiated effect phenomenon whereby the use of one drug intensifies the effect of a second drug

preferred provider organization a group of physicians who market their professional services to an insurance company at predetermined fees

primary care physician the physician who sees a patient on a regular basis, rather than a specialist who sees the patient only for a specific condition or procedure

problem drinking alcohol use pattern in which a drinker's behavior creates personal difficulties or difficulties for other people

procreation reproduction

prodromal stage stage of an infectious disease process in which only general symptoms appear

professional nurses registered nurses who hold a bachelor's degree in nursing from a college or university

progesterone ovarian hormone that continues the development of the uterine wall that was initiated by estrogen

progressive resistance exercises muscular strength training exercises that use traditional barbells and dumbbells with fixed resistances

proof twice the percentage of alcohol by volume in a beverage; 100 proof alcohol is 50% alcohol

prostaglandin inhibitors drugs that block the production of prostaglandins, thus eliminating the hormonal stimulation of smooth muscles

prostaglandins chemical substances that stimulate smooth muscle contractions

prosthodontics dental specialty that focuses on the construction and fitting of artificial appliances to replace missing teeth

proteins compounds composed of chains of amino acids; primary components of muscle and connective tissue

protooncogenes normal genes that hold the potential of becoming cancer-causing oncogenes

psychoactive drug any substance capable of altering one's feelings, moods, or perceptions

psychogenic disorders illnesses with observable symptoms that are generated by stress but are not associated with tissue change

psychological dependence need to consume a drug for emotional reasons; also called *habituation*

psychosocial sexuality masculine and feminine aspects of sexuality

psychosomatic disorders physical illnesses of the body generated by the effects of stress

puberty achievement of reproductive ability

pulmonary pertaining to the lungs and breathing

pulmonary emphysema irreversible disease process in which the alveoli are destroyed

purging use of vomiting or laxatives to remove undigested food from the body

putrefaction decomposition of organic matter

Q

quackery marketing of unreliable and ineffective services, products, or information under the guise of curing disease or improving health

R

radiation sickness illness characterized by fatigue, nausea, weight loss, fever, bleeding from mouth and gums, hair loss, and immune deficiencies, resulting from overexposure to ionizing radiation

radon gas a naturally occurring radioactive gas produced by the decay of uranium

range of motion distance through which a joint can be moved; measured in degrees

rape an act of violence against another person wherein that person is forced to engage in sexual activities

recovery stage stage of an infectious disease at which the body's immune system has overcome the infectious agent and recovery is under way; convalescence stage

recycling ability to convert disposable items into reusable materials

reflexology massage applied to specific areas of the feet to treat illness and disease in other areas of the body

refractory errors incorrect patterns of light wave transmission through the structures of the eye

refractory phase that portion of the male's resolution stage during which sexual arousal cannot occur

regulatory genes genes within the cell that control cellular replication or doubling

rehabilitation return of function to a previous level

relaxation response physiological state of opposition to the fight-or-flight response of the general adaptation syndrome

relaxation training the use of various techniques to produce a state of relaxation

remediation development of alternative forms of function to replace those which had been lost or were poorly developed

resolution stage fourth stage of the sexual response pattern; the return of the body to a preexcitement state

retinal hemorrhage uncontrolled bleeding from arteries within the eye's retina

rheumatic heart disease chronic damage to the heart (especially heart valves) resulting from a streptococcal infection within the heart; a complication associated with rheumatic fever

rheumatoid arthritis the result of autoimmune deterioration of the joints

rigor mortis rigidity of the body that occurs after death

role of health mission of health within a person's life cycle

rubella German (or 3-day) measles

rubeola red or common measles

S

sadism sexual excitement achieved while inflicting injury or humiliation on another person

sadomasochism combination of sadism and masochism into one sexual activity

salt sensitive descriptive of people whose bodies overreact to the presence of sodium by retaining fluid and thus increasing blood pressure

satiety state in which there is no longer a desire to eat; fullness

satiety value food's ability to satisfy feelings of hunger

saturated fats fats that are difficult for the body to use; they are in solid form at room temperature; primarily animal fats

sclerotic changes thickening or hardening of tissues

screenings relatively superficial evaluations designed to identify deviations from normal

secondary bacterial infection bacterial infection that develops as a consequence of a primary infection

sediments fine particles of soil that are washed into a body of water, become suspended, and eventually settle to the bottom

self-actualization highest level of personality development; self-actualized people recognize their roles in life and use personal strengths to reach their fullest potential

self-care movement trend toward individuals taking increased responsibility for prevention or management of certain health conditions

self-esteem the quality of feeling good about yourself and your abilities

self-limiting capable of not progressing beyond a specific point; self-correcting

semen secretion containing sperm and nutrients discharged from the male urethra at ejaculation

sensory modalities vision, hearing, taste, touch, and smell; pathways for stimuli to register within the body

serum lipid analysis analysis of fat substances in the bloodstream; includes cholesterol and triglyceride measurements

set point a genetically programmed range of body weight beyond which a person finds it difficult to gain or lose additional weight

sex flush reddish skin response that results from increasing sexual arousal

sex reassignment operation surgical procedure designed to remove the external genitalia and replace them with genitalia appropriate to the opposite gender

sexual fantasies fantasies with sexual themes; sexual daydreams or imaginary events

sexual harassment unwanted attention of a sexual nature that creates embarrassment or stress

sexual victimization sexual abuse of children, family members, or subordinates by a person in a position of power

sexuality the quality of being sexual; can be viewed from many biological and psychosocial perspectives

sexually transmitted diseases (STDs) infectious diseases that are spread primarily through intimate sexual contact

shaft body of the penis

shingles viral infection affecting the nerve endings of the skin

shock profound collapse of many vital body functions; evident during acute alcohol intoxication and other serious health emergencies

sidestream smoke the smoke that comes from the burning end of a cigarette, pipe, or cigar

singlehood the state of not being married

six dimensions of health important areas of health in which specific strengths or limitations will be found: physical, emotional, social, intellectual, spiritual, and occupational

skinfold measurement measurement to determine the thickness of the fat layer that lies immediately beneath the skin

sliding scale method of payment by which patient fees are scaled according to income levels

smegma cellular discharge that can accumulate beneath the clitoral hood and the foreskin of an uncircumcised penis

smog air pollution composed of a combination of smoke, photochemical compounds, and fog

smokeless tobacco tobacco products (chewing tobacco and snuff) that are chewed or sucked rather than smoked

snuff finely shredded smokeless tobacco; used for dipping

spermatogenesis process of sperm production

spermicides chemicals capable of killing sperm

stalking a crime involving an assailant's planned efforts to pursue an intended victim

starch complex carbohydrate; a polysaccharide; a compound of long-chain glucose units

static stretching the slow lengthening of a muscle group to an extended level of stretch followed by holding the extended position for a recommended time period

sterilization generally permanent birth control techniques that surgically disrupt the normal passage of ova or sperm

stewardship acceptance of responsibility for the wise use and protection of the Earth's natural resources

stillborn baby that is dead at the time of birth

stimulants psychoactive drugs that stimulate the function of the central nervous system

stress the physiological and psychological state of disruption caused by the presence of an unanticipated, disruptive, or stimulating event

stress test examination and analysis of heart-lung function while the body is undergoing physical exercise; generally accomplished when the client walks or runs on a treadmill device while being monitored by a cardiograph

stressors factors or events, real or imagined, that elicit a state of stress

subcutaneous fat fat layer immediately beneath the skin

sudden cardiac death immediate death resulting from a sudden change in the rhythm of the heart

surrogate parenting one of several arrangements in which a woman becomes pregnant and gives birth for an infertile couple

sustainable environment an environment capable of supporting habitation; made possible by the efforts of individuals, organizations, and all levels of government

sympto-thermal method method of periodic abstinence that combines the basal body temperature method and the cervical mucus method

synapse location at which an electrical impulse from one neuron is transmitted to an adjacent neuron

synergistic drug effect heightened, exaggerated effect produced by the concurrent use of two or more drugs

synesthesia perceptual process in which a stimulus produces a response from a different sensory modality

systolic pressure blood pressure against blood vessel walls when the heart contracts

T

tar particulate phase of tobacco smoke with nicotine and water removed

target heart rate (THR) number of times per minute that the heart must contract to produce a training effect

technical nurses registered nurses (RNs) who hold diplomas or associate degrees from schools of nursing or university nursing programs

teratogenic capable of producing birth defects

testes male reproductive structures that produce sperm and the gonadal hormone testosterone

testosterone male sex hormone that stimulates tissue development

thorax the chest; portion of the torso above the diaphragm and within the rib cage

titration determining a particular level of a drug within the body

tolerance an acquired reaction to a drug; continued intake of the same dose has diminished results

total person holistic view of the person, incorporating the dynamic interplay of physical, emotional, social, intellectual, spiritual, and occupational factors

toxic shock syndrome (TSS) potentially fatal condition resulting from the proliferation of certain bacteria in the vagina, whose toxins enter the blood circulation

trace elements minerals whose presence in the body occurs in very small amounts; micronutrient elements

training effect significant positive effect that exercise has on the heart, lungs, and blood vessels

transcenders self-actualized people who have achieved a quality of being ordinarily associated with higher levels of spiritual growth

transcervical balloon tuboplasty the use of inflatable balloon catheters to open blocked fallopian tubes; a procedure used for some women with fertility problems

transient ischemic attack (TIA) temporary spasm of a cerebral artery that produces symptoms similar to those of a minor stroke; often a forewarning of a true cerebrovascular accident

transition the third and last phase of the first stage of labor; full dilation of the cervix

transsexualism the profound rejection of the gender to which the individual has been born

transvestism recurrent, persistent cross-dressing as a source of sexual excitement

trimester three-month period of time; human pregnancies encompass three trimesters

tropical oils oils extracted from coconut, palm, and palm kernel that contain much higher levels of saturated fat then other vegetable oils

tubal ligation sterilization procedure in which the fallopian tubes are cut and the ends tied back or cauterized

tumescence state of being swollen or enlarged

tumor mass of cells; may be cancerous (malignant) or noncancerous (benign)

type I alcoholism inherited predisposition supported by environmental factors favoring alcoholism

type II alcoholism male-limited alcoholism; an inherited form of alcoholism passed from father to son

U

unbalanced diet diet lacking adequate representation from each of the five food groups

underweight condition in which body weight is below desirable weight

unintentional injuries injuries that occur without anyone's intending that harm be done

urethra passageway through which urine leaves the urinary bladder

urethritis infection of the urethra

V

vacuum aspiration abortion procedure in which the cervix is dilated and vacuum pressure is used to remove the uterine contents

vaginal contraceptive film (VCF) spermicide-containing film that clings to the cervical opening

variant different from the statistical average

vas deferens (pl. vasa deferentia) passageway through which sperm move from the epididymis to the ejaculatory duct

vascular system body's blood vessels; arteries, arterioles, capillaries, venules, and veins

vasectomy surgical procedure in which the vasa deferentia are cut to prevent the passage of sperm from the testicles; the most common form of male sterilization

vasocongestion retention of blood within a particular tissue

vegan vegetarian diet vegetarian diet that excludes the use of all animal products, including eggs and dairy products

very-low-density lipoprotein (VLDL) the type of lipoprotein that transports cholesterol and other lipid material from the liver into the bloodstream

vicariously formed stimuli erotic stimuli that originate in one's imagination

virulent capable of causing disease

vitamins organic compounds that facilitate the action of enzymes

voyeurism watching others undressing or engaging in sexual activities

vulval tissues tissues surrounding the vaginal opening

W

warm-up physical and mental preparation for exercise

wellness a broadly based process used to achieve a highly developed level of health

will legal document that describes how a person wishes his or her estate to be disposed of after death

withdrawal illness uncomfortable, perhaps toxic response of the body as it attempts to maintain homeostasis in the absence of a drug; also called *abstinence syndrome*

work movement of mass over distance

Y

yeast single-cell plant responsible for the fermentation of plant products

young adult years segment of the life cycle from ages 18 to 22; a transitional period between adolescence and adulthood

yo-yo syndrome The repeated weight loss, followed by weight gain, experienced by many dieters

Z

zero tolerance laws laws that severely restrict the right to drive for underage drinkers who have been convicted of driving under the influence of *any* alcohol

zoophilia sexual contact with animals as a preferred source of sexual excitement; bestiality

EXAM PREP

Chapter 1   Shaping Your Health

MULTIPLE CHOICE

1. What health strategy involves following specific eating plans or exercise programs?
   A. Health screenings
   B. Education activities
   C. Behavior changes
   D. Regimentation

2. Why is it necessary to formulate an initial adult identity?
   A. So you can answer the question, "Who am I?"
   B. To have a productive and satisfying life
   C. It will help you move through other stages of development
   D. All of the above

3. Which developmental task involves using your own resources to follow a particular path?
   A. Forming an initial adult identity
   B. Assuming responsibility
   C. Establishing independence
   D. Developing social skills

4. Which of the following statements is *false*?
   A. The deeper the emotional relationships a person has, the better.
   B. Maintaining and improving your health is an important responsibility.
   C. The need to interact socially will at times negatively influence your health.
   D. Development of social skills can enhance your independence from your family.

5. What is *generativity?*
   A. The process of generating wealth and status in midlife
   B. The process of repaying society for its past support
   C. The negative attitude one generation holds for another
   D. None of the above

6. Which of the following are developmental tasks for the elderly?
   A. Accepting the physical decline of aging
   B. Maintaining high levels of physical function
   C. Establishing a sense of integrity
   D. All of the above

7. Which of the following is *not* a dimension of health?
   A. Transitional dimension of health
   B. Emotional dimension of health
   C. Holistic dimension of health
   D. Both A and C

8. Which dimension of health do some professionals believe to be the "core of wellness"?
   A. Emotional
   B. Spiritual
   C. Social
   D. Intellectual

9. Why is the occupational dimension of health important?
   A. Because you won't be happy unless you make a lot of money after graduation.
   B. Because both external and internal rewards from work affect your happiness.
   C. Because when people feel good about their work, they are more likely to live a healthier lifestyle.
   D. Both B and C

10. Which of the following is a strategy for changing your behavior?
    A. Make a personal contract to accomplish your goals.
    B. "Go it alone!" It is better not to involve family or friends.
    C. Don't reward yourself until you get to the final outcome.
    D. Don't let any obstacles occur or you will fail.

CRITICAL THINKING

1. What is health?

2. What is meant by the term *wellness?*

3. How does *empowerment* affect overall health and well-being?

4. Which dimensions of your health would you like to improve, and why?

5. How do you plan to successfully complete your developmental tasks?

Chapter 2   Achieving Emotional Maturity

MULTIPLE CHOICE

1. Emotionally well people:
   A. Experience the full range of human emotions, but are not overcome by them.
   B. Are only concerned with their own well-being.
   C. Set goals that are far and above what they can realistically accomplish.
   D. Trust only those who have proven their worth.

2. What factors shape self-esteem?
   A. Warm and supportive physical contact
   B. Religious indoctrination leading to guilt
   C. Failure to be successful in early undertakings
   D. All of the above

3. What three traits show a person's *hardiness?*
   A. Success, direction, and ability
   B. Commitment, control, and challenge
   C. Commitment, self-control, and self-esteem
   D. None of the above

4. Which of the following statements most accurately describes adults in midlife?
   A. Most experience a period of yearning for their youth called *midlife crisis.*
   B. Most experience a multitude of problems that fill them with melancholy and despair.
   C. Most have less to think about than they did when they were younger.
   D. Most see themselves as being in the prime of life.

5. Which of the following factors affects the quality of life of older adults?
   A. Sexual intimacy
   B. Marital status
   C. Economic status
   D. All of the above

6. What type of depression may occur after the death of a spouse or some other period of difficulty?
   A. Primary depression
   B. Reactive depression
   C. Chemically induced depression
   D. None of the above

7. Which is the most mature form of conflict resolution?
   A. Dialogue
   B. Submission
   C. Persuasion
   D. Aggression

8. What is the first step toward taking a proactive approach to life?
   A. Undertaking new experiences
   B. Taking risks
   C. Accepting mental pictures
   D. None of the above

9. Which of the following are motivational needs defined by Maslow?
   A. Physiological needs
   B. Economic needs
   C. Sexual needs
   D. Material needs

10. Which of the following statements describes creative individuals?
    A. They are intuitive and open to new experiences.
    B. They are less interested in detail than in meaning and implications.
    C. They are flexible.
    D. All of the above

CRITICAL THINKING

1. What is meant by a "normal range of emotions"?

2. What are some ways to overcome feelings of loneliness and shyness?

3. What are the warning signs of suicide, and how should they be treated?

4. What is the four-step process that allows one to control the outcomes of experiences and learn about one's emotional resources?

5. How do faith and spirituality affect emotional well-being?

Chapter 3   Managing Stress

MULTIPLE CHOICE

1. An event that produces stress is called a:
   A. Response
   B. Stressor
   C. Type B
   D. None of the above
2. Positive stress is called:
   A. Eustress
   B. Distress
   C. Type R stress
   D. None of the above
3. Which of the following is *not* a stage in Selye's general adaptation syndrome model?
   A. Alarm reaction stage
   B. Relaxation stage
   C. Resistance stage
   D. Exhaustion stage
4. Which part of the body is responsible for the interconnection between the nervous system and the endocrine system?
   A. Hypothalamus
   B. Pituitary gland
   C. Adrenal gland
   D. None of the above
5. When the body perceives stress, a number of responses are brought about by the epinephrine (adrenaline) and corticoids released. Which of the following is an expected response?
   A. Decreased cardiac and pulmonary function
   B. Increased digestive activity
   C. Decreased fat use
   D. Altered immune system response
6. PMR, or progressive muscular relaxation, is:
   A. A procedure of alternately contracting and relaxing muscle groups.

B. A correct way of breathing, by relaxing the diaphragm.
   C. An Eastern relaxation technique that employs the use of a mantra.
   D. A form of self-hypnosis that costs between $250 to $400 to learn.
7. Which of the following diseases have some origin in unresolved stress?
   A. Irritable bowel syndrome
   B. Allergies
   C. Asthma
   D. All of the above
8. Which of the following personality traits fosters high levels of stress?
   A. Self-confidence and practicality
   B. Anger and cynicism
   C. Both A and B
   D. Neither A nor B
9. Stress is best described as:
   A. Something completely beyond your control.
   B. The leading cause of cynicism.
   C. A physical and emotional response to change.
   D. A realistic and positive outlook on life.
10. What three areas of the body prepare the body to respond to stressors?
    A. Circulatory system, lymphatic system, and brain
    B. Brain, nervous system, and endocrine system
    C. Brain, muscular tissue, and nervous system
    D. Heart, lungs, and brain

CRITICAL THINKING

1. What is stress? Give an example of a stressful situation and how the person might feel.

2. Can stress be positive? Give an example.

3. What physiological reactions occur in the body because of stress?

4. How can repeated stress, if not dealt with properly, affect long-term health?

5. What are some healthy ways to deal with stress? Which would you choose to adopt, and why?

Chapter 4   Becoming Physically Fit

MULTIPLE CHOICE

1. Which of the following is *not* a benefit of physical fitness?
   A. The person can engage in various tasks and leisure activities.
   B. Body systems function efficiently to resist disease.
   C. Body systems are healthy enough to respond to emergency (threatening) situations.
   D. All of the above are benefits.

2. Which of the following areas of physical fitness do exercise physiologists say is most important?
   A. Muscular strength
   B. Muscular endurance
   C. Cardiorespiratory endurance
   D. Flexibility

3. Anaerobic, or oxygen-deprived, energy production:
   A. Is the result of low-intensity activity.
   B. Is the result of short-duration activities that quickly cause muscle fatigue.
   C. Is the result of activities such as walking, distance jogging, and bicycle touring.
   D. None of the above

4. Which of the following types of training exercises are based on the *overload principle?*
   A. Isometric exercises
   B. Progressive resistance exercises
   C. Isokinetic exercises
   D. All of the above

5. Of the following statements, which accurately describes flexibility?
   A. It is relatively the same throughout your body.
   B. Not every joint in your body is equally flexible.
   C. Nothing alters the flexibility of a particular joint.
   D. Gender and age do not affect flexibility.

6. Which of the following statements is true about aging?
   A. Aging is predictable and the same for every person.
   B. The greatest change is in areas of the simplest function.
   C. Change often occurs suddenly and without warning.
   D. Two people of the same age may experience deterioration of different body systems.

7. The American College of Sports Medicine recommends five significant areas to consider for achievement of cardiorespiratory fitness. Which of these is *not* one of the areas?
   A. Mode of activity
   B. Frequency of training
   C. Intensity of training
   D. Popularity of activity

8. What is target heart rate (THR)?
   A. An intensity level of between 60% and 90% of maximum heart rate
   B. An intensity level of between 70% and 100% of maximum heart rate
   C. The maximum number of times your heart should contract each minute to give your respiratory system a work overload
   D. The rate at which you become so fatigued that you must stop exercising

9. What are the three basic parts of a good training session?
   A. Running, weightlifting, stretching
   B. Warm-up, workout, cooldown
   C. Warm-up, stretching, cooldown
   D. Mental warm-up, socialize, workout

10. Which of these is an abnormal sign to be aware of, during or after exercise?
    A. A delay of over 1 hour in your body's return to a fully relaxed, comfortable state after exercise
    B. Difficulty sleeping
    C. Noticeable breathing difficulties or chest pains
    D. All of the above

CRITICAL THINKING

1. What are the components of a well-designed fitness program for older adults?

2. How serious is low back pain, and what should a person do to alleviate or prevent it?

3. Explain what steps you would take to develop a cardiorespiratory fitness program, taking into account all five areas recommended by the American College of Sports Medicine.

4. Describe some of the newest trends in physical activity (such as rollerblading, water exercise, or "street jam"). Which most appeals to you, and why?

5. Why is steroid use dangerous?

Chapter 5 Understanding Nutrition and Your Diet

MULTIPLE CHOICE

1. What three nutrients provide the body with calories?
   A. Sugar, amino acids, and supplements
   B. Carbohydrates, fats, and proteins
   C. Tropical oils, food additives, and carbohydrates
   D. None of the above

2. Which of the following statements accurately describes carbohydrates?
   A. They occur in two forms only, depending on the number of proteins that make up the molecule.
   B. About 20% of our calories comes from carbohydrates.
   C. Carbohydrates are combinations of sugar units, or saccharides.
   D. Each gram of carbohydrate contains 400 calories.

3. Which of the following statements is *false?*
   A. Fats are important nutrients in our diets.
   B. Fats make it impossible for our bodies to absorb vitamins A, D, E, and K.
   C. Fat insulates our bodies, helping us retain heat.
   D. Most of the fat we eat is "hidden" in food.

4. What are vitamins?
   A. Inorganic materials necessary for tissue repair and disease prevention
   B. Pills that can be taken each morning to give the body energy all day
   C. Organic compounds that are required in small amounts for normal growth, reproduction, and maintenance of health
   D. Nutrients that provide more than half our body weight

5. Which of the following nutrients could the body not live without for over a week?
   A. Minerals
   B. Fiber
   C. Vitamins
   D. Water

6. Which of the following is a recommendation based on the USDA Food Guide Pyramid?
   A. Adults should eat two to four servings from the fruit group each day.
   B. Three to five servings from the vegetable group each day are recommended for an adult.
   C. Adults should consume two to three servings from the milk, yogurt, and cheese group each day.
   D. All of the above

7. What are phytochemicals?
   A. Physiologically active components that function as antioxidants and may deactivate carcinogens
   B. The additives used in foods that preserve freshness or enhance flavor, color, or texture
   C. The chemicals used to enrich breads and cereals
   D. None of the above

8. What kind of vegetarian eats milk products but not eggs?
   A. Ovolactovegetarian
   B. Macrobiotic vegetarian
   C. Lactovegetarian
   D. Vegan vegetarian

9. What factors may influence nutritional changes as a person ages?
   A. Changes to the structure and function of the body resulting from age
   B. The progressive lowering of the body's basal metabolism
   C. Both A and B
   D. Neither A nor B

10. Which of the following is a suggested step toward increasing the availability of food?
    A. Increase the yield of land under cultivation.
    B. Increase the amount of land under cultivation.
    C. Use water more efficiently for the production of food.
    D. All of the above

CRITICAL THINKING

1. Based on your personal assessment of your current diet, are you getting all the nutrients you need? In which areas do you need to improve?

2. What role does cholesterol play in the diet?

3. Explain the difference between *water-soluble* and *fat-soluble* vitamins and the characteristics of each.

4. Would you consider becoming a vegetarian? Why or why not?

5. What is *nutrient density?* Why is it important to consider this concept when making food choices?

Chapter 6   Maintaining a Healthy Weight

MULTIPLE CHOICE

1. Which weight measurement technique precisely measures relative amounts of fat and lean body mass by comparing underwater weight with out-of-water weight?
   A. Skinfold measurements
   B. Body mass index (BMI)
   C. Electrical impedance
   D. Hydrostatic weighing

2. Which may be the simplest method of determining a person's amount of body fat?
   A. Appearance
   B. Height-weight tables
   C. Body mass index (BMI)
   D. Waist-to-hip ratio

3. What influences obesity?
   A. Environment
   B. Genetics
   C. Both environment and genetics
   D. None of the above

4. Which area(s) within the hypothalamus tell the body when it should begin and end food consumption?
   A. Feeding and satiety centers
   B. Central nervous system (CNS)
   C. Thyroid and pituitary glands
   D. None of the above

5. Which of the following statements describes "brown fat"?
   A. It is located in small amounts in the upper back between the shoulder blades.
   B. There is a renewed interest in the study of it.
   C. It burns calories as heat without generating energy units that are stored in fat cells.
   D. All of the above

6. Which of Sheldon's three body types is characterized by a tall, slender build?
   A. Ectomorph
   B. Mesomorph
   C. Endomorph
   D. None of the above

7. What is hypercellular obesity?
   A. The increase of fat cells later in life as a result of being overfed in infancy or substantially gaining weight in childhood or adolescence
   B. When fat cells increase in size as a result of long-term positive caloric balance in adulthood
   C. Excessive fat around the waist, which can contribute to the onset of diabetes mellitus
   D. None of the above

8. What would most experts cite as the most important reason for the widespread problem of obesity?
   A. Family dietary practices
   B. Endocrine influence
   C. Infant feeding patterns
   D. None of the above

9. What is basal metabolic rate (BMR)?
   A. The rate of caloric intake to caloric output
   B. The minimum amount of energy the body requires to carry on all vital functions
   C. The rate of a food's thermic output
   D. None of the above

10. Which weight management technique involves the use of pharmaceuticals?
    A. Balanced diets supported by portion control
    B. Fad diets
    C. Hunger/satiety-influencing products
    D. Self-help weight reduction programs

CRITICAL THINKING

1. What factors influence your body image and self-concept?

2. What steps might you take to successfully control your weight throughout your lifetime?

3. Why is dieting alone not a good technique for achieving and maintaining weight loss?

4. What are reasons someone might develop anorexia nervosa or bulimia? How should a person be treated for these disorders?

5. What does it mean to exercise or eat compulsively?

Chapter 7   Choosing a Drug-Free Lifestyle

MULTIPLE CHOICE

1. Which of these is an aspect of addictive behavior?
   A. Exposure
   B. Compulsion
   C. Loss of control
   D. All of the above
2. What kind of drugs alter the user's feelings, behaviors, or moods?
   A. Medicines
   B. Over-the-counter drugs
   C. Psychoactive drugs
   D. Steroids
3. Which type of dependence creates *full* withdrawal symptoms when the drug use is stopped?
   A. Psychological
   B. Physical
   C. Cross-tolerant
   D. None of the above
4. What are neurotransmitters?
   A. Chemical messengers that transmit electrical impulses
   B. Organic messengers that transmit the chemicals in drugs directly to the brain
   C. Hallucinogenic drugs that are currently popular with college students
   D. None of the above
5. How do drugs "work"?
   A. By blocking the production of a neurotransmitter
   B. By forcing the continued release of a neurotransmitter
   C. Either A or B
   D. Neither A nor B

6. Which type of psychoactive drug *excites* the activity of the central nervous system (CNS)?
   A. Inhalants
   B. Hallucinogens
   C. Narcotics
   D. None of the above
7. What is "crack"?
   A. Powdered cocaine that is alkalized in benzene or ether and smoked through a waterpipe
   B. A small, rocklike crystalline material made from cocaine hydrochloride and baking soda
   C. A white powder that is snorted in "lines" through a rolled dollar bill or tube
   D. A pure form of methamphetamine that looks like rock candy
8. Which type of psychoactive drug *slows down* the function of the central nervous system (CNS)?
   A. Inhalants
   B. Hallucinogens
   C. Cannabis
   D. Depressants
9. What is THC?
   A. A hallucinogen derived from the peyote cactus plant
   B. A drug popular in the 1960s
   C. The active ingredient in marijuana
   D. A new "designer" drug
10. Which drugs are among the most dependence-producing?
    A. Inhalants
    B. Hallucinogens
    C. Depressants
    D. Narcotics

CRITICAL THINKING

1. What is the difference between drug *misuse* and drug *abuse*?

2. How has cocaine use affected poor urban areas?

3. What are possible long-term effects of marijuana use?

4. What is a synergistic effect, and why is it dangerous?

5. What do you think about the legalization of drugs and about drug testing?

Chapter 8 Taking Control of Alcohol Use

MULTIPLE CHOICE

1. What is *binge drinking?*
   A. The practice of drinking and then purging
   B. A harmless activity popular among college students
   C. The practice of consuming five drinks in a row, at least once during the previous 2-week period
   D. The practice of consuming two drinks in a row, at least once a day

2. What is the alcohol content of a bottle of 140-proof gin?
   A. 140% of the fluid in the bottle
   B. 70% of the fluid in the bottle
   C. 14% of the fluid in the bottle
   D. 1.4% of the fluid in the bottle

3. What type of drug is alcohol?
   A. Stimulant
   B. Hallucinogen
   C. Depressant
   D. Narcotic

4. What should be done with people who become unconscious resulting from alcohol consumption?
   A. They should be given a cold shower to wake them up.
   B. They should be made to drink coffee.
   C. They should be taken to bed and left undisturbed for several hours.
   D. They should be put on their side and monitored frequently.

5. Which of the following leading causes of accidental death has connections to alcohol use?
   A. Motor vehicle collisions
   B. Falls
   C. Drownings
   D. All of the above

6. Which of the following is a good guideline to follow for responsibly hosting a party?
   A. Make alcohol the primary entertainment, especially with a keg or other popular way to serve alcohol.
   B. Ridicule those who are too afraid to drink.
   C. If friends say they are just fine to drive home even though they have been drinking, let them go.
   D. None of the above

7. Which alcohol awareness group promotes responsible party hosting among university students?
   A. AA
   B. MADD
   C. BACCHUS
   D. SADD

8. What is the main difference between problem drinking and alcoholism?
   A. Problem drinkers stay away from hard liquor.
   B. Alcoholics usually don't engage in binge drinking.
   C. Alcoholism involves a physical addiction to alcohol.
   D. Problem drinking is easier to detect.

9. Which support group appeals to the children of alcoholics?
   A. Al-Anon
   B. AA
   C. Alateen
   D. MADD

10. Which new drug, approved by the FDA in 1995, is being used to treat alcoholism?
    A. Naltrexone
    B. Antabuse
    C. Heroin
    D. Maltodextrine

CRITICAL THINKING

1. Why do people drink alcohol?

2. What physiological differences in women make them more susceptible to the effects of alcohol?

3. What are the possible effects of drinking alcohol while pregnant?

4. What role does alcohol use play in violent crime, family violence, and suicide?

5. Explain *denial*, *enabling*, and *codependence* as they occur with alcoholism.

Chapter 9   Rejecting Tobacco Use

MULTIPLE CHOICE

1. Which factor most affects a person's decision to smoke?
   A. Gender
   B. Age
   C. Education
   D. Race

2. What are psychosocial factors of tobacco dependence?
   A. Manipulation
   B. Advertising
   C. Modeling
   D. Both A and C

3. What consumer group is the FDA focusing its education efforts on to discourage increased tobacco use?
   A. Women
   B. African-American men who attend predominately black universities
   C. Teens
   D. Older adults who began smoking before health risks were known

4. Which phase of tobacco use includes nicotine, water, and a variety of powerful chemical compounds known collectively as *tar?*
   A. Active phase
   B. Particulate phase
   C. Gaseous phase
   D. Nicotine phase

5. What signals the beginning of lung cancer?
   A. Changes in the basal cell layer resulting from constant irritation by accumulating tar in the airways
   B. An inability to breathe normally
   C. A "smoker's cough"
   D. Mucus swept up to the throat by cilia, where it is swallowed and removed through the digestive system

6. What is COLD?
   A. Chronic obstructive lung disease
   B. A chronic disease in which air flow in and out of the lungs becomes progressively limited
   C. A disease state made up of chronic bronchitis and pulmonary emphysema
   D. All of the above

7. Which of the following statements is *false?*
   A. It is strongly recommended that women who smoke not use oral contraceptives.
   B. Chewing tobacco and snuff generate blood levels of nicotine in amounts equivalent to those seen in cigarette smokers.
   C. Contrary to some claims, secondhand smoke is not a serious health threat.
   D. Children of parents who smoke are twice as likely to develop bronchitis or pneumonia during the first year of life.

8. Which of the following statements is *true?*
   A. Chewing tobacco is a safe alternative to smoking.
   B. Sidestream smoke makes up only 15% of our exposure to involuntary smoking.
   C. Spouses of smokers may have a 30% greater risk of lung cancer.
   D. The only effective way to quit smoking is to go "cold turkey."

9. Which is more effective as a means of quitting smoking?
   A. Nicotine-containing chewing gum
   B. Transdermal patch
   C. Neither A nor B work
   D. Both A and B are equally effective

10. What is the main debate concerning smoking today?
    A. The validity of health warnings
    B. The rights of the nonsmoker vs. the rights of the smoker
    C. The rights of young adults to buy cigarettes
    D. None of the above

CRITICAL THINKING

1. What advertising tactics do tobacco companies use to offset the potential decline in sales from reports of health risks?

2. In what ways is tobacco addictive?

3. How does smoking adversely affect health?

4. Why should a pregnant or breastfeeding woman refrain from smoking?

5. Do you think smoking should continue to be banned from public places? Why or why not?

Chapter 10   Reducing Your Risk of Cardiovascular Disease

MULTIPLE CHOICE

1. Why has the rate of death caused by cardiovascular disease declined?
   A. Changing American lifestyles
   B. Medical advances in diagnosis and treatment
   C. A breakthrough new drug
   D. Both A and B

2. What is the nation's number one "killer"?
   A. AIDS
   B. Lung disease
   C. Cancer
   D. Cardiovascular disease

3. Which of the following is a function of the blood?
   A. Regulation of water content of body cells and fluids
   B. Transportation of nutrients, oxygen, wastes, and hormones
   C. Buffering to help maintain appropriate pH balance
   D. All of the above

4. What are three cardiovascular risk factors that cannot be changed?
   A. Age, gender, body composition
   B. Heredity, weight, glandular production
   C. Age, heredity, and metabolism
   D. None of the above

5. What is a risk factor that can be changed?
   A. Cigarette/tobacco use
   B. Physical inactivity
   C. High blood pressure
   D. All of the above

6. Which disease predisposes people to developing heart disease?
   A. Cancer
   B. Epilepsy
   C. Diabetes
   D. Multiple sclerosis

7. Which form of cardiovascular disease involves damage to the vessels that supply blood to the heart muscle?
   A. Hypertension
   B. Stroke
   C. Coronary heart disease
   D. Congenital heart disease

8. What is cholesterol?
   A. The oil used to fry food
   B. A soft, fatlike material manufactured by the body
   C. A material necessary for reproduction of blood
   D. None of the above

9. What is hypertension?
   A. A consistently elevated blood pressure
   B. Stress on arterial walls resulting from plaque build-up
   C. The tendency for blood to clot
   D. Abnormally low blood pressure

10. What is the name of the cardiovascular disease that begins as a streptococcal infection of the throat?
    A. Peripheral artery disease
    B. Rheumatic heart disease
    C. Phlebitis
    D. Congestive heart failure

CRITICAL THINKING

1. What components make up the cardiovascular system? How does the system work?

2. Do you exhibit any risk factors for cardiovascular disease? What steps can you take to change them, if they can be changed?

3. What is the difference between HDLs and LDLs?

4. How can hypertension be prevented?

5. What are the different causes of stroke?

Chapter 11   Living with Cancer and Chronic Conditions

MULTIPLE CHOICE

1. What changes characterize cancer cells?
   A. Their normal behavior ceases.
   B. They become severely dysfunctional.
   C. Neither A nor B
   D. Both A and B

2. What are protooncogenes?
   A. Genes that repair damaged cells
   B. Genes that suppress the immune system
   C. Genes that have the potential to become cancerous
   D. Abnormal genes

3. What is the Human Genome Project?
   A. The testing of new cancer-fighting drugs
   B. A scientific study of genes
   C. A secret military project that exposed World War II troops to carcinogens
   D. The study of cancer-producing viruses

4. Which type of cancer is found in cells of the blood and blood-forming tissues?
   A. Lymphoma
   B. Neuroblastoma
   C. Carcinoma
   D. Leukemia

5. Which is the most common site of the body to develop cancer in women?
   A. Breast
   B. Uterus
   C. Lung
   D. Skin

6. Which test greatly improves the chances of preventing cervical cancer?
   A. Mammography
   B. MRI
   C. Pap test
   D. Biopsy

7. Which type of cancer is referred to as the "silent" cancer because of its vague symptoms?
   A. Ovarian
   B. Prostate
   C. Vaginal
   D. Lung

8. Which traditional method of cancer treatment has had many successful advances in recent years?
   A. Surgery
   B. Chiropractic manipulation
   C. Chemotherapy
   D. Radiation

9. Which chronic disease most often appears in early adulthood and continues intermittently for the next 20 to 25 years?
   A. Diabetes mellitus
   B. Lupus
   C. Multiple sclerosis
   D. Asthma

10. Which type of asthma is caused by stress or as a consequence of frequent respiratory tract infections?
    A. Extrinsic
    B. Intrinsic
    C. EIA
    D. Childhood-onset asthma

CRITICAL THINKING

1. What social and environmental factors contribute to the onset of cancer?

2. What steps can women take to prevent cancer or to detect the early stages of cancer?

3. What steps can men take to prevent cancer or to detect the early stages of cancer?

4. What are the seven warning signs of cancer?

5. What are the differences and similarities between insulin-dependent and non–insulin-dependent diabetes?

Chapter 12   Preventing Infectious Diseases

MULTIPLE CHOICE

1. What is a pathogen?
   A. A disease-causing agent
   B. A virus, bacterium, or fungus
   C. Neither A nor B
   D. Both A and B
2. What is the function of a reservoir in the chain of infection?
   A. To cause disease
   B. To offer a favorable environment in which an infectious agent can thrive
   C. To act as a portal of exit
   D. To transmit the agent from person to person
3. Which term describes insects, animals, or birds that carry diseases from human to human?
   A. Vectors
   B. Pathogens
   C. Reservoirs
   D. Agents
4. During which of the following stages of infection is the infected person *most* contagious?
   A. Prodromal stage
   B. Clinical stage
   C. Decline stage
   D. Incubation stage
5. Which type of immunity is the result of vaccination or immunization?
   A. Naturally acquired immunity
   B. Artificially acquired immunity
   C. Passively acquired immunity
   D. None of the above
6. Which viral infection has mental fatigue and depression as side effects?
   A. Influenza
   B. Common cold
   C. Mononucleosis
   D. Pneumonia
7. What is chronic fatigue syndrome (CFS)?
   A. A mononucleosis-like condition most commonly seen in women in their thirties and forties
   B. A condition that may be linked to neurally mediated hypotension
   C. A condition that may be a psychological disorder
   D. All of the above
8. How is Lyme disease transmitted?
   A. Through droplet spread
   B. Through fecal-oral spread
   C. Through the deer tick nymph
   D. Through inhalation
9. Which sexually transmitted disease occurs as blisterlike lesions on the genitals or lips?
   A. Herpes simplex
   B. Gonorrhea
   C. Syphilis
   D. Human papillomavirus
10. Of the following STDs, which has no cure?
    A. Vaginal infections
    B. Cystitis and urethritis
    C. Herpes simplex
    D. Gonorrhea

CRITICAL THINKING

1. What are the two main components to the body's protective defense? How do they work?

2. Why do the elderly and people with additional health complications need to take extra precaution to avoid contracting influenza?

3. Why should people pay close attention to their immunization history, especially college-aged students?

4. What precautions should women take when using tampons to avoid toxic shock syndrome?

5. How is AIDS transmitted, and what precautions can be taken to avoid contracting it?

Chapter 13   Understanding Sexuality

MULTIPLE CHOICE

1. Which basis for biological sexuality refers to the growing embryo's development of gonads?
   A. Genetic
   B. Gonadal
   C. Structural
   D. None of the above
2. At which age are typical children able to correctly identify their gender?
   A. 4 years
   B. 2 years
   C. 18 months
   D. 6 months
3. What part of the testis produces sperm?
   A. Seminiferous tubules
   B. Scrotum
   C. Epididymis
   D. Interstitial cells
4. Which is the most sensitive part of the female body?
   A. Mons pubis
   B. Vagina
   C. Clitoris
   D. Prepuce
5. During which phase of the menstrual cycle does ovulation occur?
   A. Menstrual
   B. Proliferative
   C. Secretory
   D. None of the above
6. Which phase of the sexual response pattern prevents men from having multiple orgasms?
   A. Excitement
   B. Plateau
   C. Orgasmic
   D. Refractory

7. Which of the following statements is not true about celibacy?
   A. Celibate people may have intimate relationships without sex.
   B. It is defined as the self-imposed avoidance of sexual contact.
   C. Psychological complications often result from a celibate lifestyle.
   D. All are true.
8. Which type of oral-genital stimulation involves kissing and licking the vulva of the female?
   A. Foreplay
   B. Fellatio
   C. Cunnilingus
   D. None of the above
9. Which type of love is enduring and capable of sustaining long-term mutual growth?
   A. Infatuation
   B. Passionate love
   C. Companionate love
   D. Devotional love
10. Which of the following statements is not true of cohabitation?
   A. It is an alternative to marriage.
   B. It can sometimes exist between people sharing a platonic relationship.
   C. Approximately half of all cohabiting couples will disband.
   D. Couples who cohabit are more likely to get married than those in a more traditional dating relationship.

CRITICAL THINKING

1. How do biological and psychosocial factors contribute to the complex expression of our sexuality?

2. How has a blending of feminine and masculine qualities benefitted society?

3. Why might the "withdrawal" method of contraception not work?

4. What changes, both physiological and psychological, might menopause create in a woman's life?

5. What effect does the aging process have on the sexual response pattern?

Chapter 14   Managing Your Fertility

MULTIPLE CHOICE

1. Which form of birth control *does not* prevent STDs?
   A. Withdrawal
   B. Calendar method
   C. IUD
   D. All of the above

2. Which two forms of birth control, when used together, provide a high degree of contraceptive protection *and* disease control?
   A. IUD and spermicides
   B. Spermicides and condoms
   C. Calendar method and spermicides
   D. Oral contraceptive and spermicides

3. Which of the following statements is *not* true of oral contraceptives?
   A. The use of antibiotics lowers their contraceptive effectiveness.
   B. They regulate a woman's menstrual cycle.
   C. The user may experience more frequent vaginal infections, weight gain, mild headaches, and mild depression.
   D. They are useful in the prevention of STDs.

4. What are "minipills"?
   A. Smaller versions of the regular oral contraceptive that can be swallowed more easily
   B. The placebo pills taken between cycles
   C. Oral contraceptives that contain no estrogen— only low-dose progesterone
   D. Less expensive versions of the pill that are slightly less effective

5. What is Depo-Provera?
   A. An injectable contraceptive
   B. A subdermal implant contraceptive
   C. A type of diaphragm
   D. A brand of oral contraceptive

6. Which type of abortion is performed in the earliest stages of the first trimester?

   A. Menstrual extraction
   B. Dilation and curettage
   C. Dilation and evacuation
   D. Hypertonic saline procedure

7. What is RU-486?
   A. The "morning after" pill
   B. The process of using prostaglandin to influence muscle contractions that expel uterine contents
   C. A hypertonic saline solution
   D. A drug that blocks the action of progesterone, thus producing an early abortion

8. What is the first thing a parent should do on arriving home?
   A. Collapse in front of the television.
   B. Hug or hold his or her young children for at least a few minutes.
   C. Begin making dinner.
   D. Encourage children to do their chores.

9. Which of the following is an obstacle to pregnancy?
   A. 200 to 500 million sperm cells are deposited in each ejaculation.
   B. Sperm cells are capable of moving quickly.
   C. The acidic level of the vagina is destructive to sperm.
   D. Once inside the fallopian tubes, sperm can live for days.

10. Which type of artificial fertilization involves transferring fertilized ova from a laboratory dish into the fallopian tubes?
    A. In vitro fertilization and embryo transfer (IVF-ET)
    B. Gamete intrafallopian transfer (GIFT)
    C. Zygote intrafallopian transfer (ZIFT)
    D. Surrogate parenting

CRITICAL THINKING

1. What factors should you consider when choosing a method of birth control?

2. Which of the available methods of birth control would you be most likely to use, if you needed to?

3. What are the guidelines set forth under *Roe v. Wade,* the landmark 1973 Supreme Court case?

4. What serious questions need to be considered before deciding to have children?

5. Describe the birth process from beginning to end.

Chapter 15   Making Consumer and Health Care Choices

MULTIPLE CHOICE

1. Which of the following statements is *false?*
   - A. The accuracy of health information from friends and family members may be questionable.
   - B. The mass media routinely supply public service messages that give valuable health-related information.
   - C. Never trust the labels and directions on prescription medication; it is usually misleading and intended to make you buy more of the product.
   - D. Folk wisdom is on occasion supported by scientific evidence.

2. Which health resource has the most effective way of distributing information to the public by mail?
   - A. On-line computer services
   - B. Voluntary health agencies
   - C. Government agencies
   - D. Qualified health educators

3. What is the difference between allopathy and osteopathy?
   - A. Osteopaths engage in quackery.
   - B. Allopathic physicians are board-certified; osteopaths are not.
   - C. Osteopaths perceive themselves as being more holistic.
   - D. Only osteopaths function as primary care physicians.

4. Which type of health care professional provides services relating to understanding behavior patterns or perceptions but does not dispense drugs?
   - A. Dentist
   - B. Psychiatrist
   - C. Podiatrist
   - D. Psychologist

5. What does an optician do?
   - A. Specializes in vision problems due to refractory errors
   - B. Provides prescriptions for eyewear products
   - C. Grinds lenses according to a precise prescription
   - D. Specializes in vision care with a base in general medicine

6. What type of nursing position is helping to provide communities with additional primary care providers?
   - A. Nurse practitioner
   - B. Registered nurse
   - C. Licensed practical nurse
   - D. Technical nurse

7. The established amount that the insuree must pay before the insurer reimburses for services is:
   - A. Fixed indemnity
   - B. Coinsurance
   - C. Deductible
   - D. Exclusion

8. What are Medicare and Medicaid?
   - A. Preferred provider organizations (PPOs)
   - B. Independent practice associations (IPAs)
   - C. Health maintenance organizations (HMOs)
   - D. Forms of governmental insurance

9. Which is the most frequently prescribed drug in the United States?
   - A. Prozac (for depression)
   - B. Vasotec (for high blood pressure)
   - C. Mevacor (for high cholesterol)
   - D. Zantac (for ulcers)

10. Which of the following is a sign of quackery?
    - A. Makes promises of quick, dramatic, painless, or drugless treatment
    - B. Claims a product provides treatment for multiple illnesses
    - C. States that the treatment is secret or not yet available in this country
    - D. All of the above

CRITICAL THINKING

1. What are some pros and cons of obtaining health information from mass media?

2. What are some sources of health information available to you?

3. What are some alternative health care practices? Would you be willing to try them?

4. How can self-care benefit both individuals and the health care industry as a whole?

5. What are the advantages and disadvantages of HMOs?

Chapter 16 Protecting Your Safety

MULTIPLE CHOICE

1. Which form of violence received national attention because of the deaths in 1994 of Nicole Brown Simpson and Ronald Goldman?
   A. Child abuse
   B. Carjacking
   C. Domestic violence
   D. Elder abuse

2. Who is most often a victim of partner abuse?
   A. Prostitutes
   B. Teenage girls
   C. Spouses or former spouses of the assailant
   D. Men

3. Which form of child abuse occurs most frequently?
   A. Neglect
   B. Physical
   C. Psychological
   D. Sexual

4. What may be the "single greatest crime problem in America today"?
   A. Youth violence
   B. Hate crimes
   C. Bank robberies
   D. Organized crime

5. Aside from the physical harm of rape, what other effects may occur?
   A. Posttraumatic stress syndrome
   B. Guilt
   C. Emotional damage resulting from "broken trust"
   D. All of the above

6. Which of the following constitutes sexual harassment?
   A. Excessive pressure for dates
   B. Sexually explicit humor
   C. Unwanted physical contact
   D. All of the above

7. Which of the following can help increase safety around your home?
   A. Make sure your name is spelled correctly in the phone book.
   B. Try to live in apartments on the first floor.
   C. Require repair people to show valid identification.
   D. Leave windows unlocked in case you need to escape in a hurry.

8. Over half of all murders result from:
   A. Random crime
   B. Domestic abuse
   C. Arguments between acquaintances or relatives
   D. None of the above

9. Which of the following persons is a highly probable candidate for death by motor vehicle accident?
   A. Male, 55–65 years of age, driving in rainy conditions on a weekend afternoon
   B. Female, 35–45 years of age, driving on a freeway with the noise of children playing in the back seat
   C. Female, 65–75 years of age, driving in rush-hour traffic
   D. Male, 15–25 years of age, driving on a two-lane rural road on a Saturday night

10. Which of the following resources will help improve your safety on campus?
   A. University-approved escorts
   B. Campus security departments
   C. Campus counseling center
   D. All of the above

CRITICAL THINKING

1. What factors may have contributed to a drop in U.S. homicide rates?

2. How should suspected child abuse be properly handled?

3. What is rape? What is acquaintance rape? What is date rape?

4. How can you increase your personal safety?

5. What steps can you take to protect children and the elderly?

Chapter 17   Controlling Environmental Influences

MULTIPLE CHOICE

1. Each year, the population of the world grows by:
   - A. 90 million people
   - B. 90,000 people
   - C. 90%
   - D. 90 billion people

2. What is the leading source of air pollution?
   - A. Kuwait oil fires
   - B. Chemical production plants
   - C. Internal combustion engines
   - D. Coal-fired power plants

3. What has caused the greenhouse effect?
   - A. A progressive increase in carbon dioxide in the atmosphere
   - B. A hole in the ozone layer
   - C. A slight warming of the Earth's surface
   - D. All of the above

4. What substances produce acid rain when they combine with moisture in the atmosphere?
   - A. Coal and hydrogen
   - B. Hydrocarbons and particulate matter
   - C. Chlorofluorocarbons
   - D. Nitrogen and sulfur

5. Which type of pollution disproportionately affects children of low-income families?
   - A. Radon gas
   - B. Lead
   - C. Subsidence inversion
   - D. Radiation inversion

6. What is eutrophication?
   - A. A biological imbalance that causes fish to die in great numbers from lack of oxygen
   - B. The overabundance of aquatic plants that results when water is rich in nitrates and phosphates
   - C. Both A and B
   - D. Neither A nor B

7. Which of the following is the name of a hydrocarbon found in the water supply that has been linked to cancer?
   - A. Chlorine
   - B. PCB
   - C. DDT
   - D. EPA

8. Which of the following sources of water pollution comes from power plants?
   - A. Oil spills
   - B. Thermal pollution
   - C. Sediments
   - D. None of the above

9. Which type of solid waste disposal is discouraged or illegal in many urban areas?
   - A. Ocean dumping
   - B. Incineration
   - C. Sanitary landfill
   - D. Open dumping

10. Which of the following devices generates electromagnetic fields?
    - A. Water bed heater
    - B. Electric razor
    - C. Cellular phone
    - D. All of the above

CRITICAL THINKING

1. How do different types of air pollution adversely affect us?

2. Why are metals, such as mercury, arsenic, and copper, particularly dangerous when they pollute our water supply?

3. What factors have kept recycling from being fully adopted in many areas?

4. What are some concerns related to nuclear energy?

5. What steps can you take to improve your environment and reduce your exposure to harmful environmental pollutants?

Chapter 18   Accepting Dying and Death

MULTIPLE CHOICE

1. Which of the following is a criterion by which death may be determined?
   A. Lack of heartbeat and breathing
   B. Lack of central nervous system function
   C. Presence of rigor mortis
   D. All of the above
2. Which type of euthanasia is illegal in the United States?
   A. Direct euthanasia
   B. Indirect euthanasia
   C. Both A and B
   D. Neither A nor B
3. What does the physician's order "DNR" stand for?
   A. Death not recorded
   B. Do not resuscitate
   C. Do not release
   D. Do not recognize
4. Which psychological stage for dying people serves as the earliest temporary defense mechanism?
   A. Denial
   B. Anger
   C. Bargaining
   D. None of the above
5. Which of the following describes the appropriate way to act toward someone who is dying?
   A. Refrain from crying so as not to upset them
   B. Remain optimistic even when there is no hope for recovery
   C. Try to be genuine and honest
   D. Try to distract the person from talking about death

6. Adults coping with the death of a child should:
   A. Have another child and name that child after the deceased.
   B. Move to a different home for a change of environment.
   C. Give themselves time and space to grieve.
   D. All of the above
7. Which of the following is *not* a normal, healthy expression of grief over the loss of a loved one?
   A. Physical discomfort
   B. Sense of numbness
   C. Guilt
   D. Extreme hostility
8. How long do periods of grief usually last?
   A. A few weeks
   B. 2 to 5 years
   C. A few months to a year
   D. 10 years or more
9. What is a wake?
   A. An established time for friends and family to share emotions and experiences about the deceased
   B. A formaldehyde-based fluid used to replace blood components during embalming
   C. A container for ashes from cremation
   D. None of the above
10. Which of the following is the word for a notice of death printed in a newspaper?
    A. Eulogy
    B. Epitaph
    C. Obituary notice
    D. None of the above

CRITICAL THINKING

1. What are living wills and medical power of attorney documents? Why would it be prudent to have these documents?

2. How do the emotional stages of dying described by Elisabeth Kübler-Ross affect those close to the dying person?

3. Describe what might occur during an out-of-body experience.

4. How does a hospice differ from a traditional hospital with respect to care of the terminally ill?

5. In what ways do death rituals aid people in dealing with death?

ANSWERS

Chapter 1
1. C; 2. D; 3. C; 4. A; 5. B; 6. D; 7. D; 8. B; 9. D; 10. A

Chapter 2
1. A; 2. D; 3. B; 4. D; 5. D; 6. B; 7. A; 8. D-Constructing mental pictures is the answer; 9. A; 10. D

Chapter 3
1. B; 2. A; 3. B; 4. A; 5. D; 6. A; 7. D; 8. B; 9. C; 10. B

Chapter 4
1. D; 2. C; 3. B; 4. D; 5. B; 6. D; 7. D; 8. A; 9. B; 10. D

Chapter 5
1. B; 2. C; 3. B; 4. C; 5. D; 6. D; 7. A; 8. C; 9. C; 10. D

Chapter 6
1. D; 2. A; 3. C; 4. A; 5. D; 6. A; 7. A; 8. D-Inactivity is the answer; 9. B; 10. C

Chapter 7
1. D; 2. C; 3. B; 4. A; 5. C; 6. D-Stimulants is the answer; 7. B; 8. D; 9. C; 10. D

Chapter 8
1. C; 2. B; 3. C; 4. D; 5. D; 6. D; 7. C; 8. C; 9. C; 10. A

Chapter 9
1. C; 2. D; 3. C; 4. B; 5. A; 6. D; 7. C; 8. C; 9. A; 10. B

Chapter 10
1. D; 2. D; 3. D; 4. D-Age, gender, and heredity is the answer; 5. D; 6. C; 7. C; 8. B; 9. A; 10. B

Chapter 11
1. D; 2. C; 3. B; 4. D; 5. C; 6. C; 7. A; 8. C; 9. C; 10. B

Chapter 12
1. C; 2. B; 3. A; 4. B; 5. B; 6. C; 7. D; 8. C; 9. A; 10. C

Chapter 13
1. B; 2. C; 3. A; 4. C; 5. B; 6. D; 7. C; 8. C; 9. C; 10. D

Chapter 14
1. D; 2. B; 3. D; 4. C; 5. A; 6. A; 7. D; 8. B; 9. C; 10. C

Chapter 15
1. C; 2. C; 3. C; 4. D; 5. C; 6. A; 7. C; 8. D; 9. D; 10. D

Chapter 16
1. C; 2. C; 3. A; 4. A; 5. D; 6. D; 7. C; 8. C; 9. D; 10. D

Chapter 17
1. A; 2. C; 3. A; 4. D; 5. B; 6. B; 7. B; 8. B; 9. D; 10. D

Chapter 18
1. D; 2. A; 3. B; 4. A; 5. C; 6. C; 7. D; 8. C; 9. A; 10. C

Credits

....

Credits

Chapter 1: p. 2 (Star Box), Source: Guyton R, et al: College students and national health objectives for the year 2000: a summary report, *Journal of American College Health,* July 1989, 38:9–14.

Chapter 2: p. 26, From Study Guide for *Psychology applied to modern life; adjustment in the 90s,* by W. Weiten and M. Loyd. Copyright © 1997, 1994, 1991, 1986, 1983 Brooks/Cole Publishing, Pacific Grove, CA 93950, a division of International Thomsom Publishing Inc. By permission of the publisher. **p. 29 (Star Box),** From Depression is a sign of illness, not a sign of weakness, *Ball State University Campus Update,* Dec 12, 1988, p. 1; **p. 31 (Star Box),** From Blumenthal SJ: Suicide: a guide to risk factors: assessment and treatment of suicidal patients, *Medical Clinics of North America* 72:937–971, 1988; **p. 36 (Figure 2–2),** "HIERARCHY OF NEEDS" from MOTIVATION AND PERSONALITY, by ABRAHAM H. MASLOW. Revised by Robert Frager, James Fadiman, Cynthia McReynolds, and Ruth Cox. Copyright © 1954, 1987, Harper and Row, Publishers, Inc. Copyright © 1970 by Abraham H. Maslow. Reprinted by permission of Addison Wesley Educational.

Chapter 4: pp. 69, 77 (Star Boxes), From Prentice WE: *Fitness for college and life,* ed 4, St. Louis, 1994, McGraw Hill; **pp. 74–75,** Data from the National Fitness Foundation; **p. 84,** Copyright 1984, *USA Today,* excerpted with permission, art by Donald O'Connor, **pp. 85–86 (Star Boxes),** Copyright 1986, *USA Today* excerpted with permission.

Chapter 5: pp. 95–95, From *Nutrition for a healthy life,* courtesy of Marcy Leeds; **p. 98 (Figure 5–1),** Adapted from Procter & Gamble, 1989; **pp. 100–106, 109 (Tables 5–1, 5–2, 5–3, 5–4, 5–6),** From Wardlaw G, Insel P: *Perspectives in nutrition,* ed 3, St. Louis, 1996, McGraw Hill; **pp. 106–108 (Table 5–5),** Modified from Food and Nutrition Board, National Research Council: *Recommended dietary allowances,* ed 10, Washington, DC, 11989, National Academy of Sciences; **p. 108 (Figure 5–2),** US Department of Agriculture/US Department of Health and Human Services, August, 1992; **pp. 112–113 (Star Box),** Consumer Reports, Consumer Union; **pp. 115–116 (Figure 5–3, A-B),** Source: Food and Drug Administration, and Wardlaw G. Insel P: *Perspectives in nutrition,* ed 3, St. Louis, 1996, McGraw Hill; **pp. 117 (Health Action Guide), 118 (Table 5–7),** US Department of Health and Human Services, Public Health Service: *The Surgeon General's report on nutrition and health,* Washington, DC, 1988, US Government Printing Office; **p. 117 (Star Box),** From *Nutrition and your health: dietary guidelines for Americans,* ed 4, 1995, USDA, Home & Garden Bulletin No. 232; **p. 119 (Health Action Guide),** © 1986, American Diabetic Association, HEALTH FOOD CHOICES, used with permission; **p. 120 (Figure 5–5),** National Dairy Council, Rosemont, IL.

Chapter 6: p. 128 (Star Box), C. Everett Koop Foundation, American Diabetes Association; **p. 129 (Table 6–1),** Reprinted with permission of Metropolitan Life Insurance Company; **p. 130 (Table 6–2),** US Department of Agriculture; **p. 131**

(Figure 6–1), Modified from George A. Bray; **p. 137 (Table 6–4),** Based on data from Bannister EW, Brown SR: The relative energy requirements of physical activity. In HB Falls, editor: *Exercise Physiology,* New York, 1968, Academic Press Inc.; Howley ET, Glover ME: The caloric costs of running and walking a mile for men and women, *Medicine and Science in Sports* 6:235, 1984; and Passmore R, Durnin JVGA: Human energy expenditure, *Physiological Reviews* 35:801, 1955; **p. 141 (Health Action Guide),** © 1987, *USA Today,* excerpted with permission; **pp. 142–143 (Table 6–5),** Adapted from Guthrie H: *Introductory nutrition,* ed 7, St. Louis, 1989, McGraw Hill, pp. 226–227.

Chapter 7: p. 155 (Figure 7–1), Source: National Institute on Drug Abuse, 1990, survey; **p. 158 (Star Box),** Source: Interagency Drug Alcohol Council: Why people use drugs, Ft. Wayne, IN, The Council; **p. 160 (Table 7–1),** Modified from Muncie Star © 1987. Reprinted with permission; **p. 162 (Table 7–2),** Sources: C Lecos: The latest caffeine scoreboard, *FDA Consumer,* March 1984, p. 14; Measuring your life with coffee spoons, *Tufts University Diet and Nutrition Letter,* April 1984, pp. 3–6; and Expert Panel on Food Safety and Nutrition, Institute of Food Technologists; Evaluation of caffeine safety, from the Institute of Food Technologists, 221 N. LaSalle Street, Chicago, IL 60601, 1986; **p. 163 (Figure 7–2),** Source: American Management Association Survey.

Chapter 8: p. 182 (Table 8–1), US Department of Health and Human Services: Alcohol and health: fourth special report to the US Congress, Washington, DC, 1981, DHS Pub No ADM 81–1080; **p. 183 (Figures 8–1 and 8–2),** Source: Presley CA, Melman PW: *Alcohol and drugs on American college campuses: a report to college presidents,* June 1992, US Department of Education, Drug Prevention in Higher Education Program (FIPSE Grant), Southern Illinois University Student Health Program Wellness Center; **p. 184 (Table 8–2),** US Department of Transportation, National Highway Safety Administration: Adapted from alcohol and the impaired driver (AMA); **p. 187 (Figure 8–3),** From Wardlaw G: *Perspectives in nutrition,* ed 3, St. Louis, 1996, McGraw Hill; **p. 191 (Health Action Guide),** Modified from brochure of the Indiana Alcohol Countermeasure Program; **p. 196 (Star Box),** Modified from Woititz JG: *Adult children of alcoholics,* Pompano Beach, FL, 1983, Health Communications, Inc. In Pinger R, Payne W, Hahn D, Hahn E: *Drugs: issues for today,* St. Louis, 1991, McGraw Hill.

Chapter 10: pp. 229 (Figure 10–1), 230 (Star Box), 244 (Health Action Guide), Reproduced with permission, 1995 Heart and Stroke Facts, Copyright American Heart Association; **p. 238 (Health Action Guide),** Reproduced with permission, © 1988, American Heart Association: Heart Facts; **p. 239 (Table 10–1),** Report of the Expert Panel on Detection, Evaluation and Treatment of High Blood Cholesterol in Adults, US Department of Health and Human Services (DHS: NIH Pub No 89–2925), 1989, Washington, DC, US Government Printing Office.

Chapter 11: p. 252 (Figure 11–1), National Cancer Institute: *Horizons of cancer research,* NIH Pub

No 89–3011, © 1989; **pp. 253 (Figure 11–2), 254, 258, 260, 265 (Health Action Guides), 263 (Star Box),** Reprinted with permission of the American Cancer Society, Inc.; **p. 262 (Health Action Guide),** American Academy of Dermatology; **p. 266 (Table 11–2),** From Hasler CM: *Nutri-News,* St. Louis, 1995, McGraw Hill; **p. 271 (Health Action Guide),** Courtesy of Allergy and Asthma Network, Mothers of Asthmatics, Inc.

Chapter 12: p. 284, Sources: Centers for Disease Control and Prevention and American Academy of Pediatrics; **p. 288 (Table 12–3),** Courtesy of the National Institute of Allergy and Infectious Diseases; **p. 298,** Centers for Disease Control and Prevention, Atlanta.

Chapter 13: p. 331, Modified from *USA Today;* **p. 334 (Health Action Guide),** Adapted from Haas K, Haas A: *Understanding sexuality,* ed 3, St. Louis, 1993, McGraw Hill.

Chapter 14: pp. 346–347 (Table 14–1), Modified from Lisken L, et al: Youth in the 1980s: social and health concerns, Population Reports, Series M, No. 9, Population Information Program, Johns Hopkins University, November-December 1985; **p. 348,** From Haas I, Haas A: *Understanding sexuality,* ed 3, St. Louis, 1993, McGraw Hill.

Chapter 15: p. 381 (Figure 15–1), First Databank, The Hearst Corporation; **p. 384 (Health Action Guide),** Source: Pell AR: *Making the Most of Medicare,* DCI Publishing, 1990, in *in-synch,* Erie, PA, Spring, 1994, Erie Insurance Group; **p. 389 (Figure 15–2),** Source: SAMSHA News, Vol I, #4, p. 3.

Chapter 16: p. 407 (Figure 16–1), Courtesy of the National Committee to Prevent Child Abuse, Chicago, IL; **p. 413 (Health Action Guide),** From the American College Health Association; **p. 416 (Health Action Guide),** Adapted from Pynoos J, Cohen E: *Creative ideas for a safe and livable home,* Washington, DC, American Association of Retired Persons, 1992; and Van Tassel D: *Home, safe home,* St. Louis, 1996, GenCare Health Systems.

Chapter 17: pp. 424–425, Modified from *Being green: some tips on how to help the earth,* Scripps Howard News Service; **p. 425 (Figure 17–1),** Source: UN Population Fund; **p. 426 (Figure 17–2),** World Resources, 1988–1989; **p. 429 (Table 17–1),** Source: Water Pollution Control Federation; **p. 437 (Star Box),** From McGrath M, Dadd DL: *Nontoxic, Natural, and Earthwise,* Los Angeles, 1990, Jeremy P. Tarcher.

Chapter 18: p. 451 (Star Box), Reprinted by permission of Choice in Dying, formerly Concern for Dying/Society for the Right to Die, 1035 30th Street NW, Washington, DC 20007; **p. 460 (Figure 18–1),** The National Kidney Foundation Uniform Donor Card is reprinted with permission from the National Kidney Foundation, Inc. Copyright 1970, 1991, New York, NY.

Photo Credits

Chapter 1: p. 19, Stewart Halperin.

Chapter 2: pp. 34, 41, Stewart Halperin.

Chapter 3: pp. 43, 47, Stewart Halperin; **pp. 48, 54,** Ed Self/Photographic Services, Ball State University.

Chapter 4: pp. 68, 82, Ed Self/Photographic Services, Ball State University; **pp. 71, 74–75, 77, 91,** Stewart Halperin.

Chapter 5: pp. 92, 94, 125, Stewart Halperin; **p. 97,** NutraSweet, Monsanto Corp.; **p. 113,** Ed Self/Photographic Services, Ball State University.

Chapter 6: p. 132, Linsley Photographics; **p. 136,** Steward Halperin; *p. 139,* CLG Photographics.

Chapter 7: p. 175, Stewart Halperin; **p. 167,** From Drug Enforcement Administration: Drugs of Abuse, US Department of Justice; **p. 170,** Charles Gupton/The Stock Market; **p. 172,** courtesy of Partnership for a Drug Free America.

Chapter 8: p. 180, Stewart Halperin; **p. 188,** George Steinmetz.

Chapter 9: pp. 203, 207, 215, 219, Stewart Halperin; **p. 206,** Ed Self/Photographic Services, Ball State University; **p. 213,** Courtesy of American Cancer Society.

Chapter 10: p. 235, Richard Hirneisen/The Stock Shop.

Chapter 11: pp. 261, 262, From Thibodeau G, Patton K: *Anatomy & physiology,* ed 3, St. Louis, 1996, Mosby; **p. 262,** From Habif TP: *Clinical dermatology,* ed 3, St. Louis, 1996, Mosby; **pp. 264, 270,** CLG Photographics.

Chapter 12: p. 290, courtesy of Dr. Farrar: *Slide atlas of infectious diseases,* 2/e; **p. 294,** courtesy of Beth and William Kenk; **pp. 300, 301,** Centers for Disease Control and Prevention.

Chapter 14: p. 349, Courtesy of Ortho Pharmaceutical Corp.; **p. 350,** Courtesy of Apothocus, Inc.; **pp. 351 (left), 355,** Stewart Halperin; **pp. 351 (right), 353 (top),** Laura J. Edwards; **p. 353 (bottom),** Courtesy of Alza Corporation; **p. 353 (left),** Linsley Photographics; **p. 357,** Courtesy of Wyeth-Ayerst Laboratories; **p. 363,** SPL/Photo Researchers; **p. 365,** Science Photo Library/Photo Researchers.

Chapter 16: pp. 406, 412, CLG Photographics.

Chapter 17: p. 431, Norbert Wu; **p. 433,** Greig Granna/Stock Boston.

Chapter 18: p. 450, The Gamma Liaison Network; **p. 454,** CLG Photographics.

Index

A

A personality type, 53
AA. *See* Alcoholics Anonymous
AAI, 284, 285
Abortion, 359–61, 373
Abortion pill, 360. *See also* Morning-after pill
Absorption of alcohol, 182
Abstinence birth control, 346–47, 346*t*
Accidents
  alcohol use and, 188–89
  causes of death and, 2*t*
  falls, 188
  learning activities, 408
  unintentional injury, 414–16
ACE inhibitors, 248
Acid rain, 427, 428
ACOAs. *See* Adult Children of Alcoholics
Acquired immunity (AI), 283, 285
ACTH. *See* Adrenocorticotropic hormone
Action on Smoking and Health, 225
Acupressure, 264
Acupuncture, 264, 384
Acute alcohol intoxication, 185–86
Acute rhinitis, 287–88, 288*t*
Acyclovir, 300
ADA, 20
Adaptive thermogenesis, 133
ADD
  amphetamines for, 159, 162
  tobacco use and, 215
Adenocarcinomas, 252, *253*
Adipose tissue
  in diabetes II, 133
  in midlife adults, 72
Adoption, 374
Adrenaline, 50, 51
Adrenocorticotropic hormone (ACTH)
  nicotine and, 205
  in stress response, 48, 50, 51
Adult adjustments
  midlife
    aging in, 71–73
    developmental tasks for, 7–8, 16–17
    emotional maturity and, 27–28
    job stress and, 60–62
    midlife crisis in, 28
    student identity tasks in, *5*, 16–17
Adult Children of Alcoholics (ACOAs), 195–96
Advertising, 179, 196, 197, 379
Aerobic energy, 68, 69
Aerobic exercises
  athletic shoes for, 85
  bench, 76
  benefits of, 80–81
  for cardiorespiratory system, 68, 73
  crosstraining with, 83
  fitness assessment and, 74
  reduction of cervical cancers and, 68
Aerosols, abuse of, 157, 168
Africa
  appetite suppression and, 135
  hepatitis B in, 293
  infectious diseases and, 293
  nutrition and, 135
  tobacco use and, 206
African-Americans
  alcohol use/crime and, 199

cardiovascular risk factors of, 233
college enrollment of, 19
hypertension in, 247–48
pancreatic cancer in, 261
Aggressive behaviors, 166
Aging
  acceptance of, 8
  cardiovascular risk factors and, 233
  changes of, 71–73
  in elderly, 73
  flexibility in, 70
  sexuality and, 329
AIDS. *See also* Sexually transmitted diseases
  artificial insemination screening for, 368
  drug abuse and, 164
  hot lines for, 296
  pathology of, 293–96, 295*t*
  prevalence of, 2, 229, *229*
  prevention of, 296–97, 306, 307
  transmission of, 280, 282
  treatment of, 297
Air pollution, 423–29, *426*, 444–45
Al-Anon organizations, 194, 195–96
Alcohol Alert, 180
Alcohol consumption, 179–200
  action guides for, 186, 191
  assessments and
    alcoholism, 155, 157, 179–80, 184, 190–95, 205
    binge type, 180–81, *180*, 181
    drinker classification, 182*t*
    drinking patterns, 179–80, 182*t*, 190–91
    moderate use redefined, 180
    multicultural use of, 179
    personal, 13, 187, 197
    questionnaire for, 13
    women, 180, 184, 195–96
  bans on, 82
  disease/illness and
    acute intoxication, 185–86
    barbiturates, 164
    blackouts, 191, 192
    cancers, 265, 266*t*
    cardiovascular risk factors, 232
    chronic diseases, 191–93
    depression, 192, 194
    fetal alcohol syndrome, 186–88, *188*, 189
    health problems and, 186–89, *186*
    migraine/cluster headaches and, 50
    naltrexone, 195
    stress origins and, 44
    suicide and, 189
  driving and, 180, 189, 190–91, 193, 200
  HealthQuest Activities, 184
  learning activities, 195
  organizations and
    ACOAs, 195–96
    BACCHUS/MADD/SADD, 190
  physiology of, 182–85, *187*
  social issues and, 183, 188–89, 195–97
    accidents, 188–89
    advertising, 179, 196
    codependence, 194
    crime/violence, 180, 189, 199–200
    host responsibility, 189
    reduction of, 11
    responsible drinking, 189–90, 200
    safety, 188–89

types/content of
  beverage classification, 184*t*
  beverage making, 180–81, 182*t*
  distilled beverages, 182, 184*t*
  proof defined, 182
Alcohol hot lines, 171
Alcoholics Anonymous (AA), 156, 171, 194–95
Allopathy, 383
Alternative Medicine: Expanding Medical Horizons, 385–86
Alternative practitioners, 384–85, 386
Alternative therapies, 264–65, 384–86
Alveoli, 214
Alzheimer's disease, 268, 269
America, North. *See* North America
American Cancer Society (ACS), 211, 267
American College Health Association, 2
American College of Radiology, 267
American College of Sports Medicine (ACSM), 76–79
American Heart Association, 231–36
American history, 20
American literature, 20
Americans with Disabilities Act (ADA), 20
Amino acids, 97–99
Amotivational syndrome, 167
Amphetamines, 160–62
  abuse of, 157, 159–60, 160*t*
  for attention deficit disorder, 160
  designer drugs and, 166
  for narcolepsy, 160
  testing for, 169
Amyl nitrite, 168
Anaerobic energy, 68, 69
Analgesics
  caffeine content in, 162*t*
  over-the-counter, 394–95
Anatomical donation, 459
Androgyny, 314–15
Anesthetic gases, 168
Aneurysms, cerebral, 242
Angel dust. *See* Phencyclidine
Anger, 53
Angina pectoris, 238–40
Angiogenesis potential, 251
Angioplasty, *240*, 240
Angry heart condition, 53
Anorexia, 145, 146
Antagonistic effect, 168
Antibodies, 285–86
Antidepressants, 50
Anxiety, 193, 194
Appetite control, 133, 144
Appetite suppressants
  ephedrine, 144
  phen-fen, 144
  side effects, 144
Aquired immunodeficiency syndrome. *See* AIDS
Archery
  alcohol bans and, 82
  calories used in, 137*t*
  fitness limits of, 73
Arm hang exercises, 74
Artery disease, peripheral, 244, 245
Arthritis, 80
Artificial hearts, 240–41
Artificial insemination, 368

Page numbers in *italics* indicate illustrations; *t* indicates tables.

Artificially acquired immunity (AAI), 284, 285
Asia and Asians
    college enrollment of, 19
    exercise and, 81
    hepatitis B in, 293
    hypertension and, 247
    infectious diseases and, 293
    stress management and, 55
    tobacco use and, 206
Asphyxiation, 186
Aspirin, 73
Assault, 403, 410
Asthma, 271
Atherosclerosis, 236–39, 237
Athletic organizations, 169–70
Athletic shoes, 85
Atria, 230, 230
AT&T, 61–62
Attention deficit disorder (ADD)
    amphetamines for, 160, 161
    tobacco use and, 215
Autoimmune diseases
    multiple sclerosis, 270–71
    systemic lupus erythematosus, 272
Avonex, 271
Axons, 159
Ayurveda, 265, 384, 385
Azidothymidine (AZT), 296

B

B-cell immune response, 283, 283–84, 285–86
BAC, 184–85
BACCHUS, 190
Back pain
    biking for, 79
    chronic, 277
    flexibility and, 70, 71
    in older adults, 79
    tobacco use and, 214
Bacterial infections, 280–81, 281t
Ballistic stretching, 70, 71
Barbiturates, 164–65
    abuse of, 157
    alcohol abuse and, 165
    stimulants and, 164
    testing for, 169
Basal body temperature method, 346t, 347–48
Basal cell layer, tobacco effects on, 212
Basal metabolic rate (BMR), 137–38, 139
Baseball, 137t
Baseline data, 15
Basketball, 76, 137t
Beans, 109t, 111
Beer, 182, 183, 184t, 196
Behaviors
    assessments for, 12–15
    changes for health, 11, 16, 17
    modeling, 207–8
    motivational systems and, 16
Bench aerobics, 76
Benson, Herbert, 53–54
Benzodiazepines, 169
Benzopyrene, 167
Beta blockers, 239, 248
Beta endorphins, 205
Betaseron, 271
Biking
    ACSM recommendations for, 76
    for back pain, 79
    bicyclist's nipples, 80
    calories used in, 137t
    cardiorespiratory system and, 68, 73
    fitness clubs and, 82–83
Billboards, 179, 196
Billings cervical mucus method, 348–49
Binge drinking, 179–80, 180, 181, 192
Biofeedback, 265
Birth, 365–68, 366. See also Pregnancy
    premature, 203
Birth control, 370–71. See also Contraceptives
    basal body temperature method, 346t, 347–48

Billings cervical mucus method, 348–49
    calendar abstinence, 346t, 347–48
    vs. contraception, 344–45
    effectiveness rates in, 346t
    questionnaire for, 14
    symptothermal method, 349
    withdrawal method, 345, 346t
Birth control, oral contraceptives. See Oral
        contraceptives
Birth defects, 165
Birth weights, 203
Bisexuality, 337
Blackouts, alcohol, 191, 192
Blacks. See African-Americans
Blood
    heart function and, 231
Blood alcohol concentration (BAC), 184–85
Blood pressure, 232
Blue babies, 242–43
BMI, 130, 131, 131, 132
BMR, 137–38, 139
Body composition, 70–71
Body image, 128, 132
Body mass index (BMI), 130, 130t, 131, 131, 132
Bodybuilding, 82–83
Bone marrow growth regulators, 264
Bone mass
    in elderly, 73
    in midlife adults, 72
    tobacco use and, 214
Bone structure, 73
Boost Alcohol Consciousness Concerning
        the Health of University Students
        (BACCHUS), 190
Bosnia, 409
Bowling
    fitness limits of, 73
Boxing, 137t
Bra exercise supports, 80
Brandy, 184t
Brazelton, T.B., 362
Breads, 109t, 111
Breast cancers
    estrogen therapy and, 72, 255
    fats and, 255
    obesity and, 128
    oral contraceptives and, 255
    pathology of, 251, 252, 254, 255–57, 259
Breast examinations, questionnaire for, 14
Breast exercise supports, 80
Breastfeeding
    tobacco use and, 215
    weight gains and, 134
Breasts, nipple irritations in, 80
Breathing, 185
Bronchitis, chronic, 213
Brown fat, 133
Buddhism, rituals/funerals in, 457
Bulimia nervosa, 145–46
Burial arrangements, 457, 458, 459
Burns, 188–89
Butyl nitrite, 168

C

Caffeine, 159, 160, 160t
    abuse of, 157, 159–60, 160t, 162t
    bone loss and, 214
    quitting, 11
    smoking and, 214
Calcium channel blockers, 239
Calcium supplements, 72
Calendar abstinence birth control, 346, 346t
Calipers, 130, 131, 132
Calories
    in alcoholic beverages, 182
    balance, 136, 136
    defined, 93–94
    energy consumption and, 136–39, 137t
    weight control and, 128, 129
Cambodia, rituals/funerals in, 457
Camel cigarettes advertising, 208

Campus crime. See Crime, campus
Canada
    health insurance in, 393
    tobacco use warnings in, 203
Canadians, diets and, 99
Cancers, 250–78
    action guides for, 254, 260, 262
    alcohol consumption and, 266, 266t
    alternative therapies for, 264–65
    assessments for, 256
    benign tumors, 251–52
    breast. See Breast cancers
    carcinogens defined, 251
    causes of death and, 2t
    cervical, 252, 254, 256, 257, 258
    checkup guides for, 254
    colon/rectum, 251, 254, 260–61
    diagnosis of, 263–66
    HealthQuest Activities, 254
    learning activities, 259
    leukemia, 251, 253
    liver, 252
    lung, 251, 252, 253, 253–55
    lymphomas, 253
    melanoma, 261–62, 262
    metastasis, 251, 252
    obesity and, 128
    ovarian, 258–59
    pancreas, 261
    pathophysiology of, 250–53
    prostate, 254, 259–60
    resources for patients with, 267
    risk reduction for, 265–66
    silent, 259
    skin, 252, 256, 261, 261–63, 263t
    testes, 254, 260
    tobacco use and, 211–12, 212, 213
    treatment of, 263–65
    types of, 252–53, 253
    uterine, 254, 257
    vaginal, 257–58
Candlelighters Childhood Cancer Foundation, 267
Cannabis, 166–67
    abuse of, 166–67
    testing for, 169
Canoeing, 137t
Cape Canaveral, 61
Carbohydrates, 93
Carbon monoxide
    air pollution and, 427
    pregnancy and, 214–15
    tobacco use and, 203, 210, 211
Cardiorespiratory fitness
    benefits of, 69
Carcinogens
    defined, 251
    marijuana and, 167
Carcinomas, 252, 253
Cardiac nodes, 230, 230
Cardiopulmonary fitness
    assessment for, 74–76, 88–89
    program for, 73–80
    stress response and, 51–52
Cardiopulmonary resuscitation (CPR)
    education for, 3
    elderly fitness programs and, 79
    for emergency treatment, 239
Cardiovascular diseases, 229–48
    action guides for, 238
    aging and, 233
    alcohol use and, 240
    angina pectoris and, 238–40
    angioplasty and, 240, 240
    artificial hearts and, 240–41
    assessments in, 232
    atherosclerosis and, 236–39, 237
    blue babies and, 242–43
    causes of death, 2t
    cholesterol/lipoproteins and, 237, 239t
    congenital heart disease, 242–43
    congestive heart failure, 244–45

coronary arteriography, 239–40, 241
coronary artery heart disease, 236–45
emergency treatment for, 239
heart catheterization and, 239–40
heart transplants and, 240–41
hypertension and, 241–42, 247–48
learning activities, 236
murmurs, 244, 245
myocardial infarction, 237
normal function and, 229–31
peripheral artery disease, 244, 245
prevalence of, 229, 229, 230
rheumatic heart disease and, 243–44
risk factors in, 231–36, 247–48
stroke, 242
tobacco use and, 210–11, 215–16
transient ischemic attack, 242, 243
women and, 234
Carpal tunnel syndrome, 60–61
CAT scans
body composition by, 130
stroke and, 242, 243
Catheterization, heart, 239–40
Caucasians
alcohol use/crime and, 199
breast cancer incidence in, 255
Cell-mediated immunity, 283
Cements, abuse of, 168
Central nervous system (CNS)
alcohol effects on, 182
appetite and, 133
caffeine effects on, 214
cocaine effects on, 164
drug effects on, 159
in stress response, 50
tobacco effects on, 210, 214
Cereals, 109t, 111
Cerebral aneurysms, 242
Cerebral cortex, 50
Cerebral hemorrhages, 242
Cerebrovascular occlusions, 242, 243
Cervical cancers, 68, 252, 254, 256, 257, 258
Cervical caps, 346t, 352, 355
Cesarean deliveries, 368, 369
Champagne, 184t
Cheese, 50
Chemical wastes, 434–35
Chemotherapy, 264
Chernobyl nuclear power plant, 437
Chickenpox, 285
Child abuse, 403, 406, 411
Child physical fitness, 83
Children of Alcoholics Foundation, Inc., 195
Chile, health objectives in, 11
China
exercise and, 81
humor in, 32
maternal deaths in, 356
nutrition in, 121
rituals/funerals in, 457
Chippers, 205
Chiropractic cancer therapy, 264
Chiropractic services, 384
Chlordane, 430–31
Chlordiazepoxides, 164
Chlorinated hydrocarbons, 430–31
Chlorofluorocarbons, 427
Chloroform, 168
Chocolate, 50
Cholesterol levels, 96–97, 100
cardiovascular diseases and, 232, 235, 237, 239t
effects of, 96–97, 100
health screenings for, 3
high/low density lipoproteins and, 237, 239t
Chronic bronchitis, 213
Chronic diseases, 273
alcoholism and, 191–93
defined, 250, 251
description of, 266–72
pain management in, 275–78
Chronic fatigue syndrome, 290

Chronic obstructive pulmonary disease
causes of death and, 2t
Chronic obstructive lung disease (COLD)
tobacco use and, 203, 213, 213, 214
Cider, hard, 184t
Cigarette preferences, 202
Cigar smoking, 203
Cilia, 212, 213
Circulation, 68, 69
Clean Water Act, 1994, 431
Cleaning activities, 137t
Clear cell cancers, 258
Climbing, 137t
Clotting, 52
Cluster headaches, 50
Coca leaves, 135
Cocaine
abuse of, 157, 162–64, 163
appetite suppression and, 135
dependencies and, 205
Cocaine Anonymous, 171
Cocaine hot lines, 171
Cocktail alcohol content, 184t
Cocoa
caffeine content in, 162t, 214
tobacco CNS effects of, 214
Codeine
sources of, 157
testing for, 169
Codependence, 193–94
Coffee
appetite suppression and, 135
caffeine content in, 162t, 214
tobacco CNS effects, 214
Cognac alcohol content, 184t
Cognitive ability
accidents and, 188–89
alcohol use and, 181–82, 183–84, 185, 186, 199
crime/violence and, 180, 189, 199–200
current concerns and, 195–96
suicide and, 189
Cohabitation, 335–36
COLD. See Chronic obstructive lung disease
Cold, common, 162t, 286–87, 288t
learning activities, 287
Collateral circulation, 68, 69
Colon cancer
aerobic fitness and, 68
obesity and, 128
physiology of, 251, 254, 260–61
Combined pill contraceptives, 347t, 354–55
Communication, 31
Computer workstations, 60–61
Computerized axial tomography scans
body composition by, 130
stroke and, 242, 243
Condoms
action guides for, 352
effectiveness of, 346t
female, 346t
male, 346t, 350–51
STDs and, 298
Conflict skills, 32–33
Congenital heart disease, 242–43
Congenital rubella syndrome (CRS), 243
Congestive heart failure, 214, 244–45
Connective tissue disorders
multiple sclerosis, 270–71
systemic lupus erythematosus, 272
Consumer advocacy groups, 382
Consumer protection agencies, 382
Consumerism, 379–401
assessments in, 15, 380
cosmetics, 395
fraud and quackery and, 395–96
health care costs/insurance, 388–93
health care providers, 383–88
health information on the Internet, 399–400
information sources, 379–83
over-the-counter drugs, 394–95
prescription drugs, 393–95

self-help, 388
Contraception
vs. birth control, 344–45
Contraceptives
cervical caps, 346t, 352, 355
combined pills, 347t, 354–55
condoms/female, 346t
condoms/male, 346t, 350–51
Depo-Provera, 347t
diaphragms, 346t, 351, 351–52
effectiveness rates in, 344–45, 346t–347t
injectable, 357
IUD, 346t, 352–54, 353
minipills, 347t, 357
morning-after pills, 356
oral contraindications, 356
oral effectiveness, 347t, 354–57
spermicides, 346t, 349–50, 350
STDs and, 298
sterilization, 357–59, 358
subdermal implants, 347t, 357
tobacco use and, 215–16
triphasic pills, 347t, 355
tubal ligation, 347t
vasectomy, 347t
Cooking, 137t
Copolymer 1, 271
Coronary arteries, 230, 230, 231
Coronary arteriography, 239–40, 241
Coronary heart disease
caffeine and, 214
types of, 236–45
Correction fluids, 168
Corticoids, 48, 50, 51
Cosmetics, 395
Costs. See Health care costs
CPR. See Cardiopulmonary resuscitation
Crack, 163, 163–64
abuse of, 162–63
dependencies and, 205
Crank. See Methamphetamines
Creative expression, 36–37
Cremation, 459
Crime
alcohol use and, 180, 189, 199–200
binge drinking and, 180
campus safety and, 199–200, 416–18
child abuse, 403, 406, 411
concerns of late 1990s, 2
domestic, 403, 405–7
elder abuse, 403, 406–7
gangs/youth, 407–8
guns and, 408
hate crimes, 408–9
intentional injury, 403–10
personal safety assessments for, 404
residential safety and, 414–15
sexual victimization, 410–14
stalking, 409–10
victims and alcohol use, 199–200
Crisis drug hot lines, 171
Critical personality types, 53
Croatia, hate crimes in, 409
Cross-country skiing
ACSM recommendations for, 76
cardiorespiratory fitness and, 73
CRS. See Congenital rubella syndrome
Crystal. See Methamphetamines
Curanderismo cultures, 20
Curl-up exercises, 75
Curricula, multicultural, 19–21
CVD. See Cardiovascular diseases
Cyberspace sex, 340–42
Cynicism, 53
Cystitis, 303

D

Dairy products, 109t, 111
Dancing
ACSM recommendations for, 76
calories used in, 137t

cardiorespiratory system and, 67, 68, 73
fitness clubs and, 83
Darvon, 168
Date rape, 180, 411, 413
Dating, 329–30
D&C. *See* Dilation and curettage
ddC, 296
DDI, 296
DDT, 430–31
Death and dying
　awareness of, 449
　from cancers, 2*t*
　cardiovascular causes of, 2*t*
　of children, 453–54
　clinical definition of, 449
　costs of services and, 460
　elderly and, 8
　emotional stages of, 452
　euthanasia, 449–52
　fear of, 9
　grief process and, 455–56
　hospice care and, 454–55
　of infant/unborn child, 464–66
　interaction with the dying, 453
　learning activities, 462
　near-death experiences, 452–53
　organ donation, 461
　personal preparation for, 458, 460–61
　rituals/funerals and, 456–60
　teaching children about, 453
　top 10 causes of, 2*t*
Demerol, 157, 168
Denial, 193
Dentists, 386
Department of Agriculture, U.S., 121
Depressants, 164
　abuse of, 157
　alcohol as, 182, 199
Depression
　action guides for, 30
　alcoholism and, 192, 194
　emotional maturity and, 29-30
　stress origins and, 44
DES, 258, 356
Designated drivers, 189, 194
Designer drugs, 166
Developmental tasks
　for college students, 5–7, *5*, 16–17
　for elderly, 8–9, 16–17
　for midlife adults, 7–8, 16–17
Diabetes mellitus
　cardiovascular risk factors and, 232, 233–34, 235–36
　learning activity, 259
　physical fitness and, 80
　type I
　　appetite suppressants and, 144
　　pathophysiology of, 269, 270
　type II
　　appetite suppressants and, 144
　　genetic origins of, 133
　　overweight trends in, 128, 133
　　pathophysiology of, 266–67, *268*, 269
Diaphragms, 346*t*, *351*, 351–52
Diaries, for behavioral changes, 16
Diastolic pressure, 241
Diazepam, 165
Dietary thermogenesis, 137
Diets, 124
　additives in, 114
　assessments in, 2, 110, 122, 123
　breads, cereals, rice group, 109*t*, 111
　for cancer risk reduction, 265, 266*t*
　dairy products group, 109*t*, 111
　fast foods and, 111–13
　fats, oils, sweets group, 109*t*, 111
　food supplements, 120
　labels, 114, 115, *115*
　meats, beans, fish, eggs, nuts group, 109*t*, 111
　multicultural, 121
　nutrient density and, 120, *120*

nutrition in, 93–126, 115–16, *118*, 118*t*
　obesity and feeding patterns, 134
　phytochemicals in, 113
　salt and cardiovascular diseases, 242, 243
　vegetable group, 109, 109*t*
　vegetarian/semivegetarian, 117–20, 125–26
Digestive function, 50–51
Digging activities, 137*t*
Dilation and curettage, 360
Dilation and evacuation, 360, *360*
Dilbert, United Feature Syndicate, Inc., 61
Diphtheria, 280, 284, 284*t*, 306
Disabled persons' exercises, 76
Distilled spirits, 182, 184*t*, 185
Distress, 44
Diuretics, 162*t*
Diverticulitis, 44
Divorce, 333–34
Doctors. *See* Physicians
DOM. *See* Designer drugs
Domestic violence, 199, 403, 405–7
　learning activity, 408
Downsizing, 60–62
Drinker classification, 182*t*
Drivers, designated, 189
Driving
　alcohol consumption and, 180, 189, 190–91, 193, 200
　BAC, 181–82, 183–84, 185
Drowning, 188
Drug abuse, 155–77
　abuse/misuse, 157–58
　AIDS and, 164
　assessments for, 13, 158, 171
　　drug classifications, 159–68
　　drug-free lifestyles, 155–77
　　questionnaire for, 13
　effects of
　　addiction, 156–57, 168
　　additive behavior, 155–56
　　central nervous system, 159
　　combination effects, 168
　　psychological dependence, 157
　HealthQuest Activity, 163
　learning activities, 172
　treatment for, 156
　　National Council on Alcoholism and Drug Dependence, 196
　　society's response to, 169–70
　　support services for, 170, 173
　　terminology for, 156–58
　　testing for, 169–70
　types of
　　amphetamines, 159–62
　　barbiturates, 164
　　caffeine, 159, 160, 162*t*
　　cannabis, 166–67
　　cocaine, 162–64, *163*
　　crack, *163*, 163–64
　　depressants, 164
　　designer drugs, 166
　　gateway drugs, 169
　　hallucinogens, 155, 157, 165–66
　　ice, 162
　　inhalants, 168
　　LSD, 166
　　marijuana, 155
　　narcotics, 167–68
　　phencyclidine, 166
　　prescription, 175–77
　　psychoactive drugs, 155, 157, 160*t*–161*t*
　　stimulants, 159–63
　　tranquilizers, 165
Drug abuse hot lines, 171
Drug testing, 169–70
Drugs, 156–57
　cross-tolerance, 157
　medicine defined, 156
　over-the-counter, 394–95
　prescription, 393–95
　　abuse of, 175–77

generic *vs.* brand name of, 394
　research and development of, 393–94
　psychological dependence on, 157
　tolerance for, 157
Dying. *See* Death and dying

·· **E** ··

Eating disorders, exercise and, 146
Ebola, 307
Ecstasy. *See* Designer drugs
Ectomorph body type, 134
Eggs, 109*t*, 111
Elderly
　abuse of, 403, 406–7
　accident prevention for, 415–17
　ACSM exercises for, 76
　aging process of, 73
　back pain and, 79
　cardiopulmonary resuscitation and, 79
　emotional maturity and, 28
　exercises for, 79
　nutrition for, 120–21
Electrical impedance, 130, 131
Electromagnetic radiation, 436–37
El Niño, 440
Embolus, 242, *243*
Emergency medical care
　for acute alcohol intoxication, 185–86
　cardiopulmonary resuscitation for, 239
　for cardiovascular diseases, 239
Emotional health, 10, 44–63
Emotional maturity, 25–38
　action guides for, 27, 30
　active life approach to, 33–34
　affronts to, 28–30
　aging and, 27
　assessments for, 26, 39
　characteristics of, 25–27
　conflict skills and, 32–33
　creative expression and, 36–37
　depression and, 29–30
　in elderly, 28
　enhancement of, 31–34, 40–42
　faith and, 35–36
　hardiness and, 27
　humor and, 31–32
　improving communication and, 31
　loneliness and, 29
　Maslow's hierarchy of needs, 34–35, *36*
　mental picture skills and, 34
　in midlife adults, 27–28
　normal emotional range, 25
　problems in, 28–31
　reflections of, 34–38
　self-esteem and, 25–27, *33*, 33–34
　shyness and, 30
　spiritual development and, 35–36, 40–42
　suicide and, 30–31
Emphysema, 203, 213–14
Empowerment, 4, 16, 17
Enabling, 193
Endocrine dysfunction obesity, 134
Endocrine system
　osteoporosis and, 72
　in stress response, 50
Endomorph body type, 134
Energy consumption, 72, 135–39, 137*t*
Environmental protection, 440–41
　action guides for, 429
　air pollution, 423–29, *426*, 444–45
　air quality standards, 426
　chemical wastes, 434–35
　concerns of late 1990s, 2
　herbicides, 435
　indoor pollution, 428–29
　learning activities, 436
　land pollution, 432–35
　noise pollution, 438
　personal assessments for, 424–25
　pesticides, 435
　radiation, 435–38

recycling, 432–34, *434*
solutions for, 438–41
telecommuting and, 444–45
temperature inversions, 427–28
water pollution, 429*t*, 429–32
wetlands pollution, 431
Environmental Protection Agency (EPA), 427, 428
Environmental tobacco smoke. *See* Passive smoke
Enzymes, 99
EPA, 427, 428
Epinephrine, 50, 51
Ergot compounds, 50
ERT. *See* Estrogen replacement therapy
Escape drinking, 192
Estrogen replacement therapy
breast cancer and, 72, 255
heart disease and, 234
osteoporosis and, 72
Ether, 168
Ethnic violence
alcohol use/crime and, 199
Europe
meals per day in, 135
nutrition and, 135
Eustress, 44
Exercise equipment, 69–70, 82
Exercises
action guides for, 76
assessments for, 12, 74–76, 88–89
calories used in, 137*t*, 137–38
for cancer risk reduction, 265–66
cardiovascular risk factors and, 232, 234
danger signals for, 87
eating disorders and, 146
isokinetic, 69–70
isometric, 68, 69, *70*
issues for students, 2
for older adults, 78–79
osteoporosis and, 72
for pregnancy, 90–91
progressive resistance, 69
warm-up to cooldown, 78

F

Fad diets, 139
Faith
assessment for, 13
emotional maturity and, 35–36
overall health and, 10
spiritual development and, 35–36, 40–42
Falls, 188
Family history, 188, 193. *See also* Hereditary conditions
Family support, 16
FAS. *See* Fetal alcohol syndrome
Fast foods, 111–13
learning activity, 94
Fats
action guide for, 97
in alcoholic beverages, 182
assessments in, 93–97
breast cancers and, 255
brown, 133
low-fat, 97
nutrition and, 93–97, 109*t*, 111
use in stress response, 52
weight control and, 133–34, 138–42, 142*t*–143*t*, 148
FDA. *See* Food and Drug Administration
Fear
of death, 9
stress disorders and, 51
Feline leukemia virus, 251
Fenfluramine, 133, 144
Fermentation, 182–83
Fertility
aging in midlife adults and, 72
fertilization, 362–63
hallucinogen abuse and, 165
Fetal alcohol syndrome (FAS), 186–88, *188*, 189
Fetal development, 362–68

exercises and, 90–91
tobacco use and, 203, 214–15
Fiber, 104, 107
Fibrocystic breast disease, 214
Fight-or-flight response, 48, 51
Fire safety, 416, 417
Firearms, 414–15
Fires, 188–89
First aid, 185–86
Fish, 109*t*, 111
Fishing, 73, 137*t*
Fixed indemnity benefits, 389–90
Flashbacks, 166
Flexibility, 70
Folic acid, 100
Folklore, 20, 379
Food and Agricultural Organization of the United Nations, 121
Food and Drug Administration (FDA)
naltrexone and, 195
nicotine ruling of, 209
smoking issues and, 209
Foods
additives, 114
fast foods and, 111–13
groups
assessments in, 110
breads, cereals, rice, 109*t*, 111
dairy products, 109*t*, 111
fats, oils, sweets, 109*t*, 111
fruits, 107–11, 108*t*, 109*t*
meats, beans, fish, eggs, nuts, 109*t*, 111
vegetables, 109, 109*t*
health guidelines for, 115–16, *118*, 118*t*
labels, 114, 115, *115*
HealthQuest Activity, 114
multicultural, 121
nutrient density, 120, *120*
phytochemicals, 113
vegetarian/semivegetarian diets, 117–20, 125–26
Football
ACSM recommendations for, 76
calories used in, 137*t*
steroid use and, 83
Fortune 500 companies, 169–70
Fractures, 214
France, humor in, 32
Fraud, 395–96
Freebasing, 163
Friendship
sexuality and, 330–31
support and, 16
Fruits, food group, 107–11, 108*t*, 109*t*
Fungus infections, 280–81, 281*t*

G

Gait, 73
Galloway, Jeff, 85
Gamblers Anonymous, 156
Gamete intrafallopian transfer (GIFT), 369
Gangs, 407–8
Gardening, 137*t*
Gases, 157
Gasoline, 168
Gastric resection, 144
Gastrointestinal disorders, 44
Gastroplasty, 144
Gateway drugs, 169
Gender risk factors
female
breast cancer, 255
cardiovascular diseases, 232
hypertension, 248
male
alcohol use/crime, 199
cardiovascular risk factors, 233, 234
pancreatic cancer, 261
General adaptation syndrome, 47–48
Generativity, 7–8, 16–17
Genetics

in alcoholism, 191–93
ALL-1, AF-9/leukemia cancers, 251
BRCA1, BRCA2/breast cancers, 251
in cancers, 250–51
diabetes II, 133
MSH1, MSH2/colon cancers, 251
in osteoarthritis, 72–73
p16/lung cancers, 251
regulatory genes, 250, 251
repair genes, 250
Germany, 81
Glandular obesity, 134
Glucose function, 52
Glues, 157, 168
Goals for change, 11–16
Goblet cells, 212
Golf
calories used in, 137*t*
fitness limits of, 73
Gonorrhea, 299
Government agencies
consumer information from, 383
mandatory drug testing by, 169–70
Government health insurance, 388–93
Grain alcohol, 182
Great Britain
humor in, 32
nutrition and, 135
Greenhouse effect, 426, *426*
Guilt feelings, 192, 194
Guns, 199, 408
riflery, 82
Gymnastics, 137*t*

H

Haemophilus influenzae, 284, 284*t*, 285
Hallucinogens, 155, 157, 165–66
Handball
ACSM recommendations for, 76
calories used in, 137*t*
Hantavirus pulmonary syndrome, 291–92
Hash
abuse of, 167
testing for, 169
Hate crimes, 408–9
Headaches, 50
Health
alcohol use control in, 179–200
assessments in, 2, 11–17
behavioral changes and, 11–16
concerns of late 1990s, 2, 2*t*
consumerism and, 379–401
definitions of, 2–3, 9–11, 17
discussion topics, 21
drug-free lifestyles and, 155–77
emotional maturity in, 10, 25–38
information on the Internet, 399–400
intellectual dimension of, 10
learning activities, 394
nutrition in, 93–126
objectives for 2010, 1, 3
occupational dimension of, 10–11
physical fitness in, 10, 67–91
promotion, 3
role/composition, 9
social dimension of, 10
spiritual dimension of, 10
stress management in, 44–63
tobacco use control in, 202–26
weight maintenance and, 128–52
Health agencies, 382–83
Health care costs, 2, 388–93, 389*t*
pregnancy and, 374–75
Health care providers, 383–88
Health educators, 383
Health for All, 4
Health insurance, 2, 388–93, 389*t*
pregnancy and, 374–75
Health maintenance organizations (HMOs), 390–91
Health on the Net Foundation, 399–400

Health practitioners, 381
Health products, 393-95
Health reference publications, 382
Healthy body weight, 129t, 129–30
Hearing
    in elderly, 73
    noise-induced problems in, 438
Heart
    angry heart condition, 53
    cancer and, 68
    catheterization of, 239–40
    function of, 230, 230–31
    HealthQuest Activities, 233
    learning activities, 236
    obesity and, 128
    physical fitness and, 79
    stress origins and, 44
    tobacco use and, 203
Heart murmurs, 244, 245
Heart transplants, 240–41
Heart-regulating drugs, 52
Hemorrhages
    cerebral, 242
    retinal, 241
Hepatitis, 292
Hepatitis B, 284, 284t, 285, 293, 306
Hepatomas, 252, 253
Herbalism, 20
Herbicides, 435
Hereditary conditions
    in alcoholism, 191–93
    assessments for, 14
    in breast cancers, 251
    in cancers, 250–51
    in cardiovascular diseases, 233
    in colon cancers, 251
    in diabetes II, 133
    in leukemia, 251
    in lung cancers, 251
    in obesity, 132–34
    in osteoarthritis, 72–73
    questionnaire for, 14
Heroin
    dependencies and, 205
    sources of, 157
    testing for, 169
Herpes simplex, 256, 300, 299–301
HGE. See Human granulocytic ehrlichiosis
High blood pressure. See Hypertension
Highball mixed drinks, 184t
High-density lipoproteins (HDLs), 237, 239t
Hiking
    ACSM recommendations for, 76
    calories used in, 137t
    college clubs and, 82
Hindus, rituals/funerals and, 457
Hispanics
    alcohol use/crime and, 199
    college enrollment of, 19
    health view of, 20
    hypertension and, 247
History, 20
HIV. See also Sexually transmitted diseases
    cancers and, 251
    causes of death and, 2t
    drug abuse and, 164
    pathology of, 285, 293–96, 295t
    prevention of, 296–97, 306, 307, 351, 352
    screenings for, 3
    transmission of, 280, 282
    treatment of, 296
HMOs, 390–91
Hockey, 137t
Hodgkin's disease, 267
Holistic health, 3, 16, 17
Home pregnancy tests, 364
Home safety, 414–15, 416, 417
Homeopathy, 265
Homeostasis
    decline, 71, 73
    stress and, 48

Homicide, 2t, 199, 403
Homosexuality, 336–37
    HIV risk factors, 306
Horseback riding, 137t
Hospice care, 454–55
Host responsibility, 189
Hot lines. See also Organizations of support
    for AIDS/HIV, 296
    for alcohol, 171
    for drug crisis, 171
HPV, 257, 299
Human Genome Project, 251
Human granulocytic ehrlichiosis (HGE), 291
Human immunodeficiency virus. See HIV
Human papillomavirus (HPV), 257, 299
Humor
    emotional maturity and, 31–32
    multicultural, 32
Humoral immunity, 283
Hunger, social issues and, 2
Hunting, 73
Hurry sickness, 53
Hydrostatic weighing, 131
Hygiene, 14
Hypercellular obesity, 134, 135
Hyperparathyroidism, 72
Hypertension
    cardiovascular risk factors and, 241–42, 247–48
    obesity and, 128
    physical fitness and, 80
    from stress, 44, 51
Hypertonic saline procedure, 360
Hypertrophic obesity, 134, 135
Hypochondriasis, 72
Hypothalamus, 50, 51

I

Ice. See Methamphetamines
Ice beer, 182
Ice hockey, 137t
Immune system
    alcohol use damage to, 186
    B-cells and, 283, 283–84, 285–86
    infectious diseases and, 283, 283–84, 285–87, 286
    stress disorders in, 51–53
    stress management and, 53
Immunizations, 284t, 284–85, 306–7
Immunotherapy
    for asthma, 271
    for cancer, 264
In vitro fertilization-embryo transfer
        (IVF-ET), 368–69
Independence development, 6, 16–17
India
    hepatitis B in, 293
    rituals/funerals in, 457
Infants
    birth defects, 165
    birth process and, 365–68, 366
    birth weights, 203
    fetal alcohol effects, 188
    miscarriage and, 464–66
    obesity and feeding patterns, 134
Infectious diseases, 280–307
    immune response to, 283, 283–84, 285–87, 286
    immunizations for, 284–85, 306–7
    transmission of, 280–83, 281, 281t
Infertility, 214, 368–70. See also Pregnancy
Influenza, 280
    cold vs., 288t
    defined, 287–88, 288t
Information, consumer sources of, 379–401
Infrared light transmission, 130
Inhalant abuse, 157, 168
Injectable contraceptives, 357
Injuries
    intentional, 403–10
    unintentional, 414–16
Inner city environments, 199
Insecticides, 168
Insemination, artificial, 368

Insomnia, 45
Insurance. See Health insurance
Integrity development, 9, 16–17
Intellectual health, 10
Interferon, 264, 271
Interleukin-2, 264
International Olympic Committee, 82
Internet, 20, 399–400
Intimacy
    development of, 5, 7, 16–17
    sexuality and, 332
Intrauterine devices (IUDs), 346t, 352–54, 353
Ionizing radiation, 435–38
Irritable bowel syndrome, 44
Isokinetic exercises, 69–70
Isometric exercises, 68, 69, 70
Israel, 32
Italy, 179
IUDs, 346t, 352–54, 354t, 353

J

Japanese
    breast cancer and, 255
    exercise and, 81
    rituals/funerals in, 457
    stress management and, 55
Job stress, 60–62
Jock itch, 281
Jogging
    calories used in, 137t
    cardiorespiratory system and, 68
    college clubs and, 82
Johnson, Edmund, 54
Joint cartilage, 72
Joint flexibility, 70
Journals, for behavioral changes, 16
Judo, 137t

K

Kepone, 430–31
Kerosene abuse, 168
Kevorkian, Jack, 450
Kidney diseases. See Renal diseases
Knitting activity, 137t
Ku Klux Klan, 409
Kübler-Ross, Elisabeth, 452

L

La Niña, 440
Labels, 379, 381
Labor, 365–68, 366
Lacrosse, 137t
Land pollution, 432–35
Landfills, 432–34
Larynx, 213
Latin America, 206
Laws
    abortion and, 359
    alcohol use and, 179
    host negligence/alcohol use and, 189
    smoking issues and, 225
    zero tolerance alcohol, 192
Lead toxicity, 427, 428
Lebanese cultures
    hospitality, 11
Legal issues. See Laws
Leptin, 132
Leukemia, 251, 252
Libraries, 382
Librium
    abuse of, 165
    testing for, 169
Lifestyles
    assessments of, 11–17
    changes for health, 11, 16, 17
    stress and, 57–58
    theory Z people, 35
Lifting, 79
Light beer, 182
Lipoprotein levels, 237, 239t
Liqueurs, 184t

Literature curricula, 20
Liver cancers, 252
Living wills, 451
Locus of control, 7
Loneliness, 29
Love drug. *See* Designer drugs
Love, sexuality and, 330–31
Low back pain
    flexibility and, 70–71
    onset in older adults, 79
Low-density lipoproteins (LDLs), 237, 239*t*
Low-impact aerobic exercise, 81
LSD, 165
Ludes. *See* Methaqualone
Lung cancers, 203, 251, 252, *253*, 253–55
Lupus erythematosus, systemic, 271–72
Lyme disease, 282, 291, 306
Lymphomas, cancers in, 253
Lysergic acid diethylamide (LSD), 166

M

MADD, 169, 190
Magazine advertising, 179, 196
Magic cultural traditions, 20
Magnetic resonance imaging (MRI)
    body composition by, 130
    for breast cancer, 255, 259
    for strokes, 242, 243
Mainstream smoke. *See* Passive smoke
Male itch, 281
Malignant neoplasms, 2*t*
Malt beer. *See* Beer
Mammograms, 254, 255
Manhattan mixed drinks, 184*t*
Manipulation behaviors, 208
Marching activity, 137*t*
Marijuana
    abuse of, 157, 166–67
    benzopyrene and, 167
    testing for, 169
Marriage
    sexuality and, 332–33
    unintended pregnancy and, 373
Martinis, 184*t*
Maslow's hierarchy of needs, 34–35, *36*
Mass media, 380–81
Mastectomy, 255, 259
MDA. *See* Designer drugs
MDMA. *See* Designer drugs
Measles, 284*t*, 285, 290–91
Meats, 109*t*, 111
Mecca, rituals/funerals and, 457
Medicaid, 391–92, 393
Medical examinations, 2
Medicare, 391–92
Medicine
    allopathic, 383
    alternative, 384–86
    physicians, 383–84
    specialities in, 384–87
Medigap, 392
Melanomas
    cancerous, 261–62, *262*
    defined, 252, *253*
    indicator moles and, 263
Men
    alcohol use/crime and, 199
    cardiovascular risk factors and, 233, 234
    male itch, 281
    pancreatic cancer in, 261
    reproductive systems of, 315–17, *316*
Menopause, 321–22
    osteoporosis and, 72
Menstrual extraction, 359
Menstruation, 319–22
Mental health
    emotional health defined, 9
    emotional maturity in, 25–38
    issues for students, 2
    job stress and, 60–62
    spiritual health and, 10, 13
    stress management for, 44–63
Mental picture skills, 33–34
Meperidine, 168
Mescaline, 157, 165
Mesomorph body type, 134
Metabolic rate, 51
Metastasis, 251, 252
Meth, 162
Methadone abuse, 157, 168
Methamphetamines, 162–63
Methaqualone, 165, 169
Mexico
    curricula and, 20
    diets and, 99
    drug-free lifestyles and, 165
Mice, 291–92
Middle Eastern cultures, 11
Midlife adults
    aging in, 71–73
    developmental tasks for, 7–8, 16–17
    emotional maturity and, 27–28
    job stress and, 60–62
    midlife crisis in, 28
Mifepristone, 360
Migraine headaches, 50
Minerals, 102, 103*t*–106*t*, 107*t*, 108*t*, 109*t*
    adult recommendations, 107*t*, 108*t*
    in alcoholic beverages, 182
Minipill contraceptives, 347*t*, 357
Miscarriages, 464–66
Mixed drinks, 184*t*
Modeling behaviors, 207–8
Monoclonal antibodies, 264
Mononucleosis, 289, *290*
Monosodium glutamate (MSG), 50
Moody, Raymond, 452
Morning drinking, 191
Morning-after pill, 356
Morphine, 157, 170
Mortality. *See also* Death and dying
    alcohol use and, 185
    in burns, 188–89
    job stress and, 61
    leading causes in, 188
    top 10 causes of, 2*t*
Mothers Against Drunk Driving (MADD), 169, 190
Motivational systems, 16
Motor vehicle safety, 188, 415–16, 420
Mowing activity, 137*t*
MPPP. *See* Designer drugs
MRI. *See* Magnetic resonance imaging
MS. *See* Multiple sclerosis
MSG. *See* Monosodium glutamate
Mucous membranes, 186
Mucus, 212, 213
Multicultural community
    alcohol consumption, 179
    assessments and, 17
    breast cancer and, 255
    changes in, 19–21
    curricula and, 19–21
    death rituals and, 456–60
    diets/nutrition in, 99, 121, 135
    diversity in colleges and, 19–21
    drug-free lifestyles and, 165
    emotional maturity and, 32
    environmental influences and, 433
    exercise in, 81
    health objectives in, 11
    humor and, 32
    hypertension and, 247–48
    infectious diseases and, 293
    maternal death and, 356
    obesity and, 135
    stress management and, 55
    tobacco use and, 206
Multiple sclerosis (MS), 270–71
Mumps, 284*t*, 285, 290–91
Muscle injury, 214
Muscle relaxation, 50, 54–55
Muscle strength
    assessment for, 74–76
    in elderly, 73
    endurance, 70–71
    in physical fitness, 68–71
    tissue breakdown and, 52
Muslims, rituals/funerals and, 457
Myanmar, rituals/funerals in, 457
Myocardial infarction, 237
    angry heart condition, 53
    tobacco use and, 211, 216

N

NAI. *See* Naturally acquired immunity
Naltrexone, 195
Naps, 87
Narcolepsy, 162, 163
Narcotics abuse, 167–68
Narcotics Anonymous, 169, 171
National Cancer Institute, Cancer Information Service, 267
National Clearinghouse for Alcohol and Drug Information, 171
National Coalition for Cancer Survivorship, 267
National Cocaine Hot Line, 171
National Collegiate Athletic Association (NCAA), 83
National Council on Alcoholism and Drug Dependence, 196
National Federation of State High School Association Target Programs, 171
National Health Information Clearinghouse, 171
National Household Survey on Drug Abuse, 167
National Institute on Alcohol Abuse and Alcoholism (NIAAA), 180
National Institute on Alcohol and Drug Abuse Hot Line, 171
National Institutes of Health, 264
National Weight Control Registry, 139
Native Americans
    college enrollment of, 19
    drug-free lifestyles and, 165
    holistic health view of, 20
    hypertension and, 247
Naturally acquired immunity (NAI), 284, 285
Naturopathy, 265
NCAA, 83
Near-death experiences, 452–53
Neonates, 464–66. *See also* Infants
Neo-Nazi groups, 409
Neoplasms, 2*t*
Netherlands, 255
Neuroblastomas, 252, *253*
Neurons, 159
Neurophysiology, 132, 133
Neurotransmitters, 159, 160
Neutron activation, 130
New England Journal of Medicine, 184
Nicotine
    FDA and, 209
    physiology and, 205–7
    as psychotropic agent, 210
Nitrite-containing foods, 50
Nitrogen compounds, 427
Nitroglycerin, 239
Nitrous oxide, 168
Nomograms, 130, 131, *131*
Nonnarcotic pain relievers, 50
Nonspecific urethritis (NSU), 297, 299
Nonsteroidal anti-inflammatory agents, 73
Norepinephrine, 210
North America
    maternal deaths in, 356
    nutrition and, 135
North Carolina, 225
NSU, 297, 299
Nuclear accidents, 437–38
Nutrition, 93–126
    additives/labeling
        additives, 114
        labels, 114–15, *115*
        phytochemicals and, 113

assessments/guides to
  action guides for, 117, 119
  good habits of, 11
  guidelines for, 2, 107–11, 108t, 109t, 115–16, 116
  overall, 13, 122, 123
  questionnaire for, 13
diet types
  disease reduction diets, 118t
  fad diets, 139
  multicultural diets, 99, 121
  nontraditional, 116–20
  vegetarian/semivegetarian, 125–26
  vegetarian/vegan, 117–20
  water, 102, 105t
eating out, 114
  fast foods, 111–13
essentials of
  bread, cereal, rice, pasta, 111
  carbohydrates, 93
  fiber, 104, 107
  food groups and, 107–11, 108t, 109t
  fruits, 107, 109
  meat, poultry, fish, dry beans, eggs, nuts, 111
  milk, yogurt, cheese, 111
  minerals, 102, 103t–106t, 107t, 108t, 109t
  nutrient density and, 120, 120
  proteins, 97–98
  types/sources of, 93–106, 101t–102t, 103t–104t, 105t–106t, 107t, 108t
  vegetables, 109
  vitamins, 99, 100t–102t, 106t, 107t, 108t, 109t
learning activities, 94
problem areas in
  alcoholism, 192
  cholesterol, 96–97, 100
  fats, 93–97, 111
  oils, 111
  older adults, 120–21
  sweets, 111
  tobacco use and, 214
Nuts, 109t, 111

O

Obesity, 132–36
  appetite center, 133
  body type in, 134
  cancers and, 128
  cardiovascular risk factors and, 233, 236
  determination of, 128–29
  endocrine balance and, 134
  genetic basis of, 132–33
  health risks of, 128
  infant-adult feeding patterns and, 134
  multicultures and, 135
  neurophysiological causes of, 132, 133
  pregnancy and, 134
  set point theory in, 133
  types of, 128
Occupational safety
  cancers and, 265
  overall health and, 10–11
  radiation and, 435–38
  smoking issues and, 225
Occupational Safety and Health Administration, 225
Oil spills, 431
Oils, dietary, 96, 98, 109t, 111
Older adults
  exercises for, 79
  nutrition for, 120–21
On Death and Dying, 452
Oncogenes, 250, 251
On-line computer services, 381
Opiates, 169
Optometrists, 387
Oral contraceptives
  breast cancer and, 255
  combined pill, 347t, 354–55
  contraindications for, 356

effectiveness of, 347t, 354–57
  morning-after pill, 356
  STDs and, 298
  tobacco use and, 215–16
  triphasic pill, 347t, 355
Organizations of support
  for AIDS/HIV, 296
  for alcoholism, 156, 180, 190, 194, 195–96
  for cancers, 211, 267
  for cardiovascular diseases, 231–36
  for consumer protection, 382
  for drug abuse, 156, 169, 170, 171
  for drug testing, 169–70
  for eating disorders, 147
  for food assistance, 121
  for gambling, 156
  for health maintenance, 171, 264, 390–91
  for infertility, 370
  for rape, 412
Oriental poppy derivatives, 157, 168
Orlistat, 144
Orthodontics, 386
OSHA, 225
Osteoarthritis, 72–73
Osteopathy, 383
Osteoporosis
  exercises and, 72
  midlife adults and, 72, 73
  tobacco use and, 214
OTC Drugs. See Over-the-counter drugs
Ovarian cancers
  aerobic fitness reduction of, 68
  pathophysiology of, 258–59
  Taxol for, 259
Overload principle, 68, 69
Over-the-counter drugs, 156, 395t, 394–95
Ovral, 356
Oxidation, 184, 185
Oxidizing agents, 265
Oxygen, 52
Oxygen debt, 68, 69
Oxygen uptake, 73
Ozone, 426–27, 428

P

PAD, 244, 245
PAI, 284, 285
Pain management
  caffeine content in, 162t
  in chronic diseases, 275–78
Paint thinners, 168
Painting, 137t
Paints, 168
Pancreatic cancers
  in African-Americans, 261
  caffeine and, 214
Pap tests, 254, 257
Paranoia, 166
Paraphilias, 337
Parasitic worms, 280–81, 281t
Parenting, 361–62, 368–70, 373–75
  single, 336
  surrogate, 369
Parents Against Drugs, 169
Parents for a Drug-Free Youth, 169
Parents' Resource Institute for Drug Education (PRIDE), 171
Parties, host responsibility/alcohol use and, 189
Parturition. See Birth
Passive smoke, 216–17
Passively acquired immunity (PAI), 284, 285
Pasta, 111
Pathogens, 280
PCP. See Phencyclidine
Pelvic inflammatory disease (PID), 299
  diaphragms and, 351
  IUDs and, 353
  spermicides and, 350
Periodontal disease, 216
Peripheral artery disease (PAD), 244, 245
Personal health plans, 11–17

Personality traits, 53
Personality types
  critical, 53
  theory Z people, 35
  type A, 53
  type B, 53
  type R, 44
Pertussis, 280, 306
Pesticides, 430–31, 435
Petroleum products, 157, 168
Peyote
  abuse of, 157
  appetite suppression and, 135
  Native Americans and, 165
Phencyclidine
  abuse of, 166
  testing for, 169
Phentermine, 144
Phenylpropanolamine (PPA), 144, 145
Physical abuse, 194
Physical fitness, 67–91
  action guides, 76, 87
  aerobic exercises, 80, 81
  aging and, 71
  alcohol effects on, 82
  assessments for, 12, 74–76, 88–89
  body composition and, 70–71
  bodybuilding and, 82–83
  cardiorespiratory, 67–68, 73–80
  children and, 83
  crosstraining, 83
  danger signs and, 86
  defined, 67
  for elderly, 73, 78
  equipment for, 82
  female breast supports and, 80
  flexibility, 70
  fluid replacement and, 81
  health/fitness clubs, 82
  HealthQuest Activities, 67
  improvement of, 15
  low back pain and, 79
  maintenance for elderly, 8
  medical examinations and, 79
  in midlife adults, 71–72
  multicultural, 81
  muscular endurance, 70
  muscular strength, 68–70, 70, 79
  in overall health, 9
  pregnancy and, 90–91
  program for, 73–80
  questionnaire for, 12, 14
  questions/answers, 79–86
  shoes for, 85–86
  sleep and, 86–87
  steroids and, 83, 84
Physicians, 383–84
  allied health care professionals, 387–88
  alternative practitioners, 384–86
  nurse professionals, 387
  podiatrists, 387
  primary care, 383
  psychologists, 386–87
  restricted providers, 386–87
  specialities, 384–86
Pictures, positive mental, 33–34, 33
PID. See Pelvic inflammatory disease
Pipe smoking, 203
Pituitary gland, 50, 51
Placenta, 186, 189
Plastic cements, 168
Platelets, 211
PMR. See Progressive muscle relaxation
Pneumonia
  causes of death and, 2t
  defined, 289
Polio, 284t
Pollution
  air, 423–29, 426, 444–45
  chemical wastes, 434–35
  concerns of late 1990s, 2

herbicides, 435
indoor, 428–29
land, 432–35
pesticides, 435
radiation, 435–38
recycling and, 432–34, *434*
telecommuting and, 444–45
temperature inversions, 427–28
water, 429–32, 429*t*
wetlands, 431
Population control, 2
Population growth, 423, *425*
POS plans, 391
Positive caloric balance, 128, 129
Positive thinking, 33–34, *33*
Postmenopause, 72
Posttraumatic stress syndrome, 411
Posture, 73
Potentiated effect, 168
Power naps, 87
Power of attorney, 451
PPA, 144, 145
PPO. *See* Health insurance
Pregnancy
    ACSM exercises for, 76
    alcohol use in, 180
    caffeine risks in, 214
    exercises and, 90–91
    fetal alcohol syndrome in, 186–88, *188*, 189
    physiology of, 362–65
    tobacco risks in, 214–15
    unintended, 373–75
    vitamin requirements for, 106*t*
    weight gains in, 134–35
Premature births, 203
Premenopause, 72
Prenatal care, 374
Prescription drugs, 175–77, 393–95
PRIDE, 171
Primary care physicians, 383
Progressive muscle relaxation (PMR), 54–55
Progressive resistance exercises, 69
Proof, level of alcohol, 182
Property destruction, 180
Propoxyphene, 167–68
Prostaglandin procedure, 360–61
Prostate cancers, 254, 259–60
Prostate-specific antigen (PSA) blood
    tests, 260
Prosthodontics, 385–86
Proteins, 97–99, 182
Protooncogenes, 250, 251
Protozoa, 280–81, 281*t*
Prozac
    appetite effects of, 133, 144
    usage of, 381
Psilocybin, 165
Psychedelic drugs. *See* Hallucinogens
Psychoactive drugs, 155, 157, 160*t*-161*t*, 214
Psychological counseling
    costs of, 170, 173
    for drug abuse, 170–73
    for eating disorders, 146–47
Psychological dependence
    drug abuse and, 157
    tobacco use and, 205
Psychosis, 191
Psychosomatic disorders, 52, 53
Pubic lice, 301, *301*
Public Health Service, U.S., 296
Pulmonary emphysema, 213
Pulmonary function, 51–52
Pulmonary hypertension, 144
Pulse, 186
Purging. *See* Bulimia nervosa

Q

Quaaludes. *See* Methaqualone
Quackery, 399–400
Quetelet index (QI). *See* Body mass index
Quieting Reflex, The, 55

R

Rabies, 280
Race, 199
Racquetball
    ACSM recommendations for, 76
    calories used in, 137*t*
    equipment/information for, 82
Radiation. *See also* Nuclear accidents
    for cancer, 264
    sickness, 435–36, 437
    testing on citizens of, 438
Radner, Gilda, 258–59
Radon gas, 428–29
Raking, 137*t*
Range of motion exercises, 69
Rape
    binge drinking and, 180
    date, 411, 413
    help for, 403, 412
    morning-after pill and, 356
    myths about, 410
    prevention guidelines for, 411, 413
Reaction time, 73
Recovery programs, 195
Rectum/colon cancers, 251, 254, 260–61
Recycling, 432–34
Red wines, 50
Reese, J. Lynn, 85
Reflexology, 265, 384
Regulatory genes, 250, 251
Rehabilitation
    for alcoholism, 194–95
    for elderly, 8
Relaxation
    assessments for, 14–15
    questionnaire for, 14–15
    response, 54
Relaxation Response, The, 54
Religion. *See also* Spiritual development
    cultural traditions and, 20
    mental health and, 40–41
Religious ceremonies, 165
    rituals/funerals, 456–60
Remediation, 8
Renal diseases
    stress and, 44
Repair genes, 250
Repetitive strain injuries (RSIs), 61
Reproductive systems, 315–22, *316, 318*
Resource Center: American College of
    Obstetricians and Gynecologists, 267
Respiratory system, 73
Responsibility development, *5,* 6, 16–17
Rest. *See also* Sleep
    assessments for, 14–15
    issues for students, 2
    for migraine headaches, 50
    questionnaire for, 14–15
Retinal hemorrhages, 241
Reward systems, 16
Rheumatic heart disease, 243–44
Rice, 109*t*, 111
Rickettsia, 280–81, 281*t*
Riflery, 82
Ringworm, 281
Robbery, 403
    victims of, 199
Roe vs. Wade, 359
Rollerblading
    ACSM recommendations for, 76
    cardiorespiratory fitness and, 73
Rope climbing, 68
Roussel-Uclaf company, 360
Rowing
    ACSM recommendations for, 76
    cardiorespiratory fitness and, 73
RU 486 (mifepristone), 360
Rubella
    congenital, 243, 285
    immunizations for, 284*t*
Rum, 184*t*

S

Runner's nipples, 80
Running
    ACSM recommendations for, 76
    athletic shoes for, 85
    calories used in, 137*t*
    cardiorespiratory system and, 67, 68, 73
    equipment/information for, 82

SADD, 190
Safety
    alcohol use and, 188–89, 199–200
    binge drinking and, 180
    campus, 417
    causes of death and, 2*t*
    child abuse, 403, 406, 411
    concerns of late 1990s, 2
    domestic, 403, 405–7
    elder abuse, 403, 406–7
    fire, 416, 417
    firearms, 408, 415
    gangs/youth and, 407–8
    hate crimes, 408–9
    intentional injuries, 403–10
    motor vehicle, 415–16, 420
    personal assessments for, 13–14, 404
    questionnaire for, 13–14
    recreational, 414
    residential, 414–15, 416
    sexual victimization, 410–14
    stalking, 409–10
    unintentional injuries, 414–16
Sailing, 137*t*
Saliva, 213
Salivation, 51
Salt, 242, 243
San Antonio College, 20
Sarcomas, 252, *253*
Saturated fats. *See* Fats
Saunas, 82
Sclerotic changes, 252, 253
Secular Organizations for Sobriety (SOS), 194
Secular recovery programs, 194
Self-antigens, 272
Self-care movement, 388
Self-esteem
    alcoholism and, 192, 194
    body image and, 128
    learning activities, 27
    positive mental pictures for, 33–34, *33*
Self-help, 14, 53, 388
Self-hypnosis, 53
Selye, Hans, 44
Sensory modalities, 73
Septum, 230, *230*
Serbia, 409
Set point theory, 133
*7th Special Report to the U.S. Congress on Alcohol and
    Health,* 188, 189
Sex Addicts Anonymous, 156
Sexual orientation, 336–37
Sexual victimization, 410–14
    alcohol use and, 194, 199–200
    assault, 410–13
    of children, 411
    commercialization and, 413–414
    rape, 403, 410–13
    safety and, 413–14
    sexual harassment, 412–13
    stalking, 409–10
Sexuality, 311–42
    assessments and, 327, 331
    action guides for, 334
    behaviors, 325–29
        paraphilias, 337
    biology/psychology of
        behaviors, 325–29
        biology of, 311–12
        psychosocial, 312–14
        reproductive systems, 315–22, *316, 318*
        response patterns, 321–25

function and
  aging, 72, 329–30
  hallucinogen abuse, 165
learning activities, 335
relationships and
  breakups, 333–34
  cohabitation, 335–36
  cyberspace sex, 340–42
  dating, 329–30
  divorce, 333–34
  friendship, 330–31
  intimacy, 332
  love, 330
  marriage, 332–33
  unhealthy, 330
types of
  androgyny, 314–15
  sexual orientation, 336–37
  single parenthood, 336
  singlehood, 334–35, 335t
Sexually transmitted diseases (STDs). See also
    AIDS, HIV
  assessments for, 298
  chlamydia, 297, 299
  condoms and, 351
  contraceptives and, 298
  cystitis, 303
  gonorrhea, 299
  herpes simplex, 299–301, 300
  immune response to, 283–84, 283, 285–87, 286
  immunizations for, 284–85
  learning activities, 287
  nonspecific urethritis, 297, 299
  PID and, 299
  pubic lice, 301
  spermicides and, 350
  syphilis, 301, 302
  transmission of, 2, 280–81, 282–83
  urethritis, 303
  vaginal infections, 301–3
Shallow breathing, 186
Sheldon body types, 134
Shock, 186, 189
Shoes, 85–86
Shooting sports, 82
Shyness, 30
Sick building syndrome, 428
Sidestream smoke. See Passive smoke
Silent cancers, 259
Single parenthood, 336
Singlehood, 334–35, 335t
Sit and reach exercises, 74
Skating
  calories used in, 137t
  cardiorespiratory fitness and, 73
Skiing, 137t
Skin cancers, 252, 256, 261–63, 261, 263t
Skin discoloration, 186
Skin disorders, 214
SLE, 272
Sleep
  assessments for, 14–15
  developing good patterns for, 11
  learning activities, 87
  physical fitness and, 86–87
  questionnaire for, 14–15
Smallpox, 280
Smell, 214
Smoke pollution, 428–29
Smokeless tobacco use, 216
Smoking. See Tobacco use
Sobering process, 185
Soccer, 137t
Social behaviors, 192, 199
Social skills
  assessment of, 12
  for overall health, 10
  questionnaire for, 12
  tasks for students, 5, 6–7, 16–17
Soft drinks
  caffeine content in, 162t

calories in, 81
CNS effects of, 214
Softball, 76
Solvents, 168
Somatotype, 134
Sopor. See Methaqualone
SOS, 195
Soviet Union
  Chernobyl nuclear power plant in, 437
  hate crimes in, 409
Specific dynamic action, 137
Specificity of adaptation, 48
Speed. See Methamphetamines
Speedballs, 164
Spermicides, 346t, 349–50, 350
Spiritual development
  assessment of, 13
  emotional maturity and, 35–37
  importance of, 35–37, 40–42
  overall health and, 10
  theory Z people, 35
Sports drinks, 81
Spouse abuse. See Domestic violence
Spray products, 168
Sprinting, 68
Squash activities, 137t
Sri Lanka, 457
Stalking, 409–10
State laws. See Laws
Static stretching, 70, 71
STDs. See Sexually transmitted diseases
Step training, 76
Sterilization, 357–59, 358
Steroids, 83
Stimulants
  abuse of, 157
  barbiturates and, 164
  caffeine content in, 162t
  classification of, 159–64
STP. See Designer drugs
Strength-building equipment, 70
Stress management, 44–63
  assessments for, 12, 45, 46, 49, 59
    realistic perspectives, 57–58
  corticoids and, 48, 50, 51
  HealthQuest Activities, 52
  learning activities, 57
  multicultural community and, 55
  origins and
    alcohol consumption, 44
    computer workstations and, 60
    depression, 44
    noise pollution, 438
    personality types, 53
    stressors, 44–47
    technology and, 60
    work-related, 60–62
  physiology of
    back pain, 52
    cardiovascular risk factors, 232, 236
    central nervous system and, 50
    cerebral cortex and, 50
    disease and, 44–45, 51, 52–53, 232, 236
    endocrine system and, 50
    epinephrine and, 50
    immune system and, 50, 51, 52–53
    physiological responses and, 44, 48–52, 49
    psychoimmunity, 52–53
    sensory modalities and, 50
  stages of
    alarm reaction, 48
    exhaustion, 48
    recovery, 48
    resistance, 48
  techniques for
    action guides, 47, 54
    aerobic exercises, 56
    biking, 56
    biofeedback, 56
    diaphragmatic breathing, 55–56, 56
    emotional responses, 51

exercises, 56, 62
fitness clubs, 82–83
progressive muscle relation, 54–55
self-hypnosis, 53
transcendental meditation, 56
varied, 11, 53–58, 60–62
yoga, 55
Stretching, 70, 71
Stroebel, Charles, 55
Stroke, 44, 241–42
Students Against Drunk Driving
    (SADD), 190
Subdermal implants, 347t, 357, 357
Substance abuse
  alcohol, 179–200
  drugs, 155–77
  issues in, 2
  tobacco, 202–26
Suicide, 403
  alcohol use and, 189, 199–200
  causes of death and, 2t
  drug abuse and, 164
  emotional maturity and, 30–31
  warning signs of, 31
Sulfur compounds, 427
Sun exposure risks, 265–66
Support organizations. See Organizations
    of support
Suppressor genes, 250
Surgery
  abuse of painkillers after, 168
  for cancer, 264
  coronary artery bypass, 239–40, 241
  for ovarian cancer diagnosis, 259
  recovery and tobacco use, 214
Surrogate parenting, 369
Surviving: Support Group, 267
Sweating stress response, 48
Sweets, 109t, 111
Sweet/sour mixed drinks, 184t
Swimming
  ACSM recommendations for, 76, 77
  for back pain, 79
  calories used in, 137t
  cardiorespiratory system and, 68, 73
  for stress management, 56
Symptothermal birth control, 349
Synapse, 159
Synergistic drug effect, 168, 169
Synesthesia, 165
Syphilis, 301, 302
Systemic lupus erythematosus, 272
Systolic pressure, 241

T

Table tennis, 137t
Target heart rate (THR), 76–77
Taxol, 259
T-cells, 283, 283–84, 285–86
Tea
  appetite suppression and, 135
  caffeine content in, 162t
  CNS effects and, 214
Technology, 60–62
Television, 179, 196
Telomerase, 251
Temperature inversions, 427–28
Tennis
  ACSM recommendations for, 76
  calories used in, 137t
  equipment/information for, 82
Tension headaches, 50
Terminology, 2–4
Test anxiety, 47
Testes cancers, 254, 260
Testicle examinations, 14
Testosterone, 83
Tetanus, 280, 285, 306
Tetrahydrocannabinol (THC), 167, 169
Theory Z people, 35
Therapeutic touch, 265

Third World countries, 121
Thorax, 230, 231
3TC, 296
Thrombus, 242
TIA, 242, 243
Ticks, 291
Time management
   fitness clubs and, 82
   in stress reduction, 54
Tissue change, 72
Tissue damage, 52
TM, 56
TMJ dysfunction, 51
Tobacco use, 202–26
   assessments for, 13, 204, 222
   behaviors and, 207–9
   diseases and, 203, 210–14
      aging changes, 73
      back pain, 214
      breast cancer, 255
      caffeine, 214
      cancers, 210–11, *212*, 213, 265
      cardiovascular, 210–11, 215–16, 232–34
      education and, 202
      lung cancers and, 253–55
      medical examinations, 79
      pregnancy, 203
   issues/trends in
      Action on Smoking and Health, 225
      advertising and, 202–3, 208–9
      in America, 202–3
      issues for students, 2
      multicultural, 206
      nonsmokers *vs.* smokers, 220, 224–26
      passive smoking, 216–17
      psychosocial factors, 207–9
      questions of rights, 220, 224–26
      tobacco industry, 203, 207
      usage trends, 155
   learning activities, 209
   physiology and, 205–6, 209–10
      appetite suppression, 135
      dependencies, 203, 205
      effects on basal cell layer, 212
      nicotine in, 205–7, 210
   quitting, 11
      fitness clubs, 83
      reducing, 217–20
      weight control, 219
   types of
      cigar smoking, 203
      low tar/nicotine levels, 202
      pipe smoking, 203
      smokeless, 216
Tonic mixed drinks, 184*t*
Toughlove support group, 171
Toxic shock syndrome (TSS), 292–93
TPA, 242
Trace minerals, 102, 103*t*–104*t*, 107
Track sports, 83
Tranquilizers
   abuse of, 157, 165
   testing for, 169
Transcendental meditation (TM), 56
Transcenders, 35
Transcervical balloon tuboplasty, 368
Transient ischemic attack (TIA), 242, 243
Transplants, heart, 240–41
Triphasic pill contraceptives, 347*t*, 355
Tropical oils, 96, 98
TSS, 292–93
Tubal ligation, 347*t*
Tuberculosis, 280, 288–89
Tumors
   benign, 251–52
   necrosis factor, 264
Typhoid, 280

U

Ulcerative colitis, 52
Ulcers

stress origins and, 44
Ultrasound, 259
Unconsciousness, 185
Underwater weighing. *See* Hydrostatic
   weighing
United States
   drug-free lifestyles and, 165
   health insurance in, 388–93
   health objectives in, 11
   humor in, 32
   nutrition in, 99
   violence in, 408
United States Department of Agriculture
   (USDA), 121
Upper body strength, 75
Urban environments, 199
Urethritis, 303
U.S. Public Health Service, 296
USA Today, 199, 202
USDA, 121
Uterine cancers, 68, 254, 257

V

Vacuum aspiration, 359
Vaginal cancers, 257–58
Vaginal contraceptive film (VCF), 349–50, *350*
Vaginal infections, 302–3
Valium, 165, 169
Vascular systems, 229–30
Vasectomy, 347*t*
VCF, 349–50, *350*
Vegetables, 109, 109*t*
Vegetarian/semivegetarian diets, 117–20, 125–26
Ventricles, 230, *230*
Vertebral compression, 72
Vietnam, rituals/funerals in, 457
Violence
   alcohol use and, 180, 189, 199–200
   binge drinking and, 180
   campus safety and, 417
   child abuse, 403, 406, 411
   concerns of late 1990s, 2
   domestic, 403, 405–7
   elder abuse, 403, 406–7
   gangs/youth, 407–8
   guns and, 408
   hate crimes, 408–9
   intentional injuries, 403–10
   in other cultures, 408
   personal safety assessments for, 404
   residential safety and, 414–15
   sexual victimization, 410–14
   stalking, 409–10
Viruses
   cancers and, 251, 256
   transmission of, 280–81, 281*t*
Vision
   in elderly, 73
   in midlife adults, 72
Visualization therapy, 265
Vital Options, 267
Vitamins
   in alcoholic beverages, 182
   fat soluble, 100*t*
   osteoporosis/vitamin D, 72
   for pregnancy, 106*t*
   recommendations, 99, 100*t*–102*t*, 106*t*,
      107*t*, 108*t*, 109*t*
   water soluble, 101*t*–102*t*, 107*t*
Vodka, 184*t*
Volleyball, 137*t*
Volunteer health agencies, 382–83
Vomiting, 186

W

Waist-to-hip ratio (WHR), 129–30, 129*t*
Walking
   ACSM recommendations for, 76
   for back pain, 79
   calories used in, 137*t*
   cardiorespiratory system and, 68, 73

Waste recycling, 432–34
Water
   for fluid replacement, 81
   major minerals and, 105*t*–106*t*
   nutrition and, 102, 104, 105*t*
Water exercises, 76
Water pollution, 429–32, 429*t*
Weight
   cancers and, 265
   cardiovascular risk factors and, 232
   inactivity and, 135–36
Weight control, 128–52
   action guides for, 141
   activity requirements and, 137, 137*t*
   anorexia nervosa, 145–47
   appearance and, 132
   assessments for, 140, 149
   basal metabolism, 136–38
   body image, 128, 150
   body mass index, 130, 131, 131*t*, 132*t*
   bulimia nervosa, 145–47
   caloric balance, 136, *136*
   compulsive eating/exercise, 146
   diets/techniques for, 139–45, 142*t*, 143*t*, 147
   eating disorders and, 145–47
   electrical impedance, 130
   energy needs and, 135–36
   fad diets, 139
   fasting, 140
   gaining weight, 151–52
   goals for, 11
   HealthQuest Activities, 138
   height/weight determinations, 128, 129*t*, 130,
      130*t*, 150
   hydrostatic weighing, 131–32
   image/self-concept, 128
   learning activities, 147
   liposuction for, 145
   low calorie/fat/serving, 140–41
   multicultures and, 135
   obesity, 128–29, 132–36, 150
   physical intervention for, 142–44
   self-concept and, 128
   self-help programs for, 141
   skinfold measurements, 130, *132*, 150
   surgery for, 144–45
   thermic effect of food, 137–38
   tobacco use and, 214
   undernutrition, 147–48
   underweight problems and, 128, 150
Weight control aids, 162*t*
Weight gains, in pregnancy, 134–35
Weight lifting, 68–71
   cardiorespiratory system and, 68
   fitness clubs and, 82
   steroids and, 83
Weight training
   calories used in, 137*t*
   cardiorespiratory fitness and, 73
Wellness
   defined, 3–4, 16, 17
   fitness clubs and, 83
Western history, 20
Western literature, 20
Wetlands pollution, 431
Whirlpools, 82
Whiskey, 184*t*
Whooping cough, 280, 284,
   284*t*, 306
Wills, 451
Wines
   advertising, 196
   calories in, 182
   migraine headaches and, 50
   types of, 184*t*
Withdrawal
   alcoholism and, 192, 194–95
   cold turkey, 168, 169
   illness, 157
Withdrawal birth control, 345, 346*t*
Woititz, Janet Geringer, 195

Women
    advertising and, 196, 202–3
    alcohol use in, 180, 184, 195–96
    aspirin therapy and, 240
    breast cancer incidence in, 255
    cardiovascular diseases in, 232
    crime and, 199–200
    hypertension in, 248
    pregnancy and, 180, 185, 187–88, *188*, 189
    reproductive systems of, 317–22, *318*
    tobacco use in, 202–3
    trends of, 195

Work-related stress, 60–62, 72
World Health Organization (WHO)
    on cancers, 253
    definitions by, 2–3, 16, 17
World hunger, 2
World literature, 20
World population growth, 423, *425*
World Wide Web, 20
Wrestling, 137*t*
Writing, 137*t*

X

XTC. *See* Designer drugs

Y

Yoga, 55
You Must Relax, 54
Yo-yo weight syndrome, 133

Z

Zantac, 393
Zero tolerance laws, 192, 193

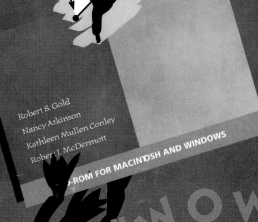